SPARKLING GEMS
FROM THE GREEK

1-800-413-2132

SPARKLING GEMS FROM THE GREEK

365 Greek Word Studies for Every Day of the Year
To Sharpen Your Understanding of God's Word

Rick Renner

TEACH ALL NATIONS

A book company anointed to take God's Word
to you and to the nations of the world.

A division of
RICK RENNER MINISTRIES

Sparkling Gems From the Greek
ISBN 0-9725454-2-5
Copyright © 2003 by Rick Renner
P. O. Box 702040
Tulsa, OK 74170-2040

14th Printing

Editorial Consultant: Cynthia D. Hansen

Endorsements

(in alphabetical order)

Rick Renner has given us a treasure. *Sparkling Gems From the Greek* is a magnificent daily devotional that opens the door of understanding and rich revelation in God's Word. This is the daily devotional that will take you deep into the substance and meaning of scriptures and will thrill your soul. Thank you, Rick — you have done it again. You have brought fresh insight to scriptures that bring the Word to life. This is a book I will cherish.

Dennis Burke
Dennis Burke Ministries
Fort Worth, Texas

When I read the first page of Rick Renner's daily devotional, I sensed the wisdom and anointing of God. Rick has painstakingly revealed the wisdom of God for us to victoriously live life on a daily basis. Now you can "study to shew thyself approved unto God, a workman that needeth not to be ashamed, rightly dividing the word of truth" (2 Timothy 2:15).

Happy Caldwell
Senior Pastor, Agape Church
Little Rock, Arkansas

In his *Sparkling Gems From the Greek,* Rick Renner has done an outstanding job of acquainting non-Greek readers with the essential language of the New Testament. By tracing these basic Greek terms back to their original roots, Rick adds a great deal to our understanding of the richness and depth of what at first glance appears to be the disarmingly simple language of the New Testament. Rick makes it clear that whereas no translation can exactly reproduce the original meaning, nevertheless, through an understanding of the original language and the broad range of meaning that many of the words in that language possess, it is more readily possible to penetrate and comprehend the meaning of the original language.

Dr. John S. Catlin
Chairman, Classics and Letters
Department
University of Oklahoma

Although some have used the Greek language in an intimidating way, Rick makes the wonderful truths of God's Word inviting and enriching. Far from taking a stodgy, hyper-academic approach, Rick presents powerful spiritual truths with great simplicity and clarity. He uses dynamic Bible principles that are extremely practical, relevant, and readily applicable. As I read the Gems, I was encouraged, enlightened, and challenged to act on these excellent spiritual insights. If you want your spiritual life raised to a new level, this book will be a wonderful catalyst for you, and a great asset for promoting maturity and growth in the Body of Christ.

Tony Cooke
Tony Cooke Ministries
Broken Arrow, Oklahoma

Until Rick Renner came on the scene, the only Greek I knew owned a restaurant in downtown Chicago! But now, hotter than a sizzling gyros sandwich off the Windy City's Halstead Street, comes *Sparkling Gems From the Greek.* Rick Renner has a tremendous God-given ability to help anyone who has the desire to gain depth in the Word of God. Every day of the year, you can enjoy a feast of the Renner-selected scripture passages. Bite into *Sparkling Gems From the Greek.* It's *delicious*!

William (Van) Crouch
President
Van Crouch Communications
Chicago, Illinois

Rick Renner is a Bible scholar who takes the revelation of God's Word and changes lives. He understands what it means to put the Word to the test, and he writes out of faith-demanding circumstances. You will be strengthened with fresh insights from God's Word as you read *Sparkling Gems From the Greek.*

Billy Joe Daugherty
Pastor, Victory Christian Center
Tulsa, Oklahoma

I am a firm believer in the fact that there are answers awaiting you in the Presence of God. Any amount of time that you spend in His Presence is *never* wasted. That's why Rick Renner's devotional, *Sparkling Gems From the Greek,* is so timely. There's nothing like beginning each day the *right way* — basking in God's Presence, meditating on His Word, and focusing solely on heavenly things.

Being a no-nonsense "man of the Word" like Rick, I like the fact that this devotional is practical and has a strong biblical foundation. It covers true-to-life issues such as spiritual boredom, the desire to escape from "dead-end" places, the requirements for maintaining an attitude for success, and how to think like a spiritual billionaire. The bottom line is that this devotional will help you change the way you *think* so you can change the way you *live.*

Dr. Creflo A. Dollar
Senior Pastor and CEO
World Changers Ministries
Atlanta, Georgia

I have been carrying and reading this devotional all over America and have found it truly wonderful, with great and fresh insights into the Word. Some who walk in the "high places" spiritually find it difficult to minister effectively to the common man, but not so in this case. Rick Renner's approach makes it easy for us all to gain tremendous revelation through his *Sparkling Gems From the Greek.* Just imagine — if one word from God can change our world forever, what can the true revelation of that one word do as we apply it and are impacted by it in our everyday lives?

Phil Driscoll
Mighty Horn Ministries
Chattanooga, Tennessee

If you have ever desired a closer relationship with the Lord and wanted to fully understand the meaning and intent behind the scriptures in the Bible, this devotional is for you! *Sparkling Gems From the Greek* is a powerful devotional by Rick Renner that I believe will not only minister life to you and your everyday circumstances, but will also deepen your hunger for more of God and His awesome Word.

Sometimes Greek can be a little intimidating, and for a lot of people it has become just that...Greek! But not this book! Rick has a phenomenal understanding of the Greek language. He has compiled his years of study and put it into a daily devotional that is simple and easy for anyone to understand. He takes Greek from the Word of God and seamlessly turns it into a revelation word from God. Some people need only a word from God on Sunday, but this wonderful devotional gives you a word from God every day of your life. I like that!

Sparkling Gems From the Greek is a book that I feel is needed in the world we live in today, and I highly recommend it to you. I thoroughly enjoyed reading it and I believe that you will too! I especially enjoyed the "Prayer for Today" and the "Confession for Today" at the close of each day's study. So sit down and relax; you're going to have a great time reading this devotional. It's not just a word from Rick — it's a word from God!

Rev. Jesse Duplantis
Jesse Duplantis Ministries
New Orleans, Louisiana

Rick Renner has written an insightful and inspiring devotional that will help you win victory one day at a time. *Sparkling Gems From the Greek* is a great way to begin your day. I heartily recommend it.

Willie George
Senior Pastor
Church on the Move
Tulsa, Oklahoma

Sparkling Gems From the Greek takes the hard work of academic research and places the best gleanings in the hands of all believers. Rick Renner successfully combines solid scholarship with a passion for God to help us face life with an unshakeable faith founded on Scripture.

Pastor Ted Haggard
New Life Church
Colorado Springs, Colorado

Sparkling Gems From the Greek is an exciting new approach that marries a faith-filled devotional with bite-sized morsels of Greek word studies. I highly recommend *Sparkling Gems From the Greek.* The daily devotions will exhort you, teach you, and bless you.

Rev. Kenneth Hagin, Jr.
Pastor, RHEMA Bible Church
Executive Vice President
Kenneth Hagin Ministries
Tulsa, Oklahoma

I have known Rick Renner for years and have watched as God rewarded his faithfulness by repeatedly promoting him. I think of Rick as the "apostle to Russia" for our day. I've had a peek at his new book, *Sparkling Gems From the Greek*, and this is Rick as I love to hear him — mining practical, life-changing revelations from his exhaustive study of the Greek language. I look forward to discovering Rick's Gems on a daily basis. This is an important book, a treasure! I can't wait to get my copy — and *you* must have one too!

Marilyn Hickey
International Bible Teacher
Marilyn Hickey Ministries
Denver, Colorado

Rick Renner has done it again! He has written a book that is so fascinating and so intriguing that you can't wait to get to the next page. It is a daily devotional, but I don't know anyone who is going to be content to read just one day at a time. The urge is to get to day 365 as fast as you can! Rick Renner is the only person we know of who can expound on the Greek and yet make it simple enough for anyone to understand it. This is a precious gift for any person's home library. A diamond sparkles more brightly that any other gem, and this book is really a diamond!

Charles and Frances Hunter
Hunter Ministries
Kingwood, Texas

This devotional is totally awesome and a wonderful resource for those of us who do not know how to read Greek. The ability the Lord has given Rick to explain the Greek words in such a colorful, easy-to-understand, easy-to-apply manner is a gift from God to the Body of Christ. *Sparkling Gems From the Greek* is definitely a must for every minister's library!

Dr. Jim Kaseman
President, Jim Kaseman Ministries
Association of Faith Churches and
    Ministers
Branson, Missouri

The breadth of the subject matter in this book sets it apart from the traditional devotional. From peace to preparing for battle, from dealing with the devil to preparing for success and meditating on the love God has for us, Rick's book is truly filled with "Sparkling Gems," just as the title indicates. The book is not only a tremendous learning tool but a daily practical guide to living life as God intended and in a way that is consistent with His principles. You will find great study subjects to help you grow, as well as daily confessions and very practical daily living suggestions to guide you. No person interested in walking a daily walk with God should be without this book.

Mike King
Attorney
Winters, King & Associates
Tulsa, Oklahoma

Rick Renner is real, radical, and anointed — and so are his books. They are easy to read and full of the truth that makes you free — especially this one! It will change your life!

Mylon LeFevre
Musician, Evangelist
Fort Worth, Texas

Rick Renner is brilliant and anointed. His ability to translate from the Greek provides a richer understanding of the scriptures. Like other precious stones, the gems Rick mines and shares with us have facets that reflect the Light in ways we perhaps have not seen before. *Sparkling Gems From the Greek* is a devotional that will take you deeper in your walk with God. Prepare yourself to partake of the rich treasury of God's Word through Rick's treasure hunt!

Joyce Meyer
Joyce Meyer Ministries
Fenton, Missouri

Rick Renner is not only one of the most outstanding apostles of today, but he is also one of the most sound biblical teachers in the Body of Christ. His books and teaching ministry have been an inspiration to me and thousands of others like me. I believe that you will find a "Sparkling Gem" for every day of the year in his daily devotional. I highly recommend this book and believe that it is one of the best daily devotionals today!

Pastor Ray McCauley
Pastor, RHEMA Bible Church
Johannesburg, South Africa

Rick Renner has written a daily devotional with more than 1,000 Greek word studies that will enrich your walk with God. It is filled with information that every believer will benefit from, and I highly recommend it! What a great way to start your day!

Pat Robertson
Founder/President, CBN
Regent University
Virginia Beach, Virginia

Wow! *Sparkling Gems From the Greek* is the most comprehensive devotional study of substance available to the Body of Christ today. Rick Renner continues to help us remain accurate in our pursuit of the Master. I not only highly recommend it — I also teach it!

Robb Thompson
Senior Pastor
Family Harvest Church
President
Family Harvest International
Tinley Park, Illinois

In *Sparkling Gems From the Greek,* each new day in your life will be filled with exciting insight from the Greek that makes the Bible come alive in a new way. I believe this devotional is not only a great book, but truly a must for any Christian seeking insight into Scripture and wanting to grow spiritually.

Dr. Duane Vander Klok
Senior Pastor
Resurrection Life Church
Grandville, Michigan

Sparkling Gems From the Greek is one of the finest devotional and inspirational works ever written. God Almighty has breathed His anointing upon these pages to heal and to deliver hope and intimacy to His people. This inspired work is so needed for this generation. It is my personal recommendation to every believer who desires to meet with God in a personal way.

Bob Weiner
Weiner Ministries International
Gainesville, Florida

Rick Renner has created a masterpiece. The rich nuances of each Greek word make this devotional a book that affords the reader the opportunity to grow closer to God in every area of life. It will increase your consecration and your faith; it will help you to tap into God's divine guidance system and to be transformed by His power. It will be well worth it to invest in *Sparkling Gems From the Greek*.

Dr. Douglas J. Wingate
President
Life Christian University
Tampa, Florida

Just as an attorney uses the laws of the land to counsel and represent a client, Rick Renner has masterfully used his knowledge of God's Law to create this sparkling collection of daily devotions to counsel and encourage the reader. *Sparkling Gems From the Greek* will challenge you, teach you, rebuke you, and comfort you. Pick it up, open it, read it, apply it!

Tom Winters
Attorney
Winters, King & Associates
Tulsa, Oklahoma

Rick's new devotional *Sparkling Gems From the Greek* is the best way I know of to begin each day with the Lord. It gives you both a thought and a scripture on which to base your meditation. I believe this book is also great for ministers, adult class teachers, and Bible teachers because it provides a great foundation for sermons and lessons. I plan on using many of the Gems in my own sermons. If you are like me, you can use all the help you can get! Thanks, Rick, for making this new book available.

Bob Yandian
Pastor, Grace Fellowship
Tulsa, Oklahoma

Dedication

It is with great pleasure that I dedicate
Sparkling Gems From the Greek
to my dearly loved wife, Denise.

To Denise —

From the time Jesus brought us together as a husband-and-wife team
so many years ago, you have stood by my side as my best friend,
my greatest supporter, and the most significant partner I have in ministry.
You have been my companion in travels that have led us
across the face of the earth more times than we can count.
And through it all, you have become an able minister of the Gospel
for whom I have the greatest esteem and respect.

Thank you for answering the call of God
to take the Gospel with me to the ends of the earth.
Thank you for marrying me, for rearing our sons with me,
and for being my counselor, my comrade, and my partner in this life.
I am so thankful that you will be with me
to the end of our lives on this earth.

No human being is more important in my life than you.

Thank you for everything you are and for all that you do.

Table of Contents

Acknowledgments

A work of this magnitude requires the gifts and collaboration of many people. It would be improper to publish such a work without acknowledging those special people whose time, talent, and effort helped to produce *Sparkling Gems From the Greek*. As you read and learn from this book, you will be receiving not only from the teaching God has entrusted to me but also from the labors of others who helped produce this volume.

First, I would like to thank my wife, Denise, and our three sons, Paul, Philip, and Joel, for their patience during the months that I have worked nonstop on this monumental project. Your kindness and patience with me during the many days I wrote this book are greatly appreciated. The multitude of times that I asked you to sit down and listen to what I had written and the many suggestions you gave me are a very important part of this book.

Second, I wish to thank the entire staff of Rick Renner Ministries in America, in England, and in the former Soviet Union for your steadfast prayers as I worked so many long hours on this book. If it had not been for the wonderful team God has given to me, I would have been unable to devote myself so completely to this task. Thank you for staying at your post and being faithful. You will reap a reward in Heaven for what you are doing for the Kingdom of God and for the excellent attitude with which you are doing it.

Third, I wish to thank my editor, Cindy Hansen, not only for being an outstanding editor, but also for her spiritual sensitivity to the material that passes her desk for editing. You are without a doubt one of the finest editors I've ever worked with, and you are tremendously appreciated by Denise and me. We believe in the gifts and callings that God has placed in your life. Your name may not be on the cover, but your touch is throughout this book, and for this I am very thankful.

Fourth, I wish to express my thanks to Angel Ausdemore for her resolute, steadfast, unwavering commitment to keep up with the pace of this project. Your attitude has been outstanding, and I am certain that Jesus has observed the manner in which you have served Him as you have helped in the editorial process. I also wish to thank Jane Janosky and Terri Young for the many hours you invested into this project.

Fifth, I wish to express my deepest, heartfelt thanks to Pavel Zolotarev, my Moscow graphic designer, who typeset this entire book. This was a colossal job for a man who speaks Russian as his primary language, and I am very proud of your work. Not only did you do a good job, but you did it with excellence. Thank you for the many hours that you invested into *Sparkling Gems From the Greek*. I am thankful you are on my team, and I am grateful to be a spiritual father to you.

Sixth, I wish to thank Bob Gilbert and Jeremy Rhodes for handling all the negotiations regarding the publishing of this book. There would be no book if it were not for the part you played in this process, and I am very grateful for what you have contributed to the publishing of this work.

Seventh, I desire to express my profound gratitude to all the Christian leaders worldwide who took time out of their busy schedules to read parts of the original manuscript. Thank you for giving me your valuable suggestions and kind endorsements.

Rick Renner

Foreword

It is not often, if ever, one finds a book of such practical value as Rick Renner's *Sparkling Gems From the Greek*. This book is well named because it literally sparkles with 365 "gems" of divine truths, not just from the English Bible but also from the Greek New Testament. I know of no other book where you will find:

◆ 365 potential sermons.
◆ 365 choice devotional thoughts.
◆ 365 transforming truths.
◆ 365 lectures for special occasions.
◆ 365 golden nuggets upon which to meditate.
◆ 365 spiritual meals to feed the hungry soul.

I have from eight to ten thousand volumes in my library, but no books that are so monumental in their wealth of biblical truths. Furthermore, this book's value is greatly augmented by the clarity and simplicity with which the truth is articulated.

More importantly, we need to understand that the Bible is God talking to us personally, provided the Bible is permitted to speak in the language in which it was originally written by holy men of God (2 Peter 1:20,21) — the wonderful Greek tongue. Such is the case with *Sparkling Gems From the Greek*. This book contains the very words of the living God by which one must live if he is to live at all (Matthew 4:4). Jeremiah experienced this living word, shouting in his spirit these words, "Thy words were found, and I did eat them; and thy word was unto me the joy and rejoicing of mine heart…" (Jeremiah 15:16).

This is the way I feel after feasting from *Sparkling Gems From the Greek*. I know I have indeed found the very word of the living God, and I rejoice with exceeding great joy. How, then, could I fail to recommend this book to anyone who hungers for the life-giving bread of our once crucified, now risen, reigning and soon coming King? I would be of gross ingratitude if I did not commend and recommend it to the whole wide world. And so I do.

Soli Deo Gloria.

Dr. Bill Bennett
Professor of Homiletics and Pastoral Ministries,
    Chaplain, Southeastern Baptist Theological Seminary
Wake Forest, North Carolina
Founder and President of Mentoring Men for the Master
General Director of Alpha Ministries International, India
BA, Wake Forest University; MA, M. Div., Duke University
Doctor of Theology, New Orleans Seminary

Preface

As I write the preface to this book, it is very late at night, and I am looking out my window at the beautiful golden-domed towers of the Moscow Kremlin. My heart is filled with gratefulness to God for calling my family and me here and for allowing us to give our lives to these people who have enriched us more than we could ever express. This is truly one of the greatest honors God has given to our family.

As I sit here in the heart of the Russian capital, I am also thinking of what a great honor it is to minister to you through *Sparkling Gems From the Greek*. As I write this preface, I have just put the final strokes on this daily devotional. Writing this book has been a dream of mine for many years, and I am thankful that God has enabled me to bring this dream to pass. My prayer is that these 365 daily devotions containing more than 1,000 different Greek word studies will richly bless every person with a hungry heart into whose hands it falls.

Although I have studied the Greek New Testament for many years, I am still a vigorous student of the New Testament in its original language and continually discover many new truths and wonderful insights that bring change to my own life. Throughout my decades-long treasure hunt in the Greek New Testament and my continuous extracting of new "gems," I have often thought of Matthew 13:52, where Jesus says, "...Therefore every scribe which is instructed unto the kingdom of heaven is like unto a man that is an householder, which bringeth forth out of his treasure things new and old." I know from personal experience that as we give our attention to the Word of God, the Holy Spirit adds new insights to the old ones and causes our understanding of God and His Word to be marvelously expanded.

In the writing of this devotional, I relate well to the scribe described in Matthew 13:52. Many of the Greek word studies you will read in this book are old to me; yet so many of them are brand new. Often I think that I have unearthed every gem that can possibly be found in a particular verse of the New Testament. But then the next time I study that same verse, the Holy Spirit wonderfully opens my eyes and illuminates my mind to show me truths that I previously overlooked. I have invested thousands of hours into prayer and study and the writing of the book you hold in your hands. It is my heartfelt, sincere prayer that God will use this book to take you to a higher place in Him.

As you will see, this book can be used as a daily devotional or, with the help of the Greek word index in the back of the book, it can also be used as a Greek reference tool for your own personal study. And as you read *Sparkling Gems From the Greek*, ask the Holy Spirit to assist you in comprehending these truths, for although you utilize your mind to search and study facts, history, and language, the Holy Spirit is the only One who can illuminate your mind and impart divine revelation to your spirit.

As a word of explanation: In the pages to follow, you will often see a paraphrased, interpretive translation of the specific New Testament verse or verses that are being discussed in a particular Gem. These are not intended to be word-for-word translations; rather, they are designed to give you a fuller and expanded understanding of the meaning behind the scripture under discussion. I first tried to capture the picture presented by each word and each verse. Then I endeavored to carry that picture into a contemporary, interpretive translation in order to give you a broader comprehension of what God is trying to say to you through that particular scripture.

As you use *Sparkling Gems From the Greek*, dig deep into the rich treasures of God's Word so you may extract as many precious gems of truth as possible. Now it's time for you to get started!

Rick Renner
Moscow, Russia
October 12, 2003

Preface

All scripture is given by inspiration of God, and is profitable for doctrine, for reproof, for correction, for instruction in righteousness: that the man of God may be perfect, throughly furnished unto all good works.

— 2 Timothy 3:16,17

SPARKLING GEMS FROM THE GREEK

365 Greek Word Studies for Every Day of the Year
To Sharpen Your Understanding of God's Word

Rick Renner

JANUARY 1

❧❧❧

Let God's Peace Serve as an Umpire For Your Mind and Emotions!

And let the peace of God rule in your hearts,
to the which also ye are called in one body; and be ye thankful.
— Colossians 3:15

*H*ave you ever had one of those days when there was so much confusion whirling around your head that you felt like screaming, "STOP"?

From time to time, everyone has that kind of a day. And when you do, your temptation is probably either to get in the flesh and react to someone in an ugly way or to get depressed, go to bed, and forget about it all. However, you know that neither choice will help you solve the problems you are facing.

Rather than throw in the towel and give way to these emotions that want to get the best of you, why not stop right now and make a decision to let the Word of God rule you today? When I say "rule" you, I'm talking about God's supernatural peace *dominating* and *governing* every emotion and situation that confronts you. If you don't make this decision and follow through with it, worry, fear, insecurity, doubt, and a whole host of other emotions will assuredly try to take control. And there is no worse roller-coaster ride than when you are being knocked all over the place by emotions that are out of control!

Instead, let the peace of God rule in your heart, as Paul wrote in Colossians 3:15. He said, "And let the peace of God rule in your hearts, to the which also ye are called in one body; and be ye thankful." I especially want you to notice the word "rule" in this verse. It is from the Greek word *brabeuo*, which in ancient times was used to describe the *umpire* or *referee* who moderated and judged the athletic competitions that were so popular in the ancient world.

Paul uses this word to tell us that the peace of God can work like an umpire or referee in our hearts, minds, and emotions. When detrimental emotions attempt to exert control over us or try to throw us into an emotional frenzy, we can stop it from happening by making the choice to let God's peace rise up from deep inside us like an umpire or referee to moderate our emotions. As we do, we will be kept under the control of that divine peace as it rules in our hearts. When this divine umpire called "peace" steps into the game, it suddenly begins to call the shots and make all the decisions instead of fretfulness, anxiety, and worry.

Colossians 3:15 could be translated:

"Let the peace of God call the shots in your life...."
"Let the peace of God be the umpire in your life and actions...."
"Let the peace of God act as referee in your emotions and your decisions...."

Even though it's true that everyone has hard days and difficult weeks, you don't have to surrender to those emotions that try to steal your joy, disturb your relationships, and rob you of your victory. When you feel overwhelmed by problems or emotions that are hitting you from every direction, just stop a moment and deliberately set your heart and mind on Jesus and the Word of God. *As you do this, the wonderful, conquering, dominating, supernatural peace of God will rise up from your spirit and take control!*

Lord, I don't want to let my emotions get the best of me today, so I ask that Your peace would rise up like a mighty umpire and referee in my heart, mind, and emotions. Help me recognize those moments when unhelpful emotions try to sneak up on me. I ask You to teach me how to put those emotions aside and release Your supernatural peace that is resident in my heart — the peace that is always ready at every moment to moderate every thought and emotion that tries to pass into my life!

I pray this in Jesus' name!

MY CONFESSION FOR TODAY

I confess that God's supernatural peace dominates me. When I am tempted to get upset and my emotions try to take control of me, I put these emotions aside and allow the Spirit of God to release a supernatural, dominating, moderating peace to rule my heart, mind, and emotions!

I declare this by faith in Jesus' name!

QUESTIONS FOR YOU TO CONSIDER

1. Do you recognize moments when your emotions try to throw you into an emotional tizzy and steal your peace and joy?
2. Have you asked God to help you overcome these moments?
3. What steps can you take to quiet yourself so you can focus on God's Word and allow the peace of God to rise up and referee what is going on inside your heart, mind, and emotions?

JANUARY 2

*Could You Use a Little Extra Strength
To Make It Through Your Day?*

For I know that this shall turn to my salvation
through your prayer, and the supply of the Spirit of Jesus Christ.
— Philippians 1:19

At times everyone gets physically tired and mentally exhausted. However, some believers, regardless of how long or how hard they work, seem to have the knack, fortitude, determination, and will to keep going strong, even when everyone else can barely take one more step.

Have you ever met someone like this? Have you wondered, *How in the world can that person keep going the way he does?*

Could it be that this person has learned how to tap into a supernatural Source of power? Well, the same inexhaustible supply of power is available to you! In Philippians 1:19, Paul talked about this kind of power: "For I know that this shall turn to my salvation through your prayer, and *the supply of the Spirit of Jesus Christ.*"

I especially want you to notice the word "supply" in this verse. It is the Greek word *epichoregeo*. To those who read Greek, this word seems like a strange choice for Paul. However, after reflecting on the original usage of this word, it makes this verse very exciting! The word *epichoregeo* is an old word that literally means *on behalf of the choir.* I know this sounds peculiar, so let me explain where this word came from and why Paul uses it here.

Thousands of years ago in classical Greece, a huge choral and dramatic company practiced endlessly for a huge, important theatrical performance. After they put in a great amount of time, effort, energy, and practice, it was finally time for the show to go on the road. But there was one major problem — they ran out of money!

These people had given their lives to this production. They had committed all their resources to making sure the performance succeeded. But because they ran out of financing, it meant the show was over — *finished*! They were washed up before the show ever officially got started. From all appearances, it was the end of the road for them and their dream.

At that exact moment, a wealthy man heard of their crisis, stepped into the middle of their situation, and made a huge financial contribution *on behalf of the choir.* This contribution "supplied" all they needed to get back in business again! In fact, the gift the man gave was so enormous that it was more than they needed or knew how to spend! This man's contribution was excessively large, abundant, overflowing, and overwhelming.

This is where we get the word "supply" in Philippians 1:19 that now describes the enormous contribution of the Spirit that Jesus Christ wants to give to you and me!

In light of this, Philippians 1:19 could be taken to mean:

"I am certain that this situation will ultimately turn around and result in my deliverance. I'm sure of it — first, because you are praying for me; and second, because of the special contribution of the Spirit that Jesus Christ is donating for my present cause."

This means when you've run out of steam; when you've given your best effort and you don't feel like you have another ounce of energy left to give; when it looks like your resources are drained and you are unable to take one more step unless someone steps in to help you — that is exactly the moment when Jesus Christ becomes your personal Benefactor! Like the wealthy man in the story above, Jesus steps into your life at that moment to donate a massive, overwhelming, generous contribution of the Spirit's grace and power for your cause!

Jesus is your wealthy Benefactor. He has more strength and power to give you than you'll ever be able to use! If you are weak, He has precisely what you need to get up, get recharged, and get going again! If you'll open your heart to Him right now, Jesus will give you a brand-new contribution of the Spirit's power — and it will be more than enough to get you on your feet and back on the road again!

So when your natural human will is too tired to keep going and you've exhausted all your resources, let Jesus reinforce you with a new "supply of the Spirit" that will give you all the strength you will ever need. *Just open your heart to the Holy Spirit's help today. Allow Him to fill you with a supply of power so large, you could never even begin to use it all!*

MY PRAYER FOR TODAY

Lord, I realize I don't have enough strength by myself to do what You have asked me to do. Today I'm asking You to donate a new supply of Your Spirit into my life. Right now, I open my heart and ask You to fill every nook and cranny of my life with the power of the Holy Spirit so I can get back on my feet again and fulfill what You have told me to do!

I pray this in Jesus' name!

MY CONFESSION FOR TODAY

I declare by faith that I am refilled and recharged with the Spirit of God. There is no lack of strength in me because Jesus continuously provides a huge supply of the Spirit in my life that empowers me to achieve everything I need to do. There is no excuse for me to fail or to stop short of the goals God has given me for my life, because in the Spirit of God there is enough supernatural strength and power to energize me to finish my divine assignment!

I declare this by faith in Jesus' name!

QUESTIONS FOR YOU TO CONSIDER

1. Do you ever run into times in your life when you feel like you've hit a wall and you can't go any further?
2. How do you normally respond to times like these?
3. Compare the results of your past responses to these difficult times to what would happen if you took the time to talk to Jesus about your need for supernatural strength.

JANUARY 3

Isn't It Time for You To Hit the Rewind Button?

Wherefore I put thee in remembrance that thou stir up the gift of God,
which is in thee by the putting on of my hands.
— 2 Timothy 1:6

Have you ever experienced the delivering and rescuing power of God? I'm talking about those moments when your situation looks completely hopeless — but suddenly God's amazing grace intervenes and your situation is miraculously changed! Can you think of moments like this in your past?

It's amazing that when we are confronted with a new challenge, we often fail to remember God's faithfulness in the past. Our perspective gets blurry because of the problems we are currently facing, and we forget that we've gone through similar or worse circumstances before. The looming mountain of problems before us looks so big that we momentarily fail to remember all the other mountains we've already faced and overcome with the help of God.

When Paul wrote his second letter to Timothy, the younger man was facing the biggest mountain of his life. Nero had become the emperor of the Roman Empire. Because of his tyrannical rule, believers were being persecuted and were even dying for their faith. In the midst of all the panic, Timothy was tempted to fear for his life and his future. He must have wondered, *Is God going to be faithful to me in this terrible hour?*

So in Second Timothy 1:5, Paul tells Timothy, "When I call to remembrance the unfeigned faith that is in thee, which dwelt first in thy grandmother Lois, and thy mother Eunice, and I am persuaded that in thee also." Paul wanted to remind Timothy about something very important!

God's faithfulness was a part of Timothy's family heritage. His grandmother trusted the Lord — *and the Lord had never failed her or let her down.* His mother trusted the Lord — *and the Lord had never failed her or let her down either.* Because Timothy was dealing with great stress and difficulty, Paul took the opportunity to remind him that just as God had never failed his grandmother or mother, neither would He abandon Timothy in his difficult hour.

Then Paul told him, "…I put thee in remembrance that thou stir up the gift of God, which is in thee by the putting on of my hands" (2 Timothy 1:6). I want you to particularly focus on the phrase, "I put thee in remembrance." It is taken from the Greek word *anamimnesko*, a compound of the words *ana* and *mimnesko.* Pay close attention, because this is very important! The word *ana* means *again* or *to repeat something.* The second part of the word *mimnesko* means *to be reminded of something,* such as memories.

When these two words are joined together as in this verse, it means *to regather* or *to recollect memories.* The little prefix *ana* carries the idea of *replaying* these memories over and over again in your mind, the way you would hit the rewind button on your video player so you can back up and watch one part of a movie over and over again.

This means there are some memories we should never forget! For example, we should constantly hit the rewind button in our minds and "replay" the times that God has been faithful to us in the past — delivering us, healing us, and rescuing us time and time again. We should "replay" those scenes in our minds until we never forget His faithfulness to us!

You could translate Second Timothy 1:6 in the following way:

"I am putting you in memory of all these things, so that by your remembering them, you might stir up the gift of God that is in you.…"

Paul reminds Timothy (and us) to take our eyes off these times of trouble or the present crisis and to *remember* God's delivering and rescuing power in the past. If we really looked at our past, we'd find that we have faced other moments more severe than the one we're facing right now — and God never failed us or let us down. In fact, He delivered us and turned those situations around!

Don't ever forget what God has already done for you, for those memories will stir you up and encourage you to face your present dilemma with faith. Just as God has always been faithful to you in the past, He will be faithful to you right now.

Never forget how:

◆ God has *healed* you.
◆ God has *delivered* you.
◆ God has *saved* you.
◆ God has *guided* and *directed* you.
◆ God has *brought you through* difficult trials.
◆ God has *provided* for you during hard financial times.
◆ God has *protected* you from the snare of the enemy.

These kinds of memories are powerful and will stir up your faith today!

So the next time the devil tells you there is no way you'll survive what you're facing, take the time to get alone with the Lord. Then hit the rewind button, and ask the Holy Spirit to help you regather and recollect all those past events when God came through for you! As you replay those memories over and over in your mind, your faith will rise to a new level of confidence. You'll be able to look your problems right in the face and say, *"God's record with me has always been faithfulness, and I know He'll be faithful to me now as well!"*

MY PRAYER FOR TODAY

Lord, You have always been faithful. I thank You that even in my present situation, You are going to be faithful again. Please help me recall all the times in the past when You delivered and rescued me from other situations that also looked hopeless. Thank You for helping me keep those awesome experiences alive and fresh in my mind and heart. I thank You for always being faithful to me!

I pray this in Jesus' name!

MY CONFESSION FOR TODAY

I confess that God has never failed me or let me down. He has always delivered me from difficult times, and He will rescue and deliver me now as well. Today I will dwell on those past moments when God did for me what everyone thought was impossible! Just as He intervened on my behalf in the past, He will intervene on my behalf again! I will not succumb to fear, doubt, or failure. With God's help, I will conquer what the enemy meant for my downfall and defeat!

I declare this by faith in Jesus' name!

QUESTIONS FOR YOU TO CONSIDER

1. As you think about God's faithfulness in your life, how does it affect the way you perceive the problems you are dealing with right now?
2. What are some of the seemingly impossible situations you faced in the past that God delivered you from?
3. What steps can you take to trust God more fully to deliver you from your present situation as He has done for you in the past?

JANUARY 4

❧❧❧

How Often Should We Pray?

Praying always with all prayer and supplication in the Spirit,
and watching thereunto with all perseverance and supplication for all saints.
— Ephesians 6:18

*H*ow is your prayer life? Is prayer a central and significant part of your life, or is it something you only do when you are with other believers? Is prayer a daily discipline for you, or do you mainly pray when you get in trouble? Do you pray when you are home alone, or do you find that you only pray and worship the Lord when you come to church and are in the presence of other worshiping and praying people?

To pray regularly requires discipline. Unfortunately, most people are "on-again, off-again" when it comes to prayer. They are faithful for a while, but then they fall out of prayer because they are too tired to get up early, or they become distracted by other things.

But how often are we supposed to pray? Ephesians 6:18 gives us the answer! It says, "Praying *always* with all prayer and supplication in the Spirit, and watching thereunto with all perseverance and supplication for all saints."

The word "always" is taken from the Greek phrase *en panti kairo.* The word *en* would be better translated *at.* The word *panti* means *each and every.* You could say that this word *panti* is an all-encompassing word that embraces everything, including the smallest and most minute of details. The last word in this Greek phrase is the word *kairo,* the Greek word for *times* or *seasons.* When all three of these words are used together in one phrase (*en panti kairo*) as in Ephesians 6:18, they could be more accurately translated *at each and every occasion.*

Ephesians 6:18 conveys this idea:

"Pray anytime there's an opportunity — no matter where you are or what you're doing. Use every occasion, every season, every possible moment to pray...."

This clearly tells us that prayer is not optional for the Christian who is serious about his or her spiritual life. According to this scripture, believers are to make prayer a top priority. Yet, unfortunately, prayer is largely disregarded by the average Christian today.

If prayer isn't a priority in your life right now, why not make it a priority starting today? You might say, *"But I don't have time to pray."* You have time to do whatever you really want to do. If it's truly in your heart to pray, you can find the time. And if your schedule is as busy as you think it is, take Ephesians 6:18 to heart. Grab any available time you can find, and make it your prayer time. Why not start this day out right? *Make a quality decision to make prayer your first order of business!*

MY PRAYER FOR TODAY

Lord, I ask You to help me become consistent in prayer. I admit that other things have distracted me from being in Your Presence, but I ask You to forgive me for this and to give me the strength to say no to those things that keep pulling me away from time in prayer. Thank You for helping me to make this a high priority in my life. I know that with Your help, I can learn to discipline myself to pray. Thank You for helping me get started on the right path today!

I pray this in Jesus' name!

MY CONFESSION FOR TODAY

With God's help, I have the power to say no to the distractions that keep trying to steal my time with God. Prayer is a top priority in my life; therefore, I am consistent and habitual in my prayer time. Nothing is a higher priority than the time I spend every day with God. From this moment onward, I will be as faithful as can be when it comes to this issue of prayer!

I declare this by faith in Jesus' name!

QUESTIONS FOR YOU TO CONSIDER

1. Have you been "on-again, off-again" in your prayer life? What keeps distracting you from being consistent in your prayer life?
2. What type of event in your life consistently jolts you out of prayerlessness and into a time of praying?
3. What changes do you need to make in your life or environment to assure that your prayer life becomes disciplined and consistent?

JANUARY 5

Do Not Grieve the Holy Spirit!

And grieve not the holy Spirit of God,
whereby ye are sealed unto the day of redemption.
— Ephesians 4:30

Many years ago, when I first studied the word "grieve" in Ephesians 4:30, I ran to my bookshelf and pulled out my Greek New Testament to discover exactly what the word "grieve" meant. I found that this word was taken from the Greek word *lupete*. This surprised me, because the word *lupete* is from the word *lupe*, which denotes a *pain* or *grief* that can only be experienced between two people who deeply love each other.

This word *lupe* would normally be used to picture a husband or wife who has discovered his or her mate has been unfaithful. As a result of this unfaithfulness, the betrayed spouse is *shocked, devastated, hurt, wounded,* and *grieved* because of the pain that accompanies unfaithfulness.

This tells us, first of all, that the relationship that exists between us and the Holy Spirit is precious! The Holy Spirit is deeply in love with us. Just as someone in love thinks about, dreams of, and cherishes the one he loves, the Holy Spirit longs for us, thinks about us, desires to be close to us, and wants to reveal Himself to us.

But when we act like the world, talk like the world, behave like the world, and respond the same way the world does, we cause the Spirit of God to feel shock, hurt, and grief. You see, when we deliberately do what is wrong, we drag Him right into the mire of sin with us, because He lives in us and goes wherever we go.

The Holy Spirit convicted us of sin and brought us to Jesus; then He indwelt us, sanctified us, empowered us, and faithfully remains alongside to help us. So when we deliberately enter into sin, it *grieves* Him. Just as a husband or wife would feel who has just discovered that his or her spouse has committed adultery, the Holy Spirit is *shocked* when we dishonor His Presence in our lives.

One scholar has translated Ephesians 4:30 in the following way:

"Stop deeply wounding and causing such extreme emotional pain to the Spirit of God, by whom you have been sealed until the day of your redemption."

We need to realize how precious the Holy Spirit is in our lives and honor Him by making sure we live holy and upright lives. If our behavior has been wrong, we should confess our sin and receive cleansing by the blood of Jesus so we can be restored to fellowship with the Spirit of God.

So before you get started with your daily duties today, stop and ask, *"Holy Spirit, is there anything in my life that causes You grief? If there is, please reveal it to me so I can change."*

MY PRAYER FOR TODAY

Lord, I ask You to forgive me for allowing attitudes and actions in my life that are dishonoring to You. I want to please You more than ever before, so I ask You to help me recognize those negative things in my life that cause You pain. Help me to permanently walk free of them. From the depths of my heart, I thank You for all You have done inside me. Starting right now, I want to live every moment of my life with the intent to please You and to never cause You grief again.

I pray this in Jesus' name!

MY CONFESSION FOR TODAY

Starting today, I make the choice to walk away from everything in my life that is displeasing and desecrating to the Holy Spirit's Presence within me. I walk away from every negative thought, word, and deed that has tried to operate in me and that is dishonoring to Him. I turn the other direction to walk a new walk and talk a new talk that shows respect and love for the Spirit of God who dwells inside me.

I declare this by faith in Jesus' name!

QUESTIONS FOR YOU TO CONSIDER

1. Are there any wrong attitudes or actions in your life that grieve the Holy Spirit? If so, write them down and then pray about them.

2. Are there any relationships in your life that have a negative effect on your relationship with the Lord?
3. For you to get right and stay right with God, what changes do you need to make in your life?

JANUARY 6

Dealing With Wrong Attitudes
The Right Way

Wherefore lay apart all filthiness and superfluity of naughtiness,
and receive with meekness the engrafted word, which is able to save your souls.
— James 1:21

Today I would like to draw your attention to the words "lay apart" in the verse above. These words are taken from the Greek word *apotithimi,* a compound of the words *apo* and *tithimi.* The word *apo* means *away,* and the word *tithimi* means *to place* or *to lay something down.* When these two words are compounded together, it gives a picture of someone who is *laying something down* at the same time he is *pushing it far away* from himself. Therefore, this compound word means *to lay something down and to push it far away and beyond reach.*

An example would be a person who is about to sinfully indulge in eating too much pie but suddenly realizes what he is doing. So instead of diving into the extra piece of pie and eating it, he chooses instead to lay it back down on the table; then he deliberately shoves it away from himself lest he should overindulge one time too many! He lays it down, and he pushes it away. This is the idea of the word *apotithimi* James uses when he tells us to "lay apart" all filthiness in our lives. But there is another very important meaning to this word in the New Testament!

In New Testament times, the word *apotithimi* was frequently used to describe someone taking off his dirty clothes at the end of the day. How do you deal with your dirty clothes at the end of the day? *You take them off and put them away in the clothes hamper!* Now James uses this illustration to explain how you must deal with wrong attitudes and actions in your own life. *Just as you wouldn't go to bed in dirty clothes at night, neither should you go to bed with wrong attitudes.* You must deal with them like an old set of filthy clothes. *You have to decide to get rid of those bad attitudes!*

James 1:21 could be interpreted to mean:

"You must make the choice to remove those filthy, stinking garments from your life, to permanently lay them down and then deliberately push them out of your range forever...."

Also, it's important to realize that dirty clothes don't fall off your body by accident! To get them off, you have to push the buttons through the button holes, unzip the zipper, and slip the clothes off your arms and legs one piece at a time. Dirty clothes don't automatically come off just because you realize they are dirty. They will only come off if you do something to remove them! This is *exactly* what James has in mind when he tells us to "lay apart" all filthiness from our lives.

When James says to "lay apart" all filthiness from our lives, he is telling us to first acknowledge what is wrong and then to take appropriate measures to remove those areas from our lives. If you are going to get free and stay free, it won't happen by accident. You must start taking steps to remove those negative things from your life — to lay them down and push them so far away that you'll never be able to reach them again!

Are you struggling with a sin today? Does a wrong attitude keep trying to conquer your life? If so, you must begin to look at that sin or wrong attitude like an old set of filthy clothes that isn't worthy for you to wear anymore. Make the decision to step out of every destructive area of your life that has held you captive. *Once you make that decision, the Holy Spirit will give you the power to carry it out!*

MY PRAYER FOR TODAY

Lord, help me step out of the sins and bad attitudes that have held me captive for so long. Help me know the right steps to take to remove these destructive and unworthy things from my life. You want me to be free, and I desire to be free. With Your help, I know I can be permanently set free from these negative things, stepping out of them and pushing them so far away that I will never pick them up again!

I pray this in Jesus' name!

MY CONFESSION FOR TODAY

The Word of God reveals those areas in my life that are unclean and that need to change. Rather than act like a victim who cannot do anything about myself or my circumstance, today I start the process of acknowledging my sin and removing these attitudes, actions, and sins that are unworthy of the new creation I am today in Christ. I can be free, and I will be free. I will be ALL that God intended for me to be!

I declare this by faith in Jesus' name!

QUESTIONS FOR YOU TO CONSIDER

1. Do you recognize wrong attitudes or patterns of behavior in your life that you know need to change?
2. Are you willing to make the necessary adjustments to walk free from the sins, attitudes, habits, and bondages that have been clinging to you?
3. If your answer is yes, what steps do you need to take to start walking toward your freedom?

Does a wrong attitude keep trying to conquer your life? If so, you must begin to look at that sin or wrong attitude like an old set of filthy clothes that isn't worthy for you to wear anymore.

JANUARY 7

❧⚶❧

How To Remedy Spiritual Boredom in Your Life!

But be ye doers of the word, and not hearers only,
deceiving your own selves.
— James 1:22

Do you ever get bored with church or with your spiritual life? If you say, "Yes, I get bored with my spiritual life all the time," I want to help you understand the root of that spiritual boredom.

There is one primary reason why people get spiritually bored. It is very simple: *Knowledge without application eventually becomes boring and unfulfilling — every time.*

If all you do is sit and listen, listen, and *listen* to the Word without ever taking steps to apply it to your life, you'll soon reach a place where you've heard, heard, and heard so much of the Word that you are sick of hearing it! Instead of anticipating what you might receive from the Lord, you'll think, *Oh, no, another sermon!*

But the problem isn't the Word! God's Word was meant to be acted on. So if you just sit and listen to more and more sermons, gathering more and more information but never acting on what you've heard, you'll eventually become so oversaturated that you won't want to hear any more!

If this describes you, it is likely that you are tired of hearing the same ol' Word over and over again. You probably wish someone would come along to preach or teach you something that you've never heard before. You might even find yourself roaming from church to church, seeking someone or something to spice up your spiritual life. However, the problem is not the church, your pastor, or the kind of preaching you are hearing. The problem is *you*!

You are bored because you're not doing the Word that you've heard preached. Let me tell you the truth: If you will simply do what you have already been told to do, you won't have time to be bored!

Applying the Word you already know will necessitate that you have a serious prayer life. It will require great discipline; it will demand that you learn to crucify your flesh. In fact, walking in the kind of obedience that God expects of you will take every ounce of your focus. You'll be so busy trying to obey what you've already heard preached that you'll never have a moment to be bored!

This is why James 1:22 tells us: "But be ye doers of the word, and not hearers only, deceiving your own selves." Notice especially the words "hearers only" in the verse above. These words are taken from the Greek word *akroates*, which was used in classical Greek times to describe *people who audited a class rather than taking it for credit.*

In other words, these people didn't attend the class to receive credit for the course. They were simply there to hear the lecture, think about what was taught, and then later discuss it with their friends. But they had no intention of actually applying what they heard!

In addition to being intellectually stimulating, these lectures could be quite entertaining. So these "hearers only" would roam from meeting to meeting because they loved special speakers and the excitement of hearing something they hadn't heard before. Sometimes they followed their favorite speakers from city to city.

Although the "hearers only" had no intention of applying anything they heard, they loved to gather new information that made them look knowledgeable in the eyes of other people. It was their delight to attend meetings in order to be with the crowd, to have a good laugh, or simply to hear something new. But they never put any action to what they heard, because they were "hearers only." They weren't listening to the messages they heard to get credit for it, but simply to have a good time!

This means James 1:22 conveys this idea:

"Don't be like those who attend meetings and listen to sermons for the sole purpose of being with the crowd or of gathering information that makes them look smart in other people's eyes...."

Since this is the background to the phrase "hearers only" used in James 1:22, we must take a good look at ourselves and ask:

✦ *Am I serious about the Word of God and its application in my life?*
✦ *Or am I simply an "auditor" who has no intention of doing the Word?*
✦ *Am I doing something with the Word I've heard preached, or am I among those who hear the Word but do not act on what they have heard?*
✦ *Does God consider me to be a hearer or a doer of the Word?*

The fact is, many people attend church regularly, go to special meetings, read books, listen to teaching tapes, and watch nonstop Christian television. They've seen a lot, heard a lot, and they really do know a lot — yet they do nothing with what they have heard. That's why they eventually become bored with spiritual matters. They haven't acted on what they've heard or put into practice the information they've gathered; therefore, they've become *oversaturated* and *spiritually numb*.

Don't let this happen to you. Make the decision to be a "doer of the Word and not a hearer only." Receive deep into your heart the truths you've heard preached over the years and let them begin to work in your life. You can be sure of this one thing: *If you determine to obey every scriptural truth that's ever been preached to you, you'll never have time to become spiritually bored again!*

MY PRAYER FOR TODAY

Lord, I ask You to help me become a doer of the Word and not a hearer only. Forgive me for the times I've heard the Word of God preached in power and even said "Amen" to the message, yet failed to walk out the truth I heard or to make it a part of my life. Starting today, I make the decision to be a doer of the Word of God. Holy Spirit, give me the strength and divine energy I need to take the Word I hear or read and put it into practice in my life!

I pray this in Jesus' name!

MY CONFESSION FOR TODAY

I declare that I am a doer of the Word of God. I am among those who hear the Word and immediately apply it to their lives. I experience the power of God's Spirit in my life because of my obedience to walk in what God has revealed to me.

I declare this by faith in Jesus' name!

1. *Be honest!* Have you been "spiritually bored" recently?
2. If Jesus were to ask you the reason for your boredom, what would you tell Him?
3. Make a list of steps you could take to eliminate spiritual boredom from your life.

JANUARY 8

It's Time for You To Act Fast!

And others save with fear....
— Jude 1:23

Have you ever known fellow believers who got caught up in sinful lifestyles that had the power to destroy their lives? How did it affect you when you saw them making those harmful decisions? I don't know about you, but I find it heartbreaking when I see someone I love doing things that are self-destructive and harmful to his or her walk with God. *Doesn't it affect you this same way?*

Jude tells us what our attitude should be toward fellow believers who get caught up in the world again. We must realize that these fellow believers are in grave danger of reaping the consequences of sin and that those consequences are very serious. Therefore, we must act *decisively* when we see this happen to someone we love.

In Jude 1:23, Jude tells us, "And others save with fear...." That word "save" is taken from the Greek word *sodzo*. In this particular verse, it is used in the present imperative tense, which means the Greek calls for *immediate, fast, and continuous action*. This is *not* a mild suggestion that Jude is making to his readers. This is a strong *command* to take action and to do it as *fast* as possible.

The word "fear" is from the Greek word *phobos*. In this particular case, it evokes *a fear* or *a strong dose of respect for something that is life-threatening, dangerous,* or *alarming.* Jude uses this word "fear" to let us know that believers who continue in sin place themselves in a very precarious, dangerous, and alarming situation. *This is no game.* Sin in the life of a believer is *extremely* serious. Therefore, Jude commands us to *act immediately* when we see a fellow brother or sister compromising his or her walk with the Lord.

With the full meaning of these Greek words,
Jude 1:23 could be translated:

"Because of the alarmingly dangerous state that some believers are in, I urge you to take immediate and fast-acting measures to see them delivered and rescued. And if they don't quickly respond, don't stop! You need to keep up your sense of urgency until you are convinced that they are rescued from this precarious situation...."

There is no doubt about it! This verse places a heavy *responsibility* on us to do whatever we can to bring this deceived person back to a place of safety. Jude speaks in a commanding tone of voice to let us know that we don't have a choice in this matter. We must *act fast, act deliberately,* and be *continuous* and *unending* in our efforts until we are certain that these straying brothers and sisters are back in safe territory again.

So if you know a friend or loved one who is allowing serious sin to continue in his life, pray for him. Then go to him and express your concerns in love. Love that person enough to speak the truth to him. Act fast on his behalf, and do what you can to save him. Otherwise, he may eventually make mistakes that will bring disaster and destruction upon his life.

That's why Jude commands us to take action right now. *The possible consequences are too serious to ignore. We must do everything within our power to save and rescue believers caught in the snare of sin as quickly as possible.*

MY PRAYER FOR TODAY

Lord, help me know exactly what to say and what to do when I see fellow brothers or sisters who are headed in a wrong spiritual direction. Give me Your heart, Your wisdom, and Your boldness to speak the words I need to speak. Help me love them enough to speak the truth to them. I realize the consequences of sin are great, so please help me do everything within my ability to see them rescued as soon as possible.

I pray this in Jesus' name!

MY CONFESSION FOR TODAY

I confess that I am moved to action when I see fellow believers caught in sin. I pray and believe for their deliverance. I go to them in love to express my concerns to them. I love them enough to speak the truth. I act fast on their behalf and do what I can to save them.

I declare this by faith in Jesus' name!

QUESTIONS FOR YOU TO CONSIDER

1. Are there people in your life who are headed in a wrong spiritual direction? Who are those people? Have you spent time in prayer asking God for a real "turnaround" in their lives?
2. Have you taken the time to go to them so you can express your concerns? Or have you asked the Lord to give you ideas of how you can approach them in a non-threatening way so they will listen to you instead of tuning you out?
3. If you were in their situation, wouldn't you want someone to care enough that they would come to you to express their concerns? If this is what you would hope others would do for you, don't you think it is the least that you can do for someone else?

Sin in the life of a believer is *extremely* serious. Therefore, Jude commands us to *act immediately* when we see a fellow brother or sister compromising his or her walk with the Lord.

JANUARY 9

❦

Have You Said 'Thank You' Today?

[I] cease not to give thanks for you,
making mention of you in my prayers.
— Ephesians 1:16

When was the last time you gave thanks from your heart for the loved ones God has placed in your life? The phrase "give thanks" in Ephesians 1:16 comes from the Greek word *eucharisteo*, a compound of the words *eu* and *charis*. The word *eu* means *good* or *well*. It denotes a general *good disposition* or *an overwhelmingly good feeling* about something. The word *charis* is the Greek word for *grace* or *freely granted favor*.

When these two words are compounded into one, they form the word *eucharisteo*. This compound word describes *an outpouring of grace and of wonderful feelings that freely flow from the heart in response to someone or something*. This is the word Paul used when he "gave thanks" for the Ephesian church. In fact, in nearly all his epistles, Paul used *eucharisteo* when he "gave thanks" for people he loved.

For instance, Paul used this word in Ephesians 1:16 when he said, "[I] cease not to give thanks for you…." This means that when Paul thought of the Ephesian church, wonderful feelings of thankfulness would well up in his heart for them.

The Greek carries this idea in Ephesians 1:16:

"Thanking God for you is so easy — it just flows out of my heart every time I think of you. In fact, I never take a break from letting God know how I feel about you."

In Colossians 1:3, Paul uses the same Greek word when he says, "We *give thanks* to God and the Father of our Lord Jesus Christ, praying always for you." In First Thessalonians 1:2, he again uses the same Greek word when he prays similarly for the Thessalonian believers: "We *give thanks* to God always for you all, making mention of you in our prayers." In Second Thessalonians 1:3, he uses this word again when he writes, "We are bound to *thank God* always for you…."

The fact that Paul used the word *eucharisteo* when he prayed for his dearest friends reminds us that we must be thankful for the relationships God has put in our lives. Whenever we think of our closest circle of friends, a deep sense of gratefulness, thankfulness, and appreciation should well up within us!

So when you're praying for others, stop for a moment and reflect on all God has done in your life through those who are closest to you. *When you realize how valuable those relationships have been to you, you'll be able to freely, joyfully, and unreservedly thank God for such precious friends!*

MY PRAYER FOR TODAY

Lord, You have blessed me with the most wonderful friends — and today I want to thank You for putting such great people in my life. Long-term, real friends are such a treasure, so I want to start this day by thanking You for these gifts of precious relationships. Help me never lose sight of how much I need these people. Help me also to never fail to show them how much I love and appreciate them!

I pray this in Jesus' name!

I am thankful for the relationships God has placed in my life. They are a blessing to me, and I am a blessing to them. God brought us together, and Satan will not tear us apart. I will learn to love them more dearly, forgive them more quickly, and show them the same patience I want them to show me. I am richly blessed with some of the best friends I could ever ask for!

I declare this by faith in Jesus' name!

QUESTIONS FOR YOU TO CONSIDER

1. How long has it been since you stopped to thank God for the people He has placed in your life?
2. When you pray, do you focus only on the "problem people" who bother you and steal your peace, or do you always make certain to take the time to thank God for the faithful ones?
3. Write down a list of all the people God has specially used to help you in life. Then stop to tell the Lord how grateful you are that He sent each one of them into your life.

JANUARY 10

Learning To 'Follow the Leader'

For as many as are led by the Spirit of God,
they are the sons of God.
— Romans 8:14

When I was a small boy, my siblings and I used to play a game called "Follow the Leader." I always wanted to be the leader, but my older sister always claimed that coveted leadership role. As leader, she had the right to tell us what to do, what games we would or would not play, who would clean the house, who would take out the trash, who would vacuum the carpets, and so on. No wonder my older sister always wanted to be the leader!

I always think of this when I read Romans 8:14. It says, "For as many as are led by the Spirit of God, they are the sons of God." In Greek, the sentence structure is reversed so that it reads, *"For as many as by the Spirit are being led, they are the sons of God."* This version puts the Holy Spirit at the first of the verse, and we are placed behind Him — just as children stay behind the leader as they play "Follow the Leader"!

The Greek word for "led" is the word *ago,* which simply means *to lead.* It was often used to depict animals that were led by a rope tied around their necks. Once tied to that rope, these animals willfully followed wherever their owner *led* them.

How interesting that Paul used this word! It tells us that we should be willing to let the Holy Spirit lead us in every part of our lives. We should be so surrendered to Him that wherever He tells us to go or whatever He tells us to do, we should simply be obedient and follow.

However, it must also be pointed out that this word *ago* is also the root for the Greek word *agon,* which is where we get the word *agony.* Even in Greek, the word *agon* describes *an intense conflict, such as a struggle in a wrestling match or a struggle of the human will.* This illustrates the fact that although the Holy Spirit wants to lead us, our human will doesn't like the idea of being led. You see, it's the nature of the flesh to want to go its own way, so when we choose to walk in the Spirit and let Him dictate our lives, His leadership over us creates a struggle between our will and our flesh.

Just for a moment, think of how many times a child is tempted to rebel against his parents. Or consider the many times our flesh has rebelled against exercise or a diet that we've imposed on ourselves. There's no doubt about it — the human will and the flesh are strong. These parts of us have a very difficult time surrendering control to someone else — and that includes being *led* by the Holy Spirit!

When I was a child and we played "Follow the Leader," I didn't like being led by my sister and being told what to do. I wanted to be in charge myself so I could call the shots as I saw them! Maybe that's how you've been feeling about your own life. But as a child of God, you have to learn to stay in your place — behind the Holy Spirit, following His lead.

Romans 8:14 really means:

"Those who follow the leadership of the Holy Spirit, they are the sons of God."

**However, because the word *agonidzo* is used,
Romans 8:14 also carries this idea:**

"Following the leadership of the Holy Spirit is one of the privileges of being a son of God, although it may be agonizing to learn how to defer to Him and to really let Him be your Leader."

If you want to learn to live a Spirit-led life, there is no way around it — you have to deal with your flesh. The flesh wants control, so you must mortify or defeat the flesh and allow the Holy Spirit to have His way. The struggle may seem great, but it's the only way to live a supernatural Christian life!

Make it your goal to learn how to discern the Holy Spirit's leading. Become His constant "tag-along," watching to see what He's doing, where He's going, and how He's leading. Stay sensitive to Him so you can pick up His "nudge" in your heart. *Then once you know what He wants you to do, just fall in step behind Him and "follow the Leader"!*

MY PRAYER FOR TODAY

Lord, I want to learn how to follow the leading of the Holy Spirit. I know that You sent Him to be a Leader and a Guide for my life, so today I open my heart to Him. I ask You to help me learn to recognize the Holy Spirit's voice and to know what He is leading me to do. With all my heart, I request that You help me become sensitive to Him so that He can lead me in all the paths You have designed for my life.

I pray this in Jesus' name!

QUESTIONS FOR YOU TO CONSIDER

1. Can you recall times in the past when you *emphatically* knew that the Holy Spirit was supernaturally leading you to do something?
2. What were you doing at that time in your spiritual life that made it easier for you to recognize and follow the leading of the Holy Spirit?
3. In order for you to be consistently led by the Holy Spirit, what actions do you need to take to keep yourself sensitive enough to hear His voice and to discern His leading?

JANUARY 11

When Your Attitude Stinks So Badly That It Affects Everyone Around You!

Wherefore lay apart all filthiness and superfluity of naughtiness,
and receive with meekness the engrafted word,
which is able to save your souls.
— James 1:21

Today I want to speak to you from James 1:21. I want you to particularly look at the words "filthiness and superfluity of naughtiness." Since James tells us that we must remove and discard from our lives whatever is meant by these two concepts, it is *imperative* that we understand *exactly* what he is talking about.

The Greek word for "filthiness" is the word *raparian*. This Greek word describes filth that is *obnoxiously filthy*. The man pictured in James 2:2 is described in this same way. In this verse, James described two categories of people who attended the Early Church — those who were nice in appearance and those who were filthy dirty. About these categories, James wrote, "For if there come unto your assembly a man with a gold ring, and in goodly apparel, and there come also a man in vile raiment."

That word *vile* at the end of this verse and the word *filthiness* in James 1:21 come from the same Greek word. In James 2:2, the Greek word *raparian* portrays a man whose body and clothes are so encrusted with filth that he emits a disgusting odor to everyone nearby. Have you ever smelled a person who stank that badly? Take just one whiff of that kind of stench, and you'll never want to smell it again!

This is the same Greek word James uses in James 1:21 when he describes believers who have bad attitudes! In other words, when a believer is being pessimistic, downbeat, negative, uncooperative, gloomy, cynical, or indifferent, it just flat stinks! *Whew!* Nothing stinks worse than an attitude of a grumpy and pessimistic person. In fact, a person with a bad attitude emits such a distasteful aroma that it will literally drive people away from him! This person has to make the decision to "lay apart all filthiness" — which in this case is not referring to dirty clothes, but the stinking and repulsive attitudes he carries in his life.

**Because James uses the word *raparian* in James 1:21,
the verse could be translated:**

"In light of what I've told you, it's time for you to remove those stinking, foul-smelling, putrid, rank garments...."

When my wife and I were young in the ministry, a man attended our church who never learned proper hygiene when he was growing up. His hair was dirty; his face was unshaved; his skin was encrusted with dirt; and his clothes smelled like something had died in them.

Because we loved this man, we decided to take him into our home to teach him hygiene. We grabbed our noses, held our breath, and took him to our house so he could get cleaned up. I coaxed him into the shower, and afterwards he came out looking nice and clean. But then he reached over, picked up his same old, dirty clothes, and put them back on again!

As I watched this newly cleaned man put on his filthy clothes, I thought, *That's just what a lot of Christians do!* Jesus' blood washes and cleanses us, and God gives us a new robe of righteousness. But many people were reared in negative, faithless environments and were never taught God's Word. These Christians have walked in these negative attitudes for so long that it has become a part of their thinking. Yes, Jesus has washed and cleansed them by His blood and showered them with His grace and power. But those wrong attitudes have been a part of their lives for so long that they are still tempted to reach down, pick them up again, put them on, snap them back in place, and keep acting the same old way they did before they were saved.

These people are inwardly changed, but their old thinking patterns have become a bad habit. Therefore, they still wear those old, filthy attitudes, even though those negative attitudes are no longer consistent with the clean, new condition of their inner man.

For people who fit this description, it will take a strong act of determination for them to stay free of those old encumbrances. That's why it's so important to understand the words "lay apart" (*see* January 6). In Greek, these words describe someone *deliberately laying down* wrong attitudes and then pushing them *so far out of range* that he isn't able to reach down to pick them up again.

Before you get too busy today, why don't you take a few minutes to ask the Holy Spirit to show you if there are any stinking attitudes from the past that you're still carrying around in your life? *I guarantee you that He will reveal them to you — and then He will give you the power to remove these foul-smelling, negative attitudes from your life!*

MY PRAYER FOR TODAY

Lord, I thank You for washing me with the blood of Jesus and for making me brand new. Forgive me for clinging to my old ways of thinking and of doing things. Today I ask You to help me drop those old habits and attitudes and to never pick them up again. By myself, this would be almost impossible, but I know that by Your power, I can walk free. Right now, I release those old attitudes and habits that I've been carrying around with me for so long. I ask You to help me think and behave in a way that's consistent with the new creature in Jesus Christ You have made me to be!

I pray this in Jesus' name!

I declare by faith that I am free from wrong habits and attitudes from my past. I have laid them down, and I am free of them forever. Now I have the mind of Christ, the power of the Spirit, and the fruit of Jesus Christ working inside my life.

I declare this by faith in Jesus' name!

QUESTIONS FOR YOU TO CONSIDER

1. What attitudes have you been harboring that are repulsive or offensive to God and that you know need to change? Make a list so you can pray about these wrong attitudes.
2. What do you need to do to drop those foul-smelling attitudes from your life?
3. Is there a person you need to forgive or a past situation you need to forget in order to really be free? Be honest with yourself as you search your heart.

JANUARY 12

A Unique Receptacle
Specially Made for the Power of God!

Finally, my brethren, be strong in the Lord,
and in the power of his might.
— Ephesians 6:10

*C*ould you use some extra strength today? I want to draw your attention to the word "strong" in Ephesians 6:10. It is the Greek word *endunamao,* a compound of the words *en* and *dunamis.* The word *en* means *in.* The word *dunamis* means *explosive strength, ability,* and *power.* It's where we get the word *dynamite.*

Thus, this word *endunamao* presents the picture of an *explosive power that is being deposited into some type of container, vessel, or other form of receptacle.* The very nature of this word *endunamao* means that there necessarily must be some type of *receiver* for this power to be deposited *into.*

This is where we come into the picture! We are specially designed by God to be the receptacles of divine power. When Paul tells us to be strong in the Lord, he is essentially saying, "Receive a supernatural, strengthening, internal deposit of power into your inner man." God is the Giver, and we are the *receptacles* into which this power is to be deposited.

Paul knew you and I would desperately need supernatural power in order to successfully combat the attacks the enemy would bring against us. That's why he urges us to open our spirits, souls, and bodies to God so we can receive this supernatural strength.

Ephesians 6:10 could be translated to mean:

"...Be infused with supernatural strength and ability...."
"...Be empowered with this special touch of God's strength...."
"...Receive this inner strengthening...."

God wants you and me to have this supernatural strength and ability! We are the special receptacles or containers He created to possess this phenomenal power. Think of how wonderful it is that God specially fashioned you and me to be the containers for the power of God!

So if you're feeling a need for extra strength today, open your heart right now and allow God to give you a fresh infilling of His explosive, Holy Spirit power!

MY PRAYER FOR TODAY

Lord, it is clear that You want me to be filled with Your power and strength today, so I open my heart right now and ask You to fill me with Your Spirit. Thank You for creating me to be the receptacle for this wonderful power — and by faith, I receive a fresh infilling of Your Spirit right now!

I pray this in Jesus' name!

MY CONFESSION FOR TODAY

I declare by faith that I am filled with the Spirit of God. I am specially made by God to be the container of the Holy Spirit. He lives in me; He fills me; and He empowers me to conquer every attack that the devil tries to bring against me. God knew I needed this power and therefore gave it to me. I boldly confess that I am FILLED with the supernatural, wonderworking, and dynamic power of the Holy Spirit!

I declare this by faith in Jesus' name!

QUESTIONS FOR YOU TO CONSIDER

1. Do you feel a need for more strength and power in your life today?
2. Have you asked the Lord to refill you with the power of the Holy Spirit? Why don't you take a few minutes right now to open your heart and let the Lord fill you with a new surge of divine power?
3. What steps can you take today to avail yourself to a special touch of the Holy Spirit's strength?

We are the special receptacles or containers God created to possess this phenomenal power. Just think of it! He specially fashioned you and me to be the containers for His divine power.

JANUARY 13

❧

Where Should You Go When You Get Discouraged?

Not forsaking the assembling of ourselves together,
as the manner of some is....
— Hebrews 10:25

*P*eople tend to skip church and stay away from other believers when they get discouraged. Maybe you know someone who has done this. Maybe you've even done it yourself at a time in your life when you felt discouraged or depressed.

There are a myriad of reasons why people stay away from church when they are discouraged. Perhaps they're embarrassed that their faith isn't working as fast as they think it should. Perhaps they're ashamed that they're still struggling with problems they think should have been conquered long ago. They don't want anyone to know they're still wrestling with the same old problems, so they disappear from sight.

Don't let embarrassment or discouragement keep you away from other believers. You need their strength! You need their testimony! You need their encouragement! You need to hear them say, *"You can do it! You can make it!"*

That's why Hebrews 10:25 says, "Not forsaking the assembling of ourselves together, as the manner of some is...." The word "forsaking" is taken from the Greek word *egkatakeipontes*. It's a compound of three different Greek words: *eg, kata,* and *leipo.* The first word, *eg* (actually from the Greek word *ek*), means *out. Kata,* the second part of the word, means *down.* The third word, *leipo,* means *behind.* These three words compounded together simply mean *out, down, and behind.*

These words describe *someone who is extremely discouraged, defeated, and depressed.* Maybe he feels depressed because it looks like everyone is succeeding but him. Or maybe this is someone who is simply weary from fighting a very long battle. Regardless of the reason why, this word describes a person who feels *left out, down, depressed, and far behind everyone else.*

The moment people begin to feel like they are failing or falling short of everyone else is often the moment when Satan tells them, *"Oh, just stay home from church today. You don't need to go down there with all those rejoicing people. You know that you don't feel like being with them today, so why not just stay home by yourself? You don't need them. You can just read the Bible at home!"*

Satan knows that if he can get you to fall out of fellowship with other believers — *at the very moment when you need fellowship and encouragement the most* — then he can probably keep you down and defeated. Yes, it's true that you can read the Bible at home by yourself, and you need to do this. But fellowship with other believers is essential for everyone, and that includes you! You receive encouragement from other believers that you can't get anywhere else.

That is why church is the last place the devil wants you to go when you're feeling low! He knows if you go to church, you will be touched by the Presence of the Lord; you will get encouraged by other believers; and in the end, you'll crawl out of that hole the enemy has put you in and rise up to a place of heavenly victory!

The devil works overtime to try to tempt you to skip church, stay home, and do something else instead. *But, friend, why isolate yourself when you are in the greatest need of encouragement?*

Hebrews 10:25 could be translated:

"When you're feeling down and depressed — like a failure who is falling behind everyone else — that isn't the time to stay away from other believers, as some are in the habit of doing...."

Instead of letting the devil and your flesh get the best of you in moments of weakness, here's my suggestion: *In addition to praying and reading the Word at home when you're feeling down and out, go find another believer or a group of believers who can build you up in faith and encourage you in the Lord.* After fellowshiping with people of faith, you'll feel recharged to go back and face those challenges with a winning attitude!

MY PRAYER FOR TODAY

Lord, I ask You to help me push my flesh and my feelings aside when I am tempted to be down and depressed. Your Word promises that I'll be encouraged if I fellowship with the saints, so I ask You to help me shove my lying emotions out of the way, get out of my house, and stop focusing on my defeat. Give me the strength of will to go attach myself to a band of believers who will encourage me to stand up, stand tall, and fight like someone who has the armor and the power of God working in my life!

I pray this in Jesus' name!

MY CONFESSION FOR TODAY

I declare that Satan does not have the power to keep me down and depressed! When life comes against me and the devil tries to tell me that I have no hope of ever getting out of my problems, I run to people of faith so I can get encouraged! I don't fall out of fellowship, and I don't stay away from church. I am faithful in my church attendance, and I receive encouragement every time I get in God's Presence and rub shoulders with the people of God!

I declare this by faith in Jesus' name!

QUESTIONS FOR YOU TO CONSIDER

1. When you get discouraged, where do you go for help, strength, and encouragement?
2. Has the devil successfully tempted you to stay away from other believers?
3. How can you get more involved with a faith community that can give you needed encouragement to help you win the battles you've been waging?

Satan knows that if he can get you to fall out of fellowship with other believers — *at the very moment when you need fellowship and encouragement the most* — then he can probably keep you down and defeated.

JANUARY 14

Preparing the Troops
For Battle!

Not forsaking the assembling of ourselves together, as the manner of some is;
but exhorting one another....
— Hebrews 10:25

Tthe word "exhorting" is a powerful little word! It's the Greek word *parakaleo*, a compound of the words *para* and *kaleo*. *Para* means *alongside* and *kaleo* means *to call, to beckon*, or *to speak to someone*. When these two words are compounded together, it depicts *someone who is right alongside of a person, urging him, beseeching him, begging him to make some kind of correct decision.*

In the ancient Greek world, this word was often used by military leaders before they sent their troops into battle. Rather than hide from the painful reality of war, the leaders would summon their troops together and speak straightforwardly with them about the potential dangers of the battlefield. The leaders would also tell their troops about the glories of winning a major victory.

Rather than ignore the clear-cut dangers of battle, these officers came right alongside their troops and urged, exhorted, beseeched, begged, and pleaded with them *to stand tall; throw their shoulders back; look the enemy straight on, eyeball to eyeball; and face their battles bravely.*

Walking by faith and doing the will of God sometimes places us in the midst of spiritual battles. Sometimes these battles aren't won quickly.

If you know someone who is discouraged because his fight isn't won yet, speak to that person truthfully and in a straightforward manner the way a commanding officer would speak to his troops. Remind the person of others who have stood the test of time and won their battles. And be sure to remind him of the sweetness of victory when the battle is over. He needs to hear a passionate, heartfelt word of exhortation from you!

The word "exhort" in Hebrews 10:25 could mean:

"When you're feeling down and out — like a failure who is falling behind everyone else — that isn't the time for you to stay away from other believers, as some are in the habit of doing. That is the very time that you need to come together for the sake of encouragement so you can face your battles more bravely...."

Do you know people who need some encouragement today? Instead of letting the day slip by before you know it, why not take the time *right now* to call those individuals and encourage them? If you can't call them, how about *writing them a note* that will help them focus on victory?

Think back to all those moments in your own life when someone came alongside of you to encourage you. Didn't it make a big difference in your life? Now it's your turn to return this blessing to someone else.

So determine today to be a real comrade in the Lord to another Christian soldier. Make it your aim to speak words of encouragement to those around you today. *If you see someone who is discouraged, or if you know someone who has been struggling in his or her faith, go out of your way to encourage the troops!*

MY PRAYER FOR TODAY

Lord, today I want to be used by You to encourage someone! I ask You to lead me to those You want me to encourage. Show me what to say, how much to say, and when to say it. Teach me to recognize the needs in other people and not to focus only on my own needs.

I pray this in Jesus' name!

MY CONFESSION FOR TODAY

I confess that I am going to be a major blessing in someone's life today. The Holy Spirit is going to open my eyes and show me exactly whom I am supposed to encourage. With the help of the Spirit, I will speak the right words at the right time, and I will say only as much as I need to say. When this day concludes, someone will thank God for the way I stepped into his or her life to be a source of encouragement!

I declare this by faith in Jesus' name!

QUESTIONS FOR YOU TO CONSIDER

1. Have you been so focused on your own challenges that you've failed to recognize the needs of others who are around you?
2. Can you think of some people in your life who need encouragement and extra strength today?
3. Can you make a list of practical ways you can reach out to encourage these individuals and let them know you are thinking of them today?

JANUARY 15

It's Time To Get Creative In 'Doing the Word'

But be ye doers of the word, and not hearers only,
deceiving your own selves.
— James 1:22

*L*et's talk about what James meant when he said, "But be ye doers of the word...." The word "doers" is taken from the Greek word *poietes,* the same Greek word used for *a poet.* This word carries with it the idea of *creativity,* such as a poet whose personality includes a creative flair. James is telling us that if we can't easily think of a way to *do* what has been preached to us, we must get creative! We must find ways to *do* the Word.

Ephesians 2:10 is another place where a form of this word *poietes* is used. Paul writes, "For we are his *workmanship*, created in Christ Jesus unto good works...." The word "workmanship" is the Greek word *poiema*, which comes from the same root word as *poietes*.

This tells us that when we were saved, God put forth all His best efforts and creative powers to marvelously fashion and create us in Jesus Christ. Because the word *poiema* is used in Ephesians 2:10, it unmistakably means that God wielded His fullest, greatest, and most creative powers when we were born again. We weren't just mildly saved; rather, God took us into His hands and marvelously made us new in Jesus Christ as He released His most powerful creative forces and made us a workmanship that would be worthy to bear His name.

Whether the word *poietes* is used to depict a poet, as mentioned above, or (in another form) to describe God's creative power, as in Ephesians 2:10, it always depicts someone *putting forth his fullest creative abilities to achieve something.* Now James uses this word *poietes* in James 1:22 to tell us that we must put forth our fullest efforts and most creative abilities in doing what we have heard preached! We cannot passively hope that the Word becomes a part of our lives; we have to get *creative* and find ways to make the Word a practical part of our lives.

Thus, you could translate these words in James 1:22 to mean:

"If you can't easily think of ways to do what you've heard preached, it's time for you to get creative! Put all your heart and soul into finding a way to act on what you've heard...."

You could also translate it to read:

"It's time for you to get creative in the ways you do the Word of God...."

It could be that you're thinking, *But I don't know how to do what has been preached to me!*

Don't worry — the Lord isn't short on *creativity*! If you will listen, the Holy Spirit will say, "Here's an opportunity to apply what you've been hearing. Do it!" If you have a heart to truly act on the Word of God, the Holy Spirit will show you ways to do it.

Seek the Lord and allow Him to show you how:

✦ To pray for the sick.
✦ To share Jesus with your lost friends.
✦ To bake a cake and take it to the lady next door.
✦ To help your neighbor repair his car.

Spiritual maturity isn't measured by the number of meetings you've attended, how many speakers you've heard, how many books you've read, or how many tapes you've listened to in the past year. You have to take that Word you've heard and find a way to make it work in your life. God is looking for people who actually do what they've heard preached!

So if you can't seem to think of practical ways to apply the Word to your life, ask the Holy Spirit to help you. Here's one thing you can be sure of: *The Holy Spirit is never short on ideas about how you can become a "doer" of the Word!*

MY PRAYER FOR TODAY

Lord, I ask You to help me think of new ways to do the Word of God. You have all the fresh ideas I'll ever need, so I am looking to You to show me how to put the Word into practice in my life. You are full of creative power and fresh ideas, so please open my eyes and show me how I can serve, how I can bless someone else, or any other way I can become obedient to do the Word that has been revealed so powerfully to my life.

I pray this in Jesus' name!

I declare that I never run short of ideas on how to walk out the Word that has been preached to me. I do what I've heard; I obey what I've read; and I get better and better every day at finding ways to put into operation the Word that God has so graciously brought into my life.

I declare this by faith in Jesus' name!

QUESTIONS FOR YOU TO CONSIDER

1. Have you asked the Holy Spirit to show you creative ideas for applying the Word to your life?
2. Can you think of specific people you could be serving and sharing the love of Jesus with? For instance, could you share Jesus with your lost friends, bake a cake for the lady next door, or help your neighbor repair his car?
3. What other ways can you become a "doer" of the Word that has been preached to you?

JANUARY 16

Have You Paid Attention To Yourself Lately?

Take heed unto thyself....
— 1 Timothy 4:16

*A*re you constantly serving others without giving yourself needed times of rest and refreshing? Or do you remember that you have spiritual needs too?*

When Paul wrote First Timothy 4:16, Timothy was a young pastor working ferociously to see his ministry succeed. Timothy was serving as the pastor of the giant church of Ephesus — the world's largest church at that time. In the process, he was learning to deal with all the problems that go along with serving as the senior pastor of such a large church.

Timothy was discovering that taking care of a large church was an all-consuming task. He was giving every ounce of himself to serve the needs of that church and to make sure it was well taken care of. In fact, he was so busy taking care of everything and everyone else that he was forgetting to take care of himself!

Have you ever been guilty of running around and taking care of everyone else except yourself? Have you ever gotten so busy helping others that you forfeited your own vital time with God? *Be honest!* Have you ever done this so regularly that you began to feel drained, and you knew it was because you weren't taking care of your own spiritual needs?

That's why Paul admonished Timothy, "Take heed unto thyself...." This phrase "take heed" comes from the Greek word *epecho,* which is a compound of the words *ep* and *echo.* The word *ep* means *on,* and the word *echo* means *to have* or *to hold.* When these two words are compounded into one word, it means *to grab hold of something very tightly.* In other words, the word *epecho* describes *an extremely firm grip.*

It's so easy to get distracted by other things that scream for your attention. However, if your relationship with God suffers because you are trying to help everyone else, it will just be a matter of time until you run dry, lose your energy and passion, and have nothing more to offer. This is exactly what was happening to Timothy! If he was to continue serving as an effective minister to other people, he had to set aside some private time to develop his own relationship with God.

Paul's words to Timothy could be translated:

"Get ahold of yourself...."
"Make your own spiritual life a priority...."
"Don't get so busy that you forget you have spiritual needs too...."

It's good to serve the Lord and to be willing to work. You should be faithful at whatever He has called you to do. But you should never get so busy that you forget your own spiritual needs and thus end up running dry of spiritual power. Take Paul's words to heart. Never forget to *"take heed unto thyself"*!

If you are going to serve God and do His will for years to come, it is essential that you make your own spiritual life your first priority. After all, you can only give what you have inside you. If you run dry because you never spend time with the Lord, it won't be long until you have nothing left to give to anyone!

So if you wish to continue being effective for God's Kingdom, it is mandatory that you don't forget about your own spiritual need to grow and to be refreshed by the Word. As Paul's words could be understood, *"Don't get so busy that you forget you have spiritual needs too!"*

MY PRAYER FOR TODAY

Lord, help me remember not to neglect my own spiritual life. My time with You is vital if I am to remain spiritually fresh and empowered to serve others. When life gets so busy that I think there is no time to spend with You, help me refocus and reschedule my life so that my relationship with You remains my greatest priority. And after I've been refreshed by Your Word and Your Presence, help me then to minister the fullness of Your Spirit and Your love to those around me.

I pray this in Jesus' name!

MY CONFESSION FOR TODAY

I boldly proclaim by faith that my spiritual life is my number-one priority. I pay attention to my walk with God, and I do everything I can do to make sure my spiritual life is alive, growing, and constantly reaching out for more of the Lord. I am sensitive to God's Spirit. I am attuned to His Word. As a result of putting my own spiritual life first, I am filled with enough power and love to adequately serve the needs of those who are around me.

I declare this by faith in Jesus' name!

QUESTIONS FOR YOU TO CONSIDER

1. How much time do you personally spend alone with God every day?
2. Have you gotten so busy serving the Lord that you have neglected your own walk with Him? If so, write down any problems you may be facing in different areas of your life because of this neglect.
3. What steps do you need to take to reverse this situation and refocus on your relationship with Jesus?

JANUARY 17

What Should You Do When Your Plans Seem Hindered?

Wherefore we would have come unto you,
even I Paul, once and again; but Satan hindered us.
— 1 Thessalonians 2:18

Have you ever pursued something that you believed was God's will, yet obstacles seemed to keep you from doing what you thought you were supposed to do? If you have, don't feel alone, because many people have been in that same position! Even the apostle Paul felt this way from time to time! *But what should you do in times like these?*

Today I want you to particularly notice the word "hindered" in the verse above. It comes from the Greek word *egkopto,* an old word that was originally used to describe *a road so deteriorated and broken up that it was impassable.*

Have you ever driven down a road on your way to your destination, only to discover that the road you're driving on is too full of ruts and holes to continue your journey? As a result, you have to turn around, go back, and find another route to get where you are going. Well, that is exactly the image the word *egkopto* portrays to us!

Paul uses this word to describe hindering forces that kept him from going to see the Thessalonians. There is no doubt that this means Paul was on his way to see them — not once, he says, but twice. But the journey became so filled with danger and unexpected bumps that Paul had to turn around, go back, and rethink his strategy on how he was going to get to the church at Thessalonica. Can you think of a time when you encountered something like this in your own journey?

But the word *egkopto* means even more than this! It was also used in Greek times in an *athletic* sense. It was used to portray the moment when *a runner comes alongside another runner and literally elbows him out of the race.* Although the second runner was running a good race, *he is shoved out of the way* by the aggression of his fellow runner. As a result of this action, the runner who was elbowed loses the leading edge he previously held.

This categorically means that Paul understood Satan's tactics. The enemy had tried to make use of dangerous and unexpected bumps along the way to throw Paul off track and to elbow him out of his spiritual race. In fact, Paul was convinced that Satan had specifically engineered these unforeseen and unanticipated hassles to keep him from getting to the Thessalonian church.

When these two ideas are combined together, the primary idea of the word "hindered" becomes that of *an impasse so severe that it prohibits you from going where you need to go* or *an aggressor who unkindly elbows you off course in your spiritual race.*

Paul is actually saying:

"...Satan created an impasse that kept me from coming to see you."
"...Satan put obstructions in my path to prevent me from getting to you."
"...Satan cut in on me and prohibited me from visiting you as I wanted to do."
"...Satan tried to elbow his way in on me to keep me from coming to see you."

When something happens that seems to prohibit you from doing the will of God, remember that you are not the first to encounter such difficulties. Others have been in the same quandary. In time, however, the devil's attack ceased, and the way for them to move ahead became clear. In the same way, you can be sure that God is going to empower you and give you the wisdom you need to get where you need to go!

Don't despair — the story isn't over yet! Don't throw in the towel and give in just because you've hit some kind of impasse. The devil has never had the last word on anything, and he isn't going to have the last word on this situation either. *Regardless of what the devil has tried to do, it's time for you to remember that what God promised SHALL come to pass as you hold fast to your faith in Him!*

MY PRAYER FOR TODAY

Lord, I've run into an impasse, and I don't know how to get past it by myself. I have done everything I know to do, but the problem continues to persist in my life. Today I am asking You for the strength I need to keep pushing forward and to overcome the obstacles that Satan has set in my path. I know that greater is He who is in me than he that is in the world, so today I fervently ask that the power of God residing within me be released to overcome each attack the devil has tried to bring against me.

I pray this in Jesus' name!

MY CONFESSION FOR TODAY

I know I am not the first to encounter difficulties. Therefore, I confess that with God's help, the devil's attack will cease and the way for me to move ahead will become clear. God is going to give me the exact wisdom I need to get where I need to go! I am not going to give in just because I've hit some kind of impasse. The devil has never had the last word on anything, and he isn't going to have the last word on this situation either!

I declare this by faith in Jesus' name!

QUESTIONS FOR YOU TO CONSIDER

1. Can you think of times in your life when you've experienced impasses that eventually moved out of the way?
2. What actions did you take that caused those devilish assaults and roadblocks to dissipate?
3. Have you asked the Holy Spirit to show you the real root cause of any current impasse you're facing, as well as the steps you can take to close the door to the devil and reverse your situation?

JANUARY 18

*The Dead-End Places
Of Life*

> But we had the sentence of death in ourselves,
> that we should not trust in ourselves,
> but in God which raiseth the dead.
> — 2 Corinthians 1:9

*A*lthough we don't like to admit it, we all occasionally run into dead-end places in our lives where we don't know what to say, what to do, where to turn, or even how to pray. Sometimes it seems like we've hit a dead-end — in other words, it seems like everything is *finished, over,* and *done with*! If you've ever been in a place like this, you know what a *hard place* this can be!

Through these kinds of experiences, you and I discover that in our own strength, we are no match for some of life's problems. That's why we must learn to depend on the power and wisdom of God!

The apostle Paul tells us that he, too, went through this kind of learning experience when he found himself face-to-face with life-threatening situations in his own ministry. In Second Corinthians 1:9, he says, "But we had the sentence of death in ourselves, that we should not trust in ourselves, but in God which raiseth the dead." Paul was definitely at one of those dead-end places that we're talking about today. In fact, the situation he faced was so acute that he compared it to a sentence of death. That's dramatic language!

Notice the word "sentence" in the verse above. It is taken from the Greek word *krino*. This word *krino* normally refers to a jury who just handed down their *final sentence* in a court of law. You could say that the word *krino* denotes a *verdict* or a *sentence* pronounced as the result of a court trial.

After all the evidence is presented and the judge has examined all the facts, a *final verdict* is issued by the court. This is exactly the word that Paul uses in this dramatic verse. In using such a word, Paul is telling us that so much evidence and so many problems were stacked up against him and his companions, by all appearances it looked like there was no way for them to escape or even to survive. It looked like they had hit a dead-end; everything for them seemed to be *finished, over,* and *done with*!

- ✦ *Have you ever had a time in your life when it looked like it was the end of the road for you and your dreams?*
- ✦ *Did you think there was no way out?*
- ✦ *Did it look like there were so many problems stacked against you that you'd never survive what you were facing?*

This is *precisely* what Paul must have felt when he was facing overwhelming problems in Asia. He used the Greek word *krino* to let us know that as far as he was concerned, there was only one possible outcome for his life — *death*!

In essence, Second Corinthians 1:9 could be translated:

"As far as we were concerned, the final verdict was in, and the verdict demanded our deaths...."

But in spite of how it looked, Paul didn't die, nor did he fail at fulfilling the job God had given him. It may have looked like it was the end of the road, but it was really the beginning of a new supernatural flow of divine power into Paul's life. That's why he went on to say that through it all, he learned not to trust in himself, but in God who raises the dead.

Paul had been under such intense pressure that he felt death was unavoidable. Then right from the midst of this horrible situation, God's power was released and Paul was rescued! Paul said it was as if he and his companions had been *raised from the dead.*

When you don't know what else to do and when you have no one else to turn to, that's usually when God's resurrection power begins to operate in you to the greatest measure! You see, there's no such thing as *no hope.* As long as there is a loving Heavenly Father you can call on, there is still hope for you! If you learn to rely on Him, that dead-end place in your life that you're facing right now can become a new beginning!

So call out to your Heavenly Father right now. Expect Him to release His resurrection power on your behalf to turn your dead-end situation around!

MY PRAYER FOR TODAY

Lord, I have found that in my own strength, I am no match for life's problems. I thank You for revealing this to me today. From this day forward, please help me turn to You immediately when I come up against a dead-end place in my life. I ask You, Lord, to help me fully surrender each of these areas to You so You can have full access to them and raise them, one by one, from the dead. Please show me Your life-giving power today.

I pray this in Jesus' name!

MY CONFESSION FOR TODAY

I confess that God's resurrection power is released on my behalf to turn all dead-end situations in my life around! I do not trust in my own efforts or human thinking but in God and His life-giving power. I choose to partake of this power today by releasing every dead-end place to the Lord. I trust Him to perfect that which concerns me, and I look to see His power made manifest this day in my life!

I declare this by faith in Jesus' name!

QUESTIONS FOR YOU TO CONSIDER

1. Can you think of other people who faced impossible situations, but later experienced the delivering power of God that changed their situation?
2. Can you name Bible characters who learned to rely on God and experienced the same delivering power?
3. What kind of faith confessions can you start speaking to get your faith in gear and to release God's supernatural power into your situation?

JANUARY 19

Comrades
In the Lord Jesus Christ

I charge you by the Lord that this epistle
be read unto all the holy brethren.
— 1 Thessalonians 5:27

Throughout Paul's writings in the New Testament, he uses the word "brethren" when he writes to the churches. This word comes from the Greek word *adelphos*, which is one of the oldest words in the New Testament. In the *King James Version*, it is usually translated as the word "brethren." However, it actually has a much deeper meaning than this.

In its very oldest sense, the word *adelphos* ("brother") was used by physicians in the medical world to describe *two people who were born from the same womb*. So when the early Greeks addressed each other as "brethren," they meant to convey the idea: *"You and I are brothers! We came out of the same womb of humanity. We have the same feelings; we have similar emotions; and we deal with the same problems in life. In every respect, we are truly brothers!"*

In part, this was Paul's thinking when he addressed his readers as "brethren." By using this terminology, he brought himself right down to the level of his readers to identify with their position in life and with their personal struggles and victories. They were truly brothers — born from the womb of God, related by the blood of Jesus Christ, and members of the same spiritual family.

But the word "brethren" also had another very significant meaning during New Testament times, a meaning that it doesn't have in our world today. It was used during the time of Alexander the Great to describe faithful *soldiers*. These fighting men were true *brothers*, *comrades*, and *partners* who were united to fight the same fight, handle the same weapons, and win the same wars!

From time to time, Alexander the Great would hold huge public ceremonies where he would give awards to soldiers who had gone the extra mile in battle. When the most coveted awards were given, Alexander the Great would beckon the most faithful soldiers on stage to stand next to him. Before an audience of adoring soldiers, Alexander would embrace each faithful soldier and publicly declare, "Alexander the Great is proud to be the brother of this soldier!"

That word "brother" was this same Greek word *adelphos,* but in this instance, it referred to military men who were *brothers in battle.* This was the highest and greatest compliment that could be given to a solider during the time of Alexander the Great.

Thus, to be a "brother" meant that a person was a true *comrade.* Through the thick and thin of battle, these soldiers stood together, achieving a special level of brotherhood known only by those who stay united together in the heat of the fray. This was also part of what Paul had in mind when he wrote to the Early Church.

When Paul called his fellow Christians "brothers," he was telling them:

"In addition to being blood brothers, we are all in a similar fight, slugging it out against the same enemy — and this common fight makes us real comrades...."

I'm sure that Paul's readers were probably struggling in their personal lives, just as we do today, but they hadn't given up the fight. They were still on the front lines, slugging it out and plodding along, one step at a time. They were the kind of believers who are worth knowing and worthy to be called brothers because they possessed an ongoing commitment to stay faithful in the battle and committed to the cause.

No matter how well or how badly these believers were doing in the midst of their fight, at least they were *still fighting*! Others had given up, but they had not. As long as they remained faithful to the fight and refused to relinquish their stand of faith, Paul viewed them as exceptionally fine soldiers — the kind of soldiers anyone would be happy to associate with!

The word "brother" emphatically declares that it's not really how well you fight in life that counts. What really counts is that you keep on fighting! So don't give up on yourself, and don't give up on those believers around you who seem to be struggling. As long as they keep on trying — as long as they stay in the battle — they're worthy of your friendship! *You should be proud to be associated with people of such a spiritual caliber!*

MY PRAYER FOR TODAY

Lord, I ask You to help me see myself and other Christian brothers and sisters as soldiers in the army of God. Help me develop an attitude of determination that refuses to surrender to hardship or to throw in the towel in the face of difficulty. At the same time that this attitude is being developed inside me, use me to help fortify the same determined attitude in other Christian soldiers who face hostile forces that have come to steal their victory and joy.

I pray this in Jesus' name!

MY CONFESSION FOR TODAY

I confess that regardless of how much resistance the devil is trying to bring against my life, I will never surrender to defeat. Others may give up, but not I! As long as I am alive, I will stay in the fight. I refuse to relinquish my stand of faith. I am an exceptionally fine soldier — exactly the kind other Christian soldiers should be happy to associate with — because I am committed and determined to fight until my victory is complete!

I declare this by faith in Jesus' name!

QUESTIONS FOR YOU TO CONSIDER

1. Can you name five people who have been real "comrades" in your life?
2. In your mind, what qualifies a person to be a bona fide friend?
3. What practical things can you do to become a better friend to those you love, and how can you start this process today?

JANUARY 20

Never Forget That You Are More Than a Conqueror!

Nay, in all these things
we are more than conquerors through him that loved us.
— Romans 8:37

How do you see yourself? As a champion who wins nearly every fight? Or as a loser — someone who struggles along, never seeming to conquer a single problem? How you perceive yourself is very important because it will ultimately affect the way other people see you.

Have you ever met someone who had a bad self-image or who always seemed to carry an air of inferiority around with him? It isn't hard to discern this attitude in people. They feel so badly about themselves that they *exude* their negative perception of themselves and their sense of insecurity. On the other hand, if you've ever met individuals who are self-confident and self-assured, you know that it's easy to recognize their confidence. Why? Because a confident person exudes confidence.

It is simply a fact that you will inevitably *project* what you feel about yourself to others. So this question about how you see yourself is very important. If you see yourself as a champion who wins every fight, that is exactly how others will see you. But if you see yourself as someone who struggles and wrestles with a bad self-image — that is precisely how others will perceive you.

So let's turn to Romans 8:37 to see what the Word of God has to say about us. In this verse, Paul declares that "...we are more than conquerors through him that loved us." I want to especially draw your attention to the phrase "more than conquerors." It comes from the Greek word *hupernikos*, a compound of the words *huper* and *nikos*. By joining the words *huper* and *nikos* together into one word, Paul is making one fabulous, jammed-packed, power-filled statement about you and me!

The words "more than" are derived from the Greek word *huper*, which literally means *over, above, and beyond*. It depicts *something that is way beyond measure*. It carries the idea of *superiority — something that is utmost, paramount, foremost, first-rate, first-class, and top-notch; greater, higher, and better than; superior to; preeminent, dominant, and incomparable; more than a match for; unsurpassed, unequaled, and unrivaled by any person or thing.*

Now Paul uses this same word to denote what kind of conquerors we are in Jesus Christ. We are *huper-conquerors!* Paul uses this word *huper* to dramatize our victory.

This is what Paul meant to get across in Romans 8:37:

"We are greater conquerors, superior conquerors, higher and better conquerors!"
"We are more than a match for any foe!"
"We are utmost conquerors, paramount conquerors, top-notch conquerors, unsurpassed conquerors, unequaled and unrivaled conquerors!"

But we must continue to the next part of the verse, where Paul calls us "conquerors." The word "conqueror" is from the Greek word *nikos*. The word *nikos* describes *an overcomer; a conqueror, champion, victor,* or *master.* It is the picture of *an overwhelming, prevailing force.* However, the word *nikos* alone wasn't strong enough to make Paul's point, so he joined the words *huper* and *nikos* together to make his point even stronger!

When you put these two words together, they form the word *hupernikos,* which declares that in Jesus Christ, you are *an overwhelming conqueror, a paramount victor,* or *an enormous overcomer.* This word is so power-packed that one could interpret it as *a phenomenal, walloping, conquering force!*

That's precisely who you are in Jesus Christ! So stop looking at yourself as a struggling loser. Regardless of your past experiences, you must begin to look at yourself through God's eyes and in the light of Romans 8:37. This verse declares that you are always the winner and never a loser! And when you begin to see yourself the way God sees you, it will change the way others see you too.

Resolve right now to see yourself the way the Word of God does — as a walloping and conquering force! You are more than a match for any adversary or foe that would come against you today!

MY PRAYER FOR TODAY

Lord, I thank You for making me a phenomenal, walloping, conquering force! Because of what Jesus has done for me, I am no longer a struggling loser. Instead, I possess the power to be an enormous overcomer! Holy Spirit, I ask You to help me take my eyes off my past failures so I can focus on the power of the resurrection that lives inside me.

I pray this in Jesus' name!

MY CONFESSION FOR TODAY

I boldly declare that in Jesus Christ, I am a conqueror who is utmost, paramount, foremost, first-rate, first-class, and top-notch; greater, higher, and better than; superior to; preeminent, dominant, incomparable; more than a match for; unsurpassed, unequaled, and unrivaled by any challenge that would ever try to come against me!

I declare this by faith in Jesus' name!

QUESTIONS FOR YOU TO CONSIDER

1. How do you honestly see yourself in life — as a winner or a loser?
2. Think about the Christians you know who exude boldness and confidence in the Lord. What do those people do to maintain that sense of confidence on a consistent basis?

3. What steps can you take to begin to see yourself as God sees you according to His Word?

January 21

*A Spirit of Wisdom
And Revelation for You*

That the God of our Lord Jesus Christ, the Father of glory,
may give unto you the spirit of wisdom and revelation
in the knowledge of him.
— Ephesians 1:17

Would you like to receive guidance from the Holy Spirit to help you make some important decisions today?* If so, Paul's prayer to the Ephesian church in Ephesians 1:17 is an important scripture for you to apply to your own life.

The word "wisdom" in this verse is from the Greek word *sophias*. It is an old Greek word that was used to describe *insight* or *wisdom not naturally attained*. In other words, this is not natural human wisdom — this is *special insight*.

The word "revelation" is from the word *apokalupsis*. It refers to *something that has been veiled or hidden for a long time and then suddenly, almost instantaneously, becomes clear and visible to the mind or eye*. It is like pulling the curtains out of the way so you can see what has always been just outside your window. The scene was always there for you to enjoy, but the curtains blocked your ability to see the real picture. But when the curtains are drawn apart, you can suddenly see what has been hidden from your view. The moment you see beyond the curtain for the first time and observe what has been there all along but not evident to you — *that* is what the Bible calls a "revelation."

Now apply the meaning of this word to the realm of spiritual truths. The truths we now grasp and enjoy were always there in the realm of the Spirit, but they were veiled — *hidden* to us. It wasn't the time for these truths to be revealed yet, so they remained obscured from our sight, even though they were always there. But once the right time came and the Holy Spirit removed the veil that obstructed our view, our minds instantly saw and understood. When this occurred, you and I had a *revelation!*

Can you remember times in your past when you suddenly saw something in the Bible you had never seen before? That truth had been there all along, but it had been hidden to your eyes. Then suddenly one day, it was as if someone pulled the covers off that verse, and it literally jumped off the pages in front of you. You saw it! You *understood* it! You had a *revelation!*

It is a fact that truths remain hidden until God chooses to reveal them to us. This is why Paul prayed for God "to give" the Ephesian church a spirit of wisdom and revelation. The phrase "to give" is the Greek word *didomi,* which means *to hand something over completely to someone else*. It could also be translated *to impart*.

Because the Ephesian church needed wisdom beyond their own human understanding, Paul asked God to give them what they needed: *special insight that is not naturally attained.* Then Paul clarified what he meant by adding the word "revelation." One expositor has said the verse could be better translated to "give unto you a spirit of wisdom, *even revelation!*"

Taking all this into consideration, Ephesians 1:17 could be translated:

"That the God of our Lord Jesus Christ, the Father of glory, may give you special insight — I'm talking about wisdom that is not naturally attained. This is the divine moment when the curtains are drawn back, and you are supernaturally enabled to see what you could never see by yourself...."

God had all the answers the Ephesian believers needed. By themselves, they would never have been smart enough to figure it all out. So Paul besought God to impart to them the wisdom they needed. Then Paul clarified that this kind of wisdom would only come to them *by revelation* — which only God can give.

If you need direction and guidance today, stop right now and pray Paul's prayer in Ephesians 1:17 for your own life. Ask God to give you "a spirit of wisdom and revelation." God has all the answers you need, and they're not as far from you as you may think. In one moment, He can remove the veil of ignorance and help you see clearly the things you need to understand. *All you have to do is ASK!*

MY PRAYER FOR TODAY

Lord, I ask You to give me the insight and wisdom I need for this moment in my life. There is so much I need to know, but I am unable to figure it all out by myself. Today I ask that the Holy Spirit would take away the veil that has obscured my view. I ask that my eyes be opened to see exactly what I need to know. I ask You to give me a real revelation about my life, my situation, and the truth I need to know right now.

I pray this in Jesus' name!

MY CONFESSION FOR TODAY

I boldly declare that God gives me "a spirit of wisdom and revelation" regarding the truth I need in my life right now. God has all the answers I need — answers I will not find with my own natural reasoning. At the right moment, the Holy Spirit will remove the veil of ignorance that has blinded my view and help me see clearly the things I need to understand.

I declare this by faith in Jesus' name!

QUESTIONS FOR YOU TO CONSIDER

1. Can you remember a time in your life when a light bulb went off in your spirit and you saw a new revelation from God that you'd never seen before?
2. What difficult issues in your life have you been trying to work out in your own strength? Write them down.
3. Are you ready to surrender those issues to God and ask Him to reveal to you the answers you need?

JANUARY 22

❧❦❧

A Time To Forcefully
Speak the Truth in Love

And others save with fear,
pulling them out of the fire....
— Jude 1:23

What does the Bible say about how we should respond to believers who continue to practice sin? If you are personally aware of individuals like this, what steps or action should
you take to rescue him or her?

✦ *What attitude does God expect you to have regarding these people's sin?*
✦ *What kind of action does God expect you to take to see them delivered?*
✦ *What approach should you take regarding the sin they are living in?*
✦ *What is the proper outlook for you to have concerning their situation?*

The answer to these questions is found in Jude 1:23. In this verse, Jude compellingly tells us,
"And others save with fear, pulling them out of the fire...."

First of all, Jude tells us to "save [them] with fear." This word "fear" is the Greek word *phobos*. It
suggests *a fear or a strong dose of respect for something that is life-threatening, dangerous, or alarming.*
Because Jude uses this key Greek word, it tells us what kind of *attitude* we should have regarding sin. Sin
is *dangerous, alarming,* and even *life-threatening* to a person's spiritual life. Therefore, sin must not be tolerated, nor should the effects of sin be watered down. In short, we should have no stomach for sin.

Next, Jude 1:23 tells us what action we must take when we find a fellow believer who is getting
caught up in sin. This verse tells us that we must act fast to "pull them out of the fire." The word
"pull" comes from the Greek word *harpadzo.* This is an extremely strong and aggressive word that
presents the picture of *snatching someone out of a dangerous situation.* In fact, it would be better translated *to seize.*

The word *harpadzo* is the very word used in Colossians 1:13 when Paul writes, "Who hath
delivered us from the power of darkness, and hath translated us into the kingdom of his dear son."
That word "delivered" is also from the Greek word *harpadzo.*

In Colossians 1:13, this word portrays that moment when Jesus Christ broke Satan's power
over our lives and snatched us out of the kingdom of darkness. One Greek expositor says the word
harpadzo in Colossians 1:13 carries this idea: *"He grabbed us by the back of our necks and snatched us
out of danger, just in the nick of time...."* This Greek word *harpadzo* contains *passion, fervency, urgency,*
and *action.*

Because these words are used in Jude 1:23,
it could be translated:

*"Because of the alarmingly dangerous state that some believers are in, I urge you to take
immediate and fast-acting measures to see them delivered and rescued. And if they don't
quickly respond, don't stop! You need to keep up your sense of urgency until you are convinced*

that they are rescued and snatched out of the fires of destruction. If you must, go all the way to grab them by the back of their necks and jerk them out of those flames...."

Jude uses the word *harpadzo* to tell you that sometimes people are so deceived about what they're doing, they don't want to change. Even if you tell them that they are headed for trouble, they may not believe it! In these cases, your sweet words and tender pleading with them may not work. That means you may have to get forceful in the way you tell these people the truth. Your words must reach out and seize their hearts.

Think back for a minute to Lot, the nephew of Abraham. Lot got so caught up in the sin of Sodom and Gomorrah that when the angels told him the two cities were about to be destroyed, he wanted to stay anyway! The angels had to take him by the hand and *make* him leave! They had to forcibly *remove* him from that situation; otherwise, he would have been destroyed. The angels literally *dragged* Lot out of the city against his will (Genesis 19:16).

Likewise, we must do everything within our power to *snatch* people from spiritually dangerous predicaments. Although they may not feel the heat of the fire at the moment or realize the seriousness of their spiritual condition, we must speak forcefully and truthfully to them in order to *seize* their hearts and set them free.

We're not in the business of kidnapping people or taking them out of situations against their will. But we are to pray for fellow believers who are caught in sin and don't realize the dangerous nature of their situation. We must also go to them and do all we can to "pull them out of the fires" of destruction they're about to release into their lives.

If you know someone who is drifting away from his relationship with the Lord, pray for a door to open that will allow you to speak the truth in love and pull him out of impending destruction. Just think about it — if you were the one about to make a major spiritual error, wouldn't you want your true friends to speak the truth in love to you? *So believe God for an open door. He'll show you how and when to speak the truth.*

MY PRAYER FOR TODAY

Lord, I ask You to give me Your heart for brothers and sisters who are living in sin. Forgive me for the times I have been insensitive to the dangerous nature of sin. Help me to be passionate and fervent in prayer for them and to keep praying for them until their deliverance is complete and they are fully restored. Help me consider the way I would want others to pray for me if I were in the same situation.

I pray this in Jesus' name!

MY CONFESSION FOR TODAY

I confess that I will do everything within my power to snatch people from spiritually dangerous predicaments. Although they may not feel the heat of the fire at the moment or realize the seriousness of their spiritual condition, I will obey the Word of God and speak truthfully to them in order to seize their hearts and set them free. I believe that God will open a door and show me how and when I am to speak the truth.

I declare this by faith in Jesus' name!

QUESTIONS FOR YOU TO CONSIDER

1. Is there anyone in your life right now who comes to mind as someone who is in danger of being consumed in the "fire" of sin?
2. Realizing the seriousness of sin and deception, how would you want someone to confront you if you were in that person's situation?
3. In what ways could God use you to bring the truth in love to this person in order to set him or her free?

JANUARY 23

How To Be
A Spiritual Billionaire

Let the word of Christ dwell in you richly....
— Colossians 3:16

When I was growing up, I spent a lot of time at my grandparents' house. Grandpa was an immigrant fresh from Germany. Before his life in America, he had always known poverty. Grandma had also known many hardships and had always had to scrape by to survive financially.

Every afternoon, Grandpa and Grandma would go into their living room, turn on the television, and take their seats; then with great pleasure, they would watch the television program called "Let's Make a Deal!" When the program concluded, they would always spend a few minutes daydreaming about what they'd do if they suddenly *struck it rich* and inherited a large amount of money.

I loved to listen to my grandparents as they fantasized about paying off all their bills, purchasing a new house, contributing huge sums of money to the church, and bequeathing money to their children and grandchildren. They'd also talk about how they would show extraordinary generosity toward people who were disadvantaged in life. For Grandpa and Grandma, the supreme dream was what life would be like if they suddenly *struck it rich*!

If you are also among those who dream of *striking it rich* someday, I want to tell you that you don't have to fantasize about being rich anymore! If you are a child of God, *you've already struck it rich*! You have been given a treasure that will make boundless wealth accessible to you for the rest of your life. You are already a spiritual billionaire; however, for you to derive benefit from what God has provided, you have to learn how to tap into these vast resources.

In Colossians 3:16, the apostle Paul wrote, "Let the word of Christ dwell in you richly...." Today I want us to look at the word "richly" in this verse. It comes from the Greek word *plousios,* a very old Greek word that describes:

+ *incredible abundance*
+ *extreme wealth*
+ *enormous affluence*

✦ *great prosperity*
✦ *immense riches*
✦ *magnificent opulence*
✦ *extravagant lavishness*

Paul uses the word *plousios* in Colossians 3:16 to let us know that if we will receive the Word of God in the right way — if we give it a warm reception and make it feel *at home* in our lives — it will *enrich* us spiritually. Thus, the word *plousios* means that the Word of God can make us spiritual "billionaires"!

Colossians 3:16 conveys the following idea:

"Let the Word of God dwell in you richly! Throw open the doors, roll out the red carpet, and give it a grand reception! If you'll let the Word dwell in you in this way, it will produce an amazing amount of spiritual wealth in your life...."

You may ask, *"How can the Word make us spiritually rich?"* Paul continues to tell us what the Word can produce in us if we allow it to do so. He says, "Let the word of Christ dwell in you richly in all wisdom; teaching and admonishing one another in psalms and hymns and spiritual songs, singing with grace in your hearts to the Lord" (Colossians 3:16).

These words describe people so full of the Word of God that their entire being is affected. Their hearts are full of joy; their minds are flooded with wisdom and understanding; and their mouths are singing songs to the Lord. This describes people who have *struck it rich spiritually*!

It is a fact that when the Word of God really comes to feel at home in you, dwelling lavishly inside your heart, it enriches you with the wisdom, the gifts, and the power you need for today. You become so filled with the riches of God that you automatically find yourself admonishing and encouraging other people in their faith. When the Word dwells in you richly, there's always a song of rejoicing in your heart! When you are filled with the Word to this extent, those inward spiritual riches will easily flow out of you to bring life to everyone around you.

By using the word "richly" in this verse, Paul is painting a picture of what the Word of God will produce for you if you allow it to take up residency in you and become a vital part of your life. So if you're tired of striving with no results — if you're tired of feeling spiritually weak and worn out with nothing to offer — stop right where you are today. Don't take another step without making the decision to let God's Word play a more important role in your life.

As you do, the Word of God will *enrich* you with spiritual wisdom and insight. It will put victory in your heart and a song in your mouth! It will turn you into a *spiritual billionaire*! It will enrich your life so much that you'll always have something spiritually to donate, to bequeath, or to freely share with someone else!

MY PRAYER FOR TODAY

Lord, I ask You to help me become so full of the Word of God that my entire being is affected by its life-giving truth. As I dwell on Your Word and let it live inside me, my heart will be filled with joy, my mind will be flooded with wisdom and understanding, and my mouth will be filled with songs. Lord, I know that Your Word will take me to the richest spiritual place I've ever known in my life. So help me make Your Word feel at home in my heart so I can start living each day like I've struck it spiritually rich!

I pray this in Jesus' name!

I confess that the Word of God enriches me with spiritual wisdom and insight. It puts victory in my heart and a song in my mouth! As I meditate on the Word, it enriches my life, and I always have something spiritually to donate, to bequeath, or to freely share with others. I am so filled with the riches of God's Word that I automatically find myself admonishing and encouraging other people in their faith.

I declare this by faith in Jesus' name!

QUESTIONS FOR YOU TO CONSIDER

1. How can you roll out the red carpet and give God's Word a grand reception today?
2. Do you want the wisdom, gifts, and power of God to be more active in your life so you can minister more effectively to those around you?
3. What can you do differently in your private times with the Lord to "let the Word of Christ dwell in you richly"?

January 24

You Are Never Alone!

Wherefore seeing we also are compassed about
with so great a cloud of witnesses....
— Hebrews 12:1

*A*t times you may have wondered, *Has anyone else ever experienced the kinds of problems I'm experiencing right now, or am I out here all alone?*

No, you're not alone! Hebrews 11 records the remarkable feats of faith accomplished by various people in the Old Testament. These were people who had to fight and struggle as they waited for the object of their faith to manifest. Their walk of faith was a great, great challenge.

Because these Old Testament saints stayed with what God had told them to do and never gave up, they eventually saw His blessings begin to operate in their lives. Nevertheless, nearly all of them endured great, difficult hardships and challenges before their victory came.

To let us know that we're not alone in our own walk of faith, the writer of Hebrews says, "Wherefore seeing we also are compassed about with so great a cloud of witnesses, let us lay aside every weight, and the sin which doth so easily beset us, and let us run with patience the race that is set before us" (Hebrews 12:1).

Notice that it says, "Wherefore seeing we also are compassed about with so great a cloud of witnesses...." The phrase "compassed about" is taken from the word *peikeimenai*, which is a compound of the words *peri* and *keimai*. The word *peri* means *around* or *to be completely encircled by something.* The second part of the word *keimai* means *to lie down.* When these two words are compounded into one word, they mean *to lie around,* as if something has been *piled high* and is *lying all around you on every side.* This is the portrayal of being *completely encircled* by something that is *stacked high* on every side!

Therefore, this verse carries the following idea:

"Wherefore seeing we have lying all around us on every side...."
"Wherefore seeing these biblical examples are piled up and lying all around us...."

The Bible is piled high with examples of people — *people just like you* — who stood in faith and endured difficulties in order to do the will of God. You are surrounded on every side with powerful examples of people who were challenged in their faith, yet who held fast to the Word of God. And as a result, these godly people saw God's promises come to pass in their lives!

You are not alone!

✦ Look at Noah and the fight he endured.
✦ Look at Abraham and the fight he endured.
✦ Look at Sarah and the fight she endured.
✦ Look at Jacob and the fight he endured.
✦ Look at Joseph and the fight he endured.
✦ Look at Moses and the fight he endured.
✦ Look at Gideon, Barak, Samson, Jepthah, David, Samuel, and the prophets and the fight they all endured.

Take some time today to read some of these examples from the Old Testament — and then turn to the New Testament to see the many examples of faithful people who are also listed there. The Bible is packed full of examples of those who heard from God, who took His Word deep into their hearts, and who refused to stop until they saw the fulfillment of what God had promised them. Like you, they faced hardships and challenges. But no matter what obstacles stood in their way, they kept going and never stopped until God's plan for their lives was accomplished.

According to Hebrews 12:1, there are so many people who fit this description that they are literally lying all around you. And don't think you can only look to the Bible for these godly examples. If you look closely, you'll see that there are huge numbers of these "never-give-up" kind of people living on this earth right now as well. *You are not alone in your walk of faith!*

Don't let the devil tell you that you're the only one who has faced this kind of circumstance, because many have gone before you who have faced the same battles and won great victories. If you'll commit a few minutes of your time to read Hebrews 11, I believe you'll find that your battle isn't worse than the battles these saints fought and won. Reading these verses will encourage your heart!

Don't give up and throw in the towel! Hard times will pass, and you will see the Word of God bring you the victory you desire. *When you're tempted to get discouraged, just remember the many examples piled up all around you of people who endured and later won their prize!*

MY PRAYER FOR TODAY

Lord, Your Word says nothing is impossible to those who believe, so I am releasing my faith in Your promises. I fully believe that what You did for those faithful believers, You will also do for me!

I pray this in Jesus' name!

I confess that I have victory over the challenges I face in life! I know that many have faced the same battles I'm facing and victoriously won their fight. My battle isn't worse than the battles others have faced, so I boldly declare that I will be triumphant in my fight, just as they were triumphant in theirs! It is a fact that hard times will pass — and when they do, I will see the Word of God bring me the victory that I declare and desire! It is not a matter of IF I will win, but only a question of WHEN I will win!

I declare this by faith in Jesus' name!

QUESTIONS FOR YOU TO CONSIDER

1. What are some of your past victories that you can encourage yourself with as you fight your current fight of faith?
2. In each of those past struggles, what helped you to stay in the fight until you won?
3. List some examples of people in your life and in the Bible who held fast to God's promises as they faced great difficulties until their victory was finally won.

JANUARY 25

*Staying Untangled
From the World*

No man that warreth entangleth himself
with the affairs of this life....
— 2 Timothy 2:4

Have you ever wondered, *How do I know if I'm becoming too materialistic? How do I recognize when natural possessions have become too important to me?*

Today let's answer those questions! In Second Timothy 2:4, Paul wrote, "No man that warreth entangleth himself with the affairs of this life...." The word "entangleth" in this verse comes from the Greek word *empleko*. This Greek word can be used several different ways, but it is often used to describe *a person entangled in his lower garments* or *a person who is caught in some type of vine.*

For instance, this is the same Greek word that is used in Matthew 27:29 to describe how the Roman soldiers assembled Jesus' crown of thorns! That verse says, "And when they had *platted* a crown of thorns, they put it upon his head...." The word "platted" is this same Greek word *empleko*. It may be the clearest and best example of this word in the entire New Testament.

Think for a moment: How did the soldiers "plait" a crown of thorns? The soldiers took vines loaded with sharp, dangerous thorns; then they carefully wove together those razor-sharp, prickly, jagged vines until they formed a tightly woven, dangerous circle resembling the shape of a crown. It was this kind of crown that the soldiers violently shoved down upon Jesus' head in Matthew 27:29.

What I want you to see is that this word "entangleth" describes *something that has been woven together.* By using this word, Paul tells us that, as committed Christians, we don't have the privilege of getting too involved or intertwined with matters that are relatively unimportant in light of eternity.

The word *empleko* was also used to describe a runner whose garments become *entangled* in his legs. Although the runner was running a good race, his floppy, dangling garments have now become ensnared and entangled in his legs — and as a result, they break his pace and hinder his race. So here we find that the word *empleko* Paul uses in Second Timothy 2:4 can also describe someone who has become *ensnared* or *entangled* in something and thus hindered.

This means that Second Timothy 2:4 can be translated:

"No one serving as a soldier permits himself to get entwined, ensnared, and entangled in the affairs of this life...."

But now let's go back to the question about *materialism.* There is nothing wrong with owning nice things. In fact, God wants to bless us with nice things. But we are not to allow material possessions to become so ingrained in our hearts that they become the central focus of our lives. Our souls, emotions, and desires are not to become so *ensnared, entangled,* and *caught up* in the things of the world that we become *meshed together* with them.

How do you know if you've become materialistic? How do you know if natural possessions mean too much to you? Well, could you give them up if the Lord asked you to? Or have they become so woven into the very fabric of your life that you are now *entangled* in them? Only you and the Holy Spirit know the answers to these questions.

Do everything in your power to keep the temporal things of this world in the right perspective. Keep them in your hands but out of your heart. *Ask the Holy Spirit to show you areas of your life that need to be "untangled" and brought back into balance. Then after He speaks to you, it's up to you to STAY untangled from those natural affairs of life!*

MY PRAYER FOR TODAY

Lord, I ask You to help me keep my heart free from the things of the world. You have called me to be a committed and focused Christian soldier. I cannot permit anything to ensnare and entrap me, thus distracting me from the good fight of faith You've called me to fight and win. You are the revealer of the secrets of men's hearts, so today I am looking to You to reveal to me any areas in my soul where I have allowed something to entrap me so greatly that it threatens to eliminate me from the fight.

I pray this in Jesus' name!

MY CONFESSION FOR TODAY

I boldly declare that my heart and soul are free to follow Jesus Christ! My worldly possessions are in my hands, but they are not in my heart. I will remain free of materialism, worry, and other worldly concerns, and I will stay focused on the task Jesus Christ has assigned to me!

I declare this by faith in Jesus' name!

1. Have you allowed any of your material possessions to ensnare or trap you? Why don't you make a list of these things?
2. What steps can you take to get untangled in your heart from these possessions?
3. Do you trust God enough to release all your worldly possessions into His hands?

JANUARY 26

A Fight Always Follows Illumination

But call to remembrance the former days,
in which, after ye were illuminated,
ye endured a great fight of afflictions....
— Hebrews 10:32

Have you ever received a word from the Lord that gave you the exact direction you needed? If so, let me guess what happened next. Suddenly — *BOOM*! It seemed like all hell broke loose! The craziest circumstances erupted, seeming to directly challenge and assault that word you had just received from God!

If I've just described what you've gone through or what you are going through right now, *be encouraged*! You must be right on track! A spiritual fight usually does occur when you've been specially illuminated to the plan God has for your life.

In Hebrews 10:32, the Bible says, "But call to remembrance the former days, in which, after ye were illuminated, ye endured a great fight of afflictions...." Today I want us to look at three key words in this verse: "great," "fight," and "afflictions." These words describe what you and I might experience after the Lord has given us a word of instruction to illuminate us regarding His plan for our lives.

First, let's look at the word "great." In Greek, it's the word *mega*, and it describes *something very big*. For instance, the word *mega* is where we get the word megaphone, an instrument for making a *very big* noise. This word *mega* is used by people when they speak of *mega*-bills, *mega*-problems, *mega*-work, and so on. By using this word, the writer of Hebrews tells us that spiritual conflicts accompanying a word of divine direction are normally not small — they're usually *mega*! They're *BIG*!

The second word I want you to see is the word "fight." It comes from the Greek word *athlesis* and refers to a *committed athlete*. This undoubtedly tells you that when you receive a word from the Lord, it may throw you into one of the greatest challenges of your entire life! You'll feel like you've just entered the ring and are competing for the prize!

Finally, we come to the third word, "afflictions." It is the Greek word *pathema* and usually refers to *mental pressure* or to *suffering that affects the mind*. This isn't talking about mental sickness; rather, it points to a war in your soul or an attack on your mind.

Hebrews 10:32 could thus be taken to mean:

"After you were illuminated, you endured a mega-sized ordeal that threw you into the biggest fight you ever faced in your life. But the most critical part of the struggle resulted from the unremitting assaults that literally battered your mind...."

You can be sure that if you take a stance of faith in response to a word you received from God, every possible negative thought will come against your mind. Not only will the devil try to use people and circumstances to thwart the plan, but he will also affect your mind with all kinds of negative thoughts and accusations. He'll do everything he can to talk you out of doing what God has called you to do.

Don't be surprised by this! You must remember that Jesus experienced this type of attack as He hung on the Cross. As He selflessly laid down His own life on the Cross, the soldiers and other criminals hurled their horrible, slanderous statements at Him. But Jesus pushed aside all the assaults that came against His soul and endured, committing His life and destiny into the Father's hands.

So if you have received a word from God for your life, let me ask you:

✦ Did you go through a mega-ordeal yourself after you were illuminated to God's plan?
✦ Did you feel you were thrown into a fight that came to challenge what God had told you?
✦ Did you find that the devil tried to assault your mind and emotions with lies, accusations, and fears?

If you have been in this place I'm talking about — or if this is exactly where you are right now — then *be encouraged!* This is probably your clearest signal that you've received a real word from the Lord. You must be right on track, because the devil is terribly concerned about what will happen if you act on what God has revealed to you.

Don't back down. Don't surrender to the enemy's vicious lies in your mind, his attacks against your body, his challenges to your finances, or his assaults on your relationships. Regardless of how much resistance he tries to bring against you, don't you dare back up on that word God gave you!

If you hadn't received a true word from the Lord, there would be nothing for the devil to challenge! *The fight you face is the greatest evidence you're right on track! Just hang on, and don't give up! You're clearly headed in the right direction!*

MY PRAYER FOR TODAY

Lord, as I take a stand of faith in response to that word I have received from You for my life, I realize that Satan may try to use negative thoughts to war against my mind. Thank You for alerting me to the fact that the devil may even try to use people and circumstances to thwart Your plan for my life. But I also thank You that Satan cannot stop Your plan from coming to pass! With Your Spirit illuminating my mind, I know I will be able to discern the attacks of the enemy and successfully resist each and every attack!

I pray this in Jesus' name!

MY CONFESSION FOR TODAY

I boldly declare that I won't back down! I won't surrender to Satan's vicious lies — his attacks against my body, his challenges to my finances, and his assaults against my relationships. Regardless of how much resistance he tries to bring against me, I will not back up on the word that God gave me. I will stand fast, holding tightly to what God has promised, and the devil will be the one to throw in the towel and surrender! I will resist him until he flees and leaves me!

I declare this by faith in Jesus' name!

QUESTIONS FOR YOU TO CONSIDER

1. What are some past instances when you received direction for your life that you knew was from God?
2. Were you bombarded with negative thoughts and pressures that tried to make you doubt the direction God gave you? How did you react?
3. In the future, how can you respond according to the Word when these negative thoughts and pressures come against God's direction for your life?

JANUARY 27

Is It Time To Make a Change In Your Environment?

Wherefore seeing we also are compassed about
with so great a cloud of witnesses, let us lay aside every weight,
and the sin which doth so easily beset us....
— Hebrews 12:1

*Y*our biggest potential enemy in life (besides your own wrong thinking and the devil himself) is the environment in which you live. For instance, if you constantly live in an atmosphere of doubt and unbelief, it's just a fact that you'll have a much more difficult time maintaining a walk of strong faith. That doubt-filled *environment* will try to rub off on you!

It's just a fact that your environment tends to affect you and the way you think. For example, if you used to smoke or if you used to have a drinking problem, it's obviously not a smart idea for you to hang around smokers or drinkers — *unless*, that is, you want to be influenced to return to your old habits. Hanging around people who still do these things may lure you to pick up a cigarette to take a smoke or to allow yourself one more small drink.

However, those little allowances may possibly be the very hook that the devil uses to drag you back into the bondage from which Jesus Christ already delivered you. That's why it's vital for you to understand that the environment surrounding you is very important!

With this in mind, look at the phrase "...the sin which doth so easily beset us...." What kind of sin is this verse talking about? The words "so easily beset us" are from the Greek word *euperistatos*, a compound of three words: *eu*, *peri*, and *statos*. Let's look at all three of these words.

The word *eu* usually means *well*, but in this case it carries the idea of *something that feels well* or *something that is comfortable*. The Greek word *peri* means *around* or *being completely surrounded*. The word *statos* is from the root word *istimi*, meaning *to stand*. When these three words are compounded, the new word describes *something that comfortably stands all around you, such as a comfortable environment.*

So this phrase in Hebrews 12:1 could be understood to say:

"...Lay aside the sin and the environment that so comfortably envelops you...."

Sometimes in order to make necessary changes in your life, you must physically *remove yourself* from an unprofitable situation. If you're not strong enough in your faith to stay there without being affected, you need to get up and get out of that unbelieving, negative environment — *the one you've been comfortably living in for a long, long time.* If you're not strong enough to overcome it, it will unquestionably try to reach out and drag you back into your old behavior again.

If God's admonition to lay aside every weight applies to you, then obey Him and make a break from that unhealthy environment! Perhaps old friends, old places, or wrong believing are trying to exert a bad influence on you and you're not resisting that influence too well. *If that's the case, get out of there!* For you, that environment is *sin* if it keeps you from fulfilling your potential in Jesus Christ.

Be honest as you consider your workplace, your friends, and your living conditions. Ask yourself, *Is this environment conducive to my walk in Christ, or is it dragging me back down into the mire I was delivered from?*

Your friends and your job are not so important that you should let them destroy your spiritual life. If you cannot successfully handle the environment you're in, get out of there. Then watch the Lord provide a better job and better friends than you've ever had in your life!

Your Christian life is serious business. Don't let your environment fill you with doubt and knock you out of your spiritual race! If you can't handle your environment victoriously, initiate a plan of action to change it today!

MY PRAYER FOR TODAY

Lord, I want to stay in an environment that will keep my faith alive and strong. Help me recognize those relationships and places I should avoid to keep my faith from being negatively affected. As You show me places, people, and things I should avoid, give me the strength I need to do what is right — and give me the wisdom I need to know how to avoid those places and people!

I pray this in Jesus' name!

MY CONFESSION FOR TODAY

I confess that I will physically remove myself from unprofitable situations that are not positive for my faith. I make the choice to get up and get out of unbelieving, negative environments that tend to pull me down. I am laying aside every weight, and I am making a break from all unhealthy environments! With God's help, I make right choices and right friends. I do everything I can to stay in environments that help me keep my faith alive and well.

I declare this by faith in Jesus' name!

QUESTIONS FOR YOU TO CONSIDER

1. Have you been in any relationships or environments that you should have avoided? How did they affect your walk with God?

2. Are there any unprofitable situations or relationships that you need to remove yourself from now?

3. What steps can you take to start making better choices of friends and environments? What do you think the Lord wants you to do with your current relationships and places that you frequent?

JANUARY 28

You're Not a Spiritual Orphan!

I will not leave you comfortless:
I will come to you.
— John 14:18

Have you ever felt isolated or alone in this world? If you have, just remember — you are *never* alone! Imagine how alone the disciples felt when Jesus informed them that He would soon ascend to Heaven and leave them behind on the earth!

What do you think the disciples felt when Jesus told them this? They must have wondered, *What will life be like without Jesus? How will we continue without the Master walking right alongside of us?* But it was time for Jesus to ascend to the Father and to take His place as our Great High Priest.

It was natural for the disciples to feel sorrowful. To them, it must have seemed like the end of their wonderful encounter with the Lord and with the power of God. Living and walking with Jesus was more than they had ever hoped for in this world. With Jesus at their side, their lives had been filled with adventure, excitement, joy, victory, power, healings, and miracles.

Feelings of insecurity and uncertainty would have been normal for any human beings who found themselves in the disciples' position. They had grown dependent upon the physical, visible presence of Jesus — something we've never experienced and therefore cannot fully comprehend. The thought of Jesus leaving this earth probably made the disciples feel spiritually forsaken and abandoned.

In the midst of these fears, Jesus promised His disciples, "I will not leave you comfortless…" (John 14:18). Today I want us to look at the word "comfortless" in this verse. It is taken from the Greek word *orphanos,* which is where we get the word *orphan.*

In New Testament times, the word *orphanos* described *children left without a father or mother.* In today's world, the word *orphan* has exactly the same meaning. It refers to *a child who is abandoned due to the death or desertion of a father or mother.* Once orphaned, the child is deprived of parental care, supervision, and protection — *unless* that child is placed in the custody of a blood relative or a new guardian who assumes a parental role in that child's life.

However, in New Testament times the word *orphanos* was also used in a broader sense to describe *students who had been abandoned by their teacher.* Just as children are dependent on their parents, these students were reliant on their teacher to teach them, to guide them, and to prepare them for life. But once the teacher abandoned them, they felt *deserted, forsaken, discarded, and thrown away.*

In both cases, the word *orphanos* is used to carry the same idea, whether it refers to children abandoned by their parents or students discarded by their teacher. It gives the picture of *younger, less educated, less knowledgeable people feeling deserted by those they trusted and looked to for guidance.*

Jesus was a spiritual father to the disciples. He knew they were completely reliant upon Him. They couldn't make it on their own in the world without Him. This is why He promised them, *"I will not leave you like orphans."*

Jesus' words could be translated to express this idea:

"I will not leave you behind like orphans who have been deserted by their parents, nor will I desert you like an unfaithful teacher who walks out on his students and leaves them with no supervision or help...."

Jesus knew the disciples couldn't make it on their own in the world. That's why He sent the Holy Spirit into the world to be their new Guardian and Teacher.

You can't make it on your own in this world either — but you don't have to, because Jesus did not abandon you! He did not desert you, walk out on you, or throw you away. When He ascended to the Father, He sent the Holy Spirit to care for you, to guide you, and to teach you. Jesus did not leave you as an orphan in this world!

So meditate on this truth today, and let it sink deep into your heart: *I'm not alone! I'm not a spiritual orphan. Jesus has given me the Holy Spirit to comfort, guide, counsel, and strengthen me in every situation of life!*

MY PRAYER FOR TODAY

Lord, I thank You that I am not a spiritual orphan in this world. You didn't abandon me or leave me to figure out everything on my own. You sent the Holy Spirit to be my Teacher and Guide. So right now I open my heart wide to the Holy Spirit, so He can be the Helper You sent Him to be in my life. I give You thanks for sending this divine Helper, and I ask You to teach me how to lean upon Him more and more in the course of my life.

I pray this in Jesus' name!

MY CONFESSION FOR TODAY

I boldly declare that the Holy Spirit is my Helper, my Teacher, and my Guide. Everything Jesus did for the disciples, the Holy Spirit now does for me. He leads me, He teaches me, and He shows me everything the Father wants me to know. I am not a spiritual orphan! I am a child of God who is fully befriended, indwelt, empowered, and led by the Spirit of God.

I declare this by faith in Jesus' name!

QUESTIONS FOR YOU TO CONSIDER

1. Can you think of a critical moment in your life when you felt abandoned and alone and turned to God for comfort and support?
2. What are some of the ways the Father has comforted you in the past?
3. Are you allowing the Holy Spirit to be your Comforter, Strengthener, and Guide?

JANUARY 29

❦

Royal Ambassadors
For Christ

Now then we are ambassadors for Christ....
— 2 Corinthians 5:20

*D*id you know that you have a high-ranking, esteemed, celebrated, impressive, and influential job in the Kingdom of God? It's true! You are so important to the Kingdom of God that all of Heaven is standing behind you, just waiting to back you up, defend you, provide for you, help and assist you, and join forces with your actions of faith! In short, Heaven is just waiting to act on your behalf. Why? Because you are an *ambassador* for Christ to this world!

In Second Corinthians 5:20, Paul wrote, "Now then we are ambassadors for Christ...." The word "ambassador" comes from the Greek word *presbeuo*. It describes *an ambassador* or *one who fulfills the duties of an ambassador.* How wonderful that Paul would use this word to describe you and me!

In New Testament times and in today's world, the word "ambassador" has the same meaning. An "ambassador" can be defined as:

- ✦ An envoy sent to represent a nation to a foreign land.
- ✦ A diplomatic agent of the highest rank accredited to a foreign government or king.
- ✦ A representative temporarily sent to a foreign country to represent the king or country that sent him.
- ✦ An authorized messenger who has the power to make decisions and to represent the will of the government, nation, or king he represents.
- ✦ An official representative who is authorized to speak on behalf of his sender.

According to Paul's words in Second Corinthians 5:20, we are heavenly delegates — "ambassadors" who have been sent forth as Heaven's *representatives* to planet earth! As ambassadors for Christ, we are *the voice of Heaven.* As His representatives, we are authorized *to speak and act* on behalf of the Lord. And as Heaven's ambassadors, we are fully backed, fully funded, *fully defended, and fully assisted* by the authority and resources of Heaven!

Paul's words in Second Corinthians 5:20 therefore mean:

"We are sent forth and temporarily stationed here as the fully authorized representatives of Jesus Christ! As His ambassadors, we are here to be His voice and His will — a true representation of who He really is. As His official representatives sent here to do His business, we are fully backed up by all the power and resources of Heaven...."

Don't ever think that you are unimportant to the plan of God. *You are an ambassador!* You represent Jesus Christ to your family, to your place of employment, and to your neighborhood. You have been invested with royal powers, including the name of Jesus and the authority of His blood, and you may call upon Heaven to assist you at any given moment! All angelic powers and all the vast resources stored in the treasury of Heaven are available for your use when you are representing Heaven to this world!

So wherever you go today and whatever you do, remember the One you are representing. If you need special help from above in order to represent the Lord in a positive way, remember that as an ambassador of Christ, all of Heaven is standing by to fully support you!

As your day gets started, stop for a moment and think about who you really are in Jesus Christ. *You are a royal ambassador for the King of Kings Himself!*

MY PRAYER FOR TODAY

Lord, I thank You for the tremendous privilege of representing You on this earth! Please forgive me for the times I have overlooked the honor of being a child of God. I am sorry for the moments when I've been negative about myself, talked badly about myself, and did not acknowledge who You have made me to be in Jesus Christ. Today I am asking the Holy Spirit to help me see and truly perceive that You have made me to be an ambassador in this world!

I pray this in Jesus' name!

MY CONFESSION FOR TODAY

I confess that I am important to the plan of God. I am an ambassador! I represent Jesus Christ to my family, to my place of employment, and to my neighborhood. I have been invested with royal powers, including the name of Jesus and the authority of the blood, and I may call upon Heaven to assist me at any given moment! All angelic powers and all the vast resources stored in the treasury of Heaven are available for my use when I am representing Jesus to this world!

I declare this by faith in Jesus' name!

QUESTIONS FOR YOU TO CONSIDER

1. Have you ever viewed yourself as an ambassador of Jesus Christ?
2. Have you asked the Father to give you a revelation of your rightful place as an ambassador for Jesus Christ?
3. In what ways can you act as an ambassador for Jesus where you live and work?

You have been invested with royal powers, including the name of Jesus and the authority of His blood, and you may call upon Heaven to assist you at any given moment! All angelic powers and all the vast resources stored in the treasury of Heaven are available for your use when you are representing Heaven to this world!

JANUARY 30

❧❧❧

Is It Ever Right To Hate Something?

And others save with fear, pulling them out of the fire;
hating even the garment spotted by the flesh.
— Jude 1:23

I don't know about you, but I believe the word "hate" is a very strong word that should only rarely be used. When our children were young, Denise and I forbade our children to use this word. Even if we strongly disliked something or someone, we never allowed ourselves or our children to use the word "hate" to describe this strong dislike. It was simply too strong an expression to describe how we or our children felt about something or someone.

But there is a proper time and place for *hate*! Jude 1:23 gives us an example of one of those times. It says, "…Hating even the garment spotted by the flesh."

The word "hate" in this verse is taken from the word *miseo*. It is one of the strongest, fiercest words in the Greek New Testament. In fact, it is so strong that it actually carries the idea of a *hatred* that can turn *violent*. So when Jude tells us to "hate" the garments spotted by the flesh, he isn't talking about a mere dislike of something; he is talking about a *radical, violent aversion* to something.

The Greek word *miseo* is the same Greek word that is used in Revelation 2:6 and 2:15, when Jesus declares that He "hates" the deeds of the Nicolaitans. Because the word *miseo* is used in these verses, the Bible categorically tells us that Jesus had no taste for what the Nicolaitans were doing. In Jesus' opinion, their deeds and teachings were *repugnant, disgusting, revolting, repulsive, and nauseating*. The Lord Jesus possessed *a deep-seated aversion* to their activities and found their deeds *abhorrent*.

Now Jude uses this Greek word *miseo* in Jude 1:23 when he writes, "…Hating even the garment spotted by the flesh." There is no doubt about it. Jude is letting us know that we should have a *strong* aversion to sin — so strong that it allows absolutely no tolerance for sin in our lives or in the lives of other believers.

This part of verse 23 could be taken to mean:

"When it comes to sin in your life or in the lives of others, you should have no stomach for it at all. In fact, your feelings about sin should be so strong that you possess an aversion and repugnance to it.…"

Our aversion to sin should be so fierce that Jude says we are to hate "…even the garment spotted by the flesh." The word "garment" (from the Greek word *chiton*) was used in ancient times to describe *a person's undergarment.* You see, the outer robe may be changed to look fresh and clean while the *undergarment* remains just as *dirty* as ever! A new, clean robe may hide the truth that a person's undergarment is filthy — but this disguise doesn't alter the fact that he has a deeper problem to deal with!

Sin isn't just a superficial, outward problem. If we allow wrong attitudes and behavior to continue in our lives, this moral decay will eventually *permeate* deeper than the surface and *penetrate* even to the deepest, most hidden parts of our souls. The defilement may begin as an outward problem, the same way loose dirt can soil a man's outer garment. But if this filth is never dealt with, it will begin to work its way through every area of a person's life until he is *completely defiled.*

When this happens, Jude says the person has been "spotted by the flesh." The word "spotted" is the word *spilos.* It means *to stain, defile,* or *contaminate.* This person could have dealt with his moral problems before the problem got so serious. However, through neglect he allowed that filth to contaminate his entire life.

Thus, the second part of this verse conveys this idea:

"...And don't just deal with the superficial issues of sin by cloaking yourself with a garment that hides the true picture. Be honest with yourself about your true situations. And be hard on sin, refusing to allow it access to the deeper parts of your life. If sin sinks that deep below the surface, it won't be long until you are completely contaminated and affected by it."

It is imperative that we understand the consequences of sin and learn to hate even the smallest hint of its presence in our lives. If we don't deal with sin while it's still a small, superficial problem, it will become a much deeper problem — and much more difficult to deal with!

So before you do anything else today, ask the Holy Spirit to open your eyes to those areas of your life that need attention and correction. He will lovingly point them out to you and then show you how to change!

MY PRAYER FOR TODAY

Lord, help me see sin the way You see it so that I have no stomach for it in my life. I know that as long as I view sin only as a mistake or a weakness, I will be tempted to tolerate it. So I ask You to teach me to see sin exactly the way You do so my desire for change will grow. Holy Spirit, help me see the truth and know the proper steps I need to take in order to make those needed changes.

I pray this in Jesus' name!

MY CONFESSION FOR TODAY

I confess that I understand the consequences of sin and that I hate even the smallest hint of sin in my life. I will deal with sin while it is still a small, superficial problem so that it never becomes a much deeper problem. The Holy Spirit opens my eyes to those areas of my life that need attention and correction. He lovingly shows me what needs to change, and I willingly obey Him as He shows me how to change.

I declare this by faith in Jesus' name!

QUESTIONS FOR YOU TO CONSIDER

1. Have you had any ongoing battles with particular sins? Make a list of the areas you've been struggling with, and be honest with yourself.
2. Have you asked the Lord to help you overcome and change in these areas of your life?
3. What can you begin to do differently that will help you walk free of these sins once and for all?

JANUARY 31

❧❧❧

Unshackled From The Tyranny and Cruelty of Sin!

But God be thanked, that ye were the servants of sin,
but ye have obeyed from the heart that form of doctrine
which was delivered you.
— Romans 6:17

Would you like to more fully appreciate how the grace of God has changed you? Why not take a little time today to recall what your spiritual condition was like before His grace touched your life? As you do that, I think you'll realize that before Jesus Christ came into your heart, life was doomed to failure. In fact, it was so unpromising that Romans 6:17 says you were in reality a "servant" to sin.

When Paul writes that we were previously the servants of sin, he uses the Greek word *doulos*, one of the most wretched expressions for a slave in the ancient Greek language. It described a servant who was so totally sold into slavery that he had no destiny of his own; rather, he was perpetually obligated to do the bidding of his owner — fulfilling the whims, impulses, quirks, urges, and desires of his master for the rest of his life.

In other words, the word *doulos* depicts *one whose very existence is to fulfill the commands of his master.* Or as one expositor explained, the word portrays *one whose will is completely swallowed up in the will of another.*

This is the word Paul uses to describe our slavery to sin before Jesus came into our lives. Paul is saying that prior to our salvation experience, we were completely consumed, swallowed up, devoured, and engulfed in the will of Satan. We may have thought we were in charge of our lives; we may have assumed we were "calling the shots" ourselves. But in reality, you and I were in the grip of sin, and our sin nature was controlling our lives and destinies. We were like captives sold into the depravity of slavery. As the slaves of sin, our destinies were being masterminded by an unseen, diabolical spirit that wanted to destroy us.

**Because of the word *doulos* in Romans 6:17,
one section of this verse could be taken to read:**

"...In the past you were the wretched slaves of sin — sold out entirely to sin — and you had no 'say-so' about your life, your future, or your desires. At that time, your entire existence on earth was centered around fulfilling the whims, impulses, quirks, urges, and desires of your master — sin...."

Our prior slavery to Satan was so deeply rooted in our nature that we became inseparable from the sinful nature that so constantly worked in us and controlled us. Indeed, this pervading demonic presence in our lives was so absolute and supreme that Paul described it this way in Ephesians 2:2: "Wherein in time past ye walked according to the course of this world, according to the prince of the power of the air, the spirit that now worketh in the children of disobedience."

In Greek, the word "worketh" is the word *energeo*. The word *energeo* denotes a force that is *energizing*. In fact, this is where we get the word *energy*.

By choosing to use this word, the Holy Spirit is vividly portraying how destitute our spiritual condition was before you and I were born again. It plainly means that prior to our salvation experience, we were *energized* by the spirit that works in all the sons of disobedience. The devil himself used to have authorization to accomplish his destructive will in our lives. Because we were his *slaves,* he could do whatever he wanted with us.

But when Jesus Christ came into our lives, we were immediately emancipated — *totally set free!* Because of this, we are no longer servants to sin; now we are servants of the Almighty God.

The evil spirits that once exacted every ounce of your being and required your all-inclusive servitude no longer possess the authorization to control you or to dictate your destiny. Now Jesus is your Lord. Now it is the Spirit of God who works in you and supernaturally energizes you to fulfill God's will in your life. You have a new Master, and His name is *Jesus!* You have a new Source of energy on the inside — the power of the *Holy Spirit!*

Refuse to let sin have its way in your life any longer. Yes, you were a servant to sin in the past, but now you are a servant of Jesus Christ. So tell the devil to hit the road and take his temptations elsewhere! It's time for you to yield to the Holy Spirit so He can mightily release His divine power in you and give you the energy you need to live a life of obedience to God!

MY PRAYER FOR TODAY

Lord, I thank You for coming into my life and for breaking the power of sin that used to hold me captive. I remember the futility I felt as I tried to change myself but couldn't do it. But when You came into my life, everything changed! I praise You for loving me so much that You left Heaven and descended into a world filled with sin and depravity. You did that for me, and I thank You so much!

I pray this in Jesus' name!

MY CONFESSION FOR TODAY

I confess that I am free because of the death and resurrection of Jesus Christ. The shedding of His blood paid the ransom for me. The hold Satan used to have on me is broken, and I am liberated and set free! Now God's divine power operates mightily in me, and I have authority over the enemy who used to control me!

I declare this by faith in Jesus' name!

QUESTIONS FOR YOU TO CONSIDER

1. What were some of the sinful impulses and desires you were set free from when Jesus came into your life?
2. Are you continuing to walk in the freedom from sin that Jesus Christ gave you?
3. Why not take time right now to ask the Holy Spirit to release His divine power in you so you can walk in greater obedience to the will of God?

FEBRUARY 1

❧❀❧

Does God's Word Feel at Home in Your Life?

Let the word of Christ dwell in you richly ....
— Colossians 3:16

Many years ago when I was speaking in a particular church, the pastor informed me that because the church couldn't afford a hotel for me, I'd be staying that week with a family from his church. When I arrived at this family's home, the host met me at the front door, showed me my bedroom, and pointed out the bathroom and kitchen. Then the entire family ignored me for the rest of the week!

If I asked the family members a question, they pretended not to hear me. When it was time to eat, they informed me that it wasn't their responsibility to feed me and that I could just take care of myself because they weren't there to nurse me.

Words cannot describe how *uncomfortable* I was in that home! Everything that family did let me know that they wished I wasn't there. When that week concluded, I was so happy to move out of that miserable predicament! I pledged that I would *never* let myself be put in that kind of situation again.

How about you? Have you ever stayed as a guest in a home where the people made you feel very unwelcome and unwanted?

I remember that when this happened, I was studying Colossians 3:16, where it says, "Let the word of Christ dwell in you richly...." The chilly reception I felt in that home caused me to look at my own heart and ask, *What kind of reception have I given the Word of God in my life?* I wanted to know:

✦ *Have I given God's Word the kind of reception it deserves, or have I ignored it and given it the "cold shoulder"?*
✦ *Does God's Word feel at home in my life, or does it feel unwanted?*
✦ *Have I rolled out the red carpet and given God's Word a grand reception, making it clear that I love the Word and am privileged to have it dwelling in my heart?*

In Colossians 3:16, Paul tells us that the word of Christ should "dwell" in us richly. I decided to go get my Greek New Testament and study the word "dwell" so I could determine what kind of reception I had given God's Word in my own life.

I found that the word "dwell" is taken from the word *enoikeo*. The word *enoikeo* is a compound of the words *en* and *oikos*. The word *en* means *in*, and the word *oikos* is the Greek word for *a house*. When the two words are compounded together, they form the word *enoikeo*, which means *to dwell in a house*. This is the same Greek word used in both New Testament literature and secular literature to signify someone who takes up *permanent residency* in a home. The person is so at home and contented in this new location that he has chosen to make it his *permanent dwelling place* for the rest of his life.

So when Paul tells us to let the word of Christ "dwell" in us, he is beseeching us to give God's Word such a grand, welcoming reception that it literally feels *at home* in us and therefore comes to take up permanent residency!

Does the Word have this kind of place in your life? Does it really "dwell" in you richly? Does it feel *at home* and *comfortable* in your life? Or is the Word of God treated like a stranger that is occasionally welcomed into your life as a visitor? *Be honest!*

Why not make today *the* day that the Word of God comes to take up permanent residency in your life? *Throw the door open, roll out the red carpet, and welcome the Word of God as a new, permanent resident in your heart!*

MY PRAYER FOR TODAY

Lord, how can I ever thank You enough for the power of Your Word? I am so honored that You would place such a gift in my life. Help me to appreciate it, value it, and give it the kind of reception it deserves. I want to make Your Word a top priority in my life; I want it to feel welcomed, wanted, and deeply loved. Starting today, I open my heart wider than ever before and ask that Your Word come to richly dwell inside me!

I pray this in Jesus' name!

MY CONFESSION FOR TODAY

I confess that the Word of God dwells richly in me. It has such a grand reception in my life that it literally feels at home in me. Because I give it this place of prominence in my life, it produces phenomenal amounts of spiritual wealth in my life. I have so many spiritual riches inside me that they continually flow forth to enrich those around me.

I declare this by faith in Jesus' name!

QUESTIONS FOR YOU TO CONSIDER

1. Is God's Word a priority in your life or just a sideline issue?
2. How can you better give God's Word a grand, welcoming reception in your life?
3. What steps can you take to make God's Word feel so *at home* in your life that it takes up permanent residency?

When Paul tells us to let the word of Christ "dwell" in us, he is beseeching us to give God's Word such a grand, welcoming reception that it literally feels *at home* in us and therefore comes to take up permanent residency! Does the Word have this kind of place in your life? Or is the Word of God treated like a stranger that is occasionally welcomed into your life as a visitor? *Be honest!*

FEBRUARY 2

The Greatest Price Ever Paid To Set a Slave Free!

Who gave himself for us,
that he might redeem us from all iniquity,
and purify unto himself a peculiar people,
zealous of good works.
— Titus 2:14

T he word "redeem" used in the verse above is one of the most important words in the entire New Testament, so today I want us to look more deeply into its historical roots. Since Jesus redeemed us, we need to know all the powerful images that are contained in this key New Testament word!

In New Testament times, slaves could be very *costly*. When a slave purchaser came to the slave market to look for a new slave, he would meander through the aisles of the marketplace, his eyes roaming over all the slaves for sale as he searched for the one he wanted. After pinpointing the slave who seemed to fit his needs, the purchaser was then allowed to inspect the slave's condition. The purpose of this inspection was similar to that of a test drive when a person is checking out a car before he purchases it. Just as every buyer wants to be sure he's getting a good product, every slave buyer wanted to check out the merchandise before he put his money on the table.

The inspection included physically beating the slave to see how he responded to abuse, so the purchaser would know how much "wear and tear" the slave could take on the job. The buyer was also allowed to pull open the slave's mouth and look at his teeth to see if they were rotten or in good shape as he tried to establish the slave's physical health before making an offer to purchase him.

If the buyer decided to proceed with the purchase after the inspection was complete, it was then time for the next stage of the process — that moment when the slave was put on the auction block. When the auctioneer knew that a buyer really had his eye set on a specific slave, he would take that as a signal to push the price for that slave as high as possible. And if the buyer continued to show interest in that same slave, that would let the auctioneer know he could demand a completely unreasonable price and probably get it!

All of these images are contained in the word "redemption," which comes from the Greek word *lutroo*. This is the word used in Titus 2:14, where Paul says, "…That he might redeem us from all iniquity…." This Greek word depicts *a person who paid a very high price to obtain the slave of his choice*. Once the price was offered and accepted, that slave became his personal property.

However, the word *lutroo* was used in another very significant way that also has to do with the concept of redemption. At times, a caring and compassionate individual would come to the slave market for the sole purpose of purchasing slaves *out of* slavery to liberate and set them free! In this case, the payment offered was viewed as a *ransom* — paid to obtain freedom for slaves.

Because Paul uses the word *lutroo* to denote the redemptive work of Jesus Christ on our behalf, it tells us several important things:

1. Jesus came into the world, Satan's slave market, because He was looking for us.
2. Jesus knew He wanted us and wouldn't be satisfied until the purchase was complete.
3. Jesus was willing to pay *any* price demanded to purchase us from the slave market.
4. Jesus purchased us with His own blood so we would become His own personal property.
5. Jesus paid the price with His blood, purchased us for Himself, and gave us a liberating freedom that can only be known because of His work in our lives!

Our freedom from Satan's power was extremely expensive. The price Jesus paid for us was the highest price ever paid for a slave. What was the ransom that Jesus paid in order to procure our freedom from Satan's ownership? *His own blood!*

This means that the word *lutroo* in Titus 2:14 conveys this idea:

"Who gave Himself for us, that He might purchase us out of the slave market to become His own personal property — yes, He was willing to pay the ransom price to see us liberated and set free...."

It was the shedding of Jesus' own blood that guaranteed our deliverance and lasting freedom from the demonic powers that had previously held us captive. The word *lutroo* unmistakably means Jesus paid the ransom that set you and me free! *He bought us with His own blood!* As Hebrews 9:12 says, "Neither by the blood of goats and calves, but by his own blood he entered in once into the holy place, having obtained eternal redemption for us."

Jesus gave Himself as the ransom to set you free from sin. Someone had to enter Satan's slave market, so Jesus chose to go. Someone had to offer a price, so Jesus offered to pay the price for your freedom with His own blood. Someone had to finalize the deal, so Jesus willingly paid the price with His own life on the Cross.

MY PRAYER FOR TODAY

Lord, I want to thank You for loving me so much that You gave Your precious blood on the Cross for me. I was so lost and so hopeless, but You came for me — and when You came into my life, everything in me changed. Hope, joy, and peace came into my heart, and today I am completely different from the person I used to be. All this happened because of Your shed blood, Jesus, so today I want to take this moment to thank You for doing what no one else could do for me!

I pray this in Jesus' name!

MY CONFESSION FOR TODAY

I declare that Jesus' blood purchased my deliverance and lasting freedom from the demonic powers that had previously held me captive. Jesus loves me so much that He was willing to do for me what no one else was willing to do. He went into the slave market, found me, and bought me for Himself. For the rest of my life, I will live to serve and glorify Him.

I declare this by faith in Jesus' name!

FEBRUARY 3

Do Whatever Is Necessary To Keep Envy and Strife Out of Your Life!

For where envying and strife is,
there is confusion and every evil work.
— James 3:16

Tʜe devil knows that *envy* and *strife* destroy relationships and long-term friendships. He is aware that if he can create envy and strife between you and the ones you love, he can ruin those special relationships that God intended to be a blessing in your life. *Do you have any relationships in your life right now that are under this kind of demonic assault?*

The devil doesn't just target friendships with this type of assault. He also knows how to get in between you and your church family, a ministry you love and support, or even the organization or place of business where you work. The enemy doesn't care *whom* he divides — he simply wants to *divide*! Since envy and strife are some of the tools he uses to do this, it is crucial that you understand how to recognize *envy* and *strife* and how to stand against them!

In James 3:16, the Bible says, "For where envying and strife is, there is confusion and every evil work." I want you to notice the word "envy" in this verse. It is taken from the Greek word *zelos*, and it denotes *a fierce desire to promote one's own ideas and convictions to the exclusion of everyone else.* This word *zelos* is where we get the word *zealot*, which describes a person who is so *fixated, obsessed,* and *fanatical* about his own cause that others perceive him as an *extremist* on the threshold of becoming *militant.*

In the case of James 3:16, this word presents a picture of a believer who is so obsessed, gripped, and preoccupied with his own view of things that he can't see or hear the view of anyone else. In fact, his militant perspective has made him lopsided in his thinking. He never takes a softer line but holds out until all the other parties admit defeat and agree with his point of view.

Therefore, the word "envy" in James 3:16 could be translated this way:

"For where there is a fierce desire to promote one's own ideas and convictions to the elimination of everyone else...."

If this kind of attitude continues, it will naturally lead to the next step in this horrible sequence of events. This is where *strife* comes into the picture! Notice that James goes on to say, "For where envying and *strife* is...."

The word "strife" is taken from the Greek word *eritheia*. It was used by the ancient Greeks to stand for *a political party*. This Greek word is often translated as a *party spirit* because of its linkage to political systems and political parties. Therefore, in order for us to understand why James used this word, we need to stop and think about the way political parties are formed and how they function.

Political parties are formed by a group of people who have similar values and views. After the party is formed, the participants develop a unified agenda; once the agenda is decided on, they create a platform. From that platform, the people begin to push their agenda and ideas, fighting fiercely to see that their party's platform is accepted and eventually put in the position of ruling and calling the shots.

In the same way, some Christians become so clouded by their ambition to see their own views adopted that they have no tolerance for anyone who sees things differently than they do. These people usually gravitate to other believers who hold similar views.

Once these "like-minded" Christians find each other, they naturally begin to take sides, forming a kind of allegiance. Then they begin to form agendas and develop plans to see their views pushed, promoted, and accepted. As a result, people who once stood shoulder to shoulder often end up standing on different sides of a fight with their relationships ruined and filled with hurt.

When envy and strife have made it this far, the next step in this sequence of events becomes inevitable. James 3:16 continues, "For where envying and strife is, there is *confusion*...."

The word "confusion" is taken from the word *akatastasia*. It was used in New Testament times to describe *civil disobedience, disorder,* and *anarchy* in a city, state, or government. By using this word, James explicitly tells us that when situations of strife and discord are allowed to persist, an atmosphere of anarchy sets in and begins to destroy the relationships once loved and cherished. Rational thinking is replaced by raw emotions, and people end up getting hurt.

James wants to make sure we understand what this kind of conduct eventually produces if this behavior isn't stopped. He goes on to say, "For where envying and strife is, there is confusion and every evil work."

The word "evil" is from the word *phaulos,* describing something that is *terribly bad* or *exceedingly vile*. We get the word "foul" from this Greek word. James is saying that where envy and strife are permitted to operate, thus producing confusion and anarchy in relationships, they ultimately yield a foul-smelling situation!

These various Greek words in James 3:16 convey this idea:

"For where there is a fierce desire to promote one's own ideas and convictions to the exclusion of everyone else's, it produces divisions so great that people end up taking sides and forming differing parties with conflicting agendas. This is a terrible event, because it creates great unrest among people who should be united. Ultimately, the whole situation becomes a stinking mess!"

But understand this: You can help stop this from happening by choosing to consider other people's opinions to be just as important as your own! Instead of pushing your own agenda, why not stop and listen to what others have to say? They may have something powerful to contribute, but if you can't hear them, you'll never benefit from their perspective.

You don't have to yield to envy and strife! When the opportunity for strife arises, you can beat Satan at his own game by choosing to make room for the ideas, thoughts, and opinions of others. Even if you don't agree with what they say, at least you can demonstrate that you value their right to have a differing opinion. By maintaining an attitude of staying on the same side with your fellow believers, you can put the devil on the run and keep your relationships alive, healthy, and long-lasting!

MY PRAYER FOR TODAY

Lord, I ask You to forgive me for the times I have allowed strife to get into my heart. Also, please forgive me for those occasions when I have been the origin of strife and fighting. Help me grow in discernment so I can quickly recognize when the devil is trying to create division. Show me how to be a peacekeeper and a source of harmony rather than a player in the midst of others' wrong attitudes.

I pray this in Jesus' name!

MY CONFESSION FOR TODAY

I confess that I do not yield to envy and strife! When the opportunity for strife arises, I beat Satan at his own game by choosing to respectfully make room for the ideas, thoughts, and opinions of others. Even if I don't agree with what they say, I let them know that I value their right to have a differing opinion. I maintain an attitude of staying on the same side with my fellow believers; therefore, I put the devil on the run and keep him OUT of my relationships!

I declare this by faith in Jesus' name!

QUESTIONS FOR YOU TO CONSIDER

1. Do your coworkers, friends, and family members find you open-hearted to their suggestions, or do they find it difficult to express themselves honestly in front of you?
2. When the opportunity for strife arises, what can you do to circumvent it and promote peace?
3. Can you recall moments when you were so sure you were right, only to discover that someone else's idea was really much better than yours?

Even if you don't agree with what others say, at least you can demonstrate that you value their right to have a differing opinion. By maintaining an attitude of staying on the same side with your fellow believers, you can put the devil on the run and keep your relationships alive, healthy, and long-lasting!

February 4

⚜

Don't Ignore the Last Words!

Finally, my brethren, be strong in the Lord,
and in the power of his might.
— Ephesians 6:10

*I*n the sixth chapter of Ephesians, the apostle Paul writes his great text about spiritual warfare and spiritual weapons. But before Paul goes into a detailed explanation of our spiritual armor, he first passionately beseeches us, "Finally, my brethren, be strong in the Lord…."

The word "finally" is one of the most important words in this text. It is taken from the Greek phrase *tou loipou* and would be better translated *for the rest of the matter; in conclusion;* or *in summation.* The phrase *tou loipou* is used in other Greek manuscripts of that same period to depict something so extremely important that it is placed at the very end of the letter. This way if the reader remembers nothing else in the letter, he will be more likely to remember this one thing.

**With this in mind, the word "finally"
in Ephesians 6:10 carries this idea:**

"In conclusion, I have saved the most important issue of this epistle until the end of the letter, so if you remember nothing else I have said, you will remember this. I want this to stand out in your mind!…"

This is a remarkable statement! The book of Ephesians contains some of the deepest theological teaching in the New Testament. Let me mention just a few of these theological points. Paul writes about:

✦ The election of the saints (Ephesians 1:4)
✦ The predestination work of God (Ephesians 1:5)
✦ The adoption of the sons of God (Ephesians 1:5)
✦ The dispensation of the fullness of times (Ephesians 1:10)
✦ The sealing of the Holy Spirit (Ephesians 1:13)
✦ The earnest of the Holy Spirit (Ephesians 1:14)
✦ The power of God that is available to every believer (Ephesians 1:19)
✦ The grace of God (Ephesians 2:1-10)
✦ The eternal plan of God (Ephesians 3:10-11)
✦ The fivefold ministry gifts (Ephesians 4:11-13)
✦ The infilling with the Spirit (Ephesians 5:18-19)
✦ *And the list goes on and on.*

But in addition to these important theological points, the book of Ephesians also includes some of the most practical instructions in the New Testament regarding such issues as:

✦ The relationship between believers (Ephesians 4:25-5:2)
✦ The relationship between believers and the world (Ephesians 5:3-16)
✦ The relationship between husbands and wives (Ephesians 5:22-33)
✦ The relationship between parents and children (Ephesians 6:1-4)
✦ The relationship between employers and employees (Ephesians 6:5-9)

Yet when you come to the end of this epistle that is so jam-packed with theological and practical truths, Paul says, "Finally…" and then begins to speak to us about *spiritual warfare*!

Why is this? Because like so many in the Church world today, the Ephesian believers had gathered together a vast accumulation of spiritual knowledge, information, and facts; nevertheless, this alone was not enough to keep the devil under their feet where he belonged! As we read through chapter 4, we can see that the devil was apparently attacking the Ephesian church and was having some success!

That's why Paul had to instruct these believers to put away lying, steal no more, let no corrupt communication out of their mouths, grieve not the Holy Spirit, and put aside all anger and malice (Ephesians 4:25-31). Does this sound like a church full of victorious people to you? The Ephesian believers were members of the largest church of that day, yet they were not fully experiencing the overcoming, abundant life that Jesus Christ had come to offer them.

Consider your own life. Are you experiencing victory in most areas of your life, or are you suffering defeat in key areas? Have you ignored the fact that spiritual warfare is real? Have you gathered lots of spiritual information, knowledge, and facts, yet forgotten to put on the whole armor of God?

Praise God for all the knowledge you've gained, but now it's time to turn your intellectual knowledge of God's Word into the sword of the Spirit. Then you must raise it high and brandish it against the onslaughts the enemy has been trying to bring against you. It's also time for you to turn your knowledge about faith into a shield that withstands every demonic attack! That's why Paul said, "Finally…." In case the Ephesian believers didn't remember anything else, he wanted them to remember that they *had* to have spiritual weapons to keep the devil under their feet.

How about you? Are you dressed in the whole armor of God today?

MY PRAYER FOR TODAY

Lord, help me not to get so brain-heavy with facts, knowledge, and information that I forget I must have more than brain power. I am asking You to help me focus on my spiritual side and to stay equipped with the spiritual weapons You have provided for me, for I know that knowledge alone is not enough to keep the devil under my feet. Today I choose to pick up those weapons and to walk in the whole armor of God!

I pray this in Jesus' name!

MY CONFESSION FOR TODAY

I confess that I have spiritual weapons to defeat the enemy! I walk in those weapons and use them every time the devil tries to attack my life or the lives of those I love. Because I have the whole armor of God, I am fit and equipped to shove back every assault the devil may try to bring against me. God has more than adequately outfitted me with every weapon I need to maintain the victory Jesus obtained for me.

I declare this by faith in Jesus' name!

QUESTIONS FOR YOU TO CONSIDER

1. When you take a serious look at your life, do you think you're doing all you can to keep the devil out of your affairs?

2. Are there any areas of your life that are "targets" for the devil right now because of something you're doing that you shouldn't be doing?

3. How long has it been since you read Ephesians 6:10-18 and really meditated on those verses about spiritual weapons? Don't you think you should take some time to do it today?

FEBRUARY 5

A Divine Stream Of Supernatural Revelation

But as it is written, Eye hath not seen, nor ear heard,
neither have entered into the heart of man,
the things which God hath prepared for them that love him.
But God hath revealed them unto us by his Spirit:
for the Spirit searcheth all things, yea, the deep things of God.
— 1 Corinthians 2:9,10

I remember one January day several years ago when I was aroused from my sleep very early in the morning, and I sensed that the Holy Spirit was awaking me because there was something He wanted to tell me. At first, I thought I was just having a difficult time sleeping, so I tried to shrug it off and go back to sleep. But the longer I lay there in my bed, the more I became aware that it was God who was stirring up my spirit. There was something He wanted to say to me.

For months preceding that time, I had been seeking answers to some very important questions about the steps we needed to take in order to fulfill the assignment God had given us. I had spent hundreds of hours thinking over the questions I faced. I had worked my ink pen over endless pages that were scrawled with my notes. Yet I couldn't find the right answer to the questions that were constantly on my mind. I had prayed and prayed about it, but it seemed that the correct answers kept evading me. Then in the early hours of that January morning, the answers *suddenly* came!

I walked back and forth in our apartment as I prayed. Finally, I went into the dining room and lay my head on the dining table to pray more earnestly. I said, *"Holy Spirit, what is it that You want to reveal to me this morning? What is it that You want to communicate to me?"*

Suddenly — and very unexpectedly — it seemed as if the spiritual realm miraculously opened, and a stream of information descended from Heaven and began to pour the answers I needed directly into my mind! As that information began surging into my mind, I *instantly* saw the solutions for which I had been seeking for so long! It was as if the Holy Spirit said, *"Let Me pull the curtains off your mind, so you can see everything you've been desiring to see. I will remove the veil of ignorance that has blinded your sight. When I do this, the ignorance will be removed and you'll instantly know every answer you've been seeking!"*

This was not the first time I'd had that experience. The Holy Spirit had revealed many things to me through the years — and I know He will continue to be my unlimited Source of divine revelation for the rest of the time I live on this earth. He will do the same for any person who genuinely seeks to know God's will for his or her life, for this is the right of every child of God.

Regarding the Holy Spirit's supernatural revelation to believers, the apostle Paul wrote, "But as it is written, Eye hath not seen, nor ear heard, neither have entered into the heart of man, the things which God hath prepared for them that love him. But God hath revealed them unto us by his Spirit: for the Spirit searcheth all things, yea, the deep things of God" (1 Corinthians 2:9,10).

Paul begins this verse by talking about man's inability to understand the deep things of God by himself. It could have been translated, *"The heart of man could never dream, imagine, or conjure up the things God hath prepared for them that love Him."* The human mind, by itself, cannot fathom, even in its wildest imagination, the wonderful things God has prepared for His people! If this is so, then how can you and I ever comprehend what God has planned for *us*?

Paul tells us the answer in the above verse: "But God hath revealed them unto us by His Spirit…." This means the day of ignorance is gone! Because the Holy Spirit has come, we can now know all the things God has planned and prepared for us!

Notice that Paul says, "But God hath *revealed* them unto us by his Spirit…." The word "revealed" is the word *apokalupto*, which means *to unveil, to reveal,* or *to uncover.* It is actually a picture of *something that is veiled or hidden at the moment when its veil or covering is suddenly removed.* As a result, what was hidden for so long now comes into plain view. And God does all of this *by His Spirit* — just as He did for me on that early morning in January!

When the Holy Spirit lifts the cover and removes the veil that has blocked your view of God's plans for you, the eyes of your spirit *suddenly* see and perceive truths that were previously veiled. This is what the Bible calls a *revelation.* In one instant, everything comes into clear view, answering all your questions and giving you the direction you've been seeking for a long time.

The word *apokalupsis* suggests this meaning for First Corinthians 2:9,10:

"…God has supernaturally pulled back the veil that previously obscured your view and blocked God's plan from your sight. It was the Holy Spirit who actually carried out this operation and made all of these once-concealed things now visible to you…."

Truthfully, God gave us our brains so we could use them, and we need to learn how to use them well. But there are some things the mind alone will *never* perceive. If we are ever going to see those spiritual truths, we will have to have a spiritual experience that opens our eyes to them.

If you have been seeking answers that your mind can't find, why not go to the ultimate Source of divine revelation? God holds all the answers you seek. As you sincerely ask in faith and genuinely open your heart so the Holy Spirit can speak to you, He will tell you everything He wants you to know!

MY PRAYER FOR TODAY

Lord, now I understand that I've been trying to find answers I'll never discover by myself. The things I long to know can only be revealed by You, so today I ask You to pull back the veil that has concealed those things I long to understand. I know that when You get involved, my eyes will be opened and my ignorance will evaporate. I sincerely ask You in faith to speak to me and to show me those things I need to know.

I pray this in Jesus' name!

QUESTIONS FOR YOU TO CONSIDER

1. Have you been seeking God for answers that seem elusive to you?
2. Why not make a list of the questions for which you're seeking answers?
3. Have you sincerely asked in faith for answers to your questions and then genuinely opened your heart to God so He can speak to you?

FEBRUARY 6

What Does It Mean To Have a 'Sound Mind'?

For God hath not given us the spirit of fear;
but of power, and of love, and of a sound mind.
— 2 Timothy 1:7

*I*n moments of stress, pressure, or fear or when you're so exhausted you can't think straight, have you ever been tempted to say, *"Dear God, what is wrong with me? I feel like I'm losing my mind"*?

If you've ever felt this way before or if you're tempted to think like this right now, let me assure you: You're not going crazy! God's Word declares that you have been given a *sound mind* that works even in the craziest and most difficult situations!

Let me give you an example from the Bible. When Paul wrote the book of Second Timothy, it was a very difficult time for the Early Church. Due to Nero's insanity, he was persecuting believers everywhere — and his methods of persecution were gruesome and cruel. At that time, Timothy was the pastor of the church of Ephesus. He knew that Nero's secret police would take special pleasure in killing him in some barbaric way if they ever got their hands on him.

As Timothy considered the threat against his life, a spirit of fear tried to grab hold of him. That's why Paul told Timothy in Second Timothy 1:7, "For God hath not given us the spirit of fear; but of power, and of love, and of a sound mind."

I want to especially point your focus to the words "sound mind." This phrase is taken from the Greek word *sophroneo*, which is a compound word combining *sodzo* and *phroneo*. The Greek word *sodzo* means to be *saved* or *delivered*. It suggests something that is *delivered, rescued, revived, salvaged, and protected* and is now *safe and secure*. One expositor suggests that the word *sodzo* could actually depict a person who was on the verge of death but then was *revived* and *resuscitated* because new life was breathed into him.

The second part of the phrase "sound mind" comes from the Greek word *phroneo*, which carries the idea of a person's *intelligence* or *total frame of thinking* — including his *rationale, logic,* and *emotions*. The word *phroneo* refers to *every part of the human mind, including all the processes that are engaged in making the mind function and come to conclusions.*

When the words *sodzo* and *phroneo* are compounded into one word, they form the word *sophroneo*, which pictures *a mind that has been delivered, rescued, revived, salvaged, and protected and is now safe and secure*. Thus, even if your mind is tempted to succumb to fear, as was the case with Timothy, you can allow God's Word and the Holy Spirit to work in you to deliver, rescue, revive, and salvage your mind. This means your rationale, logic, and emotions can be shielded from the illogically absurd, ridiculous, unfounded, and crazy thoughts that have tried to grip your mind in the past. All *you* have to do is grab hold of God's Word and His Spirit.

The word *sophroneo* in Second Timothy 1:7 could be translated:

"God has not given you a spirit of fear, but of power and of love — He has given you a mind that has been delivered, rescued, revived, salvaged, protected, and brought into a place of safety and security so that it is no longer affected by illogical, unfounded, and absurd thoughts."

You see, when your mind is guarded by the Word of God, you think differently. When the Word of God is allowed to work in your mind, it safeguards your emotions; it defends your mind from demonic assault; and it shields you from arrows the enemy may try to shoot in your direction in order to arouse a spirit of fear inside you.

Why is it important for you to understand this? Because when you begin to live a life of faith — when you reach out to do the impossible — the enemy will try to assault you mentally and emotionally in an attempt to stop your progress. For instance, he may speak to your mind, saying things like, *You can't do this! This doesn't make sense! Are you crazy?*

So what do you do when the devil tries to convince you that you're losing your mind? What do you do if you're confused due to stressful situations and so tempted to fear that you can't think straight? Go get alone with the Lord and give Him your concerns. As you focus on Jesus and release all those burdens, you'll find that your mind is working fine! Second Timothy 1:7 promises you a sound mind; therefore, you have the right and privilege to tell the devil to shut up and then to declare by faith that your mind is *sound, safe,* and *secure*!

MY PRAYER FOR TODAY

Lord, I thank You by faith that I am NOT going crazy and I am NOT losing my mind. The stress and pressure I've been facing is going to pass, and I know You will bring me through these challenging times. You promised me a sound mind, and that is exactly what You have given me. I can't ever thank You enough or fully express my gratitude for the power, love, and sound mind You have given to me that will carry me safely through these times!

I pray this in Jesus' name!

QUESTIONS FOR YOU TO CONSIDER

1. Have you ever had a moment in your life when you were tempted to think that you were going crazy or that you were losing your mind?
2. What kind of circumstances were you facing in your life at that time?
3. What actions did you take during that difficult time that helped bring you back in touch with the "sound mind" that rightfully belongs to you?

FEBRUARY 7

It's Time for You To Stop Acting Like You're a Victim!

And having spoiled principalities and powers,
he made a shew of them openly, triumphing over them in it.
— Colossians 2:15

We can count on the fact that there are unseen evil forces that have been assigned to kill, steal, and destroy everything good in our lives. The Bible clearly teaches that these devilish forces band together to commit acts of aggression against the saints — and that includes you and me!

This truth is quite evident in Scripture, for Paul wrote many verses about spiritual weapons, spiritual armor, and how we are to resist these unseen, demonic forces. Yet it is *very important* that we approach this subject with the right attitude!

Because of Jesus' death on the Cross and His resurrection from the dead, the forces of hell are *already* defeated. However, even though they have been legally stripped of their authority and power, they continue to roam around this earth, carrying out evil deeds like criminals, bandits, hooligans, and thugs. And just like criminals who refuse to submit to the law, these evil spirits will continue to operate in this world until some believer uses his God-given authority to enforce their defeat!

We need to get ahold of this truth: These demonic forces are legally stripped of their authority and are defeated! We are not puny, struggling believers who are somehow trying to learn how to cope with the devil's attacks against us. We're not merely trying to learn how to scrape by or survive. Jesus' death and resurrection gave us the legal authority to keep Satan under our feet, so we must always make sure we approach spiritual warfare as *victors* and not *victims*.

Let's look at Colossians 2:15 to gain a greater revelation of the victory Jesus has already accomplished for you and me through His death, burial, and resurrection. Paul tells us that Jesus "…made a shew of them *openly*…." The word "openly" is taken from the word *parresia*, a word that is used throughout the books of the New Testament to denote *boldness* or *confidence*.

By using the word *parresia*, Paul declares that when Jesus was finishing His dealings with Satan, His victory over the devil was no "quiet affair." Quite the contrary! Jesus *boldly*, *confidently*, and *loudly* exposed and displayed this now-defunct foe to Heaven's hosts. Make no mistake! When Jesus "made a shew of them openly," it was quite a spectacular show!

The verse continues, "…He made a shew of them openly, *triumphing over them in it*." The word "triumph" is taken from the Greek word *triambeuo*, which is a technical word used to describe *a general* or *an emperor returning home from a grand victory in the enemy's territory*. Specifically, the word "triumph" was used to describe the emperor's triumphal parade when he returned home.

When a returning emperor or general came striding through the gates on his big, powerful, and beautiful horse, he was accompanied by his fellow victorious warriors, who also appeared glorious after their triumphant battle. As the parade followed, the weaponry and treasures seized from the enemy's territory were grandly displayed for all to see.

The grand finale to this triumphal procession was the foreign ruler himself. This ruler had been beaten and bound in chains and was now being forced to walk in disgrace, shame, dishonor, embarrassment, and humiliation as crowds of people came to celebrate his defeat and to get a "peek" at a once-powerful but now totally defeated opponent.

So when Colossians 2:15 declares that Jesus triumphed over evil powers, it is explicitly declaring that Jesus took the enemy apart piece by piece as He thoroughly "spoiled principalities and powers." *When Jesus was finished with those demonic forces, they were utterly plundered — "stripped to bare nakedness" and left with nothing in hand to retaliate!*

**Because of the words *parresia* and *triumbeuo*,
Colossians 2:15 conveys this idea:**

> *"…He gallantly strode into Heaven to celebrate His victory and the defeat of Satan and his forces. As part of His triumphal process, He flaunted the spoils seized from the hand of the enemy. Yet the greatest spectacle of all occurred when the enemy himself was openly put on display as bound, disgraced, disabled, defeated, humiliated, and stripped bare…."*

Jesus' victory over Satan was a momentous affair! When Jesus returned, He was *totally* triumphant! The party Heaven threw that day was enormous! All of Heaven's hosts came to celebrate Jesus' victory and Satan's downfall and demise! Right there in front of everyone, Jesus displayed the devil and his cohorts, so all could know that this enemy no longer had the legitimate right or the necessary arms to prolong his rule of terrorism.

Once again, Satan is not a force we are *trying* to defeat; he is *already* defeated. But because very few believers know how to effectively use their God-given authority to resist Satan, he tries to continue illegally operating and doing damage to the souls of men and even to the creation itself.

No matter what demonic strategy may come against you this day or how many demons are assembled together for your destruction, you *never* have to go down defeated. Jesus *plundered* the enemy when He rose from the dead. So when you look into the mirror, you need to learn to see yourself as one who *already* has the victory. You *already* possess the authority necessary to keep Satan under your feet where he belongs. Remember, you are no longer a victim — *you are a victor*!

MY PRAYER FOR TODAY

Lord, I thank You for the victory You obtained by Your resurrection from the dead! No one else could have done what You did for us. You invaded hell; broke the power of its demonic forces; seized their artillery; and bound the devil. And because You did all this, You set us free! You are our great Victor, our great Champion, and You are the Lord of all lords. Thank You for cleansing me with Your blood and granting me the honor to be called a child of God and a joint heir with You.

I pray this in Jesus' name!

MY CONFESSION FOR TODAY

I confess that Satan is not a force I am trying to defeat because he is already defeated. I use my God-given authority to resist him, and he flees from me. No matter what demonic strategy may come against me this day or how many demons may try to assemble together for my destruction, I NEVER have to go down in defeat. When I look into the mirror, I see someone who already has the victory. I possess the authority necessary to keep Satan under my feet where he belongs!

I declare this by faith in Jesus' name!

QUESTIONS FOR YOU TO CONSIDER

1. Do you approach life like you are a victorious champion, or a struggling victim?
2. Do you quickly give in to defeat, or do you dig in your heels and refuse to go down defeated?
3. What changes could you make in your thoughts, words, and attitudes to help you maintain a more victorious approach to life?

Because of Jesus' death on the Cross and His resurrection from the dead, the forces of hell are *already* defeated. However, even though they have been legally stripped of their authority and power, they continue to roam around this earth, carrying out evil deeds like criminals, bandits, hooligans, and thugs. And just like criminals who refuse to submit to the law, these evil spirits will continue to operate in this world until some believer uses his God-given authority to enforce their defeat!

FEBRUARY 8

※❧❦❧※

The Holy Spirit Wants To Place A Razor-Sharp Sword in Your Hands

And take the helmet of salvation,
and the sword of the Spirit, which is the word of God.
— Ephesians 6:17

How would you like God to give you a weapon that can rip to shreds the devil's strategies against you? Well, that's exactly what He has done! Ephesians 6:17 declares that God has given you "...the sword of the Spirit, which is the word of God"!

I want you to look at the word "sword" in this verse. It is the Greek word *machaira* — a word that exacted fear in the minds of those who heard it! You see, this wasn't just a sword, but a weapon of murder that caused the victim horrid pain as he lay bleeding to death.

Just for your knowledge, there were various types of swords used by the Roman army during New Testament times. For instance, there was a huge *double-handed sword* — a sword so massive that it could only be utilized with the use of *two hands*. This sword could not be used in real combat because it was too huge. Instead, it was used during sword practice sessions because it helped develop stronger muscles as soldiers swung it against a post that represented an enemy.

There was also a long sword that was used for fighting in a battle, similar to the sword we are familiar with today. This sword was very effective in battle, but it more often wounded the enemy than it killed him. Because it was long, it was most often swung at an enemy from the side, thus scraping or cutting a gouge into the side or limbs of an adversary.

But the weapon referred to in Ephesians 6:17, coming from the Greek word *machaira*, was neither of these swords. This sword was an exceptionally brutal weapon. Although it could be up to nineteen inches in length, most often it was shorter and shaped like a dagger-type sword.

Just as a dagger is inserted into a victim at close range, this sword was used only in close combat. It was razor sharp on both sides of the blade. The tip of the sword often turned upward; sometimes it was even twisted, similar to a cork screw. Because this dagger-type sword was razor sharp, it could easily be thrust into the abdomen of an adversary. And if it had a cork-screw tip, the attacker could shred the insides of a victim by twisting the sword.

All these characteristics made the *machaira* a very deadly and frightful weapon. This two-edged, dagger-type sword inflicted a wound far worse than any other sword that was available to the Roman soldier at that time. Although the other swords were deadly, this one was a terror to the imagination!

By using the word *machaira* in Ephesians 6:17, the apostle Paul is saying that God has given the Church of Jesus Christ a weapon that is frightful to the devil and his forces. Why is this weapon so horrific to the kingdom of darkness? Because it has the razor-sharp power to slash our demonic foes to shreds!

Because the word *machaira* denoted a sword that was dagger-shaped, it tells us that the "sword of the Spirit" is a weapon that is normally employed in closer combat. Let's take this one step further, so we can understand why this is so.

Notice that this verse calls it "the sword of the Spirit, which is the word of God." The term "word" is taken from the Greek word *rhema*, which describes *something that is spoken clearly and vividly, in unmistakable terms and in undeniable language.* In the New Testament, the word *rhema* carries the idea of a *quickened word.*

Here's an example of a *rhema* or a *quickened word*: You are praying about a situation when suddenly a Bible verse rises from within your heart. In that moment, you know that God has supernaturally made you aware of a verse you can stand on and claim for your situation. When this happens, it's as if the Holy Spirit has put a sword in your hand — a spiritual dagger — that you can insert into the heart of the enemy to bring about his defeat.

There are many examples of God giving someone this kind of *quickened word* in the Bible, but the best one is found in Luke 4, where Jesus is being tempted by the devil in the wilderness. Over and over again, the devil tempted and tested Jesus. But with each temptation, a scripture was *quickened* inside Jesus, and He would speak forth that scripture to the devil, brandishing it like a sword against His enemy. Each time Jesus used a verse that the Spirit had *quickened* to Him, the sword of the Word dealt a serious blow to the enemy — causing the devil to eventually flee in defeat.

Because of the words *machaira* and *rhema*,
Ephesians 6:17 conveys this impression:

"The Spirit will place a razor-sharp sword at your disposal anytime the enemy gets too close. This sword's power will be available the very moment the Spirit quickens a specific word for a specific situation you are facing."

When you receive a *rhema* from the Lord, the Holy Spirit drops a word or scripture into your heart, causing it to come alive supernaturally and impart special power and authority to you. This quickened word is so powerful that it is like a sword has been placed in your hands! That's why Paul calls it "the sword of the Spirit, which is the word of God."

The next time you find yourself in close combat with the enemy, take the time to get quiet in your heart and listen. The Holy Spirit will reach up from within your spirit and *quicken* to you a scripture that has the exact power you need for the situation you find yourself in at that moment. In other words, the Holy Spirit will give you a *rhema* — a specific word for a specific time and a specific purpose.

When that happens, you have just received real "sword power" in the realm of the Spirit. It's time for you to *insert, twist,* and *do damage* to the devil. Then you can watch in jubilation as he hits the road and flees!

MY PRAYER FOR TODAY

Lord, I know that Your Spirit has the very answer I need for any situation I may confront in life. When He speaks to my heart, it places a razor-sharp sword in my hands that I can use against my spiritual enemies. Help me keep a sensitive ear to the Holy Spirit so I can recognize those moments when He is trying to give me a "rhema" that will put the devil on the run!

I pray this in Jesus' name!

MY CONFESSION FOR TODAY

I confess that I can hear the Holy Spirit's voice when He drops a word into my heart at the exact moment I need it. Those quickened words impart special power and authority to me.

They are so powerful that it is as if a sword has been placed in my hands! When I receive that kind of word from the Lord, I insert it, twist it, and do as much damage as possible to the devil until he's sorry he ever messed with me!

I declare this by faith in Jesus' name!

QUESTIONS FOR YOU TO CONSIDER

1. Can you think of times in your life when you needed a *rhema* for the situation you were facing?
2. Did you turn to the Holy Spirit in those situations to listen for a quickened word?
3. What steps can you take to help make the Scriptures more readily available in your life? How would that change the situation you are in now?

FEBRUARY 9

If You're Feeling Unwanted, Abandoned, Or Rejected, It's Time To Rejoice!

And base things of the world,
and things which are despised, hath God chosen....
— 1 Corinthians 1:28

Have you ever felt unwanted, abandoned, or rejected? If your answer is yes, I relate to your feelings entirely. There was a time in my life when I felt very inferior to everyone else, even though I had no reason to feel this way.

Because I was sick for a prolonged period of time when I was in junior high school, I missed a great deal of school. I especially felt the pain of this loss when it came to the subject of mathematics. As a result, I missed all the essential elements of mathematics that my fellow students were learning. When I finally returned to school, I was far behind everyone else.

As I started my first algebra class in junior high school, my teacher ridiculed me for not understanding the basic elements of mathematics that everyone else in class seemed to understand. I tried to explain my situation, but she responded by calling me "Stupid." In fact, every day when she called the roll, instead of calling my name, she'd say, "Stupid Renner," and I'd always answer, "Here, Ma'am."

My teacher's words negatively affected my self-image when I was a young junior high student. Other students laughed at me and thought it was funny to call me "Stupid." Outside of class, they started to call me by the same name until, finally, the word "stupid" became my nickname that many of the kids used that school year when they spoke to me. Everywhere I turned at school, people yelled out, *"Stupid...hey, Stupid!"* I allowed this petty name-calling to create feelings of inferiority in my life that affected me for several years.

Everyone remembers feeling unwanted and rejected at some time or another in his or her life. Some people recover from these experiences; however, the devil has used memories of rejection to keep others in an emotional prison for the rest of their lives. These are the people who never feel wanted and accepted, nor do they feel like they can measure up to other people.

It could be that I'm describing something *you* have experienced in the past. Perhaps it is a recent event that is still very fresh in your memory.

Personally, I am thankful that what happened to me had no long-term effect on my life; in fact, today I even laugh about it. However, I know many people who were devastated by rejection at some point in their lives and never recovered from it.

I've had many other opportunities to feel rejected since my junior high years. For instance, after my family and I moved to the former Soviet Union in 1991, we poured our whole lives into this land. We invested our monies, energies, and nearly every ounce of our strength into establishing churches, broadcasting the Word on television, and enriching the lives of the people in this region of the world. But time and again I've been shocked by the editorials and newspaper articles that accuse me and our ministry of being criminals, cult leaders, a dangerous sect, and so on.

Regardless of who we are, we all deal with these issues from time to time. Therefore, it is essential that you and I make a decision about how we are going to react when something occurs that makes us feel *unwanted*, *abandoned*, or *rejected*. Personally, I have always turned to First Corinthians 1:28 when I've felt tossed aside by friends, by the world, or even by the Church. This scripture has always been a source of strength to me, for it says, "And base things of the world, and things which are despised, hath God chosen...."

When Paul wrote that verse, he was writing to the Corinthian believers, who were being *ostracized* and deemed *stupid* by the unbelieving community in the city of Corinth. The unbelieving citizens didn't understand the Christian faith. But instead of trying to understand, they just decided that Christians were stupid and out of touch with society. In fact, their disdain for Christians was so intense that Paul said they "despised" the Corinthian church.

The word "despised" is the Greek word *exoutheneo*. This Greek word means *to make light of, to despise, to treat with contempt, to disregard, and to neglect*. It pictures *someone low and detestable whom others perceive as hideous, disgusting, despicable and nauseating*. In fact, this word describes a person who is such an outcast and so low in other people's opinions that they don't even consider him worth recognition. People just want to shut their eyes and pretend this person isn't there — to ignore him and to go their own way. But notice the end of the above verse: It boldly announces that the people whom the world rejects are the very ones whom God has chosen!

First Corinthians 1:28 could be translated:

"God has picked out people who are laughable, and through them He is confounding those who think they are high and mighty. Low-class, second-rate, common, average, run-of-the-mill people — those so low that the world doesn't even think they're worth the time of day — these are the ones whom God has chosen...."

Have you noticed that the lost and unbelieving world still tries to ignore believers and pretend they're not there? This is nothing new. In the verse above, the Greek tense indicates that the lost world's terrible opinion of Christians will continue to prevail.

In First John 5:19, the Bible explains why the world refuses to acknowledge those of us who are believers: "...*The whole world lieth in wickedness*." As long as the world lies in the grip of wickedness, we may as well accept the fact that the unbelieving world will mock and make fun of us, no matter what we do to try to change their opinion. *It's just the way a lost world is going to act!*

Rather than let other people affect your self-image and confidence, you need to know who you are in Jesus Christ and hold your head up high. You have no reason to be embarrassed or ashamed. From the beginning of time, the lost world has ridiculed, made fun of, sarcastically accused, and debased the people of God. *There is nothing new about this at all.*

The devil may try to use your friends, your family, your business associates, or your school teachers to make fun of you and drag you down, but you don't have to let the devil's plan work against you. In times like these, remember that Jesus was also "despised and rejected of men" (Isaiah 53:3).

You are in good company with Jesus! So if the world makes light of you or treats you with contempt — if it disregards, neglects, and overlooks you — take heart! *You are exactly the kind of person God wants to use!* He has big plans to use you as a demonstration of His almighty power to your friends, to your family, to your business associates, and to the unbelieving world!

MY PRAYER FOR TODAY

Lord, I am so thankful that You chose me! Even though the devil has tried to use people to tell me that I would never be worth anything, You wanted me and sought me out until I finally heard Your voice and surrendered to Your call. I am so grateful that the opinion of the world about me wasn't true. I'm so glad that You pursued me with such a mighty love and that You refused to give up on me. What else can I say to express my heart to You? I can only say, "Thank You, Jesus!"

I pray this in Jesus' name!

MY CONFESSION FOR TODAY

I confess that because I am in Christ Jesus, I have no reason to be ashamed of who I am. I do not allow other people to affect my self-image and confidence. Because I know who I am in Jesus Christ, I hold my head high and refuse to be embarrassed or to let anyone make me think I am inferior or less than who Jesus made me to be! I am exactly the kind of person God wants to use. He has BIG plans to use me in a mighty way!

I declare this by faith in Jesus' name!

QUESTIONS FOR YOU TO CONSIDER

1. Can you remember a time when you felt despised and rejected? Have you forgiven your offender for making you feel low-class, second-rate, unwanted, abandoned, and rejected?
2. Isn't it comforting to know that God has not only provided a way out of rejection and bitterness for you through forgiveness, but He has also elevated and honored you by choosing you to fulfill His high call on your life?
3. How does it make you feel when you realize that God chooses people who, like Jesus, have felt "despised and rejected of men" so He can demonstrate His power and glory to the world?

FEBRUARY 10

God Will Make Sure You Get Rewarded For Your Work of Faith

Cast not away therefore your confidence,
which hath great recompence of reward.
— Hebrews 10:35

God has all kinds of ways to pay you for staying in faith and doing what He has called you to do. But one thing is for sure — Hebrews 10:35 proves that God wants you to receive a blessing for the services you have rendered in His Kingdom!

The phrase "recompense of reward" is from the Greek word *misthapodosia.* The word *mistha* is the word for *money, a person's salary,* or *a payment that is due.* It was primarily used in an industrial or commercial context to denote a payment, salary, or reward that was given for a job performed. However, when it becomes the word *misthpodosia,* it doesn't just refer to a payment, but to a *recompense, reimbursement, settlement,* or *reparation.*

The first part of this word is the Greek word *mistha,* which communicates several vital ideas to us. First, as noted above, *mistha* communicates the idea of *being paid for present labor.* When any person does a good job, he *expects* to pick up a paycheck for the work he accomplished. It is appropriate for him to expect payment. That paycheck reflects the effort he put into his job. Because he was faithful to do what he was hired to do, he has *earned* that money. Therefore, it is normal for him to *expect* to be paid.

But now this word is used to tell us that God *rewards* or *pays* those who are faithful to assignments He has given them. This refutes the common misconception people have that if they serve God, they will suffer loss or lack for the rest of their lives. These people think they'd do better in life by *not* serving God.

But why would we think God is going to do less than a human employer would do? Don't we expect a human employer to reward employees properly? Because the verse above uses the word *mistha,* it emphatically asserts that God is going to take good care of those who do His will. This means that *faith really does pay!*

But in Hebrews 10:35, the word used isn't just *mistha;* it is expanded even further into the word *misthapodosia.* This compound word means *reimbursement for expenses you spent to do the job; a settlement to take care of injuries or losses;* or *reparations to cover all that vanished due to war.*

God is mindful of the time, love, patience, and money you have invested as you have worked for Him. Hebrews 6:10 says God never overlooks or fails to remember what you have done for Him. If you've worked long hours on His behalf; if you've invested your personal energies into the work of His Kingdom; if you've given 100 percent of your heart and soul to your assigned task; or if you've given sacrificially of your finances — God has never forgotten any of these things. That is why Hebrews 6:10 says, "For God is not unrighteous to forget your work and labour of love, which ye have shewed toward his name…."

The word *misthapodosia* suggests that God will be sure to remember it all — and He will see to it that you are fully *reimbursed* for everything you spent to accomplish the assignment He gave to you. He will make a *settlement* with you for past expenses that would make anyone want to rejoice! God will make sure you get *reparations* for any damage you've experienced because of the battles you've fought for Him.

Because the word *misthapodosia* is used,
Hebrews 10:35 carries the following idea:

"…God will see to it that you are paid and fully reimbursed for expenses you have spent to do His will; He will make a settlement that takes care of all injuries or losses you may have incurred; He will make sure that you get reparations to cover all that has been damaged or destroyed due to the attacks of the enemy or because of the adversarial situations you have faced."

Hebrews 10:35 makes it clear that God is *fair* and *equitable* in His dealings. You may have given your best and worked with all your heart and might to fulfill an assignment He gave you. You may have invested your whole heart into that assignment or lost something along the way that was precious to you. If so, God will make certain that you are *paid* and *reimbursed*. God never disregards what you have done for Him.

God's *payments* and *reimbursements* for what you have done may come to you in different forms, but you can be certain that it will be *equitable* for what you have invested. For instance, He may pay you by giving you:

◆ *New victories in different areas of your life.*
◆ *Success in your business or ministry.*
◆ *A greater anointing than you've ever had.*
◆ *An increase of financial prosperity.*
◆ *A long-term friendship you'll be able to count on for years to come.*

According to Philippians 4:19, God has no shortage of riches in Heaven — and those riches are reserved to meet your current needs. There is no need to be beggarly in how much you expect to be blessed. Those riches are reserved for *you*, so raise your level of expectation! Throw open your arms! It's time for you to receive the harvest you *earned* through a lot of hard work and effort!

If something has been telling your mind that it isn't right to expect God to reward you for your faith in this life, tell that religious spirit to get away from you in Jesus' name! Open your heart right now and expect God to pay you for services rendered in your walk of faith!

MY PRAYER FOR TODAY

Lord, I am thankful that You reward us when we are faithful to fulfill the assignments You've given us to do. I know that by serving You, I will never suffer real loss or lack because You always take good care of those who do Your will. I trust that You will see to it that I am fully reimbursed for everything I've spent to complete my assigned tasks. I believe that You will make a settlement for past expenses that will make me shout with joy! You've never overlooked what I've done for You in the past, and I trust that You will take care of me now as well.

I pray this in Jesus' name!

MY CONFESSION FOR TODAY

I confess that God is mindful of the time, love, patience, and money I have invested as I've served Him. Hebrews 6:10 says God never overlooks or fails to remember what I have done for Him. This means I can rest assured that as I work long hours on His behalf; invest my personal energies; give 100 percent of my heart and soul to my assigned task; and give sacrificially of my finances, God will never forget any of it. He rewards those who diligently seek Him, so I'm a candidate for one of His rewards! Therefore, I will not get tired; I will not give in to discouragement; and I will keep pressing forward to do what God has called me to do, believing that He will take care of me all the way through to the end!

I declare this by faith in Jesus' name!

QUESTIONS FOR YOU TO CONSIDER

1. Can you recollect some of the rewards God has given you in the past for being faithful?
2. Are you diligently putting your heart and soul into what God has called you to do right now and expecting Him to reward you for your faithful labor?
3. Since God is mindful of everything you invest in your work for Him, can you think of some ways you could invest more into His Kingdom?

FEBRUARY 11

Set the Spiritual Hostages Free!

…For this purpose the Son of God was manifested,
that he might destroy the works of the devil.
— 1 John 3:8

Multitudes of people in this world today are held hostage in their minds by the devil. They are incarcerated, locked up, and caged in their minds and emotions, held like slaves, prisoners, or detainees who are under arrest and live at the mercy of their conqueror.

I couldn't begin to count the people I've met through the years who fit that description. Although they belong to Jesus and legally have every right to freedom, they remain in spiritual bondage, at least in some measure, in certain areas of their lives. Whether they persisted in a particular sin or failed to do something they should have done (such as read the Word, pray, or stay in fellowship with other saints), their minds were pried open wide enough for Satan to find an inroad and take that part of their minds captive.

You see, the mind is the primary area Satan seeks to attack. He knows that once he succeeds in planting a stronghold of deception in some area of a person's mind, from that lofty position he can then begin to control and manipulate that person. The Bible calls this kind of deception in the mind a "stronghold" (2 Corinthians 10:4). It is a "stronghold" because once a lie is planted in someone's head, it is very hard to remove!

But First John 3:8 says that Jesus came into the world "…that he might *destroy* the works of the devil"! I want you to particularly notice the word "destroy" in this verse. It is taken from the Greek word *luo,* which refers to the act of *untying* or *unloosing* something. It was used in classical Greek literature to refer to people being *delivered, released,* or *freed* from difficulties, burdens, or needs.

In the New Testament, the word *luo* was used to depict the *untying* of the thongs of a shoe or sandal in Mark 1:7; the *unfastening* of a donkey's colt in Matthew 21:2; the *loosening, unraveling,* and *removal* of Lazarus' grave clothes in John 11:44; and the *taking away* of Paul's chains in Acts 22:30. But the Greek word *luo* also means *to break* or *to destroy,* as in Revelation 5:2, where the Bible says that Jesus is worthy to "loose" (or *break*) the seals referred to in the book of Revelation.

One of the clearest examples of the word *luo* is found in Luke 3:16, when John the Baptist says, "…But one mightier than I cometh, the latchet of whose shoes I am not worthy to unloose…." The word *luo* is translated here "to unloose." It is the picture of someone who reaches down to *unloose* the tight strings of a sandal; then he begins to *unwrap* those strings from the shoe until finally the shoe becomes so *loosened* that it easily slips off his foot.

Now let's look at First John 3:8, the verse we are focusing on today. Here the Bible uses the word *luo* when it says, "…For this purpose the Son of God was manifested, that he might *destroy* the works of the devil." This tells us that when Jesus Christ came into the world, He came to *untie* and *unloose* Satan's binding powers over us. His objective was to *disentangle* us from Satan's control; to *unfasten* us from the demonic shackles that held us captive; to *unravel* the chains Satan used to keep us in his grip; and to *break* and *destroy* all the fetters Satan had used to hold us hostage.

**Because the word *luo* is used in First John 3:8,
it could be taken to mean:**

"…For this purpose the Son of God was manifested, that He might untie people from all the works of the devil, unraveling Satan's hold on them — until the devil's works in people's lives are utterly destroyed and his hostages are set free."

Through His death and resurrection, Jesus' redemptive work destroyed the power of the enemy and our liberty was fully purchased. You see, setting people free from Satan's power has always been Jesus' primary concern. First John 3:8 declares that this was the *purpose* that the Son of God was manifested on this earth. Since this is His concern, it should also be ours.

So many people in this world today are incarcerated, locked up and caged in their minds and emotions. They are held like slaves or prisoners, living at the mercy of their conqueror. Therefore, it is time for you to learn how to recognize the devil's strategies in other people's minds and lives. Jesus came to set people free, and God wants to use *you* to take the delivering power of God to them so the works of the devil can be destroyed in their lives.

The mind may be the devil's preferred battlefield, but you can make sure he loses every skirmish! *Just determine today to be a willing vessel God can use to free spiritual hostages from demonic oppression!*

MY PRAYER FOR TODAY

Lord, please help me to be conscious of the people I meet who are bound by the devil in their minds. I know that You want to use me to touch them and to bring them the freedom that can be found only in You. I am so sorry for the times I get so busy that I fail to recognize opportunities to speak Your name and to share Your love with people who are lost and bound. Please help me to become consistently alert to the people for whom You died and to go out of my way to tell them the Good News that will deliver them and set them free.

I pray this in Jesus' name!

QUESTIONS FOR YOU TO CONSIDER

1. Can you think of people you know or have known who live like spiritual hostages?
2. Has the Holy Spirit ever told you to minister to any of these individuals? How did you respond to His instructions and what was the result?
3. Why not make a list of the people you know who need to be set free from Satan's bondage and then ask the Holy Spirit to show you how to bring freedom to them?

FEBRUARY 12

He's Still the Lord Of the Wind and the Waves!

And there arose a great storm of wind,
and the waves beat into the ship, so that it was now full....
And He [Jesus] arose, and rebuked the wind, and said unto the sea,
Peace, be still. And the wind ceased, and there was a great calm.
— Mark 4:37,39

*A*nytime you are on the front lines of battle doing something significant for the Kingdom of God, the enemy's attacks against your life will escalate. I'm not telling you this to scare you, but to mentally equip you. That way when the attacks come, you won't be taken by surprise!

Being mentally prepared for a spiritual attack is very important. If you are familiar with the devil's tactics, his assaults won't take you off guard or by surprise when they intensify against you. You'll be able to recognize and resist every demonic attack, rejoicing in the Lord because you know what's happening.

Jesus came under this kind of intense attack when He was crossing the Sea of Galilee with His disciples on His way to cast a legion of demons out of the demoniac of Gadara. This demon-possessed man was an important weapon in Satan's arsenal. Through the actions of the demoniac of Gadara, the devil had held the countryside hostage with fear for a very long time. The demoniac was so legendary that people throughout the entire coastland region knew of him.

The devil knew that if Jesus crossed the Sea of Galilee that night and reached the other side, He would cast the demons out of that man. When that happened, Satan would lose the weapon he had long used to terrorize the whole countryside.

So as Jesus and His disciples crossed the Sea of Galilee that night, violent and destructive winds seemed to come from out of nowhere to capsize Jesus' boat and drown Him and His disciples in the middle of the sea. Mark 4:37 says, "And there arose a great storm of wind...."

The phrase "there arose" is taken from the Greek word *ginomai,* which in this case describes *something that happens unexpectedly* or *something that catches one off-guard.* This plainly tells us that Jesus and His disciples did *not* expect bad weather that night. The Greek word *ginomai* emphatically means that this event completely took the disciples *by surprise.*

To let us know the size of this storm, Mark uses the Greek word *mega,* which denotes *something of massive proportions.* It is where we get the idea of *mega-bills, mega-work,* and *megaphone.* Because Mark uses the word *mega,* it alerts us to the fact that this was a *mega-storm* with *mega-winds*!

The word "wind" is the Greek word *lalaipsi,* which means this was a *turbulent or terribly violent wind.* This word can also be translated *hurricane, cyclone, tempest, gale, windstorm, a furious tempest,* or *a fierce squall.* Therefore, we know the storm that came against Jesus that night was no small breeze. It was a formidable, crushing, overpowering type of storm.

One very important fact must be pointed out: This was a *windstorm.* There is no mention of rain at all because this was a storm of *wind.* Jesus and His disciples could *feel* its effects as the wind blew against them and their boat. They could *see* the raging waves that were tossed to and fro by this violent wind. However, the windstorm that had come to overturn their boat in the middle of Sea of Galilee and to kill them before they reached the other side was *invisible.*

The Greek words in Mark 4:37 gives this idea:

"And suddenly and unexpectantly — as if it came from out of nowhere — there arose a gale of wind. It was a ferocious tempest with winds that were terribly violent, turbulent, and overpowering...."

Here was Jesus — on the brink of one of the greatest miracles of His ministry. At the same time, there was the devil, fearing that he was about to lose one of his most highly prized weapons of terrorism. It was at this exact moment that this violent, destructive turbulence came down upon Jesus and His disciples.

The occurrence of the storm at this exact moment was no accident. The devil didn't want Jesus to reclaim one of his most prized captives. This was a preemptive strike of the devil to undo the work of God.

But that night in the midst of the storm, Jesus arose and took authority over the situation. The Bible says that when He exercised His authority over this unseen turbulence, "...the wind ceased, and there was a great calm" (Mark 4:39). In doing this, Jesus demonstrated that He was the Lord of the wind and the waves. This potentially deadly situation provided a great opportunity for the disciples to learn that Jesus Christ is truly Lord over all!

Rest assured — Satan will certainly try to attack you with unexpected turbulence from time to time. His attacks against you will probably escalate whenever you're right on the edge of a breakthrough, as was the case with Jesus that night. But just as that event provided an opportunity for Jesus to demonstrate His power and authority, you need to see each demonic attack against you as an opportunity to rise up, take authority, and demonstrate who you are in Jesus Christ!

Mentally and spiritually prepare yourself to deal with the devil's attacks. Put on the whole armor of God. Rise up and take authority in Jesus' name over the wind and the waves that come against you and your family. *Never forget that this is your golden opportunity to see a demonstration of God's power in your life!*

MY PRAYER FOR TODAY

Lord, thank You for teaching me that Satan often attacks right when I'm on the verge of a major breakthrough. This knowledge helps me so much because it causes me to recognize that Satan loves to make all hell break loose in my life just before a big victory. Now that I know this, please help me keep this in mind when a turbulent wind blows into my life. Help me to look at that storm and say, "I know that the devil must be upset; otherwise, he wouldn't be messing with me right now. I must be right on track with God!" With this understanding, I will keep pressing ahead, regardless of what I see, feel, or hear.

I pray this in Jesus' name!

MY CONFESSION FOR TODAY

I declare that every attack of the devil is my opportunity to see a demonstration of the power of God. What the devil meant for my harm, God will turn for my good. This is my opportunity to rise up, speak the name of Jesus, use my God-given authority, and declare to the spiritual realm that the Lord of lords whom I serve is by far the One with the most spiritual power!

I declare this by faith in Jesus' name!

QUESTIONS FOR YOU TO CONSIDER

1. Do you recall some storms in your past that you had to stand against until the victory finally came?
2. How did you react to the last storm in your life? Did you rise up and take authority over the situation?
3. In what ways are you mentally and spiritually preparing yourself for future attacks?

You can be quite certain that Satan will try to attack you with unexpected turbulence from time to time. His attacks against you will probably escalate whenever you're right on the edge of a major breakthrough. You therefore need to see each demonic attack against you as an opportunity to rise up, take authority, and demonstrate who you are in Jesus Christ!

FEBRUARY 13

❧❧❧

'X' Marks the Spot!

But we have this treasure in earthen vessels,
that the excellency of the power may be of God, and not of us.
— 2 Corinthians 4:7

When I was a small boy, the guys in our neighborhood loved to play like they were pirates. My friends and I would draw detailed maps with palm trees, waterfalls, lagoons, and, of course, *buried treasure!* The location of the buried treasure was always specified with a huge "X." As we acted out our game and pretended to look for hidden treasure, we'd remind each other that *"X" marked the spot* of the buried treasure.

Treasure hunters are always scouring the earth to look for treasures and relics left by previous civilizations and generations. But the greatest treasure in the whole universe is right inside you! I'm talking about a cache of wealth so immense that its reserves can never be completely dug out, explored, discovered, or discerned. These are spiritual assets beyond your wildest imagination!

The apostle Paul wrote about this astonishing treasure in Second Corinthians 4:7, where he said, "But we have this treasure in earthen vessels, that the excellency of the power may be of God, and not of us." The first thing Paul does in this verse is tell us *where* this treasure is buried.

Notice that Paul says, "But we have…." The words "we have" in Greek is *echomen*, which is taken from the Greek word *echo*. The word *echo* means *to have, to hold, to possess,* or *to keep.* It is the picture of someone who "has" something in his possession because it belongs to him. It is rightfully his, and he has the right to keep it.

But when Paul uses this word in this verse, he speaks in the plural, including himself and all believers. His words could be translated, *"We hold and possess as our very own…."* He is describing something that is already in the hands of all believers — something that legally belongs to them and that they have a right to claim! The word "treasure" is the Greek word *thesauros*, a word that describes *a treasure, a treasury, a treasure chamber,* or *a place of safekeeping where riches and fortunes are kept.* It presents the idea of *a specially built room designed to be the repository for massive riches and wealth.* By using this word, Paul declares that we as believers are the possessors of riches beyond belief. Moreover, we are the chambers, repositories, or treasuries where God has placed this fortune. Because the word *echomen* ("we have") precedes the word *thesauros,* this phrase could be translated, *"We already have and hold this wealth in our possession."* Therefore, it is not something we are *trying* to obtain; it is something we already *possess.*

However, Paul says that this treasure is contained in "earthen vessels" — a phrase he uses to refer to our human bodies. The phrase "earthen vessels" comes from the Greek word *ostrakinos*, a word used to describe *small, cheap, and easily broken pottery made of inferior materials.* This kind of pottery was *weak, fragile, and valueless* — so cheaply made that it would never have been seen in wealthier homes. These "bargain-basement" dishes were primarily used in the lower-class neighborhoods, purchased by people who couldn't afford to acquire better merchandise. Because the dishes were made of imperfect materials, they usually had defects.

As time passed, it is interesting that this word *ostrakinos* came to represent *anything inferior, low-grade, mediocre, shoddy, second-rate, or substandard.* Furthermore, it is where we get the phrase "to ostracize."

When people "ostracize" a person, it means they regard him as *substandard* — too *unfit* to be a part of their group. They speak derogatorily of him, poke fun at him, and belittle him in front of others. The person being "ostracized" most likely feels as though he has been *cut out* of the group — shunned, ignored, and treated like something that is shoddy and deficient.

Shoddy, deficient, substandard pottery is exactly the kind of "earthen vessels" Paul had in mind when he wrote Second Corinthians 4:7. He used the illustration of these cheaply made dishes to announce the location of the secret chamber where God placed His greatest treasure on planet earth!

✦ *Where is the secret chamber in which God has put His greatest treasure?*
✦ *Where are the earthen vessels Paul refers to in this verse?*

By connecting the Greek words *echomen, thesauros,* and *ostrakinos,* Paul says that *we* are the location of this divine treasure! If "X" marks the spot, then the "X" is marked on us! As amazing as this is to consider, it is true that God has placed His greatest gift on earth *on the inside of us*!

This means that Second Corinthians 4:7 communicates this idea:

"We possess treasure within ourselves! And not only do we possess treasure, but our easily broken, inferior, temporary bodies are themselves the treasure chambers where this astonishing cache is kept.…"

Paul uses these Greek words, almost in amazement, to joyfully announce that the human body is the residence of the Holy Spirit — God's powerful gift to every believer. Even though our human bodies *are* fragile and eventually die, it pleased God to deposit this gift inside us. Think about how incredible this is! The human body is so fragile that:

✦ A wrong diet can kill it.
✦ Working too hard can break it.
✦ Too much pressure can damage it.
✦ And even after caring tenderly for it your entire lifetime, it still eventually dies.
✦ *Yet God placed His greatest treasure inside us anyway!*

Get ahold of this picture in your heart: You are a treasure hunter's greatest dream. You have the treasure map. "X" marks the spot for the hidden treasure, but this time you don't have to go searching for the hidden treasure because the "X" is written on you! You are the hiding place for God's greatest treasure — the third Person of the Godhead, the Holy Spirit!

So meditate on this truth today: *You are valuable and precious in God's sight.* Even though in the natural you may seem weak, fragile, and valueless, God has chosen your human body as the place to hide His greatest treasure. Now you can say, "When God looks at me, 'X' really does mark the spot!"

MY PRAYER FOR TODAY

Lord, how can I ever say thank You enough for putting Your Spirit inside me! It is so amazing to think that You would want to live inside someone like me. Yet this was Your choice, and for this I am eternally grateful. Help me live a life that is worthy of Your Presence inside me. Forgive me for times when I've treated You wrongly by defiling my mind or my body with things that are not worthy of You. Help me stay constantly aware that I am a carrier of the greatest gift the world has ever known.

I pray this in Jesus' name!

I joyfully declare that I carry the Presence of God in my life. I am the temple of the Holy Spirit — a treasury where God has placed His power, His gifts, His grace, His fruit, and His character. Resident within me is enough power and answers to change both my environment and the environment of anyone to whom God uses me to speak the words of life.

I declare this by faith in Jesus' name!

QUESTIONS FOR YOU TO CONSIDER

1. Are you daily aware of the wonderful Presence of God that is always resident inside you?
2. Do you look at yourself with disgust, or do you see your body as a wonderfully made treasure chamber for the Holy Spirit?
3. Since the Holy Spirit lives inside you, how should this affect the way you live your life?

FEBRUARY 14

The Holy Spirit Earnestly Yearns for You!

Do ye think that the scripture saith in vain,
the spirit that dwelleth in us lusteth to envy?
— James 4:5

Has there ever been anything you wanted so badly that you just couldn't get it off your mind? Every time you tried to think about something else, your mind just kept drifting back over and over again to that thing you desired. Finally, your urge to possess it became so intense that every fiber of your being wanted to reach out and capture it before anyone else had a chance to snatch it first!

Let me use a different illustration to make this point. If a drug addict or an alcoholic abruptly decides to stop doing drugs or drinking after many years of chemical abuse, what happens? Unless that person has a miraculous deliverance, it probably won't be too long before his body begins to crave those chemicals. In fact, his appetite for drugs or alcohol might get so forceful that he doubles over in agony. That's how much his body yearns for a "fix" of what it has habitually received in the past.

In the New Testament, the images above would be depicted by the Greek word *epipotheo*, which is a compound of the words *epi* and *potheo*. The word *epi* means *over*, and the word *potheo* is the word for *desire*. But when these two words are compounded together, the new word *epipotheo* portrays *an intense desire, a craving, a hunger, an ache, a yearning for something, a longing or pining for something*. More specifically, it describes *an intense, abnormal, excessive yearning*.

Usually this word is used to indicate an intense yearning for something that is morally wrong and sinful. It is the pitiful picture of someone, such as a drug addict or an alcoholic, who needs his "fix" so seriously that he is doubled over, racked with pain, and crying out, *"Please, someone, give me what I need!"*

Remarkably, this Greek word *epipotheo* is the same word found in James 4:5 to describe the desire of the Holy Spirit when it says, "...The spirit that dwelleth in us *lusteth* to envy...."

The word "lust" in this verse is from this same Greek word *epipotheo*. Only this time the word is not used to describe the painful addiction of a drug addict or alcoholic; rather, it depicts the Spirit of God! There is obviously some object that the Spirit of God craves. In fact, this Greek word pictures Him as desiring it so desperately that He is like one who needs some type of "fix" to satisfy an addiction. He is crying out, "I have to have it! I can't wait any longer! Give me what I crave! Give me what I am aching and yearning to have!"

But what does this mean? What is James 4:5 saying to us? What does the Holy Spirit yearn for so sincerely that the Bible would picture Him in this way?

In James 4:5, the Bible reveals the intense yearning the Holy Spirit possesses to have *us* entirely for Himself. That should be no surprise to us. He is our Indweller, our Sealer, our Sanctifier, and our Source of power. His attention, His gifts, His power, and His Word are all directed toward us. He is in love with us!

The Holy Spirit is so in love with us that He wants more, more, more, and more of us. Every day He wants our time, our attention, our devotion, and our fellowship. If we deny the Holy Spirit of what He wants from us, He cries out, "I need you! I must have you! I want to fill you, empower you, and flood you with My divine life!"

James 4:5 conveys this compelling idea:

"...The Spirit has an all-consuming and passionate desire to have more and more of us. In fact, this desire to possess us is so strong that He literally yearns, craves, and pines after us."

Never forget that the Holy Spirit is a Divine Lover who lives on the inside of us. He passionately yearns to fulfill His responsibility to the Father to help, teach, guide, and empower us. The word *epipotheo* emphatically means that when it comes to you and me, the Holy Spirit can never get enough!

The Holy Spirit desires to possess you — *all of you*. Because of this intense desire, He is focused on changing you, empowering you, conforming you to the image of Jesus Christ, and helping you fulfill God's plan for your life.

Learn how to yield to the Holy Spirit. Allow Him to have more and more of you each day. *Satisfy the yearning of this Divine Lover. Let the Holy Spirit love you! Let Him control you! Let Him exercise His authority in your life and flood you with His divine desire!*

MY PRAYER FOR TODAY

Lord, help me to be mindful that the Holy Spirit lives inside me and wants to possess more and more of me every day. Please help me learn how to surrender to the Spirit's power and to yield to His sanctifying Presence. I know that as I yield to Him, He will fill me full of every good thing I need to live a happy and successful life in this world. I want to begin today by opening myself to the Holy Spirit completely. Holy Spirit, I ask You to fill me anew right now.

I pray this in Jesus' name!

QUESTIONS FOR YOU TO CONSIDER

1. Have you ever experienced the deep love that the Holy Spirit has for you?
2. When you had this experience, where were you and what was happening in your life?
3. In order for you to continually experience the deep love of the Holy Spirit, what do you need to do?

FEBRUARY 15

Be a 'Holy Terror' To the Kingdom of Darkness!

For though we walk in the flesh,
we do not war after the flesh.
— 2 Corinthians 10:3

You have been delivered from Satan's power through the victorious, redemptive work of Jesus Christ. Make sure you keep that wonderful truth in mind the next time you have to deal with the devil's attack on your life. And don't try to defeat a spiritual enemy with fleshly weapons and techniques because fleshly weapons are for fighting fleshly adversaries; they were never intended to defeat a spiritual foe. Spiritual adversaries must be fought with spiritual weapons!

Paul makes this point in Second Corinthians 10:3 when he says, "For though we walk in the flesh, we do not war after the flesh." The word "walk" in this verse is taken from the Greek word *peripateo*. This is a compound of the word *peri*, which means *around*, and *pateo*, which means *to walk*. When these two words are compounded together, the new word means *to walk around* or *to habitually live and carry on in one general territory*. It is the picture of a person who has walked in one general path for so long that he can now almost walk that path blindfolded. He knows that area well because he has habitually lived and functioned there.

By using the word *peripateo* in Second Corinthians 10:3, Paul is making a very strong statement about his humanity. He's saying, "Nearly everything I do, I do in the flesh. I eat in the flesh; I sleep in the flesh; I think in the flesh; I study in the flesh. My life is primarily lived in this earthly realm." Although he was a spiritual man, he still lived in a body made of flesh.

Paul knew that he was locked into his fleshly body and couldn't get out of it — nor could he trade it for another! I'm sure he would have taken that option if it had been available because he had been brutally beaten and terribly abused during the course of his ministry. His physical body permanently bore the scars, marks, wounds, and disfigurement of those beatings (*see* 2 Corinthians 11:23-25 and Galatians 6:17). Having a body free of scars and disfiguring wounds would have seemed like a terrific prospect to Paul!

In addition to the beatings he had endured, Paul was naturally a man of small stature. In fact, the name Paul means "little one." Although he was an intellectual giant who was highly educated, cultured, and even skillful in the political arena before he came to Christ, he did not have a striking physical appearance. Even historians record that he was a small and unimposing man.

It seems that the appearance of Paul's body was even an issue in the Corinthian church. Those who were against his ministry and wanted to eliminate him used his physical appearance as a reason to discredit him. In response to this, Paul wrote and said: "...In presence [I] am base among you..." (2 Corinthians 10:1). Because his adversaries were judging him according to the flesh, he asked them: "Do ye look on things after the outward appearance?..." (2 Corinthians 10:7). Finally, Paul actually quoted what they were saying about him: "For his letters, say they, are weighty and powerful; but his bodily presence is weak..." (2 Corinthians 10:10).

Notice that Paul never argues with them about the condition of his body. In fact, it seems that he agrees with them, even stating, "I am base among you." But whereas some may have judged him according to the flesh, Paul's confidence was not in the flesh but in the spirit. That is why he told them, "For though we walk in the flesh, we do not war after the flesh" (2 Corinthians 10:3).

I think this message is important because we live in a day when people tend to judge themselves by the appearance of their bodies. If they are skinny, they feel good about themselves. But if they gain just a little weight, they are tempted to think that they are ugly and disgusting. Because of modern movies and advertisements, people are continually inundated with thousands of subliminal messages that say, "If you're not skinny and youthful-looking, you don't rate!"

Amazingly, even believers get caught up in judging themselves by their outward appearance. Although it's true that we should do what we can to stay in good shape physically, there are millions of people who are in great physical shape but couldn't win a spiritual battle if their lives depended on it!

You see, physical muscles make you look great in the natural, but mere flesh and blood has no effect on the devil or the spiritual realm. Spiritual battles are not to be fought or won with flesh, because the flesh is no match for spiritual foes. This disadvantage of the flesh is the reason God has supplied spiritual weapons for the believer.

Paul was aware of the weakness and futility of his flesh. He knew that when it came to dealing with the devil, he had to turn his attention to the realm of the Spirit where supernatural assistance was available and spiritual weapons existed for him to use against the devil. He knew his greatest weapons did not lie in his mind, his talents, or his flesh, but in spiritual weapons that exist in the realm of God's Spirit.

In Acts 19, a group of exorcists, whom the Bible identifies as the seven sons of a man named Sceva, attempted to cast an evil spirit out of a demon-possessed man. But when they commanded the evil spirit to come out of that man, the spirit answered them: "...Jesus I know, and Paul I know; but who are ye?" (Acts 19:14,15).

Think of it! That evil spirit knew who Jesus was *and* who Paul was! Even though Paul lived in a small body that had been mercilessly beaten and abused, he was so powerful in the spiritual realm that hell knew his name! Perhaps the limitations of Paul's flesh turned out to be to his advantage! Because he couldn't lean on his flesh, he had to learn how to function in the realm of the Spirit — and that's the reason the evil spirits knew who he was!

That's exactly what you need to do as well. Yes, you may live in a fleshly body that has all kinds of limitations, but you can go forth with spiritual weapons to do warfare in the Spirit! Regardless of what you look like in the natural realm, you can be a holy terror to the devil in the spiritual realm. So reach out and take the loinbelt of truth, the shoes of peace, the breastplate of righteousness, the shield of faith, the helmet of salvation, and the sword of the Spirit, which is the Word of God. When you're clothed in the whole armor of God, you can win the victory over the kingdom of darkness every time!

MY PRAYER FOR TODAY

Lord, help me remember that real spiritual battles are fought and won in the Spirit. I'm so often tempted to focus on my physical appearance and the condition of my body. I even frequently judge myself by how physically "in shape" I am. But the fight I need to win isn't going to be won by my physical appearance. Yes, I want to be in good physical shape, and I ask You to help me achieve that goal. But please keep me from getting distracted by the less-than-pleasurable aspects of my physical body. Help me stay focused on the spiritual realm where the real battle is being waged.

I pray this in Jesus' name!

MY CONFESSION FOR TODAY

I proclaim that regardless of what I look like in the natural realm, I am a menace to the devil in the spiritual realm. In that sphere, I am anointed and powerful, with the ability to pull down strongholds from peoples' lives and minds. I am so mighty in the Spirit that the devil and his forces flee when I resist them!

I declare this by faith in Jesus' name!

QUESTIONS FOR YOU TO CONSIDER

1. Do you tend to accept or reject yourself on the basis of how much you weigh or how you look physically? *Be honest!*
2. Do you spend as much time focusing on your spiritual development as you do fretting and complaining about your physical appearance?
3. How much do you think you could grow spiritually this year if you invested the same amount of time you now spend worrying about your body in developing yourself *spiritually?*

Physical muscles make you look great in the natural, but mere flesh and blood has no effect on the devil or the spiritual realm.

FEBRUARY 16

❧

Don't Put Out The Spirit's Fire!

Quench not the Spirit.
— 1 Thessalonians 5:19

Have you ever sensed the Holy Spirit leading you to do something, but because of fear you were afraid to do it? Even though you were sure it was God's Spirit who was speaking to you, did you grit your teeth, dig in your heels, and decide that you would *not* do what He was leading you to do or say?

If the answer is *yes*, it's time for you to stop doing that! The Holy Spirit is trying to use you to help someone or to accomplish some feat according to His plans and purposes. Don't let the devil or a spirit of fear talk you out of experiencing the joy of being used by the Holy Spirit. This is exactly why Paul admonished us, "Quench not the Spirit" (1 Thessalonians 5:19).

The word "quench" in this verse is taken from the Greek word *sbennumi*. The word *sbennumi* means *to extinguish, smother, suppress, douse, put out, snuff out,* or *to quell.* It most often means *to extinguish a fire by dousing it with water.* In some places, it means *to evaporate* or *to dry up.*

There's no doubt about what Paul is trying to tell us. If we ignore the Holy Spirit's voice long enough and often enough, eventually we will become spiritually hardened and will no longer be able to hear Him when He does try to speak to us. It will be like His voice *evaporates* or *dries up,* and we will hear it no more.

You need to know that your own actions, fears, insecurities, and disobedience to the voice of the Holy Spirit can thwart the plan of God for your life! The Holy Spirit is willing and ready to give you a divine assignment, but you hinder His wonderful plans by ignoring and denying His right to use you time and time again.

If you've ever seen a campfire, you know that its flames can burn very bright and hot. But what happens if someone keeps throwing water on the coals? Initially it will only *dampen* the heat of the flames. But if the person continues to throw water on the flames, eventually that water will *quench, smother,* or *put out* the fire altogether.

Has the Holy Spirit been speaking to your heart, tenderly directing you to do something? Have you obeyed Him and done what He has prompted you to do — or have you turned a deaf ear to His voice? Let me encourage you:

✦ *Don't ignore the Holy Spirit's leading!*
✦ *Don't disregard His voice!*
✦ *Don't close your ears when He is speaking to you!*
✦ *Don't pass up an opportunity for the Holy Spirit to use you!*
✦ *Don't avoid moments when God wants to pour His power through you!*
✦ *Don't throw water on the flames until you quench the Spirit!*

Instead of continually shutting your ears to the Holy Spirit's voice and dousing the flames of the Spirit in your heart, it's time for you to say, "Yes, Lord, I'll do what You say. I'll go where You send me. I'll obey what You tell me to do!" When you adopt this attitude, you start putting fuel back on the fire again! Every time you say, "Yes, Lord," and follow through with obedience, you stoke the coals and cause the Holy Spirit's fire to burn more brightly in your life.

The primary reason we don't obey the prompting of the Holy Spirit is that we are afraid of what may or may not happen if we step out in faith to do what He has asked us to do. But we need to learn to trust the Holy Spirit. He will never lead us to do something that is wrong or harmful; He will never fail us or let us down.

Determine in your heart today to obey whatever the Spirit of God tells you to do. As you stay true to that decision, you'll see God do marvelous things through you. *He will use you to set people free from whatever holds them in bondage — all because you determined to do what the Holy Spirit led you to do!*

MY PRAYER FOR TODAY

Lord, help me to quickly obey when the Spirit of God prompts me to do something. The last thing I want to do is throw water on the flames of the Spirit in my heart. Forgive me for suffocating the life of the Holy Spirit in me by refusing to do what He tells me to do. From this point onward, I make the choice to quickly obey, but I need Your strength to do this. So today I am asking You to fill me anew with brand-new courage to step out in faith, to quickly obey, and to leave the results with You!

I pray this in Jesus' name!

MY CONFESSION FOR TODAY

I confess that I am quick to obey the voice of the Holy Spirit. When He tugs at my heart, pointing me in a specific direction or leading me to minister to a certain person, I do not hold back, hesitate, or resist. Instead, I say, "Lord, I'll do whatever You want me to do!" I then step out in faith and watch as His power is demonstrated to me and through me!

I declare this by faith in Jesus' name!

QUESTIONS FOR YOU TO CONSIDER

1. Can you think of a time when the Spirit of God prompted you to do something, but you dug in your heels and refused to do it?
2. How did you feel afterwards, knowing that you had resisted the voice of the Holy Spirit?
3. How will you respond the next time the Holy Spirit tells you to do something?

Instead of continually shutting your ears to the Holy Spirit's voice and dousing the flames of the Spirit in your heart, it's time for you to say, "Yes, Lord, I'll do what You say. I'll go where You send me. I'll obey what You tell me to do!"

FEBRUARY 17

A Great Cloud of Witnesses

Wherefore seeing we also are compassed about
with so great a cloud of witnesses....
— Hebrews 12:1

Do you see the word "cloud" in the verse above? It is taken from the Greek word *nephos*. It describes *clouds* — just like the clouds you see in the sky. When most people read this verse, they imagine big, fluffy white clouds with Old Testament saints scattered mystically throughout the glorious white billows. But is this really the picture that Hebrews 12:1 means to convey to us?

The Greek word *nephos,* translated "clouds," has an additional meaning that is very exciting when understood in this context. In ancient, classical Greek times, the word "clouds" was used to describe *the highest seats in the bleachers of a stadium.* The seats at the very top of the stadium were called *the clouds* because they were so high up in the air. If you had gone to a sports competition with a ticket for one of these seats, your usher might have said, *"Your seat is in the clouds today."* This meant you'd be seated in the highest row available in the bleachers.

We have seen before (*see* January 24) that the phrase "compassed about" is taken from the word *peikeimenai,* which is a compound of the words *peri* and *keimai.* The word *peri* means *around, as to be completely encircled by something.* The second part of the word, *keimai,* means *to lie down.* When these two words are compounded into one word, they mean *to lie around,* as if something has been *piled high* and is *lying all around you on every side.* This portrays the idea of *being completely encircled* by something that is *stacked high* on every side.

Thus, this verse carries the following idea: "Wherefore seeing we have lying all around us on every side...." or "Wherefore seeing these biblical examples who are piled up and lying all around us...." But to make this point even stronger, the Holy Spirit uses the word "clouds." Why is this so vital?

In Hebrews 12:1, the Holy Spirit is emphasizing:

"You're not alone! The grandstands of Heaven all the way up to the 'clouds,' the highest seats in the bleachers, are piled high with people who stood the test of time and eventually saw their faith manifested...."

Let me stress again that the Greek word *nephos* ("clouds") depicted the highest seats in a sports stadium. This is a powerful image because it jogs our memory to the fact that our walk of faith will remove us from the spectator sections and will put us right in the middle of the fight!

The devil hates it when people take a stand of faith or when they do something that benefits the Kingdom of God and drives back darkness. Like an opponent would do in a natural fight, Satan may try to wrestle you, pin you down, or even try to knock you out of the race altogether.

So when you have become illuminated with direction for your life, business, family, or ministry, you need to know that the contest has just begun. You are on the field. All eyes are on you. The fight of faith is on! But if you'll look up into the bleachers of Heaven for just a moment, you'll see that they are stacked all the way to the "clouds" with people just like you!

Just as you are taking steps of obedience now, the bleachers of Heaven are *filled* with people who have already faced the enemy and won their fight. They *faced the impossible*; they *accomplished the unthinkable*; and they stand as *proof* that you can make it too. They're all cheering you on to victory! Just listen with the ears of faith, and you'll hear them saying, *"Go for it! You can do it! Your faith will carry you through!"*

MY PRAYER FOR TODAY

Lord, thank You for reminding me that I am not the first to walk by faith. Others have walked this walk before me, and they did it with power and with grace. If they were able to do it, I know I can do it too, but I must have Your assistance to make it all the way through. So today I look to You to give me everything I inwardly need to keep marching ahead in order to achieve the things You have ordained for me!

I pray this in Jesus' name!

MY CONFESSION FOR TODAY

I confess that I can do whatever God asks me to do! He wouldn't ask me if He didn't think I could do it. Rather than doubt my abilities, I confess that His ability is working inside me. I lean on the Holy Spirit — His mind, His power, and His grace — and these divine forces enable me to successfully achieve the things He has designed for me to do today.

I declare this by faith in Jesus' name!

QUESTIONS FOR YOU TO CONSIDER

1. How has your life changed since God spoke to you and gave you a specific assignment?
2. What should you do to stir yourself up and get encouraged when you are in the middle of a battle?
3. Who are your favorite Old Testament characters? Can you say why they are your favorites or why you find yourself relating to them so much?

When you have become illuminated with direction for your life, business, family, or ministry, you need to know that the contest has just begun. You are on the field. All eyes are on you. The fight of faith is on! But if you'll look up into the bleachers of Heaven for just a moment, you'll see that they are stacked all the way to the "clouds" with people just like you!

FEBRUARY 18

God Uses the Weak To Baffle Those Who Think They Are So High and Mighty

*…God hath chosen the weak things of the world
to confound the things which are mighty.*
— 1 Corinthians 1:27

Consider for a moment just how incredible it was that God chose David to fight the giant Goliath. David was just a young boy when God called him. He was so young in age and immature in physical development that the Bible says, "And when the Philistine looked about, and saw David, he disdained him: for he was but a youth, and ruddy, and of a fair countenance" (1 Samuel 17:42). Goliath took it as a joke when he saw who had been sent to fight with him. The giant *laughed* when he saw whom God had chosen!

First Samuel 17:43 tells us what Goliath said: "…Am I a dog, that thou comest to me with staves? And the Philistine cursed David by his gods." Who would have ever dreamed that God would select a young, inexperienced boy like David to bring down this giant? It may have looked laughable in the eyes of the world, but this young boy who fearlessly faced Goliath in battle was the exact person God had chosen!

With that in mind, consider what Paul says in First Corinthians 1:27: "But God hath chosen the foolish things of the world to *confound* the wise; and *God hath chosen the weak things of the world* to confound the things which are mighty." The word "weak" is the Greek word *asthene*. It refers to something that is *weak, base, feeble, puny,* or *powerless*. This word *asthene* describes *something that is so substandard, second-rate, low-grade and inferior that it's almost laughable*!

When Paul wrote this epistle, the Corinthian church was the laughingstock of the city. In fact, believers were viewed as the laughingstock of the entire Roman Empire. Governmental authorities considered Christians to be a weak, puny, pathetic, useless group of religious idiots. They were literally the butt of all the jokes and were viewed as societal rubbish.

Yet these same Christians turned the world upside down in their day and evangelized the Roman Empire! Through their steadfast endurance and commitment to Jesus Christ, they liberated Rome from pagan religion and paved the way for the Gospel to go into the whole world.

The unbelieving world today views the Church very much in the same way. You see, the devil fears believers because He knows the power and authority they possess. That's why he uses the entertainment industry, educational institutions, and other human agencies to try to belittle the Church and make it look irrelevant, inconsequential, and trivial.

The enemy does everything he can to give the impression that we are minor-league players — a worthless waste of time. He knows the power God has placed at our disposal, so he attempts to discredit us in the eyes of the world. Therefore, if we perceive that the Church today is the butt of jokes and viewed in a derogatory fashion, we just need to realize that this perception is nothing new.

Paul told the Corinthians, "…God hath chosen the weak things of the world to *confound* the things which are mighty." The word "confound" is *kataishuno*, which means *to put to shame, to embarrass, to confuse, to frustrate,* or *to baffle*. The word "mighty" is the word *dunatoi*, describing *people who have political power.* When you keep in mind that the political arm of the Roman Empire was trying to wipe out the Early Church, it becomes clear that this verse packs a powerful message!

First Corinthians 1:27 communicates this message to us:

"...God has chosen those whom the world considers to be puny and powerless — even laughable. These are the very ones God will use to confuse, frustrate, and baffle the political powers of the world!"

It took awhile for the Church of Jesus Christ to *put to shame* all the evil forces that had come against it. But in the end, that's what happened! The Church eventually emerged in power and changed the face of history. The common, regular, run-of-the-mill people whom God had chosen were so mighty and powerful in the Lord that they "conquered the world" for Christianity in their day!

So quit seeing yourself as someone who is substandard, second-rate, low-grade, or inferior. You are filled with the Spirit of God and have the call of God on your life! Who cares what the world thinks? Even if your gifts and talents seem small in comparison to what others possess, that doesn't mean you're eliminated from God's list of candidates.

In fact, your feelings of weakness and inadequacy actually qualify you as a candidate in God's service! God is looking for people just like you, because He knows He will receive the glory for what He does through you. *You're exactly the kind of person God wants to use!*

MY PRAYER FOR TODAY

Lord, help me see myself with the full potential I have in Jesus Christ. My temptation is to see myself according to my past, but starting today I ask You to help me see myself through the promises of Your Word. I know that with Your grace and power, I can rise above any weakness or infirmity that has hindered me in the past. I turn to Your grace, and I ask You to release Your power in me so I can step into the reality of the person You have made me to be!

I pray this in Jesus' name!

MY CONFESSION FOR TODAY

I confess that I am NOT substandard, second-rate, low-grade, or inferior. I am filled with the Spirit of God, and I have the call of God on my life. Even if my gifts and talents seem small in comparison to others, I have all that I need in order to do what God has asked me to do. God wants to use me to baffle the "know-it-alls" and to bewilder people who are more talented than I but who do not trust in the Lord. He wants to get glory because of what He does through me!

I declare this by faith in Jesus' name!

QUESTIONS FOR YOU TO CONSIDER

1. If nothing could hinder you from fulfilling your dreams, what dream would you most want to fulfill in your life?
2. Do you really believe that God can help you fulfill such a mighty dream?
3. In what ways do you need to change the way you think about yourself in order for you to become the kind of person who carries out this kind of dream?

FEBRUARY 19

Diligence Is Required
For Success in God

But without faith it is impossible to please him:
for he that cometh to God must believe that he is,
and that he is a rewarder of them that diligently seek him.
— Hebrews 11:6

Some people are just lazy, which is why they never see anything accomplished with their lives. They blame their lack of success on this, that, and everything but themselves. But God is no respecter of persons. What He does for one, He will do for all. The key factors that make the difference are not about God, but about *a person's level of determination* and *his or her willingness to do whatever is necessary to achieve a goal.*

It may be a hard fact to face, but ultimately we are all responsible for our success or our lack of success. We all possess the same promises, the same faith, the same power, the same Spirit, and the same Jesus who sits at the right hand of God to make intercession for us (Hebrews 7:25). The main thing that determines who succeeds and who doesn't succeed is *attitude.*

You have to *want* success in order to get it. It doesn't float on clouds, and it takes hard work to achieve it. Because most people are willing to do only average work, they reap average results. To achieve super results, one must do super work, be deeply committed to the task, and be willing to do whatever is necessary to realize goals and aspirations.

Hebrews 11:6 says that God "...is a rewarder of them that *diligently* seek him." According to this verse, even God rewards diligence. In fact, He only rewards those who diligently seek Him, which means people with a lazy, lethargic, do-nothing, "take-it-easy" attitude will never be greatly rewarded by the Lord. This verse says that God rewards the *diligent seeker.*

Diligence is required for any success. The phrase "diligently seek" in Hebrews 11:6 is taken from the Greek word *ekzeteo,* and it carries an entire range of power-packed meanings. It means *to zealously seek for something with all of one's heart, strength, and might.* It presents the picture of *one who seeks something so passionately and determinedly that he literally exhausts all his power in his search.*

Because the word *ekzeteo* portrays such an earnest effort, the idea of being *hard-working, attentive, busy, constant,* and *persistent in one's devotion to what he or she is doing* is also included.

This tells us that Hebrews 11:6 means:

"God is a rewarder of those who put all their heart, strength, and might into seeking Him. Those who are so committed in their search that they are willing to exhaust all their natural powers in their search for Him — they are the ones who will find what they are seeking!"

You see, you have to be diligent to be rewarded by God, so it should be no surprise that diligence is going to be required in order for you to succeed in every sphere of life. It's just a fact that a lazy, neglectful attitude will never get you where you need to go. If you take your life assignment lightly — if you approach it with a casual, easygoing, take-it-easy, relaxed attitude — you'll never go far in the fulfillment of your call or dream. Live like a slug, and you'll eat dirt the rest of your life!

If you're serious about succeeding in life, you'll have to adjust your level of commitment and give your *full attention* to what God has called you to do. Diligence cannot be a sideline issue. Your assigned task must have your full consideration, your undivided attention, and your mental and spiritual concentration. You must immerse yourself in faith, prayer, and meditation regarding God's call on your life. *Distractions are not allowed.*

It takes hard work to achieve *any* goal, and complaining about that hard work won't make it any easier. *So be constant in your commitment. Refuse to relent! Stay stubborn and unbending even in the face of opposition until your objective is achieved. Your consistency and determination will push the powers of hell aside and obtain the victory you desire!*

MY PRAYER FOR TODAY

Lord, I ask You to please help me become more serious as I adjust my level of commitment to a higher level. Help me give full attention to what You have called me to do. I realize that diligence cannot be a sideline issue in my life. In order for me to succeed at what You have asked me to do, I must give it my full consideration, my undivided attention, and my mental and spiritual concentration. But I can only keep pressing toward this higher level of commitment if I have the divine energy of the Holy Spirit propelling me forward. As I reach upward to become all that You want me to be, I ask You for divine assistance.

I pray this in Jesus' name!

MY CONFESSION FOR TODAY

I agree that God is no respecter of persons. What He does for one, He will do for all. Every believer possesses the same promises, the same faith, the same power, the same Spirit, and the same Jesus who sits at the right hand of God to make intercession for us. These promises belong to me today! Because I choose to put my whole heart into my assigned task and to do more than average work, I know I will reap more than average results! I am deeply committed to the task and willing to do whatever is necessary to realize the goals and aspirations God has given to me.

I declare this by faith in Jesus' name!

QUESTIONS FOR YOU TO CONSIDER

1. Do you believe you are diligently seeking after the Lord in a way that will bring success into every realm of your life?
2. As you honestly evaluate your life, what areas in your life need more diligence? Write them down and make them a matter of prayer.
3. Would other people say that you are determined and committed or that you only give half your heart to the projects assigned to you?

FEBRUARY 20

How Do You Make A Dead Man See?

And when he [the Holy Spirit] is come,
he will reprove the world of sin....
— John 16:8

Do you remember times as a child when you did something wrong and thought no one was watching — but then you got caught? Do you remember how it felt to realize that someone had been watching you all along? What horror and dread to be caught in the middle of the act!

You couldn't lie your way out of such a situation, especially when someone was watching you the whole time. You were unmistakably guilty and couldn't escape facing your sin. Can you remember what it was like to feel so exposed?

This is what a sinner feels like the first time the Holy Spirit convicts him of sin. Before that happens, it is amazing how long that same sinner can live without conviction or sorrow for his behavior, almost numb to any sense of the wrongness of his actions.

The Bible says that sin makes people hardhearted, spiritually blind, and past feeling (Ephesians 4:18,19). Add this to the fact that they are spiritually dead and therefore unable to respond to God, and you will better understand why lost people can do what they do over and over again.

But all these factors change instantaneously when the Holy Spirit touches the human soul and exposes its sinful condition. A sinner feels exposed, naked, embarrassed, and *confronted* when the Holy Spirit wakes him up to his real spiritual condition.

In John 16:8, Jesus spoke of this exposing work of the Holy Spirit. He told the disciples, "And when he [the Holy Spirit] is come, he will reprove the world of sin...."

Notice that Jesus said the Holy Spirit would *reprove* the world of sin. The word "reprove" is the Greek word *elegcho*. It means *to expose, to convict,* or *to cross-examine for the purpose of conviction,* as when convicting a lawbreaker in a court of law. In this case, it is the image of a lawyer who brings forth *evidence* that is *indisputable* and *undeniable*. The accused person's actions are *irrefutably brought to light* and, as a result, the offender is *exposed* and *convicted.*

This tells us that by the time the Holy Spirit is finished dealing with a lost, sinful soul, the unsaved person will feel exposed and convicted. As the Holy Spirit enables him to hear the Word of God for the first time, that Word is so razor sharp that it penetrates his soul until he feels as if he has been cross-examined on a witness stand. Finally, the court is adjourned, the verdict is announced, and he is declared guilty.

John 15:8 expresses this idea about the "convicting" work of the Holy Spirit:

"But when He [the Holy Spirit] is come, He will present such convincing evidence about the world's sin that the entire world will stand guilty and convicted — so exposed that they will feel they have nowhere to hide from the facts...."

A major part of the work of the Holy Spirit is to convict sinners of their lost condition. The whole world stands guilty before God (Romans 3:19), but until the Holy Spirit does His convicting work, the world doesn't realize it is guilty. That is why this special "convicting" work of the Spirit is so essential. Without it, mankind would remain comfortable in his sin — but as the Holy Spirit convicts, man becomes aware of his sinful condition and his need for God.

Jesus taught, "No man can come to me, except the Father which hath sent me draw him..." (John 6:44). No one argues that God draws us to Him through the work of the Holy Spirit. Jesus reminded us of this when He said, "And when he is come, he will reprove the world of sin..." (John 16:8). It is just a fact that without the work of the Holy Spirit to expose our sinful condition, we would still be in darkness today, eternally lost and without God.

Let me give you an example of what I am talking about. Have you ever tried to share Christ with family members or friends and felt as if you were "hitting a brick wall"? You shared, talked, and pled with them to receive Christ; yet it seemed like they just couldn't hear what you were saying. Even though they knew they were sinners, they didn't seem to be convicted by this knowledge. Ignoring that horrible fact, they pressed on as though they were numb to or ignorant of the degree of spiritual decay in their lives.

The Bible says that the lost person is "dead in trespasses and sins" (Ephesians 2:1). How can you make a dead man see or feel? How can you convince a dead man that he needs to change? It is impossible for a dead man to respond because dead people don't feel anything. They especially don't feel the conviction of sin. It requires a special, supernatural work of the Holy Spirit to rouse the human consciousness to its sinful condition.

Thanks to the Holy Spirit's call that touched our souls, we were awakened to our sinfulness. Once we were brought to this horrible place of undeniable conviction where we recognized that we were sinners, the Holy Spirit then beckoned us to come to Jesus. At that divine moment, our souls heard Him say, "...Awake thou that sleepest, and arise from the dead, and Christ shall give thee light" (Ephesians 5:14).

As you begin to share Christ with your family and friends, first stop and ask the Holy Spirit to go before you, to touch their hearts, and to open their eyes and ears to the truth so they might be supernaturally roused from the spiritual deadness that clutches their lives. Let the Holy Spirit be your Partner, for without His help, a sinner is unable to see the truth. But when the Holy Spirit's convicting work begins, the sinner's eyes are opened to his true spiritual condition, and he realizes that there is no escape from the facts. The only answer for a sinner in this case is to come to Jesus!

There is no greater miracle than a sinner who sees the light for the first time and then receives Jesus Christ as the Lord of his life. *And there is no greater blessing than to know that, with the help of the Holy Spirit's convicting power, you helped a dead man see!*

MY PRAYER FOR TODAY

Lord, thank You for the convicting power of the Holy Spirit, for it was this act of the Spirit that first brought me to the place of my salvation. When I do wrong and the Holy Spirit convicts me of what I have done, help me be sensitive enough to recognize that He is pricking my heart to get my attention. Help me slow down to see what He is wanting to show me and to take the necessary time to properly repent and deal with the issues He is wanting me to change.

I pray this in Jesus' name!

MY CONFESSION FOR TODAY

I confess that I am sensitive to the Holy Spirit and live a life that pleases Him. But when I fail to do what is right, I am sensitive to His voice and quickly repent for the wrong I have done. My heart's desire is to please Him, and I will do everything I can to live a life that honors His Presence inside me.

I declare this by faith in Jesus' name!

QUESTIONS FOR YOU TO CONSIDER

1. How has the convicting power of the Holy Spirit transformed you since you first received Jesus as Lord?
2. Who are five people you can ask the Holy Spirit to touch today with His convicting power of repentance and salvation?
3. Have you thanked the Lord recently for the Holy Spirit's work in your heart to convict you of sin and keep you pure and powerful for the Lord's use?

FEBRUARY 21

Effective Spiritual Weapons Require Effective Spiritual Strategies

For the weapons of our warfare are not carnal,
but mighty through God to the pulling down of strong holds.
— 2 Corinthians 10:4

*I*n this powerful verse, Paul speaks to us about the subject of spiritual warfare. In fact, this is one of the foundational verses on this subject, so it is vital to understand what Paul is talking about. Today I want to especially draw your attention to three words in this power-packed scripture. Pay special attention to the words *weapons, warfare,* and *carnal.*

First, Paul tells us that we have "weapons." These spiritual armaments have been provided by God and are at our disposal. They are both offensive and defensive weapons and can be found in Ephesians 6:13-18, where Paul lists them one by one and explains what each piece represents.

Second, Paul uses the word "warfare." The word "warfare" is taken from the word *stratos.* By choosing to use this word, the Holy Spirit alerts us to some very important facts about spiritual warfare.

The word *stratos* is where we derive the word *strategy.* This informs us that spiritual warfare does not occur accidentally but is something that is *strategically planned.* Just as any army plans its line of attack before a battle begins, the devil plans a line of attack, decides which methods he will use, and chooses the approach he wants to take as he cautiously charts a well-thought-out assault.

But the word *stratos* doesn't just describe the devil's strategies. It also tells us that if we will listen to the Holy Spirit, He will give us a strategy that is superior to any schemes of the devil. The devil is not the only one with a strategy. The Holy Spirit always holds the key to every victory, and He wants to provide us with a divinely-inspired strategy that will render null and void the works of the devil every time!

The Old Testament is filled with examples of divinely-inspired strategies. Consider the case of Joshua and the children of Israel as they stood before the walls of Jericho (Joshua 6:1-27). What strategy did the Lord give them? They were to walk around the walls of Jericho once a day for six days and seven times on the seventh day. Then after the seventh time around the wall on the last day, they were to blow trumpets made of rams' horns. None of this sounded "reasonable" to the natural mind, but the effects of that God-given strategy are still renowned today!

Or consider the time Jehoshaphat sent out a praise team before the army to sing and to worship the Lord (2 Chronicles 20:20-25). What army would send singers and musicians to the frontlines of battle in front of its armed soldiers? Yet as they sang praises to God and played their instruments, the Lord supernaturally set ambushments and the enemies were smitten.

That day the children of Israel walked away from the battle without losing a single fighter. Not only that, but they were also weighed down with gold, silver, jewels, and other riches in abundance! There was so much plunder that it took them three days to gather it! How did they win this famous battle? They received a strategy from the Lord and then followed it accurately. The results of that strategy are legendary.

In both of these cases, the line of attack made no sense to the natural mind, but it released so much power that it completely crushed the foe. So don't be surprised if the Holy Spirit gives you a strategy that doesn't make sense when you first hear it! Remember, He operates on a higher level than you, and He knows what you don't know. Therefore, He may tell you to do something that seems odd to you at first. But you can be sure that Spirit-inspired strategies always work!

Imagine an army that is fully equipped with weapons of warfare but has no strategy about how to use those weapons against the enemy. Even with all those weapons and artillery at their disposal, an army in this condition would utterly fail.

Likewise, although it's crucial that you put on the whole armor of God, that's just the first step. You must then have a strategy on how to use those weapons and how to attack! Until you receive a strategy from the Lord on how to use your spiritual weapons, they will be of little help in driving back the forces of hell that have come against you.

This leads to the word "carnal." In Greek, this word is *sarkos*, which describes *anything that is of the flesh, fleshly made, or fleshly conjured up* or *anything that is natural or of an unspiritual nature.* Paul uses this word when he writes, "For the weapons of our warfare are not *carnal....*"

In effect, Paul is saying, *"Don't look to your flesh for the weapons or strategies I'm describing to you because they do not arise out of natural talent, mental exercises, or human efforts. These are spiritual weapons and spiritual strategies, and they come from the spiritual realm."*

When you put all these Greek words together, ### Second Corinthians 10:4 carries this idea:

"Our God-given weapons are to be used in connection with a divine strategy. But don't look to the flesh to find that strategy, for the battle plan you need is not going to arise out of your own natural talent, mental exercises, or human effort."

If you want to receive the strategy needed to assure your victory, you must turn your attention to the *realm of the Spirit*, for it is from this realm that you will hear from God. You must spend time praying in the Spirit and reading the Word. By yourself, you will never conceive a plan that will deliver you.

Just as spiritual weapons come from God, so do spiritual strategies. So use your head as much as you can, and think through every step. But as you seek God, stay open for Him to graciously give you a supernatural strategy for destroying the work of the devil. And don't be surprised if God tells you to do something that seems a little odd. Since the beginning of time, God has been giving effective strategies that seem strange to the mind of man!

MY PRAYER FOR TODAY

Lord, I know that today I'm going to need a supernatural strategy to do what I need to do. My own natural mind is working all the time to come up with solutions. I'm doing the best I can do, but now I need extra help. I need a divine strategy — a divine idea so powerful and effective that no force will be able to resist it! I know that these kinds of strategies are imparted by the Holy Spirit, so right now I open my heart wide to Him. Holy Spirit, I ask You to drop a supernatural idea into my spirit and soul. Please help me to properly discern it, understand it, and then follow through with obedience.

I pray this in Jesus' name!

MY CONFESSION FOR TODAY

I declare by faith that the Holy Spirit gives me the strategies and ideas I need. I am willing and ready to do whatever He tells me to do. The Spirit of God was sent into this world to be my Helper and my Guide, and I know I can fully rely on Him. I must have His direction, or I won't know what to do. So today He will speak to my heart; I will perceive what He tells me to do; and then I will obediently carry out His good plan for me!

I declare this by faith in Jesus' name!

QUESTIONS FOR YOU TO CONSIDER

1. Has the Holy Spirit ever told you to do something that seemed odd to your natural mind but resulted in His power being mightily demonstrated in a situation?
2. Have you found that your natural talent, mental reasonings, and human effort are helpless to win the battles you are facing today?
3. God is ready to give you the battle plan you need to have victory in your life. Are you willing to spend the time in prayer that is required for you to receive that plan?

Don't be surprised if the Holy Spirit gives you a strategy that doesn't make sense when you first hear it. Remember, He operates on a higher level than you, and He knows what you do not know.

FEBRUARY 22

You Have a Two-Edged Sword!

For the word of God is quick, and powerful,
and sharper than any twoedged sword....
— Hebrews 4:12

What is the significance of the "two-edged sword" referred to in Hebrews 4:12? If you start looking, you'll find out this phrase regarding a "two-edged sword" appears all over the New Testament, so it must be pretty important.

For instance, when the apostle John received his vision of Jesus on the isle of Patmos, he said, "And he had in his right hand seven stars: and out of his mouth went a sharp twoedged sword: and his countenance was as the sun shineth in his strength" (Revelation 1:16). Notice that this "two-edged sword" came out of Jesus' mouth! Why would Jesus have a sword in His mouth? Shouldn't the sword have been in His *hand*?

The phrase "two-edged" is taken from the Greek word *distomos* and is unquestionably one of the oddest words in the entire New Testament. Why is it so odd? Because it is a compound of the word *di,* meaning *two,* and the word *stomos,* which is the Greek word for one's *mouth.* Thus, when these two words are compounded into one (*distomos*), they describe something that is *two-mouthed*! Don't you agree that this seems a little strange? So why would the Bible refer to the Word of God repeatedly as a "two-edged sword" or, literally, a *"two-mouthed sword"*?

The Word of God is like a sword that has two edges, cutting both ways and doing terrible damage to an aggressor. Ephesians 6:17 calls it "the sword of the Spirit, which is the word of God" (*see* February 8). As noted, the term "word" is taken from the Greek word *rhema,* which describes *something that is spoken clearly, vividly, in unmistakable terms and undeniable language.* In the New Testament, the word *rhema* carries the idea of a *quickened word.*

Here's an example of a *rhema* or a *quickened word:* You are praying about a situation, and suddenly a Bible verse rises up from inside your heart. At that moment, you are consciously aware that God has given you a verse to stand on and to claim for your situation. You've received a word that came right *out of the mouth of God* and dropped into your spirit! That word from God was so sharp that it cut right through your questions, intellect, and natural logic and lodged deep within your heart.

After you meditated on that *rhema,* or that quickened word from God, it suddenly began to release its power inside you. Soon you couldn't contain it any longer! Everything within you wanted *to declare* what God had said to you. You wanted *to say* it. You want to release it *out of your mouth*! And when you did, those powerful words were sent forth like a mighty blade to drive back the forces of hell that had been marshaled against you, your family, your business, your ministry, your finances, your relationship, or your body.

First, that word came out of the mouth of God. Next, it came out of *your* mouth! When it came out of your mouth, it became a sharp, "two-edged" — or literally, a "two-mouthed" — sword. One edge of this sword came into existence when the Word initially proceeded *out of God's mouth.* The second edge of this sword was added when the Word of God proceeded *out of YOUR mouth*!

The Word of God remains a one-bladed sword when it comes out of God's mouth and drops into your heart but is never released from your own mouth by faith. That supernatural word simply lies dormant in your heart, never becoming the two-edged sword God designed it to be.

But something happens in the realm of the Spirit when you finally rise up and begin to speak forth that word. The moment it comes out of your mouth, a second edge is added to the blade! Nothing is more powerful than a word that comes first from God's mouth and then from your mouth. You and God have come into agreement, and that agreement releases His mighty power into the situation at hand!

So begin to willfully take the Word into your spirit by meditating on it and giving it a place of top priority. This is how you take the first necessary step in giving the Word a "second edge" in your life. Then when you are confronted by a challenge from the demonic realm, the Holy Spirit will be able to reach down into the reservoir of God's Word you have stored up on the inside of you and pull up the exact scripture you need for that moment.

As that quickened *rhema* word from God begins to first fill your heart and mind and then come out of your mouth, it becomes that "two-mouthed sword" described in the Scriptures. *That's* when demons start to tremble in terror!

MY PRAYER FOR TODAY

Lord, I know that Your Word has the power to defeat every adversary in my life. As I take it into my heart and get it deep into my soul, I know it will empower me to speak Your Word with mighty strength and authority. Forgive me for the times I have just skimmed over Your Word rather than planting it deep in my heart. I realize that the answers I seek are in Your Word — and that Your Word, when spoken from my mouth, releases authority against the devices the devil tries to use against me. So today, Lord, I make the decision to plant Your Word deep in my spirit man and then to speak it and release its power in my life!

I pray this in Jesus' name!

MY CONFESSION FOR TODAY

I confess that God's Word is a mighty and sharp two-edged sword that releases His power when I speak it out of my mouth. I read the Word; I take it deeply into my heart; and then I release its power from my mouth to thwart the enemy's strategies and bring victory into every situation I'm facing today!

I declare this by faith in Jesus' name!

QUESTIONS FOR YOU TO CONSIDER

1. Can you remember a time when a specific scripture suddenly sprang up from down deep inside you, causing you to feel super-charged and empowered by God's Spirit?
2. When God speaks to you, do you first meditate on that *rhema* word and then let it come out of your mouth, or do you forget to speak that quickened word out loud and thus fail to release its power?
3. According to what you read today, what happens when you and God begin to speak the same thing?

FEBRUARY 23

❧❀❧

The Holy Spirit — A Partner Who Wants To Take Responsibility For You in This Life!

The grace of the Lord Jesus Christ, and the love of God,
and the communion of the Holy Ghost, be with you all. Amen.
— 2 Corinthians 13:14

*M*ost all of us would say we want to live a victorious Christian life. But without daily communion with the Holy Spirit, it's impossible to attain that goal. Communion with the Holy Spirit is the launching pad for a life of supernatural power and consistency.

In Second Corinthians 13:14, Paul says, "The grace of the Lord Jesus Christ, and the love of God, and the communion of the Holy Ghost, be with you all. Amen." I want you to notice the word "communion" in this verse, because *communion with the Spirit* is what we are talking about today. The word "communion" is the Greek word *koinonia,* a word that has a whole flavor of meanings, but one primary meaning is that of *partnership.*

An example of *koinonia* conveying the idea of partnership can be found in Luke 5:7 after Jesus supplied a miraculous catch of fish. After the fishermen had fished all night and caught nothing, Jesus told them to cast their nets on the other side. When they obeyed, they caught such a massive amount of fish that the nets began to break!

Peter knew he couldn't handle this miraculous catch by himself, so he called to other fishermen in nearby boats to come and assist him. Luke 5:7 says, "And they beckoned unto their *partners,* which were in the other ship, that they should come and help them. And they came, and filled both the ships, so that they began to sink."

Do you see the word "partners" in this verse? It is a form of this word *koinonia.* However, in Luke 5:7 it refers to real, legitimate business partners. One scholar says that this word used in this context lets us know that Peter was no small-time fisherman. He owned an entire fishing enterprise, and those men in the other boats were his *business associates* or his *company partners.* Whether these other fishermen were co-owners or employees who worked for Peter, they were all working together on the same job and were focused on a joint venture to catch and sell fish.

Keeping this in mind,
Second Corinthians 13:14 could convey the following idea:

"…and the PARTNERSHIP of the Holy Spirit be with you all."

If you stop and think about it, this really makes a lot of sense. When Jesus' earthly ministry was in operation, He and the Holy Spirit always worked together. Jesus was *conceived* of the Holy Spirit (Luke 1:35); *empowered* by the Holy Spirit (Matthew 3:16); and *led* by the Holy Spirit (Matthew 4:1). Jesus also healed people by the power of the Holy Spirit (Acts 10:38); cast out demons by the power of the Holy Spirit (Matthew 12:28); was *resurrected* from the dead by the power of the Holy Spirit (Romans 8:11); and was seated at God's right hand in the heavenly places through the power of the Holy Spirit (Ephesians 1:19,20).

Every time we see Jesus in the Gospels, He is working hand in hand with the Holy Spirit. In fact, Jesus even said He wouldn't initiate anything by Himself, indicating His total dependence on the Spirit of God (John 5:30). Well, if Jesus needed this kind of ongoing partnership with the Holy Spirit in order to accomplish His divine role in the earth, we certainly have to have it as well!

But there is yet another idea conveyed by the word "communion" (*koinonia*) — that is, the idea of *taking responsibility for someone*. An example of this is found in Philippians 4:14, when Paul wrote to the Philippians and commended them for the generous gift they sent for his ministry. He told them, "Notwithstanding ye have well done, that ye did *communicate* with my affliction." The word "communicate" here is another use of the word *koinonia*.

At the time Paul wrote the Philippian letter, he was in prison in Rome. Over the years, he had traveled and preached, raised up churches, worked with leaders, and given his life for the Church. But of all the churches Paul had poured his life into, none of them helped him financially the way they should have.

In order to cover his expenses, Paul worked as a tentmaker during the day; then he preached and trained leaders during the evenings. This wasn't the best plan, but because no one would support him, it was what he had to do. He was pouring his heart and soul into churches that were not financially helping him bear his load.

Paul was in prison in Rome when he received a special delivery letter from the Philippians. In that package, he found a sizable offering that the Philippian church had sent to support him during his time of difficulty. In other words, the Philippian church didn't just say, "We'll pray for your situation, Brother," and then forget about Paul. Instead, they understood their responsibility to help him, so they took up an offering to support him and to communicate their love for him. In other words, they took *responsibility* for him. Paul uses the Greek word *koinonia* to convey this meaning — the same word he uses in Second Corinthians 13:14 when he writes about the "communion of the Holy Spirit."

Thus, Second Corinthians 13:14 could also be read this way:

"...and the RESPONSIBILITY of the Holy Spirit be with you all."

This means that just as the Holy Spirit wants to become your Partner, He also wants to assume great responsibility for you in this world. If you wish, He'll stand by and watch you try to do it all alone. But if you'll open your heart to the Spirit of God, He will assume a more active role in your life. He wants you to know that you are not alone — and that He will take *responsibility* for you!

If the cry of your heart is to know the *partnership* and the *responsibility* of the Holy Spirit — not merely as mental doctrines, but as constant, daily realities in your life — then decide today to get to know the Holy Spirit as your intimate Friend. Make Him your Partner. Allow Him to help you fulfill the responsibilities of your calling in Christ.

Begin today to develop a walk of daily communion with the Greater One within. Let Him be all He wants to be in your life — your Source of wisdom, power, and strength to launch you forth into victory!

MY PRAYER FOR TODAY

Holy Spirit, I want to thank You for being my Partner in this world. I need Your partnership. I know that without You, I am so limited in what I am able to do. You see what I can't see; You know what I don't know; You have wisdom and insight that I don't have. I simply must have Your help if I am going to do what God has asked me to do. I ask You to please forgive me for all the times I have gotten in such a hurry that I didn't take time to fellowship with

You. From this moment on, I promise I will do my best to consult You before I make a decision or take a single step!

I pray this in Jesus' name!

MY CONFESSION FOR TODAY

I confess that I am led by the Spirit of God. I am careful not to make big decisions without consulting Him first. The Holy Spirit is my Leader, my Teacher, and my Guide; therefore, I look to Him to help me make the right decisions and take the right actions in every sphere of my life — my family, my business, and my ministry. Every day I experience more and more victory because I allow the Holy Spirit to direct all my steps.

I declare this by faith in Jesus' name!

QUESTIONS FOR YOU TO CONSIDER

1. Have you asked the Spirit of God to be your Partner in life and to take responsibility for all your cares and concerns?
2. What can you do to make the Holy Spirit a closer, more active Partner in every area of life?
3. Have you spent quality time in communion with the Holy Spirit today, being still and simply knowing that He is your God?

FEBRUARY 24

It's Time for You To Lay Aside Every Unnecessary Weight

Wherefore seeing we are compassed about
with so great a cloud of witnesses,
let us lay aside every weight....
— Hebrews 12:1

What is it that keeps hindering you from living a life of obedience? Do you struggle with a particular sin, habit, attitude, or fear that keeps you from running your race of faith the way you ought? If so, you probably already know what it is, and I'd guess that you've already prayed, prayed, and *prayed* for victory in overcoming that problem because you really do want to please God.

Every now and then, we all tolerate things in our lives that make it difficult for us to please God. And when we know we're not pleasing God, we typically aren't happy with ourselves either. This is one reason that Hebrews 12:1 tells us to "...lay aside every weight...."

The words "lay aside" are taken from the Greek word *apotithimi*, a compound of the words *apo* and *tithimi*. As noted in the *Sparkling Gem* for January 6, the word *apo* means *away* and the word *tithimi* means *to place* or *to lay something down*. When these two words are compounded together, it gives a picture of someone who is *laying something down* while at the same time he is pushing it *far away* from himself. It means *to lay something down and to push it far away and beyond reach*. Thus, this word implies *a deliberate decision to make a permanent change of attitude and behavior*.

Removing wrong attitudes and actions from our lives will *not* occur accidentally. We must *decide* to change — *to remove, to lay aside, and to put away* attitudes and actions that don't please God and adversely affect our walk of faith.

Hebrews 12:1 refers to these incorrect attitudes and actions as "weights." The word "weight" is from the Greek word *ogkos* — a word that describes a *burden* or *something so heavy and cumbersome that it impedes a runner from running his race as he should*.

This word was particularly used in the athletic world to signify the actions of an athlete who would deliberately strip himself of excess weight before participating in a competition. This stripping process included the loss of excess flesh through dieting and exercise. Then on the day of the actual competition, he stripped off nearly all his clothes so no extra weight would slow him down. He had his eye on the prize, so he was determined to strip off all "weight" that might potentially keep him from being the best athlete he could be.

This sends a strong message to us! If we want to please God, satisfy ourselves, and do something significant with our lives, we have to choose to remove anything from our lives that would hinder those objectives.

The athlete of the ancient world didn't become "unweighted" by accident. He dropped all excess weight on purpose. He dieted; he exercised; and he shed every other unnecessary weight he could find to shed. This stripping process demanded his attention, his decision, and his devotion. It wasn't going to happen by accident, so he had to initiate the process of removal.

What if those athletes had tried to run their race with loads of extra weight? They certainly wouldn't have been able to run very far! This is exactly what sinful habits and attitudes do to your walk with the Lord. If you don't *remove* them, they will eventually *weigh* you down and knock you out of your race of faith!

The Holy Spirit is urging you and me to take a good look at our lives and then remove everything that weighs us down and keeps us from a life of obedience. *We must be honest with ourselves and with God.*

Do you have a habit or a wrong attitude that binds you? Are you plagued by a fear that weighs you down and keeps you from fulfilling your potential in Christ? Make a rock-solid, quality decision today to grab hold of those unnecessary burdens and *remove, lay aside, and permanently put them away* from your life.

Once you make that decision, you'll find yourself running your race of faith with much more ease as you press on to victory!

MY PRAYER FOR TODAY

Lord, I know that You're on my side and that You want to help me. So today I'm asking You to help me lay aside the attitudes, negative thought patterns, and bad habits that keep pulling me back down into miserable defeat. I'm exhausted from trying to live for You while dragging along these old weights behind me at the same time. I need to drop them and leave them behind! So today I am asking You to help me make the big break. Help me make this the day I permanently drop all the unnecessary weights that hinder me and walk away from them forever!

I pray this in Jesus' name!

MY CONFESSION FOR TODAY

I confess that I live a life of obedience! Sin, bad habits, negative attitudes, and fear have no influence in my life. Because I am free of these things, I am able to run my race of faith without any hindrances caused by my own actions. Because I want to please God, I do not tolerate things in my life that make it difficult for me to walk by faith or to please God. Absolutely nothing is more important to me than knowing God's will and doing it in a way that brings pleasure to the Lord!

I declare this by faith in Jesus' name!

QUESTIONS FOR YOU TO CONSIDER

1. What is the first thing that comes to mind when you think of a "weight" that has been keeping you from running your race with grace and ease lately?
2. How can you strip yourself today of that "weight" so you can stay in the race to win God's prize for your life?
3. Write down three ways you can please God, satisfy yourself, and do something significant in your life this week.

FEBRUARY 25

You Are a Shrine For the Holy Spirit

What? know ye not that your body
is the temple of the Holy Ghost which is in you,
which ye have of God, and ye are not your own?
For ye are bought with a price: therefore glorify God
in your body, and in your spirit, which are God's.
— 1 Corinthians 6:19,20

*R*ussia is a nation with more than one thousand years of Russian Orthodox religious history. One of the greatest signs of this religious history is located right in the heart of Moscow — a gigantic white marble cathedral with golden domes that is called "Christ the Savior." I've traveled the world and seen a lot in my life, but when it comes to decorative architecture, this building is by far one of the most splendid I've ever seen. Its interior is highly adorned with ornamentations of gold, silver, and precious stones. It is embellished like no other building I've ever seen anywhere else.

When we hear the word "shrine," this is normally the type of image that passes through our minds. We see arched and vaulted ceilings, marble, granite, gold, silver, hand-carved etchings, and lots and lots of smoke from incense being burned as a part of worship. Shrines are not comfortable places where we'd want to live, but their ornamentation is certainly impressive. A shrine is a beautiful place to visit, but we wouldn't want to live there!

The Greek word *naos* is the word for *a temple* or *a highly decorated shrine*, like the one illustrated in the story above. This Greek word is the very word the apostle Paul used when he told the Corinthians, "…Know ye not that your body is the temple of the Holy Ghost which is in you…?" (1 Corinthians 6:19).

Because the Corinthians were Greek and had grown up in a classical Greek culture, they had seen temples their entire lives. So when Paul used this word *naos*, it would have been natural for images like the ones above to flash through their minds. They knew that the word *naos* always depicted *a highly decorated shrine*. The temples of their times were beautiful buildings with tall, vaulted ceilings, marble columns, granite floors, hand-carved woodwork overlaid with gold and silver, and burning incense billowing into the air around the front of the altar.

Shrines like the one I described above are imposing and impressive; however, they're *not* comfortable. But when the Holy Spirit came into your heart, He made a home that was so comfortable, He was actually happy to come live inside you! He moved in, settled down, and permanently took up residency in your heart — *His new home!*

You see, when you got saved, the ultimate miracle was performed inside your heart. The Holy Spirit took your spirit, which had been dead in trespasses and sin, and raised it to new life. His work inside you was so glorious that when it was all finished, He declared you to be His own workmanship (Ephesians 2:10). At that moment, your spirit became *a marvelous temple of God*!

What does all this mean?

✦ When we were born again, we were inwardly created to become a dwelling place of God.
✦ Our bodies are not mere shacks or mud huts; rather, we are inwardly fashioned to be magnificent dwelling places for the Spirit of God.
✦ Because the fruit of the Spirit, the gifts of the Spirit, and the grace of God are working inside us, we are inwardly embellished with rich spiritual ornamentation.
✦ Our inner man is now a temple that is so marvelous, no human eye has ever seen anything like it!

If you've been dealing with a poor self-image, grab hold of this truth, because this is the greatest self-image booster that exists! Inwardly you are so beautiful and magnificent that Almighty God wanted to live inside you! What kind of home do you think God would require? A shabby shack made of dirt and sticks? No! He has built for Himself a beautiful temple within your heart — and that is who you are right now! *Now live like the magnificently decorated cathedral of God's Spirit that you are!*

MY PRAYER FOR TODAY

Lord, I am so excited to think that You made my heart Your home. It is so overwhelming to think that You want to live inside me. Help me see myself as Your dwelling place and to honor Your Presence inside me by the kind of life I lead. I want to bless You and honor You, so please help me do the right things that bring You the greatest pleasure and joy.

I pray this in Jesus' name!

MY CONFESSION FOR TODAY

I gratefully acknowledge that my body is the temple of the Holy Spirit. Yes, the Holy Spirit lives inside me. My heart is not a hotel where He occasionally visits; rather, my heart has become His home. He has invested His power, His gifts, His fruit, and the life of Jesus Christ in me. Inwardly I am highly adorned with the goodness of God. My spirit is so marvelously created in Christ Jesus that God Himself is comfortable to live inside me!

I declare this by faith in Jesus' name!

QUESTIONS FOR YOU TO CONSIDER

1. Are you living like the magnificently decorated cathedral of God's Spirit that you are?
2. How can you make use of the rich ornamentation you have on the inside of you: the fruit of the Spirit, the gifts of the Spirit, and the grace of God?
3. How would you behave differently if you truly believed that the Holy Spirit has permanently moved into your life and redecorated the place?

FEBRUARY 26

Take Advantage Of All Kinds of Prayer

Praying always with all prayer....
— Ephesians 6:18

*I*f you want to grow in your spiritual walk, you need to make prayer a central part of your life. But in order for prayer to be the great adventure God wants it to be in your life, you must understand that there are all kinds of ways to pray. Don't get stuck with just one form of prayer! The Bible tells us that there are several kinds of prayer, and you need to learn to use every kind of prayer that's available to you.

Ephesians 6:18 says, "Praying always with all prayer...." The first thing I want you to notice is that this verse commands us to pray "always." As noted in the *Sparkling Gem* for January 4, the word "always" is taken from the Greek phrase *en panti kairo*. The word *en* would be better translated *at.* The word *panti* means *each and every.*

You could say that this word *panti* is an all-encompassing word that embraces *everything*, including *the smallest and most minute of details*. The last word in this Greek phrase is the word *kairo,* the Greek word for *times* or *seasons.* When all three of these words are used together in one phrase (*en panti kairo*) as in Ephesians 6:18, they could be more accurately translated *at each and every occasion.*

But I want you to notice that this verse goes on to say that you are to pray "with *all* prayer." This phrase is taken from the Greek phrase *dia pases proseuches* and would be better translated *"with all kinds of prayer."* To assist the Church in maintaining a victorious position in life, God has given His people various kinds of powerful prayer.

Other translations of Ephesians 6:18 include:

"Use every kind of prayer...." (*Goodspeed*)
"Pray...with all manner of prayer...." (*AMP*)

"Pray...with all kinds of prayers...." (NIV)
"Pray...with all kinds of prayers that are available for you to use...." (REV)

Most people don't realize there are different kinds of prayer. But according to this verse, God has actually made many forms of prayer available to us to use as needed, such as the prayer of faith, the prayer of intercession, the prayer of consecration, and the prayer of agreement.

Sometimes life can be difficult and challenging. For one thing, the devil doesn't want you to be blessed or successful in your endeavors. So in order to face the inevitable attacks that arise against your marriage, finances, body, job, and career, you must come to realize that prayer is indispensable. You cannot succeed as a Christian without an active and effective prayer life.

No matter how anointed, skilled, or gifted you may be or how bold and courageous you think you are, you simply cannot maintain a victorious position in life apart from prayer. Without prayer, you can be sure of absolute and total defeat. But as you develop a lifestyle of prayer, taking advantage of every form of prayer available to you, you will find that victory is yours in the midst of every challenge!

The various kinds of prayer have all been given to you for your benefit and spiritual growth. So take the time to study the Word and learn how to pray with "all kinds of prayer." *Don't let this day go by without spending quality time in prayer with the Heavenly Father. There is victory waiting on the other side!*

MY PRAYER FOR TODAY

Lord, forgive me for the times I get so busy that I neglect my prayer life. I really want this inconsistency in my life to be broken; I want my prayer life to get stronger and more stable. I realize that when I don't spend time alone with You, I make it difficult for You to tell me what You want me to know. Inconsistency is a work of the flesh, so I am asking You to help me break this pattern and learn how to make prayer one of the most important pillars of my life.

I pray this in Jesus' name!

MY CONFESSION FOR TODAY

I declare by faith that prayer is a central and significant part of my life. God has great spiritual adventures planned for me, and He wants to reveal them to me during my time of prayer. I am steadfast, immovable, and consistent in my time with God. Nothing is as important to me as those moments I enjoy with Him. As I spend time with Him each day, He refreshes my spirit and enlightens my mind with the knowledge that He wants me to know. My prayer time is a key to the success God is giving me in my life.

I declare this by faith in Jesus' name!

QUESTIONS FOR YOU TO CONSIDER

1. Do you find yourself praying "at each and every occasion" during the day?
2. How can you remind yourself to pray throughout the day?
3. In what types of situations would it be appropriate to pray the following kinds of prayers: the prayer of faith for your own life, the prayer of thanksgiving, the prayer of intercession, and the prayer of worship?

FEBRUARY 27

❧❦❧

A Picture of Who You Used To Be!

Wherein in time past ye walked according to the course of this world,
according to the prince of the power of the air,
the spirit that now worketh in the children of disobedience.
— Ephesians 2:2

Do you ever look through old photographs to reminisce about the past? When browsing through those old images, does it ever make you drift back to moments in the past that are precious to you or perhaps not so pleasant? Photographs are reminders of who we were back then, what we once looked like, what we once did, and so on.

Ephesians 2:2 is like looking at a photograph of what you were like before Jesus Christ came into your life. It says, "Wherein in time past ye walked according to the course of this world, according to the prince of the power of the air, the spirit that now worketh in the children of disobedience." The *King James Version* says, "Wherein in time past...." But the Greek could be better translated, "*Back then....*"

Paul was reminding his readers of what they were like before the grace of God touched their hearts. With this one statement, he reached into his pocketbook, pulled out a stack of old photographs, and began flipping through them, searching for one old photo that would remind them of their past. When Paul wrote Ephesians 2:2, it was like he held that old photo up in the air and said, "Hey, look at this! Do you remember what you looked like back then?"

Then Paul reminds his readers, "Back then...you *walked* according to the course of this world." The word "walked" is the Greek word *peripateo*, a compound of the words *peri* and *pateo*. The word *peri* means *around* and the word *pateo* means *to walk*. When these are joined together, it means *to walk around habitually in one general area all the time*. The Greek grammar implies that it is a path from which these people cannot deviate. You might say they are trapped on this path — bound to walk it again and again. They are *locked* in this one general sphere and can't find their way out by themselves.

The verse goes on to say, "Back then...you walked *according to*...." That phrase "according to" is from the Greek word *kata,* which portrays something that is *forceful* or *dominating*. By using this little word, Paul reminds us that before we met the Lord, we *"habitually walked around under the dominating influence of this world, unable to alter the path we were taking."* Although unaware of our condition, we were spiritual prisoners that were *dominated* and *manipulated* by the influence of a lost society.

But Paul goes on to say, "Back then...you walked according to the *course* of this world...." The word "course" is from the Greek word *aiona,* a word that describes *a specific, allotted period of time*, such as an age, a specific era, or a generation. It often denotes *the influence of a particular generation* or a period of time, like a decade, a century, or even a millennium.

The word *aiona* also denotes the *spirit* of a period; for instance, the 1920s were typified as "the Roaring Twenties." The *spirit* of the 1960s and 1970s was typified as a "rebellious" period because of drug use and the strong reaction against the Vietnam War. Many times in Greek literature, this word *aiona* carries this same meaning of *the spirit of the age.*

Then Paul adds the next word: "Back then...you walked according to the course of this *world*...." This word "world" in Greek is *kosmos*, a word that depicts *something that is fashioned or ordered*. In this verse, it denotes systems and institutions in society, such as fashion, education, or entertainment. Because Paul uses the word *kosmos*, he paints a picture of people who have no standard like God's Word by which to live; therefore, they are guided by the constantly changing ethics and whims of the times. Sadly, education, entertainment, and fashion are the forces that guide the lost world.

You could rephrase Ephesians 2:2 this way:

"Don't you remember what you used to be like? Why, back then you habitually walked around trapped and unable to get off the track you were stuck on — totally unaware that you were being dominated and manipulated by the constantly fluctuating thinking of the day, by the whims of the times, and by whatever society was giving its approval to at that moment...."

That is who you *were*, but that is not who you *are* today! Now you are a child of God who has been redeemed, sanctified, and indwelt by the Spirit of God. But think for a moment of all the people you know who still don't know Jesus Christ. That means they still fit into this category! They are still trapped, unable to get off the treadmill they are stuck on!

Don't you think it's time for you to tell those people the Good News about Jesus Christ? Aren't you glad someone told you? They may not act thrilled when you first approach them, but after a while the message will begin to sink in, and they'll be so thankful you told them the Good News!

MY PRAYER FOR TODAY

Lord, as I read this today, it makes me so thankful that I am not the person I used to be! Thank You for sending someone to me to share the Good News of the Gospel. My life has been transformed, and now I'm on the path that You planned for My life. I ask You to forgive me for not telling others about the saving message of Jesus Christ. I have freely received, and now I have a responsibility to freely give. So today I thank You that I have all the power I need to be a witness to my lost family and friends!

I pray this in Jesus' name!

MY CONFESSION FOR TODAY

I confess that I am a witness for Jesus Christ. When I was filled with the Holy Spirit, I received power to tell my friends and family about the Good News of the Gospel. I have no reason to be afraid of their reaction, and I refuse to allow a spirit of fear to keep me from giving them the truth that will set them free!

I declare this by faith in Jesus' name!

QUESTIONS FOR YOU TO CONSIDER

1. Have you ever stopped to think about what you were like before you were saved?
2. Seeing God's saving work in your own life and how far He has brought you, is there anyone in particular you can think of who needs to hear your testimony of God's grace and saving power?

3. Have you thanked God yet today for saving you from being completely dominated by the enemy and the world's system?

FEBRUARY 28

❧❧❧

Your Redemption Is a Done Deal!

Christ hath redeemed us from the curse of the law,
being made a curse for us: for it is written,
Cursed is every one that hangeth on a tree.
— Galatians 3:13

Don't you wish you could be free from sin and its consequences once and for all? Well, according to Galatians 3:13, you already are! You just haven't comprehended it yet! Let me give you an illustration of this before we dive into Galatians 3:13.

A friend of mine had a goat that he dearly loved. Very late one night, he received a telephone call from the local police, who informed him that his goat had wandered away from home, had been hit by a car, and now lay dead in a ditch by the side of the road.

My friend was grieved and broken-hearted, but he knew he needed to retrieve the dead goat. When he approached the ditch where the goat lay, he saw that the goat was very much alive! Its legs were bound with rope, which let my friend know that someone had kidnapped the goat and then dumped it in the ditch on the side of the road.

Jubilantly, he leaped into the bottom of the ditch, pulled out his pocketknife, cut the ropes, slapped the goat on its backside, and said, "Get up!" But the goat just lay there with its legs still clinging to each other as if they were still bound with rope. He hit her a second time, then a third time. Then he yelled at her one last time, "Get up!"

My friend mused to himself, *Bless this dumb ol' goat! It's free and doesn't even know it!* He reached down and pulled apart the goat's legs; then he lifted it and set it on its feet. Only then did the goat realize it wasn't bound anymore.

When I heard this story, it made me think about us as believers. We don't need to *get* free — we *are* free! Jesus' work on the Cross totally purchased our redemption and freedom.

Although Jesus broke the bonds of slavery and the devil has no legal hold on believers anymore, most believers still lay on their sides in the bottom of the ditch, wishing they could get free. The chains that hold them are an illusion, because Jesus already paid the price for their release!

Galatians 3:13 gives us a glorious picture of the redemption Jesus Christ purchased for us. The word "redeem" that Paul used in this verse is derived from the Greek word *exagoridzo*. It is a compound of the words *ex* and *agoridzo*. The word *ex* is a preposition that means *out*. The word *agoridzo* was the Greek word most notably used to describe *the slave market* — a disgusting place where human beings were bought, sold, and traded like animals.

But when the words *ex* and *agoridzo* are compounded together, it pictures a *buyer* or *redeemer* who has gone to the slave market to purchase a slave for the solitary purpose of bringing him out of that place of slavery so he can be set free. Therefore, this particular word for "redeem" conveys the thought of *permanent removal from captivity.*

Exagoridzo is the very word Paul used in Galatians 3:13, where he says, "Christ hath redeemed us from the curse of the law…." Because this word is used in connection with Jesus redeeming us from the curse of the law, Paul is telling us plainly that Jesus' sacrificial death didn't only pay *the penalty* for our sin; His death *removed us* from living under the curse henceforth!

Paul continues to tell us that Jesus' work of redemption was the reason He came into the world: "But when the fulness of the time was come, God sent forth his Son, made of a woman, made under the law, to redeem them that were under the law, that we might receive the adoption of sons" (Galatians 4:4,5).

As you get started on your day, take time to rejoice that God's purpose in sending Jesus was not only to inspect your condition of slavery and locate you in your depravity — His ultimate plan was to buy you *out* of that miserable condition and then to place you in His family as His own child. You are forever removed from the curse of sin and the law. God accomplished that plan through Jesus Christ's death and resurrection. *It's a done deal!*

You're a purchased possession, bought out of bondage by the Son of God, never to be a slave to sin again. So make a quality decision to walk in the reality of that marvelous fact!

MY PRAYER FOR TODAY

Lord, I thank You that my redemption is a done deal! It's not something I'm trying to get; it's something You've already purchased and accomplished in my life. Help me renew every area of my mind so I can enjoy the liberty You purchased for me. Give me a desire to experience Your freedom in every sphere of my life and a determination to reject any form of bondage that tries to hang on to me!

I pray this in Jesus' name!

MY CONFESSION FOR TODAY

I confess that I am free! Sin has no more hold on me! Bondages and habits from the past have no more legitimate right to exercise their control over me! I rejoice that God sent Jesus to buy me out of my slavery and place me in His family as His own child. I declare that I am forever removed from the curse of sin. I agree that it's a done deal!

I declare this by faith in Jesus' name!

QUESTIONS FOR YOU TO CONSIDER

1. Have you ever felt like that goat, mentally and emotionally paralyzed by the fear of being "kidnapped" by some kind of bondage in your life?
2. How would you act differently if you truly believed that you are no longer under the power of sin and its consequences once and for all?
3. How has the realization of what Jesus accomplished through His death and resurrection changed your opinion of yourself as God's child?

FEBRUARY 29
(LEAP YEAR)

Whose Side Are You On?

...A friend of the world is the enemy of God.
— James 4:4

When a Christian who has walked with God and knows the things of the Spirit decides to step back into the world — *intentionally* or *unintentionally* — this is a *very* serious matter to God. When I say serious, I'm talking about a situation so grave that it eventually causes God to take an aggressive and antagonistic stance toward that believer! This is why James 4:4 says, "...A friend of the world is the enemy of God."

Notice that James refers to believers who have become a "friend" of the world. The word "friend" is from the Greek word *phileo*, a word that has many different facets, including the ideas of *fondness, friendship,* or *love.* This is the Greek word someone would use if he wanted to express *affection* or even *romance.* And when used to depict *friends,* this word is the picture of *very close friends* who are *fond of* and *familiar* with each other.

From the word *phileo* we get the word *philema,* which means *to kiss.* In the ancient world, *a kiss* was a form of greeting that was reserved for family members, friends, fellow church members, or any other esteemed and cherished people in one's life. A kiss like this would never be given to a stranger, but to someone for whom a person felt deep *affection* or with whom he had some kind of *relationship.*

This leads us to the next usage of the word *phileo.* In some places, it portrayed *a person who was under some type of commitment or obligation due to a relationship.* This relationship could be family-related, business-related, socially-related, or friendship-related. Regardless of the basis for the relationship, it is one that includes obligations, such as the obligations that exist in a marriage, between business partners, or even between friends. These relationships carry responsibilities. The word *phileo* could be used to describe these types of *relationships* and the *obligations* that result from entering into them.

So when James talks about believers who have become "a friend of the world" (the Greek word *phileo*), he is talking about Christians who have drifted so far back into the world that they now *feel close* to the world; they have *affection* and *fondness* for it. The *connection* and *sense of familiarity* they have with the world is so intense that they feel an *obligation* to the world or to their worldly friends.

These believers have exchanged their once-deep affection for the Lord for a renewed allegiance to the world from which they were rescued. Because they now have a strong affection for the world, it lets us know that these believers have been drifting for a long time. Backsliding like this doesn't happen overnight. It is clear that a slow, methodical, seducing process has lured them away from Christ and back into a relationship with the world. Now their sense of obligation to the world is greater than their sense of obligation to the Lord.

James solemnly declares that any believer who has slipped back into this type of serious relationship with the world becomes the "enemy" of God. The word "enemy" is from the Greek word *echthros,* a word that appears more than 450 times in the Old Testament Septuagint to describe *hate, hatred, hostility, an enemy,* or *an opponent.* One example of its usage in the New Testament is Luke 23:12, where it portrays the *animosity, antagonism, enmity, rivalry,* and *competition* that existed between Herod Antipas and Pilate. These two men were definitely *not* on the same side!

What does this mean to you and me? It tells us that God is jealous when a believer transfers his devotion back to the world. In fact, this creates strong jealousy in the heart of God for that believer. God sees that believer's relationship with the world as a violation of His own relationship with him. Just as a spouse would feel violated if he discovered that his mate had secretly carried on an intimate relationship with someone else, God feels betrayed when a believer transfers his affection away from Him and back to the world. In these cases, God takes an antagonistic view toward the improper relationship and begins to set things in motion to see that relationship end!

Because God wants that believer to refocus his affection where it ought to be, His grace moves in to intervene. It may not feel like help at the time, but God, who is intensely jealous for His people, sees Himself as a Contender for that believer's affection and devotion! He will therefore do what He must to get the attention of His wayward child so He can turn him around and bring him back to where he ought to be!

Backsliding is serious business! When you try to split your heart between the Lord and the world, it simply won't work! There's too much animosity between a holy God and the world from which you were rescued. So don't let yourself head back in the direction of the world, because God won't just sit back and watch it happen. He will come after you like the most serious Competitor in the whole universe!

MY PRAYER FOR TODAY

Lord, I pray that my passion for You will grow stronger and stronger and that I will remain untainted from the world. Please show me if there are any places in me that are drawn to things that displease You. It may be hard for me to hear, but if there is anything in me that seeks to slip back into the life from which You delivered me, please reveal it to me. If my affection for anything else in this world is greater than my affection for You, please show me!

I pray this in Jesus' name!

MY CONFESSION FOR TODAY

I declare by faith that I am more deeply in love with Jesus Christ today than at any previous moment in my life. My affection for Him is so deep that I will never turn back to the life from which I've been delivered. I have no relational obligations greater than the sense of obligation that I feel for Jesus Christ. He saved me, redeemed me, delivered me, and changed me — and I vow to serve Him for the rest of my life!

I declare this by faith in Jesus' name!

QUESTIONS FOR YOU TO CONSIDER

1. Can you think of any areas in your life where your devotion to the world is greater than your devotion to the Lord?
2. Have there been times recently when you have felt the "pull" of the world trying to seduce you back into the life from which you were delivered?
3. What do you need to do to reject that "pull" and stay free?

MARCH 1

༄

God's Power Is Yours For the Taking!

Finally, my brethren, be strong in the Lord,
and in the power of his might.
— Ephesians 6:10

Many years ago, I was preaching in a series of meetings about the power of the Holy Spirit. At the end of one of the services, an invitation was given for people to come forward who wanted to be filled with the Spirit. I watched with great joy as nearly one hundred people filled the altar of that church. They slipped down on their knees at the steps of the stage, lowered their heads in prayer, and began to ask the Lord to touch them, to fill them, and in some cases, to refill them with a fresh infilling of power.

As I stepped off the stage to pray for the people, the host informed me that he would be praying for them that night. I moved aside to let him take the lead, but it was a decision I soon regretted. I watched as this leader moved among those dear people, patting them on the back and telling them, *"You have to pray louder. You have to pray harder. You have to plead if you want to be filled. You have to tarry a little longer."*

In a matter of minutes, the atmosphere at that altar mutated into a sad scene as those precious people began to beg and plead for something that God graciously and freely wanted to give them. A precious work of grace was turned into an ugly work of the flesh — and as a result, few of them received anything from God that night.

Later I asked the host, "How long have these people been praying to be filled with the Spirit?" He answered that some had been waiting as long as twenty years; some had been waiting fifteen years; and others had been seeking for a "mere" year or two. I was aghast! I thought, *Why has it taken so long for these believers to be filled with the Holy Spirit when this is something God has made so accessible to every believer?*

You see, the fresh touch of power each of us need today is as close as the air we breathe. God designed us to be the receptacles for this power (*see* January 12), so He wants us to receive it. He knows we need it to walk in victory, to exercise authority in our lives, and to overcome the works of the devil.

But where do we get that supernatural power? Paul answers this question in Ephesians 6:10, where he says, "Finally, my brethren, be strong in the Lord, and in the power of his might." I want you to especially look at that phrase "be strong in the Lord."

The phrase "in the Lord" is a Greek phrase that means that this special infusion of dynamic, supernatural power can be found in only one place — *in the Lord*. The fact that Paul wrote in this particular Greek case is very important, because it tells us that this power is *locked up* in the Person of Jesus Christ and that it can't be found anywhere else.

You can't obtain this supernatural power by reading books or listening to tapes. The books and tapes can *direct* you to the place where it can be found, but the power itself can only be obtained through a personal relationship with the Lord Jesus Christ. This power is locked up *"in the Lord."*

Now, let me take this one step further so I can explain why it's so easy and uncomplicated for you to receive a new infilling of God's power in your life. This same *locative case* that describes the power of God being *locked up* inside Jesus Christ is used *nine times* in Ephesians 1, where Paul uses it to declare that we are perpetually and infinitely *locked up* inside the Person of Jesus Christ. In verses 3, 4, 6, 7, 10 (twice), 11, and 13 (twice), Paul says that we are *in Him, in Christ, in whom,* or *in the Beloved.* Because these phrases are in the locative case, Paul is saying we have actually been placed *inside Jesus Christ;* He has become our realm of existence and the place of our habitation.

Just as you live at a certain physical address, you also have a spiritual address. You permanently reside *inside* the Son of God! He is your permanent home — a home from which you will never move because you are *locked up* and securely placed *inside Him* perpetually!

Stay with me, because this now leads us to the reason that the supernatural power of God we desperately need is so easy to receive!

The reason God's power is so accessible to us is that both we and this divine power are gloriously *locked up* inside the same place! The power is located *inside the Lord,* and we are also located *inside the Lord.* We may not always be mentally aware of it, but we are constantly rubbing elbows with this divine power on a day-to-day, hour-to-hour, and minute-to-minute basis.

Let me use a simple illustration to help you get the point of what I'm communicating to you today. The fact that we reside inside Jesus along with God's power can be somewhat likened to water and fish sharing the same space in an aquarium. The water and fish are definitely different in substance, but they both reside in the same tank. The tank serves as the "home" for these two substances that are held simultaneously within its walls. Therefore, the fish doesn't have to release its faith to *get into* the water, for it already perpetually *lives in* the water.

The very fact that we are locked up inside the Lord along with the Holy Spirit's supernatural power means that we are never far away from a new surge of superhuman power into our human spirits. A fresh surge of this power into us is as accessible as our very next breath of air! It's just as normal for us to receive a new infilling of the Spirit as it is for a fish to freely swim around in its tank.

In fact, God has designed our lives in Christ in such a way that it would be very difficult for us *not* to freely receive this impartation of superhuman, supernatural strength for the fight. However, if we are to experience this ever-available, ever-near power, we must open our hearts to it and ask God to release it into our lives. Then by *faith* we must reach out to embrace it.

This means there is no need to beg, plead, or beat yourself up in prayer to somehow prove that you are good enough to receive this divine power. If you know Jesus Christ, you are already locked up in the same place with the power of God. In fact, you're rubbing elbows with it all the time. It's no more difficult to receive than it is for a fish to start swimming! It's yours for the taking!

You are surrounded by God's supernatural power *right now.* At this very moment, you are immersed in that divine power. *Supernatural inner strength and ability is yours for the taking — so take it by faith!*

MY PRAYER FOR TODAY

Lord, how can I ever thank You enough for making Your power so available to me? I need this power so much in my life, and I'm grateful You have made it so easy for me to receive it. Therefore, I open my heart right now by faith, and I ask You to give me a fresh infilling of Your Spirit.

I pray this in Jesus' name!

I confess that a fresh infilling of the Holy Spirit's supernatural power is never far away from me. A fresh surge of this power is as accessible to me as my very next breath of air! It's just as normal for me to receive a new infilling of the Spirit as it is for a fish to freely swim around in its tank. In fact, it's difficult for me NOT to receive this impartation of superhuman, supernatural strength for the fight! Because my heart is open to receive it, I ask God to release it into my life, and by faith I now receive this divine power. It's mine for the taking!

I declare this by faith in Jesus' name!

QUESTIONS FOR YOU TO CONSIDER

1. When was the last time you received a fresh surge of supernatural power in your life?
2. Do you freely receive a touch from the Lord, or do you feel like you have to beg and plead in order to convince Him to give you a fresh touch of His power?
3. How will today's *Sparkling Gem* make a difference in your way of thinking?

MARCH 2

Stopping Satan At His Own Game

Lest Satan should get an advantage of us:
for we are not ignorant of his devices.
— 2 Corinthians 2:11

I don't like talking about the devil, but time after time the Bible warns us that the devil is like a roaring lion who roams about, seeking whom he can destroy (1 Peter 5:8). Whether we like it or not, the devil is a real personality who is looking for ways to destroy our lives. Since the Bible frequently warns us about this sinister enemy, we need to know:

✦ *How the devil operates.*
✦ *How to identify the devil's attacks at their very onset.*
✦ *How to block and stop his devilish assaults.*
✦ *How to prevent repeat attacks from occurring in the future.*

In Second Corinthians 2:11, the apostle Paul wrote a verse that is teeming with insight to answer these questions. He wrote, "Lest Satan should get an advantage of us: for we are not ignorant of his devices."

Paul clearly understood that Satan was constantly seeking ways to take advantage of people. The word "advantage" in this verse is the Greek word *pleonekteo*. This word means *to outwit; to trick; to take advantage of someone through some sinister or sneaky means.* It is a compound of the word *pleon,* which means *more,* and the word *echo,* which means *to have.* Together, these words form the word *pleonekto,* which denotes *a desire to have more, more, and more.* It is a form of the word *pleonexia,* the Greek word for *greediness.* In this case in Second Corinthians 2:11, it pictures *someone whose lust for something is so intense that he will take any actions required to obtain what he wants.*

Because Paul used this word about Satan, we are alerted to the fact that Satan desperately wants something in his control. He wants *us!* The devil will use any method necessary to take advantage of us and get us under his control. He will deviously and artfully endeavor to outwit us, trick us, dominate us, and ultimately take us as his hostages. That is why Paul said, "...We are not *ignorant* of his devices."

When you have an enemy who hates you this much and who wants to destroy you, you can't afford to be ignorant. In Paul's case, he and his team were invading new territory with the Gospel all the time. Paul knew that Satan wanted to hinder and even stop them and that it was therefore essential for him to understand the way the devil operated. He had to be able to discern whether he was facing a mere human problem or a planned demonic attack.

Likewise, you need to know if the storm you're facing right now is just a natural problem that will blow over, or if are you facing demonic turbulence sent from hell to disrupt God's plan for your life. You can't just shut your eyes and hope the problem will work out by itself. If this is an attack from the devil and you do nothing to stop it, it will not simply go away. On the contrary, it will actually increase and become more intense. That's why being able to recognize Satan's game is so important!

The word "ignorant" in Second Corinthians 2:11 is the Greek word *agnoeo,* and it refers to one's *ignorance* or *lack of certain facts.* However, it also includes *making mistakes or errors due to a lack of understanding.* It is the picture of an *uneducated person* who, due to a lack of knowledge, is prone to arrive at mistaken conclusions. The word *agnoeo* depicts someone who is *in the dark* or *without a clue.* Because this person lacks understanding, his conclusions are *faulty, erroneous,* and *misguided.* This is where we get the word *agnostic,* the official name used to describe individuals who claim they don't know what they believe. So when someone claims to be *agnostic,* he is literally claiming to be *ignorant!*

An example of this kind of ignorance is often seen when a person is diagnosed with a terminal disease sent from the devil, yet the person believes his sickness comes from God. Because the sick person is *ignorant* of the fact that Satan and *not* God is the author of sickness and disease, he mistakenly concludes that his sickness must be God's will for his life. This ignorance is so devastating that it could possibly lead to that individual's premature death. Do you see how dangerous it is to remain ignorant about how the devil operates?

This is the reason Paul says, "...We are *not ignorant* of Satan's devices." Paul and his companions had carefully observed how the devil operates and the primary methods he uses to attack. As a result, they knew how to recognize the onset of an attack when Satan started maneuvering to frustrate their plans. Paul and his team were definitely not *in the dark* about the devil; hence, the enemy found it much more difficult to take advantage of them.

Paul had to learn these things because he faced problems with people, religious leaders, governmental leaders, and even with friends. He was thrown in prison, cast into the sea, and beaten during moments of persecution. Traps were constantly being set for his capture, and he constantly had to be on the lookout for people who tried to use him and take advantage of him. Paul couldn't afford to be *in the dark* spiritually about the way Satan operated — and neither can *you!*

But notice what Paul says next: "...We are not ignorant of Satan's *devices.*" The word "devices" is the Greek word *noemata,* derived from the word *nous.* The word *nous* is the word for *the mind* or *the intellect.* However, when the word *nous* becomes the word *noemata,* it describes *a mind that is scheming, calculating, conniving, devious, shrewd, sly,* or *clever.* This is very significant because it alerts us to the reality that Satan isn't just *hoping* to hinder us; he is incessantly scheming and conniving to injure or deliberately mess up a person's plans, health, marriage, business, and family. The enemy doesn't really care how he accomplishes his evil plan; he just wants to find ways to ruin whatever that person holds dear.

Thus, the word *noemata* denotes *Satan's insidious, malevolent plot to attack and victimize human beings,* clearly demonstrating that the devil loves to captivate and ultimately destroy human beings. If this devilish process is not aborted by the power of God, it is only a matter of time before Satan puts the last touches on his plan to take captive a person, family, church, ministry, business, organization, or even an entire nation!

When you put all of these words together, it expresses this idea:

"Satan can forget it if he thinks he is going to pull the wool over our eyes! We know how he operates, and we understand the way he schemes and connives to take us out."

So don't shut your eyes and ignore the fact that the devil wants to bring about your downfall. Instead, open your eyes and allow the Holy Spirit to teach you how to recognize the devil's operations so you won't fall prey to him any longer. Then you'll be able to say, *"Devil, I know this is you attacking me, so I am telling you to leave now in Jesus' name!"*

MY PRAYER FOR TODAY

Lord, I thank You for opening my eyes and illuminating my understanding to recognize Satan's attacks against my life. Thank You also for giving me the understanding to know how to stand against these demonic attacks. I am so grateful that You have sent the Holy Spirit to be my Teacher and Guide and to equip me to stand against every assault that comes against my life, my family, my church, my business, and all my relationships. Armed with the power and insight of the Spirit, I never have to allow the enemy to take advantage of me again. So I open my heart today, and I ask the Holy Spirit to teach me everything I need to know to stand against the wiles the devil wants to employ against me.

I pray this in Jesus' name!

MY CONFESSION FOR TODAY

I declare that I am not ignorant of Satan's devices. Because the Holy Spirit is my Teacher, I know how to recognize the onset of Satan's attack as he starts maneuvering to frustrate my plans. I am not in the dark about the devil; therefore, the enemy finds it very difficult to take advantage of me. Because my mind has been illuminated to see how the devil operates, his evil plots against my life are aborted by the power of God! I will not be taken down by any strategy the enemy tries to use against me.

I declare this by faith in Jesus' name!

QUESTIONS FOR YOU TO CONSIDER

1. Are you aware of areas in your personal life where you are currently falling prey to the cunning plots of the devil? Can you think of some ways you have been susceptible in the past to his repeated tactics?

2. Have you really looked at Satan's repeat attacks on your life to see what you can learn about the way he attacks you?

3. Since awareness of your enemy is so important, what are some ways you can be more prepared for his attacks, all of which are designed to bring ruin in your life?

MARCH 3

'Filthy Stinking Rich!'

…In every thing ye are enriched by him, in all utterance,
and in all knowledge; even as the testimony of Christ was confirmed in you.
— 1 Corinthians 1:5,6

My dictionary says that the word "rich" means *to have goods, property, and money in abundance; to have possession of abundant resource, material goods, and significant wealth; to have more than enough to gratify one's normal needs or desires.*

Who wouldn't enjoy being "rich" enough to satisfy his own needs and desires? Who wouldn't like to have so much wealth that he could give large amounts of money and special gifts to family, friends, and loved ones? What person wouldn't enjoy being able to financially help someone who has suffered due to difficult circumstances?

The dream of being "rich" has consumed human beings since the very beginning of man's life on this earth. In fact, this insatiable desire and voracious appetite for wealth has driven both men and nations to lie, to steal, to fight, and even to murder and kill. However, if you are a child of God, you don't have to lie, steal, fight, murder, or kill to be rich! You are already "rich" beyond your wildest imagination! Even though you may not have tapped into your riches yet, those resources are nonetheless at your disposal — and they will make you feel like you're *filthy stinking rich*!

The apostle Paul told the Corinthians about these riches when he wrote, "…In every thing ye are enriched by him, in all utterance, and in all knowledge; even as the testimony of Christ was confirmed in you" (1 Corinthians 1:5,6). The word "enriched" is the Greek word *plousios,* which describes *extreme or vast material wealth.* In fact, the word *plousios* is where we get the term "plutocrat," referring to a person who is so prosperous that he is unable to ascertain the full extent of his own wealth. Because his investments, his companies, and the percentage of interest he earns on his portfolio all grow so rapidly, it is impossible for his accountants and bookkeepers to keep track of how much wealth he actually possesses.

Can you imagine being so rich that no one can figure out how much you own or control? Well, that is the description of a *"plutocrat"*!

Now Paul uses this same word *plousios* in First Corinthians 1:5 when he says we are "enriched by him.…" The Greek word for "by" in this verse is the word *en*; and in this verse, it can be translated either *in him* or *by him.* This conveys two very powerful truths to you and me:

1. The day we were born again and placed *into Jesus Christ* was the richest day of our lives. On that day, we literally became *joint heirs* with Jesus Christ, with a legal right to all the promises of God! Indeed, that was a rich day for all of us! In light of this, First Corinthians 1:5 could be interpreted, *"...We were made rich the day we were placed into Him...."*

2. But the Greek word *en* could also emphasize the point that just as we were enriched the day we got saved, this enrichment process continues throughout our lives as we walk with God. The verse could thus be interpreted, *"...We are continually being enriched as a result of being in Him...."*

Because the word *plousios* is used,
this verse conveys the following idea:

"...You are invested with great spiritual riches because you are in Him, and that's not all! The longer you remain in Him, you just keep getting blessed with more and more wealth that comes from being in Him."

Of course, Paul is talking about *spiritual* riches, not *worldly* riches. As time progressed, the word *plousios* came to depict riches in a more general sense, including the riches of honor, wisdom, mercy, and so on. First Corinthians 1:5 uses the word *plousios* to happily proclaim that the Corinthian church was "enriched" with gifts of the Spirit, such as the gifts of utterance and knowledge: *the word of knowledge, the word of wisdom, discerning of spirits, prophecy, tongues,* and *interpretation of tongues.*

The church of Corinth was loaded with these kinds of spiritual gifts. In fact, these gifts were in such mighty manifestation in Corinth that Paul had to write and tell them how to administrate such a huge abundance of spiritual gifts (*see* 1 Corinthians chapters 12-14). It appears that the Corinthian believers had more of these gifts in manifestation than any other church of that time. In a real sense, they were *extremely wealthy* in spiritual manifestations that had come to them as a result of being in Christ.

The Corinthians had been enriched when they first came to Christ, becoming joint heirs with Jesus Christ and inheritors of the promises of God. But by remaining in Jesus, they were constantly made richer and richer as the gifts of the Spirit began to operate mightily among them.

In the same way, the gifts of the Spirit bring spiritual riches into our lives. In fact, the more these gifts operate, the richer we become spiritually!

So don't settle for spiritual poverty. You have every right to expect an abundance of manifested promises, power, and spiritual gifts in your life. These spiritual riches are yours by virtue of your relationship with Jesus. The day you were placed in Him, they legally became yours! In God's eyes, you are a *spiritual plutocrat* — so loaded with spiritual assets and treasures that you'll never be able to fully explore or exhaust all of them in your lifetime!

MY PRAYER FOR TODAY

Lord, I'm so glad You saved and delivered me from the life I used to lead. Thank You for making me a joint heir with Jesus and for allowing me to have access to the riches of Heaven! I ask You to forgive me for the times I've lived so far below what You provided for me. I sincerely ask You to help me explore the spiritual riches I possess. Help me to release those riches so my own life can be enriched and so You can use me to enrich the lives of people around me.

I pray this in Jesus' name!

MY CONFESSION FOR TODAY

I boldly declare that the day I was born again and placed into Jesus Christ was the richest day of my life. On that day, I literally became a joint heir with Jesus Christ and obtained the legal right to claim all the promises of God! From that day until now, I have been constantly enriched by His Presence in my life. I no longer have to settle for spiritual poverty, because I have every right to expect an abundance of manifested promises, power, and spiritual gifts in my life. I possess more spiritual treasure than I'll ever be able to explore or fully exhaust!

I declare this by faith in Jesus' name!

QUESTIONS FOR YOU TO CONSIDER

1. Do you see yourself as spiritually rich or spiritually poor?
2. What spiritual gifts operate in your life, and how have they enriched you and others?
3. Have you been hungering for and seeking God concerning the spiritual gifts He desires for you to operate in (1 Corinthians 14:1)?

MARCH 4

Laziness and Slothfulness —
Don't Allow Either in Your Life!

That ye be not slothful, but followers of them
who through faith and patience inherit the promises.
— Hebrews 6:12

I'll never forget the day when the Lord suddenly spoke to my heart as I was praying and shocked me by what He told me. I heard the Holy Spirit say, "Rick, if you're going to do what I've called you to do, it's time for you to remove *slothfulness* from your life!"

I was shaken when I heard those words. I had always been such a hard worker and couldn't imagine why the Lord would tell me that I needed to remove *laziness* from my life. I sat quietly for a moment and thought about the Holy Spirit's message to me. It upset me to think the Lord would think of me as *lazy*.

But in reality, the Lord hadn't spoken a word to me about laziness. He had spoken to me about *slothfulness*. Until that day, I had always thought *slothfulness* and *laziness* were the same thing, but they are not.

I said to the Lord, "You know how hard I've been working in the ministry. I know You're aware of how many hours I spend writing books, developing materials, traveling, teaching seminars, and preaching in more than four hundred different services every year. How could You ever accuse me of being lazy, Lord?"

The Holy Spirit gently answered me, "I didn't say a word to you about *laziness*. You're a good worker, and I would not accuse you of laziness. But you are *slothful*, and I want you to eradicate this *slothfulness* from your life!"

For the first time in my life, I realized there is a difference between laziness and slothfulness. Because Hebrews 6:12 speaks of slothfulness, I turned there first to begin my study as I sought to discover what the word "slothful" really meant. It says, "That ye be not slothful, but followers of them who through faith and patience inherit the promises."

To my utter amazement, I discovered that "slothful" doesn't have anything to do with laziness! It comes from the Greek word *nothros* and describes *something that is dull, monotonous, or unexciting; something that is slow and sluggish;* or *something that has lost its speed or momentum.* This "something" is still moving, but it isn't moving with the same velocity and aggressiveness it once had. It has lost the drive, thrust, impetus, pace, and speed it once possessed. This word therefore presents the idea of someone who was once zealous about something but whose zeal has now dissipated, replaced instead by *neutrality.*

The Greek word *nothros* could be typified by a candle that no longer burns brightly as it once did; now its flame has dwindled to a mere flicker of its original intensity. The candle still gives light, but not the way it once did. Thus, the word *nothros* doesn't present the picture of laziness; rather, it speaks of someone who has lost his zeal or his intense conviction about a matter that once was of great importance to him. It denotes a person who has become *disinterested* and whose zeal has been replaced with a *middle-of-the-road, take-it-or-leave it* mentality.

Because of this word *nothros,*
Hebrews 6:12 could be interpreted this way:

"Quit being slothful — quit acting like someone who has lost his enthusiasm and excitement and has now sunk into a state of being slow, boring, monotonous, sluggish, dull, and uninterested...."

When I grasped what the word "slothful" really meant, I began wishing the Lord had accused me of laziness! I saw that "slothfulness" has nothing to do with the amount of energy you or I put out to do a job. Instead, it speaks of an *inward* condition. Even though it may look like we're going somewhere on the outside, inwardly we're stuck in "neutral" and going nowhere.

In my case, I was doing a lot for the Lord at that time; however, right in the midst of all that activity, I was becoming hardened to the things of the Spirit. I was losing the edge I once possessed. When the Lord told me to remove slothfulness from my life, He was calling me to eradicate any hint of spiritual neutrality and to reclaim the red-hot position I'd previously held in my walk with Him.

If you are serious about serving and pleasing God, you must view the loss of your passion, momentum, and desire as totally unacceptable. If slothfulness has slowly wormed its way into your life, this spiritual problem can be corrected. You *can* get back on track again! By repenting and deciding to turn from slothfulness and neutrality, you can remove this hindrance from your life. So if you've lost your momentum in running your spiritual race, *don't stay in neutral!* If you continue in that sorry state, it will only be a matter of time before you look back and realize how much ground you've lost.

Don't let another day go by without repenting of your slothfulness and stirring up your inner desire to fulfill all God has called you to do. Shift back into high gear, and go after God's best for all you're worth!

MY PRAYER FOR TODAY

Lord, help me understand how totally unacceptable it is for me to lose my passion, momentum, and desire. I ask You to forgive me for allowing any hint of slothfulness to operate in my life. Today I repent and deliberately turn from slothfulness. Holy Spirit, I turn to You now and ask You to stir and reignite the fire in my heart. Please help me regain the zeal, the thrust, and the fire I once possessed. Help me to keep that fire burning this time, never to lose it again.

I pray this in Jesus' name!

MY CONFESSION FOR TODAY

I declare by faith that I am NOT spiritually neutral for Jesus Christ. The Holy Spirit burns brightly in my life, and I am more excited about serving Jesus Christ than at any other time in my life! The fire of God is burning brightly inside me, evident for all to see. I am an example of what it means to be passionate, committed, and on fire about the things of God. I am stirred up and ready to take on any assignment God gives me — and I will do it with all my heart.

I declare this by faith in Jesus' name!

QUESTIONS FOR YOU TO CONSIDER

1. Can you detect any spiritual neutrality in your life?
2. What are the signs that let you know you have become neutral? Write them down so you can pray about them.
3. If you have become spiritually neutral, what steps are you going to take to start reversing this condition?

MARCH 5

Does Jesus Find You To Be Therapeutic, Refreshing, or Disgusting?

So then because thou art lukewarm, and neither cold nor hot,
I will spue thee out of my mouth.
— Revelation 3:16

*I*n Russia, it is a tradition for people to visit the sauna. People especially love to do this in the middle of the winter. This tradition is hundreds of years old, dating back to the time when people didn't have running water in their villages or homes. People would join all their friends at the local sauna once a week not only to get clean but to spend an evening of fellowship.

Today everyone has running water in their homes in Russia; nevertheless, people still go to the sauna, for it remains a very important part of Russian culture. And because I live in Russia, I frequently go to the local sauna with brothers from the church for an evening of fellowship and prayer.

After we have all sat in sweltering hot temperatures, I watch in shock as the Russian men leap into huge tubs of bitterly cold water. Or sometimes while we're on a ministry trip, we'll stay at a farm and I'll take a sauna with the brothers from the local church. These brothers will run out of the building; dive head first into the snow; roll around in it for a few minutes, screaming and shouting; and then dash back into the sauna where it's nice and warm. They tell me that the purpose for this practice is to get their blood moving!

I enjoy going to the sauna with my fellow brothers in the Lord, but I refuse to leap into sub-zero cold water or dive into snow when it's already forty degrees below zero outside! I don't care if it *is* good for the circulation; I will not do it! I find it much more enjoyable to rest in a tub of lukewarm water that is relaxing. Going from sweltering "hot" to freezing "cold" is just too much for me!

When I refuse to go from one extreme temperature to the other and even ask for lukewarm water to be poured into a tub especially for me, the men sometimes joke with me, reminding me about Jesus' words to the Laodiceans in Revelation 3:16: "So then because thou art lukewarm, and neither cold nor hot, I will spue thee out of my mouth."

The city of Laodicea was built in a region that was full of seismic activity and had experienced many earthquakes. As often happens in a seismic area, vents came up from the depths of the earth, allowing boiling hot water to reach the surface. In the nearby city of Hierapolis, these hot springs were famous. People came from great distances to bathe in those waters, believing they had medicinal powers. An experience in those waters was viewed to be therapeutic and effective in improving one's health.

Another city named Colosse was not too far away. As Hierapolis was known for its hot springs, Colosse was known for its cold waters. Just as people journeyed to Hierapolis to bathe in the hot springs for health purposes, people would travel great distances to vacation in Colosse, where they could invigorate themselves by taking frequent dips into the famous, refreshing, cool-to-freezing waters of that city.

Laodicea may have been the biggest and richest city in the area, but it had neither hot nor cold water. Therefore, the people of Laodicea had to leave their luxurious homes and travel to Colosse if they wanted to enjoy fresh, cool water. On the other hand, those who desired to soak in the hot springs had to travel six miles to Hierapolis.

Once in an attempt to bring the hot water from Hierapolis to Laodicea, a huge construction project was commenced. The goal of those who initiated the project was to build pipes that would channel the hot water six miles from Hierapolis to the city of Laodicea. The pipes effectively delivered the water — a real feat of construction at that time. Sadly, however, the water lost its heat along the way. By the time the water reached Laodicea, it was not only lukewarm, but it had developed a sickening, nauseating taste. The taste was so revolting that no one wanted to drink it!

So when Jesus told the Laodiceans, "…Because thou art lukewarm, and neither cold nor hot, I will spue thee out of my mouth," this was a message that carried a strong punch. He was telling them, "Because you have become so dead, dull, sickening and nauseating — because no spiritually refreshing waters flow from you and you have no healing properties left — I will spue thee out of My mouth!"

The word "spue" is the Greek word *emeo*, and it means *to vomit, to spit out, to regurgitate*. This picture of Jesus threatening to "spue" the Laodiceans out of His mouth doesn't mean He was *rejecting* them or *disinheriting* them. It just reveals how utterly distasteful a spiritually lukewarm condition is to Jesus. The fact that these believers were lukewarm means they weren't good for anything; they were neither cool and refreshing, nor were they hot and healing. They were just stuck in the middle, like something that has lost both its flavor and its heat along the way.

These words in Revelation 3:16 could be interpreted:

"Because you've lost your temperature and become lukewarm — because no refreshing waters flow out of you and you have no healing properties left — I find your taste in My mouth to be disgusting! I can't bear it anymore, and I have no choice but to spit you out!"

That's how God feels about a lukewarm spiritual walk. You see, with God there is no middle ground. But if you have allowed your walk with God to become lukewarm, you can reverse that abominable condition! God has tossed the ball in your court, and now it's up to you. He is calling you to repent of your lukewarm attitude. *Go after the things of God with all your heart, soul, and strength!*

MY PRAYER FOR TODAY

Lord, I never want to be lukewarm so that You find me to be an unpleasant taste in Your mouth. Instead, I ask You to help me be a fountain from which healing waters flow to the sick and a source of refreshment to anyone who needs strength and encouragement. Help me to never allow a lukewarm attitude to take hold in my life! If there is any area of my life where I've already slipped into a lukewarm state, please reveal it to me so I can repent and get back to where I ought to be!

I pray this in Jesus' name!

MY CONFESSION FOR TODAY

I confess that I am a fountain of healing and a source of refreshment to everyone who comes into my life. When people come near me, they receive exactly what they need. Healing flows from me to everyone who needs a healing touch. Those who are spiritually tired become refreshed when they spend time with me. I allow no middle ground in my life — no neutrality, no lukewarm attitude — and I am therefore continually filled with everything needed to meet the needs of people who come across my path.

I declare this by faith in Jesus' name!

QUESTIONS FOR YOU TO CONSIDER

1. What are some signs of a lukewarm spiritual condition in your life?
2. Can you recall a time when you were "hot" for the Lord? What were you doing at that time that caused you to be so on fire for Jesus?
3. If you have slipped away from that wonderful time in your walk with the Lord, can you recall what changed the condition of your heart? What can you do to get back there again? Write down your answers so you can see them and pray about them.

MARCH 6

❧

It's Time for You
To Start Acting Like God!

Be ye therefore followers of God, as dear children.
— Ephesians 5:1

Have you ever been in a situation that made you so uncomfortable, you wished you could turn and run, but you knew you had to stay? Did you throw a fit and cry in front of everyone, alerting them to the fact that you were upset? Or did you speak to yourself, telling your emotions to get a grip and to be controlled? Did you make the choice to grit your teeth, put a smile on your face, and *act* like you were happy to be there, although truthfully that wasn't what you felt at all?

Let me give you two more common scenarios to consider. Have you ever been depressed, but because you were with other people, you had no choice but to smile, laugh, and *act* as if everything was fine? Or can you remember a moment when you were having a very upsetting or emotional talk with someone in your household — and suddenly the phone rang? Did you notice how your voice changed from sounding gloomy to sounding like a cheerful welcoming committee when you answered the telephone? *"Hello! I'm so glad to hear from you. How are you?"*

To disguise what you really were feeling in these different situations, you were required *to act*. All of us have found ourselves in similar situations.

Acting is an ability that every human being possesses. Children know how to act; teenagers know how to act; husbands and wives know how to act; and employees know how to act. If needed, every person on the planet knows how to switch into an acting mode! *Acting is something that everyone can do.*

In Ephesians 5:1, the apostle Paul wrote these words: "Be ye therefore followers of God, as dear children." The word "followers" is the Greek word *mimetes*. The word *mimetes* means *to imitate someone* or *to mimic what you see someone else doing*. It was also used to describe *actors* or *performing arts artists* who *acted* on the stage for their profession. In addition, *mimetes* frequently depicted the *modeling* of a parent, teacher, champion, or hero. When a person was known for his high moral character, others were encouraged to *emulate* or *copy* that person.

The word *mimetes* is frequently used in the New Testament. For instance, Paul used the word *mimetes* when he told the Corinthians, "Wherefore I beseech you, be ye *followers* of me." (1 Corinthians 4:16). This verse could be translated, *"I'm urging you to act like me! Watch what I do, and duplicate in your own life everything you see in me...."*

In Second Thessalonians 3:7, Paul used the word *mimetes* when he told the Thessalonians, "For yourselves know how ye ought to *follow* us...." This could be translated, *"It would behoove you to follow our example — to imitate and mimic us with the goal of replicating the things you observe in our lives."*

Hebrews 13:7 also uses the word *mimetes*. It says, "Remember them which have the rule over you, who have spoken unto you the word of God: whose faith *follow*, considering the end of their conversation." The last section of that verse could be translated, *"...You need to carefully model your faith after theirs — doing what they do, saying what they say, acting like they act — considering the great maturity and fruit produced by their lives."*

Because Paul uses this word in Ephesians 5:1, he is telling us to model our lives after God. Just as a professional actor is committed to capturing the emotions, looks, voice, character, and even the appearance of the person he is portraying, we are to put our whole heart and soul into imitating God in every sphere of our lives. This means we must make a decision to act like God!

But let's go back a little to see how Paul begins this verse. He says, "Be ye therefore...." The Greek word used here is the word *ginomai*; however, here it appears as the word *ginesthe* and would be better translated: *"Be constantly in the process of becoming...."* It expresses the idea of someone who has *started* some action in his life and is now *continuing* to work on it. He hasn't arrived at his goal yet, but he is committed to keep working on it and to stay in the process of *becoming*.

Successfully *acting* like God is not something you will attain the first time you try. For you to capture the emotions, looks, voice, and character of God — in other words, to successfully *replicate* Him in your life — will require commitment and time. Don't expect to arrive at this high level of duplication overnight. Instead, resolve to start where you are today; then do more tomorrow. Keep it up until you finally begin to *think* like God, *talk* like God, *sound* like God, and *carry yourself in the confidence* of God!

**When all of this is put together in Ephesians 5:1,
it could be interpreted:**

"Be constantly in the process of becoming more like God — making it your aim to act like Him, to duplicate Him, and to exactly copy Him in every area of your life...."

I noted already that children, parents, husbands, wives, students, and employees have the ability *to act.* Very early in life, people learn that they must *act* a certain way in order to get what they want. If their behavior is wrong, they know that they must *act* differently. Changing behavior requires a decision to do things differently — to speak differently, to think differently, and to act differently. It all starts with a decision.

Why don't you make a decision to put your unsanctified emotions, thoughts, feelings, and behavior aside, and start *acting* like God? What would happen to your life, your family, your church, your community, your nation, and the world if you did that? What would happen if you approached every problem acting as God does when *He* approaches problems? What difference would it make in your life if you acted like God every time you have to deal with an unloving person?

In all these cases, your world would be dramatically affected if you acted like God. Problems would appear very small, and you'd believe you could overcome every one of them. You'd have sufficient love, patience, and forgiveness for every unloving person.

So why don't you make the decision to take up acting? Resolve today that in every situation, you're going to imitate your Heavenly Father, the greatest Role Model of all. And remember, when you face a challenge, you don't have to sit around wondering what God would say or do. His "script" — His anointed Word — is always available to help you learn how to act like Him!

MY PRAYER FOR TODAY

Lord, help me make the decision to put my unsanctified emotions, thoughts, feelings, and behavior aside and to start acting like You. I know that if I approached every problem "acting" like You, it would make a huge difference in my life. You see everything from a viewpoint of power and victory, so please help me to see like You, think like You, and act like You. Help me make the decision to change my way of thinking — to learn how to respond as You do to every situation I am confronted with in life.

I pray this in Jesus' name!

MY CONFESSION FOR TODAY

I declare by faith that I am going to take up acting! In every situation I face, I am going to imitate the character of my Heavenly Father, successfully replicating Him in every sphere of my life. I know it will require a great deal of time and commitment for me to arrive at this high level of duplication, but I resolve to start where I am today and then do more each day from this moment forward. And I'll keep up my efforts to act like God until I finally begin to think like Him, talk like Him, sound like Him, and carry myself in His confidence!

I declare this by faith in Jesus' name!

QUESTIONS FOR YOU TO CONSIDER

1. What would happen if you approached every problem acting as God does when He approaches problems?
2. What difference would it make in your life if you acted like God every time you dealt with an unloving person?
3. When you are faced with a difficult situation, do you ask yourself what God would say or do?

MARCH 7

A Guaranteed Way To Infuriate the Holy Spirit!

Do ye think that the scripture saith in vain,
The spirit that dwelleth in us lusteth to envy?
— James 4:5

I know you want to please the Spirit of God with your life, so today I want to tell you about something that is guaranteed *not* to please Him. By knowing this, you can avoid grieving Him and can concentrate your attention on doing those things that are sure to bring Him pleasure.

James 4:5 says, "Do ye think that the scripture saith in vain, the spirit that dwelleth in us lusteth to envy?" I want to draw your attention to the word "envy" in this verse. But first I want to back up and speak to you about the "lust" that the Holy Spirit feels for you and me.

I noted in the February 14 *Sparkling Gem* that the word "lust" is the Greek word *epipotheo*, a word that portrays *an intense desire; a craving; a hunger; an ache; a yearning for something; a longing or pining for something.* Usually this word is used to indicate an intense yearning for something that is morally wrong and sinful. But in James 4:5, this Greek word describes the intense yearning that the Holy Spirit possesses to have us entirely for Himself. Because the word *epipotheo* is used to depict the Spirit's longing to have us, it expresses the deep love and affection that the Spirit of God has for every believer.

However, James goes on to tell us that in addition to this intense yearning for us, the Holy Spirit also experiences "envy" regarding you and me. The word "envy" in James 4:5 is the Greek word *phthnos*, a word that describes *a person who is jealous about something; a person who feels rivalry or envy;* or *a person who holds a grudge because of someone else's behavior*. It also carries the idea of *ill will* and *malice*.

This word *phthnos* is the very word that would have been used to illustrate the emotions a young man experiences when he discovers his spouse is being romantically pursued by someone else. Because James uses this word to depict the Holy Spirit, we need to stop and think about what it means for a few moments.

Anger, resentment, rage, envy, jealousy — these are the emotions a man feels in such a situation! He takes this threat to his marital relationship very personally and holds a *grudge* against the pursuer. Every time the husband thinks about what that romantic bandit is trying to do, feelings of *malice* and *ill will* toward the violator rise up in his soul.

Even more significantly, a man who really loves his wife is not going to sit by and watch his wife be stolen! The envy and jealousy he feels will move him to *action* — to do everything in his power to win back his wife and permanently eliminate his competitor.

Because the husband is envious, he does all he can to see his relationship with his wife restored. All of these ideas are conveyed by the Greek word *phthnos* used in James 4:5 when the Bible tells us about the "envy" of the Holy Spirit.

One scholar says the picture contained in the Greek word *phthnos* could be understood this way:

"The Spirit takes it very personally when we share our lives with the world. He wants us so entirely for Himself that if the world tries to take us away, it infuriates Him. You need to know that in these cases, the Holy Spirit will not idly sit by and watch it happen. He'll do something to change the situation!"

Not only does it infuriate the Holy Spirit when believers turn their devotion to the world, but it drives Him to intense jealousy. At this point, He will release His full rage against that unholy relationship, moving on the scene like a Divine Lover who has come to defend and rescue the relationship He holds so dear. This is something you can be sure of: If you commit more of your heart, soul, and attention to worldly things than you give to the Spirit of God, He will *not* take it lightly.

Never forget that the Holy Spirit is a Divine Lover. He is preoccupied with you. He wants to possess you totally, and He desires that your affection be set wholly on Him. That's why the Holy Spirit feels like a lover who has been robbed if you walk and talk like an unbeliever or give your life to the things of this world. He jealously desires His relationship with you to be restored. He has divine malice toward the worldliness that has usurped His role in your life.

The Holy Spirit is *not* a passive Partner. He aggressively and actively pursues you. He fiercely wants more of you. When you give part of yourself to something or someone else's control, the Holy Spirit wants to seize that part of your life and bring it back under His divine control. He even has malice toward your preoccupation with things in this natural realm.

So make your relationship with the Holy Spirit your top priority. Don't give Him a reason to feel betrayed by or envious of other things in your life that have taken His place. Get to know the Holy Spirit's voice in your spirit so He can help you set your life in order. Make sure *every* area of your life is under His loving control!

MY PRAYER FOR TODAY

Lord, if I ever turn my devotion to the world, please move on the scene like a Divine Lover who has come to defend and rescue that relationship You hold so dear. Help me never to forget that You are preoccupied with me and want to possess me totally. I know that You want my desires and affection to be set on You, so if I begin to walk and talk like an unbeliever and give my life to the things of this world, please nudge me and bring conviction to my heart to change. And if I refuse to listen, I ask You to please move with divine malice toward those things that have usurped Your role in my life.

I pray this in Jesus' name!

MY CONFESSION FOR TODAY

I confess that I respect the Holy Spirit's Presence in my life; therefore, I am careful in the way I think, the way I speak, and the way I connect with the world around me. I do not grieve the Spirit of God by allowing worldliness to become a part of my life. He fiercely wants more of me, and I want more of Him. The Holy Spirit is the top priority in my life, and I never do anything that would make Him feel wounded, grieved, or envious. I live a life that pleases Him!

I declare this by faith in Jesus' name!

QUESTIONS FOR YOU TO CONSIDER

1. Is your relationship with the Holy Spirit the top priority in your life?
2. Have you allowed anything in your life to usurp the position that only the Holy Spirit should have?
3. Why not take inventory of your "love life" today, asking the Holy Spirit to show you areas in your life where you have allowed your affection to be diverted from Him to other things?

MARCH 8

Relax From the Stresses of Life!

And to you who are troubled rest with us....
— 2 Thessalonians 1:7

*I*f you have been under a lot of stress, pressure, and anxiety lately, I think Paul's words in Second Thessalonians 1:7 are meant just for you! Read carefully, because you're going to find real encouragement and instruction today that will help you find peace in the midst of trouble.

When Paul wrote the book of Second Thessalonians, the believers in the city of Thessalonica were undergoing horrifying persecution. The persecution in this city was worse than it was in other places because Christians were being hunted both by pagan idol worshipers and by unbelieving Jews who detested the Gospel message. As a result of these threatening conditions, members of the Thessalonian church were suffering, and some even paid the price of dying for the Gospel. However, in spite of these afflictions and pressures from outside forces, this congregation refused to surrender to defeat.

When Paul addressed these believers in Second Thessalonians, they had already been under this stress and pressure for a long period of time. The assaults against them had been like a stream of unrelenting poundings from which they had no pause. Naturally, they were *exhausted — extremely tired, worn out, and fatigued*. It had been a very long time since they had put up their feet and taken a break! The idea of unwinding or lightening up almost seemed like a fantasy. But everyone needs to rest at some point!

If you've been going through a prolonged period of hardship due to persecution, your business, your family, your relationships, your finances, or your children, you still must learn how to rest in the Lord, even in the middle of that difficult situation you are facing. If you don't, the battle will wear you out!

That's why Paul told the Thessalonians, "And to you who are troubled rest with us...." The word "troubled" tells us the extent of their hardships. It is the Greek word *thlipsis*, a word Paul often employs when he describes *difficult events* that he and his team have encountered. This word is so strong that it is impossible to misunderstand the *intensity* of these persecutions. It conveys the idea of a *heavy-pressure situation*. In fact, one scholar commented that the word *thlipsis* was first used to describe *the specific act of tying a victim with a rope, laying him on his back, and then placing a huge boulder on top of him until his body was crushed*. As time progressed, this word came to describe *any situation that was crushing or debilitating*.

One example of this can be found in Second Corinthians 1:8, where Paul writes, "For we would not, brethren, have you ignorant of our trouble which came to us in Asia...." The word "trouble" in this verse is also from the word *thlipsis*. It could be translated, *"We would not, brethren, have you ignorant of the horribly tight, life-threatening squeeze that came to us in Asia...."* By using this word, Paul lets us know that his time in Asia was one of the most grueling nightmares he had ever undergone. In fact, when he was in the midst of the situation, he didn't even know if he would survive it!

Now this is exactly the word Paul uses when he writes to the Thessalonian believers and says, "To those of you who are *troubled....*" The word "troubled" alerts us to the fact that they were not just *mildly* suffering; they were *horrifically* suffering — and as noted earlier, this suffering had gone on for a very long time. But because Paul had been in these types of adverse circumstances himself on different occasions and had victoriously survived, he knew that for the Thessalonians to outlast these difficulties, they needed to take a break from the pressure! That is why he told them, "...*Rest* with us."

The word "rest" come from the Greek word *anesis,* which means *to let up*, *to relax*, *to stop being stressed*, or *to find relief*. One scholar comments that the word *anesis* was used in the secular Greek world to denote *the release of a bowstring that has been under great pressure*. It was also used figuratively to mean *relaxation from the stresses of life* and *freedom to have a little recreation*. By using this word, Paul urges the believers in the city of Thessalonica to find *relief* from the constant stress they are undergoing as a result of opposition to their faith. Paul exhorts them *to let it go*, *shake it off*, and learn how to *relax*, even in the midst of difficult circumstances.

An interpretive translation of this verse could be:

"To you who are still going through difficulties right now, it's time for you to let up, take a breather, and relax. We know what it's like to be under pressure, but no one can stay under that

kind of stress continuously. So join us in learning how to loosen up a bit. Shake off your troubles, and allow yourself a little relaxation and time for recreation...."

I realize that when you're dealing with problems, a vacation is the last thing on your mind! You just want to survive the challenge and make a transition into the next phase of your life — and to do it as soon as possible! You may even feel that it's irresponsible for you to put up your feet and relax for a while. But even God rested on the seventh day!

Take Paul's counsel to heart, and allow yourself a little relaxation and time for recreation — time away from your problems. When it's time to come back and face those problems again, you'll be refreshed and recharged with renewed vision. You'll see that challenge with new eyes, and you'll face it with new strength. Yes, I know it's hard to allow yourself the time to do what I'm suggesting. But, friend, *your survival depends on it.* If you don't take a break from that constant stress, it will keep wearing you down until you become easy prey for the devil.

So say goodbye to your problems today. Take a break, and allow yourself a little time to rest, relax, and recuperate!

MY PRAYER FOR TODAY

Lord, I admit that I've been carrying the worries, stresses, and pressures of life for too long. Before I do anything else, I want to cast these burdens over onto You today. I am tempted to worry that the problems I'm facing won't work out, but taking them into my own hands and worrying about them isn't going to make the situation any better. So I repent for letting myself become consumed with worry about things I cannot change, and I turn them all over to You today. Please help me stay free of anxiety as I learn to relax and enjoy life a little more than I've been enjoying it lately!

I pray this in Jesus' name!

MY CONFESSION FOR TODAY

I confess that I need to set aside time for relaxation and recreation. Starting today, I'm going to take a break from my problems. I am casting my burdens on the Lord; as a result, I know I will be refreshed, recharged, and given a renewed vision. After a little rest, I will see my challenge with new eyes, and I'll face it with new strength. I know my survival depends on this, so today I choose to take a break from the constant stress I've been dealing with before I get worn down and become easy prey for the devil. God will give me the strength and energy I need to get up and get going so I can complete the work He has entrusted into my hands.

I declare this by faith in Jesus' name!

QUESTIONS FOR YOU TO CONSIDER

1. When was the last time you took some time to rest and relax from the pressures in your life?
2. What are some signs in your life that you need to take time to rest and gain a fresh perspective about the situations you're facing right now?
3. What are some of the best ways you've discovered that help you rest and recuperate during a stressful time in your life?

MARCH 9

❧

'Perilous Times'
In the Last Days

This know also, that in the last days
perilous times shall come.
— 2 Timothy 3:1

*T*he Bible makes it unmistakably plain that in the last days, the world will be filled with difficulties, the like of which have never before been known in the history of mankind. In fact, the Holy Spirit was so committed to making sure we understand what will occur in the last days that in Second Timothy 3:1, it is as if He points His prophetic finger two thousand years into the future and specifically foretells what will occur at the end of the age.

Paul wrote these words by inspiration of the Holy Spirit in Second Timothy 3:1: "This know also, that in the last days perilous times shall come." Notice that this verse begins by saying, "This *know*...." The word "know" is the Greek word *ginosko,* the Greek word for *knowledge.* But in this verse, it is used in the present imperative tense, which means it is a strong command to recognize that there is something that *must be known, must be recognized,* and *must be acknowledged.* Having this knowledge is not optional; it is *mandatory.*

The verse continues, "This know also, that in *the last days*...." The word "last" in this verse is from the word *eschatos,* which points to *the ultimate end of a thing* — such as the last month of the year; the last week of the month; the last day of a week; or the very extreme end of the age. In other words, the word *eschatos* doesn't merely describe the last days in general, but the very *last* of the last days. It was used in classical Greek literature to depict *a place furthest away,* such as the very *ends* of the earth. In this sense, it also signified something that is *final.*

With this word *eschatos,* the Holy Spirit through Paul takes us right into the *end of the age* to enlighten our eyes and help us see what the world environment will be like in the concluding moments of the age. Paul goes on to say that "perilous" times will mark that final age. "Perilous" is the Greek word *chalepos* — a word used to describe *ugly words that, when spoken, are hurtful and emotionally hard to bear.* It is also used in various pieces of literatures to depict *wild, vicious, uncontrollable animals that are unpredictable and dangerous.* It always carries the idea of an action, place, person, or thing that is *harsh, harmful,* and filled with *high risk.*

This is the very word used in Matthew 8:28 to portray the two demon-possessed men who were so legendary in the country of the Gadarenes. It says, "And when he was come to the other side into the country of the Gadarenes, there met him two possessed with devils, coming out of the tombs, *exceeding fierce,* so that no man might pass by that way." The words "exceeding fierce" is this same word *chalepos.* This means the two demon-possessed men were like wild, vicious, and uncontrollable animals, completely unpredictable and dangerous. Simply being in the region near these men placed one's life in jeopardy because these demonized men were *chalepos* — *harsh and harmful,* presenting a *high risk* to anyone in the region.

Taking the definitions of all these words into consideration,
Second Timothy 3:1 could be taken to mean:

"You emphatically must know what I am about to tell you! In the very last part of the last days, in the very end of the age, hurtful, harmful, dangerous, unpredictable, uncontrollable, high-risk periods of time will come."

Considering the events that have shaken the world in recent years, we shouldn't be shocked to hear that this is the meaning of Second Timothy 3:1. Dangerous, harmful, high-risk periods of time have already arrived! We are living in a generation that faces world threats no other generation has ever known. As always, the Holy Spirit was correct in what He was trying to tell us.

But why did the Holy Spirit forewarn us about these events? Were His prophetic warnings intended to scare or to fill us with fear? *No!* The Holy Spirit, as He always has done, wanted to prepare God's people so they could be spiritually alert and ready to minister to people who suffer harm as a result of the events that will grip the world at the end of the age.

According to Second Timothy 3:1, we are living in an age that will be marked by "perilous" world events. Let us therefore be wise, protecting our minds, our family members, and every other area of our lives by renewing our minds with the Word of God. Rather than hide in fear, let's get *God's* perspective about what we should be doing to help people who have been victimized by this age. Let's move out with the power of God and be ready to minister to those who have suffered harm because of the times in which we live!

MY PRAYER FOR TODAY

Lord, You designed me to live in these last days according to Your great plan. Because You are in charge of my life, I know it's no mistake that I am alive in this generation. Since these days are filled with greater risk than any other generation has ever known, I need faith to face these times victoriously. I need wisdom to minister to others who are wounded and hurt. So today I ask You to help me embrace this time as a part of my destiny and to become strong in faith so I can reach out to those who are near me and who need spiritual assistance! Help me to recognize their need and to know exactly how I should respond to help them.

I pray this in Jesus' name!

MY CONFESSION FOR TODAY

I declare by faith that I am chosen and equipped to live in this last generation. The Word of God protects my mind, my family, and everything that is a part of my life. I will renew my mind with the Word of God and get God's perspective about what His role is for me in these last days. Therefore, I will be a blessing and a help to people who have been victimized by these difficult and trying times. Rather than hide in fear, I will move out with the power of God and stay ever-ready to minister to those who have suffered harm because of the times in which we live!

I declare this by faith in Jesus' name!

QUESTIONS FOR YOU TO CONSIDER

1. Are you heeding the warning of the Holy Spirit to be spiritually alert in these last days?
2. If God were to ask you to minister to someone who is suffering, do you feel prepared to help that person? How can you become better prepared?
3. Do you feel overcome with fear or filled with faith as you contemplate what it will take to face the special challenges of our generation?

MARCH 10

*Hang In There
And Don't Give Up!*

My brethren, count it all joy when ye fall into divers temptations;
knowing this, that the trying of your faith worketh patience.
But let patience have her perfect work,
that ye may be perfect and entire, wanting nothing.
— James 1:2-4

*I*n the earliest years of the Church, the believers faced unremitting persecution. Every day they were confronted by hostile powers that were arrayed against them. Culture, pagan religion, government, unsaved family and friends — all these forces were arrayed against them, putting constant pressure on them to forfeit their faith and return to their old ways.

Even if you are facing great challenges today, it doesn't begin to match the pressure these brothers and sisters felt. I don't want to make light of the struggles you're going through, but the truth is, very few people alive today have faced the level of intense opposition that these early believers faced.

Think about it — do you personally know anyone who has been thrown into the arena to be mauled and eaten by hungry lions? Do you know anyone who has been burned at the stake for his faith? Or can you think of any friends of yours who have been forced into imprisonment because of their faith in Jesus Christ?

Now, these scenarios do happen today to believers who live in anti-Christian parts of the world, and we definitely need to hold them up in prayer. Let's not forget about them, nor about those who suffer for the Gospel in countries that are blessed with freedom. It is a statistical fact that since the year 1900, more than 29 million believers have died worldwide for their faith in Jesus Christ. In fact, large numbers of people currently die for Jesus every single day. By the time we get up, get dressed, and arrive at work to clock in for the day, someone, somewhere, has already laid down his life for the Gospel.

This puts a different light on the problems we face in the free world. Our problems are related to relationships, finances, family issues, health issues, and other problems of a personal nature. The stress that believers experience in free parts of the world is often related to having too much work to do; being under pressure due to the intense nature of their jobs; or trying to figure out how to handle their busy schedules. Although no one in his or her neighborhood or local church is currently being fed to hungry lions, the stresses and pressures a believer feels can nonetheless be very severe.

So no matter where you live or what you're facing, remember that it's essential to have the right attitude toward high-pressure situations! The Early Church called "patience" the "queen of all virtues." They believed that if they possessed this one virtue, they could survive anything that ever came against them. It is this same virtue that is sustaining believers today who live in godless regions of the world — and this virtue is exactly what *you* need to victoriously outlast the pressures and ordeals you may be dealing with today.

James was writing to believers who were undergoing the kind of hardships described above. He told them, "But let patience have her perfect work, that ye may be perfect and entire, wanting nothing."

The word "patience" is the Greek word *hupomeno* — a compound of the words *hupo* and *meno*. The word *hupo* means *under*, as *to be underneath something*. The word *meno* means *to stay* or *to abide*.

You could say that the word *meno* means *to remain in one's spot; to keep a position; to resolve to maintain some territory that has been gained*. It is the state of mind that says, "This is my spot, and I'm not moving!"

The determination inherent within the word *hupomeno* is clearly seen when it was used in a military sense to picture soldiers who were ordered to maintain their positions even in the face of fierce combat. Their order was *to stand their ground and defend what had been gained*. To keep that ground, they had to be courageous to do whatever was required — *no matter how hard or difficult the assignment*. Their goal was to see that they survived every attack and held their position until they had outlived and outlasted the resistance. These soldiers had to indefinitely and defiantly stick it out until the enemy realized they couldn't be beaten and decided to retreat and go elsewhere.

Thus, the word *hupomeno* conveys the idea of being *steadfast, consistent, unwavering*, and *unflinching*. It is the attitude that declares, "I don't care how heavy the load gets or how much pressure I'm under, I am not budging one inch! This is *my* spot, and I'm telling you right now that there isn't enough pressure in the whole world to make me move and give it up!"

Although the *King James Version* translates this word "patience," a more accurate rendering would be *endurance*. One scholar calls it *staying power*, whereas another contemporary translator calls it *hang-in-there power*. Both of these translations adequately express the right idea about *hupomeno*. This is an attitude that never gives up! It *holds out, holds on, outlasts*, and *perseveres*.

Revelation 1:9 uses the word *hupomeno* when it refers to "the patience of Jesus Christ." In Second Thessalonians 3:5, this word is also used in the phrase, "the patient waiting for Christ," which could be translated, *"...The patience of Jesus Christ — that attitude that hangs in there, never giving up, refusing to surrender to obstacles, and turning down every opportunity to quit."* This word illustrates the patient endurance Jesus demonstrated during His trial, scourging, and crucifixion. Even though the assignment was the most difficult task ever given to anyone, Jesus stayed with it all the way to the end.

Keeping all this in mind,
James 1:4 could be interpreted:

"But let patience have her perfect work — I'm talking about the kind of attitude that hangs in there, never giving up, refusing to surrender to obstacles and turning down every opportunity to quit...."

The Early Church called patience the "queen of all virtues" for good reason. They knew that as long as they had this character quality working in their lives, it wasn't a question of *if* they would win their battles — it was only a question of *when* they would win their battles.

Hupomeno — that is, *endurance, staying power, hang-in-there power* — is one of the major weapons you need to outlast any difficulty or time of stress and pressure that comes your way. So if you're going through some rough circumstances at the moment, be encouraged! It's a fleeting and temporary condition that will soon change! It's time for you to get your eyes off your challenges and to stop fixating on your problems. *Make up your mind that you're going to stand your ground and hang in there. It won't be long until the problems flee — and when they do, you'll be so glad you didn't give up!*

MY PRAYER FOR TODAY

Lord, help me stand my ground and defend what I have gained, no matter how difficult it might be to do this. I know that with Your supernatural help, I can outlive and outlast the resistance. With Your Spirit's power working inside me, I know I can indefinitely and defiantly stick it out until the enemy realizes he cannot beat me and decides to retreat!

I pray this in Jesus' name!

MY CONFESSION FOR TODAY

I confess that I am steadfast, consistent, unwavering, and unflinching. I don't care how heavy the load gets or how much pressure I'm under, I am not budging one inch! This is my spot, and there isn't enough pressure in the whole world to make me move and give it up! I have supernatural endurance — staying power, hang-in-there power — and an attitude that holds out, holds on, outlasts, and perseveres until the victory is won and the goal is reached!

I declare this by faith in Jesus' name!

QUESTIONS FOR YOU TO CONSIDER

1. What is the biggest difficulty and pressure you are facing in your life right now?
2. Have you determined to stay put, never giving up and never budging, until the devil gives up on his attack to defeat you?
3. Can you recall some difficulties in the past where you stood your ground and refused to give up until the victory came? How did you do it?

MARCH 11

❧⟡❧

Why Not Bring Others Into the Project?

For I say, through the grace given unto me,
to every man that is among you, not to think of himself
more highly than he ought to think; but to think soberly,
according as God hath dealt to every man the measure of faith.
— Romans 12:3

When a person is a brand-new leader, he often mistakenly assumes that being a leader means he has to know it all. As a result, he puts himself under unnecessary stress, trying to project himself as one who knows everything. His need to appear as an "expert" at everything reveals an immature understanding of what true leadership is all about.

When a leader keeps everything in his own hands and doesn't allow anyone else to do anything, this leads to frustration for the team members working with him. It is especially frustrating when there are people surrounding the leader who *know* the answers, who *are experts* in their fields, and who really *could* help. But they have to silently sit by and just watch the leader struggle as he tries to be "Mr. Super Leader," never asking his team for help.

No one has all the answers! The smartest leaders in the world are those who realize both their gifts and their limitations. A leader is being wise when he recognizes his need for gifted, talented, willing-minded people to chip in and help him effectively do what he is called to do. No one can do it all alone.

If you will open your eyes and look around, you'll find that God has graciously surrounded you with the very people you need. They are just waiting for your invitation to help you nurture your God-given dreams, visions, and projects and bring them to fulfillment.

In Romans 12:3, Paul spoke about our need for others in our lives. He said, "For I say, through the grace given unto me, to every man that is among you, not to think of himself more highly than he ought to think; but to think soberly, according as God hath dealt to every man the measure of faith."

If anyone could have thought highly of himself, it was Paul — *and he would have been correct*! He formerly had been a lawyer, politician, and Pharisee. No doubt he was also once very wealthy. Now Paul could claim that he had seen Jesus and had been taught by Him (Galatians 1:12). In regard to his own apostleship, he acknowledged that his apostleship to the Gentiles was "mighty" (Galatians 2:8). In fact, it was so mighty that when those who were appointed as apostles before Paul saw the great grace in his life, they extended to him the right hand of fellowship and invited him into their inner sanctum. In Second Peter 3:16, Peter writes that the profound nature of Paul's revelation was so extraordinary that even he wrestled to comprehend it all.

Yet Paul is the one who admonishes us *not* to think too highly of ourselves but to learn to view ourselves "soberly." The word "soberly" is the Greek word *sophroneo*, and it means *to be of sound mind; to be reasonable; to be balanced and levelheaded in the way one thinks; to maintain a proper appraisal, measurement, or value; to think clearly about one's limitations.* In other words, we are not to pretend to be more than we are!

Although Paul stood in a class by himself and could boast of unprecedented accomplishments, he recognized his need for other members of the team. That's why he leaned so heavily on Timothy, Titus, Luke, Barnabas, Silas, Sosthenes, and others. The understanding of his own limitations is the reason Paul could rejoice that others were on his team. Thus, he could write with no sense of being threatened by someone else, "I planted, but Apollos watered…." Apollos contributed a part that Paul would never have brought into the project. Paul was a dynamic planter, but Apollos was an excellent nurturer. Paul needed all his team members to bring his job to maturity.

Of course, you need to recognize your own God-given abilities and use them. God wants you to develop your gifts and use your talents to become the very best you can be. But when you come to the edge of your limitations, realize that it's all right for you to say:

✦ "This is too much for me!"
✦ "This a project that I'm not anointed to do!"
✦ "This demands gifts and talents that I don't possess!"
✦ "This is a time for someone else to take the lead!"
✦ "This assignment is going to take teamwork, because I can't do it by myself."

God intended for you to be a part of a team! If you try to act like you can do everything on your own, you're going to find it quite humiliating when you fail miserably in front of everyone.

Trying to tackle a huge project all by yourself is the surest way to end up embarrassed in front of others. When you fail and fall flat on your face, you'll regret that you didn't say, "I think someone else can do this job better than I can. This is simply not where I'm most gifted. Who can help me out with this project?"

So instead of thinking too highly of yourself and attempting to go it alone with every project you undertake, be smart! Develop a team mentality. Bring others into the project with you as the Lord leads. Recognize your limitations, and seek out those who have the gifts and talents you need.

Rather than try to figure everything out by yourself, let the people around you contribute their thoughts, views, and insights. Let them use the talents and abilities God gave them. You can accomplish a whole lot more as a team than you can do by yourself.

The next time you set out to accomplish a task God has assigned to you, remember — there are other members of the Body of Christ too! You're not the only one who is called and has faith. God has gifted His entire Body with faith and spiritual gifts. *Rather than trying to do it all by yourself, think "soberly." Recognize your limitations, and allow other people to be used by God too!*

MY PRAYER FOR TODAY

Lord, give me the grace to recognize both my abilities and limitations. Help me be unafraid to admit when I've overstepped my bounds and tried to tackle something bigger than my abilities. In those moments, please enable me to ask others to join the project and to help me do what I cannot accomplish by myself. I really need You to help me overcome my weaknesses and my fears that others may be better gifted than I am. I know You have placed people all around me to be blessings in my life, so today I am turning to You. Help me recognize these people and receive them as the blessings You intend for them to be.

I pray this in Jesus' name!

MY CONFESSION FOR TODAY

I confess that I am part of a team as God intended for me to be! I don't think too highly of myself, nor do I attempt to go it alone with every project I undertake. I have a team mentality. I recognize my limitations and seek out those who have the gifts and talents I need. Rather than try to figure out everything by myself, I let the people around me contribute their thoughts, views, and insights. I want them to use the talents and abilities God gave them, because we can do a whole lot more as a team than I can do by myself.

I declare this by faith in Jesus' name!

QUESTIONS FOR YOU TO CONSIDER

1. Do you feel secure enough to say, "This project is too big for me; I need someone else to step in and help me"?
2. If you were really honest with yourself, would you have to confess that at times you've put a lot of pressure on yourself to do everything when there were others who could have pitched in and helped?
3. Are you the kind of person who includes others, or do you shut out other people, giving them no chance to contribute their gifts, talents, or ideas?

Recognize your limitations, and seek out those who have the gifts and talents you need. You can accomplish a whole lot more as a team than you can do by yourself.

MARCH 12

❧❧❧

You Are One Of God's Pillars!

Therefore, my beloved brethren, be ye stedfast, unmoveable,
always abounding in the work of the Lord....
—1 Corinthians 15:58

Have you ever looked at someone and thought, *Wow, that person is such a rock!* What does it mean to you when you think of someone as a "rock"? That's a strong statement, so it would be well worth your time to think it through and decide what characteristic makes a person a "rock" to you, to someone else, or to a church, business, or organization. Even more importantly, would others call *you* a "rock"?

In First Corinthians 15:58, Paul writes, "Therefore, my beloved brethren, be ye stedfast, unmoveable, always abounding in the work of the Lord...." I want you to look at the word "stedfast" in this verse, because it illustrates what kind of person God considers to be a "rock" in His family.

What does it mean to be *steadfast*? This word "steadfast" is the Greek word *edraios,* which has several meanings:

✦ It means to be *stationary*, such as *something that sits in one place for a long, long time.*
✦ It describes *something that is firm and steady.*
✦ It was frequently used in connection with *foundations or support structures in buildings.*
✦ It portrays *something that is strong, unbendable, unbreakable, and permanent,* such as *a well-built foundation for a large building or a strong column that holds up a roof.*

So when Paul urges us to be "steadfast," he's calling on us to be totally reliable — not shaky or undependable. We should be *stationary* in the roles God has called us to fulfill in the Body of Christ. We shouldn't be quickly shaken or easily lured to some other place or some other task. We must be like *pillars, foundations,* or *supports* in the house of God.

When you take the Greek word *edraios* into consideration,
it means First Corinthians 15:58 could be interpreted:

"...Be reliable; dependable; not easily excited, shaken, or affected...."

What is the purpose of a huge stone pillar in a building? Its purpose is to support the roof or some other important section of the building, correct? What would happen if you suddenly jerked that pillar out of its place? You'd find out very quickly that the pillar had been essential to holding up the place! Remove that pillar, and the entire building would collapse into a heap of rubble, creating a horrible, terrible mess!

When God tells you to be "steadfast," He is asking you to be a "rock" in His house — like a pillar that faithfully stands in its place and helps to hold things together. He wants you to be so dependable that people lean on you, counting on the fact that you'll always be there to help keep things together. And when events occur that shake up everyone's world a bit, God wants people to look to you as one who isn't easily excited, shaken, or affected.

Now that you know the kind of "rock" God needs you to be, would you say that you qualify to be called a "rock" today? Would others call you a "rock," or would they say you are up again, down again; easily excited; and not too dependable? If you got real honest with yourself, would you judge yourself to be steady, sturdy, and reliable — or unpredictable and undependable?

Don't view yourself as small, insignificant, or unimportant. God needs you, and other people are depending on you. It's time for you to realize that God meant for you to be a part of the foundation of the Body of Christ! You can be a "rock" in His family and a person on whom others can lean and depend.

If you're thinking differently than this, you need to change your thinking. Instead of focusing on how insignificant you are in God's great plan for these last days, start focusing on becoming steadfast, immovable, and always abounding in the work the Lord has assigned to *you*!

MY PRAYER FOR TODAY

Lord, I want to be the person You and others can depend on. Forgive me for any instability in my life, and help me overcome every weakness in my character. Just as I have looked for others to be "rocks" in my life, I want to be a "rock" to other people. I have a lot of room for development in my life, but I am willing to be changed. I want to be taught, corrected, and taken to a higher level. Today I ask You to do whatever is necessary to make me the strong and reliable kind of person You want me to be! Please do Your special work inside me!

I pray this in Jesus' name!

MY CONFESSION FOR TODAY

I confess that God's Word overcomes the weaknesses in my personality and character. God calls me to be "steadfast" — and I AM steadfast. God and people see me like a pillar that stands in its place and helps to hold things together. I am so dependable that people can lean on me, counting on the fact that I will always be there to help keep things together. When events occur that shake up the world around me, I am not easily excited, shaken, or affected. Praise God, I am becoming more and more dependable all the time! When people hear my name, they think of someone on whom they can rely!

I declare this by faith in Jesus' name!

QUESTIONS FOR YOU TO CONSIDER

1. Can you think of five people who have been "rocks" in your life? Why not go out of your way to let those people know how much you appreciate them?
2. What strengths did those people exhibit that made you think so highly of them?
3. Is there anyone who needs your strength right now? What can you do to be a "rock" to that person in his time of need?

Don't view yourself as small, insignificant, or unimportant. God needs you, and other people are depending on you.

MARCH 13

❧❦❧

Who Said You Had To Deserve What God Gives You?

Thou therefore, my son,
be strong in the grace that is in Christ Jesus.
— 2 Timothy 2:1

Timothy was the pastor of the world's largest church of that time — the church of Ephesus. It was also the most famous church in the world. Started by Paul, this illustrious congregation included the apostle John as a church member. Mary, the mother of Jesus, was also a member of the church in her old age. It was a church like none other before or after it.

What a privilege it was for Timothy to become the pastor of this well-known and powerful congregation! After working side by side with the apostle Paul for many years, he had finally become the leader of his own work. It was a huge assignment for a young man, but after working with Paul all those years, Timothy was ready to step into his own pulpit as the senior pastor of the cherished Ephesian church. As far as we know, it was the first time in his life he served in such a position.

By the time Paul wrote the book of Second Timothy, however, things weren't going so well in the city of Ephesus. Nero was persecuting the church, and, as a result, church members were deserting the Lord in order to save their lives. Leaders in the church were waging war with each other over doctrinal issues; others didn't like Timothy and consequently rebelled against his leadership. This young pastor must have felt like he had a mess on his hands! After receiving the honor of becoming senior pastor of the world's largest church, he may have felt like he was failing at his job.

Have you ever felt like you were failing with an assignment that was given to you? Or perhaps you feel like you were dealt an unfair hand — that a major assignment was transferred to you just at the point when all hell was about to break loose. Maybe you believe that there was nothing you could have done to change the negative developments that followed. But even if you can logically explain why everything fell apart under your guard, do you still feel responsible for this failure?

It is quite possible that this is how Timothy felt as he presided over the huge church of Ephesus and watched the developing internal problems, such as the defections and the decline in attendance. Many of these things would have occurred regardless of who was senior pastor, but I'm certain Timothy struggled with feeling like he was a dismal failure. *He needed a touch from God! He needed strength to stay there and to do what God wanted him to do.*

That is why Paul wrote, "Thou therefore, my son, be strong in the grace that is in Christ Jesus" (2 Timothy 2:1). The word "strong" is the Greek word *endunamao*, and it means *to be empowered* or *to be made strong*. If you refer to the January 12 *Sparkling Gem*, you will see that this is a compound of the words *en* and *dunamis*. The word *en* means *in*. The word *dunamis* means *explosive strength, ability*, and *power*. It's where we get the word *dynamite*.

Thus, this word *endunamao* presents the picture of *an explosive power being deposited into some type of container or vessel, or some other form of receptacle*. In this case, the destination of this power was Timothy! He needed power, so Paul told him, "Be strong." It's almost as though Paul was saying,

"Timothy, it's time for you to receive the supernatural, dynamic, explosive power that you need! You were designed for this power...."

Because Timothy was struggling with feelings of failure, he probably didn't feel worthy to receive a supernatural touch. This is why Paul said, "Thou therefore, my son, be strong *in the grace* that is in Christ Jesus."

The supernatural strengthening you need doesn't come because you deserve it. God makes His supernatural power available to you and me for *free!* That is why Paul goes on to say, "...Be strong in the *grace...."* The phrase "in the grace" is important, because it could be translated, *"...Be strong BY MEANS OF the grace that is in Christ Jesus...."*

God's grace makes this strength available to *every* Christian soldier! This is good news! God's grace never runs out! His power is available to anyone who releases his or her faith to receive it. And because it's available by grace — for free — a person doesn't have to feel worthy to receive it!

As long as there is still grace, there is still a free, supernatural, empowering, inner strengthening available to you — *if* you reach out and take it. You have to receive a new touch of God's power *freely* — by means of God's grace. The devil will always be around to tell you that you're not good enough, not worthy enough, not faithful enough to deserve anything from God. But who said you have to deserve anything God gives you? Because Jesus died for you and washed you with His blood, you are a candidate for everything that God possesses!

So quit beating yourself over the head, telling yourself how bad you are and how terribly you've failed. If you really did mess up the assignment God gave you, just repent! Then open your heart and ask the Lord to give you a new touch of power so you can get up and start moving again! And if the devil tells you that you're not worthy to receive a new touch, just answer him: *"Devil, I'm going to lay hold of the steady current of God's power that comes to me as a result of His grace, and there's not a thing you can do to stop it!"*

MY PRAYER FOR TODAY

Lord, I have been made worthy by the blood of Jesus Christ to receive every good thing You have planned and prepared for me. Forgive me for the times I have placed limitations on Your ability to bless me because I thought I wasn't good enough. It is clear that You want to bless me IN SPITE of me! You are so good to do all the wonderful things You do in my life. Today I thank You for choosing to bless me with the extra strength I so desperately need in my life right now. Thank You for making this power completely available for free!

I pray this in Jesus' name!

MY CONFESSION FOR TODAY

I declare that thoughts of unworthiness have no place in me. What Jesus does for me, He does for free — just because He loves me. I do not have to worry that I'm not good enough to receive of His goodness, because my feelings don't have a thing to do with His good pleasure to bless my life. He wants to bless me regardless of anything I do, because it is God's nature to bless and to do good in my life. Today I receive the power God wants to give me by His grace. I receive it without hesitation, knowing that this is His good pleasure for me!

I declare this by faith in Jesus' name!

1. Name ten things God has done for you that you don't feel you deserved. Write them down and really meditate on the grace of God that has been demonstrated in your life.
2. Did the Lord bless you in spite of your feelings of unworthiness?
3. If you need a touch from the Lord today, why don't you take a few minutes right now to open your heart and let Him fill you to overflowing?

MARCH 14

Payday Is on the Way!

Cast not away therefore your confidence,
which hath great recompence of reward.
— Hebrews 10:35

*I*f you have ever invested time, money, energy, and commitment into God's Kingdom that no one knew about except you and the Lord, it did *not* go unnoticed. The Lord saw it all. And according to Hebrews 10:35, He plans on reimbursing you in full!

The phrase "recompense of reward" is from the Greek word *misthapodosia*, and it carries the idea of *being reimbursed for an expense that a person has paid out of his own pocket in order to get his job done.* Here's a situation that is an example of this definition: A company sends an employee on a business trip. Because the company gives the employee no credit card or cash for the journey, the employee uses his own credit cards and puts his own money on the table. He willingly uses his own resources, at least temporarily, to cover these costs and needs for the organization. (For more on the word *misthapodosia, see* February 10.)

Of course, it's always nice when an employee can use a company credit card or corporate cash to handle these travel needs. But because neither cash nor a credit card was available at the time, the employee has no choice but to cover the cost himself and then expect the company to reimburse him later for these expenses. Once the trip is over, it's time for him to tally up the total amount owed. Then he can be *recompensed* for what he willingly contributed at a difficult or inconvenient moment.

Now the Greek word *misthapodosia* — which essentially conveys the ideas described above — is brought into play in Hebrews 10:35, where the Bible declares: "Cast not away therefore your confidence, which hath great recompence of reward."

The word "confidence" is the Greek word *parresia*, which refers to *bold, frank, forthright speech.* This bold kind of speech is often translated in the New Testament as the word "confidence." Indeed, it does depict *a confident kind of speaking* — a daring to speak exactly what one believes or thinks with no hesitation or intimidation. Because this kind of speech is so *bold*, it frequently incites a volatile reaction.

An example of this can be found in First Thessalonians 2:2, where Paul writes, "But even after that we had suffered before, and were shamefully entreated, as ye know, at Philippi, we were bold in our God to speak unto you the gospel of God with much contention." The phrase "bold in our God to speak" is from the word *parresia*. Paul inserts the words "in our God" to let us know he was so bold that only God could have enabled him to be that *audacious*. His preaching caused a great stir; therefore, the verse could be translated, *"...we were emboldened in God to publicly speak the Gospel and to be very outspoken and forthright in the way we proclaimed it, even though we were thrown into a serious fight with opposing forces that were very hostile to what we were doing and saying."*

Similarly, the word "confidence" used in Hebrews 10:35 also refers to *very bold, frank speech* — communication that is so strong, listeners may perceive the speaker to be arrogant, haughty, or over-confident. So apparently the believers to whom Hebrews 10:35 was written were speaking something that was *very bold* and *extraordinarily frank*. What words were they speaking? *They were speaking words of faith!*

Apparently these Hebrew Christians had been speaking those words a long time — and they had been waiting and waiting for those faith-filled words to come to pass. After investing their lives, their time, their energy, and their faith into their walk with God, they wanted to see some action! Because their answers hadn't come yet, they were tempted to throw it all away as though the manifestation was never going to come to pass. That's why the verse screams at them, "Cast not away your confidence...." God was saying to them, *"Don't throw away your bold confessions of faith!"*

Why did they need to hang on and continue believing and speaking words of faith? The verse tells us why: because their confidence — their bold confessions of faith — had great *recompense of reward*. As discussed above, the word "recompense" is *misthapodosia*.

God wanted these Hebrew Christians to know:

"...I know what you've done to serve Me. I am aware of the time, energy, effort, work, and money you have spent to do the job I sent you to do. Go ahead and tally up what is owed you, and boldly declare that you will be reimbursed. I will see to it that you recoup everything you spent along the way. You'll get everything that you've spent and that you've been declaring by faith!"

You may be tempted to feel like you've wasted years waiting for your calling or your dream to come to pass. The devil may try to beguile you into thinking your bold confessions of faith are mere fantasies that are never going to happen. But God's Word promises He will reward you for all you've sacrificed and invested along the way. He has heard every faith declaration you have made, and He will reward you and reimburse you for all the time, energy, commitment, and money you've given over the years!

MY PRAYER FOR TODAY

Lord, I am so thankful that You are always mindful of the time, money, and talents — as well as the blood, sweat, and tears — that I've poured into my life assignment. Sometimes when it gets hard or when I get physically or emotionally exhausted, I am tempted to think no one sees or appreciates what I have done. But You have seen it all, and You are going to be faithful to see that I am rewarded for what I have done. I thank You for being so steadfast and faithful and for promising that I will be recompensed for everything I've done with a right heart!

I pray this in Jesus' name!

MY CONFESSION FOR TODAY

I boldly declare that God is going to reward me! God's Word promises that He sees what I have done and that He will see to it that I am fully recompensed for all I have done in His name. Because I am convinced that God will take care of me, I boldly, frankly, and confidently declare that my payday is on the way! He knows about everything I have done in faith, and He will reward and reimburse me for all the time, energy, commitment, and money I've given to His work over the years!

I declare this by faith in Jesus' name!

QUESTIONS FOR YOU TO CONSIDER

1. What are some of the desires of your heart that you've recently been boldly confessing by faith so God can bring them to pass in your life?
2. What is the biggest manifestation of faith you've ever experienced in your own life?
3. How long did you have to wait before it came to pass?

MARCH 15

Are You Wearing Your Killer Shoes?

Stand therefore, having your loins girt about with truth,
and having on the breastplate of righteousness; and your feet shod
with the preparation of the gospel of peace.
— Ephesians 6:14,15

*I*f you had seen the shoes of a Roman soldier, you'd have wanted to make sure you didn't fall in front of him or get in his way where he might accidentally step on you. Those weren't normal shoes — they were *killer shoes*!

Paul refers to these killer shoes in Ephesians 6:15 as he talks about the spiritual weapons God has given to the Church. Just as God has given each believer a sword (*see* February 22), He has also clothed every believer with the shoes of peace.

Now, I realize that these shoes may sound like a passive, peaceful part of our spiritual armor. However, these are actually *killer shoes*, such as those worn by a Roman soldier.

The shoes of a Roman soldier were *vicious weapons*. They began at the top of the legs near the knees and extended down to the feet. The portions that covered the knees to the feet were called the "greaves." They were made of metal and were specially shaped to wrap around the calves of a soldier's legs. The greaves were uncomfortable but essential for the safekeeping of a soldier's legs.

The shoe itself was made of heavy pieces of leather or metal, tied together with leather straps that were intermingled with bits of metal. The bottoms were manufactured of heavy leather or pieces of metal. The bottom of the shoes were affixed with sharp, dangerous, protruding spikes. These spikes had several purposes, which we will get to in just a moment. In addition, two sharply pointed spikes extended beyond the front of each shoe.

Let me explain to you the reasons for all this gear on a soldier's legs and feet. First, the greaves — the metal that covered the Roman soldier's legs from his knees to the top of his feet — were designed to protect the soldier's calves when he was required to march through rocky and thorny terrain. If he'd had no protection on his legs, he would have surely been gashed and cut by the environment.

Thus, the greaves gave the soldier protection so he could keep walking, regardless of the obstacles he encountered. The metal barriers also gave him defensive protection in those moments when an adversary kicked him in the shins, trying to break his legs. Because the soldier's calves were covered with these greaves, his legs could not be broken and the enemy's attacks were in vain.

Now let's talk about the spikes on the bottom of the soldier's shoes. These were intended to hold him "in place" when in battle. His opponent might try to push him around, but the spikes on the bottom of his shoes helped keep him in his place, making the soldier virtually immovable. Additionally, those spikes on the bottom and front of the shoes served as weapons of brutality and murder. One good kick with those shoes, and an enemy would be dead. Just a few seconds of stomping on a fallen adversary would have eradicated that foe forever!

When Paul writes about these shoes in Ephesians 6:15, he says, "...And your feet shod with the preparation of the gospel of peace." Notice that he connects *peace* with these killer weapons! In just a moment, you'll understand why.

The word "shod" is derived from the word *hupodeomai* — a compound of the words *hupo* and *deo*. The word *hupo* means *under*, and *deo* means *to bind*. Taken together as one word, it conveys the idea of *binding something very tightly on the bottom of one's feet*. Therefore, this is not the picture of a loosely fitting shoe but of a shoe that has been tied onto the bottom of the foot *extremely tightly*.

Just as the greaves of a Roman soldier protected him from the environment and from the blows of his enemy, the peace of God — when it is operating in your life — protects and defends you from the hassles and assaults of the devil. The enemy may try to disrupt you, distract you, and steal your attention by causing negative events to whirl all around you, but his attempts will fail because the peace of God, like a protective greave, stops you from being hurt and enables you to keep marching forward!

Just as those spikes held a Roman soldier securely in place when his enemy tried to push him around, the peace of God will hold you in place when the devil tries to push *you* around! And as the soldier used those spikes to kick and to kill his opponent, there is no need for you to ever stop moving ahead just because the devil tries to block your path. If he is foolish enough to try to get in front of you, just keep walking! Stomp all along the way! By the time you're finished using your shoes of peace, you won't have much of a devil problem to deal with anymore!

Paul uses this illustration to tell us that we must firmly tie *God's peace* onto our lives (*see* January 1 to read more about the supernatural peace of God). If we only give peace a loosely fitting position in our lives, it won't be long before the affairs of life knock our peace out of place. Hence, we must *bind* peace onto our minds and emotions in the same way Roman soldiers made sure to *bind* their shoes very tightly onto their feet.

But wait — there's one more important point. Paul continued, "And your feet shod with *the preparation*...." The word "preparation" is the Greek word *etoimasin*, and it presents the idea of *readiness or preparation.* When used in connection with Roman soldiers, the word *etoimasin* portrayed *men of war who had their shoes tied on very tightly to ensure a firm footing.* Once they had the assurance that their shoes were going to stay in place, they were ready to march out onto the battlefield and confront the enemy.

When peace is in place in your life, it gives you the assurance you need to step out in faith and make the moves God is leading you to make. But before you take those steps, you need to be sure His peace is operating in your life. This mighty and powerful piece of your spiritual weaponry is essential because, without it, the devil can try to kick, punch, pull, and distract you. But with that conquering peace firmly tied to your mind and emotions, you will be empowered to keep marching ahead, impervious to the devil's attempts to take you down!

MY PRAYER FOR TODAY

Lord, I thank You for the peace You have placed in my life. This powerful spiritual weapon protects me from the assaults of life, enabling me to stand fixed, even in the face of the occasional storms that try to blow into my life, my family, my church, my friendships, and my business. How can I ever express how much I need this peace or how grateful I am to You for covering me with this protective shield that fortifies me and makes me strong? When adverse situations arise against me, help me remember to immediately release this divine force to safeguard my life.

I pray this in Jesus' name!

MY CONFESSION FOR TODAY

I confess that God's peace rules my mind and emotions, protecting me from the ups and downs of life. When storms are trying to rage against me and situations are hostile toward me, God's peace covers and safeguards me from all harm. Because divine peace is operating in me, I am not easily moved, quickly shaken, or terrified by any events that occur around about me. This mighty and powerful piece of spiritual weaponry is mine to use day and night. Therefore, although the devil may try to kick, punch, pull, and distract me, that conquering peace empowers me to keep marching ahead, oblivious to the devil's attempts to take me down!

I declare this by faith in Jesus' name!

QUESTIONS FOR YOU TO CONSIDER

1. Have there been some very difficult times in your life when the peace of God protected you from the turmoil that was happening around you?
2. Do you recall how you felt when you were enveloped in this supernatural peace? Think about it.
3. If the devil is trying to shove you around emotionally right now, what can you do to stay in the peace of God?

MARCH 16

❧❧❧

Whose Faith Are You Following?

That ye be not slothful, but followers of them
who through faith and patience inherit the promises.
— Hebrews 6:12

*L*et me ask you a question today: Who is the most influential spiritual leader in your life right now? Is there one leader whom you respect and admire so exceptionally that you would want to emulate him and try to be like him in your own life? Is there one certain leader producing the type of fruit you long to see generated in your own personal life? If so, who is that leader?

You may wonder if it's right to follow someone so closely that you actually start emulating them. But the Bible is replete with scriptures that instruct us to be followers of spiritual leaders. One such scripture is Hebrew 6:12: "That ye be not slothful, but followers of them who through faith and patience inherit the promises."

Notice that this scripture says we are to be "...*followers* of them who through faith and patience inherit the promises." The word "followers" is taken from the Greek word *mimetes*, from which we get the English word "imitate." Other words that are derived from *mimetes* are "mimic" and "mime." However, the best translation of this word is actually the word "actor." (For more on the word *mimetes*, see March 6.)

Therefore, the command to "follow" isn't referring to a casual type of following; rather, it implies an intentional study of the deeds, words, actions, and thoughts of another person in an attempt to fully understand that person and then to replicate his attributes in one's own life. This type of *following* enables a person to think like his subject, walk like his subject, mimic his subject's movements, make the vocal intonations of his subject, and act like his subject in a masterful way. However, this can only be achieved by those seriously committed to the act of *replication*. Such a commitment to act, mimic, or replicate a respected leader is the result of true discipleship.

Therefore, you could actually translate this phrase:

"...But skillfully and convincingly act like those who through faith and patience inherit the promises."

A good actor studies the character and life of another and then portrays that person on a stage or on film. The actor obtains every bit of information he possibly can about the person in order to better portray him in his acting role. Then the actor begins to practice acting just like that person — trying to talk like him, think like him, and even walk and dress like him. If the actor acts long enough and consistently enough, the character role he is playing can actually become a part of the actor's own identity. That's the power of acting!

The writer of Hebrews understood the power of imitation. That's why he said in essence, "If you want to walk in faith, find someone who successfully walks in faith. Watch what he says, how he behaves, and how he lives — and then act like him! Do what he does; say what he says; and behave like he behaves. Be an imitator of those who through faith and patience have inherited the promises!"

You may ask, "But isn't it hypocritical to act like I feel great when I really feel bad?" Absolutely not! Acting and imitating is foundational to the Christian life. It is for this very reason you are instructed to "...put ye on the Lord Jesus Christ, and make not provision for the flesh..." (Romans 13:14). When you wake up in the morning, you may not feel like smiling, talking, or saying anything nice to anyone. But because you want to please the Lord, what do you do? You choose to be nice, to smile, to speak kindly; in other words, you choose to put on the Lord Jesus Christ. You make the decision *to act* differently than you naturally feel.

Putting on Christ is a daily mindset — a daily, hour-by-hour determination. So wake up and declare that you have the mind of Christ! Find some godly people who live according to who they truly are in the Spirit — new creations with the nature, character, desires, and behavior of Jesus Christ. Study their lives, and follow their example. *In other words, ACT like those who through faith and patience inherit the promises!*

MY PRAYER FOR TODAY

Lord, I need an example that I can follow and imitate! Your Word commands me to imitate strong and successful spiritual leaders, so I am asking You to help me find that exact leader whom You want me to follow and imitate. Give me the grace to do what he does, say what he says, and act the way he acts, until finally I no longer have to act because I have become like the person I have been imitating. Holy Spirit, I want to be obedient to God's Word. Since God tells me to mimic those who through faith and patience inherit the promises of God, I'm asking You to please help me recognize the people whom I should look to as spiritual examples in my walk with God.

I pray this in Jesus' name!

MY CONFESSION FOR TODAY

I confess that I do not have to find my way by myself! By locating godly examples, I can imitate these people's lives and produce the same fruit they produce in their lives. So right now I choose to follow the examples of those who have preceded me — acting like them and replicating both their acts and their godly fruit in my life. God's Word says this is what I am to do, so I will do it as I am commanded. The Holy Spirit will help me know exactly who should be the supreme examples in my life, and He will help me follow their example as I ought to do.

I declare this by faith in Jesus' name!

QUESTIONS FOR YOU TO CONSIDER

1. Who is the most influential spiritual leader in your life right now? Have you ever taken the time to let that leader know that you appreciate him?
2. What have you done to establish a relationship with that leader? Write down ideas regarding what you can do to strengthen your relationship with him.
3. What in particular do you respect about this leader, and what fruit is demonstrated in his life that you want to see reproduced in your own life? Take the time to really think about this question, and write down your answers.

MARCH 17

֎֎֎

Stick Your Neck Out —
Commit Yourself to Someone!

And the things that thou hast heard of me among many witnesses,
the same commit thou to faithful men, who shall be able to teach others also.
— 2 Timothy 2:2

*C*an you think of an occasion when you were hurt by someone so badly that you were tempted to think, *That's it! I'll never give my heart to anyone like that ever again! This hurts too much to go through this a second time. I've had all the abuse I can take, and I'll never put my neck back on the chopping block again!*

I think everyone has been through heart-wrenching experiences of betrayal, disloyalty, deception, and unfaithfulness in his or her relationships with others. Sometimes people put on one face in front of you but show a totally different side when they are out of your presence. Maybe it was a close friend you thought would be faithful to you forever; but then that person walked out on you, stabbing you in the back as he exited! Or perhaps you had a trusted friend whom you confided in, but he violated your trust by repeating all the private things you had shared with him.

There's no doubt about it — it hurts when you find out that certain people in your life have been unfaithful, especially if they were people who you sincerely believed would be loyal to the end. These feelings of hurt must be exactly what Timothy felt as he was serving as senior pastor of the church of Ephesus. After investing his life into his group of leaders for three years — *spending time with them, loving them, caring for them, teaching them, forgiving them, and literally pouring his whole heart and soul into them, as pastors are required to do* — Timothy correctly expected a return on his investment. In other words, he expected those leaders to stay with him forever!

The return Timothy anticipated from his leaders was *commitment* and *faithfulness*. For those same men to deny him their loyalty after all he had poured into them was a flagrant violation of relationship, yet that is precisely what they did. The majority of those leaders walked out of the church and deserted Timothy.

It is a historical fact that because of Nero's persecutions against the Church, masses of believers left the Ephesian church and returned to their old pagan temples. The fires of persecution had revealed the genuine level of these people's commitment to Jesus. When they realized they might die for their faith, they reevaluated their commitment and deserted the Lord, the Church, and their pastor in order to save their lives.

Many of those who left the church of Ephesus were the leaders Timothy had trained and poured his life into. Timothy thought he could count on these leaders to serve at his side in both good and hard times. But now hard times had come, and the ones he had assumed he could trust walked out and abandoned him.

As a result, Timothy had a severe deficit of leaders whom he could rely on and was facing the task of selecting new leaders. So Paul tells him, "And the things that thou hast heard of me among many witnesses, the same commit thou to faithful men…."

These are pretty heavy instructions for Paul to give his young disciple! Timothy had already been "burned" once after giving his life to a group of people. He knew what it felt like to have people he trusted stab him in the back. Nevertheless, Paul now tells Timothy to choose a new group and start all over again!

At that moment, Timothy's emotional pain must have been enormous. I'm sure Paul's words were hard for him to hear. Just as you and I have felt in the past, he probably thought, *Forget it! I've already been through this pain once, and I don't like the idea of going through it again. I'll just pastor this church by myself!*

But it's not possible to do any monumental job alone. Therefore, if a person has been hurt, he eventually has to get over it, choose new leaders and friends, and start over again. That is why Paul told him, "And the things that thou hast heard of me among many witnesses, the same *commit thou* to faithful men...."

The word "commit" comes from the Greek compound word *paratithimi*, a compound of the words *para* and *tithimi*. The word *para* is a Greek word that means *alongside*. It refers to something that is *near* or *close by*. But in Second Timothy 2:2, it presents a picture of *close relationships*.

The second part of the word is the Greek word *tithimi*, meaning *to place, to lay something down,* or *to position something*. When the words *para* and *tithimi* are compounded together, creating the word *paratithimi*, it means *to come close in order to make some type of deposit,* like a person who goes to the bank to place a deposit into the repository for safekeeping. Significantly, this is now the word Paul uses when he tells Timothy to "commit" himself to a new group of leaders.

Timothy clearly understood Paul's instruction. He was to pick a new group of leaders, come closely alongside of them, and deposit his life into them. The Greek word *para* made it plain that this was not something that could be done from a distance. Timothy would be required to push aside his hurt and pain and to make himself vulnerable to a new group of leaders; in other words, he had to give his heart a second time.

Because of Timothy's past experience with leaders who had defected, this order from Paul may have been one of the scariest thoughts the younger minister had ever had. Timothy may have thought, *Wait a minute! I already poured my life into one group of people. But when I needed them — when I needed to draw on that deposit — they were gone! My last deposit in people didn't work out too well. They hurt me. I don't know if I'm willing to make that kind of investment in people again!*

Timothy may have asked himself, *Isn't this taking things one step too far? Does God really expect me to stick out my neck all over again after I've been hurt?* But that is *exactly* what Paul was telling him to do — and it's what you must do as well! *Stick out your neck and your heart, and try again!*

The use of the word *paratithimi* meant that Paul wanted Timothy to understand this message:

"...You need to choose some new people who have proven themselves faithful. Pull up alongside those people; get as close to them as you can so you can deposit everything you are and everything you know into them."

Timothy's future depended on how well he was able to connect and work with other people. The same is true with *your* future. Rather than allow the pain from past experiences to paralyze you today, you must do what Paul commanded Timothy to do: Put the past away; decide to quit focusing on how others have failed you; and begin to search for a new group of people or friends so you can start over again. If you don't do this, the devil will have the victory over you — paralyzing and immobilizing you, effectively preventing you and your gifts from ever being fully realized. *Don't give the devil the pleasure of that victory!*

It's time for you to grab hold of the power of God and to emerge out of your place of hiding! It may be true that a person or a group of people hurt you in the past, but there are friends out there who are just waiting for you. They are the ones who will be faithful and steadfast all the way to the end. Ask the Holy Spirit to open your eyes and direct you to them. Once you connect with them, you'll be so thankful that you didn't hide from relationships for the rest of your life and that you took the bold step to start all over again!

MY PRAYER FOR TODAY

Lord, help me overcome the hurts and disappointment I've experienced because of people who proved to be unfaithful. When I am tempted to judge those who have wronged me, help me remember those whom I myself have wronged in the past. Just as I never intended to hurt anyone, help me realize that my offenders probably didn't intend to hurt me either. As I was forgiven then, I am asking You now to help me forgive — and not just to forgive, but to stick out my neck again and begin to rebuild my life with other people in the Body of Christ!

I pray this in Jesus' name!

MY CONFESSION FOR TODAY

I confess that I don't hold grudges or bitterness against anyone who has wronged me in the past. Just as I've been forgiven, I freely forgive. As others gave me a second chance, I give people the benefit of the doubt and allow them to prove themselves even if they've done something to hurt me. The devil can't paralyze me with fears of being hurt again, because I refuse to allow that kind of fear to operate inside me. I have too much to do to let the devil immobilize me with something that happened to me in the past, so I confess right now that I am freed from every past hurt and I am moving forward to possess all that God has for me!

I declare this by faith in Jesus' name!

QUESTIONS FOR YOU TO CONSIDER

1. Has anyone ever let you down so badly that you felt like you never wanted to stick out your neck and risk getting hurt again?
2. Have you ever been the source of this type of pain to someone else? If your answer is yes, did you ever go back to that person to repent for being the source of his or her pain?
3. What can you do differently in your relationships today to make sure that never happens again?

You must decide to quit focusing on how others have failed you and begin to search for a new group of people or friends so you can start over again. If you don't do this, the devil will have the victory over you — paralyzing and immobilizing you, effectively preventing you and your gifts from ever being fully realized.

MARCH 18

❧❧❧

Don't Be A 'Bone out of Joint'!

From which some having swerved
have turned aside unto vain jangling.
— 1 Timothy 1:6

*H*ave you ever been in a situation where you found it hard to submit graciously to the orders of the person in authority over you? Maybe you thought that the orders were unfair or that you had a better idea. Or can you think of a moment when a fellow employee, staff member, or volunteer became so obstinate, disagreeable, or uncooperative that it made everyone else feel uneasy?

We've probably all had experiences in which one person's belligerence caused us and those around us to feel ill at ease. This uneasy circumstance is particularly awkward when everyone else is in agreement and willing to do what is being asked, but one person decides to defy those in authority. Refusing to budge, unwilling to give an inch, this kind of person can put the entire group and project "on hold" because a stubborn, quarrelsome, provoking, "pig-headed" attitude stalemates everything!

Can you think of a person you know who acts like this? Have *you* ever been that person I'm describing? Can you remember an instance when you were the one who acted like a "bone out of joint" with the rest of the team?

Today I want us to look at the phrase "a bone out of joint" and see what it means. I'm taking this phrase from First Timothy 1:6, so let's go there first to see how Paul used it and how it applies to you and me today.

When the book of First Timothy was written, young Timothy had only recently stepped into the position of senior pastor. In the early months of his pastoral ministry, he was simultaneously enjoying phenomenal successes and huge challenges. The successes had to do with the growth his church was experiencing. However, Timothy also had to deal with rebellious leaders who didn't like him or who thought he was too young to be the pastor of such a large church. These leaders had no desire to submit to Timothy's authority or follow his vision.

The attitudes of these argumentative leaders became so rank that Paul wrote to Timothy about this problem. Referring to the belligerent people under Timothy's authority, Paul said, "From which some having swerved have turned aside unto vain jangling" (1 Timothy 1:6).

I want you to especially pay close attention to the words "turned aside." These words come from the Greek word *ektrepo*, which means *to turn* or *to twist*. This word was also a medical term used in the medical world to denote *a bone that had slipped out of joint*. So when Paul used this word to picture these argumentative and stubborn leaders, he was making a powerful statement about them and their bad attitudes. He was calling them "a bone out of joint"!

When a person has a bone that is out of joint, it's a very difficult, painful experience. Although that bone is still located inside his body and isn't broken, it isn't properly connected. Therefore, it becomes a major source of pain and irritation, sending signals of pain throughout the entire body. If you've ever had an out-of-joint bone in your body, you know how excruciatingly painful it can be.

Nearly every movement of the body is affected as that out-of-joint bone screams misery throughout your entire central nervous system!

This is exactly the image Paul had in mind when he used the word *ektrepo* to describe the unruly, difficult church members Timothy was trying to work with. Although these people were saved and valuable to God, they had become a source of pain and irritation to the pastor and ultimately to the entire church because of their rebellious attitude and refusal to cooperate. The strife they had caused in the church was a distraction that pulled Timothy from what he needed to be doing, constantly demanding that he try to bring peace. All these problems resulted from the rebellious attitudes of a few people who didn't want to follow the senior leadership of the Ephesian church. In the end, they became "out of joint," not only with their pastor but with the entire congregation.

Paul's words in First Timothy 1:6 could be interpreted:

*"Some among you have become like a bone out of joint —
a source of real pain and irritation to the whole body."*

A sincere act of repentance can snap "out-of-joint" people back into their rightful place so they can begin to function properly and become productive members of the church. But no one can make them repent and get their attitude right. It's a decision only *they* have the power to make. Once they make this decision, they can again become a benefit and a joy to everyone around them.

Do you know anyone who fits this "out-of-joint" description? Is it you? If it *is* you, it's time for you to reevaluate your attitude and the issues you have allowed to become so divisive in your life. Are those issues really so important that you should let them make you a "thorn in the side" of everyone else in the group? Is it possible that you've allowed the enemy to use you to bring division? Have you become a source of distraction, pulling the group's attention from where it ought to be?

If you've become a "bone out of joint" in your home, in the workplace, in your church, or in any other area of your life, do everything you can to snap yourself back into the godly attitude and behavior you ought to be displaying. *Get back in place,* for you have a divine call to fulfill! Your gifts and cooperation are needed by those who are running their spiritual race alongside you!

MY PRAYER FOR TODAY

Lord, help me to never be viewed as an argumentative, belligerent, disagreeable person by those who know me — especially by those who are working with me toward a common goal. If I've done anything to be perceived this way, I am sincerely asking You to forgive me right now. But I know that I don't just need Your forgiveness; I also need to ask for forgiveness from those who felt uncomfortable with my wrong behavior so my relationship with them can be made right. I need Your help to keep a right attitude, Lord, so I am asking You to help me to stay open-minded and correctable. Help me to always maintain a humble spirit and to strive to get along with the key people You have placed in my life.

I pray this in Jesus' name!

MY CONFESSION FOR TODAY

I confess that I have a teachable, correctable spirit. People love to work with me because I strive to be cooperative and to show appreciation for those who are working with me toward a common goal. When an idea is presented that is new or different to me, I think carefully before I open my mouth to respond. Even if I disagree, I don't show disrespect for anyone in the group. I realize that I am not always right and that others may be correct, so I make room for others to express themselves and to speak their hearts, and I honor their right to hold a position that is different from mine.

I declare this by faith in Jesus' name!

QUESTIONS FOR YOU TO CONSIDER

1. Can you recall an experience when you were in a group where someone's belligerent attitude made everyone feel uneasy? What did you learn from that experience?
2. When that happened, how did it affect the entire group?
3. If you have ever been that "bone out of joint," did you later apologize and ask for forgiveness? If not, don't you think it's time that you went back to those who were involved and make things right?

MARCH 19

The Necessary Attitude for Success

Therefore, my beloved brethren, be ye stedfast, unmoveable,
always abounding in the work of the Lord....
— 1 Corinthians 15:58

*T*oday I want to talk to you about an attitude you must possess if you wish to achieve success in your life. If you study the lives of achievers and history-makers, you will find that all of them remarkably share certain attitudes that helped them reach success. However, the attitude I wish to speak to you about today is so essential that it should be considered non-negotiable, especially if you wish to do anything significant with your life.

This non-negotiable attitude is found in First Corinthians 15:58, where Paul urges us, "Therefore, my beloved brethren, be ye stedfast, unmoveable, always abounding in the work of the Lord...." The word "stedfast" in this verse is dealt with in the March 12 *Sparkling Gem*, but today I want you to consider the word "unmoveable." This word refers to one of the most critically important attitudes for those who want to please God and do something noteworthy in their lives.

The word "immovable" is the Greek word *ametakinetos*, which has several meanings:

✦ It means *not easily excited, shaken, or affected.*
✦ It describes *something that is not changeable or unpredictable.*
✦ It was also frequently used in connection with *stone structures* or to refer to *people who are known to have a strong and unbending character.*
✦ Thus, this word portrays *something that is solid, unbending, and not easily excited,*

shaken, or affected; a person, building, or place that is constant, stable, enduring, and dependable.*

In other words, this is not a flighty, fickle, "here-today, gone-tomorrow," "on-again, off-again" type of person; rather, this is someone who is constant, stable, and dependable. Because the word *ametakinetos* describes something *immovable*, it carries the idea of someone whose attitude can be described as:

✦ Rock-solid
✦ Fixed
✦ Grounded
✦ Established
✦ Rooted
✦ Anchored
✦ Unvarying
✦ Permanent
✦ Stable

When you start a new project or step out in faith to do something new, there will always be obstacles that try to get in your way. If you aren't determined to be tougher than the problems that arise, it won't be long until you throw in the towel and give up. That's why this word *ametakinetos* is so vital. It is an attitude that says, *"I'm not moving until I see my dream come to pass!"*

Anyone who wants to be great or to do great things must learn to be constant, stable, dependable, inflexible, unbending, and unyielding in the face of challenges. This is a common characteristic shared by all great achievers.

First Corinthians 15:58 could be translated:

"...Be constant, stable, enduring, and dependable — one who is always abounding in the work of the Lord...."

When you know God has called you to do something, you have to develop this kind of *rock-solid, immovable attitude* about that task or project because one thing is certain: Satan *will* attempt to sidetrack you. That's what the enemy does to *anyone* whom God calls to do a job!

The devil will try to use people's negative words, a lack of finances, adverse circumstances, discouragement, and a host of other tactics to move you off course from your intended goal. That's why you have to make up your mind to be *fixed*, *rooted*, *grounded*, *anchored*, and *unwavering* in your commitment to accomplish the task God has set before you!

So don't allow yourself to be inconsistent and wavering in your commitment to accomplish your God-given assignment. Remember — others around you are watching your example. In this world where a lackadaisical, "who cares?" attitude predominates, people need to see what true commitment looks like!

Be steadfast and immovable in the place where God has called you. Make the rock-solid decision that you will be a "permanent fixture" within your divine call until your task is completed with excellence, regardless of what it costs you!

MY PRAYER FOR TODAY

Lord, as I step out in faith to do something new, I realize there will always be obstacles that try to get in my way. So today I am asking You to help me stay tougher than any problems that may arise. Help me maintain the attitude that says, "I'm not moving until I see my dream come to pass!" I understand that if I am going to do great things for You, I must be constant, stable, dependable, inflexible, unbending, and unyielding in the face of challenges. With Your help, I know this is exactly the kind of person I will be!

I pray this in Jesus' name!

MY CONFESSION FOR TODAY

I declare that I am steadfast and immovable! I have a non-negotiable attitude of absolute determination to do what God has called me to do. I am fixed, solid, grounded, established, anchored, unvarying, permanent, and stable in my tenacity to grab hold of all that God has destined for me to accomplish with my life. I will not stop, give in, give up, or surrender to anything that tries to discourage me or to throw me off track. I am committed to stay in the race until I've made it all the way to the end.

I declare this by faith in Jesus' name!

QUESTIONS FOR YOU TO CONSIDER

1. If others were asked what they think about you, would they say you are flighty and fickle or stable, consistent, and solid?
2. If you were looking for someone you could depend on to do a job, would you want to choose someone like you?
3. If you've been consistently unstable in the past, can you think of ways to correct this in your life?

MARCH 20

❧❧❧

Refuse To Ever Let Go Of Your Dream!

Let us hold fast the profession of our faith without wavering;
(for he is faithful that promised;).
— Hebrews 10:23

What do you want God to accomplish through you in this life? What are the dreams you think about every night when your head hits the pillow, or every day when no one else is around? Do you daydream about what you'd like to become or do in the years that lie ahead? Have you considered the possibility that these daydreams may in fact be the will of God for your life — dreams He placed deep down inside your spirit that are starting to be awakened? Is it possible that this is the timing for God's dream for your life to be ignited in your soul?

Dreams are powerful. They usually seem impossible at first, but those who dare to do the impossible are the ones who eventually see the impossible come to pass in their lives. Everything great starts as a dream. Consider the example of Thomas Edison, who worked so long and furiously to realize his dream of the light bulb. Although Edison failed literally thousands of times in the earliest pursuits of his dream, he learned from every failure and pushed forward. Finally, his dream came to pass, and it changed the course of human history.

What if this brilliant man had given up and given in to discouragement? I'm sure someone else along the way would have invented the light bulb, but Edison wouldn't have had the great honor of being a part of it.

There are myriads of Bible examples of individuals who had a dream. For instance, let's consider the dream God gave Abraham — called the father of our faith — regarding a new land and a new people. When God first spoke to him about the son He would give him, Abraham and his wife had long been infertile and unable to conceive a child. The thought of having a baby probably seemed like an unattainable fantasy to them. They could have asked themselves, *Is this really the plan of God for our lives, or is this a hallucination?*

God also promised Abraham a new land but didn't tell him where it was located. In their efforts to find that land, Abraham and Sarah were stricken with colossal challenges, problematic circumstances, and horrible internal family problems. First, Abraham's father died. Then they lost their nephew Lot to Sodom and Gomorrah. Abraham also took Hagar as a second wife, producing a son that didn't belong to Sarah and a great deal of jealousy and strife. In addition, Abraham and Sarah experienced a terrible famine in their promised territory that forced them to leave due to a lack of food. Traveling to Egypt in search for food, they soon found themselves evicted from that land as well.

At any moment, it would have been so easy for Abraham and Sarah to say, "Enough is enough! Pack it up — we're going back home to the city of Ur!" But instead of giving in to defeat and discouragement, they held tightly to the dreams God had put in their hearts and kept pursuing those dreams until they had witnessed their fulfillment.

If you want to see the dream God has given you fulfilled in *your* life, it is *imperative* that you have this same attitude. As Hebrews 10:23 says, "Let us hold fast the profession of our faith without wavering; (for he is faithful that promised;)."

I want you to particularly notice the phrase "hold fast." Abraham and Sarah "held fast" to their dream, and that is what you must do as well. The phrase "hold fast" is taken from the Greek word *katecho*, which is a compound of the two words *kata* and *echo*. The first word, *kata*, carries the idea of *something that comes downward*.

You could say the word *kata* carries the force of *something that comes down so hard and so heavily, it is overpowering and dominating to the point of being subjugating*. When this force arrives on the scene, it *conquers, subdues, and immediately begins expressing its overwhelming, influencing power*.

The second part of the word *katecho* is the word *echo*, which simply means *I have* and carries the notion of *possession*. This is the picture of someone who has sought and searched for one particular thing his entire life. After years of seeking and searching, he finally finds the object of his dreams. Joyfully he rushes forward to *seize it and hold it tight*. He *wraps his arms around that object*, making it his very own. Finally, he can say, *"I have it! At long last it is mine!"*

When *kata* and *echo* are compounded into the word *katecho*, it literally means *to embrace something tightly*. However, because of the word *kata*, we know that this is the image of *someone who finds the object of his dreams and then holds it down — taking control of it, dominating it — even sitting on it so it doesn't slip away!*

The phrase "hold fast" is so strong that it can actually be translated *to suppress*. It is used this exact way in Romans 1:18, where Paul tells us about ungodly men "...who hold [or suppress] the truth in unrighteousness." In other words, because these ungodly men don't like the truth, they "sit on it" or "put a lid on it" in an effort to keep others from hearing the truth and getting set free. But in Hebrews 10:23, this same idea is used positively to describe you sitting on your word from God and refusing to let it slip out and get away from you!

This is the attitude you must have if you want to see your God-given dream come to pass. You have to wrap your arms around that word from God and never stop believing and pursuing your dream until it comes to pass. If you'll *katecho* your dream, it won't be able to get away from you, nor will anyone else be able to take it away from you!

The word *katecho* in Hebrews 10:23 could be interpreted this way:

"And let us hold fast to our confession, tightly wrapping our arms around it and embracing it with all our might, rejecting all attempts of anyone who tries to steal it from us...."

When you finally discover God's will for your life — when His plan finally begins to awaken in your heart and you know exactly what you are to do — *hold fast* to that dream. Tightly embrace what God has shown you. Seize it — wrap your arms of faith around it. *Hold it down, and hold it tight!*

Whenever you are tempted to get discouraged, give up, and release your dream, remember Abraham and Sarah. Although it took them awhile to receive their dream of a son, and although they had to overcome titanic hurdles along the way, they refused to let go of that dream and eventually saw it come to pass. In the end, they discovered that their dream was not a hallucination; it really was a word from God!

If you'll hold tight and refuse to let go of YOUR dream, it will just be a matter of time until you see it come to pass! Place all your weight on top of that dream so that NOTHING can steal it away from you!

MY PRAYER FOR TODAY

Lord, I am well aware that events will occur in life that will tempt me to release the dream You put in my heart. So right now I ask You to fill me with the courage I need to refuse to let go of my dream. Even though my mind and the circumstances around me may send signals that the dream will never come to pass, I know that You are faithful to what You have promised. Help me wrap my arms of faith around Your promises and never let go until I see them come into manifestation!

I pray this in Jesus' name!

MY CONFESSION FOR TODAY

I boldly declare that my word from God will come to pass! It may take a little while for it to happen, but I will firmly hang on to the promise God has given me. And because I refuse to let the dream slip from my heart, I stand by faith and declare that it is only a matter of time until I see the manifestation of what I'm believing God for!

I declare this by faith in Jesus' name!

QUESTIONS FOR YOU TO CONSIDER

1. What can you learn about faith by looking at the lives of Abraham and Sarah?
2. In what ways does your own walk of faith compare with Abraham and Sarah's walk of faith?
3. Can you think of a time in your past when you claimed a promise, hung on to it in the face of opposition, and later saw that promise come to pass? What was the blessing you received by faith?

MARCH 21

Doing Things Decently and in Order

Let all things be done decently and in order.
— 1 Corinthians 14:40

How does God want us to worship Him? This is a question that has been asked by different denominations throughout the centuries.

In the church I grew up in, I remember what we thought of any church that had "wild" church services. We deemed those people "incorrect" because their services weren't conducted "decently and in order" — at least not according to *our* perspective.

But over the years, I have come to learn that "decently and in order" can mean different things to different people. What is acceptable to one group may be outrageous and offensive to another group. What is deemed holy, sweet, and touching by one group might be viewed as dead and dull to another. Everyone has his or her own opinions about what is appropriate or inappropriate in worship.

The Body of Christ is composed of too many different groups to list them all here, such as Catholics, Orthodox, Baptists, Episcopalians, Methodists, Pentecostals, and Charismatics. It therefore shouldn't surprise us that Christians have differing opinions about the right and wrong way to worship God. It also shouldn't surprise us that most people assume that *their* form of worship is the most scriptural.

So who is right and who is wrong? Is there only one correct form of worship? Could there possibly be room for a variety of different expressions of worship in the Kingdom of God? And are we ready to honestly ask ourselves, *Are my opinions about worship influenced only by the Bible, or am I also influenced by my culture and upbringing? What are the guidelines set forth in Scripture?*

You may personally believe that praise and worship with instruments, clapping, dancing, and all kinds of celebration is the right approach to worship. Or you may be a person who loves a quieter, more structured form of worship with hymns and organ music. Either way, you may have a host of scriptures to back up your conviction and support your view of what worship ought to be.

However, the New Testament basically gives us only one rule to follow in regard to this question of what is acceptable and appropriate in worship. That rule is found in First Corinthians 14:40, where the apostle Paul tells us, "Let all things be done decently and in order."

The word "decently" is the Greek word *euschemonos*. Other than this verse, the word *euschemonos* is only found two other times in the New Testament — in Romans 13:13 and in First Thessalonians 4:12. In both of these places, it is translated *to do something honestly* or *to walk honestly*. It carries the notion of something that is done *properly* as opposed to *improperly*. It has to do with *intent* and *motivation* more than outward action, although such a good intention always results in right actions.

The word "order" is the Greek word *taksis*. It carries the idea of *something done in a fitting way* or *something done according to order*. The Jewish historian Josephus used the word *taksis* when he recorded the *orderly way* in which the Roman army erected their camps — indicating their camps were *orderly, organized,* and *well-planned*. The commanders didn't engage in last-minute planning. Their camps were not hastily thrown together but rather set up in an *organized* and *thoughtful* manner.

Josephus also uses the word *taksis* to describe the way the Essene Jews were respectful of others. These Jews would wait until others were finished speaking before they'd take their turn and speak out. In Josephus' depiction of this behavior among the Essenes, he used the word *taksis* to picture people who were *respectful, deferential, courteous, accommodating, well-mannered, and polite*.

Taking these meanings into account,
First Corinthians 14:40 could be translated:

"Let everything be done in a fitting and proper manner that is organized, well-planned, respectful, well-mannered, and polite."

This throws open the door to all kinds of worship! It can be quiet, loud, soft, or bold. The important thing is that the time of worship would not be something thrown together at the last minute with no thought or organization. After all, we're talking about believers coming together to worship the Almighty God! Therefore, when we plan corporate worship, it should be well thought out and organized. Additionally, our time of worship together should be well-mannered, respectful, and polite.

A group of believers can be bold, loud, and well-mannered all at the same time. They can also be soft and quiet while at the same time rude and offensive. The style, use of instruments, and volume level are not the biggest questions in God's mind. The big question in His mind is this: *What is their intent and motivation?* If the group's intent and motivation is correct, their worship will be accompanied by an attitude that reflects the character of Jesus Christ.

So don't get upset if others worship a little differently from how you are accustomed to worshiping. Jesus is listening to their *hearts*. He is watching to see how much energy and forethought they put into the plan before they enter into His Presence. Their form of worship may be different than yours, but if they are worshiping God from a pure heart and with their entire being, you can rest assured that their worship is acceptable to Him!

The truth is, God is more interested in the condition of your heart than the style of worship you use in the format of your church service. So instead of focusing on who has the best form of worship, concentrate on whether YOU have an open, pure heart before God!

MY PRAYER FOR TODAY

Lord, I want to have an appreciation for the entire Body of Christ and not hold others in judgment because they worship differently than I do. Please forgive me for the times I've been so judgmental, narrow-minded, and closed to anyone who does things differently than what I am accustomed to doing. Help me see the wonderful flavors You have placed in Your Church and to learn to appreciate and enjoy the wonderful blend and varieties that exist in Your family!

I pray this in Jesus' name!

MY CONFESSION FOR TODAY

I confess that I am tolerant and nonjudgmental toward those who worship God differently than my friends and I. As long as they worship Jesus and do it with all their hearts, I thank God for them. I choose to do everything within my power to show respect for and to honor the way others feel most comfortable in their worship of God. If God sees their hearts and receives their worship, I am in no position to judge or condemn. For the rest of my life, I will no longer take a contentious position against those who represent parts of the Church that are different from mine.

I declare this by faith in Jesus' name!

QUESTIONS FOR YOU TO CONSIDER

1. Have you been opinionated and judgmental about other people's forms of worship?
2. After reading today's *Sparkling Gem*, what attitude do you think is right for you to have toward other people's different forms of worship?
3. According to First Corinthians 14:40, what is the most important thing for you to be concerned about in the way a church worships God?

MARCH 22

How Is Your Memory Working?

I thank God, whom I serve from my forefathers with pure conscience,
that without ceasing I have remembrance of thee in my prayers night and day.
— 2 Timothy 1:3

When Paul wrote these words, he was sitting in prison in Rome. Having been judged by the courts and sentenced to death, he was living his final days in prison as he awaited the day of his execution. The method of execution had been decreed: He was to die by beheading.

Paul knew that in just a short time, soldiers would enter his cell, bind him in chains, and then take him to the place of his beheading. As he anticipated this coming hour, Paul received a letter from Timothy. Reading the letter, he perceived that his young disciple was in trouble. A spirit of fear was attempting to operate in Timothy due to the horrific persecution that was sweeping like waves across his city. In addition, Timothy was fighting feelings of hurt and devastation because the leaders he trusted had abandoned him in this difficult hour.

Paul knew that this might be his last opportunity on earth to encourage the younger man of God, so he wrote back to Timothy and told him, "I thank God, whom I serve from my forefathers with pure conscience, that without ceasing I have remembrance of thee in my prayers night and day" (2 Timothy 1:3).

This word "remembrance" comes from the Greek word *mneia*. In some places in literature, this word denoted *a written record used to record and memorialize a person's actions*. In other places, it signified *a statue, monument,* or *memorial.* An example of this latter meaning is found in Acts 10:3,4. As Cornelius prays, an angel appears to him and says, "Thy prayers and thy alms are come up for a *memorial* before God." This word "memorial" is from the same Greek root as the word "remembrance" that Paul used in Second Timothy 1:3.

What do all these various meanings have to do with Paul's prayer for Timothy? What images does Paul intend to communicate by using this very special word?

First, this word tells us that Paul intended to use his prayer time to make sure Heaven was fully aware of all the achievements being accomplished by Timothy. Before Paul began to lift up Timothy's present need, he'd take the time to tell Heaven everything he thought and felt for this young man of God. By doing this, Paul *memorialized* Timothy in the annals of Heaven! Paul set the record straight and made sure Heaven was aware of what this young disciple was doing in Jesus' name.

We need to learn from Paul's example. Before you begin to pray for a person's need, first take a few minutes to review his acts of faith! Remind the Lord of all that person has done for the Kingdom of God. Put the Lord in remembrance of the way he has served, the time he has given, the money he has sown, and the way he has endured to do His will. Make sure you start your prayer time by *setting the record straight* and *memorializing* that person in the Presence of the Lord.

Second, the use of this word tells us that Paul prayed so fiercely and fervently for Timothy that his prayers left a lasting impression in Heaven. Like a statue or memorial permanently stands for generations *to remind us* of what someone did in the past, Paul's prayers for Timothy were monumental in Heaven. Figuratively speaking, Paul prayed so much for Timothy that he filled the throne room of God with pictures, images, statues, and memorials of the younger man. Everywhere God looked, He saw an image of Timothy! In other words, God was continually confronted with the needs of Paul's young disciple through the apostle's continual prayers.

How would you like for someone to pray for you this much? Would it bless you to know that one person is so dedicated to praying for you that he has filled Heaven with your image — to the point that everywhere God looks, He is met head-on with your needs and your desires?

Let me turn the question around now and ask this: Is there anyone you're praying for right now? If the answer is yes, go for it with all your heart, knowing that your prayers are painting pictures and erecting statues of that person and his need before God. Because of your prayers for your loved one, God will consistently be reminded of his need and will move mightily on his behalf.

**These Greek meanings tell us
that it is almost as if Paul was telling Timothy:**

"Timothy, my intention is to pray, pray, pray, and pray for you until I have set the record straight about your activities and until I have stacked the throne room of God with your name! Anywhere God looks, I want Him to see a living memorial of you! I don't want God

to ever forget you; therefore, I am loading Heaven with statues, monuments, and memorials of you. My prayers for you will stand as an everlasting memorial before God!"

The fact is that many lives have been spared because of a mother or grandmother who prayed. Even long after these faithful prayer warriors die and go to Heaven, their prayers continue to exert power in life. Why is this so? Because prayers are permanent and everlasting. God never forgets a prayer that is prayed in faith. That prayer stands in His Presence as an everlasting memorial — like a huge edifice or marble statue!

Don't wait another day! Go ahead and start stacking Heaven with some of your own everlasting memorials. Open the door for God's blessings to flow into the lives of those for whom you pray. And be assured — your prayers of faith on behalf of others will NEVER be forgotten by God!

MY PRAYER FOR TODAY

Lord, I thank You so much for people who have prayed for me. I know their prayers were a vital force to keep Heaven in remembrance of the needs and situations I was facing in life at the time. Forgive me for not being more grateful for people who loved me enough to pray. Now I ask You to help me faithfully pray for those You place on my heart, just as others have prayed for me. Help me keep Heaven in remembrance of these people and their needs.

I pray this in Jesus' name!

MY CONFESSION FOR TODAY

I declare that I am faithful to pray for the people I love! Just as others have prayed for me, I take time to pray for those whom God places on my heart, even mentioning them by name to the Lord. My prayers are powerful and effective for them, causing Heaven to be constantly confronted by the situations and needs they are facing right now. I make a difference in their lives by taking time to pray!

I declare this by faith in Jesus' name!

QUESTIONS FOR YOU TO CONSIDER

1. Do you know anyone who fervently prayed for you and who is partially responsible for where you are in life right now because of his or her prayers?
2. Don't you think it's time for you to return the favor by consistently praying for someone else?
3. Why don't you make a prayer list of people you can begin to pray for every day? Take time to really think about who you should include on that list; then write down their names on a piece of paper, and keep the list in a place where you can refer to it when you pray.

The fact is that many lives have been spared because of a mother or grandmother who prayed. Even after these faithful prayer warriors die and go to Heaven, their prayers continue to exert power in life.

MARCH 23

❧❦❧

Do You Have the Right To Demand Anything From God?

If ye abide in me, and my words abide in you,
ye shall ask what ye will, and it shall be done unto you.
— John 15:7

*E*xactly how bold can you dare to be in prayer? Do you have the right to come into the Presence of God and make certain demands of Him? What are your rights, your limitations, and your boundaries when it comes to the issue of prayer?

Jesus used an attention-grabbing word in John 15:7 when He was speaking to the disciples about prayer. The *King James Version* says, "…Ask what ye will, and it shall be done unto you." The Greek word "ask" destroys any religious suggestion that we are lowly worms who have no right to come into the Presence of God. It also destroys the picture that we must pitifully beg and plead for the things we need of the Lord. You see, the word "ask" is the Greek word *aiteo*, a word that means *to be adamant in requesting and demanding assistance to meet tangible needs, such as food, shelter, money, and so forth.*

Although this word *aiteo* means *to demand* or *to insist*, it does *not* give a believer license to be arrogant or rude in his approach to God. In fact, in the New Testament, the word *aiteo* is used to portray a person addressing a superior. The person may *insist* or *demand* that a certain need be met, but he approaches and speaks to his superior with respect and honor. Additionally, the word *aiteo* expresses the idea that one possesses a *full expectation* to receive what was *firmly requested.*

There is no doubt that this word describes someone who prays authoritatively, in a sense *demanding* something from God. This person knows what he needs and is so filled with faith that he isn't afraid to boldly come into God's Presence to ask and expect to receive what he has requested.

Some people are disturbed by this idea of "demanding" something from God. However, they wouldn't find this particular concept of prayer so disturbing if they kept it in context with the entire verse.

The first part of John 15:7 gives the key: "If ye abide in me, and my words abide in you…." Jesus knew that if His words take up permanent residency in your heart and mind, you will never ask for something that is out of line with His will for your life. His Word will so transform your mind that your prayers will always be in accordance with what He has already said. In fact, this transformation process is what gives you the confidence to boldly come into God's Presence and make your requests known! You ask boldly because you already know it is what He wants to do!

When you know you are praying according to the will of God, you don't have to sheepishly utter your requests. Rather, you can boldly assert your faith and *expect* God to move on your behalf! To tell the truth, God *wants* you to act boldly and courageously in prayer! He wants you to *seize* His will for your life and demand that it come into manifestation! He's just waiting for you to ask!

And don't think that you can *only* come to God for spiritual blessings. As noted earlier, the word *aiteo* used in John 15:7 primarily has to do with requesting things of a physical and material nature, such as food, clothes, shelter, money, and so forth. Jesus plainly stated in Matthew 6:33 that if we seek the Kingdom of God first, God will see to it that all the material things we need are provided. On the other hand, James 4:2 teaches that believers often do not have what they need because they don't ask!

Philippians 4:6 says, "Be careful for nothing; but in every thing by prayer and supplication with thanksgiving let your requests be made known unto God." The word translated "request" is also the word *aiteo*. By using *aiteo* in this verse, Paul also urges us to be *bold, authoritative,* and *commanding.* However, he underscores the point that our approach to God must not be rude and arrogant but rather filled with *gratefulness* and *thanksgiving.* This means we should have a thankful, grateful heart as we come to make our requests known.

As you allow God's Word to take an authoritative role in your heart and mind and you give that Word the freedom to transform your thinking, your mind will become renewed to God's will. When that happens, it will cause you to pray in accordance with His plan for your life. Once you are in this position, you are ready to experience this *aiteo* kind of prayer. *That's when you can begin to boldly, courageously, and confidently move into higher realms of prayer to obtain the petition you desire of God! As you make your bold requests known to God, take the time to show your respect by thanking Him for all He has done in your life!*

MY PRAYER FOR TODAY

Lord, I'm so glad that I can be bold and straight to the point when I come into Your Presence. I am so thankful that You want me to boldly present my needs to You and expect You to answer my requests. Jesus told me to boldly ask, so it is right for me to do just that! Today I come before You to tell You about some big needs I have in my life — and because I know You want to bless and help me, I am releasing my faith, fully expecting to receive what I request of You today!

I pray this in Jesus' name!

MY CONFESSION FOR TODAY

I confess that I am bold when I come to God in prayer. Because Jesus beckons me to come to the Father with bold, frank, and confident requests, I make my needs known to God and fully expect Him to answer me. He is my Father, and I am His child. He WANTS me to be bold enough to ask Him to meet my needs, and He promises never to withhold any good thing from me!

I declare this by faith in Jesus' name!

QUESTIONS FOR YOU TO CONSIDER

1. Have you ever felt like you needed to beg and plead for God to do something in your life?
2. How is the teaching in this *Sparkling Gem* going to change your prayer life?
3. Can you think of one thing you can boldly ask God to do for you today?

MARCH 24

✦✦✦

The Most Essential Weapon In Your Spiritual Arsenal

Stand therefore, having your loins girt about with truth….
— Ephesians 6:14

Roman soldiers were dressed in beautiful armor! From head to toe, they were covered with various pieces of weaponry that were designed to protect them and equip them for fighting. But of all these pieces, one piece was more important than all the others. That vital and most important piece of weaponry was the Roman soldier's loinbelt.

A loinbelt didn't look important. Certainly no soldier would have written home and told his parents, "Wow, I've got the most incredible loinbelt!" He might have told them about his shield, his sword, or his breastplate, but no one got excited about the loinbelt. Nevertheless, it was the Roman soldier's most important piece of weaponry. Why was this so? Because the loinbelt held many of the other pieces of weaponry together. If a soldier's loinbelt wasn't in place, he was in *big* trouble.

This is even true with modern clothing. For example, the belt I wear around my waist is not something people notice. They might mention my tie, my suit, my shirt, my sweater, and even my shoes. But to date, I've never had anyone walk up to me and say with excitement, "Wow, what a belt!" However, my belt *is* very important! If I removed it, I'd find out how important it is, because my pants would fall off! That makes my belt quite a vital part of my attire!

In the same way, the Roman soldier's loinbelt was the piece of armor that held all the other pieces together. His sword hung in a scabbard that was clipped to the side of his loinbelt. When not in use, his shield was hung on a special clip on the other side of his loinbelt. The pouch that carried his arrows rested on a small ledge attached to his loinbelt on his backside. Even his breastplate was attached in some places to his loinbelt.

Accordingly, the soldier's ability to use his other pieces of weaponry depended on his loinbelt. If he had no loinbelt, he had no place to attach his massive shield or to hang his sword. Without a loinbelt, there was nothing to rest his lance upon and nothing to keep his breastplate from flapping in the wind. The armor of a Roman soldier would literally come apart, piece by piece, if he didn't have the loinbelt around his waist.

You can see why the loinbelt was absolutely essential to the Roman soldier in order for him to be confident in battle. With that belt securely fastened, he could be assured that all the other pieces of his equipment would stay in place, enabling him to move quickly and fight with great fury.

Thus, the loinbelt was the most vital part of all the weaponry the Roman soldier wore. Now consider all this in light of Ephesians 6:14, where Paul says, "Stand therefore, *having your loins girt about with truth*…." For the child of God, the loinbelt of his spiritual armor is the written Word of God — the truth.

When God's Word has a central place in your life, you will have a sense of righteousness that covers you like a mighty breastplate. When God's Word is operating in your life, it gives you the sword you need — that *rhema* word quickened to your heart by the Holy Spirit (*see* February 22).

When God's Word dominates your thinking, it gives you peace that protects you from the attacks of the adversary and shields your mind like a powerful helmet.

As long as the loinbelt of truth — the Word of God — is central in your life, the rest of your spiritual armor will be effective. But the moment you begin to ignore God's Word and cease to apply it to your life on a daily basis, you'll start to lose your sense of righteousness and peace. You'll find that the devil will start attacking your mind more and more, trying to fill it with lies and vain imaginations. You see, when you remove God's Word from its rightful place at the very core of your life, it won't be long until you will begin to spiritually come apart at the seams!

If you want to stay clothed in your spiritual armor, you must begin by taking up God's Word and permanently affixing it to your life. You have to give the Word a central place and dominant role in your life, allowing it to be the "loinbelt" that holds the rest of your weaponry together.

So as you go about your daily routine today and every day, keep your "loinbelt of truth" fully attached and operative in every situation you face. Let the Bible be the governor, the law, the ruler, the "final say-so" in your life!

MY PRAYER FOR TODAY

Lord, I know that Your Word is the most important weapon You have given to me. Forgive me for the times I have not made it a priority in my life. Today I make the decision to never ignore Your Word again. Holy Spirit, help me stay true to this decision. Please remind me every day to open my Bible and take the time needed to wrap that Word around my life!

I pray this in Jesus' name!

MY CONFESSION FOR TODAY

Because God's Word has a central place in my life, I have a sense of righteousness that covers me like a mighty breastplate. God's Word is operating in my life, giving me a powerful sword to wield against the enemy — that rhema word quickened by the Spirit of God to my heart in my time of need. And because God's Word also dominates my thinking, I have peace that protects me from the attacks of the adversary and shields my mind like a powerful helmet.

I declare this by faith in Jesus' name!

QUESTIONS FOR YOU TO CONSIDER

1. Does the Word of God really have a central role in your life, or is reading your Bible something you do once in a while when it's convenient to you?
2. Was there a time in your life when you devoured the Word of God? What kind of fruit did that period of time produce in your life? Take the time to write down your answers and really think about them.
3. What changes do you need to make in your schedule now to give God's Word the central place it ought to have in your life?

MARCH 25

୧ଊଋଵ

Keep the Devil Where He Belongs —
Under Your Feet!

And the God of peace shall bruise Satan
under your feet shortly....
— Romans 16:20

*A*re you tired of the devil blocking your way and causing all kinds of disruptions and problems in your life, such as problems in your relationships, financial woes, or health problems? How would you like to lift your foot high and then slam it down as hard as you can on top of the devil — pounding, hammering, trouncing, crushing, and smattering him to bits under your feet? *Does that sound like something you wish you could do?*

Believe it or not, the apostle Paul encourages you to do exactly that! In Romans 16:20 he writes, "And the God of peace shall *bruise* Satan under your feet shortly...." The word "bruise" is taken from the Greek word *suntribo*, a word that significantly presents this notion of trampling the devil under your feet. The word was historically used to denote *the act of smashing grapes into wine*. However, it was also used to refer to *the act of snapping, breaking, and crushing bones*. In fact, it pictures *bones that have been utterly crushed beyond recognition*.

This word *suntribo* is used in Mark 5:4 where the Bible tells us about the demon-possessed man of the Gadarenes. It says, "Because that he had been often bound with fetters and chains, and the chains had been plucked asunder by him, and the fetters *broken in pieces*...." The phrase "broken in pieces" is this same word *suntribo*. Although bound in chains and fetters, the demonized man was sufficiently energized by the demons to be able to crush those fetters to pieces.

The use of the word *suntribo* in this verse portrays a demon-possessed man releasing so much rage and violence that he was able to *obliterate, smash, demolish*, and *reduce those fetters to nothing*. When he was finished, the fetters fell to the ground in a heap, twisted and deformed — so broken that they would never be used to hold anyone captive again.

Now Paul uses this same word in Romans 16:20 when he says we are to "bruise" Satan under our feet. However, notice that Paul says we are to bruise him under our feet "shortly." This word "shortly" is extremely important because it takes the whole picture to the next level. It tells us what attitude we must demonstrate the next time the devil tries to get in our way or block our path.

The word "shortly" comes from a military term that described the way Roman soldiers marched in formation. They were instructed by their commanders, "You are Roman soldiers! Lift your feet high, stomp loud, and let everyone know you are coming through town. The sound of the stomping and pounding of your feet is the signal to let everyone know they need to get out of your way. And if someone is foolish enough to stand in your way — even if someone falls down in front of you — don't you dare stop to ask them to move! Just keep marching, stomping, and pounding, even if it means you have to walk right over them!"

So when Paul uses the word "shortly," he is referring to the pounding, stomping, crushing steps of a Roman soldier. And remember, Roman soldiers wore shoes that were spiked with nails on the bottom (*see* March 15). When a challenger stood in front of them — or if a person fell in their path — these soldiers would simply ignore the obstacle and keep marching, stomping, and pounding along their way, leaving the challenger or unfortunate person completely obliterated and trampled beyond recognition — an ugly, bloody sight.

What does all this mean for you and me today? It means the next time the devil tries to get in your way or block your path, you shouldn't stop to politely ask him to move. If the enemy is stupid enough to challenge you and tries to hinder your plans, God tells you what to do in this verse: *"Just keep walking! If the devil tries to stop you, just raise your feet high, pound down as hard as you can, and stomp all over him as you march forward. Crush and bruise him beyond recognition!"*

However, it is important to point out that this *smashing* and *crushing* of Satan must be done in cooperation with God. Alone you are no match for this archenemy. That's the reason Paul says, *"…The God of peace* shall bruise Satan *under your feet…."* In other words, this is a joint partnership between you and God. By yourself, you could never keep Satan subdued. But with God as your Partner, the devil has no chance of ever slipping out from under your heel!

Romans 16:20 suggests this idea:

"The God of peace will smash and completely obliterate Satan under your feet! If Satan tries to get in your way or to block your path, then it's time for you to act like a soldier — lift your feet high, stomp and pound down hard, crushing the enemy under your feet and leaving him in a heap, trampled beyond recognition, as you march on…."

The glorious truth is that Jesus already completely destroyed Satan's power over you through His death and resurrection. The devil was utterly *smashed, crushed,* and *bruised* when Jesus was victoriously raised from the dead (*see* January 31, February 11, February 28). Your God-given mission now is to reinforce the victory already won and to demonstrate just how miserably defeated Satan already is!

The enemy may try to lord himself over you; he may attempt to exert his foul influence over your life. However, he is merely using empty threats and illusions to feed fear into your mind.

Never forget — the only place that rightfully belongs to the devil is the small space of ground right under your feet! Jesus accomplished a total, complete, and perfect work through the Cross of Calvary and His resurrection from the dead. That means your healing, your miracle, or your financial blessing already belongs to you! The victory is already yours!

MY PRAYER FOR TODAY

Lord, the next time the devil tries to get in my way or to block my path, help me to raise my feet high, pound down as hard as I can, and stomp all over him as I march forward unhindered to do Your will. I thank You that because of Your victory, Satan has no right to exercise this kind of control over my life anymore! With You working as my Partner, I can stare that old enemy in the face and command him to move. And if he tries to put up a fight, I can push him out of the way and walk on through!

I pray this in Jesus' name!

MY CONFESSION FOR TODAY

I boldly declare that Jesus destroyed Satan's power over me! Through Jesus' death and resurrection, the devil was utterly smashed, crushed, and bruised. Now my God-given mission is to reinforce that glorious victory and to demonstrate just how miserably defeated Satan already is. The enemy may try to lord himself over me, but he has no authority to exercise any control in my life!

I declare this by faith in Jesus' name!

QUESTIONS FOR YOU TO CONSIDER

1. Do you see yourself as a victorious soldier in the army of God?
2. Are your problems under your feet today, or do you feel like you are constantly under the heel of your problems?
3. What are you going to do to turn this situation around? Write down ideas about what actions you can take to start winning the victory over the devil's attacks in your life.

MARCH 26

The Lord Will Reckon With You When He Comes!

After a long time the lord of those servants cometh,
and reckoneth with them.
— Matthew 25:19

No one likes to think about judgment, but there is a day in all our futures when we will stand before the judgment seat of Christ to give account for our lives. Paul makes this very clear in Second Corinthians 5:9 and 10, where he writes, "Wherefore we labour, that, whether present or absent, we may be accepted of him. For we must all appear before the judgment seat of Christ; that every one may receive the things done in his body, according to that he hath done, whether it be good or bad."

The judgment seat of Christ is a subject rarely taught today, but simply because it is ignored doesn't mean it has ceased to exist. Some assert there will be no judgment for believers. However, these people are misinformed, for Paul makes it unmistakably clear that every person will stand before Jesus on that Day and give account for his or her life.

Our attitude changes dramatically when we live with the awareness that one day we will stand before the Lord "eyeball to eyeball" and answer for how responsibly or irresponsibly we lived our lives. There will be no fast talking on that day, because every lie and excuse will evaporate in His glorious light.

For this reason, I do my best to live every day of my life with the thought that one day I will answer for what I do. I make the most of every minute, walk in love to the best of my ability, use the gifts and talents God has given me, and strive to obediently and successfully fulfill every task the Lord has given to me.

In Matthew 25, Jesus taught a parable to let us know that a day of reckoning is coming for all of us. After distributing measurements of money to three different servants, a certain lord (or employer) left on a long journey. When he came back, he wanted to see what his three servants had done with the money he had given them, so he called them in for a review.

The *King James Version* of verse 19 says, "After a long time the lord of those servants cometh, and reckoneth with them." Just as this lord returned in the parable, Jesus is coming back again one day not so far away. Just as this lord reckoned with his servants, Jesus will reckon with us when He returns. Therefore, we need to know what the Bible means when it says Jesus will "reckon" with us.

The word "reckon" comes from the Greek phrase *sunairei logon meta*. It is a commercial term that means *to compare accounts*. It is also a bookkeeping phrase that means *to look at the record, to study the facts, to compare accounts,* or *to settle an account.* This phrase would normally be used to portray an accountant who is putting together a profit-and-loss statement for his boss. He isn't just skimming the surface; he is digging deep to analyze the real financial status of the corporation.

It's very significant that Jesus used this word because it tells us the Lord is never satisfied with taking a shallow look at what we have done for Him! Neither will He just accept our word for it; rather, He will search and dig until He obtains a real picture of what we did or didn't do for Him. In the end, Jesus' examination of the facts will result in a very thorough investigation as He looks at what we have done and then compares it to what He asked us to do.

The only other place this Greek phrase is used in the New Testament is in Matthew 18:23 and 24, where it is used twice in one parable. It says, "Therefore is the kingdom of heaven likened unto a certain king, which would *take account* of his servants. And when he had begun *to reckon*, one was brought unto him, which owed him ten thousands talents."

As in Matthew 25, this parable pictures a king — a superior power — who calls his servants in for *a review* of what they have or haven't done. By thoroughly studying and examining the facts, he obtains a real picture of their situation. Armed with this knowledge, the king calls his servants to stand before him and give *account* for what they have done.

In using these Greek words, the Holy Spirit makes it hard for us to miss the point that a day is coming in the future when we are going to stand before Jesus to answer for our lives. On that day, we will look into His eyes and hear Him say, "Did you do what I asked you to do?"

Revelation 20:12 tells us that there are all kinds of record books in Heaven. One of them is called the Book of Life, but this scripture also says there are "books" that will be opened, containing records of what we did and didn't do on this earth. These records must be very important, for they are saved in the archives of Heaven itself. And in each of our futures, there will come a day of reckoning when those books are opened. On that day, the Lord Jesus will look over the "profit-and-loss statement" for our lives, comparing what we did to what we were actually supposed to do.

This judgment will not be in regard to our salvation, for if we are at the judgment seat of Christ, we are already eternally saved. However, that day *will* determine our reward. Those who fulfilled the assignment Jesus gave them will receive a reward (1 Corinthians 3:14). Those who were *not* obedient will still be saved, but they will have no reward to show for their lives (1 Corinthians 3:15).

Matthew 25:19 could be interpreted:

"And when the lord of those servants returned, he called them up for a review — intending to thoroughly look at all the facts, to examine all the accounts, to determine the real status of what they had and had not done, and to make them accountable to him for what he discovered."

Life is very serious, friend. Jesus expects us to do something with the gifts, talents, abilities, and assignments that He has entrusted to us. Therefore, since we know that a day of reckoning awaits us, let's do everything we can to please Jesus. Let's live in the constant awareness that one day we will stand before Him to answer for what we did in this life.

Consider this question: If you were required to stand before Jesus today and to answer for your personal record, what would the records reflect about *you*?

Starting today, why not put your whole heart into doing what He asked you to do? Decide to step out in faith to use your gifts, talents, and abilities. Choose to put aside those fears that have kept you from a life of obedience; then move forward by faith to do what God has asked you to do. As long as you're doing everything you can to please Jesus and to walk in obedience, you have no reason to fear that day when you stand before Him and give account for what you have done!

MY PRAYER FOR TODAY

Lord, help me live with the awareness that a day of reckoning is in my future. Your Word makes it clear that on the day I stand before You, I will answer for what I did in this life. I will give account for the gifts, talents, abilities, ideas, and assignments You entrusted to me. On that day, I want to look into Your face with confidence, so help me NOW to faithfully use the abilities You've given me to execute every task You have asked me to do!

I pray this in Jesus' name!

MY CONFESSION FOR TODAY

I boldly acknowledge that a day of reckoning is coming in my future. On that day, I will give account for what I did or didn't do in this life. Therefore, I will use the gifts, talents, and abilities Jesus has given to me. I will faithfully execute every assignment He has asked me to do. I will do everything within my power to please Jesus in the way that I serve Him. I will make sure that my conscience is clear with God and with myself.

I declare this by faith in Jesus' name!

QUESTIONS FOR YOU TO CONSIDER

1. Do you ever think about the day that you will stand before Jesus to give account for your life?
2. Does that thought give you peace, or does it bother you because you know you haven't been obedient to pursue what God has asked you to do?
3. What do you need to do differently in your life to have peace about this question?

A day is coming in the future when we will stand before Jesus to answer for our lives. On that day, we will look into His eyes and hear Him say, "Did you do what I asked you to do?"

MARCH 27

❧❧❧

Run Like You Are In the Race of Your Life!

Know ye not that they which run in a race run all,
but one receiveth the prize? So run, that ye may obtain.
— 1 Corinthians 9:24

The main goal of all believers should be to find God's plan for their lives and then to go after it with all their might and strength. But most Christians have never even awakened to the fact that God has a special race for them to run! This is why Paul asked the Corinthians, "Know ye not that they which run in a race run all, but only one receiveth the prize? So run, that ye may obtain."

Paul teaches us here that we are in a "race." The word "race" is the Greek word *stadion*, which later became our word *stadium*. However, it first described a race course that was 600 feet in length or one-eighth of a Roman mile — the exact length that was used in the Olympics of the ancient world and in the Isthmian Games that were held near the city of Corinth. Because Paul was highly educated, he knew precisely what he was doing when he used a word that described the Olympic race course of his day.

As noted above, eventually the word *stadion* became the word for a *stadium*, a place where athletic competitions were held. Since this is the picture Paul has in his mind as he uses the word "race," let's stop to consider the Olympic competitions and competitors of that time.

The winners of the Olympic competitions were rewarded both materially and with great honor; however, if you study the Olympic champions in the ancient world, you will see that the primary emphasis of reward was not on material wealth, but on the distinguished honor bestowed on the winners. These people were only able to achieve victory in the Olympic games by being disciplined, balanced, and committed to excellence; for these qualities, they were held in high regard. They became revered as heroes, gods, or icons in their society. Respect, honor, notoriety, and fame became their lifelong reward.

In addition to these ideas, it is also important to note that the word "race," from the Greek word *stadion,* depicted *the huge arena where athletic competitions were held.* Paul uses this word to tell us that when we enter the race of faith, it puts us in the center of the arena. People see us as we walk by faith. They know of our struggles, and they watch as spectators to see if we will win our battles.

We must always keep in mind, therefore, that we're not running a private race of faith, but a race that has influence on many people's lives. Hence, Paul urges us to run our race in a way that encourages the bystanders who are watching from the sidelines to jump into the race themselves and pursue *their* destiny in God!

By using these ideas, Paul was communicating to the Corinthians (and to us) that we need to see ourselves as spiritual Olympic competitors! This life we lead is no game; it is the most serious competition we will ever face in this world. The rewards of a life well lived are enormous. Not only will God materially reward us as we are faithful to His call, but He also reserves eternal rewards of honor and glory for those of us who run our race well in this life (Romans 2:10).

It is interesting that Paul says, "...They which run in a race run all...." Notice particularly the emphasis "run all." It means *every* believer is in some kind of race. A believer may not have awakened to the race he is in yet, or perhaps the race hasn't yet been revealed to him. Nevertheless, the fact remains that God has a specific plan for every individual.

Our task is to find the divine plan for our lives; to get in shape so we can start running our race; and then to run like mad so we can finish in first place! That's why Paul exhorted us, "...Run, that ye may *obtain*" (1 Corinthians 9:24).

You see, runners have one thought foremost in their minds — *the finish line!* With this analogy in mind, Paul tells you to run your spiritual race with all your might, keeping your focus on the goal — the divine call on your life as God has revealed it to you. You may ask, "How long am I supposed to keep running and trying to reach my God-given goals?" The answer is until you "obtain" what God called you to do!

The word "obtain" is the Greek word *katalambano*, which is a compound of two words, *kata* and *lambano*. The word *kata* describes *something that is coming downward*, and the word *lambano* means *to take* or *to seize something*. When compounded together into one word, *katalambano* means *to grab hold of, to seize, to wrestle, to pull down, and to finally make a desired object your very own*. This is the picture of someone who finally sees what he wants — and instead of letting that goal he desires slip away, he pounces on it, seizing it and latching hold of it with all his might!

Paul uses this word *katalambano* to depict the attitude of a runner who is running with all his energy, straining forward as he keeps his focus fixed on the finish line. At last the runner reaches the goal, and the prize is now his! He gave that race all he had to give, and it paid off! Had he approached the race with a casual, lazy attitude, the prize would have gone to another. But because he ran to *obtain* that prize, in the end that's exactly what he did!

There is no doubt that you have a divine purpose for your life, something God has called *you* to do. God has marvelous ideas and plans for your life! The question is this: *Do you want to fulfill His plans for you?* If your answer is truly *yes*, then set your heart on your goal. Don't be half-hearted, mealy-mouthed, touchy, or easily discouraged. It's time for you to develop some *resolve!*

Do you see yourself as someone who is running the spiritual Olympic event of his or her life? Or are you simply "jogging for Jesus"? If you're serious about fulfilling God's plan for your life, it's time to shift into high gear and to start putting all your spiritual, mental, and physical energies into getting the job done. You have to remove all distractions and commit yourself to a life of discipline, balance, and devotion.

Your attitude must be, *"I'm going to run this race, and I'm going to WIN it! I'm not going to live my whole life missing out on what God has for me! No matter what inconvenience I endure, what price I have to pay, or what adjustments I have to make, I am going to faithfully run my race so that one day I can obtain the prize — the fulfillment of God's call on my life!"*

MY PRAYER FOR TODAY

Lord, I want to set my eyes on the finish line and never lose my focus until I know that I've accomplished the task You have given me to do. I know it's going to take all my spiritual, mental, and physical energies to get this job done. So I am turning to You now, Holy Spirit, and I'm asking You to empower me and to help me make it all the way to the completion of the dream You have given to me!

I pray this in Jesus' name!

MY CONFESSION FOR TODAY

I declare that I have a divine purpose in life! I am not half-hearted, mealy-mouthed, touchy, or easily discouraged. I am like a runner who is seriously running a race. Because I'm serious about achieving God's plan for my life, I am shifting into high gear and putting all my spiritual, mental, and physical energies into getting the job done.

I declare this by faith in Jesus' name!

QUESTIONS FOR YOU TO CONSIDER

1. Do you know what race you are supposed to be running in your life?
2. Are you running that race with 100 percent of your effort, or are you just half-heartedly jogging along in your life?
3. For you to achieve what God has told you to do, what changes of attitude and behavior do you need to make in your life? Write these changes down so you can pray about them!

MARCH 28

Are You an 'Amateur' Or a 'Professional'?

And if a man also strive for masteries,
yet is he not crowned, except he strive lawfully.
— 2 Timothy 2:5

*I*t is a fact that hardships nearly always reveal the real level of a person's commitment to Jesus Christ. When everything is going well and there are no challenges, it's easy to serve God. But when things get tough and people are faced with hard decisions, this is the golden moment when the real level of their commitment is revealed –– when they have to decide, *Will I remain faithful in the hard times?* You can be certain that if a flaw exists in their commitment to Jesus, difficult episodes in life will bring that defect to the surface.

In the former Soviet Union, I know many people who paid a very high price for their faith in Jesus Christ. The rulers of that past time sent many believers to prison; deported others to slave labor camps; and incarcerated still others in psychiatric hospitals, where they were treated as mental patients because they believed in God. The Soviet leadership found all sorts of ways to disdain, humiliate, and mock Christians for being different. It was therefore a very serious matter to believe in Jesus Christ, requiring a life commitment.

This is really true about all levels of life. For instance, you may say that you are committed to your spouse, a friend, to your employer, or even to your church. But what if problems emerge in those relationships that make you feel uncomfortable? What if being faithful requires you to stick with someone who is suddenly unpopular? Will you remain faithful to that relationship if problems arise in it? Will you stick to your commitment and keep your word — or will you tuck your tail and run from the stress, tossing the relationship to the wind?

You see, hard times really do reveal the truth about who people are! Doesn't it make you grateful for the people who have stayed with you through the high moments and low moments, through thick and thin, through the good times and the bad times? Friends like these are very rare, so make sure you never take them for granted. They have proven the sincerity of their commitment to you by sticking with you through it all.

In Second Timothy, many people were defecting from the faith because hard times had come. Staying faithful to Jesus meant they might face persecution, beatings, imprisonment, or even death. Before the persecution commenced, the church at Ephesus was growing rapidly. But now it was declining as the newly arrived adversities exposed the genuine level of people's faith.

In the midst of these trying times, Paul wrote to Timothy about the attitude that is essential to survive difficult times. Although Paul was making a statement, he was also asking a very pointed question. He said, "And if a man also strive for masteries, yet is he not crowned, except he strive lawfully."

The word "strive" is the Greek word *athlesis*, which always describes *athletic activities* or *sporting events*. It also notably depicted *professional athletes*. As time passed, it expressed the idea of *any event in life that demands one's labor or sweat and tears*. It indicated *exertion, effort, and commitment*. It could refer to either *physical exertion* or *mental exertion*.

Just as in our world today, there were both amateur and professional athletes at the time Paul wrote this letter. If someone was an amateur, he wasn't a serious contender and would not participate in the harshest competitions. However, if he was a professional athlete, he was so committed that he was ready to compete, no matter how intense the opposition or how difficult the circumstances. This is the idea Paul is conveying when he used the word *athlesis* in this verse.

Paul was in essence asking:

◆ Are you an amateur who serves the Lord just for fun?
◆ Have you committed yourself to go all the way to the end, regardless of the fight that ensues?
◆ Are you serving the Lord only because it's popular and enjoyable for the moment?
◆ Are you a professional that is willing to pay any price, undergo any kind of hardship, bear up under any pressure, and endure it all until you come out the winner?
◆ *Are you really committed?*

If you're not committed, you'll never make it to the end. But if you do, Paul says there is a "crown" waiting for you. That word "crown" is the word *stephanos*, and it refers to a *victor's crown*. In the ancient games, it was a wreath of leaves placed on the head of the winning athlete. As far as value goes, it wasn't worth anything — but what it represented was worth the struggle! An athlete who walked away with the victor's crown was *honored* for the rest of his life. The memory of his achievement would be etched into society, ensuring that he would never be overlooked or forgotten during the course of his life.

If you are a serious contender for doing the will of God — if you don't allow anything to stop you, no matter what challenges the devil and life may try to throw at you — you *will* walk away with the respect and honor of others at the end of the battle. They will see that the sincerity of your faith was genuine and proven, surviving the hard times. Yours wasn't a flawed faith that tucked its tail and ran in tough times. No, you stuck it out and showed who you really are! As a result, people will never forget that you stood true to your commitment!

Isn't it true that you remember and almost stand in awe of people:

✦ Who stayed faithful to their friends, even through hard times?
✦ Who kept their commitment to their spouse, even though their marriage was hurting?
✦ Who remained faithful to their pastor in spite of the hard times in the church?
✦ Who stuck by their principles and refused to bend to the pressures that came to break them?

Let's face it — people who fit into these categories are pretty rare in today's world. But they are champions to the rest of us! They are examples of what we should try to become. Although they endured a lot to keep their commitments, as a result they stand as heroes to those who have observed their spiritual race. Their crown in this life is the special place of honor that has been etched in other people's minds because of their accomplishments. They proved to be professional believers — *not* just amateurs who were along for the ride until it cost them something!

What kind of believer are you today, friend? Are you a professional, or are you an amateur?

You must come to a place of honesty in your spiritual walk where you are willing to ask yourself these questions. You see, it's fun to serve the Lord when it's easy and convenient. *But what if God asks you to step out of your life of ease to accept a bigger challenge? That's the moment of discovery when you find out what kind of spiritual athlete you really are!*

MY PRAYER FOR TODAY

Lord, I want You to see me as a professional! Therefore, I choose to put away amateurish Christian attitudes and behaviors! For me to be all You want me to be, I understand that it's going to require more of me. Right now I am making up my mind to move to a higher level of commitment with God, to give Him all that I have, and to never stop until the job is done and the assignment is complete! Help me move into the "professional league" as a believer and to leave the life of the amateur behind forever!

I pray this in Jesus' name!

MY CONFESSION FOR TODAY

I confess that I am a serious contender for doing the will of God! In spite of what the devil and life may try to throw at me, I will walk away as the winner. I will survive hard times and thus prove the sincerity of my faith. Mine isn't a flawed faith that tucks its tail and runs. I am the kind of Christian who sticks it out to the end!

I declare this by faith in Jesus' name!

QUESTIONS FOR YOU TO CONSIDER

1. Does your level of commitment reveal that you are an amateur or a professional Christian?

2. Do you face hardships bravely, or do you tuck your tail and run when things get tough?

3. What would other people say about your level of commitment? Why not ask a few friends to tell you what they think, giving them the right to be totally honest with you?

MARCH 29

The Supernatural Intercessory Ministry Of the Holy Spirit

Likewise the Spirit also helpeth our infirmities:
for we know not what we should pray for as we ought: but the Spirit itself
maketh intercession for us with groanings which cannot be uttered.
— Romans 8:26

*T*o whom do you go for help when you feel trapped, cornered, or pinned against the wall because of a situation you've fallen into? In moments like that, do you feel overwhelmed with a sense of desperation, or do you know where to turn for help?

I want to speak to you about the supernatural intercessory ministry of the Holy Spirit. But today I'm not talking about prayer when I use the phrase "intercessory ministry." I am talking about a very special, unique work of the Holy Spirit that is available to help you every day — especially in times when you're feeling backed into a corner by situations in life.

Romans 8:26 says, "Likewise the Spirit also helpeth our infirmities: for we know not what we should pray for as we ought: but the Spirit itself maketh intercession for us with groanings which cannot be uttered." I would like to draw your attention to the word "intercession" in the middle of this verse. It is the Greek word *huperentugchano*, an old word that does not appear to exist outside early Christian literature. It is the picture of one who comes upon someone who has fallen into some kind of quandary. Upon discovering the trapped person's dilemma, he swiftly swings into action to rescue and deliver the one who is in trouble. Therefore, the word *huperentugchano* conveys the idea of *a rescue operation*.

Paul uses this word here to tell us about a special work of divine intercession — a special ministry performed by the Holy Spirit Himself when He sees that you are at a loss for words or that you are trapped in a situation and don't know how to get out. Suddenly and supernaturally, the Holy Spirit falls into that place with you. Now you are no longer facing the challenge by yourself, for the Holy Spirit has stepped into your dilemma and is initiating a rescue plan to get you out of that mess!

The Holy Spirit feels everything you feel. He understands the complete inadequacy you are experiencing. He knows about every battle you are facing. He willingly joins you in your circumstances, sharing your emotions and frustrations. Then He begins to put a supernatural plan of rescue into operation to get you out of your mess!

The middle phrase of Romans 8:26 conveys this idea:

"...The Spirit Himself falls into our difficulty with us, initiating a supernatural rescue operation to get us out of the mess we've fallen into...."

So the next time you get into trouble, there's no need for you to sweat it out by yourself. The Holy Spirit is standing by, just waiting for you to ask for His assistance. Helping you is a part of His ministry, so never hesitate to say, "Holy Spirit, help me!" This is what the intercessory ministry of the Holy Spirit is all about!

What challenges are you facing today? What problems seem bigger than your ability to handle by yourself?

Come to grips with your need for supernatural assistance, and open your heart to the Holy Spirit's help today. As you do, you will liberate Him to release His mighty power in you. An answer to every problem is just around the corner as you allow the Holy Spirit to work His supernatural ministry of intercession in your life!

MY PRAYER FOR TODAY

Lord, I thank You that the Holy Spirit joins me in the challenges I am facing in my life today. You sent Him to be my Helper, my Guide, my Teacher, and my Intercessor — the One who meets my problems head-on and helps me to overcome them! Rather than try to work out those problems by myself, I open my heart today for the Holy Spirit to join me as my divine Partner so I can be more than a conqueror in every situation!

I pray this in Jesus' name!

MY CONFESSION FOR TODAY

I confess that the Holy Spirit is my leading Partner in this life. When I need help, He is right by my side, ready to help me and to pull me through each challenge that I face. I know His voice; I partner with Him; and as a result, I enjoy continuous victory in my life.

I declare this by faith in Jesus' name!

QUESTIONS FOR YOU TO CONSIDER

1. Can you think of a time when you have experienced the supernatural help of the Holy Spirit?
2. What immediate change occurred when you sensed the Holy Spirit join you in that situation?
3. Do you need the Holy Spirit's supernatural assistance with any challenges that you're facing right now? Why don't you write down those areas and talk to the Lord about them today?

The Holy Spirit feels everything you feel. He understands the complete inadequacy you are experiencing in your life right now.

MARCH 30

❧❧❧

Don't Get in a Hurry!

But as we were allowed of God to be put in trust with the gospel,
even so we speak; not as pleasing men, but God, which trieth our hearts.
— 1 Thessalonians 2:4

H
ave you ever wondered, *God, how long am I going to have to wait for that promotion I deserve? Is there a reason that the promotion I want keeps getting delayed? What is happening in my life, Lord?*

We always seems concerned about making things happen faster, but God doesn't work in the same time frame we do. There are some things that are more important to God than giving us a promotion when we want it or making sure we get a pay raise when we think we deserve it.

Now, God does reward us for our faithfulness, but sometimes He takes a little longer than we might like to promote us in order to make sure we're really ready for that next big assignment. It's hard on the flesh while we wait, yet it is actually the mercy of God at work. You see, during that time of waiting, the imperfections that would have ruined us are exposed so God can remove them. Then He can move us up into the new position with no concern that a hidden flaw will cause us to fall flat on our faces.

We know from Acts 9:20-25 that when Paul first became a Christian, he tried to barge right into a public ministry. But he wasn't ready for that yet and therefore created some problems and a lack of peace in the Early Church. Although saved and called, he simply wasn't ready to be promoted into such a visible position of leadership. It was going to take some time for God to prepare Paul for the kind of ministry and anointing he was going to carry in his life.

Paul referred to this process when he wrote to the Thessalonians. He said, "But as we were allowed of God to be put in trust with the gospel, even so we speak; not as pleasing men, but God, which trieth our hearts" (1 Thessalonians 2:4). This verse is packed full of insight regarding Paul's own experience of being prepared, tested, and finally promoted into his own public ministry.

Notice first that Paul says, "But as we were allowed of God...." The word "allowed" is the Greek word *dokimadzo*, a word that *means to test; to examine; to inspect; to scrutinize; to determine the quality or sincerity of a thing*. Because the object scrutinized has passed the test, it can now be viewed as *genuine* and *sincere*.

This word *dokimadzo* was also used to illustrate the test used to determine real and counterfeit coinage. After a scrutinizing test was performed, the bona fide coinage would stand up to the test and the counterfeit would fail. The strictness conveyed by the word *dokimadzo* is evident by an early use of this word to picture the refining of metal by fire to remove its impurities. First, the metal was placed in a fire that burned at a certain degree of heat; then it was placed in a fire burning at an even higher degree; and finally, it was placed in a blazing fire that burned at the highest degree of all. Three such tests were needed in order to remove from the metal all the unseen impurities that were hidden from the naked eye.

From the viewpoint of the naked eye, the metal probably looked strong and ready to be used even prior to those tests. But unseen defects were resident in the metal that would have shown up later as a break, a fracture, or some kind of malfunction. Before a person could be assured that the metal was free of defects and thus ready to be used, these three purifying tests at three different degrees of blazing hot fire were required. The fire was hot and the process was lengthy, but the tests were necessary in order to achieve the desired result.

Because Paul uses the word *dokimadzo,* he testifies to us:

"It was a lengthy process and I went through a lot of refining fires to get to this place, but finally I passed the test and God saw that I was genuinely ready...."

So don't be discouraged if it takes time for your dream to become a reality in your life! God never gets in a hurry, because godly character is more important to Him than gifts, talents, or temporary success in the eyes of other people. He wants to use you, but He also wants you to be ready to be used!

Right now you may need some time to prepare, change, and grow. That way when God finally promotes you, you'll have what you need both naturally and spiritually to STAY established in that God-ordained position as you fulfill your assignment with excellence.

MY PRAYER FOR TODAY

Lord, thank You for considering my character so carefully. I know that You want to change me and conform me into the image of Jesus more than anything else. I often feel rushed to get things moving, but I know that You are looking to see if I have the character I need so I can successfully do what You've called me to do. I yield my heart to You and ask You to do Your work inside me. Change me so You can use me as You wish!

I pray this in Jesus' name!

MY CONFESSION FOR TODAY

I declare by faith that I am being changed so God can use me to the degree He desires! Yes, I have areas in my life that need to be transformed, but because I renew my mind with the Word of God and spend time in prayer, God is free to work on me and get me ready for the big job He has designed for my life. I know that as I stay open and willing to change, my character WILL be transformed into the image of Jesus so I can complete my task successfully and to the glory of God!

I declare this by faith in Jesus' name!

QUESTIONS FOR YOU TO CONSIDER

1. Do you think you're ready for a big new promotion?
2. If it seems like your promotion has gotten delayed again and again, do you have any idea why this might be happening?
3. Are there any areas of weakness in your life that could hinder you once you step into a more visible and demanding role? What are those areas you need to work on?

MARCH 31

❧

Jesus' Last Lesson For the Disciples

And I will pray the Father,
and he shall give you another comforter....
— John 14:16

I've often heard Christians ask, "I wonder what it must have been like to walk with Jesus. Wouldn't it be wonderful to walk with Him and to hear His voice and talk to Him?" But believers who ask these kinds of questions don't understand the ministry of the Holy Spirit. If they did, they'd know that having the Holy Spirit with them is just like having Jesus right at their side!

Because Jesus was about to depart from the world, He knew it was absolutely essential that the disciples learn how to rely entirely on the Spirit of God and to follow His leadership. Therefore, Jesus used His last moments to teach the disciples how to follow the Holy Spirit's leadership in the same way they had followed Him.

It must have seemed strange to the disciples as they listened to Jesus speak about the Holy Spirit. They had been accustomed to Jesus' physically and visibly leading them, but now they were learning that the Spirit of God would become their Leader. This would be a Leader they couldn't see, couldn't touch, and couldn't audibly hear; yet they were supposed to follow Him just as they had followed Jesus. They were probably thinking, *What is the Holy Spirit's leadership going to be like in our lives? Does He act and think differently than Jesus? What is it going to be like to follow the Spirit of God?*

Knowing that these were normal questions to ask, Jesus used His final moments with the disciples to dispel all fear and insecurity they might have felt about following the Holy Spirit's leadership. This is why Jesus was so careful to use key words when He spoke to them about the coming of the Holy Spirit. In John 14:16, for example, Jesus said, "And I will pray the Father, and he shall give you *another* comforter...."

Notice that word "another." I want to draw your attention to this very important word today. In Greek, there are two possible words for *another*. The first is the Greek word *allos*, and the second is the Greek word *heteros*. The word *allos* means *one of the very same kind; same character; same everything;* or *a duplicate*. The second word, *heteros*, means *one of another kind* or *one of a different kind*. This word *heteros* forms the first part of the word *heterosexual*, which, of course, describes someone who has sexual relations with a person of the opposite sex.

The Greek word used in John 14:16 is the first word, *allos*. The word *allos* emphatically means that the Holy Spirit would be like Jesus in every way. This conveys a very strong and important message about the Holy Spirit. Jesus wanted the disciples to know that the Holy Spirit was just like Him. Following the Holy Spirit wouldn't be any different than following Him, except the Spirit's leadership would be invisible rather than physical and visible, as Jesus' leadership had been.

**One translator says the word *allos* in John 14:16
could be translated to mean:**

*"I will pray to the Father, and He will send you Someone who is just like Me in every way.
He will be identical to Me in the way He speaks, the way He thinks, the way He operates,*

the way He see things, and the way He does things. He will be exactly like Me in every way. If the Holy Spirit is here, it will be just as if I am here because We think, behave, and operate exactly the same...."

Earlier in John 14, Philip told the Lord, "...Shew us the Father, and it sufficeth us" (v. 8). Jesus answered, "...Have I been so long time with you, and yet hast thou not known me, Philip? he that hath seen me hath seen the Father; and how sayest thou then, Shew us the Father" (v. 9).

Jesus was the exact image of the Father when He walked on this earth. Hebrews 1:3 (*AMP*) declares, "He is the sole expression of the glory of God [the Light-being, the out-raying or radiance of the divine], and He is the perfect imprint *and* very image of [God's] nature...." This means Jesus reflected the character of His Heavenly Father in every way. That is why Jesus told Philip, "...He that hath seen me hath seen the Father...."

If you see Jesus, you see the Father. By looking at Jesus, you can discover the Father's will. Jesus did and said exactly what the Father would do and say. His life, attitudes, and actions were the absolute manifested will of the Father, for the two were united in nature, in character, in thought, and in deed.

As Jesus teaches the disciples about the Holy Spirit, He takes this truth one step further. Just as Jesus is the *exact image* of the Father in every way, now Jesus unmistakably tells the disciples that when the Holy Spirit comes, He will *exactly* represent Jesus in every word. That's why the word *allos* is used to make this point. It leaves no room for doubt that the Holy Spirit will be exactly like Jesus.

The word *allos* tells us the Holy Spirit perfectly represents the life and nature of Jesus Christ. Jesus did only what the Heavenly Father would do, and now the Holy Spirit will do only what Jesus would do. As Jesus' Representative on earth, the Holy Spirit never acts on His own or out of character with the life of Jesus Christ.

You see, the Spirit of God was sent to bring us the life of Jesus. Just as Jesus told Philip, "If you've seen Me, you've seen the Father," now He is telling us, "If you have the Holy Spirit, it will be just as if you have Me."

You and I must stop looking backward and grieving over what we missed by not living two thousands years ago. Instead, we must learn to let the Holy Spirit lead and guide us, just as He did in the Early Church. Jesus' physical absence didn't stop the early believers from performing miracles, raising the dead, casting out demons, healing the sick, or bringing multitudes to a saving knowledge of Jesus Christ. Because the Holy Spirit was with them, the ministry of Jesus continued uninterrupted in their midst.

Why don't you start opening your heart to the work of the Spirit today? He wants to represent Jesus to you, your church, your family, your business, and your city, just as He did to believers who lived during the time of the book of Acts. Remember, if you have the Holy Spirit working alongside you, it's just like having Jesus right there at your side!

MY PRAYER FOR TODAY

Lord, help me learn how to work with the Holy Spirit! I don't want to waste time grieving over what I missed by not living two thousands years ago, so I ask You to teach me how to let the Spirit lead and guide me. Your Word teaches that because the Holy Spirit is with me, the ministry of Jesus can continue uninterrupted in my life today. Holy Spirit, I ask You to bring me into a greater knowledge of how to work with You so that the ministry of Jesus can continue through me!

I pray this in Jesus' name!

MY CONFESSION FOR TODAY

I declare by faith that the Holy Spirit works mightily in my life. I know His voice; I discern His leading; and I boldly do what He tells me to do. Because I am obedient to His voice, the life of Jesus Christ is manifested in me. Having the Holy Spirit work with me is just like having Jesus right by my side all the time. Just as Jesus worked miracles in the book of Acts through the apostles, the Holy Spirit works miracles through me today — healing the sick, casting out demons, and bringing salvation to the lost through Jesus Christ!

I declare this by faith in Jesus' name!

QUESTIONS FOR YOU TO CONSIDER

1. Can you say that the Holy Spirit is working powerfully in your life right now? If you say yes, what is the evidence that lets you know He is working mightily through you? Ponder this question, and write down your answers on a piece of paper.
2. When you read the Gospels, does it seem like you're reading about the same Jesus who works in your life today — or about a historical Jesus who did things you've never experienced?
3. What actions and changes do you need to take so the Holy Spirit can become a supernatural Partner in your life?

The Holy Spirit would be the disciples' new Leader. This would be a Leader they couldn't see, couldn't touch, and couldn't audibly hear; yet they were supposed to follow Him just as faithfully as they had followed Jesus. They were probably thinking, *What is the Holy Spirit's leadership going to be like in our lives? Does He act and think differently than Jesus? What is it going to be like to follow the Spirit of God?*

Because the month of April is normally the time that Easter is celebrated, I have dedicated all the *Sparkling Gems* for the entire month of April to the following subjects:

✦ *Jesus' final hours with His disciples*
✦ *Jesus' prayer in the Garden of Gethsemane*
✦ *Jesus' arrest in the Garden of Gethsemane*
✦ *Jesus' trial before Pontius Pilate*
✦ *Jesus' appearance before King Herod*
✦ *Jesus' scourging and beating*
✦ *Jesus' crown of thorns*
✦ *Jesus' crucifixion*
✦ *Jesus' burial*
✦ *Jesus' resurrection*

I believe that the information that follows in April's *Sparkling Gems* will be revelational and life-changing for you. My prayer is that these Gems will give you insights into these events that you have never seen or heard before.

APRIL 1

❧❦❧

How the Devil Turned
A Friend Into a Betrayer!

And supper being ended, the devil having now put
into the heart of Judas Iscariot, Simon's son, to betray him.
— John 13:2

Have you ever felt *betrayed* by a friend or by someone you dearly loved? When it happened, were you *shocked*? Did it feel like that person put a knife in your back by violating your trust and revealing things that should have been kept in confidence? Did you marvel that such a trusted friend could turn out to be so disloyal? Did you wonder, *How in the world could a person so dear and close be used so viciously by the devil to attack me in this way?*

It's painful when a friend betrays you. It's even worse when the person is your best friend or someone you've known and trusted for many years.

Betrayal is something that has happened to people since the beginning of time. It is simply a fact that the devil is a master at distorting and ruining relationships. He knows how to lure people into situations where they end up feeling offended or hurt; then he coaxes them to nurture their offense until it mutates into strife that separates even the best of friends and family.

Don't forget — Satan was kicked out of Heaven because of his unique ability to create confusion, discord, and strife. Heaven is as perfect as an environment can be; yet in that perfect environment, the devil was still able to affect one-third of the angels with his slanderous allegations against God. Angels who had worshiped together for eons of time now stood opposed to each other over issues the devil had conjured up in their minds.

That should tell you how clever the devil is at creating discord and strife! If the devil is persuasive enough to do this with angels, think how much easier it is for him to deceive people who live in a far-from-perfect environment and who wrestle daily with their own imperfections and self-images!

Satan watches for that opportune moment when a person is tired, weary, or exasperated; then he waits until someone does something that person doesn't understand or agree with. Suddenly it is as if the devil shoots a fiery arrow of rage straight into the person's emotions! Before long, strife, bitterness, unforgiveness, and division begin to mount. Friends who once stood side by side and cherished each other now stand facing each other as hostile rivals.

If this sounds familiar, be encouraged! This same scenario happened *to Jesus*! After working with Judas Iscariot for three years, the devil found his way into Judas' soul, turning him so sour against Jesus that this disciple became His betrayer. But we need to ask, *What opened the door for this deception to occur inside Judas?*

In John 13:2, the Bible gives us a very powerful insight into the way the devil establishes a foothold in people's minds. Back in John 12:3-7, Mary brought a pound of spikenard and poured it on Jesus' feet. Judas thought her act of love was a waste of money and took issue with Jesus about it. But Jesus told Judas to leave Mary alone and allowed her to continue. John 13:2 then tells us, "And supper being ended, the devil having now put into the heart of Judas Iscariot, Simon's son, to betray him."

What was the exact moment that Satan put this thought into Judas' heart? Apparently, it was when Judas became offended with Jesus about the spikenard. Perhaps Judas didn't agree with Jesus' decision, or maybe he didn't like the fact that Jesus told him to leave Mary alone. Whatever the reason, it was at that moment of disagreement that the devil found an open door into Judas' heart.

Especially notice the phrase "...the devil having now put into the heart of Judas Iscariot...." The words "put into" come from the Greek word *ballo*, which means *to throw, to cast, to thrust,* or *to inject*. This word *ballo* carries the idea of *a very fast action of throwing, thrusting, or injecting something forward*, such as the throwing of a ball or rock, or the forward thrusting of a sharp knife.

It is significant that this word was used in this context, because it tells us how quickly the devil moved to inject a seed of betrayal into Judas' heart. When the seed of betrayal was injected, it went so deep that it turned Judas — one of Jesus' closest associates — into a deceiver and a betrayer. Judas became the epitome of a disloyal and unfaithful friend.

When Satan finally penetrated Judas' mind and emotions with this seed of betrayal, he injected it so hard and fast that it became *deeply embedded* or *lodged* in Judas' soul.

John 13:2 could therefore be translated:

"...the devil having now thrust into...."
"...the devil having now inserted into...."
"...the devil having now forcibly hurled into...."
"...the devil having now embedded into...."

There is no doubt that the word *ballo* means the devil *quickly seized* an opportunity *to inject* a seed of betrayal into Judas' heart. He was so offended by Jesus that a window to his heart and emotions opened, even if only for a brief moment. When the devil saw that opening, he moved like lightning to penetrate Judas' mind and emotions in order to sour a long-term relationship and turn a trusted friend into a betrayer.

Judas was used as Satan's instrument because he allowed the enemy to drive a wedge between him and Jesus. Rather than let go of the disagreement and forget about it, Judas let the issue become a big deal in his mind — something so blown out of proportion that the devil was able to use the offense to lure him into the ultimate act of disloyalty. Because Judas didn't take his thoughts captive, the devil succeeded in tainting his view of Jesus. This then led to a disastrous effect on Judas' relationship with Him.

It is important that you learn how to recognize those times when the devil tries to inject a seed of division into your heart. He wants to drive a wedge between you and the people you love. Rather than let him get away with this evil tactic, make a decision to resist every temptation to get angry and offended. By resisting these thoughts, you can take a stand against the devil and protect your relationships.

Learn from the example of Judas Iscariot. Determine that you will never let any issue get so blown out of proportion that it turns you into a disloyal, lying, betraying friend. And if you are hurting right now because someone has recently betrayed and hurt you, choose the route of forgiveness! Remember, what you sow is what you reap — and if you sow forgiveness now, you will reap forgiveness from others when you need it in the future!

MY PRAYER FOR TODAY

Lord, please forgive me for the times I've allowed the devil to put a wedge between me and the people You have placed in my life. Help me go to them and ask forgiveness for the things

I did wrong. Help me also to extend patience, forgiveness, and love to others who have done wrong to me or who will wrong me in the future. I never want the devil to be in charge of my emotions or my thought life, so I am asking You to help me think clearly and to know how to recognize those times when the devil tries to upset me and ruin my relationships.

I pray this in Jesus' name!

MY CONFESSION FOR TODAY

I confess that my mind is free of offense, unforgiveness, and strife. Because I walk in mercy and forgiveness, the devil has no entrance or open door to find his way into my mind and emotions. The Spirit of God dominates my thinking and helps me see things very clearly!

I declare this by faith in Jesus' name!

QUESTIONS FOR YOU TO CONSIDER

1. Have you ever been aware of a moment when the devil was trying to sow a seed of discord into your soul against someone you dearly loved?
2. Did you know that you faced a choice — that you could either overlook what the person had done to offend you, or you could let the offense get lodged deep down inside your soul?
3. Did you let the devil divide you and that person you loved, or did you win the victory by making the choice that you would not allow the devil to disrupt such an important long-term relationship?

APRIL 2

Have You Ever Felt 'Agony' Over Situations You Have Faced in Life?

And there appeared an angel unto him from heaven,
strengthening him. And being in an agony he prayed more earnestly:
and his sweat was as it were great drops of blood
falling down to the ground.
— Luke 22:43,44

H ave you ever wondered where all your friends were at a time when you really needed them? They pledged they would be faithful, but when you needed them, they were nowhere to be found! Did you feel abandoned in that moment of need? Jesus Himself was confronted with that same situation when He was in the Garden of Gethsemane on the night before His crucifixion.

After Jesus was finished serving Communion to His disciples in the upper room, the Bible tells us that He went to the Garden of Gethsemane with His disciples. Knowing the Cross and the grave was before Him, Jesus felt a need to spend time in intercession so He might have the strength needed to face what lay before Him. He also requested that Peter, James, and John come apart to pray with Him.

Rarely, if ever, did Jesus need His friends' assistance; most of the time, they needed His! But in this intense moment, Jesus really felt a need to have the three disciples who were closest to Him pray with Him. Jesus asked these disciples to pray for just one hour. But instead of faithfully praying when Jesus desperately needed their support, they kept falling asleep!

The mental and spiritual battle Jesus was experiencing that night in the Garden of Gethsemane was intense. In fact, Luke 22:44 says, "And being in an agony he prayed more earnestly: and his sweat was as it were great drops of blood falling down to the ground."

Today I want you to especially notice the word "agony" in this verse. It comes from the Greek word *agonidzo*, a word that refers to *a struggle, a fight, great exertion,* or *effort*. It is where we get the word *agony* — a word often used in the New Testament to convey the ideas of *anguish, pain, distress,* and *conflict*. The word *agonidzo* itself comes from the word *agon*, which is the word that depicted the *athletic conflicts and competitions* that were so famous in the ancient world.

The Holy Spirit used this word to picture Jesus in the Garden of Gethsemane on the night of His betrayal. This tells us that Jesus was thrown into *a great struggle* and *fight* that night. Knowing that the Cross and the grave were before Him, He cried out, "Father, if thou be willing, remove this cup from me..." (Luke 22:42).

The spiritual pressure that bore down upon Jesus' soul was so overwhelming that the Bible says it was *agonidzo*, or *agony*. It was so strenuous that it involved all of Jesus' spirit, soul, and body. He was in the greatest fight He had ever known up to that moment.

Jesus' intense level of agony is depicted in the phrase, "...he prayed more *earnestly*...." The word "earnestly" is the Greek word *ektenes*, a Greek word that means *to be extended* or *to be stretched out*. A person in this kind of agony might drop to the ground, writhing in pain and rolling this way and that way. This word *ektenes* presents the picture of a person who is pushed to the limit and can't be stretched much more. He is on the brink of all he can possibly endure.

Jesus' emotional state was so intense that it says "...his sweat was as it were great drops of blood falling down to the ground." The "sweat" is the Greek word *idros*. The word "drops" is the Greek word *thrombos*, a medical word that points to *blood that is unusually thickly clotted*. When these two words are joined, they depict a medical condition called *hematidrosis* — a condition that occurs only in individuals who are in a highly emotional state.

Because the mind is under such great mental and emotional pressure, it sends signals of stress throughout the human body. These signals become so strong that the body reacts as if it were under actual physical pressure. As a result, the first and second layer of skin separate, causing a vacuum to form between them. Thickly clotted blood seeps from this vacuum, oozing through the pores of the skin. Once the blood seeps through, it mingles with the sufferer's sweat that pours from his skin as a result of his intense inner struggle. In the end, the blood and sweat mix together and flow down the victim's face like droplets to the ground.

This was the worst spiritual combat Jesus had ever endured up to this time. Where were His disciples when He needed them? They were *sleeping*! He needed His closest friends — yet they couldn't even pray for one hour! So God provided strength for Jesus in another way, which we will see in tomorrow's *Sparkling Gem*.

Have you ever felt a need for help but found your friends couldn't be counted on? Did you find your friends sleeping on the job when you felt a deep need for help and support? Were you in a situation that caused you to feel intense agony or pushed to the limit? Are you in that kind of situation right now?

Maybe you've never sweat blood and tears. But more than likely, you have struggled in your soul at one time or another because of problems with your marriage, your children, your relationships, your ministry, or your finances. If you've ever felt like you were constantly living in a "pressure cooker," you know that continuous pressure is hard to deal with — *especially* if you have no one to lean on for strength, encouragement, and help.

If you are experiencing one of those times right now, Jesus understands because He faced the same situation in the Garden of Gethsemane. Hebrews 2:18 says, "For in that he himself hath suffered being tempted, he is able to succour them that are tempted." Because of what Jesus experienced, He is able to understand everything you are thinking and feeling today. So take a few minutes to pray, and talk to Jesus about the situations you are facing. *He empathizes completely, and He will give you the strength you need to make it today!*

MY PRAYER FOR TODAY

Lord, I need a little relief from the stress and pressure I've been under lately. I'm so thankful You understand what I'm feeling and going through in my life right now. Sometimes I feel so lonely in my situation. Even when my friends want to help, I don't know how to express myself. But I know that You understand me, even when I can't get the right words out of my mouth. So, Lord, today I am asking You to come alongside me in a special way. Undergird me with Your strength, power, and wisdom. Thank You for understanding me and for helping me today!

I pray this in Jesus' name!

MY CONFESSION FOR TODAY

I boldly confess that Jesus Christ understands and empathizes with me and the situations I am facing right now. Because He understands, I go to Him and talk to Him, knowing that He hears me when I pray. And not only does He listen to me, but He also answers the prayers and the cries of my heart. I do not have to face my challenges today alone because Jesus is with me, empowering me to stand tall, to stand firm, and to hold my head high! With Him as my Helper, I will not only survive but will thrive and prosper in spite of what the devil has tried to do to me.

I declare this by faith in Jesus' name!

QUESTIONS FOR YOU TO CONSIDER

1. Have you ever found yourself in a situation where you were pushed to the limit of what you thought you could endure?
2. In that situation, did you turn to the Lord for strength and comfort and talk to Him about it?
3. In what way did the Lord bring strength and comfort to your soul when there may not have been another person there to help you?

APRIL 3

❦

Supernatural Assistance When You Don't Know Where To Turn for Help!

And there appeared an angel unto him
from heaven, strengthening him.
— Luke 22:43

I'll never forget the time years ago that our ministry was under a great assault. For no reason we could logically explain, the financial gifts of our partners seemed to dry up and dwindle away for a number of months. After this drought had gone on for several months, our situation became so serious that I didn't know how we were going to pay for our television broadcasts that covered the length and breadth of the former Soviet Union. It was time to pay the bills, and I didn't have the money.

As I walked through the city of Moscow that cold winter night, I broke inside from the pressure I had been feeling. I stopped at Red Square, leaned against a rail, and literally wept, not even caring about the people who passed by me. I felt so frustrated because I didn't know what to do. We had drained everything we had to keep those broadcasts on the air. Millions of people watched our television programs, and those hungry souls were depending on us. God had entrusted me with taking His Word to these former Soviet nations, and I took that responsibility seriously. But because our finances had dwindled, I found myself in an extremely hard spot.

After riding on the subway system for several hours while I tried to pull my thoughts together, I felt myself sinking deeper into a feeling of desperation. The reality was that if something didn't happen to quickly change the situation, I would have to cancel our program, and all those millions who waited for it each week would lose the teaching of God's Word.

I had just come up from the subway on my way to the television meeting when I leaned against that rail in Red Square and wept before the Lord. I felt so alone, so trapped, so unable to fix my problem. There didn't seem to be anyone I could call or turn to who could comprehend the enormity of what I was tackling in the spiritual realm that night.

I cried out, *"Lord, why has this happened? Is there a reason our supporters have temporarily stopped their support? Have we done anything that opened a door for the devil to disrupt our finances? Please tell me what I am supposed to do right now about this situation. What about the millions of people who are waiting for Your Word? Do we just disappear from television and leave them wondering what happened to us?"*

All of a sudden, it felt like a divine force entered me! Strength and courage flooded into my soul. I knew God was touching me, giving me a new supernatural boost of courage and faith to face this moment victoriously. Within minutes, my tears disappeared, my desperation vanished, and I began to celebrate the victory! Although I still didn't have the cash in hand to cover all the television bills, I knew the battle had been won in the Spirit. As it turned out, the money didn't come in all at once, but the valve had been turned on again and the gifts of our partners began to flow back into the ministry. I thank God for the supernatural assistance He gave me that night!

Have you ever known a time when you felt alone in the challenge you were facing? On the night of Jesus' betrayal, He must have felt that way. He asked His closest disciples — Peter, James, and John — to come apart and pray with Him in those last hours. But every time He came back to check on the three men, they were sleeping. Jesus was experiencing a great spiritual battle and extreme pressure that night (*see* April 2); that's why He wanted His closest disciples to assist Him in prayer. However, that night they were not found faithful.

But when Jesus could find no one to stand with Him in His hour of need, God provided supernatural assistance! Luke 22:43 says, "And there appeared an angel unto him from heaven, strengthening him." This supernatural strength made up for any lack of support from His three closest disciples.

When Luke writes that the angel "strengthened" him, he uses the Greek word *enischuo*. This is a compound of the words *en* and *ischuos*. The word *en* means *in*, and the word *ischuos* is the word for *might* or *strength*. Normally in New Testament times, the word *ischuos* was used to denote *men with great muscular abilities*, similar to the bodybuilders in today's world. But when these two words *en* and *ischuos* are compounded together, the new word means *to impart strength; to empower someone; to fill a person with heartiness;* or *to give someone a renewed vitality*. A person may have been feeling exhausted and depleted, but he suddenly gets a blast of energy so robust that he is *instantly recharged*! Now he is ready to get up, get with it, and get going again!

This means that when Jesus' disciples and friends couldn't be depended on in His hour of need, God provided an angel that *imparted strength, empowered,* and *recharged* Jesus, *renewing His vitality* with the strength needed to victoriously face the most difficult hour in His life! After being super-charged, Jesus was ready to face the Cross. He awakened His disciples and said, "Rise up, let us go; lo, he that betrayeth me is at hand" (Mark 14:42).

Maybe you've had a time in your life when you felt trapped and alone. Perhaps you thought your friends would help you, but now you feel like they let you down at a time when you really needed them. Don't let desperation take over! Your friends may have fallen asleep on the job, but God hasn't fallen asleep! He is absolutely committed to seeing you through the situation you are facing right now. And if necessary, He will provide supernatural assistance to recharge you and keep you moving full steam ahead. You may be tempted to feel isolated and alone, but if your spirit's eyes were opened just for a moment, you would see that you are not alone at all! He is surrounding you with the Holy Spirit's power, angels, and anything else needed to keep you going forward!

So remember — regardless of the particular battle or situation you are facing in life, God will always come to your assistance. If no one else is faithful, God will see to it that you receive the strength and power you need to victoriously overcome in every circumstance. Supernatural assistance is yours today!

MY PRAYER FOR TODAY

Lord, I thank You for this word from You that has spoken so directly into my life today. It's true that I feel very alone and trapped in the situation I'm facing right now. I don't know what to do, what step to take, what to say, or where to turn. I've tried to give the problem to You, but in some way I've continued to carry part of the load by myself, and it is starting to break me. Right now — at this very moment — I am throwing the full weight of my burden and cares on Your huge shoulders! I thank You for taking this burden from me and for filling me with the strength I need to press through this time in my life!

I pray this in Jesus' name!

MY CONFESSION FOR TODAY

I confess that God is committed to seeing me through the situation I am facing right now. He is providing all the supernatural assistance I need to get recharged and to keep me moving full steam ahead! Even though I am tempted to feel isolated and alone, I am not alone! God is filling me with power; He is surrounding me with angels; and He is ready to provide me with anything else I need to keep moving forward to fulfill His will for my life!

I declare this by faith in Jesus' name!

QUESTIONS FOR YOU TO CONSIDER

1. Can you recall some very desperate situations in your life when you felt trapped — like there was no way out — but suddenly the Lord filled you with strength and brought you through victoriously?
2. Can you think of two times in your life when you were absolutely aware that God was supernaturally filling you with the special strength you needed for that exact moment? If so, why don't you take a few minutes to write down those memories and think about God's faithfulness to you?
3. Has there ever been a particular situation in your life when you sensed the presence of angels on the scene, ministering on your behalf?

APRIL 4

How Many Soldiers Does It Take To Arrest One Man?

Judas then, having received a band of men and officers
from the chief priests and Pharisees, cometh thither
with lanterns and torches and weapons.
— John 18:3

*J*esus has the greatest power in the whole universe! When He walked the earth, He healed the sick, cast out demons, raised the dead, walked on water, changed water into wine, and multiplied loaves and fishes. In fact, Jesus performed so many miracles that the apostle John said, "And there are also many other things which Jesus did, the which, if they should be written every one, I suppose that even the world itself could not contain the books that should be written..." (John 21:25).

Satan was terrified of Jesus. That's why the enemy inspired Herod the Great to try to kill the infant Messiah by slaughtering all the babies in Bethlehem and the surrounding region (Matthew 2:16). When that failed, the devil tried to wipe out Jesus by attempting to seduce Him with temptations in the wilderness. And when *that* failed, the devil tried to kill Jesus on numerous occasions using angry religious people!

Do you recall the many times religious leaders tried and failed to catch Jesus? The Gospels are filled with examples when He supernaturally slipped out of the hands of His aggressors. (*See* Luke 4:30, John 7:30, John 8:59, and John 10:39.)

Now it was time for Satan's next attempt using Judas Iscariot — and it seems that the devil was worried he wouldn't succeed again! Thus, the enemy inspired Judas to lead a massive group of Roman soldiers and temple police to arrest Jesus. There were far too many soldiers in this group to capture just one individual — *unless that individual was the Son of God*!

The religious leaders the devil was using were also filled with hate toward Jesus. Considering how many times Jesus had previously slipped out of their hands, they must have worried that He might slip away this time too.

After serving Communion to His disciples, Jesus retreated to the Garden of Gethsemane to pray. John 18:2 tells us that it was Jesus' custom to go there to pray with His disciples. Therefore, Judas knew precisely where to find Jesus that night when it was time to lead the soldiers and temple police to arrest Him.

John 18:3 says, "Judas then, having received a band of men and officers from the chief priests and Pharisees, cometh thither with lanterns and torches and weapons." This verse says Judas received "...a band of men and officers from the chief priests and Pharisees...." I want you to understand exactly who this "band of men" and these "officers from the chief priests" were so you can see the full picture of what happened that night on the Mount of Olives. I believe you will be flabbergasted when you realize the gigantic numbers of armed men who came looking for Jesus that night!

The soldiers Judas brought with him to the Garden of Gethsemane were soldiers who served at the Tower of Antonia — a tower that had been built by the Hasmonean rulers. Later it was renamed the "Tower of Antonia" by King Herod in honor of one of his greatest patrons, Marc Antony (yes, the same Marc Antony who fell in love with the Egyptian queen Cleopatra!).

The Tower of Antonia was a massive edifice that was built on a rock and rose seventy-five feet into the air. Its sides had been completely smoothed flat to make it difficult for enemies to scale its walls. Although it had many towers, the highest one was located on the southeast corner, giving the watchman an uninhibited view of the temple area as well as much of Jerusalem.

Inside this massive complex was a large inner courtyard for exercising the Roman cohort — comprised of 300 to 600 specially trained soldiers — that was stationed there. These troops were poised to act defensively in the event of an insurgency or riot. In fact, a staircase led from the tower into the temple, enabling the troops to enter the temple in a matter of minutes should a disturbance develop there. One writer has noted that there was even a secret passageway from the tower to the inner court of the priests, making it possible for troops to reach even that holy, off-limits location.

John 18:3 records that there was "a band of men" in the Garden that night. The Greek word for "a band of men" is *spira*. This is the word that describes *a military cohort* — the group of 300 to 600 soldiers mentioned above. These extremely well-trained soldiers were equipped with the finest weaponry of the day.

John 18:3 also tells us that on the night Jesus was arrested, this band of soldiers was accompanied by "...officers from the chief priests and Pharisees...." The word "officers" is from the Greek word *huperetas*. The word *huperetas* has several meanings in New Testament times, but in this case, it described the "police officers" who worked on the temple grounds. Once a judgment was given from the religious court of law, it was the responsibility of the temple police to execute these judgments. This fearsome armed force worked daily with the cohort stationed at the Tower of Antonia and reported to the chief priests, the Pharisees, and the Sanhedrin. These were the "officers" who accompanied the Roman soldiers to the Garden of Gethsemane.

We can therefore conclude that when the Roman soldiers and temple police arrived to arrest Jesus, the hillside where the Garden was located was literally covered with Roman soldiers and highly trained militia from the Temple Mount. I want you to really see what a huge crowd of armed men came that night, so let's look at what the other Gospels tell us about this same incident.

Matthew 26:47 says it was "a great multitude" of soldiers, using the Greek words *ochlos polus* to indicate that it was *a huge multitude* of armed men. Mark 14:43 calls it "a great multitude," using the Greek word *ochlos,* indicating that it was *a massive crowd.* Luke 22:47 also uses the word *ochlos* to indicate the band of soldiers that came that night was *enormous.*

It makes one wonder what Judas had told the chief priests about Jesus that made them think they needed a small army to arrest Him! Did Judas forewarn them that Jesus and His disciples might put up a fight? Or is it possible that the chief priests were nervous that Jesus might use His supernatural power to resist them?

Certainly Jesus was known for His power! After all, He had ministered for three years — healing the sick, cleansing lepers, casting out demons, raising the dead, walking on water, changing water into wine, and multiplying loaves and fishes. The stories of Jesus' power must have already been legendary even during His lifetime here on earth!

Even Herod heard of Jesus' powers and longed to be an eyewitness himself of the miracles He performed (*see* Luke 23:8). We saw what the apostle John said about this in John 21:25: The world itself couldn't contain all the books it would take to record every one of Jesus' miracles. So it's not too hard to imagine that the majority of people in Jesus' day had heard stories of the extraordinary power that flowed through Him.

It thrills my heart to think of the power of Jesus Christ! Even more thrilling is the knowledge that the same power that flowed through Him when He walked on this earth now flows through you and me. The same Holy Spirit who anointed Jesus to fulfill His ministry has been sent to empower you and me to do the same works He did! In fact, Jesus prophesied that we would do even greater works (John 14:12). This is the kind of power that operates in you and me!

Anytime the devil tries to insinuate that you're not a serious threat to be feared, you need to rise up and remind him of Who lives inside you! Tell the devil (and remind yourself at the same time) that the Greater One lives inside you (1 John 4:4) and that you are a world overcomer (1 John 5:4). Remind yourself every day that the same power that raised Jesus from the dead now lives inside you and is at your disposal 24 hours a day. And the next time you're faced with a situation that requires power, open your heart and let it flow — because the anointing that was on Jesus now rests on you!

MY PRAYER FOR TODAY

Lord, I am so thankful You possess the greatest power in the whole universe! I'm not serving a dead god; I'm serving a living Lord who is interceding for me at the right hand of the Father at this very moment. Jesus, I come to You as my great High Priest, and I ask You today to fill me with Your power 24 hours a day, 365 days a year. I don't want to just intellectually know about You; I want to truly know You. I want to experience Your power and walk in Your ways!

I pray this in Jesus' name!

I declare by faith that the Greater One lives inside me. I am a world overcomer! The same power that raised Jesus from the dead now lives inside me and is at my disposal 24 hours a day. When I'm faced with a situation that requires power, I open my heart and release the immense power of Jesus Christ that is stored up deep inside me. This power is continuously resident in my heart and is more than enough to face and overcome any obstacle the devil ever tries to throw in my way!

I declare this by faith in Jesus' name!

QUESTIONS FOR YOU TO CONSIDER

1. Do you live with a constant awareness of God's power living inside you?
2. What are some scriptures you can confess about the power of God that is available to you? It would be good for you to write them down and put them in a visible place so you can be reminded of them every day.
3. Can you think of some times in your life when the anointing of God was upon you so strongly that you were consciously aware of that mighty power flowing through you to others? If someone asked you what it felt like when the anointing was flowing through you, how would you describe it to them?

APRIL 5

A Full Moon, Lanterns,
Torches, and Weapons!

Judas then, having received a band of men and officers
from the chief priests and Pharisees, cometh thither
with lanterns and torches and weapons.
— John 18:3

Have you ever had an experience with someone who had a wrong perception of you? When you heard what that person thought of you, were you shocked to hear it? Did you wonder, *How could anyone ever think something like that about me?*

The more well-known you become, the more that people hear all kinds of rumors about you — most of which are completely untrue. You know how rumors work. When one person hears a rumor, he passes it along to another person, who then repeats it to someone else — and so it goes from one person to the next, growing more and more ridiculous with each telling. Finally, an entire story is being told that has no truth in it whatsoever; unfortunately, when people hear it, they believe it! *This is one reason Christians need to be very careful not to participate in gossip.*

I don't know what stories were being repeated about Jesus, but they must have been pretty wild. After all, when the Roman soldiers and temple police came to arrest Him in the Garden of Gethsemane, they were armed to the maximum! They also brought enough search lamps and lights to light up the entire Mount of Olives. What had they heard that made them think they needed to be so heavily equipped in order to find Jesus and the three disciples who were praying with Him that night?

Judas had obviously prepared them for the worst. He had seen Jesus perform innumerable miracles, so he knew very well about the massive power that operated through Him. Judas had also been present many times when religious leaders tried unsuccessfully to catch Jesus as He seemed to vanish, supernaturally slipping through the crowd to safety. So many times Jesus' enemies thought they had Him, but then suddenly — boom! He was gone!

When the troops arrived that night, they must have been operating on the basis of these stories. John 18:3 tells us, "Judas then, having received a band of men and officers from the chief priests and Pharisees, cometh thither with lanterns and torches and weapons." Today I want to draw your attention to the words "lanterns," "torches," and "weapons." When you see the impact of these words, you'll understand that the soldiers who had come to arrest Jesus were acting on presumptions about Him that were totally inaccurate!

In the first place, Passover occurred at the time of a full moon, so the night was already very well lighted at this time of year. But Judas didn't want to take a risk that Jesus and His disciples wouldn't be found; therefore, Judas obviously instructed these armed forces to be equipped to search, hunt, and track them down with the aid of "lanterns" and "torches."

The word "lantern" comes from the Greek word *lampas*. This word refers to *a bright and shining light*. It portrays something like a lampstand — a light that is intended to "light up" a room so you can see things better. A *lampas* was actually the equivalent of a first-century flashlight. Its light was so brilliant that it penetrated darkened areas and revealed things hidden in darkness.

In addition to these lamps, John 18:3 tells us that the soldiers also carried "torches." The word "torch" is from the Greek word *phanos*, a word that describes *a long-burning oil lamp*. The "lamps" mentioned above were brilliant but short-lived. These "torches," however, were oil-based, had a long wick, and could burn all night if necessary. The fact that these soldiers came with these torches strongly suggests that the soldiers and police were prepared to search all night. So when they came to the Garden of Gethsemane that night, they had enough bright shining lights (*lampas*) and long-burning oil lamps (*phanos*) to hunt for Jesus all night long.

Several hundred troops scoured the hillside, carrying brightly lighted lamps as they searched for Jesus. This was the scene that occurred that night. Were the soldiers apprehensive that Jesus and His disciples might hide from them?

A great number of caverns, holes, and caves were scattered all over the hill where the Garden of Gethsemane was located. The hillside was also a place of many graves with large tombstones, behind which a person could hide. Finally, the hill offered prime hiding spots in its many great olive trees with twisted branches. So why in the world would 300 to 600 soldiers, plus the temple police, need so many brilliantly lit lights to find Jesus unless they thought He would try to hide or escape from them?

John 18:3 also tells us that the soldiers and temple police brought "weapons" with them. The Greek word for "weapons" is *hoplos*, the very word that depicts *the full weaponry of a Roman soldier* referred to in Ephesians 6:13-18. This means the soldiers came attired in full weaponry — belt, breastplate, greaves, spikes, shoes, oblong shield, a brass helmet, a sword, and a lance. These 300 to 600 troops were ready for a *huge* skirmish and confrontation!

But there's still more to this story! In addition to the weapons the Roman soldiers bore that night, the temple police also came ready to put up a fight. Mark 14:43 says, "And immediately, while he yet spake, cometh Judas, one of the twelve, and with him a great multitude with swords and staves, from the chief priests and the scribes and the elders."

I want you to notice those words "swords" and "staves." The word "sword" is the Greek word *machaira*. It refers to *the most deadly type of sword*, one that was more often than not used for stabbing someone at close range. *Does this mean the temple police were ready to stab and draw blood that night?*

The word "stave" is from the Greek word *zhulos*. The word *zhulos* describes *a thick, heavy stick made of wood*. You might say it was a heavy-duty, dangerous, hard-hitting club intended to beat someone. When you look at the combined list of weapons brought to the Garden of Gethsemane that night, you will readily understand that these Roman soldiers and temple police were prepared to be militarily engaged!

As noted earlier, the stories being repeated about Jesus must have been pretty wild! What makes this even wilder is the likely prospect that Judas Iscariot was the one who fanned the flames of these rumors! He was right alongside the soldiers with all their lanterns, torches, and weapons.

Is it possible that after Judas had walked with Jesus for three years, he himself had never really come to know the real Jesus? Did Judas himself have a false perception of how Jesus would respond in such an event? It makes one wonder what kind of relationship Judas had with Jesus to perceive Him so inaccurately. The next two *Sparkling Gems* will sufficiently answer this question regarding the kind of relationship Judas *really* had with Jesus.

As you know, Jesus willfully went with the soldiers that night. He and His disciples did *not* hide or put up a fight. After being supernaturally empowered by the angel God sent to help Him, Jesus rose up and went out to greet Judas and the troops. However, I'm personally convinced that when Jesus saw Judas surrounded by hundreds upon hundreds of soldiers and temple officers with lanterns, torches, and weapons, it must have stunned Him! I think Jesus was surprised to learn just how erroneously Judas perceived Him.

The next time you hear that someone has a wrong perception about you, don't let it ruffle your feathers too much. Remember all the times you've had a wrong perception about someone else! You were just so sure that your opinion about that person was right, but then you discovered you were so wrong! If you've perceived others incorrectly at times, why should it surprise you when the same thing occasionally happens to you?

If you ever find yourself in this position, consider it an opportunity to show people who you really are! Notice that Jesus didn't say to those who came for Him in the Garden, "How dare you think so badly about Me!" Instead of arguing or trying to prove a point, He simply surrendered, went with the soldiers, and gave His life for the very men who arrested Him. The response Jesus made with His life was the greatest comeback He could have demonstrated to them!

So when people misunderstand you, back off and take some time to think and pray about the matter before you proceed. Don't let the devil get you all upset because you were misunderstood. This may be the greatest chance you'll ever have to show people the truth about who you really are!

MY PRAYER FOR TODAY

Lord, help me learn how to avoid misjudging and misperceiving other people. I know that when I misjudge someone, it affects my opinion of that person in a way that can open a door to the devil in our relationship with each other. I don't want to give the devil an inch in any of my relationships, so I need You to help me think cautiously, to take time to get to know people, and to give them the benefit of the doubt when I don't understand something they say or do. Help me give people the same mercy I would expect them to give me. And help me get started on this path today!

I pray this in Jesus' name!

MY CONFESSION FOR TODAY

I confess that it doesn't ruffle my feathers or upset me when I hear that someone has a wrong perception about me. I know I've made this same mistake about others in the past, so I am filled with mercy for those who misjudge or have misconceptions about who I am. I choose to be thankful for this situation and to see it as my opportunity to show people who I really am. I also take this opportunity to see what needs to be changed in my life and then to make the necessary adjustments so people never misperceive me in this way again!

I declare this by faith in Jesus' name!

QUESTIONS FOR YOU TO CONSIDER

1. Can you think of any times when you had misconceptions about someone else but later discovered that you were wrong about that person?
2. In light of that experience, do you believe you are now more cautious about what you think and say about others?
3. Since you know from personal experience how easy it is to have a false perception of someone, in what way does this help you when you discover someone has a wrong perception of *you*?

APRIL 6

The Judas Kiss

And he that betrayed him had given them a token, saying,
Whomsoever I shall kiss, that same is he; take him,
and lead him away safely. And as soon as he was come,
he goeth straightway to him, and saith,
Master, master; and kissed him.
— Mark 14:44,45

*H*ave you ever been stabbed in the back by someone you thought was a true friend? You had walked with him and spent much time with him; you had shared your thoughts and even your secrets with him, thinking that everything you said would be held in confidence between the two of you. Then you discovered that the commitment you felt for that person was not what he felt for you. Can you recall any hurtful moments in your life like this?

This is what happened to Jesus on the night Judas betrayed Him. It was no accidental betrayal, but one that was premeditated and meticulously implemented. Before Judas led the soldiers and temple police to the Garden of Gethsemane, he met with the religious leaders and negotiated a deal for Jesus' capture. During these meetings, he disclosed information about where Jesus prayed and where He met with His disciples. Judas must have also told them about Jesus' phenomenal power, which explains why so many troops came with weapons to arrest Jesus that night. It was in those meetings with the religious leaders that Judas agreed to receive a payment of thirty pieces of silver for delivering Jesus into their hands.

Because many of the soldiers and temple police had never seen Jesus before, Judas devised a special signal that would alert them to know who Jesus was. Mark 14:44 calls this special signal a "token," from the Greek word *sussemon,* meaning *a signal previously agreed upon.* This makes it emphatically clear that the kiss Judas gave Jesus was nothing more than a signal devised to let the troops know they needed to move swiftly to make their arrest.

Judas must have been very confused. On the one hand, he warned the religious leaders about Jesus' supernatural power so strongly that the soldiers arrived on the scene prepared to put up a serious fight with weapons of murder. But on the other hand, Judas told them that he thought he could deliver Jesus into their hands with a mere kiss!

These two conflicting pictures provide an excellent example to demonstrate the kind of confusion created inside a person who walks in deception. Deception is a powerful force that twists and distorts one's ability to see things clearly. Deceived people misperceive, misunderstand, misrepresent, and misjudge — and later don't even understand why they did what they did.

The different mixed signals Judas was giving about Jesus make it evident that Judas was both deceived and confused. He told the soldiers and temple police, "…Whomsoever I shall kiss, that same is he; take him, and lead him away safely." The word "kiss" is the Greek word *phileo.* This well-known Greek word is used to show *strong emotion, affection, and love.* Later, it came to represent such strong affection that it was used only between people who had *a strong bond* or *a deeply felt obligation* to each other, such as husbands and wives or family members. Later on, it came to be used as a form of greeting between especially dear and cherished friends.

During the time that the Gospels were written, the word *phileo* would have depicted *friends who were bound by some kind of obligation or covenant and who cherished each other very deeply.* On the basis of this deep emotion, it also became the Greek word for *a kiss* as a man would give his wife, as parents and children might give to each other, or as a brother or sister might give to his or her siblings.

In Mark 14:44, this word depicts not just a kiss of friendship, but a symbol of *deep love, affection, obligation, covenant, and relationship.* Giving this kind of kiss was a powerful symbol to everyone who saw it. Strangers would never greet each other with a kiss, for it was a greeting reserved only for the most special of relationships. This is why Paul later told the Early Church in Rome to "salute one another with an holy kiss…" (Romans 16:16). It was a symbol in that day of deep affection, commitment, and covenant.

Judas knew beforehand that he could give Jesus such a kiss. This lets us know that he and Jesus were not strangers but had a unique, friendly relationship. As the bookkeeper and treasurer of the ministry, Judas had assuredly met often with Jesus to discuss ministry finances and disbursement of funds. It seems that during their three-year working relationship, they became dear and cherished friends — so close that Judas had the privilege of giving Jesus *a kiss* of friendship, a privilege reserved only for the intimate few.

On the very night of Jesus' betrayal, He served Communion to all His disciples, including Judas Iscariot. That Communion was a reaffirmation of His covenant to all twelve of them. Jesus understood what it meant to be in covenant. He knew He would have to lay down His life to empower that covenant and make it real. And just as Jesus reaffirmed His covenant to the other disciples that night, He also confirmed it to Judas. Jesus extended His genuine love and commitment to Judas as He offered him the bread and wine, and Judas feigned commitment by accepting the bread and the wine as symbols of the covenant.

However, Judas' loyalty to Jesus was fatally flawed. As noted above, that night Judas told the troops and temple police, "…Whomsoever I shall kiss, that same is he; take him, and lead him away safely."

Betraying Jesus with a kiss was about as low as a person could go. It was like saying, "You and I are friends forever. Now please turn around so I can sink my dagger into your back!" You see, the kiss Judas gave was a false kiss that revealed insincerity, bogus love, and a phony commitment. The fact that it was premeditated made it even worse. This was no last-minute, accidental betrayal; it was well-planned and very deliberate. Judas played the game all the way to the end, working closely with Jesus and remaining a part of His inner circle. Then at the preappointed time, Judas drove in the dagger as deep as he could!

When I travel and speak with people, I repeatedly hear stories of those who have felt betrayed by someone they dearly loved and trusted. Although they never gave the other person a kiss as a symbol of their affection, they opened their hearts, shared their secrets, and gave a part of themselves to him or her. Then later they discovered that the person they loved and trusted wasn't as he or she seemed. That kind of discovery can be a very traumatic and emotional ordeal.

Have you ever experienced betrayal somewhere along the way from a friend or associate you thought was a true friend — only to find out later that he or she wasn't? Did you wonder, *How could this person behave like this after we've been together for so many years?*

Something was evidently wrong in the relationship from the beginning. Maybe you subconsciously knew something was wrong, but you loved the person so much that you didn't want to see what your heart was telling you. Or perhaps you really were blind to what was happening right under your nose.

When someone becomes a betrayer, you can be certain that: 1) the person was never who you thought he or she was to begin with, or 2) you sensed something wasn't right but allowed yourself to go ahead with the relationship anyway.

Does either of these scenarios describe you? Have you been burned by someone you trusted? If you allow your hurt to fester and grow inside you, it will only make you bitter and ugly. It's time for you to forgive and let go of that offense so you can move on with your life.

Jesus always knew that Judas would be His betrayer; nevertheless, Jesus loved Judas, working closely with him and even sharing Communion with him on the same night of his betrayal!

You may ask, *Why did Jesus extend so much of Himself to someone He knew would be disloyal to Him?* Let me answer this question by posing a few questions to you:

- ✦ Have you ever been disloyal and unfaithful to Jesus?
- ✦ Have you ever violated His authority in your life by disobeying Him?
- ✦ Have you ever dragged Him into unholy situations that you got yourself into?
- ✦ Have you ever betrayed or denied Him in your own life?

If you're honest, your answer to all four of these questions will be "Yes, I've done that!" Jesus knew you would do these things even before He called you and saved you. But did He throw you out, reject you, or disown you? No, He forgave you, and He is still forgiving you now. Aren't you glad that Jesus has so much patience with you? Aren't you grateful He gives you so many chances to get things right?

So just learn from the experience, and determine to never let a Judas be your best friend again. Then allow the Holy Spirit to lead you to the finest friends you've ever had in your life! Yes, it has been painful, but if you'll allow this experience to work for you and not against you, it will make you a stronger and better person. And when you come out on the other side, you'll be in a position to understand what others are going through who have been hurt by betrayal so you can be a help and a blessing to them!

MY PRAYER FOR TODAY

Lord, forgive me for the times I've been a Judas! I am so sorry for the times I've been unfaithful or hurtful to people who thought they could trust me. I truly repent for repeating things that were told to me in confidence, for I know it would have hurt me deeply if someone had done the same thing to me. Help me go back to those whom I have hurt and ask for their forgiveness. Please restore my fellowship with those people, and help me never to repeat this wrong behavior again!

I pray this in Jesus' name!

MY CONFESSION FOR TODAY

I confess that I use wisdom in the way I choose my closest friends. Because the Holy Spirit is constantly illuminating my mind with insight, I discern who is a real friend and who isn't. Even more, I confess that I am a real friend and not a betrayer of the people who are dear to me. When the devil tempts me to open my mouth and repeat things that were told to me in confidence, I do not do it! I am a friend who can be trusted. I will never be known as a betrayer to the friends God has brought into my life!

I declare this by faith in Jesus' name!

QUESTIONS FOR YOU TO CONSIDER

1. Has a close friend or associate ever betrayed you? How did you deal with this in your life?
2. Having experienced betrayal yourself, have you become even more committed to being a loyal friend and associate yourself?
3. Knowing what you have learned from that experience when you were betrayed by someone close to you, what would you do differently now if you found yourself in that same situation?

Have you ever experienced betrayal somewhere along the way from a friend or associate you thought was a true friend — only to find out later that he or she wasn't?

APRIL 7

Have Disagreements Revealed Your Level of Submission to Authority?

And he that betrayed him had given them a token, saying,
Whomsoever I shall kiss, that same is he; take him,
and lead him away safely. And as soon as he was come,
he goeth straightway to him, and saith,
Master, master; and kissed him.
— Mark 14:44,45

When I was a young man and just getting started in the ministry, God positioned me under a great man of God who could read Greek and exegete New Testament verses, yet was also strongly anointed by the Spirit of God. To me, this minister had the best combination possible — brains and anointing all mixed together in one package! The first time I heard him preach, my jaw dropped open! His preaching reminded me of the way Jesus baffled the scribes when they heard Him teach with such great authority. I immediately knew that I needed to be under this man's anointing and to receive from his life.

God opened the door for me to be trained by this great man of God, and for two years I worked side by side with him every day — carrying his books and traveling to his meetings with him. I literally met with him seven days a week so he could teach and train me. It was amazing that a man of this caliber would put so much of himself into someone as young as I was, but he did it because he believed in the call of God on my life. This man imparted the tools, the skills, and the understanding I needed to become a man of God who could both grow in the things of the Spirit and establish a ministry that was balanced between the Word and the Spirit.

Everything was great between this minister and me — until one day when I got offended. The reason for the offense is not important, but the situation revealed that I had a flaw in my understanding of authority and submission.

This was an expensive lesson that God has used throughout the years of my ministry as I have worked with others who are themselves learning the hard lessons of submission and authority. Because of what I experienced, I understand the temptation people occasionally feel to think too highly of themselves and to run off and leave their spiritual mentors.

That is exactly what I did to this man who had been so gracious to me. After he had poured his life into me, teaching and training me, I left him when we had our first major disagreement. Although I called him my pastor, the conflict between us revealed that I had never really given him a place of authority in my life. He had been a great example to me, and I respected him as the best teacher I had ever heard. Yet I had obviously never received him as God's authority in my life; if I had, I never would have done what I did to him.

Unfortunately, the true level of one's commitment isn't tested by good times, but by times of conflict and disagreement. It's easy to walk together when you agree with the one you call your spiritual authority and you're having a good time together. But what happens when you disagree or experience a conflict in your relationship? This is the critical moment when the truth about your level of submission will become observable.

When Judas Iscariot came to the Garden of Gethsemane the night he betrayed Jesus, he said something that revealed he had never been truly submitted to Him. The truth about Judas' recognition of and submission to Jesus' authority was exposed that night, just as my submission to that minister was also proven to be defective. Mark 14:45 says, "And as soon as he [Judas] was come, he goeth straightway to him, and saith, Master, master; and kissed him."

Notice that Judas called Jesus, "Master, master." These words reveal the type of relationship that *really* existed in Judas' heart toward Jesus. These words also reveal the reason the devil was able to use Judas, and not one of the other disciples, to betray Jesus.

The word "master" comes from the Greek word *didaskalos*, which means *teacher*. When it is translated "master," as in this verse, it is intended to give the idea of *one who is a fabulous, masterful teacher*. This is the Greek equivalent of the Hebrew word *rabbi*. Of course, a *rabbi* is a teacher who is honored and respected because of his understanding of and ability to explain the Scriptures. When Judas approached Jesus in the Garden that night, this is exactly the title he used when he referred to Jesus. He called Him, "Master, master." It literally meant, "Teacher, teacher."

Titles are very important, because they define relationships. For instance, the words *Daddy* and *Mother* define the unique relationship between a child and a parent. The word *Boss* defines the relationship between an employee and his employer — a relationship much different than the one that exists between the employee and his fellow employees. The words *Mr. President* define the relationship between the nation and its leader. The word *Pastor* defines the relationship between a church and its pastor.

A world without titles would be a world with confusion, for titles give rank, order, and definition to relationships. Jesus Himself told the disciples, "Ye call me Master and Lord: and ye say well; for so I am" (John 13:13).

Even Jesus acknowledged it was correct for His disciples to call Him "Lord" and "Master." In fact, there isn't a single occurrence in the Gospels where they called Him "Jesus." They were always respectful, honoring, and deferential when they spoke of Him or to Him.

But I want you to notice what title Judas *didn't* use that night — he didn't call Jesus "Lord." The word for "Lord" expresses the idea of One who has ultimate and supreme authority in your life. If you called someone "Lord," it meant you were submitted to that person's authority and yielded every realm of your life to his management, direction, and control.

Had Judas called Jesus "Lord" that night, it would have meant that Judas had surrendered his life to Jesus' control and was submitted to His authority. But Judas *didn't* use the word "Lord"; he used the word for "Teacher," which revealed that Jesus had never really become God's authority in Judas' life. The truth is, Judas had only received Jesus as a teacher, a rabbi, and a gifted communicator, but never as "Lord."

As happens in all relationships where submission to authority is required, the moment finally came that proved the true level of Judas' submission to Jesus. When the test came, Judas failed it. There was a fatal flaw in his relationship with Jesus. In the end, it became apparent to everyone that even though he honored and followed Jesus as a Master Teacher, Jesus had never been his Lord. Thus, Judas' side of his relationship with Jesus had been artificial from the very beginning.

Jesus knew what was in the heart of Judas, yet continued to work closely with him, extending mind-blowing mercy, amazing grace, and astounding patience toward him! Jesus graciously extended His time and attention to Judas to correct the fatal flaws in the disciple's character and to get things right. But even with all of Jesus' love and patience, the ball was in Judas' court. He was the one who ultimately determined the level of relationship that would exist between him and Jesus. Jesus was willing to be his "Lord" — but Judas was never truly willing to be in submission to Jesus' authority. Instead, Judas only authorized Jesus to be a gifted Teacher in his life.

I have learned over the years that it takes time to really get to know who people are. The apostle Paul urged us not to lay hands on people suddenly for this very reason (1 Timothy 5:22).

So don't be too shocked if you discover someone whom you thought was with you all the way isn't really with you at all. *If this ever happens to you, remember that it happened to Jesus too.* Just as God used Jesus to extend mercy, grace, and patience to Judas Iscariot, God may be using you now to give an unfaithful person a chance to have a change of heart so he can become a faithful person.

Can God count on you to be His extension of kindness to that person? Are you to be His mercy outstretched to give that person a magnificent opportunity to make a true turnaround in his heart, mind, and character?

When I wronged my pastor so many years ago, my actions uncovered a flaw inside me that needed correction. It revealed that I didn't understand what submission to authority really meant. In retrospect, I'm so thankful that this happened, for God used it to expose a defect in my character that needed to be eradicated. To change me, He tapped a great man of God on the shoulder and instructed him to love me, forgive me, and teach me. Because he was willing to be God's outstretched hand of mercy in my life, I *was* corrected, delivered, and changed. I can never thank God enough for placing me under a person who cared enough for me that he stuck with me and brought correction into my life.

Are *you* supposed to be that kind of person to someone close to you right now? It's so easy to fixate on the kiss of betrayal, but just think about how much God loves that "problem person" in your life! He is trying to help him by giving him a friend like you!

If that person chooses *not* to respond to the mercy, grace, and patience that is being poured out to him through you, he will have to live with the results of his decisions. Just make sure that you fulfill what God is requiring of *you* in this relationship. It may seem difficult to do, but you need to be thankful that God has kindly entrusted you with the responsibility of giving that person one last chance!

MY PRAYER FOR TODAY

Lord, thank You for the spiritual authorities You have placed in my life. Help me learn how to honor them, respect them, and truly submit to their spiritual authority. If there is any defect in my character that would cause me to rebel or to act in an ungodly fashion, please expose it in me now so I can deal with it and change! I want to make sure that my commitments are real and not artificially contrived, so please work in me and bring to light every area that needs work and attention!

I pray this in Jesus' name!

MY CONFESSION FOR TODAY

I confess that God uses me to extend mercy, grace, and patience to unfaithful people, giving them a chance to have a change of heart, to truly turn around, and to become faithful in their relationships with others. I am God's mercy outstretched. He has tapped me on the shoulder and instructed me to love, to forgive, and to help those who need it. I refuse to fixate on the kiss of betrayal; rather, I choose to be thankful that God has entrusted me with the responsibility to give those individuals one last chance!

I declare this by faith in Jesus' name!

QUESTIONS FOR YOU TO CONSIDER

1. Can you think of a time when God used a spiritual authority to bring correction into your life or to reveal your lack of submission?
2. Was this a difficult experience in your life, or did you find it easy to receive correction? What did you learn from that experience?
3. Has God put a person in your life who has the right to speak to you about areas of adjustments you may need to make? If so, who is that person?

APRIL 8

When Roman Soldiers Were Knocked Flat by the Power of God!

Jesus therefore, knowing all things that should come upon him,
went forth, and said unto them, Whom seek ye? They answered him,
Jesus of Nazareth. Jesus saith unto them, I am he….
As soon then as he had said unto them,
I am he, they went backward, and fell to the ground.
— John 18:4-6

Just as the Roman soldiers and temple police were preparing to arrest Jesus, a supernatural power was suddenly released that was so strong, it literally knocked an entire band of 300 to 600 soldiers backward and down on the ground! It was as if an invisible bomb had been detonated. So much explosive strength was released that the power knocked the soldiers flat on their backs! Where did this discharge of power come from, and what released it?

After Jesus received Judas' kiss of betrayal, He stepped forward and asked the crowd of militia, "…Whom seek ye? They answered him, Jesus of Nazareth. Jesus saith unto them, I am he…. As soon then as he had said unto them, I am he, *they went backward, and fell to the ground*" (John 18:4-6).

Notice how Jesus identified himself. He told them, "…I am he…." These mighty words come from the Greek words *ego eimi*, which is more accurately translated, "I AM!" It was not the first time Jesus used this phrase to identify Himself; He also used it in John 8:58 and John 13:19. When the hearers of that day heard those words *ego eimi*, they immediately recognized them as the very words God used to identify Himself when He spoke to Moses on Mount Horeb in Exodus 3:14.

But let's look at the two additional examples of the word *ego eimi* in the Gospel of John. In John 8:58, Jesus said, "Verily, verily, I say unto you, Before Abraham was, I am." Those final words in the verse, "I am," are the Greek words *ego eimi* and should be translated, "I AM!"

In John 13:19, Jesus said, "Now I tell you before it come, that, when it is come to pass, ye may believe that I am he." If you read the *King James Version,* you will notice the word "he" is italicized, meaning it was supplied by the *King James* translators and is not in the original. The Greek simply says, "...Ye may believe that I AM!" In both of these cited texts, Jesus strongly and boldly affirmed that He was the Great "I AM" of the Old Testament.

Now in John 18:5 and 6, Jesus uses the words *ego eimi* again. The soldiers wanted to know, *"Who are you?"* They probably expected him to answer, "Jesus of Nazareth" — but instead, He answered, "I AM!" John 18:6 tells us, *"As soon then as he had said unto them, I am he, they went backward, and fell to the ground."* A more accurate rendering would be *"As soon then as he said unto them, I AM, they went backward and fell to the ground."*

The words "went backward" come from the Greek word *aperchomai.* In this case, the words depict the soldiers and temple police *staggering* and *stumbling backward,* as if some force has hit them and is pushing them backward. The word "fell" is the Greek word *pipto,* which means *to fall.* It was used often to depict *a person who fell so hard, it appeared that they fell dead* or *fell like a corpse.*

The members of this militia that came to arrest Jesus were knocked flat by some kind of force! In fact, the verse says they went backward and fell "to the ground." The words "to the ground" are taken from the Greek word *chamai,* which depicts these soldiers falling abruptly and hitting the ground *hard.* Some force unexpectedly, suddenly, and forcefully knocked these troops and temple police flat!

Think of it — 300 to 600 Roman soldiers and a large number of trained temple police had all come laden with weapons, swords, and clubs to help them capture Jesus. After they announced that they were searching for Jesus of Nazareth, Jesus answered them with the words, "I AM" — thus identifying Himself as the "I AM" of the Old Testament. And when Jesus spoke those words, a great blast of God's power was unleashed — so strong that it literally thrust the troops and police backward, causing them to stagger, wobble, and stumble as they hit the ground hard.

What a shock it must have been for those military men! They discovered that the mere words of Jesus were enough to overwhelm and overpower them! The tales they had heard about Jesus' power were correct! Of course He really was strong enough to overcome an army. After all, He was the Great "I AM!"

After Jesus proved He couldn't be taken by force, He willfully surrendered to them, knowing that it was all a part of the Father's plan for the redemption of mankind. But it's important to understand that *no one took Him.* It was Jesus' *voluntary choice* to go with the troops.

The Jesus we serve is powerful! There is no force strong enough to resist His power. No sickness, financial turmoil, relational problems, political force — *absolutely nothing* has enough power to resist the supernatural power of Jesus Christ! When the Great "I AM" opens His mouth and speaks, every power that attempts to defy Him or His Word is pushed backward and shaken until it staggers, stumbles, and falls to the ground!

What is your need today? Why not present those needs to Jesus, the Great "I AM"? Let Him speak to your heart, directing you to His Word. Once you see the promise you need, get your mouth into agreement with His Word, and you, too, will see the power of God unleashed against the forces that try to defy you!

MY PRAYER FOR TODAY

Lord, I am so glad that You are the Great "I AM" and that You have power over every force in the universe. When You speak, demons tremble, sickness flees, poverty is vanquished, and your Kingdom rules and reigns! Because You live inside me, Your power is resident in me and ready to set me free from any force that tries to come against me. I stand on Your Word, Lord. I speak it out loud by faith and therefore expect to see mountains move out of the way for me!

I pray this in Jesus' name!

MY CONFESSION FOR TODAY

I declare that there is no force strong enough to resist God's power in my life. No sickness, financial turmoil, relational problems, political force — absolutely NOTHING has enough power to resist the supernatural power of Jesus Christ that is resident in me! When I open my mouth and speak the Word of God, every power that attempts to defy His Word is pushed backward and shaken till it staggers, stumbles, and falls to the ground. When my mouth gets into agreement with God's Word, I see His power unleashed against the forces that try to come against me!

I declare this by faith in Jesus' name!

QUESTIONS FOR YOU TO CONSIDER

1. Do you have a mountain in your life right now that is so big, only God's power can move it out of the way?
2. Can you think of a time in your life when you spoke God's Word and saw almost instantaneous results in the physical and material realm?
3. If you are not facing a mountain right now, how might you spiritually prepare yourself for one in the future?

The Jesus we serve is powerful! There is no force strong enough to resist His power. No sickness, financial turmoil, relational problems, political force — *absolutely nothing* has enough power to resist the supernatural power of Jesus Christ! When the Great "I AM" opens His mouth and speaks, every power that attempts to defy Him or His Word is pushed backwards and shaken until it staggers, stumbles, and falls to the ground!

APRIL 9

❧

*Peter Swings for the Head —
But Gets an Ear!*

Then Simon Peter having a sword drew it,
and smote the high priest's servant,
and cut off his right ear. The servant's name was Malchus.
— John 18:10

When they which were about him saw what would follow,
they said unto him, Lord, shall we smite with the sword?
And one of them smote the servant of the high priest,
and cut off his right ear.
— Luke 22:49,50

Can you think of a time when you became so impatient while waiting on the Lord that you decided to take matters into your own hands to get things moving a little faster? When you later realized that you had made a big mess of things, were you regretful that you didn't wait a little longer before taking action?

At one time or another, all of us have been guilty of acting rashly and thoughtlessly. For example, just think of how many times you've said something you later regretted! Oh, how you wished you could have retracted those words, but it was too late! Or perhaps you've been guilty of acting spontaneously on an issue before you had enough time to really think things through.

Or have you ever gotten so angry at someone that you popped off and vocalized your dissent before the other person was finished talking? When you later realized that the person wasn't saying what you thought, did you feel like a fool for popping off too quickly? Did you have to apologize for making a rash statement, all the while wishing you had just kept your mouth shut a few minutes longer?

Hotheaded moments rarely produce good fruit. In fact, when we act rashly, we usually end up loathing the stupidity of our words and actions. The truth is, we all need a good dose of patience — a fruit that is produced inside us by the Spirit of God. We desperately need patience in our lives!

Perhaps no story better demonstrates the mess that impatience produces than that night in the Garden of Gethsemane when Peter seized a sword, swung it with all his might, and lopped off the ear of the high priest's servant.

When Jesus spoke and identified Himself as the great "I AM," the soldiers and temple police were knocked to the ground — their eyes dazed, their heads whirling and spinning, and their bodies stunned by the power of God. The power that was released hit them so hard and so fast that they were on their backs before they knew what hit them!

While these soldiers were still flat on their backs, Peter suddenly decided to take matters into his own hands. He must have seen it as his great chance to show himself brave and to take advantage of the moment, but what he did was simply shocking! It is the perfect picture of someone acting before thinking things all the way through.

Peter's spontaneous, hasty behavior earned him a place in history that no one has ever forgotten. However, to see the full picture of what happened that night, it is essential to piece the story together from both Luke and John's Gospel, for each Gospel writer tells a different part of the story.

While the soldiers and temple police were lying horizontal on their backs, Peter looked around and realized that the armed men were disabled. So he reached down and took a sword, and with sword in hand, he gleefully asked, "…Lord, shall we smite with the sword?" (Luke 22:49).

Before Jesus had an opportunity to answer, Peter swung into action and did something outrageous and utterly bizarre! He gripped the sword and impulsively swung down, slicing right past the head of the high priest's servant. Imagine how shocked Jesus must have been to see Peter lop this poor man's ear right off and then to watch the severed ear fall into the dirt on the ground! John 18:10 tells us that Peter "…smote the high priest's servant, and cut off his right ear…."

Let's look at these words to see exactly what happened in that impulsive moment when Peter swung this sword. The word "smote" is the Greek word *epaio*, from the word *paio*, and it means *to strike*, as a person who viciously strikes someone with a dangerous tool, weapon, or instrument. It can also be translated *to sting*, like a scorpion that strongly injects its stinger into a victim. In addition, it means *to beat with the fist*. In this verse, the word is used to picture *the force* of Peter's swinging action. This tells us that Peter put all his strength into the swinging of his borrowed sword, fully intending to cause some kind of bodily impairment.

Do you think Peter was aiming for the servant's ear? Why would anyone attack an ear? Furthermore, it wouldn't take this much force to cut off an ear. No, I believe Peter was aiming for the man's head and missed, swiping the man's ear by mistake. When that sword missed its target, it slipped down the side of the servant's head and took his ear with it.

When John 18:10 says Peter "cut off" his right ear, the words "cut off" are from the Greek word *apokopto*, which is a compound of the words *apo* and *kopto*. The word *apo* means *away*, and the word *kopto* means *to cut downward*. Put together, it describes *a downward swing that cuts something off*. In this case, Peter swung downward so hard that he completely removed the ear of the servant of the high priest. Some try to insinuate that Peter merely nipped this man's ear, but the Greek shows that the swing of Peter's sword caused its complete removal. The Greek word for "ear" is *otarion*, and it refers to *the entire outer ear*. The Bible is so detailed about the events that occurred that night, it even tells us it was the servant's *right* ear. The servant of the high priest lost his entire right ear when Peter swung in his direction!

John 18:10 tells us the servant's name was *Malchus*. Who was this Malchus? Did Peter indiscriminately select Malchus as his target that night? Was there a particular reason Peter chose this man as the focus of his wrath?

The name Malchus has two meanings: *ruler* and *counselor*. We do not know that this was his original name; it may have been a name given to him because of his close position to the high priest, who at that time was a man named Caiaphas. Caiaphas was a member of the Sadducees, a sect that was particularly opposed to the reality of supernatural happenings, viewing most supernatural events of the Old Testament as myths and legends. This is one reason Caiaphas was so antagonistic to the ministry of Jesus, which, of course, was overflowing with miraculous events every day.

When Peter saw Malchus in the Garden of Gethsemane, it no doubt brought back memories of the many times he had seen Malchus standing at the side of the high priest. Although this man is referred to as the servant of the high priest, he in fact was the high priest's personal assistant. This was a very prominent position in the religious order of the priesthood. As a high-ranking officer of the religious court, Malchus was regally dressed and carried himself with pride and dignity. To Peter's eye, he probably represented everything that belonged to the realm of the priesthood, an order of religious men that had instigated numerous problems for Jesus and the disciples.

Because Malchus was present at the time of Jesus' arrest, we may conclude that he was sent as the personal representative of the high priest to officially oversee the activities connected with Jesus' arrest. Few scholars believe that Peter singled him out by chance. Although the following thought can't be said with absolute certainty, Malchus may have become the intended target because of Peter's deep resentment and long-held grudge toward the high priest and his entourage, all of whom had been continually critical of Jesus' ministry.

I must point out that the healing of Malchus' ear was the last miracle Jesus performed during His earthly ministry. What a statement this makes to us about Jesus! Just before He goes to the Cross, He reaches out to help a publicly declared and avowed foe! This man was part of a group that had been menacing and antagonistic toward Jesus. But Jesus didn't say, *"Finally, one of you guys got what you deserve!"* Instead, He reached out to the man in his need, touched him, and *supernaturally* healed him. Keep in mind that the high priest, a Sadducee, was vehemently opposed to Jesus' supernatural ministry. Yet it was the high priest's own servant who received *a supernatural touch* from Jesus!

What a contrast Jesus' actions were to Peter's behavior! More than likely, Peter acted out of a long-held offense, but Jesus demonstrated love and genuine care even to those who opposed Him during His life and who were instrumental in leading Him to His crucifixion.

So don't follow Peter's example; instead, pray for the grace to be like Jesus! *Decide today to let the Holy Spirit empower you to reach out to your offenders and opponents and to love them the way Jesus would love them!*

MY PRAYER FOR TODAY

Lord, I ask You to help me be more like Jesus! Help me release the grudges and deeply-held resentments that I am tempted to carry toward people. Instead of rejoicing when they get in trouble or when something bad happens to them, help me to reach out to them, to see what I can do to help, and to become the hand of God in their lives. Forgive me that I haven't already acted as Jesus would act, and help me learn how to put any negative emotions aside so I can reach out to them in the name of Jesus!

I pray this in Jesus' name!

MY CONFESSION FOR TODAY

I confess that I do not hold grudges, nor do I allow deep-seated resentments to reside in my heart, mind, and emotions. I have the mind of Christ, and I think just like Jesus thinks. What Jesus does is what I do. What Jesus says is what I say. How Jesus behaves is how I behave. Because the Holy Spirit is working to produce the life of Jesus Christ in me, I can be the extended hand of Jesus to everyone around me, including those who have been opposed to me.

I declare this by faith in Jesus' name!

1. Can you think of five times in your life when you acted rashly and later regretted that action in your life?
2. What did you learn from these incidents, and how might you respond differently the next time?
3. When you find yourself reacting with impatience, do you ask the Holy Spirit to help you become more patient? If you haven't done this recently, why don't you stop what you're doing right now and ask the Holy Spirit to help you in this area of your life today?

APRIL 10

༄༅

Jesus Cleans Up Peter's Mess!

When they which were about him saw what would follow,
they said unto him, Lord, shall we smite with the sword?
And one of them smote the servant of the high priest,
and cut off his right ear. And Jesus answered, and said,
Suffer ye thus far. And he touched his ear, and healed him.
— Luke 22:49-51

*H*ave you ever had a time when it nearly broke your heart to see what a mess a friend had made of his life? Because you loved your friend so much, you were willing to do anything necessary to assist him in getting his life back in order again. Although you knew it would be difficult, you were nonetheless willing to step into his disorder, chaos, and confusion to help him because you knew he'd never get out of his mess by himself.

Let's see what Jesus did for Peter that night in the Garden of Gethsemane after Peter chopped off the ear of Malchus, the servant of the high priest. There is something we can learn from the example Jesus gave us that night.

What Peter did to Malchus was not only scandalous — it was against the law and therefore punishable. Peter's action was criminal! Peter's wrongdoing was sufficient to ruin his entire life, since he could have been sentenced for physically injuring a fellow citizen. And this wasn't just any citizen. As the servant of the high priest, Malchus was an extremely well-known man in the city of Jerusalem. Peter certainly would have been imprisoned for injuring a person of such stature.

Jesus had just been sweating blood from the intense spiritual battle He fought in prayer in the Garden. Then He had received the kiss of betrayal from a friend and was therefore facing the prospect of the Cross and three days in the grave. Now a new problem had been thrust upon Him.

Because of Peter's impetuous, unauthorized behavior, Jesus had to put everything on hold for a moment so He could step forward and fix the mess Peter had created!

As blood poured from the side of Malchus' head and dripped from the blade Peter held in his hand, Jesus asked the soldiers, "...Suffer ye thus far..." (Luke 22:51). This was the equivalent of saying, *"Let Me just do one more thing before you take Me!"*

Then Jesus reached out to Malchus and "...touched his ear, and healed him." Rather than allow Himself to be taken away while Peter was still subject to arrest, imprisonment, and possible execution, Jesus stopped the entire process to fix the mess Peter made that night.

The Bible says that Jesus "touched" the servant. The Greek word for "touch" is *aptomai*, a word that means *to firmly grasp* or *to hold tightly.* This is very important, for it lets us know that Jesus didn't just lightly touch Malchus; He firmly grabbed the servant's head and held him tightly.

This is important because it tells us the tenacity with which Jesus prayed! When He laid His hands on people, they *knew* that hands had been laid on them!

The Bible doesn't tell us whether Jesus touched the stump that remained from the severed ear and grew a new ear or grabbed the old ear from the ground and miraculously set it back in its place. Regardless of how the miracle occurred, however, the word *aptomai* ("touched") lets us know that Jesus was aggressive in the way He touched the man.

As a result of Jesus' touch, Malchus was completely "healed" (v. 51). The word "healed" is the Greek word *iaomai*, which means *to cure, to restore,* or *to heal.* Jesus completely restored Malchus' ear before the soldiers bound Him and led Him out of the Garden.

That night in the Garden of Gethsemane, Jesus' very words knocked 300 to 600 soldiers off their feet and flat on their backs. He didn't need Peter's help. He didn't request Peter's intervention. Nevertheless, Peter suddenly jumped in the middle of God's business and tried to create a revolt. Yet rather than walk off and leave Peter in the mess he had made by his own doings, Jesus stopped everything that was happening and intervened on his behalf. Jesus took the time to heal Malchus' ear for two primary reasons: 1) because He *is* a Healer and 2) because He didn't want Peter to be arrested for his impulsive actions.

The next time you think you are too busy or too important to get involved in a friend's problem, remember this example that Jesus gave us on the night of His arrest. That night Jesus had a lot on His mind, but He still stopped everything to help a friend. He could have said, *"Peter, you've made this mess by yourself; now you can fix it by yourself."* But it was clear that Peter would never get out of this trouble without assistance, so Jesus stepped in to help Peter get things back in order again.

When you are tempted to be judgmental about other people's self-imposed problems, it would be good for you to remember the many times God's mercy has intervened to save you from messy situations that you created yourself. Even though you deserved to get in trouble, God loved you enough to come right alongside you and help you pull things together so you could get out of that mess. Now whenever you see others in trouble, you have the opportunity to be an extension of God's mercy to them.

Put everything on hold for a few minutes so you can reach out to a friend in trouble; then do whatever you can to help restore the situation. If this was important enough for Jesus to do, then you have time to do it too! *Make it a priority today to be a faithful friend to the end, just as Jesus was to Peter in the Garden of Gethsemane!*

MY PRAYER FOR TODAY

Lord, I am so thankful for the many times You have stepped into my life to clean up the messes I've created by myself. Had I been more patient and waited on You, I could have avoided the problems that stole my time, my thoughts, my energies, and my money. Forgive me for being impetuous, and help me learn to wait on You. When I see others make the same mistakes I've made, help me remember the times You have helped me so I can respond with a heart filled with compassion and not with judgment, reaching out to help them recover from the mistakes they have made!

I pray this in Jesus' name!

MY CONFESSION FOR TODAY

I confess that I am merciful and compassionate to people who have messed up their lives. Their problems are my opportunities to allow God to use me in their lives by helping them recover from their mistakes. God loves these people so much that He wants to send me alongside them to assist, teach, and do whatever I can to help them get back on their feet again. I have been so touched by God's mercy myself that judgment and condemnation cannot operate inside me! Rather than lecture people about their mistakes so they feel even worse about what they have done, I am God's mercy extended to support them in their time of trouble!

I declare this by faith in Jesus' name!

QUESTIONS FOR YOU TO CONSIDER

1. Can you recollect a time in your life when you were so impatient with what was happening in your life that you took matters in your own hands to speed them up a bit — only to find out that you made things much worse?
2. Can you think of other people who need God to supernaturally intervene to fix the messes they have made? Have you asked God if He wants to use you to help them find a way out of this difficult time they are facing right now?
3. When you consider Jesus' attitude toward those who are undeserving, how does it affect your attitude toward others who find themselves in some kind of self-made trouble?

When you are tempted to be judgmental about other people's self-imposed problems, it would be good for you to remember the many times God's mercy has intervened to save you from messy situations that you created yourself. Even though you deserved to get in trouble, God loved you enough to come right alongside you and help you pull things together so you could get out of that mess.

APRIL 11

❧❧❧

Twelve Legions of Angels

Thinkest thou that I cannot now pray to my Father,
and he shall presently give me more than twelve legions of angels?
— Matthew 26:53

*H*ow much strength do you think one angel possesses? Today I'd like for us to consider the full impact of Jesus' words in Matthew 26:53, where He said, "Thinkest thou that I cannot now pray to my Father, and he shall presently give me more than twelve legions of angels?"

Let's look at three questions:

✦ *What is a "legion"?*
✦ *How many angels would there be in twelve legions?*
✦ *What would be the combined strength of this number of angels?*

It is important to know the answers to these questions, because the answers reveal the full might that was available to Jesus had He requested supernatural help in the Garden of Gethsemane. Actually, when we take into account the power that was already demonstrated in the Garden and then add the potential assistance and impact of twelve legions of angels, it becomes obvious that there was no human force on earth strong enough to take Jesus against His will. The only way He was going to be taken was if He allowed Himself to be taken! This is why He later told Pilate, "…Thou couldest have no power at all against me, except it were given thee from above…" (John 19:11).

Let's begin with our first question: *What is a "legion"?* The word "legion" is a military term that was taken from the Roman army. A legion denoted a group of at least 6,000 Roman soldiers, although the total number could be higher. This means that anytime we read about a legion of anything, we can know it always refers to at least 6,000 of something.

An amazing example of this is found in Mark 5:9, where the Bible tells us that the demon-possessed man of the Gadarenes had a legion of demons. That means this man had an infestation of at least 6,000 demons residing inside him!

Let's now contemplate the second question: *How many angels would there be in twelve legions?* Since the word "legion" refers to *at least* 6,000, it means a legion of angels would be *at least* 6,000 angels. However, Jesus said the Father would give Him "more than" twelve legions of angels if He requested it. Because it would be pure speculation to try to figure out how many "more than" twelve legions would be, let's just stick with the figure of twelve legions to see how many angels that entails.

One legion is 6,000 angels, so if you simply multiply that number by twelve, you'll discover that twelve legions of angels would include a minimum of *72,000 angels*. But Jesus said the Father would give Him *more than* twelve legions of angels; therefore, you can conclude that there were potentially many additional thousands of angels available to Jesus the night He was arrested!

Finally, let's look at our third question: *What would be the combined strength in this number of angels?* Angels are powerful! In fact, Isaiah 37:36 records that a single angel obliterated 185,000 men in one night. So if a single angel had that kind of power, how much combined strength would there be in twelve legions of angels?

Since a single angel was able to obliterate 185,000 men in one night, it would mean the combined strength in a legion of 6,000 angels would be enough to destroy 1,110,000,000 men (that is, one billion, one hundred ten million men) — and that's just the combined power in *one* legion of angels!

Now let's multiply this same number 185,000 by twelve legions, or at least 72,000 angels, which was the number of angels Jesus said was available to Him on the night of His arrest. When we do, we find that there was enough combined strength at Jesus' disposal to have annihilated at least 13,320,000,000 men (that is, thirteen billion, three hundred twenty million men) — which is more than twice the number of people living on the earth right now!

Jesus didn't need Peter's little sword that night. Had He chosen to do so, Jesus could have summoned 72,000 magnificent, mighty, dazzling, glorious, overwhelmingly powerful angels to the Garden to obliterate the Roman soldiers and the temple police who had come to arrest Him. In fact, the combined strength in twelve legions of angels could have wiped out the entire human race! But Jesus *didn't* call on the supernatural help that was available to Him. Why? Because He knew it was time for Him to voluntarily lay down His life for the sin of the human race.

Learn a lesson from Jesus and from the apostle Peter. Jesus didn't need Peter's undersized, insignificant sword to deal with His situation. What good would a single sword have been against all the troops assembled in the Garden that night anyway? Peter's actions were a perfect example of how the flesh tries in vain to solve its own problems but cannot. Jesus had all the power that was required to conquer those troops.

As you face your own challenges in life, always keep in mind that Jesus has the power to fix any problem you'll ever come across. Before you jump in and make things worse by taking matters into your own hands, remember the story of Peter! The next time you're tempted to "grab a sword and start swinging," take a few minutes to remind yourself that Jesus can handle the problem without your intervention. Before you do anything else, *pray* and ask the Lord what you are supposed to do. Then after you receive your answer and follow His instructions, just watch His supernatural power swing into action to solve the dilemma you are facing!

MY PRAYER FOR TODAY

Lord, I am so glad You have the power to put an end to my problems! So many times I've acted just like Peter, swinging furiously in the strength of my own flesh as I've tried to solve my problems without Your help. Forgive me for wasting so much time and energy! Today I ask You to speak to my heart and tell me what I am supposed to do; then help me follow Your instructions to the letter. Give me the patience to wait while You supernaturally work behind the scenes to resolve my questions.

I pray this in Jesus' name!

MY CONFESSION FOR TODAY

I boldly and joyfully affirm that Jesus Christ has all the power needed to fix my problems! I am not smart enough by myself to figure out how to get out of my messes, so I turn to Him to give me wisdom, insight, power, and the answers I need to get from where I am to where I need to be. His power works mightily through me, and that divine power is being released right now to tackle the challenges I face in life and bring me to a peaceful place of resolution in every situation.

I declare this by faith in Jesus' name!

QUESTIONS FOR YOU TO CONSIDER

1. Has there ever been a moment in your life when you got in a hurry and acted too fast — and then later regretted your actions?
2. When you candidly examine your life, do you find that the same problems keep resurfacing again and again? Does this indicate that you are trying to solve those problems in the strength of your flesh instead of relying on the power of Jesus to help you?
3. How does today's *Sparkling Gem* cause you to look differently at your challenges? What are you going to do differently as a result of what you have read and learned today?

APRIL 12

Who Was the Naked Boy In the Garden of Gethsemane?

And there followed him a certain young man,
having a linen cloth cast about his naked body;
and the young men laid hold on him:
and he left the linen cloth, and fled from them naked.
— Mark 14:51,52

*J*ust about the time Jesus was finished healing the ear of the servant of the high priest named Malchus, the Gospel of Mark tells us a naked young man was found in the Garden of Gethsemane. Mark 14:51,52 says, "And there followed him a certain young man, having a linen cloth cast about his naked body; and the young men laid hold on him: and he left the linen cloth, and fled from them naked."

Who was this young man? Why was he following Jesus? Why was he naked? Why was he draped in a linen cloth instead of wearing normal clothes? And why was the Holy Spirit so careful to include this unique story in Mark's account of the Gospel? *What is the significance of this event?*

The key to identifying this young man lies in the "linen cloth" he had lightly draped about his body. The particular Greek word that is used for this "linen cloth" is used in only one other event in the New Testament — to depict the "linen cloth" in which the body of Jesus was wrapped for burial (*see* Matthew 27:59, Mark 15:46, and Luke 23:53). Thus, the only reference we have for this kind of cloth in the New Testament is that of a burial shroud used for covering a dead body in the grave.

Some scholars have tried to say this naked young man was Mark himself. They assume that when Mark heard about Jesus' arrest, he quickly jumped out of bed and dashed to the Garden of Gethsemane. But the Garden was remotely located, and no one could have run there so quickly. It is simply a physical impossibility.

Others have speculated that Mark threw off his clothes in an attempt to shock and distract the soldiers so Jesus could escape. This idea is preposterous. Others have tried with similar vain attempts to assert that this naked young man was the apostle John. But why would John be walking naked in the Garden of Gethsemane?

As I said, the answer to this naked young man's identity lies in the cloth he had wrapped around his body. You see, when a body was prepared for burial, it was washed, ceremonially cleaned, and buried naked in a linen cloth exactly like the one described here in the Gospel of Mark. Furthermore, the Garden of Gethsemane was situated on the side of the Mount of Olives. Toward the base of that mount is a heavily populated cemetery, with many of its graves going back to the time of Jesus.

When Jesus said, "I AM," the power that was released was so tremendous that it knocked the soldiers backward (*see* April 8). But evidently it also caused a rumbling in the local cemetery! When that blast of power was released, a young boy, draped in a linen burial cloth in accordance with the tradition of that time, crawled out from his tomb — *raised from the dead*!

The reason he "followed" Jesus was to get a glimpse of the One who had resurrected him. The word "followed" here means *to continuously follow*. This tells us that this resurrected young man trailed the soldiers as they took Jesus through the Garden on the way to His trial. When the soldiers discovered the young man who was following Jesus, they tried to apprehend him. But when they reached out to grab him, he broke free from their grip and fled, leaving the linen cloth in their possession.

Today, I want you to reflect again on the amazing power that was active at the time of Jesus' arrest in the Garden of Gethsemane. He later told Pilate, "…Thou couldest have no power at all against me, except it were given thee from above…" (John 19:11). Indeed, there was so much power present that *no one* could have withstood Jesus had He chosen to resist. Jesus was not taken by the will of man; He was delivered by the will of the Father.

Think how marvelous it is that Jesus freely gave His life for you and me! So much power was at work in Him even at the time of His arrest that no one had sufficient power to forcibly take Him. The only reason Jesus was taken was that He chose to willingly lay down His life for you and for me. *So take a little time today to stop and thank Him for being so willing to go to the Cross to take your sin on Himself!*

MY PRAYER FOR TODAY

Lord, You are so amazing! How can I ever thank You enough for coming into this world to give Your life for me? I'm sorry for the times I get so busy that I fail to remember the incredible love You willfully demonstrated to me by going to the Cross. You didn't have to do it, but You did it for me. I thank You from the depths of my heart for loving me so completely!

I pray this in Jesus' name!

MY CONFESSION FOR TODAY

I boldly declare that God values me! He loves me so much that He sent Jesus into the world to take my place on the Cross. He took my sin; He carried my sickness; and He bore my shame. Because of Jesus' work of redemption on the Cross, today I am saved, I am healed, and I am not ashamed!

I declare this by faith in Jesus' name!

QUESTIONS FOR YOU TO CONSIDER

1. When you consider how much of God's power was available to Jesus in the Garden of Gethsemane, how does this affect your level of expectation for His power to work in your life right now?
2. Have you ever witnessed God's power working mightily in your life when no natural help was available? If so, when was it, and what happened?
3. What did you learn from today's *Sparkling Gem* that was brand new to you?

APRIL 13

Led Like a Sheep To Its Slaughter

And they that had laid hold on Jesus
led him away to Caiaphas the high priest,
where the scribes and the elders were assembled.
— Matthew 26:57

*A*fter Jesus demonstrated His phenomenal power, He permitted the soldiers to take Him into custody. In a certain sense, this was simply an *act,* for He had already vividly proven that they didn't have adequate power to take Him. Just one word and He could put them on their backs, yet the Bible says that they "laid hold on Jesus" and "led him away."

The words "laid hold" are from the Greek word *kratos.* In this case, this word means *to seize, to take hold of, to firmly grip,* and *to apprehend.* Used in this context, it primarily carries the idea of *making a forceful arrest.* Once Jesus demonstrated that He could not be taken by force, He then allowed the soldiers to seize Him.

Once Jesus was in their hands, Matthew 26:57 tells us that they "led him away." This phrase comes from the Greek word *apago* — the same word used to picture *a shepherd who ties a rope about the neck of his sheep and then leads it down the path to where it needs to go.* This word pictures exactly what happened to Jesus that night in the Garden of Gethsemane. He wasn't gagged and dragged to the high priest as one who was putting up a fight or resisting arrest. Instead, the Greek word *apago* plainly tells us that the soldiers lightly slipped a rope about Jesus' neck and led Him down the path as He followed behind, just like a sheep being led by a shepherd. Thus, the Roman soldiers and temple police led Him as a sheep to slaughter, just as Isaiah 53:7 had prophesied many centuries earlier. Specifically on that night, however, the soldiers led Jesus to Caiaphas the high priest.

Let's see what we can learn about Caiaphas. We know that Caiaphas was appointed high priest in the year 18 AD. As high priest, he became so prominent in Israel that even when his term as high priest ended, he wielded great influence in the business of the nation, including its spiritual, political, and financial affairs. Flavius Josephus, the famous Jewish historian, reported that five of Caiaphas' sons later served in the office of the high priest.

As a young man, Caiaphas married Anna, the daughter of Annas, who was serving as high priest at that time. Annas served as Israel's high priest for nine years. The title of high priest had fallen into the jurisdiction of this family, and they held this high-ranking position firmly in their grip, passing it among the various members of the family and thus keeping the reins of power in their hands. It was a spiritual monarchy. The holders of this coveted title retained great political power, controlled public opinion, and owned vast wealth.

After Annas passed the title of high priest to his son-in-law Caiaphas, Annas continued to exercise control over the nation through his son-in-law. This influence is evident in Luke 3:2, where the Bible says, "Annas and Caiaphas being the high priests...." It was impossible for two people to serve as high priests at the same time; nonetheless, Annas held his former title and much of his former authority. He was so influential to the very end of Jesus' ministry that the Roman soldiers and temple police who arrested Jesus in the Garden of Gethsemane led Jesus to Annas first before delivering him to Caiaphas, the current high priest (John 18:13).

Both Annas and Caiaphas were Sadducees, a group of religious leaders who were more liberal in doctrine and had a tendency not to believe in supernatural events. In fact, they regarded most supernatural occurrences in the Old Testament as myths.

The constant reports of Jesus' supernatural powers and miracles, as well as the reputation He was gaining throughout the nation, caused Caiaphas, Annas, and the other members of the Sanhedrin to view Jesus as a threat. These religious leaders were control freaks in the truest sense of the word, and it was an affront to them that Jesus' ministry was beyond their control and jurisdiction. Then they heard the verified report that Lazarus had actually been resurrected from the dead! This incident drove them over the edge, causing them to decide to do away with Jesus by committing murder.

These leaders were so filled with rage about Lazarus' resurrection and were so worried about Jesus' growing popularity that they held a secret council to determine whether or not Jesus had to be killed. Once that decision was made, Caiaphas was the one who was principally responsible for scheming how to bring His death to pass.

As high priest and the official head of the Sanhedrin, Caiaphas was also responsible for arranging Jesus' illegal trial before the Jewish authorities. At first, he charged Jesus with the sin of blasphemy. However, because Jesus wouldn't contest the accusation Caiaphas brought against Him, the high priest then delivered Him to the Roman authorities, who found Jesus guilty of treason for claiming to be the king of the Jews.

Caiaphas was so powerful that even after the death of Jesus, he continued to persecute believers in the Early Church. For instance, after the crippled man at the Beautiful Gate was healed (*see* Acts 3), Peter and John were seized and brought before the council (Acts 4:6). Caiaphas was the high priest at this time and continued to serve as high priest until he was removed in 36 AD.

This emphatically tells us that Caiaphas was also the high priest who interrogated Stephen in Acts 7:1. In addition, he was the high priest we read about who gave Saul of Tarsus written permission that authorized him to arrest believers in Jerusalem and later in Damascus (Acts 9:1,2).

Because of the political events in the year 36 AD, Caiaphas was finally removed from the office of high priest. Of the nineteen men who served as high priests in the first century, this evil man ruled the longest. The title of high priest, however, remained in the family after Caiaphas stepped down, this time passed on to his brother-in-law Jonathan, another son of Annas.

Consider this: Jesus had never sinned (2 Corinthians 5:21); no guile had ever been found in His mouth (1 Peter 2:22); and His entire life was devoted to doing good and to healing all who were oppressed of the devil (Acts 10:38). Therefore, it seems entirely unjust that He would be led like a sheep into the midst of the spiritual vipers who were ruling in Jerusalem. According to the flesh, one could have argued that this wasn't fair; however, Jesus never questioned the Father's will or balked at the assignment that was required of Him.

The apostle Peter wrote this regarding Jesus: "Who, when he was reviled, reviled not again; when he suffered, he threatened not; but committed himself to him that judgeth righteously" (1 Peter 2:23). The word "committed" is the Greek word *paradidomi,* a compound of the words *para* and *didomi.* The word *para* means *alongside* and carries the idea of *coming close alongside to someone or to some object.* The word *didomi* means *to give.* When compounded together, it presents the idea of *entrusting something to someone.* The prefix *para* suggests that this is someone to whom you have drawn *very close.* It can be translated *to commit, to yield, to commend, to transmit, to deliver,* or *to hand something over to someone else.*

The Lord Jesus yielded Himself to the Father who judges righteously when He found Himself in this unjust situation. In that difficult hour, He drew close to the Father and fully entrusted Himself and His future into the hands of the Father. Jesus knew He was in the Father's will, so He chose to entrust Himself into the Father's care and to leave the results in His control.

If you are in a situation that seems unfair or unjust and there is nothing you can do to change it, you must draw as close to the Father as you can and commit yourself into His loving care. You know He wants the best for you, even though you have found yourself in a predicament that seems so undeserved. Your options are to get angry and bitter and turn sour toward life, or to choose to believe that God is in control and working on your behalf, even if you don't see anything good happening at the present moment.

When Jesus was arrested and taken to Caiaphas to be severely mistreated, there was no escape for Him. He had no choice but to trust the Father. *What other choice do you have today?*

MY PRAYER FOR TODAY

Lord, in times when I find myself stuck in a situation I don't like or enjoy, help me lift my eyes and look to You for strength. I know that You love me and are looking out for my life, so in those moments when I am tempted to be nervous or afraid, I ask You to help me rest in the knowledge that You will take care of me.

I pray this in Jesus' name!

MY CONFESSION FOR TODAY

I declare by faith that I am kept by the peace of God. Even when I find myself in situations that seem unjust, undeserving, and unfair, God is secretly working to turn things around for my good. He loves me; He cares for me; and He wants to see the very best for my life.

Therefore, I entrust my job, my income, my marriage, my children, my health, and everything else in my life into the hands of my Heavenly Father!

I declare this by faith in Jesus' name!

QUESTIONS FOR YOU TO CONSIDER

1. Have you ever found yourself trapped in a situation that seemed unfair? What did you do to stay in peace and to avoid fear and anxiety?
2. If you were counseling a friend who was caught up in an undeserved situation, what steps would you suggest that your friend take in order to stay in peace?
3. If you were to lead someone in a prayer of commitment to God, how would you word that particular prayer? Why don't you take a few minutes to pray this same prayer for yourself?

APRIL 14

Has Anyone Ever Spit in Your Face?

Then did they spit in his face, and buffeted him....
— Matthew 26:67

Some years ago, I visited another church in our city to hear a special speaker who had come from afar. That evening at the meeting, the local church I was visiting announced they would be starting a building program. As I sat in there, God's Spirit spoke to my heart and instructed me to sow a sacrificial seed into their new building program. It was a time when we desperately needed money for our own building program, so anything I sowed would be sacrificial. However, the amount the Lord put in my heart was significant.

What made it even harder for me to give this gift was that this church had acted maliciously toward our church in the past. They had lied about us, scoffed at us, and even prayed for our downfall. *And now the Lord was telling me to sow a large gift into this same church?*

Throughout that entire service, I argued with the Lord. The issue really wasn't the money, although we could have used the money ourselves at that moment. The issue I was wrestling with was giving a gift to this church that had treated us with contempt for so long.

Finally, the Spirit of God asked me, *Are you willing to sow a seed for peace with this church?* That clinched it! I pulled my checkbook out of my pocket to write what I considered to be a sizable gift for this other church. Writing that check was difficult, but once it was written, my heart simply flooded with joy because I had been obedient. There is no joy to compare with the joy that comes from being obedient!

One week later, the pastor to whom I gave the gift was at a meeting with his staff and church leaders. The pastor told his leaders, "Look at this puny little check Pastor Rick gave us! Couldn't he have done any better than this?" When I heard how he viewed the sizable gift I'd given, I was quite shocked. But when I heard what this pastor did next, I was literally stunned. He devoted the next part of his staff meeting to discussing all the things he didn't like about me and our church. He poked fun at us, ridiculed us, mocked us, and put us down in front of his people. Instead of being thankful for the gift we gave, he once more demonstrated utter disrespect and contempt for us.

When I heard about this event, it hurt so badly that it cut deep into my heart. How could anyone say the gift we gave was puny? It would be considered significant in any nation of the world. But what hurt the most was that the pastor had put us down and publicly made fun of us in front of his staff and leadership. I remember feeling as if I had been spit on — and as the years passed, this same pastor spit on us many more times.

For instance, when we dedicated our church building — the first church to be built in sixty years in our city — it was a moment of great rejoicing. But soon after our dedication, this man stood before a large convention of several thousand people and sneered at our new facility. For a second time, he injected a dagger into my heart! At a time when this pastor could have been rejoicing with us, he chose to make it another opportunity to spit in our faces.

How about you? Can you think of an instance in your life when you did something good for someone, but that person didn't appreciate what you did? Was he so unappreciative that you felt as if he'd spit in your face? Were you stunned by his behavior? How did you act in response to that situation?

I think nearly everyone has felt taken advantage of and spit on at some point or another. But imagine how Jesus must have felt the night He was taken to the high priest where He was *literally* spit on by the guards and temple police! For three years, Jesus preached, taught, and healed the sick. But now He was being led like a sheep to the spiritual butcher of Jerusalem, the high priest Caiaphas, and to the scribes and elders who had assembled to wait for His arrival.

In the trial that took place before the high priest and his elders, the religious leaders charged Jesus with the crime of declaring Himself the Messiah. Jesus replied by telling them that they would indeed one day see Him sitting on the right hand of power and coming with clouds of glory (Matthew 26:64). Upon hearing this, the high priest ripped his clothes and screamed, *"Blasphemy!"* as all the scribes and elders lifted their voices in anger, demanding that Jesus die (Matthew 26:66).

Then these religious scribes and elders did the *unthinkable*! Matthew 26:67,68 says, "Then did they spit in his face, and buffeted him; and others smote him with the palms of their hands, saying, Prophesy unto us, thou Christ, Who is he that smote thee?"

Notice that it wasn't just a few who spit in his face that night; the Bible says, "...*they* spit in his face...." The word "they" refers to all the scribes and elders who were assembled for the meeting that night. One scholar notes that there could have been one hundred or more men in this crowd! And one by one, each of these so-called spiritual leaders, clothed in their religious garments, walked up to Jesus and spit in His face!

In that culture and time, spitting in one's face was considered to be the strongest thing you could do to show utter disgust, repugnance, dislike, or hatred for someone. When someone spattered his spit on another person's face, that spit was meant to humiliate, demean, debase, and shame that person. To make it worse, the offender would usually spit hard and close to the person's face, making it all the more humiliating.

By the time Caiaphas and his scribes and elders had finished taking turns spitting on Jesus, their spit was most likely dripping down from His forehead into His eyes; dribbling down His nose, His cheekbones, and His chin; and even oozing down onto His clothes. This was an extremely humiliating scene! And remember, the men who were acting so hatefully toward Jesus were religious leaders! Their hideous conduct was something Jesus definitely didn't deserve. And what makes this entire scene even more amazing is that Malchus — the servant whom Jesus had just healed — was in all probability standing at the side of Caiaphas and watching it all happen!

These religious leaders didn't stop with just humiliating Jesus. After spitting on Him, they each doubled up their fists and whacked Him violently in the face! Matthew 26:67 says, "Then did they spit in his face, *and buffeted him....*" The word "buffet" is the Greek word *kolaphidzo*, which means *to strike with the fist.* It is normally used to picture a person who is *violently beaten.*

As if it wasn't insulting enough to spit on Jesus, approximately one hundred men viciously and cruelly struck Him with their fists. Not only was this brutal — it was sadistic! Humiliating Jesus with their spit and curses didn't satisfy the hatred of these men; they wouldn't be satisfied until they knew He had been physically maltreated. To ensure that this goal was accomplished, their own fists became their weapons of abuse.

It appears that these scribes and elders were so paranoid about Jesus getting more attention than themselves that they simply wanted to destroy Him. Every time they spit on Him, they were spitting on the anointing. Every time they struck Him, they were leveling a punch against the anointing. They hated Jesus and the anointing that operated through Him to such an extent that they voted to murder Him. But first they wanted to take some time to personally make sure He suffered before He died. What a strange way to render "thanks" to One who had done so much for them!

When I get disappointed at the way others respond to me or to what I have done for them, I often think of what happened to Jesus on that night when He came before these Jewish leaders. John 1:11 tells us, "He came unto his own, and his own received him not." Although these men who spit on and hit Jesus refused to acknowledge Him, He still went to the Cross and died for them. His love for them was unwavering — unshaken and unaffected by their wrong actions.

As you think of how people have wronged you, does it affect your desire to love them? What have these conflicts revealed about *you*? Is your love for those unkind people consistent, unwavering, unshaken, and unaffected? Or have the conflicts revealed you have a fickle love that you quickly turn off when people don't respond to you the way you wished they would?

The same Holy Spirit who lived in Jesus now lives in you. Just as the Spirit of God empowered Jesus to love people consistently, regardless of what they did or didn't do, the Holy Spirit can empower you to do the same. *So why don't you take a few minutes today to pray about the people who have let you down or disappointed you? Then forgive those people, and decide to love them the way Jesus loved those who wronged Him!*

MY PRAYER FOR TODAY

Lord, thank You for being such a good example of love that is unshaken and unaffected by other people's actions. You have loved me with a consistent love, even in times when I've acted badly and didn't deserve it. Thank You so much for loving me in spite of the things I've done and the things I've permitted to go on in my life. Today I want to ask You to help me love others just as consistently as You have loved me. Forgive me for being on-again, off-again in my love. Help me become rock-solid and unwavering in my love for others, including those who haven't treated me too nicely. I know that with Your help, I can love them steadfastly no matter what they do!

I pray this in Jesus' name!

MY CONFESSION FOR TODAY

I confess that what other people have done to me doesn't affect my desire or my commitment to love them. My love for people is consistent, unwavering, unshaken, and unaffected. The same Holy Spirit who lived in Jesus now lives in me — and just as the Spirit of God empowered Jesus to love everyone consistently, now the Holy Spirit empowers me to do the same!

I declare this by faith in Jesus' name!

QUESTIONS FOR YOU TO CONSIDER

1. Has there ever been a time in your life when you felt like someone you tried to help later turned around and "spit in your face"?
2. Did that conflict reveal that your love for them was consistent, unwavering, unshaken, and unaffected — or that you have a fickle love that is quickly turned off when people don't respond to you the way you wished they would?
3. The next time someone treats you this way, how do you think you should respond to him or her?

APRIL 15

Playing Games at Jesus' Expense!

Then did they spit in his face, and buffeted him;
and others smote him with the palms of their hands,
saying, Prophesy unto us, thou Christ, Who is he that smote thee?
— Matthew 26:67,68

And the men that held Jesus mocked him, and smote him.
And when they had blindfolded him, they struck him on the face,
and asked him, saying, Prophesy, who is it that smote thee?
— Luke 22:63,64

*I*f we're going to get the full picture of what happened in Caiaphas' chamber that night when the religious leaders were spitting on Jesus and striking Him in the face with their fists, we need to pull all the pieces of this picture together from both the Gospel of Matthew and Luke.

Luke 22:63 says, "And the men that held Jesus mocked him, and smote him." I want you to particularly see the word "mock" in this verse. It comes from the Greek word *empaidzo*, which meant *to play a game*. It was often used for *playing a game with children* or for *amusing a crowd by impersonating someone in a silly and exaggerated way*. For instance, this word might be used in a game of charades when someone intends to *comically portray someone or even make fun of someone*. This gives us an important piece of the story that Matthew didn't include in his Gospel account.

Even before He had to endure the spitting and vicious beating of the scribes and elders that night, Jesus was also severely beaten by "the men that held" Him. This doesn't refer to the scribes and elders, but to the temple police and guards who kept watch over Jesus before Caiaphas examined Him.

In addition to everything else that was going on that night, these guards decided they would take advantage of the moment too. The Bible doesn't tell us how these men mimicked and impersonated Jesus that night, but the use of the Greek word *empaidzo* categorically lets us know that these men turned a few minutes of that nightmarish night into a stage of comedy at Jesus' expense. They put on quite a show, hamming it up as they almost certainly pretended to be Jesus and the people He ministered to. Perhaps they laid hands on each other as if they were healing the sick; or lay on the floor and quivered, as if they were being liberated from devils; or wobbled around, acting as if they had been blind but now could suddenly see. Whatever these guards did to mock Jesus, it was a game of charades to mimic and make fun of Him.

When they were finished making sport of Jesus, Luke tells us that these guards "smote him." The word for "smote" is from the word *dero*, a word used frequently to refer to *the grueling and barbaric practice of beating a slave*. This word is so dreadful that it is also often translated *to flay*, such as *to flay the flesh from an animal or human being*. The usage of this word tells us that even before the scribes and elders got their hands on Jesus, the guards had already put Him through a terrible ordeal.

Immediately after the guards were finished playing their charades and brutally beating Jesus, the scribes and elders began to spit in His face and whack Him on the head with their fists (*see* April 14). But the elders didn't stop there. They blindfolded Jesus and began to strike Him on the head *again*, taking their humiliation of Him to the next level. This represented Jesus' third beating.

If we only read Luke's account, we might conclude that this third beating was also at the hands of the guards. However, when we compare and connect Luke's account with Matthew's account, it becomes clear that by this time Jesus had already been transferred into the hands of Caiaphas and his scribes and elders. What we read next in Luke 22:64 occurred *after* these religious leaders had already spit on Him and hit Him (Matthew 26:67).

Luke 22:64 says, "And when they had blindfolded him, they struck him on the face, and asked him, saying, Prophesy, who is it that smote thee?" The word "blindfolded" comes from the Greek word *perikalupto*, which means *to wrap a veil or garment about someone, thus hiding his eyes so he can't see*. We don't know where the blindfold came from. It could have been a piece of Jesus' own clothing or a garment borrowed from one of the scribes and elders. But by the time they finished wrapping Jesus' head in that cloth, He was completely blinded from seeing what was happening around him.

Just as the guards played charades at Jesus' expense, now Caiaphas with the scribes and elders played blindman's bluff at His expense! Once Jesus was blindfolded, "they *struck* him on the face." The word "struck" is from the Greek word *paio*, which describes *a strike that stings*. A more precise translation might be *"they slapped him on the face."* This is the reason the Greek word *paio* was used, for it referred to a slap that caused a terrible sting.

After slapping Jesus, the scribes and elders would badger Him, saying, "…Prophesy, who is it that smote thee?" Here we find that these so-called religious leaders got so caught up in their sick behavior that they sadistically enjoyed the pain they were putting Jesus through. They slapped Him over and again, telling Him, *"Come on, prophet! If You're so good at prophesying and knowing things supernaturally, tell us which one of us just slapped You!"*

Finally, Luke 22:65 tells us, "And many other things blasphemously spake they against him." The word "blasphemy" is from the Greek word *blasphemeo*, meaning *to slander; to accuse; to speak against; to speak derogatory words for the purpose of injuring or harming one's reputation.* It also signifies *profane, foul, unclean language.*

When Luke says they "blasphemously spake," he is talking about Caiaphas with his scribes and elders! Once these religious leaders "took off the lid," every foul thing that was hiding inside them came to the top. It was as if a monster had been let out, and they couldn't get it back in its cage!

Jesus had told these religious leaders earlier, "Woe unto you, scribes and Pharisees, hypocrites! For ye are like unto whited sepulchres, which indeed appear beautiful outward, but are within full of dead men's bones, and of all uncleaness" (Matthew 23:27). In the end, the death and uncleanness in their souls came raging to the top as they screamed and yelled at Jesus using profane, foul, unclean language.

I'm sure that if the people of Israel had been allowed to sneak a peek into that room that night, they would have been horrified to see their supposedly godly leaders slapping Jesus, spitting on Him, slapping Him again, and then screaming curses right in His face! Here these leaders were — all dressed up in their religious garb, but inwardly so rotten that they could not hide their true nature anymore.

So let me ask you two questions:

✦ Are you serious in your relationship with Jesus Christ, or are you, like those who held Him that night, simply playing games with Him?
✦ When other people start playing around with *your* mind and emotions, are you able to follow Jesus' example by holding your peace and loving them in spite of the torture they are putting you through?

Let's covenant together from this day forward to never be like the backslidden religious leaders in this story. How terrible it is to outwardly look beautiful but to inwardly be so ugly! To avoid this scenario in our own lives, we must make the commitment to be serious in our relationship with Jesus and absolutely *refuse* to play games with God.

And should you ever find yourself in a predicament similar to the one Jesus faced — in other words, if people are emotionally abusing you or taking advantage of you — then call out to God to strengthen you! He will give you the wisdom to know when you should speak, when you should be quiet, and exactly what steps you must take. When you find yourself in this kind of tight place, just be certain to guard your mouth and to let the Holy Spirit dictate your emotions so you can demonstrate the love of God to those whom the devil is trying to use against you.

Jesus is the perfect Example of how we must behave in all situations. Although He was blasphemed, reviled, and cursed, He never fought back or allowed Himself to be dragged into a war of words. For this reason, Peter exhorted us to follow in Jesus' steps: "For even hereunto were ye called: because Christ also suffered for us, leaving us an example, that ye should follow his steps: who did no sin, neither was guile found in his mouth" (1 Peter 2:21,22).

Today you can make the decision to come up to a higher level in your commitment to Jesus Christ. You can refuse to play games with God or to deceive yourself any longer about your own spiritual condition. The truth about what is in you will eventually come out anyway, so take an honest look at your soul now to make sure there are no hidden flaws that will later come rising up to the surface!

Why don't you open your heart right now and let the Holy Spirit shine His glorious light into the crevices of your soul? Allow Him to reveal those areas of your life where you need to get to work!

MY PRAYER FOR TODAY

Lord, I never want to play games with You. I am asking You right now to forgive me for any time that I have lied to You and to myself, deceiving myself into believing that things were all right in my life when, in fact, they were not inwardly good at all. Please shine Your light deep into my soul to show me any areas of my life that need immediate attention. And, Lord, I also ask that You give me a strong desire to read through all four of the Gospels so I might better know the life of Jesus and how I can be more like Him.

I pray this in Jesus' name!

MY CONFESSION FOR TODAY

I declare by faith that God gives me the wisdom to know how to respond when I am in a difficult predicament. I know when I should speak, when I should be quiet, and exactly what steps I must take. When I find myself in a tight place, I don't give way to my emotions. Instead, I guard my mouth and let the Spirit dictate my emotions so I can demonstrate the love of God even to those whom the devil is trying to use against me!

I declare this by faith in Jesus' name!

QUESTIONS FOR YOU TO CONSIDER

1. Do you have areas in your life where you are playing games with God and deceiving yourself about your own spiritual condition? Isn't it time for you to get honest with God and with yourself about these problem areas?
2. Have you ever experienced times when the monster in your flesh that you hadn't yet dealt with came crawling to the top, causing you to behave in a way that was shocking even to yourself?
3. Since reading the Gospels is the best way to learn how to become more like Jesus, don't you think it would be a good idea for you to carefully read all four Gospels from beginning to end?

APRIL 16

Being Confident of God's Plan

And when they had bound him, they led him away,
and delivered him to Pontius Pilate the governor.
— Matthew 27:2

Have you ever found yourself in a situation where you felt like you were surrounded and besieged by control freaks who were obsessed with keeping everything that moved under their monitoring control? If you've been in a situation like this before, you know how hard it is to function in that kind of environment.

Well, at the time of Jesus' ministry on earth, Israel was overwhelmed with scads of leaders who were obsessed with the notion of holding on to the reins of power. This paranoia was so epidemic that it had spread to both the religious and political world. The high priest, along with his scribes and elders, were suspicious and paranoid of anyone who appeared to be growing in popularity. The political leaders installed by Rome to preside over Israel were just as paranoid, looking behind every nook and cranny for opponents and constantly struggling every day of their lives to keep power in their grip.

Israel was under the enemy control of Rome, an occupying force that the Jews despised. They hated the Romans for their pagan tendencies, for pushing Roman language and culture on them, for the taxes they were required to pay to Rome — and that's just a few of the reasons the Jews hated the Romans.

Because of the political turmoil in Israel, few political leaders from Rome held power for very long, and those who succeeded did so using cruelty and brutality. The land was full of revolts, rebellions, insurgencies, assassinations, and endless political upheavals. The ability to rule long in this environment required a ruthless, self-concerned leader who was willing to do anything necessary to maintain a position of power. This leads us to *Pontius Pilate*, who was just that type of man.

After Herod Archelaus was removed from power (*see* April 18 to find out more about the three sons of Herod the Great), Judea was placed in the care of a Roman procurator. This was a natural course of events, for the Roman Empire was already divided into approximately forty provinces, each governed by a procurator — a position that was the equivalent of a *governor*. It was normal for a procurator to serve in his position for twelve to thirty-six months. However, Pilate governed Judea for ten years, beginning in the year 26 AD and concluding in the year 36 AD. This ten-year span of time is critical, for it means Pilate was governor of Judea throughout the entire length of Jesus' ministry. The Jewish historian, Flavius Josephus, noted that Pilate was ruthless and unsympathetic and that he failed to comprehend and appreciate how important the Jew's religious beliefs and convictions were to them.

In addition to the normal responsibilities a procurator possessed, Pilate also ruled as the supreme authority in legal matters. As an expert at Roman law, many decisions were brought to him for final judgment. Because of this high-ranking legal position, he had the final say-so in nearly all legal affairs for the territory of Judea. However, even though Pilate held this awesome legal power in his hands, he dreaded cases having to do with religion and often permitted such cases to be passed into the court of the Sanhedrin, over which Caiaphas the high priest presided.

Pilate lived at Herod's palace, located in Caesarea. Because it was the official residence of the procurator, a military force of about 3,000 Roman soldiers was stationed there to protect the Roman governor. Pilate disliked the city of Jerusalem and recoiled from making visits there. But at the time of the feasts when the city of Jerusalem was filled with guests, travelers, and strangers, there was a greater potential of unrest, turbulence, and disorder, so Pilate and his troops would come into the city of Jerusalem to guard and protect the peace of the population. This was the reason Pilate was in the city of Jerusalem at the time of Jesus' crucifixion.

As a highly political man, Pilate knew how to play the political game. The Jews he ruled were also well-versed at playing the political game with him. In fact, so many complaints had been filed in Rome about Pilate's unkind and ruthless style of ruling that the threat of an additional complaint was often all that was needed for the Jews to manipulate Pilate to do their bidding. This no doubt affected Pilate's decision to crucify Jesus.

That day the high priest, the Sanhedrin, and the entire mob, insisted that Jesus be crucified. Pilate wanted to know the reason for this demand, so they answered him, "…We found this fellow perverting the nation, and forbidding to give tribute to Caesar, saying that He himself is Christ a King" (Luke 23:2).

Pilate knew the Jews were jealous of Jesus. But politically the charges they brought against Jesus put him in a very bad position. What if the news reached Rome that Jesus had perverted the nation, teaching the people to withhold their taxes and claiming to be a counter King in place of the Roman emperor? It would be political suicide for Pilate to do nothing about that kind of situation. The Jewish leaders were well aware of this when they fabricated these charges against Jesus. They knew exactly what political strings to pull to get Pilate to do what they wanted — and they were pulling every string they held in their hands.

The Jewish people loathed Pilate for his cruelty and inadequate care of his subjects. The kind of brutality that made him so infamous and hated can be seen in Luke 13:1, where it mentions that Pilate slaughtered a number of Galileans and then mixed their blood together with the sacrifices. Appalling and sick as this act may sound, it is in accordance with many other vicious actions instigated under Pilate's rule as procurator of Judea.

Another example of Pilate's callousness can be seen in an incident that occurred when a prophet claimed to possess a supernatural gift that enabled him to locate consecrated vessels, which he alleged had been secretly hidden by Moses. When this prophet announced that he would unearth these vessels, Samaritans turned out in large numbers to observe the event. Pilate, who thought the entire affair was a disguise for some other political or military activity, dispatched Roman forces to assault and massacre the crowd that had gathered. In the end, it became apparent that nothing political had been intended.

The Samaritans felt such great loss for those who died, they formally requested that the governor of Syria intervene in this case. Their complaints of Pilate became so numerous that he was eventually summoned to Rome to give account for his actions before the Emperor Tiberius himself. But before Pilate could reach Rome to counter the charges that were brought against him, the Emperor Tiberius had died.

Outside the Gospels, Pilate is not mentioned again in the New Testament. Historical records show that the procurator of Syria brought some sort of accusations against Pilate in the year 36 AD. These indictments resulted in his removal from office and exile to Gaul (modern-day France). Eusebius, the well-known early Christian historian, later wrote that Pilate fell into misfortune under the wicked Emperor Caligula and lost many privileges. According to Eusebius, this man Pilate — who was ultimately responsible for the trial, judgment, crucifixion, and burial of Jesus and who had ruled Judea ruthlessly and mercilessly for ten years — finally committed suicide.

With this history now behind us, let's look at Matthew 27:2. It says regarding Jesus, "And when they had bound him, they led him away, and delivered him to Pontius Pilate the governor." The word "bound" is the Greek word *desantes*, from the word *deo*, the same word that would be used to describe *the binding, tying up, or securing of an animal*. I am confident that this was precisely the connotation Matthew had in mind, for the next phrase uses a word that was common in the world of animal caretakers.

The verse tells us that they "led him away." These words come from the Greek word *apago*. The word *apago* is used for *a shepherd who ties a rope about the neck of his sheep and then leads it down the path to where it needs to go (see* April 13). Just as the soldiers had led Jesus to Caiaphas, now they slipped a rope about His neck and walked the "Lamb of God" to Pontius Pilate.

The Bible says that once Jesus was in Pilate's jurisdiction, they then "...delivered him to Pontius Pilate the governor." The word "delivered" is the word *paradidomi*, the same word we saw when Jesus *committed* Himself to the Father who judges righteously (*see* April 13). However, in this case, the meaning would more likely be *to commit, to yield, to transmit, to deliver,* or *to hand something over to someone else.*

This means that when the high priest ordered Jesus to be taken to Pilate, he officially made the issue Pilate's problem. The high priest took Jesus to Pilate; delivered Him fully into Pilate's hands; and then left Pilate with the responsibility of finding Him guilty and crucifying Him.

Matthew 27:11 says, "And Jesus stood before the governor: and the governor asked him, saying, Art thou the King of the Jews? And Jesus said unto him, Thou sayest." Pilate asked a direct question, but Jesus refused to directly answer him. Matthew 27:12 goes on to say, "And when he was accused of the chief priests and elders, he answered nothing." So for a second time, Jesus refused to answer or refute the charges that were brought up against Him.

Matthew 27:13,14 tells us what happened next: "Then said Pilate unto him, Hearest thou not how many things they witness against thee? And he answered him to never a word; insomuch that the governor marvelled greatly." Notice the Bible says Pilate "marveled greatly" at Jesus' silence. In Greek, this phrase is the word *thaumadzo*, which means *to wonder; to be at a loss of words; to be shocked and amazed.*

Pilate was dumbfounded by Jesus' silence because Roman law permitted prisoners three chances to open their mouths to defend themselves. If a prisoner passed up those three chances to speak in his defense, he would be automatically charged as "guilty." In Matthew 27:11, Jesus passed up His *first chance.* In Matthew 27:12, He passed up His *second chance.* Now in Matthew 27:14, Jesus passes up His *final chance* to defend Himself.

At the very end of this time of interrogation, Pilate asked Jesus, "...Art thou the King of the Jews? And he answered him and said, Thou sayest it" (Luke 23:3). John's Gospel tells us that Jesus added, "...My kingdom is not of this world: if my kingdom were of this world, then would my servants fight, that I should not be delivered to the Jews: but now is my kingdom not from hence" (John 18:36). After hearing these answers, "then said Pilate to the chief priests and to the people, I find no fault in this man" (Luke 23:4).

As you will see in tomorrow's *Sparkling Gem,* Pilate searched diligently for a loophole so he wouldn't have to kill Jesus. John 19:12 says, "And from thenceforth Pilate sought to release him...." But nothing Pilate could do was able to stop the plan from being implemented. Even Jesus passed up His three chances to defend Himself, because He knew the Cross was a part of the Father's plan.

When Jesus finally answered Pilate's question, He still didn't defend Himself, knowing it was the appointed time for Him to be slain as the Lamb of God who would take away the sins of the world. But Pilate didn't want to crucify Him. In fact, the Roman governor began looking for a loophole — for some way out of putting this Man to death.

But Pilate's search for a way out was in vain; the plan *couldn't* be changed because it was time for the Son of God to offer the permanent sacrifice for sin. As Hebrews 9:12 says, "Neither by the blood of goats and calves, but by his own blood he entered in once into the holy place, having obtained eternal redemption for us."

Are you certain of God's plan for your life? Consider whether or not you are able to say with conviction: "I know what God has called me to do, and I'm willing to go where He tells me to go and pay any price I have to pay. My greatest priority and obsession is to do the will of the Father!" If you are *not* able to say this yet, ask the Holy Spirit to help you grow to the point where doing God's will, regardless of the cost, becomes the most important thing in your life. *Even if the life of obedience takes you through hard places as it did with Jesus, the end result will be resurrection and victory!*

MY PRAYER FOR TODAY

Lord, I want to be so confident of Your plan for my life that I refuse to let anything move me! Just as Jesus refused to be swayed away from Your plan for Him, I want to be fixed and committed to do exactly what I've been born to do. Help me know Your plan for my life — and once I really understand it, please give me the strength, power, and conviction to stand by that plan until I see it come to pass in my life!

I pray this in Jesus' name!

MY CONFESSION FOR TODAY

I boldly declare that God has a wonderful plan for my life! God's Spirit is revealing that plan to me right now. I am willing to do what He's called me to do; I'm willing to go where He tells me to go; and I'm willing to pay any price I have to pay to accomplish the life-assignment God has preordained for me! My greatest priority and obsession is to do the will of the Father!

I declare this by faith in Jesus' name!

QUESTIONS FOR YOU TO CONSIDER

1. Are you able to verbalize or write down God's plan for your life? If so, try right now to speak out loud or write out plainly on paper what God has put in your heart about His plans for you.
2. Do you believe you possess the fortitude you need to stand firm in the face of any hardship or opposition that might come to challenge you as you follow God's plan?
3. What steps do you need to take right now so you can grow strong enough spiritually to overcome any pressures that might try to coax you into giving up God's plan for your life?

Pilate was dumbfounded by Jesus' silence because Roman law permitted prisoners three chances to open their mouths to defend themselves. If a prisoner passed up those three chances to speak in his defense, he would be automatically charged as "guilty." In Matthew 27:11, Jesus passed up His *first chance*. In Matthew 27:12, He passed up His *second chance*. Now in Matthew 27:14, Jesus passes up His *final chance* to defend Himself.

APRIL 17

ཀྵ

Pilate Looks for a Loophole

When Pilate heard of Galilee,
he asked whether the man were a Galilean.
And as soon as he knew that he belonged unto Herod's jurisdiction,
he sent him to Herod,
who himself also was at Jerusalem at that time.
— Luke 23:6,7

*P*ilate had never had a problem with causing bloodshed in the past, so it seems strange that he balked at the thought of crucifying Jesus. As governor and the chief legal authority of the land, Pilate had been invested by Rome with the power to decide who would and wouldn't live. This Roman governor was infamous for his cold-hearted, insensitive, and cruel style of leadership and had never found it difficult to order the death of a criminal — until now.

There was something inside Pilate that recoiled at the idea of crucifying Jesus. The Bible doesn't state exactly why Pilate didn't want to crucify Him, but it makes one wonder what he saw in Jesus' eyes when he interrogated Him. We do know Pilate was shocked at the manner in which Jesus carried Himself, for Matthew 27:14 tells us that Pilate "marveled greatly" at Jesus.

The words "marveled greatly" are from the Greek word *thaumadzo* which means *to wonder, to be at a loss of words, to be shocked and amazed.* A man like this Jesus had never stood before Pilate before, and the governor was obviously disturbed at the thought of murdering Him.

In fact, Pilate was so disturbed that he decided to probe deeper by asking questions. He was looking for a loophole that would enable him to escape this trap the Jews had set both for Jesus and for himself as well. Indeed, the Jewish leaders had carefully schemed a trap with three potential results, all of which would make them very happy. The threefold purpose of this trap was as follows:

1. To see Jesus judged by the Roman court, thus ruining His reputation and guaranteeing His crucifixion, while at the same time vindicating themselves in the eyes of the people.

To ensure that this happened, the Jewish leaders falsified charges that made Jesus appear to be a bona fide political offender. These were the charges: 1) that He had perverted the whole nation — a religious charge that was the responsibility of the Sanhedrin to judge; 2) that He had commanded people not to pay their taxes to Rome; and 3) that He claimed to be king (*see* Luke 23:2). According to Roman law, Jesus should be crucified for claiming to be king. If these charges were proven true, Pilate was bound by law to crucify Him. If this is what followed, the first purpose of their scheme would have worked.

2. To see Pilate wiped out and permanently removed from power on the charge that he was unfaithful to the Roman emperor because he would not crucify a man who claimed to be a rival king to the emperor.

Had Pilate declined to crucify Jesus, this rejection would have given the Jewish leaders the ammunition they needed to prove to Rome that this governor should be removed from power because he was a traitor to the emperor. News would have reached the emperor of Rome that Pilate had permitted a rival king to live, and Pilate would have been charged with treason (*see* John 19:12).

It is interesting that this same charge was brought against Jesus. It was a charge that most assuredly would have led to Pilate's own death or banishment. If Jesus was allowed to go free by the Roman court, the Jewish leadership would have been thrilled, for then they would have had a legal reason to expel Pilate from their land. Thus, the second purpose of their scheme would have worked.

3. To take Jesus back into their own court in the Sanhedrin if Pilate would not crucify Him, where they had the religious authority to stone Him to death for claiming to be the Son of God.

The truth is, the Jewish leaders never needed to deliver Jesus to Pilate because the court of the Sanhedrin already had the religious authority to kill Jesus by stoning for claiming to be the Son of God. Even if Pilate refused to crucify Jesus, they fully intended to kill Him anyway (*see* John 19:7).

So we see that the trip to Pilate's court of law was designed to turn Jesus' arrest into a political catastrophe that would possibly help the Jewish leaders get rid of Pilate as well. But if Jesus had been freed by the Roman court, they intended to kill Him anyway. This was the third part of their scheme.

The solution to this mess was easy! All Pilate had to do was crucify Jesus; then he would have happy Jewish elders on his hands; no charges of treason leveled against him in Rome; strengthened ties to the religious community; and a guarantee of remaining in power. Pilate just had to say, "CRUCIFY HIM!" and this political game would be over. But he couldn't bring himself to utter those words!

Instead, Pilate gave Jesus three opportunities to speak up in His own defense. But Jesus said nothing. Isaiah 53:7 (*NKJV*) says, "...As a sheep before its shearers is silent, so He opened not His mouth." According to the law, Jesus should have automatically been declared "guilty" because He passed up three chances to defend Himself. But this time Pilate simply could not permit himself to follow the due course of judicial process. He sought instead to find a way out of this dilemma.

As noted above, perhaps Pilate saw something in Jesus' eyes that affected him. Maybe Jesus' kind and gracious behavior grabbed Pilate's heart. Others have speculated that Pilate's wife may have secretly been a follower of Jesus who told her husband about His goodness and the miracles that had followed His life. Matthew 27:19 reports that Pilate's wife was so upset about Jesus' impending death that she even had upsetting dreams about Him in the night. She sent word about her dreams to Pilate, begging him not to crucify Jesus.

As Pilate probed deeper in his interrogation, he discovered that Jesus was from Galilee. At long last, Pilate could breathe a sigh of relief. He had found the loophole that shifted the full weight of the decision to his old enemy, Herod! Galilee was under the legal jurisdiction of Herod. What a coincidence! Herod just "happened" to be in Jerusalem that week to participate in the Feast of Passover!

Pilate promptly ordered Jesus to be transferred to the other side of the city to the residence where Herod was staying with his royal entourage. The Bible tells us, "And when Herod saw Jesus, he was exceeding glad: for he was desirous to see him of a long season, because he had heard many things of him; and he hoped to have seen some miracle done by him" (Luke 23:8). However, it didn't take long for Herod to get angry with Jesus and return Him to Pilate!

What do you think went through Jesus' mind as He stood before first a Roman governor, then a Jewish king — only to be shipped back to the Roman governor again? Have you been feeling knocked around and passed from one authority figure to another at home, at church, in the workplace, or in the governmental system? If so, you can feel free to talk to Jesus about it, because He really understands the predicament you find yourself in right now!

Hebrews 4:15,16 says, "For we have not an high priest which cannot be touched with the feelings of our infirmities; but was in all points tempted like as we are, yet without sin. Let us therefore come boldly unto the throne of grace, that we may obtain mercy, and find grace to help in time of need." Since Jesus understands your dilemma, I advise you to speak freely to Him about the emotional ups and downs you feel as a result of your situation. His throne is a throne of grace — a place where you can obtain mercy and find grace to help in your time of need.

So go before God's throne today. He will hear you, answer you, and give you the power and wisdom you need to press through this time in your life!

MY PRAYER FOR TODAY

Lord, I am so glad You understand when I feel confused about the person I am supposed to report to and to whom I am supposed to be accountable at work and at church. Sometimes I feel like my leaders send me back and forth, not knowing what to do with me or to whom I am supposed to report, which makes it hard for me to do my job. I know that those who are over me have their own challenges, so I want to be helpful to them, not judgmental of them. Please give me the wisdom to know how to behave in a godly manner in this environment.

I pray this in Jesus' name!

MY CONFESSION FOR TODAY

I confess that I have the mind of Christ for my situation. I am not in confusion; rather, I walk in peace in every situation. Because Jesus has been in my same place, I go to Him to tell Him about my situation, and He gives me all the mercy and grace I need to be successful in this place where He has called me!

I declare this by faith in Jesus' name!

QUESTIONS FOR YOU TO CONSIDER

1. Do you feel like you are knocked around from one authority to another at your job or in your position at church? Are you confused about whom you are really supposed to be accountable to?
2. Have you ever asked for clarification regarding this matter? If you didn't understand what you were told, did you seek further clarification to avoid confusion?
3. If you've done all you can to properly report to the authorities who are over you and they still don't like the way you are reporting to them, have you prayed and asked the Lord to help you become what your authorities need you to be?

Have you been feeling knocked around and passed from one authority figure to another at home, at church, in the workplace, or in the governmental system? If so, you can feel free to talk to Jesus about it, because He really understands the predicament you find yourself in right now!

APRIL 18

⚜

Herod Finally Meets Jesus!

And when Herod saw Jesus, he was exceeding glad:
for he was desirous to see him of a long season,
because he had heard many things of him;
and he hoped to have seen some miracle done by him.
— Luke 23:8

*A*fter Pilate discovered Jesus was from Galilee, the jurisdiction of Herod, the Roman governor quickly sent Jesus off to see Herod. At that time, Herod was in Jerusalem to celebrate the Feast of Passover with the Jewish people. But before we get into Herod's excited anticipation to meet Jesus, let's first see which Herod this verse is talking about.

Several men named Herod ruled in Israel over the years. The first and most famous was "Herod the Great," who was made the first governor of Galilee when he was twenty-five years old. His kingship was launched by the order of Octavius and Marc Antony — the same Marc Antony who had a famous relationship with Cleopatra, the Queen of Egypt. Flavius Josephus, the well-known Jewish historian, recorded that Herod the Great died in 4 BC.

After the death of Herod the Great, his territory was divided among his three sons. These three sons (also named "Herod") were as follows:

Herod Archelaus

Herod Archelaus was made governor of Samaria, Judea, and Idumea in 4 BC when his father died, and he ruled until approximately 6 AD. This makes him the Herod who was ruling when Mary, Joseph, and Jesus returned from their flight to Egypt (*see* Matthew 2:22).

When Herod Archelaus ascended to the throne in 4 BC, things almost immediately went sour for him. The first problem he confronted was a rebellion incited among Jewish students by their teachers. Because the Ten Commandments forbid graven images, these teachers encouraged their students to tear down and destroy the imperial golden eagle that Rome had ordered to be hung on the entrance to the temple. As punishment, Herod Archelaus ordered these teachers and students to be burned alive. The massacre continued until three thousand Jews had been slaughtered during the Feast of Passover. Soon Herod Archelaus journeyed to Rome to be crowned by the Emperor Augustus. However, fresh riots ensued in his absence, resulting in more than two thousand people being crucified.

The Gospel of Matthew indicates that Joseph and Mary were troubled about settling in the territories ruled by Herod Archelaus and therefore made their home in Galilee (Matthew 2:22). Herod Archelaus was so despised that the Jews and Samaritans, usually foes, united together and corporately appealed to Rome to request that he should be removed from power. In 6 AD, Herod Archelaus was banished to Gaul (modern-day France) and died before the year 18.

Herod Philip

Herod Philip was educated in Rome, along with his brothers Herod Archelaus and Herod Antipas. When his father, Herod the Great, died in 4 BC, Herod Philip became governor of the distant regions in the northeast territories of his father's kingdom. These territories included:

✦ Gaulanitis — known today as the Golan Heights.
✦ Batanaea — the territory east of the Jordan River and the Sea of Galilee.
✦ Trachonitis and Auranitis (or Hauran) — the southern part of modern-day Syria.

The Jews were a minority among Herod Philip's subjects. Most people under his rule were of Syrian or Arabian ancestry, but he had Greek and Roman subjects as well, usually living in the cities. Herod Philip died in the year 34 AD after having ruled his kingdom for thirty-seven years. Since he left no heir, the Roman Emperor Tiberius directed his territories to be added to the region of Syria.

Flavius Josephus wrote that Herod Philip was moderate and quiet in the conduct of his life and government. When Tiberius died in 37 AD, his successor, Caligula, restored the principality almost in its entirety and appointed Herod Philip's nephew, Herod Agrippa, as the new ruler — *but he's another story that we won't get into today*!

Herod Antipas

This leads us to the third son of Herod the Great — *Herod Antipas*, the same Herod before whom Jesus appeared in Luke 23:8 and who had long desired to personally meet Jesus. What do we know of this Herod?

Herod Antipas was assigned tetrarch of Galilee and Peraea (located on the east bank of the Jordan). The Roman emperor Augustus affirmed this decision, and the reign of Herod Antipas began in the year 4 BC when his father died.

The name "Antipas" is a compound of two Greek words, *anti* and *pas*. The word *anti* means *against,* and the word *pas* means *all* or *everyone*. Once compounded into one word, it means *one who is against everything and everyone*. This name alone should tell us something about the personality of this wicked ruler.

In the year 17 AD, Herod Antipas founded Tiberias, a new capitol he built to honor the Roman emperor, Tiberius. However, the building of this city caused an enormous disturbance among his Jewish subjects when they discovered it was being constructed on top of an old Jewish graveyard. Because these graves had been desecrated, devout Jews refused to enter Tiberias for a very long time.

Herod Antipas tried to style himself in a way that would appeal to the Jewish people, even participating in national Jewish celebrations. But the people were not convinced by this act and viewed him as an insincere fraud. Even Jesus compared Herod Antipas to a fox — an animal that was considered to be the epitome of trickery and that was usually unclean and infected with sickness. In other words, when Jesus called Herod a fox, it was the equivalent of saying he was a sneaky, lying, deceiving, dishonest, infected, and sick individual. Those were pretty strong words for Jesus!

Herod Antipas' first marriage was to the daughter of an Arabian leader. However, he divorced this woman so he could marry the ex-wife of his half-brother, a woman named *Herodias*. Taking the ex-wife of one's brother was not uncommon, but Herodias was also the daughter of another half-brother, Aristobulus. In Roman law, marriage to one's niece was also permitted, but marriage to a woman who was both one's sister-in-law and one's niece was most unusual. This unusual marriage drew the attention and criticism of John the Baptist. The Gospel of Mark records that John the Baptist died because of the public stand he took against Herod Antipas' second marriage.

In the year 37, Herod Antipas' new wife, Herodias, disagreed when her brother Agrippa became king in place of Herod Philip. She thought that the royal title should not be given to Herod Agrippa but to her husband and made plans accordingly for Herod Antipas to be appointed king. Adamantly disagreeing with Herodias, the Roman emperor exiled both her and her husband to live the rest of their lives in Gaul, which is modern-day France.

Luke 23:8 tells us that Herod Antipas was eager to finally meet Jesus: "And when Herod saw Jesus, he was exceeding glad: for he was desirous to see him of a long season, because he had heard many things of him; and he hoped to have seen some miracle done by him." Notice this verse says "And when Herod *saw* Jesus...." The word "saw" is from the Greek word *horao*, meaning *to see; to behold; to delightfully view; a scrutinizing look;* or *to look with the intent to examine.*

This word *horao* paints a very important picture for us of exactly what happened when Jesus finally stood before Herod Antipas. It conveys the idea that Herod was *excited* and *delighted* to finally behold the miracle-worker he had heard so much about. Once Jesus stood before him, Herod literally *looked Him over, scrutinizing and examining every detail* of the Man who appeared before him.

The next part of the verse confirms the exhilaration and jubilation Herod Antipas felt about seeing Jesus. It says, "he was *exceeding glad*...." The Greek text uses two words, *echari lian*. The word *echari* is from the word *chairo*, the Greek word for *joy*. The Greek word *lian* means *much, great,* or *exceedingly*. These two words together suggest *extreme excitement* or someone who is *ecstatic* about something. In other words, Herod Antipas was so "hyper" about having the chance to meet Jesus that he was nearly jumping up and down on the inside!

This should tell us how well known Jesus had become during His ministry. If Herod Antipas was this excited to meet Him, it's no wonder that the scribes and elders were apprehensive about His widespread popularity. Even the nobility longed for a chance to see Jesus' miracles!

That's why the next part of the verse says, "...for he was desirous to see him of a long season, because he had heard many things of him...." The word "desirous" is the Greek word *thelo*, which means *to will* or *to wish*. However, the construction used in this Greek phrase intensifies the *wish*, making it a *very strong wish or desire*. According to this verse, Herod had this strong desire for "a long season" — a phrase taken from the Greek words *ek hikanos chronos*. The word *hikanos* means *many, considerable,* or *much*. The word *chronos* means *time*, such as *a season, epoch, era*, or *any specified duration of time*. These words together could be translated *for many years, for a long time*, or *for many seasons*.

Why had Herod Antipas longed to see Jesus for many years? The verse says, "...because he had heard many things of him...." Jesus was a name that the Herod household had heard for years! I'm sure all three Herod boys — *Archelaus, Philip*, and *Antipas* — heard tales about:

✦ Jesus' supernatural birth.
✦ The kings from the east who had come to acknowledge Him.
✦ The attempt of their father, Herod the Great, to kill Jesus by ordering all the babies in Bethlehem to be murdered.
✦ Jesus and His parents slipping into Egypt and waiting for the right moment to come back into Israel.
✦ The ministry of Jesus touching the nation with healing and delivering power.

Stories of Jesus must have been very familiar to the Herod household. Herod Antipas had longed for a chance to meet this famous personality for many years. Jesus was a living legend, and now He was standing in his presence!

At the end of this verse, we discover the reason Herod Antipas was most excited to meet Jesus. The verse continues to tell us, "...he hoped to have seen some miracle done by him." The Greek word for "hoped" is *elpidzo*, meaning *to hope*, but the construction used in this verse is similar to the word *thelo*, noted above, which means *to wish*. Just as Herod's *wish* to see Jesus was *a very strong wish*, now his *hope* to see some miracle performed by Jesus was *a very strong hope* or *an earnest expectation*.

Herod was expecting to "...*have seen* some miracle done by him." The word "see" is the Greek word *horao*, the same word used in the first part of this verse when we are told that Herod was *excited to see* Jesus. Now this word is used to let us know Herod was *euphoric* about his chance to see some "miracle" done by Jesus.

The word "miracle" is the Greek word *semeion*, which is *a sign, a mark, or a token that verifies or authenticates an alleged report*. It is used in the Gospels primarily to depict *miracles and supernatural events*, which means the purpose of such miracles and supernatural events is *to verify and authenticate* the message of the Gospel.

But Luke 23:9 tells us that Jesus did not work miracles on demand for Herod, nor did He answer the large number of questions that Herod put to Him that day. As a result of His silence, the following verse tells us, "And the chief priests and scribes stood and vehemently accused him" (v. 10).

Notice that the chief priests and scribes followed Jesus from Pilate's palace to Herod's residence. When Jesus performed no miracle for Herod, the scribes and elders, most of whom belonged to the sect of the Sadducees who didn't believe in the supernatural, seized the moment to start screaming and yelling uncontrollably. The word "vehemently" is the Greek word *eutonus*, meaning *at full pitch, at full volume, strenuously,* or *vigorously*. In other words, these religious leaders weren't just slightly raising their voices; they were what we might call "screaming their heads off"! Most likely they were screaming accusations right in Jesus' face, saying things like, *"Some miracle worker You are! You have no power! You're a fraud! If You can work miracles, why don't You work one right now! You're nothing but a charlatan!"*

That day Herod was left with the impression that Jesus was nothing more than a spiritual fraud. Because Jesus didn't perform on demand as Herod wished, this governor's expectations were dashed, causing him to unleash his rage against Jesus. In the short time that followed, Jesus took the full brunt of this wicked ruler's wrath.

I'm sure you've been in situations when you've been railed at because you failed to meet someone's demands. Can you think of a time when something like this happened to you? How did you respond? Did you yell and scream back at that person when he vented his anger at you, or were you able to remain quiet and controlled as Jesus did that day before Herod Antipas and the chief priests and elders?

Life will occasionally take you through difficult places. One of those hard places is when you discover that people are disappointed with your performance. If you find yourself in this kind of predicament, remember that Jesus failed to meet the expectations of Herod Antipas (although that was probably the *only* person whose expectations Jesus ever failed to meet)! *When you find yourself in such a place, go hide yourself away for a few minutes and call out to the Lord. He has been there; He understands; and He will help you know how you must respond!*

MY PRAYER FOR TODAY

Lord, help me control myself when a project into which I've put my whole heart and soul goes unappreciated and rejected by my boss, my parents, my pastor, my fellow workers, or my friends. Help me take advantage of moments like these to learn how to be quiet and controlled. Please use these times in my life to help me mature and to learn how to keep my mouth shut. I know You understand the emotions that accompany this kind of disappointment, so who else can I turn to but You to help me in these kinds of ordeals?

I pray this in Jesus' name!

I confess that I am self-controlled when people get angry or upset with me. Even when others vent their anger by yelling and screaming, I don't yell and scream back at them. In these moments, the Spirit of God rules my heart, mind, and emotions, and I am able to remain quiet and controlled. When I find myself in this situation, I hide myself away in prayer for a few minutes and call out to the Lord. He helps me understand the right way and the right time to respond.

I declare this by faith in Jesus' name!

QUESTIONS FOR YOU TO CONSIDER

1. Can you recall a time when after putting forth your very best efforts, you discovered that those efforts weren't appreciated or considered acceptable by those you were trying to please?
2. When those you were trying to satisfy informed you about how displeased they were with your performance, did you graciously listen and learn, or did you put up a fight in your self-defense?
3. Looking back on that situation and knowing what you know now, how would you respond differently if you could turn the clock back and do it all over again?

APRIL 19

ᏚᏋᏒᎧᏒᎧ

Herod Antipas Mocks the King of Glory!

And Herod with his men of war set him at nought,
and mocked him, and arrayed him in a gorgeous robe,
and sent him again to Pilate.
— Luke 23:11

On that day when Jesus refused to meet Herod's expectations, Luke 23:10 tells us the chief priests and scribes were so infuriated that they stood up and "...vehemently accused him." That word "vehemently" means *at full pitch, at full volume, strenuously,* or *vigorously.* That means those men must have been screaming like crazy maniacs who were totally out of control! They were most likely saying something like, *"Some miracle worker! You have no power! You're a fraud! If You can work miracles, why don't You work one right now? You're nothing but a charlatan!"*

Once the screaming match stopped and the volume of their voices was turned down enough for Herod's voice to be heard, Herod gave the official order for himself and his men of war to deliberately humiliate, mock, make fun of, and heckle Jesus. Suddenly the people in that room in Herod's residence turned into a booing, hissing, mocking, laughing mob, with all their venom directed toward

Jesus. Luke 23:11 tells us about this event, saying, "And Herod with his men of war set him at nought, and mocked him, and arrayed him in a gorgeous robe, and sent him again to Pilate."

Notice that Herod was gathered there that day with "his men of war." Who were these men of war, and why were they at Herod's side when Jesus stood before him? The word for "men of war" in Greek is *strateuma*. This Greek word could signify *a small detachment of Roman soldiers*, but most likely it suggests that these men were Herod's personal bodyguards, selected from a larger group of soldiers because they were exceptionally trained and prepared to fight and defend if called upon — thus, the reason the *King James Version* refers to them as "men of war."

The Bible informs us that Herod, with the assistance of his bodyguards, took Jesus and "set him at nought." This phrase is developed from the Greek word *exoutheneo*, a compound of the words *ek* and *outhen*. The word *ek* means *out*, and the word *outhen* is a later form of the word *ouden*, which means *nothing*. Taken together, it means *to make one out to be nothing*. It can be translated *to make light of, to belittle, to disdain, to disregard, to despise,* or *to treat with maliciousness and contempt*.

Jesus had already endured the insane yelling and screaming that the chief priests and elders unleashed on Him. But now Herod and his bodyguards entered center stage to start their own brand of humiliating Jesus. Luke uses the word *exoutheneo* to let us know that they were *malicious* and *vindictive* and that their behavior was *nasty* and *ugly*. Then Luke tells us that Herod and his men "mocked him." This gives us an idea of how low they sank in their ridiculing of Jesus.

The word "mocked" is the Greek word *empaidzo*, the same word used to portray the mocking behavior of the soldiers who guarded Jesus before He was taken into Caiaphas' high court (*see* April 15). The word *empaidzo* meant *to play a game*. It was often used for *playing a game with children* or *to amuse a crowd by impersonating someone in a silly and exaggerated way*. It might be used in *a game of charades* when someone intends *to comically portray or even make fun of someone*.

Herod Antipas was a Roman governor — supposedly an educated, cultured, and refined man. He was surrounded by finely trained Roman soldiers who were supposed to be professional in their conduct and appearance. But these men of war, along with their king, descended deep into depravity as they began to put on quite a show impersonating Jesus and the people He ministered to. They probably hammed it up, acting as if they were healing the sick; lying on the floor and quivering as if they were being liberated from devils; groping around as if they were blind and then pretending to suddenly be able to see. It was all a game of charades intended to mimic and make fun of Jesus.

Then Luke tells us, "…they arrayed him in a gorgeous robe…." The word "arrayed" is the Greek word *periballo*, which means *to throw about* or *to drape about*, as to drape around one's shoulders. The words "gorgeous robe" are the words *esthes* and *lampros*. The word *esthes* describes *a robe or garment*, while the word *lampros* depicts *something that is resplendent, glistening, or magnificent*. It was frequently used to depict *a garment made of sumptuous, brightly colored materials*.

It is doubtful that this was the garment of a soldier, for even a bodyguard of Herod would not be arrayed in such resplendent garments. In all likelihood, this was a garment worn by a politician, for when candidates were running for public office, they wore beautiful and brightly colored clothes. More specifically, however, this was almost certainly one of Herod's own sumptuous garments that he permitted to be draped around Jesus' shoulders so they could pretend to adore Him as king as part of their mockery of Him.

Although Herod apparently enjoyed this maltreatment and abuse of Jesus, Luke 23:14,15 says he could find no crime in Jesus worthy of death. Therefore, after the conclusion of these events, Herod "…sent him again to Pilate" (Luke 23:11).

When Herod sent Jesus back to Pilate, he sent Him clothed in this regal robe. One scholar notes that since this garment was one usually worn by a candidate running for office, Herod's decision to send Jesus to Pilate in this robe was the equivalent of saying, "This is no king! It's only another candidate, a pretender, who thinks he's running for some kind of office!"

When I read of what Jesus endured during the time before He was sent to be crucified, it simply overwhelms me. Jesus committed no sin and no crime, nor was any guile ever found in His mouth; yet He was judged more severely than the worst of criminals. Even hardened criminals would not have been put through such grueling treatment. And just think — all this happened *before* He was nailed to that wooden Cross — the lowest, most painful, debasing manner in which a criminal could be executed in the ancient world!

Before you do anything else today, why don't you take a few minutes to stop and thank Jesus for everything He went through to purchase your redemption? Salvation may have been a free gift to you, but purchasing salvation was *not* free for Jesus. It cost Him His life and His blood. This is why Paul wrote, "In whom we have redemption through his blood, the forgiveness of sins, according to the riches of his grace" (Ephesians 1:7).

And here's one more suggestion for you: Rather than keep the Good News of Jesus Christ to yourself, why don't you find an opportunity today to tell someone else all that Jesus did so he or she can be saved? *God's Spirit might use you to lead someone to a saving knowledge of Jesus this very day!*

MY PRAYER FOR TODAY

Lord, I want to take this moment to say thank You for everything You went through for me. It is amazing that You loved me so much that You were willing to endure all of this for me. I know that my salvation was purchased with Your blood and that I could never pay for my salvation. But I want to tell You that I will serve You faithfully for the rest of my days as a way to show You my gratitude! Jesus, thank You for loving me so much!

I pray this in Jesus' name!

MY CONFESSION FOR TODAY

I confess that I am redeemed by the blood of Jesus Christ! God loved me so much that He sent His only begotten Son to take away my sin, my sickness, my pain, my lack of peace, and my suffering on the Cross. Because of Jesus, today I am forgiven; I am healed; I am free of pain; I am filled with peace; and I am a joint heir with Him!

I declare this by faith in Jesus' name!

QUESTIONS FOR YOU TO CONSIDER

1. What did you learn new from today's *Sparkling Gem*?
2. Have you ever felt mocked for your faith? If so, how did you respond to those who mocked you?
3. Can you think of someone you can share the Gospel with today? If your answer is yes, who is that person?

APRIL 20

❧❧❧

'Not Guilty'

[Pilate] said unto them, Ye have brought this man unto me,
as one that perverteth the people: and, behold, I, having examined him before you,
have found no fault in this man touching the things whereof ye accuse him:
No, nor yet Herod: for I sent you to him;
and, lo, nothing worthy of death is done unto him.
I will therefore chastise him, and release him.
— Luke 23:14-16

When Jesus was returned to Pilate's court, Pilate assembled the chief priests and rulers; then he told them, "Ye have brought this man unto me, as one that perverteth the people: and, behold, I, having examined him before you, have found no fault in this man touching the things whereof ye accuse him: No, nor yet Herod: for I sent you to him; and, lo, nothing worthy of death is done unto him. I will therefore chastise him, and release him."

Notice Pilate said he had "examined" Jesus. This Greek word, *anakrinas,* means *to examine closely, to scrutinize,* or *to judge judicially.* You must recall that Pilate was the chief legal authority of the land. He knew Roman law and was invested with power to see that Roman law was kept. From a judicial standpoint, he couldn't find a single crime Jesus had committed. Perhaps Jesus had broken some Jewish religious law, but Pilate wasn't a Jew and couldn't care less about Jewish law. From a purely legal standpoint, Jesus wasn't guilty. To add weight to his action, Pilate backed his view by saying, "Herod has arrived at the same conclusion as I have: This Man has committed no legal offense."

Knowing that the religious leaders were bent on seeing the shedding of Jesus' blood, Pilate offered to chastise Jesus, hoping this would appease the bloody appetite of the mob. Had this offer been accepted, the beating would have been minor; however, it would have been viewed as a warning that Jesus needed to limit His activities.

Then Pilate announced that after Jesus was chastised, he would "release" Him. When the mob heard the word "release," they jumped on the chance to reverse Pilate's decision. You see, it was a custom at this particular time of the year for one prisoner to be "released" from prison as a favor to the people. Because Israel hated being occupied by Rome, many Jewish sons fought like "freedom fighters" to overthrow Roman rule. Therefore, each year when it came time for this big event, all of Jerusalem waited with anticipation to see which prisoner would be released.

By choosing to "release" Jesus at this moment, it was as if Pilate was making the choice himself which prisoner would be released — and his choice was Jesus. When the people heard of Pilate's decision, they cried out, "…Away with this man, and release unto us Barabbas: (who for a certain sedition made in the city, and for murder, was cast into prison)" (Luke 23:18,19).

Who was Barabbas? He was a notorious rabble-rouser who had been proven guilty of "sedition" in the city of Jerusalem. What is "sedition"? It comes from *stasis,* the old Greek word for *treason,* which refers to *the deliberate attempt to overthrow the government or to kill a head of state.*

It is interesting that treason was the very charge the Jewish leaders brought against Jesus when they accused Him of claiming to be king! However, in the case of Barabbas, the charge was *real,* for he had led a volatile insurrection against the government that resulted in a massacre. Nevertheless, Barabbas' act of bravery, although illegal and murderous, made him a hero in the minds of the local population.

Luke informs us that this Barabbas was so dangerous that they "cast" him into prison. The word "cast" is the Greek word *ballo,* meaning *to throw,* which suggests the Roman authorities wasted no time in *hurling* this low-level bandit into jail for the role he played in this bloody uprising. The Roman authorities wanted him off the streets and locked up forever!

Luke 23:20,21 says, "Pilate therefore, willing to release Jesus, spake again to them. But they cried, saying, Crucify him, crucify him." The word "willing" is the Greek word *thelo.* It would be better translated, *"Pilate therefore, wishing, longing, or desiring to release Jesus...."* Pilate searched for a way to set Jesus free, but the multitude screamed for crucifixion.

This was the first time crucifixion had been specially demanded by the crowd. Luke says the angry mob "cried" for Jesus to be crucified. The word "cried" is the word *epiphoneo,* and it means *to shout, to scream, to yell, to shriek,* or *to screech.* The Greek tense means they were hysterically *screaming* and *shrieking* at the top of their voices — totally out of control and without pause.

Pilate appealed to them again, "...Why, what evil hath he done? I have found no cause of death in him: I will therefore chastise him, and let him go" (Luke 23:22). Again the Roman governor hoped that a beating might satisfy the people's bloody hunger, but "...they were instant with loud voices, requiring that he might be crucified. And the voices of them and of the chief priests prevailed"(v. 23).

The words "they were instant" is the Greek word *epikeima,* a compound of the words *epi* and *keimai.* The word *epi* means *upon,* and the word *keimai* means *to lay something down.* When compounded together, this word meant that the people began *to pile evidence on top* of Pilate, nearly *burying him* in reasons why Jesus had to be crucified. To finish this quarrel, they threatened him, saying, "...If thou let this man go, thou art not Caesar's friend: whosoever maketh himself a king speaketh against Caesar" (John 19:12).

Pilate was taken aback by the threat of treason these Jewish leaders were bringing against him. Once he heard these words, he knew they had him in a trap — and there was only one way legally for him to get out of the mess he was in. He had to make a choice: He could either set Jesus free and sacrifice his own political career, or he could deliver Jesus to be crucified and thus save himself.

When confronted with these two stark choices, Pilate decided to sacrifice Jesus and save himself. But as he turned Jesus over to the masses, Pilate first wanted to make it clear to everyone who was listening that he didn't agree with what they were doing. This is why Matthew 27:24 tells us, "When Pilate saw that he could prevail nothing, but that rather a tumult was made, he took water, and washed his hands before the multitude, saying, I am innocent of the blood of this just person: see ye to it."

Pay careful attention to the fact that Pilate "...took water, and washed his hands...." Water, of course, is symbolic of a cleansing agent, and hands are symbolic of our lives. For instance, with our hands we touch people, we work, we make money — in fact, nearly everything we do in life, we do with our hands. This is why Paul told us to "lift up holy hands" when we pray and worship (1 Timothy 2:8). When we lift our hands to God, it is the same as lifting our entire lives before Him, because our hands represent our lives.

In Bible times, the washing of hands was a ritual often used symbolically for the removal of one's guilt. So when Pilate washed his hands in that basin of water and publicly declared, "I am clear of all guilt regarding the blood of this just person!" he was demonstrating what he believed to be his total innocence in this matter.

As long as Pontius Pilate thought he could stand with Jesus and keep his own position as well, he protected Jesus. But the moment Pilate realized that saving Jesus would mean he would have to sacrifice his own position in life, he quickly changed his tune and gave in to the demands of the unsaved mob who were screaming all around him.

Can you think of times in your own life when your walk with Jesus put you in an unpopular position with your peers? What did you do when you realized your commitment to the Lord was going to jeopardize your job or your status with your friends? Did you sacrifice your friendship and your status, or did you sacrifice your commitment to the Lord?

Let's make a decision today to never make the mistake of sacrificing our relationship with Jesus for other people or other things. Instead, let's resolve to stand by Jesus regardless of the situation or the personal cost we may have to pay for staying faithful to Him.

Remember what Jesus said: "Whoever finds his life will lose it, and whoever loses his life for my sake will find it" (Matthew 10:39 *NIV*). When we hang on to the wrong things, our wrong choices always costs us the most. On the other hand, when we let go of things we count dear and choose to give everything we have to Jesus, we always end up with more! *So let's be sure to stand by Jesus regardless of what we may have to temporarily lose or lay down!*

MY PRAYER FOR TODAY

Lord, forgive me for the times I've denied You and the principles of Your Word because I was afraid I'd jeopardize my popularity if I remained faithful to You. I am truly sorry for this, and I repent for my wrong behavior today. The next time I'm put on the spot and required to make this kind of choice, please help me put aside any worry about saving my own popularity or reputation and make the decision that honors You.

I pray this in Jesus' name!

MY CONFESSION FOR TODAY

I confess that living for Jesus Christ is the most important thing in my life. I will stand for Him, live for Him, speak up for Him, and never back down. Regardless of the pressure that comes to push me away from this rock-solid position, I will not move from my wholehearted commitment to Jesus. His power strengthens me and helps me remain strong even in the face of opposition and conflict!

I declare this by faith in Jesus' name!

QUESTIONS FOR YOU TO CONSIDER

1. Can you think of a time when you sacrificed your relationship with Jesus in order to save yourself a little pain from ridicule or rejection?
2. How did you feel after you did this? Were you regretful that you didn't stand tall in your commitment to the Lord?
3. What are you going to do the next time you find yourself in such a situation? What do you need to start doing now to make sure you will be strong enough to resist that temptation the next time you face it?

APRIL 21

❧❧❧

Scourged!

...And when he had scourged Jesus,
he delivered him to be crucified.
— Matthew 27:26

What was it like for a prisoner to be scourged in New Testament times? From what materials was a scourge made? How did it feel when the straps of a scourge whipped across a person's back and body? What effects did a scourging have on the human body?

Matthew 27:26 tells us that Pilate "had scourged Jesus" before he delivered Him to be crucified, so we need to understand what it meant to be "scourged." The word "scourged" is the Greek word *phragello*, and it was one of the most horrific words used in the ancient world because of the terrible images that immediately came to mind when a person heard this word. Let me tell you a little about the process of scourging and what it did to the human body. I believe this explanation is important so you can understand more completely what Jesus endured *before* He was taken to be crucified.

When a decision was made to scourge an individual, the victim was first stripped *completely* naked so his entire flesh would be open and uncovered to the beating action of the torturer's whip. Then the victim was bound to a two-foot-high scourging post. His hands were tied over his head to a metal ring, and his wrists were securely shackled to the metal ring to restrain his body from movement. When in this locked position, the victim couldn't wiggle or move, trying to avoid or dodge the lashes that were being laid across his back.

Romans were professionals at scourging; they took special delight in the fact that they were the "best" at punishing a victim with this brutal act. Once the victim was harnessed to the post and stretched over it, the Roman soldier began to put him through unimaginable torture. One writer notes that the mere anticipation of the first blow caused the victim's body to grow rigid, the muscles to knot in his stomach, the color to drain from his cheeks, and his lips to draw tight against his teeth as he waited for the first sadistic blow that would begin the tearing open of his body.

The scourge itself consisted of a short, wooden handle with several 18- to 24-inch-long straps of leather protruding from it. The ends of these pieces of leather were equipped with sharp, rugged pieces of metal, wire, glass, and jagged fragments of bone. This was considered to be one of the most feared and deadly weapons of the Roman world. It was so ghastly that the mere threat of scourging could calm a crowd or bend the will of the strongest rebel. Not even the most hardened criminal wanted to be submitted to the vicious beating of a Roman scourge.

Most often, two torturers were utilized to carry out this punishment, simultaneously lashing the victim from both sides. As these dual whips struck the victim, the leather straps with their jagged, sharp, cutting objects descended and extended over his entire back. Each piece of metal, wire, bone, or glass cut deeply through the victim's skin and into his flesh, shredding his muscles and sinews.

Every time the whip pounded across the victim, those straps of leather curled tortuously around his torso, biting painfully and deeply into the skin of his abdomen and upper chest. As each stroke lacerated the sufferer, he tried to thrash about but was unable to move because his wrists were held so firmly to the metal ring above his head. Helpless to escape the whip, he would scream for mercy that this anguish might come to an end.

Every time the torturers struck a victim, the straps of leather attached to the wooden handle would cause multiple lashes as the pieces of metal, glass, wire, and bone sank into the flesh and then raked across the victim's body. Then the torturer would jerk back, pulling hard in order to tear whole pieces of human flesh from the body. The victim's back, buttocks, back of the legs, stomach, upper chest, and face would soon be disfigured by the slashing blows of the whip.

Historical records describe a victim's back as being so mutilated after a Roman scourging that his spine would actually be exposed. Others recorded how the bowels of a victim would actually spill out through the open wounds created by the whip. The Early Church historian Eusebius wrote: "The veins were laid bare, and the very muscles, sinews, and bowels of the victim were open to exposure."

The Roman torturer would so aggressively strike his victim that he wouldn't even take the time to untangle the bloody, flesh-filled straps as he lashed the whip across the victim's mangled body over and over again. If the scourging wasn't stopped, the slicing of the whip would eventually flay the victim's flesh off his body.

With so many blood vessels sliced open by the whip, the victim would begin to experience a profuse loss of blood and bodily fluids. The heart would pump harder and harder, struggling to get blood to the parts of the body that were profusely bleeding. But it was like pumping water through an open water hydrant; there was nothing left to stop the blood from pouring through the victim's open wounds.

This loss of blood caused the victim's blood pressure to drop drastically. Because of the massive loss of bodily fluids, he would experience excruciating thirst, often fainting from the pain and eventually going into shock. Frequently the victim's heartbeat would become so irregular that he would go into cardiac arrest.

This was a Roman scourging.

According to Jewish law in Deuteronomy 25:3, the Jews were permitted to give forty lashes to a victim, but because the fortieth lash usually proved fatal, the number of lashes given was reduced to thirty-nine, as Paul noted in Second Corinthians 11:24. But the Romans had no limit to the number of lashes they could give a victim, and the scourging Jesus experienced was at the hands of Romans, not Jews. Therefore, it is entirely possible that when the torturer pulled out his scourge to beat Jesus, he may have laid more than forty lashes across His body. In fact, this is even probable in light of the explosive outrage the Jews felt for Jesus and the terrible mocking He had already suffered at the hands of Roman soldiers.

So when the Bible tells us that Jesus was scourged, we now know exactly what type of beating that Jesus received that night. What toll did the cruel Roman whip exact on Jesus' body? The New Testament doesn't tell us exactly what Jesus looked like after He was scourged, but Isaiah 52:14 says, "As many were astonied at thee; his visage was so marred more than any man, and his form more than the sons of men."

If we take this scripture literally for what it says, we can conclude that Jesus' physical body was marred nearly beyond recognition. As appalling as this sounds, it was only the overture to what was to follow. Matthew 27:26 continues to tell us, "...and when he had scourged Jesus, *he delivered him to be crucified.*" This scourging was only the preparation for Jesus' crucifixion!

Every time I think about the scourging Jesus received that day, I think of the promise God makes to us in Isaiah 53:5. This verse says, "But he was wounded for our transgressions, he was bruised for our iniquities: the chastisement of our peace was upon him; and with his stripes we are healed." In this verse, God declares that the price for our healing would be paid by those stripes that were laid across Jesus' back.

In First Peter 2:24, the apostle Peter quoted Isaiah 53:5. He told his readers, "…By whose stripes ye were healed." The word "stripes" used in this verse is *molopsi,* which describes *a full-body bruise.* It refers to *a terrible lashing that draws blood and that produces discoloration and swelling of the entire body.* When Peter wrote this verse, he wasn't speaking by revelation but by memory, for he vividly remembered what happened to Jesus that night and what His physical appearance looked like after His scourging.

After graphically reminding us of the beating, bleeding, and bruising that Jesus endured, Peter jubilantly declared that it was by these same stripes that we are "healed." The word "healed" is the Greek word *iaomai* — a word that clearly refers to *physical healing,* as it is a word borrowed from the medical term to describe *the physical healing or curing of the human body.*

For those who think this promise refers to spiritual healing only, the Greek word emphatically speaks of *the healing of a physical condition.* This is a real promise of bodily healing that belongs to all who have been washed in the blood of Jesus Christ!

Jesus' broken body was the payment God demanded to guarantee our physical healing! Just as Jesus willfully took our sins and died on the Cross in our place, He also willfully took our sicknesses and pains on Himself when they tied Him to the scourging post and laid those lashes across His body. That horrific scourging paid for our healing!

If you need healing in your body, you have every right to go to God and ask for healing to come flooding into your system. It's time for you to dig in your heels and hold fast to the promise of God's Word, releasing your faith for the healing that belongs to you. (I encourage you to read the *Sparkling Gem* for March 23, for it discusses your legal right to ask God to give you what He has promised).

Jesus went through this agony for you, so don't let the devil tell you that it's God's will for you to be sick or weakly. *Considering the pain Jesus endured to bear your sicknesses that day, isn't that enough evidence to convince you how much He wants you to be physically well?*

MY PRAYER FOR TODAY

Lord, I am moved by what I've learned today. I had no idea how much pain You endured to pay the price for my physical healing. Forgive me for the times I've tolerated sickness and didn't even pray to be healed. Now I understand that Your desire to see me healed is so great that You paid a price far beyond anything I will ever be able to comprehend. Since my physical well-being is that important to You, starting today I determine to walk in divine health and healing. I am taking a stand of faith to walk in healing and to fully possess the health You bought for me that day when You were so severely beaten!

I pray this in Jesus' name!

MY CONFESSION FOR TODAY

I boldly confess that I am healed by the stripes of Jesus Christ. The agony He endured was for me and my health. I don't have to be sick; I don't have to be weak; and I don't have to live at the mercy of affliction anymore. The stripes on Jesus' body were for me, so today I release my faith and commit that I will not be satisfied with anything less than God's best — divine healing and health every day of my life!

I declare this by faith in Jesus' name!

QUESTIONS FOR YOU TO CONSIDER

1. What did you learn new today about the scourging Jesus endured for you?
2. In light of the fact that Jesus suffered all that He did to purchase your physical healing, are you now ready to dig in your heels and hold fast to God's promise of healing until divine health has become a part of your life?
3. What other scriptures can you claim for your healing? Why don't you write those scriptures on a piece of paper and put them in a visible place where you can read them every day? Even better, why not memorize them so you can quote them to yourself?

APRIL 22

Scorned!

Then the soldiers of the governor took Jesus into the common hall,
and gathered unto him the whole band of soldiers.
And they stripped him, and put on him a scarlet robe.
And when they had platted a crown of thorns,
they put it upon his head, and a reed in his right hand:
and they bowed the knee before him,
and mocked him, saying, Hail, King of the Jews!
— Matthew 27:27-29

*A*fter Jesus was scourged, Pilate delivered Him to the Roman soldiers so they could initiate the crucifixion process. However, first these soldiers dragged Jesus through the worst mockery and humiliation of all. Matthew 27:27-29 describes what Jesus went through at this stage of His ordeal: "Then the soldiers of the governor took Jesus into the common hall, and gathered unto him the whole band of soldiers. And they stripped him, and put on him a scarlet robe. And when they had platted a crown of thorns, they put it upon his head, and a reed in his right hand: and they bowed the knee before him, and mocked him, saying, Hail, King of the Jews!"

Verse 27 says the soldiers "…took Jesus into the common hall, and gathered unto him the whole band of soldiers." The "common hall" was the open courtyard in Pilate's palace. Since Pilate rotated between several official royal residences in Jerusalem, this could have been his palace at the Tower of Antonia (*see* April 4). It also could have been his residence at the magnificent palace of Herod, located on the highest part of Mount Zion. All we know for sure is that the courtyard was so large, it was able to hold "the whole band of soldiers." This phrase comes from the Greek word *spira*, referring to a *cohort* or *a group of 300 to 600 Roman soldiers*.

Hundreds of soldiers filled the courtyard of Pilate's residence to participate in the events that followed. Matthew 27:28 says, "And they stripped him, and put on him a scarlet robe." First, the soldiers "stripped him." The word "stripped" is the Greek word *ekduo,* which means *to totally unclothe* or *to fully undress.* Nakedness was viewed as a disgrace, a shame, and an embarrassment in the Jewish world. Public nakedness was associated with pagans — with their worship, their idols, and their statues.

As children of God, the Israelites honored the human body, made in the image of God; thus, to publicly parade someone's naked body was a great offense. We can know, then, that when Jesus was stripped naked in front of 300 to 600 soldiers, it went against the grain of His entire moral view of what was right and wrong.

Once Jesus stood naked before them, the soldiers then "...put on him a scarlet robe." The Greek phrase is *chlamuda kokkinen,* from the word *chlamus* and *kokkinos.* The word *chlamus* is the Greek word for *a robe* or *a cloak.* It could refer to a soldier's cloak, but the next word makes it more probable that this was an old cloak of Pilate. You see, the word "scarlet" is the Greek word *kokkinos,* a word that describes *a robe that has been dyed a deep crimson or scarlet color,* which is suggestive of *the deeply colored crimson and scarlet robes worn by royalty or nobility.* Did this cohort of Roman soldiers who worked at Pilate's residence pull an old royal robe from Pilate's closet and bring it to the courtyard for the party? It seems that this is the case.

As Matthew continues the account, we find out what happened next: After the soldiers "...had *platted* a crown of thorns, they put it upon his head...." The word "platted" is the Greek word *empleko* (*see* January 25). Thorns grew everywhere, including in the imperial grounds of Pilate. These thorns were long and sharp like nails. The soldiers took vines that were loaded with sharp and dangerous thorns; then they carefully wove together those razor-sharp, prickly, jagged vines until they formed a tightly woven, dangerous circle that resembled the shape of a crown.

Afterward, the soldiers "...put it upon his head...." It was this kind of crown that the soldiers violently pushed down upon Jesus' head. Matthew uses the Greek word *epitithimi,* a word that implies they *forcefully shoved* this crown of thorns onto Jesus' head. These thorns would have been extremely painful and caused blood to flow profusely from His brow. Because the thorns were so jagged, they would have created terrible wounds as they scraped across Jesus' skull bone and literally tore the flesh from His skull.

Matthew called it a "crown" of thorns. The word "crown" is from the Greek word *stephanos,* the word that described a coveted *victor's crown.* These soldiers intended to use this mock crown to make fun of Jesus. Little did they know that Jesus was preparing to win the greatest victory in history!

After forcing the crown of thorns down onto Jesus' brow, the soldiers put "...a *reed* in his right hand...." There were many beautiful ponds and fountains in Pilate's inner courtyard where long, tall, hard "reeds" grew. While Jesus sat there before them clothed in a royal robe and crown of thorns, one of the soldiers must have realized that the picture was not quite complete and pulled a "reed" from one of the ponds or fountains to put in Jesus' hand. This reed represented the ruler's staff, as seen in the famous statue called "Ave Caesar," which depicted Caesar holding a staff or scepter in his hand. The same image, also showing a scepter in the right hand of the emperor, appeared on coins that were minted in the emperor's honor and in wide circulation.

With a discarded royal robe about Jesus' shoulders, a crown of thorns set so deeply into His head that blood drenched His face, and a reed from Pilate's ponds or fountains stuck in His right hand, "...they bowed the knee before him, and mocked him, saying, Hail, King of the Jews!" The word "bowed" is the Greek word *gonupeteo,* meaning *to fall down upon one's knees.* One by one, the cohort of soldiers passed before Jesus, dramatically and comically dropping to their knees in front of Him as they laughed at and mocked Him.

The word "mocked" is the Greek word *empaidzo*, the same word used to describe the mocking of Herod and his bodyguards (*see* April 19). As Pilate's soldiers mocked Jesus, they said to Him, "Hail, King of the Jews!" The word "hail" was an acknowledgment of honor used when saluting Caesar. Thus, the soldiers shouted out this mock salute to Jesus as they would to a king to whom honor was due.

Matthew 27:30 goes on to tell us, "And they spit upon him, and took the reed, and smote him on the head." The word "they" refers to the entire cohort of soldiers who were present in Pilate's court-yard that night. So as each soldier passed by Jesus, he would first mockingly bow before Him; then he'd lean forward to spit right in Jesus' blood-drenched face. Next the soldier would grab the reed from Jesus' hand and strike Him hard on His already wounded head. Finally, he would stick the reed back in Jesus' hand to make Him ready for the next soldier to repeat the whole process.

The Greek clearly means that *the soldiers repeatedly struck Jesus again and again on the head.* Here was another beating that Jesus endured, but this time it was with the slapping action of a hard reed. This must have been excruciatingly painful for Jesus, since His body was already lacerated from the scourging and His head was deeply gashed by the cruel crown of thorns.

When all 300 to 600 soldiers were finished spitting and striking Jesus with the reed, Matthew 27:31 tells us that "…they took the robe off from him, and put his own raiment on him, and led him away to crucify him." The robe wrapped around Jesus had no doubt had time to mesh into His wounds, for it took a great amount of time for so many soldiers to parade before Him. Therefore, it must have been terrifically painful for Jesus when they jerked this robe off His back and the material ripped free from the dried blood that had coagulated on His open wounds.

But this would be the last act of torture Jesus would endure in this stage of His ordeal. After putting His own clothes back on Him, the soldiers led Him from the palace to the place of execution.

As the soldiers mocked Jesus that day, hailing Him as king in derision and ridicule, they were unaware that they were actually bowing their knees to the One before whom they would one day stand and give an account for their actions. When that day comes, bowing before Jesus will be no laughing matter, for *everyone* — including those very soldiers who mocked Jesus — will confess that Jesus is Lord!

Yes, a day is soon coming when the human race will bow their knees to acknowledge and declare that Jesus is the King of kings. Philippians 2:10,11 talks about that day: "That at the name of Jesus every knee should bow, of things in heaven, and things in earth, and things under the earth; and that every tongue should confess that Jesus Christ is Lord, to the glory of God the Father."

If you have a friend who doesn't know Jesus yet, don't you think it's time for you to introduce that friend to Jesus Christ? Your friend will one day bow before Him anyway; the question is, from which place will he bow before Jesus — from Heaven, from earth, or from hell?

Everyone in Heaven will bow low before Jesus on that day, as will everyone who is alive on earth at His coming and everyone who has gone to hell because they didn't bow before Him while they lived on this earth. So the big question is not *if* a person will bow before Him, but *from which place* will he choose to bow before Him?

Isn't it your responsibility to help lead your friends and acquaintances to Jesus? God's Spirit will empower you to speak the Gospel to them. If you pray before you speak to them, the Holy Spirit will prepare their hearts to hear the message. *Why not stop today and ask the Lord to help you speak the truth to those friends, acquaintances, and fellow workers whom you interact with every day?*

MY PRAYER FOR TODAY

Lord, open my eyes to those around me who are unsaved and in need of salvation. You died for them because You want them to be saved. I know that You are trusting me to tell them the Good News that they can be saved. Please empower me strongly with Your Spirit, giving me the boldness I need, to step out from behind intimidation and to tell them the truth that will save them from an eternity in hell. Help me to start telling them the Good News immediately, before it is too late.

I pray this in Jesus' name!

MY CONFESSION FOR TODAY

I declare by faith that I am a strong witness for Jesus Christ. My eyes are opened and my spirit is attentive to recognize opportunities to speak the Gospel to people who are unsaved. When I speak to them, they listen with an open heart and want to hear what I have to say. Because of my bold witness, my family, friends, acquaintances, and fellow workers are getting saved!

I declare this by faith in Jesus' name!

QUESTIONS FOR YOU TO CONSIDER

1. How long has it been since you shared the Good News of Jesus Christ with your family, friends, acquaintances, or fellow workers?
2. Since the people in your life will bow their knees before Jesus at some point in the future anyway, don't you agree that you should help them do it now so they won't have to bow their knees to Him one day from hell?
3. How long has it been since you've bowed your own knees to pray or to worship Jesus? Don't you think it would be a good idea for you to make this a part of your daily spiritual routine?

A day is soon coming when the human race will bow their knees to acknowledge and declare that Jesus is the King of kings. If you have a friend who doesn't know Jesus, don't you think it's time for you to introduce that friend to Jesus Christ? Your friend will one day bow before Him anyway; the question is, from which place will he bow before Jesus — from Heaven, from earth, or from hell?

APRIL 23

ᘛᕈᕆᘚ

Golgotha: The Place of the Skull

And as they came out, they found a man of Cyrene,
Simon by name: him they compelled to bear his cross.
And when they were come unto a place called Golgotha,
that is to say, a place of a skull.
— Matthew 27:32,33

When the soldiers brought Jesus out from the residence of Pilate, Jesus was already carrying the crossbeam that would serve as the upper portion of His Cross.

Most Roman crosses were shaped like a "T." The upright post had a notched groove at the top into which the crossbeam was placed after a victim had been tied or nailed to it. The crossbeam, normally weighing about one hundred pounds, was carried on the back of the victim to the place of execution.

According to Roman law, once a criminal was convicted, he was to carry his own cross to the place of execution if his crucifixion was to occur somewhere other than the place of the trial. The purpose for exposing criminals heading for crucifixion to passersby was to remind those who watched of Roman military power. At the place of execution, vultures flew overhead, just waiting to swoop down and start devouring the dying carcasses left hanging on the crosses. In the nearby wilderness, wild dogs anxiously waited for the newest dead bodies, dumped by the executioners, to become their next meal.

After the person was declared guilty, a crossbeam would be laid across his back and a herald would walk ahead of him, proclaiming his crime. A sign with the person's crime written on it would also be made, later to be hung on the cross above his head. Sometimes the sign bearing the person's crime would be hung from his neck, so all the spectators who lined the streets to watch him walk by would know what crime he committed. This was the very type of sign that was publicly displayed on the Cross above Jesus' head, with the crime He was charged with — "King of the Jews" — written in Hebrew, Greek, and Latin.

Carrying such a heavy weight for a long distance would be difficult for any man, but especially for one who had been as severely beaten as Jesus. The heavy crossbeam on which He was destined to be nailed pressed into His torn back as He carried it to the place of execution. Although the Bible does not state the reason why, we may assume that the Roman soldiers forced Simon of Cyrene to help because Jesus was so drained and exhausted from the abuse He had suffered.

Little is known of Simon of Cyrene, except that he was from Cyrene, the capital of the province of Libya that was situated approximately eleven miles south of the Mediterranean Sea. Matthew 27:32 informs us that the Roman soldiers "compelled him to bear his cross." The word "compelled" is the Greek word *aggareuo*. It means *to compel; to coerce; to constrain; to make;* or *to force someone into some kind of compulsory service.*

Matthew 27:33 says, "And when they were come unto a place called Golgotha, that is to say, a place of a skull." This scripture has been the center of controversy for several hundred years, for many have attempted to use this verse to geographically identify the exact location of Jesus' crucifixion. Some denominations allege that the place of Jesus' crucifixion was inside modern-day

Jerusalem, while others assert that the name Golgotha refers to a site outside the city that from a distance looks like a skull. However, the earliest writings of the Church fathers say this phrase "a place of a skull" refers to something very different!

An early Christian leader named Origen, who lived from 185-253 AD, recorded that Jesus was crucified on the spot where Adam was buried and where his skull had been found. Whether or not this is true, there *was* an early Christian belief that Jesus had been crucified near Adam's burial place. As this early story goes, when the earthquake occurred as Jesus hung on the Cross (Matthew 27:51), His blood ran down the Cross into the crack in the rock below and fell on the skull of Adam. This history is so entrenched in early Christian tradition that Jerome referred to it in a letter in 386 AD.

Interestingly, Jewish tradition states that Adam's skull was buried near the city of Jerusalem by Noah's son, Shem. Tradition says this burial place was guarded by Melchizedek, who was the priest-king of Salem (Jerusalem) during the time of Abraham (*see* Genesis 14:18). Unknown to most Western believers, this history is so accepted that it is considered a major theme of Orthodox doctrine, and the skull of Adam appears consistently at the base of the Cross in both paintings and icons. If you ever see a skull at the base of a crucifix, you can know that it symbolizes Adam's skull that was allegedly found buried at the site of Jesus' crucifixion.

These extremely interesting facts, although unprovable, have retained strong support throughout 2,000 years of Christian history. If it were true, it would be quite amazing that the Second Adam, Jesus Christ, died for the sins of the world exactly on the spot where the first Adam, the original sinner, was buried. If Jesus' blood ran down the crack in the stone and fell upon Adam's skull, as tradition says, it would be very symbolic of Jesus' blood covering the sins of the human race that originated with Adam.

But what can we definitely know about the place of Jesus' crucifixion?

We definitely know that Jesus was crucified like a criminal by the Roman government just outside the walls of the ancient city of Jerusalem. Whether or not He was crucified at the place of Adam's skull is interesting but not important. What is vital for us to know and understand is that Jesus died for the sins of the entire human race — and that includes you and me!

Today we may not be able to say with certainty exactly where Jesus was crucified, but in our hearts and minds we should meditate on the scriptures that speak of His crucifixion. Sometimes life moves so fast that we tend to forget the enormous price that was paid for our redemption. Salvation may have been given to us as a free gift, but it was purchased with the precious blood of Jesus Christ. *Thank God for the Cross!*

This question of where Jesus was crucified is a good example of the way people tend to get distracted by unimportant issues and, as a result, miss the main point God wants to get across to them. People have argued and debated for centuries about the accurate location of the crucifixion when the truth they should have been focusing on is that Jesus was crucified for their salvation! The apostle Paul wrote, "...Christ died for our sins according to the scriptures; and that he was buried, and that he rose again on the third day according to the scriptures" (1 Corinthians 15:3,4). Of this, we can be sure!

Aren't you thankful that Jesus' blood purchased the forgiveness for all of mankind's sin? It is true that through Adam's disobedience, sin entered the world and death was passed on to all men. But just as sin entered the world through Adam, the gift of God came into the world through the obedience of Jesus Christ. Now the grace of God and the free gift of righteousness abounds to all who have called upon Jesus Christ to be the Lord of their lives (*see* Romans 5:12-21). *Now every believer has the glorious privilege of reigning in life as a joint heir with Jesus Himself!*

MY PRAYER FOR TODAY

Lord, how can I ever adequately say thank You for all that You did for me at the Cross? I was so undeserving, but You came and gave Your life for me, taking away my sin and removing the punishment that should have passed to me. I thank You from the depths of my heart for doing what no one else could do for me. Had it not been for You, I would be eternally lost, so I just want to say thank You for laying down Your life that I might be free!

I pray this in Jesus' name!

MY CONFESSION FOR TODAY

I confess that I am washed in the blood of Jesus Christ. His blood covered my sin, washed me whiter than snow, and gave me rightstanding with God. I have no need to be ashamed of my past sins, because I am a new creature in Christ Jesus — marvelously made brand new in Him. Old things have passed away, and all things have become new because I am in Jesus Christ. That's who I am!

I declare this by faith in Jesus' name!

QUESTIONS FOR YOU TO CONSIDER

1. How often do you reflect on the work of Christ on the Cross?
2. Have you ever taken time to think of what it must have been like for Jesus to take the sins of the whole world upon Himself?
3. How would it affect you if you read each Gospel's account of the crucifixion over and over again for an entire month? Why don't you commit to doing this and see what God does in your heart as you read, reread, and meditate on these important scriptures?

APRIL 24

❧

Crucified!

They gave him vinegar to drink mingled with gall:
and when he had tasted thereof, he would not drink.
And they crucified him....
— Matthew 27:34,35

When Jesus arrived at Golgotha, the Bible says, "They gave him vinegar to drink mingled with gall...." According to Jewish law, if a man was about to be executed, he could request a narcotic, mingled together with wine, which would help alleviate the pain of his execution. The word "gall" in this verse refers to this special painkiller that was mingled together with wine for this purpose.

There was a group of kind women in Jerusalem who made it their good deed to help anesthetize the pain of people who were dying horrific deaths. These women wanted to eliminate as much pain and misery as possible for the scores of people being crucified by the Romans. Therefore, they produced the homemade painkiller that Matthew tells us about in this verse.

Jesus was offered this anesthetic twice — once before His crucifixion and once while He was dying on the Cross (*see* Matthew 27:34,48). In both instances, Jesus turned down the offer and refused to drink it, for He knew that He was to fully consume this cup the Father had given Him to drink.

Verse 35 begins, "And they crucified him...." The word "crucified" is the Greek word *staurao*, from the word *stauros*, which describes *an upright, pointed stake that was used for the punishment of criminals.* This word was used to describe those who were *hung up, impaled,* or *beheaded and then publicly displayed.* It was always used in connection with *public execution.* The point of hanging a criminal publicly was to bring further humiliation and additional punishment to the accused.

Crucifixion was indisputably one of the cruelest and most barbaric forms of punishment in the ancient world. Flavius Josephus, the Jewish historian, described crucifixion as "the most wretched of deaths." It was viewed with such horror that in one of Seneca's letters to Lucilius, Seneca wrote that suicide was preferable to crucifixion.

Different parts of the world had different kinds of crucifixion. For example, in the East the victim was beheaded and then hung in public display. Among the Jews, the victim was first stoned to death and then hung on a tree. Deuteronomy 21:22,23 commanded, "And if a man have committed a sin worthy of death, and he be to be put to death, and thou hang him on a tree: his body shall not remain all night upon the tree, but thou shalt in any wise bury him that day; (for he that is hanged is accursed of God;)...."

But at the time Jesus was crucified, the grueling act of crucifixion was entirely in the hands of the Roman authorities. This punishment was reserved for the most serious offenders, usually for those who had committed some kind of treason or who had participated in or sponsored state terrorism.

Because Israel hated the occupying Roman troops, insurrections frequently arose among the populace. As a deterrent to stop people from participating in revolts, crucifixion was regularly practiced in Jerusalem. By publicly crucifying those who attempted to overthrow the government, the Romans sent a strong signal of fear to those who might be tempted to follow in their steps.

Once the offender reached the place where the crucifixion was to occur, he was laid on the crossbeam he carried (*see* April 23) with his arms outstretched. Then a soldier would drive a five-inch (12.5-centimeter) iron nail through each of his wrists into the crossbeam. After being nailed to the crossbeam, the victim was hoisted up by rope, and the crossbeam was dropped into a notch on top of the upright post.

When the crossbeam dropped into the groove, the victim suffered excruciating pain as his hands and wrists were wrenched by the sudden jerking motion. Then the weight of the victim's body caused his arms to be pulled out of their arm sockets. Josephus writes that the Roman soldiers "out of rage and hatred amused themselves by nailing their prisoners in different postures." Crucifixion was truly a vicious ordeal.

When the victim was nailed to his cross, the nails were not driven through the palms of his hands, but through his wrists. Once the wrists were secured in place, the feet came next. First, the victim's legs would be positioned so that the feet were pointed downward with the soles pressed against the post on which the victim was suspended. A long nail would then be driven between the bones of the feet, lodged firmly enough between those bones to prevent it from tearing through the feet as the victim arched upward, gasping for breath.

In order for the victim to breathe, he had to push himself up by his feet, which were nailed to the vertical beam. However, because the pressure on his feet became unbearable, it wasn't possible for him to remain long in this position, so eventually he would collapse back into the hanging position.

As the victim pushed up and collapsed back down again and again over a long period of time, his shoulders eventually dislocated and popped out of joint. Soon the out-of-joint shoulders were followed by the elbows and wrists. These various dislocations caused the arms to be extended up to nine inches longer than usual, resulting in terrible cramps in the victim's arm muscles and making it impossible for him to push himself upward any longer to breathe. When he was finally too exhausted and could no longer push himself upward on the nail lodged in his feet, the process of asphyxiation began.

Jesus experienced all of this torture. When He dropped down with the full weight of His body on the nails that were driven through His wrists, it sent excruciating pain up His arms, registering horrific pain in His brain. Added to this torture was the agony caused by the constant grating of Jesus' recently scourged back against the upright post every time He pushed up to breathe and then collapsed back to a hanging position.

Due to extreme loss of blood and hyperventilation, the victim would begin to experience severe dehydration. We can see this process in Jesus' own crucifixion when He cried out, "…I thirst" (John 19:28). After several hours of this torment, the victim's heart would begin to fail. Next his lungs would collapse, and excess fluids would begin filling the lining of his heart and lungs, adding to the slow process of asphyxiation.

When the Roman soldier came to determine whether or not Jesus was alive or dead, he thrust his spear into Jesus' side. One expert pointed out that if Jesus had been alive when the soldier did this, the soldier would have heard a loud sucking sound caused by air being inhaled past the freshly made wound in the chest. But the Bible tells us that water and blood mixed together came pouring forth from the wound the spear had made — evidence that Jesus' heart and lungs had shut down and were filled with fluid. This was enough to assure the soldier that Jesus was already dead.

It was customary for Roman soldiers to break the lower leg bones of a person being crucified, making it impossible for the victim to push himself upward to breathe and thus causing him to asphyxiate at a much quicker rate. However, because of the blood and water that gushed from Jesus' side, He was already considered dead. Since there was no reason for the soldiers to hasten Jesus' death, His legs were never broken.

This, my friend, is a brief taste of Roman crucifixion.

The above description of crucifixion was exactly what Jesus experienced on the Cross when He died for you and me. This is why Paul wrote, "And being found in fashion as a man, he humbled himself, and became obedient unto death, even the death of the cross" (Philippians 2:8). In Greek the emphasis is on the word "even," from the Greek word *de*, which dramatizes the point that Jesus lowered Himself to such an extent that He died *even* the death of a Cross — the lowest, most humiliating, debasing, shameful, painful method of death in the ancient world!

Now you understand why the kind women of Jerusalem prepared homemade painkillers for those being crucified. The agony associated with crucifixion is the reason they offered Jesus this "gall" once before the crucifixion began and again as He hung on the Cross.

Meanwhile, the soldiers near the foot of the Cross "…parted his garments, casting lots…" (Matthew 27:35). They didn't understand the great price of redemption that was being paid at that moment as Jesus hung asphyxiating to death, His lungs filling with fluids so He couldn't breathe.

According to Roman custom, the soldiers who carried out the crucifixion had a right to the victim's clothes. Jewish law required that the person being crucified would be stripped naked. So there Jesus hung, completely open and naked before the world, while His crucifiers literally distributed His clothes among themselves!

Making this distribution of clothes even cheaper was the fact that the soldiers "cast lots" for His garments. The Gospel of John records that "...when they had crucified Jesus, took his garments, and made four parts, to every soldier a part; and also his coat: now the coat was without seam, woven from the top throughout. They said therefore among themselves, Let us not rend it, but cast lots for it..." (John 19:23,24).

This account informs us that four soldiers were present at Jesus' crucifixion. The four parts of His clothing that were distributed among them were His head gear, sandals, girdle, and the *tallith* — the outer garment that had fringes on the bottom. His "coat," which was "without seam," was a handmade garment that was sewn together from top to bottom. Because it was specially handmade, this coat was a very expensive piece of clothing. This was the reason the soldiers chose to cast lots for it rather than tear it into four parts and spoil it.

When the Bible refers to "casting lots," it indicates a game during which the soldiers wrote their names on pieces of parchment or wood or on stones and then dropped all four pieces with their names written on them into some kind of container. Because the Roman soldiers who helped crucify Jesus were remotely located, it is probable that one of them pulled off his helmet and held it out to the other soldiers. After the others dropped their names in the helmet, the soldier shook it to mix up the four written names and then randomly withdrew the name of the winner.

It is simply remarkable that all of this was taking place as Jesus was pushing down on that huge nail lodged in His feet so He could gasp for breath before sagging back down into a hanging position. As Jesus' strength continued to drain away and the full consequence of man's sin was being realized in Him, the soldiers at the foot of the Cross played a game to see who would get His finest piece of clothing!

Matthew 27:36 says, "And sitting down they watched him there." The Greek word for "watch" is the word *tereo,* which means *to guard.* The Greek tense means *to consistently guard* or *to consistently be on the watch.* It was the responsibility of these soldiers to keep things in order, to keep watch over the crucifixion site, and to make sure no one came to rescue Jesus from the Cross. So as they cast lots and played games, the soldiers were also keeping watch out of the corners of their eyes to make certain no one touched Jesus as He hung dying on the Cross.

When I read about the crucifixion of Jesus, it makes me want to repent for the callousness with which the world looks upon the Cross today. In our society, the cross has become a fashion item, decorated with gems, rhinestones, gold, and silver. Beautiful crosses of jewelry adorn women's ears and dangle at the bottom of gold chains and necklaces. The symbol of the cross is even tattooed on people's flesh!

The reason this is so disturbing to me is that in beautifying the Cross to make it pleasing to look upon, people have forgotten that it wasn't beautiful or lavishly decorated at all. In fact, the Cross of Jesus Christ was *shocking* and *appalling.*

Jesus' totally naked body was flaunted in humiliation before a watching world. His flesh was ripped to shreds; His body was bruised from head to toe; He had to heave His body upward for every breath He breathed; and His nervous system sent constant signals of excruciating pain to His brain. Blood drenched Jesus' face and streamed from His hands, His feet, and from the countless cuts and gaping wounds the scourging had left upon His body. In reality, the Cross of Jesus Christ was a disgusting, repulsive, nauseating, stomach-turning sight — so entirely different from the attractive crosses people wear today as a part of their jewelry or attire.

At this time of the year, it would be good for all of us as believers to take a little time to remember what the Cross of Jesus Christ was really like. If we don't deliberately choose to meditate on what He went through, we will never fully appreciate the price He paid for us. How tragic it would be if we lost sight of the pain and the price of redemption!

When we fail to remember what it cost Jesus to save us, we tend to treat our salvation cheaply and with disregard. That's why the apostle Peter wrote, "Forasmuch as ye know that ye were not redeemed with corruptible things, as silver and gold, from your vain conversation received by tradition from your fathers; but with the precious blood of Christ, as of a lamb without blemish and without spot" (1 Peter 1:18,19).

The kind women of Jerusalem wanted to anesthetize Jesus to remove His pain. He refused their painkiller and entered into the experience of the Cross with all His faculties. Let's not allow the world to anesthetize us, causing us to overlook or forget the real price that was paid on the Cross.

Why not take time today to let the reality of the Cross sink deep into your heart and soul? As you do, you'll find that it will cause you to love Jesus so much more than you love Him right now!

MY PRAYER FOR TODAY

Lord, help me never to forget the price You paid on the Cross for my salvation. Please forgive me for the times my life starts moving so fast that I fail to remember what You did for me. No one else could have taken my place. No one else could have paid the price for my sin. So You went to the Cross, bearing my sin, my sickness, my pain, and my lack of peace. That Cross was the place where the price was paid for my deliverance. Today I want to thank You from the very depths of my heart for doing this for me!

I pray this in Jesus' name!

MY CONFESSION FOR TODAY

I boldly and thankfully confess that the blood of Jesus Christ was shed for me! That precious blood covered my sin and washed me clean, and today it gives me a rightstanding before God. Because of the Cross, I am redeemed from sin, sickness, pain, and torment. Satan no longer has a right to lay any claim on me! From a grateful heart, I will faithfully serve Jesus the rest of my days!

I declare this by faith in Jesus' name!

QUESTIONS FOR YOU TO CONSIDER

1. How long has it been since you've really looked at the Cross and considered what Jesus did for you on Calvary?
2. Can you remember the day you turned to the Lord, repented of your sin, and gave your life to Jesus? When was that day in your life? Where were you when it happened?

3. Do you have family members, friends, associates, or fellow workers who are unsaved? Have you ever told them the best news in the world — that Jesus died for them so they could be saved and their lives changed forever? If you haven't told them yet, why not?

APRIL 25

The Day the Veil Was Rent And the Earth Shook

Jesus, when he had cried again with a loud voice,
yielded up the ghost. And, behold, the veil of the temple
was rent in twain from the top to the bottom;
and the earth did quake, and the rocks rent.
— Matthew 27:50,51

Matthew, Mark, and Luke all record that on the day Jesus was crucified, the sky turned eerily dark at the sixth hour of the day. Matthew 27:45 says, "Now from the sixth hour there was darkness over all the land unto the ninth hour."

Notice the choice of words Matthew uses to describe this event. First, he says that "there was darkness." The words "there was" are from the Greek word *ginomai*, which describes an event that *slowly crept up on them* before they knew what was happening. Suddenly and unexpectedly, the clouds started rolling over the land, becoming darker and darker until finally an ominous, dark gloom filled the entire sky and loomed over the landscape. The word "dark" is the Greek word *skotos*, used all over the New Testament to depict something *very dark*.

Verse 45 says that this sudden and unexplainable darkness covered all the "land." The word "land" is the word *ges*, the Greek word for *the earth*, and it refers to *the entire earth*, not just a small geographical region. The Greek word *ges* emphatically tells us that the whole world literally became simultaneously darkened.

The historians Phlegon, Thaddus, and Julius Africanus all referred to the darkness that covered the earth at the time of Jesus' crucifixion. Critics of the Bible have attempted to explain away this supernatural darkness by alleging that it was due to an eclipse of the sun. This is impossible, however, for the Passover occurred at the time of a full moon.

The Bible informs us that the darkening of the sky started at the sixth hour (*see* Matthew 27:45; Mark 15:33; Luke 23:45). This is significant, for the sixth hour (noontime) was the very moment that the high priest Caiaphas, arrayed in his full priestly garments, began the procession in which he would enter the temple to slaughter a pure, spotless Passover lamb. This darkness that covered the land lasted until the ninth hour — the exact moment the high priest would be making his entrance into the Holy of Holies to offer the blood of the Passover lamb to cover the sins of the nation.

It was at this moment that Jesus cried out, "It is finished!" (John 19:30). As He heaved upward to breathe for the last time, Jesus gathered enough air to speak forth a victory shout! His assignment was complete! After proclaiming those words with His last ounce of strength, Matthew 27:50 tells us that He "…yielded up the ghost."

What Matthew tells us next is simply *amazing*! He writes, "And, behold, the veil of the temple was rent in twain from the top to the bottom…." The word "behold" is the Greek word *idou*. This is a very difficult word to translate, for it carries such intense feeling and emotion. The *King James Version* most often translates this word as *behold*. But in our contemporary world, it might be better rendered, *Wow!*

This word *idou* carries the idea of *shock, amazement, and wonder*. It's almost as if Matthew says, *"Wow! Can you believe it? The veil of the temple itself rent in twain from top to bottom!"* Matthew wrote about this event many years after the fact, yet he was still so dumbfounded by what happened that day that he exclaimed in effect, *"Wow! Look what happened next!"*

There were two veils inside the temple — one at the entrance to the Holy Place and a second at the entrance to the Holy of Holies. Only the high priest was allowed to pass through the second veil once a year. That second veil was sixty feet high, thirty feet wide, and an entire handbreadth in thickness! One early Jewish writing states that the veil was so heavy, it took three hundred priests to move or manipulate it. It would have been impossible humanly speaking to tear such a veil.

At the exact moment Jesus was breathing His last breath on the Cross at Golgotha, Caiaphas the high priest was standing at his station in the inner court of the temple, preparing to offer the blood of a spotless Passover lamb. At the very instant Caiaphas stepped up to kill the Passover sacrifice, Jesus exclaimed, "It is finished!" At that same instant, miles away from Golgotha inside the temple at Jerusalem, an inexplicable, mystifying supernatural event occurred. The massive, fortified veil that stood before the Holy of Holies was suddenly split in half from the top all the way to the bottom!

The sound of that veil splitting must have been deafening as it ripped and tore, starting from the top and going all the way down to the floor. It was as if invisible, divine hands had reached out to grab it, rip it to shreds, and discard it.

Imagine how shocked Caiaphas must have been when he heard the ripping sounds above his head and then watched as the veil was torn in half, leaving two sides of the once-massive curtain lying collapsed to his right and his left. Just think what must have gone through this evil high priest's mind when he saw that the way to the Holy of Holies was opened — and that God's Presence was no longer there!

You see, when Jesus was lifted up on that Cross, that Cross became the eternal mercy seat on which the blood of the final sacrifice was sprinkled. Once that sacrifice was made, it was no longer necessary for a high priest to continually make sacrifices year after year, for Jesus' blood had now settled the issue forever!

For this cause, God Himself ripped the veil of the temple in half, declaring that the way to the Holy of Holies was now available to everyone who came to Him through the blood of Jesus! This is why the apostle Paul wrote that Jesus "…hath broken down the middle wall of partition between us" (Ephesians 2:14).

Jesus' death was such a dramatic event that even the earth reacted to it. Matthew 27:51 says, "…the earth did quake, and the rocks rent." The word "earth" is the word *ges*, the same word seen in verse 45 (*see* above) that describes *the whole earth*. The word "quake" is the Greek word *seiso*, which means *to shake, to agitate,* or *to create a commotion*. It is where we get the word for a *seismograph*, the apparatus that registers the intensity of an earthquake. It is interesting to note that Origen, the early Christian leader, recorded that there were "great earthquakes" at the time of Jesus' crucifixion.

I find it so amazing that although Israel rejected Jesus and the Roman authorities crucified Him, creation *always* recognized Him! During His life on this earth, the waves obeyed Him; water turned to wine at His command; fishes and bread multiplied at His touch; the atoms in water solidified so He could walk across it; and the wind ceased when He spoke to it. So it should come as no surprise that Jesus' death was a traumatic event for creation. The earth shook, trembled, and shuddered at the death of its Creator, for it instantly felt its loss.

The earth shuddered so violently when Jesus died that even "…the rocks rent…." The word "rocks" is *petra*, referring to *large rocks*. The other word that could have been used for "rocks" is the word *lithos*, which meant *small stones*. But Matthew tells us that *huge, large rocks* were "rent" by the shaking of the earth. The word "rent" is *schidzo*, meaning *to rend, to tear, to violently tear asunder, or to terribly fracture*. This was a *serious* earthquake! It makes me realize all over again the incredible significance of the death of Jesus Christ!

When Jesus' blood was accepted at the Cross as final payment for man's sin, the need to habitually offer sacrifices year after year was eliminated. The Holy of Holies, a place limited only to the high priest once a year, has now become open and accessible to all of us! As "believer-priests," each of us can now enjoy the Presence of God every day. This is why Hebrews 10:19,22 says, "Having therefore, brethren, boldness to enter into the holiest by the blood of Jesus…. Let us draw near with a true heart in full assurance of faith, having our hearts sprinkled from an evil conscience…."

Since the way to the Holy of Holies has been thrown wide open to us, we need to take a few minutes each day to enter into the Presence of God to worship Him and to make our requests known. Because of what Jesus did, we can now "…come boldly unto the throne of grace, that we may obtain mercy, and find grace to help in time of need" (Hebrews 4:16). *Since this is God's promise to us, let's drop everything we're doing and come boldly before that throne of grace for a few minutes today!*

MY PRAYER FOR TODAY

Lord, I thank You for destroying the veil that separated me from Your Presence. By taking away the veil, You made it possible for me to come boldly before Your throne of grace to obtain mercy and receive help in my time of need. Because of what You did for me, today I am coming boldly to tell You what I need in my life. I present my case to You, and I thank You in advance for helping me just as You promised in Your Word.

I pray this in Jesus' name!

MY CONFESSION FOR TODAY

I confess that I have a God-given right to come directly into the Presence of God. Jesus removed the wall of separation — and because of what He did, I have no reason to feel unworthy or beggarly when I come before the Lord. Indeed, I am washed by the blood of Jesus, and God beckons me to come to Him with confident expectation. Therefore, I boldly come and make my requests known to God, and He answers me when I pray.

I declare this by faith in Jesus' name!

QUESTIONS FOR YOU TO CONSIDER

1. When you come to God in prayer, do you feel bold and courageous or afraid and ashamed?

2. Is there any sin in your life that is causing you to avoid coming into God's Presence every day? *Be honest!*

3. What is that one request you would like God to give you if you could go to Him and make your request today? Why don't you go ahead and make your request, because God is just waiting for you to ask Him!

APRIL 26

Two Friends Bury Jesus

And after this Joseph of Arimathaea, being a disciple of Jesus,
but secretly for fear of the Jews, besought Pilate
that he might take away the body of Jesus: and Pilate gave him leave.
He came therefore, and took the body of Jesus.
And there came also Nicodemus, which at the first came
to Jesus by night, and brought a mixture of myrrh and aloes,
about an hundred pound weight.
Then took they the body of Jesus, and wound it in linen clothes
with the spices, as the manner of the Jews is to bury.
— John 19:38-40

When it was time for Jesus' body to be brought down from the Cross, Pilate received a surprise visit from a high-ranking member of the Sanhedrin who was a secret follower of Jesus. His name was Joseph, from the city of Arimathea; thus, we know this man as *Joseph of Arimathea*. He was accompanied by another high-ranking member of the Sanhedrin who was also a secret disciple of Jesus. This second man's relationship with Jesus began with a secret visit in the middle of the night, recorded in John 3:1-21. That second admirer was *Nicodemus*.

Let's begin with Joseph of Arimathea and see what we know of him. To obtain an accurate picture of this man, we must turn to Mark 15:42-43, which says, "And now when the even was come, because it was the preparation, that is, the day before the sabbath, Joseph of Arimathaea, an honourable counseller, which also waited for the kingdom of God, came, and went in boldly unto Pilate, and craved the body of Jesus."

This verse tells us that Joseph of Arimathea was an "honorable counselor." The Greek word for "honorable" is *euschemon*, a compound of the words *eu*, meaning *well* or *good*, and the word *schema*, meaning *form*, often referring to *an outward appearance*. When compounded together, it means *a good outward appearance*. It refers to *people who have a good reputation, who have a good standing in society*, or *who are prominent, influential, and wealthy*. The word "counselor" is the Greek word *bouleutes*, the word for *a member of the Sanhedrin*. This is the same word used to describe *Roman senators*. By using this word *bouleutes*, Mark tells us that Joseph of Arimathea's position in the land of Israel was one of great honor and respect.

The above verse also tells us that he "waited for the kingdom of God." The Greek word for "waited" is *prosdechomai*. Other examples of this word are found in Acts 24:15, where it describes *a hope* or *expectation.* In Romans 16:2, Paul uses this word to tell the Roman church *to receive* Phebe, suggesting that they *fully receive* and *embrace* her. In Hebrews 10:34, it is translated *to take,* and it means *to fully and completely take something without reservation of hesitation.* So when Mark 15:43 tells us Joseph of Arimathea "…waited for the kingdom of God…," this doesn't refer to a do-nothing, "hang-around-and-see-what-happens" kind of waiting. Joseph was earnestly looking for and anticipating the Kingdom. He was inwardly ready *to take it, to fully receive it, and to embrace it without any reservation or hesitation.*

This explains why Joseph was attracted to the ministry of Jesus. Because of his deep hunger and longing to see the Kingdom of God, he ventured out to see this Jesus of Nazareth. *Spiritual hunger is always a prerequisite to receiving the Kingdom of God,* and Joseph of Arimathea possessed that hunger. His willingness to think "outside the circle" of how others in the Sanhedrin thought no doubt made him unique in the supreme council. However, it appears that the other members of the council shut their eyes and tolerated him due to his prominent position and extreme wealth.

Next Mark tells us that Joseph of Arimathea went "boldly unto Pilate." Although he was undoubtedly known for his spiritual hunger, John 19:38 informs us that this Joseph had never publicly announced that he was a follower of Jesus "for fear of the Jews."

As a member of the Sanhedrin, Joseph was well aware of the exultation the supreme council members felt over Jesus' death. If it became known that Joseph was the one who took the body and buried it, it could place him in considerable jeopardy. Therefore, going to Pilate to request that he might remove the body of Jesus before the Sabbath began was an act of bravery on Joseph's part.

Joseph's desire to take the body of Jesus and prepare it for burial was so powerful that Mark 15:43 says he "craved the body of Jesus." The word "craved" is the Greek word *aiteo,* a word that means *to be adamant in requesting and demanding something.* In the New Testament, the word *aiteo* is used to portray *a person addressing a superior,* as in this case when Joseph of Arimathea appealed to Pilate. The person may *insist* or *demand* that a need be met, but he approaches and speaks to his superior with *respect.* Therefore, although Joseph showed respect toward Pilate's position, he also presented a strong demand to the governor, adamantly insisting that Jesus' body be released to him.

The word "body" is the Greek word *ptoma,* which always referred to *a dead body* and is often translated as the word "corpse." The Roman custom was to leave the body hanging on the cross until it rotted or until the vultures had picked away at it. Afterward, they discarded of the corpse in the wilderness, where it was eaten by wild dogs. The Jews, however, held the human body in great honor because it was made in the image of God. Even those who were executed by the Jews were respected in the way they were handled after death. Thus, it was not permitted for a Jew's body to hang on a cross after sunset or to be left to rot or for the birds to devour.

Mark 15:44,45 says, "And Pilate marvelled if he were already dead: and calling unto him the centurion, he asked him whether he had been any while dead. And when he knew it of the centurion, he gave the body to Joseph."

At this point, *Nicodemus enters the picture.* The third chapter of John gives the greatest insight into Nicodemus. It says, "There was a man of the Pharisees, named Nicodemus, a ruler of the Jews: the same came to Jesus by night and said unto him, Rabbi, we know that thou art a teacher come from God: for no man can do these miracles that thou doest, except God be with him" (vv. 1,2).

John 3:1 tells us that Nicodemus was a "Pharisee." The word "Pharisee" means *the separated ones.* This means they viewed themselves separated by God for His purposes; thus, they were extremely committed and even fanatical in their service to God.

During the time Jesus lived, the Pharisees were the most respected and esteemed religious leaders in Israel. The Pharisees believed in the supernatural and earnestly waited for the arrival of the Messiah, contrary to the Sadducees who did *not* believe in the supernatural and did *not* wait for the Messiah's coming. The Pharisees held strictly to the Law, whereas the Sadducees took a more liberal approach to the Law that the Pharisees found unacceptable. Flavius Josephus, the famous Jewish historian, was a Pharisee, as was Gamaliel (*see* Acts 5:34) and the apostle Paul before he was converted to Christ on the road to Damascus (*see* Philippians 3:5).

Verse 1 goes on to tell us that Nicodemus was "a ruler of the Jews." The word "ruler" is the Greek word *archon,* which means *the chief one, ruler,* or *prince.* This word was used to *denote the rulers of local synagogues and members of the Sanhedrin* who were the *highest authorities* in the land. Due to this high-ranking position, Nicodemus, like Joseph of Arimathea, was *prominent, influential,* and *wealthy.*

Nicodemus' notoriety among the Jews in Jerusalem was the reason he visited Jesus by night. Nicodemus' fame most likely created a stir every time he passed through the city. Therefore, he wanted to avoid visiting Jesus by day, as it would draw attention to the fact that he was spending time with a teacher the Sanhedrin viewed to be a maverick and out of their control. Consequently, Nicodemus came to Jesus by night when his visit would not be observable.

What he told Jesus during this visit reveals much about the spiritual hunger that Nicodemus possessed. First, he called Jesus "Rabbi." The word itself means *great,* but it was used as a title of respect that was used only in reference to the great teachers of the Law. The Pharisees loved to be called "Rabbi," for they viewed themselves as the chief keepers of the Law.

For Nicodemus to call Jesus "Rabbi" was remarkable indeed. The Jewish leader would never have used that title unless he had already heard Jesus interpret the Law and thereby judged His ability to do so. The fact that Nicodemus called Jesus by this privileged title, given only to those who were viewed as the greatest theologians in Israel, tells us that he was very impressed with Jesus' knowledge of the Scriptures.

This means that Nicodemus, like Joseph of Arimathea, was open-minded enough to receive from people who were "outside the circle" of what most religious people viewed as acceptable. In fact, Nicodemus was so hungry to find a touch of God that it appears he himself visited Jesus' meetings that had just been conducted in the city of Jerusalem.

John 2:23 says, "Now when he [Jesus] was in Jerusalem at the passover, in the feast day, many believed in his name, when they saw the miracles which he did." When Nicodemus visited with Jesus, he referred to these miracles, saying in John 3:2, "...Rabbi, we know that thou art a teacher come from God: for no man can do these miracles that thou doest, except God be with him."

It seems that Nicodemus had come close enough to these miracle meetings to personally view the miracles. This must have been the occasion when he heard Jesus teach and deemed Him worthy of the title "Rabbi." As a Pharisee, Nicodemus believed in the supernatural. He was so moved by the miracles and so convinced of their legitimacy that he wanted to personally meet Jesus and ask Him questions. In the conversation that followed, Jesus told Nicodemus, "...Verily, verily, I say unto thee, Except a man be born again, he cannot see the kingdom of God" (John 3:3). The famous conversation that followed has been read, quoted, and preached all over the world for two thousand years.

After Joseph of Arimathea received permission to remove Jesus' body from the Cross, he took the body to begin preparations for burial. John 19:39 tells us what happened next: "And there came also Nicodemus, which at the first came to Jesus by night, and brought a mixture of myrrh and aloes, about an hundred pound weight."

This verse tells us Nicodemus "...brought a mixture of myrrh and aloes, about an hundred pound weight...." "Myrrh" was an expensive yellowish-brown, sweet-smelling gum resin that was obtained from a tree and had a bitter taste. It was chiefly used as a chemical for embalming the dead. "Aloes" was a sweet-smelling fragrance derived from the juice pressed from the leaves of a tree found in the Middle East. It was used to ceremonially cleanse, to purify, and to counteract the terrible smell of the corpse as it decomposed. Like myrrh, this substance was also very expensive and rare — yet the Bible tells us that Nicodemus "brought a mixture" of both substances — about a hundred pounds' worth!

Nicodemus' cost for this offering of love must have been out of sight! Only a rich man could have purchased such a massive combination of these costly, uncommon substances. Nicodemus obviously intended to fully cover the body of Jesus, so he spared no cost in preparing the body for burial, demonstrating his love for Jesus right up to the very end.

John goes on to tell us, "Then took they the body of Jesus, and wound it in linen clothes with the spices, as the manner of the Jews is to bury" (v. 40). The word for "linen" is the Greek word *othonion*, which describes *a cloth made of very fine and extremely expensive materials* that was fabricated primarily in Egypt. Nobles in that day were known to pay very high prices to have robes made for their wives from this material.

When Lazarus came forth from the tomb after being resurrected by Jesus, he was "...bound hand and foot with graveclothes: and his face was bound about with a napkin..." (John 11:44). This shows that Lazarus was bound with bandages made of strips of material. However, the word *othonion* tends to suggest that Jesus was carefully laid in a large linen sheet of fine weave. Specially prepared spices were then mingled between the folds of this high-priced garment in which Jesus' dead body was wrapped.

This is an amazing story of two men who dearly loved Jesus. Although Joseph and Nicodemus lived in circumstances that made it difficult for them to publicly follow Jesus, they chose to follow Him to their fullest capability. When Jesus died, they continued to demonstrate their deep love for Him, treating His dead body with tender care and using their personal wealth to bury Him with honor. As far as they understood at the time, this was their last opportunity to show Jesus how much they loved Him, and they were going to take full advantage of it!

Jesus taught, "For where your treasure is, there will your heart be also" (Matthew 6:21). When these two men used their wealth to bury Jesus, they illustrated that their heart was with Jesus. He was their highest priority, so they invested their assets in showing their love for Him. They literally sowed their money into the ground when they bathed Jesus in one hundred pounds of those rare substances, wrapped Him in an expensive cloth, and then buried Him in a rich man's tomb.

If people were to look at the way you spend your finances, would they be able to see that Jesus is the highest priority in your life? Do you treat Him with honor and respect in the way you serve Him, or is He the last priority on your list? According to the words of Jesus, what you do with your finances really does tell the truth about what you love the most. So what would He say that your finances reveal about how much you love Him?

As Joseph of Arimathea and Nicodemus honored Jesus in death, let's commit to honor Him with everything we possess as we serve Him every day of our lives. *Right now, let's make the choice to upgrade our giving, our living, and every other way that we are privileged to serve Jesus!*

MY PRAYER FOR TODAY

Lord, I want to become a better and bigger giver! I love You with all my heart, and I want to demonstrate my love with my finances. Your Word says where my treasure is, that is where my heart is also. What I do with my treasure reveals what is precious to me and the true condition of my heart. Therefore, I want to give more to You; I want to live better for You; and I want to serve You more fully than ever before. I am making the decision today to make You and Your Kingdom the highest priority when it comes to how I spend my personal finances!

I pray this in Jesus' name!

MY CONFESSION FOR TODAY

I boldly declare that Jesus Christ and His Kingdom are the highest priorities in my life. I faithfully tithe and give special offerings to help advance the message of Jesus Christ around the world. There is no higher priority in my life than getting the Gospel to the ends of the earth, so I use my finances wisely and carefully, making certain that I am able to give my maximum gift to Jesus. Because I give so faithfully, I am blessed!

I declare this by faith in Jesus' name!

QUESTIONS FOR YOU TO CONSIDER

1. If Jesus were to look at your finances to determine what is the greatest priority in your life, would He be able to say that He and His Kingdom were most important to you, or would He see that He is somewhere lower on your list of priorities?
2. Are you faithful in the giving of your tithe, or are you sporadic in the way you honor God with your money?
3. In order to become faithful with your tithe and offering, what changes do you need to make in your spending habits? Why don't you think it over and then make the needed adjustments so you can start treating Jesus like He is the most important priority in your life?

APRIL 27

Buried!

Now in the place where he was crucified there was a garden;
And in the garden a new sepulchre, wherein was never man yet laid.
There laid they Jesus therefore because of the Jews' preparation day;
for the sepulchre was nigh at hand.
— John 19:41,42

John's Gospel tells us that near the crucifixion site, there was a garden. The Greek word for "garden" is *kepos*, and it refers *to any garden with trees and spices*. It can also be translated as *an orchard*. The same word is used in John 18:1 to describe *the Garden of Gethsemane*, which was *an olive tree orchard*.

All four Gospels suggest that this tomb was near the place where Jesus was crucified, but John 19:42 says, "…The sepulchre was nigh at hand." The word "nigh" is the Greek word *aggus*, meaning *nearby*. Most crucifixions were performed along a roadside. Evidently this garden was located in an orchard-like place, just down the road from where Jesus was crucified.

John 19:41 tells us that in the garden was "…a new sepulchre, wherein was never man yet laid." The word "new" is the Greek word *kainos*, meaning *fresh* or *unused*. This doesn't necessarily mean that the tomb had recently been made but that it was a tomb that had never been used — thus, the reason John writes, "…Wherein was never man yet laid."

Matthew, Mark, and Luke all record that this tomb belonged to Joseph of Arimathea, suggesting that it was the tomb he had prepared for his own burial. The fact that it was a tomb "hewn out in the rock" (Matthew 27:60; Mark 15:46; Luke 23:53) confirms the personal wealth of Joseph of Arimathea. Only royalty or wealthy individuals could afford to have their tombs carved out of a wall of stone or in the side of a mountain. Poorer men were buried in simple graves.

The word "hewn" in Matthew, Mark, and Luke comes from the Greek word *laxeuo*, meaning not only *to cut out*, but *to polish*. It implies that it was *a special tomb, a highly developed tomb, a refined tomb,* or *a tomb that was splendid and expensive*. Isaiah 53:9 had prophesied that the Messiah would be buried in a rich man's tomb, and the word *laxeuo* strongly suggests that this was indeed the expensive tomb of a very rich man.

John 19:42 says, "There laid they Jesus…." The word "laid" comes from the word *tithimi*, which means *to set, to lay, to place, to deposit,* or *to set in place*. As used here, it portrays the careful and thoughtful placing of Jesus' body in its resting place inside the tomb. Luke 23:55 tells us that after Jesus' body was placed in the tomb, the women who came with Him from Galilee, "…beheld the sepulchre, and how his body was laid." The word "beheld" in Greek is *theaomai*, from which we get the word *theater*. The word *theaomai* means *to gaze upon, to fully see,* or *to look at intently*. This is very important, for it proves the women *inspected* the tomb, *gazing upon* the dead body of Jesus *to see* that it had been honorably laid in place.

Mark 15:47 identifies these women as Mary Magdalene and Mary the mother of Joses and says that these women "…beheld where he was laid" at the tomb. The imperfect tense is used in Mark's account, alerting us to the fact that these women took their time in making sure Jesus was properly laid there. It could be translated, "*they carefully contemplated where he was laid*." If Jesus had still been alive, those who buried Him would have known it, for they spent substantial time preparing His body for burial. Then after His dead body was deposited into the tomb, they lingered there, checking once again to see that the body was treated with the greatest love and attention.

Once they were certain everything was done correctly, Joseph of Arimathea "…rolled a great stone to the door of the sepulchre, and departed" (Matthew 27:60; Mark 15:46). It was rare to find a stone entrance to a Jewish tomb in biblical times; most Jewish tombs had doors with certain types of hinges. A large stone rolled before the tomb would be much more difficult to move, making the burial site more permanent.

However, the chief priests and Pharisees weren't so sure that the site was secure. Fearing that Jesus' disciples would come to steal the body and claim that Jesus had been resurrected, the Jewish leaders came to Pilate and said, "…Sir, we remember that that deceiver said, while he was yet alive, After three days I will rise again. Command therefore that the sepulchre be made sure until the third day, lest his disciples come by night, and steal him away, and say unto the people, He is risen from the dead: so the last error shall be worse than the first" (Matthew 27:63,64).

When the chief priests and Pharisees asked that "…the sepulchre be *made sure…*," the Greek word *sphragidzo* is used. This word described *a legal seal* that was placed on documents, letters, possessions, or, in this case, a tomb. Its purpose was *to authenticate that the sealed item had been properly inspected before sealing and that all the contents were in order.* As long as the seal remained unbroken, *it guaranteed that the contents inside were safe and sound.* In this case, the word *sphragidzo* is used to signify *the sealing of the tomb.* In all probability, it was a string that was stretched across the stone at the entrance of the tomb, which was then sealed on both sides by Pilate's legal authorities.

Before sealing the tomb, however, these authorities were first required to inspect the inside of the tomb to see that the body of Jesus was in its place. After guaranteeing that the corpse was where it was supposed to be, they rolled the stone back in place and then *sealed* it with the official seal of the governor of Rome.

After hearing the suspicions of the chief priests and Pharisees, "Pilate said unto them, Ye have a watch: go your way, make it as sure as ye can" (Matthew 27:65). The word "watch" is the Greek word *coustodia,* from which we get the word *custodian.* This was a group of four Roman soldiers whose shift changed every three hours. The changing shifts assured that the tomb would be guarded twenty-four hours a day by soldiers who were awake, attentive, and fully alert. When Pilate said, "Ye have a watch…," a better rendering would be, *"Here — I'm giving you a set of soldiers; take them and guard the tomb."*

Matthew 27:66 says, "So they went, and made the sepulchre sure, sealing the stone, and setting a watch." Wasting no time, the chief priests and elders hastened to the tomb with their government-issued soldiers and the special officers assigned to inspect the tomb before placing Pilate's seal upon it. After a full inspection had been made, the stone was put back in place, and the soldiers stood guard to protect the tomb from anyone who would attempt to touch it or remove its contents. Every three hours, new guards arrived to replace the old ones. These armed soldiers guarded the entrance to Jesus' tomb so firmly that *no one* would have been able to come near it.

The purpose of the seal was to authenticate that Jesus was dead; therefore, we can know that His body was thoroughly inspected again for proof of death. There is no doubt that Jesus was dead, for He was examined again and again, even as He lay in the tomb. Some critics have claimed that Jesus' body was inspected only by His own disciples and that they could have lied about Him being dead. However, the body of Jesus was also examined by an officer from Pilate's court. We can also be fairly certain that the chief priests and elders who accompanied the soldiers to the burial site demanded the right to view His dead body as well so they could verify that He was truly dead.

When Jesus came out of that grave several days later, it was no hoax or fabricated story. In addition to all the people who saw Him die on the Cross, the following individuals and groups verified that His dead body was in the tomb before the stone was permanently sealed by an officer from the Roman court of law:

- ✦ Joseph of Arimathea carefully laid Him inside the tomb.
- ✦ Nicodemus provided the embalming solutions, assisted in embalming Him, and helped Joseph of Arimathea lay Him in His place in the tomb.
- ✦ Mary Magdalene and Mary the mother of Joses lovingly examined His body and carefully contemplated every aspect of the burial site to ensure everything was done properly and respectfully.
- ✦ Rome's official officer ordered the stone rolled back; then he went into the tomb and examined the body of Jesus to verify that it was Jesus and that He was really dead.
- ✦ The chief priests and elders entered the tomb with Rome's official officer so they could look upon Jesus' dead body and put an end to their worries that He had somehow survived.

✦ Roman guards checked the contents of the tomb because they wanted to know for sure a body was there. They didn't want to be guarding an empty tomb that would later be used as a claim of resurrection, while they got blamed for the disappearance of Jesus' body.

✦ After all of these inspections were complete, Rome's official officer ordered the stone rolled back in its place. While the chief priests, elders, and Roman guards watched, he secured the site and sealed it shut with the seal of the governor of Rome.

Regardless of these efforts to secure the site and to keep Jesus inside the grave, it was impossible for death to hold Him. When preaching on the day of Pentecost, Peter proclaimed to the people of Jerusalem, "…Ye have taken, and by wicked hands have crucified and slain [Jesus]: whom God hath raised up, having loosed the pains of death: because it was not possible that he should be holden of it" (Acts 2:23,24).

Today the tomb in Jerusalem is empty because Jesus arose on the third day! Now He is seated on His throne at the right hand of the Father on High, where He ever lives to make intercession for you and for me (Hebrews 7:25).

Since He has become your High Priest and lives to make intercession for you, there is no need for you to struggle alone. *Jesus is sitting at the Father's right hand, waiting for you to come boldly to Him for help and assistance. There is no mountain He cannot move, so go to Him today to make your requests known!*

MY PRAYER FOR TODAY

Lord, I refuse to struggle in my own strength any longer, acting like I can handle every problem and challenge in my life by myself. You were raised from the dead to become my High Priest. I am so sorry for the times You have waited in vain for me to come to You because I lingered, thinking I didn't need Your help. Starting right now, I am changing this in my life — and when I have a need, I'm going to come straight to You because You are there waiting to help me!

I pray this in Jesus' name!

MY CONFESSION FOR TODAY

I boldly declare that Jesus is my High Priest and that He hears me when I pray. I go to Him and tell Him about my needs and challenges, and He answers me! He gives me strength, power, wisdom, and all the guidance I need to make right decisions and choices. As a result of Jesus' help, I am strong; I am wise; and I make right decisions and choices in my life today.

I declare this by faith in Jesus' name!

QUESTIONS FOR YOU TO CONSIDER

1. How long has it been since you truly contemplated the fact that Jesus died and was buried in a sealed tomb? What effect does this truth have on your life?

2. Do you really have a revelation in your heart that Jesus died and was raised from the dead? Can you imagine what it was like at that burial site the day life came flooding into His dead body and He was physically raised from the bonds of death?

3. Are you struggling with your problems all alone, or do you turn to Jesus, your great High Priest, for help with all your problems or challenges? Do you have any specific needs you should be taking to Him right now?

APRIL 28

Resurrection Morning!

In the end of the sabbath, as it began to dawn
toward the first day of the week, came Mary Magdalene
and the other Mary to see the sepulchre.
And, behold, there was a great earthquake:
for the angel of the Lord descended from heaven, and came
and rolled back the stone from the door, and sat upon it.
— Matthew 28:1,2

Jesus is *alive!* His resurrection is not merely a philosophical renaissance of His ideas and teachings — He was literally raised from the dead! The power of God exploded inside that tomb, reconnected Jesus' spirit with His dead body, flooded His corpse with life, and He arose! So much power was released behind the sealed entrance of His tomb that the earth itself reverberated and shuddered from the explosion. Then an angel rolled the stone from the entrance to the tomb, and Jesus physically walked through the door of that tomb *alive*!

This is no legend nor fairy tale. *This is the foundation of our faith!* So today let's examine the events surrounding the resurrection of Jesus Christ. He was resurrected from the dead sometime between the close of Sabbath sunset on Saturday evening and before the women came to the tomb early on Sunday morning. The only actual eyewitnesses to the resurrection itself were the angels who were present and the four Roman soldiers who had been stationed there at Pilate's command (Matthew 27:66; *see* April 27). However, Matthew, Mark, Luke, and John all record the events that followed on the morning of His resurrection.

When first reading all four accounts of what happened that morning, it may appear that a contradiction exists between the details told in the various Gospels. But when they are chronologically aligned, the picture becomes very clear and the impression of contradiction is wiped away.

Let me give you an example of what appears to be a contradiction. The Gospel of Matthew says there was *one angel outside the tomb*. The Gospel of Mark says there was *one angel inside the tomb*. The Gospel of Luke says there were *two angels inside the tomb*. John says *nothing* about angels, but does say that when Mary returned later in the day, she saw *two angels inside the tomb* who were positioned at the head and foot of the place where the body of Jesus had been laid.

So who is telling the right story? How many angels were there? As I said, to see the entire scenario that transpired that day, the events in all four Gospels must be must properly sequenced chronologically. So let's get started!

Matthew 28:1 says, "In the end of the sabbath, as it began to dawn toward the first day of the week, came Mary Magdalene and the other Mary to see the sepulchre." In addition to Mary Magdalene and the other Mary, the mother of James, Luke 24:10 tells us that "Joanna" and "other women" came to the tomb. Luke 8:3 tells us that this "Joanna" was the wife of Herod's steward — evidently a wealthy woman who was a financial supporter of Jesus' ministry. According to Luke 23:55 and 56, many of these women were present when Jesus was placed inside the tomb, but returned home to prepare "spices and ointments" so they could anoint His body for burial when they returned after the Sabbath day.

These women had no way of knowing that the chief priests and elders had gone to Pilate the day after Jesus was buried to request a watch of four Roman soldiers to guard the tomb and an official from the Roman court to "seal" the tomb. *How would these women have known of this?* They were at home, preparing spices and ointments.

Yet while these women were preparing to return to anoint Jesus' dead body, the tomb was being officially sealed shut and Roman soldiers had been ordered to guard the tomb twenty-four hours a day. Had the women known that the tomb was legally sealed and couldn't be opened, they wouldn't have returned to the tomb, for it was legally impossible for them to request the stone to be removed.

Mark 16:2-4 says, "And very early in the morning the first day of the week, they came unto the sepulchre at the rising of the sun. And they said among themselves, Who shall roll us away the stone from the door of the sepulchre? And when they looked, they saw that the stone was rolled away: for it was very great."

Ignorant of the fact that the tomb couldn't legally be opened, the women proceeded to the tomb for the purpose of anointing Jesus' body. As they drew near to the garden where the tomb was located, they wondered among themselves who would remove the stone for them. However, Matthew 28:2 says, "And, behold, there was a great earthquake…."

This earthquake didn't occur at the time when the women approached the tomb; rather, it occurred simultaneously with the moment of Jesus' resurrection, sometime after the Saturday sunset and before the women arrived at the garden. When describing the magnitude of the earthquake, Matthew uses the word "behold." In Greek, this is the word *idou*. The *King James Version* translates it *behold,* but in our day, it might be better translated, *Wow!* This word carries the idea of *shock, amazement,* and *wonder,* so when Matthew says, "And, behold, there was a great earthquake," he literally means, *"Wow! Can you believe it?…"* The word *idou* could also carry this idea: *"Whew! Listen to the amazing thing that happened next…."* Although Matthew writes his Gospel many years after the fact, he still experiences *amazement* when he thinks of this event!

Matthew tells us that there was "a great earthquake." The word "great" is the Greek word *mega,* leaving no room for doubt as to the magnitude of this event. The word *mega* always suggests something *huge, massive,* or *enormous.* The word "earthquake" is the Greek word *seimos,* the word for *a literal earthquake* (*see* April 25). Just as creation shook when its Creator died on the Cross, now the earth exploded with exultation at the resurrection of Jesus!

Mark 16:4 says that when the women arrived at the tomb, they found "…the stone was rolled away: for it was very great." The word "very" is the Greek word *sphodra,* meaning *very, exceedingly,* or *extremely.* The word "great" is that word *mega,* meaning *huge, massive,* or *enormous.* In other words, this was no normal stone; the authorities placed *an extremely, exceedingly massive stone* in front of the entrance to Jesus' tomb. Yet when the women arrived, it had been removed!

Matthew 28:2 tells us how the stone was removed. It says that "…the angel of the Lord descended from heaven, and came and rolled back the stone from the door, and sat upon it." The word "sat" is the Greek word *kathemai,* which means *to sit down.* Some have suggested that the ability of the angel to sit on top of such a huge stone may also denote his immense size — in other words, he was so huge that he could sit on top of the enormous stone as if it were a chair. If this were the case, the removal of the stone would have been a simple feat. Matthew informs us that not only was the angel strong, but "his countenance was like lightning, and his raiment white as snow" (v. 3).

The immense size, power, and brilliance of this angel explains why the Roman guards fled the scene. Matthew 28:4 tells us, "And for fear of him the keepers did shake, and became as dead men." The word "fear" is the Greek word *phobos*, which means *to fear*. In this case, it was such a *panic-stricken fear* that it caused the guards to "shake."

This word "shake" is derived from the Greek word *seio,* the identical root word for an *earthquake*. The mighty Roman soldiers trembled and quaked at the sight of the angel. In fact, they "…became as dead men." The words "dead men" is the Greek word *nekros* — the word for *a corpse*. The soldiers were so terrified at the appearance of the angel that they fell to the ground, violently trembling and so paralyzed with fear that they were unable to move. When they were finally able to move again, these guards fled the scene — and when the women arrived at the garden, they were nowhere to be found!

Luke 24:3 tells us that with the stone removed, these women passed right by the angel who sat on top of the huge stone and crossed the threshold into the tomb. It says, "And they entered in, and found not the body of the Lord Jesus." *But what did they find inside the tomb besides the vacant spot where Jesus had laid?* Mark 16:5 tells us: "And entering into the sepulchre, they saw a young man sitting on the right side, clothed in a long white garment; and they were affrighted."

First, these women saw an angel sitting on top of the stone at the entrance of the tomb. Now inside the tomb, they see another angel whose appearance is like a young man. The words "young man" are from the Greek word *neanikos,* referring to *a young man who is filled with vigor and energy and who is in the prime of his life*. This illustrates the *vitality, strength,* and *ever-youthful appearance* of angels. The Bible also tells us that this angel was "…clothed in a long white garment…." The word "clothed" pictures *a garment draped about his shoulders*, as a mighty warrior or ruler would be dressed. The word "garment" is from the Greek word *stole,* which represents *the long flowing robe that adorned royalty, commanders, kings, priests, and other people of high distinction*.

As these women stood in an empty tomb, Luke 24:4 tells us that "…they were much perplexed thereabout…." This Greek word for "perplexed" is *aporeo,* which means *to lose one's way*. It is the picture of someone who is so confused that he can't figure out where he is, what he's doing, or what is happening around him. This person is completely *bewildered* by surrounding events.

Of course these women were perplexed! They came expecting to see the stone in front of the tomb, but it was *removed*. Sitting on top of the massive stone was *a dazzling angel*. To get into the tomb, they had to pass by that angel — but once in the tomb, they discovered there was *no dead body*. Then suddenly they looked over to the right side of the tomb and saw *a second angel*, dressed in a long, white robe like a warrior, ruler, priest, or king. The women didn't expect to encounter any of these unusual events that morning. It would have been normal for their heads to be whirling with questions!

Then Luke 24:4 tells us that all of a sudden "…two men stood by them in shining garments." The words "stood by" are from the Greek word *epistemi,* which means *to come upon suddenly; to take one by surprise; to burst upon the scene; to suddenly step up;* or *to unexpectedly appear*. In other words, while the women tried to figure out what they were seeing, the angel sitting on top of the stone decided to join the group inside the tomb. Suddenly to the women's amazement, *two* angels were standing inside the tomb in "shining garments"!

The word "shining" is *astrapto,* depicting something that *shines* or *flashes like lightning*. It may refer to the angels' shining appearance.

Luke 24:5-8 says, "And as they were afraid, and bowed down their faces to the earth, they [the angels] said unto them, Why seek ye the living among the dead? He is not here, but is risen: remember how he spake unto you when he was yet in Galilee, saying, The Son of man must be delivered into the hands of sinful men, and be crucified, and the third day rise again. And they remembered his words."

After the two angels proclaimed the joyful news of Jesus' resurrection, they instructed the women, "But go your way, tell his disciples and Peter that he goeth before you into Galilee: there shall ye see him, as he said unto you" (Mark 16:7). Matthew 28:8 says they "...did run to bring his disciples word." Mark 16:8 says, "And they went out quickly, and fled from the sepulchre...." Luke 24:9,10 says that the women returned and "...told these things unto the apostles."

Can you imagine how flustered these women must have been as they tried to tell the apostles what they had seen and heard that morning? Luke 24:11 says, "And their words seemed to them as idle tales, and they believed them not." The words "idle tales" are from the Greek word *leros*, which means *nonsense, idle talk, babble,* or *delirium.* In other words, the women's presentation of the Gospel probably wasn't extremely clear, but it stirred enough interest in Peter and John to make them get up and go find out for themselves about Jesus!

When we've had a supernatural encounter with the Lord, it isn't always easy to put that experience into words. This is a frustration all of us who know the Lord have felt at one time or another. However, we can't let that keep us from spreading the good news of what Jesus Christ has done in our lives. We should never forget that although these women seemed to be speaking nonsense and babble, their words were all that was needed to spark an interest in those men that made them get up and go find out about Jesus themselves.

As you share Jesus Christ with your family and friends, it is your job to "give it your best shot." Tell the Good News the best way you know how! But don't overlook the fact that the Holy Spirit is also speaking to their hearts at the same time you are speaking to their ears. The Spirit of God will use you and your witness to stir hunger deep in their hearts. But long after you are finished talking, God will still be dealing with them. And when they come to Jesus, they won't remember if you sounded confusing the day you presented the Gospel to them. They will be thankful that you loved them enough to care for their souls!

So get up and get going! Open your mouth, and start telling the Good News that Jesus Christ is alive and well!

MY PRAYER FOR TODAY

Lord, I am concerned for my family, friends, acquaintances, and fellow workers who still don't know You as their personal Savior. I've been concerned that if I tried to talk to them, I wouldn't make sense, so I've shied away from witnessing to them. But I know You can make sense out of anything I say. Today I am leaning on You to help me witness to people in my life. I need You to speak to their hearts at the same time I'm speaking to their ears! Please help me tell them about Your saving grace!

I pray this in Jesus' name!

MY CONFESSION FOR TODAY

I confess that I am a witness for Jesus Christ! I open my mouth and speak the truth in love, and people want to hear what I have to tell them. This is the best news in the whole world —

and when I tell it, people get excited and want to give their lives to Jesus. I am not afraid to speak up, to speak out, and to speak on behalf of my precious Savior. What He has done for me, He will do for others, for He is not a respecter of persons. Therefore, I will boldly tell of the grace of God and what He has done for me!

I declare this by faith in Jesus' name!

QUESTIONS FOR YOU TO CONSIDER

1. Have you had times when you wanted to tell someone about an experience you've had with the Lord, but you felt frustrated because you couldn't find the right words to explain your experience to them?
2. If you suddenly found yourself in front of someone who was dying and who needed to give his heart to Jesus, would you know how to lead that person to the Lord? If your answer is yes, how would you do it? What would you tell him?
3. If your answer to the above question is "No, I wouldn't know how to lead someone to Jesus," don't you think it's time for you to start learning how to do this? How could you go about learning how to more effectively witness for the Lord?

APRIL 29

Peter and John Run to the Tomb

Peter therefore went forth, and that other disciple,
and came to the sepulchre. So they ran both together:
and the other disciple did outrun Peter,
and came first to the sepulchre.
— John 20:3,4

*B*y the time the women reached the apostles, they must have sounded very *confused*! On one hand, they reported that the angels said Jesus was alive from the dead. On the other hand, they were confused and operating in fear, so they exclaimed, "…They have taken away the Lord out of the sepulchre, and we know not where they have laid him" (John 20:2).

Fear always produces confusion, and these women were so confused that the apostles didn't take what they said seriously. Luke 24:11 says, "And their words seemed to them as idle tales, and they believed them not." The words "idle tales" are from the Greek word *leros,* which means *nonsense, idle talk, babble,* or *delirium* (*see* April 28). Who did these women think removed Jesus from the tomb? Which story was true? Was He resurrected and alive as the women first told the apostles, or was He stolen away?

John 20:3,4 says, "Peter therefore went forth, and that other disciple, and came to the sepulchre. So they ran both together: and the other disciple John did outrun Peter, and came first to the sepulchre." When the Bible says Peter and John "went forth," the Greek tense indicates that their feet were moving before the conversation with the women concluded. When they heard that something had happened at the tomb, both men were on the move to get there as quickly as possible.

We also know from John 20:11 that Mary Magdalene soon followed Peter and John back to the tomb, for she was present at the site and remained there after Peter and John returned to the apostles.

I find it interesting that when Peter and John raced to the tomb to see whatever it was that the women were trying to communicate to them, none of the other apostles joined them. The others apparently just sat and watched Peter and John put on their clothes and start running, but they didn't join the two men. Instead, the rest of the apostles probably stayed behind to discuss what they had heard and to debate about what it meant.

Because Peter and John ran to the garden, they experienced something the other apostles missed by staying home. *It is simply a fact that if you want to experience Jesus Christ and His power, you must get up from where you are and start moving in His direction.*

John outran Peter to the garden where the tomb was located. As soon as he arrived, John 20:5 tells us, "And he stooping down, and looking in, saw the linen clothes lying; yet went he not in." The Greek word for "stooping down" is *parakupto*. It means *to peer into; to peep into; to bend low to take a closer look; to stoop down to see something better.*

John bent down so he could take a close peek into the tomb, and he "…saw the linen clothes lying…." The word "saw" is the Greek word *blepo*, which means *to see*. It was just enough of *a glance* to see the linen clothes lying there. The words "linen clothes" is the same identical word used in John 19:40 (*see* April 26) when referring to the expensive Egyptian-made garment in which Joseph of Arimathea and Nicodemus had buried Jesus. If Jesus had been stolen, whoever took Him would have taken this expensive garment as well, but John saw that these linen clothes had been left lying in the tomb.

Graves were a place of respect for the Jews, which may explain the reason John was hesitant to enter the tomb. It is also quite possible that he observed the broken seals and realized that it looked like an unlawful entry had occurred. Perhaps he was thinking twice before he found himself connected to an alleged potential crime scene. Regardless of why John hesitated, the Bible tells us that Peter didn't hesitate but promptly barged right into the tomb to check it out for himself: "Then cometh Simon Peter following him, and went into the sepulchre, and seeth the linen clothes lie, and the napkin, that was about his head, not lying with the linen clothes, but wrapped together in a place by itself" (John 20:6,7).

John only glanced into the interior of the tomb, but the above verse says Peter went into the sepulcher and "…seeth the linen clothes lie." The word "seeth" is the Greek word *theaomai*, from which we get our word *theater*. It means *to fully see* or *fully observe*, like a patron who carefully watches every act of a play at the theater.

When Peter entered that tomb, he surveyed it like a professional surveyor. He looked over every nook and cranny, paying special attention to the linen clothes and the way they were left there. He saw "…the napkin, that was about his head, not lying with the linen clothes, but wrapped together in a place by itself." The word "napkin" is *soudarion,* and it refers to *a napkin that could be used for wiping perspiration from one's face.* This word was also used in connection with *a burial cloth that was gently placed upon the face of the dead at burial.*

When Lazarus came out of the tomb, Jesus instructed that his grave clothes be removed along with the *soudarion,* or napkin, from his face (John 11:44). Apparently Jesus' entire body was wrapped in a large white linen sheet (*see* April 26), but His face was covered with such a napkin in traditional Jewish burial style.

The most fascinating fact about this facial cloth was that it was "…wrapped in a place by itself." The word "wrapped" is the Greek word *entulisso*, which means *to neatly fold; to nicely arrange;* or *to arrange in an orderly fashion.* The reason this word is so interesting is that it tells us Jesus was calm and completely in control of His faculties when He was raised from the dead. He removed the expensive Egyptian-made burial cloth from His body, sat upright, and then removed the burial napkin from His face. Sitting in that upright position, He neatly folded the burial cloth and gently laid it down to one side, separate from the linen clothes He probably laid down on His other side. Now as Peter gazed at the scene inside the tomb, he could see the empty spot where Jesus had sat between these two pieces of burial clothing after He was raised from the dead.

John 20:8 says, "Then went in also that other disciple, which came first to the sepulchre, and he saw, and believed." This verse says that when John saw the empty stone slab where Jesus' body had previously lain and the burial clothes lying to the right and to the left, forming the empty spot where Jesus sat after He was resurrected, John then "believed." I find it truly amazing that even though Peter had spent a longer time than John inside the tomb, he was still uncertain as to the meaning of it all. Luke 24:12 says that Peter "…departed, wondering in himself at that which was come to pass." John, on the other hand, left the tomb believing Jesus was alive.

Later that evening, Jesus would appear to all the apostles and breathe the Spirit of God into them, giving them the new birth (John 20:22). But at this moment, because the Holy Spirit was not yet resident in them as their Teacher, there was much they could not understand. Even though Jesus had told them He would die and be raised from the dead, they simply were not yet able to comprehend it. That's why John 20:9 says, "For as yet they knew not the scripture, that he must rise again from the dead."

Although the apostles had heard this scripture from Jesus Himself, the reality and full impact of its truth had not registered in their hearts. After this historical and momentous day, the Bible tells us, "Then the disciples went away again unto their own home" (v. 10).

It is remarkable to me that Peter could stand in the middle of Jesus' empty tomb and still leave uncertain about what it meant. How in the world would it be possible to be in the very room where Jesus' dead body had lain, to see the neatly folded napkin, to recognize the spot where He sat upright between those garments, and to still not be able to figure out that Jesus was now alive?

Yet it starts making sense when I think about it. God has done so many unquestionable miracles for you and me as well. How many times have we walked away unaffected by the power and miracles we've seen and experienced? God has delivered us, saved us, and rescued us from harm time and time again; yet we still tend to wonder if God is really with us or not. How in the world could we ever question the faithfulness of God after all He has already done for us?

We need to make sure we don't remain unaffected by the miracle-working power of God that has worked in our lives. Instead, we should make the decision to fully embrace every good thing God does for us — to soak it up so entirely that it changes us and our outlook on life. God is good! He has been good to every one of us. If we fail to remember this, it is only because we are not opening our eyes to see His hand of protection, provision, and safety all around us.

So make the choice today to recognize what God has done in your life. Remember to thank Him for it, and then never forget it!

MY PRAYER FOR TODAY

Lord, it is true that You have worked so many miracles in my life. If I were to try to recount all the times You have saved me, delivered me, rescued me, gotten me out of trouble, put me on a right path, and blessed me when I didn't deserve it, I wouldn't have enough time to recite them all! So how could I ever question that You would be with me right now in my present challenge? Of course You are with me and will help me. Forgive me for being so hard-hearted as to forget what You have already done for me. And I thank You right now that You are going to help me this time too!

I pray this in Jesus' name!

MY CONFESSION FOR TODAY

I confess that I am not forgetful of the many ways God has worked in my life. I am mindful of His mercy and grace and I praise Him for it every day. I am a living testimony of His power. He is my Redeemer, my Healer, my Deliverer, and my Provider. He is the One who rescues me from harm and who meets my every need. I am fully supplied in every area of my life because of the promises God has made to me in His Word!

I declare this by faith in Jesus' name!

QUESTIONS FOR YOU TO CONSIDER

1. Be honest! Haven't you had times in your life when you were like Peter? In other words, have you ever been standing right in the middle of God's gracious provision when a new challenge caused you to wonder if He was going to be faithful to help you make it through in victory?

2. Why don't you take a few minutes right now to reflect on the miracles God has done in your life? Make a list, and see how many instances of supernatural provision you are able to write down.

3. Since you have a responsibility to tell others what God has done for you, why don't you find an opportunity today to tell someone one good thing God has done for you? Then ask that person to tell you one moment when he is sure God did something supernatural for him. You may be surprised at how people respond to this question!

How in the world could we ever question the faithfulness of God after all He has already done for us? We need to make sure we don't remain unaffected by the miracle-working power of God that has worked in our lives. Instead, we should make the decision to fully embrace every good thing God does for us — to soak it up so entirely that it changes us and our outlook on life forever.

APRIL 30

⁂

Jesus Appears to Mary Magdalene

But Mary stood without at the sepulchre weeping:
and as she wept, she stooped down, and looked into the sepulchre,
and seeth two angels in white sitting, the one at the head,
and the other at the feet, where the body of Jesus had lain.
And they say unto her, Woman, why weepest thou?...
— John 20:11-13

When Peter and John left the garden, Mary Magdalene remained behind. She had followed the two men, possibly hoping to obtain a clearer understanding of what she had experienced that day. All she knew was that her day started with a desire to come to the tomb to anoint the body of Jesus. But when she arrived, the stone was rolled away, and an angel was sitting on top of the great stone (Matthew 28:2)! Then when she entered the tomb, she first discovered another angel (Mark 16:5) and then suddenly found herself in the presence of *two* angels inside the tomb (Luke 24:4)!

The angels had told Mary, "He is not here, but is risen..." (Luke 24:6). *But if Jesus was risen as the angels had said, where was He? How could she find Him?*

Feeling dejected and alone, Mary stood outside the tomb weeping. The Greek tense means *continually weeping*, highlighting the fact she was extremely troubled about the inexplicable events that were happening. Most of all, she wanted to know what had happened to Jesus. John writes, "...she stooped down, and looked into the sepulchre...." The word "stooped down" is *parakupto,* the same word used in John 20:5 to portray John taking a *peek into* the tomb. Now it was Mary's turn to bend low and peer into the empty sepulcher — but when she looked inside, she saw something she didn't expect!

John tells us, "...She stooped down, and looked into the sepulchre, and seeth two angels in white sitting, the one at the head, and the other at the feet, where the body of Jesus had lain" (John 20:11,12). The word "seeth" is the Greek word *theaomai,* which tells us assuredly that Mary *fixed her eyes* on the angels and *determined to look them over and to take in the whole experience.* First, she saw that the two angels were "in white." This agrees with all the other experiences of angels that eventful day. All of them had been dressed in shining white with a lightning-bright appearance. All the angels seen that day also wore the same type of robe — like the long, flowing regal robes worn by warriors, kings, priests, or any other person of great power and authority. The usage of the word *theaomai* ("seeth") tells us that this time Mary *visibly studied* every single detail of the angels she saw in the tomb.

John goes on to inform us that Mary saw these angels "...sitting, the one at the head, and the other at the feet, where the body of Jesus had lain." This statement is in perfect agreement with the interior of a rock-hewn tomb during biblical times. Past the entrance of such a tomb, a smaller separate room with a table-shaped pedestal, also carved from stone, was usually located to one side. On this rock slab the body was laid to rest after being dressed in burial clothes and perfumed by loved ones. The head would be slightly elevated, causing the trunk of the corpse to lie in a sloping downward position with the feet resting against a small ledge or in a groove, either of which were designed to keep the body from slipping from the slab.

When Mary saw the angels, she noted that one was seated at the top of the burial slab and the other was seated at the foot. In between these angels, she could see the empty place where she had personally viewed Jesus several days earlier. Luke 23:55 tells us that after Jesus' body was placed in the tomb, Mary Magdalene and other women who came from Galilee "...beheld the sepulchre, and how his body was laid." The word "beheld" (*theaomai*) means *to gaze upon, to fully see, to look at intently.* These women *inspected* the tomb, *gazing upon* the dead body of Jesus *to see* that it had been honorably laid in place. Because Mark 15:47 uses the imperfect tense to tell us how the women looked upon Jesus' dead body, it means these women took plenty of time to make certain He was properly laid there. Now Mary saw the same spot where she had so carefully labored days before, but the dead body she cherished was no longer there.

As Mary looked and wept, the angels asked her, "...Woman, why weepest thou? She saith unto them, Because they have taken away my Lord, and I know not where they have laid him. And when she had thus said, she turned herself back, and saw Jesus standing, and knew not that it was Jesus" (John 20:13,14).

Stricken with sorrow, Mary withdrew from the tomb just in time to see a man standing nearby. Due to Jesus' changed appearance, she was unable to recognize Him. Verse 15 tells us what happened next: "Jesus saith unto her, Woman, why weepest thou? whom seekest thou? She, supposing him to be the gardener, saith unto him, Sir, if thou have borne him hence, tell me where thou hast laid him, and I will take him away."

At that very moment, Jesus tenderly said, "Mary." Upon hearing that voice and recognizing the old familiar way in which He called her name, "...she turned herself, and saith unto him, Rabboni; which is to say, Master" (v. 16). Although Jesus' appearance was different now, Mary knew Him by His voice. This reminds me of John 10:27, when Jesus told His disciples, "My sheep hear my voice...." Mary knew His voice and recognized that it was her Shepherd who stood before her.

In Revelation 1, John tells us about his vision on the island of Patmos. In the midst of this phenomenal divine visitation, he says, "I was in the Spirit on the Lord's day, and heard behind me a great voice, as of a trumpet.... and I turned to see the voice that spake with me..." (Revelation 1:10,12). Like Mary, when John heard that voice, he recognized it as the voice of Jesus. This is why John writes, "...I turned to see the voice that spake with me."

Of course, it is impossible to "see" a voice, but John recognized the sound of that voice and turned to match the face with the voice he heard. He knew it was Jesus. But as Mary had also discovered, Jesus' physical appearance looked radically different from the Jesus whom John had known in His earthly form. But the voice of Jesus never changed, and John immediately recognized it.

It appears that Mary reached out to cling to Jesus with her hands, but Jesus forbade her, saying, "...Touch me not; for I am not yet ascended to my Father: but go to my brethren, and say unto them, I ascend unto my Father, and your Father; and to my God, and your God" (John 20:17). With this one statement, Jesus let it be known that everything had changed because of the Cross. *Now a new relationship with God was available to the apostles and to all who would call upon the name of Jesus Christ!* John 20:18 goes on to say, "Mary Magdalene came and told the disciples that she had seen the Lord, and that he had spoken these things unto her."

Today we rejoice that Jesus is alive! Because of what He did for us at the Cross, now we have access to God the Father. This was the purpose of the Cross: To redeem mankind and to put man back in right relationship and fellowship with his Heavenly Father. Jesus paid it all! He finished the work of redemption so that today we can be in right relationship with God by accepting the work of Christ on Calvary by faith.

I encourage you to be bold in recognizing the voice of Jesus. If you belong to Him, then you do know His voice. Mary knew His voice; John knew His voice; and your born-again spirit knows His voice. *If you'll take the time to listen, you will hear the voice of Jesus calling out to you just as He tenderly called out to Mary that day in the garden. He knows you by name, and He wants to enjoy close fellowship with you. So take the time to listen!*

MY PRAYER FOR TODAY

Lord, thank You for being my Good Shepherd! I am so thankful You speak to me and lead me through life. I'm sorry I haven't listened to You so many times when You have tried to warn me, help me, and guide me. I have lost so much because I didn't listen when You spoke. But rather than focus on my past losses, I determine to do everything within my ability to hear You now and to obediently follow what You tell me to do!

I pray this in Jesus' name!

MY CONFESSION FOR TODAY

I boldly confess that I know the voice of Jesus! He is my Shepherd, and I am His sheep. He promises that I will know His voice and that the voice of a stranger I will not follow. Therefore, I declare by faith that I recognize the voice of Jesus when He speaks to me. I am not hesitant to follow, but I am bold and quick to obey what He speaks to my heart.

I declare this by faith in Jesus' name!

QUESTIONS FOR YOU TO CONSIDER

1. How long has it been since you heard the voice of Jesus tenderly speak to your heart?
2. It takes time to develop any relationship, so are you giving time to your relationship with Jesus so you can get to know Him better and allow Him the opportunity to speak to you about your life?
3. Are there certain times or places in your daily routine when you are able to hear Jesus speak more clearly to you than at other times? For instance, do you hear Him best when you're alone at home, driving your car, worshiping at church, or having a private time of prayer?

This was the purpose of the Cross: To redeem mankind and to put man back in right relationship and fellowship with his Heavenly Father. Jesus finished the work of redemption so that today we can be in right relationship with God by accepting His work on Calvary by faith. *Jesus paid it all!*

MAY 1

⋙ ❧ ⋘

The Post-Resurrection Appearances of Jesus Christ

And when he had said this, he breathed on them,
And saith unto them, Receive ye the Holy Ghost.
— John 20:22

*O*n Resurrection Day itself, Jesus appeared to the disciples at various times and places. It was simply a physical impossibility for Him to be at so many different places in one day. These appearances therefore revealed that Jesus' glorified body didn't have the same limitations His earthly body possessed before His resurrection and glorification. The Bible makes it plain that in His glorified condition, He was able to appear, to disappear, to travel great distances, and to even supernaturally pass through a wall or the locked door of a house (John 20:26).

On the same day Jesus was raised from the dead, He not only appeared to Mary Magdalene outside the garden tomb (John 20:14-17), but to two disciples as they walked from Jerusalem to the city of Emmaus (Luke 24:13-31). When the three men sat down to eat together, Jesus blessed the food. After hearing the way He blessed the food, the two disciples instantly recognized it was the Lord — just as He suddenly "…vanished out of their sight" (v. 31).

That same evening, Jesus supernaturally traveled through the walls of a house where the eleven disciples were gathered, miraculously appearing right in front of them. John 20:19 tells us about this amazing event: "Then the same day at evening, being the first day of the week, when the doors were shut where the disciples were assembled for fear of the Jews…."

This verse says that when the disciples gathered for dinner, they made certain "…the doors were shut…." The word "door" is *thura*, which lets us know this was a door that was *large* and *solid*. But as if this were not enough, the verse tells us that these doors "were shut."

The word "shut" is the Greek word *kleio*, meaning *locked*. Doors of this kind were usually locked with a heavy bolt that slid through rings attached to the door and the frame — like the dead-bolts we use in doors today, only heavier. This door would be difficult, if not impossible, to break down. The fact that it was locked "for fear of the Jews" tells us that the disciples had moved into a mode of self-preservation and protection.

With rumors of Jesus' resurrection already filling the city of Jerusalem, there was no certainty that the leaders who crucified Jesus wouldn't try to arrest the rest of the apostles and do the same to them as they had to Jesus. We know that the Roman guards who fled the resurrection site "…shewed unto the chief priests all the things that were done" (Matthew 28:11). To prevent the people of Israel from knowing the truth of Jesus' resurrection, the chief priests and elders bribed the soldiers to keep their mouths shut about what they had seen. Verse 12 tells us, "And when they were assembled with the elders, and had taken counsel, they gave large money unto the soldiers."

The chief priests and elders fabricated a story and told the soldiers what they were to say when people asked them what happened: "…Say ye, His disciples came by night, and stole him away while we slept" (v. 13).

The soldiers' admission that they had slept on the job would deem them worthy of punishment in Pilate's sight, so the religious leaders further assured them, "And if this come to the governor's ears, we will persuade him, and secure you" (v. 14). The soldiers listened to the religious leaders' plan and were satisfied with the amount of money being offered to them to keep silent. Verse 15 then says, "So they took the money, and did as they were taught...."

Once the chief priests and elders had bought the testimony of the Roman guards, they were positioned to make some serious arrests. First, we know that they were already asserting that the disciples had stolen the body of Jesus. But to steal the body, they had to either overpower the Roman guards or creep past them as they slept. Either way, this would be deemed a terrible dishonor to the guards' reputation. And if the disciples were caught, they'd potentially be put to death for this action.

To open the tomb, the governor's seal had to be broken. Breaking that seal was an offense that required the death sentence, for this was a breach of the empire's power. No doubt the same angry mobs who cheered while Jesus carried His crossbeam to Golgotha were still in the city. The city was already in turmoil due to such strange happenings — the sky turning dark in the middle of the day with no natural explanation; the veil of the temple rent in half; the various earthquakes shaking the entire surrounding territory. It wouldn't take too much to put the whole city on edge and turn them against the disciples. *This is why the disciples were locked behind closed doors that evening.*

But although the doors were sealed tightly shut, Jesus supernaturally passed right through solid matter and appeared in the midst of the disciples. John 20:19 says Jesus came "...and stood in the midst, and saith unto them, Peace be unto you."

No doubt this sudden appearance must have *terrified* the disciples. Luke 24:37 tells us that "...they were terrified and affrighted, and supposed that they had seen a spirit." This is why Jesus told them, "...Why are ye troubled? and why do thoughts arise in your hearts? Behold my hands and my feet, that it is I myself: handle me, and see; for a spirit hath not flesh and bones, as ye see me have" (vv. 38,39).

Notice Jesus said, "...Handle me...." This is the Greek word *psilaphao*, and it literally means *to touch, to squeeze,* or *to feel.* He gave the disciples permission to examine His resurrected body to see that it was a real body and not a spirit.

All of a sudden Jesus asked them, "...Have ye here any meat?" The following verses say, "And they gave him a piece of a broiled fish, and of an honeycomb. And he took it, and did eat before them" (Luke 24:42,43). After eating the fish and honeycomb, Jesus began to speak to them from the Scriptures, pointing out key Old Testament prophecies having to do with Himself. Luke 24:45 says, "Then opened he their understanding, that they might understand the scriptures." Jesus explained to the disciples that repentance would have to be preached in His name among all the nations, but that it was to begin in Jerusalem. This is when He told them, "...As my Father hath sent me, even so send I you" (John 20:21).

The disciple Thomas had not been present in the room that night when Jesus passed through solid matter and entered into the room. Later that evening Thomas joined them and heard the news, but by that time Jesus was already gone. He scoffed at the other disciples and said, "...Except I shall see in his hands the print of the nails, and put my finger into the print of the nails, and thrust my hand into his side, I will not believe" (John 20:25).

Eight days later, the disciples were behind locked doors again, but this time Thomas was with them. John 20:26,27 says, "...Then came Jesus, the doors being shut, and stood in the midst, and said, Peace be unto you. Then saith he to Thomas, Reach hither thy finger, and behold my hands; and reach hither thy hand, and thrust it into my side: and be not faithless, but believing." Of course, after this event, Thomas believed!

Jesus appeared to His disciples again, this time at the Sea of Tiberias. Peter, Thomas Didymus, Nathanael, the sons of Zebedee, and two other disciples followed Peter to the seacoast to go fishing. But after fishing all night, the disciples had caught nothing.

Then in the morning, Jesus stood on the shore and called to them to cast their nets on the other side of the boat. Although they weren't sure who was instructing them, the disciples obeyed anyway — and caught so many fish that they weren't even able to pull their nets into the boat! That's when they recognized that the Man who had instructed them was the Lord (John 21:2-7).

Before the evening was finished, Jesus had sat around a campfire with them, eaten fish with them, and spent time fellowshipping with them. John 21:14 says, "This is now the third time that Jesus shewed himself to his disciples, after that he was risen from the dead."

Then finally, the disciples gathered together on the same mountain in Galilee where Jesus had first ordained them. He appeared to them there, and gave them the Great Commission. He told them, "…All power is given unto me in heaven and in earth. Go ye therefore, and teach all nations, baptizing them in the name of the Father, and of the Son, and of the Holy Ghost: teaching them to observe all things whatsoever I have commanded you: and, lo, I am with you alway, even unto the end of the world. Amen" (Matthew 28:18-20).

In addition to these appearances recorded in the Gospels, First Corinthians 15:5-7 says, "And that he was seen of Cephas, then of the twelve: after that, he was seen of above five hundred brethren at once; of whom the greater part remain unto this present, but some are fallen asleep. After that, he was seen of James; then of all the apostles." Acts 1:3 says "…He shewed himself alive after his passion by many infallible proofs, being seen of them forty days, and speaking of the things pertaining to the kingdom of God."

How about you? Do you experience Jesus Christ in the daily activities of your life, or is Jesus just relegated to church services and Sunday school? From what you just read today, you now know that Jesus was "in the midst" of His disciples after His resurrection. They ate with Him, talked to Him, and fellowshipped with Him. Jesus even helped them catch fish! The resurrected Jesus drew near to His disciples — but is He near to you as you go about the activities of your daily life?

Even though Jesus is seated right now at the right hand of the Father on High, you can know Him intimately through the ministry of the Holy Spirit. The Holy Spirit is the Great Revealer of Jesus Christ. *Just ask the Holy Spirit to show you Jesus, and He will be faithful to make Jesus real to you!*

MY PRAYER FOR TODAY

Lord, I want You to be so real in my life. I know that You are willing to make Yourself known and felt in any part of my life that I will surrender to You. So I choose right now to surrender more of me so I can experience more of You in every sphere of my existence. Jesus, please have Your way in my life. Do whatever You deem necessary to make me the kind of person I need to be to know and experience You better.

I pray this in Jesus' name!

MY CONFESSION FOR TODAY

I confess that the Presence of Jesus Christ is felt in almost every area of my life. I am surrendering more and more of me to Him every day, and as a result, I am expecting a stronger Presence of God in my life. As I give more of me to Him, He gives more of Himself to me!

I declare this by faith in Jesus' name!

QUESTIONS FOR YOU TO CONSIDER

1. Do you experience the reality of Jesus in the everyday activities of your life?
2. Can you think of a particular instance when you sensed the Presence of God in your life much more strongly than usual?
3. Do you recall what that experience did for you? Did it help you draw closer to the Lord or produce permanent changes in your life? If so, what were those changes?

MAY 2

Let God Breathe Into Your Life!

All scripture is given by inspiration of God,
and is profitable for doctrine,
for reproof, for correction, for instruction in righteousness.
— 2 Timothy 3:16

Would you be interested in getting plugged into a power source that will permeate you with extraordinary energy, vitality, strength, and wisdom to assist you in overcoming any challenge that comes against you? Of course you would like to have that kind of help! The amazing thing is that you already have it at your disposal! However, you may not have learned yet how to tap into this power source to receive its full benefits.

Right there in your home or apartment is a source of power beyond your wildest imagination. It's probably sitting on a shelf, situated nicely on a table, or perhaps even kept in the magazine rack in the bathroom. Or maybe you keep this source of power in the drawer of your desk at work or on the back seat of your car.

You may have guessed by now that I'm talking about your Bible, which is one of the greatest sources of power on earth! If you learn how to tap into God's Word and let its power flow into you, it will equip you with wisdom, answers, and the power to overcome in every single situation in life.

When Timothy felt attacked on every side by difficult situations he was facing in the city of Ephesus, he wrote to Paul, seeking answers and help to his various dilemmas. Expecting counsel and advice from Paul, he received a letter from Paul that contained these precious words: "All scripture is given by inspiration of God..." (2 Timothy 3:16).

Especially notice the word "inspiration" in this verse, for this word is a powerhouse when you really understand what it means! It comes from the Greek word *theopneustos*, a compound of the words *theos* and *pneuma*. The Greek word *theos* is the word for *God*; however, the real secret to this powerhouse is the second half of the word, *pneuma*, which comes from the Greek root *pneu*.

The root *pneu* communicates the idea of *the dynamic movement of air*. For instance, it can mean *to blow*, as *to blow air* or *to blow air through an instrument to produce a distinct musical sound*. There are also places where it is translated *to breathe* or *to emit a fragrance*. Finally, this root word can be used to denote *the projection of emotions*, such as *anger, courage,* or *goodwill*.

But when the root *pneu* becomes *pneuma*, as in this verse, it carries a more profound range of meanings, including *life, force, life-force, energy, dynamism, and power*. The Jews considered the *pneuma* to be the *powerful force* of God that created the universe and all living things, and the *force that continues to sustain creation*. In the Old Testament, the *pneuma* of God would sometimes move mightily upon a person, *enabling* him to do supernatural feats.

When this word *pneuma* is compounded together with the word *theos*, it forms the word *theopneustos*, which is where we get the word *inspiration*. Together, these words literally mean *God-breathed*. The word *theopneustos* — or "inspiration" — is the picture of *God breathing or emitting His own substance into something*. Just as a musician would blow on an instrument to produce a distinct sound, God mightily moved on those who wrote the Scriptures, and they temporarily became the instrument through whom God expressed His heart and will. They were the writers, but God was the Great Musician who breathed upon them, His instruments. Thus, the Bible is God's message delivered through human writers to you and me.

Just as the word *pneuma* can carry the idea of *a fragrance*, the Word was breathed out from God and thus carries *His very essence and fragrance* within it. Since the word *pneuma* can also portray *the projection of emotions*, this tells us that God projected the totality of His emotion into the written Word when He inspired its writing. Therefore, the Word not only conveys an intellectual message, but it has *God's heart* in it as well.

It's important to understand that the *pneuma* of God didn't create the Scripture and then depart from it. This power — the same *pneuma* power that originally created and continues to sustain the universe — is still working inside the Word, upholding and empowering it to be just as strong as it was the day it was penned by "God-breathed" writers.

Let me give you this very simple example of the word *theopneustos*. If I hold a deflated balloon that is without form to my lips and breathe into it, the balloon will inflate. The blowing of *my breath* into that deflated little piece of rubber causes it to fill up so that its true form becomes visible. When the balloon is fully inflated, I tie a knot at the base to trap the air within. Now the air that filled up the balloon and caused it to take form is the same substance that empowers it to *sustain* its form. It was my breath that created its form, and it is my breath that now sustains it. And if the molecules inside the balloon were analyzed, it would be found that a part of me is held inside in the form of the air I breathed into it.

Now let's apply this to the Bible. When God was ready to speak to mankind, He held up human language to His mouth and breathed into it. After breathing His *pneuma* power into the language to produce life-giving words, God moved upon the hearts of those He had called to write His Book, and men began to write under divine inspiration. As God continued to breathe on words and phrases and sentences, His Word began to form and take shape until finally it had become the Bible as we know it today.

Today the same breath of God that caused the Word to materialize in written form is now held inside the Bible. It was God's own breath that caused this Word to manifest in the first place, and now His own Presence, His breath — His "molecules," if you will — are permanently held inside the Word of God itself. In other words, God didn't just inspire the writing of the Bible. God Himself — *His life, His life-force, His essence, power, energy, dynamism, and power* — is contained inside the Word.

Think about it — the Bible you own that is sitting on a shelf, stored away in your desk drawer, sitting on the back seat of your automobile, situated nicely on your coffee table, or placed on the nightstand next to your bed contains the very *life, essence, energy,* and *dynamism* of God Himself! If you'll get hungry for more of God and determine to meditate on this truth long enough to tap into it, God Himself will come pouring out of the Bible into your life and situation. The *pneuma* held inside the Word will blow mightily upon you and upon the situations that surround you — and when that happens, *everything* will change!

Because of the word *theopneustos*,
Second Timothy 3:16 carries this idea:

"All scripture came into existence because God Himself breathed upon men, who then wrote as this divine breath moved upon them — and thus, the Word took shape and came into existence...."

The supernatural breath and life of God that is held within His written Word is the reason Paul went on to say that the Word is "profitable." The word "profitable" is the Greek word *ophelimos*, and it means *helpful, profitable, useful, beneficial,* or *something that is to one's advantage.* Paul goes on to list all the ways that God's Word brings benefit to the one who reads it, meditates on it, and taps into its *pneuma*.

So when Paul wrote to Timothy, "All scripture is given by inspiration of God...," he was reminding the younger man that because Timothy had the Word, he possessed the greatest source of power and energy that exists! If he would get into the Word — tapping deeply into its internal resource and allowing the life of God in that Word to flow up, out, and into his life — enough power would be released to change every difficult situation he was facing.

That is why Paul said the Word is "profitable." Wouldn't you agree that this kind of power operating in your life would be to *your* advantage as well?

Once you understand the meaning of this word "inspiration," you realize that the Bible is not just a Book *about* God; it is a Book that actually *contains* God. His own breath and Spirit are contained *within* it. That's a very good reason why you should spend time studying and meditating on God's Word. By studying and meditating *on* the Word, you will learn to unlock the power contained *within* it. And when you have unlocked that door, the power of God will come pouring into your life and into the situations you are facing. *Believe me when I tell you that when this power begins to operate, it will definitely be to your advantage!*

MY PRAYER FOR TODAY

Lord, I've been asking You for power and strength, not realizing that I have the source of Your power and strength sitting right in my house. Forgive me for not spending enough time in my Bible to tap into the power that is held within it. Starting today, I want to make Your Word a priority in my life. When I am tempted to be lazy and to put off reading my Bible, please help me say no to my flesh. Help me choose to pick up my Bible and read it whether I feel like it or not, taking it deep into my heart and letting the power inside the Word begin to work in me and in my situation.

I pray this in Jesus' name!

MY CONFESSION FOR TODAY

I confess that I have determined to read and meditate on the Word of God on a regular basis. The power of the Word works mightily inside me because I take it deeply into my heart. It transforms my thinking, renews my vision, forces darkness out of my mind, and blows like a mighty force into every part of my life. There is nothing stronger at my disposal than God's Word, so I make it a priority in my life!

I declare this by faith in Jesus' name!

QUESTIONS FOR YOU TO CONSIDER

1. Can you think of an instance in your life when you literally felt the power of God's Word flow into you and energize you to deal with a situation you were facing? If so, when was that and what was the end result of the power you felt so strongly that day?

2. Does God's Word have a say-so in your life, or is the Bible just a book you carry to church and read only when you hear a sermon being preached?

3. How much time do you spend reading your Bible in a given week? Do your Bible-reading habits reveal that you are digging deep to get everything out of the Word you possibly can? Or are you reading just enough to barely get by — certainly not enough for its power to be released inside you?

MAY 3

The Right Way To Die!

I have fought a good fight, I have finished my course,
I have kept the faith.
— 2 Timothy 4:7

When I was just old enough to get a job, I heard about a job opening at the huge cemetery just down the street from where my family lived. The old caretaker needed someone to mow the cemetery lawn. So one day I walked down to the cemetery and knocked on the door at the caretaker's residence. When he came to the door, I said, "Sir, I understand there's a job opening here. I've come to apply for that position."

The old man, who had been the caretaker for more than forty years, looked me over and asked me a few questions. Then he told me to report to work on the following Monday.

That following Monday I started my short career at the local graveyard — *my first real job*! Every day after school, I quickly dashed down the hallway to put my books in my locker, and then rushed across town to the cemetery, pulled out my lawnmower, and went to the next section of the cemetery that needed to be mowed. *Five days a week, I lived and worked among the dead!*

Each day, I mowed and edged the weeds around new graves, old graves, mausoleums, and one section of the cemetery that was so old, no one could decipher the inscriptions on the limestone markers any longer. When it was time to bury someone, I helped dig the grave, lower the casket, and fill the grave with dirt. When the flowers wilted that loved ones had placed on the graves, I was the one who gathered up the dead flowers and took them to the garbage. I helped put up the tent that loved ones stood under during gravesite rites, and then I helped take it down.

Working in a graveyard had a very strong effect on my life in those formative years. God used that time in the graveyard to make me think about the seriousness and temporal nature of life in general, as well as what I was going to do with my own life.

As I walked between the tombstones, I'd look at them and ask myself, *Who were these people? What did they do with their lives? Did they contribute anything to the world, or did they just live, die, and then disappear into these graves?* Every day I thought about these questions. It made me determine that I would not pass from this earth without doing something significant for God with my life. I resolved that when I died, no one would have to ask, "Gee, I wonder who he was and what he did with his life?" To me, it was totally unacceptable that I would end up like so many others had — as just another name on another tombstone.

People don't like to think about dying, yet death is a reality each of us ultimately has to face. We may hope and wait for Jesus' return in our lifetime. But if He doesn't come before we die, then a day will come in all our futures when we will be laid in a coffin. Family and friends will come to our funeral services; the casket lid will be closed for the last time; and we will be lowered into a grave that will then get packed with dirt. Later our graves will have grass growing on top of them — and a young boy will push the lawnmower over them as a part of his job, just as I did years ago.

Like it or not, there is a funeral in all our futures unless Jesus comes while we are still alive. This thought may sound morbid, but if you live with this unavoidable fact before you at all times, it will help you to live a more balanced and committed life. Why is that? Because when you live thinking only of today, everything seems monumental. Yet the truth is, most of the things that steal our peace, hinder us from doing what God wants us to do, disrupt our joy, and hurt our relationships won't matter anymore when we die and stand before Jesus. *The only thing that will matter then is what Jesus will say to us when we stand before Him and look into His eyes.*

The apostle Paul told us, "For we must all appear before the judgment seat of Christ; that every one may receive the things done in his body, according to that he hath done, whether it be good or bad" (2 Corinthians 5:10). Because Paul lived with the awareness of that moment when he would stand before Jesus, he was able to keep pushing ahead even when times became exceedingly difficult. He knew that eventually life would pass and the difficult trials would end, and he would stand before Jesus to give account for his life.

This is why Paul wrote, "For our light affliction, which is but for a moment, worketh for us a far more exceeding and eternal weight of glory" (2 Corinthians 4:17).

I love this verse, because it sheds light on Paul's attitude toward life and afflictions. He didn't like afflictions and he stood against them, but he refused to over-magnify them, choosing instead to view them as "light afflictions."

Would *you* call Paul's problems "light afflictions"? He faced rejection from some of his closest friends and, even worse, by many of the churches in Asia (2 Timothy 1:15). He had been severely beaten several times (2 Corinthians 11:24,25). He had been shipwrecked three times (2 Corinthians 11:25). He had lived through perils in the city, in the wilderness, and at sea. He had been in peril of robbers, of heathens, and of false brethren and had endured periods of hunger, thirst, and sleeplessness (2 Corinthians 11:26,27).

These were monumental problems, yet Paul refused to let them be monumental in his life. Instead, he deemed them "small stuff" — mere distractions compared to the eternal glory that awaited him.

What enabled Paul to press ahead when he was being assaulted so viciously? How could he maintain such a victorious attitude? How is it that he never surrendered to weariness, exhaustion, or to the devil's attacks?

These questions can all be answered by the foremost desire of Paul's heart: That he would one day hear Jesus say to him, "Well done, thou good and faithful servant." Paul's driving motivation was his anticipation to hear Jesus say those words and to know that he had finished his race well. This is why Paul said, "But none of these things move me, neither count I my life dear unto myself, so that I might finish my course with joy…" (Acts 20:24).

At the end of his life, he wrote to Timothy and triumphantly declared, "I have fought a good fight…" (2 Timothy 4:7). The words "fought" and "fight" are from the Greek word *agonidzo*. This word means *a struggle, a fight, a combat,* or *a fierce competition,* and it is where we get the word *agony.* By using this word, Paul tells us that some of his ministry has been *a real struggle — difficult, fierce, and agonizing.* Yet Paul never budged an inch! He stayed in the fight and was faithful to his call!

This verse could literally be translated, "A good fight — that's what I fought!" That proclamation has the sense of victory and exhilaration. These are the sentiments of a man who has no regrets. He is proud of the contest in which he has been engaged. Regardless of all the others who have dropped out of the fight, Paul can say, "I stayed in there. *A good fight* — that's what I fought!"

Then Paul goes on to tell us, "…I have finished my course…." This word "course" is the Greek word *dromos,* which always describes *a foot race* or *a running track.* Also, notice that he referred to his life assignment as "*my* course." Paul knew precisely what race he was called to run, and he didn't attempt to run anyone else's course. In spite of all the things that tried to slow him down, knock him out of the race, and defeat him, he refused to quit running! No matter what happened, Paul just stayed right on track — true to the course God had given him. Thus, this part of the verse could be translated, "*My race — I ran it with all my might, never stopping until I knew I had reached the goal and finished it!*"

Lastly, Paul writes, "…I have kept the faith." The Greek word for "kept" is the word *tereo.* It is the same Greek word used to depict *a watch of soldiers who were positioned to protect something important.* The job of these soldiers was *to stand guard* and *to keep watch.* They were to be faithful and remain committed to their charge of keeping watch regardless of the kind of assault or the number of attackers they might encounter.

This is the word Paul uses when he says, "I have kept the faith." Even though he encountered difficulties and challenges, he never left his post or surrendered to the assaults and attacks that came against him. Through it all, Paul kept watch over the mission and the message God gave him!

When you put all of this together, Second Timothy 4:7 could be understood to say this:

"A good fight — that's what I fought! My race — I ran it with all my might, never stopping until I knew I had reached the goal and finished it! The faith — I protected it, guarded it, and watched over it with all my heart and strength. In spite of the assaults and attacks, I stayed true to my assignment!"

This soldier of the Lord has everything to shout about! His ministry may have been difficult, but *he made it!* Paul never gave an inch to the enemy. Now as he faces his own death, he isn't fearful; rather, he rejoices because *he knows he has done well.* He's ready to depart this earth and to be forever with his Lord! Looking toward that moment when he will finally stand before Jesus, Paul confidently writes, "Henceforth there is laid up for me a crown of righteousness, which the Lord, the righteous judge, shall give me at that day: and not to me only, but unto all them also that love his appearing" (2 Timothy 4:8).

When you are tempted to be sidetracked and distracted by the problems of life, try to find a few minutes to be alone with the Lord. Remind yourself that all your problems are fleeting and that they will soon pass. But your obedience to God is eternal, so there is nothing more important than doing what God has told you to do.

When you stand before Jesus, all the challenges you faced will be forgotten, and just one question will remain. Jesus will want to know, "Did you do what I asked you to do, or did you get distracted and let the cares of life stop you from fulfilling your assignment?"

It will help you live a more balanced and committed life if you will keep everything that happens to you in perspective of that day when you stand before Jesus. Don't you want to look into His face with confidence? Of course you do. So take the attitude of the apostle Paul. Decide to deliberately view your problems as nothing but "light affliction" that won't last too long. On the other hand, what you do with God's call on your life *will* last forever, so don't let those measly little problems prevent you from pushing onward toward the high calling of God!

Just as the apostle Paul finished his race with joy, you can finish *your* course with joy and victory as well. *Determine today that you will be a soldier of the Lord who can look back one day and be proud of the fight you fought, the race you ran, and the faith you kept — a soldier with no regrets!*

MY PRAYER FOR TODAY

Lord, help me to keep my focus and to not allow the challenges I face to distract me from fulfilling Your will for my life. I know that the enemy keeps surrounding me with distractions because You have called me to do something important. Rather than let these nuisances break me and steal my joy, help me keep my eyes focused on that day when I will stand before You. I ask that Your Spirit will supernaturally energize me to push beyond the obstacles and keep pressing forward to the high calling You have designed for my life!

I pray this in Jesus' name!

MY CONFESSION FOR TODAY

I boldly declare that I am a winner and not a loser. I don't throw in the towel and quit when it gets hard; instead, I dig in my heels and refuse to surrender the territory that God has called me to conquer and possess. I live my life seriously and with balance and commitment. Because of God's Spirit inside me, I am tougher than any challenge and stronger than any foe. I fight a good fight and run a good race — and I successfully guard over and hold tight to the assignment God has given to my life!

I declare this by faith in Jesus' name!

QUESTIONS FOR YOU TO CONSIDER

1. Have you ever thought about what people will say about you after you have died? Will they know of the contribution you made in life, or will they ask, "Gee, I wonder who that person was and what he (or she) did?"

2. Can you verbalize what God has called you to do with your life? If someone asked you to describe your life assignment, would you be able to intelligently answer his question?

3. If you have allowed the challenges of life to distract you and throw you off schedule in doing God's will, don't you agree that it's time for you to get back on track again?

MAY 4

Is Jesus Christ a Fairy Tale to You, Or Do You Really Know Him?

...In every thing ye are enriched by him, in all utterance, and in all knowledge;
Even as the testimony of Christ was confirmed in you.
— 1 Corinthians 1:5,6

*T*he State Hermitage, which is the most famous of all Russian museums, is located on the banks of the Neva River in St. Petersburg, Russia. Within its walls is a huge collection of religious paintings that were collected from the time of Catherine the Great. This museum, the former Winter Palace of the Russian czars, is fabulous beyond description and attracts millions of visitors who come to view this world-renowned art collection and to see the opulence in which the czars lived.

The first time I visited the Hermitage was near the end of the Soviet Union; thus, communism and atheism were still dominant in the nations that comprised the former USSR. As I walked past the section of paintings by Rembrandt, I saw the painting of Lazarus being raised from the dead by Jesus. The painting was so moving that it drew me nearer to observe the painting from up close. Then I read the plaque on the base of the frame, which said, "The Fairy Tale of Jesus Christ Raising Lazarus From the Dead." I was stunned that Lazarus' resurrection was referred to as a fairy tale.

But as I moved from that painting of Jesus to others that depicted scenes from Jesus' life, I realized that they were all officially identified by State authorities as various "fairy tales of Jesus Christ." Communists wanted to discredit the Gospel. By calling the works of Jesus "fairy tales," they were attempting to put the Gospel on the same level as Peter Pan or as Little Red Riding Hood.

However, my experience in the museum that day caused my mind to start thinking in another direction. I began to consider how so much about Jesus Christ really is a fairy tale to many people, including Christians who read their Bible and love the Lord. When they read about the miracles He performed, they relegate His miracle-working power to a limited historical time frame that is long past and to a people who are no longer alive. They then conclude that they cannot expect such miracles today. Thus, the only thing they really know regarding Jesus' power is what they have read in the Bible. Never having personally witnessed His miracle-working power, they can only fantasize and try to imagine what His miracles must have been like. As a result, much of what they know about Jesus is purely mental, imaginary, or speculative — similar to the way they might view the hero in a fairy tale or legend.

But God never intended for Jesus to be only a historical figure who did something in the past. Jesus is alive *today*, and through the ministry of the Holy Spirit and His gifts, Jesus brings His supernatural reality right into the midst of the local church! This is why Paul told the Corinthians, "...In everything you are enriched by him, in all utterance, and in all knowledge; even as the testimony of Christ was confirmed in you" (1 Corinthians 1:5,6).

The Corinthian church was so abundantly endowed with spiritual gifts that Paul says they were "enriched" by Jesus with gifts of utterance and knowledge. "Utterance gifts" would include the vocal gifts, such as tongues, interpretation, and prophecy. Knowledge gifts would include the revelation gifts, such as the word of wisdom, the word of knowledge, and discerning of spirits. Prophecy could also fall into this category.

According to Paul, the Corinthian believers were loaded with these types of gifts. In fact, they had so many of these gifts in operation that Paul used the word "enriched" to express the extent to which these gifts were operating in that particular local church. The word "enriched" is from the Greek word *plousios*, and it means *to make extremely rich* (*see* January 23). It describes *incredible abundance, extreme wealth, immense riches, magnificent opulence, and extravagant lavishness.*

This Greek word denoted people whose wealth was growing so fast that they were never able to quite figure out how much fortune they possessed. With their wealth, they ruled and controlled society. Hence came the word "plutocrat," which is used in today's world to portray a person who is endowed with great wealth, opulence, fortune, and power.

When Paul uses the word *plousios* to express how many gifts of the Spirit were in operation in Corinth, he is telling us that this church was *filthy rich* with spiritual gifts and manifestations. In fact, Paul went on to say, "So that ye come behind in no gift; waiting for the coming of our Lord Jesus Christ" (1 Corinthians 1:7). The words "come behind" are taken from the Greek word *hustereo*, meaning *to fall short, to be inferior, to be left behind, to lack,* or *to come in second place.* Paul uses this word to say, *"In regard to spiritual gifts, you are second to none when it comes to the manifestations of the gifts of the Spirit. No one has more gifts of the Spirit in operation than you do."*

Paul told them that these gifts were vital, for they "confirmed" the "testimony" of Christ among them (1 Corinthians 1:6). The word "confirmed" is the Greek word *bebaioo*, which means *to make firm, concrete, or stable; to authenticate; to verify; to guarantee;* or *to prove to be true.* The word "testimony," from the Greek word *maturios*, describes *a personal testimony that is so strong, it could stand up to scrutiny in a court of law.* But when a "testimony" (*maturios*) is "confirmed" (*bebaioo*), it is extra powerful! Now we not only have a witness — that is, a person or a group of people who possess concrete knowledge and facts — but we also have confirming evidence brought forth to validate their knowledge and verify that their report is bona fide truth.

Now let's connect this concept to the gifts of the Spirit in the Corinthian church. According to Paul's account, the believers in that church were *enriched, loaded, and mightily endowed* with the gifts of the Spirit. These gifts, he said, *confirmed the testimony* of Jesus Christ in their midst. What did they know of Jesus Christ? What was the testimony they possessed and proclaimed about Jesus Christ? From a historical perspective, they had been taught and therefore knew that:

✦ Jesus was a Prophet.
✦ Jesus was a Healer.
✦ Jesus was a Miracle-Worker.

However, the Corinthian church didn't just intellectually know these things about Jesus because of books they had read. They *experientially knew Him* in this way because the gifts of the Spirit literally *energized* and *authenticated* what they intellectually knew of Jesus.

By means of the Spirit's manifestations, Jesus the Prophet operated before them all in their church services. They didn't need to fantasize about what Jesus the Prophet was like, because Jesus the Prophet regularly operated in their midst through the gift of prophecy. They didn't have to try to imagine what it had been like when Jesus healed the sick, because the gifts of healing mightily functioned among them, causing them to experientially *know* Jesus the Healer. There was no reason for them to speculate about what it must have been like to see Jesus' miracles, for they consistently had the working of miracles operating in their church services, making Jesus the Miracle-Worker *a reality* to them. The gifts of the Spirit lifted Jesus right off the pages of history and brought Him into the midst of the Corinthian church services.

First Corinthians 1:6 could be translated:

"Everything you've heard and believed about Jesus Christ has been authenticated, proven beyond a shadow of a doubt, verified, and guaranteed to be true because of the gifts of the Spirit."

What does all this have to do with you and your relationship with God today? If there is no operation of the Holy Spirit's gifts in your life or in the church you attend, an entire supernatural element of Jesus Christ is missing from your life. God never intended for your salvation to exist only on an intellectual level. He gave the Holy Spirit to the Church to bring the overflowing, abundant life of Jesus Christ right into the life of His people! There is a whole level of understanding Jesus — who He is and how He operates — that can only be comprehended by observing and participating in the working of the gifts of the Holy Spirit.

The Holy Spirit wants to confirm everything you know about Jesus. He wants you to know Jesus the Prophet, Jesus the Healer, and Jesus the Miracle-Worker. When these gifts operate through you or on your behalf through someone else, they give testimony to the fact that Jesus is still alive, still healing, and still working miracles today. Thus, by means of these marvelous spiritual gifts, the Holy Spirit both teaches you and speaks on behalf of Jesus Christ.

So are you ready for the Jesus of the Bible to step off the pages of history and into your life or into the life of your church? If the answer is yes, ask the Holy Spirit to start moving supernaturally in your midst. And if you sense an inner nudge to step out in faith and let God use *you* in spiritual gifts, don't hesitate to obey. That's the Holy Spirit talking to you! *Perhaps it's your turn to step forth and allow the Spirit of God to work supernaturally through you!*

MY PRAYER FOR TODAY

Lord, I thank You for the ministry of the Holy Spirit and for His powerful gifts that make Jesus so real to me. Help me understand my need for the Spirit's gifts. Arouse a spiritual hunger inside me that makes me earnestly yearn to experience more of these gifts in my life and in my church. I know You gave the gifts of the Spirit because we need them, so today I am choosing to open my heart so I can experience more of Your power as these supernatural gifts begin to flow through me.

I pray this in Jesus' name!

MY CONFESSION FOR TODAY

I confess that I am a vessel for the gifts of the Holy Spirit. These gifts operate through me and bring the living reality of Jesus Christ to me and to those who are around me. I am not afraid to obey what the Holy Spirit prompts me to say. I am not hesitant to act when the Spirit prompts me to step out in faith. Because I obey the leading of the Spirit, God's power mightily flows through me to others who are in need.

I declare this by faith in Jesus' name!

QUESTIONS FOR YOU TO CONSIDER

1. Have you ever thought that the miracles of the Bible were for a different time, not something you were supposed to experience on a consistent basis in your life or in your church?

2. Can you ever recall a time in your life when the gifts of the Spirit operated through you? If so, what was that experience like?

3. In order for you to become a more yielded vessel so the Holy Spirit can use you, what changes do you need to make personally in the way you think and the way you believe?

MAY 5

❧

Rejuvenated by the Spirit of God!

But if the Spirit of him that raised up Jesus from the dead dwell in you,
he that raised up Christ from the dead shall also quicken your mortal bodies
by his Spirit that dwelleth in you.
— Romans 8:11

Recently I was thinking of the pressures and stresses that affect so many people's lives. People live their lives in their cars as they spend endless hours on expressways each day. They take their kids back and forth to school and to sports events; they go to church functions, to the grocery store, and back and forth to work. This constant movement puts a lot of stress on the mind and body. Yet there seems to be no option but to constantly try to keep up with the hectic pace!

Then when you finally get home in the evening, you can't really rest. After all, the bills must be paid; the house must be maintained; the yard needs mowing; dishes need washing; dinner needs to be cooked; groceries have to be put away; the children need special attention and discipline. Walking through the door of the house at the end of the work day does not mean your work is finished. You have switched to a different kind of work.

Then there are still church responsibilities. You want to be faithful to your church and serve in as many areas as possible. Church is important and should be treated as such. But often you have expended so much energy on all the other important matters of life that when you finally get around to church, you feel exhausted and unmotivated. This makes you feel *guilty* and even *condemned* for not being more excited about serving the Lord in a practical way at church. But it isn't really a question of desire; it's a question of energy. Already your body and mind have almost been pushed to the brink!

Then there are family responsibilities. If you have an elderly person in your family, you know that this requires attention and energy too. *Of course you want to do this!* This isn't an obligation; it is a *privilege* to take care of older family members. Nevertheless, it still takes time and energy. And if you live in an area where you are close to cousins, aunts, uncles, brothers, sisters, and grandparents, you must also work all these precious people into the schedule. Birthdays, anniversaries, funerals, weddings — all of these are part of your family responsibilities that require your time, energy, and finances.

How about your friendship responsibilities? Friendships require time and attention. As a good friend, you want to be there for your friend's good times and bad times. You probably believe that you shoud be available when they need to talk about a problem. You want to spend time with your friends because you need and enjoy their fellowship. But all this requires time and energy as well.

Don't forget your financial challenges and pressures. Life is expensive. Car insurance, life insurance, house payments, credit card payments, groceries, electricity and air-conditioning bills, expenses for the kids to play sports or go to summer camp, clothes for growing children, repairs on the car — and on and on it goes. Plus, you *must* be faithful in paying your tithes to your church, and you want to give special offerings to other ministries too.

One of Satan's greatest weapons is discouragement, and he knows exactly when to use it. He waits until you are tired, weak, and susceptible to his lies. Then he hits you hard in your emotions, trying to tell you that you are accomplishing nothing valuable in life.

In those moments when I feel physically exhausted and yet I see no pause in my schedule, I turn to Romans 8:11 for encouragement. It says, "But if the Spirit of him that raised up Jesus from the dead dwell in you, he that raised up Christ from the dead shall also quicken your mortal bodies by his Spirit that dwelleth in you."

I especially focus on the phrase that says, "...he that raised up Christ from the dead shall also quicken your mortal bodies...." Our mortal bodies simply have limitations, and there is nothing we can do about it. These limitations are one of the reasons we become physically tired. But in those moments when we need extra strength to keep going, this verse promises that the Holy Spirit will "quicken" our mortal bodies.

The word "quicken" is the Greek word *zoopoieo,* from the word *zoe* and *poieo.* The word *zoe* is the Greek word for *life,* and it often describes *the life of God.* The word *poieo* means *to do.* When these two words are compounded together, it means *to make alive with life.* It carries the idea *to revitalize, to rejuvenate,* or *to refresh with new life*!

This means that if you will yield to the Holy Spirit who dwells in you, He will supernaturally revitalize you. He will rejuvenate you. He will refresh you with a brand-new surge of supernatural life. He will fill you with so much resurrection power that you will be ready to get up and go again!

MY PRAYER FOR TODAY

Lord, I admit that I need a fresh surge of supernatural power in my life right now. I ask You to release the resurrection power of Jesus Christ that resides in my spirit. Let it flow up into my body and mind so I can be rejuvenated and recharged with enough power to fulfill all the responsibilities and duties that lie before me. I know that in my own strength, I can't do everything that is required of me in the days ahead. But I also know that with Your supernatural power working in me, I will be able to do everything You have asked me to do!

I pray this in Jesus' name!

MY CONFESSION FOR TODAY

I confess that God's Spirit is quickening my mortal flesh and rejuvenating me with enough strength to fulfill all the duties and responsibilities that lie ahead of me. I am not weak. I am not tired. I am refreshed. I am strengthened. I am filled with power. Because the Holy Spirit dwells in me, there is not a single moment when I don't have everything that I need!

I declare this by faith in Jesus' name!

QUESTIONS FOR YOU TO CONSIDER

1. Have you been feeling a little depleted lately? If so, have you asked the Holy Spirit to release resurrection power in you so that you can be supernaturally rejuvenated?
2. Can you think of one particular time when you were physically exhausted, but in one instant you were so filled with life and power that your weakness left and you were magnificently empowered?
3. Instead of shutting this book and running to your next thing to do, why don't you take a few minutes and ask the Holy Spirit to fill you with power right now?

MAY 6

Isolation — A Tool The Devil Uses To Discourage People

And let us consider one another to provoke
unto love and to good works.
— Hebrews 10:24

*M*y wife and I heard from various sources that a young missionary girl was depressed and discouraged. We were both shocked when we heard it because she always seemed so "up" about everything. She always flashed a big smile on her face; her voice was vivacious; and she seemed full of energy. When we were told that she was struggling with depression, we immediately made an appointment to talk to her and to see how we might encourage her in the Lord.

We asked this young woman, "Are you all right? Is there anything going on with you that we need to know about?"

She answered, "I'll be all right. It's just that I give, give, give and give every ounce of my strength to people, and it just seems like no one ever gives back to me. I've been pretty lonely, and that has made me feel very discouraged."

With some people, it is easy to know when they are discouraged. But when people are vivacious, life-giving, and effervescent like this young lady, it becomes more difficult to discern when they are struggling with discouraging thoughts. People like this project such confidence and victory that we tend to forget they have feelings just like everyone else. Unfortunately, we often wrongly assume they don't need anything when, in fact, they are very needy.

This is why you should pray for sensitivity to recognize the needs of those around you. In fact, it would be a good idea to stop right now and ask the Lord to give you the sensitivity to recognize those times when the people in your life need an encouraging word.

This precious young lady was ministering to everyone around her, but she herself was feeling isolated and secluded. Because she was perceived to be so strong, no one dreamed that she was discouraged. As a result, no one reached out to her until discouragement was already a reality she struggled with in her life.

Everyone needs encouragement! That's why the writer of Hebrews exhorts us to "...consider one another to provoke unto love and to good works" (Hebrews 10:24). The word "consider" is the Greek word *katanoeo*, a compound of the words *kata* and *noeo*. The word *kata* is a preposition that means *down*. It describes something that is moving *downward* and can also describe *a dominating force*. The second part of the word is the Greek word *noeo*, from the word *nous*, which refers to *the mind*. When these two words are linked together, it means *to thoroughly consider something; to think something through from the top to the bottom; to think hard about something;* or *to deeply ponder a matter*. In other words, the word *katanoneo* does not represent a momentary shallow thought. A person engaged in this type of thought process is focused and concentrated. His attention has been completely captured, and he is seriously contemplating the matter at hand.

So when God urges us to "consider one another," He is saying we are to be so concerned about each other's welfare that we take time to regularly and seriously contemplate how we might encourage one another. If we truly care about the people in our lives, we should notice when their countenance has changed, when they don't seem as "up" as usual, or when they begin to skip church services. Because of our genuine care for others, we should make it our aim to think through from beginning to end the question of how we might become a greater source of blessing and strength for others.

The local church is designed by God to be a spiritual family where people sincerely love and are mindful of each other's needs. We should not only know each other's dream and desires, but we should pray often for those dreams to come to pass and check to see how things are progressing.

Church should be a place where everyone is committed to being a blessing to one another. If each member of a local church family took this approach, observing and contemplating each other's needs this thoroughly, it would be very hard for discouragement to find its way into the family of God. In fact, a situation like the one described above with the young missionary girl would almost be unheard of! Instead, Christians would be able to perceive when someone was starting to sink and begin to lift that person back up to a place of strength!

Therefore, Hebrews 10:24 could be taken to mean:

"Carefully observe one another, contemplating each other's situation and needs, diagnosing the other person's situation, and contemplating how you can stir him or her to love and good deeds."

We all like to be cared for and appreciated, but let's not forget that there are others around us who need encouragement just as much as we do. We shouldn't be led by our eyes only! Everyone who smiles isn't always happy.

If you'll be sensitive to the Holy Spirit and truly be concerned about the people who are close to you, God will show you when they need a special word to lift their spirits. Think how much it means to you when someone deliberately goes way out of his or her normal daily routine to let you know you are appreciated. Isn't it powerful when someone does this for you? Well, just as you need people who will love you, be sensitive to your needs, and support you when you are struggling through challenges or feeling tired and worn out, the people you encounter in your daily life have those same exact needs.

It's time to let the Holy Spirit use you to be a source of encouragement to others — and you can start by letting Him use you to be a blessing to someone today!

MY PRAYER FOR TODAY

Lord, forgive me for being so self-centered that I forget to think about other people's needs. I get so fixated on my own problems that I forget I am not the only person in the world who is struggling with a situation. Help me to take my eyes off myself and to look around me to see who needs a special word of encouragement. Holy Spirit, open my eyes and help me be sensitive in my spirit to recognize people who need a tender touch. So many times I've freely received help from others. Now I want to freely give what I have received.

I pray this in Jesus' name!

MY CONFESSION FOR TODAY

I declare by faith that I am sensitive to the needs of others. God uses me to encourage people who are around me. As I become more Christ-like, I am less aware of me and more aware of those who are around me. Because God's Spirit lives inside me, all the wonderful fruit of the Spirit — love, joy, peace, patience, gentleness, goodness, faith, meekness, and temperance — reside in me and flow through me to others. I am aware of others. I think of them; I ask about them; I pray for them; and I treat them with the greatest love, care, and attention.

I declare this by faith in Jesus' name!

QUESTIONS FOR YOU TO CONSIDER

1. Have you ever felt isolated and lonely and wished that someone would reach out to check on you? If yes, did anyone ever check on you, or did you feel abandoned in your time of need?
2. How long has it been since you deviated from your normal course of affairs to go check on someone else and let that person know you have been thinking about him or her?
3. What can you do today to specially communicate that you are concerned about someone else's welfare? Write down several ideas, such as sending flowers, writing a note, calling someone on the telephone, etc.

Let's not forget that there are others around us who need encouragement just as much as we do. We shouldn't be led by our eyes only! Everyone who smiles isn't always happy.

MAY 7

True Profession
Is From the Heart

Let us hold fast the profession of our faith without wavering;
(for he is faithful that promised;).
— Hebrews 10:23

Years ago, I was staying at a pastor's house while I was preaching in his church. The first day I slept in his home, I became very frustrated early the next morning. About 5 a.m., the telephone started ringing — and it rang and rang and rang. I began to count the rings — thirty rings, forty rings, forty-five rings. Finally on the fiftieth ring, I got up, put on my clothes, and walked down the hallway to the kitchen, mumbling to myself, "If no one else cares enough to get up and answer this telephone, I'll do it!"

I picked up the receiver and said, "Hello." But to my amazement, the phone just kept on ringing, even though I was holding the receiver in my hand! Then I noticed that the ringing wasn't coming from the telephone at all, but from something to my right that was covered with a big white sheet. I pulled the sheet back to look, and there in a big cage was a Grey African parrot looking back at me! It had been mimicking the ringing of the telephone! That parrot sounded just like a telephone, but it was *not* a telephone!

As I walked back down the hallway to my bedroom, I started thinking about how that parrot reminded me of some people I knew! I'm talking about people who made what sounded like great faith confessions, but who weren't really in faith at all. Their words sounded right, but they weren't doing anything but parroting what they had heard someone else say or do. Because there was no faith backing up their words, their confessions were no more real than the ringing telephone coming from the beak of that parrot!

In Hebrews 10:23, the Bible says, "Let us hold fast the profession of our faith...." Today I'd like to draw your attention to the word "profession." It comes from the Greek word *homologia*, which is a compound of the words *homo* and *logos*. The Greek word *homo* means *one of the very same kind*. The second part of the word, *logos*, is the Greek word for *words*. When these two words are joined together, they form the word *homologia*, which seems at first to mean *to say the same thing*.

The *King James Version* translates the word *homologia* as the word "profession." However, this is really inadequate to fully understand what the word *homologia* means. To capture the comprehensive meaning of the word *homologia*, it is essential to further consider the word *logos*. As noted above, it means *words*.

Let me give you an illustration of the word *homologia*. I am a writer and have written many books. My words are my thoughts, my convictions, and my beliefs printed on paper. If you read my books and agree with what I have written — with my words — then in essence you are in agreement with me, for those words *are* me! They are what I think, what I believe, and what I have expressed.

Ultimately, if you like my books and agree with what I've written, you are coming into agreement with me, the author. If you take my viewpoint and begin to hold it as your own conviction, it won't be long until you and I are *aligned* in our thinking and believing.

After my words have gotten deeply into your heart and you have fully embraced them, those words will soon become your own conviction. Then when you share that information with others, you will no longer be just repeating — or parroting — what you have read in my book. Instead, you will be speaking from the platform of your own heart about what you believe. At that point, you and I will be genuinely aligned in our viewpoints and convictions, talking the same language!

The word "profession" used in Hebrews 10:23 (or "confession," as it is translated in other scriptures), from the Greek word *homologia*, is not the picture of a person who simply repeats what someone else says. This is an individual who has gotten God's Word into his heart and who has come into agreement or alignment with what God says. This person sees a matter like God sees it; hears it like God hears it; feels it like God feels it. Now his heart and God's heart are so unified on the issue that their hearts are nearly beating in syncopation with each other. Thus, when the believer opens his mouth to "confess" God's Word, his confession is no longer powerless, empty chatter; instead, it comes from a very deep place of conviction inside his heart.

In light of this, Hebrews 10:23 carries this idea:

"Let us come into agreement with God and then begin to speak what He says, holding tightly to what we confess and refusing to let anyone take it from us...."

Real confessions are made out of words from God that have been sown *into the heart*. After a period of meditating and renewing the mind, you finally begin to see it the way that God sees it. You really believe what God believes! And from that place of heartfelt conviction, you then begin to speak and to declare your faith!

You see, when a believer gets God's Word so deep into his heart that he comes into alignment with it, he is no longer simply muttering empty words or parroting something he has heard when he speaks. Now he speaks boldly from a legitimate place of faith!

Many people make the mistake of going through life repeating what they have heard someone else say without ever developing any depth of faith or understanding behind their words. They say the right things, but because these words come only out of their mouths and not out of their hearts, their confession doesn't produce results.

Your faith and your mouth must be connected. A mechanical profession doesn't come from the heart; therefore, it doesn't bring forth any fruit. True profession must come from your heart *before* it comes out of your mouth.

How do you avoid making mechanical, mindless confessions?

✦ *First, make certain you have chosen to believe what God says.* Commit your mind, heart, and all your strength to believing the Word of God, no matter how crazy it may sound to your natural mind.

✦ *Then ask the Holy Spirit to make God's Word real to you* — so real, in fact, that should anyone even imply that what God said isn't true, you'd think that person was out of his mind!

✦ *Finally, pick up your Bible and do some serious study and meditation. Sow that Word into your heart until you and God are aligned on the issue. After that alignment comes into being, it's time for you to open your mouth and start declaring the Word of God over your situation!*

Today I want to encourage you to get into God's Word. Take it deep into your heart and mind, and meditate on it until you and God begin to think alike! Once that Word becomes so real inside you that it becomes *your* word, it's time for you to open your mouth and speak to any mountain that stands in your way. As you do, that mountain will be removed!

A faith confession can only be a real mountain-moving confession when it comes from the heart before it comes out of the mouth. If you have planted God's Word in your heart so that it is now your word as well, you have no need to tarry any longer! *Open your mouth, and begin to confess what God has promised you!*

MY PRAYER FOR TODAY

Lord, I want to get Your Word so deep into my heart that it becomes MY word! I want to see things the way You see them, hear things the way You hear them, and feel things the way You feel them. I want to get so aligned with You that our hearts beat in syncopation together. I thank You that once Your Word gets that deeply rooted in my heart, my spoken words will release rivers of power and authority against the works of the devil that he has designed for my destruction! I thank You that just as Your words created the universe, my spoken words of faith create a change in my atmosphere!

I pray this in Jesus' name!

MY CONFESSION FOR TODAY

I boldly confess that God's Word is deeply rooted inside my heart and soul. My mind is being renewed to the truth, and I am being changed. What I used to think, I no longer think; what I used to believe, I no longer believe. Now I base my life on the eternal truths contained in God's Word. I take the Word deep into my heart and soul where it inwardly transforms me. When I open my mouth to speak, I don't speak empty, mindless words; instead, my words come from a deeply held conviction and therefore release power to set the answers I need in motion!

I declare this by faith in Jesus' name!

QUESTIONS FOR YOU TO CONSIDER

1. Have there been times when you have found yourself so aligned with God's Word that when you spoke, the words you released literally caused a change in your situation? What was that situation, and what happened when you spoke forth words of faith?
2. On the other hand, can you remember a time when you just mindlessly parroted what someone else said and nothing happened? What did you learn from that experience?
3. From what you have read today, what must you do in order to be able to speak a true confession of faith?

Your faith and your mouth must be connected. A mere mechanical profession doesn't come from the heart; therefore, it doesn't bring forth any fruit. A true profession must come from your heart *before* it comes out of your mouth.

MAY 8

Don't Do What You're Tempted To Do When Someone Gets Ugly With You!

And the servant of the Lord must not strive;
but be gentle unto all men, apt to teach, patient.
— 2 Timothy 2:24

*H*ave you ever found yourself in a predicament where you were trying to help someone who resisted you, spoke disrespectfully to you, and just flat out acted ugly? In that instant, did you find your blood boiling, your temperature rising, and your emotions agitated? Were you so angry that you felt like you would detonate? *Be honest!* Did you feel tempted to fly into a rage, lecture the ingrate derogatorily for his attitude, or even slap him right across the face?

It's natural to feel exasperated when someone you are trying to help doesn't respond appropriately to the assistance you are offering. But yielding to your own emotions and getting in the flesh won't make the situation any better. In fact, it will only make the situation worse! So hold your tongue, stay seated in your chair, and keep your head on straight when you find yourself in a situation like this!

Many years ago, Denise and I had one particular employee who was extremely gifted — but he was one of the most difficult people to work with I've ever met in my life. This man was rude, insubordinate, critical of others, and regularly late to work. On the other hand, he was very talented and produced great results in his job. One day I wanted to fire him; the next day, I wanted to reward him. It was such an emotional mixture! How I wished this employee would just calm down, talk nicely to people, and learn how to get along with others!

From time to time, I had to sit down and talk to this man about his attitude. But dealing with him was so excruciatingly laborious. I *dreaded* those moments when I knew I had to sit down to talk to him. Here I was, trying to help this employee — but rather than receive correction graciously and thank me for trying to take him to a higher level, he would argue, debate, or try to turn the conversation around and point his finger at other people. It simply exasperated me, yet I knew that God wanted me to work with and teach this man; therefore, I had to remain self-controlled and not allow myself to get caught up in the flesh and knock him flat!

Have you ever felt this way before? Can you remember a time when you tried to help your child, but your child's response was belligerent and unreceptive to you? Or can you recall a time when you worked with a fellow employee whose attitude toward the boss was so bad that he or she deserved to be fired for it? Or perhaps you can remember someone at church who had a critical attitude toward the pastor and got involved in ugly backbiting and gossip. *I hope it wasn't you!*

When Timothy was serving as pastor of the Ephesian church, he had some insubordinate people in church leadership positions. Apparently he had written to Paul about this problem, because when Paul wrote his second letter to Timothy, he addressed the problem, telling Timothy what kind of attitude he needed to maintain when dealing with people who had bad attitudes. Paul said, "And the servant of the Lord must not strive; but be gentle unto all men, apt to teach, patient" (2 Timothy 2:24).

The word "strive" is the Greek word *machomai*, and it means *to quarrel, dispute, argue,* or *to get into strife or contention with someone else.* At first, this Greek word was used to picture *armed combatants who exchanged blows with deadly weapons.* Later, it came to denote men *who fought hand to hand* — striking, punching, wrangling, and rolling on the ground as they slugged it out with each other. But by the time of the New Testament when Paul used the word *machomai* in this verse, it depicted *people who were at odds with each other bickering, squabbling, and slugging it out — not with swords or fists, but with their words.* So Paul urges Timothy (and all of us) not to allow ourselves to get dragged into a war of words when we are trying to correct people who have bad attitudes.

Next, Paul tells us that we must be "gentle." This is the Greek word *epios*, which means to be *mild-mannered, kind, temperate, calm,* or *gentle.* We find this word used by Paul in First Thessalonians 2:7, where he reminds the Thessalonians of how he had behaved among them. He writes, "But we were *gentle* among you, even as a nurse cherisheth her children."

It is important that we see how Paul uses the word *epios* in the context of caring for little children. This suggests that now Paul is telling Timothy to realize that he is dealing with immature people whom he must treat like children. Parents are to teach and discipline their children without "flying off the handle" every time their children are rude or disrespectful. Now Timothy must assume this kind of parental, correcting, teaching role in the way he deals with these who are acting inappropriately in his church.

When people behave disrespectfully toward their boss, their department director, their pastor, or their parents, they are demonstrating that they are not smart and certainly not mature. When you see this, it should send up a red flag before you to let you know the maturity level you are dealing with in the lives of these individuals. Even if they are called to the ministry; even if they have been to Bible school; even if they have been members of your church for a long time — the fact that they would act disrespectfully toward authority reveals that these people are still young in terms of maturity.

You should thank God that this came to light. Had you moved these individuals upward into a higher place of visibility while they were still at this deficient level of maturity, it would have been a big problem for you later. But now you can see that they're not ready for a higher place of responsibility. You can also visibly discern the areas in which you need to help them so they can maximize their potential in the Lord.

Second Timothy 2:24 could be translated to read:

"And the servant of the Lord must not get caught up in a war of words — wrangling, wrestling, bickering, squabbling, arguing, and verbally slugging it out with his contenders. Instead, he must be calm, steady, temperate, kind, and gentle in the way he responds...."

So when you try to bring correction into someone's life who is under your authority and that person doesn't initially respond the way he should, don't let it ruffle your feathers or throw you into a state of exasperation. Certainly you shouldn't allow yourself to get so caught up in emotions that you descend to their level and start acting just like them!

This is a time for you to "put on your parent-teacher hat." Lovingly deal with that person like a child or a young person who needs to be taught how to respond to authority and who needs guidance and correction from someone who loves him.

And what should you do if you get stirred up and enter into the fray of flesh, allowing yourself to get entrenched in a war of words? Thank God that your own level of maturity has been exposed! Not only does that other person need to grow, but this situation has revealed a flaw in your own character, drawing attention to an obvious area in your own life that needs attention, correction, and a higher level of maturity. *So as you pray for that other person to grow, don't forget to include yourself on your prayer list!*

MY PRAYER FOR TODAY

Lord, please help me to be calm, kind, and gentle when I find it necessary to correct people who are under my care. Forgive me for any time that I've allowed myself to become angry and exasperated and for those times when I have said things I shouldn't have allowed myself to speak. Help me act like a real leader, taking a parental-teacher role. I know I am called to help take people to a higher level in their work, their attitudes, and their lives. So help me to be more like You in the way I deal with people who are under my authority and care. As I learn to bring correction to others the way You bring correction into MY life, I will become a good example and the kind of leader You have called me to be.

I pray this in Jesus' name!

MY CONFESSION FOR TODAY

I confess that I have the mind of Christ for every situation I face in life. When it is necessary for me to speak correction to a member of my team, I speak with compassion and love from my heart. I desire the best for every person whom God has placed under my authority and care. Therefore, when I deal with these individuals, I approach them from a standpoint of how I can best help them grow, help them develop, and help them become all God has called them to be. I don't get angry, frustrated, or exasperated if they get upset; instead, I remain calm, kind, and gentle as I deal with the people whom God has entrusted to my care.

I declare this by faith in Jesus' name!

QUESTIONS FOR YOU TO CONSIDER

1. As you read this today, did your mind drift back to a past situation when you had to correct someone who didn't respond in the right way to your correction? If so, how did you react to that person's wrong response?
2. Can you think of a time when someone in authority over you tried to correct you, but you responded in an insubordinate and closed-hearted manner, making it difficult for that person to correct you?
3. As you reflect on times in the past when you've had to correct someone, what do you think you could do differently to help people more easily receive your correction in the future? Is there anything in your style of bringing correction that should be changed so people don't feel intimidated but rather feel embraced and loved by what you are telling them?

Have you ever found yourself in a predicament where you were trying to help someone who resisted you, spoke disrespectfully to you, and just flat out acted ugly?

MAY 9

Are You Dressed In the Whole Armor of God?

Put on the whole armor of God, that ye may be able
to stand against the wiles of the devil.
— Ephesians 6:11

Not far from our personal residence is Moscow's Great Kremlin Palace. Its massive red brick walls rise to the sky with bell towers and clock towers. Its huge, famous ruby-red stars can be seen from all directions in the city of Moscow. One entire side of the Kremlin is surrounded by the beautiful and historical Red Square, which includes St. Basil's Cathedral and Lenin's tomb. Another side of the Kremlin is encompassed with the lovely, tree-lined Alexandrovski Gardens.

At the far end of that Garden is a tall tower through which thousands of tourists enter every year to visit the State Armory Museum, one of the most fabulous museums in the entire world. As a person enters the State Armory Museum, he quickly becomes mesmerized as he walks past glass-enclosed dresses spun of pure silver that formerly adorned Russian queens. He can't help but be stunned by the dazzling crowns and regalia worn by the Russian monarchy.

As the onlooker is led along the museum corridors, he looks in amazement at thrones made of ivory, covered with diamonds or spiked with precious stones. With fascination he gapes at the gold-covered, diamond-encrusted carriages that once transported various branches of the Russian royal family.

But a favorite part of the museum, especially for men, is the section that displays the heavy metal armor that was once worn in battle hundreds of years ago. Behind walls of glass, one can look at hundreds of years of metal armor, including a huge horse that is dressed in heavy metal armor from medieval times. Every time I see this armor section of the museum, I think of Paul's words in Ephesians 6:11: "Put on the whole armor of God, that ye may be able to stand against the wiles of the devil."

The phrase "whole armor" is taken from the Greek word *panoplia*, and it refers to *a Roman soldier who is fully dressed in his armor from head to toe*. It is the word *pan*, which means *all*, combined with the word *hoplos*, which is the Greek word for *armor*. Together they form the word *panoplia*, which was officially recognized as the word to describe *the full attire and weaponry of a Roman soldier*.

Although not all-inclusive, the following list is the basic military hardware each soldier possessed:

✦ **Loinbelt**
This was the central piece of weaponry that held much of the other pieces of armor in place. In Ephesians 6:14, Paul tells us that the believer is equipped with a loinbelt of truth, referring to the written Word of God.

✦ **Breastplate**
This was a crucial piece of weaponry that defended the heart and the central organs of the body against attack. In Ephesians 6:14, Paul informs us that in our spiritual arsenal, we have at our disposal the "breastplate of righteousness."

319

✦ **Greaves**

These specially formed pieces of metal were wrapped around the soldier's lower legs to protect him from being bruised and scraped and to defend his lower extremities from being hit hard and broken. In Ephesians 6:15, Paul refers to this vital piece of weaponry when he tells us that our feet are "…shod with the preparation of the gospel of peace."

✦ **Shoes**

These heavy-duty shoes of a Roman soldier were covered with thick leather on the top and fitted with hobnails on the tip of the toe and the back of the heel. They were also heavily spiked with hobnails on their undersides. Paul makes reference to these shoes in Ephesians 6:15 when he talks about our feet being "…shod with the preparation of the gospel of peace."

✦ **Shield**

The shield that the Roman soldier used in battle was long, door-shaped, and covered with leather hide. It was lubricated every day by the soldier to keep it soft and flexible so arrows that struck the shield would slide off and fall to the ground rather than penetrate it. In Ephesians 6:16, Paul declares that as a believer, you are specially outfitted with a "…shield of faith, wherewith ye shall be able to quench all the fiery darts of the wicked."

✦ **Helmet**

The helmet of a Roman soldier, made either of brass or some other type of metal, was especially fitted to the shape of the soldier's head, thus protecting the head from receiving a mortal wound from an arrow, a sword, or an ax. In Ephesians 6:17, Paul proclaims the good news that God has provided every believer with "the helmet of salvation" to protect him against the mental assaults of the enemy.

✦ **Sword**

The Roman soldier's sword, shaped similarly to a long dagger that was intended to be used in close battle, was absolutely indispensable to his ability to attack, overcome, and defeat his adversary. In Ephesians 6:17, we are taught by Paul that every believer has "…the sword of the Spirit, which is the word of God." This sword is God's Word, specially quickened inside us to use in times when we are in close combat with the adversary.

✦ **Lance**

The lance gave the Roman soldier the ability to strike his enemy from a distance; therefore, no Roman soldier would be caught without his lance. Although Paul does not specifically mention the lance in his list of weaponry in Ephesians 6, it is suggested in verse 18 when Paul writes, "Praying always…." With the lance of prayer, each believer is able to assault the enemy from a distance, doing him so much damage that he is paralyzed in his attempts to come any nearer!

Because of Paul's many imprisonments, this was an easy illustration for Paul to use. Standing next to these illustrious soldiers during his prison internments, Paul could see the Roman soldier's *loinbelt; huge breastplate; brutal shoes affixed with spikes; massive, full-length shield; intricate helmet; piercing sword; and long, specially tooled lance that could be thrown a tremendous distance to hit the enemy from afar.*

Everything the soldier needed to successfully combat his adversary was at his disposal. Likewise, we have been given the whole armor of God — *everything* we need to successfully combat opposing forces. *Nothing is lacking!* Every piece of armor has great significance for us in our battle against an unseen enemy.

God has provided everything you need to successfully stand up to the devil, to resist him, and to defeat him. Will you choose to obey or ignore Paul's urgent command to "put on the whole armor of God"? *Your success against an enemy that seeks every opportunity to destroy you depends on the choice you make!*

MY PRAYER FOR TODAY

Lord, how can I ever thank You enough for providing me with everything I need to successfully stand against each and every attack the devil tries to bring against my life? I thank You for loving me enough to equip me with these kinds of spiritual weapons. Because of what You have provided for me, I can stand fast, confident that I can withstand every assault, drive out the enemy, and win every battle. Without You, this would be impossible; but with Your power and the weapons You have provided for me, I am amply supplied with everything I need to push the enemy out of my way and out of my life!

I pray this in Jesus' name!

MY CONFESSION FOR TODAY

I joyfully declare that I am dressed in the whole armor of God. There isn't a part of me that hasn't been supernaturally clothed and protected by the defensive and offensive weapons God has provided for me. I proceed with my loinbelt of truth; I walk in my shoes of peace; I boldly wear my breastplate of righteousness; I hold up my shield of faith; I am clad in my helmet of salvation; I make use of my sword of the Spirit; and I have a lance of intercession that deals a blow to the enemy from a distance every time I aggressively pray!

I declare this by faith in Jesus' name!

QUESTIONS FOR YOU TO CONSIDER

1. How long has it been since you took time to stop and reflect on all the weaponry that God has provided for your defense and offense against the enemy?
2. Have you ever taken time to deeply study the spiritual weapons that God has supernaturally provided for you? If yes, what other steps can you take and what other books can you read to become better acquainted with this subject?
3. What did you learn from reading today's *Sparkling Gem* that you never realized before? After you think this question through and come up with the answer, why not share it with someone else today?

We have been given the whole armor of God — everything we need to successfully combat opposing forces. *Nothing is lacking!*

MAY 10

❧

Peace That Passes Understanding

And the peace of God, which passeth all understanding,
shall keep your hearts and minds through Christ Jesus.
— Philippians 4:7

*A*re you tired of letting the devil get you all stirred up? Has it been easy for the enemy to throw you into a frenzy of panic and anxiety? Maybe it doesn't happen continually to you, but every once in a while, something happens or someone says something that pushes a button inside you and throws you into a tizzy! When this occurs, do you say and do things you later regret? Do you feel sorry that you allowed the devil to get to you again?

If what I just described sounds familiar, I have help for you today! In Philippians 4:7, the apostle Paul writes, "And the peace of God, which passeth all understanding, shall keep your hearts and minds through Christ Jesus."

As we begin our study today, I want to draw your attention to the word "passeth" in the verse above. It is the Greek word *huperecho*, which is a compound of the words *huper* and *echo*. The word *huper* literally means *over, above, and beyond*. It depicts something that is *way beyond measure*. It carries the idea of *superiority; something that is utmost, paramount, foremost, first-rate, first-class, and top-notch; greater, higher, and better than; superior to; preeminent, dominant, and incomparable; more than a match for; unsurpassed* or *unequaled*. The second part of the word "passeth" is the Greek word *echo*, which means *I have*, as someone who *holds something* in his possession. It can be translated *to keep; to possess; to have; to hold;* or even *to acquire*.

When these words are compounded into one, they form the word *huperecho*, which Paul uses in Philippians 4:7. This Greek word denotes a peace *so superior that it is held high above* all other types of peace. This is a peace that *transcends, outdoes, surpasses, excels, rises above, goes beyond and over the top of* any other kind of peace. The implication is that people may try to find peace in other places, but there is no peace like the peace of God. The peace of God *completely outshines* every other attempt to produce peace, causing it to stand in a category by itself. There is absolutely nothing in the world that can compare with the peace of God.

Paul continues to tell us that this peace surpasses and excels above "all understanding." The word "understanding" is the Greek word *nous*, the classical Greek word for *the mind*. This word refers to *the ability to think, to reason, to understand,* and *to comprehend*. It also depicts *the mind as the source of all human emotions*. In Greek, the word "mind" represents *the inner powers of a person* and thus *the place from which a person rules and controls his environment and the world around him*. The Greek word emphatically depicts the mind as the *central control center* for a human being. Therefore, it was understood that *the condition of the mind is what determined the condition of one's life*.

Then Paul tells us what this powerful peace will produce in our lives! He says that this peace "…shall *keep* your hearts and minds…." The word "keep" is the Greek word *phroureo*, a military term that expresses the idea of soldiers who stood faithfully at their post at the city gates *to guard* and *control* all who went *in* and *out* of the city. They served as *gate monitors*, and no one entered or exited the city without their approval.

The apostle Paul uses this word *phroureo* to explicitly tell us that God's peace, if allowed to work in our lives, will stand at the gates of our hearts and minds, *acting like a guard to control and monitor everything that tries to enter our hearts, minds, and emotions.* When God's peace is ruling us, nothing can get past that divine "guard" and slip into our hearts and minds without its approval!

This is the good news you've been waiting for! It means you can refuse to allow the devil to access you, throw you into a state of panic and anxiety, or push any button inside you any longer. When the peace of God is standing guard at the entrance of your heart and mind, the devil has lost his access to your thought life and your emotions!

**Taking these Greek words together,
Philippians 4:7 could be understood in the following way:**

"And the peace of God — a peace so wonderful that it cannot be compared to any other type of peace; a peace that stands in a category by itself and rises far above and goes beyond anything the human mind could ever think, reason, imagine, or produce by itself — will stand at the entrance of your heart and mind, working like a guard to control, monitor, and screen everything that tries to access your mind, heart, and emotions."

By using this word, Paul tells us that the *peace of God* will keep and guard your heart and mind! God's peace will surround your heart and mind just as a band of Roman soldiers would keep dangerous nuisances from entering a city or from breaking into special, private places. In the same way, peace keeps fretfulness, anxiety, worry, and all the other wiles of the devil from breaking into *your* life. When this peace is active in your life, it surpasses all natural understanding. It protects, guards, keeps, and defends you.

Nothing compares to this powerful, protective, guarding peace that God has positioned to stand at the entrance of your heart and mind! When this peace operates in you, it dominates your mind and your life. Since what is inside you is that which rules you, peace rises up and conquers your entire being. It stands at the gate of your heart and mind, disabling the devil's ability to disturb you by preventing his attacks from bypassing and slipping into your mind. The devil may try his best to find access to your mind and emotions, but this guarding peace will paralyze his efforts.

So make sure Philippians 4:7 is a reality in your life. In every situation you face today and every day, let God's supernatural peace rise up to dominate your heart and protect your mind and emotions. *If you're tired of the devil getting you all stirred up and throwing you into a tizzy, it's time for you to let this supernatural peace go to work and start monitoring, guarding, and approving what does and does not get access to you!*

MY PRAYER FOR TODAY

Lord, I thank You for placing Your wonderful, powerful, protective peace in my life. I am grateful that You have positioned it to stand at the entrance of my heart and mind and that it dominates my mind and controls my life. Because what is inside me is what rules me, I choose to let this peace rise up and conquer me. With this peace standing at the gate of my heart and mind, I know it will disable the devil's ability to attack my emotions and will not permit his lies and accusations to slip into my mind! Thank You for loving me enough to put this powerful peace in my life!

I pray this in Jesus' name!

MY CONFESSION FOR TODAY

I confess that I am guarded and protected by the powerful peace of God that works in my life. It rises up to dominate my mind; it controls my thinking; and it determines the condition of my life and the environment where I live and work. I am unaffected by the circumstances that surround me, for this supernatural peace stands at the gate of my mind and emotions to monitor everything that tries to access me. Because no fretting, anxiety, panic, or worry is allowed to enter me, I remain free, calm, and peaceful — even in difficult situations that in the past would have upset me!

I declare this by faith in Jesus' name!

QUESTIONS FOR YOU TO CONSIDER

1. Have you noticed specific events or moments in your life when the devil seems to be able to access your mind and emotions to upset your peace and throw you into one of these regrettable fits I've described to you today? If your answer is yes, do you know the "buttons" he pushes to throw you into this state that you detest?
2. What can you do to slow your reactions down long enough to let the peace of God rise up and conquer your emotions so you don't end up saying and doing things you later regret?
3. Why don't you really think this through and ask the Holy Spirit to help you come up with some ideas you can write down and pray about?

MAY 11

Cast All Your Care on the Lord!

Casting all your care upon him; for he careth for you.
— 1 Peter 5:7

When we were constructing a huge church facility many years ago in the Republic of Latvia — a former Soviet nation where our family once lived and worked — worry and anxiety tried so hard to control me. In fact, worry nearly broke me until I really came to understand and embrace the meaning of First Peter 5:7.

At the time, no credit was available for building churches in that nation. This meant we had to believe for all the finances to come in quickly so we could pay cash as we constructed the massive facility. Then the local authorities gave us a deadline by which the building had to be complete and occupied; otherwise, there was a possibility we could lose everything we had invested. With this kind of pressure on me, I found myself continually worrying that we wouldn't have enough money to finish the project on time. I was constantly fighting thoughts about losing the building if we didn't make the deadline that the government had given us.

I would lie in bed at night, rolling this way and that way, turning again and again, unable to sleep because my stomach was churning with acid and my mind was spinning with doubts, worries, fears, reservations, and concerns. My heart pounded harder and harder each day and night as anxiety reached out its demonic fingers to grab hold of my emotions and twist them into a mangled mess of panic. My wife would tell me to quit worrying and start trusting the Lord, but instead of appreciating her advice, I only got angry that she wasn't worrying with me!

Finally one night, I got up, walked down the hallway to my study, opened my Bible, and read these words: "Casting all your care upon him; for he careth for you" (1 Peter 5:7). I had read this verse thousands of times in my life, but that night it was as if it reached out from the pages of the Bible and grabbed hold of my attention. I read it and read it and read it again. At last, I picked up my Greek New Testament and began to dig deeper into the verse. What I discovered in that verse changed my life and set me free from worry, anxiety, fretting, and fear!

That night, I saw that the word "casting" used in First Peter 5:7 was the Greek word *epiripto*, a compound of the words *epi* and *ripto*. The word *epi* means *upon*, as *on top of something*. The word *ripto* means *to hurl, to throw,* or *to cast,* and it often means *to violently throw* or *to fling something with great force.*

The only other place this word *epiripto* is used in the New Testament is in Luke 19:35, where the Bible says, "And they brought him to Jesus: and *they cast* their garments upon the colt, and they set Jesus there on." It is important to note this passage, for it correctly conveys the idea of the word *epiripto*, which in secular literature often pictured *the flinging of a garment, bag, or excess weight off the shoulders of a traveler and onto the back of some other beast, such as a donkey, camel, or horse.*

We are not designed to carry the burden of worry, fretting, and anxiety. This load is simply too much for the human body and the central nervous system to tolerate. We may be able to manage it for a while, but eventually the physical body and mind will begin to break under this type of perpetual pressure. In fact, the medical world has confirmed that the major source of sickness in the Western Hemisphere is stress and pressure. Man was simply not fashioned to carry pressures, stresses, anxieties, and worries; this is the reason his body breaks down when it undergoes these negative influences for too long.

If *you* are struggling with sickness or depression, your condition very possibly could be related to stress and pressure. In First Peter 5:7, it is almost as if Jesus is calling out to you and saying, *"Your shoulders are not big enough to carry the burdens you're trying to bear by yourself. This load will eventually break you — so please let ME be your beast of burden! Take that load and heave it with all your might. Fling it over onto MY back, and let ME carry it for you!"* Just as Luke 19:35 says *they cast* their garments upon the back of the donkey, now you need to cast your burdens over on the Lord and let Him carry those burdens for you!

But exactly what problems and cares are we to throw over onto the shoulders of the Lord? The apostle Peter says we are to cast all of "our cares" upon Jesus. The word "cares" is the Greek word *merimna*, which means *anxiety.* However, in principle it described *any affliction, difficulty, hardship, misfortune, trouble, or complicated circumstance that arises as a result of problems that develop in our lives.* It could refer to problems that are financial, marital, job-related, family-related, business-oriented, or anything else that concerns us.

This means anything that causes you worry or anxiety — *regardless of why it happened* — is what you need to throw over onto the shoulders of Jesus Christ! Nothing is too big or small to talk to the Lord about, Peter says, because He "careth for you." The word "careth" is taken from the Greek word *melei*, which means *to be concerned; to be thoughtful; to be interested; to be aware; to notice;* or *to give painful and meticulous attention.* Peter uses this word to assure us that Jesus really does care about us and the things that are heavy on our hearts. In fact, He gives meticulous attention to what is happening to us. He is interested in every facet of our lives.

So don't ever let the devil tell you that your problems are too stupid, small, or insignificant to bring to Jesus. The Lord is interested in *everything* that concerns you!

Because of the Greek words used in First Peter 5:7, this verse carries the following idea:

"Take that heavy burden, difficulty, or challenge you are carrying — the one that has arisen due to circumstances that have created hardship and struggles in your life — and fling those worries and anxieties over onto the back of the Lord! Let Him carry them for you! The Lord is extremely interested in every facet of your life and is genuinely concerned about your welfare."

When I saw these Greek words and perceived how deeply Jesus cared about the burdens that were on my heart, I realized I was carrying a load I didn't have to bear by myself. Jesus was standing right at my side, longing to help me and inviting me to shift the weight from my shoulders to His shoulders. By faith, I heaved those financial cares onto the back of Jesus — and when I did, I was set free from the stress, anxiety, and pressure that had been weighing me down at that time in my life.

You don't have to carry the whole weight of the world by yourself. Jesus loves you so much and is so deeply concerned about you and the difficulties you are facing that He calls out to you today, "Roll those burdens over on Me. Let Me carry them for you so you can be free!"

If you are lugging around worries, cares, and concerns about your family, your business, your church, or any other area of your life, why not stop right now and say, *"Jesus, I'm yielding every one of these concerns to You today. I cast my burden on You, and I thank You for setting me free!"*

MY PRAYER FOR TODAY

Lord, I thank You for what I've read today. I regret having carried these burdens and worries so long by myself when, in fact, You were always ready to take them from me and to carry them on my behalf. But it's never too late to do what is right, so right now I make the decision to yield to You every one of these matters that are bothering me. Thank You for coming alongside me to take these weights from my shoulders. Because You are so loving and attentive to me, I can now go free!

I pray this in Jesus' name!

MY CONFESSION FOR TODAY

I confess that Jesus is standing right at my side, yearning to help me and inviting me to shift the weight from my shoulders to His shoulders so I can go free! By faith I have already cast my cares onto Jesus. As a result, I am liberated from stress, anxiety, worries, pressures, and all the other things that have been bothering me!

I declare this by faith in Jesus' name!

QUESTIONS FOR YOU TO CONSIDER

1. Do you habitually worry and fret about certain things? What are the issues that weigh on your mind more than anything else?
2. Are you able to cast these cares over onto the Lord, or do you keep stirring yourself up with thoughts of fear, reigniting the fretting and the worry all over again even after you have already released those cares to the Lord?

3. What triggers worry, fretting, and anxiety in you? Have you noticed key words, phrases, or events when worry and fretting begin to operate inside you? Recognizing those moments may help you prevent them from reoccurring, so consider well what kinds of situations arouse these emotions in you.

MAY 12

What Should You Do When You Get Offended?

> Then said he unto the disciples,
> It is impossible but that offences will come....
> — Luke 17:1

*E*very so often, everyone has an opportunity to get offended. In fact, Jesus said, "...It is impossible but that offences will come..." (Luke 17:1). The word "impossible" is the word *anendektos*, meaning *something that is impossible, inadmissible, unallowable, or unthinkable*. One scholar notes that it could be translated, "*It is simply unthinkable that you would allow yourself to dream that you could live this life without an opportunity to become offended....*"

But what is an offense? The word "offense" comes from the Greek word *skandalon*, from which we get the word *scandal*. This is a powerful picture that you must understand! The word *skandalon* originally described the small piece of wood that was used to keep the door of an animal trap propped open. A piece of food was placed inside the trap to lure the animal inside. When the animal entered the trap and accidentally bumped the *skandalon*, or the small piece of wood, the *skandalon* collapsed, causing the trap door to slam shut and the animal to be caught inside with no way to escape.

However, the New Testament also uses the word *skandalon* to refer to *a stone or an obstacle that caused one to trip, to stumble, to lose his footing, to waver, to falter, and to fall down*. In First Peter 2:8, the word *skandalon* is used to describe how unbelievers react to the Gospel when they don't want to hear it or believe it. Peter said, "And a stone of stumbling, and a rock of offence, even to them which stumble at the word...." Rather than accept the message and be saved, these people stumble when they hear the truth, tripping over the message that could set them free.

But in Luke 17:1, Jesus used the word *skandalon* to warn us about events that happen in life with the potential to trip us up. Sometimes Satan baits us with something — drawing us into a trap in which he knows we'll become offended. When we bump into a moment of offense, the trap slams down shut — and like an animal that is trapped in a cage and can't get out, we suddenly find ourselves caught in a miserable situation, trapped in detrimental and negative emotions!

This means Luke 17:1 could be translated:

"It is simply unthinkable that you would allow yourself to dream that you could live this life without an opportunity to be lured into a situation that could potentially snare you in the feelings of offense...."

If this is really what Jesus meant, we need to know the nature of the bait Satan uses to get to us. What is the "offense" the devil uses to trap most people?

An offense usually occurs when you see, hear, or experience a behavior that is so different from what you expected that it causes you to falter, totter, and wobble in your soul. In fact, you are so stunned by what you have observed or by a failed expectation that you lose your footing emotionally. Before you know it, you are dumbfounded and flabbergasted about something. Then your shock turns into disbelief; your disbelief into disappointment; and your disappointment into offense.

We've all experienced this kind of disappointment at some point in our lives. According to Jesus' words in Luke 17:1, the opportunity to be offended comes to every one of us. As long as we live and breathe, we must combat this nuisance and refuse to allow it to have a place in our hearts and minds. Even worse, we've all been the source of offense at some point or another. It may not have been intentional on our part; in fact, we may not have even known we offended anyone until the person later came and informed us of what we did.

In light of all this, I'd like you to consider these questions:

◆ *Have you ever offended someone?*
◆ *When you found out about the cause of offense, were you shocked?*
◆ *When the news finally reached you that you had offended that person, were you surprised to hear how he or she perceived what you did or said?*

Through the years, I've learned to do the best I can to avoid being a source of offense to anyone. At the same time, I try not to be too shocked if I find out that someone, somewhere, has gotten offended. Because people come from different backgrounds, wake up in bad moods, have a bad day at work, don't physically feel well, and go through a whole host of other negative experiences in their lives, their *interpretation* of our actions and words may be very different from our original *intention*.

We can be almost 99-percent sure that someone along the way will misunderstand what we do or misinterpret something we say. Therefore, as Christians, we must: 1) do everything in our power to communicate correct messages to one another; and 2) do everything in our power to bring healing and restoration whenever misunderstanding and offense occurs between ourselves and someone else.

If you discover that you have been a source of offense to someone else, take the mature path and go ask that person to forgive you. And don't get defensive, for that will only make the problem worse. It may even lead to a deeper conflict, so just say you are sorry and move on!

Do everything you can to bury that offense and destroy what the devil is trying to do between you. Make it your personal aim to help that other person overcome what he *thinks* you did or said. Sometimes it is more important to help the other person attain a position of peace than it is to prove who is right or wrong!

MY PRAYER FOR TODAY

Lord, I want to repent for ever being a source of offense to anyone. I am asking You to forgive me for fighting to prove my point in the past when I should have just gone to that other person and apologized, asking for his forgiveness. If I ever find out I've offended someone again, please help me deal with it more maturely than I have in the past. Jesus, I also need You to help me remember that when others do things that make me sad or that disappoint me, they probably didn't mean to do it. Help me give them the same mercy and grace that I hope others will give me.

I pray this in Jesus' name!

MY CONFESSION FOR TODAY

I confess that I am a source of blessing and not a cause of offense! I do everything in my power to communicate correct messages, and I immediately move to bring healing and restoration whenever misunderstanding and offense has occurred between myself and someone else. I do everything I can to bury that offense and to destroy what the devil is trying to do. I make it my aim to walk in the Spirit, to speak the love of God into every situation, and to refuse to let the devil use me to cause others to trip and fall.

I declare this by faith in Jesus' name!

QUESTIONS FOR YOU TO CONSIDER

1. Can you think of an occasion when you unintentionally offended someone, and you were totally shocked when you heard how he or she perceived what you said or did?
2. Have you ever been offended by someone, only to find out later that the person never intended to offend you and was genuinely sorry when he or she found out how you felt about it?
3. What do you think is the most mature way a person can respond when he or she is tempted to get caught in the trap of offense? How do you think *you* should deal with a potential offense when someone hurts your feelings or lets you down?

MAY 13

Dip and Dye!

Go ye therefore, and teach all nations, baptizing them
in the name of the Father, and of the Son, and of the Holy Ghost.
— Matthew 28:19

O ne year our Moscow pastoral staff had a debate over whether or not it was right or wrong to dye Easter eggs for the annual Easter celebration. In the Russian Orthodox Church, Easter eggs are a very big part of tradition. Therefore, I wanted to include Easter eggs in our church celebration in order to help those from an Orthodox background feel more comfortable in their new Protestant surroundings. My goal was for our children's ministry to dip, dye, and decorate several thousand eggs — one for each member of the congregation — and then to publicly present them on stage to the church before giving one to every person in attendance.

Because the children would be presenting the eggs on stage, I knew this special presentation would attract their unsaved parents to the service, allowing the parents to hear the Gospel for the first time. Some of the pastoral staff thought this was a great idea, but others thought it was inappropriate to use a symbol that also had alleged ties to paganism from the past.

At the same time we were debating this question, I was preparing to preach a message about water baptism. To prepare for my message, I pulled out my Greek New Testament, opened it to Matthew 28:19, and began to look at the Greek word for "baptism." I honestly thought, *What new revelation could I possibly learn about the word "baptism" after studying it for so many years? But I'll open all my books and give it a shot to see if there's anything about this word I've never seen before.*

Wow! Was I ever shocked at what I discovered that day! After all those years of studying, I saw something I had never seen before about *baptidzo,* the Greek word for "baptism." I saw that this word *baptidzo* originally meant *to dip and to dye.* For instance, in very early cases, *baptidzo* described the process of dipping a cloth or garment into a vat of color to dye it; leaving it there long enough for the material to soak up the new color; and then pulling that garment out of the dye with a permanently changed outward appearance. When I saw this, I just about leaped out of my chair with excitement!

In Second Corinthians 5:17, Paul wrote, "Therefore if any man be in Christ, he is a new creature: old things are passed away; behold, all things are become new." A person who comes to Jesus Christ can be likened to an old garment that needs to be dipped into a vat of dye so its color can be changed. However, the person isn't dipped into a vat of colored dye, but into the precious blood of the Lamb! This person is so totally transformed by Jesus' blood that he becomes a new creature. His countenance is so changed that he even looks different. You could say that this new believer has been "dipped and dyed"!

What a new light this shed on baptism! Paul wrote, "Therefore we are buried with him by baptism into death: that like as Christ was raised up from the dead by the glory of the Father, even so we also should walk in newness of life" (Romans 6:4). Water baptism is a symbolic proclamation of the fact that believers have been buried with Christ and raised with Him. When a believer is placed in the baptismal waters, it symbolizes being immersed in one condition and coming out looking brand new. In other words, it is a picture of what happened to that person when he got saved! This outward symbol represents the fact that he has been dipped in the blood of the Lamb, and now his entire life has been newly colored and transformed to be like Jesus!

When I saw this meaning in the word *baptidzo,* I told my pastoral staff, "This year we're going to let the children dye Easter eggs. Then we're going to use this as a teaching tool to show them what happens when a person is born again!" I instructed the teachers to tell the children that each egg represented a person who has been saved and dipped in the blood of Jesus Christ — newly colored, transformed, and changed forever.

The time came for the children to dye and decorate those eggs. As they dipped those eggs, they imagined that they were baptizing people who were newly saved. It turned out to be quite a hallelujah time! Each Easter egg became a declaration to those children that several thousand new people would soon be saved and water baptized!

Aren't you thankful that Jesus totally transformed your life? Don't you see things differently from the way you used to see them? Hasn't your entire outlook on life been altered? In a certain sense, couldn't you say that there is new light and color since Jesus came into your life? Just go ahead and rejoice in the fact that you have been dipped and dyed in the blood of Jesus and that you'll never be the same again!

MY PRAYER FOR TODAY

Lord, I am so grateful that You accepted me when I was dead in sin and washed me with Your precious blood. When I was placed inside You, everything old passed away and everything in me became brand new. For this great gift of life and salvation, I want to serve You the rest of my days. I am so thankful to You for giving me a new view of life and a whole new reason to live. When You came to dwell in me through the Person of the Holy Spirit, the drab, dark days of sin passed away, and a new world of light and color filled my life. For this, I am forever thankful!

I pray this in Jesus' name!

MY CONFESSION FOR TODAY

I boldly declare that I am a new creature in Jesus Christ. Old things have passed away, and all things have become new! I am not who I used to be anymore. I don't think like that old man; I don't see like that old man; I don't talk like that old man; and I don't behave like that old man anymore. Now I am in Jesus Christ, and I think like Him, see like Him, talk like Him, and behave like Him. I have come alive with vibrant life because of His resurrection power that works inside me!

I declare this by faith in Jesus' name!

QUESTIONS FOR YOU TO CONSIDER

1. Can you name the ways your life radically changed after Jesus Christ came into your heart? Make a list of ten ways your life changed after you got saved.
2. When you first got saved, can you remember how the world looked different to you? What seemed to be the most different?
3. Have you obeyed the Lord and been water baptized? If not, when do you plan to take this fundamental step of obedience that Jesus demands of every serious believer?

MAY 14

What Are You Teaching Your Children at Home?

One that ruleth well his own house,
having his children in subjection with all gravity.
— 1 Timothy 3:4

*A*s parents, we have a responsibility to train and prepare our children to be successful in life, and there is no better classroom for teaching them the responsibilities of life than in our own homes. God expects us to teach our children how to conduct themselves, how to respond to authority, how to cooperate with others, how to work as a part of a team, and how to successfully execute daily responsibilities. By giving our children this kind of training, we prepare them for the real world where they will one day be employed and make a living.

331

This issue of properly training our children is extremely important. In First Timothy 3:4, the apostle Paul wrote that leaders are to set the example in this area for everyone else in the church. A leader must be "one that ruleth well his own house, having his children in subjection with all gravity."

Today I want to focus on what Paul said about how children should behave. What he says applies to all children, for there are no double standards. We are commanded by God to train, teach, prepare, and equip our sons and daughters to victoriously enter the arena of life.

Paul says that our children should be "…in subjection with all gravity." The word "subjection" comes from the Greek word *hupotasso*. It means *to set things in order* or *to be subject to someone else*, and it strongly suggests the idea of *obedience to authority*. One expositor notes that this word implies a subjection to authority that can happen voluntarily or that can be required by force. It is important that Paul uses this word when speaking to parents, for it affirms that parents have the right to exercise godly authority over their children. If children don't voluntarily submit, parents have every right before God to force their children to obey.

Further confirming the strength of the word *hupotasso*, this word was a military term that was used to describe *soldiers who were under the command or authority of a superior officer*. As with all soldiers, they knew who their superior was; they understood how to respond to that superior officer; they knew their own place, function, and assignment in the army; and they understood both the rewards for obedience and the penalty for disobedience and disrespect. Let's consider how this example of a soldier in the military applies to the training of our own children.

First, a soldier never questions who his authority is. He knows from the first day who is in charge and to whom he reports. Having this knowledge clears away any confusion about whom he is accountable to. He has been given clear instructions about who is the boss, and this sets things in order so he never has to wonder who is really in charge.

Likewise, parents need to make it clear from the time a child is young that Dad and Mom are the ultimate authority in the home. When a parent doesn't exercise authority and lets a child get away with whatever he or she wants, it brings confusion into the home.

Set things straight by making it known to your children that you are assuming your godly role as the leader of your home. By teaching your children to respond correctly to your authority at home, you are preparing them to respond properly to their future employers.

A soldier understands his daily responsibilities. For example, no soldier in the army wakes up and says, "Gee, I wonder what the sergeant will ask me to do today?" The soldier knows that certain responsibilities are regular and routine. He understands that he is expected to fulfill these basic duties each day — duties such as making his bed, combing his hair, grooming his face, shining his shoes, and wearing clothes that are pressed.

Likewise, your children need daily duties to teach them responsibility. By using the word *hupotasso*, Paul is telling us that, like soldiers, children need daily discipline — including responsibilities that are *required* and *expected* of them each day. This kind of "basic training" helps children understand the realities of work, the responsibilities of life, and how to be a part of a team.

It is my personal view that it's *wrong* for a parent to make a child's bed, clean up his room, pick up his mess after he showers, and wash his dishes after he eats while he sits and watches television. This kind of "schoolroom" represents an unrealistic picture of life for the child. In the real world, no one will do everything for him when he's an adult. He'll get a big shock when he goes out into the world and suddenly discovers that no one is going to be easy on him in the workplace and that he has to carry his own weight of responsibility.

If a soldier fails in performing his basic duties, he knows beforehand that it will result in some kind of penalty. By using the word "subjection" (*hupotasso*), Paul embraces this picture of military order that includes rewards for a job well done and penalties for poor performance.

Rewards are very important as you teach your children. Rewards become goals and aspirations to help motivate a child to achieve bigger and better results. Teaching this to your child at home will help him later when he gets a job and wants a bigger salary. He will understand that to receive better wages, he will have to put out better work. Teaching our sons and daughters that nothing comes free in life is imperative if we want them to be blessed as adults.

But as important as it is to give your children rewards for a *good* performance, it is also important to give them penalties for a *poor* performance. Why should a bad job be rewarded? Will your children be rewarded for a bad performance when they go out into the workplace and get a job? Of course not! Therefore, it is part of your parental responsibility to ingrain into your children the principle that good work reaps a good reward, but poor work produces undesirable consequences. That doesn't mean you have to berate them for unsatisfactory work. You just need to take the time to lovingly explain and demonstrate how different levels of work are rewarded differently.

It is amazing that all these concepts are concealed in the Greek word *hupotasso*, translated in First Timothy 3:4 as the word "subjection." Unfortunately, we live in a day when parents are afraid to be the authority in the home as God has called them to be. But you have no need to be afraid. God has designated you to be a leader and a teacher for your children. If *you* don't assume this place of responsibility and teach them the necessary principles for success, who *will* prepare them for life?

So follow God's pattern of parenting. Give your children responsibilities to regularly perform. Make sure they understand the rewards and penalties for not doing what is expected. Do everything you can to help prepare your children for a successful, disciplined life. When they grow up and begin to work in the real world, they will thank you for investing your time and love into preparing them for life!

MY PRAYER FOR TODAY

Lord, I thank You for speaking to me about teaching my children the responsibilities of life. I want my children to be godly and successful, so I want to lead them and teach them from the Word of God. I know that my personal example is the strongest message I have to preach to my children, so help me be real and authentic, not hypocritical in my Christian life. Parenting is such a huge responsibility that I must have Your help to do it properly. I look to You and Your Word to guide me as I rear the children You have placed in my care.

I pray this in Jesus' name!

MY CONFESSION FOR TODAY

I declare by faith that I am a godly parent and I lead my children in the way of righteousness! I am not afraid to step up to the plate and take my leadership role. I do it boldly, proudly, and reverently, realizing that this is one of the greatest honors and responsibilities of my life. I recognize that my children are gifts from God, and I treat them with the greatest respect as I teach them how to become successful young adults. With the help of God's Spirit and the guidance of His Word, I am doing exactly what I must for my children to be anointed, godly, and blessed.

I declare this by faith in Jesus' name!

1. What impact did your own parents make on your life? Did they prepare you for life, or did you go out into the world feeling like you were totally unequipped for living on your own?

2. What are you doing right now to teach your own children how to be prepared for life? Do you require daily duties of them and hold them accountable for how well they perform the jobs you have assigned to them?

3. As you look at your own children and their attitude toward life, toward work, and toward authority figures, what changes could you make in your own leadership style in order to produce better results in your children?

MAY 15

The Most Common Word For Prayer in the New Testament

Praying always with all prayer and supplication
in the Spirit, and watching thereunto
with all perseverance and supplication for all saints.
— Ephesians 6:18

The most common Greek word translated "prayer" in the New Testament is the word *proseuche*. This particular word and its various forms is used approximately 127 times in the New Testament. It is the word that Paul uses in Ephesians 6:18, when he says, "Praying always with all prayer...." The word "prayer" in this verse is a translation of the word *proseuche*. Today I would like to tell you about this word and what it means for you and me.

The word *proseuche* is a compound of the words *pros* and *euche*. The word *pros* is a preposition that means *toward*, and it can denote *a sense of closeness*. For example, one scholar says the word *pros* is used to portray the intimate relationship that exists between the members of the Godhead. John 1:1 says, "In the beginning was the Word, and the Word was *with* God...." The word "with" is taken from the word *pros*. By using this word to describe the relationship between the Father and the Son, the Holy Spirit is telling us that theirs is an intimate relationship. One expositor has translated the verse, "In the beginning was the Word, and the Word was *face to face* with God...."

The word *pros* is used in Ephesians 6:12 to picture our *close contact* with unseen, demonic spirits that have been marshaled against us. Nearly everywhere it is used in the New Testament, the word *pros* carries the meaning of *close, up-front, intimate contact with someone else*.

The second part of the word *proseuche* is taken from the word *euche*. The word *euche* is an old Greek word that describes *a wish, desire, prayer*, or *vow*. It was originally used to depict a person who made some kind of vow to God because of some need or desire in his or her life. This individual would vow to give something of great value to God in exchange for a favorable answer to prayer.

A perfect illustration of this word can be found in the Old Testament story of Hannah, the mother of Samuel. Hannah deeply desired a child but was not able to become pregnant. Out of great desperation and anguish of spirit, she prayed and made a solemn vow to the Lord. First Samuel 1:11 tells us, "And she vowed a vow, and said, O Lord of hosts, if thou wilt indeed look on the affliction of thine handmaid, and remember me, and not forget thine handmaid, but wilt give unto thine handmaid a man child, then I will give him unto the Lord all the days of his life...."

First Samuel 1:19,20 goes on to tell us, "And they [Elkanah and his wife Hannah] rose up in the morning early, and worshipped before the Lord, and returned, and came to their house to Ramah: and Elkanah knew Hannah his wife; and the Lord remembered her. Wherefore it came to pass, when the time was come about after Hannah had conceived, that she bare a son...."

In exchange for God's gift of this son, Hannah vowed that her young boy would be devoted to the work of the ministry. By making this commitment, she gave her most valued and prized possession in exchange for answered prayer. Technically, this was a *euche* — she made a vow to give something to God in exchange for answered prayer.

In Greek culture, before prayer was verbalized and offered to a "god," a commemorative altar was set up and thanksgiving was offered on that altar. Such offerings of praise and thanksgiving were called *votive offerings* (from the word "vow"). These votive offerings were similar to a pledge. The person would promise that once his prayer had been answered, he would be back to give additional thanksgiving to God. These votive offerings of praise and worship were elaborate and well-planned. Giving thanks to a deity was a significant event, so it was done in a serious and grandiose manner to outwardly demonstrate a thankful heart.

All of this is included in the background of the word *proseuche*, the word used more than any other for "prayer" in the New Testament. Keep in mind, the majority of Paul's readers were Greek in origin and knew the cultural background of this word; hence, they understood its full ramifications. *What a picture of prayer this is!*

This tells us several important things about prayer. First, the word *proseuche* tells us that prayer should bring us face to face and into close contact with God. Prayer is more than a mechanical act or a formula to follow; it is a vehicle to bring us to a place whereby we may enjoy *a close, intimate relationship with God.*

The idea of *sacrifice* is also associated with this word for "prayer." It portrayed an individual who desired to see his prayer answered so desperately that he was willing to surrender everything he owned in exchange for answered prayer. Clearly, this describes an altar of sacrifice and consecration in prayer whereby a believer's life is yielded entirely to God.

Although the Holy Spirit may convict our hearts of areas that need to be surrendered to His sanctifying power, He will never forcibly take anything from us. Thus, this particular word for prayer tells of a place of decision, a place of consecration, an altar where we freely vow to give our lives to God in exchange for His life. Because the word *proseuche* carries this meaning of surrender and sacrifice, we can know that God obviously desires to do more than merely bless us — He wants to change us! He wants us to come to a place of consecration where we meet with Him face to face and surrender every area of our lives to Him, and in exchange, we are touched and changed by His power and Presence.

Thanksgiving was also a vital part of this common word for "prayer." This tells us that genuine prayer, when offered in faith, will include thanksgiving to God in advance for hearing and answering the prayer. Thus, when we come to the Lord in prayer, it is imperative that we never stop short of thanking Him for answering our prayers and requests before we ever see the answers manifested.

I think you can see that the word for "prayer" used most often in the New Testament is more than simply a prayer request. This word demands *surrender, consecration,* and *thanksgiving* from us. The idea of the word *proseuche* is this: *"Come face to face with God, and surrender your life in exchange for His. Maintain an attitude of consecration as an ongoing part of your life, and be sure to give Him thanks in advance for moving on your behalf...."*

The possible references for the word *proseuche* are far too many to list right now, but I suggest that you study for yourself many of the 127 places where it is used in the New Testament. However, be sure you don't just study this subject of prayer — *you also need to do it!*

MY PRAYER FOR TODAY

Lord, I come before You right now with the specific petition that is on my heart. I know that You want to answer my prayers and fulfill my requests, but You also want me to surrender more of myself to You. Before I ask You to meet my needs today, I first want to consecrate myself more fully to You. Forgive me for hanging on to parts of my life that I've needed to surrender to You. Right now I yield these areas of my life to You, and I ask You in exchange to please fill me with more of You. I thank You in advance for answering that prayer. I also thank You for hearing my specific prayer request and for fulfilling the needs I am confronted with today.

I pray this in Jesus' name!

MY CONFESSION FOR TODAY

I confess that I am surrendered and yielded to the Lord. Every part of my life is becoming more yielded to Him every day. As the Holy Spirit shows me areas that I need to release to Him, I do it quickly and without delay. Because I have given my life to Him, He is filling me with more and more of Himself. He hears me when I pray; He accepts my thanksgiving; and He fulfills the needs that I present to Him today!

I declare this by faith in Jesus' name!

QUESTIONS FOR YOU TO CONSIDER

1. How often do you come before the Lord for a time of intimate prayer and worship? Do you set aside time to spend with God once a day, a couple of times a week — or do you only experience His Presence during worship when you attend church services?
2. Can you recall a time when God dealt with your heart about something you needed to yield to Him? When you finally relinquished it into His hands, how quickly did you experience an answer to your specific prayer requests?
3. Is there anything you need to yield to the Lord in your life right now? Write down whatever comes to mind that you need to release to Him.

We must never stop short of thanking God for answering our prayers and requests before we ever see the answers manifested.

MAY 16

❦

There's a Time for You To Be Inflexible and Unmoving!

Let us hold fast the profession of our faith without wavering;
(for he is faithful that promised;).
— Hebrews 10:23

Maybe you've been muttering to yourself, "Come on! I've waited and waited for my dream to come to pass. God hasn't done anything I thought He was going to do. I've seen others blessed; I've seen others healed; but I'm still sitting here with the same old unanswered prayers. I'm sick of it all! I'm not going to believe and wait any longer. Forget it — I'm letting it all go!"

If this sounds like you, I want to encourage you to take a look at Hebrews 10:23. It says, "Let us hold fast the profession of our faith without wavering...."

We already looked at the words "hold fast" (*see* March 20) and "profession" (*see* May 7), but today I want to take you one step further and draw your attention to the word "waver" in this powerful verse of Scripture. The word "waver" is taken from the Greek *aklines*, which conveys the picture of *something that does not bend* or *something that is fixed and unmoving* and is therefore *stable* and *enduring*.

Interestingly, if you remove the *a* from the word *aklines,* you are left with the word *klines*, which pictures *a person who is bowed down.* With shoulders sloped and body bent over, this person is so tired that he can barely stand. Ultimately, he becomes so exhausted that he throws in the towel and gives up. In fact, the word *klines* is the same root in Greek for *a couch* or *a bed.* So when a person is *klines,* his "give-up" attitude causes him to head for the couch or bed where he lays down, stagnates, and vegetates.

But as noted above, when the *a* is added to the front of the word, it forms the word *aklines,* which is just the opposite of a lazy person! Instead, this portrays an attitude that is *unbending, unchanging, fixed, stable, and unmoving.* In other words, this person has too much invested to go to bed on his faith. He therefore refuses to budge an inch on what he is believing to see or to receive!

Hebrews 10:23 could be interpreted to mean:
(*refer to* March 20 and May 7)

"Let us come into agreement with God and begin to speak what He says, tightly wrapping our arms around the promise we are confessing — embracing it with all our might, holding tightly to it, rejecting all attempts of anyone who tries to steal it from us, not allowing ourselves to be fickle in our commitment, but determined to be inflexible and unmoving from that which we believe and confess...."

Many people give up hope and quit believing because they get tired of waiting. The devil whispers in their ears and tells them, *"This thing you're believing for isn't ever going to happen! If it was going to happen, it would have already happened by now! This is just a fantasy. You are wasting your time and throwing away precious years of your life. Why don't you forget it, let it go, and move on with your life?"*

As long as you are energized by faith, you'll keep moving in a forward direction. But the day you let loose of your faith and back off your position, it won't be too long until a spiritual sadness will come over your life. Spiritually speaking, your shoulders will slope; your head will drop; and you'll feel like someone pulled the plug on your energy level. Your eyes will drift toward the couch or bed, and soon you'll end up completely going to bed on your faith!

Don't let that happen to you! What God promises, He *will* perform. It may take awhile for that promise to come into manifestation, but eventually it will come. In the meantime, you must choose to believe that He will do what He has promised. That is the key! You must set your heart and commit your will, making an irrevocable decision to believe His Word regardless of how you feel, what you think in your natural mind, what others say, or how circumstances look.

It is time for you to make the decision that you have too much invested to turn back now! Dig in your heels; drive down your stake; and tell the devil that you are *not* going to move from your position of faith! Aggressively choose to believe that what God has promised, He will always do. Once you've made that kind of life-changing decision, it's only a matter of time before you'll be rejoicing!

When you finally put your foot down, the devil will stop uttering his lying accusations and he will flee from you. You will be mightily blessed and very thankful that you didn't give up when you see the confession of your faith finally begin to come into manifestation!

MY PRAYER FOR TODAY

Lord, I've tolerated the devil's lies long enough. Today I am making the decision to put my foot down. I'm going to tell the enemy to shut his mouth and flee from me! I have made my choice that I will stand by Your promise and will never retreat from what You have told me to believe and confess. You are not a man that You should lie, and I believe Your Word to be true for my life. Holy Spirit, give me the strength I need to stay fixed, immovable, and steadfast until I finally see the manifestation of those things that I believe!

I pray this in Jesus' name!

MY CONFESSION FOR TODAY

I confess that I don't waver or bend and that I am fixed and unmoving as I stand on the promises of God. What God promises, He will perform. It may take awhile for that promise to come into manifestation, but I know it is on the way right now! I dig in my heels; I drive down my stake; and I tell the devil that I am NOT going to move from my position of faith!

I declare this by faith in Jesus' name!

QUESTIONS FOR YOU TO CONSIDER

1. Think of three times when you were tempted to quit believing on the verge of the manifestation of your answer. Write these experiences down; then take a few minutes to thank God that you didn't quit believing just before the blessing came!
2. Can you name specific promises from God's Word that you are currently believing to come into manifestation in your life?

3. Can you remember a time when you gave in to the devil's lies and threw in the towel on your fight of faith, only to discover just a little later that you would have received your answer if only you had held on a little longer?

MAY 17

When You're Discouraged And Ready To Give Up, Here's What You Should Do!

But call to remembrance the former days, in which,
after ye were illuminated, ye endured a great fight of afflictions.
— Hebrews 10:32

What should you do when you're feeling discouraged and dangerously close to doubting God's integrity — when you start thinking He just might not come through for you? Hebrews 10:32 tells us what we are to do when we find ourselves in this situation. It says, "But call to remembrance the former days, in which, after ye were illuminated...."

This verse was written to believers who were so discouraged that they were tempted to give up and throw away their strong position of faith. They had been waiting a long time to see God's promises come to pass, and they had begun to feel like their answer would never come. But just when they were about to give up, they read this verse that reminded them of when they were first "illuminated."

The word "illuminated" comes from the Greek word *photidzo*, which means *to lighten up, to shine, to illuminate, to make visible,* or *to radiate.* It gives the impression of *a brilliant flash of light* that leaves a permanent and lasting impression. We get "*photo*graphy" from this word, which calls to mind the blinding flash on a camera. This word is used here in order to help these struggling believers put their present hardships "on pause" for a few minutes so they can remember what they experienced when they heard the Word of God for the first time and were "illuminated."

Maybe you can remember a time in your own life when it was as if someone suddenly flipped the light switch and turned on the light, removing the darkness from your eyes so you could see things clearly? That's exactly how I felt when the Spirit of God finally revealed the truth of the baptism in the Holy Spirit to me. I *saw* it! I *understood* it! I was *illuminated* by that truth. The Spirit's brilliant flash of light upon my mind was so strong that it made a permanent and lasting impression on my life. In fact, I've never been the same since!

Can you think of a time in your life when the Holy Spirit "illuminated" you regarding some truth? Perhaps He illuminated you regarding healing. Did it feel like your eyes were finally opened and you understood the work of the Cross in a new and different light? Or perhaps you were illuminated about the power of giving. After struggling with giving for all those years, it was like someone pulled back the veil that blinded your understanding — and *boom*! You *saw* it! You were *illuminated* about giving, and the light of that truth made a permanent and lasting impression on your life!

Do you remember the first time the Word of God shot through your being like a bolt of lightning? You saw the truth, and it brought perfect order out of the chaos in your life! How about the first time God spoke to your heart about His dream of greatness for your life? Do you remember the joy you felt?

When you get discouraged and are tempted to give up — when times are tough and your faith isn't finding its fulfillment as quickly as you desire — you must decide to put everything on hold. Tell your mind to be silent; command your emotions to be stilled; and *remember* when you were first *illuminated* to the truths of God's Word.

That is precisely why Hebrews 10:32 urges us, "But call to remembrance the former days, in which, after ye were illuminated…." The words "former days" is from the Greek word *proteron*. This word points the readers back to *earlier times* when they first met the Lord and when they were filled to overflowing with joy, hope, and faith. But now, years have passed. These believers have gone through a lot of struggles, and weariness has set in. Many of their prayers remain unanswered; the devil is telling them that none of the answers they are waiting to see manifested will ever come to pass; and they are tempted to quit.

Sometimes when you are discouraged, it's good to hit the rewind button in your mind and drift backward to earlier experiences with the Lord when faith was simple and life was uncomplicated. Do you remember how precious those days were? Do you recall how changed you were by the power of God? Do you remember the laughter and joy you experienced? It's good for you to rehearse those experiences because they stir you up, encourage you, and summon strength for the battle you are facing right now.

**In light of these Greek words,
Hebrews 10:32 conveys this idea:**

"You need to remember and never forget what it was like back in the early days — how your eyes were opened and you really saw the truth for the first time…."

Your divine calling, your God-given dream, must be an illumination in your heart that you can call to remembrance over and over again. Call to remembrance how God first spoke to you, and meditate on the promise He made to you. This will help you get past the weariness that's trying to pull you down. *Keep your dream shining brilliantly in your heart and mind — a powerful illumination and revelation that lights your way through any darkness the enemy might bring against you!*

MY PRAYER FOR TODAY

Lord, help me to never forget those early experiences I had with You after I first got saved. I'm so sorry I've allowed the complexities of life to steal my joy, and today I ask You to help me return to the simplicity of faith I once enjoyed. I admit I've been discouraged, but today I am deciding to get encouraged! Thank You for helping me to refocus and to remember that Your Word is unchanging and Your promises are true!

I pray this in Jesus' name!

MY CONFESSION FOR TODAY

I boldly confess that discouragement has no place in me! God's Word is true; the devil is a liar; and my circumstances are not permanent. And with God's power, I will rise above the situations I face today! I decide it; I declare it; and I pronounce it to be true!

I declare this by faith in Jesus' name!

1. What thoughts stir in your heart when you stop and remember the early days after you first came to the Lord? Can you remember how precious and exciting it was back in those days?
2. What one word would you use to describe what your Christian life was like in those early days after you were first illuminated?
3. Can you recall a time when you were specially "illuminated" by the Spirit of God regarding some Bible truth? What was that truth, and how did this "illumination" affect your life?

MAY 18

Intellectual Power Alone Is Not Sufficient To Do the Job

And I, brethren, when I came to you,
came not with excellency of speech or of wisdom,
declaring unto you the testimony of God.
For I determined not to know any thing among you,
save Jesus Christ, and him crucified.
— 1 Corinthians 2:1,2

*A*fter Paul was finished preaching to the intellectual leaders in Athens, he left the city feeling disappointed and sad. He preached in the great amphitheater on Mars Hill to a packed audience of intellectual pagans who yearned to hear his strange message about resurrection from the dead (*see* Acts 17:22).

In his sermon, Paul did everything perfect from a cultural standpoint. He used a idol from their city as an example of his message — something that showed them honor and surely must have gotten their attention (*see* Acts 17:23). He quoted their poets and philosophers (Acts 17:28), reaching out to them with their own culture and proving that he was a man of learning, worthy of addressing such an intellectual audience. With this mixture of culture, brain power, and the Word, Paul attempted to reach the leaders in Athens.

From a natural standpoint, Paul's message was *brilliant*. Seminaries, schools of theology, and Bible school instructors would applaud any student who preached a message as exceptional as Paul's sermon was that day. The message is a superb example for missionaries who invade new cultures as they preach the Gospel in the farthest extremes of the world. It excels at demonstrating how to use culture to reach a group that has never heard the Gospel before.

Yet when Paul finished preaching that day and the meeting was dismissed, the results of his masterpiece were dismal and depressing. The Bible says, "And when they heard of the resurrection of the dead, some mocked: and others said, We will hear thee again of this matter" (Acts 17:32).

After the meeting, it appears that a group of people stayed in Paul's company, of which a small, unspecified number became believers (v. 34).

When Paul walked out of Athens on the road to Corinth, he must have thought about what happened in Athens. Why weren't more saved? How could they walk out mocking after such a masterful message was preached? It was the perfect sermon — the right mix of brains, culture, and the Word — so why hadn't it produced a better effect? As he pondered on these questions, he came to a *conclusion!* That conclusion is contained in First Corinthians 2:1-4.

In verse 1, Paul writes to the Corinthians, "And I, brethren, when I came to you, came not with excellency of speech or of wisdom, declaring unto you the testimony of God." Paul had nothing against excellency of speech, wisdom, or brain power, but in Athens he had taken a purely intellectual approach to preaching, and he was less than satisfied with the results. Afterward, Paul determined that he would never again lean entirely upon the power of his intellect to accomplish the job of preaching.

Athens was a very religious city (*see* Acts 17:22) in which pagan religions and temples filled with the supernatural were in abundant supply. For instance, Athens had the Temple of Dionysius, a temple where prophecies and supernatural manifestations were regularly heard and witnessed. Athens also had the famous Temple of Asklepios. This was a temple where people came to be supernaturally healed by the Greek god of healing, whose image had a serpent wrapped around his legs. There were many other temples in Athens where supernatural occurrences were reported. These supernatural events were seen to be *the proof* that these religions were true.

Because of this, the Athenians didn't just intellectually believe their religions; they had seen supernatural proof that made them believe. Although the supernatural activities in these temples were demonic, it was nevertheless real supernatural activity.

Thus, Paul's mistake in Athens was that he forgot to *demonstrate the supernatural!* In a city like that, it wasn't enough to come with words only. If the Athenians were ever to believe in Jesus, it was essential to preach the Gospel with the power of signs and wonders following.

If you carefully read Acts 17, you will find this is the one element that was missing from Paul's message. So as he approached Corinth — another very supernatural city — Paul resolved that he would never again make the mistake of preaching without supernatural signs and wonders. This is why he said, "And my speech and my preaching [to the Corinthians after Paul left Athens] was not with enticing words of man's wisdom, but in demonstration of the Spirit and of power" (1 Corinthians 2:4).

The word "enticing" is the Greek word *peitho*, which means *to persuade, to entice,* or *to convince*. However, this word also carries the notion of *craftily trying to coax someone to believe.* In addition, it expresses the idea of someone who is trying *to sweet-talk* a person into taking some type of action. Apparently, Paul looks upon his ministry in Athens as a futile attempt to intellectually sweet-talk the Athenian intellectuals into faith. Because it failed so miserably, he declares he will never do it again!

He writes that he will never again try to entice a crowd with "man's wisdom." The word "wisdom" is the Greek word *sophos* — the word for *wisdom that is attained naturally.* Although this kind of wisdom is respected, rare, and honored in society, it is nonetheless insufficient to produce the power that is needed for the preaching of the Gospel.

In conclusion, Paul declares that from henceforth he will preach with a "…demonstration of the Spirit and of power" (v. 4). The word "demonstration" comes from the Greek word *apodeiknumi* — a word that indisputably refers to *something that is outwardly seen* or *something visible that authenticates, proves, and guarantees the message to be true.* It means *to display* or even *to show off.*

When preaching to a crowd like this, it was mandatory to do it with the vindicating power of supernatural signs and wonders. Because this was a society dominated by superstition and demonic activity, the people needed *supernatural proof to authenticate* the fact that God was behind the message being preached to them. This demonstration of power would get their attention more than anything else. Their thinking was similar to that of Nicodemus in John 3:2, when he told Jesus: "…Rabbi, we know that thou art a teacher come from God: for no man can do these miracles that thou doest, except God be with him."

From that point onward, Paul determined to have a supernatural ministry. No, he didn't abandon his brains, nor did he stop using culture to help him connect to the hearts of the people. But Paul never again preached without the authority of signs and wonders to verify that he was God's man and that the message he preached was God's message. All those who saw the mighty "demonstration of the Spirit and of power" that operated through Paul in his ministry knew that God was speaking to them!

As you share Jesus with your friends, family, fellow employees, or acquaintances, you should certainly present the Gospel in an intellectual format that can be easily understood. But don't be remiss and forget that the supernatural working power of the Holy Spirit is available to confirm the message you are telling your friends, family, and acquaintances. *If you've made the mistake of trying to present the Gospel only through the power of your intellect, you now have an opportunity to repent and ask the Holy Spirit to come alongside to help you do a better job!*

MY PRAYER FOR TODAY

Lord, I want to tell You that I am sorry for the many times I've tried to present the Gospel to others in the power of my intellect and flesh, failing to let the Holy Spirit confirm the Word with signs following. I have been timid and shy about moving in the power of God, but I know it's time for me to push that timidity aside. To the best of my ability and with sincerity of heart, I am telling You today that I want Your Gospel-proving power to flow through me.

I pray this in Jesus' name!

MY CONFESSION FOR TODAY

I declare by faith that I am not timid or afraid! God wants to pour His power through me, and I am receptive and open to His using me in this wonderful way. People need the power of God, and God wants to use me to bring His miraculous touch into their lives. I am bold and confident — and I am growing bolder and more confident every day!

I declare this by faith in Jesus' name!

QUESTIONS FOR YOU TO CONSIDER

1. Have you ever felt that your presentation of the Gospel to unbelievers lacked power?
2. Is there a reason you are timid about letting the Holy Spirit and His gifts work through you when presenting the Gospel to unbelievers? If yes, what is that reason, and what steps do you need to take to start getting rid of this fear?

3. What kind of difference do you honestly think it would make if signs and wonders accompanied you every time you spoke the Gospel to people who are unsaved? For instance, do you think that a supernatural healing of their sick bodies would get their attention more quickly?

MAY 19

Is Jesus Testing You?

When Jesus then lifted up his eyes, and saw a great company
come unto him, he saith unto Philip, Whence shall we buy bread,
that these may eat? And this he said to prove him:
for he himself knew what he would do.
— John 6:5,6

*A*fter ministering to multitudes for numerous days, Jesus and His disciples privately retreated to the top of a mountainside just outside Jerusalem. It was the time of the feast, and before He and the twelve entered the city, "...Jesus went up into a mountain, and there he sat with his disciples" (John 6:3).

The word "sat" is the Greek word *kathemai*, implying that they *reclined* on the slopes of the mountainside. Certainly they must have been tired, because they had been ministering to multitudes of people who were following them for many days. So before Jesus and His men entered Jerusalem to resume their ministry activities, they took a break on top of a mountain apart from the crowd, where they could enjoy a cool, refreshing breeze and a welcome rest.

Suddenly, "...Jesus then lifted up his eyes, and saw a great company come unto him..." (John 6:5). The word "saw" is from the word *theaomai*, our word for a *theater*. It means *to really look*, like a patron who attends a play and carefully watches every act, listening attentively to every word because he doesn't want to miss anything important in the play. By using this word, John lets us know that Jesus carefully looked out at this crowd in amazement — observing the entire scene, analyzing the size of the crowd, and determining what needed to be done for them.

The words "great company" in Greek are the words *polus ochlos*. These are exactly the same words used to describe the massive number of soldiers who came to arrest Jesus in the Garden of Gethsemane (*see* April 4). This was a *massive crowd* of people.

As that vast crowd marched toward Jesus on the mountainside, Jesus turned to Philip and asked, "...Whence shall we buy bread, that these may eat?" (John 6:5). The word "buy" is the Greek word *agoradzo*, from the word *agora*, which describes *a marketplace*. When it becomes the word *agoradzo*, as it appears in this verse, it means *to purchase something at the marketplace*. But this was a strange question for Jesus to put to Philip, because they were seated on top of a remote mountain where there were no markets!

In fact, Mark 6:36 tells us the disciples were worried about where to buy food for this crowd. In fact, they pleaded with Jesus, "Send them away, that they may go into the country round about, and into the villages, and buy themselves bread...."

There was simply no place nearby to purchase bread for the people on that mountaintop. Even if there had been a local shop nearby, it wouldn't have been possible to purchase enough bread to feed a crowd that size — a crowd of "five thousand men" (John 6:10), plus "women and children" (Matthew 14:21). Yet in spite of the huge crowd and the impossibility of the situation, Jesus asked Philip, "…Whence shall we buy bread, that these may eat?"

John 6:6 goes on to tell us the reason Jesus asked this question: "And this he said to prove him: for he himself knew what he would do." The word "prove" is the word *peiradzo*, which means to *put to the test, to test in order to prove,* or *to test in order to expose the truth about the quality of a substance.* An example of this is how the word *peiradzo* was used to describe the purifying fires placed under molten metal. The metal may have looked strong, but only a blazing fire could *expose* all the hidden defects. Once the defects were exposed, they could be scraped off and removed, but without the test of fire they would remain undetectable. This test wasn't just done for the sake of testing, but to assure that the metal would be purer, finer, and stronger. In other words, the purpose of the test was to make the item *better*.

Jesus asked Philip this question to *expose* any deficiency in His disciple's faith. You see, these disciples had lived in the presence of Jesus and had seen Him perform every kind of creative miracle, including turning water into wine, cleansing lepers, and even raising the dead. Miracles were nothing novel to them. But at this moment, they were being confronted with a problem that was totally different from anything they had faced before — *they needed food to feed a multitude*!

It is amazing to me that after seeing Jesus perform possibly thousands of miracles, the disciples didn't immediately say, "Lord, we trust that You can provide for all these people!" Instead, they went on a food search and frantically tried to solve this problem by themselves.

Philip certainly didn't consider a supernatural solution. In verse 7, he and the other disciples began to "grasp at straws" as they went looking for a way to solve this problem through natural means. Philip told Jesus, "…Two hundred pennyworth of bread is not sufficient for them, that every one of them may take a little" (v. 7). Philip didn't realize God's stores of supernatural provision are always *more* than enough!

It is simply a fact that new challenges often expose a deficiency in our faith and accentuate any weak area in our lives. Jesus knew exactly how He was going to meet the need, but He asked Philip the question so Philip's lack of faith would be exposed — and so the disciples would see that there was still room for improvement in regard to the level of their faith!

Don't be surprised if Jesus asks you to do something that seems impossible to your natural mind. When He tells you that He expects you to take a leap of faith and accomplish what others say can't be done, His request may expose the fact that you need to work a little more on your faith! What a blessing that Jesus would ask us to do things that reveal who we really are — for only then will we really discover the areas of our faith that need improvement!

So the next time Jesus gives you a fabulous, impossible-looking job to do, rejoice if it reveals a little shakiness in your ability to believe. Now you know that you have a deficiency in your faith walk — and you can start today to do something about it!

MY PRAYER FOR TODAY

Lord, I want to thank You for allowing me to be a part of Your great plans. You could use someone else, but You have chosen to use me. For this, I am so thankful to You. If there is any faith deficiency in me, please expose it NOW so I can get it fixed and be prepared for any assignment You give to me in the future!

I pray this in Jesus' name!

MY CONFESSION FOR TODAY

I confess that I am ready for God to use me! My faith is growing. It's getting stronger, and the deficiency in my faith is being reduced day by day. There was a time when I was weak, but now God's Word is making me stronger. There was a time when I would have doubted and feared, but now I am filled with faith. In fact, I'm excited about taking on ANY assignment Jesus Christ wants to give me!

I declare this by faith in Jesus' name!

QUESTIONS FOR YOU TO CONSIDER

1. Has Jesus ever asked you to do something that seemed impossible? How did you first react to the Lord when He put the big question to you and asked you to do something that seemed so impossible to do?
2. When you stepped out to do what He asked, what happened? Did you see His miraculous power at work and learn that God can do the impossible?
3. What should you be doing right now to improve the level of your faith so you have no deficiency the next time Jesus asks you to do something that is impossible in the natural?

MAY 20

The 'Kratos' Power of God!

Finally, my brethren, be strong in the Lord,
and in the power of his might.
— Ephesians 6:10

I n Ephesians 6:10, the apostle Paul gives us some very important insight into the kind of power God has made available to every believer — including you! This is really important for you to understand because it describes the kind of power that God wants to operate through you, so be sure to carefully read every word of this *Sparkling Gem*.

First, let me remind you that Ephesians 6:10 is a verse about the supernatural power God has made available for our fight with unseen, demonic powers that come to war against the soul. The word "strong" used at the first of this verse is taken from the word *endunamao*, which describes *a power whose purpose is to infuse a believer with an excessive dose of inward strength*. This particular type of *endunamao* power is so strong that it can withstand any attack and successfully oppose any kind of force (*see* January 12).

A historical study of this word proves its supernatural nature. It was used by early writers from the Greek classical periods to denote special individuals, like Hercules, who had been handpicked by the gods and supernaturally invested with superhuman strength in order to accomplish a superhuman task. Now Paul uses this word *endunamao* to tell us that God has made this kind of supernatural strength available to believers in Jesus Christ!

Let's see what else Paul tells us about this power. In Ephesians 6:10, he says, "Finally, my brethren, be strong in the Lord, and in the power of his might." Especially notice the words "power" and "might." Today we will look at the word "power," and tomorrow we will look at the word "might."

The word "power" is taken from the Greek word *kratos*, and it describes what I have come to call *demonstrated power*. In other words, *kratos* power is not a power that one merely adheres to and believes in intellectually. Rather, this *kratos* power is a power that is *demonstrative, eruptive,* and *tangible*. It almost always comes with some type of external, outward manifestation that one can actually see with his or her eyes. This means that *kratos* power is not a hypothetical power; this is *real* power!

Ephesians 1:19,20 declares that when God raised Jesus from the dead, He used this very same *kratos* power to do the job! It says, "And what is the exceeding greatness of his power to us-ward who believe, according to the working of his mighty power [*kratos*], which he wrought in Christ when he raised him from the dead...."

The *King James Version* is a bit reversed from the original Greek. The Greek says, "...according to the power of his might...." *Why is this difference so important?* Because the phrase "the power of his might" is the same identical phrase used in Ephesians 6:10 to denote the power that is working behind the scenes to energize us! This power that God used when He raised Jesus from the dead is the same, exact, identical power that is now at work in us. *That means we have resurrection power working in our lives!*

Kratos power is so overwhelming that the Roman soldiers who guarded Jesus' tomb on that resurrection morning fainted and crumbled to the ground beneath the full load of this divine force. And the soldiers continued to lie prostrate on the ground, paralyzed and unable to move, until the resurrection was complete.

This *kratos* power was indomitable, overpowering, and irresistible on that day long ago. Flooding the grave where Jesus' dead body lay, this conquering power permeated every dead cell and fiber of His body with divine life until it was impossible for death to hold Him any longer!

God's *kratos* power was so overwhelming that, had we been present at the resurrection, we would have felt the ground trembling as this electrifying force entered the tomb where Jesus' body lay. The power that raised Jesus from the dead was an eruptive power, a demonstrated power, an outwardly visible power. *It was the strongest kind of power known to God or man.*

And now Paul uses this very word to describe the power that is available for our use! With this empowering Presence of the Holy Spirit working in our lives, we can *expect* the very same power that raised Jesus from the dead to operate in us! Remember, this is a demonstrated or outwardly manifested kind of power, so when this power begins to operate in us, it immediately seeks an avenue of release so it can *demonstrate* itself.

So turn up your level of expectation! Start anticipating that this mighty power of God will begin to flow through you!

MY PRAYER FOR TODAY

Lord, I thank You for making such power available to me. Now I see that I have no excuse to ever complain that I am weak, for You have placed at my disposal the very power of the resurrection itself. Teach me how to tap into that power so it can be released in my life. I know that this power is the answer for many people's needs and that You want it to flow through me. Holy Spirit, as my Great Teacher, please teach me how to open my heart wide so the river of Your divine goodness can flow through me.

I pray this in Jesus' name!

MY CONFESSION FOR TODAY

I confess that God's indomitable, overpowering, conquering, and irresistible power flows through me! The very power that raised Jesus from the dead resides and operates in my life. It is an eruptive power; it is a demonstrated power; and it is an outwardly visible power — the strongest kind of power known to God or man. With this empowering Presence of the Holy Spirit working in me, I expect the power that raised Jesus from the dead to operate in my life. I deliberately turn up my level of expectation and anticipate this mighty power of God to begin to flow through me!

I declare this by faith in Jesus' name!

QUESTIONS FOR YOU TO CONSIDER

1. If you were asked to give a personal testimony regarding a time in your life when you actually experienced a special touch of God's supernatural power, what experience would you talk about? Could you relate more than one experience?
2. What do you imagine it was like for the soldiers on resurrection morning? What do you think they felt, saw, or heard as the power of God surged into that tomb and raised Jesus from the dead?
3. If you could choose to witness any kind of miracle, what kind would you want to see?

MAY 21

The 'Ischuos' Power of God!

Finally, my brethren, be strong in the Lord,
and in the power of his might.
— Ephesians 6:10

*I*n yesterday's *Sparkling Gem*, we began looking at the kinds of power that God has made available to every believer. As noted yesterday, He has provided two kinds of power for every Christian. The first is *kratos* power, which is a demonstrative, eruptive, manifested power. But today we will look at a second word in Ephesians 6:10 that describes a second kind of power made available to the believer.

In Ephesians 6:10, Paul says, "Finally, my brethren, be strong in the Lord, and in the power of his might." The word "might" is taken from the word *ischuos*, and it conveys the picture of *a very, very strong man, such as a bodybuilder* or *a mighty man with great muscular capabilities*. Now Paul applies this picture of a strong, muscular man, not to himself, but to *God*. Paul pictures God as One who is *able, mighty, and muscular*.

Let me ask you — is there anyone more powerful than God? Is there any force in the universe equal to the muscular ability of God? Consider this:

✦ With one stroke of the hand, God's mighty arm released so much creative power that the entire universe was flung into being.

✦ With one stroke of the hand, God's mighty arm discharged such incredible force that the civilized world of Noah's day was flooded and an entire period of civilization was wiped out.

✦ With one stroke of God's mighty arm, Egypt's rebellion against Him was crushed beyond recognition, and the children of Israel were set free.

✦ With one stroke of God's mighty arm, the wicked powers of the heavenlies were forcibly shoved aside, and although it was physically and medically impossible, Jesus was conceived and miraculously born from a virgin's womb.

✦ With one stroke of God's mighty arm, His power surged into the throes of hell itself, where it ripped Jesus out of the pangs of death, stripped demonic principalities and powers naked, and made a public display of their embarrassing defeat.

✦ When the mighty arm of God moved on the day of Pentecost, the Holy Spirit came as a "rushing mighty wind" and filled the Upper Room with His awesome power, supernaturally enabling the disciples to preach the Word with signs and wonders following.

Where is this powerful, mighty ability of God working today? *In you and me!* Paul says, "Finally, my brethren, be strong in the Lord, and in *the power of his might*."

Remember, the word *kratos* is the demonstrated, outwardly manifested, eruptive power of God, which now operates in every believer. But the *ischuos* we have looked at today is the force that works behind the *kratos* power! Why is *kratos* power so strong and demonstrative (as in the resurrection of Jesus from the dead)? Because God's muscles (*ischuos*) are backing it up!

These words in Ephesians 6:10 are so powerful
that they convey this idea:

"Be strong in the Lord and in the powerful, outwardly demonstrated ability that works in you as a result of God's great muscular ability that is working behind the scenes."

All that God is, all the power He possesses, and all the energy of His muscular, mighty ability now energizes the *kratos* power that is at work within you. With this power at your disposal today, you can confront the unseen demonic spirits that come to wage war against your flesh and your soul — and you can win every time! Since this power is available to you today, you are ready to lay hands on the sick, pray with power and authority, speak the word of faith in every situation, and see mountains move on your behalf!

So the next time you run into a problem that seems a little overwhelming, remind yourself that "…greater is he that is in you than he that is in the world" (1 John 4:4). You have no need to be afraid and no need to shrink back in timidity, for there's enough power at work in you to resist any force that comes against you and to supernaturally remedy anything that needs to be changed!

MY PRAYER FOR TODAY

Lord, I am so thankful that Your muscles are the backup for the power that operates in my life! Just as Your mighty arm created the universe, divided the Red Sea, destroyed the Egyptians, ripped Jesus from the throes of hell, and raised Him from the dead, I know that now this mighty power also works in me. Help me learn how to flow with this power and allow it to be released through my life so I can be a bigger blessing to people who are around me.

I pray this in Jesus' name!

MY CONFESSION FOR TODAY

I boldly confess that all that God is, all the power He possesses, and all the energy of His muscular, mighty ability now energizes me! With this power at my disposal, I confront every spirit that comes to wage war against me. I lay hands on the sick and see them recover; I pray with power and authority; I speak the word of faith to every situation I face. Therefore, mountains move on my behalf! Greater is He who is in me than he that is in the world. I have no need to be afraid, and I don't shrink back in timidity, because there's enough power at work in me to resist any force that comes against me and to supernaturally remedy anything that is out of God's order in my life!

I declare this by faith in Jesus' name!

QUESTIONS FOR YOU TO CONSIDER

1. Can you name a time in your life when you suddenly felt so *energized* and *quickened* by the Spirit of God that it was as if a river of power flowed through you to help you get something important accomplished? When did that happen, and what triggered the release of that power?
2. Do you deliberately pray for God's power to operate in your life? If so, do you expect your prayer to be answered? If you don't pray for God's power to be operative in your life, why not?
3. Why don't you take a few minutes to remember the miracles you have personally witnessed in your life?

With God's power at your disposal, you can confront the unseen demonic spirits that come to wage war against your flesh and your soul — *and you can win every time*! Since this power is available to you today, you are ready to lay hands on the sick, pray with power and authority, speak the word of faith in every situation, and see mountains move on your behalf!

MAY 22

Learning How To Be Quiet When Others Are Speaking

Wherefore, my beloved brethren, let every man be swift to hear,
slow to speak, slow to wrath.
— James 1:19

O ne of the biggest lessons to learn in life is to know when you need to be quiet and when you need to speak up. For instance, if someone over you in authority is trying to tell you something, that's a time for you to be quiet and listen to what the authority is attempting to tell you. In order to really hear what he or she is trying to communicate, *you have to stop talking!* Listening and talking at the same time almost always guarantees that you are going to miss important facts and details.

In James 1:19, the Bible says, "Wherefore, my beloved brethren, let every man be swift to hear, slow to speak, slow to wrath." The word "swift" in this verse is the Greek word *tachus*. It can be used to depict *a runner who runs as fast as he can so he can reach the finish line before his competitors.* Because this runner fiercely wants to win the race, he puts everything else out of his mind, focuses on the finish line, and then presses forward to obtain the first-place prize.

**Because of the word *tachus*,
the first part of James 1:19 could be rendered:**

"Wherefore, my beloved brethren, set your focus on becoming a good listener — and do it with all your might, as if you are in a competition to win the race of being the best listener...."

James is telling us that we should desire to win "first place" when it comes to listening! Because the word *tachus* depicts a runner that is totally *focused* on reaching the finish line, James lets us know that it takes *effort* to slow our minds down so we can hear what other people are trying to communicate to us. I am referring to that moment when we deliberately quiet our minds and shut our mouths in order to *intentionally listen to* and *digest* what someone else is endeavoring to tell us. This is a challenge for any of us who have busy minds and a lot of details in our lives to think about.

Take me, for example. If I don't make the choice to slow down and really *focus* on what someone is telling me, I know I will miss much of what he or she is trying to communicate. My mind is busy all the time. I have a church to pastor, a ministry to oversee, and television programs to film. I go on ministry trips that take me all over the world. I am constantly writing books. Besides all that, I am a husband and father. I rarely have a moment when I don't have some important matter pressing heavily on my mind.

I've learned that I must discipline myself to listen to what people are saying to me. Otherwise, they'll think I'm listening when, in reality, I'm about a million miles away in my thoughts. Just because I'm looking into their eyes doesn't mean I'm really listening. If I'm going to hear what they're communicating, I have to push everything else out of my mind and deliberately *focus* on what they're saying. This is a matter of discipline that I've had to work at developing in my life.

I made a decision years ago that if a person believes he has something important enough to say to me, the least I can do is give him the courtesy of listening. Even if I don't agree with what he's saying or want to do what he's asking, I should respect him enough to hear him out. To pretend I'm listening when I'm not is simply rude.

Through the years I've had to train myself to be a listener. To make sure I've really heard the point being made to me, I often stop and repeat the conversation to the person speaking to me. I ask the person:

- ✦ "Is this what you're trying to tell me?"
- ✦ "Is this the point you're making to me today?"
- ✦ "Is this what you want me to get from this conversation?"
- ✦ "Is this what you want me to do after we're done talking?"
- ✦ "Is this how I need to respond?"
- ✦ "Is there anything else I need to know about this?"

If I've missed anything important in the conversation or misunderstood what that person was attempting to tell me, I discover it by asking these kinds of questions. At the same time, the person speaking to me is assured that he has had my complete and total attention. When my conversation with that person is finished, I should understand exactly what he was communicating because I *focused* on him and *listened* to what he was telling me.

Those who cultivate and develop the skill of listening make good team players because they're better able to understand other people's opinions and positions. These people have a good foundation for success because *listening is the first step of communication.*

If you realize that you need to become a better listener, I urge you to make the decision to cultivate and develop this discipline in your life. You *can* be a first-place runner when it comes to listening to others. Remember, listening is the first step of communication, and communication is a prerequisite for success in your dealings with both God and man!

So make it a top priority to become a superb listener. Learn how to digest the information other people are trying so desperately to communicate to you!

MY PRAYER FOR TODAY

Lord, it is true that I need to learn how to be a better listener. Forgive me for the times I've inconvenienced others and messed up their plans because I didn't carefully listen to the instructions that everyone else obviously understood. I recognize that this is a flaw in my life. Starting today, I want to discipline myself to become a top-notch listener. For me to do this, I know I'll have to break the habit of thinking about other things when people are trying to talk to me. So I'm turning to You to help me silence my mind, listen to others, digest what they are saying, and become a better team player!

I pray this in Jesus' name!

MY CONFESSION FOR TODAY

I confess that I am quick to hear what others are trying to tell me, and I don't interrupt them when they are speaking. I am a first-place runner when it comes to listening to others. Because God's Spirit is helping me, I am getting better and better in this area of my life. As a result, I am an effective team player, and others enjoy working with me.

I declare this by faith in Jesus' name!

1. Have you ever tried to talk to someone who you knew wasn't really listening to you? How did it make you feel? Did you think that person really cared about what you were saying to him or her?

2. Are you a good listener? Are you able to remember what others have told you? If your answer is no, what are you going to do to develop better listening skills?

3. Can you think of someone at work, at church, or in your family who constantly makes mistakes because he doesn't clearly listen to the instructions that are given to him? What kind of inconvenience does this create for everyone?

MAY 23

When Are You Supposed To Help Bear Someone Else's Burden?

Bear ye one another's burdens,
and so fulfil the law of Christ.
— Galatians 6:2

Not so long ago, a precious woman in our congregation came to church looking sad and depressed. It was unusual to see her this way, because she was normally cheerful and full of faith. She sat in her chair, dropped her head, and began to weep. I wanted to go to her right then, but she had come into the service late, and I was on stage getting ready to step up to the pulpit to preach.

As I delivered my message, I kept glancing in her direction to see if she was still crying. Her head remained clutched in her hands, and I could see that she was sobbing about something that was greatly burdening her heart. When the service concluded, I went with my pastoral staff into the foyer to shake hands with people who were leaving the service. Soon she appeared in the line with heavy red eyes and a countenance that told me she was heartbroken over something.

I pulled her out of the line and called for my precious wife. Soon the two of them were sitting alone at the far end of the foyer where they could talk without anyone overhearing the conversation. The woman told Denise that her husband, who had been delivered from alcoholism, had started to drink again. That weekend he had been violent toward her and verbally abusive toward the children, acting like the old man he used to be. The woman's heart was simply crushed, but by the time she and Denise were finished talking and praying together, her face had lightened up, her countenance had changed, and it was evident that God had stirred hope in her heart for her family.

I often think of how many church members come to church burdened by the cares of life. Perhaps the burdens they carry are due to finances, marriage, friendships, a problem at work, a child who is rebellious or who is running from God, a death in the family — the list of potential problems people face goes on and on.

It saddens me to think of the vast number of churchgoers who come into their church services feeling the weight of the world on their shoulders. These people wish that someone would help them or pray with them, but no one ever asks how they are doing. Never having an opportunity to tell anyone what is happening in their lives, they frequently leave a service just as burdened as they were when they first walked through the church doors.

Have you ever been so burdened by the cares of life that you thought you might be crushed by the weight of it all? Did you wish someone would crawl under that load and help you carry it? Perhaps you can remember times when you cried out to God, *Please send someone to help me with these things that I'm dealing with in my life right now!*

In Galatians 6:2, the apostle Paul tells us, "Bear ye one another's burdens, and so fulfil the law of Christ." Answer this question: *When are we supposed to help bear someone else's burden?*

The word "burden" in this verse comes from the Greek word *baros*. It refers to *a weight that is heavy or crushing*. In fact, the word *baros* describes such a *crushing weight* that Paul used this same word in Second Corinthians 1:8 when he wrote about the terrible problems he and his traveling companions underwent in Asia. Paul wrote that these difficulties were of such a stressful nature that the men literally felt as if they were "pressed out of measure." In Second Corinthians 5:4, he used the word *baros* once more when he said, "...[We] do groan, being *burdened*...." Again, this word refers to a load so heavy that it causes a person to feel that he is *burdened* or *weighed down*.

The word *baros* could refer to either a *physical* or a *spiritual* problem. For instance, this type of pressing burden could be a habitual sin that has plagued you and weighed you down year after year. Satan may try to use these kinds of weaknesses and faults to hinder or completely abort God's plan for your life. That's why it's so important that these "burdens" be dealt with and defeated. If you are unable to do it alone, you need to seek the help of others to pull you through to a place of victory.

The point Paul is making here is that when a fellow believer is under a crushing weight — when he is under so much pressure that he feels like he'll break if someone doesn't get under that load and help him carry it — it is our Christian responsibility to help bear his burden, "...and so fulfil the law of Christ" (Galatians 6:2).

In Galatians 6:2, the Greek expresses the following:

"When someone is burdened by crushing cares and difficult events in life that are too much for one person to carry all by himself, crawl up under that burden and help that person carry it, and so fulfill the law of Christ."

I want to encourage you today to be sensitive to the needs of others who are around you. When you go to church, go to work, or even spend time with your family and friends, ask the Holy Spirit to help you see when people are carrying too much by themselves. If you discern that they are burdened, go to them and ask, *How can I pray for you today? What is happening in your life?*

God may use you to bring real relief and freedom into someone's situation. Perhaps just providing a listening ear is all that is needed to help that person get through his or her dilemma.

On the other hand, if an overwhelming problem, weakness, habit, or sin is pressing down on your life, you need to be humble enough to say, *Hey, I need someone to pray with me! This is too much for me to do completely by myself!* It may be difficult for you to open your heart and reveal your need, but it will be far more difficult for you to carry it alone until you eventually become emotionally devastated by that burden.

As brothers and sisters in the Lord, we need to do everything we can to step deeply into people's lives in order to encourage and refresh them spiritually and to help them get through their problems. When we see someone struggling, we must be bold enough to ask that person how we can help! *When we work together as a Body in this way, every need will be addressed and met!*

MY PRAYER FOR TODAY

Lord, I am asking You to help me be sensitive to the needs of other people. Help me to stop being so self-consumed with my own concerns that I am negligent in recognizing the needs of people around me who need help and prayer. Holy Spirit, help me see through the masks people tend to wear to cover up what is really happening in their lives. Give me the wisdom to know how to approach people who need strength and encouragement.

I pray this in Jesus' name!

MY CONFESSION FOR TODAY

I confess that I am sensitive to the needs of people who are around me. I see when they hurt; I recognize the times when they're struggling; and I am a blessing to them in their time of need. God's Spirit is helping me to become a better minister and servant to help meet the needs in other people's lives. I am attentive, caring, and Christ-like in the way I deal with others. What Jesus does for me is what I am becoming to other people.

I declare this by faith in Jesus' name!

QUESTIONS FOR YOU TO CONSIDER

1. Have there been situations in your life when you thought you might break under the weight you were trying to carry by yourself? When that happened, did anyone come to you and ask how he or she might help or pray for your needs?
2. Have you ever gone to others to see how you could help them through the situations they were enduring? Or have you been too self-consumed to remember that other people have needs too?
3. Do you know of individuals you should check on today to see what you can do to help them through a situation they are facing? In what ways can you be a strength or an encouragement to them?

When a fellow believer is under a crushing weight — when he is under so much pressure that he feels like he'll break if someone doesn't get under that load and help him carry it — it is our Christian responsibility to help bear his burden, "...and so fulfil the law of Christ" (Galatians 6:2).

MAY 24

❧

It's Time for You To Become Responsible!

For every man shall bear his own burden.
— Galatians 6:5

When Denise and I were first married and were just getting started in the ministry, our heart desire was to help people who were in need. Word of our efforts to help people soon spread throughout our city, and it seemed like there was always a long line of people approaching us to request help for all kinds of needs. Some of the needs were serious and legitimate, but soon we recognized that some people just wanted to take advantage of our goodwill.

That latter category included those who didn't want to get a job. These people had myriads of excuses for why they couldn't go to work, and they came up with fantastic reasons to explain why everyone else should be paying their bills. At first, Denise and I didn't realize that we were the newest gullible victims they had discovered to help them freeload. But after a while we looked at each other and said, "Wait a minute! These people aren't serious. They're just looking for someone to pay their bills so they can get a free ride in life."

Most needs you become aware of will be legitimate needs. However, there is a category of people who live like leeches on the goodwill of others. Helping people like this with financial assistance really doesn't help them at all. You are simply helping to prolong the way they are living and empowering them to keep being irresponsible. Why should they get a job if they can keep getting someone to pay their bills and relieve them of their responsibilities?

In Galatians 6:5, Paul makes a statement which at first sounds like a contradiction to Galatians 6:2 (*see* May 23). It says, "For every man shall bear his own burden." *What about this verse?* Is it in conflict with Galatians 6:2? Are we supposed to help bear each other's burdens, or is each person supposed to bear his or her own burdens? *Do these verses contradict each other?*

The word "burden" in Galatians 6:5 is completely different from the one in Galatians 6:2. In Galatians 6:2, the word is *baros*, but in Galatians 6:5 it is the Greek word *phortion*. These words are completely unrelated to each other and don't even look the same! The second word, *phortion*, is a military term that was used to indicate *the expected amount of weight that every soldier was expected to carry in his bag, kit, or backpack*. In the secular world, it was used to denote *the normal responsibility that every man must carry for himself*. Because it is a load we are expected to carry, it really is the idea of *a person's individual responsibility in life*.

You see, there is a certain amount of responsibility we are required to carry by ourselves. For instance, no one can do our work for us, and no one can make our decisions for us. Our bills are our responsibility to pay; our children are ours to raise; our dog is ours to feed; our yard is ours to mow; and our kitchen is ours to clean.

If you haven't discovered it yet, let me inform you that there are many freeloaders in the Body of Christ who would love to shirk these responsibilities and find someone else to do everything for them. These are the people Paul was referring to when he said, "For every man shall bear his own burden."

In Galatians 6:5, the Greek expresses the following idea:

"For every man is accountable for a certain level of personal responsibility in life, and he cannot look to anyone else to free him of these obligations that are his to take care of himself."

So when Paul addresses these two kind of burdens in Galatians 6:2 and Galatians 6:5, he is describing: 1) a crushing burden that is too much for you to bear by yourself and that necessitates the help of someone else; and 2) the daily duties and obligations you must bear by yourself as a responsible adult.

If you know someone who shirks responsibilities, it's time for you to start helping that person accept responsibility for his own life! If you know someone who is freeloading on the goodwill of others, God may want to use you to tell him to stop it!

People like that need to grow up and act like adults! So make sure that you don't empower and prolong their irresponsible existence by giving them everything they ask for. Saying no may be hard for you to do, but doing it a couple of times will help them realize they have lost their free ride, awaken them to reality, and thus put them on a right track!

It is very important that you think soberly about these things. Your actions are so important because your response will either help or hurt people. If they have sincere needs that they cannot overcome alone, you need to pray about what God wants you to do to help them. But if your analysis of the situation reveals that they are needy because they won't do what is necessary to fix the problem, it may be God's will that you tell them no.

If you seek the help of the Lord, He will show you what to do in every situation. So ask the Holy Spirit today to give you the mind of Christ for every situation that is presented to you. *If you will listen carefully, God's Spirit will advise you about what you should do.*

MY PRAYER FOR TODAY

Lord, what I have read today is very hard for me personally. I know some people who need to grow up and start taking on more of the responsibilities of life. I must admit that I've gone to their rescue too many times and that I've probably enabled them to continue their wrong behavior and inappropriate lifestyle. Saying no is so hard for me to do, but I am asking You to help me stop empowering them to keep living irresponsibly as they have been doing. Holy Spirit, please give me Your mind and Your power, and help me to do what is right on this issue.

I pray this in Jesus' name!

MY CONFESSION FOR TODAY

I confess that I have the mind of Christ to help me know when I am to help and when I am to say no. The Holy Spirit speaks to my heart and shows me what to do in every situation. God's Spirit advises me about what I should do. I am obedient to Him and am NOT led by my emotions.

I declare this by faith in Jesus' name!

QUESTIONS FOR YOU TO CONSIDER

1. Is there anyone you've been harming by giving him so much help that he hasn't had to assume responsibility for himself?

2. What change is required in your own heart and character to cause you to respond correctly to that person who has been living irresponsibly?
3. Is it hard for you to say no? Can you identify the reason it is so hard for you?

MAY 25

❦

It's Wearisome To Work With the Dead!

This is a true saying, If a man desire the office of a bishop,
he desireth a good work.
— 1 Timothy 3:1

One of the greatest frustrations I've experienced through the years is working with people who have great potential but are apathetic about life. It's even more frustrating when these people grew up in Christian homes and should therefore have been taught to pursue a higher standard for life.

But many people weren't raised according to a high standard of excellence as my parents raised me. Therefore, they don't possess a deep desire to be excellent in everything they do. They grew up in an environment where low-level thinking was viewed as normal, so that's the standard they've accepted for their own lives. However, a person who comes from a low-level background hurts only himself when he uses that as an excuse for staying mediocre.

It's so frustrating when you give people the opportunity to learn, to adapt, and to better themselves, but they don't take advantage of these opportunities and therefore never experience needed change. You can send them to school, educate them, and even pay for them to fly halfway around the world in order to learn new and better techniques. But if they don't possess the inner drive to become better and more professional, it doesn't matter how much time or money you throw at them. It's all a waste unless they have *desire*.

This is the reason the apostle Paul put "desire" at the top of the list when he wrote to Timothy and instructed him on how to choose leaders for his church in Ephesus. In First Timothy 3:1, Paul said, "This is a true saying, If a man desire the office of a bishop, he desireth a good work." According to this verse, desire is not only an important quality to possess, it is a requirement for any believer who wants to fulfill God's plan for his or her life!

The word "desire" comes from the Greek word *orego*, which means *to stretch forward* or *to reach toward*. It denotes *the longing, cravings, urge, burning desire, or yearning ambition to achieve something or to become something*. It portrays a person so fixed on the object of his desire that his whole being is stretched forward to take hold of that goal or object.

In other words, this word doesn't portray a person who just "thinks" about becoming something; this is a person who is *determined* to become something! He has put his whole heart, soul, and body into his dream, and he won't take no for an answer! He will do whatever is required; he will change anything in his character that needs to be changed and do anything he must do to achieve his goal.

It takes only a few personal experiences with desireless people to make it perfectly clear why Paul put this quality at the top of the list of character requirements for leaders. There is nothing more dreadful or irritating than to work with someone who is gifted and talented but who doesn't even possess enough initiative to get up and do his job!

As I said, one of my greatest frustrations — and this is true of every leader — is in trying to help, nurture, and develop people who have great potential but are apathetic about life. Desireless people stroll through life at their own pace, accepting standards and practices that would *never* be accepted in the business or secular world. They are like *dead people*!

You push, shove, beg, plead, and pray for people that fit this description to get involved. Finally, they respond to your constant requests to do something at work or in the church. They even do it for a while — at least until they feel a little opposition or are just too tired! At that point, they give up. These people don't have enough *desire* to make it through the obstacles they face along the way. This is another reason a potential leader must demonstrate this quality of strong inward *desire*.

Obstacles will come as you grow in the Lord. From time to time, hindrances will try to knock you out of your spiritual race. If you don't have a strong desire to be used by God and to become someone important in the work of His Kingdom, it won't take too many of these obstacles and hindrances to make you give up and back out of your commitments. That's why it's essential to develop an inner desire strong enough to overcome the forces that come against you along the way.

You need to know that even though every person has a dream for success, that doesn't mean every person will attain it. It takes great effort and hard work to achieve success in any realm of life. Many people who dream of success will never experience it because they don't desire it enough; therefore, they aren't willing to put forth the effort to make it happen.

As a result, a large portion of the lost world looks at the Church as a pathetic entity made up of a bunch of nincompoops who aren't serious about what they do or say. This lack of desire is the reason why so much of what is done in the Christian world is of such inferior quality. A person who is satisfied with little will never achieve much. On the other hand, *a person who is full of desire for excellence will never be satisfied with a low-level performance in his or her life.*

But how about you? Do you have enough desire to get up and do something with your life? Do your actions demonstrate that you are fixed on a goal God has given you? How much time do you waste watching television when you could be reading, studying, working, and developing yourself into someone better? You'll never become someone great or achieve anything special by doing what everyone else does. If you want to stand above the rest of the crowd, you'll have to do more than what others do. If you don't have desire, you'll never make it!

So ask the Holy Spirit to stir up strong desire in your heart to become all that God has called you to be and fulfill all that He has told you to do. Keep developing your desire until it's strong enough to overcome the forces that come against you along the way. Stretch forward with your whole being and take hold of your goal!

MY PRAYER FOR TODAY

Lord, thank You for speaking to me so strongly today about my personal level of desire. For me to be what You have called me to be, I know that I have to develop a stronger inner desire than I am demonstrating in my life at this moment. Holy Spirit, please stir my heart so fiercely that I won't be satisfied with my current level of life. Please give me a godly discontentment with the level I've already achieved so I'll be motivated to keep reaching for higher levels in my personal life!

I pray this in Jesus' name!

MY CONFESSION FOR TODAY

I confess that I am filled with desire! I am fixed on the goal God has given me to achieve, and my actions demonstrate that I am committed to achieving God's plan for my life. I read, study, work, and develop myself regularly so I can become better and achieve higher results. Because I will never become someone great or achieve anything special by doing what everyone else does, I do more than what others do. Because I have desire, I will make it!

I declare this by faith in Jesus' name!

QUESTIONS FOR YOU TO CONSIDER

1. What are you doing to develop yourself so you can reach the goal God has given you? Are you studying, reading, or serving and learning at the side of someone who is already doing what you want to do?
2. What will be required of you in order for you to see your dream come to pass?
3. If you keep doing exactly what you're doing right now, what will be your status in life two years from now?

MAY 26

Don't Hold Anything Back!

So being affectionately desirous of you,
we were willing to have imparted unto you,
not the gospel of God only, but also our own souls,
because ye were dear unto us.
— 1 Thessalonians 2:8

One common failure among ministers is to teach people the Word yet neglect to model the principles so the people will know how to live it in their personal lives. But true discipleship is not complete until there is an example to follow. When people receive the Word only as an intellectual exercise, their heads may become filled with knowledge, but that knowledge won't become workable in their lives until they have access to someone who models the message before them.

For example, Jesus modeled His message before His disciples. He lived with them, walked with them, worked with them, traveled with them, and spent nearly every minute of three whole years with them. As a result of working with Jesus so closely, the disciples not only received Jesus' message, but they also saw the way He lived it as He modeled an example before them.

We know that modeling the Word was also a part of Paul's teaching style. In First Thessalonians 2:8, the apostle Paul wrote, "…We were willing to have imparted unto you, not the gospel of God only, but also our own souls…." In this statement, Paul gave us the dynamic, life-changing principle that we must teach the Word *and* use our lives to model the message!

Certainly Paul taught publicly — and there was probably no better teacher than he in New Testament times. He was the "crème-de-la-crème" of New Testament theologians. Paul could have lectured for multiplied hours from the vast wealth of information and revelation stored up in his incredible intellect — and I'm sure that from time to time he did this.

But Paul didn't *just* lecture and preach. He gave the people not only the Gospel, but also his own soul. His "soul" was his life, his emotions, his view of things, his lifestyle. He lived so openly before the Church that he was able to *model* his message before them.

Paul even told the Thessalonians, "For yourselves know how ye ought to follow us…" (2 Thessalonians 3:7). The words "ye ought" are taken from the Greek word *dei* — a strong word indicating the Thessalonians understood that Paul was giving them compelling advice they *should* obey. In other words, Paul's readers understood that even though the apostle did not directly command them to obey, they were to strictly follow the advice he was giving them.

Paul continues to tell the Thessalonians, "…Ye ought to *follow* us…." The word "follow" is the Greek word *mimeomai*, an old Greek word for an *actor* or a *mimic*. Therefore, Paul's command to "follow" isn't referring to a casual type of following; rather, it implies *an intentional study of the life, deeds, actions, and thoughts of another person in an attempt to fully understand that person and then to replicate his attributes in one's own life*. This type of *following* enables one to think like his subject, walk like his subject, mimic his subject's movements, make the vocal intonations of his subject, and to act like his subject in a masterful way. However, this can only be achieved by those seriously committed to the act of *replication*. Mimicking, replicating, and acting like another person are the results of true discipleship.

**When you put all these words together,
Second Thessalonians 3:7 could be translated:**

"It would behoove you to follow our example — to imitate and mimic us with the goal of replicating what you observe in our lives…."

Paul was committed to sharing not only the Word, but his *life* with those to whom he ministered. He told the elders from Ephesus, "And how I kept back nothing that was profitable unto you, but have shewed you, and have taught you publickly, and from house to house" (Acts 20:20). From his testimony in this verse, we know that Paul publicly taught the Word; however, he also showed the people he taught how to *live* the Word! He gave them the entire package, which was *the Word and his life combined together*!

When the Word is packaged with a personal, living example, it is powerful! Nothing is more powerful than a message backed up by a person who applies that message to his daily life.

There is an unfortunate alarm among Christian leaders that if their followers become too familiar with them, the people will lose respect for them and their anointing. However, Jesus' disciples were very familiar with His lifestyle, and it didn't hurt their respect or honor for Him at all. Quite the contrary, Jesus' life became the greatest message He ever preached to His disciples!

Paul also wasn't fearful that the Thessalonians would lose respect by knowing him too well. Quite the contrary, he urged them to follow him and his lifestyle so closely that they would be able to duplicate his life themselves. The personal example of his own life showed them that they could walk in the power of the Word just as he was doing. Watching the Word work in Paul's life only made the message that much more powerful to the Thessalonians.

As you work with new believers or people who are under your spiritual influence, be sure to let them get close enough to see that the Word you preach really works. It's great to give them Bible lessons, but they need an example they can follow. If you are concerned that allowing people to get close to you will affect their respect for you, then you need to be honest about those areas of your life that you fear may discredit you in their eyes!

Ask the Holy Spirit to help you walk in the reality of what you preach and teach. Ask Him to give you the boldness, confidence, and grace to let the key leaders under your authority get close enough to see how the Word works in your own life. *If you're really walking in the reality of what you preach, allowing people to get close to you will only demonstrate that you are the real thing — and that will increase their level of respect for you!*

MY PRAYER FOR TODAY

Lord, I thank You for placing me under people who helped me grow when I was a young Christian. Their influence was important in my spiritual development, so I thank You for them right now — for their patience, their love, their kindness, and their willingness to let me get close enough to really learn how to walk with You. Now it's time for me to do this for someone else, so please lead me to a young disciple whom I can begin to show how to walk in the power and authority of Your Word.

I pray this in Jesus' name!

MY CONFESSION FOR TODAY

I confess that I am a good example to other believers. Because I walk in the truth of what I preach, my life makes the message even stronger. People need a good example they can follow, and that means they need me! The Holy Spirit empowers me to preach, to teach, and to boldly model my life before others with confidence and grace!

I declare this by faith in Jesus' name!

QUESTIONS FOR YOU TO CONSIDER

1. When you first came to the Lord, who had the greatest personal impact on your spiritual development? What kind of access did you have to these individuals, and why was their influence so important to your growth?
2. Is there anyone you are helping by giving him or her this kind of access to *your* life right now? Since it was so effective for you, don't you think you ought to return the favor by letting God use you this same way in someone else's life?
3. Be honest! Is there any area of your life that you are afraid for people to know about? Does that out-of-order area cause you to keep people from getting too close to you?

MAY 27

How Would You Like To Receive a Fresh Anointing?

…I shall be anointed with fresh oil.
— Psalm 92:10

How would you like to receive a fresh anointing of the Holy Spirit on your life today? If your answer is yes, why don't you go before the Great Anointer and allow Him to give you that fresh anointing? This is precisely what David was referring to when he said, "…I shall be anointed with fresh oil" (Psalm 92:10).

The word "anoint" that is used primarily in the Old Testament Septuagint and the Greek New Testament comes from the Greek word *chrio*. This word originally denoted *the smearing or rubbing of oil or perfume upon an individual.* For example, if a patient came to see his physician because he had sore muscles, the physician would pour oil upon his own hands; then he would begin to *deeply rub that oil into* the sore muscles of his patient. That penetrating application of oil would be denoted by the Greek word *chrio.* So technically speaking, the word "anoint" has to do with the rubbing or smearing of oil upon someone else.

When I hear the word "anoint," I immediately think not only of the oil, but of the hands of the Anointer! Oil was very expensive in biblical times; therefore, rather than tip the bottle of oil downward and freely pour it upon the recipient, a person would first pour the oil into his hands and then apply it to the other person. For this reason, I refer to the anointing as a "hands-on" situation. It took someone's hands to apply the oil.

Let's consider this concept in the context of God anointing our lives. God Himself — the Great Anointer — filled His hands with the essence of the Spirit and then laid His mighty hands upon our lives, pressing the Spirit's power and anointing ever deeper into us. So when we speak of a person who is anointed, we are actually acknowledging that the hand of God is on that person. The strong presence of the anointing that we see or feel is a signal to let us know that God's hand is personally resting on that individual's life.

Therefore, if you would like a fresh anointing of the Holy Spirit upon your life, you must come before the Great Anointer! He alone can give you what you need. Open your heart to God, and allow Him to lay His hand upon your life in a new way. *I guarantee you, a strong anointing will follow!*

MY PRAYER FOR TODAY

Lord, I am asking You to lay Your hand upon me in a brand-new way today. Rub the oil of Your Spirit deep into my life — and let the powerful fragrance of the anointing be felt, sensed, and seen by others who are near me. I want to carry Your power and demonstrate the aroma of Your Presence, so please lay Your hand on me today and let the anointing deeply penetrate me!

I pray this in Jesus' name!

MY CONFESSION FOR TODAY

I confess that God's hand is on my life. Because of this, the Spirit of the Lord rests mightily upon me. Just as He anointed Jesus, I am also anointed to preach the Gospel to the poor; to heal the brokenhearted; to preach deliverance to the captives; to give recovery of sight to the blind; and to preach the acceptable year of the Lord. I carry the power of Jesus Christ, and I give off the aroma of God's Presence!

I declare this by faith in Jesus' name!

QUESTIONS FOR YOU TO CONSIDER

1. Can you recall a moment when you really *knew* the hand of God came upon you? When that happened, what were the immediate results?
2. How long has it been since you experienced a fresh anointing of the Spirit? Where were you when God's hand last came upon you in a dramatic and spectacular fashion?
3. If someone were to ask you to explain the anointing to them, what would you say? After thinking about this, try to write your answer down so you'll be better prepared the next time someone asks you this question.

MAY 28

The Shield of Faith!

Above all, taking the shield of faith, wherewith ye shall be able
to quench all the fiery darts of the wicked.
— Ephesians 6:16

When Paul wrote his letter to the church of Ephesus, he gave a full description of the spiritual weaponry God has provided for every believer. In Ephesians 6:16, he referred to the shield of faith. He said, "Above all, taking the shield of faith, wherewith ye shall be able to quench all the fiery darts of the wicked."

With the imagery of a Roman soldier before him, Paul used the Roman soldier's shield to illustrate the shield of faith that God has provided for you and me. The word "shield" is the Greek word *thureos*, which was used by the Greeks and Romans to depict *an oblong door that was wide in width and long in length.* The reason the Roman soldiers used this word to describe their battle shields was that the shields were *door-shaped.* They were wide in width and long in length; just like the *door* of a house.

Because it was wide and long, this shield completely covered the Roman soldier! This is why the Holy Spirit chose to use the word *thureos* as the illustration of faith. He is telling us that God has given us enough faith to make certain we are completely covered for every situation — just like the shield that completely covered a Roman soldier!

In Romans 12:3, Paul wrote, "...God hath dealt to every man the measure of faith." How much faith has God given you? He has given you enough faith to make sure you are covered for any event that comes along in life!

So you don't need to worry or fret that God has given more faith to others than He has given to you. Rest assured in the fact that God has imparted enough faith to you to make sure you are covered from head to toe! That faith, like a wide and long shield, is adequate to cover any need that will ever come along in your life!

In the majority of cases, the Roman soldier's shield was composed of multiple layers of thick animal hide that had been tightly woven together. Usually six layers of animal hide were specially tanned and then woven together so tightly that they became nearly as strong as steel. One piece of leather is tough, but imagine how tough and durable *six* layers of leather would be! Because of how it was made, the shield of the Roman soldier was *extremely* tough and *exceptionally* durable!

However, the Roman soldier's leather shield could become stiff and breakable over a period of time if it wasn't properly taken care of. Therefore, it was necessary for him to know how to take care of it.

In order to keep those shields in good shape, the soldiers were given a daily schedule to maintain excellent condition of their shields. Each morning when the soldier was awakened, he would reach for a small vial of oil. After saturating a piece of cloth with oil, he would begin to rub, rub, and *rub* that heavy ointment into the leather portion of the shield to keep it soft, supple, and pliable.

Any soldier who neglected this daily application of oil and allowed his shield to go without the necessary care was in effect inviting certain death. If not correctly cared for and properly maintained, the leather portion of the shield would harden, crack when put under pressure, and finally fall to pieces. Therefore, the end result of a soldier's failure to care for his shield was the loss of his own life.

Paul says that this shield is representative of our *faith*. This tells us that our faith, like the shield in Paul's illustration, requires *frequent anointings* of the Holy Spirit. Without a fresh touch of God's Spirit upon our lives, our faith will become hard, stiff, and brittle.

What happens when you ignore your faith and allow it to go undeveloped? What is the result of never seeking a fresh anointing of God's Spirit to come upon your life? When a challenge comes your way, your faith won't be soft, supple, and pliable enough to stand up under attack. A faith that is ignored nearly always breaks and falls to pieces in the midst of confrontation.

So don't assume that your faith is always in top-notch shape! Instead, play it safe and assume that your faith always needs a fresh anointing. By taking this approach, you will always seek to do what is necessary to keep your faith alive, active, and well!

MY PRAYER FOR TODAY

Lord, I want to thank You for giving me spiritual weapons! Today I am especially grateful that You have equipped me with a shield of faith that covers me from head to toe. Because You have been so gracious to provide everything I need, there is never a reason that Satan's fiery darts should get through to me. So I ask You to help me hold my faith up high, keep it out in front, and march forward without any fear of what Satan might try to do to me!

I pray this in Jesus' name!

MY CONFESSION FOR TODAY

I confess that I am dressed in the whole armor of God! There isn't a part of me that hasn't been covered by the spiritual weaponry God has placed at my disposal. My shield of faith is working fine! It is anointed; it is strong; it is ready for any confrontation; and it will cause any dart that the enemy tries to throw at me to ricochet off without doing harm!

I declare this by faith in Jesus' name!

QUESTIONS FOR YOU TO CONSIDER

1. If you were really honest with God and yourself, how would you evaluate the way you maintain, develop, use, and grow in your faith? Are you using your faith as you once did, or have you slowly backed away from the strong stance of faith you once possessed?
2. When an attack comes against you, do you stand strong in the face of it, or do you tend to fall to pieces? If your answer is the latter, what does this tell you about the way you are maintaining your faith?
3. What do you think you need to do to keep your faith in top-notch shape?

MAY 29

*Never Forget To Look
At the Children!*

One that ruleth well his own house,
having his children in subjection with all gravity.
— 1 Timothy 3:4

*O*nce while traveling on an airplane, I sat next to a lady who had taught public school for thirty-five years. I asked her, "What can you tell about a family by the way a child behaves in school?"

She answered, "Everything! I can usually tell by the way a child acts if his or her home is peaceful or tormented; if the parents pay attention to their kids or ignore them; and if the father and mother have a good relationship. Almost everything can be determined by watching a child's behavior. It's usually a mirror of what's happening at home."

Of course, I know there are unique situations in which parents do everything right in raising their child, yet the child still becomes indifferent toward God and develops a rebellious and disrespectful attitude toward others. But often rebellious children are a symptom of a deeper problem in the family. If only one of the children in a family is rebellious and unmanageable, you might be able to dismiss the situation as a freak development or an attack of the devil. But if every child exhibits the same disturbing behavioral problems, you can surmise that something is not right in that home.

Paul considered the condition of the home so important that he wrote that a leader must have "...his children in subjection with all gravity" (1 Timothy 3:4). This is important to understand, because what happens in a person's home is usually the true picture about what kind of leader he is going to be. So when I personally look for new leaders or for people who will represent me and my ministry, I look at their children to see if they are respectful and understand authority. If the children aren't being taught this at home, it may be a sign that this parent doesn't value the things I count as important.

But what age of children are we talking about? The word "children" that Paul uses in First Timothy 3:4 is the Greek word *tekna*, the word used to describe *children who are still under parental guidance at home.* After a child grows into a young adult and leaves home, the parent is no longer responsible; however, as long as the child remains at home and under the authority of his or her parents, those parents have a God-given parental responsibility to teach that child how to live and how to act toward others.

Paul says in this verse that a leader's children should have "gravity." The word "gravity" is the Greek word *semnotes*. It presents the idea of *a person who carries himself with dignity and treats other people with courtesy and respect.*

Through the years, I've learned that the way a person's children speak to each other and to others outside the home is very revealing about what's really happening behind closed doors in that home. As noted above, children usually mirror the true situation in a home. In other words, how they speak, carry themselves, and treat others usually reflects the quality of relationships in their home.

If parents are constantly arguing and screaming at each other until it has become a pattern and a way of life, the children will usually speak to each other exactly the same way in that home. When siblings engage in chronic patterns of strife, name-calling, and mutual accusation, these destructive patterns probably exist in their parents' marital relationship as well. Children repeat what they see their parents do.

I'll never forget the time I was called upon to mediate a very difficult situation between a husband and wife whose marital problems could no longer be hidden. On the surface, they always smiled and acted deeply in love. However, the behavior of their children let me know that serious problems existed in that marital relationship.

Those kids frequently told each other:

+ *"I hate you!"*
+ *"I wish you were dead!"*
+ *"I can't stand you!"*
+ *"I'll be so glad when you grow up and move out of this house!"*
+ *"I think you stink!"*

It was very revealing to me that the children spoke so freely to each other like this and that no one at home stopped it. It told me that it was probably the kind of language spoken by everyone in the home — *including Dad and Mom.*

Then the true story came to light, and the facade of marital bliss this couple tried to project was removed. The truth was that this husband and wife fought like cats and dogs. He yelled and she screamed; he threatened and she threw objects. That house had been filled with strife, discord, quarreling, and squabbling for many years. This long-term destructive behavior was exactly what those kids mirrored in their own behavior and conversations with each other.

If a home is filled with love, respect, and teamwork, this is also evident in the way the children conduct themselves. For instance, just recently a leader and his family came to our home for dinner. I watched that leader's children interact with each other all evening while they were at our home. By watching those children, I knew exactly what I needed to know about this family. Those children possessed a respect and courtesy for each other and for other people that had been passed down to them by their parents' example.

When children are disrespectful toward authority and resentful when they're asked to do something they think is too low for them to do, it usually means they come from a home where a servant mentality is nonexistent. If their parents were true servants, their children would reflect that servant mentality themselves. Leaders who are servants most often have children who are servants.

So if you're looking for someone to serve in your church or to hire for a job, never forget to take a good look at the potential candidate's children. If you see a house full of children who are content to sit and watch other people work, be careful. You may be inviting someone who lacks a servant's heart into your team of leaders. Certainly there are exceptions to the rule, but you will most often find that what you see in the children is what you'll experience with the parent as well.

I am certain this *Sparkling Gem* has raised questions for you. My prayer is that it raises a warning flag to make you think twice about your own children and to cause you to move more slowly when choosing a leader who has disrespectful children. *I'm NOT saying that a potential leader whose children are rude and disorderly can't be used. But you should enter that relationship with both eyes wide open.*

If your own children are disrespectful toward each other and toward authority, maybe you need to ask the Lord to help you analyze the real situation in your life and your home so He can show you what is out of order. *Then once He reveals it to you, determine to start taking the proper steps to put things in good shape!*

MY PRAYER FOR TODAY

Lord, thank You for speaking to me through today's Sparkling Gem. I ask You to help me truthfully evaluate the situation in my life and honestly analyze how I am doing at rearing my children. It is difficult for me to be honest with myself about my performance as a parent, so I need You to give me the grace to see the truth as You see it. After You show me where I have erred, please quickly teach me how to bring correction into the situation. I am willing to be corrected, and I am waiting for You to help me clearly see the situation. I determine this day to do whatever is required to put my home in good working order.

I pray this in Jesus' name!

MY CONFESSION FOR TODAY

I confess that I am growing and developing as a parent. My parental skills are getting better and better all the time. My home is filled with love; my children speak with kindness and respect; and I am rearing them to be godly leaders for the next generation. With God's Word as my guide and the Holy Spirit as my Teacher, I am leading my family in a way that pleases God and that is an example to others.

I declare this by faith in Jesus' name!

1. When considering the behavior of your children, would you say they are respectful or disrespectful toward authority?
2. Do your children play one parent against the other parent — going to the second parent to get approval for what they want to do after the other parent has already denied their request? If yes, what does this communicate to you?
3. Do your children speak kindly to each other and respectfully toward their parents? If the answer is no, what does this reveal about you as a parent?

MAY 30

Two Kinds of Strongholds

(For the weapons of our warfare are not carnal,
but mighty through God to the pulling down of strong holds;)
Casting down imaginations....
— 2 Corinthians 10:4,5

*I*f you want to be free from every stronghold of the enemy in your life, you have to understand that there are two kinds of strongholds: *rational* and *irrational*. The rational strongholds are the most difficult to deal with — because they usually make sense!

Paul refers to these rational strongholds when he says, "Casting down *imaginations*...." The word "imaginations" is taken from the Greek word *logismos*, which is where we get the word "logic," as in "logical thinking." Thank God for a good, sound mind, but even a sound mind must be submitted to the sanctifying work of the Holy Spirit. Otherwise, your mind will develop a stronghold of natural reasoning that starts to dictate all kinds of lies to your life. I call these *rational strongholds*.

The reason I call them *rational strongholds* is that they are strongholds in the mind that make sense! You see, your logical mind will always try to talk you out of obeying God. In fact, if you don't take charge of your mind, it will begin to completely dominate and control your obedience to God. It will tell you that you can't afford to obey the Lord and that it isn't a good time to step out in faith. Your natural mind will come up with a whole host of logical reasons to explain why you shouldn't do what the Spirit of God is telling you to do.

Second, there are *irrational strongholds*. These primarily have to do with completely unrealistic fears and worries, such as a fear of contracting a terminal disease, a fear of dying early in life, an abnormal fear of rejection, and so forth. These types of irrational strongholds in the mind, emotions, and imagination will normally play their course and then dissipate. But if harassing thoughts persist in your mind and insist on controlling you mentally and emotionally, you must deal with them straightforwardly with the Word of God.

In Second Corinthians 10:5, Paul says, "Casting down imaginations, and every high thing that exalteth itself against the knowledge of God, and bringing into captivity every thought to the obedience of Christ." Notice that Paul doesn't say one thing about bringing the *devil* into captivity. Rather, he tells you to take every *thought* into captivity to the obedience of Christ.

The devil tries to invade your life through lies that he plants in your brain. If you don't take your thoughts captive, it will be just a matter of time before the devil starts using those lies to create mental and emotional strongholds for the purpose of keeping you in bondage. But if you take *your thoughts* captive, then your thoughts cannot take *you* captive!

Whether those strongholds are rational or irrational, you can take authority over them and cast them down! So quit listening to every ol' lie that devil tries to sink into your brain, and start taking those thoughts into captivity to the obedience of Christ! *Pull down every mental or emotional stronghold in your life with the supernatural weapons of warfare God has given you!*

MY PRAYER FOR TODAY

Lord, help me to see any area of my life that is dominated by rational or irrational strongholds. Forgive me for allowing the devil to sink his lies into my mind, and help me now to uproot and cast down every one of his lies. I know that Your Word will renew my mind to think in accordance with You, so I am asking You today to help me make Your Word a priority in my life!

I pray this in Jesus' name!

MY CONFESSION FOR TODAY

I boldly declare that my mind is free from the devil's lies! I think God's thoughts; I meditate on God's Word; and my brain is spot-free from the rational and irrational strongholds that Satan would like to plant inside me. Because of God's Word working in me, I am completely free!

I declare this by faith in Jesus' name!

QUESTIONS FOR YOU TO CONSIDER

1. Can you think of three areas in which the devil has tried to penetrate your mind and take you captive with ridiculous, irrational lies?
2. Can you identify times in your life when the devil has tried to seize control of your mind with logical, rational strongholds in order to keep you from stepping out to do what God has asked you to do?
3. What steps can you start taking right now to cast these thoughts down so you can get free of these lies and move forward with God's plan?

Thank God for a good, sound mind, but even a sound mind must be submitted to the sanctifying work of the Holy Spirit. Otherwise, your mind will develop a stronghold of natural reasoning that starts to dictate all kinds of lies to your life.

MAY 31

❧❧❧

Darkness Cannot Overcome the Light!

And the light shineth in darkness;
and the darkness comprehended it not.
— John 1:5

I know of no great Christian leader who hasn't faced some kind of opposition as he or she sought to do God's will. But the truth is that darkness does not have the power to overcome light! Every believer can overcome any attack if he or she won't quit first!

John 1:5 says, "And the light shineth in darkness; and the darkness comprehended it not." The word "comprehended" is the Greek word *katalambano*. It is a compound of the words *kata* and *lambano*. The word *kata* carries the force of something that is *dominating* or *subjugating*. The word *lambano* means *to seize or grab hold of*. When the two words are compounded, they mean *to seize, to pull down, to tackle, to conquer,* or *to hold under one's power*. Therefore, this verse could be translated, "*Darkness does not have the ability to suppress or to hold the light under its domain.*"

This doesn't mean that darkness won't *attempt* to overcome the light. However, its efforts will be frustrated and unsuccessful because the light of God always prevails, even in what seems to be the darkest hour or the bleakest situation. Darkness simply doesn't have the power or ability to put out God's light. Since you are a child of the light (Ephesians 5:8), this means darkness doesn't have the ability to put out *your* light either!

First John 5:4 says, "For whatsoever is born of God overcometh the world: and this is the victory that overcometh the world, even our faith." The word "overcometh" is the Greek word *nikos*. It means *to conquer*. It was used to portray athletes who had gained the mastery of the competition and ultimately reigned supreme as champions over the games.

The Holy Spirit was careful in His selection of this word *nikos*. This word communicates vivid images that pertain to our walk of faith and victory. First, it tells us that when we begin the walk of faith, we enter into a real-life competition. The decision to walk by faith puts us right smack dab in the center of the ring where the contest immediately begins.

This is so important to understand, because too often we wrongly presume that if we walk by faith, we will be removed from all problems. But our faith pits us directly opposite the devil's powers. He hates our faith because he knows what it can do! For this reason, Satan may try to go for a knock-out punch. But even if he knocks us flat, he can't keep us down on the ground!

The apostle Paul testified to this when he said that he was "...cast down, but not destroyed" (2 Corinthians 4:9). One translation says, *We occasionally get knocked down, but never get knocked out!* Those who are born of God have the supernatural ability to keep getting up again, no matter how many times they fall! Remember, John wrote, "For whatsoever is born of God *overcometh* the world...."

Because the word "overcometh" is the Greek word *nikos*, it tells us that we are the ultimate champions and describes our superior position as children of God over the world. We are fully armed with everything we need to be super-conquerors in this life!

As the "god of this world" (2 Corinthians 4:4), the devil may try to use the world around us to do battle with us. But regardless of what weapon Satan uses or how he attempts to combat you and me, First John 5:4 declares that we have a faith that *overcomes* the world! This means we have a faith that *overrides* and *supercedes* any organization, any event, any circumstance, or any difficult dilemma Satan would try to employ against us. He may be the "god of this world," but we have a weapon so powerful that we can shoot him down every time he shows up uninvited.

John 1:5 makes it absolutely clear that *darkness does not have the ability to suppress or to hold the light under its domain.* Darkness may try to prevent the light from shining, but it never holds back the light permanently. Eventually it always comes shining through.

This is true of you and your dream, vision, or calling as well. You may feel hindered from time to time in your attempts to fulfill the call God has given you, but don't despair. Those hindrances won't last long. The only way the devil can steal your dream, vision, or calling is if you surrender to him first! *If you hold on and refuse to give up, your faith will overcome every encumbrance the devil tries to set in your path!*

MY PRAYER FOR TODAY

Lord, I thank You that darkness doesn't have the power to overcome me! It may try, but Your Word guarantees that darkness doesn't have the ability to overcome the light! I am so thankful that I am Your child and that I live on the winning side! When the devil tries to discourage me, help me remember that in the end, we win!

I pray this in Jesus' name!

MY CONFESSION FOR TODAY

I boldly confess that even if I occasionally get knocked down, I never get knocked out! I possess the supernatural ability to keep getting up again because I am born of God and I overcome the world. Regardless of what weapon Satan uses or how he attempts to combat me, my faith overrides and supercedes any event, any circumstance, and any difficult dilemma Satan would try to employ against me.

I declare this by faith in Jesus' name!

QUESTIONS FOR YOU TO CONSIDER

1. In what ways has Satan tried to use the world around you to hinder what God has called you to do? For instance, has he tried to create a lack of finances to slow you down? What unsuccessful attempts has he made against you and your dream?
2. What did you do to resist those past attacks?
3. If you sense that the devil is trying to assault you right now, in what ways are you resisting his assaults?

Our faith pits us directly opposite the devil's powers. He hates our faith because he knows what powerful things it can achieve!

JUNE 1

❧

If You Pray Wrongly, You Can Be Sure Your Prayers Won't Be Answered!

> ...Ye have not, because ye ask not.
> Ye ask, and receive not, because ye ask amiss....
> — James 4:2,3

W̲e've all encountered moments in our spiritual lives when we prayed with no results. Apparently the people to whom James was writing his epistle were having the same experience. Just as you have probably asked yourself at one time or another, it appears that these believers were also asking, "Why aren't our prayers being answered?" We can surmise that they were asking this question because James provided an answer in James 4:3: "Ye ask, and receive not, because ye ask amiss...."

The Greek word for "amiss" is *kakos*, which describes *something that is bad or wrong.* As James uses it in this verse, it depicts *a person who is asking wrongly, badly, or inappropriately.* You could say that this person is simply not hitting the mark in his request. Although he prays with the greatest fervor, he is not hitting the target with what he is asking. This person is apparently asking God to do something that is not in agreement with His Word. Therefore, regardless of how long or how passionately the person asks, God will not answer his request with a positive answer because it is not in agreement with the Word.

Or perhaps this person is asking for the right thing, but because he is so fretful and filled with fear and anxiety, he doesn't ask in faith. Rather than praying from a position of faith, he cries out to the Lord in fear and anxiety. But fear doesn't move God — *faith* does. Hence, although this person may be asking for the right thing, he is asking from a wrong spirit. Thus, he is asking *badly* or *inappropriately.*

This means *what we ask* and *how we ask* are both of vital importance if we are going to get our prayers answered!

A literal translation of this verse would be as follows:

"...You ask, and receive not, because you are asking wrongly, badly, inappropriately...."

Especially when I was younger in the Lord, I made the mistake of asking things wrongly when I prayed. Perhaps my intentions were right, but my prayers were not in agreement with the truths revealed in the Bible. There were other moments when I finally got my prayers in agreement with the Word of God, but I was so motivated by anxiety and fear that I couldn't ask in faith. Consumed with worry, I pounded the floor as I prayed, yelling and screaming out for God to move on my behalf. But because I was so filled with fear regarding the situation I was praying about, all my pounding, yelling, and screaming didn't do a bit of good. I was praying from a wrong spirit — out of fear rather than out of faith — so all of that effort resulted only in a sore throat!

Have you ever had the experience of asking the *right thing* in the *wrong way*? Praying scripturally and in faith is essential if you want your requests to be answered positively.

First John 5:14 says, "And this is the confidence that we have in him, that, if we ask any thing according to his will, he heareth us." The word "confidence" is the Greek word *parresia*. It describes *confidence, boldness,* or *assurance.* It pictures a person so confident that when he speaks, he has no doubt about what he is saying. He knows what he is saying is correct or appropriate; therefore, he becomes very bold. In the context of prayer, this word presents the picture of a believer who is so confident he is right in what he is asking that he asks *unashamedly* and *confidently.*

What can give you this kind of confidence? The verse goes on to tell you: "…If we ask any thing according to his will, he heareth us." So when you 1) know God's will and 2) ask Him to do something that is in agreement with His will, you can be 100-percent sure that God will hear you and that your request will be positively answered!

This means you have solid ground on which to stand as you pray in agreement with the revealed will of God, the Bible. Since your request is in agreement with what God has already revealed in His Word, you know you can be bold when you make your request! And there is no need for you to pray out of fear and anxiety either. Just quiet down, and let the Word of God fill you with peace; *then* ask in faith.

First John 5:14 guarantees that if you ask anything that is in agreement with His will, God *will* hear you. In fact, verse 15 goes on to promise you, "And if we know that he hear us, whatsoever we ask, we know that we have the petitions that we desired of him."

Knowing *what to pray* and *how to pray* is vitally important. So always keep this in mind as you get ready to make your requests known to God: *God listens for His Word, and He responds to faith.* When He hears His Word prayed from a heart of faith, He is compelled to act.

The success of your prayer life is up to you, friend, so don't ask "amiss" when you pray. Make sure you are asking correctly and in an appropriate spirit of faith. *As you learn to pray in line with God's Word from a heart filled with faith, the answers you seek will manifest in your life more quickly and more fully than ever before!*

MY PRAYER FOR TODAY

Lord, I can remember times in my past when I've prayed the right thing the wrong way, and it resulted in unanswered prayer. I ask You to help me ask correctly when I pray, and to ask in a spirit of faith and not in a spirit of fear, dread, or anxiety. I never realized before now how important it is to ask in the right way. Holy Spirit, I ask You to help me ask correctly and pray appropriately from this moment forward. Whenever I start praying wrongly or out of a wrong spirit, please stop me. I ask You to correct me and teach me how to pray in line with Your Word from a heart of faith!

I pray this in Jesus' name!

MY CONFESSION FOR TODAY

I confess that God's Word is my guide to help me ask correctly when I pray. I declare that I am motivated by faith and not by fear, dread, or anxiety when I pray. Because I ask according to God's will, He hears me when I pray. Because He hears me, I know that I have the petitions I ask of Him. God acts promptly to answer my prayers because I ask with a heart filled with faith in accordance with His will. Because I make sure that what I pray is correct and how I pray is appropriate, I am receiving more and more results from my prayers all the time!

I declare this by faith in Jesus' name!

QUESTIONS FOR YOU TO CONSIDER

1. Can you think of a time in your life when you were so filled with fear that you couldn't pray in faith, even though you prayed the right words? Did you wonder why your prayer wasn't answered? Do you now understand how important it is for you to pray in an appropriate spirit of faith?

2. What results have you received in the past when you prayed in a spirit of faith and asked God to do something that was in agreement with His Word?

3. Can you list two things you have learned from today's *Sparkling Gem*? If these two points have helped you, can you think of one person with whom you can share these truths today in order to encourage him or her the same way you've been encouraged?

JUNE 2

Are You Tired of Waiting For Your Fruit-Producing Season?

Rooted and built up in him, and stablished in the faith,
as ye have been taught, abounding therein with thanksgiving.
— Colossians 2:7

*H*ave you ever been so frustrated at waiting for a fruitful time in your life that you said to the Lord, *"When is the fruit-producing season ever going to start in my life? I've worked, believed, and waited, but I am a little tired of waiting to see the fruit I long to see in my life. How long do I have to wait, Lord?"*

I encourage you today to stay on track and refuse to give up, because you're about to reach the greatest period of fruitfulness you've ever known. Before a fruit-producing tree reaches a time in its growth when it blossoms and bears fruit, first it sends its roots down deep into the earth where it can draw on a constant source of nourishment. Then as it continues to be nourished from below, it begins to send its limbs upward and outward.

During the life of that tree, it must endure the elements of every season — the heat, the cold, the sleet, the rain, and the snow — before it ever blossoms. Because those roots are deeply tapped into a continuous source of strength, nourishment, and energy, the tree is able to outlast all the seasons and eventually become a fruit-producing tree.

Psalm 1:3 uses the example of a tree to declare that when a person is rooted in God's Word, he is "...like a tree planted by the rivers of water, that bringeth forth his fruit in his season; his leaf also shall not wither; and whatsoever he doeth shall prosper."

If you are wondering how long it is going to take before your fruit-producing season finally arrives, don't get too discouraged! The bigger the tree, the greater the need for that tree to send its roots down deep into the earth to draw nourishment and to give it a firm footing against the wind, the weather, and the elements of the different seasons. That continual nourishment will also protect the tree from pestilence that may try to attack it through the years.

In light of this, consider what the apostle Paul wrote in Colossians 2:7: "Rooted and built up in him, and stablished in the faith, as ye have been taught, abounding therein with thanksgiving." I want you to especially notice the word "rooted" in this verse. It comes from the Greek word *ridzo*, which means *to be firmly and deeply rooted, making the object fixed, steady, stable, and strong*. This is the picture of a strong tree whose roots go down deep and reach its source of nourishment. The tree is also held securely in place by those roots, regardless of the weather or the environmental opposition that comes against it.

Rather than complain that it's taking too long for your fruit-producing season to arrive, you need to thank God for this time in your life! Take this time to send your roots down deep and tap into the strength of God's Word and God's Spirit. If your roots are securely fixed in Jesus Christ, you will outlast every season, every foul climate, and every storm. Eventually you will enter into the finest fruit-producing season of your life, your ministry, your family, or your business.

Honestly, you need to thank God that things haven't happened faster in your life! Have you ever seen someone who reached success too quickly? That person usually loses his success just as quickly as he gained it because he didn't have the roots and the experience necessary to maintain the success he gained. When people achieve success too quickly, it often means they don't have the roots, the depth, and the sure foundation to bear them up in the difficult times they will encounter as they go through the seasons of life.

So take this time to work on your personal life, your mind, your thinking, your discipline, your finances, your weight, your relationships, and your behavior. While you are waiting for that fruit-producing season to come to pass in your life, use this time to put off the old man and to put on the new man (Colossians 3:9,10). Spend this phase of your life wisely by renewing your mind to the Word of God (Ephesians 4:23) and being certain your affections are set on things above, not on things of this earth (Colossians 3:2).

If you use your time wisely, there will be no wasted time in your life. But if you just sit around and complain that it's taking too long to get where you want to go, you *will* waste time. Sitting and complaining doesn't make anything happen faster — and it often further delays the manifestation of the answer you've been waiting for.

So refuse to belong to those who are grumpy and complaining all the time. Instead, look at this time in your life as a blessing sent from Heaven to help you get yourself rooted deeply in Jesus Christ! Then send your limbs upward and outward as you tap into the power of God. *Eventually you'll begin to see blossoms budding in your life, signaling that you are about to enter your long-awaited season of bringing forth much fruit!*

MY PRAYER FOR TODAY

Lord, I thank You for not sending success to me too quickly. I know that if I had achieved success earlier, I wouldn't have been ready for it. In fact, I might have destroyed it due to my own lack of experience and my immaturity. Help me embrace this time in my life as a time of preparation. Help me to truthfully analyze every part of my life in order to see what areas need to be more deeply rooted in You. I want my roots to go down so deeply that no storms of life and no attacks from the devil will be able to move me from the place where You have called me.

Help me to stay so fixed, firm, strong, and stable that once I enter the fruit-producing season, I will never leave it!

I pray this in Jesus' name!

MY CONFESSION FOR TODAY

I confess that I am firmly and deeply rooted in God's Word. As a result, I am fixed, steady, stable, and strong like a tree whose roots go down deep. I am tapped into the life of Jesus Christ, and He has become my Source of nourishment. I am held so securely in place that I am unaffected by the storms of life and the pestilence that the devil tries to use to attack me. I will outlast every season, every foul climate, and every storm. I am about to enter into the finest fruit-producing season of my life, my ministry, my family, and my business. My fruit-producing season is getting ready to begin!

I declare this by faith in Jesus' name!

QUESTIONS FOR YOU TO CONSIDER

1. Have you ever seen people quickly reach success, but it seemed that they lost their success just as quickly as they attained it? Can you name specific individuals who come to mind as examples?
2. What were the reasons these individuals gained and lost success so quickly? Reflect on this question for a while; then write down your observations.
3. What do you need to be doing differently in your own life to make sure you don't ever fall into the category of those who quickly gained and quickly lost success?

JUNE 3

You Are Sealed and Guaranteed by God's Spirit!

In whom also after that ye believed,
ye were sealed with that holy Spirit of promise.
— Ephesians 1:13

I couldn't believe what I had just heard on the telephone! A beautiful and very expensive piece of Russian porcelain that we had sent to a dear friend in the United States had arrived broken in pieces! It was so broken that it couldn't be put back together again. What made this situation even worse was that this was already our *third* attempt to mail this piece of porcelain — and every single time we had tried, it had arrived broken!

We were so frustrated with these attempts to mail this porcelain that we decided to personally carry it on the airplane with us the next time we flew our transatlantic flight to see this friend on the other side of the world. Although it was a huge piece of porcelain and very difficult to carry, the only way we could be assured that it would arrive safely was to personally and gently carry this delicate object ourselves. Finally, the day came when we boxed up the large porcelain, packing lots of stuffing around it. We brought that bulky box with its fragile cargo onto each airplane that carried us to our destination. When we finally delivered the exquisite gift to our friend, she rejoiced to see that it had finally arrived at her house without a single broken piece and without a scratch!

If you've ever received something in the mail that was broken, you can probably relate to this story. Or have you ever ordered something by mail that you were so excited to receive but that was a big disappointment when it arrived? When you opened the package, did you find out it was so poorly made that you had to return it to the sender?

Or have you ever ordered a product with the promise of a certain delivery date, only to have the arrival of the package delayed so many times that you nearly lost your temper with the company from whom you ordered it? All these scenarios can leave you feeling very frustrated and disappointed, can't they?

Well, in the first chapter of Ephesians, Paul lets us know that God Himself is waiting for a special delivery package! He is so excited to receive this package that He has personally done everything necessary to ensure that it will arrive intact, complete, with no defects, and without a single piece of it being broken or scratched. He has also done everything necessary to make sure it arrives right on time!

Notice that Ephesians 1:13 says, "...In whom also after that ye believed, ye were *sealed* with that holy Spirit of promise." Today I want to draw your attention to the word "sealed." This word comes from the Greek word *sphragidzo. This is extremely important.*

Seals were used in New Testament times to guarantee that the contents of a package were *complete* and *not defective*. Such a seal would only be placed on a package if the product had been *thoroughly examined* and *inspected* to make sure it was *fully intact* and *complete*. If it were broken, defective, or faulty, the guarantor would not put his seal upon it. *The seal was proof that the product was impeccable.*

Such seals were also put on parcels before being mailed to their final destination. Parcels bearing such "seals" were usually sent by extremely wealthy individuals. These seals, which bore the insignia of a particular wealthy or famous person, meant that this package was to be *treated with the utmost, tender care.*

To seal such a package, the sender poured hot wax onto the flap of the envelope or the string that bound the box. Afterward, he pressed his insignia into the wax, leaving a visible, distinctive mark. This insignia alerted everyone that the package was the possession of a wealthy or powerful person. Therefore, the "seal" guaranteed that the package would make it to its final destination.

Well, the Bible says *you* are "sealed" with the Holy Spirit of promise. This means there is *nothing incomplete or defective* about you. When God made you new, the last thing He did was check you out, thoroughly examining and inspecting you *before* placing His final seal of approval on your heart.

In Ephesians 1:13, Paul says that if you belong to the Lord, you have been "sealed" with the Holy Spirit. For God to "seal" you with His Spirit means that you are God-approved! Your contents are intact and in order. You should never again view yourself as if you are "damaged goods." You're *not* damaged! You are *approved, endorsed, recognized, affirmed, sanctified,* and *notarized* by the Spirit of God. You have the seal of God's approval, so start acting as if you're special. God thinks you are *very* special!

The "seal of the Holy Spirit" is also the guarantee that you're going to make it to your final destination. God is the One who inspected and packaged you. He also put His guarantee on you to ensure that you're delivered to His ordained destination for your life. That means you should never complain that you're not going to make it. *Of course you're going to make it. God will see to it!*

When demons see the seal of God on your life, they know they are not to mess around with that package. *You're a special package, to be treated with special care.* Angels watch over you and guard your safe passage from one place to the next. Evil forces may attempt to delay the timing of your arrival, *but the seal of God in your heart guarantees that you'll get there.*

An interpretive translation of Ephesians 1:13 could be the following:

"...The moment you believed, God thoroughly examined and inspected you to make sure that you were fully intact and complete. Because He found nothing in you broken, defective, or faulty, God put His seal upon you — the ultimate proof that He found you to be impeccable. That seal meant you were approved, endorsed, recognized, affirmed, sanctified, and notarized by the Spirit of God. It was His guarantee that you are going to make it to your final destination."

This should tell you how intensely God longs for your arrival in Heaven! He Himself has inspected you, sealed you, and guaranteed you. Now He watches over you to see that you make it all the way into His Presence, where He eagerly anticipates that day when He will see you face to face. *So whenever the devil speaks to your mind or your flesh screams that you're not going to make it, rebuke those lies and point to the seal God has placed on your life!*

MY PRAYER FOR TODAY

Lord, I am so thankful today that You have sealed and guaranteed me! Forgive me for those times when I speak badly of myself, judge and condemn myself, or put myself down in front of others. I should be proud of and thankful for who I am, because the blood of Jesus has cleansed and redeemed me. You were so convinced that I was free of defects that You sealed me with Your Spirit, giving me Your ultimate seal of approval. Help me appreciate the great work You have done inside me! Thank You for guaranteeing, overseeing, and assuring me that no force on earth and no demonic powers can stop me from arriving at my ultimate heavenly destination!

I pray this in Jesus' name!

MY CONFESSION FOR TODAY

I confess that I am "sealed" with the Holy Spirit. My contents are intact and in order. I am approved, endorsed, recognized, affirmed, sanctified, and notarized by the Spirit of God. Because God has "sealed" me, it is guaranteed that I am going to make it to my final destination. When demons see the seal of God on me, they know they are not to mess around with me! I am a special package, to be treated with special care. Angels watch over me and guard my safe passage from one place to the next. Evil forces may attempt to mess with me, but the seal of God guarantees that I'll arrive safely and complete!

I declare this by faith in Jesus' name!

QUESTIONS FOR YOU TO CONSIDER

1. Do you view yourself as "damaged goods," or do you see yourself as approved, endorsed, recognized, affirmed, sanctified, and notarized by the Spirit of God?
2. If you don't view yourself the way God does, what scriptures can you begin to

memorize, meditate on, and confess to renew your mind to the truth of who Jesus Christ has made you to be? Why not make a list of those scriptures and put them in a visible place where you can frequently be reminded of them?

3. Do you know some believers who are struggling with their self-image and could use a little boost from a friend to help them think higher of themselves? If so, why don't you take a little time today to go out of your way and let them know that they are approved and endorsed by God?

JUNE 4

God Isn't Looking for Aristocrats, Cultured, or High-Born People

For ye see your calling, brethren, how that not many wise men
after the flesh, not many mighty, not many noble, are called:
But God hath chosen the foolish things
of the world to confound the wise....
— 1 Corinthians 1:26,27

*T*hrough the ages, God has always delighted in choosing normal people to do His business. If you consider yourself to be a normal, average kind of person, that means you are just the kind of person God is looking to use!

First Corinthians 1:26 says, "For ye see your calling, brethren, how that not many wise men after the flesh, not many mighty, *not many noble*...." Do you see the word "noble" in this verse? It comes from the Greek compound word *eugenes*. The first part of the word is the Greek prefix *eu*, which means *well* or *good*. The second part of the word is the Greek word *genes*, from which we get our English word for the human *gene*. When these two words are compounded together, the new word portrays *people who are well-born or who have excellent genes*.

In ancient Greece, the word *eugenes* meant *men of high descent*, such as sons of kings, politicians, or others from the upper crust of society. It referred to *individuals whose ancestors had been powerful, wealthy, rich, or famous*. These were high-born, blue-blooded, cultured, refined, courtly, pedigreed, aristocratic people who sustained their lofty positions in society based on their birth.

Examples of this class of people would be members of royalty who held their exalted positions in society whether or not they personally merited those positions. They were born into the upper crust and stayed there simply because of their family name or relations.

Modern examples of *eugenes* are sons and daughters of kings and queens who retain their royal posts simply because of the blood that runs in their veins. Other examples would be the sons and daughters of famous and beloved politicians. Although the offspring themselves may not have accomplished anything significant, their famous last name has sealed their fame and place in society. They were born with a "name" that gives them lifetime guarantees and access to privileges that are not available to common people with unknown names.

But the word *eugenes* can also refer to people who carry the seed of genius as a result of the good *genes* with which they were born. An example of this category of *eugenes* would be the family of Albert Einstein.

Some years ago, I was visiting a pastor in New York City who told me an interesting story about a visit he had with the niece of Albert Einstein. He was amazed to discover she had five earned doctorates and held several prominent positions in universities in New York City. Like her uncle Albert, she was endowed with genius in her *genes*, and it carried her all the way to the top of every field in which she became involved.

Let me give you another example of "good genes" as portrayed by the Greek word *eugenes*. Before the Russian revolution, noble families owned the lands and controlled the territory of Russia. In 1917 when the Red Army seized power, all of Russia's rich decoration and regal royalty came to an abrupt end. The nobility was killed or fled to foreign countries. It looked as if history had buried them forever.

Thank God, today the communist regime is gone. In its place, a brand-new rich Russian class is emerging. People often ask, *"Who are these new super-rich Russians?"* It is interesting to note that many of them have the same family names of the old ruling class that dominated Russia before the 1917 revolution. The nobility that runs in their veins is too strong to be held down. Once again, it is taking them to the top of society.

The Russian nobility were endowed with powerful *genes*. These *genes* have been passed down to the present generation. Now the offspring of the Russian nobles are reassuming positions of power that were once occupied by their grandparents. This tendency to rule and reign is in their *genes*.

The word *eugenes* describes both kinds of people — those born into famous families who enjoy the inherent privileges of their last name, and those who carry a streak of genius, talent, or superiority in their genes. These are "the upper crust" — the ruling class or aristocracy of the world.

However, Paul says that God hasn't specialized in calling this category of people. Take a look at world history, and you'll see that God *hasn't* primarily specialized in using kings, queens, royalty, politicians, scientists, philosophers, writers, movie stars, or celebrities to advance His Kingdom. From the onset of time, God has reached into the hearts of *ordinary* men and women. These are the ones who most often accomplish mighty feats through His grace and power.

So if God isn't looking for the upper crust of society, He must be looking to "the lower crust" — in other words, *to the ordinary, usual, regular, routine, run-of-the-mill, standard, typical kind of people.* This means that if you come from a normal, average background, you are possibly the very one God wants to use!

Yes, God has called the rich and famous as well, but it is the regular folks who most often find themselves chosen by God to carry out His will in the earth. He specializes in using ordinary people, just like you and me. That is why Paul goes on to say, "But God hath chosen the *foolish things* of the world to confound the wise...."

The word "foolish" is from the Greek word *moraino*. The word "moron" also comes from this Greek word. My thesaurus gives these other synonyms for a "moron": *idiot, imbecile, halfwit, numskull, dimwit, dunce, blockhead, dope, ignoramus, lamebrain, jerk,* or *twerp*!

The truth is, no one is an idiot in God's view. But the world often views people whom God chooses as being *nitwits, lamebrains, and idiots.* It is worth noting that the word *moraino* was used in Paul's time to depict people whom the world scorned, made fun of, and treated with contempt.

Because much of the Early Church was comprised of servants and slaves, most of the people in the local congregations were very uneducated, uncultured, clumsy, crude, awkward, and unpolished. It wasn't that they were stupid. They had simply never been exposed to or taught about manners, culture, and refined behavior. Reared and treated as servants since birth, they'd never had a need to know these skills.

However, the early Christians' lack of polish made them look stupid in the world's eyes. In fact, the Roman Empire at first looked upon Christianity as the religion of stupid, poor people because it grew so rapidly among the lower slave classes.

Yet Paul says, "...God hath chosen the foolish things of the world to confound the wise...." The word "confound" is the Greek word *kataishuno*. It means *to put to shame, to embarrass, to confuse, to frustrate, to baffle*. The word "wise" is again the word *sophos*, referring to those who *are naturally brilliant, intellectually sharp, or especially enlightened*. Paul is saying that God calls people whom the world considers *morons* in order to put to shame, embarrass, confuse, frustrate, and baffle those who think they're so smart!

So if anyone has ever called you an idiot — if you've ever been called a stupid imbecile, a jerk, or a twerp — it's time for you to rejoice! *This makes you a candidate to be used for God's glory!*

The following expanded version of First Corinthians 1:26,27 gives a fuller picture of the Greek words used in this verse:

"For you see your calling, brothers, how not many of you were especially bright, educated, or enlightened according to the world's standards; not many of you were impressive; not many came from high-ranking families or from the upper crust of society. Instead, God selected people who are idiots in the world's view; in fact, the world sees them as imbeciles, jerks, real twerps. Yet God is using them to utterly confound those who seem smart in the world's eyes...."

Therefore, even though you may not have any genius residing in your genes nor any nobility running in your blood, that isn't a strike against you! You can't lay claim to these factors as excuses for not being used by God! God isn't looking for people who are geniuses or well-born, high-class blue bloods. He's looking for *anyone* who will say *yes* to His call! So if you consider yourself to be just a regular ol' person, it's time for you to start rejoicing again! *You are exactly the kind of person God wants to use!*

MY PRAYER FOR TODAY

Lord, help me stop making excuses for why I think God shouldn't use me! It's time for me to stop ignoring the call of God and to accept the fact that He has laid His hand upon me and wants to use me in this world. Forgive me for putting this off for so long, but today I accept Your call. I reject all excuses for any further delay, and I gladly embrace what You are telling me to do!

I pray this in Jesus' name!

MY CONFESSION FOR TODAY

I boldly confess that I am exactly the kind of person Jesus Christ wants to use! I may not have the blue blood of nobility flowing through my veins, but I have been touched, cleansed, and redeemed by the blood of Jesus Christ. That blood qualifies me! With the Word as my guide and the Holy Spirit as my Teacher, I have everything I need to do anything Jesus ever requires of me. I am quick to obey; I do not hesitate; and I am faithful to carry out every assignment that He gives me!

I boldly declare this in Jesus' name!

QUESTIONS FOR YOU TO CONSIDER

1. Thinking back on those who were most mightily used by God throughout the ages, do you know from which class of society most of them came?
2. Now think about those whom God is greatly using to touch the world and confound society today. What class of society do most of these people come from? What kind of education did most of them have when God first started using them in a notable way? How many of them have blue blood running in their veins or would be deemed geniuses by the great universities of the world?
3. What does this tell you about God's ability to use *you*?

JUNE 5

You Are No Accident, Because God Chose You!

According as he hath chosen us in him
before the foundation of the world, that we should be holy
and without blame before him in love.
— Ephesians 1:4

From time to time, someone says, "My parents didn't plan me. I was an accident no one expected." People use this as an excuse for not accepting more responsibility in life, claiming that they are accidents who came into the world by mistake and aren't even supposed to be here!

Well, I want to tell you that even though we may have been a surprise to our parents, we were *not* a surprise to God! The Bible teaches that long before you or I were ever conceived in our mothers' wombs, God already knew us and was calling us to be His children with a special purpose to fulfill in this world.

In Psalm 139:15 and 16, David declares that God's eyes were fixed on us not only when we were in the earliest stages of being formed in our mother's womb, but even *before* we were conceived. David said concerning himself (and us), "My substance was not hid from thee, when I was made in secret, and curiously wrought in the lowest parts of the earth. Thine eyes did see my substance, yet being unperfect; and in thy book all my members were written, which in continuance were fashioned, when as yet there was none of them."

According to David, God knew us when we were nothing more than mere "substance" in the earliest stages of being formed in our mothers' wombs. God was so intricately aware of us that He took note as our arms, hands, fingers, legs, feet, and toes were being formed. In fact, this verse says He even knew us "...when as yet there was none of them" in existence! Think of it! Long before we were conceived, God already knew of us — and by faith He could see us being conceived, formed, and born into this world. This means there isn't a single human being on the earth who was a surprise to God, and that includes *you*!

Those of us who are believers were also saved by no accident. Paul writes, "According as he hath chosen us in him before the foundation of the world...." The word "chosen" in Greek is *eklego* — a compound of the words *ek* and *lego*. The word *ek* means *out*, and the word *lego* means *I say*. Together these words literally mean *Out, I say!* It can also mean *to call out, to select, to elect,* or *to personally choose*.

In classical Greek writings, this word *eklego* referred to a person or a group of people who were *selected* for a specific purpose. For example, the word *eklego* was used for the selection of men for military service. It was also used to denote soldiers who were *chosen out of* the entire military to go on a special mission or to do a special task. Finally, it was used for politicians who were *elected* by the general public to hold a public position or to execute a special job on behalf of the community.

In every case where the word *eklego* is used to portray the election or selection of individuals, it conveys the idea of *the great privilege and honor of being chosen*. It also strongly speaks of *the responsibility placed on those who are chosen to walk, act, and live in a way that is honorable to their calling*. Because of the great privilege of being elected to a higher position or selected to perform a special task, those who are "chosen" bear a responsibility to walk and act in accordance with the calling that has been extended to them. They should look upon themselves as chosen, honored, esteemed, and respected — special representatives of the one who elected them!

So when Paul says that God "...hath chosen us in him before the foundation of the world...," he is saying that God looked out to the horizon of human history — *and He saw us*! And when God saw us, His voice echoed forth from Heaven: *"Out, I say!"* In that flash, our destinies were divinely sealed! We were separated by God from a lost and dying world, and He called us to be His own.

Just as the word *eklego* in classical Greek times depicted the military selection of young men to leave their homes and come serve in the military, God looked out at the human race and personally *selected, elected,* and specially *chose us* to come away from the world and be permanently enlisted as His sons and daughters! Now as children of the King, we bear the awesome responsibility of walking worthily of the high calling we have received!

Look at when this selection took place. Paul says it occurred "...before the foundation of the world...." The word "foundation" is the Greek word *katabole*, a compound of the words *kata* and *bole*. The word *kata* means *down*, and the word *bole* means *to hurl* or *to throw*. These two words together mean *to forcibly hurl something down*, and it refers to *the act of creation*.

Thus, before God ever spoke the earth into existence — before His booming voice ever called out for the first layers of the earth's crust to be put into place — He had already spoken our names! He selected and elected us *before* the very first layers of the earth were created.

**In light of these Greek meanings,
Ephesians 1:4 could be phrased to read:**

"When God saw us, He said, 'Out, I say!' In that moment, He separated us from the rest of the world and enlisted us in His service. And think of it! He did all of this before He ever hurled the first layers of the earth's crust into existence...."

So if your flesh ever tries to rant and rave that you're not worthy enough to be used or that you're just an accident, you need to take authority over your flesh and tell it to shut its stupid mouth! Then you need to declare, "God chose me, and He planned a great future for me. He wants to use me. I'm not going to listen anymore to this foul garbage from my lying flesh and unrenewed emotions. I have an awesome destiny! In fact, I'm a significant part of God's plan!"

Don't listen to your filthy, stinking, lying, fibbing flesh anymore! God has been waiting for your arrival for a very long time! It's time for you to accept His assignment and make the necessary changes to flow with His program. He's calling out to you all the time, saying, *"Get up and jump in the race! I want you. I'm calling you to be a part of My team."*

There is too much at stake for you to make the mistake of sitting around and feeling sorry for yourself. You'll only begin to experience true significance when you accept the fact that God has chosen you, and when you begin to live up to the glorious calling He has placed on your life! No matter how large or small the task, no matter how big or tiny the assignment, joy and satisfaction will be yours when you start accomplishing what God brought you into this world to do.

This is what imparts *true significance* to any person's life. No satisfaction compares with this satisfaction. Those who contribute nothing to life are usually the ones who struggle with a sense of purposelessness.

Even if you think your gifts are small in comparison to others, *you can still use them*! If you use the gifts God gave you, they will increase. And the more proficient you become at using those gifts, the more valuable you will become to your family, your church, your business, and your friends. On the other hand, you will cause your life to be inconsequential if you ignore the gifts God gave you and minimize the life assignment He has entrusted to you.

A person's life becomes *pointless* when he or she contributes nothing to the world. *Don't let that describe YOUR life!* God didn't bring you into the world so you would live a pointless and inconsequential life! He has a purpose for your life. *He wants to use you!* He wants you to be a significant part of His plan!

MY PRAYER FOR TODAY

Lord, I am so glad that You knew me and called me even before I was conceived in my mother's womb. According to Your Word, I am no mistake; therefore, I ask You to help me start looking at my life with respect, esteem, and honor. You called me, and You have an awesome plan for my life. I ask You to help me uncover that plan so I can get started on the road of obedience toward the fulfillment of what You brought me into this world to do!

I pray this in Jesus' name!

MY CONFESSION FOR TODAY

I boldly declare that I am no accident and no mistake! God knew me before the earth was created; He called me before I was formed in my mother's womb; and He has long awaited my arrival on planet earth! God has a plan for me! I am purposeful; I am respectful of myself; and I walk in a way that honors the One who called and anointed me to be enlisted in His service!

I declare this by faith in Jesus' name!

QUESTIONS FOR YOU TO CONSIDER

1. Have you ever been tempted to think that your life was pointless and inconsequential? What happens in your life most often that triggers these negative emotions?
2. Can you think of a time when you were supernaturally illuminated to the call of God on your life? When that happened, what did you understand was the chief purpose that God had for you in this lifetime?
3. If you have been struggling with feelings of purposelessness or of inferiority toward other people, what are you going to do to stop these negative emotions from affecting you in an adverse way?

JUNE 6

What Jesus Thinks of Laziness

And cast ye the unprofitable servant into outer darkness:
there shall be weeping and gnashing of teeth.
— Matthew 25:30

*M*y grandfather was a German immigrant who spoke no English when he arrived at Ellis Island in New York's harbor, so he had to work very hard to achieve anything in his new life in America. Because he had no time to go to school to learn English, the best job he could get was to work as a janitor. In the course of his janitorial duties, my grandfather pulled discarded tin cans out of the kitchen garbage in the tall skyscraper he cleaned every night. The cans had pictures of vegetables and fruit on them, and he found out that by comparing the words on the cans to the pictures, he could start teaching himself how to read and speak English.

As the years passed, my grandfather worked hard to educate himself and eventually received highest honors in his field of engineering. As he raised his son — my father — Grandfather went on to instill the principles of diligence and hard work into him. Afterward, my father passed those same principles on to me.

Through the years, our family has been very devoted to any task we've been given, believing that we have a responsibility to do the best job possible for the people we are called to serve. Because of this work ethic that was instilled in me by my parents, I find laziness to be completely intolerable. I refuse to permit lazy people to be a part of my team!

This intolerance for laziness must also have been the attitude that Jesus felt about lazy people. In His parable of the talents, Jesus told us of a master who, before embarking on a long journey, entrusted his money into the hands of three servants. The master expected the servants to increase what he had given them. However, Matthew 25:19-23 tells us that when this master returned, he found that only the first two servants had increased what He had entrusted to them.

In verse 21, the Bible tells us the master returned and discovered that the first servant *doubled* his investment. When the master saw this *increase*, he said, "...Well done, thou good and faithful servant: thou hast been faithful over a few things, I will make thee ruler over many things: enter thou into the joy of thy lord." In verse 23, the master was similarly thrilled when he found out the second servant had *doubled* his investment as well: "His lord said unto him, Well done, good and faithful servant; thou hast been faithful over a few things, I will make thee ruler over many things: enter thou into the joy of thy lord."

But why did the master call their success a "few things"? Their accomplishment wasn't small. In fact, it was *huge*. Yet the master said to the first two servants, "…Thou hast been faithful over a few things…." His words "over a few things" seem to indicate that what they had done wasn't such a big deal after all. I'm sure the servants were dumbfounded. What did their master mean? Was he *belittling* what they had accomplished?

What the first two servants had achieved was fantastic, but it was just the *beginning*. They had proven themselves to be hardworking and capable. They had demonstrated responsibility. The master now knew they could be trusted with true riches. Because these two stewards had proven themselves faithful, the master saw a bright future ahead for them. As is always true with God, faithfulness resulted in promotion and greater responsibilities. The first two stewards had passed a test on a lower level. Now their master was satisfied to thrust them upward into even more monumental life assignments.

But when the master came to the third servant and saw that he had done *nothing* with the money given to him, he told the servant, "…Thou knewest that I reap where I sowed not, and gather where I have not strawed: Thou oughtest therefore to have put my money to the exchangers, and then at my coming I should have received mine own with usury" (vv. 26,27).

It is obvious that this third servant was not ignorant of the master's expectation. He *knew* that the master expected increase from him. In fact, he told them, "Thou knewest." This means the third servant couldn't pretend to be ignorant. He *knew* that the master expected him to do something significant with what had been entrusted to him.

This master would accept *no excuses* for a lack of increase. It didn't matter how difficult the situation, how many odds were against his servants, or how impossible it seemed, the master still expected *increase*. His servants understood that this was his expectation. Thus, the servant who did *nothing* with his talent found himself in a horrible predicament.

His master called him, "Thou wicked and slothful servant" (Matthew 25:26). As if this isn't bad enough, in Matthew 25:30 his master called him "the unprofitable servant." Before we go any further, let's stop to examine these words, for they vividly express Jesus' personal sentiment toward people who possess great potential but never develop it due to laziness.

Let's look first at Matthew 25:26, where Jesus calls the non-productive servant "thou wicked and slothful servant." The words "wicked and slothful" are taken from the single Greek word *okneros*. This word means *lazy* or *idle*. It carries the idea of *a person who has a do-nothing, lethargic, lackadaisical, apathetic, indifferent, lukewarm attitude toward life.*

This is a strong word, chosen by the Holy Spirit to tell us how strongly Jesus feels about those who are *apathetic* and *lethargic* about their spiritual lives and life assignments. Jesus has no taste for *lackadaisical* people. People who are *lukewarm* about their God-given abilities or who are *indifferent* about their assignments leave a sickening taste in the Lord's mouth. He loves the person, but He strongly dislikes the lazy attitudes that keep them from reaching their maximum potential.

In Matthew 25:30, Jesus continues by calling this non-productive servant "the unprofitable servant." The word "unprofitable" is from the Greek word *achreios*, which literally means *useless*. A literal translation in today's vernacular would be *the good-for-nothing servant*.

This word describes a person whose existence in life is absolutely *pointless*. He is an aimless, purposeless person who contributes nothing to life. This person's value has never been realized because he does nothing but take up space on the face of the planet. But like everyone else, this person had a choice. He *could* have become something significant if he had used what was entrusted to him and had done what God asked him to do.

As I read these words of Jesus, it makes me personally thankful that my parents taught me good work ethics and ingrained in me the importance of doing a more than satisfactory job for anyone I am called to serve. This pertains to serving God, serving people, serving my congregation, or serving any purpose that is entrusted to my care. Jesus expects the best I can do. I know that if I do anything less than my best, I have not done what He expects of me. Jesus' parable in Matthew 25 shouts this message to all of us!

Do you need to come up to a higher level by working on your work ethic? If so, make the decision to do so today. Jesus expects you to do the best you can do. Are you giving Him your best at church? Are you giving Him your best at the workplace, doing your job with the highest level of ability you possess? If Jesus came to evaluate your work, would He find it effective and satisfactory, or defective and lacking?

Never forget that Colossians 3:17 commands you: "And whatsoever ye do in word or deed, do all in the name of the Lord Jesus, giving thanks to God and the Father by him." Why don't you take a few minutes today to ask Jesus to help you be better at your job, to give more effort than you've ever given before, and to help you adjust your attitude so you can become a high-level performer at whatever task is assigned to you?

MY PRAYER FOR TODAY

Lord, I am sorry for any laziness that I've allowed in my life. Yes, I know I can do so much more than I've done. I haven't applied myself with all my heart and strength; instead, I've permitted myself to slip by at a mediocre level. I have done enough to keep my job, but I haven't done enough to deserve a promotion or a salary increase. Forgive me for complaining that I don't make enough money when the truth is that I haven't done my best work. I sincerely ask You to help me change my attitude and to increase my level of work performance.

I pray this in Jesus' name!

MY CONFESSION FOR TODAY

I confess that I am a good worker and that I have a great attitude! I am exactly the kind of person God can use and bless — and I am exactly the kind of employee that my employer is thrilled to have in his department, organization, or business. I work so hard and do such good work that I bring many blessings and benefits to those who are over me in authority. Because I am around, I make them look better! God rewards me for being faithful. My striving toward excellence today will lead to my promotion and financial increase tomorrow!

I declare this by faith in Jesus' name!

QUESTIONS FOR YOU TO CONSIDER

1. If Jesus were to come and personally inspect your attitude toward work and your actual work performance, what kind of evaluation do you think He would give

you? (You may as well be honest, because Jesus *is* watching your attitude and your work all the time!)

2. If you were looking for someone to promote, would you want to promote someone who had an attitude like yours or who worked like you do? If your answer is yes, thank God for it! If your answer is no, why wouldn't you want to promote someone like you?

3. What do you think are the top ten attitudes that make an employer so satisfied with an employee that he would want to promote him to a higher position? It would be a good idea to write down these "top ten attitudes" and then take some time to think about what you can do to better maintain these attitudes in your own life.

JUNE 7

Weeping and Gnashing of Teeth

And cast ye the unprofitable servant into outer darkness:
there shall be weeping and gnashing of teeth.
— Matthew 25:30

When I was a boy growing up in the church, I would frequently hear preachers use the phrase "weeping and gnashing of teeth" as a part of their sermons, especially if they were preaching on the subject of eternal damnation. Every time I heard the phrase "weeping and gnashing of teeth," I wondered, *What does that phrase mean? What is weeping and gnashing of teeth?*

The answer to this question is found in the story of the master who gave talents to three of his servants. As we already saw in yesterday's *Sparkling Gem*, Jesus called the lazy servant in that parable a "wicked and slothful servant." The words "wicked and slothful" both come from the single Greek word *okneros*. This word means *lazy* or *idle*. It carries the idea of *a person who has a do-nothing, lethargic, lackadaisical, apathetic, indifferent, lukewarm attitude toward life.*

Jesus used this parable to teach those of us who are His followers what He expects of us. The master in the parable vividly illustrates Jesus' sentiments toward people who have great potential but who are too lazy to get up, get out of the house, and do something to develop the potential that has been entrusted to them. Friend, we need to pay careful attention to the message in this parable, because *how Jesus sees things is how we must see things!*

Notice that the master in this parable said, "Take therefore the talent from him, and give it unto him which hath ten talents" (v. 28). This would be the response of any employer who discovered a time-waster on his staff. Rather than throw away more time waiting for an unprofitable, nonproductive person to get with the program, a smart employer will take his responsibility from him and give it to someone he knows can get the job done right!

Jesus continued, "For unto everyone that hath shall be given, and he shall have abundance: but from him that hath not shall be taken away even that which he hath" (v. 29). Here again we find a powerful truth: *Those who are good performers and whom the boss can trust to get things done will always have a very full plate of responsibility.* The employer trusts this employee's ability and appreciates his willingness to do whatever necessary to complete the assigned task with excellence. Therefore, he keeps piling more and more on this person whom he knows he can trust! This is precisely what Jesus meant when he said, "For unto everyone that hath shall be given, and he shall have abundance...."

But Jesus also said, "...But from him that hath not shall be taken even that which he hath." A good way to make sure that you get no pay increase or promotion and possibly even get fired is to do a poor job. Poor jobs should not be rewarded.

Rewards are given to those who deserve them. If a person consistently fails to do his job correctly or on time, or if he consistently does his assigned task with a grumpy, complaining attitude, he shouldn't be surprised when the new and bigger assignments are delegated to someone else besides him!

This leads us to Jesus' statement about "weeping and gnashing of teeth" in Matthew 25:30. It says, "And cast ye the unprofitable servant into outer darkness: there shall be weeping and gnashing of teeth." The word "unprofitable" is the Greek word *achreios*, which literally means *useless*. A literal translation in today's vernacular would be *the good-for-nothing servant.*

But notice that the master in this parable said to "cast" this servant "into outer darkness." The word "cast" is the word *ekballo*, from the words *ek* and *ballo*. The word *ek* means *out*, and the word *ballo* means *to throw*. Together these words mean *to expel, to throw out, to drive out,* or *to kick out*. This word pictures the master saying, *"Throw him out...";* *"Kick the guy out of the organization...";* *"Expel him as quickly as you can...";* *"Toss him out of here...."* The Greek expresses such total intolerance for laziness and non-productivity that the master wants the unprofitable servant gone as quickly as possible!

The master said to cast the unprofitable servant into "outer darkness." Let me explain this to you, because it is very important to the truth in this parable.

It is a fact that in New Testament times, almost every large city had huge stone city walls that protected the city from intruders and from lions who roamed the countryside. The residents of the city often dumped their garbage over the top of the walls in certain parts of the city, allowing the trash to fall and build up around the base of the huge stone walls. Because this garbage included unused food, lions from the countryside would come to the base of the city walls late at night — when it was very dark — to pillage the trash and look for food.

These huge piles of trash became sites where authorities tried to determine the guilt or innocence of individuals suspected of crimes but not concretely proven to be guilty. The authorities would tie the suspected criminal with rope and lower him to the base of the city walls during the darkest hours of the night — right into the midst of the garbage where the lions roamed every night. If they found the suspect alive the next morning, he was judged to be innocent of his crime. If he had been devoured, it was assumed that he had been guilty of the crime of which he had been accused.

Even if the victim *was* found alive the next morning, he was usually insane or on the verge of total insanity. In fact, his teeth were usually ground down by his own nervous gnashing and grinding of his teeth as the lions prowled and roared all around him all night long. This is where we get the phrase "weeping and gnashing of teeth." It was derived from this experience of suffering agony and even insanity as a result of being cast into outer darkness.

Why would Jesus use this example to depict the unprofitable servant who was kicked out of the business or organization? Well, just imagine what this person would feel like after being kicked out for doing a poor job. Later he would see others doing exactly what he had once been asked to do but what he had refused or failed to do because he was too lazy. That experience would be *pure agony* for him! It would be so difficult to watch someone else in his position — doing what he used to do, getting the promotion he could have gotten, achieving the greatness he should have achieved. To know that all of this could have been his if he hadn't forfeited it through his own wrong attitude and laziness — that would be *agony* for anyone!

So many people have had great ideas, but because they pondered the idea for too long without acting on it, someone else finally came up with the same idea — and then went out and did something about it! The person who originally came up with the idea sees someone else prospering with the idea he had first. How do you think that makes him feel? He knows it could have been him experiencing that prosperity and success, *but now it's too late.* His hesitation to act or his laziness prevented him from getting up and putting that idea into action; as a result, the opportunity passed on to someone who was willing to *do* something with the idea.

Do you know anyone who has experienced such agony due to his own lack of faith to step out and act on his dream? *Do you fit this description yourself?*

I pray that I haven't just described you! The last thing Jesus wants is for you to experience "weeping and gnashing of teeth." But honestly, friend, it's up to you. If you do nothing with the abilities and opportunities God gives you, you can be certain that those privileged opportunities for success will pass to someone who is willing to do something with them. The opportunity can be yours, or it can be taken from you. But if it *is* taken from you, it will be agony to your soul when you see someone else standing in your dream.

That's why I am begging you — please don't make this mistake! God has given you gifts, callings, and dreams to fulfill. Now it's up to you to step out in faith and DO something with what He has given you!

MY PRAYER FOR TODAY

Lord, help me understand how to act on the ideas You have placed in my heart. I don't want to be like the unprofitable servant who was thrown into outer darkness and experienced weeping and gnashing of teeth. I want to stand in the reality of the dream You have put in my heart. Please give me wisdom and courage to step out and begin to fulfill the dream You birthed so deeply inside my soul. I need You, Holy Spirit. I ask You to stir up Your courage inside me and help me to get moving!

I pray this in Jesus' name!

MY CONFESSION FOR TODAY

I confess that I'm not lazy or afraid to step out in faith. I am filled with God's wonderful ideas, and I will do what He has put in my heart. I am not hesitant or fearful but rather bold, courageous, and ready to go! God is my Helper; therefore, I will not be afraid. I will not fear what man can do to me, for the Lord is with me! He directs my mind; He guides my steps; and His Word lights my path before me.

I declare this by faith in Jesus' name!

QUESTIONS FOR YOU TO CONSIDER

1. Have you ever experienced "weeping and gnashing of teeth" from watching someone else step into your dream or your position because you failed to do it first?

2. If your answer is yes, did you ask Jesus to forgive you for being so faithless, afraid, hesitant, or lazy? If you haven't asked Him to forgive you yet, don't you think it would be a good idea to find a quiet place where you can really talk to the Lord about this?

3. If you have truly repented of your past actions, Jesus has forgiven you. Are you open for Him to give you another dream or opportunity when He sees that you're ready for the next assignment?

JUNE 8

You Can Make a Difference In Someone Else's Life!

And of some have compassion, making a difference.
— Jude 1:22

*I*f you are burdened for someone who isn't serving God the way he used to, it's time for you to do something about it. Worrying won't change a thing! But turning that worry into action can make a big difference in the outcome of that other person's life.

You can make a difference in someone else's life! That is precisely why Jude 1:22 tells us, "And of some have compassion, making a difference." Do you see the word "compassion" in this verse? This important word is taken from the Greek word *eleao*, which in this case refers to *deep-seated and unsettling emotions a person feels when he has seen or heard something that is terribly sad or upsetting.*

These are the kinds of emotions that well up inside you when you see a child whose stomach is bloated from malnutrition and starvation. You might also feel these emotions when you see a person who is emaciated and dying of terminal cancer or a destitute family that is forced to live on the streets with no food and money.

Jude's purpose in using the Greek word *eleao* is very plain. He is doing exactly what television programs do when they flash pictures of starving children with bloated stomachs on the television screen in front of us. The producers of these programs show us these kinds of worst-scenario pictures in order to stir us to *action*.

These pictures of desperate misery from Third World countries are flashed in front of us while emotionally moving music plays in the background. Then the celebrity host on the program says in an impassioned voice, *"Pick up your phone and call today. Your call could save the life of a child."*

These kinds of television programs are designed to stir up emotional feelings of pity. The producers of the programs realize that simply stating a need verbally would never get our attention; we're just too mentally busy in today's society. Therefore, they make the need as graphic as they possibly can, knowing that pictures speak a thousand words and are much more effective in arousing pity from our hearts.

However, arousing pity is *not* the ultimate aim of these programs. The horrifying pictures and emotional musical background are designed to convince you to pick up your telephone, call the phone number on the television screen, and make a donation to help the cause of the sponsoring organization. This compulsion *to act* and *to do something* is the moment when *pity* is transformed into *compassion*. By itself, pity would simply feel sorry about the situation. But compassion cannot sit by and idly watch the scenario grow worse. *Compassion reaches out to act immediately and to do something about the situation.*

It is unmistakably clear that Jude wants to elicit an emotional response from his readers. He wants them to graphically see and understand the seriousness of believers who have backslidden into a life of sin and disobedience. He wants his readers to "feel" for these critically ill spiritual patients. In fact, he wants them to "feel" their condition so intensely that he says, "And of some have compassion...." In other words, Jude is telling his readers to *take that pity and turn it into action*!

You see, when genuine compassion begins to flow from your heart, you cannot sit idly by and simply feel sorry about a person's situation. Real compassion says, "I have to get up and do something about this!"

Because Jude uses the word "compassion," he is telling us that the spiritual condition of a backslidden believer is just as real and serious as the plight of a starving child, a dying man, or a destitute family. If you will allow the love of God to flow through you, it won't be long until compassion for these erring believers begins to flow from you to them. Then you will be compelled to see them set free from their bondage! *That compulsion is the activity of compassion!*

You may think, "Yes, but those believers knew better! If they had stayed faithful in their walk with the Lord, they wouldn't be in the mess they are in right now. Isn't it their fault that they're in trouble?"

The answer to this question may be "Yes, they are to blame for their condition." However, consider this: Wouldn't you have compassion on a homosexual who contracted AIDS due to his own illicit sexual activity? Although his own actions got him into his mess, wouldn't it still grab hold of your heart when you saw his wasting body? Wouldn't his helpless condition make you wish there was a cure for AIDS?

In the same way, even though a sinning believer may have gotten himself into trouble because of his own actions, we must not therefore shut off the flow of God's compassion that resides within us. Believers who have become spiritually deceived need a touch of God's power more than they ever did before! Therefore, we cannot let the enemy sow hardheartedness in our hearts toward people who have become spiritually ill or backslidden. Their plight is very serious, and they need our help and prayers of intercession!

If you know people who fit this description, it's time for you to let the supernatural compassion of Jesus Christ begin to flow out of your heart toward them. These error-ridden believers need a divine touch from God that will open their eyes and bring them back to the Lord. By releasing a flow of this powerful force toward them, you could set in motion the very deliverance these individuals need from the powers of darkness that bind their souls and keep them in deception.

This is why Jude urges us to release this delivering flow of compassion when he says, "And of some have compassion...." This kind of compassion is a mighty force that reaches even into the flames of judgment to snatch people from destruction. Why not open the bowels of your heart and allow this supernatural flow of compassion to start flowing through you today? *Just think — by opening your heart and letting compassion flow through you toward these people, you could be the very one God uses to bring them back home again!*

MY PRAYER FOR TODAY

Lord, please forgive me for being hardhearted, condemning, and judgmental toward people who have needed my prayers and intercession. Instead of wasting all my time judging them,

I could have been praying for them. Now I see my mistake, and I truly repent for it. Starting today, I pledge to change my attitude — to open my heart and let the compassion of Jesus Christ flow through me to help set their deliverance in motion. Let Your compassion begin flowing through me today!

I pray this in Jesus' name!

MY CONFESSION FOR TODAY

I boldly confess that compassion flows through me like a river! Condemnation and judgment have no place in my life, in my thinking, or in the way I relate to other people. I am filled with the love of God, and I allow that love to touch others who are near me. The bowels of my heart release the compassion of Jesus Christ, touching the lives of people caught in the deception of sin and darkness and setting them free!

I declare this by faith in Jesus' name!

QUESTIONS FOR YOU TO CONSIDER

1. Do you know anyone who is no longer walking with God and for whom you need to be praying and interceding right now?
2. Have you acted in a judgmental way toward a sinning or erring believer — someone who really needs your prayers and intercession, *not* your condemnation? If your answer is yes, I suggest that you take a few minutes to get your heart right with God and then begin to regularly pray for his or her deliverance.
3. Have you ever been caught in a deception, but someone loved you through it until you were set free and put back on a straight course? Who was that person who stood with you through that ordeal? Did you ever take the time to express your gratefulness for his or her love and patience toward you during that time?

JUNE 9

Spiritual Warfare Is Real!

For we wrestle not against flesh and blood,
but against principalities, against powers,
against the rulers of the darkness of this world,
against spiritual wickedness in high places.
— Ephesians 6:12

Spiritual warfare is real! The devil and his demon spirits are not myths or fantasies. These are real beings that hate the human race and therefore roam about seeking whom they might destroy and devour. That's why it is vitally important to know how to best protect yourself against their attacks!

Most of the attacks the devil wages against you will occur in your mind. He knows that your mind is the central control center for your life; therefore, if he can take control of one small area of your mind, he can begin to expand outward into other weak areas that need to be strengthened by the Holy Spirit and the Word of God. By poisoning your mind with unbelief and lying strongholds, the devil can then manipulate not only your mind, but also your emotions and your body. There is no doubt about it — the mind is the strategic center where the battle is won or lost in spiritual warfare!

The devil wants to get access into your life — and if he finds that access, you may be headed for quite a conflict! You can see why it is so important that you keep every door shut; then the enemy won't be able to find any entrance through which he can begin to wage warfare against you.

However, the devil will often put up quite a fight even when he *doesn't* find an entrance into our lives. That's why we need to know exactly what the Bible says about spiritual warfare.

In Ephesians 6:12, Paul told us, "For we wrestle not against flesh and blood, but against principalities, against powers, against the rulers of the darkness of this world, against spiritual wickedness in high places." I want to especially draw your attention to the word "wrestle" in this verse, for this word is the key to understanding how intense spiritual warfare can become!

The word "wrestle" is from the old Greek word *pale*, which refers to *struggling, wrestling,* or *hand-to-hand combat.* However, the word *pale* is also the Greek word from which the Greeks derived their name for the *Palastra* — a huge palace of combat sports that was situated in the center of most larger, ancient cities.

The Palastra was a huge building that outwardly looked like a palace but was dedicated to the cultivation of athletic skills. Every morning, afternoon, and night, the most committed, determined, and daring athletes of the day could be found in this fabulous building, working out and training for their respective sports. Three kinds of athletes primarily worked out at the Palastra: *boxers, wrestlers,* and *pankratists.*

Let me tell you a little about how these sports functioned in the first century when Paul wrote this verse, because it forms the backdrop to the word "wrestle" in Ephesians 6:12. The first and most feared combat sport was *boxing.* But the boxers from the first century were not like our boxers today. Their sport was *extremely violent* — so violent that they were not permitted to box without wearing helmets. Without the protection of helmets, their heads would have been *crushed*! In fact, this sport was so severe that few boxers ever lived to retire from their profession. Most of them died in the ring. Of all the sports, the ancients viewed boxing as the most hazardous and deadly.

In this brutal and barbaric sport, the ancient boxers wore gloves ribbed with steel and spiked with nails. At times the steel wrapped around their gloves was serrated, like the blade of a hunting knife, in order to make deep gashes in the opponent's skin. In addition to this, they used extremely heavy gloves that made every punch more damaging. It is quite usual to find artwork from the time of the ancient Greeks that includes boxers whose faces, ears, and noses are totally deformed from being struck by these dangerous gloves.

Making this sport even more dangerous was the fact that there were *no rules* — except that a boxer couldn't clench his opponent's fist. That was the only rule of the game! There were no "rounds" like there are in boxing today. The fight just went on and on until one of the two surrendered or died in the ring.

Next, there were *wrestlers*! Wrestling was also a deadly sport in the first century. In fact, most wrestlers chose to fight to the death rather than walk out of the ring in humiliation and defeat. As you see, it was an ugly, bloody sport. In order to make an opponent surrender, it was quite normal to strangle him into submission. Choking was another acceptable practice in wrestling. Like boxing, wrestling was an extremely violent and bloody sport that tolerated every imaginable tactic: breaking fingers, breaking ribs by a waist lock, gashing the face, gouging out the eyes, and so on. Wrestling was a bitter struggle to the very end.

The third combat sport was *pankration*, from the Greek words *pan* and *kratos*. The word *pan* means *all*, and *kration* is from the word *kratos*, which means *power*. When these two words were put together, they formed the word *pankration*, which means *all powerful*. These fighters were the fiercest, toughest, and most committed of all! In this sport, they were permitted to kick, punch, bite, gouge, strike, break fingers, break legs, and to do any other horrible thing you could imagine. There was no part of the human body that was off limits. They could do anything they wanted to any part of their competitor's body, for there were basically no rules.

An early inscription from a father to his sons who participated in pankration says this: "If you should hear your son has died, you can believe it. But if you hear he has been defeated and chose to retire, do not believe it!" Why? Because like the other combat sports, pankration was *extremely violent*. While participating in this sport, more professional pankratists died than surrendered or were simply defeated.

I realize that these are very graphic images, but they are also very important images, for they are all contained in the word "wrestle" that Paul uses in Ephesians 6:12. In the day when Paul wrote this letter, everyone who saw the Greek word *pale* ("wrestle") saw all these images in their minds. You can see, then, that this was a powerful, pungent word for Paul to use when he started to describe our conflict with unseen, demonic powers that Satan has marshaled together to try to destroy us. By using the word "wrestle" from the Greek word *pale*, Paul was telling every reader (and us) that spiritual warfare can be *a bitter struggle* and *an intense conflict*.

This first phrase in Ephesians 6:12 really carries this idea:

"For our wrestling — that is, our intense struggle, fierce combat, contest, challenge, and ongoing conflict — is not really with flesh and blood, but with...."

Then Paul goes on to describe the different levels of demonic powers that exist in Satan's kingdom. As we look at what Paul said, I want you to see that this conflict can be fierce! I don't mean to alarm you, but you need to know that the devil is serious in his attempts to destroy you — and if you haven't prepared yourself spiritually to thwart such attacks, you may find yourself in a real quandary.

You see, our adversary is *real*. There are foul forces of darkness that work covertly behind most disasters and many moral failures. *However, these demonic spirits can't do anything unless our flesh cooperates with them!* They may come to tempt, to seduce, to deceive, and to assault the mind — but unless they find a partner to listen or cooperate with them, their evil attempts are futile and powerless.

Therefore, the greatest key to winning every battle the devil wages against you is to keep your mind dominated by the Word of God. As you do that, your flesh will be kept under the control of the Holy Spirit, which will block the majority of the enemy's attacks against your mind! This is why Peter urges us to "...gird up the loins of your mind..." (1 Peter 1:13).

Remember, the devil knows that if he can take control of one small area of your mind, he can begin to expand outward into other weak areas of your life. Therefore, don't you think it's time for you to start reading your Bible and filling your mind with God's thoughts? There is no better mental protection against the enemy's strategies than to fill your brain with God's Word! It will strengthen you and keep your mind free from unbelief and lying strongholds.

So take God's Word deep into your mind, and stop the devil from finding access into your life. Do everything you can to shut every door. Don't give the enemy *any* entrance through which he can begin to wage warfare against you!

MY PRAYER FOR TODAY

Lord, I don't want to ever give the devil access to my mind. I ask for forgiveness for the times I've permitted wrong thinking to go on inside me when I knew it was wrong. Now I understand that these are the areas through which the devil seeks to find entrance into my life. Starting today, I am asking You to help me locate each "open door" in my mind; then help me seal those doors shut by the power of Your Spirit and Your Word!

I pray this in Jesus' name!

MY CONFESSION FOR TODAY

I confess that my mind is dominated by the Word of God and that I am under the control of the Holy Spirit! I gird up the loins of my mind by reading my Bible and filling my mind with God's thoughts. God's Word strengthens me and keeps my mind free from unbelief and lying strongholds. I take God's Word deep into my mind, and it stops the devil from finding access into my life!

I declare this by faith in Jesus' name!

QUESTIONS FOR YOU TO CONSIDER

1. Can you think of any "open doors" in your mind right now through which the devil finds access into your life? Write down the "open doors" you need to shut immediately in order to stop the enemy's attacks.
2. Now that you have identified these areas, what are you going to do to seal them shut so the devil's access to your life is stopped?
3. Are you able to do this on your own, or do you need to ask someone to help you with prayer and daily encouragement? If you need help, ask the Holy Spirit to show you whom you should talk to. Then boldly go to that person and ask for his or her assistance.

Remember, the devil knows that if he can take control of one small area of your mind, he can begin to expand outward into other weak areas of your life. Therefore, don't you think it's time for you to start reading your Bible and filling your mind with God's thoughts? There is no better mental protection against the enemy's strategies than to fill your brain with God's Word! It will strengthen you and keep your mind free from unbelief and lying strongholds.

JUNE 10

The Rank and File
Of Satan's Kingdom

For we wrestle not against flesh and blood,
but against principalities, against powers,
against the rulers of the darkness of this world,
against spiritual wickedness in high places.
— Ephesians 6:12

I realize that many people tend to think that screaming, yelling, screeching, stomping, and shouting are required to defeat the devil. However, these actions will accomplish nothing if those same people are not living a consecrated and holy life.

It is simply a fact that if we have deliberately or by negligence allowed sinful strongholds to secretly remain in our lives, then we have left gaping holes through which Satan may continue to insert his schemes into our lives. Negligence in dealing with these secret places may give Satan the very loopholes he needs to orchestrate our defeat!

This business of spiritual warfare is serious! We must do all we can to shut every door to our souls through which the devil might attempt to access our lives. Because this issue *is* so serious, we would do well to pay attention when the Bible offers us information about the enemy of our souls. The devil has destroyed too many Christians who were ignorant of his devices!

In Ephesians 6:12, the apostle Paul presents a divine revelation he received that describes how Satan's kingdom has been militarily aligned. He writes, "For we wrestle not against flesh and blood, but against principalities, against powers, against the rulers of the darkness of this world, against spiritual wickedness in high places."

Notice that at the top of this list, Paul mentions a group of evil spirits he calls "principalities." This word is taken from the Greek word *archai*, an old word that is used symbolically to denote *ancient times*. It is also used to depict *individuals who hold the highest and loftiest position of rank and authority*. By using the word *archai*, Paul emphatically tells us that at the very top of Satan's kingdom are powerful evil beings that have held their lofty positions of power and authority since ancient times — probably ever since the fall of Lucifer.

Paul goes on to tell us that below principalities is a second group of evil beings he refers to as "powers." This word "powers" is taken from the Greek word *exousia*, and it denotes *delegated authority*. This describes a lower, second-level group of evil beings — demon spirits — who have received *delegated authority* from Satan to carry out all manner of evil in whatever way they desire to do it. These evil forces are second in command in Satan's dark kingdom.

Continuing in his description of Satan's rank and file in descending order, Paul mentions "the rulers of the darkness of this world." This amazing phrase is taken from the word *kosmokrateros* and is a compound of the words *kosmos* and *kratos*. The word *kosmos* denotes *order* or *arrangement*, whereas the word *kratos* has to do with *raw power*. Thus, the compounded word *kosmokrateros* depicts *raw power that has been harnessed and put into some kind of order*.

This word *kosmokrateros* was at times used to picture *military training camps where young men were assembled, trained, and turned into a mighty army.* These young men were like raw power when they first arrived in the training camp. However, as the military training progressed and the new recruits were taught discipline and order, all that raw manpower was converted into an organized, disciplined army. This is the word Paul now uses in his description of Satan's kingdom. *What does it mean?*

It tells you and me that Satan is so serious about doing damage to the human race that he deals with demon spirits as though they are *troops*! He puts them in rank and file, gives them orders and assignments, and then sends them out like military soldiers who are committed to kill. Just as men in a human army are equipped and trained in their methods of destruction, so, too, are these demon spirits. And once these demons are trained and ready to start their assault, Satan sends them forth to do their devious work against human beings.

Paul makes reference to this dispatch of evil spirits when he writes next about "spiritual wickedness in high places." The word "wickedness" is taken from the word *poneros*, and it is used to depict *something that is bad, vile, malevolent, vicious, impious, and malignant.* This tells us the ultimate aim of Satan's dark domain: These evil spirits are sent forth to afflict humanity in *bad, vile, malevolent, and vicious* ways!

Satan uses all these evil forces in his attacks against mankind. Nevertheless, we believers have far more authority and power than the devil and his forces. You and I have the Greater One living within us! As members of the Church of Jesus Christ, we are loaded with heaps and heaps of raw power, for the Church has no shortage of power, nor is it deficient in God-given authority. We have more power and more authority than all these evil forces combined!

What we lack is *order* and *discipline*. We must learn to see ourselves as the army of God and to view the local church as the training center where we are taught to do God's business. Then we must heed the call of Jesus and be dispatched into the dark world to preach the Gospel and to drive these evil forces from people's lives. We must buckle down and begin to view ourselves as the troops of Jesus Christ!

Being organized and disciplined includes living a holy and consecrated life. There is no room for slackness in the life of a real Christian soldier. To deal with these forces that are being dispatched to destroy us and the world around us, it is required that we walk with God and listen to the voice of His Spirit. We must gird up the loins of our minds and fill our thoughts with the Word of God. Satan's troops are serious — and if we're not serious about our contest with them, it will only be a matter of time until they discover our weakness and strike with all their force to bring us down.

Determine to see yourself as a soldier in the army of God. Don't allow *anything* to remain in your life that would hinder your fight of faith. Be disciplined, committed, and organized. Take advantage of all the weapons described in Ephesians 6:13-18. *Then get ready to witness the awesome demonstration of God's power in your life as you prevail against Satan's rank and file!*

MY PRAYER FOR TODAY

Lord, help me start seeing myself as a mighty soldier in the army of God. You have provided every weapon I need to prevail against the enemies that come against my life, my family, my business, my friends, and my church. I want to stand tall and firm against the wicked plots the devil tries to exert against people's lives whom I love and need. Holy Spirit, give me the power and strength I need to successfully resist every attack and to drive all dark forces from my life and from the lives of those close to me!

I pray this in Jesus' name!

MY CONFESSION FOR TODAY

I confess that I live a holy and consecrated life! There is no room for slackness in my life. I am serious about serving God as a real Christian soldier. I do everything that is required for me to walk with God and to hear the voice of His Spirit when He speaks to me. I am very serious about winning every conflict with evil forces. Because of my strong commitment to this fight of faith, I am more than a match for anything the devil tries to throw at me!

I declare this by faith in Jesus' name!

QUESTIONS FOR YOU TO CONSIDER

1. What did you learn by reading today's *Sparkling Gem*?
2. Do you see yourself as a soldier in the army of God?
3. Do you view your local church as a place for you to be trained, taught, and disciplined in order to become a better Christian soldier?

JUNE 11

Your Faith Will Put You On Center Stage!

Partly, whilst ye were made a gazingstock
both by reproaches and afflictions;
and partly, whilst ye became companions
of them that were so used.
— Hebrews 10:33

Have you ever taken a stand of faith that made you the biggest joke in your church, among your friends, in your city, or in your state? When people heard what you believed that God told you, did they laugh? Did they find the dream God gave you to be one of the most amusing things they had ever heard, endlessly joking about it at your expense? Did you find their response humiliating and hurtful, or were you able to shove it aside and keep marching forward with the orders Jesus gave you?

When the writer of Hebrews wrote his letter, the Jewish believers to whom he was writing had been walking by faith for many years. He reminded them of how people first responded when they started their walk of faith. He said, "Partly, whilst ye were made a gazingstock both by reproaches and afflictions; and partly, whilst ye became companions of them that were so used" (Hebrews 10:33).

Do you see the word "gazingstock" in this verse? It comes from the Greek word *theatron*, from which we get the word *theater*. It means *to observe, to watch, to study, to scrutinize,* or *to bring upon the stage for all to see.* It is a picture of spectators taking their seats in the theater to watch how the play goes, all the way through Act I, Act II, Act III, and Act IV. However, if we look at this word in the context of this verse, we can see that this audience isn't watching to see how *good* the show is; they are watching in order to catch the players making a mistake!

This crowd is on the edge of their seats, anticipating the first time one of the actors makes a mistake or forgets a line so they can laugh at him, scorn him, ridicule him, and make fun of him. In fact, one expositor says the Greek word *theatron* in this verse means *to bring on to the stage in order to scorn, to scoff at, to shame, to sneer at, and to publicly humiliate*.

It is so important that this word was used here, for the Holy Spirit is alerting us to the fact that whether you and I like it or not, when we take a step of faith or a new stand on the Word of God, it almost always puts us "center stage"! We may not be known by thousands, but our faith confession or our announced plans will become the dinner conversation among friends, family, associates, and foes. Everyone will seem to develop an opinion as to whether we are overstepping our boundaries by taking on something too big for us, or whether we will be able to fulfill our dream.

You'll be amazed at how many of the people you thought would believe in you and support you instead buy a ticket to the show with everyone else, taking a seat in the theater to watch how well you fare with your new grand announcement! It's just a fact that there will always be spectators who stand by, eagerly anticipating the moment they can laugh at you or say, "We told you so!" when you make your first mistake in your walk of faith. Unfortunately, many times these spectators are not unbelievers, but *believers*!

Because the word *theatron* is used in this verse,
an expanded translation of this verse could read this way:

"You were made a theater...."
"You became a spectacle of entertainment...."
"On account of your faith, you became the best show in town...."

Hebrews 10:33 also uses two other very important words that are key for you to understand. These are the words "reproaches" and "afflictions." The word "reproach" is the Greek word *oneidismos*, and it refers *to insults hurled at you from other people*. This is precisely what they did to Jesus when He was on the Cross. That Cross literally put Jesus on the center stage of the universe. Rather than applauding Him for what He was doing for mankind, the people "reproached" Him. In other words, they threw *insults* and *slanderous accusations* at Him.

When you take a strong stand by faith or when the Holy Spirit convicts you about staying true to a principle in God's Word, Satan will do everything within his power to coax you to move off that stance of faith. He'll use family members, friends, associates, and even circumstances to thwart the plan of God for your life. The devil will use people you know and love to say things that simply shock you! This is his attempt to get you to back off the promise you have received. But if you are certain you are doing what God told you to do, don't budge an inch, no matter how much verbal opposition you encounter!

But Paul says that in addition to the verbal abuse that people may hurl at you, the devil will also try to use "afflictions" to stop you! The word "afflictions" is from the Greek word *thlipsis*, which refers to *a tight squeeze* or *terrible pressure*. This describes how the devil will try to use circumstances and events in life to put you under so much pressure that you eventually break, throwing in the towel and giving up. This word *thlipsis* indicates that the devil may try to use everything around you to shut you down when you step out in faith to obey what God has instructed you to do.

Satan doesn't hide in the closet and pop out at night to personally attack us while we're sleeping! Because he is the "god of this world" (2 Corinthians 4:4), he uses the world to do battle with us. In other words, he uses people, events, situations, circumstances, and difficult dilemmas to obstruct us from reaching our goals.

But regardless of what weapon the enemy uses or how he attempts to combat you and me, we have a faith that overrides and supercedes any organization, any event, any circumstance, or any difficult dilemma Satan would try to employ against us. He may be the "god of this world," but we have a weapon so powerful that we can shoot him down every time he shows up uninvited!

So when you find yourself on center stage in front of people who are watching your walk of faith as if it were the newest show in town, don't let this situation take you by surprise or throw you off track from your assignment. *Ignore it.* And if problems emerge as you step out in faith, don't let that shake you either. You shouldn't automatically assume that problems are indicators you are doing something wrong. They may be indicators that you are doing something *right* and that Satan hates it!

Ask the Spirit of God to help you stay on track. Don't budge an inch, and refuse to yield or give *any* territory to the devil. It's time for you to stay put, ignore the opposition, and *hold tight*!

MY PRAYER FOR TODAY

Lord, help me keep my eyes and ears fixed on You and not on what I see and hear coming from people and circumstances around me. I believe that Your Word is true; therefore, I am standing firm on Your promise to me. Regardless of what people say or do, I choose to follow You! Please help me to stay put and to ignore other people's verbal accusations as I hold tightly to Your Word.

I pray this in Jesus' name!

MY CONFESSION FOR TODAY

I boldly declare that I will not move from the promise Jesus made to me! His Word is true, and His timing is right. Therefore, I am staying put until I see the manifestation of what I have believed! Although the devil tries to use people and circumstances to move me, I refuse to be moved from what Jesus has promised me!

I declare this by faith in Jesus' name!

QUESTIONS FOR YOU TO CONSIDER

1. Can you think of a time when you took a step of faith that put you on center stage in most people's minds? Did you feel like everyone bought a ticket to the show and took their seats to watch, to scrutinize, and to criticize?

2. As you sincerely review your own past, can you think of a time in your life when you became the cynic and critic of someone who took a step of faith? If your answer is yes, is it possible that you are now reaping what you sowed and that you need to repent for being critical in the past of others who took similar steps of faith?

3. Do you have a faith-filled circle of friends who are standing with you and who are supporting you as you take this step of faith? Can you name those friends who are standing with you?

JUNE 12

❧

Don't Ignore the Fruit Growing On the Branches of the Tree!

Wherefore by their fruits ye shall know them.
— Matthew 7:20

*J*esus taught very strongly that when considering people for any leading position, it is necessary that we first carefully look at the fruit in that person's life. Even if the person is willing and eager to serve, the fruit in his personal life and attitude is exactly what you're going to get when you put him into a position of leadership. *So don't ignore what you see!*

One of the greatest mistakes I've made through the years is to ignore obviously bad symptoms in a person's life because I so wanted to see that person use his gifts and reach his maximum potential. But I learned the hard way that we cannot overlook the fruit in a person's life when considering him or her for a position of leadership. Talents and gifts are important, but they do not supercede the importance of a person's character.

In Matthew 7:20, Jesus told us, "Wherefore by their fruits ye shall know them." The word "fruit" is the Greek word *karpos* — the Greek word that describes *the physical fruit of plants or trees*. However, the word *karpos* is also used to depict *the fruit borne by a person's life*. This fruit might include *a person's deeds, actions, moral character, and behavior, or the output of the person's work*. In essence, Jesus used the word *karpos* to tell us that the various by-products of a person's life ultimately reveal what is *inside* that person.

Jesus taught that we can ascertain much about a person by looking at the fruit in his life. In fact, Jesus said it is possible to "know" people by their fruit. The word "know" is the Greek word *epignosis*, a compound of the words *epi* and *gnosis*. The word *epi* means *upon*; the word *gnosis* means *to know* and is the Greek word for *knowledge*. When you compound these two words together, they form the word that means *to come upon or to happen upon some kind of knowledge* and carries the idea of *making a discovery*.

In light of this, we must be very careful to look at the fruit of people's lives when considering them for key positions in our churches, ministries, businesses, or organizations. You can make quite a discovery about people if you'll just take the time to carefully observe their lives! If you want to know what is inside a person, just observe his attitudes and how he relates to other people. His *fruit* will tell you the truth about who he really is. Good fruit belongs to good trees, and bad fruit belongs to bad trees. It's that simple. The fruit *never* lies.

For so many years, I made the mistake of being impressed with the tree while failing to take a serious look at the fruit. I learned the hard way that even though the tree may be tall, stout, and strong, that impressive-looking tree may produce deadly fruit. Or perhaps the tree is destined to produce good fruit in the future, but the time for picking its fruit hasn't come yet.

Timing is very important when it comes to harvesting good fruit. It's simply a fact that if you pick fruit before it's ready, it will produce a bitter taste. For example, if you pick apples too early, their taste is sour, bitter, and sharp. By picking an apple before it's ripe, you ruin what would have been a perfectly good apple.

It's the same with people. If you pull someone off the pew and plop him into a leadership position before he's ripe, it won't be an enjoyable experience for either you or that person. If he isn't ripe yet, there's nothing you can do to make him ripen faster. So be careful not to push this kind of person into a position he isn't ready to handle; if you do, both of you will end up regretting a sour experience.

John Mark is a good example of what I'm talking about. This young man had so much potential that Paul and Barnabas took him with them when they first began their journeys (Acts 13:5). But Acts 13:13 tells us that for some reason, John Mark abandoned the apostles at an early stage of the trip and returned home to Jerusalem.

The Bible doesn't tell us exactly why John Mark left. Perhaps he was homesick and therefore returned home. Maybe he was simply immature and unfaithful. Whatever caused John Mark to decide to leave, the experience left such a bitter taste in Paul's mouth that when Barnabas wanted to take this young man on the next trip, Paul *refused*.

Paul's memories of John Mark were so bitter that he fought with Barnabas about it. Paul even broke up his partnership with Barnabas rather than be subjected to another bad experience with this young man. But then something truly amazing happened. Years later when Paul was in a Roman prison preparing to die, he wrote to Timothy and said, "Take Mark, and bring him with thee: for he is profitable to me for the ministry" (2 Timothy 4:11).

This "Mark" that Paul mentioned is the same John Mark whom Paul earlier refused to take as a part of his team. Now years have passed, and John Mark has grown and matured. By the time Paul wrote those words to Timothy, he considered this young man not only ready to be used, but "profitable for the ministry"!

When John Mark went on that first trip with Paul and Barnabas many years earlier, he was simply not ready to be used as a part of such a significant leadership team. As is often the case, the problem years before wasn't whether or not John Mark was "called"; it was a matter of timing. He wasn't mature enough to take part in such heavy-duty ministry at that earlier time. But now years had passed, and Mark had not only become ready, but *profitable* to the work of God.

John Mark was like an apple that had been picked too early. He went on that first ministry trip before his fruit was ripe or ready for picking. But the truth is, that wasn't entirely John Mark's fault. Those who chose him to be a part of that first team made a mistake by selecting him too soon. They needed to accept part of the responsibility for putting an immature person into the ministry before he was ready.

It is true that Mark did wrong by abandoning the apostles to return home prematurely. However, this probably wouldn't have happened if the leaders had tested him properly instead of rushing through the process in order to use him. Although Mark may have been talented and gifted, he wasn't ready for that kind of responsibility in the ministry. *He was an apple picked before it was ripe!*

So open your eyes, and let the Holy Spirit help you observe the fruit a person produces in his life. If you see a disturbing symptom, don't overlook the warning signs that are flashing all around you, hoping that these things will somehow mysteriously go away. Pay attention to what you see and hear, because what you see and the attitude that person emits is most likely what he will produce once you take him into your team.

And as you contemplate the fruit produced by others, don't forget to let the Holy Spirit speak to you about the fruit you are producing in your own life! Would others say the fruit they taste from your life is sweet or bitter? Are you a blessing, or are you a curse? A good tree produces good fruit, and a bad tree produces bad fruit. So what kind of fruit do you produce? *Always remember — the fruit never lies!*

MY PRAYER FOR TODAY

Lord, help me take a truthful look at the fruit produced in my life. After seeing the truth and coming to recognize areas of my life that produce bad fruit, please help me purge those bad places from my character so I can start producing good fruit in every part of my life. Without You, I can never be everything I need to be — but with Your help, I can become just like Jesus! So today I am asking You to help me get started purging and cleansing every part of my life that produces less-than-pleasing fruit.

I pray this in Jesus' name!

MY CONFESSION FOR TODAY

I confess that I am a producer of good fruit! People see the character of Jesus Christ in me, and I demonstrate His love to everyone around me. Every day I am drawing closer to the Lord and becoming more like Jesus. The fruit produced by my life is so sweet that it causes others to draw near that they might experience the goodness of God as demonstrated through me.

I declare this by faith in Jesus' name!

QUESTIONS FOR YOU TO CONSIDER

1. Have you ever known a person who produced fruit so bitter that you wanted to stay away from him? What kind of bitter fruit did that person produce?
2. Have you ever known individuals who produced such sweet fruit in their lives that you cherished every opportunity to be close to them? How would you describe the good fruit these individuals produced with their lives?
3. If you were someone else looking at your own life, would you rate the fruit demonstrated by your life as good or bad fruit? Explain your answer.

If you pull someone off the pew and plop him into a leadership position before he's ripe, it won't be an enjoyable experience for either you or that person. If he isn't ripe yet, there's nothing you can do to make him ripen faster. So be careful not to push this kind of person into a position he isn't ready to handle; if you do, both of you will end up regretting a sour experience.

JUNE 13

❧

How Badly Do You Want To Win Your Race?

Know ye not that they which run in a race run all,
but only one receiveth the prize? So run, that ye may obtain.
— 1 Corinthians 9:24

When runners run in a race, they have one thing foremost in their mind — the finish line! It was with this thought in mind that the apostle Paul wrote and told the Corinthians, "Know ye not that they which run in a race run all, but only one receiveth the prize? So run, that ye may obtain" (1 Corinthians 9:24).

The word "run" is the Greek word *trecho*, which means *to run* and indicates a *constant and continuous pace*. This word *trecho* often depicted runners who ran a foot race in a huge stadium before adoring crowds of fans. In order for the runner to run successfully and finish triumphantly, every ounce of his strength and his complete attention were required. Paul had this example in mind as he wrote this verse.

Just as it takes full concentration and a stride that is paced for a runner to run a long distance, Paul now uses the word *trecho* to tell us that if we are going to run our race as God expects, it will require 100 percent of our attention and will mandate that we learn how to run at a constant and continuous pace. In other words, we can't try today, stop tomorrow, and then give it another shot a week later. We must be constant and consistent. Once we are in the race, we must run ferociously. On the other hand, to stay in the race on a long-term basis, we must learn to pace ourselves so we can stay consistent and avoid wearing ourselves out!

Paul tells us that we are to run until we "obtain." The word "obtain" is the Greek word *katalambano*, which is a compound of the words *kata* and *lambano*. The word *kata* describes something that is coming *downward*, and the word *lambano* means *to take* or *to seize* something. When compounded together into one word, it becomes *katalambano* — a very powerful word indeed!

For example, the word *katalambano* can picture someone who has found something he has searched for his entire life. Rather than lose it or pass up the opportunity to possess it, he pounces on it with all his might, latching hold of it and seizing it with joy! Or once again, this word can portray a runner who runs fiercely, using every last ounce of his energy as he strains forward toward the finish line. At last he reaches the goal and crosses the finish line. The prize is now his! He won the reward because he put his whole heart, soul, and body into obtaining it!

**In light of the words *trecho* and *katalambano*
found in this verse, First Corinthians 9:24 carries this idea:**

"Don't you know that those who compete in a foot race run with all their might and strength against the other runners, but only one wins the competition and takes the prize? In light of this, run with all the might you can muster! Go the distance, and pace yourself to make sure you have enough energy to get to the finish line, where you will finally latch hold of and possess that which you have been so passionately pursuing!"

At the end of Paul's own life, he wrote, "I have finished my course" (2 Timothy 4:7). He triumphantly exclaimed that he had done it! His race was finished! He had given his spiritual race all he had to give; he had run with all the might he could muster; and he had run so consistently over the years that he had finished a winner! All those years of being concentrated and focused finally paid off! If Paul had approached his race with an attitude of lazy complacency, the prize would have gone to another. But because he had "run to obtain," he *obtained*!

Paul looked at his divine destiny that lay before him like a runner looks at the finish line. Rather than approach his spiritual race lazily and half-heartedly, Paul did everything within his power to preach the Gospel. If it meant getting a job on the side in order to be able to preach, that's what Paul did (Acts 18:3). If it meant becoming as a Jew in order to able to preach to the Jews, that's what Paul did (1 Corinthians 9:20). And if it meant becoming as those without law to win those who were without law, that's what Paul did (1 Corinthians 9:21). He became all things to all men in order that he might win some to the Lord (1 Corinthians 9:22).

Paul suffered hardship, persecution, lack, cold, hunger, nakedness, homelessness, trouble from false brethren, trouble from true brethren — in the city, in the wilderness, and even at sea. He was beaten, afflicted by persecution, and troubled by religious people. Yet Paul never lost sight of the fact that he was called of God and that he would one day account for what he did with that calling. The finish line was always before him! He kept one thing foremost in his mind and preeminent in his thinking: *I must obtain the prize. I must fulfill the purpose for which I was born. I must achieve the plan of God for my life.*

Likewise, if you want to achieve God's will for your life, there isn't room for any other attitude than one of boldness and determination to keep running toward the goal with your eyes fixed on the finish line! This alone will take you through every obstacle and attack of the enemy and ultimately bring you to the place God desires for your life.

Like Paul, you must have resolve, strength of will, determination, backbone, high morale, courage, devotedness, persistence, tenacity, and an unrelenting mindset. You must put your foot down and take your stand as a no-nonsense kind of person who puts your whole heart into your calling. Sitting around hoping for something to happen isn't going to produce anything! You have to jump in the race, fix your eyes on the goal, and run with all your might to the finish line so you can take the prize!

It's time for you to "take the bull by the horns" and then hold on for dear life all the way to the goal! Make the decision that you are going to run the race, go the distance, and *finish first place*! *Only you can make this choice, so why not get started today?*

MY PRAYER FOR TODAY

Lord, I ask You to help me become more fixed and focused on the goal You have given for my life. I don't want to allow distractions to pull me away from Your plan any longer. I want to shut my eyes and ears to the voices that beckon me to slow down and then set my face toward the purpose for which I was born. I can only do this with the help of Your Spirit, so today I turn to You to empower me to do this and to carry it all the way through to completion!

I pray this in Jesus' name!

MY CONFESSION FOR TODAY

I confess that I am fixed and focused on God's plan for my life. I have set my face like flint; I am unflinching and unstoppable in my pursuit toward the goals God has set for me. I have strength of will, determination, a strong backbone, high morale, courage, devotedness, persistence, tenacity, and an unrelenting mindset. I have put my foot down and taken my stand. I am in the race; I have fixed my eyes on the goal; and I run with all my might so I can take the prize!

I declare this by faith in Jesus' name!

QUESTIONS FOR YOU TO CONSIDER

1. How well are you running your race of faith right now? Are you consistent, or are you on-again, off-again in the way you are pursuing God's plan for your life?
2. If you keep running at the pace you're running right now, how long will it take you to get to where God wants you to be? Is it even possible to reach God's destination for you at your present pace?
3. What do you need to do to become more focused and less distracted? What do you need to remove from your life to help you stay on track and keep your sight fixed on the goal before you?

JUNE 14

A True Story To Demonstrate
The Danger of 'Cracks' in Your Life

Wherefore let him that thinketh
he standeth take heed lest he fall.
— 1 Corinthians 10:12

*T*here is an incredible story from history that demonstrates the danger of "cracks" in your spiritual life. The story comes from the city of Sardis, where one of the seven churches in the book of Revelation was located (*see* Revelation 3:1-6).

The city of Sardis was located very high on top of sheer cliffs that were almost impossible to climb. Because of their city's high and remote location, the residents believed it couldn't be penetrated or taken captive by a foreign enemy. It was this overconfidence that led to the demise of Sardis on more than one occasion.

Because those who lived in Sardis believed they were impenetrable, they felt sure that foreign aggressors couldn't make war on them. As a result, they became proud, cocky, overconfident, lazy, and complacent. As this apathy took over, the residents smugly concluded that there was no other city as secure as theirs. As a result of this haughty attitude, they stopped giving attention to the foundations and walls of their spiraling city. Thus, while the people's pride and overconfidence kept growing stronger and stronger over the years, they failed to notice that the foundations and walls of their city had begun to deteriorate and form massive cracks at the base of the walls.

At first the cracks were small and unnoticeable; but as time progressed, those tiny cracks grew bigger, deeper, and wider. Finally, the gaps in the walls became so wide that a human body could easily slip through them — but the people didn't even realize that they were no longer secure! Due to the massive fractures in the walls and foundations, it had become very easy for an enemy to climb up the sides of the mountain, slip through the cracks, and march right into the city. Yet the city residents were completely unaware of the problem!

One night while the city of Sardis was sleeping, an enemy army scaled up the cliffs and slithered through the cracks in the foundations and walls of the city. It took only a few minutes for the enemy soldiers to creep through those fractures and silently make their way up to the top of the city walls. The invading army then settled into military positions with weapons fixed on the main routes of the interior so no one in Sardis could make a move without facing retaliation.

When the residents of Sardis awakened the next morning and ventured out into the streets, they were thrown into a state of panic and shock when they realized that they were surrounded on every side by an enemy force. Enemy forces had infiltrated into their midst before they knew those forces were even near!

Unfortunately, the city of Sardis is like so many of us. We become so busy with life, so tossed about by everyday cares, or perhaps so confident of our own abilities, that we become unaware of our own spiritual need. We go on in life as though we have no need to deal with the foundations of our lives, not realizing that tiny cracks are starting to form.

This kind of negligent thinking is usually accompanied by prayerlessness and insensitivity to the Spirit of God. A Christian who is too busy to get into the Presence of God is a Christian who will soon find himself in trouble, just like the city of Sardis.

This is why the apostle Paul said, "Wherefore let him that thinketh he standeth take heed lest he fall" (1 Corinthians 10:12). The word "thinketh" is from the Greek word *dokeo*, which in this case means *to be of the opinion, to reckon, to suppose,* or *to think,* as it is translated here in the *King James Version*. In this verse, the word *dokeo* expresses the idea of what a person *thinks* or *supposes* about himself. There is nothing here to verify that the individual's opinion is correct; only that it is the prevailing opinion he has regarding himself. In just a moment, you'll see why this is so important for you to understand!

Next, Paul says, "Wherefore let him that thinketh he standeth...." The word "standeth" comes from the Greek word *istemi*, which simply means *to stand, to stand fast, to stand firm,* or *to stand upright*. But when the words *dokeo* and *istemi* are combined together as Paul uses them in this verse, it means, "Wherefore let anyone who has the self-imposed opinion of himself that he is standing strong and firm...." Then Paul adds the next critically important words: "...take heed lest he fall."

The words "take heed" are from the Greek word *blepo*, which means *to watch, to see, to behold,* or *to be aware*. The Greek tense indicates the need not only *to watch,* but *to be continually watchful*. Paul is urging us to live in an uninterrupted state of watchfulness regarding our spiritual lives and the firm stance of faith that we claim to possess!

Why does he insist that we be so watchful? He goes on to say, "Wherefore let him that thinketh he standeth take heed lest he fall." The word "fall" is *pipto*, which means *to fall*. In the New Testament, it is used to depict someone who *falls into a terrible predicament or into a worse state than he was in before*. It can also depict someone who *falls into sin; falls into ruin;* or *falls into some type of failure*. The word *pipto* that Paul uses in this verse emphatically describes *a downfall from a formerly presumed high and haughty position*. Therefore, it isn't just a little stumbling that Paul is referring to; it is a downward plummet that causes one to sorrowfully crash!

When you put all of this together,
First Corinthians 10:12 could be translated:

"If anyone has the opinion of himself that he is standing strong and firm, he needs to be continually watchful and always on his guard lest he trip, stumble, and fall from his over-confident position and take a nose-dive downward to a serious crash!"

We must never become so smug that we fall into complacency. The day we allow that to happen, we are in big trouble! Like the city of Sardis, we may end up with huge cracks we aren't even aware of. That is exactly when the enemy will slip in to take us captive in different areas of our lives. Therefore, we must match our *confidence* with *watchfulness*!

Unfortunately, it appears that the *church* in Sardis precisely mirrored the *city* of Sardis. Jesus told them, "…I know thy works, that thou hast a name that thou livest, and are dead" (Revelation 3:1). At one time the church in Sardis had a great name and a testimony of being spiritually alive and vibrant. But because the believers in that church got too busy and failed to give heed to the foundational things in their lives, cracks began to form spiritually over time. Eventually the devil found a way to slip into that church to ruin its name and influence. Because of spiritual negligence, this church body lost its vitality until Jesus even said it was "dead."

In Revelation 3:2, Jesus told them, "Be watchful, and strengthen the things that remain, that are ready to die: for I have not found thy works perfect before God." I love this verse, for it alerts us to the fact that it is never too late to do something to fix the problem! Jesus said, *"Locate the problem! Find a solution! Strengthen what you have! Do it before it's too late!"*

If you have a part of your life that is broken, cracked, or splintered, there is still hope that it can be restored. It may require emergency care to get it on life support for now, but it can be *resuscitated* and brought *back to life* again. Preventative medicine is always better than corrective surgery, so learn to take the right steps to avoid these problems.

It may seem like it takes a lot of time to stay watchful and prayerful about your spiritual life, but I assure you that it is less expensive and less painful than it is to crash spiritually and then have to fix things in your life that never had to be broken in the first place!

MY PRAYER FOR TODAY

Lord, help me stay watchful regarding the condition of my spiritual life! I recognize that sometimes I get too busy and fail to pray, wrongly presuming that I am strong enough to be able to survive in a state of prayerlessness. Especially after what I've read today, I realize that this kind of smugness and pride has always gotten me into trouble. Therefore, I turn from apathy and the wrong kind of confidence, and I turn to the Cross! Please examine my heart and help me identify those areas of my life that need to be fixed or corrected. Once You reveal to me what needs to be changed, please give me the power to apply the needed correction.

I pray this in Jesus' name!

MY CONFESSION FOR TODAY

I declare by faith that I am sensitive to the Spirit of God! The Holy Spirit shows me every area of my life that is weak and that needs attention. When the Holy Spirit speaks to me, I am quick to listen and quick to obey. I urgently act to bring correction to every weakness in my character and my spiritual life where the enemy might try to penetrate. Therefore, the devil has no access to me!

I declare this by faith in Jesus' name!

QUESTIONS FOR YOU TO CONSIDER

1. Are you aware of any areas in your life that have deteriorated and need attention? It could be your marriage, your finances, your relationships, or a whole host of other vital areas of your life. Are there cracks in any of these areas through which the devil may try to sneak up on you and take you captive?
2. If your answer is yes, what do you need to do to seal those cracks and strengthen those areas so the devil cannot successfully lay siege to your life?
3. Can you think of one area in your life that was fractured in the past, but through God's grace is now healed and sealed from any future attacks of the devil?

JUNE 15

Don't Throw Holy Things to the Dogs!

Give not that which is holy unto the dogs,
neither cast ye your pearls before swine,
lest they trample them under their feet,
and turn again and rend you.
— Matthew 7:6

Sometimes we try in vain to help people who don't appreciate the help we are offering them. When we try to help people like this, they are so ungrateful that it almost feels like they spit in our faces. When we give them helpful hints about how to do something better or attempt to warn them of a catastrophe that is headed in their direction, these people are so bullheaded that they refuse to listen!

When my wife and I were young in the ministry, we embraced everyone and gave our whole hearts to anyone who said they needed help. Often we invested ourselves, our time, and our money into people who didn't have a job and didn't even want to work, but who knew how to pull on our heart-strings to help them. Eventually my wife and I learned the hard lesson, as everyone must, that there comes a time when we have to stop throwing away our time and attention on people who don't care.

Yes, these people are precious, and you need to treat each of them as a unique creation of God. But your gifts are also precious, and you need to be valued and appreciated as well. If you have given again and again to the same people, but they consistently refuse to appreciate or value what you have given them, you need to respect *yourself* enough to quit giving away the precious things of your life to people who don't even care.

In Matthew 7:6, Jesus said, "Give not that which is holy unto the dogs, neither cast ye your pearls before swine, lest they trample them under their feet, and turn again and rend you." When I was younger, this verse bothered me terribly because I didn't like the idea of thinking of people as "dogs" and "swine." Yet these are the words that Jesus used to describe the behavior of a certain category of people. Why did He use such strong words? What message was Jesus trying to give us when He said, "Give not that which is holy unto the dogs..."?

Let's look at this verse today. Jesus said, "Give not that which is holy unto the dogs, neither cast ye your pearls before swine..." (Matthew 7:6). The word "give" is the Greek word *didomi*, which means *to give*, but here it is used with a negative, and the tense used in the Greek grammar should be taken as a command. This means the verse should be translated, *"Never give...."* It emphatically declares that this is something that should *never* be done!

The word "holy" is the word *hagios*, which refers to *something that is so hallowed that you would consider it to be very precious.* So Jesus' words should be translated, *"Never give what is hallowed and precious to the dogs...."* Once again, there is no room for misunderstanding here — Jesus said this should *never* be done!

When the Lord referred to "that which is holy," he was speaking of those precious and holy things that God has done *inside* you. It may be the hard lessons you've learned as you've submitted to the dealings of God in your life; the insights you've gained over the years; or the wisdom you have amassed as the result of years of experience. It may also refer to the spiritual gifts that operate in your life. All these things are *holy* and *valuable.* It's impossible to put a price tag on that which has cost you your life. *Who can measure the tears, pain, and energy spent to gain those revelations and the lessons you have learned?*

When you open your heart and share these holy things with someone else, you are opening the door to your most private treasures. When you begin to share details, secrets, insights, and wisdom that you've learned through the hard knocks of life and from the Spirit of God, it is a precious gift you are giving. You should never underestimate the tremendous value God places on the experience and wisdom you've gained. These are *holy* things.

Every time you break open the Word of God and share the principles, lessons, and insights you've gained as you have dealt with your own heart and sought to do God's will, you are giving out *precious* things to those who listen. This is why Jesus ordered that you are *"never* to give that which is hallowed and precious to the dogs."

But who are the dogs that Jesus is referring to in this verse? The word "dogs" comes from the Greek word *kunun*, which is the same word used to describe the *vicious, wild, unclean dogs* that roamed the countryside just outside the city of Jerusalem. These dogs were famous for pillaging the garbage dump outside the city where unclaimed dead bodies were thrown to rot or to be eaten by dogs and hungry vultures (*see* April 23).

These dogs were not tamed pets, but an out-of-control, wild, dangerous, wandering, nomadic collection of diseased, mangy dogs. Even worse, they were always trying to get into people's houses and gardens where they could find better food. To prevent the dogs from getting in where they weren't supposed to be, walls often had to be built as defenses to keep them out!

Sadly, there are some people who behave just like dogs, and apparently Jesus had encountered some of them. That is the reason He used the example of wild dogs to depict this category of people.

Jesus was referring to a type of people who are undomesticated and untamed. These are people who refuse to submit to anyone's authority. They roam about like nomads, wandering from one church to the next, using and abusing one pastor after another. Out of control and beyond the reach of anyone's authority, these people are constantly trying to get into places where they shouldn't be allowed.

Jesus' choice of words in this verse
conveys this idea:

"Never give that which is hallowed and precious to wild, dangerous, out-of-control, wandering, nomadic, diseased, and mangy dogs...."

This tells you and me that before we open our hearts and begin to share our deepest experiences and most precious inner treasures — before we draw certain individuals close to us and invest our time and energy into them — we need to be certain that these are people who are serious about their walk with God. Our time and our treasures are too precious to throw them at the feet of people who don't care and who won't apply what we are trying to tell them.

Have you been putting your time and energy into someone who is bullheaded and resists you every step of the way? Does that person stubbornly defy your suggestions and act offended every time you try to help him? If so, maybe it's time for you to turn your attention to someone else who is openhearted and who truly has a genuine desire to learn from you.

As I noted earlier, eventually there comes a time when you must stop wasting your time and attention on people who don't care. You can pray for them, love them, and believe for God to work in their lives. But if they don't demonstrate a sincere desire to learn, to receive from you, and to soak up the rich wisdom you are trying to impart into their lives, it's time for you to stop trying to make them receive what they need and turn your attention elsewhere. That doesn't mean you cease to love these people, but it does mean their reactions to you have revealed the true level of the relationship.

Open your eyes! The Holy Spirit will lead you to someone who is hungry and ready to learn! Release the person you've been trying to push and to force into changing against his will. If that person doesn't want to change, you can't make it happen. Instead, let the Lord lead you to those who are already praying and crying out for God to send someone like you to them!

MY PRAYER FOR TODAY

Lord, I am asking You to help me discern when the holy things I share are being appreciated and valued, and when I am being ignored by those I am trying to help. Forgive me for investing too much of myself into people who aren't committed to applying what I have to teach them. I just wanted the best for them, and that's why it's been so hard for me to let them go. But today I am making a decision to start viewing myself, my experience, and my wisdom as treasures to be valued and held in esteem. From this moment onward, I ask You to help me invest these treasures into people who will listen, take what I have to share deeply into their hearts, and then apply those truths to their lives.

I pray this in Jesus' name!

MY CONFESSION FOR TODAY

I confess that God has done wonderful things in my life that are a great blessing to others! I have something to share because Jesus has taught me so much. I am careful about what I say, and I allow the Holy Spirit to lead me to those I can open my heart to and pour out these treasures. God is helping me to be wiser about what I share and with whom I share it!

I declare this by faith in Jesus' name!

1. Can you relate to today's *Sparkling Gem?* Have you ever opened up and poured out your heart to someone who you later discovered really did take what you said to heart? How did that experience affect you?
2. Have you ever kept hanging on to someone who was less concerned about his own spiritual growth than you were?
3. Have you ever been guilty of the negative attitudes and actions I've described today? Can you think of a time when someone tried to help and teach you, but out of pride you stubbornly resisted the help God was trying to freely offer you through that person?

JUNE 16

Pearls and Pigs!

Give not that which is holy unto the dogs,
neither cast ye your pearls before swine,
lest they trample them under their feet,
and turn again and rend you.
— Matthew 7:6

Once I was on a farm where the farmer had a hog that was so huge, I could hardly believe my eyes when I saw it! It just lay there on the ground, flicking its ears and shaking its rolls of fat in an attempt to shoo away the flies. I was simply amazed at the enormous size of that hog. I wondered, *How can it even stand up?*

I asked the owner, "Does that pig do anything except lie here?"

The owner answered, "It hardly moves until it's time to eat. But when it's dinnertime, that pig nearly jumps to its feet, snorting with joy and excitement at the prospect of eating a meal!"

When I heard this, it made me think of what Jesus said about pigs in Matthew 7:6. He told us, "...Neither cast ye your pearls before swine, lest they trample them under their feet, and turn again and rend you."

I always thought this was a strange verse, because pearls and pigs in the same verse seem like such a bizarre mixture! But Jesus had a purpose for using this example, so we need to take a look and see why He made this statement and what it means for you and me.

First, Jesus said, "...neither *cast* ye...." The word "cast" is from the Greek word *ballo*, and it means *to throw* or *to cast*. But the Greek is so strong that it could be translated, "...*NEVER cast your pearls before swine*...." In other words, this word conveys a strong prohibition to *never* do something! As we saw in yesterday's *Sparkling Gem*, Jesus wasn't giving a suggestion here; He was giving an *order* that this particular action should *never* be taken!

The word "pearls" is the Greek word *margarites*. You may find it interesting to know that this is where we get the names *Margaret* and *Margarita*. Since Jesus uses the example of *pearls* in this verse, let's talk about pearls for a moment.

Pearls are not easily found. To obtain the richest and most beautiful pearls, a diver must dive again and again and again and again. Then after lifting the shells from the sea floor, he must force open the mouth of each shell and dig through the tough meat of the muscle, poking and searching for the tiny white pearl that was formed over a long period of time. These pearls are precious, rare, valuable, and hard to obtain.

This is how you should view the things God has done in your life. You can't put a price on what you have learned through your life experiences as you've walked with Him. Like precious pearls, those life lessons are inestimable in their value because they cost you something. They weren't the result of shallow swimming. *You had to go deep into God to obtain those spiritual treasures.*

Each time you open the door to those treasures and begin to share them with someone else, you need to remember that you're sharing your *pearls* with that person. The counsel and advice you're giving may be free to him, but it has cost you everything! So if what you are sharing isn't appreciated, *stop giving that person your pearls*!

This is why Jesus said, "…neither cast ye your pearls before swine.…" And remember, the Greek more accurately says, "*never* cast your pearls before swine.…" But do you see the word "before"? It is the Greek word *emprothen*, and it means *to present something to someone else*. An example would be if I publicly honored a person by *presenting* him with a special gift. To show honor, I would come to him dressed properly and thoughtfully; then I would give that person a gift that cost me something in order to demonstrate the great honor in which I held him.

By using this word, Jesus tells us in Matthew 7:6 that we shouldn't waste our time, energy, or money or put too much thought into honoring individuals who don't even care about what we are doing for them! There's no reason to get all dressed up, to put hours of contemplation into how to help them, or to open our hearts and tell them deep truths and lessons that have cost us much in life. Why would we ever want to do all that for people who don't even care?

Jesus uses the example of "swine" or "pigs" to describe this category of people who couldn't care less about what you are trying to tell them. The word "swine" is from the Greek word *choipos*, and it can be translated as *pig, sow, swine,* or *hog*. Of course, pigs were very well known in Jesus' day — and in Jewish circles, they were considered to be the lowest, basest, and the most unclean of filthy, stinking animals. For Jesus to refer to people as swine was a very powerful and graphic depiction!

Pigs are consumers. They take, take, and take. They eat and then want more. They never think to ask where the food came from, who paid for it, or what process was required to produce it. They are just mindless, careless consumers.

If you've ever been to a pigpen, you know that pigs do nothing but lie on their sides and jump up just in time to eat. They never contribute anything to the farm until they're dead. Covered in their own mess, waddling around in their own filth, pigs just wait to be fed again and again.

When the bell rings and it's time for the pigs to eat, they fight and kick to see who can get to the food first. Slopping up the food, slobbering all over themselves, they "eat just like pigs." Driven to have their need for food met, pigs never stop to say thank you to the person who brought it to them. Not one "thank you" is heard — *not even one*!

This is exactly like people who don't appreciate the holy things that are freely given to them from the depths of another person's life. It's sad to say, but many believers live and act just like pigs because they are careless, mindless consumers of other people's time and energy. They never think about how a person obtained his wisdom, what it cost for him to obtain it, or how many years it took for him to come to his present place of growth in God. These people who act like pigs just take and take and take. And after they have drained that person of all his strength, they don't even take the time to say thank you for what they have consumed!

Jesus' words in Matthew 7:6 convey this idea:

"Never invest too much time, energy, or money into people who don't even care about what you are doing for them! I'm commanding you not to share your 'pearls' — those precious details, experiences, and parts of your life that have cost you so much — with people who live and act like ungrateful pigs...."

As I noted earlier, when Denise and I first began in the ministry, we thought our door and telephone had to be available to people twenty-four hours a day, seven days a week. Because of this, people came to us all the time. Some of them really needed help, but it didn't take us too long to learn that some people just wanted *us — our* time and *our* energy. They didn't have any intention of changing or doing anything we suggested. It was almost as if they were sent on a mission designed to drain us dry of everything we had inside of us.

Once these people were finished with us, they'd leave to find someone else. We were just the ones they attached themselves to for that moment. As long as they could get just a little more out of us, they stuck around. But when they had drained us dry, they were off to find a new victim.

Do you see why Jesus used such a strong example? This is exactly what the Lord was referring to when He said such people would "...trample them [our pearls] under their feet...." You see, Jesus wants us to value ourselves and what we have to share so highly that we carefully choose the people with whom we share our treasures.

What is absolutely amazing to me is that Jesus said this ungrateful group of people will most likely "turn again and rend you" in the end. Pastors and leaders from all over the world could tell you about people whom they have tried to help, but who later turned and accused *them* of being unloving! People like that take all they can from a person; then later they turn against that same person!

It is *extremely* hard to understand how someone you have tried so hard to help can act so ugly! Nevertheless, that is frequently the case. As soon as you say, *"Enough is enough!"* and turn your attention elsewhere, this type of person begins to accuse: *"You are so unloving. You don't love me the way you used to love me. If you were a good Christian, you'd listen to me when I talk. You just don't care."*

You may assume that these people would *know* they are loved. The reason you have endured so long in your efforts to help them is that you *do* love them. If you didn't love them, you would have let go of your relationship with them a long time ago. Only love could have kept you going after they had disappointed you time after time.

But if those individuals aren't serious by now, they probably never will be serious. So there comes a time when *you* have to stop behaving like a beggar. You shouldn't have to beg anyone to follow you. You need to think more highly of yourself — and those whom you are trying to help need to think more highly of you as well.

People must never take you and the pearls of your life for granted. If that starts happening, stop giving to them until their attitude changes. If their attitude *never* changes, let go of those unfruitful relationships and find someone who *will* appreciate what you are trying to accomplish in his or her life. You may be fearful to let go of those individuals at first because you've put so much time and energy into them. But I assure you, there are other fish in the sea. You are *not* locked into a few certain individuals. Lots of potential leaders exist in the Body of Christ, just waiting for someone to tap into their God-given abilities.

It's time for you to quit acting like the world rises and falls on whether or not one person gets with the program. Move on to someone who will *contribute* to the program instead of being only a "taker" and a consumer of your time and energy.

But what if *you* are the one who has been acting like a mindless consumer of other people's time, talents, gifts, and money? If that is the case, it's time for you to stop acting like a pig! *If you're really a child of God, the Holy Spirit who dwells within you wants to teach you how to start living on a much higher level!*

MY PRAYER FOR TODAY

Lord, I want to thank You for forgiving me for all the times in my past when others did so much for me that I didn't appreciate. I was too young and too foolish to really appreciate what was being done for me, but now I understand. So today I want to thank You for everything that has been done for me. I thank You for every person You have sent to love me, to be patient with me, and to be used so mightily in my life. Now I ask You to help me be a blessing and a help to someone else who is just as I once was!

I pray this in Jesus' name!

MY CONFESSION FOR TODAY

I confess that the pearls in my life are precious and have the power to help other people. I open my heart to share them with people who are serious about listening and growing. Because I'm putting so much time and energy into these people, they are going to grow in the Lord and become something truly great! They possess lots of potential, and their God-given gifts, talents, and abilities will be developed and released because God used me in their lives!

I declare this by faith in Jesus' name!

QUESTIONS FOR YOU TO CONSIDER

1. As you read this *Sparkling Gem* today, did you find yourself thinking of specific individuals who always *take* but never *give* anything back in return? What kind of impression do these people leave on others? Is it positive or negative?
2. Can you think of times in your life when you freely took from someone else, never even stopping to think what it cost that person to give so much to you? Have you ever taken the time to go back to that person and thank him for what he so graciously did for you?
3. Is there anyone in your life right now who continually takes from you but seems to have no intention of changing? If so, how long are you going to let this situation go on?

JUNE 17

❦

Has Satan Ever Tried To Use You As a Source of Strife?

But if ye have bitter envying and strife in your hearts,
glory not, and lie not against the truth.
— James 3:14

*M*any years ago, I worked as an associate pastor in a large Southern Baptist church. The pastor I served was a wonderful man of God who taught me and gave his life to me unselfishly. I nearly adored this man — until one day, I became *offended* by something he did.

What this pastor did was very minor, and it shouldn't have affected me at all. Nevertheless, at that moment I was weak and became an open door for the devil. It is amazing how quickly a dart of the enemy, thrown into our hearts, can change our perspective! In a matter of *seconds*, my whole view of this precious man changed for the worse. Although he was older and more spiritual than I was, I suddenly thought I could see the full picture of the church ministry more clearly than he could.

Soon I found myself in the position of a judge, thinking that I was more spiritual than he and therefore more qualified to discern the voice of God. Although my actions were ungodly and destructive, I really *thought* my motives were pure as the snow. My heart toward this dear pastor became hardened, and it wasn't long until the devil was trying to use me as a source of strife in that congregation. The biggest obstacle in this situation was that I genuinely believed I was right! But in reality, I was acting in rebellion to authority, blinded to the ugliness that was raging in my soul.

The devil has always tried to use people to bring division into the church. There is nothing new about this problem. In fact, James addresses the issues of wrong attitudes and a spirit of strife in James 3:14. From the earliest inception of the New Testament church, church leaders have always had to correct people who acted just like I was acting toward my pastor. But thank God for His grace! Today that pastor is one of my dearest friends and one of my greatest mentors.

In respect to people being used by the devil to bring division, James 3:14 says, "But if ye have bitter envying and strife in your hearts, glory not, and lie not against the truth." The phrase "bitter envying" is very important. It is the Greek word *zelos*, which refers to *a fierce desire to promote your own idea to the exclusion of others' ideas*. The word "strife" is the Greek word *eritheia*, which means *rivalry* or *ambition*. It can also be translated as *a party spirit* or *a divisive spirit*.

This first part of James 3:14 could be translated:

"If you have a fierce desire to promote your own ideas to the exclusion of others' ideas...."
"If you have a spirit of competition and rivalry...."
"If you're full of selfish ambition...."
"If your actions are creating a party spirit in the church...."

In verse 15, James goes on to say, "This wisdom descendeth not from above, but is *earthly, sensual, devilish*." The word "earthly" in Greek is the word *epigeios*. It describes something from an earthly dimension, *not* from a heavenly dimension. The Greek word for "sensual" is *psuchikos*, which means *soulish*. Then James says, "This wisdom is...*devilish*." The word "devilish" comes from the Greek word *daimoniodes*, which is best translated *demonized*, depicting *a person whose mind or emotions have come under the influence of demon spirits.*

James is telling his readers:

"When a person behaves like this, it is obvious that his soul has come under the influence of demonic activity."

Consider what James 3:15 means in light of the fact that I had become the source of strife in that pastor's church. According to this scripture, I had fallen into a trap of the devil and didn't even know it! What I did to that pastor was blatantly wrong, but at the particular moment it was happening, I *really* believed I was doing what was right. I had fallen into the same trap so many people have fallen into throughout two thousand years of Church history.

Let me assure you that anytime something small becomes *a major issue*, you need to back up and reexamine what you are thinking and feeling. The devil may be trying to work in your mind and imagination to divide you from people you both love and need. Do you want to let the devil build a wall between you and the people in your life over something that won't even matter a year from now? Is that issue really so serious that you would break a long-term relationship over it? Is it possible that the devil is over-magnifying this problem in your mind and that you are getting a little out of focus over this issue?

As a result of this regretful experience that occurred so long ago, I learned to keep my heart free from all strife and offense. That is a lesson we all need to learn. If our hearts stay free of strife and offense, the door stays closed to the devil so he cannot disrupt our relationships. You need to know that when you allow a spirit of strife to operate inside you, inside your home, inside your business, or inside your church, it won't be too long until people who used to love each other are standing in opposition to each other. That is the way the spirit of strife operates, and that is the fruit it produces.

If you have taken offense or feel even the smallest temptation to get in strife with someone in your life, I strongly advise you to get into the Presence of God and allow Him to help you see things from a clearer perspective. Let the Holy Spirit remove the blur of the disagreement and remind you of how much you love that other person. Take a few minutes to be with God and to let Him search your heart and show you the truth. As you do, you will stop the devil from using you as a source of strife today!

MY PRAYER FOR TODAY

Lord, I never want to be a source of strife! Please help me keep my heart free of strife and my mind clear of accusations so I can have relationships that are pleasing to You. I want to be a blessing to people — never a vehicle the devil uses to bring confusion or hurt to anyone. I am so thankful Your love has touched me and now flows through me to others. I truly desire for Your love to flow freely through me and to bring peace where strife and chaos once reigned supreme.

I pray this in Jesus' name!

MY CONFESSION FOR TODAY

I confess that the devil doesn't have the right to work in my mind and imagination. I refuse to permit him to divide me from the people I know, love, and need. My heart is free of strife and offense, and the door is closed to the devil so he cannot disrupt my relationships. When the devil does try to distract me with the temptation of strife, the Holy Spirit removes the blur of the disagreement and reminds me of how much I love and need that other person.

I declare this by faith in Jesus' name!

QUESTIONS FOR YOU TO CONSIDER

1. Has there ever been a time in your life when you got so upset about something that it blurred your ability to think clearly about that situation? Did you slow down and get into the Presence of God before taking further action, or did you act in that moment of emotion and let the devil use you to make the situation worse?

2. What have you learned about the value of keeping your mouth shut, letting your emotions subside, and waiting before you vocalize what is making your stomach churn with fretting and anxiety?

3. What practical steps can you take to prevent the devil from over-magnifying issues in your mind and imagination? Why don't you really think about this question and then take some time to write down your preventative ideas?

JUNE 18

The Essential Attitude for Success!

Let a man so account of us, as of the ministers of Christ,
and stewards of the mysteries of God.
— 1 Corinthians 4:1

We live in a world that loves to take it easy. We want instant results — and we want them *right now*. Technology has made almost everything instantly accessible. Our entire Western lifestyle is centered around making things as easy, fast, effortless, and painless as possible.

The younger generation is so accustomed to getting everything they want that they don't understand there is a price to pay for true success. But whether they like it or not, the fact remains: True greatness, great achievements, and real success won't float to them on clouds that suddenly materialize above their heads. If anyone wants to achieve something great and significant, he or she will have to put a lot of hard work and effort into making it happen.

Let's take the apostle Paul as an example. I recently read a report that made this claim: Apart from Jesus Christ, the apostle Paul more dramatically affected Western civilization than any other man in human history. Paul achieved incredible feats with his life. His epistles have impacted world history and leaders, and what he accomplished in his life and ministry remains legendary. So let's look at this famous Christian leader and ask:

◆ *How did Paul live his life?*
◆ *What kind of attitude did he possess regarding his life mission?*
◆ *What attitude did he possess that enabled him to dramatically affect his world?*

In First Corinthians 4:1, Paul wrote, "Let a man so account of us, as of the ministers of Christ, and stewards of the mysteries of God." I believe that some very important answers to the questions above are found in this interesting statement that Paul himself wrote.

In this verse, Paul calls himself a "minister." This is the Greek word *huperetas*, a vivid term that conveys *the essential attitude necessary to get a job done* — especially the work of the ministry. However, this word doesn't apply only to ministry. It also denotes the essential attitude a person must possess to become successful in *any sphere* of life.

Interestingly, this word *huperetas*, translated "ministers" here, was used in classical Greek society to describe *low-class criminals*. The first time I studied this Greek word, it seemed so odd that Paul would use this word to describe himself and his attitude toward the ministry. I wondered:

◆ *Why would Paul use such a word?*
◆ *Is he using this word as a picture to make a point to us?*

After a lot of digging into the original Greek, I found out exactly why Paul used this word. He was a successful man who understood what it took to get a job done — and no word more vividly explains this work ethic than the Greek word *huperetas*.

Originally this word described *the very lowest class of criminals*. These criminals were *so low, so detestable*, and *so contemptible* that they were *outcast* and *removed from society*. Often they were assigned to the bottom galleys of huge shipping vessels, where they literally became the engines of those huge ships.

And the harsh assignment given to these criminals wasn't temporary either. They were sentenced to live the rest of their lives in the darkness below the deck — endlessly rowing, rowing, and rowing. Their entire existence was devoted to keeping that ship moving toward its ultimate destination! These *huperetas* were officially called "under-rowers" because they lived and rowed down in the bottom of the ship. Day after day, their job was to heave those massive oars forward and backward, pushing them through the water to make the ship move through the sea.

This is the same word the apostle Paul uses to describe the attitude that is necessary to do what God has called us to do! God has called us to take our place in His plan — to grab hold of an oar, so to speak, and begin to serve Him practically in some way. We are to keep rowing, rowing, rowing, and rowing, doing our part and fulfilling what He has asked us to do.

Some people tend to sit and watch as achievers reach out to do the impossible. But if you are going to join the ranks of those achievers, you'll have to do more than just sit around and talk about it. You'll need to say yes to what the Lord is urging you to do.

And remember, these *huperetas* who rowed the boat didn't quickly finish their assignment of rowing; it was their responsibility for a lifetime. In the same way, we need to realize that the secret dream God has put in our hearts probably won't be achieved quickly either. It may be an assignment that will last for the rest of our lives. It takes hard work and a lifelong commitment for us to achieve the great things that God wants to do through you and me!

I heartily recommend that you mentally prepare yourself for a long-term stint at doing what God is calling you to do. It will almost certainly take unbelievable strength and energy to move that vision from the realm of dreams to the realm of reality. So jump into the bottom of the boat; take your place on the rowers' bench; and begin to row with all your might! With each step of obedience you take and each day of faithfulness you live, you will come closer to the desired destination — the ultimate fulfillment of God's plans and purposes for your life.

We may live in a world that loves to take it easy and that delights in instant results. But in order to achieve the true greatness God desires for us, we will have to be determined, committed, and willing to do anything necessary to accomplish what He has for us.

No, real success *doesn't* float to you on clouds that suddenly materialize above your head. Therefore, I encourage you to make the decision to start putting a lot of hard work and effort into making your assignment successful. *It's going to take every ounce of strength you have to make your dream come to pass, so you might as well resolve to get started today!*

MY PRAYER FOR TODAY

Lord, I am determining in my heart today to jump into the bottom of the boat, grab an oar, and start rowing with all my might. Doing the minimum is never going to get me where I need to go, so right now I am making the choice to put all my energies forward to achieve what You have planned for me. Help me to be faithful, steadfast, unmoving, and unflinching in the face of opposition. Help me to tell my flesh to be silent when it tries to scream out that I'm doing too much! I choose to crucify the flesh and press forward with all the strength You give me. As I do this, I believe that You will make my dreams come to pass!

I pray this in Jesus' name!

MY CONFESSION FOR TODAY

I confess that I will see the fulfillment of the dream God has put in my heart. I am a hard worker, willing to do whatever it takes, and I have made a long-term commitment to achieve all that God wants to do through me! It will almost certainly take unbelievable strength and energy to move that vision from the realm of dreams to the realm of reality, but I can do all things through Christ who strengthens me! With God's Spirit working in me, I will see the fulfillment of my dreams!

I declare this by faith in Jesus' name!

QUESTIONS FOR YOU TO CONSIDER

1. If you keep operating at your current level of production, will you reach the goals God has given for your life?
2. *Be honest!* Has your desire to have things "easy" been a hindrance to you? Has your desire for "creature comforts" overpowered your desire to reach your goal regardless of the price you must pay or how long it takes?
3. If you continue at your present momentum, will you dramatically affect your world and environment as the apostle Paul affected his? If not, what changes do you need to make in your thinking to become a great achiever?

JUNE 19

❧❧❧

God's Delivering Power Is Yours!

For we would not, brethren, have you ignorant of our trouble
which came to us in Asia, that we were pressed out of measure,
above strength, insomuch that we despaired even of life:
But we had the sentence of death in ourselves,
that we should not trust in ourselves,
but in God which raiseth the dead.
— 2 Corinthians 1:8,9

*E*veryone has had to endure hardness at some point in life, including the apostle Paul. He describes some of the hardships he endured in Asia in Second Corinthians 1:8,9: "For we would not, brethren, have you ignorant of our trouble which came to us in Asia, that we were pressed out of measure, above strength, insomuch that we despaired even of life: But we had the sentence of death in ourselves, that we should not trust in ourselves, but in God which raiseth the dead."

Notice the first part of verse 8, where Paul says, "For we would not, brethren, have you ignorant of the *trouble* which came unto us in Asia...." The word "trouble" is the Greek word *thlipsis*, which was used to convey the idea of *a heavy-pressure situation*. In fact, at one point this word was used to depict a victim who was first tied up with rope and laid on his back; then a huge, heavy boulder was slowly lowered upon him until he was *crushed*! This, indeed, would be *a very heavy situation* for the man underneath the boulder! He would be in *a tight place, under a heavy burden*, or in *a great squeeze*.

By using this word, Paul is saying, "*We were under a heavy load — an unbelievably heavy amount of stress and pressure! We were in very tight circumstances. Our minds were being 'squeezed.' It felt like our lives were being pushed right out of us!*"

You might think Paul is referring to *physical suffering*. Of course, physical suffering is difficult, but the greatest suffering of all always occurs in the mind — *mental suffering*. A person can live with pain in his body if his mind is still in control. However, when the suffering begins to work on that person's mind, both his body and his mind could eventually break and fold.

Paul's greatest suffering was not physical, but mental. This is why he goes on to say, "...that we were pressed out of measure, above strength, insomuch that we despaired even of life" (v. 8). Particularly pay heed to that first phrase, "that we were pressed out of measure." This is the Greek phrase *kath huperbole*, and it is extremely important in Paul's testimony. It literally means *to throw beyond, to excel, to exceed*, or *to go beyond anything normal or expected*. It also describes *something that is excessive and beyond the normal range of what most would experience*.

By using this word, Paul says, "*We were under an amount of pressure that is not normal. It was FAR BEYOND anything we had ever previously experienced. It was excessive, unbelievable, unbearable, and far too much for any one human being to endure.*"

Paul goes on to tell us that this pressure was "above strength." This word "above" is also important. It is the Greek word *huper*, which always conveys the idea of *something excessive*. In order to explain how bad his situation was, Paul is piling words on top of words, all of which accurately portray how terrifically bad the ordeal in Asia was for him and his traveling companions.

It is almost as though Paul is saying, *"Normal human strength never would have been sufficient for this situation. The strength it required was far, far beyond human strength. This predicament required strength in a measure I had never previously needed. It was beyond me!"*

Then Paul says, "...insomuch that we *despaired* even of life...." The Greek word for "despaired" is the word *exaporeomai*. It was used in a technical sense to describe *no way out*. It is where we get our word *exasperated*, and it describes people who feel *trapped, caught, up against the wall, pinned down,* and *utterly hopeless*. Today we might say, "Sorry, but it looks like this is *the end of the road* for you!"

Then Paul continues in verse 9, "But we had the sentence of death in ourselves...." The word "sentence" is the Greek word *apokrima*, which in this sense speaks of *a final verdict*. Paul is saying, *"It looked to us like the verdict was in, and we were not going to survive."*

When all these different phrases and words are looked at together, it becomes very plain that Paul's primary suffering at this moment was mental, *not* physical. He is describing mental agony on a measure that few of us have ever experienced.

Because of all these Greek words, the following could be taken as an interpretive translation of these verses:

"We would not, brethren, have you ignorant of the horribly tight, life-threatening squeeze that came to us in Asia. It was unbelievable! With all the things that we have been through, this was the worst of all. It felt like our lives were being crushed! It was so difficult that I didn't know what to do. No experience I've ever been through required so much of me; in fact, I didn't have enough strength to cope with it. Toward the end of this ordeal, I was so overwhelmed that I didn't think we'd ever get out! I felt suffocated, trapped, and pinned against the wall. I really thought it was the end of the road for us! As far as we were concerned, the verdict was in, and the verdict said, 'Death.' But really, this was no great shock, because we were already feeling the effect of death and depression in our souls...."

Paul doesn't tell us exactly what happened to him and his team when they were in Asia. But whatever it was, it was the most grueling experience they had ever been through until that time.

You may ask, "Why would Paul want us to know that he had been through such difficult times? Did he want us to feel sorry for him?" *Absolutely not!* Paul wanted us to know that everyone endures hardness from time to time. Even the greatest, most well-known, celebrated spiritual leaders are confronted with situations that are devastating or challenging.

You see, even with all his knowledge, revelation, and experience, Paul was still assaulted by the devil. That assault was so aggressive that Paul wrote "we despaired even of life," describing the intense emotions he felt as he went through these extremely difficult circumstances.

But Paul *didn't* break, and he *didn't* die! Likewise, if you'll hold on and fight right where you are, *you also won't break or be destroyed*! Like Paul, you will win the victory. Then you'll be able to say that the ordeal happened in order that you would not trust in yourself, "...but in God which raiseth the dead: Who delivered us from so great a death, and doth deliver..." (2 Corinthians 1:9,10).

God's delivering power is yours! He has rescued you in the past; He will rescue you now; and He will rescue you again and again in the future. All He asks is that you "stay put" right where He called you — refusing to move, rejecting every temptation to give up, and deciding never to give in to the pressure that the devil wants to pile on top of you. *If you'll be faithful and slug it out with the power and armor of God, you'll discover that God will be with you all the way through to a successful conclusion!*

MY PRAYER FOR TODAY

Lord, You have never abandoned me, and You never will! When the devil tries to crush me with stress, I throw the weight of my cares upon You. I can't thank You enough for taking all those pressures off my shoulders and freeing me to walk in peace! My heart is simply overflowing with gratefulness for the strength and power You have released inside me. I know that with Your continued help, I shall be victorious, and these problems will flee!

I pray this in Jesus' name!

MY CONFESSION FOR TODAY

I confess that God's delivering power is mine! He has rescued me before; He will rescue me now; and He will rescue me when I need His power again in the future. I am "staying put" right where God called me. I refuse to move; I reject every temptation to give up; and I will never give in to the pressures to stop doing what God has told me to do. I will be faithful, and God will empower me to make it all the way through to my place of victory!

I declare this by faith in Jesus' name!

QUESTIONS FOR YOU TO CONSIDER

1. Can you think of a time when you underwent circumstances so difficult that you wondered if you would survive the situation? You obviously survived, so what was the one thing that most helped you get through that ordeal?
2. As you think of others who are going through hard times right now, what is the most effective thing you could do to help them get past their difficult circumstances?
3. Why don't you make a list of ten practical things you can do to encourage these people and to remind them that you are standing with them in faith until they come through this ordeal in victory?

Even with all his knowledge, revelation, and experience, Paul was still assaulted by the devil. That assault was so aggressive that Paul wrote "we despaired even of life," describing the intense emotions he felt as he went through these extremely difficult circumstances. But Paul *didn't* break, and he *didn't* die! Likewise, if you'll hold on and fight right where you are, *you also won't break or be destroyed*! Like Paul, you will win the victory.

JUNE 20

❧⸎❧

Isn't It Time for You To Tell Your Flesh To Shut Up?

Likewise reckon ye also yourselves to be dead indeed unto sin,
but alive unto God through Jesus Christ our Lord.
— Romans 6:11

*L*eft unchecked, your flesh will try to run you over, take charge of your emotions, and promote laziness in your life. It will tell you that you've done too much; that you've already done more than anyone else; that you don't need to do any more than you've already done; and that you're not as appreciated as you ought to be. Your flesh will advise you to kick back, take it easy, and cut yourself some slack. It will scream that if anyone deserves to do nothing for a while, it's *you*.

Your flesh always tries to take everything to an *extreme*. If you allow it to control you, it will carry you into a state of laziness that sedates your whole outlook and destroys your productivity. You'll lose your joy, hope, victory — even your very reason for living. In the end, you'll become weak, powerless, and devoid of the desire or energy to pursue *anything*, let alone the high calling God has for your life.

When your flesh rises up and tempts you to be slothful about your dream, your business, or your relationship with God, *what should you do*? Or when your flesh coaxes you into believing you are too poor, too stupid, too ugly, too uninteresting, or too "run of the mill" to be used by God, *how should you respond*?

Should you cry and complain that you're just not as talented as others? Should you grieve that you're not as skinny as someone else? Should you whimper that you weren't born into a more prestigious family? Should you lament that you were never able to finish your education? Will your complaining put a degree on your wall?

It's time to tell the flesh to shut its loud mouth! Then grab hold of the power of God to change *you* and the way *you* are thinking. As long as you allow that rank, stinking flesh to produce a "poor me" mentality, you will *not* make any significant contribution to the world. And that's such a pity because *God wants to use you!* Instead of letting the flesh rule you, it is time for you to do as the apostle Paul ordered in Romans 6:11 when he said, "Likewise reckon ye also yourselves to be dead indeed unto sin, but alive to God through Jesus Christ our Lord."

The word "reckon" comes from the Greek word *logidzomai*, which means *to consider, to think, to deem, to regard,* or *to count something as done.* This means the verse could be translated, *"Once and for all, deem yourselves to be dead to sin...."* But it is important to note that the Greek tense means this reckoning must be done *on a continual basis.* With this in mind, it could be translated, *"Once and for all, deem yourself dead to sin. After that, keep it up! Keep counting yourself as one who has died to sin...."*

The word "dead" comes from the word *nekros*, which is the Greek word for a *human corpse*. It is the picture of an actual dead person, whose lifeless body has no heartbeat and no breath in his lungs. This person is declared clinically dead; he is now a *corpse*. By using the word *nekros*, Paul tells us that we are to deem ourselves as dead — non-responsive to sin. We are to be just as non-responsive to sin as a dead person is to life! Dead people don't respond to anything because they are *dead*!

These powerful words in Romans 6:11 could be interpreted this way:

"Once and for all, deem yourself dead to sin. After that, keep it up! You have to keep counting yourself as one who has died to sin...."

When I served as an assistant pastor in the Southern Baptist church, the senior pastor wanted to teach me how to conduct funerals, so he took me to funeral after funeral. He wanted me to learn how to conduct myself in delicate and difficult situations. One funeral I attended was an unforgettable experience. Even now I can vividly see it as I write about it. It was a funeral conducted for an unsaved family whose son had tragically died in an accident. The sorrow and remorse in that room was so thick, it could almost be cut with a knife.

Nothing is sadder than a funeral with a family of unbelievers. They have no faith and no hope. When they lose a loved one, it is truly a catastrophe because their lack of hope overwhelms them. But even worse than attending such a funeral is to be called upon to *conduct* one!

I watched as the mother approached the casket to tell her son good-bye one last time. She was so overwhelmed with grief that she crawled *into* the casket! She clutched and held tightly to her son's dead body, pleading, *"Talk to me! Talk to me! Don't leave me like this!"* Funeral-home workers had to pull the mother out of the coffin and escort her to the limousine that awaited to take her and the rest of the family to the cemetery for the burial.

That early experience is etched forever in my memory. I've never forgotten that pitiful sight as the mother gripped that dead body in her arms and begged it to speak to her one last time. But that body was *not* going to talk to her. It was *dead*.

The empty shell that lay in that casket was the deceased, expired, finished shadow of a young man who had once lived but was now gone. There was no heartbeat, no breath in his lungs, no pulse to feel in his wrists. The clock had quit running for that man's life, and there was no turning back the clock to make it start ticking again. It was a "done deal." This man's life had *expired*. His body was *mortified*.

Well, your flesh needs to be *mortified* in the same way. As Paul says in Romans 6:11, it is time for you to *reckon, deem, consider, regard,* and *count as a done fact* that you are dead to sin and to its lying insinuations! To continually count yourself dead to sin, you may have to speak to yourself often and take authority over your flesh. Command your flesh to shut its mouth, and remind yourself that the flesh lost its power at the Cross and no longer has the right to rule and reign in your life!

You don't have to allow the flesh to lord itself over you any longer. You don't have to let your flesh and emotions give you the run-around. Instead of focusing on what you *can't* do, it's time to start thinking about what you *can* do when you become yielded to the Spirit of God.

That's why Paul went on to say that you must now start looking at yourself as one who is "...alive unto God through Jesus Christ our Lord." You see, sin is no longer your master; now you are the servant of Jesus Christ! When your body, mind, and emotions are submitted to Him, you cease to be a slave to your body and emotions. Instead, your body and emotions become *your* servant — instruments of righteousness to help you achieve the dreams God has put in your heart.

The only way you and I will ever accomplish what we were born to do is to put aside the lies of the enemy; tell our lazy, complaining flesh to keep its mouth shut; take charge of our emotions;

and yield ourselves as instruments unto God. Then as we start speaking the truth of God's Word, drawing upon His power that works in us and through us to do His will, we'll start seeing supernatural results and achievements!

God has something awesome for you to do. Absolutely *nothing* can keep you from doing what He has put in your heart — not your education, status in society, political affiliation, or physical appearance. None of these factors will have any impact on God's call on your life.

The one factor that does impact God's ability to use you is your own obedience to Him. Your heart must be willing. You must take authority over the flesh that would take you down a lazy path. And you must yield your body to God's Spirit as an instrument of righteousness. *That's when you'll find yourself on the path that leads to being used by God!*

MY PRAYER FOR TODAY

Lord, I reckon myself dead to sin! It is no longer I who live, but Christ who lives in me! Since this is who You have made me to be, I ask You to help me say no to my flesh and to temptation and then to count myself alive unto You! Holy Spirit, energize me with Your strength and power to walk in the resurrection power of Jesus Christ!

I pray this in Jesus' name!

MY CONFESSION FOR TODAY

I boldly declare that I reckon, deem, consider, regard, and count as a done fact that I am dead to sin! I take authority over the flesh and command it to shut its mouth, and I refuse to give it the right to rule and reign in my life! I am alive unto God through Jesus Christ. Sin is no longer my master; now I am the servant of Jesus Christ!

I declare this by faith in Jesus' name!

QUESTIONS FOR YOU TO CONSIDER

1. Are there areas in your life that you haven't yet reckoned to be dead? What are those areas, and what are you going to do about them? Are you going to allow those unyielded areas to keep calling the shots, or are you going to count them as dead and powerless in your life?
2. Do you have any sinful habits that used to be non-active and non-responsive and are now trying to wake up again? If yes, what are you going to do to "remortify" those areas of your life so you can stay free?
3. In what area does your flesh try the hardest to speak to you and to rule over you?

Absolutely *nothing* can keep you from doing what God has put in your heart — not your education, status in society, political affiliation, or physical appearance. None of these factors will have any impact on His call on your life.

JUNE 21

❧

Do You Need Some Convincing?

And when he is come, he will reprove...of righteousness,
because I go to my Father, and ye see me no more.
— John 16:8,10

*H*ave you ever complimented someone who responded by arguing with you — rejecting your compliment and essentially questioning your judgment in the matter? For example, after you told someone that he looked as if he had lost weight, did he respond by telling you how fat he is rather than by thanking you for the compliment? "Well, I've gained a lot of weight," the person may have said, "and I look so fat now. I wish you could have seen me three months ago when I really looked good! I don't look as good now."

This is the equivalent of throwing the compliment back in your face. It would have been far more polite and gracious to say, "Thank you. I'm so glad you noticed. I appreciate you telling me that I look better."

Here is another example that I think will make the point. A person stands before the church and sings a beautiful solo that deeply stirs your heart. At the end of the service, you make your way through the congregation to find the soloist because you want to express how much his singing moved you. After opening your heart and thanking him for allowing God to use him, the soloist responds to your compliment by saying, "Thanks for the compliment, but I thought I did a horrible job tonight. I can't believe I sang so badly. I don't know how you got anything out of it."

It's rude to respond like this to someone who is trying to thank you for being a blessing. Although you are probably not deliberately intending to be ill-mannered, your response is still equivalent to a rejection of the love, admiration, and appreciation God is expressing through someone else to you. It's the same as saying, "I appreciate the fact that you gave me that compliment, but we both know it isn't true, so you don't have to say it." In effect, you are calling the person a liar!

We sometimes respond this way to one another, not meaning to be rude. But did you know that we also do this to God almost every day? Consider, for example, what Second Corinthians 5:21 declares: "For he hath made him to be sin for us, who knew no sin; that we might be made the righteousness of God in him."

This verse says that God sent Jesus to the Cross to take upon Himself our sin, to die in our place, and to give us His standing of righteousness in God's sight. Yet if there is any subject about which Christians will get bent out of shape, it is this question of their being "righteous." Most believers are so conscious of their old sinful nature that they can't embrace the truth that they've been declared righteous! Tell them that they are righteous before God, and they will respond by telling you how bad they are.

Sinful nature always clings to the worst and to what is most negative. It will always gravitate downward, never upward. That is the nature of the mind that is not under the control of the Holy Spirit. If abandoned to your flesh, you'll never believe a good report; you'll never believe God is doing a good work in you; and you'll certainly never believe that you have been made "the righteousness of God in him."

Negative, base, sinful thinking has been a part of humanity for so long that it requires some special convincing to make us realize what God has done inside us. For us to really believe that we have rightstanding with God, it will take the work of the Holy Spirit to convince us! Otherwise, when God says, "You're My child. I have made you righteous. You are beautiful to Me," our negatively charged minds and emotions will retort, "It's not so! I'm unworthy. I'm unholy. I'm so pitiful!"

But here is the good news: Just as the Holy Spirit convicts a sinner of his sin, He is also sent to convince believers of their new rightstanding with God! Jesus told us this about the Holy Spirit: "And when he is come, he will reprove...of righteousness, because I go to my Father, and ye see me no more" (John 16:8,10).

The word "reprove" is the Greek word *elegcho*. It means *to expose* or *to convict*, such as *to convict someone of a crime or a sin*. This word was used to describe legal proceedings during which a person was examined and cross-examined in a court of law until the court issued a final ruling. If the person was deemed guilty, he was *unmistakably convicted* of his crime. In this sense, the word *elegcho* describes the work of the Spirit to completely and thoroughly convict a sinner of his sin. When the Holy Spirit is finished opening the eyes of a person to his sin, that person *knows* he is a sinner. There is no escaping the truth for the unbeliever once the Holy Spirit has revealed truth to his heart!

But the word "reprove" is also used in a positive sense *to convince* someone of something positive. Again in a legal sense, it was used to denote lawyers who worked very diligently to convince people of a new way of thinking or a new way of seeing things. Perhaps they were entrenched in a wrong mindset or had a distorted perception, so the attorneys would go to work to change their opinion. In this case, they weren't trying *to convict* someone; they were working *to convince* someone!

Referring to the Holy Spirit, Jesus said, "And when he is come, he will reprove...of righteousness..." (John 16:8). After the Holy Spirit convicts us of sin and God declares us righteous, it takes a supernatural work of God to make us comprehend our new condition in Jesus Christ. This realization is just as supernatural as the moment we recognized we were lost. Only this time, we are being *supernaturally awakened* to the fact that we are righteous!

I can remember when I woke up to this truth many years ago. I was driving down the street, feeling totally unrighteous while listening to a teaching tape on the subject of righteousness. Suddenly my mind began to grasp what I was hearing. It was as if someone took blinders off my eyes and earplugs out of my ears! For the first time, I was seeing and hearing the truth about my new righteousness in Christ Jesus.

This truth was going straight to my heart by the power of the Holy Spirit! I not only heard the words, but I also *understood* them. My inward man leaped for joy when the Spirit of God illumined my understanding about righteousness. He convinced me of the truth, and I was set free!

If you struggle with a poor self-image and a constant feeling of condemnation, you need the Holy Spirit to do His convincing work in *your* life. Only He can open your eyes to see who you have become in Jesus Christ. Once your eyes have been opened and you understand you are righteous, you will never again throw the truth back in God's face and argue with Him. When the Holy Spirit reminds you that you have been declared righteous, you will cry out with joy, "Thank you! That's exactly who I am!"

This means you don't have to be negative about yourself all the time. You don't have to beat yourself over the head, constantly reminding yourself of how unworthy you are, because Jesus made you worthy! He made you righteous!

On the other hand, if you *don't* have a grasp of this God-given righteousness, a negative self-image will most likely rule your life, inhibiting your ability to pray with the confident trust that God will answer your prayer. That sense of unworthiness will cause a cloud of heaviness to hang over your life, hindering your ability to walk in the joy and victory of the Lord.

So don't you think it's time to let the Holy Spirit open your eyes and ears to see and hear the truth about who God has made you to be? It may seem hard to believe that you're righteous, and it may take a lot of convincing for you to finally believe it. *But the Holy Spirit was sent to be the Great Convincer! He is on the job and is ready right now to start convincing you of the truth regarding who you are in Christ!*

MY PRAYER FOR TODAY

Lord, I need the Holy Spirit to open my eyes and convince me that I've become righteous through the blood of Jesus Christ. I've read and heard this truth, and I know it intellectually, but I need a revelation of it in my heart. So Holy Spirit, go to work in my heart. Open the eyes and ears of my spirit to see and to hear that I am the righteousness of God in Jesus Christ. Free me from religious thinking that holds me in bondage to feelings of unworthiness. Please do it today!

I pray this in Jesus' name!

MY CONFESSION FOR TODAY

I confess that I am the righteousness of God in Jesus Christ. Jesus became sin for me so I could become the righteousness of God in Him. The Holy Spirit is the Great Convincer, and He is busy convincing me that I am free from defects and from sin, no longer the person I used to be. Because Jesus' blood touched, washed, and cleansed me, I am now free!

I declare this by faith in Jesus' name!

QUESTIONS FOR YOU TO CONSIDER

1. Are you consciously aware that you are the righteousness of God in Christ Jesus?
2. Do you struggle with feelings of unworthiness, sinfulness, and shame, even though you are a child of God? If your answer is yes, what steps can you take to walk out of those lying emotions that try to hold you captive?
3. Can you remember an instance in your life when you suddenly and supernaturally were illuminated with the understanding that you had been declared the righteousness of God in Christ Jesus? When did that happen, and what was the immediate result of this revelation in your life?

If you struggle with a poor self-image and a constant feeling of condemnation, you need the Holy Spirit to do His convincing work in *your* life. Only He can open your eyes to see who you have become in Jesus Christ.

JUNE 22

❧

Don't Throw Away Your Confidence!

Cast not away therefore your confidence,
which hath great recompence of reward.
— Hebrews 10:35

*H*ave you ever gotten so exhausted from waiting for God's promise to come to pass that you were tempted to say, "Forget it! I've waited long enough! I'm not going to sit here and wait any longer. I've given enough of my life to this, and I'm tired of it. I'm going to toss the whole thing away and move on with my life!"

If this is a temptation for you, then you need to read Hebrews 10:35 — God's strong warning that urges us never to quit and never to give up. This verse says, "Cast not away therefore your confidence, which hath great recompence of reward."

The words "cast not away" are taken from the Greek word *apoballo*, which is a compound of the words *apo* and *ballo*. The word *apo* means *away*, and the word *ballo* means *to throw something*, such as a ball, rock, or some other object. When these two words are compounded together, the new word means *to throw away; to discard;* or *to get rid of something no longer desired, needed, or wanted*.

A vivid example of the word *apoballo* is used in Mark 10:50. Jesus had just finished His ministry in the city of Jericho, and He and His disciples were about to leave the city, along with a great number of people who were following Him. As Jesus passed down the road, he walked right past a blind man named Bartimaeus.

Mark 10:47,48 says, "And when he [Bartimaeus] heard that it was Jesus of Nazareth, he began to cry out, and say, Jesus, thou son of David, have mercy on me. And many charged him that he should hold his peace: but he cried the more a great deal, Thou son of David, have mercy on me." Jesus was so struck by Bartimaeus' insistence that Mark 10:49 tells us, "And Jesus stood still, and commanded him to be called...."

The word *apoballo* is found in the next verse. It says, "And he, casting away his garment, rose, and came to Jesus" (Mark 10:50). The words "casting away" are from the word *apoballo*. It means that Bartimaeus didn't simply take off his garment and lay it aside; rather, he quickly jerked it off his body and hurled it down to the ground. He tore himself free of that garment!

You see, Bartimaeus' garment was so tightly wrapped about his body that it restricted him from getting to Jesus. To free himself, he took hold of that garment and *threw it out of the way*. He *discarded* it. It was a nuisance that was hindering his mobility, so *he pitched it out of the way*. That garment constricted his movement and stopped him from going where he wanted to be, so he grabbed hold of it and *cast it away*.

Blind Bartimaeus wanted to quickly get up and get to Jesus, but he was so annoyed, aggravated, and exasperated by the garment that was hindering his movement that *he removed it* and got it free from his legs so he could move. The Greek word *apoballo* describes this removal process in Mark 10:50.

Why is this example of blind Bartimaeus so important? Because the verse we started with today was written to believers who had suffered much for their faith. They endured hardships but still remained faithful to the call of God and to their firm belief in God's promises. But by the time the book of Hebrews was written and they read this verse for the first time, they had already been believing for God to turn their tragedies into victories for multiple years. It is quite possible that they began to wonder:

◆ *Is God ever going to turn our mourning into rejoicing?*
◆ *Is He really going to turn our ashes into beauty?*
◆ *How much longer do we have to wait for the promises of God to come to pass?*
◆ *Did we misunderstand the promises of God?*
◆ *Are we waiting for something that is never going to happen?*

This is why Hebrews 10:35 warns these believers, "Cast not away therefore your confidence...." Because the words "cast not away" are from the word *apoballo*, this verse suggests that they were so tired and frustrated with waiting for God's promise to come to pass that they were tempted to chuck "this whole faith thing" and forget the promises of God they had been holding on to for so many years. They were beginning to think that living by faith was what had restricted, bound, and kept them in the same place all those years.

The use of the word *apoballo* suggests that the Hebrew Christians were thinking, *If we hadn't stood so firmly on the Word of God all these years, at least we could have done something else with our lives. Let's just forget the promise God gave us. We've held on long enough! Let's just toss it aside and forget about it. At least then we can begin to move on with our lives and do something different. Enough of this fantasy that God is going to do something miraculous for us! Let's chuck this promise that has held us back and move on with our lives!*

Hebrews 10:35 is God's response to these kinds of lying thoughts, accusations, and doubts. God cries out to them to hold tight and to never let go of the promises He had made to each of them. And God is saying the same thing to us today!

The word "confidence" is the Greek word *paressia*. This word means *boldness* and depicts *a very bold, frank, outspoken kind of language*. It carries the meaning of *being forthright, blunt, direct, and straight to the point*. In this verse, it refers to the *bold, brave, fearless declarations and faith confessions regarding God's promises* that these believers had been making.

They had been professing, declaring, and laying claim to the promises of God's Word for their personal lives. They had done it boldly, audibly, and publicly. What they believed, they had declared loudly! However, now that the results weren't forthcoming and they were growing tired, they were feeling tempted to toss it all away and count it as nonsense. But this verse urged them to hold tight and to keep believing! And now *you* must hang on to God's promises just as these Hebrew Christians were told to do.

Hebrews 10:35 could be rendered to read:

"Don't discard, dispel, dismiss, dump, or cast off your bold declaration of faith, because it has great recompense of reward."

Today I am urging you — don't let the devil talk you into tossing away your faith. You've waited too long and have invested too much of your life into this promise for you to walk away from it now. If you walk away from what God promised you after waiting all these years, it will mean that all those years were for nothing!

The manifestation of your dreams is probably just around the corner. That is why the devil is working overtime right now to discourage you! He wants you to discard your faith now because he knows that if you hang on much longer, you'll see your dreams come true! *So it's time for you to hang tight, hold on, and keep believing, because it won't be much longer until you are standing in the middle of your dreams!*

MY PRAYER FOR TODAY

Lord, help me hold on tightly to the promises You have given me in Your Word. When I get physically tired or spiritually weary, please refill me with Your Spirit and recharge me with Your power so I can keep believing until I finally see the manifestation of my prayers. I know that You are faithful and that Your Word never fails, so help me remain steadfast until I see all Your promises come true in my own life. With the assistance of Your Spirit and Your power, I can and I WILL stand firm to the end.

I pray this in Jesus' name!

MY CONFESSION FOR TODAY

I confess that I have a faith that is unwavering! I stand firmly and solidly on the truths God has given me. The storms of life may come against me and the devil may try to move me, but I am not moving off the promises in God's Word! Those promises belong to me, and I claim them right now by faith! I am strong, and I am filled with the Spirit's power! Hell moves out of the way for me, because I take my stand on God's Word and refuse to move!

I declare this by faith in Jesus' name!

QUESTIONS FOR YOU TO CONSIDER

1. Have you ever had the heartbreaking experience of seeing a believer toss away his faith after he had believed and waited for many years for something to come to pass?
2. After that believer walked away from his long-held stance of faith, did his life improve or deteriorate?
3. If that person you are thinking about is you, how has your life progressed since you let go of the promise God made to you? Have you regretted that you didn't stand firm a little longer? If so, why don't you go to the Lord and repent so you can "reapprehend" that word from God and start pursuing it again?

Don't let the devil talk you into tossing away your faith. You've waited too long and have invested too much of your life into this promise for you to walk away from it now. If you walk away from what God promised you after waiting all these years, it will mean that all those years were for nothing!

JUNE 23

❧❧❧

Is It Possible for a Christian To Become the Enemy of God?

Ye adulterers and adulteresses,
know ye not that the friendship of the world
is enmity with God? whosoever therefore will be
a friend of the world is the enemy of God.
— James 4:4

How does God view a believer who once walked with Him and knew the power of the Holy Spirit but has now become so entangled in the world that he hardly ever picks up his Bible to read it, rarely prays, and comes to church only if it "fits" into his schedule of things to do? *How does God look on it when a believer departs from the red-hot spiritual passion he once possessed and turns his devotion to other things?*

James 4:4 says, "Ye adulterers and adulteresses, know ye not that the friendship of the world is enmity with God? whosoever therefore will be a friend of the world is the enemy of God." This verse tells us exactly how God feels about a believer who wanders away from Him.

I want you to notice the word "is" in this verse. It is from the Greek word *kathistemi*, which means *to constitute* or *to render.* This is very important, for it alerts us to the fact that when a believer chooses to take a worldly path, he sets himself in *direct opposition* to the godly path God desires for him. As a result of the choices he has made, he has *rendered, constituted,* or *caused* himself to become the "enemy" of God.

I know that the word "enemy" is strong, so let's see what it means. The word "enemy" is the Greek word *echthros.* This word is usually used to describe *enemies in a war* or *enemies in a military conflict.* It is the picture of two nations who are in opposition to one another and have therefore engaged in a military conflict. They are warring nations. They feel *hostility, antagonism,* and even *animosity* toward each other.

In Luke 23:12, the word *echthros* is used to communicate the *enmity* and *animosity* that existed between Pilate and Herod Antipas before they became allies at the time of Jesus' crucifixion. Prior to forming their new alliance, Pilate and Herod Antipas were *fiercely hostile* toward one another. Jealousy and competition raged between these two men. They were *enemies.*

So the meaning of the word *echthros* in James 4:4 is unquestionable. It is the picture of *a hostile force.* But now James uses this word to express the feelings and emotions that God possesses toward a believer who transfers his devotion and passion from Him to the world. By using this word, James tells us that if a believer chooses to make his relationship with the world a greater priority than his relationship with God, he is making a choice that will put him in direct opposition to God. In fact, the word *echthros* lets us know that God takes this decision so personally that He views it as *an act of war!* To God, this is the *ultimate violation!*

I realize that Romans 8:31 says, "...If God be for us, who can be against us?" But by the same token, if God takes a stand against us and our activities because our actions are wrong, our plans and pursuits will be frustrated and paralyzed, and we will not succeed in our endeavors. God is *not* against us being blessed or having a lot of possessions. But He *is* against whatever takes His place in our hearts. When the things of the world move from our *hands* into our *hearts*, that is the violation that concerns God the most!

In Matthew 6:24, Jesus said, "No man can serve two masters: for either he will hate the one, and love the other; or else he will hold to the one, and despise the other. Ye cannot serve God and mammon." According to these words of Jesus, it is impossible for us to give our hearts simultaneously to two masters. We must choose whom we are going to serve: *God* or *mammon*.

"Mammon" was an expression used by the Jewish community of New Testament times to express the idea of *worldliness*. So when Jesus said it was impossible to serve God and mammon, He was actually saying that it is impossible to serve both God and worldliness.

The word "serve" is the Greek word *doulos*, which describes *a servant* or *a slave*. This word was used to denote *a servant who had become a slave for the rest of his life*. This servant's lifetime responsibility was to "service" his master with all his attention, time, and energy. In other words, he catered to his master's every wish, desire, or demand. He was there to help, assist, and fulfill his master's wants and dreams to the exclusion of all else. This servant's entire existence was to "service" his master in whatever way the master asked or demanded.

Let me give you this example. When you purchase a car or a washing machine, these machines will operate for a while without your attention. However, a time comes when you must give your attention to them in order to keep them in good working order. And if you own a house or apartment, you know that a home requires all kinds of time, attention, energy, and money in order to keep it in good shape. In other words, all these natural possessions must be "serviced."

When Jesus told us, "…Ye cannot serve God and mammon," He was telling us that both God and mammon require time, attention, energy, and money. Jesus knew that there is not enough of you and me to properly "service" both God and worldliness in our lives. Hence, we must choose which master we are going to serve. Once that decision is made, we must then "…hate the one and love the other…."

To truly serve God, you must spend time with Him so you can know His voice and develop a pattern of obedience in your daily walk. It will demand your fullest attention. The work of God must be "serviced' with prayer, obedience, repentance, and worship.

If a person chooses to serve "mammon" (worldliness) instead of the Lord, he will have to turn his attention and devotion to the world. As a worldly person, he will be required to learn the ways of the world and to adapt to the thinking of the world. Serving the world and worldliness requires 100 percent of a person's attention.

Just as serving God requires your time, attention, energy, and money, the world will demand the same from you. This is why Jesus said it isn't possible to serve both God and mammon. You see, there just isn't enough of you to serve both of these masters simultaneously, so you must choose whom you are going to serve.

So let me ask you this: *Whom are you serving in your life right now? What most requires your time and attention?* Can you truthfully say you are giving God your fullest attention and that the chief priority in your life is to serve and obey Him? Or must you confess that worldly pursuits, possessions, and corporate success consume your thoughts and energies?

If you are consumed with God, these other things will take a lower place on your list of priorities. But if you are consumed with the world, material things will dominate the landscape of your mind. So just stop and ask yourself, *What do I think about more than anything else in life?* Your answer will probably tell you whom you are serving the most with your heart.

James 4:6 tells us that God takes a stand against a believer who turns his devotion to the world and becomes worldly. In fact, it says God "resists" such believers. The word "resist" is the Greek word *antitasso* — a military term that means *to militarily order one's self against someone else*. This is no accidental, fly-by-night plan of resistance but *a well-planned, prepared resistance.*

This emphatically declares that God takes it so personally when a believer turns his devotion from Him to the world that He sets Himself in opposition to that believer. Like a military commander, God reviews the situation; then He decides how to resist and frustrate the things this believer is trying to achieve and thus bring him to a place of surrender.

If this believer does not quickly surrender, repent, and come back to where he ought to be, God will continue to take a stand against his activities. The Christian can rebuke the devil all day long, but it will be to no avail, for his problem isn't the devil — his problem is God!

It doesn't matter how smart that person is, how many talents and gifts he possesses, or how hard he works to achieve his goals, things just won't work out right because God is standing in opposition to him, frustrating every step he takes in order to get his attention and help him get his priorities back in divine order.

As terrible as this resistance sounds, it is a manifestation of God's grace! By blocking our way and resisting our choices, the precious Holy Spirit endeavors to get our attention and to bring us to a sweet place of brokenness where sin is confessed and fellowship with God is restored.

You see, God is so passionate about your relationship with Him that He is unwilling to share you with the world. That doesn't mean you can't have a job or be successful. In most cases, you must have a job, and God *wants* you to be successful. But if you switch your allegiance from God to the world around you, God views that as the ultimate violation in His sight. It is the very act that causes Him to decide to rise up and to do something to bring you back to where you ought to be!

So I advise you to take a good look at your life and make sure your priorities are where they need to be! *Make sure you are more aligned with the Lord than with the world around you! Otherwise, God may step forward to deliberately frustrate your plans in order to bring you back to where you ought to be!*

MY PRAYER FOR TODAY

Lord, I am running to You! I want to be as close to You as I can possibly be! I don't want even the smallest hint of worldliness in my life. I want to be like You, to think like You, and to please You in every part of my life — my family, my job, my relationships, and my finances. Holy Spirit, if there is any part of me that has been influenced wrongly by the world, I ask You to please show it to me and help me get it corrected.

I pray this in Jesus' name!

MY CONFESSION FOR TODAY

I confess that I am on fire for Jesus Christ! I am alive to God and dead to the world around me. Nothing means more to me than pleasing Jesus. Every day of my life, I live to serve Him and to do His will. Although I live in the world, I am not of the world. I am a citizen of Heaven, living with eternity at the forefront of my mind!

I declare this by faith in Jesus' name!

1. Has there ever been a time when you unintentionally allowed your devotion to slip away from the Lord as your attention was drawn to the world around you?
2. What did you do to get back to where you needed to be with the Lord?
3. During that time when you wandered away from the Lord, did you sense that God was supernaturally working behind the scenes to get your attention and to bring you back home spiritually?

JUNE 24

Bringing Correction Into Someone Else's Life

And the servant of the Lord must not strive;
but be gentle unto all men, apt to teach, patient.
— 2 Timothy 2:24

*H*ave you ever found yourself in a situation where you are trying to help someone who isn't listening or paying attention to what you are trying to tell him? Should that happen to you in the future, don't allow yourself to get so angry that you lose your temper and say or do something you will later regret!

It's frustrating to try to help someone who stubbornly sits across the table, peers at you in total defiance, and reacts to your counsel as if you don't have any idea what you're talking about. But from time to time, everyone faces situations like this. Perhaps it happens when a parent tries to speak to his rebellious child; when an employer tries to bring correction to an employee; when a pastor speaks the truth that a church member doesn't want to hear; or when someone tries to lovingly communicate his concern to a friend who he believes is making a mistake in his life.

As you begin the process of bringing correction into a person's life, *put yourself in his shoes*. If you were the one sitting there, would it be easy or difficult for you to hear what is about to be said? Would you feel wonderful about receiving correction, or would you feel a little embarrassed?

If the person you are correcting acts closed or puts up a wall of defense at first, it may be that he's just embarrassed or reacting out of insecurity. Therefore, don't stop the conversation unless you can see that he's definitely just being combative and is completely closed to your input. In order to discern the true situation, you need to be patient and slow in judging his reaction to your correction.

When Paul wrote and instructed Timothy how to bring correction into someone's life, he stressed the need to be "patient" when giving correction. In Second Timothy 2:24, he wrote, "And the servant of the Lord must not strive; but be gentle unto all men, apt to teach, patient." The Greek word for "patient"" is *aneksikakos*. This is a compound of the words *anechomai* and *kakos*. The word *anechomai* means *to endure patiently, to bear with,* or *to have a tolerant attitude toward someone or something.* The word *kakos* is the Greek word for *evil* or for *something that is bad.*

When these two words are compounded into the word *aneksikakos* as they are in this verse, the new word portrays *an attitude that is tolerant and that bears with a bad, depraved, or an evil response.* Paul was telling us that when we attempt to bring correction into a person's life and his response is wrong or even terrible, we are not to get all flared up about it! Getting upset won't make the situation any better. Instead, we are to grab hold of the power of God, look that person in the eyes, and *bear with him* until he calms down and hears what we are saying. In other words, sometimes we just have to *put up* with a person's reaction, whether it's good *or* bad.

Because the word *aneksikakos* is used in this verse,
Second Timothy 2:24 could be rendered:

"And the servant of the Lord must not strive, but be gentle unto all men, apt to teach, patient. That means you must put up with those who don't act too thrilled when you sit down to correct or instruct them. You have to be patient and tolerantly bear with them and their reactions until they finally hear what you are trying to express to them."

In Galatians 6:1, Paul warned us, "Brethren, if a man be overtaken in a fault, ye which are spiritual, restore such an one in the spirit of meekness; considering thyself, lest thou also be tempted." When I am about to give correction, it has always been helpful for me to remember how difficult it might be to sit on the other side of the table and hear a superior correcting *me.* So before I correct someone, I first consider how I would want to be told if I had done something wrong, just as Paul suggested: "…considering thyself, lest thou also be tempted."

Before you charge into a room to correct someone, first take some time to pray and really think about the best, the most peaceful, and the most positive way to speak these words of correction or even words of rebuke. Do it in the right spirit, and don't permit yourself to get upset if you see a response that isn't exactly what you had hoped for. Just hold tight, be calm, and bear with the person you're talking to a little while as he adjusts to the idea of being corrected. If he ultimately refuses your correction and remains defiant, you may have to take a different route. But at least in the beginning, be patient with that person if he doesn't respond the way you hoped.

This is exactly what the apostle Paul is talking about when he stresses that you must be "patient" when you bring correction into someone's life. So why not ask the Holy Spirit today to help you become more temperate when people under your authority don't respond exactly as you had wished? Be patient and believe that they will eventually come around!

MY PRAYER FOR TODAY

Lord, I ask You to help me be kind and patient when it is essential for me to bring correction. Help me to not be offended if the person I'm trying to help doesn't respond at first the way I wished he would have. Help me to put myself in that person's shoes and to sympathize with how he might feel. I ask You to give me the wisdom to know what to say, when to say it, and how to say it. I also ask that You give the other person the grace to hear what I am telling him so he might see that I have his best interest at heart and that I am only trying to help him.

I pray this in Jesus' name!

MY CONFESSION FOR TODAY

I confess that I have the mind of Jesus Christ! When it is needful for me to speak correction to someone else, I do it with love, kindness, and patience. I refrain from allowing anger to rise up inside me. I am careful about the words that come out of my mouth, and I refuse to participate in vain arguing. I remain in control of myself as the Holy Spirit works mightily inside me. My words bring life to all who hear and receive them!

I declare this by faith in Jesus' name!

QUESTIONS FOR YOU TO CONSIDER

1. Can you think of a time in your own life when someone had to bring correction to you? How did you fare in the way you received it? Were you opened-hearted — or offended and defiant?
2. What did you do when you were being corrected that you wouldn't want someone to do to you if *you* were the one trying to bring correction?
3. When it's necessary to bring correction to someone, what should you do to make it easier for that person to receive your correction?

JUNE 25

What Would You Do If a Poisonous Snake Bit You?

And he shook off the beast into the fire,
and felt no harm.
— Acts 28:5

When I read about the travels of the apostle Paul, I find his story to be simply remarkable! What he had to endure to take the Gospel to the Gentiles was out of the ordinary!

For example, in Second Corinthians 11:25, Paul tells us that during the course of his ministry, he was shipwrecked three times! He writes, "…thrice I suffered shipwreck, a night and a day I have been in the deep." This verse is a bit of a mystery, because only one shipwreck is recorded in the book of Acts. Yet it is certain that too many significant events occurred during Paul's ministry for all of them to be recorded in Luke's account in the book of Acts.

Traveling by sea was a perilous and risky undertaking. Ships were not always reliable. The routes often took them through waters cluttered with sharp rocks, reefs, and debris. Even if the vessel was guided by strong and skilled leadership, currents were so strong that even the best ships could be carried directly into rocks and other dangerous obstacles.

In Acts 27, we read that Paul was traveling on board a ship that ran into rocks and broke into pieces. In that moment of crisis, Paul became God's man on board ship! He spoke the word of faith to the crew and passengers, and soon he was in charge of the entire situation.

Once marooned on the island of Melita, Paul worked with the other crew members to collect wood for a fire. Apparently a venomous viper was hidden in the sticks that he was carrying to lay on the fire. When he dropped his wood onto the flames, that snake charged out of the pile of wood and bit Paul on the hand. Acts 28:3 says, "And when Paul had gathered a bundle of sticks, and laid them on the fire, there came a viper out of the heat, and fastened on his hand."

The word "viper" is the Greek word *echidna*, and it refers to *a highly venomous snake.* The verse says that this snake "fastened on his hand." The word "fastened" is the Greek word *kathapto*, and it means *to tightly fasten.* This snake *deeply bit* the apostle Paul. Not only did it bite him, but it also injected its venom into his hand, for the word *kathapto* also meant *to introduce poison into the body.* That viper sunk its fangs deeply into Paul's flesh and then released its full load of venom into his hand. That is why Acts 28:4 says, "And when the barbarians saw the venomous beast hang on his hand, they said among themselves, No doubt this man is a murderer, whom, though he hath escaped the sea, yet vengeance suffereth not to live."

But what did Paul do? *He shook off that snake!* Acts 28:5 says, "And he shook off the beast into the fire, and felt no harm." The phrase "shook it off" is from the Greek word *apotinasso.* It is a compound of the word *apo*, meaning *off* and *away*, and the word *tinasso*, which means *to shake.* This word pictures the apostle Paul shaking his hand back and forth until finally the viper released its fangs and fell into the fire.

When the barbarian crowd saw that Paul didn't die, they assumed he was a god. In just a short time, Paul used the event to bring the whole island together for a crusade! Publius, the chief of the island, was so impressed that he took Paul into his own home for three days. While there, Paul laid hands on Publius' father, who "…lay sick of a fever and of a bloody flux…" (Acts 28:8).

The man was miraculously healed, and soon the entire island was in revival! The Bible tells us, "So when this was done, others also, which had diseases in the island, came, and were healed" (Acts 28:9). By the time Paul departed from Melita, he was so respected and honored that they loaded him down with everything necessary for the remainder of his journey!

How would you have acted if you had been in Paul's position? Suppose you became shipwrecked and lost all your human possessions. Then you found yourself marooned on an island inhabited by barbarians, where a venomous snake promptly bites you! Do you think you would have "shaken it off" as Paul did? Would you have turned your disaster into a revival? Or would you have been tempted to sit down and cry while you worried about your plans being ruined?

Paul's attitude is what kept him in the midst of revival everywhere he went. He had the opportunity to give in to his flesh and throw a pity party, just as you and I do. But because Paul chose to keep going and never stop, God's power was always available to help him in every situation.

What is hindering you today? What is the devil trying to use to latch on to your life and to distract you? Why don't you make the decision to shake it off? There's too much at stake for you to let some little thing distract you and pull you down into defeat. Turn that attack around and use it for the glory of God. *Make the devil sorry that he ever sent that poisonous viper to try to attack you!*

MY PRAYER FOR TODAY

Lord, give me the attitude that turns every attack the devil sends into an opportunity for revival! Help me walk in such strong and consistent faith that I do not flinch at ANYTHING the devil tries to do to me. Rather than give in to my flesh and let worry conquer me, help me to remember the assignment You've given to me and to remain committed to finish my course on time!

I pray this in Jesus' name!

I confess that revival happens everywhere I go! Every disaster the devil sends is my opportunity to advance the Gospel! I refuse to give in to my flesh and throw a pity party. Because I keep going and never give in or give up, God's power is always available to help me in every situation. There's too much at stake for me to let some little thing pull me down into defeat. With God's Spirit at work in me, I overcome each and every obstacle that tries to block my way!

I declare this by faith in Jesus' name!

QUESTIONS FOR YOU TO CONSIDER

1. Has there been a time when the devil tried to send a "viper" into your life to destroy you, your business, your ministry, your church, or your relationships? Who or what was that "viper," and what did you do when you realized it had already stuck its fangs into your personal affairs?
2. What did you learn from that "viper" experience? What would you do differently today than you did when that event occurred?
3. Were you able to shake off the "viper" the enemy sent your way, or did that experience send you emotionally tumbling? Were you a rock, or did you fall apart? What did your response reveal about you and what you now need to do to strengthen your inner man?

JUNE 26

Who Are You Considering Today?

And let us consider one another to provoke
unto love and to good works.
— Hebrews 10:24

Do you ever get so busy and self-consumed that you forget there are people all around you who have needs and challenges too? It's true that we are often so concerned about ourselves that we forget or bypass people who are struggling terribly, not realizing that they need a special act or word to encourage them. This is especially sad when it happens inside the church, because we are supposed to be a spiritual family who genuinely cares for one another and who helps meet each other's needs. This is why Hebrews 10:24 says, "And let us consider one another to provoke unto love and to good works."

The word "consider" is from the Greek word *katanoeo*, a compound of the words *kata* and *noeo*. The word *kata* depicts *something that is moving downward*; the word *noeo* (from the word *nous*) depicts *the mind* and means *to think*. When the two words are placed together, the new word means *to thoroughly think something through* or *to ponder something from the top all the way to the bottom*. It is the idea of *mulling something over; carefully contemplating a matter; pondering and carefully looking at a particular issue;* or *examining and fully studying a subject.*

This word pictures someone who is so concerned about someone else that he has taken the time to really consider that other person. He has observed the person's ups and downs and his highs and lows. He has studied to find out what helps that person feel encouraged and what events tend to pull him down. Because he has determined to really know and understand that other person, he invests a great deal of time and concentration into studying and getting to know that other person. This kind of knowledge doesn't come by accident, but by *determined pursuit.*

In light of this understanding, we must remember that although the local church is to be a place where we can come to worship and hear the Word of God preached and taught, it is also a place where believers should "consider one another" as this verse commands. The writer of Hebrews uses this word to convey the picture of a loving community where people are vitally concerned about each others' welfare. In fact, they are constantly observing and contemplating each other to know how to encourage and provoke each other to love and to good works.

Not only are we to *consider* one another, but the Bible goes on to say we are also to *provoke* one another unto love and good works. The word "provoke" is the Greek word *paraxusmos*. The word *para* means *alongside*, and it carries the idea of *being close*. The second part of the word is the Greek word *xusmos*, which means *to sharpen something*, such as a knife, and indicates *a very sharp situation*. When you put the two words together, the compound word describes *someone who has come alongside of someone else for the purpose of prodding and impelling that person to do something.*

You may have already guessed that "provoking" one another can be either a positive or a negative thing! One translation for this word *paraxusmos* would be *to call into combat*. Throughout the New Testament, the word *paraxusmos* is usually translated to mean *to irritate, to incite, to anger, to inflame,* or *to enrage*. Obviously, this kind of provoking is very bad! But in Hebrews 10:24, the word "provoking" is telling us that our relationships with other believers should incite us to become better, stronger, and bolder in the Lord.

How can you provoke other believers in a positive way? How can you stimulate your brother in the Lord in such a way that you make him *want* to walk in love and do good works? How can you sharpen and inspire the fellow believer who is in need of endurance?

You can come alongside that person and love him enough not to leave him in discouragement and defeat. You can *sharpen* him, *prod* him, *impel* him, and *inspire* him to keep on fighting the good fight of faith! All believers need to be provoked at times, no matter what their position is in the Body of Christ. Everyone needs a loving push in the right direction now and then!

A paraphrase of this verse might be the following:

"And constantly be observing one another, seriously contemplating, studying, and examining each other, until you know exactly how to incite and stimulate each other to love and to good works."

This verse plainly tells us that we should be extremely concerned about each other's welfare and spiritual progression. We are to get involved in the local church, not just for our own benefit, but to be a benefit to others as well. We need people who will love us, observe us, and support us when we are struggling or standing on a word from God. But at the same time, others need our assistance too.

Proverbs 17:17 says, "A friend loveth at all times, and a brother is born for adversity." This verse is telling us that real friends love us at all times and stay with us even in the midst of difficult circumstances. They will love us and stand with us no matter what we are going through, looking for ways to assist us when we are experiencing challenging times.

The local church should be a place of victory where faith is built up, the soul is encouraged, and wisdom and strength are imparted. It's a community where faith lives and triumphs through a family of believers' love and concern for one another.

There is nothing like living in an atmosphere of faith and love where you are surrounded by believers who really believe and practice the Word of God. Having friends like this gives you strength — and *being* a friend like this to someone else helps give him the strength he needs to live as an overcomer.

There is absolutely no substitute for the joy and satisfaction that comes when fellow church members go out of their way to call you, to come see you, to write you a note, or to personally check up on you — just because they have noticed that you need a little encouraging! Just knowing that someone cares enough to do that can make such a difference when you're going through a difficult time!

If you're anything like the rest of us, you're probably pretty good at provoking others in the negative sense. So why not commit yourself to becoming just as proficient in provoking your brothers and sisters in the Lord in the *positive* sense? *Make a quality decision to become an expert at provoking others unto love and good deeds!*

MY PRAYER FOR TODAY

Lord, forgive me for being so self-consumed that I have neglected to see the needs in people around me. I am sorry I've been so selfish that I haven't even recognized the times I could have been a blessing and an encouragement. I repent and I make the decision to reach out to those who are around me. Just as others have strengthened me, I want to be a source of strength to those around me!

I pray this in Jesus' name!

MY CONFESSION FOR TODAY

I confess that I take the time to carefully consider other people's needs. I observe their ups and downs and their highs and lows. I study to find out what helps them feel encouraged. I am constantly observing and contemplating others to know how to encourage and provoke them to love and to good works. God uses me to come alongside those around me to help impel them to stay on track with God and with their God-given assignments. Because I am careful to notice other people's needs and I reach out to assist them with words of strength, they are becoming better, stronger, and bolder in the Lord.

I declare this by faith in Jesus' name!

QUESTIONS FOR YOU TO CONSIDER

1. Can you think of someone whom God really used to encourage you at a critical moment in your life? What did that person do that had such a dramatic impact on you?

2. Who is that one person who needs you to be a source of strength and encouragement to him or her right now? Isn't it time that you help someone else as others have helped you in the past?
3. What practical things can you do to communicate your concern to others (for example, writing them a note, calling them on the telephone, sending flowers, etc.)? Is there something concrete you need to do today to show someone you are thinking and praying for him or her?

JUNE 27

Gird Up the Loins of Your Mind!

Wherefore gird up the loins of your mind, be sober,
and hope to the end for the grace that is to be brought
unto you at the revelation of Jesus Christ.
— 1 Peter 1:13

*T*oday I want to draw your attention to the phrase "gird up the loins of your mind" that is used in the verse above. This isn't just an interesting phrase that Peter concocted when he wrote this verse. It is an extremely powerful and graphic picture that expresses something very important that you and I need to understand and apply in our lives!

This phrase "gird up the loins" comes from the Greek word *anadzonnumi*. This word was used to describe Orientals who wore long robes. Before taking a long journey or before running in a race, they would gather up their loose robes and tuck them up under their girdle.

Most frequently this word would be used to depict a runner who was running a race. To run freely and without hindrance, he would reach down to gather the long, dangling ends of his garments and then tuck them up under his belt. With the loose ends out of the way, he could then run freely and without distraction.

But the runner would get in trouble if he ever allowed his garments to fall down and become entangled in his legs. Even though he may have been picking up his stride and running a good race up to that point, the encumbrance of dangling, loosely hanging clothes would hinder his steps. And allowing those loose ends to keep dangling would have been a sure way to lose the race!

But notice that Peter is not talking about a garment made of material; he is referring to *the loins of our minds*. You see, Peter is telling us that if we don't:

✦ deal with the loose ends that exist in our minds and emotions;
✦ correct those parts of our thinking that we know are wrong;
✦ grab hold of all those dangling areas in our thinking and put them out of the way;
✦ and remove them by the authority of the Word of God —
✦ then we are choosing to permit things to exist in our lives that will hinder our steps and slow us down in our race and in our ability to successfully walk with God!

If we want to be successful in our spiritual lives and truly walk with God, then we must start by dealing with the "loins of our minds." In other words, we must seek to deal with all the loose ends in our thinking that haven't yet been submitted to the Word of God or surrendered to the Holy Spirit's power.

If we deliberately allow wrong thinking and wrong believing to continue in our lives, we are making the same kind of mistake the runner does who deliberately allows his garment to hang down and get caught in his legs. This is why Peter admonishes us to tighten up those areas that the devil would try to grab hold of and use against us!

Are there any loose ends that you need to deal with in your life right now? If there are, I am certain you already know what those areas are! The Holy Spirit has been trying to deal with you about those areas for a long time, but have you been listening? If you continue to ignore His voice, you will pay the price of failure — of never realizing your maximum potential.

You see, God is only trying to help you when He speaks to you about the loose ends in your life. If you're smart, you'll stop everything you are doing to grab hold of those dangling ends and get them out of your way once and for all. Then you'll be able to run the race set before you with no distractions!

So what are you going to do about the loose ends in your life today? If you'll open your heart to the Holy Spirit's help, He will assist you in identifying every area that needs your attention; then He will help you grab hold of those loose ends and move them out of your way forever!

MY PRAYER FOR TODAY

Lord, I ask You to help me tie up the loose ends that I've allowed to remain in my mind and emotions. Today I am making the deliberate choice to start submitting every area of my mind and emotions to the Word of God and to the sanctifying power of the Holy Spirit. Please let the power of Your Word and Spirit flow into every area of my mind and emotions, energizing them with Your Presence so that the devil can no longer access me through these areas of my life!

I pray this in Jesus' name!

MY CONFESSION FOR TODAY

I confess that my mind and emotions are submitted to and renewed by God's Word. The devil has no access to my mind because my thought life is dominated by God's Word and by the power of the Spirit. I think God's thoughts, and I have the mind of Jesus Christ. Therefore, no entrance is available in my mind or emotions through which the devil can access me! I believe the truth; I think the truth; and I confess the truth about who Jesus Christ has made me to be!

I declare this by faith in Jesus' name!

QUESTIONS FOR YOU TO CONSIDER

1. If you take an honest look at the spiritual attacks that have assaulted your life, how many of them have been a result of your failure to renew your mind or take authority over the devil's strategies in your life? If your mind had been dominated

by the Word of God and if you had been walking in the Spirit, how might the situation have turned out differently?
2. What are you doing right now to make sure the devil can't find access to your mind and emotions again? What practical steps are you taking to make sure that you won't fall into that same trap the next time?
3. If you encounter someone who is constantly being assaulted by the enemy, what preventative steps should you advise that person to take to ensure that the next demonic attack that comes against him is ineffective?

JUNE 28

Mark 11:23 Works for the Devil Too!

For verily I say unto you, That whosoever shall say
unto this mountain, Be thou removed, and be thou cast into the sea;
and shall not doubt in his heart, but shall believe
that those things which he saith shall come to pass;
he shall have whatsoever he saith.
— Mark 11:23

The devil loves to make a playground out of people's minds and imaginations. He delights in filling their perceptions and senses with illusions that captivate them, paralyze them, and ultimately destroy them. How can believers avoid falling victim to the devil's attacks? They must make a spiritual and mental decision to take charge of every thought that enters their minds!

Taking your thoughts captive is going to require determination and energy. Once you make the decision to do it, you still have to *stick* with that decision. If you're not really committed to seizing every thought the devil tries to inject into your mind and emotions, he'll be back to strike you again and again. And if you don't stop the enemy's thoughts from invading your mind, it won't be long until your faith begins to empower those thoughts and they become a bona fide reality in your life!

Mark 11:23 is a powerful verse about faith and confession that believers claim and use around the world. But the principle in this verse works in both a positive and negative sense — or to put it another way, this principle works both in the realm of God and in the realm of the devil.

Mark 11:23 says, "For verily I say unto you, That whosoever shall say unto this mountain, Be thou removed, and be thou cast into the sea; and shall not doubt in his heart, but shall believe that those things which he saith shall come to pass; he shall have whatsoever he saith." According to what Jesus taught in this verse, you can bring to pass whatsoever you say and believe in your heart.

Did you notice that Jesus said if a person confesses something "and shall not doubt in his heart" — in other words, if he believes the words he is speaking with his mouth — he will have exactly what he says. The word "doubt" is from the Greek word *diakrinomai*, which means *to hesitate, to waver, to doubt, or to differ*. In context, Jesus is saying that when a person's heart doesn't *differ* from what his mouth is saying, the combination of his heart and mouth in agreement will always make things happen!

I call this concept "the heart-mouth connection." For instance, if you believe in your heart that Jesus purchased your healing, and you put your heartfelt faith together with the confession of your mouth, you can literally bring that healing into manifestation in your physical body.

Creative power is released when the heart and mouth get into agreement! That is why you must be careful about what you believe in your heart and say with your mouth, because when your heart and mouth get "in sync" with each other, it literally makes things come to pass!

This heart-mouth combination works on both the positive and negative sides of life. It can bring about the manifestation of healing in your body, salvation to your family, prosperity to your business, and growth to your local church. *But the devil also knows how to use this principle against you!*

The enemy knows if he can fill your mind and heart with lies that you believe and then coax you into confessing those lies with your mouth, you will make those evil images come to pass in your life! That is exactly why the devil wants to fill your mind with lies and accusations. That's why he paints so vividly on the "movie screen" in your mind. That's why he assaults your mind and emotions again and again. He knows he just has to get you to embrace these lies and to start believing them.

Once you do that, you'll soon start speaking those lies out of your mouth. And if you start speaking them with your mouth, it will only be a matter of time until they become your reality. Jesus said, "...out of the abundance of the heart the mouth speaketh" (Matthew 12:34). So according to Jesus, whatever is in your heart is eventually going to come out of your mouth!

Because great power is released when your heart and mouth start working together, it's extremely important that you put the right things into your heart. Mark 11:23 promises that whatever you believe in your heart and say with your mouth *will* come to pass. But as I said before, it doesn't just apply to Bible verses; it applies to *anything* you believe in your heart and say with your mouth. So if the devil can get you to believe and say wrong things, your own heart and mouth will cause those killer confessions to come to pass.

I know it's hard to control your mouth sometimes, but when you start to "run at the mouth" and say any ol' thing the devil puts in your head, you're playing with fire! It is a scientific fact that when you speak something *out loud*, those words are verified and empowered in your mind. That's why the devil wants you to repeat every stupid thing he puts in your mind. By repeating it out loud, you are helping him build a stronghold in the realm of your mind and imagination!

This is another reason why it's so important for you to spend time in the Word of God. As you spend time meditating in the Word, your mind becomes renewed to God's way of thinking (*see* Ephesians 4:23 and Colossians 3:10). God's Word brings a supernatural cleansing that washes your mind and emotions from the contamination of the world, the memories of past experiences, and the lies that the enemy has tried to sow into your brain.

When you make it a priority to fill your mind with truth from God's Word, the enemy can't penetrate your mind and he can't fill you with his lies. And if you're not filled with his lies, you won't be speaking and confessing things that are untrue! You see, when your mind is renewed to the Word of God, you become inwardly strengthened and very hard to deceive!

Satan knows that empty heads are much easier to deceive. That's why he loves it when he finds a believer who has made no effort to fill his mind with truth from God's Word. The devil knows he has found another empty head just waiting for him to come along and fill it — and he's happy to oblige!

Who or what is going to control your mind? God and His Word, or the enemy and his lies? Your mind is going to be filled with something, so you may as well choose the right thing to fill it. *Your choice in this matter will determine your success or your failure in life, so make sure you choose wisely!*

MY PRAYER FOR TODAY

Lord, I want my heart and mouth to say the right things! I know I need to spend more time filling my heart and mind with Your Word. I also know I need to be speaking positive confessions about myself, my family, my business, my future, my health, and every other area of my life. Your Word has the promises I need for every sphere of my life, so I ask You to help me fill my heart with the truth and line up my mouth with what Your Word promises for my life.

I pray this in Jesus' name!

MY CONFESSION FOR TODAY

I confess that I spend time meditating in the Word of God, and it renews my mind to God's way of thinking. God's Word brings a supernatural cleansing that washes my mind and emotions from the contamination of the world, the memories of past experiences, and the lies that the enemy has tried to sow into my brain. I make it a priority to fill my mind with truth from God's Word; therefore, I make it very difficult for the devil to penetrate my mind with his lies.

I declare this by faith in Jesus' name!

QUESTIONS FOR YOU TO CONSIDER

1. What negative things do you say about yourself — about your weight, your appearance, your skills, etc. — that you know you ought not to be saying?
2. Can you recall an example of how you confessed something negative for so long that your words eventually came to pass in your life?
3. How much time do you spend reading your Bible and meditating on God's Word? There is no reason to be dishonest in your answer, because God knows the truth anyway. Look at your life honestly as you answer this question.

Satan knows that empty heads are much easier to deceive. That's why he loves it when he finds a believer who has made no effort to fill his or her mind with truth from God's Word. The devil knows he has found another empty head just waiting for him to come along and fill it — and he's happy to oblige! Who or what is going to control your mind? God and His Word, or the enemy and his lies? Your mind is going to be filled with something, so you may as well choose the right thing to fill it. *Your choice in this matter will determine your success or your failure in life, so make sure you choose wisely!*

JUNE 29

❧

How To Pray for Your Pastor
Or Your Spiritual Leader

Now I beseech you, brethren, for the Lord Jesus Christ's sake,
and for the love of the Spirit, that ye strive together
with me in your prayers to God for me;
That I may be delivered from them that do not believe in Judaea;
and that my service which I have for Jerusalem
may be accepted of the saints;
That I may come unto you with joy by the will of God,
and may with you be refreshed.
— Romans 15:30-32

*B*ecause the apostle Paul's ministry demanded so much of him and because there was so much resistance to stop him, he knew he needed as much prayer support as he could get! That is why he wrote to the Romans and asked, "Now I beseech you, brethren, for the Lord Jesus Christ's sake, and for the love of the Spirit, that ye strive together with me in your prayers to God for me; that I may be delivered from them that do not believe in Judaea; and that my service which I have for Jerusalem may be accepted of the saints; that I may come unto you with joy by the will of God, and may with you be refreshed."

By studying this specific prayer request of the apostle Paul, we can gain insights about how we need to be praying for our own pastors or for those who are in spiritual authority over our lives. So let's take a few minutes to seriously look at these verses today to see what we can learn about praying for our spiritual leaders.

First, Paul makes the following request: "...that ye strive together with me in your prayers...." The words "strive together" are taken from the Greek word *sunagonidzomai*, which is a compound of the words *sun* and *agonidzo*. The word *sun* means *together* and carries the meaning of doing something *with* someone else. The word *agonidzo* means *to agonize*. It indicates *an intense agony; a violent struggle; anguish; contending with an enemy;* or *fighting in a contest*.

This tells me that Paul was in a great spiritual battle at the time he wrote this prayer request. In fact, the fight was so intense that he felt the need for others to join with him in prayer. He didn't want to face this spiritual fight alone, so he opened his heart and asked others to join with him in fighting this battle.

As you pray for your pastor or spiritual leader, remember that he or she needs your support in prayer. Just as Jesus requested Peter, James, and John to pray with Him in the Garden of Gethsemane, your pastor needs your prayer support. Yes, he can pray alone, but it will be such a help for him to know that others are standing in faith and in the Spirit with him. The apostle Paul needed this, and your pastor needs it as well.

Second, Paul specifically asked them to pray: "That I may be delivered from them that do not believe..." (v. 31). The word "delivered" is the Greek word *ruomai*, which means *to be rescued, to deliver, to snatch out of,* or *to drag out of danger*.

It may sound strange that Paul would request others to pray that he would be delivered from those who didn't believe. But Paul had gone through many experiences with "unbelievers" who resisted him, as well as with so-called "brethren" who gave him constant troubles. It is simply a fact that the devil works primarily through people. When he wants to stop the advancement of the Gospel, he often tries to resist a local church or pastor by stirring up someone in the community to be against the pastor. Sometimes the enemy even uses people inside the local church to create problems that bring division and disaster. So when you pray for your pastor, remember to pray that he will be snatched out of the traps and snares set for him by people who have wrong motives.

Third, Paul requested prayer: "…that my service which I have for Jerusalem may be accepted of the saints" (v. 31). The word "service" is the Greek word *diakonia*, which is the Greek word for *the ministry*. The word "accepted" is the Greek word *euprosdektos*, which means *to be pleasing, acceptable, or well-received*.

This is an expected prayer request from a preacher! Paul has sought God through prayer and listened to hear what the Lord is saying to his spirit because he wants to do well in his ministry. Paul desires every word to be spoken correctly, accurately, and in a way that pleases God. Furthermore, he wants people to believe in the sincerity of his motives and not to question whether he has ulterior motives for speaking to them about the Lord. Thus, he prays that his ministry to the saints in Jerusalem will be well received.

As you pray for your pastor, be sure to include this item on your prayer list! Pray that his ministry will be blessed and accepted and that people will receive him and hear his heart the way he means to convey it. He needs your prayer power working behind him as he takes specific words from God into various situations.

Fourth, Paul requested that the believers in Rome pray "that I may come unto you with joy…" (v. 32). The word "joy" is the Greek word *chara*, meaning *joy, gladness,* or *rejoicing*. This simply means Paul wanted to have joy in his ministry! He had faced many hardships that gave him opportunities to lose his joy — such as broken friendships, dashed expectations, political turmoil, church divisions, and so on. Paul's request was very simple: "Please pray that I will have and will keep my joy in the middle of everything I have to deal with in my ministry!"

Just think of the things that happen in your own life that tempt you to lose your joy. What about your pastor? Think of all the people he counsels, the marriages he tries to help, the sermons he has to prepare, and the organization he has to oversee. Then on top of all that, think of the disappointment your pastor is tempted to feel when people he has helped in the past decide to leave the church. I guarantee you that there are many opportunities for your pastor to lose his joy.

So take Paul's prayer request to heart and apply it to your pastor. Pray that your pastor will have and will hold on to his joy in spite of everything he has to deal with in his ministry!

Fifth, Paul prayed: "That I may come unto you with joy by the will of God…." The word "will" is the Greek word *thelema*, meaning the *design, purpose, plan,* or *will*. Paul wanted to be right in the middle of God's will for his life!

Just as we pray to make no mistakes and to be right where God wants us to be, Paul prayed the very same prayer! He wanted the saints to pray that he would make no mistakes and that he might always stay in the perfect plan of God.

So when you pray for your pastor, pray that he will have the wisdom to know what he is supposed to do in the various situations he faces in his ministry. Questions come at him all day long, and he needs your prayer support to make right decisions. And just as Paul requested prayer that he would be in the will of God, help your pastor by strongly praying that he will stay sensitive to the Spirit so he can avoid making costly mistakes and follow God's will for himself and for the church.

Sixth, Paul requested prayer that he might be "refreshed" (v. 32). The word "refreshed" is the Greek word *sunanapauomai*, a compound of the words *sun* and *anapauomai*. The word *sun* means *together with*, as to do or to experience something *with* someone else. The word *anapauomai* means *to calm, to soothe, to refresh,* or *to be refreshed.* When these two words are positioned together, they become the word *sunanapauomai*, which means *to be refreshed with someone else.*

Everyone needs to be refreshed from time to time — *including pastors and preachers*! People tend to think that pastors and preachers don't need the same refreshing that others need, but everyone needs to be refreshed and touched by God from time to time! Paul makes his need for refreshment known by telling his Roman readers, "I need to be refreshed just like the rest of you, so please pray that I *will* be refreshed!"

As you pray for your pastor, or for the ministries and missionaries you support, use this prayer request of the apostle Paul to guide you in your prayers. This prayer was included in the New Testament by the Holy Spirit to let us know that everyone — including ministers of the Gospel — need people to stand behind them in prayer. *So why not use this prayer as a tool to help you pray more effectively for the spiritual leaders to whom God has connected you?*

MY PRAYER FOR TODAY

Lord, I am making the decision to stand with my pastor in prayer! I want to join him as a sincere prayer partner and support him spiritually by praying for him. I ask You to deliver him from people who have wrong motives. I also pray that his ministry will be well received; that he will have joy in his ministry; that he will make right decisions and stay in the will of God; and that he will always feel strong and refreshed in his spirit, soul, and body. Please richly bless my pastor, his wife, and his family.

I pray this in Jesus' name!

MY CONFESSION FOR TODAY

I confess that I am a strong support to my pastor and his family. I regularly pray for him and for the other ministries and missionaries God has called me to support. They need my prayer power — and I stand with them in the Spirit for God's blessings to come upon their lives!

I declare this by faith in Jesus' name!

QUESTIONS FOR YOU TO CONSIDER

1. Do you spend time praying for your pastor and the needs he may be facing in his own life? If you were a pastor, don't you think that you would want your congregation to be praying for you?
2. Based on Paul's prayer request in Romans 15:30-32, what is the most important thing you can be praying for your pastor right now?
3. As you pray, do you sense the Holy Spirit prompting you to pray anything special for your pastor and his family? If so, pay close attention to that prompting, for it may be a special leading of the Holy Spirit to show you how to support him and his family in prayer, especially at this present time.

JUNE 30

❦❦❦

What God Thinks About People Who Gossip!

Let no corrupt communication proceed out of your mouth,
but that which is good to the use of edifying,
that it may minister grace unto the hearers.
— Ephesians 4:29

When I was a young man, my family attended a church where the pastor was a fabulous Bible teacher. Wednesday night services were my favorite, because that is when he would really open the Word of God and teach us. But there was one aspect of the Wednesday night services that I absolutely despised — a gossiping church member who always started running her mouth as soon as church was finished!

This woman would stand to the side, peering at others and whispering about them behind their backs. But whenever the subject of her gossip approached her little clique, she'd stop whispering and smile at him or her so nicely and graciously. I hated the hypocrisy of this gossiper's behavior and never understood how she could talk so badly about people immediately after hearing the Word of God taught with such power!

I remember how this woman always looked so elated when she found a new choice morsel of information about someone else in the church that she could start broadcasting. Yet most of what she gossiped about was based on hearsay. She didn't even know if the "tidbits" she shared were factual. As long as they were enticing to hear, she knew she'd always have a small clan of devoted listeners. But even if the things this woman gossiped about had been factual, she had no business talking about them with others.

How does God feel about people who gossip? Ephesians 4:29 says, "Let no corrupt communication proceed out of your mouth, but that which is good to the use of edifying, that it may minister grace unto the hearers." The following verse continues to say, "And grieve not the holy Spirit of God...." The implication is that when "corrupt communication" comes out of a believer's mouth, it causes the Holy Spirit to be grieved (*see* January 5).

You see, gossip is a *sin* that grieves the Holy Spirit. Did you notice that Paul calls it "corrupt communication"? This phrase comes from the Greek word *phaulos*, which refers to *something that stinks* or to *something that is rotting*, such as meat that is full of maggots. This kind of communication is *dead, decaying*, and it *stinks*. It is *offensive* to the Spirit of God, and it *grieves* Him.

Gossip is so destructive and offensive that Paul *forbids* gossip in Second Corinthians 12:20. In this verse, Paul says, "For I fear, lest, when I come, I shall not find you such as I would, and that I shall be found unto you such as ye would not: lest there be debates, envyings, wraths, strifes, backbitings, whisperings, swelling, tumults." Do you see the word "whisperings"? This is the Greek word *psithurimos* — which means *gossip*!

To make sure we know how evil gossip is, Paul lists it side by side with several other horrible attitudes and actions. He places gossip right alongside with:

Debates:

From the Greek word *eris,* which depicts a church divided by *church politics.* It could be translated as the word *quarrels* or *wranglings.*

Envyings:

From the Greek word *zelos,* which pictures *a person so self-consumed that he fiercely fights for his own cause, not considering the needs or desires of others.* It can be translated as the word *jealousy.*

Wraths:

From the Greek word *thumos,* portraying *a person who suddenly flares up and loses his control of some kind of unresolved, deep-seated anger.* This is a person who literally *boils over with anger and blows up,* erupting in an ugly outburst that negatively affects other people.

Strifes:

From the Greek word *eritheia,* depicting *a selfish desire to promote one's own way even if it means splitting and dividing the church.* This is a picture of people taking sides in the church and thus dividing, splitting, and splintering the church into opposing factions.

Backbiting:

From the Greek word *katalalia,* meaning *to talk down* or *to speak derogatorily about someone else.* It can be translated as the word *slander.*

Whisperings:

From the Greek word *psithurismos,* which expresses the idea of *a gossiper.* The reason they *whisper* is that they know this kind of talk is wrong and that they'd get in trouble for what they were saying; therefore, they *whisper* their tidbits of information to others in secret.

Swellings:

From the Greek word *phusiosis,* which carries the idea of *a person filled with pride.* In fact, it can be translated *to be puffed up.* This is a person who is puffed up in pride about something that isn't even important; nevertheless, he has allowed this thing to delude him into *a false sense of over-significance or of being better than others.* This word could also be translated as the word *arrogance.*

Tumults:

From the Greek word *akatastasia,* referring to *anarchy, chaos, insubordination,* or *to some kind of attitude or action that creates upheaval, unrest, or instability.* It describes the attitude or actions of a person who creates some type of *disastrous disturbance.*

I want you to notice that "gossip" is right smack dab in the middle of this list! What does this tell you about what God thinks of gossip and of those who are involved in the act of gossiping?

Let's be sure we understand what the word "gossip" describes! It describes a person who habitually reveals personal or sensational facts, rumors, or reports of an intimate nature that are none of his business.

For instance, gossip would include:

✦ Talking about other people's business and things that do not concern you.
✦ Repeating what someone else said, even though you don't know whether or not it's true.
✦ Talking to others as if you were an authority about matters that are other people's business, when in reality you don't know what you are talking about.

In a certain sense, gossip is like a deadly poison. It hurts people; it kills relationships; and it destroys trust. In the workplace, "gossip" usually happens between two employees who have become friends and feel like they can truly "share" with each other. They are often people who have been offended or hurt by the one who is the subject of their gossip; therefore, every rumor they hear becomes a "choice morsel" to share with the other offended party. This is what Proverbs 18:8 (*NIV*) is talking about when it says, "The words of a gossip are like choice morsels; they go down to a man's inmost parts."

Gossip is usually based on hearsay; it is usually inaccurate; it creates suspicions; and it divides people. It is so evil that I absolutely *forbid* it in our ministry.

It is interesting to note that the Greek word for gossip means *to whisper*. This means that gossip almost always takes place in secret. Just think about it — where does gossip usually takes place? If you have engaged in gossip in the past, you probably listened to someone tell you information or hearsay about other people, which you then *whispered* to someone else:

✦ In the women's bathroom at the office.
✦ In your office when the doors were closed and no one was watching or listening.
✦ In the lunch-break room when it was only you and the person to whom you were talking.
✦ In a prayer meeting, where people often whisper about others under the camouflage of "prayer."
✦ In a corner where the boss, director, pastor, or subject of your gossip couldn't hear what you were saying.

You need to know that gossipers usually attract to each other like magnets. When they get together, they see things alike and therefore begin to think they are right. Thus, they form a little faction right inside the office or church, often concluding that they are doing God's business as they meet together to discuss all the problems going on in other people's lives, even though it isn't their business to discuss or solve these problems or to meddle in other people's affairs.

Since the word "gossip" really means *to whisper*, it would be good when you are about to tell something you've heard to first ask yourself: *Would I say these things publicly? Would I say this in front of the person I am talking about?* If your answer is no, you can conclude that *you shouldn't say it privately either*.

So I urge you not to allow the devil to snag you and drag you into the sin of gossip. James 3:8 tells us that the tongue is "...an unruly evil, full of deadly poison." But you can refuse to be the source of gossip or to participate in it when it takes place. If you really love Jesus, why would you want to participate in something that will poison people's opinions and ultimately divide and hurt others? Think of it — if it were you whom people were talking about, wouldn't it be hurtful to you to discover that they were talking this way behind your back?

It's too hurtful to get into this business! If you have to whisper it, then you probably shouldn't be saying it at all. In fact, a good rule to live by is this: *If you can't say it publicly, don't say it at all!* Make the decision today to refrain from gossip and to stay away from those who practice it!

MY PRAYER FOR TODAY

Lord, I admit that I'm guilty of occasionally talking behind people's backs, and I'm wrong for doing it. I ask You to please forgive me for allowing the devil to use me in this way. I am asking You to help me keep a tight rein on my tongue and to refrain from gossiping about other people. When I find myself in a situation where the conversation turns to gossip, help me know how to graciously dismiss myself from the conversation so I can avoid participating in this sin and falling back into this trap. I repent for my activity in gossip, and I turn from it in Jesus' name!

I pray this in Jesus' name!

MY CONFESSION FOR TODAY

I confess that I will no longer participate in the sin of gossip. If it can't be said publicly, I refuse to say it. If I have to whisper it, I will not repeat it. I refrain from gossip, and I stay away from those who practice it. Gossip is a sin, and I refuse to be a part of it. My mouth speaks only what is good for the use of edifying those who hear me!

I declare this by faith in Jesus' name!

QUESTIONS FOR YOU TO CONSIDER

1. Do you find that you are tempted to repeat information about other people, even though what you are repeating has nothing to do with you and is none of your business? Be honest in your answer, because God has already observed your behavior and knows the truth!
2. Sometimes gossip happens during prayer meetings. Have you ever witnessed a moment when a prayer request turned into a gossip session, and you felt guilty for talking so badly about that person before you prayed for him or her?
3. If you've been involved in gossip, have you sensed the conviction of the Holy Spirit trying to tell you to stop this activity?

JULY 1

Are You a Revealer Or Are You a Concealer?

But the tongue can no man tame;
it is an unruly evil, full of deadly poison.
— James 3:8

*H*ave you ever felt stabbed in the back by someone who repeated secret information you had shared with him? How did you feel when you realized that person had betrayed his commitment to keep that information confidential?

Has there ever been a time when *you* were guilty of repeating something that someone shared with you, trusting that you would keep it in confidence? Or have you ever been guilty of *listening* to someone who was gossiping about someone else, thereby showing yourself to be an unfaithful friend to the person who was being discussed?

In Second Corinthians 12:20, Paul forbids gossip, using the Greek word *psithurismos,* which expresses the idea of a *gossiper.* In the *King James Version,* it is translated as the word "whisperings," because those who repeat or listen to gossip know this kind of talk is wrong and could get them in trouble; therefore, they whisper their tidbits of information in secret rather than in public. However, a better translation for *psithurismos* would be to *gossip.*

Perhaps there is nothing more distressful than the behavior of a talebearer — one who meddles in other people's affairs and repeats information that is none of his business to tell. This kind of person is continually putting his nose where it doesn't belong and often makes a situation worse because people begin to talk, talk, and talk. Usually a talebearer doesn't have all the facts; thus, he needlessly stirs up a lot of trouble as people begin to form opinions and take sides regarding situations they know very little about.

Proverbs 11:13 says, "A talebearer revealeth secrets: but he that is of a faithful spirit concealeth the matter." So here are some questions to consider:

✦ When people think of you, do they think of you as a talebearer who repeats everything you hear, or do they find you to be confidential, private, and trustworthy?
✦ Do you have the reputation of being able to conceal a matter, or do people think you are two-faced and have loose lips?
✦ Are your friends certain that if someone starts to say something negative about them, you will walk away, refusing to listen to that rumor? Or do they worry that you might listen to gossip that is being spread about them?

Every listener has the ability to walk away from a conversation. No one has the right to force dirt into another person's ears.

You have a choice! You can either pull up a chair, draw closer to the gossiper, open your ears, and let him start whispering what he has heard about what he thinks he knows — or you can choose to walk away and refuse to listen to him.

Let me ask you this: Haven't there been many times in the past when you should have said, "Excuse me, but should we be talking like this?" Or maybe you should have said, "Excuse me, but I don't believe it is right for us to talk like this, and I cannot be a part of this conversation." When you chose to listen to the gossip instead of walking away, how did you feel afterwards — clean or dirty, faithful or unfaithful and tarnished? Were you glad you listened to those words that were whispered to you behind closed doors?

When you turn and walk away from a gossiper, you literally paralyze his ability to discuss things that are not his business to discuss. You see, in order for the words of a gossip to be successful, there must be two parties involved — the *gossiper* and the *listener.* Without a listener, the gossiper's voice is silenced. If there is no one to listen, there is nothing to tell! This is exactly why Proverbs 26:20 says, "Where no wood is, there the fire goeth out: so where there is no talebearer, the strife ceaseth."

When people start to "run at the mouth" and repeat information that isn't theirs to tell, be brave enough to simply tell them: "Excuse me, but this conversation makes me uncomfortable; I don't think I want to be a part of it." By the same token, if you're tempted to talk with others about the private business of someone else, refuse to do it, even if the information is factual!

People mistakenly assume that if the information they are "telling" is accurate, then it isn't gossip. But why would gossip be more acceptable to God just because a person is repeating *accurate* information about someone else's affairs? It's still none of that person's business. Besides, even when people think they are repeating accurate information, most of the time it *isn't* accurate. But accurate or not, no one has the right to go around delving into other people's business.

Proverbs 18:8 says, "The words of a talebearer are as wounds, and they go down into the innermost parts of the belly." Why did Solomon refer to the long-term effects of gossip as "wounds"? Consider this:

✦ Gossip permanently blemishes our view of the person being discussed.
✦ Once that picture gets into our minds, it's very hard to erase it. It is simply a fact that we almost never forget a bad report we have heard about someone else.
✦ Every time we see the person about whom we heard the gossip, that rumor will be resurrected in our minds. It becomes a wound, a mark, a stain in our memory.

So make the decision today to refrain from gossiping. Be a man or woman of God, and refuse to even listen to it! The next time someone starts to "run at the mouth" and talk about things that are not his to decide or to discuss, confront that person about what he is doing. If he chooses to continue gossiping, walk away from him and maintain your integrity before God and before those who are being discussed.

So ask yourself this question: *Am I a revealer, or am I a concealer?* Don't allow yourself to fall into the trap of discussing and debating things that don't concern you. Certainly you have enough to deal with in your own life without jumping into the middle of situations where you have never been formally invited! If you'll let the Holy Spirit help you, He will show you how to walk away from gossipers and thus maintain integrity with everyone. You will be able to go through life knowing that you haven't listened to or been a participant in conversations that bring hurt and wounds to other people.

MY PRAYER FOR TODAY

Lord, I thank You for speaking to my heart today about gossip. Give me the power to tell others that I do not want to participate in talking about things that are not my business to decide or to discuss. Please forgive me for the times I've allowed myself to be caught up in conversations that didn't glorify You and that wouldn't be considered faithful by those who were being discussed. I repent for this, and today I am making the decision to walk away from such conversations from this moment forward!

I pray this in Jesus' name!

MY CONFESSION FOR TODAY

I confess that I refrain from gossiping and refuse to listen to it! I am a faithful friend, and I conceal a matter when it has been made known to me. I don't allow myself to fall into the trap of discussing and debating things that don't concern me. Because the Holy Spirit helps me, I know how to walk away from any conversation that doesn't glorify God. I do not listen to or participate in conversations that cause hurts and wounds in other people's lives.

I declare this by faith in Jesus' name!

QUESTIONS FOR YOU TO CONSIDER

1. Have you ever been guilty of tarnishing another person's opinion of someone by gossiping — telling the person information that was not yours to tell?

2. Has anyone ever told other people information about you as if he or she had the facts — but the information was incorrect? When you heard what that person said about you, how did it affect you? Were you shocked to hear what he or she believed and repeated to others?
3. What do you think makes people want to gossip? What pleasure does it give the flesh to tell nitty-gritty details about other people's personal business or affairs?

JULY 2

The Tongue Is Like a Snake!

But the tongue can no man tame;
it is an unruly evil, full of deadly poison.
— James 3:8

When I was a boy growing up in Oklahoma, I loved snakes! In fact, I had a whole collection of snakes — rat snakes, corn snakes, king snakes, garter snakes, boa constrictors, Burmese pythons, and reticulated pythons. I even had several very poisonous snakes, such as the spotted, brownish-yellow copperhead that was once a part of my collection.

Poisonous snakes behave very differently from non-poisonous snakes. Non-poisonous snakes such as boa constrictors or pythons can be domesticated, and even held and stroked. But this isn't the case with poisonous snakes because they are nervous by nature and easily agitated. They are restless creatures, ready to strike at any moment.

Because poisonous snakes are so vicious and nervous, they are almost impossible to domesticate. If you try to loosely hold or stroke a rattlesnake or a copperhead as you might do with a boa constrictor or python, you can be sure that you'll be bitten!

The venom depositories situated just above the fangs in the head of the snake are loaded with deadly venom. When poisonous snakes inject their razor-sharp fangs deep into a victim, they push down into his flesh, which causes the venom to pump through the victim's flesh and into the bloodstream. Once the venom is injected, the snake lets loose and slithers away. Meanwhile, the victim is left to suffer as the poison begins to eat away at his flesh or paralyze his nervous system, often producing death.

The reason I am writing so much about snakes is that this was exactly the picture James had in mind when he wrote James 3:8. This verse says, "But the tongue can no man tame; it is an unruly evil, full of deadly poison." When you understand the full meaning of the Greek words used in this verse, it powerfully depicts the problem of the tongue. It compares the tongue that is not controlled by the Holy Spirit to a ready-to-strike, nervous, and poisonous snake!

James begins by saying, "But the tongue can no man tame…." Pay careful attention to the word "tame," because this word accurately describes how impossible it is to control the tongue without the help of God's Spirit! The word "tame" is from the Greek word *damadzo*, which is the word that means *to domesticate, to subdue, to tame,* or *to bring under control.* It is the same exact word used in Mark 5:4 when talking about the demoniac of Gadara. Mark 5:4 tells us that this man was so wild, so frenzied, and so out of control because of the legion of demons that resided within him that "…neither could any man tame him." This word "tame" is the same Greek word that is used in James 3:8 to depict the difficulty of taming the tongue!

Let's look at the full meaning behind the word "tame" — the Greek word *damadzo*. Not only does it mean *to tame*, but it was also used to describe *animal trainers who were experts at capturing and domesticating the wildest and most ferocious of beasts*, such as lions, tigers, and bears. Normally these animals would maul or kill a person, but these skilled trainers were able to take the wildest animals and domesticate them, even turning them into house pets. The fact that this word is used in Mark 5:4 to describe the demoniac of Gadara strongly suggests that wild animal trainers had unsuccessfully attempted to subdue and tame the demoniac. This demon-possessed man was so ferocious that those who could domesticate the most ferocious of beasts were unable to subdue and tame him.

Now James uses this same word in James 3:8 to describe the tongue! By using this word, he lets us know that the tongue is as hard to subdue, tame, and domesticate as is a ferocious wild beast! In fact, the tongue is so hard to subdue that James goes on to tell us, "But the tongue can no man tame; it is an unruly evil.…"

The word "unruly" is the word *akatastatos*, describing *something that is restless*, such as a nervous, poisonous snake that is poised and is ready to strike. Because the tongue is so unstable and restless, its behavior is almost impossible to predict. It is like a snake that may appear to be docile but is actually just waiting for a victim to come along in which to inject its venom. This is precisely why James goes on to say, "But the tongue can no man tame; it is an unruly evil, full of deadly poison."

The words "full of deadly poison" come from the Greek word *thanatephoros*, which is a compound of the words *thanatos* and *phero*. The word *thanatos* is the Greek word for *death*, and the word *phero* means *to bear* or *to carry*. When these two words are compounded into one, as in this case, the new word means *death-bearing*. Like the poisonous snakes described above, the tongue is depicted as an instrument that is full of death and poison. It is also unruly — unpredictable, listless, nervous, easily agitated, and ready to inject its venom.

An interpretive translation of James 3:8 could be as follows:

"No one can successfully tame or domesticate the tongue! It is listless, nervous, easily agitated, and ready to strike. Like a poisonous snake, it is nearly always poised to strike and to deliver its load of deadly venom."

Have you ever said anything to someone that was so sharp, it sounded like you were attacking him? Afterward when you thought about what you said, were you embarrassed by your behavior? Were you shocked to realize that you could say something so ugly and derogatory? Did you have to create a recovery operation to fix the mess you created with your words of unkindness?

We are all guilty of saying ugly things from time to time simply because we all have tongues! James asserts that this "tongue" problem is a universal dilemma. The only way our tongue can be subdued, tamed, and brought under control is if we submit it to the control of the Holy Spirit. The Bible says no *man* can tame the tongue, but the Holy Spirit is *well* able to tame the tongue once it has been submitted to His sanctifying power!

You don't have to be embarrassed by unruly words that come out of your mouth any longer! Neither do you ever again have to let your lips inject venom into another person. By committing your tongue and your mouth to the Lordship of Jesus Christ, you give the Holy Spirit the authority to penetrate this realm of your life with His power and control. He will help you keep a tight rein on your mouth so you can keep from saying things you will later regret!

Why not stop right now and submit your mouth and tongue to the Lordship of Jesus? Then ask the Holy Spirit to pervade this part of your life and help you bring it under control. *The Holy Spirit is standing by, ready to help you subdue that restless, unruly tongue!*

MY PRAYER FOR TODAY

Lord, I am submitting my tongue and my mouth to the Lordship of Jesus Christ today! I am unable to control my tongue by myself, so right now I deliberately make the decision to ask You to invade this area of my life with Your power and Your control. I confess that I need Your help, Lord; I can't do it on my own. Please help me learn how to overcome in this area of my life.

I pray this in Jesus' name!

MY CONFESSION FOR TODAY

I boldly declare that my tongue is subdued, tamed, and brought under the control of the Holy Spirit. My lips speak words of kindness; my mouth releases praise; and I am known as one who says encouraging and helpful things to other people. My words are seasoned with grace, and my lips are constantly giving thanks to God! This is what my tongue speaks because it is submitted to the Lordship of Jesus Christ!

I declare this by faith in Jesus' name!

QUESTIONS FOR YOU TO CONSIDER

1. Do you relate to this teaching about the tongue being like a snake that occasionally strikes and injects deadly venom into its listeners?
2. Have you ever had the experience of saying things you later regretted — but by the time you came to regret those negative words, the damage was already done? Were you shocked as you thought back on the ugly things you said? Did you ever go back to that person and ask him or her to forgive you for acting so unlike Jesus?
3. When are you going to submit the control of your tongue and mouth to the Lord? Why don't you take a few minutes right now to get on your knees and consecrate this part of your life to Him?

The only way our tongue can be subdued, tamed, and brought under control is if we submit it to the control of the Holy Spirit. The Bible says no *man* can tame the tongue, but the Holy Spirit is *well* able to tame the tongue once it has been submitted to His sanctifying power!

JULY 3

୬ୠ୰ଌ

Is the Holy Spirit
'Tugging' at Your Heart Today?

For as many as are led by the Spirit of God,
they are the sons of God.
— Romans 8:14

When your journey of faith begins, you may not have all the answers you would like to have *before* you take your first steps of faith. For instance, when my family moved to the other side of the world so many years ago, we sincerely thought it would be a one-year investment in the USSR. But when we took the first step and arrived at that land, God gave us the next step. When we obeyed that step, He then gave us the next, and the next, and the next.

That's the way it is for all of us when we walk with the Lord. As wonderful as it would be to see the whole picture *before* we get started, He usually leads us one step at a time *after* we get started. This has certainly been true in my life. God had given me a vision for my life, but His instructions for moving toward that goal came one step at a time.

Romans 8:14 says, "For as many as are led by the Spirit of God, they are the sons of God." The word "led" is the Greek word *ago*, which described *the act of leading about an animal, such as a cow or a goat, at the end of a rope*. The owner would wrap a rope around the animal's neck and then "tug" and "pull" until the animal started to follow him. When the animal decided to cooperate and follow that gentle tug, it could then be gently "led" to where its owner wanted it to go.

Today I want to encourage you to pay careful attention to the "tugging" and "pulling" of the Holy Spirit in your heart. He is a Gentleman and does not *force* you to obey Him. He prompts you, tugs on your heart, and pulls on your spirit to get your attention. Sometimes His "tugs" may be so gentle that you almost miss them. But if you'll develop your sensitivity to the Holy Spirit, He will gently "lead" you exactly where He wants you to go with your life.

Also, don't demand that the Holy Spirit tell you the whole story first! *Trust Him!* Remember that Jesus called Him the "Spirit of Truth" (John 16:13) to help you understand that the Holy Spirit and His leading can be *trusted*! He is the "Spirit of Truth," so if He is leading you to do something, you can know He has a good reason for it. He sees and knows what you cannot see. If you will follow Him, the Holy Spirit will take you exactly where you need to go and help you reach your maximum potential in life.

As I reflect on all that has happened throughout our years of ministry, I realize that our testimony is one of being "led" by the Holy Spirit. We give Him all the glory for leading us. We weren't smart enough to accomplish everything that has been done, but the Leader we were following knew exactly how to lead us. Because we were following Him one step at a time, He led us to a high place of victory in so many areas. And we're not the only ones who have been led. Our partners have also been led by the Spirit in their giving and praying. Because they have had a heart to cooperate with God, we have seen Him do the impossible again and again and again.

As you look at your own life today, I urge you to make the decision to let the Spirit be your Leader in every area of your life. Let Him take you by the heart and give you a little "tug" and "pull" in the right direction. Then say, "Lord, I sense that You are tugging on my heart, and I'm ready to let You lead me where You want me to go."

You may not see the full picture from the onset of your journey. Certainly my wife and I could never have conceived what a huge impact would be achieved in the former USSR when we were first getting started. *But part of the excitement is letting God be in control!* Watching where He leads and seeing what He does through you will later give you cause for *great rejoicing.* You'll be so thankful that you allowed Him to be the undisputed Leader in your life!

MY PRAYER FOR TODAY

Lord, I want to be led by the Holy Spirit in all that I say and do. When the Spirit "tugs" at my heart, trying to lead me in a new direction, please stir in me the courage I need to go wherever He leads me without being fearful, nervous, or concerned. I know the Holy Spirit is the Spirit of Truth and would therefore never mislead me. Help me become fearless to obey whatever He tells me and to go wherever He leads me. I know He has my victory in mind as I follow Him where He leads. Thank You for helping me to be bold to follow!

I pray this in Jesus' name!

MY CONFESSION FOR TODAY

I confess that I am led by the Spirit of God! The Holy Spirit "tugs" and "pulls" on my heart, and I cooperate by following Him as He gently leads me where He wants me to go. He prompts me, tugs at my heart, and pulls on my spirit to get my attention. Because I am sensitive to Him, the Holy Spirit leads me one step at a time to exactly where He wants me to go with my life. He sees and knows what I cannot see. He is leading me exactly where I need to be in order to reach my maximum potential in life.

I declare this by faith in Jesus' name!

QUESTIONS FOR YOU TO CONSIDER

1. Are you aware when the Holy Spirit is tugging on your heart to lead you in a specific direction? If so, how would you describe that "tugging" to another believer who has never experienced it?
2. Have you ever started a Spirit-led project without having the entire picture before you got started? As you got started, did the Holy Spirit keep directing you step by step to where He wanted you to be?
3. Although it was challenging to be led in this way, were you afterwards glad that you obeyed the prompting of the Holy Spirit?

The Holy Spirit is a Gentleman and does not *force* you to obey Him. He prompts you, tugs on your heart, and pulls on your spirit to get your attention. Sometimes His "tugs" may be so gentle that you almost miss them.

JULY 4

❧

Our Mutual Ministry Of Exhortation

But exhort one another daily, while it is called To day;
lest any of you be hardened through the deceitfulness of sin.
— Hebrews 3:13

*I*f you want to fulfill God's plan for your life, there's one thing you must not do: *Don't forsake the daily fellowship and encouragement of other believers!* Hebrews 3:13 tells us that we need to "…exhort one another daily.…" But what does it mean to "exhort"?

The word for "exhort" that is used in this verse comes from the Greek word *parakaleo*. It is a compound of the words *para* and *kaleo*. The word *para* means *alongside*, and the word *kaleo* means *to call, to invite, to speak,* or *to beckon*. When these two words are compounded into one, it gives the picture of *someone who has come closely alongside of another person for the sake of speaking to him, consoling him, comforting him, or assisting him with instruction, counsel, or advice*.

Because it is so helpful when someone comes alongside to support you in this manner, this word is often translated in the New Testament as the word *encouragement*. Jesus used the word *paraklete*, a derivative of *parakaleo*, to describe the Holy Spirit as the "Comforter" in John 14:16.

These verses make it abundantly clear that we need to both give and receive encouragement from other believers on a daily basis. This is such a vital principle that the tense used in the Greek language calls for *continual* action. In other words, we are not to just encourage one another once a week; we are to make this a matter of lifestyle. We must get into the habit of encouraging one another, doing it so often that it becomes a daily practice!

Think how encouraging it is when someone cares enough to take you to lunch, call you on the telephone, write you a note, or go out of his way at the office or church to come to you and ask how you are doing. It is especially very strengthening to know that someone really cares about you if you're going through challenging times!

But rather than fixate only on *your* need to be encouraged, try taking your eyes off yourself to see those around you who are also in need of strength. Think of someone you know whom you can strengthen by coming alongside him to speak words of comfort, consolation, or bravery. Maybe you can take that person to lunch; call him on the telephone; drop him a note; or go out of your way to see how he is doing. Remember, you're not the only one who needs encouragement!

We all need encouragement from brothers and sisters in the Lord who will lovingly attach themselves to us — watching us, making observations about us, and finding ways to provoke us unto love and good deeds. But we must also turn around and do the same for other believers. That's what the Body of Christ is all about!

So recognize that when you're feeling down and left out, you need fellowship with people of faith more than ever. Jesus understood this principle. When He went to the Garden of Gethsemane to pray the night before His crucifixion, He asked Peter, James, and John to come pray with Him. Jesus needed their fellowship and strength that night, or He wouldn't have requested it.

Recognize your need for others — and acknowledge that others need you as well. The daily exhortation and encouragement of other believers will help you stir up your faith to hold fast to your confession until it becomes a reality. And as an added side benefit, you will experience more deeply the Presence of the Lord in your life through the joy of knowing and loving other people of like faith!

MY PRAYER FOR TODAY

Lord, I want to be a major source of blessing to people in my life! Help me to quit being so fixated on myself and to see how I can become a strength and encouragement to others who are around me. Your Word commands me to be involved in giving daily encouragement. And since I am seriously committed to obeying Your Word, I intend to find a way to encourage someone who needs strength today!

I pray this in Jesus' name!

MY CONFESSION FOR TODAY

I confess that I need to be encouraged! God's Word commands me to be encouraged daily, so I choose to believe that encouragement is what I need. I recognize my need for others, and I acknowledge that others need my encouragement as well. The daily exhortation and encouragement of other believers will stir up my faith and help me hold fast to my confession of faith!

I declare this by faith in Jesus' name!

QUESTIONS FOR YOU TO CONSIDER

1. How does it affect you when someone goes out of his way to check on you or to see how you are doing?
2. How does it affect you when no one ever asks how you are doing or what is new in your life — when it seems like everyone is ignoring the fact that you also have needs in your life?
3. Are you involved in giving strength and encouragement to others, or are you just concerned about receiving it from others? Where is your focus? Is it on yourself or on the needs of other people as well?

Rather than fixate only on *your* need to be encouraged, try taking your eyes off yourself to see those around you who are also in need of strength. Think of someone you know whom you can strengthen by coming alongside him to speak words of comfort, consolation, or bravery. Maybe you can take that person to lunch; call him on the telephone; drop him a note; or go out of your way to see how he is doing. Remember, you're not the only one who needs encouragement!

JULY 5

ᛞᚫᚾᚢᚱᛞᚫ

Going Into All the World In Order To Preach the Gospel!

Go ye therefore, and teach all nations....
— Mathew 28:19

...Go ye into all the world,
and preach the gospel to every creature.
— Mark 16:15

*T*oday I want to talk to you about the commission Jesus gave to the Church to go into all the world to preach the Gospel. In the two verses listed above, Jesus explicitly gave the directive for believers to traverse the globe to "teach all nations" the Gospel (Matthew 28:19) and to take the saving message of Jesus Christ "into all the world" (Mark 16:15). But did Jesus really expect every believer to uproot his family, leave his nation, and move to the other side of the world to fulfill this command?

By studying Matthew 28:19 and Mark 16:15, we discover that different Greek words are used in these two texts to accentuate the different parts of the world we are to reach with the Gospel. Let's look at the two words "nations" and "world" today, for in these two words we find that we needn't go far from home to fulfill the Great Commission!

First, let's look at Jesus' words in Matthew 28:19: "Go ye therefore, and teach all nations...." The word "nations" is the Greek word *ethnos*. It is where we get the word *ethnic*. In Greek, this word always describes *Gentile nations*. However, it doesn't just refer to nations that are geographically located distant from us; it also expresses the idea of *different customs, cultures, and civilizations*. This unquestionably means the Gospel is to be taken to *people from every culture, custom, civilization, race, color, or ethnicity in the world*.

The Gospel is meant for all the *ethnos* — in other words, for *all the various races and colors of human flesh, all the cultures of the world, all the civilizations that exist worldwide*. One man has translated Matthew 28:19 to read, "Go ye therefore and teach all ethnic groups, invading every race, every skin color, and every nation with its different customs and culture — ultimately taking this Gospel into every civilization that exists in the world." I personally like this translation because it tells us the Gospel is for the entire human race!

Here is the good news for you today! Because the mixture of nations has so dramatically changed in the past fifty years, you don't have to go too far from home to find different ethnic groups, skin colors, cultures, or customs. The nations are now a mixture of different cultures and customs. Just leave your house and drive down the street to a different neighborhood. You'll soon find a culture very different from your own!

Rather than shun the people from these other cultures because they are different, you need to be brave enough to go to them. Build a relationship with them so you can bring them the message of the Lordship of Jesus Christ. *They are a part of your mission field!*

But in Mark 16:15, Jesus used a different word to tell us who we are to "target" with the Gospel message. He said, "...Go ye into all the world, and preach the gospel to every creature." The word "world" in this verse is from the Greek word *kosmos*. This is very significant, for the word *kosmos* describes anything that is ordered. In Greek it is often used to denote *a particular political system; a system of fashion; a system found in any part of society, such as a circle of friends;* or *any sphere where you live and have influence.*

The apostle Paul used the word *kosmos* when he wrote that Satan was the "god of this world" (2 Corinthians 4:4). Paul wasn't speaking of the physical earth in that verse; he was telling us that Satan operates in world systems, including (but not exclusive to) some of the areas mentioned above. These world systems (*kosmos*) are the spheres Satan has invaded and where he exerts his greatest influence.

Now Jesus tells us that we are to go into all the *kosmos.* Just as Satan attempts to manipulate, dominate, and control the world through such systems, we are ordered by Jesus to go "into all the world," or into all the *kosmos* — which happens to be the very same systems through which Satan tries to control the human race. The people who live in those systems are lost, blinded by the god of this world. They need the Gospel message!

An example of these world systems may be the place where you work. "Going into all the world" may mean going to the fellow workers you see and talk to every day. The system Jesus is sending you to may be the school you attend and the circle of friends you have there. Perhaps Jesus is telling you to take the Gospel into the special clubs or societies to which you belong. Or maybe He is calling you to invade your circle of friends whom you cherish and enjoy with the saving message of the Cross. Any of these examples could be your personal *kosmos* — the place where you live, function, and have influence in other people's lives.

What does all this mean for you? It means you don't have to move to the other side of the world to preach the Gospel. Jesus never expected all believers to uproot their families and to move to foreign nations. But He *does* expect you to take the Gospel to the different ethnic groups, cultures, and civilizations that are in your city. He does expect you to invade every sphere where you have influence and to use your influence to declare the Gospel to people who live, work, and function in those places.

So where is your closest mission field? Your mission field is right down your street or on the other side of your city in a neighborhood where the culture and customs are different than your own. Your mission field is to every person whose skin color is different than yours. You are to take the Gospel to every culture, civilization, and ethnic group in the community where you live.

Whom are you called to reach? Your specific assignment is to reach every person in every group where you have influence. This means you needn't buy a plane ticket and fly to the other side of the world to do this job. Mission trips are great experiences, but you have a mission field right where you work, where you attend school, where you purchase your groceries every day — in every place where you have some level of personal influence.

Open your eyes and look around you! Jesus told the disciples that the fields of people all around them were "white already to harvest" (John 4:35). If you'll look around you, you will see that the fields around you are white unto harvest as well. People near you are struggling through life, just wishing someone would help them. They are waiting for you to come to them with the saving message of Jesus Christ, and you are the missionary God wants to send them.

Why does God want to use you to reach these people in your life? Because you already have a relationship with them. You have influence with them. They will listen to you when you tell them the Good News! *So open your heart and mind today to the Holy Spirit, and let Him use you to bring eternal change to the lost people who literally encompass your life!*

MY PRAYER FOR TODAY

Lord, I ask You to use me to reach my city and the people who are in my sphere of influence. I've made the mistake of thinking that missions work only happens on the other side of the world and have therefore missed the vast mission field that surrounds my life every day. Now that I know You are calling me to invade every culture and ethnic group, give me the power and courage to start reaching them with the Good News. And now that I know I am to invade every sphere where I have influence, help me see myself as Your missionary, sent to these people whom I know so well. I surrender to the call — and today I acknowledge that I am Your missionary to my world.

I pray this in Jesus' name!

MY CONFESSION FOR TODAY

I confess that I am God's missionary to my city and to the people I interact with in every area of life. Jesus expects me to take the Gospel to the different ethnic groups, cultures, and civilizations that are in my city and neighborhood. He expects me to invade every sphere where I have influence and to use that influence to share the Gospel with the people who live, work, and function in those places. My mission field is right down my street, and my assignment is to reach every person in every group where I have influence. So I choose this day to invest my time and energy into fulfilling that divine assignment to the glory of God!

I declare this by faith in Jesus' name!

QUESTIONS FOR YOU TO CONSIDER

1. How long has it been since you moved out of your comfortable life to reach people who are outside your culture, custom, skin color, or ethnic group? Have you been limited in your thinking to reach only people who look, think, and live like you?

2. Can you think of someone you know who doesn't know Jesus? It could be your hairdresser, your neighbor, the ladies at the local daycare, the men at the bowling alley, the people you work with every day, or the other students with whom you attend school. Since these are the types of places where you have influence, don't you think you ought to use that influential connection to bring people to Jesus?

3. Why don't you write down a list of five different people or groups to whom you can reach out with the saving message of Jesus Christ? Remember, God is expecting you to be His missionary, so think this through. After writing down your answer, pray over it and then formulate a plan you can begin to execute.

Whom are you called to reach? Your specific assignment is to reach every person in every group where you have influence.

JULY 6

❧❧❧

What Does the Word 'Preach' Mean?

…Go ye into all the world,
and preach the gospel to every creature.
— Mark 16:15

*I*n Mark 16:15, Jesus instructed believers, "…Go ye into all the world, and preach the gospel to every creature." But what did Jesus mean when He said that we were supposed to "preach"? Did He mean that every believer must have a pulpit ministry where he or she publicly stands in front of a church and preaches to a congregation? What does the word "preach" mean?

The word "preach" comes from the Greek word *kerusso*, which means *to proclaim, to declare, to announce,* or *to herald a message*. It was the message proclaimed by the *kerux*, who was *the official spokesman or herald of a king*. Because the *kerux* was *the appointed, official representative of the king or government*, his specific job was to announce with a clear and unquestionable voice the desires, dictates, orders, recent events, news, policy changes, or message that the king or government wished to express to the people.

The position of this *kerux* ("spokesman" or "herald") was viewed to be the highest, most noble, privileged position in the kingdom because his position gave him routine access to the king that was afforded only to rare individuals. To be the king's *kerux* was an honor and supreme privilege that necessitated the highest level of professionalism and excellent performance.

When the king wanted to give a message to his people, he summoned the *kerux*. The *kerux* came to the king's throne room with writing instrument and paper in hand; then he carefully and accurately penned the communication that the king desired to express to his people. After the king was finished dictating his message, the *kerux* was allowed to freely speak to the king and to ask questions of clarification to make certain he understood every point of the king's message. Because this man was speaking on behalf of the king, there was no room for mistakes in his delivery of the message. When he finally stood before the people to announce the message given to him, it had to be accurate, precise, and faithful to what the king wanted to express to his people.

As important as it was for the *kerux* to accurately understand and communicate the king's message, it was equally his responsibility to capture and convey the sentiment, heart, and emotions of the king on these various issues. Thus, the *kerux* was expected to deliver his message with emotional impact in order to properly represent both the word and the heart of the king.

Proper attire was essential for this notable position, for when the *kerux* stood before the people to speak on behalf of the king, he was also to physically represent the king in all his splendor and glory. The responsibility of publicly representing the king demanded that he dress appropriately, for a shabbily dressed *kerux* would have been an insult to the honor of the king.

And because the *kerux* was the primary connection between the people and the king, he was also required to learn how to speak to people in a kind and cultured fashion. If he was rude, his behavior would reflect negatively on the king. If he was kind and courteous, this would reflect favorably on the king. As the king's spokesman, the *kerux* understood that every word he spoke, every piece of clothing he wore, and all his actions, both public and private, would ultimately affect people's opinion of the king. Consequently, because of his great responsibility as the king's spokesman, he knew that every detail of his life was to be lived honorably, honestly, and uprightly. His personal life, as well as his public life, had to be spotless, immaculate, pristine, gleaming, and squeaky clean — *free of accusation.*

When the *kerux* had finished delivering the king's message to the people, he turned, left the platform from which he spoke, and then remained silent until the king summoned him back to the throne room to give him another message for the people. As the king's spokesman, he had no right to speak his own mind, give his own personal commentary about what the king meant, or draw any attention to himself. Such actions would be considered gross violations of his position and a guarantee that he would no longer serve as the king's spokesman.

Keeping all this in mind, let's consider again what Jesus meant when He commanded that all believers go into all the world "to preach" the Gospel. Since *kerusso* ("to preach") is the message of the *kerux* ("the king's spokesman"), it is clear that by using the word "preach," God is communicating several very powerful messages to you and to me.

First, as a believer, you must learn to see yourself as the representative of Jesus Christ. Although you may never stand before a public pulpit to preach, it is a fact that your life is your most important pulpit. What you say and do in your life reflects on the Lord Jesus Christ.

Second, as a believer, it is absolutely essential that you spend time in the Presence of the Lord so you can hear His Word and capture His heart. You should never think of the time you must spend in God's Presence praying or reading the Word as laborious or dreadful. It is a high honor that God has given you. He beckons you to come into His throne room so He can speak to you, share with you His heart, and then empower you with His Spirit to take the message to people who are desperately waiting for it. Never forget that you possess a position of great privilege.

Third, as a believer, it is imperative that you learn how to dress appropriately and how to speak kindly, courteously, and in a way that brings honor to Jesus. If your appearance communicates a low standard because you dress like a slob, never comb your hair, always look unprofessional, or allow yourself to remain overweight (yes, I know this last one affects many people, but what I am saying is true) — this is exactly the image you are imparting about Jesus Christ.

Would the president of a nation allow His spokesman to be aired on television in a sweatshirt or tennis shoes? Would a national public representative dare to go on national television to speak on behalf of the government looking like a slob? Of course not! It would be disrespectful to the office or the person the spokesman represented. Likewise, we must think about what we look like, what we sound like, and how we are perceived. We are not representing ourselves; *we are representing Jesus Christ.*

Fourth, as a believer, you must realize that your private life is just as important as your public life. If you publicly declare the Gospel, but later it is discovered that your private life is a horrible mess and a complete contradiction of what you've been preaching, this, too, will reflect poorly on the Gospel.

The lost world loathes hypocrites but enjoys it immensely when a preacher or believer is found to be a contradiction of the message he or she preaches. So never forget that as the Lord's spokesman, you are required to do everything possible to maintain a life that is spotless, immaculate, pristine, gleaming, and squeaky clean — *free of accusation.*

Fifth, as a believer and a representative of Jesus Christ, you must make a decision to refrain from making personal comments that are not your business to make. Speak what Jesus tells you to speak — but if someone tries to draw you into a debate or a conversation regarding a matter you know nothing about, just remain silent. You are not required to speak or to act like an authority regarding issues about which you are not an authority!

You see, preaching the Gospel is what you do every day of your life by the way you live and conduct yourself. It is true that public pulpit ministry is a very special gift and honor that some are called to do. But the truth is, *you* preach every day that you get up and faithfully go to work! You preach when you choose to dress modestly or when you speak kindly to your fellow employees, believers, or friends. All these things reflect on the message of the Gospel.

So as you obey Jesus' words to take the Gospel to every ethnic group, culture, custom, civilization, and sphere where you personally have influence, always be mindful of the fact that you are His *kerux* in those places. You are His personal representative, and everything you do and say preaches about Jesus Christ!

And as you go through each day, always make sure you set aside time in God's Presence to obtain His Word and capture His heart. Then you'll be able to turn to those you touch every day of your life and give them the message and heart that God has imparted to you on their behalf!

MY PRAYER FOR TODAY

Lord, I ask You to please help me become an honorable representation of who You are! I am sorry for allowing myself in the past to live a low standard that gave a wrong impression about You. Now I understand that I am Your face and Your voice to the people around me. To the best of my ability, I want to speak courteously, dress appropriately, act professionally, and live in a Christ-like manner so I can accurately portray Your Word and Your heart. I know this is going to require some changes in my life, so today I am asking You to help me as I take steps toward becoming a worthy representative who brings only honor to the King of kings.

I pray this in Jesus' name!

MY CONFESSION FOR TODAY

I confess that I am the spokesman of the Lord. As His representative, I live respectfully, honorably, and in a way that brings glory to His name. I behave professionally; I speak courteously and kindly to others; I dress appropriately as His representative; and I preach the Gospel with excellence by the way I live both my public and private life. As a believer, I accept my assignment to be one of God's messengers to my generation!

I declare this by faith in Jesus' name!

QUESTIONS FOR YOU TO CONSIDER

1. After reading today's *Sparkling Gem*, how do you feel you are doing at accurately representing Jesus Christ with your life? Does your life preach a message that brings honor or disgrace to Him?
2. Do you see any changes you need to make in the way you dress, speak, or act so you can present a better view of Jesus to those who don't know Him? If the answer is yes, what are those changes you need to make?
3. Why don't you make a list of those changes and put that list somewhere in your home where you will see it every day and be reminded to work diligently on improving those areas of your life?

JULY 7

⊱❧⊰

Are These Signs Following You?

And these signs shall follow them that believe....
— Mark 16:17

Moments before Jesus ascended to the Father, He told the disciples, "And these signs shall follow them that believe; In my name shall they cast out devils; they shall speak with new tongues; They shall take up serpents; and if they drink any deadly thing, it shall not hurt them; they shall lay hands on the sick, and they shall recover" (Mark 16:17,18).

According to Jesus, these supernatural signs are supposed to follow those who believe. Since you and I believe, that means these signs are supposed to follow you and me! So let's look carefully at this supernatural list to see precisely what Jesus said to us.

First of all, the word "signs" comes from the Greek word *semeion*, which described *the official written notice that announced the final verdict of a court*. It also described *the signature or seal applied to a document to guarantee its authenticity* and *a sign that marked key locations in a city*.

Jesus was sending His disciples into the world to preach the Gospel. As He sent them forth, He said that *God's signature* would be upon their ministry. These "signs" were to be the signature of God — the official declaration that they were sent by Heaven and that the Gospel message was true. For unbelievers, these "signs" would authenticate the fact that this was no manmade message, but a message straight from God Himself. And just as street signs point a traveler in the right direction, these signs would point the unbeliever to the Lord if he would only pay heed to them.

The specific signs that Jesus mentioned are as follows:

- ✦ They will cast out devils.
- ✦ They will speak with new tongues.
- ✦ They will take up serpents.
- ✦ If they drink any deadly poison, it will not hurt them.
- ✦ They will lay hands on the sick, and the sick will recover.

The Lord said that these signs would "follow" those who believe. The word "follow" is the Greek word *parakoloutheo*, from the words *para* and *akoloutheo*. The word *para* means *alongside*, as *to be near or in a close proximity*. The word *akoloutheo* means *to follow* or *to go somewhere with a person, as to accompany him on a trip*. When the word *para* and *akoloutheo* are joined to form one word as in this verse, it means *to tirelessly accompany someone; to constantly be at the side of an individual; to always be in close proximity with a person, like a faithful companion who is always at one's side*.

Because the word *parakoloutheo* has such a strong sense of *following someone*, it eventually came to convey the idea of *discipleship*. A true disciple faithfully follows his teacher anywhere he goes and is committed to his teacher's instruction.

This picture of commitment to another person — of someone's faithfulness to follow and his determination to never be out of step with his leader — is very significant in the context of this verse. It tells us that signs and wonders are to faithfully follow us and the Gospel message. These signs and wonders are continually to be in step with us and with the message we preach. To preach without these miraculous signs should seem very strange to us, for God intended these signs to persistently follow us and the message anywhere and everywhere we go.

These signs are God's signature that the message is true. Hence, every time the Gospel is preached — whether at church, on the mission field, in a large crusade, in the bus or subway, at your job, or at the grocery store — you should expect these supernatural signs to be present in some form. These signs should accompany you everywhere you go because they are a part of your spiritual equipment, faithful partners of the Gospel message!

But if this is true, why don't we see more of these signs following Christians? The answer to this question is found in Jesus' words in Mark 16:17. He said, "And these signs shall follow them *that believe....*"

I want to draw your attention to the word "believe." Because of the tense used with this Greek word, this verse would be better translated, *"These signs shall follow them that are constantly believing...."* In other words, these signs don't come automatically just because a person once walked the aisle and gave his heart to Jesus. These signs follow those who are *constantly believing* for them to occur. If a Christian isn't believing for these signs to be manifested or expecting them to follow him, they probably won't. Like everything else in the Kingdom of God, signs and wonders are activated by faith.

Through the years of my ministry, I have observed that people who regularly experience the miraculous are those who regularly expect to see it. Rather than being passive, they are very aggressive about pushing forward in the Spirit to see the miraculous manifested in their lives or ministries. Those who press forward and release their faith to see the supernatural are the ones who see more of it than anyone else. Because they are believing for signs and wonders, they often see them manifested in their lives.

The number of signs and wonders that follow you will be determined by how intensely you are *constantly believing* for them to be in manifestation. As noted above, everything in the Kingdom of God is activated by faith. If you're not releasing faith for the miraculous to occur, very little of the miraculous will be in manifestation in your life. If you want signs and wonders to faithfully follow you, you must be *constantly believing* for them to happen!

So when you preach and share the Gospel, *expect* things to happen!

- ✦ When you pray for the sick, *expect* them to be healed.
- ✦ When you confront someone who is demonized, *expect* that person to be set free.
- ✦ When you are in a situation that requires the miraculous, *expect* the miraculous to occur.
- ✦ When you need protection, *expect* God's hand of protection to be upon you.

If you haven't been experiencing the supernatural in your life, it may be a signal that you haven't been releasing your faith to see signs and wonders follow you. Remember, these signs *always* follow wherever the Gospel is preached and believers are believing for them to occur. This was Jesus' promise! He guaranteed that God's supernatural signature would be on anyone who preaches the Gospel and who opens the way for the supernatural to come to pass *by believing*.

Today I want to encourage you to ask the Holy Spirit to rekindle the flame in your heart to see the supernatural signature of God on your life, your church, or your ministry. God wants to show up when you preach or share the Gospel. He wants to authenticate and guarantee that the message you preach or share is truly Heaven-sent. But for the miraculous to occur, He needs you to be constantly releasing your faith — *for it is your faith that activates the supernatural*!

MY PRAYER FOR TODAY

Lord, I prayerfully admit that I haven't been expecting signs and wonders to follow me as I ought to be expecting them. From this moment onward, I release my faith for the miraculous to follow me when I preach or share the Gospel with unbelievers. Holy Spirit, let the power of God flow and confirm the message! Let God's signature be all over the Gospel that I preach. Because I am constantly releasing my faith for the miraculous to follow me wherever I go, I expect to see people healed, blind eyes opened, and captives set free by the power of God!

I pray this in Jesus' name!

MY CONFESSION FOR TODAY

I confess that signs and wonders follow me! I am intensely hungry to see the miraculous, and I am constantly believing for it to be in manifestation. Since everything in the Kingdom of God is activated by faith, I release my faith right now for supernatural signs to be manifested in my life! I am among those who are constantly believing for the miraculous to happen. When I preach the Gospel, I expect signs and wonders to follow that authenticate the message and supernaturally meet the needs of those who are listening to me!

I declare this by faith in Jesus' name!

QUESTIONS FOR YOU TO CONSIDER

1. Can you think of a time when you were sharing the Gospel and something supernatural happened, such as someone getting healed or God miraculously intervening in a situation to let an unbeliever know that God was speaking specifically to him?

2. Are you hungry for the supernatural, or have you been passive about seeing signs and wonders manifested in your life? How long has it been since you've earnestly prayed for signs and wonders to be a part of your life?

3. Do you have a desire to see the miraculous manifested in your life? If that desire has become dormant, why don't you take a little time today to ask the Holy Spirit to rekindle this desire in your heart?

If you haven't been experiencing the supernatural in your life, it may be a signal that you haven't been releasing your faith to see signs and wonders follow you. Remember, these signs *always* follow wherever the Gospel is preached and believers are believing for them to occur. This was Jesus' promise! He guaranteed that God's supernatural signature would be on anyone who preaches the Gospel and who opens the way for the supernatural to come to pass *by believing*.

JULY 8

❦

They Shall Cast Out Devils!

And these signs shall follow them that believe;
In my name shall they cast out devils....
— Mark 16:17

I have had to deal with demonic manifestations on several occasions in my ministry. I remember one time when a young Satanist teenager came forward at the end of one of my meetings in a large church. That night this young man had come to realize that Satan's powers had taken his mind captive, so he came forward to receive prayer and to be set free.

As I prayed for this one and then that one, I could visibly see from a distance that this particular young man was sending forth spiritual signals of a very strong, evil presence. As I came nearer to him, I sensed that he had been involved in some type of occult activity.

When I finally reached the young man, he looked up at me through eyes that were so tightly squeezed together, they looked like nothing more than little slits in his face. Looking into his eyes, I felt like a demon was looking back at me from behind his face. When I saw this young man's condition, I knew he was serious about being helped. It had taken a great deal of determination for him to shove that manipulating force aside and forge his way down to the front of the church auditorium.

As I laid my hands on the young man that night, his body began to violently shake as it reacted to the power of God. Trembling under the weight of God's power, he fell to the floor, crumbling down right next to my feet. Lying there under the electrifying power of God that was surging up and down his body, he cried out, as though something was trying to exit his body. As I leaned over to pray for him a second time, the horrible demonic influence that had held him captive immediately released him and fled from the scene.

This is just one instance of dealing with the demonized that I've encountered during our years in the former Soviet Union. We have had so many instances that I couldn't begin to count them. When atheism took over, the people turned to psychic phenomena to satisfy their spiritual hunger. As you can imagine, that opened the floodgates for demonic activity in thousands of people's lives.

So what do we do when we confront a demonic infestation in someone's life? *We take authority over it in Jesus' name and cast it out!*

In Mark 16:17, Jesus said, "...In my name shall they cast out devils...." The word "cast out" is the Greek word *ekballo*, which is a compound of the words *ek* and *ballo*. The word *ek* means *out*, and the word *ballo* means *to throw*. When compounded into one word, it means *to throw out, as to evict someone from a place; to drive out;* or *to expel*. Historically it was used to describe *a nation that forcibly removed its enemies out from its borders*.

The word "devils" is the Greek word *daimonion*, meaning *demons*. In Jesus' time, it was widely believed that demons thickly populated the lower, denser regions of the air and that these demons were the primary cause of most disasters and suffering that occurred in the earth. It was believed that demon spirits came into contact with humans primarily through occult practices, such as magic, spells, necromancy, or by one's participation in religious paganism, which centered around such occult activities.

It is worth noting that the world in which Jesus lived generally believed that demon spirits were the chief cause for mental sickness or insanity. The ancients also firmly believed that demon spirits were ordered and arranged with an entire hierarchy of power. This agrees completely with the picture that Paul gives us in Ephesians 6:12, where he describes the rank and file of the devil's kingdom (*see* June 10).

Today we tend to think of casting out demons in terms of ordering a demon spirit to leave a person's body or mind. Certainly this is one aspect of casting out demons, and we need to be quick to take authority over demons in this way when we recognize their activity. We see examples of Jesus expelling demons in various places in the Gospels. Examples include:

✦ Matthew 8:16, where it is written, "...and he cast out the spirits with his word...." The words "cast out" are also from the Greek word *ekballo*, meaning *to forcibly throw out*. It tells us that Jesus literally kicked these demons out of people's lives!

✦ Matthew 9:34, where even the Pharisees acknowledged Jesus' authority over demon spirits. It says, "But the Pharisees said, He casteth out devils...." These words "casteth out" are also from the word *ekballo*, which means even the Pharisees recognized that Jesus literally tossed demons out of people's lives.

✦ Matthew 10:1, which says, "And when he had called unto him his twelve disciples, he gave them power against unclean spirits, to cast them out...." Once again, the words "cast them out" are from the Greek word *ekballo*. Not only did Jesus expel demons from people's lives, but He commissioned and anointed His followers to do the same.

Mark 16:17 makes it very clear that casting out demons is a responsibility that every believer possesses. Jesus never went looking for demons, and neither should we. But when they appear, we are to act as Jesus would act — taking authority over them and kicking them out of people's lives, thus setting the people free from demonic control.

Demons were also considered to be the chief force behind occultism, sorcery, witchcraft, and paganism. Therefore, the removal of these practices was viewed to be another facet of casting out demons. This is why events like the one recorded in Acts 19:18,19 was so serious. It says, "And many that believed came, and confessed, and shewed their deeds. Many of them also which used curious arts brought their books together, and burned them before all men: and they counted the price of them, and found it fifty thousand pieces of silver."

Notice that verse 18 says these new converts came and showed their "deeds." This word "deeds" is from the Greek word *praksis*, which definitely refers to *magical arts, incantations, spells*, or *any item or activity connected with witchcraft or sorcery*. Verse 19 then speaks of those who had been involved in the "curious arts." This comes from the Greek word *periergos*, which refers to *everything connected to the practice of witchcraft or sorcery*.

This verse also tells us that the people "...brought their books together, and burned them before all men...." The word "books" is the Greek word *biblios*. Today our idea of a "book" is like the one you are reading right now. But in ancient times there were no hardbound books; instead, the word *biblios* referred to *scrolls* or *parchments*. These scrolls and parchments were extremely expensive because the information contained in them was written by hand. But because these new converts wanted to cast out all demonic activity from their lives, they "...burned them before all men...."

The word "burned" is the Greek word *katakaino*, which means *to completely burn* or *to thoroughly burn*. This was done as *a public declaration* that they were permanently removing these objects from their lives. They were kicking evil out from their midst and publicly announcing that they could never turn the clock back and return to these past activities. Once those books were burned, it meant evil had been cast out of their lives.

So when you think of casting out demons, don't think only of taking authority over a yelling, screaming demon and ordering it to leave an individual. Part of casting out demons is also removing anything associated with magical arts, incantations, spells, or any items or activities connected with witchcraft or sorcery. If you study Church history, you will find that early believers were so convinced that this was vital to the removal of evil that they defaced the pagan statues and destroyed places of pagan religious practices.

As you deal with people who have been demonized, take authority over those evil spirits and cast them out. Jesus has anointed you to do this, and you can do it. But don't forget that breaking all ties to occult practices is also a part of the process. Cleanse the person, and then cleanse the environment!

Removing every evil item in one's possession is a part of true deliverance and repentance. So be sure to burn all bridges to the past to show that you are truly casting all evil from your presence — and help those to whom you are ministering do the same!

MY PRAYER FOR TODAY

Lord, give me the courage to speak up and take authority over demons! Your Word declares that You have given me power over all unclean spirits. I am ready to use that power to bring freedom into people's lives who are bound. Help me know how to best minister to people who fall into this category so that their freedom can be full and complete!

I pray this in Jesus' name!

MY CONFESSION FOR TODAY

I boldly confess that I have authority over all evil spirits. I have no reason to be afraid of them! Jesus gave me power and authority over all the works of the devil. When I am confronted with a demonic manifestation, I speak to it, take authority over it, and cast it out in Jesus' name!

I declare this by faith in Jesus' name!

QUESTIONS FOR YOU TO CONSIDER

1. Can you think of a time when you encountered a person who you believe was genuinely demonized? What was your immediate reaction when you realized you were being confronted by an evil spiritual entity speaking through another person?
2. Have you ever taken authority over a demon spirit and commanded it to leave another person's life? If yes, what happened? If no, is there a reason you've never used the power and authority Jesus gave you to do this?
3. Had you previously considered the removal of occult items and objects as a facet of casting out demons? What do you think about this, and how does it affect your view of the objects you have in your home or apartment right now?

JULY 9

❧❧❧

They Shall Speak With New Tongues!

And these signs shall follow them that believe;
In my name shall they cast out devils;
they shall speak with new tongues.
— Mark 16:17

Regardless of the denomination to which you belong or what you have been taught to believe, it is an irrefutable fact that Jesus said believers would speak with new tongues. In fact, Jesus affirmed that speaking in new tongues would be one of the supernatural signs that would follow believers!

The first example of speaking in tongues is found in Acts 2:1-4, where the Bible says, "And when the day of Pentecost was fully come, they were all with one accord in one place. And suddenly there came a sound from heaven as of a rushing mighty wind, and it filled all the house where they were sitting. And there appeared unto them cloven tongues like as of fire, and it sat upon each of them. *And they were all filled with the Holy Ghost, and began to speak with other tongues, as the Spirit gave them utterance.*"

Of all the instances where people spoke in tongues in the book of Acts, this is the most famous example — perhaps because it was the first time this phenomenon ever occurred and thus set the pattern for believers to be filled with the Spirit and to speak in tongues. But this instance is very unique from any other instance recorded in the book of Acts, for several miracles occurred that day when believers spoke in tongues for the first time.

There is so much we could write about speaking in tongues; after all, entire books have been written and devoted to this wonderful subject. But today let's look at the specific events that occurred the first time people ever spoke in tongues.

On the Day of Pentecost, Acts 2:5,6 tells us a "multitude" was gathered in Jerusalem from every nation under Heaven. The word "multitude" is the Greek word *plethos*, which is used no less than twenty-five times in the Gospels to denote *a massive, huge crowd of people*. This is very important, for it tells us that far more foreigners were in the crowd than were believers who had been filled with the Spirit. Acts 2:9-11 tells us that in the crowd that day were Parthians, Medes, and Elamites; dwellers of Mesopotamia, Judea, Cappadocia, Pontus, Asia, Phrygia, Pamphylia, Egypt, and parts of Libya near Cyrene; strangers from Rome, both Jews and proselytes; and both Cretes and Arabians.

The believers who had just been filled with the Spirit were speaking in tongues so loudly as they exited the upper room and entered the streets that the entire crowd could hear them speaking. The crowd was amazed at what they were hearing. Acts 2:6 says they were "...confounded, because that every man heard them speak in his own language."

The word "confounded" is the Greek word *suncheo*, which means *to perplex; to stun; to bewilder; to baffle; to stupefy; to amaze; to confound;* or *to cause an astonishment that literally throws people into a state of confusion.* The word "heard" is the Greek word *akouo*, which simply means *to hear.* The word "speak" is the word *lalouton*, which means *to speak,* but the Greek tense presents the picture of people *continuously speaking* in tongues. In fact, this Greek word for "speak" is the same word used to describe *someone who speaks fluently in his own or in some other language*. This clearly shows us that the believers were *speaking nonstop in tongues* as they entered the streets that day.

But notice the end of Acts 2:6, where it says every man heard them speak "in his own language." The word "language" is the Greek word *dialektos*, which is where we get the word *dialect*. This means the believers were not heard speaking only in different languages, but with all *the specific dialects, idioms, phrases, vernacular, and regional accents* that were used in each geographical location from which the listeners came.

Consider this: There were only 120 believers speaking in tongues, and this was a massive crowd of people. So that means this small group of 120 believers must have been speaking in hundreds of different dialects! To know a language is one thing, but to know the different dialects of another language requires years of study and the highest skill. This would be amazing for a group of highly educated language specialists, but for a group of Galilaeans to speak so fluently in so many different dialects was simply unheard of — thus, the reason the listening crowd was so *baffled* and *stunned*.

Acts 2:7 lets us know that the majority of the believers who came out of the upper room speaking in tongues that day were Galilaeans, giving further cause for the international crowd to be so confounded. Galilaeans were simple people, not known for their education or wealth. Their labor, work, profession, and way of life were all primarily connected to the region of Galilee, so they had no reason to know many foreign languages. This is why the people reacted the way they did in Acts 2:7: "And they were all amazed and marvelled, saying one to another, Behold, are not all these which speak Galilaeans?"

In Acts 2:7, the word "amazed" is the Greek word *existimi*, which means *to be beside oneself* or *to be out of one's head*. It is the picture of *one who is so stunned and amazed that he stands speechless — nearly paralyzed with shock*. The word "marvelled" is the Greek word *thaumadzo*, which means *to wonder* or *to stand in awe of*. In our day, we might define it as *one who is bowled over by something he has heard, witnessed, or seen*. There is no doubt that the crowd that day was perplexed as they listened to these Galilaeans speaking in so many different languages and specific dialects.

But were the disciples supernaturally speaking in known languages that day?

Some have tried to categorically state that those who came out from the upper room that day supernaturally spoke in *known* human languages. But Paul specifically wrote that speaking in tongues is *not* speaking in a known language. In First Corinthians 14:2, Paul said, "For he that speaketh in an *unknown* tongue speaketh not unto men, but unto God: for no man understandeth him...." That word *unknown* is italicized in the *King James Version* because it doesn't appear in the Greek text; it was supplied by the translators to affirm that Paul was *not* referring to known human languages; he was writing about a supernatural prayer language that is known only to God.

According to Paul's words in First Corinthians 14:13-15, speaking in tongues is a spiritual language — *never a known language*. It is so supernatural and unknown to man that it cannot be understood, not even by the speaker himself, unless he prays for the ability to interpret what he is saying. Since this is Paul's very clear teaching about speaking in tongues, it emphatically asserts that on the Day of Pentecost, the believers did *not* speak in known human languages, but in a supernatural, unknown prayer language, just as believers speak in tongues today.

However, on the Day of Pentecost, a special miracle occurred. The believers spoke in tongues — but by the time that supernatural language reached the ears of the listeners, they "heard" a message in their own distinct dialects. This is why Acts 2:6 says that "...every man *heard* them speak in his own language." Acts 2:8 says, "And how *hear* we every man in our own tongue, wherein we were born?" And Acts 2:11 tells us that the listeners said, "…we do *hear* them speak in our tongues the wonderful works of God."

On the Day of Pentecost, the first great work of God was to fill the believers with the Holy Spirit. The second great work was to liberate their human spirits so they could pray in tongues and worship God in the Spirit. The third great work occurred when the believers spoke in other tongues and God supernaturally translated those tongues in the ears of the listeners so that each member of the audience "heard" them speaking in his or her own language.

It is amazing what happens when God's people open up to let Him work through them! When the believers in the book of Acts were filled with the Spirit and began to regularly speak in tongues, a door to supernatural power was opened. The power unleashed through speaking in tongues is evident throughout the book of Acts and is still in operation today.

There are several instances in the book of Acts where believers prayed and worshiped God in tongues. This was the norm, not the exception — a common practice that was expected to occur in the life of any person who was filled with the Spirit. And just as the early believers freely and fluently prayed in the Spirit, God has enabled us to do the same, *if* we will but open our hearts, open our mouths, and let our spirits speak to God.

How long has it been since you prayed in other tongues and allowed God's supernatural power to operate through you? Why don't you take a few minutes today to pray and praise in the Spirit? *It will bring a divine operation of the supernatural into your day!*

MY PRAYER FOR TODAY

Lord, I thank You for filling me with the Spirit and for giving me the ability to pray and to praise You in a supernatural language. My spirit longs to pray, to express itself, and to worship You. My own mind and intellect is so limited that I don't always know what to say or how to express myself. But when I pray and praise in the Spirit, I am very aware that I am praying perfectly and praising You on the highest level. Thank You for this wonderful ability. I want to pray in the Spirit and to worship You with all of my inner man!

I pray this in Jesus' name!

MY CONFESSION FOR TODAY

I confess that I am filled with the Spirit of God and that I regularly pray in the Spirit. God liberated my inner man to speak to Him on the day I was baptized in the Holy Spirit. From that time until now, I have had the ability to speak in a supernatural spiritual language. I refuse to neglect or ignore this ability God has given me; therefore, I regularly pray in tongues. As a result, I am growing stronger and more sensitive to the Holy Spirit, and I have a continual operation of divine, supernatural activity in my life!

I declare this by faith in Jesus' name!

QUESTIONS FOR YOU TO CONSIDER

1. How often do you take the time to pray in the Spirit? When you do, how much time do you devote to praying in other tongues?

2. What happens inside you when you pray in the Spirit? Do you see a greater manifestation of power, joy, victory, and personal revelation in your life? What other results do you see when you regularly pray in tongues?

3. If you have never been filled with the Spirit or spoken in other tongues, what is stopping you from receiving this glorious experience today?

JULY 10

They Shall Take Up Serpents!

And these signs shall follow them that believe;
In my name shall they cast out devils;
they shall speak with new tongues;
They shall take up serpents....
— Mark 16:17,18

*I*n the remote back hills of some states, there are religious groups who literally "take up serpents" as a part of their church services. These groups have taken Jesus' words in Mark 16:17 and 18 literally, where He said, "And these signs shall follow them that believe...they shall take up serpents...." Based on this scripture, these people have concluded that Jesus was actually ordering believers to "take up serpents" as a way to demonstrate the strength of their faith!

Back behind the pulpit and next to the wall in these churches are cages that contain rattlesnakes and other poisonous snakes. At a preappointed moment in the church service, the cages are popped open, the snakes are brought out, and those who are daring enough pass those serpents from one person to the next. But is this what Jesus was talking about when he said believers would "take up serpents"? *Of course not!*

Let's consider the times in which Jesus uttered these words. Then we can better see how these words of Jesus apply to us today.

The word "serpents" is the Greek word *ophis*, which was used to depict *snakes*. Snakes were considered to be dangerous and life-threatening creatures. People were especially afraid of snakes because the road system at this time was very much undeveloped. This meant people often had to blaze their own trail to get to some cities or remote places. Hiding in the rocks or grasses were dangerous and poisonous snakes that frequently bit travelers, causing premature death. These snakes were a concern to all travelers, especially to those traveling by foot.

In Luke 10:19, Jesus said, "Behold, I give unto you power to tread on serpents and scorpions, and over all the power of the enemy: and nothing shall by any means hurt you." When Jesus uttered these words to His disciples, it was right after He had commanded them to go into the harvest fields of the world to reap the souls of men (*see* Luke 10:2-11). This verse was Jesus' supernatural guarantee that when they went to preach, they would have divine protection against serpents, scorpions, and anything else the enemy might try to use to stop or hurt them. This is why Jesus concluded by saying, "...nothing shall by any means hurt you."

But notice that in addition to *serpents*, Jesus also mentioned *scorpions*! The scorpions in the Middle East were extremely feared because they were loaded with deadly poison. One sting from the tail of such a scorpion, and a person could be permanently paralyzed or even killed. When people took journeys by foot, the prospect of encountering a scorpion was just as scary as the thought of snakes. Scorpions hid in the rocks and in the ruts in the road. Therefore, sitting on the wrong rock or accidentally stepping on the wrong spot in the road could result in disaster.

Jesus' promise to His disciples that they would "tread upon serpents and scorpions" was very important! The word "tread" is the Greek word *pateo*, which simply means *to walk*. Jesus was telling them that even if they walked right over a scorpion or snake, they didn't need to worry because He was giving them special, supernatural protection against these natural dangers. This was a specific promise of protection for those who would be journeying long distances or through rough terrain to preach the Gospel!

To make sure the concerns of all travelers were completely covered, Jesus added, "...and nothing shall by any means hurt you." The word "hurt" is the Greek word *adikeo*, which means *to suffer injustice* or *to suffer some kind of wrong or wrongdoing*. This was the Lord's promise that we need not fear *injustice* or *wrongdoing* when we have been sent into His harvest field. In fact, the Greek uses a triple negative in this phrase. It literally says, "...and nothing (first negative), no (second negative), by no means (third negative) will injure or harm you." Jesus said this in the strongest terms available to assure followers that if they go into the whole world to preach the Gospel, they will be divinely guarded from all forms of evil.

Now let's go back to where we began today in Mark 16:17,18. Jesus said, "These signs will follow them that believe...they shall take up serpents...." What did this mean to the disciples, and how does it apply to you and me today?

For the disciples, it meant they were divinely guarded by the power of God. This divine protection was so powerful that even if they were to be bitten by a deadly snake or a highly venomous scorpion, it would have no effect on them. An example of this can be found in Acts 28:3-6 when the apostle Paul was bitten by a deadly viper. Paul simply shook off the snake into the fire and went away unharmed (*see* June 25).

You see, Jesus gave His disciples supernatural protection because He was sending them to preach the Gospel to the ends of the earth. Things that would normally injure or kill others would have no effect on them whatsoever. Since they were required to walk by foot through dangerous and rough terrain, this was a very important promise!

What does this have to do with you and me? First of all, it has *nothing* to do with passing rattlesnakes around a congregation! Although believers who do this may be sincere, they are sincerely wrong. This is foolishness and presumption. Jesus never intended for us to deliberately endanger ourselves!

But if we go in Jesus' name to carry the Gospel to parts of the world that are considered to be unsafe, it does mean that God's power will protect us! We may not deal with serpents and scorpions like the early believers did, but there may be times when we are required to fly on rickety airplanes, drive on dangerous roads, pass through highly volatile areas, or work in regions that are considered dangerous.

But as noted earlier (*see* July 7), this divine protection is activated in those of us who *believe* that God's promise of protection will work for us. Whenever we enter dangerous territory in fear, doubt, and unbelief, we are likely to get in trouble. But if we will go believing and claiming that God's protection is ours and that the enemy can't do anything to hurt us, our faith in this promise will activate it and cause it to be manifested in our lives!

The bottom line is this: *Before we ever take a mission trip, move to the mission field, or go anywhere considered dangerous for the sake of the Gospel, we need to make certain that we believe and actively claim the divine promise contained in this verse!*

MY PRAYER FOR TODAY

Lord, I believe Your Word to be true! By faith, I claim that there is nothing the enemy can do to injure or hurt me when I am traveling to take Your name to a new part of the world or to people who do not know You. Thank You for this promise of divine protection for my life! I am so grateful that You have shielded me with Your power and that the enemy cannot destroy me.

I pray this in Jesus' name!

MY CONFESSION FOR TODAY

I confess that God's power shields and protects me from every attack of the enemy! If I am required to fly on rickety airplanes, drive on dangerous roads, pass through highly volatile areas, or work in regions that are considered dangerous, I will be safe. Regardless of the conditions I am forced to face in order to take the name of Jesus to people who have never heard, God will be with me. He will protect me every step of the way. I believe and claim God's protection; therefore, the enemy cannot do anything to hurt me!

I declare this by faith in Jesus' name!

QUESTIONS FOR YOU TO CONSIDER

1. Can you think of examples when people whom you personally know were supernaturally protected by the power of God — in other words, when something catastrophic happened but had no effect on them?
2. If you know of someone who was hurt on a mission trip, do you know if that person was in faith for that trip? Was he actively believing and claiming divine protection, or did he just get up and go without first making the trip a matter of fervent prayer?
3. In light of what you have learned today, how will you change your approach to the trips on which the Lord sends you to share the Gospel with others?

If we go in Jesus' name to carry the Gospel to parts of the world that are considered to be unsafe, God's power will protect us! Regardless of the conditions we are forced to face, our faith in this promise of protection will activate it and cause it to be manifested in our lives every step of the way.

JULY 11

❧❀❧

If They Drink Any Deadly Thing, It Shall Not Hurt Them!

And these signs shall follow them that believe;
In my name shall they cast out devils;
they shall speak with new tongues;
They shall take up serpents;
and if they drink any deadly thing, it shall not hurt them....
— Mark 16:17,18

*I*n yesterday's *Sparkling Gem*, I mentioned a religious group in the remote hills of some states that "takes up serpents" and passes them around the congregation to demonstrate the strength of their faith. They believe that if their faith is strong, they will not be bitten. And if they *are* bitten, they use this as an opportunity to prove that a snake bite will have no effect on them.

But in Mark 16:18, Jesus went on to say, "…and if they drink any deadly thing, it shall not hurt them…." Based on these words, this sincerely misled group also deliberately drinks deadly poisons, such as strychnine and arsenic. Just as they take up venomous snakes to prove the strength of their faith, they intentionally subject themselves to deadly poisons for the same purpose. They actually believe Jesus intended for Christians to consume lethal chemicals to prove that when their faith is strong, such substances will have no effect on them. *But is this really what Jesus meant?* Let's look at this verse to see what Jesus was talking about!

The word "drink" is actually the Greek word *pino*, which means *to drink* or *to consume*. Although this word usually refers to *drinking*, it can also picture *a person who is consuming something*, such as meat or some other kind of food. The word "deadly" comes from the Greek word *thanasimos*, a derivative of the word *thanatos*, which is the Greek word for *death*. However the word used here in Mark 16:18 describes *something that is deadly or fatal*. The word "any" is the small word *ti*, which means *anything*. This means that Jesus wasn't referring only to liquid chemicals, but to *anything* that is deadly or fatal, including chemicals *or* foods. Hence, this part of the verse could be translated, "*…and if they consume anything that would normally be fatal….*"

Jesus continued by saying that if a believer consumes something fatal while he is on a God-sent trip, this fatal substance "shall not hurt them." The word "hurt" is the Greek word *blapto*, which means *to weaken, to disable, to hurt, to harm*, or *to injure*. It depicts *something that is probably not powerful enough to kill, but strong enough to make one sick or ill*. Because the word *thanasimos* ("deadly thing") is also used in this verse, it tells us that Jesus meant this: "*…and if they consume anything that would normally be fatal, or anything that would usually make a person sick, it will have no effect upon them….*"

Remember that Jesus was speaking to followers whom He was going to send to the farthest ends of the world. To fulfill this assignment, they would be required to eat foods they had never seen before. In fact, their journeys to pagan lands would no doubt necessitate that they eat foods they previously considered to be dirty or unclean. For them to take the Gospel to new places meant they would have to eat "mystery food" — not knowing where it came from, who killed it, how long it

...ad been dead, who cooked it, how clean or dirty the kitchen was in which it was cooked, or what effect the food was going to have on their stomachs.

Remember, the Lord had previously told His disciples, "And in the same house remain, eating and drinking such things as they give...eat such things as are set before you" (Luke 10:7,8). If the disciples had rejected what their hosts had prepared for them, they could have greatly insulted or hurt them. Therefore, Jesus said in effect, "*If your hosts have prepared the best they can give you, eat it with joy!*"

As one who travels worldwide, I can personally tell you that sometimes it is difficult to eat what is set before you! But when you look into a plate of food that looks scary, you must shut your eyes, bless that mess in Jesus' name, lift your fork from the plate, open your mouth, insert, and eat the "mystery food" by faith!

I've seen individuals come on mission trips expecting to eat the identical kinds of food they eat at home. When they discover they can't have the same food, the same restaurants, the same blend of coffee, and so on, I've seen them get very upset. But they're not at home! They are on the other side of the world where those kinds of foods don't even exist! If a person is going to take the Gospel to the ends of the earth, he must be prepared to eat food that is prepared at the ends of the earth!

This is precisely the reason Jesus told His soon-to-be world travelers that if they consumed anything deadly or sickening, it would have no effect on them. Jesus wasn't encouraging His disciples to deliberately consume poison; rather, He was assuring them of the divine protection that is available for those who take the Gospel to the ends of the earth.

But as noted earlier (*see* July 7), this promise belongs to "those who believe." If you want this promise of protection from bad foods or fatal substances, you must release your faith and activate this promise. So before you sit down to eat, take a few minutes to bless that food. Call it sanctified, and speak nutrition and health into it. Then eat the food, believing that it will only bless you and that nothing negative can happen to you as a result of eating it!

Jesus provided everything needed for those of us who would follow His call to the ends of the earth. He provided us with supernatural protection from disasters, calamities, snakes, scorpions, and all the works of the enemy. He also promised traveling mercies and protection from acts of injustice. He even guaranteed that if we accidentally consume bad foods or deadly substances, they wouldn't weaken us physically or injure our health.

It's time for you to quit worrying and start believing that Jesus meant what He said. If God is giving you an assignment that takes you to a foreign state, a distant country, or an unfamiliar culture, just keep your eyes fixed on Jesus and get going! God isn't going to send you somewhere so you can eat something deadly and die! Rebuke that spirit of fear, and release your faith! Don't let the devil keep you trapped at home because you're afraid you won't like the food. *The Gospel and the power of God is much stronger than any meat or drink!*

MY PRAYER FOR TODAY

Lord, I thank You for giving me the courage to go wherever You want me to go. I rebuke fear; I reject intimidation; and I decide by faith that I can do anything and go anywhere Jesus wants to send me. Holy Spirit, fill me with Your power and help me think with a sound mind! There's so much that Jesus has for me to do, and I don't want to waste a single minute. Thank You for helping and strengthening me!

I pray this in Jesus' name!

MY CONFESSION FOR TODAY

I boldly declare that I am protected from bad foods or fatal substances! When I sit down to eat, I take a few minutes to bless my food. I call it sanctified; I speak nutrition and health into it; and then I eat it, believing that it will only bless and strengthen my body. Jesus has provided supernatural protection from disasters, calamities, snakes, scorpions, and all the works of the enemy. He promised me traveling mercies and protection from acts of injustice. God isn't going to send me somewhere so I can die! I rebuke the spirit of fear — and I press forward into the divine life of Jesus Christ!

I boldly declare this in Jesus' name!

QUESTIONS FOR YOU TO CONSIDER

1. How do you think people in other nations are affected when after preparing their best food for their guests, they watch the guests turn up their noses and act like the food is so disgusting that they cannot consume it?
2. Do you pray over your food before you eat?
3. How does today's *Sparkling Gem* affect what you are going to do in the future concerning food that has been prepared for you?

JULY 12

They Shall Lay Hands on the Sick, And They Shall Recover!

And these signs shall follow them that believe;
In my name shall they cast out devils;
they shall speak with new tongues;
They shall take up serpents;
and if they drink any deadly thing, it shall not hurt them;
they shall lay hands on the sick, and they shall recover.
— Mark 16:17,18

*I*n Mark 16:18, Jesus said that believers would lay hands on the sick, and the sick would recover. What category of sick people was Jesus talking about? What did He mean when He said they would recover? Are there examples of this in Jesus' own ministry that we can read and learn from? Let's look deeply into this verse today to see how it applies to you and me!

First, let's look at the word "sick," because this describes the category of sick people Jesus was talking about. This is the Greek word *arroustos*, which comes from the word *arunnumi*. The word *runnumi* normally means *to be well, to be strong, to be in good health,* or *to possess a strong physical condition.* When an *a* is placed in front of this word, it reverses the condition and instead means *to be in bad health* or *to possess a weak and broken condition*. It is the image of *a person so weak and sick that he has become critically ill*. He is an *invalid*.

The following three scriptures show us examples of times when Jesus healed people who were afflicted with an *arroustos* type of sickness:

◆ Mathew 14:14 says, "And Jesus went forth, and saw a great multitude, and was moved with compassion toward them, and he healed their sick." The word "sick" in this verse is the Greek word *arroustos*. Matthew informs us that Jesus was especially drawn to those who were so weak that they were without strength. These people whom He healed that day were *invalids*.

◆ Mark 6:5 tells us, "And he could there do no mighty work, save that he laid his hands upon a few sick folk, and healed them." In Greek, the words "sick folk" also come from the Greek word *arroustos*. This lets us know that these were *extremely sick people*. Most readers presume that these were minor ailments, but the word *arroustos* tells us emphatically that these were *critically ill individuals*.

◆ Mark 6:13 says, "And they cast out many devils, and anointed with oil many that were sick, and healed them." The word "sick" is the Greek word *arroustos*, which means these individuals were *very frail* and *weak in health*.

These examples of the word *arroustos* vividly show that these were not people who were simply feeling poorly because of some small ailment; these were people who were *devastated* by sickness. They were so physically weak, so critically ill, and so lacking of strength that they had become invalids. This is the category of sick people that Jesus said believers would lay hands on, and they would recover. He wasn't talking about headaches and skin abrasions! He was talking about believers laying hands on people who are *critically ill* and who fall into the category of *invalids*.

Notice that Jesus said believers would "lay hands" on the sick. These words come from the Greek word *epitithimi*, a compound of the words *epi* and *tithimi*. The word *epi* means *upon*, and *tithmi* means *to place*. When they are joined to become the word *epitithimi*, it means *to place upon* or *to lay upon*. This word is used in Luke 4:40 to describe one event during which Jesus *placed His hands upon sick people*.

Luke 4:40 says, "Now when the sun was setting, all they that had any sick with divers diseases brought them unto him; and he laid his hands on every one of them, and healed them." That evening the people brought to Jesus "any sick." This word "sick" is different than the other examples we looked at earlier. It is the word *asthenios*, which depicts *a wide range of infirmities*. This is why it is further amplified by the phrase "any sick *with diverse diseases.*" This represents a wide range of sicknesses, but the word "diseases" lets us know that some of these people were seriously ill. This word "diseases" is the Greek word *nosos*, which always conveys the idea of *a terrible malady* or *an affliction of the most severe nature*. Often the word *nosos* depicted *a terminal illness for which there was no natural cure*. Hence, it could describe people who were *terminally ill*.

What did Jesus do for these people? He laid His hands upon them, and He healed them. In such cases, Jesus was giving the perfect example of how believers would later lay their hands on the sick — *including the terminally ill* — and see them be restored back to health as a result of their obedience.

But when you look carefully at Mark 16:18, you'll notice that Jesus promised *recovery*. That recovery could be instantaneous, or it could be a process that is prolonged over a period of time. The words "they shall" are from the Greek word *echo*, which means *to have* or *to possess*. But the tense that is used in this verse doesn't picture something that is instantaneous, but rather something that occurs *progressively*. In fact, the word "healed" doesn't speak of an instantaneous event either. It is the word *kalos*, which in this case means *to be well, to be healthy*, or *to be in good shape*. Taken together as one complete phrase, it could be translated, "…*they shall progressively feel themselves getting better and better, until finally they are well and healthy.*"

This lets us know that all healings do *not* occur instantly; some of them take place over a period of time. But Jesus' promise is that if we will follow His example and lay our hands on the sick, God's power will be released into the body of the afflicted. If we are releasing our faith and believing for healing power to flow from us to the recipient, healing virtue will be deposited into the sick person's body. Just as medicine slowly works to reverse a medical condition, the power of God that was deposited with the laying on of our hands will begin to attack the work of the devil and progressively bring that sick person back into a state of health and well-being.

Jesus promised that any believer could do this! *Any* believer, including *you*, can lay hands on the sick and see the sick get better and better until they are finally restored back to health. All that is required for God to use you in this way are three basic criteria: 1) That you have a desire for God to heal through you; 2) That you have hands to lay on sick people; and 3) That your faith is released to activate the power of God to heal. If you can fulfill these three requirements, you're ready to get into the healing ministry!

Healing the sick is part of your responsibility as a believer. You cannot do it alone, but the Holy Spirit is present to impart His power when you act in Jesus' name. So rather than look at sick people and feel pity for them, why don't you pull your hands out of your pockets and go lay them on those sick people, just as Jesus did when He was ministering on the earth? The Word of God guarantees that God will work with you to bring healing and health to those who are in need. *Why don't you get started healing the sick today?*

MY PRAYER FOR TODAY

Lord, I ask You for confidence to lay my hands on the sick. I want Your healing power to flow through me and to be deposited into sick bodies, attacking the enemy's work until finally those sick people are restored back to health again. In Your Word, it is stated that when believers lay hands on the sick, the sick would be made well again. Today I am making the decision to pull my hands out of my pockets and to place them on the sick so Your healing power can be delivered to others through me!

I pray this in Jesus' name!

MY CONFESSION FOR TODAY

I confess that God's power is released into the bodies of the afflicted when I lay my hands on them. Just as medicine slowly works to reverse a medical condition, the power of God that is deposited when I lay my hands on sick people begins to attack their affliction, causing them to be progressively restored to health and well-being. Healing the sick is part of my responsibility, so I boldly confess that I am going to lay my hands on sick people just as Jesus did when He was ministering on the earth — and I expect to see them get well!

I declare this by faith in Jesus' name!

QUESTIONS FOR YOU TO CONSIDER

1. How long has it been since you looked at your hands and really thought about how God wants His power to flow through them to heal sick people?

2. Have you ever laid your hands on the sick? When was the last time you did so? What was the result the last time you placed your hands on the sick and released your faith to see them get well?

3. If you interviewed the people you have laid hands on in the past, what percentage of them do you think eventually got well? Did you ever stop to think that their recovery may have been due to the power that was deposited into their bodies when you laid your hands on them?

JULY 13

How Would You Like To 'Take a Stroll' In the Spirit Today?

This I say then, Walk in the Spirit,
and ye shall not fulfil the lust of the flesh.
— Galatians 5:16

How would you like to "walk in the Spirit" every day of your life? Does this proposal sound like an impossibility, or do you think that constantly walking in the Spirit is a possibility you should try to achieve? To answer the question of whether or not it is possible to consistently walk in the Spirit, let's look at Paul's words in Galatians 5:16. This verse says, "This I say then, Walk in the Spirit, and ye shall not fulfil the lust of the flesh."

The word "walk" is the Greek word *peripateo*. It appears in the New Testament ninety-five times and has a very clear meaning. The word *peripateo* is a compound of the words *peri* and *pateo*. The word *peri* means *around* and suggests the idea of *something that is encircling*. In many cases it means *concerning*, but in this case it expresses the idea of *encircling*. The word *pateo* means *to walk*. It denotes *the movement of the feet*, and it can be translated *to walk, to step, to stride, to tread*, or even *to trample*. When these two words are compounded into one as they are in Galatians 5:16, it means *to habitually walk around in one general vicinity*. Thus, this word *peripateo* was often translated as the word "live."

This means that instead of being translated "walk in the Spirit," the phrase in Galatians 5:16 could be translated "*live* in the Spirit." This is a good rendering of the word *peripateo*, for indeed it suggests *a person who has walked in one region for so long that it has now become his environment, his place of daily activity, the sphere that encircles his existence*. One expositor notes that the word *peripateo* could be best explained by thinking of a person who has walked one path so habitually that he would be able to walk that path blindfolded because it is *his path, his sphere, the place where he has habitually lived and functioned*.

My wife and I recently invited a precious elderly couple whom we dearly love to come visit our family. The wife responded, "You see, Rick, I've lost most of my eyesight, so it's best if I stay home. At least at home I know where all the furniture is, so even though I can't see too well, I can still walk around."

I was saddened to hear about this dear woman's failing eyesight, but her words caused me to think of the Greek word *peripateo* in Galatians 5:16, which pictures a person who has frequented one area so repeatedly that it has become second nature to him. He needs no help to walk there, because he knows that path. *It is his path, his walk, his realm of life, and he feels very safe and comfortable there.*

In the secular literature of New Testament times, the word *peripateo* often meant *to stroll.* In fact, many Greek scholars suggest that the best way to translate Galatians 5:16 is "*stroll* in the Spirit." To stroll is *to leisurely walk.* A person who *strolls* is not an anxious, frustrated person who is fighting to do something or to get somewhere; rather, he is *restful, relaxed, unhurried, peaceful, and calm.* This wonderfully describes what it is like to walk in the Spirit. You see, when a person walks in the Spirit the stress and anxieties of life are removed, and he moves over into a realm where he can stroll along in continual rest, peace, and calmness.

Paul goes on to say that if you walk in the Spirit, "...ye shall not fulfil the lust of the flesh." The word "lust" is from the Greek word *epithumia.* The second part of the word is the Greek word *thumos,* which describes *an urge, a longing, a craving, a passion,* or *something that is excited.* The word *epi* usually means *over,* but when combined with the word *thumos,* it means *to get extremely excited for or over something.* In fact, this excitement is so vigorous that it becomes *a fervent passion,* almost like *an obsession, a mania,* or *a very strong desire.*

In Ephesians 2:3, Paul states that before we came to Jesus Christ, we walked "...in the lusts of our flesh, fulfilling the desires of the flesh...." The word "lusts" is this same word *epithumia.* The word "desires" is from the Greek word *thelema,* which denotes *one's will, intention, plan,* or *desire.* In short, it means the flesh has a mind of its own. And if allowed to do so, the flesh will become obsessed with a fleshly temptation, *fervently stirred up as it yearns to fulfill its deep, dark desires.*

But Galatians 5:16 provides the answer to the flesh. It says if you "...walk in the Spirit, ye shall not fulfil the lust of the flesh." The word "fulfil" is from the Greek work *teleo,* which means *to fulfill, to complete,* or *to reach one's goal.* But because of the tense and the strong negative that are used in the Greek phrase, Paul is telling us that if we walk in the Spirit, we have basically pulled the plug on the flesh! As a result, we have nullified the yearnings of the flesh so that they will never be fulfilled.

Because of the various words used in this verse, Galatians 5:16 conveys this idea:

"Make the path of the Spirit the place where you habitually live and walk. Become so comfortable on this spiritual path that you learn to leisurely and peacefully stroll along in that realm. Living your life in this Spirit realm is the best way to guarantee that you will not allow the yearnings of your flesh to creep out and fulfill themselves."

It is time for you to do everything you can to move up into a higher realm. Fixate on the goal of walking in the Spirit. Develop your own human spirit; do what you can to become more sensitive to the Spirit of God. When you become more spiritually sensitive, it will be easier for you to keep in step with the Holy Spirit. And as you follow Him and live to please the Lord, you will find that walking in the Spirit becomes a habit. You'll deny your flesh for so long that its voice will eventually become weaker and weaker and weaker — until, finally, it will no longer have any authority in your life.

God is calling you higher! He wants you to leave the low life you've been living and to come up to the spiritual path He has destined for you to walk on in your life. In that higher realm, you will experience love, joy, peace, longsuffering, gentleness, goodness, faith, meekness, and temperance. These are the fruit that the Holy Spirit produces! What a contrast to the rotten, decaying garbage that the flesh produces! *The Spirit always produces life!*

So resolve in your heart today to make the path of the Holy Spirit the place where you live, work, and function. Don't let it be a place you occasionally visit any longer. *Make the realm of the Spirit the place where you habitually live your entire life!*

MY PRAYER FOR TODAY

Lord, help me walk in the Spirit and not in the flesh. I realize that I must make a choice to move up into this higher realm, so today I am telling You that I want to leave the low life I've been living and come up higher. You are beckoning me to come there, and I accept Your invitation. As I start taking steps to this higher sphere of life, help me resist the yearnings of the flesh that keep trying to pull me back down! I want to become so sensitive to You that the desires of the flesh altogether cease to have any effect on my life!

I pray this in Jesus' name!

MY CONFESSION FOR TODAY

I confess that I am moving up into a higher realm! I fixate on the goal of walking in the Spirit. I am developing my own human spirit, and I am becoming more sensitive to the Spirit of God. Every day the voice of my flesh is getting weaker and weaker. I have accepted the call of God to leave the low life behind, and I am following the Spirit of God to a higher realm, where I will live in continual peace, joy, and victory!

I declare this by faith in Jesus' name!

QUESTIONS FOR YOU TO CONSIDER

1. If Jesus were to analyze your life to determine what percentage of your time is lived in the Spirit or in the flesh, what do you think He would conclude about you?
2. What steps do you need to take to start walking in the Spirit instead of being dominated by the flesh?
3. What role does praying and reading your Bible have to do with walking in the Spirit and rendering the flesh inoperative? In the past week, how much time have you spent on developing your spiritual life? Have you approached your spiritual life as if it was a high priority?

God wants you to leave the low life you've been living and to come up to the spiritual path He has destined for you to walk on in your life. In that higher realm, you will experience love, joy, peace, longsuffering, gentleness, goodness, faith, meekness, and temperance.

JULY 14

The Works of the Flesh

Now the works of the flesh are manifest....
— Galatians 5:19

I'll never forget the day I saw a terrible accident in the former Soviet republic where I lived. Right in front of me, an elderly man dashed into the middle of traffic. The oncoming cars were coming so fast that it was impossible for the drivers to put on the brakes and avoid hitting this elderly gentleman. He was hit so hard by the first car that it threw him over into the next lane of traffic. Before the traffic was finally stopped, four additional automobiles had run over the man's crumpled body, further crushing his mangled torso.

From where I was situated, I could see the whole ordeal unfold before me. The elderly man lay motionless on the pavement. People began to gather on the sides of the road to see what was happening. A police officer arrived to try to manage the crisis. To my amazement, not a single person went to see if the elderly man was dead or alive. They all assumed he was dead, so no one checked on him.

As a Christian, I felt compelled to go see if the man was alive. If he was still breathing, I wanted to pray for him. I went over to the police officer, who recognized me from my television program, and asked his permission to go see what I could do to help this man. The officer looked at me and laughed. Then he said, "Yeah, you can check on him, if you think it will help!"

I hastened over to the elderly man lying on the pavement. Blood was coming from his ears and nose. From the way his arms and legs were oddly lying, it was evident that nearly every bone in this man's body was broken. When I looked into his face, my heart ached. I could see the deep lines and the burnt reddish color that so often accompanies severe alcoholics in this part of the world. The lines in his face were deep. He looked like a wrinkled, worn-out piece of leather. It was obvious that this man's life had been one of misery. I estimated that he must have been approximately seventy years old.

Suddenly I noticed that the man was lightly breathing. I yelled to the police officer, and he quickly responded, calling for an ambulance. They loaded this man's broken body into the back of the emergency vehicle, and I watched as it drove down the road to transport him to the hospital.

The next week, the local police paid a visit to my office to inform me that the man had died. They wanted me to testify in court about the events that took place that day. Then they told me something that just shocked me — the man who died had only been *twenty-seven years old*! When the court official told me his age, I had a difficult time hearing anything else that was said in the conversation. I was completely dumbfounded that someone so young could look so old!

When the meeting concluded that day, I sat in my office, still stunned by what I had just learned. According to the appearance of that man's flesh, I had really thought he was elderly. For him to be so young and yet to look so old, I knew he had lived an unruly life. He had obviously soaked up vodka as if he were a sponge. He had degenerated to such a ruined state that he wandered right into heavy traffic that day and died.

As I pondered on all this, my thoughts went to Galatians 5:19-21, which says, "Now the works of the flesh are manifest, which are these; adultery, fornication, uncleanness, lasciviousness, idolatry, witchcraft, hatred, variance, emulations, wrath, strife, seditions, heresies, envyings, murders, drunkenness, revellings, and such like...."

When Paul writes about the works of the flesh, he uses the Greek word *ergos* for "works." This word signified *some kind of action, deed, or activity.* Very often it referred to *a person's occupation,* to *one's labor,* or to *the things produced by someone's effort or life.* It described *a person's line of work, his career, his labor,* or *his profession.* It denoted *the results of his hard work.*

Because Paul connects this word to the flesh, he is telling us something very important! Just like a person has a career or profession and works hard to achieve results, the flesh — if it is allowed to go its own way and do what it wants — will work very hard to produce fleshly results. When the flesh is not surrendered to the sanctifying power of the Holy Spirit, it will work around the clock, twenty-four hours a day, to produce fruit that is hurtful, damaging, and even deadly. This is the *occupation* of the flesh.

The word "flesh" used in Galatians 5:19 is the Greek word *sarx,* which is used mostly in Paul's epistles to depict *sinful impulses and carnal cravings.* Paul uses the phrase "works of the flesh" to give the idea that the flesh has its own mind and desires. If a believer doesn't crucify the flesh and keep it under control, it will eventually manifest those evil desires. In other words, the flesh will go to work!

Paul says, "Now the works of the flesh are *manifest....*" The word "manifest" is the Greek word *phaneros.* It means *to appear, to manifest, to become visible, to become apparent, to become seen, to be well known,* or *to become conspicuous.* By using this word, Paul tells you that if you let the flesh have its way, it will jump at the chance to manifest its evil desires and carnal cravings. In fact, the flesh is so carnal and base that if you don't stop its activity, it will even try to lead you into adultery, fornication, uncleanness, lasciviousness, idolatry, witchcraft, hatred, variance, emulations, wrath, strife, seditions, heresies, envyings, murders, drunkenness, revellings, and other similar vices.

When a little baby is first born into the world, he looks so pure, so innocent, so clean. But if that child is abandoned to the control of his flesh, he'll end up in crime, scandal, alcoholism, or drugs and become bitter, hardhearted, and filled with malice and strife. Why? Because these are the fruit that the flesh produces. This is why it is so important to teach our children and to train ourselves to mortify the deeds of the flesh and live in subjection to the control of the Holy Spirit.

The twenty-seven-year-old man whom I saw killed that afternoon was once a beautiful, pure-looking baby boy. His proud mother and father had probably carried dreams in their hearts of what their infant son would one day become. But at the age of twenty-seven, this same person looked like an old man, with deep wrinkles in his face and the appearance of a severe alcoholic. There he lay, crushed on the highway — *a wasted life.* The flesh had its way in that man's life and led him to destruction — the place where flesh always wants to go.

You may not be an alcoholic or a drug addict, but let me ask you this: Are you allowing your flesh to dominate your attitudes or your relationships? Are you giving way to the carnal impulses of bitterness or anger that the flesh wants to produce inside you? If you give in to these impulses, they will destroy your relationships, make you hardhearted, and fill you with negative attitudes that steal your joy and your peace.

You see, a life dominated by the flesh is a hard life. It is filled with excess, imbalance, extremity, laziness, self-abuse, hatred, strife, bitterness, irresponsibility, and neglect. The way of the flesh is the hardest route for any individual to take; yet the flesh cries out to be in charge, screaming to have its own way, demanding to be the boss. Unless you take your flesh to the Cross and mortify it by the power of God, it will keep screaming until you finally surrender to it and allow it to produce its ruinous effects in your life.

In the next several *Sparkling Gems*, I want us to look very carefully at the works of the flesh that Paul specifically listed in Galatians 5:19-21. But remember — if you crucify the flesh and choose instead to walk in the Spirit, you can produce fruit in your life that is just the opposite of the works of the flesh. You can yield the sweetest, most wonderful fruit imaginable. You can live in a way that is godly and beneficial and that truly makes a difference in other people's lives.

So make the decision today that you are not going to take the route of the flesh. It really is the hardest way to go! *Turn your attention to the Holy Spirit, and determine to let Him produce the life of Jesus Christ in you!*

MY PRAYER FOR TODAY

Lord, help me to mortify the deeds of the flesh and to reckon myself alive unto God! I have walked in the flesh long enough; now I want to walk in the Spirit. I no longer want the flesh to have its way in my life. Instead, I want to let the Holy Spirit produce the life of Jesus Christ in me. I know that I ultimately make the decision of what is produced in my life, so please help me to consistently say no to the flesh and to say yes to the Spirit of God!

I pray this in Jesus' name!

MY CONFESSION FOR TODAY

I confess that it is no longer I who live, but Jesus Christ lives in me! The life I now live in the flesh, I live for the Son of God, who loved me and gave Himself for me. I am His temple. I am His instrument. I refuse to allow the old flesh nature to dominate me. I willfully surrender my mind, my thoughts, my emotions, and my flesh to the sanctifying power of the Holy Spirit. As I yield to Him, He purifies me and makes me a worthy vessel for the work of God's Kingdom!

I declare this by faith in Jesus' name!

QUESTIONS FOR YOU TO CONSIDER

1. Can you think of areas in your life where you have intentionally or unintentionally allowed the flesh to retain its control over you? What are those areas, and what do you plan to do to bring them under the control of the Holy Spirit?
2. Is there any specific area in your life that has been more difficult to conquer than others — a habit, a thought, or some secret deed? Can you see how the Holy Spirit has been trying to help you bring that area of your life under control?
3. How do you respond when the Holy Spirit convicts you of wrongdoing or wrong thinking? Do you ignore His voice, or do you go before the Lord in prayer and ask Him to help you overcome it?

JULY 15

꧁꧂

Adultery, Fornication, Uncleanness, Lasciviousness

Now the works of the flesh are manifest, which are these;
Adultery, fornication, uncleanness, lasciviousness.
— Galatians 5:19

We live in a day when moral standards have deteriorated. Things that were considered sinful and shameful one generation ago are now practiced in a widespread manner throughout the Church. Rather than acknowledge their sin and repent, believers try to justify their actions as they can continue in their deeds. But no matter how painstakingly Christians may try to dress up sin, God still sees it as sin and *hates* it.

If I just gave you my personal commentary about the current status of the Church, I might make you angry at me. So instead, let me explain to you the meaning of the following Greek words from Galatians 5:19. Then you'll be able to see the works of the flesh as *God* sees them.

I will talk about these words purely from the viewpoint of their linguistic meaning. I believe the Greek definitions of these words in themselves will speak loudly enough for you to get the point. After reading these definitions, please take a few minutes to examine your own view of such actions. Determine if you see them as God sees them, or if you have been affected by a generation that has grown numb to the consequences of sin.

Adultery and Fornication:

When Paul begins his list of the works of the flesh, he begins with the sexual sins of adultery, fornication, and uncleanness. The word "adultery" and "fornication" both come from the same Greek word — the word *porneia*. This word includes all sexual activity outside of marriage — *including both adultery and homosexuality.*

When referring to a woman who has committed *adultery*, the New Testament used the word *pornos*. This is the word for *a prostitute*, and it very vividly informs us that a woman who has committed adultery has *prostituted herself.* She may not have sold herself for money; perhaps she traded her heart, her body, or her emotions for romance, for emotional support, or for a variety of other things. But regardless of why she did it, God says she has *sold herself* and entered into *the sin of prostitution.*

Don't deceive yourself into thinking that this term refers only to a professional prostitute who walks the streets at night or who works in an escort service. This word *pornos* describes *any* woman who has committed *adultery.* It leaves no room for doubt that in God's view, a woman who commits adultery has fallen into the sin of prostitution. *She is a prostitute.* One may try to give a myriad of reasons or excuses to explain why the illicit relationship occurred, but the fact is, God views such a relationship as *an act of prostitution.*

When referring to a man who has committed *adultery*, the word *porneia* depicts *a man who has had sexual intercourse with a prostitute.* Although his emotions may try to tell him that he has found the sweetheart of his dreams, the Greek word *porneia* means *he has slept with a prostitute.* A person may try as hard as he can to put a different light on this subject, but this is how God sees it. Whenever a man has sexual relations with a woman who is not his wife, God says his action is equivalent to seeking a prostitute for a cheap and dirty thrill.

I must point out that the word *pornography* comes from this same Greek word. In fact, pornography is from the Greek word *pornos* (the same word used above for *an adulteress* or *a prostitute*) and from the word *grapho*, which means *to write*. Thus, *pornography* refers to *the writings or reflections about prostitution*. This means that when an individual meditates on the writings or the photography contained in pornography, it is the equivalent of committing *mental prostitution*. Such a definition sheds new light on what Jesus said in Matthew 5:28: "But I say unto you, That whosoever looketh on a woman to lust after her hath committed adultery with her already in his heart."

What I have shared with you thus far today is not my opinion; it is the actual meaning of the Greek word "adultery" that is used throughout the New Testament. *So how does this affect your view of someone who has committed adultery? If you have committed adultery, how does this affect your view of what you have done? And how does this affect your view of pornography?*

If you are reading the *King James Version* of the New Testament, the next word in the works of the flesh is "fornication." However, this word does not appear in this text in the original Greek; it speaks only of *porneia*, the word discussed above, which includes all forms of sexual activity outside of marriage. In Greek, the next point that Paul lists is "uncleanness."

Uncleanness:

The word "uncleanness" is the Greek word *akatharsia*, which is the word *kathairo* with the prefix *a* added. The word *kathairo* means *cleansed* or *pure*, but when the *a* is added to it the condition is reversed, making the object *dirty* or *unclean*. In the New Testament, this word refers to *lewd or unclean thoughts that eventually produce lewd or unclean actions*. As it is used in the Gospels and Paul's epistles, it strongly suggests that these actions begin in the mind as unclean thoughts before they manifest as unclean deeds.

Mark 1:23 says, "And there was in their synagogue a man with an unclean spirit...." The Greek actually says that this man was "gripped by the control of an unclean spirit." It seems this man had pondered on *lewd thoughts* for so long that he had thrown open the door for these thoughts to seize and control him, so that eventually he found himself "in the clutch" of an unclean spirit. Although the text doesn't explicitly say it, the usage of the word *akatharsia* makes one wonder whether or not this demon found entrance into this man's life because he allowed his mind to dwell on things that were forbidden. Had he committed mental prostitution to such an extent that it opened the door for him to be completely controlled by spirits of uncleanness? The Bible doesn't say exactly so, but the usage of the word *akatharsia* definitely makes this a possibility.

In Mark 5:2, we find another example of a man with an unclean spirit. It says, "And when he was come out of the ship, immediately there met him out of the tombs a man with an unclean spirit." The word "unclean" is also the word *akatharsia*. Just as Mark 1:23 depicted the man in the synagogue as being "gripped by the control of an unclean spirit," this word could be translated exactly the same way in this verse. In the first five chapters of Mark, we thus have two very demonized individuals whose demon-possessed condition seems to have begun with *impure, lewd, dirty thoughts*, since this is exactly what the Greek word *akatharsia* means that is used in both texts. Did Satan lure them into the pornography of unclean ideas or into adultery, and then build a stronghold of uncleanness so robust in their minds that he was able to eventually cause unclean actions to be manifested in their lives and thus completely control them?

Never forget that Paul told us, "Know ye not, that to whom ye yield yourselves servants to obey, his servants ye are to whom ye obey..." (Romans 6:16). Whatever you give your mind to will eventually be your master. Was this the case with these two demon-possessed men in Mark 1:23 and Mark 5:2? I am not stating it emphatically, but the Greek suggests this very strongly. However, it should certainly make us want to take charge of our thought life and not allow uncleanness to have any place in our minds!

Lasciviousness:

As Paul continues listing the works of the flesh, he next mentions "lasciviousness." This strange word comes from the Greek word *aselgeia.* This Greek word describes *excess,* but it primarily refers to the *excessive consumption of food* or *wild, undisciplined living that is especially marked by unbridled sex.* The word *aselgeia* is listed as the principal sin of the cities of Sodom and Gomorrah (*see* 2 Peter 2:6) and the reason that God overthrew them.

It must be noted again that the word *aselgeia* also refers to *the excessive consumption of food.* This means that in God's mind, it is just as perverted to overindulge in food as it is to engage in sinful sexual activities! *So how does this make you feel about overeating?*

All of the works of the flesh can be forgiven — but before forgiveness comes, sin must be acknowledged. This is why we must understand exactly what these words mean. Once sin is comprehended, it can then be repented of and confessed. *This is God's requirement.*

If you have fallen into any of these works of the flesh, ask the Holy Spirit to open your eyes to see these sins as He sees them. Once you get a revelation of *His* perspective, you won't want to be the same! You'll understand the grossness of sin in God's sight, and you will want to be changed!

Once you confess your sin, God will forgive you and you can move on with your life. If your actions have violated your spouse or anyone else, pray for God's mighty grace to be upon them to forgive you. Then begin to take whatever steps are necessary to make that relationship healthier than ever before.

Dear friend, God is with you, and He wants to change your life. Open your heart and let the Holy Spirit be your Helper. He wants to help you get clean, get free, and become morally strong and stable. *With His help, you can do it!*

MY PRAYER FOR TODAY

Lord, I thank You for opening my eyes to the truth about how You see these works of the flesh. Forgive me for being too tolerant of these areas in my life. Help me to see these fleshly works the way You see them and to detest them as much as You detest them. Teach me to hate sin! Show me how to say no to ungodliness and to yield my mind and my body as instruments of righteousness. After what You have shown me today, I never want to be the same!

I pray this in Jesus' name!

MY CONFESSION FOR TODAY

I confess that I think clean thoughts and that I don't allow the devil to mess with my mind. My mind belongs to Jesus. It is filled with the Word of God. That Word renews my mind to think God's thoughts; therefore, Satan has no entrance into my mind or emotions to deceive me with thoughts of sin. I crucify my flesh, and I bring my body under the Lordship of Jesus Christ. I am no longer the servant of sin — I am the servant of righteousness!

I declare this by faith in Jesus' name!

QUESTIONS FOR YOU TO CONSIDER

1. How do you feel after reading today's *Sparkling Gem*? Has this discussion challenged any actions or secret thoughts in your life?
2. Has overeating become a part of your life? If so, how do you view overeating and gluttony now that you know it is listed in the works of the flesh? Do you view it as merely a hang-up in your life, or do you see that overeating is not only hurtful to yourself but offensive to God?
3. What steps do you need to take now that you know how God views these things?

JULY 16

Idolatry and Witchcraft

Now the works of the flesh are manifest, which are these;
Adultery, fornication, uncleanness, lasciviousness,
Idolatry, witchcraft....
— Galatians 5:19,20

When people hear the word "idolatry," they almost always visualize a great, carved stone statue of a pagan god, with wild, naked natives dancing in the light of a huge fire burning at its base. But is this what the apostle Paul had in mind when he included "idolatry" in his lists of the works of the flesh?

Idolatry:

The word "idolatry" is from the Greek word *eidololatria,* which means *the worship of idols.* However, it is a compound of the words *eidolon* and *latria.* The word *eidolon* is Greek for *a man-made idol; a heathen edifice; a pagan statue;* or *an image of a false god.* Such idols were an offense to God in the Old Testament, and they were forbidden to believers in the New Testament. God's hatred of idols is clearly demonstrated in First Samuel 5:1-4. The Philistines captured the Ark of the Covenant, which represented God's Presence, and sat it on a ledge right next to an idol of the pagan god called "Dagon." When the Philistines came into their pagan temple the next morning, the Ark of the Covenant remained high on its ledge, but the statue of Dagon lay on the ground. The Philistines put their idol back in place; but the next morning they found Dagon lying on the ground again, facing downward with its head and hands cut off. *God refused to share space with a false god!*

The second part of the word *eidololatria* ("idolatry") comes from the Greek word *latria,* derived from the word *latreuo,* which means *to work* or *to serve.* However, it primarily has the meaning of *one's extreme devotion and service to something he worships.* In a positive sense, it is used in the Old Testament Septuagint to depict *the service of the priesthood.* The priests faithfully served and fulfilled their duties in the temple, believing that part of their worship was the manner in which they served.

In Romans 1:9, Paul says, "For God is my witness, whom I serve with my spirit...." The word "serve" is the word *latreuo,* which means Paul, like the Old Testament priests, viewed his service to

God as a part of his worship. As a New Testament priest, Paul's service to God was the highest goal of his life. This is the reason he served God with all his spirit — because serving God demanded his best efforts, his best work, and his undivided attention. This was how Paul viewed his worship and service to God.

When Paul wrote Romans 12:1, he used the word *latreuo* again. This time he said, "I beseech you therefore, brethren, by the mercies of God, that ye present your bodies a living sacrifice, holy, acceptable unto God, which is your reasonable service." The words "reasonable service" are from the word *latreuo*. This implies that because of all God has done for us, it is just and fair for us to serve Him with our undivided devotion. This is one of the principal ways we worship Him. So when Paul declares that yielding our bodies as living sacrifices is our "reasonable service," he is emphatically telling us that it is reasonable for us to give our very best efforts and our complete, undivided attention to the service of God.

However, when the word *latreuo* is attached to the word *eidolon,* it forms the word *eidololatria,* which depicts *the worship of idols,* or simply put, *idolatry.* The act of idolatry transpires when an individual gives his complete and undivided attention, devotion, passion, love, or commitment to a person, project, or object other than God. When something other than God takes first place in that person's mind, he has entered, at least to some measure, into the sin of idolatry.

If you don't mortify the flesh by the power of God's Spirit, it won't be long until you are preoccupied with other things that steal the devotion and passion that should belong only to Jesus Christ. If you're not extremely careful, your family, spouse, parents, children, friends, job, dream or vision, profession, possessions, school, church activities, or even your own talents will unintentionally become the focus of your worship and service. You'll find yourself serving in your own self-consumed priesthood, giving your best effort and your undivided attention to the fulfillment of your own self-interests.

So let me ask you: *What do you think of more than anything else? What consumes most of your thoughts? What do you live for?* Your answer will probably tell you what you worship most in your life. You don't have to own a carved stone statue of a pagan god in your living room in order to be an idolater. If you are attempting to place any other person, project, or object in your life on the same level with God, you are probably committing a form of idolatry. If this is the case, it won't be long until God does something about it. Just as He shoved Dagon off that ledge and decapitated him in First Samuel 5:1-4, God will do something radical to get your attention! *He will teach you that He is not willing to share His position of Lordship in your life with anything or anyone else!*

Make sure that Jesus remains the primary focus of your life. God isn't against you possessing any of the things mentioned above —family, spouse, parents, children, friends, job, vision, profession, possessions, school, church activities, or personal talents — but God *is* against any of those things possessing *you*!

Jesus promised that if you would seek the Kingdom of God first, God will make sure you have all those other things (Matthew 6:33). Therefore, refuse to allow your flesh to take you down the road of self-worship, the worship of family, or the worship of material things to such an extent that you commit the act of idolatry.

Witchcraft:

Now let's turn to the subject of "witchcraft." Paul lists this next as one of the works of the flesh. The word "witchcraft" is from the Greek word *pharmakeia,* the Greek word for *medicines or drugs that inhibit a person's personality or change his behavior.* We would call these *mind-altering drugs.* The

Greek word *pharmakeia* is where we get the words *pharmaceutical drugs* or the word *pharmacy.* This word was used in connection with *sorcery, magic,* or *witchcraft.* But *why* was this word used in connection with witchcraft, and why would Paul use this word to depict the works of the flesh?

When the Church of Jesus Christ was being established in the first century, paganism ruled the Roman Empire. These were dark, demonic, pagan religions, of which one prominent feature was the use of drugs to alter the state of one's mind.

Heathen worshipers would come to the pagan temples to find relief from their sicknesses, mental stresses, or a myriad of other personal problems. Rather than confront the real needs of the heathen worshipers and identify real solutions for their problems, the priests of these pagan religions poured hallucinogenic drugs into vials of wine, stirred it all together, and then gave the mixture to the worshipers to drink. After the recipients were medicated and under the influence of these mind-altering drugs, the priests would send them home, telling them that they would feel better. However, once the drug wore off, the worshipers still found themselves facing the same or even worse problems.

The only way these seekers found relief from their problems was to return again and again to the pagan temples for more doses of drugs. The drugs gave the people temporary relief but offered no permanent solution. The priests were powerless to heal and incapable of solving anyone's problems. All they could do was keep dousing the worshipers with more drugs, thus temporarily altering the state of their minds and giving them a brief respite from their problems and pain. These priests were charlatans who tried to literally hypnotize people into believing their problems had gone away. But the truth is, they never dealt with the root of the problems and therefore did nothing but prolong the pain of those they pretended to help.

How does this apply to you and me today, since people in our modern-day society no longer go to pagan temples to worship? The flesh behaves the same way the pagan priests behaved in the illustration above. It doesn't know how to fix itself or anyone else. In fact, the flesh doesn't even *want* to be fixed. The flesh will try to convince a person to ignore his problem, to hide it with some superficial covering, or to drink alcohol and take drugs to make himself feel better. The alcohol and drugs may give that person a brief hiatus from reality, but when their effects wear off, he will still have the same problems to deal with that he had before.

People who refuse to look at themselves and find out what needs to change often develop chemical dependencies in their efforts to avoid seeing the truth. You see, the flesh hates confrontation. It doesn't want to look into the mirror to see the truth. If the flesh is confronted and forced to look squarely at itself, it will have to acknowledge the real problem. Rather than look the facts squarely in the face, the flesh tries to run, to hide, to sleep, to consume itself with recreational activities — anything to stay busy, to keep from slowing down long enough to think about vital issues. In other words, flesh would rather try to learn how to cope then to be crucified and changed!

I am not giving you medical advice. If your doctor has prescribed medication for you, be faithful to take your medication. However, I *am* giving you spiritual advice. Don't let your flesh tell you that you can keep covering up your problems with temporary solutions. Those temporary solutions will eventually wear off or run out, and when they do, the same ol' you will resurface again.

What will you do then? Are you going to be like the heathen worshiper who keeps running from place to place, trying to find another temporary solution? Or are you going to let the Spirit of God deal with you and change you forever?

The Holy Spirit wants to identify the root of your problem and rip that ugly thing clear out of your soul. He wants to bring *permanent change* to your life. But for you to receive this soul-cleansing work of God, you will have to make your flesh shut up and move out of the way. And after you tell your flesh to be silent, then you'll have to allow God to speak truthfully to you. This will demand that you spend time looking into the mirror of God's Word so you can see what is wrong and what needs to be changed.

If you're willing to do all this, God's Spirit will set you free. Yes, your flesh will scream in pain; but when it does, just take authority over it and tell it to be silent. It is screaming because it knows that it is losing the power it has always exercised in your life!

So for our purposes in today's world, the word "witchcraft," from the Greek word *pharmakeia*, would refer to *the flesh's attempts to avoid being confronted and changed.* In fact, the flesh would rather be told a lie than confronted with the truth! It wants someone to stroke it and to assure it, *"You don't need to change! Here, let me make you feel better! Just ignore those wrong things in your life, because if you ignore them long enough, they will somehow go away!"* Doesn't that sound just like someone on drugs?

Friend, it's time for you to quit playing these games and to let the Spirit of God really deal with you. If you've allowed your flesh to keep you on the run from your problems, or if you have committed idolatry by worshiping something or someone else more than Jesus Christ, today is the day for you to stop what you are doing and get your heart right with God. *Don't you think that right now would be a good time to do this?*

MY PRAYER FOR TODAY

Lord, I want to walk in the Spirit and to mortify the deeds of the flesh! I don't want the flesh to have the superior role in my life that it has had in the past. I know that if Your Spirit empowers me, I can say no to the flesh and to its demands to control my life. I am tired of struggling with the same old sins again and again. So right now I am asking You to help me see the truth about what needs to change in my life. Once I see the problem, give me the courage to tell that work of the flesh that it is going to die. Then help me to fully embrace the new life You are wanting to release inside me!

I pray this in Jesus' name!

MY CONFESSION FOR TODAY

I boldly declare that I am no longer dominated by the flesh; instead, I walk in the power of the Holy Spirit. There is therefore no condemnation for me! I am careful to read my Bible and to hear the truths that the Holy Spirit wants to show me. When I become aware of areas that need to be changed, I quickly ask Jesus to release His power to transform me. Instead of running from the truth, I run to the Cross to find permanent solutions for the problems I confront along the way.

I declare this by faith in Jesus' name!

QUESTIONS FOR YOU TO CONSIDER

1. Is there anything in your life that you worship more than Jesus? Don't lie to yourself about this, because Jesus knows the truth anyway. Why don't you take

a few minutes to ask the Lord to show you anything in your life that you worship more than you worship Him?

2. Have you ever known a person who refused to see the truth about himself? Instead of facing the truth and embracing change, did this person run from place to place or from person to person, trying to find assurance that he was "okay" and didn't need to change?

3. If that person is you, what are you going to do about it now that you know your flesh is causing you to run all over the place in order to avoid the truth that can set you free?

JULY 17

Hatred, Variance, Emulations, Wrath

> Now the works of the flesh are manifest, which are these;
> Adultery, fornication, uncleanness, lasciviousness,
> Idolatry, witchcraft, hatred,
> variance, emulations, wrath....
> — Galatians 5:19,20

I once heard our six-year-old son tell his nine-year-old brother, "I hate you!"

I quickly went to my son and asked him, "What did you say to your brother?"

He firmly told me, "I hate him!"

I didn't know what my older son had done to provoke this reaction, but I knew I had a responsibility to teach our sons this type of language was not acceptable in our home. I took our six-year-old into the bathroom, pulled out a bar of soap, and said, "Son, in our house, we don't use language like you just spoke to your brother. Your mouth has said some pretty ugly words, so it's time to give your mouth a bath! We're going to wash out your mouth with soap!"

Taking a bar of soap, I inserted it into his mouth, pushed it this way and that, until I knew his mouth was full of a soapy taste. Then I pulled it out and told him to spit into the sink.

My son exclaimed, "Daddy, that soap tastes so bad!"

I answered, "Yes, it tastes just as awful as those ugly words you spoke to your brother!"

Our two other sons stood outside the bathroom watching as their middle brother spit bubbles out of his mouth. I could visibly see they were inwardly resolving that they would *never* say the words "I hate you!" As far as I can determine, that was the last time those words were ever spoken in our home!

Hatred:

When Paul wrote Galatians 5:19-21, he included "hate" in his villainous list of the works of the flesh. In Greek, this word "hate" is from the word *echthra*. This word expresses the idea of *an intense hostility that one feels toward someone else*. It is often used to picture *enemies in a military conflict*. In the New Testament, it primarily denotes *a personal enemy*.

This is the very word used in Luke 23:12 to depict *the animosity, hostility, and hatred* that existed between Herod Antipas and Pilate before they became friends at the time of Jesus' trial and crucifixion. Prior to that moment, they hated each other. To say they were enemies is not even sufficient to express the deep animosity they felt for each other. They were bitter, sour, hardened enemies who despised one another — and all of this is expressed in the Greek word *echthra.*

This word *echthra* pictures *people who cannot get along with each other.* They have deep issues with each other, holding resentments, grievances, complaints, and grudges that go way back in time and have very deep roots. Something occurred along the way that caused one or both of them to be offended. Instead of letting go of the offense, they became divided, hostile, and fiercely opposed to each other. Now they are antagonistic, aggressive, and harsh. *They hate each other.* They have a grudge and are determined to hold on to it. *Doesn't that sound just like the flesh?*

If you have hatred in your heart, the Spirit of God wants you to forgive and release your offender. I realize your flesh wants your offender to feel bad, to emotionally suffer, to be paid back for his actions. Even if your flesh does finally rally around to offer a very weak version of forgiveness, it will probably still try to inflict a little punishment on your offender. You see, that is what the flesh produces! That is why it must be crucified! If you will pull the plug on the flesh and walk in the Spirit, it won't be long until that hostility and animosity is replaced with love, joy, peace, and longsuffering!

Variance:

Paul next lists "variance" as one of the works of the flesh. This old English word is the Greek word *eris,* which was used in a political context to describe *political parties that had different platforms or agendas.* For this reason, some newer translations of the New Testament translate it as a *party spirit.*

In a democratic system, people tend to align themselves politically with people of like opinions. Once they congregate, discuss the issues, and concur about their political views, they then proceed to build a platform from which they can promote their own political agenda. Once the agenda is decided upon and the competition has begun, the fighting can be fierce.

As you are well aware, political races can become very ugly. Often nasty words are spoken. False representations are sometimes publicized by opponents who wish to discredit their contenders. Lies are often told and repeated as facts. As unfortunate as this behavior is for people who are running for public office, it has been this way since ancient Greek and Roman times, and it will continue to be this way because this is the nature of the flesh!

When Paul writes to us, he uses this word *eris* to depict how flesh erupts to divide families, destroy relationships, ruin churches, and pull apart people who once stood side by side. Those who have been offended are drawn like a magnet to others who have been offended or who feel hurt. Once they discuss their feelings and realize they have similar stories or opinions, it isn't too long before they start thinking they are right and everyone else is wrong! That's when they begin the process of building their own platform from which they can divide and promote their own agenda!

The apartment where my family lives in Moscow was vacant for a very long time because the family who owned it got into a terrible family fight about how the apartment should be rented, how much they should charge for rent, what should be done with the rent money, and so on. The family members who were once so close to each other all took sides in the bitter fight, and the quarrel finally divided the family in half! Both sides had their own view and were not willing to compromise. This horrible attitude is exactly what Paul was talking about when he used the word *eris* in Galatians 5:20.

This case may sound extreme, but it happens all the time in families, churches, and businesses. The word *eris* ("variance") depicts *a bitterly mean spirit that is so consumed with its own self-interests and self-ambitions that it would rather split and divide than to admit it is wrong or give an inch to an opponent!* This is exactly why church splits occur and families frequently dissolve. Most of the issues that bring such division aren't even that important. But the flesh simply hates to surrender or compromise — to admit it is wrong or to let someone else be right. The flesh would rather blow issues all out of proportion and wreak havoc than to let someone else have his way! *Don't allow this work of the flesh to operate in you!*

Emulations:

Paul goes on to state that "emulations" is also a work of the flesh. This word "emulations" is not used much in our contemporary world, so what does it mean?

The word "emulations" comes from the Greek word *zelos,* which often denotes *enthusiasm, fervor, passion, devotion,* or *an eagerness to achieve something.* It is where we get the word *zeal.* In a negative sense, it depicts *a person who is upset because someone else achieved more or received more.* This person is therefore *jealous, envious, resentful, and filled with ill will for that other person who got what he wanted.* As a result of not getting what he desired, he is *irritated, infuriated, irate, annoyed, provoked, and fuming* that the other person did get it! In short, you could say that this person is really *incensed* and *ticked off!* He can't rejoice with the other person because he is so *jealous.*

A perfect example of the negative aspect of the word *zelos* is found in Acts 7:9, where it depicts the *jealousy* that Joseph's brothers felt for him. It says, "And the patriarchs, [Joseph's brothers] moved with envy, sold Joseph into Egypt...." The words "moved with envy" are from the word *zelos.* This indicates that the brothers were *incensed* with Joseph. After seeing him richly rewarded over and over again by his father, they couldn't bear it any longer. Rather than rejoice that their younger brother was so loved, they cringed every time Joseph received a blessing. Eventually, they were filled with so much *ill will* toward Joseph and were so overcome by their *jealousy* that they sold him into slavery.

It is very important to note that Act 7:9 says they were "moved with envy." This word *zelos —* envy or jealousy — is such a strong force that it will move you to action when it starts to operate in you. Unfortunately, it will usually move you to do things that are hurtful or that you will later regret. So don't allow "emulations" or jealousy to work inside you! It is a work of the flesh that brings great hurt and destruction.

Wrath:

Next, Paul lists "wrath" as a work of the flesh. The word "wrath" is the Greek word *thumos,* which is used throughout the New Testament to picture *a person who is literally boiling with anger about something.* Although the person tries to restrain this anger by shoving it down deeper into his soul, it intermittently flares up. When it does, it is like a volcano that suddenly blows its top — scorching everything within its reach as it hurls its load of deadly molten lava onto the entire surrounding landscape. *Have you ever seen someone blow his top like I'm describing to you right now?*

The Greek word *thumos* ("wrath") vividly paints the picture. People get hurt, offended, or upset. Rather than take the offense to the Cross and deal with it there, they choose instead to meditate on the perceived offense. The longer they think about it, the more upset they become. Soon they are inwardly boiling. They know if they don't do something quick to restrain themselves, they are going to say or do something really ugly — so they shove it back down deep inside in an attempt to keep it under control. But if those angry emotions were never properly dealt with in the first place, one day something will happen that triggers their release.

Perhaps this has happened to you. If so, you may think those vile emotions are gone, but if you never let the Lord really deal with them or the situation that created them, they are still lying dormant inside you, just waiting for the right moment to be released. Finally, when that person who made you angry in the first place does something to make you angry again, it will be like someone opens a door on the inside of you, releasing a flood of vile and rank emotions that immediately rise to the surface! That's when you'll come unglued, saying things you later regret and speaking in tones you should never use!

The word *thumos* perfectly illustrates the way the flesh tries to deal with problems. Rather than confront the problem head-on when it happens, the flesh says, "Just shove it down deep, and keep it to yourself!" The problem is, when you shove down unresolved issues, they just keep boiling and boiling deep inside. You may think that the matter is over, but the truth is, those issues are simmering and waiting for the moment of eruption. Even though the flesh is attempting to avoid confrontation, in the end its eruption creates a confrontation more scorching and hurtful than ever. It would have been far better to deal with the issue when it first happened!

I know that confronting people and problems can be challenging, but the mature path is to take care of the problems when they first occur. It is the route of the flesh to delay issues and then to erupt in madness.

If any of the works of the flesh called *hatred, variance, emulations,* or *wrath* are trying to operate in your life, it is time for you to put an end to these strongholds right now. Go to the Lord and confess that you have allowed these fleshly works to operate in your life. Ask Him to forgive you; then ask Him to fill you with the power and fortitude you need to say no to these ungodly attitudes. *With God's help, you can allow the Holy Spirit to produce His godly fruit inside you!*

MY PRAYER FOR TODAY

Lord, I am surrendering my attitudes to You today. Hatred, variance, emulations, and wrath are so hurtful to my heart and destructive to my relationships. I don't want them to be a part of me any longer. I turn from these attitudes, Lord. I repent for allowing them to have any place in my life. I confess that they are wrong and are grievous both in Your sight and to my spirit. I ask You to give me the strength I need to crucify these works of the flesh and to let the life of Jesus flow through me!

I pray this in Jesus' name!

MY CONFESSION FOR TODAY

I confess that hatred, variance, emulations, and wrath have no place inside me. God's Spirit dwells in me and helps me keep these fleshly attitudes out of my heart so I can stay free. I am filled with love; I am thrilled when other people get blessed; and I never give way to rage or wrath. It simply has no place in me. Every day I am becoming more filled and controlled by the Spirit of God!

I declare this by faith in Jesus' name!

QUESTIONS FOR YOU TO CONSIDER

1. Have you ever had one of those moments when you erupted and said hurtful things that you later regretted? Were you shocked that such ugly things could

proceed from your mouth? What was the immediate result of this behavior? Did it help the situation or make it worse?

2. When this occurred, what did you do to let people know you were sorry for your actions? If you did nothing to let them know you were sorry, what do you think you should have done? If someone did that to you, what would you expect that person to do or say to make it right with you?

3. Have you ever been a part of a church split? If yes, what was the reason for the division?

JULY 18

❧

Strife, Seditions, Heresies

Now the works of the flesh are manifest, which are these;
Adultery, fornication, uncleanness, lasciviousness,
Idolatry, witchcraft, hatred, variance, emulations,
wrath, strife, seditions, heresies.
— Galatians 5:19,20

I pray that God is opening your eyes to see the works of the flesh from a new perspective. This is clearly very important; otherwise, the Holy Spirit wouldn't have included this list in the New Testament. Each word selected by the Holy Spirit to depict the works of the flesh is pungent and powerful. There is no room for misunderstanding. The Spirit of God wants us to be able to identify the works of the flesh so we can prohibit their activity in our lives.

Strife:

As Paul continues listing the works of the flesh, he next moves to the subject of "strife." The word "strife" comes from the Greek word *eritheia*. It is very similar to the word *eris*, which is translated "variance" in the *King James Version* and was discussed in yesterday's *Sparkling Gem*.

The word *eritheia* describes a *self-seeking ambition that is more concerned about itself and the fulfillment of its own wants, desires, and pleasures than it is in meeting the same needs in others.* When *eritheia* is working in someone's life, it means that taking care of himself and getting what he wants is that person's principal concern. In fact, he is so bent on getting what he wants that he is willing to do anything, say anything, and sacrifice any standard, rules, or relationship to achieve his goals. It is *a selfish, self-focused attitude* that is engrossed with its own desires and ambitions. *It is so self-consumed that it is blinded to the desires or ambitions of other people.*

When someone has this attitude, he is bound to hurt and to offend people. It makes me think of one pastor I know in the former Soviet Union. This pastor is so committed to his own cause that he can't see anything but himself. If someone mentions a church other than his own, he immediately turns the conversation back to his own church because he can't tolerate anyone talking about anything but his own work. This characteristic of his gives the impression of *conceit*. In fact, I know of no other pastor in the city where he lives who can get along with him! Other pastors have spent years trying to build bridges to this pastor, only to have him turn around and do something hurtful and offensive to everyone who has tried to befriend him. Simply put, this man's flesh is out of control and has devastated many people.

If you hear yourself talking nonstop about your own projects, dreams, and aspirations, but you never stop to inquire about anyone else's, maybe you need to get into the Presence of God and let Him speak to you about *selfishness* in your life. Do the people in your life know all about you, but you know nothing about them? If your answer is yes, what does this tell you about your attitude toward other people? Are you mindful of others? Do you think about ways you can be a blessing to them, or do you always think of how others can be a blessing to you?

It is simply the nature of carnal flesh to be *self-consumed.* Don't let this be you! God's Spirit is inside you — and if you will yield to the Holy Spirit, He will make you compassionate and caring about the needs of others. From time to time, you will have to deliberately speak to the carnal nature and tell it to be still so the life of Jesus can flow up from your spirit to recognize and then meet the needs of those around you.

Seditions:

The word "seditions" is derived from the Greek word *dichostasia,* which is a compound of the words *dicha* and *stasis.* The word *dicha* means *apart,* as in a *separation,* and the word *stasis* means *to stand* or *to rebel.* When these are compounded into one word, it means *to stand apart, as one who rebels and steps away from someone to whom he should have been loyal.* Thus, the word "sedition" gives the impression of disloyalty.

The word *statis* is used in Matthew, Mark, and Luke to describe the insurrection that Barabbas had led in the city of Jerusalem. His rebellious deeds deemed him a terrible and notorious criminal in the mind of the Roman authorities. He had led an insurrection, *a sedition* — an act of *dichostasia.* Barabbas defied the powers, rejected their authority, and stepped away from their rule, taking other rebels with him as he went his own way. As often happens when seditious flesh has its way, Barabbas and his companions eventually united all the rebels in the city together in an attempt to overthrow the government. It was the ultimate act of *defiance* or *disloyalty* to an established authority.

Paul lists "sedition" as one of the works of the flesh. It is important for you to know that the flesh hates rules, regulations, and any order that is imposed upon it. This is why children rebel against parents, wives rebel against their husbands, churches rebel against pastors, and people in general rebel against God. Defiance and rebellion to authority is the source of most world wars, civil wars, and regional conflicts. Ninety-nine percent of the world's conflicts are due to flesh that refuses to be told what to do and thus rises up *to defy* the authority or the rules it doesn't want to accept!

This is even the reason a beautiful little baby throws his food across the room! When a baby acts like that, it makes one wonder how in the world such an innocent-looking child could behave so badly. But the reason a young child can act so defiantly is that he is wrapped in flesh — and one of the works of the flesh is to be *rebellious* and *defiant*! The flesh simply doesn't want to be told what to do!

So when you find your flesh rising up in anger because your boss, your parent, or your pastor acts like he or she has authority in your life, it's time for you to settle down and mortify the deeds of your flesh! Don't give in to your carnal desires by stepping away from your God-appointed leader. If you do, you may find yourself in a company of rebels like Barabbas, who got so caught up in his rebellion that he tried to lead an overthrow in the city of Jerusalem. Your loyalty is important; your disloyalty is hurtful and destructive. *Stick close to those whom God has called to be your leaders, and be faithful!*

Heresies:

"Heresies" is next in Paul's list of the works of the flesh. This comes from the Greek word *hairesis*. In the New Testament, it has a meaning that is unique and used differently than in secular literature. It carries the idea of *a person or group of people who are sectarian.* The word "sectarian" refers to *a group of people who adhere to the same doctrine or who ardently follow the same leader.* The adherents of a sect are usually limited in their scope and closed to outsiders, staying primarily to themselves. In New Testament times, these groups were considered to be *unauthorized* because they were not submitted to the authority of the church leadership.

In today's contemporary language, we might label these sectarian groups "cliques" — referring to groups of people who believe or conduct themselves as if they are *exclusive.* Such groups often function in secret to keep their dealings, associations, contacts, and interactions unknown to others. They give the impression that they are better or more enlightened than those outside the group or that they have a special assignment that no one else can know about. This is the reason they keep outsiders on the outside and allow so few to have an inside peek at their fellowship, meetings, conversations, or activities.

Although the word *hairesis* can describe different schools of thought, branches, or arms of a movement, it primarily suggests *a division, a faction,* or as noted, an *unauthorized group.* Because this type of group was viewed to be so disruptive to the Early Church and because it didn't fall under the spiritual covering of church leadership, the apostle Paul viewed it to be *heretical* — which, in this sense, meant *divisive.* The adherents usually followed a leader who was not the pastor but who acted as if he had spiritual authority, even though authority had never been given to him by the church leadership. This leader usually demanded the highest commitment from group members, even demanding that his followers' commitment to himself and to the group be greater than their commitment to the overall church body.

Let's face it — the flesh delights in deceiving itself into believing that it is better, more spiritual, or more enlightened than anyone else. It thrives on being puffed up, prideful, and boastful. It enjoys thinking too highly of itself. It adores being selfish, self-consumed, and self-focused, and it takes pleasure in caring for its own selfish interests. And if allowed to do so, flesh will separate into a faction, a division, or a sect. It will gravitate to others whose flesh also wants to believe they are better than others. When all that flesh gets together in one place, they will inevitably form a super-elite clique inside the church that is so tight no one else will be able to get in it — including the pastor!

Paul was against *spiritual elitism* and even forbade it! He even included it in his villainous list of the works of the flesh in Galatians 5:19-21.

Never lose sight of the fact that you are a part of the whole Body of Christ. God has not given you or anyone else a revelation or truth so special that it is only for a handful. You are a member of the Body of Christ, so act like it! Don't let your flesh deceive you into thinking that you are a member of the higher spiritual class! *Tell your flesh to come back down to reality and get busy loving and serving other brothers and sisters in the local church!*

MY PRAYER FOR TODAY

Lord, I don't want these works of the flesh to be active in my life! I stand against them in Jesus' name, and I yearn for the Holy Spirit to produce His divine fruit in me. Please help me to be sensitive to Your Spirit and to the needs of others and to stay alert for those times when my flesh is trying to take me in one of these wrong directions!

I pray this in Jesus' name!

MY CONFESSION FOR TODAY

I confess that I have the mind of Jesus Christ and I think the thoughts of God! I crucify the flesh; I mortify its deeds; and I release the resurrection life of Jesus Christ in me! Although I live in the flesh, it is no longer I who live, but Jesus Christ lives in me!

I declare this by faith in Jesus' name!

QUESTIONS FOR YOU TO CONSIDER

1. Do people in your life know all about you, yet you know very little about them? If your answer is yes, what does this tell you about your attitude toward other people? Do you spend much time thinking about how you can be a blessing to them, or do you always think about how others can be a blessing to you?
2. Consider again the fact that flesh hates to be told what to do and that it rises up to defy the authority figure or the rules it doesn't want to accept. Can you think of any areas of your life in which your flesh is rebelling against God-appointed authorities or rules right now?
3. Have you ever allowed your flesh to deceive you into thinking that you are a member of a higher spiritual class? Have you ever seen a group act like this in your church? If so, how did it affect you?

JULY 19

Envyings, Murders, Drunkenness, Revellings

Now the works of the flesh are manifest, which are these;
Adultery, fornication, uncleanness, lasciviousness,
Idolatry, witchcraft, hatred, variance,
emulations, wrath, strife, seditions, heresies,
Envyings, murders, drunkenness,
revellings, and such like....
— Galatians 5:19-21

When the Jewish leaders turned Jesus over to Pilate to be criminally tried in a court of law, Pilate knew they did it because they were jealous of the popularity that Jesus was gaining in the nation. Mark 15:10 says, "For he knew that the chief priests had delivered him for envy."

The word "envy" in the above verse is the Greek word *phthonos*. It depicts *a hostile feeling toward someone because that person has something — an advantage, a benefit, a position — that the other does not possess but would like to have.* The despicable feeling toward that person with a perceived advantage is so strong that the one who feels "envy" takes action to remove that person's advantage in the hope that it will pass on to him. This kind of envy is evil, sinister, and full of maliciousness.

Mark 15:10 tells us that Pilate could see the real motives of the chief priests. Pilate knew the real issue: The chief priests felt threatened and insecure because of Jesus' growing popularity. Pilate knew insecurity was driving the chief priests to demand that Jesus be charged with a criminal offense and that He be publicly declared guilty and crucified. Although the chief priests acted from a different pretense, the real issue was evident. They wanted to remove Jesus so that the publicity that had been focused on Him would shift back to the priesthood, where it had been before Jesus came on the scene. These horrible attitudes and appalling actions are communicated by the word "envy" in Mark 15:10.

Envy:

In Galatians 5:19-21, Paul included "envy" in the works of the flesh. As noted above, the word "envy" is the Greek word *phthonos*. This word implies *a deeply felt grudge because someone possesses what a person wishes was his own.* Because the person who feels envy has a chip on his shoulder, he begrudges what that other person possesses and is covetous of the person's belongings, accomplishments, relationships, or titles in life. Every time he sees that other person, he inwardly seethes about his success. He deeply resents that person's blessing and tries to figure out a way to seize it away from the person he envies in order to make it his own.

In the example given above, the chief priests were envious of the acclaim Jesus was gaining. To get rid of the competition, the chief priests therefore decided to kill Jesus. That is the way this type of envy reacts. It is so strong that it propels a person to take some kind of action — most often, some kind of evil action designed to do away with the person who has the advantage.

This may explain why the *King James Version* next mentions "murder." The problem is, the word "murder" doesn't appear in the Greek language! So we must ask, "Why did the King James translators insert the word 'murder' if it doesn't appear in the original Greek?" The only possible answer is that they perceived this "envy" to be so strong that it would even drive a person to "murder" in order to get what he wants.

There are examples in classical literature where the word *phthonos* is also used to represent *a person who uses others as stepping stones to get where he wants to be in terms of money, prestige, and power.* This is an unscrupulous person who uses and abuses people so he might grasp the things he desires.

Perhaps you've seen this work of the flesh manifested at the office, your place of employment, or even at your church. Have you ever witnessed a moment when a fellow employee or believer tried to snuggle up close to you, but you found out later that this person was only feigning friendship? In reality, he didn't want to be your friend; he just wanted to be close to you so he could befriend someone you knew. To get to that other person, he had to go through you. So he acted like your friend in order to gain his own advantage and then dropped you like a lead balloon.

Or perhaps someone acted as if he wanted to be your friend when in truth all he wanted was your job! This goes on in the secular world all the time, but it should not happen inside the church. Such behavior is hurtful, manipulative, and unkind. It wounds souls; it makes people feel like they have been abused; and it cheapens the concept of friendship. *No wonder Paul calls envy a work of the flesh!*

The next time you find yourself tempted to get envious over someone else's blessing or position, call upon the Spirit of God to help you mortify that deed of the flesh. Put it to silence by deliberately choosing to rejoice when someone else gets blessed! What you sow is exactly what you will reap. If you sow anger, resentment, and bitterness, that negative harvest will come back to you in the future. *But if you sow joy for those who have been blessed and who are ahead of you, a time will come when blessings will come back to you. Then people will rejoice with you about YOUR success!*

Drunkenness:

The word "drunkenness" is from the word *methe*, which refers to *strong drink* or to *drunkenness*. The consumption of wine *for the sake of intoxication* was common in the first century due to many pagan religions that employed wine as a part of their religious practices.

For example, the religion of Bacchos (whom the Greeks called Dionysos) was centered around *wine* and *intoxication*. In fact, Bacchos was called *the god of wine*. Once the worshipers were completely inebriated due to their consumption of wine, they threw off all restraints and fully yielded themselves to every temptation of the flesh. Nothing was off limits. Plunging themselves into the most vulgar sexual excesses and unnatural acts, the participants attempted to breach every known moral code, committing the grossest extremes of sin possible in order to experience a realm of excess never before tasted or known to man. That was the deliberate goal of this religion; hence, the participants were drawn into perverted and shameless orgies. While under the influence of wine, the people fornicated as the priests beat drums and clanged cymbals, adding to the rage, emotions, and uncontrolled passion of the moment.

Often drugs were mixed together with the wine, which caused the participants to convulse or to dance in frenzied circles. This frenzied condition was called *entheos* — a compound of the words *en* and *theos*. The word *en* means *in*, and *theos* is the word for *god*. Thus, if a person was *entheos*, he was "in the control of a god." Interestingly, this is where we get the word *enthusiasm*. It was believed that when a participant fell into one of these uncontrolled, frenzied moments, he had passed the moral barrier and was now caught in the control of a god or spirit. This *entheos* experience was the ultimate goal for those who participated in the religion of Bacchos.

The consumption of wine was a key factor in this pagan religion. But Bacchos was not the only religion that used wine. The use of wine was a widespread practice in nearly all the Greek and Roman religions. Recent archeological digs of ancient cities testify to the prevalent use of wine at that time. Great numbers of homes have been discovered with huge underground caverns designed to hold a vast supply of wine. In some of these sites, the houses were found to have openings in the floor through which a person could dip down into the massive wine supply below. The fact that this much wine was available to individual homes clearly demonstrates the major role that wine played in first-century society.

Paul knew that when flesh became absorbed with wine, a person lost his ability to think rationally, often leading to devastating excess. This is precisely why he told the Ephesian believers, "And be not drunk with wine, wherein is excess..." (Ephesians 5:18). This word "excess" is the Greek word *asotia*, which when literally translated means *one who has lost his ability to save or to spare himself*. This is a person who wastes his life, squanders his money, or desecrates his body because he is drunk and cannot think straight. Due to a mind that has been altered by excessive alcohol consumption, this person thinks irrationally, acts irresponsibly, and commits acts of excess that would normally not even be a temptation.

The principal pagan religion of Ephesus was the worship of Artemis. This was another religion that employed vast amounts of wine in its worship. The Bible provides a strong indication that although the believers in Ephesus had been redeemed and delivered from the temple of Artemis, they were allowing the consumption of wine to remain a common feature in their lives. Paul urged them to stop this practice, telling them to put aside the wine and to "be filled with the Spirit" in its place. Paul knew that once these believers were under the influence of God's Spirit, they would be *positively affected*! Under that influence, they would be so changed that they would start speaking to themselves in psalms, hymns, and spiritual songs, singing and making melody in their hearts to the Lord (Ephesians 5:19).

A drunken state suppresses the mind's ability to think correctly and releases the flesh to fully express itself. The believers in the first century were trying to walk free from the power of their flesh. The last thing they needed was to drink wine, inhibit their ability to think correctly, revive the flesh, and then do things that were sinful or damaging! *So Paul urged them to leave the wine alone!* The undisciplined consumption of wine only leads to the works of the flesh!

Revellings:

Last in his list of the works of the flesh is the word "revellings." This interesting word comes from the Greek word *komoi*, which describes a *festive procession* or *merry-making*. Most who see the word "revellings" imagine that it refers to drunkenness, street fights, or those who run from one drunken party to the next. Is this what you thought this word means? *Let's look at it and see what it really means in the original Greek!*

The word *komoi* ("revellings") describes a person who can't bear the thought of boredom and is therefore continually seeking different forms of amusement or entertainment. This person is actually afraid of being bored, so he constantly contemplates what he can do next to have fun or to be entertained. The word *komoi* can refer to a person who endlessly eats at parties or who seeks constant laughter and hilarity. Certainly there is nothing wrong with laughter; the problem with this person is that he is consumed with the need for comedy, light moments, fun, pleasure, entertainment, or constant eating. He lives for the next meal, the next restaurant, the next movie, the next vacation.

In Second Timothy 3:4, Paul prophesies that this kind of *hedonism* would be an especially prevalent problem in the last days. He wrote that in the last days, people would be "lovers of pleasures." These words come from the Greek word *philedonos*, which is a compound of the words *philos* and *hedone*. The word *philos* means *to love*, and the word *hedone* means *something that tastes sweet* or *something that is pleasant or enjoyable*. In classical Greece, it denoted *the exaltation of pleasure*, especially signified by the freedom to sexually express oneself. Any sexual expression was permissible as long as the parties involved agreed. In other words, there was no moral standard when *hedonism* ruled ancient Greece. Of the five times where the word *hedone* is used in the New Testament, it is used in a bad sense to describe *the unrestrained seeking of carnal pleasures*.

By using the word *philedonos* ("lovers of pleasures"), Paul tells us explicitly that in the last days people will be obsessed with pleasure — with eating, partying, and entertainment. They will be preoccupied with new methods to alleviate boredom. Life will become so soft and luxurious that people will overeat, be lazy, take unwarranted time off work, exist on borrowed money, and permit questionable moral behavior — all the while thinking that this is a normal, acceptable way to live.

Now do you see why Paul included "revellings" in his list of the works of the flesh in Galatians 5:19-21? The flesh wants to escape responsibility, thrive on fun, and avoid the seriousness of life. If you let your flesh lead you, it will waste your time, your talents, and your energies on things that are not eternal. You'll spend all your time watching television, going to movies, and eating at restaurants — and in the end, you'll have nothing to show for it but tons of credit card debt. One day you'll hold your credit card bills in your hands and realize that you are head over heels in debt because of a few fleeting moments of pleasure. *Were all those fleshly pursuits really worth the slavery to debt that you now have to live with for the next couple of years?*

You see, that is what the flesh wants to do to you. It says, *"Come on, it will feel so good if you do this. It's true that you probably shouldn't, but just one more time won't hurt. Besides, what else do you have to do? There's nothing to do at home!"*

The truth is, there is plenty to do at home! You could be reading your Bible; playing with your children; developing your relationship with your brothers and sisters; visiting your neighbors; volunteering to serve in some area of your church; mowing your yard; learning to cook; cleaning the garage; or reading a book and developing your mind. There is a host of things you could do that would be healthy for you and your family!

So the next time your flesh says *"There's nothing to do! It's so boring!"* — just take a look inside your garage; check the condition of your backyard; or peek into your clothes closet. I think you'll see that there is plenty for you to do to keep from being bored! Your flesh may recoil from doing these things, but afterward you'll feel like a champion! You'll feel so good that you didn't go into more debt for more stuff you don't need. You'll be so thankful you didn't waste your precious time doing things that don't matter. And you'll feel so victorious for accomplishing something that has needed your attention for a very long time! *Somebody say, "Amen!"*

MY PRAYER FOR TODAY

Lord, help me the next time I am tempted to get envious over someone else's blessing or position. Help me to keep my head on straight and not to allow things in my life that will recharge my flesh and stir me up to do things that are sinful or wrong. Forgive me for thinking that I constantly have to be entertained. I'm so sorry that I've wasted so much of my time and thrown away so much money on things that don't matter. I don't want to be dominated by my flesh anymore. Today I am calling on You to help me break away from my past patterns so I can start on a new and higher path!

I pray this in Jesus' name!

MY CONFESSION FOR TODAY

I confess that I am not dominated by the flesh but by the Spirit of God. I am completely committed to the Lordship of Jesus Christ and to doing what pleases Him most with my life. I refuse to let my flesh lead me astray, and I have decided to take up my cross and follow wherever Jesus leads me. I am serious about life; I am serious about doing what God wants me to do; and I am a good steward of my time, resources, and talents.

I declare this by faith in Jesus' name!

QUESTIONS FOR YOU TO CONSIDER

1. The next time you feel tempted to get envious over someone else's blessing or position, what are you going to do about it? Remember — what you sow is exactly what you will reap!
2. What changes do you need to make in your life to stop reactivating and recharging the power of your flesh? Is there any habit, hobby, preoccupation, or relationship you have that encourages you to think or to act wrong?
3. The next time your flesh says, *"There's nothing to do! It's so boring!"* what are you going to do? Will you grab a newspaper so you can see what is being shown at the local movie theater, or will you decide to do something productive and edifying?

JULY 20

❧

Do You Practice Sin in Your Life?

Envyings, murders, drunkenness, revellings,
and such like: of the which I tell you before,
as I have also told you in time past,
that they which do such things
shall not inherit the kingdom of God.
— Galatians 5:21

When I was young in the Lord and read the list in Galatians 5:19-21 of the works of the flesh, I was afterward afraid that I wouldn't be admitted into the Kingdom of God if I ever unintentionally slipped into one of these fleshly works. That's what I thought Paul meant when he said, "…they which do such things shall not inherit the kingdom of God." I wondered, *Would an occasional, unintentional act of the flesh keep me or someone else out of God's Kingdom? What does it mean when it says, "they which do such things"? If I fall into one of these vices once, does that mean it's all over for me?*

So when I first started to learn New Testament Greek, one of my top priorities was to study Galatians 5:21 to see exactly what the original Greek was saying. What I discovered brought great relief to my mind, and I believe it will bring assurance to your heart and mind as well.

When Paul says, "…They which do such things shall not inherit the kingdom of God," he uses the word "do," from the Greek word *prasso*, which means *to practice*. Had he used the Greek word *poieo*, which means *to do*, it would have referred to *an occasional act*, but Paul carefully chose to use the word *prasso*, which conclusively communicates the idea of *something that is done repeatedly or habitually*. These are the actions of *a person who has put these things into practice in his life, performing them as a matter of routine*. These actions are *his ritual, his norm, his pattern of life*. Thus, the verse could be translated, "…*Those who put these things into practice in their lives and do these things routinely as a manner of lifestyle shall not inherit the Kingdom of God.*"

For a review, let's look quickly at the following list of the works of the flesh that are not to be routinely practiced or habitually performed:

✦ **Adultery:** The Greek word *porneia* describes any sexual relationship that occurs outside the sanctified boundaries of marriage. (*See* July 15.)
✦ **Uncleanness:** The Greek word for "uncleanness" refers to lewd or unclean thoughts that eventually produce lewd or unclean actions. It strongly suggests that these actions begin in the mind as unclean thoughts before they manifest as unclean deeds. (*See* July 15.)
✦ **Lasciviousness:** This word in the Greek text describes excess, but it primarily refers to the excessive consumption of food or wild, undisciplined living that is especially marked by unbridled sex. (*See* July 15.)
✦ **Idolatry:** The Greek word *eidololatria* depicts the worship of idols, or simply put, "idolatry." The act of idolatry transpires when an individual gives his complete, undivided attention, devotion, passion, love, or commitment to a person, project, or object other than God. When something other than God takes first place in a person's mind, he has entered, at least to a measure, into the sin of idolatry. (*See* July 16.)

✦ **Witchcraft:** The word "witchcraft" is from the Greek word *pharmakeia*, the Greek word for medicines or drugs that inhibit a person's personality or change his behavior. We would call these mind-altering drugs. The Greek word *pharmakeia* is where we get the words *pharmaceutical drugs* or the word *pharmacy*. This word was used in connection with sorcery, magic, or witchcraft. However, for our purposes in today's world, the word "witchcraft" describes the flesh's attempts to avoid being confronted and changed. (*See* July 16.)

✦ **Hatred:** The Greek word *echthra* pictures people who cannot get along with each other. They have deep issues with each other, holding resentments, grievances, complaints, and grudges that go way back in time and have very deep roots. Something occurred along the way that caused one or both of them to be offended. Instead of letting it go, they are divided, hostile, and fiercely opposed to each other. They are antagonistic, aggressive, and harsh. They hate each other. They have a grudge and are determined to hold on to their offense. (*See* July 17.)

✦ **Variance:** The Greek word *eris* depicts a bitterly mean spirit that is so consumed with its own self-interests and self-ambitions that it would rather split and divide than to admit it is wrong or to give an inch to an opponent! This is exactly why churches end up divided and families frequently dissolve. Most of the issues that bring such division are not that important. Nevertheless, division occurs because the flesh simply hates to surrender, to admit that it's wrong, to let someone else be right, or to compromise. Flesh would rather blow issues all out of proportion and wreak havoc than to let someone else have his way! (*See* July 17.)

✦ **Emulations:** The Greek word *zelos* is used in a negative sense to depict a person who is upset because someone else achieved more or received more; therefore, the first person is jealous, envious, resentful, and filled with ill will for that other person who received the blessing that *he* wanted. As a result of not getting what he desired, this first person is irritated, infuriated, irate, annoyed, provoked, and fuming that the other person did get it! In short, you could say that this person is really incensed and ticked off! (*See* July 17.)

✦ **Wrath:** The Greek word *thumos* is used throughout the New Testament to picture a person who is literally boiling with anger about something. Although the person tries to restrain this anger by shoving it down deeper into his soul, it intermittently flares up. When that happens, this person is like a volcano that suddenly blows its top, scorching everything within its reach as it hurls its load of deadly molten lava onto the entire surrounding landscape! (*See* July 17.)

✦ **Strife:** The word *eritheia* describes a self-seeking ambition that is more concerned about itself and the fulfillment of its own wants, desires, and pleasures than it is in meeting the same needs in others. When *eritheia* is working in someone's life, it means that a person's principal concern is to take care of himself and to get what he wants. He is so bent on getting what he wants that he is willing to do anything, say anything, or sacrifice any standard, rule, or relationship to achieve his goals. Because this self-consumed, self-focused attitude is engrossed with its own desires and ambitions, it is blinded to the desires and ambitions of other people. (*See* July 18.)

✦ **Seditions:** The Greek word *dichostasia* means to stand apart, as one who rebels and steps away from someone to whom he should have been loyal. Thus, the word "sedition" gives the impression of disloyalty. It is the ultimate act of defiance or disloyalty to an established authority. (*See* July 18.)

✦ **Heresies:** The Greek word *hairesis* carries the idea of a group of people who adhere to the same doctrine or who ardently follow the same leader and are sectarian. The adherents of a sect are usually limited in their scope and closed to outsiders, staying primarily to themselves. In New Testament times, these groups were considered to be unauthorized because they were not submitted to the authority of the church leadership. In today's contemporary language, we would call them "cliques" — a group of people who believe or conduct themselves as if they are exclusive. (*See* July 18.)

✦ **Envyings:** The Greek word *phthonos* implies a deeply felt grudge because someone possesses what a person wishes was his own. Because this person has a chip on his shoulder, he begrudges what the other person possesses and is covetous of that person's belongings, accomplishments, relationships, or titles in life. Every time he sees that other person, he inwardly seethes about his success. He deeply resents that person's blessing and tries to figure out a way to seize it away from the person he envies in order to make it his own. (*See* July 19.)

✦ **Drunkenness:** The Greek word *methe* refers to strong drink or to drunkenness. The consumption of wine *for the sake of intoxication* was common in the first century due to many pagan religions that employed wine as a part of their religious practices. A drunken state suppresses the mind's ability to think correctly and releases the flesh to fully express itself. The believers in the first century were trying to walk free from the power of their flesh. The *last* thing they needed was to drink wine, inhibit their ability to think correctly, revive the flesh, and then do things that were sinful or damaging! This is why Paul urged them to leave the wine alone! (*See* July 19.)

✦ **Revellings:** The Greek word *komoi* describes a person who can't bear the thought of boredom and therefore constantly seeks forms of amusement or entertainment. This person is actually afraid of being bored, so he constantly contemplates what he can do next to have fun or to be entertained. The word *komoi* can refer to a person who endlessly eats at parties or who seeks constant laughter and hilarity. Although there is nothing wrong with laughter, this person is consumed with the need for comedy, light moments, fun, pleasure, entertainment, or constant eating. He lives for the next meal, the next restaurant, the next movie, the next vacation. (*See* July 19.)

✦ **And such like:** Paul ends this list with this Greek phrase, which alerts us to the fact that this list of the works of the flesh is *not* comprehensive; it is *just the beginning* of the works of the flesh! Many more examples of works of the flesh could be added to this list, but Paul uses these as examples of how the flesh behaves, ending the list once he has sufficiently made the point to his readers.

Remember, when Paul wrote, "...They which do such things shall not inherit the kingdom of God," he used a Greek tense that categorically means he is talking about those who perform these things as a manner of lifestyle or who are habitually controlled by fleshly thoughts or deeds. To such people, the works of the flesh are their ritual, their norm, their pattern of life. So I must ask you:

✦ Do you routinely commit adultery?
✦ Do you routinely live in fornication?
✦ Do you routinely allow yourself to think unclean thoughts?
✦ Do you routinely overindulge in sexual sins or gluttony?
✦ Do you routinely give your heart and devotion in idolatry to other things besides Jesus?
✦ Do you routinely run from the truth, like those who participated in witchcraft?

✦ Do you routinely allow hatred to thrive inside your heart and soul?

✦ Do you routinely exhibit a bitterly mean spirit that is consumed with its own self-interests?

✦ Do you routinely permit yourself to be jealous, resentful, and envious of what others possess?

✦ Do you routinely lose your temper, fly into a rage, and give way to destructive outbursts?

✦ Are you routinely so self-consumed that you are blinded to the desires or needs of others?

✦ Do you routinely rebel and live in defiance to authorities or show yourself to be disloyal?

✦ Do you routinely act as if you and your exclusive "clique" are superior to other people?

✦ Do you routinely begrudge other people's belongings, accomplishments, relationships, or titles in life?

✦ Do you routinely and deliberately allow your flesh to freely follow its temptations?

✦ Do you routinely live for the next moment of fleshly pleasure?

If you routinely do these things, you need to be very concerned about whether or not you are genuinely a child of God.

As you will see in tomorrow's *Sparkling Gem,* it is impossible for a real believer to continue habitually in sin. If these works of the flesh are the norm, the pattern, the routine of a person's life, it may be an indication that he was never born again — thus providing the reason he will not inherit the Kingdom of God.

If you occasionally struggle with sin, then go to God and allow Him to show you how He sees your sin. Get a revelation of what sin is — how grievous it is to the heart of God and how damaging it is to your own soul. Then ask Him to forgive you and to cleanse you — and He will! But if you routinely do many of these things as a manner of lifestyle, I believe you need to go to God and ask Him to tell you the truth about your spiritual status! *You cannot afford to make a mistake about this eternal question!*

MY PRAYER FOR TODAY

Lord, I thank You for saving me by the power of God. Help me put aside the works of the flesh once and for all. Please teach me to walk in the Spirit. I know that You have designed a powerful life for me, and I want to enter into that life in all its fullness. My heart's desire is to know You better and to walk with You, so today I am asking that Your Spirit propel me forward into this newer and higher way of living!

I pray this in Jesus' name!

MY CONFESSION FOR TODAY

I confess that I do NOT routinely perform the works of the flesh. As a genuine child of God, I live to please my Heavenly Father, and I am repulsed by sin when it tries to operate in my life. My spirit is sensitive to God, and my heart is tender to the voice of the Holy Spirit. I hate sin and its consequences, and I do everything I can to live and to stay in the Presence of God!

I declare this by faith in Jesus' name!

1. Are any of the above works of the flesh routinely performed in your life? If yes, how does today's *Sparkling Gem* affect you?
2. Has the Holy Spirit been trying to deal with you about certain works of the flesh that are operating in your life? What are those areas? Are you going to permit Him to purge those grievous actions and attitudes from your life?
3. Do you need to take some time today to get before the Lord and confess your sin? If your answer is yes, please don't leave your quiet place until you have done so. You need to respond to God while your spirit is sensitive to what He is speaking to you.

JULY 21

A True Child of God Cannot Continue To Habitually Practice Sin!

Whosoever abideth in him sinneth not:
whosoever sinneth hath not seen him, neither known him.
— 1 John 3:6

A true child of God cannot continue to habitually live a lifestyle of sin! It is *impossible*! In fact, if someone claims to be a child of God but continues in a life of sin, it is more than likely that he was never genuinely born again in the first place. You see, the Bible makes it clear that it is simply *impossible* for a bona fide child of God to continue in a life of sin! Today I want to tell you the reason why this is impossible.

First John 3:6 says, "Whosoever abideth in him sinneth not: whosoever sinneth hath not seen him, neither known him." Do you see the word "sinneth" used two times in this verse? In both cases the Greek tense indicates continuous action, which means the verse could be more accurately translated, *"He who abides in him does not go on continually, habitually sinning as a way of life; he who continually goes on routinely sinning as a way of life has not seen him, neither known him."*

I realize this is a very strong statement, but this is precisely what John said to us in this verse. According to this verse, anyone who continues to live in habitual sin does not know Jesus. It could be that this individual has come close to the Kingdom of God and has even tasted the powers of it. But the fact that he has continued uninterrupted in the practice of sin shows that he has never become a real child of God. The fact that his life never changed demonstrates that his nature was never changed. This is exactly what John wrote in First John 3:6.

John then goes on to tell us, "Whosoever is born of God doth not commit sin; for his seed remaineth in him: and he cannot sin, because he is born of God" (1 John 3:9). The tense of the word translated "commit" again indicates continuing action, which means the verse could be translated, *"Whosoever is born of God simply cannot go on continually sinning...."* And then John tells us why!

John writes, "…for his [God's] seed remaineth in him: and he cannot sin, because he is born of God." The word "seed" is the Greek word *sperma* — and yes, it is where we get the word *sperm*.

According to this phenomenal verse, God injected His own seed into you the day you gave your life to Christ! Just as the sperm of a human father carries the DNA of that father, God's seed — the Word of God — carries the life and nature of God within it. When that divine seed was implanted on the inside of you, it imparted the very nature of God Himself to your spirit.

Peter referred to this miraculous event when he wrote that you are "…born again, not of corruptible seed, but of incorruptible, by the word of God, which liveth and abideth for ever" (1 Peter 1:23). This means the day you got saved, that divine seed came rushing into your spirit, carrying the life and nature of God within it to give you a new nature. Just as a human seed produces a human life, God's divine seed immediately began to produce the life of God inside you.

In Genesis 1, God declared a spiritual law — that every living thing produces after its own kind (vv. 21,24,25): Humans produce humans; horses produce horses; plants produce plants, and so on. This principle is also true in the spiritual realm. The day that God's divine seed was planted in you, that seed transported the very nature of God Himself into your spirit, with the full expectation that His very life and nature would be reproduced on the inside of you. This is why your desires suddenly changed after you were born again. This is also why you felt so badly about sin that previously didn't bother you at all and why you became so driven to possess a holy life. You weren't the same anymore, because you had a new nature. *The nature of God Himself had been planted in you!*

This is the reason a genuinely born-again person cannot continue habitually in his past sinful patterns. His new nature will drive him to be different, to be holy, to be like God. His born-again spirit will grieve and sorrow if sins are committed, because such actions violate the new nature that has been implanted in his spirit. If a person continues in sin as though nothing happened inside him, then *nothing* is probably exactly what did happen! More than likely, he was never really born again, for if he had been born again, that new nature of God within him would not permit him to continue living habitually in sin.

What does this mean for you and me? If a person who claims to be born again continues uninterrupted in habitual sin, we can take it as a strong indicator that he has probably never really been born again. This person may have come close to the Kingdom of God; he may have even learned the lingo of the saints. But the fact that his actions are unchanged indicates that his nature has never been changed. If he had really been infused with the divine seed of God, that life-giving seed would have so changed him that he wouldn't be able to continue living as he had lived in the past.

This is why I say that people who claim to know the Lord but whose lives never reflect a change should question if they have ever really been born again. The great preacher, Charles Finney, once remarked that most people who attend church are probably *not* born again. When asked why he believed this, Finney remarked that it was impossible for true children of God to live in blatant sin as many believers do. Finney made this statement over 100 years ago. As I contemplate the amount of sin that is so prevalent in the Church today, it makes me wonder, *How many people who attend church in our own day are not genuinely born again?*

✦ Could it be that many who claim to know the Lord really aren't born again but instead have only been "enlightened" by coming closer to the Kingdom of God?
✦ If someone is really born of God, could he continue to blatantly live in sin, completely unchanged in his actions or attitudes?
✦ Doesn't John tell us that it is impossible for a person to continue in habitual sin if God's nature genuinely resides in his heart?

✦ Don't you think it is tragic that many people who come to church week after week, assuming they are saved, may not really be saved at all?

First John 3:9 plainly declares that an authentic child of God cannot routinely commit and live in uninterrupted sin. Because he has been "born of God," he is so inwardly changed that it affects him outwardly. He acts differently because he *is* different. Now God's seed resides in his spirit, and that seed is producing the life of God in him; therefore, he thinks, behaves, and acts like God's child.

On the other hand, if a person's life does *not* emulate God, perhaps it is an indication that he has never really received God's divine seed into his spirit. If he *had* been implanted with God's seed, that seed would have caused clear and visible changes in his life.

You must remember that in regard to the works of the flesh, Paul said, "...They which do such things shall not inherit the kingdom of God" (Galatians 5:21). The word "do" is the Greek word *prasso*, which means *to practice*. The Greek expresses the idea of *a person who performs these things as a matter of routine*. These actions are *his ritual, his norm, his pattern of life*. It means the verse could be translated, "...*Those who put these things into practice and who do these things routinely shall not inherit the Kingdom of God.*"

This is *not* the story of someone who has lost his salvation; rather, this is the story of someone who thought he was saved but who never really possessed genuine salvation in the first place. If he had truly been saved, he wouldn't have been able to continue living a consistent life of sin. The apostle John made this point emphatically clear in First John 3:9.

There is nothing more important than your salvation, friend. If you make a mistake about your spiritual condition, it is a mistake you will regret for all of eternity. Because this is such a vital, eternal issue, I advise you to carefully examine your own life to see if you reflect the life and nature of God.

✦ Does your life reveal that your nature has been changed?
✦ Or have you continued uninterrupted in your old attitudes and sinful actions since the time you thought you were saved?
✦ Does your daily life demonstrate clear evidence of your salvation, or have you just learned the lingo of Christians and how to behave among believers?

This question is too serious for you to make a mistake. If these questions disturb you, take the time to let the Holy Spirit speak to your heart and tell you the truth. If your life gives proof that you are saved, then rejoice! But if an honest evaluation reveals that you have only become more religious but have never really changed, perhaps you need to reconsider whether or not you have ever really been saved.

If you find that this last statement best describes you, it's time for you to make your heart right with God. Don't let pride hold you back from doing what is right. Many people will have an eternal destiny in hell because they couldn't bear the thought of publicly admitting they weren't saved. Don't let pride stop you from doing what is right. *The question of where you will spend your eternity is too important to ignore! Determine to put aside your pride so you can do what God's Spirit is urging you to do!*

MY PRAYER FOR TODAY

Lord, I thank You for placing Your divine life inside me! You have changed my whole view of life and given me new desires. I am so grateful to You for bringing about such change in me. I am truly a new creature with new desires, new longings, and new aspirations. I am so thankful that when I look at my life, I can see Your life and Your nature working in me!

I pray this in Jesus' name!

MY CONFESSION FOR TODAY

I confess that I have a new nature with new desires! I am not the person I used to be. By look-ing at me, it is evident that God's new nature is alive and working inside me. His divine seed is reproducing God's life in me so that every day I am thinking more like God, acting more like God, and possessing less tolerance for any sin that might still be active in my life. I don't have to wonder if I'm really saved, for my life gives proof that I have received a brand-new nature!

I declare this by faith in Jesus' name!

QUESTIONS FOR YOU TO CONSIDER

1. Have you ever known someone who claimed to be born again, but you never witnessed any changes in his lifestyle, behavior, attitudes, or actions? Did it make you wonder if that person was really saved?
2. If you know someone who claims to be a child of God but whose life continues uninterrupted in a lifestyle of sin, what does this person's unchanged life indi-cate to you now?
3. What changes occurred in you when you received Jesus Christ into your heart? Why don't you write down some of the biggest changes that have taken place since you were born again? It might be interesting for you to see how much your life has changed!

JULY 22

Here's What the Holy Spirit Wants To Produce in You!

But the fruit of the Spirit is love, joy, peace, longsuffering,
gentleness, goodness, faith,
Meekness, temperance: against such there is no law.
— Galatians 5:22,23

One day while visiting a remote village in southern Moldova, a precious Moldavian fam-ily invited our family to come to their home for lunch. When we arrived, we could see a huge table set up outside the house under a veranda. The veranda was covered with luscious green vines laden with the biggest grapes I had ever seen anywhere in the world.

As I sat there with Denise and our boys, I looked up to examine the green, white, red, and pur-ple grapes — mixtures of grapes I had never seen before. Soon it was time for dessert, but instead of ice cream or cake, oversized platters overflowing with grapes were placed on the table right before us. We had never seen such plump, colorful grapes, so at first we just looked at them in amazement. When we finally put them in our mouth and bit down, the juices literally flowed. That was the sweetest fruit we had ever tasted in our lives! My taste buds can almost taste them again as I write about it now.

Fruit is wonderful! It is healthy, beneficial, and delicious. This is one reason the apostle Paul used the word "fruit" to describe the wonderful things the Holy Spirit wants to produce inside our lives!

After Paul discusses the works of the flesh in Galatians 5:19-21, he begins to elaborate about the fruit that the Holy Spirit produces in a believer's life. In Galatians 5:22 and 23, he writes, "But the fruit of the Spirit is love, joy, peace, longsuffering, gentleness, goodness, faith, meekness, temperance...."

Just as Paul previously described the works of the flesh, now he tells us what the Holy Spirit wants to produce in us — and what a contrast there is between the flesh and the Spirit! The flesh produces "works" — from the Greek word *ergos*, which implies *hard work* or *hard labor*. As noted earlier (*see* July 14), a life dominated by the flesh is filled with excess, imbalance, unhealthy extremes, laziness, self-abuse, hatred, strife, bitterness, irresponsibility, and neglect. It is the hardest route for any individual, yet the flesh still cries out to be in charge, screaming to have its own way, demanding to be the boss. On the other hand, a life dominated by the Holy Spirit is filled with benefits and blessings!

Look at what the Spirit produces — *fruit*! The word "fruit" is from the Greek word *karpos*, which describes *the fruit of plants, the fruit of trees,* or *the fruit of one's body, such as a person's children or offspring*.

Regardless of whether it is a plant, an animal, or a human, all fruit is produced from some kind of seed. If there is no seed, there is no fruit — and the kind of seed that is sown determines the fruit that will be produced (Genesis 1:11,12). Apples always produce apples; oranges always produce oranges; dogs always produce dogs; cats always produce cats; humans always produce humans. The character of the seed determines the fruit.

The moment you received Jesus as your Savior by faith, God sowed His Spirit and Word into your heart like a seed, and you were spiritually born again by the incorruptible seed of the Word of God (1 Peter 1:23). And just like apples always produce apples and oranges always produce oranges, God's seed inside you immediately began to produce *God*! The kind of seed always determines the outcome of the fruit; therefore, you should expect your life to yield the fruits of the Spirit, for that is the seed God has sown into your heart.

Does a vinedresser worry that his grapevines might produce oranges? *Of course not!* He knows that grapevines only produce grapes. Does the owner of an orange grove run to the orchard to see if his tress produced watermelons? *Of course not!* He knows his tress will produce oranges because orange trees only produce oranges. If someone wants to grow watermelons, he has to plant watermelon seeds. Once those watermelon seeds are in the ground, he can rest assured that eventually he will have long vines growing juicy watermelons in his garden.

The same principle holds true in the spiritual realm. *To get what you want, you have to plant the right seed, because seed always produces fruit after its kind.*

So if God has sown His Spirit and His Word into your heart, you have every right to expect divine fruit to be produced inside you! The fruit that the Spirit produces is wonderful, godly fruit, overflowing with blessings and life. As you allow the Holy Spirit to produce these fruits in you, you'll find that people love to be near you because you're such a pleasurable experience for them. Once they partake of the love, joy, peace, longsuffering, gentleness, goodness, faith, meekness, and temperance that is evident in your life, they will want to come back for multiple servings of that luscious fruit!

So don't give way to the flesh and allow it to produce its ugly work in your life. Instead, yield to the Spirit and allow the seed of God's Spirit and Word to produce the fruit of the Spirit in your life. You are the one who makes the ultimate decision of who is going to rule you, so choose wisely today. Do you want to walk in the cruel, hard, bitter works of the flesh? Or would you prefer to mortify the deeds of the flesh and allow the Holy Spirit to produce His wonderful fruit in you? *Which path are you going to choose?*

MY PRAYER FOR TODAY

Lord, thank You for sowing Your Spirit and Word into my life. Forgive me for allowing the flesh to dominate so much of my life. Help me yield to the divine seed You have planted inside me. I know that Your life resides in me, longing to be released, so today I make the choice to let Your Spirit start working mightily inside me. Thank You for the life of God that is flowing up from my spirit right now, producing the life and the nature of Jesus Christ in me!

I pray this in Jesus' name!

MY CONFESSION FOR TODAY

I confess that the Holy Spirit lives in me and is producing His fruit in my life. The flesh no longer rules or dominates me, for I yield to the peaceful fruit of the Holy Spirit in every sphere of my life. I demonstrate love, joy, peace, longsuffering, gentleness, goodness, faith, meekness, and temperance in my life. God has sown His Spirit and His Word into my heart; therefore, I expect this divine fruit to be produced inside me.

I declare this by faith in Jesus' name!

QUESTIONS FOR YOU TO CONSIDER

1. Can you think of one person who manifests the character of Jesus Christ so much that when you are with him or her, you feel as if you have been with Jesus? What specific qualities are exhibited in the life of this person that make you feel that way?
2. What steps do you need to take so the Holy Spirit can more readily produce this godly fruit in your own life? For instance, what role do you think prayer or reading your Bible has in developing the fruit of the Spirit in your life?
3. If you were to ask others what kind of fruit they see in your life, how do you think they would answer?

The moment you received Jesus as your Savior by faith, God sowed His Spirit and Word into your heart like a seed, and you were spiritually born again by the incorruptible seed of the Word of God (1 Peter 1:23). And just like apples always produce apples and oranges always produce oranges, God's seed inside you immediately began to produce *God*!

JULY 23

꧁ ꧂

The First Fruit Is Love

But the fruit of the Spirit is love....
— Galatians 5:22

When the New Testament was being written, there were four primary Greek words to describe the concept of "love": 1) *eros,* 2) *stergo,* 3) *phileo,* and 4) *agape.* These four words conveyed four very different types of love. I want to talk to you today about these four different types of love; then I'll tell you which of these four is the type of love the Holy Spirit wants to produce in your life.

The first word for "love" in the list given above is the Greek word *eros,* which is the Greek term for *sexual love* and where we get the word *erotic.* In Greek culture, this word referred to *sensual, carnal impulses to satisfy or gratify the sexual desires of the flesh.* It shares a common root with the word *erao,* which means *to ask, to beg,* or *to demand.* This confirms that *eros* is not a giving type of love; rather, it denotes *a sexual demand.* It is not a love that seeks to give or to please someone else, but a carnal love that seeks the fulfillment of its own desires.

It is very interesting that this word never appears once in the New Testament, not even in the context of sex in marriage. Even in Greek culture, the word *eros* represented a carnal, raw, base, low-level craving, yearning, ache, or appetite for sexual fulfillment. This type of "love" is so flesh-based and so far removed from the level of love that God expects of believers that it is never included in New Testament language.

In the New Testament, regardless of whether the context is friendship, brotherhood, or romance, all believers are urged to continually operate from the perspective of *agape* love, which is a love more focused on *giving* than it is on *receiving.* Because the word *eros* primarily describes *a self-satisfying, self-gratifying, self-seeking, self-pleasing type of sexual appetite* found mainly among unbelievers or those who are focused on themselves, it is *not* the type of love that believers should aspire to in their marital lives.

The second word for "love" mentioned in the list above is the Greek word *stergo.* The word *stergo* primarily pictures *the love that exists between parents and children* or *the love that exists between members of a family.* One scholar has noted that on occasion, the word *stergo* portrayed *the love of a nation for its ruler* or even *the love of a dog for its master.* Consequently, the real idea of the word *stergo* is that of *devotion.*

Although the word *stergo* does appear in the New Testament, it is very rarely used. We find it used in a negative sense in Second Timothy 3:3, where the *King James Version* translates it "without natural affection." This suggests a time that will develop in the last days when *strong family ties* and *devotion to one's family* will deteriorate. By using this word in a negative sense, the apostle Paul warns that one of the principal signs of the last times will be the deterioration of the family and of traditional family values.

The third word for "love" is the Greek word *phileo,* which describes *affection* — such as the affection felt between a boyfriend and girlfriend or the affability shared between two friends. It carries the idea of two or more people who feel compatible, well-matched, well-suited, and complementary to each other. Although this word describes the attributes of *friendship*, it is not representative of the highest form of love, which is *agape*. Other words derived from the word *phileo* are numerous. Here are a few of them:

+ *philadelphia:* a compound of *phileo* and *adelphos*, the Greek word for *a brother*. When these two words are compounded together, it means *brotherly love*.
+ *philodonos:* a compound of *phileo* and *edone*, the Greek word for *pleasure*. When compounded together, it means *one who is a lover of pleasure*.
+ *philoxenos:* a compound of *phileo* and *xenos*, the Greek word for *strangers* or *foreigners*. When compounded together in this form, it carries the idea of *one who loves to be hospitable*.
+ *philoxenia:* similar to the word above, which means *one who loves strangers*. However, the word *philoxenia* places more emphasis on *love for the person in need of hospitality*.
+ *philanthropia:* a compound of *phileo* and *anthropos*, the Greek word for *mankind*. Compounded together, it means *one who loves or who is kind to mankind*.
+ *philarguros:* a compound of *phileo* and *arguros*, which is the Greek word for *silver*. Compounded together, it means *one who is covetous* or *one who loves money*.
+ *philosophia:* a compound of *phileo* and *sophos*, which is the famous Greek word for *wisdom*. When these two words are compounded together into one, it becomes the word *philosophy*, which is *a love of wisdom*.

The fourth word for "love" is the word chiefly used in the New Testament to depict *the love of God*. This is the Greek word *agape* — and it is this word that Paul uses in Galatians 5:22 when he writes, "But the fruit of the Spirit is love...." This is what I call high-level love, for there is no higher, finer, or more excellent love than *agape* love.

In fact, the word *agape* is so filled with deep emotion and meaning that it is one of the most difficult words to translate in the New Testament. Trying to explain this word has baffled translators for centuries; nevertheless, I will now add my attempt to clarify the meaning of this powerful word.

Agape occurs when *an individual sees, recognizes, understands, or appreciates the value of an object or a person, causing the viewer to behold this object or person in great esteem, awe, admiration, wonder, and sincere appreciation.* Such great respect is awakened in the heart of the observer for the object or person he is beholding that he is compelled to love it. In fact, his love for that person or object is so strong that it is *irresistible*.

In the New Testament, perhaps the best example of *agape* is found in John 3:16: "For God so loved the world, that he gave his only begotten Son, that whosoever believeth in him should not perish, but have everlasting life." In the phrase, "For God so loved the world," the word "love" is the word *agape*.

This means when God looked upon the human race, He stood in awe of mankind, even though man was lost in sin. God admired man; He wondered at man; He held mankind in the highest appreciation. Even though mankind was held captive by Satan at that moment, God looked upon the world and saw His own image in man. The human race was so *precious* to God and He loved man so deeply that His heart was stirred to reach out and do something to save him. In other words, God's love drove Him to action.

You see, *agape* is a love that loves so profoundly that it knows no limits or boundaries in how far, wide, high, and deep it will go to show that love to its recipient. If necessary, *agape* love will even sacrifice itself for the sake of that object or person it so deeply cherishes. *Agape* is the highest form of love — a self-sacrificial type of love that moves the lover to action. In contrast:

✦ *Eros* is a self-seeking love.
✦ *Stergo* is limited only to one's family.
✦ *Phileo* is based on mutual satisfaction and can feel disappointed.

Agape is a love that has no strings attached. It isn't looking for what it can get, but for what it can *give*. Its awe of the one who is loved is so deep that it is compelled to shower love upon that object or person regardless of the response. This is the profound love God has for the human race, for He loved man when he was still lost in sin with no ability to love Him back. God simply loved mankind without any thought or expectation of receiving love in return.

When you love with such a pure love that you expect nothing back in return, it is impossible for you to feel hurt or let down by the response of the recipients of your love. You don't love them for the purpose of getting something in return; you shower them with love simply *because* you love them. This kind of love is much higher than *eros* love that is based on selfishness; *stergo* love that is restricted by limitations; or *phileo* love that is rooted in mutual satisfaction. These three types of love are what I call low-level love, but *agape* is high-level love. It is a love that has no strings attached, a love that loves simply and purely — the God-kind of love.

In First John 3:16, we are urged to possess *agape* for each other. It says, "Hereby perceive we the love of God, because he laid down his life for us: and we ought to lay down our lives for the brethren." This plainly means that we are to love and appreciate each other just as fully and freely as God loves us.

The Father loved us to the point of self-sacrifice. Jesus' *agape* drove Him to lay down His life for us. In the same way, we are to *agape* our brothers and sisters to such a high extent that we would be willing to lay down our lives for them. If we are truly operating in *agape* and they don't respond in like fashion, it won't offend or hurt us. We are not looking for what others can do for us; we are simply focused on how to love others with no strings attached. Therefore, the way other people respond to us has no effect on our desire to shower them with *agape* love.

Further explaining the role of *agape* in our lives, John said, "My little children, let us not love in word, neither in tongue; but in deed and in truth" (v. 18). The word "love" is again the word *agape*, which tells us that when *agape* is at work, it is a force so strong that it demonstrates itself with deeds and actions. This is not an empty love that talks but does nothing. It is a love that does something, just as God loved us and then did something to save us from our lost and sinful condition.

This is the love that Paul urged us to follow after when he wrote in First Corinthians 14:1, "Follow after charity [agape love]...." The word "follow" is the Greek word *dioko*, which means *to hotly pursue*. It was a hunting term that pictured *a hunter following the tracks of an animal until he finally gets his game*. This means that attaining this high-level love doesn't come easy. If we want to attain *agape* love and regularly walk in it, *we must hotly pursue it!* It must be the *focus* and the *aim* of our lives.

If *agape* is the basis of your sexual relationship with your spouse instead of *eros*, you will always seek to serve and please your spouse rather than being self-centered and focused only on *your* needs. If *agape* is the basis of your family relationships rather than *stergo*, you will always remain devoted to your family, regardless of the disappointments that may occur along the way. And if *agape* is the basis of your friendships rather than *phileo*, you will be a faithful, immovable friend for life rather than a come-and-go friend who is faithful only as long as you get what you want out of the relationship. In fact, if *agape* is the driving motivation of your life and the force behind all your relationships, it will make you to be the best, most devoted, faithful, and reliable friend anyone has ever known.

You may ask, "But how can I possess such love? Is it really possible for me to regularly exhibit such love in my life for other people?" If you were seeking to walk in the kind of love that originates in the power of your flesh, it would be impossible, for flesh is selfish and self-focused and therefore cannot love that highly. But because the seed of God's Word has been sown into your own human spirit, the potential for this divine love is within you all the time. Now it is up to you to shove the flesh aside and release the love of God from down deep inside. If you will let the Spirit of God release it from your heart, you will discover and enjoy the fruit of the Spirit called "love." *This high-level love is already inside you. Now it's time for you to free that love and allow the Holy Spirit to manifest it in your life!*

MY PRAYER FOR TODAY

Lord, help me turn my attention to Your kind of high-level love and make it a part of my daily life. Forgive me for those times when I've fallen into low-level, "you-scratch-my-back-and-I'll-scratch-yours" love that gets easily offended. Help me climb up to the higher realms of love that You desire to be manifested in my life. Holy Spirit, it is impossible to continually walk in this kind of love in the power of my flesh, so I turn to You to awaken this divine love inside me and to help me manifest it in my life.

I pray this in Jesus' name!

MY CONFESSION FOR TODAY

I confess that I am hotly pursuing agape love in my life. I want to attain this high level of love and regularly walk in it, so I treat this fruit of the Spirit like it is one of the most important aims of my life. Because the seed of God's Spirit and Word is sown in my own human spirit, I have the potential for this divine love within me all the time. So right now I determine to shove the flesh aside and release the power of God from down deep inside. Because agape is the driving motivation of my life and the force behind all my relationships, I am the best, most devoted, faithful, and reliable friend anyone has ever known!

I declare this by faith in Jesus' name!

QUESTIONS FOR YOU TO CONSIDER

1. Can you think of one person who has loved you with real *agape* love at some point in your life? What kind of impact did that "no-strings-attached" kind of love have on you?
2. Would others say that *agape* love operates in you or that you have strings attached to your demonstrations of love?
3. What can you do to move up into God's high-level *agape* love? Think it over, and write down your ideas of what you need to do to leave behind the place of low-level love and move up to God's higher realm of *agape* love.

Agape is a love that has no strings attached. This kind of divine love isn't looking for what it can get, but for what it can *give*.

JULY 24

❧❧❧

Joy and Peace

But the fruit of the Spirit is love, joy, peace....
— Galatians 5:22

I'll never forget many years ago when a so-called "brother in the Lord" tried to destroy our ministry in the former USSR. When I finally discovered the destructive schemes he was covertly planning, I was *dumbfounded* — stunned that someone I had worked with so closely could be deviously used by the devil. It was a true "Judas Iscariot" situation.

Thanks to God's Spirit alerting us to what was happening and to staff members who sensed something was wrong in the Spirit, we probed into this man's activities and discovered what he was attempting to do. Soon I found myself on an airplane with several key members of my team, flying to another city to deal with the consequences of his dishonest, deceitful, fraudulent plans.

As we flew that day to an encounter with evil that is forever etched in my memory, my staff commented on how joyful I was in the midst of this potentially devastating situation. I must admit, even I was amazed at the joy that exuded from down deep inside me that day! I knew the joy I felt was being produced in me by the Holy Spirit, for only the Holy Spirit could give such joy in a situation as difficult as the one I was facing that day.

That experience reminded me of Paul's words to the Thessalonians in First Thessalonians 1:6. He told them, "And ye became followers of us, and of the Lord, having received the word in much affliction, with joy of the Holy Ghost." In most of Paul's writings, he associates "joy" with times of affliction. The word "affliction" used in this verse is the Greek word *thlipsis*. This word is so strong that it leaves no room for misunderstanding regarding the intensity of the afflictions the Thessalonians faced.

The word *thlipsis* conveys the idea of *a heavy-pressure situation*. One scholar says it was first used to describe the specific act of tying a victim with a rope, laying him on his back, and then placing a huge boulder on top of him until his body was crushed. Paul uses this word to alert us to moments when he or others went through grueling, crushing situations that would have been unbearable, intolerable, and impossible to survive if it had not been for the help of the Holy Spirit.

Joy:

One of the ways the Holy Spirit helps in these situations is to give us supernatural "joy." However, it's important to understand that this divine joy isn't on the same low level of mere happiness. Happiness is based on circumstantial pleasure, merriment, hilarity, exuberance, excitement, or something that causes one to feel hopeful or to be in high spirits. These fleeting emotions of happiness, although very pleasurable at the moment, usually go just as quickly as they came. All it takes is one piece of bad news, a sour look from a fellow employee, a harsh word from a spouse, or an electric bill that is larger than what was anticipated — and that emotion of happiness can disappear right before a person's eyes! But joy is unaffected by outward circumstances. In fact, it usually thrives best when times are tough! It is God's supernatural response to the devil's attacks!

The Greek word for "joy" is *chara*, derived from the word *charis*, which is the Greek word for *grace*. This is important to note, for it tells us categorically that *chara* ("joy") is produced by the *charis* ("grace") of God. This means "joy" isn't a human-based happiness that comes and goes. Rather, true "joy" is divine in origin, a fruit of the Spirit that is manifested particularly in hard times. Someone may feel happiness, merriment, hilarity, exuberance, excitement, or "high spirits," but all of these are fleeting emotions. On the other hand, "joy" is a Spirit-given expression that flourishes best when times are strenuous, daunting, and tough!

In the example given in First Thessalonians 1:6, the Thessalonians were under great stress due to persecution; yet in the midst of it all, they continued to experience great joy. In fact, the Greek strongly implies that their supernatural joy was due to the Holy Spirit working inside them. Paul even called it the "joy of the Holy Ghost."

An interpretive translation of First Thessalonians 1:6 could be the following:

"You threw your arms open wide and gladly welcomed the Word into your lives with great enthusiasm. And you did it even in the midst of mind-boggling sufferings — a level of stress and intensity that would be suffocating and crushing for most people. But while you were going through all these hardships and hassles, you were simultaneously experiencing the supreme ecstasy and joy of the Holy Spirit."

The best that the lost world has to offer is a temporary happiness. But when the seed of God has been placed inside your human spirit, that divine seed produces a "joy" that isn't based on outward events or circumstances. In fact, when times get very challenging, the supernatural life of God rises up inside you to defy that devilish pressure! This supernatural "joy" will sustain you in even the hardest of times!

Peace:

On the day when we faced that difficult ordeal with the man who was trying to destroy our ministry, there was something else I couldn't help but notice: Supernatural "peace" was ruling me and my emotions! Under such circumstances, most people would have been very upset, but I was *completely controlled, level-headed,* and *at rest.* My fellow associates kept asking me, "How can you be so peaceful in the midst of this situation?" It was simply a fact that supernatural peace had risen up from deep within my spirit, enabling me to be a rock in the middle of a terrible storm that was threatening to disrupt the outreach of our ministry.

I knew this "peace" wasn't something I was producing by myself; it was a fruit that the Holy Spirit was producing in me. Paul listed this supernatural "peace" in Galatians 5:22 when he wrote about the fruit of the Spirit. He said, "But the fruit of the Spirit is love, joy, peace...."

The word "peace" comes from the Greek word *eirene,* the Greek equivalent for the Hebrew word *shalom,* which expresses the idea of *wholeness, completeness,* or *tranquility in the soul that is unaffected by outward circumstances or pressures.* The word *eirene* strongly suggests *the rule of order in place of chaos.* When a person is dominated by *eirene* ("peace"), he has *a calm, inner stability that results in the ability to conduct himself peacefully, even in the midst of circumstances that would normally be very nerve-racking, traumatic, or upsetting.*

The Hebrew counterpart, the word *shalom,* indicates that this dominating peace ultimately gives rise to *prosperity in one's soul.* Rather than allowing the difficulties and pressures of life to break him, a person who is possessed by *eirene* ("peace") is *whole, complete, orderly, stable,* and *poised for blessing.*

The New Testament is filled with examples of this supernatural peace that the Holy Spirit produces. One classic example is found in Acts 27, when the apostle Paul found himself in a ship that was being dangerously tossed back and forth by the raging waves of the sea. In fact, the storm was so severe that Acts 27:14 and 15 says, "But not long after there arose against it a tempestuous wind, called Euroclydon. And when the ship was caught, and could not bear up into the wind, we let her drive."

Notice verse 14 says, "…There arose against it a tempestuous wind…." The word "against" is the Greek word *ballo*, which in this verse means *to throw, to dash, to hurt,* or *to rush*. It indicates that *a massive, terrible force of wind* had come against them. He continues to say it was a "tempestuous wind" — which is the Greek word *tuphonikos*, a compound of the words *tuphos* and *nikos*. The word *tuphos* means *typhoon*, and *nikos* means *to subdue* or *to conquer*. Put these two words together, and it pictures a *typhoon from which there is no escape*. This is *a storm so immense that it conquers and dominates everything in sight*. Acts 27:14 tells us that this storm was called "Euroclydon" — the term professional sailors used to describe *the deadly northeastern winter storms* that blew across the Mediterranean Sea, causing many shipwrecks that resulted in the loss of many lives every year.

This typhoon became so fierce that Acts 27:15 says, "…The ship was caught, and could not bear up into the wind…." The word "caught" is the Greek word *sunarpadzo*, which means *to seize violently* or *to seize and to carry away*. This word lets us know that the sailors had lost control of the ship. The winds were so violent that they could no longer fight them. One scholar notes that it must have felt as if a monster had seized the ship and was tearing it to pieces. The situation was so completely out of the sailors' control that they "let her drive." In other words, they chose to let the storm take them where it wanted rather than try to fight the winds that could not be conquered. Their hope was that the winds would carry them into the smoother waters near the small island of Clauda, which was a mere twenty-three miles south of Crete.

Acts 27:17 tells us that, once in the smooth waters off the shores of Clauda, the crew had much-needed repair work to do before they could continue on their dangerous journey in the winter storm. The ship had sustained a substantial amount of damage because of the fierce winds already endured on this trip. Verse 17 describes the work they undertook to prepare for the rest of the dangerous, windy trip: "Which when they had taken up, they used helps, undergirding the ship; and, fearing lest they should fall into the quicksands, strake sail, and so were driven."

The words "when they had taken up" are from the Greek word *boetheia*, which referred to *the ropes or cables used to secure the ship in one location*. Before work on the ship could commence, the ship first had to be securely tied in one spot. Once it had been secured, the crew began to repair and prepare the ship for the rest of its hazardous journey.

But notice that this verse also mentions "quicksands," which is from the Greek word *syrtis*, meaning *terror*. This referred to the sandbars that were located off the coast of North Africa. The fact that these professional sailors feared these sandbars, which were located four hundred miles south of their location at the island of Clauda, tells us that the winds they were fighting were strong enough to take them that far off their navigational course. Ships were constantly wrecked as a result of these sandbars, which were widely known to be the graveyard of countless sailors.

After all the crew's efforts to fix the ship and try to avoid the winter winds, Acts 27:18 continues to tell us, "And we being exceedingly tossed with a tempest, the next day they lightened the ship." The word "exceedingly" is from the word *sphrodros*, which means *vehemently, violently,* or *intensely*. The word "tempest" is the Greek word *cheimadzoamai*, which is the Greek word for *a storm*. But when you put these two words together into one phrase, as in this verse, it pictures *a very vehement, violent, and intense storm*.

In other words, rather than escaping the storm, the crew must have felt like they were driving right into it! It was such a serious situation that Acts 27:20 says, "And when neither sun nor stars in many days appeared, and no small tempest lay on us, all hope that we should be saved was then taken away."

But right in the midst of all this hopelessness, Paul stood up and said, "And now I exhort you to be of good cheer: for there shall be no loss of any man's life among you, but of the ship. For there stood by me this night the angel of God, whose I am, and whom I serve, saying, Fear not..." (Acts 27:22-24). Paul had heard from the Lord, which caused supernatural peace to rise up on the inside of him. Therefore, he was able to be a rock in the middle of a very serious situation. His peace brought strength to everyone on that ship!

As noted earlier, this kind of "peace" is produced by the Holy Spirit. Now think back on the meaning of the word *eirene* ("peace") in light of Paul's experience on that ship. Remember, this word expresses the idea of *wholeness, completeness,* or *tranquility in the soul that is unaffected by outward circumstances or pressures.* It strongly suggests *the rule of order in the place of chaos.* When a person is dominated by *eirene* ("peace"), he has *a calm, inner stability that results in the ability to conduct himself peacefully, even though circumstances normally would be very nerve-racking, traumatic, or upsetting.* Isn't this the exact quality Paul manifested that day on the ship?

I know that this supernatural peace of the Holy Spirit is what was working in me the day we were facing such difficulties because of that so-called brother in the Lord. That same peace has worked in me in many other difficult situations — and it will work in me many times more in the days that lie ahead!

So don't think you have to give way to upsetting emotions in difficult or challenging moments. If you'll let the Holy Spirit work in you, He will release a supernatural joy and a dominating peace from way down deep inside you. These fruits of the Spirit have the power to keep you joyful, calm, stable, and peaceful, even though you are facing circumstances that would normally push you over the edge! *Why don't you take a few minutes today to pray and ask the Holy Spirit to produce the supernatural fruits of joy and peace in you?*

MY PRAYER FOR TODAY

Lord, I am so thankful today that You haven't abandoned me to my flesh and my emotions! Because Your Spirit lives in me, I can be empowered to walk in joy and peace in any situation. Forgive me for pandering to the whims of my flesh and for allowing it to rant and rave when Your Spirit inside me is longing to cause His supernatural joy and peace to rule my life. I turn from my past habits of worry and fear, and I deliberately choose to let the Holy Spirit flood me with Your unquenchable joy and incomprehensible peace!

I pray this in Jesus' name!

MY CONFESSION FOR TODAY

I confess that I am dominated by the fruits of joy and peace. Fear and anxiety have no place in my life; neither am I ruled by the temporary, fleeting emotions of happiness. Joy strengthens me and stabilizes me in every situation. Peace rules my emotions, helping me to maintain stability and eradicate emotional chaos from my life and surroundings. I am inhabited by the Spirit of God Himself — and as I yield to Him, He is controlling me more and more!

I declare this by faith in Jesus' name!

1. Can you think of a time in your life when you should have been very upset about something, but a supernatural joy came rising up out of your spirit that sustained you during that hard time?
2. Can you also recollect a moment when the peace of God replaced the fear and worry that normally would have conquered you? What do you think would have happened that day if you hadn't been ruled by this supernatural peace?
3. Do you think you have anything to do with the fruits of joy and peace operating in your life? Can your words or actions either stop them from functioning or release them to function more freely in your life?

JULY 25

Longsuffering and Gentleness

But the fruit of the Spirit is love, joy,
peace, longsuffering, gentleness....
— Galatians 5:22

*H*ave you ever thought, *Lord, You have to help me deal with this person You've put in my life! I'm so tired of trying to help him with his rebellious attitude that I'd like to walk away and leave him forever! Please give me the patience I need to keep working with him!* Do you recognize those thoughts? Have you prayed this prayer before?

At times, we all get frustrated with someone else, and sometimes our level of frustration can rise to the boiling point. This is especially true when we are exhausted from trying to help people who don't act like they want or appreciate our help. It's so easy to be Christ-like with people who appreciate us or who show us kindness. But are we going to act just as Christ-like when people *don't* appreciate us? Will we demonstrate the life of Jesus Christ equally to those who irritate us as much as to those who make us feel good or who treat us with respect?

Whenever people fail to appreciate what you do for them, fail to listen to your counsel, or fail to value what you have contributed, your flesh likes to rant and rave about how little you're valued, respected, esteemed, and appreciated. That is often the golden moment when your soul rises up to say, "Excuse me, but I'm not a mat for people to wipe their feet on! I've invested all the time and energy I'm willing to invest in this ingrate. I refuse to help him any further!"

Parents have felt this way toward their children; teachers have felt this way toward their students; husbands and wives have felt this way toward their spouses; friends have felt this way toward their friends; and pastors have felt this way toward their congregations. The bottom line is this: Regardless of your status in life — who you're married to, where you work, or what you do — like everyone else, you need a healthy dose of "longsuffering" if you are going to successfully get along with other people in this world!

Longsuffering:

In Galatians 5:22, the apostle Paul lists "longsuffering" as another fruit that the Holy Spirit wants to produce in our lives. He writes, "But the fruit of the Spirit is love, joy, peace, longsuffering...."

The word "longsuffering" is from the Greek word *makrothumia*, which is a compound of the words *makros* and *thumos*. The word *makros* means *long*. It is where we get the word *macaroni*, which of course is *a long noodle*. The word *makros* indicates *something that is long, distant, far, remote,* or *of long duration*. The word *thumos* means *anger*, but it also embodies the idea of *swelling emotions* or *a strong and growing passion about something*. When compounded into one word, it forms the word *makrothumia*, which pictures *the patient restraint of anger* and therefore denotes *longsuffering*. It can be translated as the words *forbearance* and *patience*.

The word *makrothumia* ("longsuffering") is like a candle that has a very long wick and is therefore prepared to burn a long time. It is ready *to forbear* and *patiently wait* until someone finally comes around, makes progress, changes, or hears what you are trying to communicate or teach him or her.

In Colossians 3:12, Paul commands us, "Put on therefore, as the elect of God, holy and beloved, bowels of mercies, kindness, humbleness of mind, meekness, longsuffering." This word "longsuffering" is the word *makrothumia*. But notice Paul begins this verse by telling us, "*Put on....*" This phrase is from the Greek word *enduo*, which was used in New Testament times to denote *the putting on of a garment or a piece of clothing*.

If you are going to properly dress for the day, you have to make the choice to look into the clothes closet and choose the clothes you wish to wear. Then once that selection is made, you still have to reach into the closet, take those clothes off the hanger, and slip them onto your body! Your clothes won't jump out of the closet and onto your body without your help. If you are going to wear them, *you have to put them on!*

Paul now tells you that if you're going to be forbearing, patient, long-burning, and compassionate toward other people, you must make a choice to act in this fashion! Walking in *makrothumia* ("longsuffering") is just as much a choice as it is for you to walk in your clothes. If you don't choose to put on this fruit of the Spirit and walk in it, you won't do it!

In First Thessalonians 5:14, Paul also tells us, "Now we exhort you, brethren, warn them that are unruly, comfort the feebleminded, support the weak, be patient toward all men." The word "patient" is also the word *makrothumia*. In this case, Paul is telling us that it is just as much our responsibility to be longsuffering with people as it is our responsibility to warn the unruly, comfort the feebleminded, and support the weak. Walking in *makrothumia* ("longsuffering") is a part of our Christian responsibility. We have an obligation before God not to be short-tempered or quickly angered with people who struggle or fail; instead, we are to forbear with them and help them!

In First Corinthians 13:4, Paul uses the word *makrothumia* when he writes his famous chapter about love. He says, "Charity [or love] suffereth long...." Longsuffering is so different from the flesh, which gets easily angered, blows up, lose its temper, says things it later regrets, and doesn't want to give the same mercy that it demands others give to it. Yet we are commanded to let *makrothumia* ("longsuffering") have a key role in our lives!

Other possible interpretive translations of the word
***makrothumia* in First Corinthians 13:4 could include:**

"Love is not short-tempered or easily angered...."
"Love does not quickly blow its top, but it is patient as it waits for others...."
"Love is not irritable and impatient but is willing to wait a long time for someone to change...."

"Love is determined to wait until the other person finally comes around...."
"Love passionately burns for others and is willing to wait as long as is necessary...."

Parents need to be longsuffering toward their children; teachers need to be longsuffering toward their students; spouses need to be longsuffering toward their spouses; friends need to be long-suffering toward their friends; and pastors need to be longsuffering toward their congregations. *And each of us needs to be longsuffering with ourselves!*

If you don't allow "longsuffering" to work in you, you will end up frustrated with everyone all the time — including yourself. So decide to let the Holy Spirit supernaturally produce "longsuffering" in you today. You'll be more tolerant of others, more peaceful within yourself, and a lot more loving and patient toward those whom you love and need so much!

Gentleness:

However, "longsuffering" isn't all you need! You also need "gentleness"! This is another super-natural attribute that Paul lists as a fruit of the Holy Spirit in Galatians 5:22, where he says, "But the fruit of the Spirit is love, joy, peace, longsuffering, gentleness...."

The word "gentleness" comes from the Greek word *chrestotes*, which meant *to show kindness* or *to be friendly to others* and often depicted *rulers, governors, or people who were kind, mild, and benevolent to their subjects.* Anyone who demonstrated this quality of *chrestotes* was considered to be *compassionate, considerate, sympathetic, humane, kind,* or *gentle.* The apostle Paul uses this word to depict God's *incomprehensible kindness* for people who are unsaved (*see* Romans 11:22; Ephesians 2:7; Titus 3:4).

One scholar has noted that when the word *chrestotes* is applied to inter-human relationships, it conveys the idea of being *adaptable to others.* Rather than harshly require everyone else to adapt to his own needs and desires, when *chrestotes* is working in a believer, he seeks to become adaptable to the needs of those who are around him.

Paul was so driven to compassion about reaching the lost that he told the Corinthian church:

✦ "And unto the Jews I became as a Jew, that I might gain the Jews..." (1 Corinthians 9:20).
✦ "...To them that are under the law, as under the law, that I might gain them..." (1 Corinthians 9:20).
✦ "To them that are without law, as without law...that I might gain them..." (1 Corinthians 9:21).
✦ "To the weak became I as weak, that I might gain the weak..." (1 Corinthians 9:22).
✦ "...I am made all things to all men, that I might by all means save some..." (1 Corinthians 9:22).

You see, Paul was so interested in reaching others and meeting their needs that he was willing to become whatever he needed to be in order to reach them. In fact, he was well-known for being adaptable to people and to their needs. Paul even wrote these words about himself: "Now I Paul myself beseech you by the meekness and gentleness of Christ..." (2 Corinthians 10:1).

The word "gentleness" is the same word *chrestotes* that Paul now uses to describe himself. He made it one of the aims of his life to walk in *chrestotes*, or in *gentleness and kindness*, becoming *adaptable* to others around him so that he might minister to them and meet their needs.

This is so contrary to the flesh! Flesh says, "Excuse me, but if you don't like me the way I am, you can tough it out! This is the way I am, and if you don't like it, you can just get out of here. I'm not changing for anyone!"

But when the Holy Spirit is producing His fruit of gentleness in you, you'll hear yourself thinking and saying, "How can I be different for you? Is there any way I can change that will help you? Is there anything I can do better for you? How can I serve you and meet your needs more effectively?"

It is a supernatural work of God when we become adaptable to meet the needs of others around us. When we attain this fruit of the Spirit in our lives, we are making great progress in our walk with God. This is exactly what Jesus did for us when He laid aside His glory and took upon Himself the form of a servant, being made in the likeness of men (*see* Philippians 2:7,8). When Jesus came to earth, He denied His own comfort and adapted to human flesh that He might reach us and bring us to God!

Do you find yourself thinking about how you can reach others? Do you think of ways you can change to be a bigger blessing to people in your life? The flesh never thinks this way. It just likes to demand that everyone else change to please it! So if you are starting to consider how you can be more for those who are around you, that is a strong indication that the fruit of the Spirit called "gentleness" is starting to work in you. *And if it hasn't started to work in you yet, today would be a great day for you to ask the Holy Spirit to start producing this Christ-like attribute in your life!*

MY PRAYER FOR TODAY

Lord, I thank You that I don't have to walk in the works of the flesh. Because of Your grace, I can surrender to the power and Presence of the Holy Spirit inside me. As I surrender to the Spirit, I ask that His divine life release His supernatural fruits in me. I want to be more patient, longsuffering, and kind. I know that I need these attributes in my life and that I am lacking them right now. So rather than continue down the path I've been on, I am stopping everything right now to ask You to change me. Please produce the life of Jesus Christ and His wonderful character in me!

I pray this in Jesus' name!

MY CONFESSION FOR TODAY

I confess that I am loving, patient, and kind. I don't lose my temper. I am not quickly angered. I am forbearing of others, tolerant of their mistakes, and burning passionately to see them gain new levels of growth in their lives. Just as others have been patient and forbearing with me, I am very patient and understanding of others who are also trying to change! I am gentle, kind, and adaptable to those who are around me. As the Spirit of God works in me, I become all things to all men in order that I might gain some for the Kingdom of God!

I declare this by faith in Jesus' name!

QUESTIONS FOR YOU TO CONSIDER

1. Is there any one person with whom you are constantly losing your temper? Do you say or do things to that person you wouldn't want someone to say or do to you? Why do you think you so easily fly off the handle with that individual?
2. Have you ever asked that person to forgive you for being so unkind and ugly?
3. In what ways do you need to become more adaptable to the people around you? Have you been so busy requiring others to be adaptable to you that you have forgotten you need to adapt to others as well?

JULY 26

❧

Goodness and Faith

But the fruit of the Spirit is love, joy, peace,
longsuffering, gentleness, goodness, faith.
— Galatians 5:22

Once when I was flying from New York City to another city in the United States, I noticed the man sitting next to me had his head lowered against the seat. I could tell he was experiencing some kind of terrible throbbing pain in his head, so I asked him, "Is there any way I can pray for you?" The man peered up at me with a look of joyful surprise. I knew from his response that he was a believer! He was delighted that I had offered to pray for him, so with his permission, I reached over and laid my hands on him. Then I began to speak healing over the pain he was feeling in his head.

After prayer, I asked the man, "What do you do for a living?" He told me, "I am a wealthy businessman. I have joined together with several other very wealthy businessmen, and as a team, we travel the world over to find worthy organizations and evangelical works that need money to advance the Kingdom of God. Once we find them, we make it our business to fund them so they can operate without having to worry about raising money."

When I thought about this man and the goodness of his heart, I was reminded of the word "goodness" in Galatians 5:22, where the apostle Paul writes, "But the fruit of the Spirit is love, joy, peace, longsuffering, gentleness, goodness...." This man's desire to give is exactly what the word "goodness" is all about. His urge to help others demonstrated the fruit of goodness, which is supernaturally produced in the hearts of believers by the Holy Spirit.

Goodness:

The word "goodness" is the Greek word *agathusune*, which comes from the word *agathos*, meaning *good*. But when *agathos* becomes the word *agathusune*, it means *goodness* in the sense of *being good to someone*. This word was used to portray *a person who is generous, big-hearted, liberal, and charitable with his finances*. We would call this person *a giver*.

By reading Acts 10:38, we find that this fruit of the Spirit operated mightily in Jesus. It says, "How God anointed Jesus of Nazareth with the Holy Ghost and with power: who went about doing good, and healing all that were oppressed of the devil; for God was with him." Most people who preach from this verse focus primarily on the healing portion of this verse, but today I want to draw your attention to the phrase "doing good," because it is so crucial to this discussion.

The words "doing good" are from the word *euergeteo*, which is an old word that denoted *a benefactor, a philanthropist*, or *one who financially supported charitable works*. This word would only be used to describe *a person who possessed great financial substance and who used it to assist those who were less fortunate*.

The implication of the word *eugereteo* is that Jesus possessed a great amount of financial resources in His ministry. In addition to the offerings that were received for His ministry, Luke 8:3 tells us that a group of very wealthy women also financially supported His ministry. Also, we can infer from Judas' words in John 12:5 that Jesus' ministry had a significant philanthropic outreach to the poor and needy over which Judas had been placed in charge.

I find this very significant, for it tells me that Jesus didn't only perform supernatural works; He also used His resources to do good works in the natural realm. Jesus cared for the poor; He helped feed the needy; and He utilized the vast resources of money made available to His ministry to meet the basic needs of human beings. Thus, He set an example for us to be concerned for and involved in the meeting of basic human needs as we are able to do so.

This tells me that acting in "goodness" is a character feature of the nature of God. Luke mentioned this aspect of Jesus' nature in Acts 10:38 right along with His supernatural healing power, sounding the signal that God is just as interested in helping the poor and needy with financial assistance as He is in supernaturally healing their bodies. The truth is, helping to meet the physical needs of other people is an act of "goodness" that Jesus did and still longs to do through His people.

So when the Bible tells us that one of the fruits of the Spirit is "goodness," God is letting us know that He wants us to be selfless, using our resources to help change people's living conditions for the better. This is absolutely contrary to the flesh, which would consume every spare dollar on itself. But when the Spirit is working mightily in us, He shifts our focus from ourselves to the needs of those who are around us.

Thus, the fruit of the Spirit called "goodness" is that supernatural urge in a person to reach beyond himself to meet the natural needs of those around him. When a believer is walking in the Spirit, his eyes are supernaturally opened to see the needs of humanity, and his heart is moved to meet those needs. This is why there is no greater *benefactor* or *philanthropist* than a person who is filled with the Spirit and who is producing the fruit of the Spirit in his or her life!

Faith:

The word "faith" is the Greek word *pistis*, which is the common New Testament word for *faith*. However, in this verse it conveys the idea of *a person who is faithful, reliable, loyal, and steadfast*. It pictures *a person who is devoted, trustworthy, dependable, dedicated, constant, and unwavering*. This, of course, is contrary to the flesh, which seeks to be lazy, uncommitted, undependable, and completely unreliable.

When Paul wrote to Timothy and told him how to choose leaders, he urged Timothy to choose "faithful" men. This is also the word *pistis*, which tells us that it is mandatory for this fruit of the Spirit to be found in leaders. In fact, it is also used by Paul in First Corinthians 4:2, where Paul writes, "Moreover it is required in stewards, that a man be found faithful." That last phrase could be translated, "...*It is required...that a man be found devoted, trustworthy, dependable, dedicated, constant, and unwavering.*"

This "faith" or "faithfulness" is so esteemed by God that it is listed in First Corinthians 13:13, where Paul writes, "And now abideth faith, hope, charity...." This fruit of the Spirit is a part of the eternal nature of God. The Bible stresses that God is faithful (First Corinthians 1:9) and utterly dependable. Numbers 23:19 (*NIV*) says, "God is not a man, that he should lie, nor a son of man, that he should change his mind." Jesus Himself is the same yesterday, today, and forever (Hebrews 13:8).

If this unchanging, constant, stable, unwavering behavior is the nature of God Himself, it shouldn't surprise us that when His Spirit is allowed to freely work in our lives, He makes us faithful and steadfast, just like God. God is faithful; therefore, we should expect faithfulness to grow in *our* lives as one of the fruits of the Holy Spirit.

Does the Holy Spirit have enough freedom to produce "goodness" and "faithfulness" in your life today? Are you selfish and self-seeking, consuming every spare dollar on yourself and never showing concern for the needs of those around you? Do others know you as someone who is unstable, undependable, and unreliable? If the answer is yes to either of these latter questions, doesn't this indicate that you aren't allowing the Holy Spirit to do His work in you? If He truly had the freedom to operate in your life, the fruits of "goodness" and "faithfulness" would be evident in you. *Don't you agree?*

MY PRAYER FOR TODAY

Lord, I want You to work so mightily in me that "goodness" and "faithfulness" become an integral part of my life. Please forgive me for the times I've been flesh-bound and insensitive to the human needs that are all around me. I have walked right past people with serious needs; yet I haven't even noticed. I am convicted by this, Lord, and I'm asking You to help me shift my focus from myself to those who are around me. I also ask You to help me become so faithful that people will know they can depend on me!

I pray this in Jesus' name!

MY CONFESSION FOR TODAY

I confess that I am sensitive to the human needs of those who are around me. In addition to believing for my own needs to be met, I also believe for the financial resources to help meet the needs of others. Just as Jesus was a blessing in His generation, I am a blessing in my generation. I am stable, unwavering, and consistent in every area of my life, reflecting the life and character of Jesus Christ in all that I do!

I declare this by faith in Jesus' name!

QUESTIONS FOR YOU TO CONSIDER

1. How long has it been since you gave sacrificially to help people who are poor and needy? Are you even aware of the needs of the poor and needy in your neighborhood, city, or world?
2. What can you do right now to start "doing good" to people near you who have serious basic needs? Can you give them an offering, take them to the grocery store, or fill up their car with gas? What would Jesus do?
3. Do you have a reputation with other people of being dependable, reliable, and trustworthy?

When a believer is walking in the Spirit, his eyes are opened to see the needs of humanity, and his heart is moved to meet those needs. This is why there is no greater *benefactor* or *philanthropist* than a person who is filled with the Spirit and who is producing the fruit of the Spirit in his or her life!

JULY 27

Meekness and Temperance

But the fruit of the Spirit is love, joy, peace, longsuffering,
gentleness, goodness, faith, meekness, temperance....
— Galatians 5:22,23

*F*ew people think of "meekness" as a desirable attribute. Most assume that if a person is "meek," he must be "weak." To these people, a meek person is one who is timid, shy, bashful, or perhaps introverted.

But this a grossly incorrect view of the New Testament word for "meekness." In actual fact, "meekness" is one of the strongest attributes a person can possess, with a unique strength that has a dramatic impact on all it touches. In Galatians 5:22 and 23, meekness is listed as one of the fruits that the Holy Spirit produces in our lives. These verses tell us, "But the fruit of the Spirit is love, joy, peace, longsuffering, gentleness, goodness, faith, meekness...."

Meekness:

So what is "meekness?" The word "meekness" comes from the Greek word *prautes*, which depicts *the attitude or demeanor of a person who is forbearing, patient, and slow to respond in anger; one who remains in control of himself in the face of insults or injuries.* In the Greek language, the word *prautes* ("meekness") conveys the idea of a high and noble ideal to be aspired to in one's life. Although an injurious situation may normally produce a rash or angry outburst, a meek person is controlled by *kindness, gentleness, mildness,* or even *friendliness.*

The word "meekness" pictures a strong-willed person who has learned to submit his will to a higher authority. He isn't weak; he is *controlled.* He may in fact possess a strong will and a powerful character; he may be a person who has his own opinion. But this person has learned the secret of submitting to those who are over him. Thus, he is one who knows how to *bring his will under control.* In rare instances, the word *prautes* ("meekness") was used to describe wild animals that had become tame because it correctly conveyed the idea of *a wild, fierce will under control.*

This means when the Spirit is producing meekness in your life, you are controlled even in difficult circumstances. Rather than fly into a rage and throw a temper tantrum, you are able to remain silent and keep your emotions and temper under control. If you find yourself in a situation that you fiercely believe is wrong, you are still able to stay silent until the appropriate moment to speak or until you have been asked for your opinion. You know how to control yourself and your emotions.

In addition to these meanings, the word "meekness" was also used in a medical sense to denote *soothing medication to calm the angry mind.* A meek person doesn't project the countenance of one who is offended, upset, angry, or reactive to insults or injuries. Instead, he is so *gentle* and *mild* in his response that he becomes *soothing medicine* for the angry or upset soul, or for a troublesome or unsettling situation.

So take a moment to examine the way you respond to insults, injuries, or volatile situations. Do you find that you are often a contributor to a heated and potentially explosive atmosphere? Or does your presence bring peace into the midst of the conflict? When others say or do something that could offend you, do you quickly retort with a harsh answer, or are you able to control your emotions and temper, remaining silent until a more appropriate time to speak?

The flesh loves to rage out of control, but when meekness is being produced in you by the Holy Spirit, it will make you careful and controlled. Your very presence will become God's soothing medication for angry, upset people, and you will impart peace to situations that hitherto were unsettling and unstable.

Temperance:

Paul goes on to mention "temperance" next in his list of the fruit of the Spirit. But doesn't "temperance" have almost exactly the same meaning as the word "meekness"? What is the difference between these two fruits of the Spirit?

As noted above, the word "meekness" has to do with the attitude or demeanor of a person who can control his temper or emotions. But the word "temperance" comes from the Greek words *en* and *kratos*. The word *en* means *in*, and the word *kratos* is the Greek word for *power*. When compounded into one word, these two Greek words form the word *enkrateia*, which literally means *in control* and denotes *power over one's self*; hence, it is often translated as the word "self-control." It suggests the *control or restraint of one's passions, appetites, and desires.*

Just as a meek individual can control his attitude, a person with temperance has power over his appetites, physical urges, passions, and desires. Because the Holy Spirit has produced temperance in his life, he is able to say no to overeating, no to overindulging in fleshly activities, no to *any* excesses in the physical realm. A person with temperance maintains a life of *moderation* and *control*. The word *enkrateia* — "temperance" — could be thus translated as *restraint, moderation, discipline, balance, temperance,* or *self-control.*

You can see how opposite temperance is to the works of the flesh. If the flesh is allowed to have its way, it will over-worry, overwork, overeat, overindulge, and literally run itself to death. But when a person is controlled by the Holy Spirit, God's Spirit produces in him a discipline over the physical realm that helps him sustain his physical condition, stay in good health, remain free from sin, and live a life that is moderate and balanced.

Now that you better understand the meanings of the words "meekness" and "temperance," consider how well you're doing in allowing the Holy Spirit to produce these two spiritual fruits in *your* life. Do you demonstrate that you can control both your temper and your physical appetites and urges? Are you able to restrain your emotions and keep your flesh under control? Or would you have to honestly say that you have a hard time controlling your emotions and that your flesh is running the show?

Take a good look at yourself today to see if meekness and temperance are being produced in you. *And if the answer is no, take some time today to ask the Holy Spirit to start producing these two powerful fruits in your life!*

MY PRAYER FOR TODAY

Lord, I am so thankful that You are patient with me as I learn to walk in the Spirit and to produce the fruit of the Spirit in my life. Every day I am becoming more aware of my need to be changed. It is very evident that I cannot change myself without Your help. I know that I need meekness and temperance in my life. When I look at myself in the mirror, my physical image even tells me that temperance is greatly lacking in me. So today I am sincerely calling out and asking You to help me move up to a higher level of life. Produce these powerful, life-changing fruits in me. Change me, I pray!

I pray this in Jesus' name!

MY CONFESSION FOR TODAY

I confess that I am becoming more and more controlled in my emotions and my physical life. Restraint, moderation, temperance, discipline, self-control — all of these are becoming a part of who I am and how I behave. The nature and character of Jesus Christ are being developed in me. The spiritual fruits of meekness and temperance are changing me — bringing peace to every situation I encounter and producing health in me as I learn to be moderate in everything that I do!

I declare this by faith in Jesus' name!

QUESTIONS FOR YOU TO CONSIDER

1. Do you have the testimony of being *soothing medicine* for the angry or upset soul, or do you stir up anger and strife? Do others see you as having a *calm* and *soothing effect* on other people?
2. When you look at your life honestly, do you see *self-control*? Do you have power over yourself, or does your flesh call all the shots? Are you able to tell your flesh what to do, or does your flesh command you?
3. In what areas do you think you need more self-control? Why don't you think about this question and then make a list of those areas in your life that need to be more controlled by the Spirit of God?

JULY 28

Take My Yoke Upon You

Come unto me, all ye that labour
and are heavy laden, and I will give you rest.
Take my yoke upon you, and learn of me;
for I am meek and lowly in heart:
and ye shall find rest unto your souls.
For my yoke is easy, and my burden is light.
— Matthew 11:28-30

When our family first moved to the Soviet Union, the Soviet economy was so collapsed and the system so broken that even the most basic supplies were difficult to find. One of those hard-to-find supplies was gasoline for one's car — and not just for the car, but for any machinery that operated on gasoline. Because of this lack of fuel, few cars were driven, and people walked great distances. There was just no available fuel to put into the tanks of the cars parked inside people's garages.

At that time our family lived in a remote area on the edge of a small city where people were given small plots of land to grow gardens. One spring when it was time to plow the garden and plant seeds, I looked out the kitchen window of our house and saw something I could hardly believe! Our neighbor had taken an old harness, like one that would be normally placed around the neck of a cow, a horse, or an ox, and hooked it up to his wife! I watched in amazement as this man walked behind his wife, guiding the plow as she heaved forward with her neck and shoulders, dragging the plow through the hardened soil. The two of them were working to break up the ground so they could plant their seeds and produce their garden. They owned a small tractor, but because there was no fuel, they couldn't use it. Therefore, this couple resorted to the action I beheld that day.

I called to Denise and told her to come to the kitchen. She looked out the window with me and saw this poor woman hooked up to a harness and pulling the plow, with her husband trying to guide the sharp blade through that solid ground. Denise was speechless! What this couple was doing just outside our backyard looked so hard and difficult! We both wished we had a couple of oxen to loan them that day in order to make their job a little easier!

Many times Denise and I have worked so hard in the ministry that we felt like we had given every ounce of our strength; yet there always seemed to be so much more that we needed to give. On several occasions, I told my wife, "I guess it's time for us to hook up the plow and press through this hard ground! Let's go for it, Sweetheart!" We'd laugh and then remember the words of Jesus in Matthew 11:28-30, where He said, "Come unto me, all ye that labour and are heavy laden, and I will give you rest. Take my yoke upon you, and learn of me; for I am meek and lowly in heart: and ye shall find rest unto your souls. For my yoke is easy, and my burden is light."

The word "labour" in verse 28 is from the Greek word *kopaio*, which describes *the most wearisome kind of labor*. This is a person who is giving everything he has to a project or assignment. He is *striving, laboring, and working* with every fiber of his being. But the Greek tense describes people who have been laboring under this load without a pause for a very long time. Their work has been *wearisome, exhausting, and unending.*

The words "heavy laden" tell us why these people are so weary from their labors. These words are from the Greek word *phortidzo*, which denotes a *load or burden that is normal and expected for an individual to carry in life*. It was a military term that described the *backpack* or *bag* that every soldier was required to carry as a part of his career as a soldier. Carrying such a weight was a normal and expected requirement for soldiers. The weight of these backpacks and bags was determined by the length of the soldier's journey. If his trip was short, the weight would be less. But if the assignment mandated a longer journey, the weight of the backpack or bag would be much *heavier laden.*

This means Jesus was referring to people who had been doing their job for a very long time — and their job wasn't done yet. Their journey had not been a quick, short, and easy one, and much of it was still before them. They had quite a long distance yet to go before they reached their destination. Knowing how exhausted they were and yet how much further they had to go before they were finished, Jesus told them, "Come unto me...and I will give you rest" (v. 28).

The word "rest" is from the Greek word *anapauo*, which means *to rest, to relax, to calm,* or *to refresh*. The root is *pauo*, from which we get the word *pause*. So in Matthew 11:28, the word *anapauo* carries the meaning of *to pause, to cease, to desist,* or *to refrain*. In our modern-day language, it could be translated *to take a breather; to have a break; to have a hiatus, a lull, an interval, an interruption;* or *to take time to get away from something or some responsibility.*

Jesus never promised that He would take difficult assignments away from you. However, He did promise that if you would come to Him, He would give you the rest you need in order to be refreshed for the continuation and conclusion of the journey. So when it seems like you've given all you have, but there's still so much more for you to do before you're finished, just take a break from your journey and go to Jesus for some supernatural refreshing!

Then in Matthew 11:29, Jesus said, "Take my yoke upon you...." The word "take" is the word *airo*, meaning *to deliberately lift* or *to deliberately take up.* The fact that Jesus used the word *airo* implies that one must deliberately invite Jesus into the harness so He can help you pull the plow. The word "yoke" is the Greek word *zugos*, which describes *the wooden yoke that joined two animals together so they could combine their strength to pull a load that generally would have been too difficult for one animal to pull by itself.* This "yoke" made the team inseparable. As a result, they were stronger, and their combined strength made their task easier.

This is Jesus' offer to the weary and tired worker. Jesus offers to come alongside the worker and join him in his assignment or affairs. However, the worker — the weary soul — has to make the deliberate choice to enter into this working relationship and to come under the yoke of Jesus. He has to take the "yoke" of Jesus upon himself, reaching out by faith to lift it up and place it upon himself.

Becoming "yoked" to Jesus in your life, your ministry, your business, and your personal affairs is a premeditated, determined choice — not something that occurs accidentally. But just as two animals that are "yoked" together make a job much more easy and manageable, the strength of you and Jesus together is unbeatable! That is why the Lord went on to say, "For my yoke is easy, and my burden is light" (Matthew 11:30).

The word "easy" is the Greek word *chrestos*, meaning *pleasurable, delightful,* or *comfortable.* This means it is a *delight* to work with the Lord. When you are yoked together with Jesus, even the most difficult assignments become *pleasurable!* Situations that would normally make you uneasy become comfortable. Being "yoked" together with Him changes the atmosphere and brings peace and strength to your soul. It is the most pleasurable experience in the world!

Jesus concluded this verse by saying that being "yoked" together with Him is "light." The word "light" is the Greek word *elaphron*, describing *something that is not burdensome, but light or easy.* I can tell you from personal experience — what was once hard, wearisome, and troubling because you were doing it all alone becomes pleasurable and lighter when you are partners with Jesus!

So what about you, friend? Are you going to keep pulling that plow through that solid ground all by yourself? Or are you going to allow Jesus to become partnered with you in your endeavors? Going it alone is the hardest course you can take. *But when you choose to be yoked together with Jesus, you suddenly have the greatest Partner in the universe who will turn a once-hard situation into the most pleasurable experience of your life!*

MY PRAYER FOR TODAY

Lord, I admit that I've been trying to pull the whole load by myself, and I simply can't do it any longer. I have given every ounce of my strength; now I need You to come alongside me and help me finish the task that is before me. I'm willing to do it, but I must have Your help if I'm going to do it with all my heart and finish it all the way to the end. So today I am asking You to become "yoked" with me in my job, my business, my ministry, my family, and in all my personal affairs.

I pray this in Jesus' name!

MY CONFESSION FOR TODAY

I confess that Jesus Christ is my Partner in life. He works with me; He walks with me; and He is my biggest Helper! Because of Jesus' strategic role in my life, my attitude, my environment, my work, and everything connected to me has become better, higher, finer, and more pleasurable. My life assignment is not a burden — it is truly a delight!

I declare this by faith in Jesus' name!

QUESTIONS FOR YOU TO CONSIDER

1. Can you think of an area of your life where you need to invite Jesus to become "yoked" together with you to make your journey lighter and more enjoyable?
2. Have you been trying to do it all alone? Is this the reason you are so exhausted from your labors?
3. Do you feel alone in your endeavors, or do you sense that Jesus is hooked up with you and that He is helping you pull the load?

JULY 29

❦

Where Sin Abounds, Grace Much More Abounds!

...But where sin abounded,
grace did much more abound.
— Romans 5:20

I'll never forget the time we were being attacked on every side by the enemy. It seemed like an all-out assault had been unleashed against us. At the same time we were experiencing this attack on our ministry, the city where we lived was in political upheaval. This chaotic situation was so terrible that a bomb was detonated just a two-minute walking distance from our apartment! We could feel our building shake as the bomb exploded. It seemed as if each day was bringing new problems to the nation and more threats to our ministry.

All of this was occurring at a time when the Spirit of God had told us to launch out and take a new step of faith. It seemed like such a wrong time to take such a step of faith. Logic said, "Pull back! Protect yourself! Stop everything until the heat is off!" But the Spirit of God kept telling us,

'Dig in deeper! Keep pressing forward! Don't let up for one minute! This is a perfect opportunity for the Gospel message to be spread even further!"

Right in the middle of all that chaos, we watched as God poured out His grace on us. Although it was a dangerous and difficult time, it was also a glorious moment to be serving in the Kingdom of God! God began to do marvelous new things in the nation where we lived. In that troublesome hour, people were open and hungry to know more about the things of God. They wanted answers and were willing to listen. As a result, people were saved; spiritual darkness was pushed back in people's lives; and the Gospel was spread further than ever before! As God moved mightily in the nation, that very dark, precarious moment became a spiritually bright time as many were led into the Kingdom of God.

This simultaneous operation of darkness and grace made me think of Romans 5:20, which says, "…Where sin abounded, grace did much more abound." The word "abounded" that Paul uses to describe this abundance of sin comes from the Greek word, *pleonadzo*, which simply means *more*. It denotes *something that exists in abundance*. The Greek tense describes an *abundance that is growing larger and more expansive with the passing of time*. The implication is that sin is never stagnant but continually grows, increases, and expands. This means Romans 5:20 could be translated, "*Where sin exists in abundance and is multiplying and constantly expanding….*" This describes the growing nature of unrestrained sin.

But Paul doesn't stop there! He goes on to say, "…Where sin abounded, grace did *much more abound.*" The words "much more abound" are from the Greek word *huperperisseo*, which describes *something that is growing out of measure, beyond proportion, and out of its banks to a far-stretched extreme*. It is like a giant river that is being flooded with waters from upstream. Those waters are coming downstream so fast that the river can no longer hold the raging current in its banks. Its water rises, rises, and rises until it finally begins pouring out of its banks and begins to flood everything in sight. This is exactly the idea of the word Paul uses when he says, "…Grace did much more abound."

This means Romans 5:20 could be interpreted:

"For wherever sin exists in abundance and is multiplying and constantly expanding, that is precisely the time and place where grace is poured out in a far greater, surpassing quantity."

Regardless of where we live and what we are facing — regardless of how bad the situation around us looks to our natural eyes — the grace of God is flowing *downstream*, and God is lavishly pouring it forth in *abundant* measure! In fact, it is impossible for us to imagine, measure, or even dream of the amount of divine grace God is sending in our direction. No banks can hold the flood of grace He is sending our way! It isn't just "a lot" of grace; it is more, more, more, and *much more* grace! The flood of grace will always far surpass the flood of sin and darkness!

Satan will try to stop you from doing the will of God, but never forget that the enemy *cannot* prevail against you if you will only yield to the Lord. You will find that God is supplying more than enough grace to match whatever the enemy is trying to do. If you will surrender to that divine grace, it will rise higher and higher until it eventually floods every area in your life. Instead of seeing the destruction of the enemy, you will see the awesome outpouring of the marvelous grace of God everywhere you look!

So when a situation looks bad, as it did so many years ago when we were living amid troublesome times in our part of the world, don't be too surprised if you hear God's Spirit say, "Pour it on! Keep it up! Don't stop for a minute! Keep pressing ahead! It is in dark and difficult moments like these that I love to work the most! This is when My grace super-exceeds the darkness of the world. Wherever sin and darkness abound is where I *really* pour out My grace!"

MY PRAYER FOR TODAY

Lord, I thank You for pouring out Your grace in difficult, chaotic times. When sin abounds and darkness tries to reign, that is always when You reach out to seek and to save. Forgive me for giving way to fear and for thinking of retreating at this key moment when You are wanting to make a strategic advance. I choose to push away all my fears and to believe that You are going to do something miraculous to save the day! Let Your grace flow, Lord — pour it on! Please shine Your light in this hour of darkness!

I pray this in Jesus' name!

MY CONFESSION FOR TODAY

I confess that God's grace is poured out mightily to drive back the forces of darkness during times of difficulty and chaos. God uses these dark moments as opportunities to pour out His grace and to show others who He is! The world may reel in fear and uncertainty, but God is always near. I declare by faith that God will reveal His power and intervene with His grace to bring the solution for this difficult hour!

I declare this by faith in Jesus' name!

QUESTIONS FOR YOU TO CONSIDER

1. Have you ever had a dark moment in your life when God's grace was abundantly poured out in a measure that was far greater than anything you had ever expected or dreamed in your life?
2. Do you have any areas in your life right now where you need a fresh outpouring of God's grace to combat the darkness? If yes, what are those areas in which you need this supernatural touch?
3. Can you think of a time in history when God has sent a nation-shaping revival in the midst of troublesome times? What happened as a result of that revival?

Regardless of where we live and what we are facing — regardless of how bad the situation around us looks to our natural eyes — the grace of God is flowing *downstream*, and God is lavishly pouring it forth in *abundant* measure! In fact, it is impossible for us to imagine, measure, or even dream of the amount of divine grace God is sending in our direction. No banks can hold the flood of grace He is sending our way! It isn't just "a lot" of grace; it is more, more, more, and *much more* grace! The flood of grace will always far surpass the flood of sin and darkness!

JULY 30

❦

The Devil Has a Plan for Your Life!

The thief cometh not, but for to steal,
and to kill, and to destroy:
I am come that they might have life,
and that they might have it more abundantly.
— John 10:10

I realize that John 10:10 is a well-known verse to millions of believers around the world, but today I want to give you fresh insight into this powerful scripture. Rather than simply read it as you've read it a thousand times before, let's dig a little deeper into the Greek words behind this verse to see what we can mine from the treasures of the Greek New Testament!

Jesus said, "The thief cometh not, but for to steal, and to kill, and to destroy: I am come that they might have life, and that they might have it more abundantly" (John 10:10). According to these words of Jesus, the thief comes to steal, kill, and destroy everything good in your life. He wants to destroy your job, your joy, your happiness, your health, your finances, your marriage, and your kids. The thief just wants to ruin anything he can get his hands on!

The word "thief" comes from the Greek word *klepto*, which means *to steal*. It gives a picture of *a bandit, pickpocket, or thief who is so artful in the way he steals that his exploits of thievery are nearly undetectable*. This reminds me of the pickpockets who work the streets in certain areas of Moscow. They can slip their hands into a person's pockets, take what they want, and be long gone before that person discovers they were even there!

Jesus uses this word to let us know the devil is very cunning in the way he steals from people. He knows that if he does it outright, his actions will be recognized; therefore, he steals from people in such a deceptive way that he often accomplishes his evil goal before they even know he has stolen from them!

Often the devil injects thoughts into a person's mind to steal his peace, his joy, and even his beliefs. The word *klepto* describes *a thief's uncontrollable urge to get his hands into someone's pockets so he can take that which doesn't rightfully belong to him*. I find it very interesting that this is where we get the word *kleptomaniac*, which describes a person with a persistent, neurotic impulse to steal. Just as a kleptomaniac can't help but steal, the devil can't stop stealing because it is his impulse and his very nature to steal. This is precisely the nature and behavior of the thief Jesus told us about!

Not only does the thief come to steal, but Jesus said that he also comes "to kill." At first glance, it appears that this means *to kill, as to take someone's life*. But the Greek word is *thuo*, which means *to sacrifice*. It originally referred *to the sacrificial giving of animals on the altar*. It could mean *to sacrifice; to surrender;* or *to give up something that is precious and dear*. It was particularly used in a religious connotation to denote *the sacrifice of animals*, and it had nothing to do with killing in terms of murder.

Because Jesus uses this word to describe the work of the thief in John 10:10, He is telling us that if the thief hasn't already walked away with everything we hold precious and dear, he will then try to convince us that we need to sacrifice or give up everything he hasn't already taken from us.

The thief cannot bear the fact that you possess any kind of blessing. Therefore, if he is unsuccessful at stealing the good things from your life, he will try to cunningly convince you to give up everything you possess and love — simply because he doesn't want you to have it. He may even try to create stressful situations that cause you to conclude that your only solution is to sacrifice the things you dearly love.

Then Jesus went on to say that the thief also comes "to destroy." The word "destroy" is from the Greek word *apollumi*, meaning *to destroy*. It carries the idea of *something that is ruined, wasted, trashed, devastated, and destroyed.* By using this word, we discover that if the thief is unsuccessful in his attempts to steal from you or convince you to sacrifice what you hold dear, he will then try to ruin it!

An expanded interpretive translation
of John 10:10 could read this way:

"The thief wants to get his hands into every good thing in your life. In fact, this pickpocket is looking for any opportunity to wiggle his way so deeply into your personal affairs that he can walk off with everything you hold precious and dear. And that's not all — when he's finished stealing all your goods and possessions, he'll take his plan to rob you blind to the next level. He'll create conditions and situations so horrible that you'll see no way to solve the problem except to sacrifice everything that remains from his previous attacks. The goal of this thief is to totally waste and devastate your life. If nothing stops him, he'll leave you insolvent, flat broke, and cleaned out in every area of your life. You'll end up feeling as if you are finished and out of business! Make no mistake — the enemy's ultimate aim is to obliterate you...."

But Jesus went on to say, "...I am come that they might have life, and that they might have it more abundantly" (John 10:10). The words "they might have" are from the Greek tense that means *to have and to continually possess.* The "life" Jesus offers us is *zoe,* which suggests *a life that is filled with vitality.* The word "abundantly" is from the Greek word *periossos,* and it means *to be above, beyond what is regular, extraordinary,* or even *exceeding.* This is not just *abundance*; it is *super-abundance.*

What a comparison! The devil comes to steal, to kill, and to destroy, but Jesus comes to give life as we have never known it!

An expanded interpretive translation
of this second part of John 10:10 could be as follows:

"...But I came that they might have, keep, and constantly retain a vitality, gusto, vigor, and zest for living that springs up from deep down inside. I came that they might embrace this unrivaled, unequaled, matchless, incomparable, richly loaded and overflowing life to the ultimate maximum!"

In your walk with the Lord, you *will* experience times when the devil pushes buttons in your emotions to keep you all bound up and depressed. Other times the enemy will disguise his voice to make you think God is talking to you in order to get you off track or cause you to cast off your deepest dreams as pure imagination. But whenever these attacks occur, just tell the devil to shut up and stop dropping those dimwitted thoughts of nonsense into your head. Tell him to hit the road! Let him know you're not going to bite that bait any longer, so he might as well go fishing somewhere else. You're not a sucker anymore! You know how he works now, and you've determined that he isn't going to steal, kill, or destroy one more good thing in your life!

There's no doubt about it!

- ✦ The devil wants you to be defeated.
- ✦ The devil wants you to struggle through your entire life.

+ The devil wants you to be sick, depressed, down in the dumps, glum, and miserable.
+ The devil wants you to feel like you will never hit the target with your life.
+ But Jesus wants to give you a life that is unrivaled, unequaled, matchless, incomparable, richly loaded, and overflowing with life to the ultimate maximum!

So now that you know the devil wants to make your life a less-than-gratifying, unhappy, uneventful life — a life that no one will even notice is gone once it's over — what are you going to do about it? I urge you to put on the brakes and stop Satan from wreaking havoc in your life. *Jesus will give you the power to resist every attack and to overcome every strategy the devil ever tries to use against you!*

MY PRAYER FOR TODAY

Lord, I am so thankful that You came to give me real life! You didn't save me so I could live the rest of my life in defeat and poverty. You didn't redeem me so I could be sick, depressed, and sad. You came to give me life, and I am determined to enter into the reality of that life You promised me. Forgive me for ever allowing the devil to talk me out of the blessings You have designed for my life and my family. I'm taking my eyes off the low road, and I'm headed for the high road of blessing You have planned for me!

I pray this in Jesus' name!

MY CONFESSION FOR TODAY

I confess that Jesus Christ gives me a life that is filled with extraordinary abundance! He came that I might have, keep, and constantly retain a vitality, gusto, vigor, and zest for living that springs up from deep down inside me. He gives me a life that is not rattled or easily shaken by any outward event. I therefore embrace this unrivaled, unequaled, matchless, incomparable, richly loaded, and overflowing life that Jesus came to give me!

I declare this by faith in Jesus' name!

QUESTIONS FOR YOU TO CONSIDER

1. If an unbeliever looked at your life, would he say that you had an "abundant life" or that you lived a low-level, meager existence? What do you think "abundance" would mean to an unbeliever?
2. How do *you* gauge an "abundant life"? Do you measure abundance in terms of spirituality, finances, health, relationships, or employment? How many of these areas do you think Jesus was referring to when He spoke of living life "more abundantly"?
3. In what areas are you *not* experiencing abundant life? It would be very helpful for you to make a list of these areas so you can pray about them and begin to believe for God's abundance to flow into these parts of your life.

The word "thief" gives a picture of a bandit, pickpocket, or thief who is so artful in the way he steals that his exploits of thievery are nearly undetectable.

JULY 31

❧❧❧

Don't Deliberately Invite a Typhoon Into Your Church, Ministry, or Business!

Not a novice, lest being lifted up with pride
he fall into the condemnation of the devil.
— 1 Timothy 3:6

*M*aybe you've had an associate or a worker whom you once greatly trusted — until he or she deceived and betrayed you. If you've gone through that kind of difficult experience, you may not be too excited about trusting people again.

Every leader in the world has been through one of these experiences. Even Jesus had a thief on His team who stole money from the organization and who later betrayed Him and turned Him over to the religious authorities to be executed on a cross. If that can happen to Jesus, it's possible for it to happen to anyone. But Jesus didn't give up and quit just because there was one bad apple in His group. There were still eleven others who remained faithful. Although these eleven also made some mistakes along the way, they ultimately changed the course of human history as they carried the Gospel message to the ends of the earth.

Letting your emotions get the best of you by deciding to go on alone is not the right answer when you go through this type of experience. You need to get up, brush off the dirt, learn from your mistakes, and go for it again with all your heart. Rather than blame someone else for what has happened, just accept responsibility for where *you* may have failed. Stop moaning about the bump in the road you've hit, and allow that ordeal to become a learning experience. It's time to quit thinking about what others did wrong to you. Instead, ask what *you* did wrong that permitted the situation to arise. Ask yourself:

+ *Did I give too much authority to this person too quickly?*
+ *Did I trust someone I really didn't know very well?*
+ *Did I spend enough time with that person to really become his friend?*
+ *Did I let that person know what I expected of him?*
+ *Did I ignore signs that something was going amiss?*
+ *Did my spouse tell me something was wrong, but I wouldn't listen?*
+ *What did I learn from this experience?*

No school is more effective than the one you go through when someone you work with betrays or disappoints you. After that experience, you will better understand why Paul told Timothy not to choose unknown people for key leadership positions. In First Timothy 3:6, Paul wrote: "Not a novice, lest being lifted up with pride he fall into the condemnation of the devil."

If I were to ask you, "What is a novice?" you might answer that a novice is a new Christian. That certainly *can* be true; however, the word "novice" is much broader than this narrow interpretation. It comes from the Greek word *neophutos*, which is a compound of the words *neo* and *photos*. The word *neo* means *new*, and *photos* is the Greek word for *a plant*. Compounded together, *neophutos* means *a new plant*. In this context, it is understood to mean *a new convert* or *a new Christian*. But this word can also refer to *an old plant that is new in your garden*. In other words, it can also refer to *a transplant*.

Few pastors make the mistake of choosing brand-new converts for key positions in the church or ministry. Few business leaders would put a young, inexperienced teenager in charge of their business. However, church leaders and business people do often make the mistake of promoting people too quickly when those people come to them from other churches, organizations, or businesses. Newcomers may look good and sound good, and their talents may be urgently needed. Thus, hasty decisions are often made, and people are promoted before they are really known.

People may have years of experience, but if they are new in *your* garden — your church, ministry, organization, or business — you need to take the time to know them before you give them vast amounts of authority and responsibility. Paul explains why, saying that if you promote a person too quickly, it puts him in a position for the devil to deceive him into thinking too highly of himself. This is what Paul means when he says, "Not a novice, lest being lifted up with pride...."

The phrase "lifted up with pride" comes from the Greek word *tuphuo*, and it means *to be wrapped in smoke*, such as *a person whose vision is so blurred, he can't see things properly*. This is where we get the word *typhoon*, which refers to *a destructive storm that causes great damage*.

You see, when a person is elevated too quickly, the devil often whispers to that person, "Look how powerful you are! Even though you're new here, you've already become so visible!" Why is this so extremely dangerous? Paul continues to explain by saying, "Not a novice, lest being lifted up with pride he fall into the condemnation of the devil."

Do you see the words "he fall into"? These are from the Greek word *empipto*, which means *to fall into some kind of controversy* or *to fall into some kind of encounter*. Thus, Paul warns that when a person is promoted too high too quickly, he may become clouded by his own sense of self-importance, which causes him to stumble into an encounter with the devil that could have destructive, typhoon-like consequences not only for the person himself, but for the church, organization, or business.

Paul concludes by saying, "...lest he fall into the condemnation of the devil." The word "condemnation" is the Greek word *krima*, which means *judgment*. It can describe *an action that leads to one's judgment*. This being the case, this phrase could be translated, "...lest he fall under the same *action and judgment of the devil*."

What was the action of the devil that led to his judgment? You can find his words in Isaiah 14:12-14, where five times he declared that he would ascend into the highest places of Heaven to disrupt the position of God and to seize God's throne above the angels. Ezekiel 28:17 tells us the reason this deception filled Satan's heart. It says, "Thine heart was lifted up because of thy beauty...." You see, Lucifer became so impressed with his own beauty and radiance that he started thinking too highly of himself — and that is what led him to believe he could usurp the position of God!

This kind of situation is precisely what Paul is warning us to avoid when he urges us not to promote people to positions of authority too quickly. When this happens, Satan begins to go to work in these people's minds, telling them that they are wonderful and more powerful, gifted, and capable than anyone else. If they allow the devil's game to work in their minds, they will begin to think they should have authority that was never given to them. This is precisely the kind of wrong thinking that will release a spiritual typhoon in your church, organization, or ministry!

So if you've ever suffered after promoting someone before you really knew him — or if you've ever been hurt because you gave power to good people too quickly — you need to accept responsibility for where *you* may have failed. Learn from this experience, and then move on. *You'll be a much better leader because of what you have learned from this difficult "school of hard knocks"!*

MY PRAYER FOR TODAY

Lord, I ask You to please help me gauge how quickly others should be promoted in our church, organization, or business. I don't want to make the mistake of throwing people into situations where the devil will test them because I promoted them too quickly. Also, Lord, I ask You to please help me have a new appreciation for those who are over me and who are taking some time before promoting me. I want to be a blessing and I never want the devil to have an opportunity to blur my vision because I think too highly of myself. Thank You for loving me enough to promote me in just the right time and in just the right way.

I pray this in Jesus' name!

MY CONFESSION FOR TODAY

I confess that I use wisdom in the way I choose and promote leaders in my area of responsibility. I am careful, cautious, and hesitant about promoting people to high positions too quickly. Just as God watches and tests me before giving me greater responsibility, I watch, test, and wait to see if others are really ready before I assign them new and important tasks. Because I rely on the Holy Spirit's help in this matter, I am making fewer and fewer mistakes in choosing the right people to promote!

I declare this by faith in Jesus' name!

QUESTIONS FOR YOU TO CONSIDER

1. Have you ever seen someone promoted so quickly that it caused deep spiritual problems later on? If so, who was that person, and what did you learn by observing that heart-rending situation?
2. Have you ever watched someone whom a pastor loved, cared for, and promoted later become the chief critic of that same pastor? Was that person *you?* If yes, have you ever gone to your pastor to ask for his forgiveness?
3. If you've been feeling let down by someone you trusted, why don't you take some time today to pray and ask the Lord to help you forgive that person? After all, the prison of bitterness you've been locked in because of that past offense hurts only *you!*

Church leaders and business people often make the mistake of promoting people too quickly when those people come to them from other churches, organizations, or businesses. Newcomers may look good and sound good, and their talents may be urgently needed. Thus, hasty decisions are often made, and people are promoted before they are really known.

AUGUST 1

⚜

Instant 'in Season' And 'out of Season'!

Preach the word;
be instant in season, out of season....
— 2 Timothy 4:2

*P*aul wrote his second letter to Timothy during a very difficult season in Timothy's ministry. A few years earlier, the picture had been radically different. At that time, the church was growing and thriving. Timothy was the new young pastor whom the church loved! Those earlier years were fun and eventful, and everything was moving. What an exciting time it had been to be a Christian leader!

But by the time Second Timothy was written, the picture had changed drastically. Nero had become the emperor of the Roman Empire, and his insanity was already wreaking havoc in the lives of countless believers all over the empire. Because Ephesus was the major city of Asia Minor and the seat of the Proconsul of Rome, it had been designated as a place where Christians were to be purged and hence made an example to all believers in other parts of Asia Minor. The Roman government intended to scare them out of their Christian faith and right back into the old pagan temples.

As a result of these hard times, many believers died for their faith. Others defected from the church and returned to the old temples to save their lives. And as if all these hardships and disappointments were not mountainous enough to deal with, Timothy also had to deal with serious internal problems of rebellion among some of the members of his church leadership!

Timothy had written a letter to Paul explaining all his difficulties. Paul's response to Timothy was the book of Second Timothy. In that book, he urged Timothy to remember that he was to "...be instant in season, out of season..." (2 Timothy 4:2).

The word "instant" is the Greek word *ephistimi*, which is a compound of the words *epi* and *istimi*. The word *epi* means *upon*, and the word *istimi* means *to stand*. Compounded into one word, the new word means *to stand upon*, as to take a firm stand or a hard position. Indeed, it was a term borrowed from the military that meant *to stay at one's post*.

Timothy's post was the pulpit of his church. From that pulpit, he maintained his leadership, imparted vision, issued rebukes, taught and preached the Word, and brought correction. It was *his post*. No one else could stand in that position, because it was the position that had been assigned to him by God. Even though times were very tough and he may have been tempted to shun his responsibilities, Paul urged him, *"Stay at your post!"*

Notice that Paul told him that he was to be faithful to his post "in season, out of season." In Greek, this looks like a play on words, but it is a very powerful statement to those of us who are doing our best to serve God. The words "in season" come from the Greek word *eukairos*. The words "out of season" come from the Greek word *akairos*. Do you notice how similar these words are to each other?

The word *kairos* is the Greek word that means *seasons* or *times*. This word can be easily altered by adding different prefixes to it. For instance, if you add the word *eu* to the front of it, it becomes the word *eukairos*. The word *eu* means *good, happy, pleasing,* or *pleasurable*. This means that whe you connect the word *eu* to *kairos*, it transforms the word to *eukairos*, which means *good times, happ times, pleasing times,* or *pleasurable times*.

But you can also change the word *kairos* by adding the prefix *a*, which turns it into the word *akairos*. That little *a* may look insignificant, but it radically changes the meaning of this word. Th word *akairos* means *bad times*. So when Paul told him, "Be instant in season and out of season," h was really telling him to be faithful, whether he was having *happy times* or *bad times*!

An interpretive translation of Second Timothy 4:2 could be the following:

"Take a firm stand and resolve to stay at your post! Regardless of whether times are good or bad, that is your post — your place of responsibility — so dig in, take a firm stand, and resolve that you are going to be faithful!"

This was just the word Timothy needed to encourage him to stand tall, be brave, and remain faithfu to his assignment. His struggles passed, and he became the respected leader of the Christians in the region o Asia Minor. In the years that he served as the senior pastor of Ephesus, Timothy had many different kind of seasons — some good, some not so good. But regardless, he stayed at his post until the very end.

What kind of season are you going through right now? Is it a happy season? Or are you expe riencing hard times? Those happy seasons are such wonderful times, and you should do everything you can to enjoy them. But what are you going to do in the hard times? Are you going to be as faith ful and steadfast when you face difficult challenges as you were when things seemed a little easier?

Take Paul's words to Timothy, and apply them to yourself. This is not a time for you to run i fear or to look for someone else to take your place. *If God called you to that post, it's time for you t dig in, take a firm stand, and resolve that you are going to be faithful whether times are good or bad.*

I assure you that the bad times will eventually pass. Dark clouds never last. Eventually the sun always comes out, and the birds start singing again. Wouldn't it be a pity if you gave up and sacri ficed everything you've worked so hard to gain because of a few dark clouds?

Jesus is with you, my friend. He will give you all the strength you need to stand tall and to remain faithful. He will do His part, but only you can do your part. What is your part? *Making the choice to stay faithful to your post!*

MY PRAYER FOR TODAY

Lord, I receive this word today as strength for my life! You have called me to do something great for You, and I'm not going to let the devil or my circumstances chase me away from where I know I need to be. It's been very difficult, but this season will pass — and when it does, I'll be stronger, wiser, and more equipped for the future. I thank You for helping me to dig in, take a firm stand, and maintain the post You have assigned to me!

I pray this in Jesus' name!

MY CONFESSION FOR TODAY

I confess that I am not moving from the place where Jesus called me! The devil and various circumstances have tried hard to move me, but I have made up my mind and have resolved in my heart that I am not flinching or moving from the place where Jesus called me to give my heart! This is my post; this is my ground; and I'm going to be around until I can say I've finished my part!

I declare this by faith in Jesus' name!

QUESTIONS FOR YOU TO CONSIDER

1. Have the dark clouds been hovering over you for so long that it has made you wish you could give your assignment to someone else?
2. Have you considered how tragic it would be if you quit just before the sun started shining again? Is it possible that you are at the end of this turbulent season and that the best season of your life is just around the corner?
3. Can you think of times in your past when you thought it was all over for you, but then that difficult time passed and you came into a wonderful season of fruitfulness? Don't you believe God is able to do that again for you?

AUGUST 2

Whatsoever a Man Soweth, That Shall He Also Reap!

Be not deceived; God is not mocked:
for whatsoever a man soweth, that shall he also reap.
— Galatians 6:7

*I*t has been my pleasure to stand before my precious Russian congregation many thousands of times over the years and to boldly tell them, "Be not deceived; God is not mocked: for whatsoever a man soweth, that shall he also reap" (Galatians 6:7).

This principle is so true that Paul begins by telling us not to question its validity! He says, "Be not deceived; God is not mocked...." The word "deceived" comes from the Greek word *planao*, which means *to lead astray; to wander; to stagger; to be led off course;* or *to be affected by someone's outside influence and led in a wrong direction.* The word *planao* is usually used in the New Testament to depict the activity of false teachers who deliberately lead people from liberty into teaching that enslaves them in some kind of spiritual bondage.

When Paul wrote this verse, the language he used was a command coupled with a very strong prohibition. This means he was forbidding his readers from participating in something that seemed to have already been initiated. Because he spoke so prohibitively, it could correctly be translated, *"Stop being deceived."* He was rebuking a weakness that was already developing among the Galatians and that he wanted to halt! Could it be that false teachers were trying to tell the Galatians that the law of sowing and reaping didn't really work? It seems so.

We also live in a day and time when the law of sowing and reaping is challenged by those who do not embrace its truth. Many scoff at those who believe that God will multiply their financial seed back to them again; some even try to use their influence to persuade people to abandon their belief in such a doctrine.

Unfortunately, sometimes people who are young and unstable in the Word are caught in the middle of this war of words. A doubt sown here and there makes them question the validity of whether or not the law of sowing and reaping applies to finances. In the end, many of these new believers let go of their grip on this promise and walk away. But those deceivers who blatantly take a stand against the promise of God will one day answer for their actions.

Paul stands firm on the principle of sowing and reaping and lets his voice be heard as he states, "...God is not mocked...." The word "mocked" is the Greek word *mukteridzo*, and it means *to turn up one's nose at someone*, as if mocking or laughing at the person. The idea is of someone who arrogantly says, "Come on, you surely don't believe this stupid principle of sowing and reaping. How dumb can you be to believe that God will multiply what you sow!"

One noted scholar has commented that this type of attitude usually comes from a person who had a sour experience when he tried to apply the law of sowing and reaping to his finances. For some reason, he didn't get the results he expected, so now he acts as though this principle isn't true or applicable to anyone. Thus, he turns up his nose at the law of God, challenging the validity of it and asserting that whatsoever a man soweth is *not* always what he reaps.

Paul doesn't want this negativism and unbelief to worm its way into the thinking of the Galatian church, so he speaks loudly, firmly, and prohibitively, commanding the Galatian believers to disassociate themselves with anyone who dares to turn up his nose at the law of sowing and reaping.

Then Paul boldly declares what he believes: "...Whatsoever a man soweth, that shall he also reap." The word "soweth" is the word *speiro*, which refers to *any seed that is sown*. Notice the emphasis on *any* seed that is sown. This immediately alerts us to the fact that this law is not applicable only to finances, but to *anything* in life. It applies to love, to work, to time, to patience, to kindness, to forgiveness, to bitterness, to selfishness — and, of course, to money. All of these are potential "seeds" that we sow.

Making the definition of "soweth" even broader is the word "whatsoever," which in Greek is the word *ean*. This word literally throws open the door, for it means *whatever; whatever thing;* or *no matter what* a man sows. Again, Paul lets us know that this is a law of God that applies to every sphere of life with no exceptions. It is simply a fact: *Whatever you sow, regardless of what it is, you will reap it.*

The Greek tense does not denote a single, one-time sowing; rather, it pictures a person who continually, habitually sows. Therefore, it could be translated, *"...Whatsoever a man sows, sows, sows and sows — and keeps on habitually sowing and sowing and sowing...."* In other words, this describes a constant, steady, perpetual sowing of seed. And if you sow this seed steadily and faithfully, God's promise is that you *will* reap a harvest. The word for "reap" is in the same Greek tense, meaning that it could be translated, *"You will reap, reap, reap, and reap — and keep on habitually reaping and reaping and reaping."*

The reason most people walked away disgusted and scoffing at this promise is that they never really put it to the test! They sowed once and waited for a harvest. When nothing happened, they threw up their arms and said it didn't work. But those who keep on habitually sowing and sowing and *sowing* as a manner of lifestyle are the ones who eventually reap and reap and *reap* as the manifold blessings of God come pouring back into their lives.

The level at which you sow determines the level you will reap. Sow a little, and you'll reap a little. Sow a lot, and you'll reap a lot. Sow inconsistently, and you'll reap inconsistently. Sow regularly, and you will reap regularly.

Galatians 6:7 could be translated:

"Stop letting people lead you astray from the truth! You might try to turn up your nose at the law of God, but it won't change the law! It remains true that whatever you regularly and habitually sow — regardless of what it is — that is exactly what you will regularly and habitually reap."

Then in Galatians 6:9, Paul takes just a moment to encourage those of us who are waiting for our harvests. He says, "And let us not be weary in well doing: for in due season we shall reap, if we faint not."

Notice that Paul mentions a "due season." Even today, harvest times come at varying times for different areas, depending on the temperature, altitude, and climate of each region. For example, in one low-lying district of Israel, harvest may be in full swing while districts at higher altitudes are still weeks, or even a full month, away from their harvest time.

This principle holds true in every other realm as well. For instance, if the seed you are sowing is financial seed, remember to bathe it in prayer as it leaves your pocketbook and enters the Kingdom of God. Pray for the Holy Spirit to create a right atmosphere or climate for that seed to take root and grow. And if it takes awhile for the harvest to come back to you, remember that no farmer plants seed one day and expects to have a full wheat or corn field the next day! It takes time for seed to grow in the natural. In the same way, time may be required for the seed you have sown to spiritually mature so it can come back into your life as a multiplied blessing.

In the meantime, don't be weary in "well doing." That simply means keep it up; don't stop what you are doing; be regular; be consistent; be faithful; or be "well doing" in the sowing of your seed! The *last* thing you should do is "faint"!

That word "faint" comes from the Greek word *ekluo*, which means *to loosen up; to relax; to faint; and to lose altogether.* The devil will say, *"This doesn't work. You've tried long enough. It won't hurt if you cut back on your giving. Loosen up a little. Relax from giving so much!"*

But according to Galatians 6:9 and the Greek word *ekluo*, if you *loosen up* and *relax* in your giving, you will eventually "faint" — in other words, you'll stop giving completely. And if you do that, you will lose everything! So don't ever let the devil or anyone else ever talk you into backing out of sowing financial seeds into the Kingdom of God.

As I said earlier, the sowing of seeds applies to every area of life. If you constantly and habitually:

+ Sow *love*, you will reap *love*.
+ Sow *patience*, you will reap *patience*.
+ Sow *kindness*, you will reap *kindness*.
+ Sow *forgiveness*, you will reap *forgiveness*.
+ Sow *money*, you will reap *money*.
+ Sow *bitterness*, you will reap *bitterness*.
+ Sow *strife*, you will reap *strife*.

Friend, like it or not, this is just the way it is! It is the law of God, and there is not one thing you can do to change it. So rather than challenge the system and fail, don't you think it's time that you wise up and get with the program? *If you're going to reap what you sow, maybe you ought to figure* out what you want to reap. Then you can start planting those same kinds of seeds to assure that you'll ge‍ the harvest of your dreams!

MY PRAYER FOR TODAY

Lord, I want to be a faithful, consistent giver! I don't want to be on-again, off-again in the sowing of my financial seed. I know that this is a spiritual law that always works and will never change, so please help me renew my thinking to the truth of this law and come into a place of conformity with it. I want to habitually sow, and I want to habitually reap. Help me plant the right seeds into the right soil. Then I ask You to provide the right temperature, climate, and atmosphere to make my harvest grow!

I pray this in Jesus' name!

MY CONFESSION FOR TODAY

I confess that I am NOT a one-time sower. I continually, habitually sow my seed into the Kingdom of God. God's Word promises that "whatsoever a man sows, sows, sows, and sows, and keeps on habitually sowing and sowing and sowing, that shall he also reap, reap, reap, and reap, and keep on habitually reaping and reaping and reaping." Because I am a habitual sower, I will be a habitual reaper! The level at which I sow determines the level at which I will reap. If I sow a little, I will reap a little. If I sow a lot, I will reap a lot. If I sow inconsistently, I will reap inconsistently. If I sow regularly, I will reap regularly. Knowing this to be true, I choose to make my giving one of the most important and consistent things I do in my life!

I declare this by faith in Jesus' name!

QUESTIONS FOR YOU TO CONSIDER

1. Have you been consistent with your giving, or have you been on-again, off-again in the way you give your tithes and offerings? If you are irregularly blessed, do you think the reason may be that you irregularly sow seed? *At least it's something for you to think about!*
2. Do you faithfully give a full tithe to the work of the Lord? If yes, you can praise God for this victory in your life, for it will bless your future. If your answer is no, why are you being disobedient in this crucial area of your life?
3. In what other areas of your life are you reaping a harvest from seeds you wish you had never sown?

The level at which you sow determines the level you will reap. Sow a little, and you'll reap a little. Sow a lot, and you'll reap a lot. Sow inconsistently, and you'll reap inconsistently. Sow regularly, and you will reap regularly.

AUGUST 3

❦

A Supernatural Endowment
For Those Who Work on the Front Lines!

Truly the signs of an apostle were wrought among you
in all patience, in signs, and wonders, and mighty deeds.
— 2 Corinthians 12:12

During Paul's day, the problem of false apostles was so rampant that he felt it necessary to validate his ministry by pointing out the "signs" of an apostle that were evident in his life. In Second Corinthians 12:12, Paul gave certain indicators to help us determine whether or not a person is truly apostolic.

The word "signs" in Second Corinthians 12:12 is the Greek word *semeion*. This word was used in secular business to describe *the official written notice that announced the final verdict of a court*. It also described *the signature or seal applied to a document to guarantee its authenticity* and *a sign that marked key locations in a city*. This secular word was carried over into New Testament language, as used here by Paul.

Paul used this word to declare that certain official signs exist as the final verdict to prove a person's apostleship. These accompanying activities are like a signature or a seal that authenticates and guarantees that a person truly is an apostle. If you see these particular marks in a person's ministry, you can know that you are standing on or near bona fide apostolic territory.

Paul says, "Truly the signs of an apostle were *wrought* among you...." In this verse, Paul uses the word "apostle," taken from the Greek word *apostollos*, a compound of the words *apo* and *stello*. The word *apo* means *away*, and the word *stello* means *to send*. When compounded together, it means *to send away*. It is the idea of being *commissioned* and *dispatched* with authority and power and *sent as a personal representative* of a powerful figure or as the official representative of a government.

But notice Paul says, "Truly the signs of an apostle were *wrought* among you...." The word "wrought" is the Greek word *katergadzo*, a compound of the words *kata* and *ergos*. The word *kata* is a preposition that carries the idea of *something that is subjugating or dominating*. The word *ergos* means *work*. When compounded together, it presents the idea of *a work that is totally consuming or dominating* — a work that takes every ounce of one's being.

We know from Scripture that Paul was not afraid of work. He even referred to the work of the ministry. In addition to glorious moments when Paul experienced spectacular visions, revelations, and special demonstrations of power, he worked hard in his ministry. He referred to this very hard work when he said, "But by the grace of God I am what I am: and his grace which was bestowed upon me was not in vain; but I laboured more abundantly than they all: yet not I, but the grace of God which was with me" (1 Corinthians 15:10).

This Greek word used here for "laboured" is *kopiao* and depicts *the most difficult, most exhaustive type of work*. We could even call it *hard labor*. Because Paul used this word to describe his own work ethic, it tells us that Paul was not afraid of hard work. He was willing to do anything and everything to accomplish the task God had given to him.

So the first thing we discover in Second Corinthians 12:12 is that apostolic ministry demands the highest level of commitment and work. This isn't a calling for those who want a lifestyle in which they can take it easy. It is a demanding, all-consuming, and dominating call that requires every ounce of a person's life. Apostolic ministry includes:

- ✦ Going into territory where the Church is non-existent.
- ✦ Dealing with aggressive and hostile governments.
- ✦ Facing the opposition of false religions opposed to one's very presence.
- ✦ Pushing the evil forces of the demonic realm out of the way.
- ✦ Taking converts from the bleakness and blackness of paganism and turning them into living, breathing members of the Body of Christ.

All of this is involved in the calling of the apostle. This divine call is not for the light-hearted but for the extremely committed.

This leads us to the first sign — *the first criteria* that Paul lists as evidence of true apostleship. He writes, "Truly the signs of an apostle were wrought among you in all *patience*...."

Considering the hostile forces at work to stop apostolic ministry, it shouldn't surprise us that Paul lists *patience* as the first major sign or characteristic of apostolic ministry. The word "patience" is the Greek word *hupomeno*. It is a compound of the words *hupo* and *meno*. The word *hupo* is a preposition that means *under*, and the word *meno* means *to abide* or *to stay*. When the two are compounded together, the compound word portrays *a person who is under some type of incredibly heavy load but who refuses to stray from his position because he is committed to his task*. Regardless of the load, opposition, stress, or weight that comes against him, he is *not* going to move. He is going to stay put in his spot and not surrender it to anyone for any reason!

One expositor translates *hupomeno* as the word *endurance*. Another translates it as *staying power*. My favorite translation of the word *hupomeno* is *hang-in-there power*!

It is interesting to me that Paul lists this as a sign of apostolic ministry. We usually think of wonders and miracles as signs of apostolic ministry. But before Paul mentions anything about what we would normally deem supernatural, he first mentions a person's supernatural ability to hang in there and to stay put regardless of what forces come to stop him.

This tells me that God causes supernatural favor to rest on apostles, enabling them to stay on the front lines and out on the cutting edge. Apostles face huge challenges in order to take new territory for God's Kingdom. But because His grace is on them so strongly, they are able to endure it and stick it out, even when it becomes very difficult.

I personally know that what the devil has tried to throw against us in our ministry in the former USSR often sounds so far out and unbelievable that people wonder if what we relate about our lives in this part of the world is imaginary or the stuff of fantasy. When they hear me recount the things we've faced, they shake their heads in disbelief and amazement that we could live in such circumstances. Yet we have experienced such grace upon us to do what we are called to do that we don't even realize how terrifically difficult some of these ordeals have been. Only when we see the disbelief on others' faces and hear them express their concerns for our welfare do we realize the significance of what we have been up against.

You see, God has provided us with a supernatural grace, a divine favor, a special endowment of *hupomeno* — what others call *hang-in-there power, staying power,* or *supernatural endurance* — to do what He has called us to do. I am so grateful for this incredible endowment from Heaven on our lives, because without it, we would be unable to do what we are doing. But this divine ability works so strongly in us that we haven't just survived; we have *flourished* in our environment.

What I am describing is just as supernatural as any other kind of supernatural sign and wonder. Anyone who can do what we do day after day, week after week, month after month, and year after year — and do it joyfully and successfully — is definitely experiencing something that is truly supernatural. It is a sign from on High of a divine endowment.

My wife and I have seen the lame walk, deaf ears opened, demons expelled, and even the dead raised through the prayers of our apostolic team. But I consider *hupomeno* on our lives to be just as supernatural as any of these other signs and wonders we have experienced. In fact, I really believe it is more significant than the other signs and wonders.

Supernatural signs and wonders come and go, but the supernatural ability to endure and joyfully succeed in difficult circumstances is a grace that comes and stays continuously. This quality of patience, endurance, staying power, or hang-in-there power is part of the divine equipment for this job. *It is a divine grace that is just as supernatural as any miracle or wonder!*

You may not be called to be an apostle, but perhaps you are living in a difficult or challenging situation. God makes miraculous grace available to you to help you victoriously live for Him where you are. If you need *staying power* to stay put where He has called you; if you need *hang-in-there power* to help you hold fast in that tough place; or if you could use *a supernatural dose of endurance* to help you endure to the end — all you have to do is ask!

When this supernatural grace or endowment starts to work in you and you are suddenly empowered beyond your natural strength to endure in the midst of turmoil or adversity, you'll realize what a supernatural gift it is! So if this is the need you are facing in your life today, I urge you to stop what you are doing; then throw up your arms, lift your voice, and ask Jesus to fill you with the endurance you need. Take the time to praise Him for filling you to overflowing. *As you do, He will give you exactly the dose of staying power you need to live victoriously for Him where He has called you!*

MY PRAYER FOR TODAY

Lord, I thank You for filling me with supernatural endurance to do the job You've given me to do. In the midst of all the problems, hassles, and challenges that have come against me, I am very aware that I wouldn't be able to do it without the divine gift of endurance You have placed in my life. Others may think I am strong, but I know that much of my strength and fortitude is due to what You have done inside me. So today I give You praise, and I thank You for continuing to strengthen me until I bring this assignment to a victorious end!

I pray this in Jesus' name!

MY CONFESSION FOR TODAY

I confess that God is filling me with supernatural endurance to stay put until I have successfully done everything He has asked me to do. He gave me this assignment because He believed I could do it. He filled me with endurance to help me stay put and to be strong enough to finish it as I ought. I therefore declare that I am strong; I am filled with fortitude; and I will do precisely what God has asked me to do!

I declare this by faith in Jesus' name!

1. Have you ever experienced a time when God supernaturally filled you with a divine dose of endurance that gave you the exact amount of strength you needed at that moment?
2. If the answer is yes, what did it feel like when you received that supernatural strengthening? How did you know it occurred? What were the immediate, tangible results of that inner strengthening?
3. How is your strength level today? Have you been feeling like weariness is trying to get the best of you, or do you feel strong and ready to keep forging ahead? If you are battling fatigue, don't you agree that it would be good for you to stop today to ask the Lord to refill you with another dose of endurance?

AUGUST 4

The Helmet of Salvation

And take the helmet of salvation....
— Ephesians 6:17

*H*ow would like you to have supernatural protection wrapped so tightly around your head that it would safeguard your mind from every mental assault of the devil? Well, you may not realize it, but if you are a child of God, you have already been given this kind of safeguard to protect you from the enemy's attacks against your mind. In Ephesians 6:17, Paul writes, "And take the helmet of salvation...."

In this final chapter of Ephesians, Paul deals extensively with the subject of spiritual armor. By the time we come to verse 17, he has already talked about the loinbelt of truth, the breastplate of righteousness, the shoes of peace, and the shield of faith. Now Paul speaks to us about the helmet of salvation, using the illustration of a Roman soldier's helmet to make his point. Let's see what we can know about the helmet of a Roman soldier.

The word "helmet" in Greek is taken from the Greek word *perkephalaia*, and it is a compound of the words *peri* and *kephale*. The word *peri* means *around*, and the word *kephale* is the Greek word for *the head*. When you compound these two words into one, you discover that the word *perkephalaia* denotes *a piece of armor that fits very tightly around the head*.

The Roman soldier's helmet was a fascinating and flamboyant piece of armor, very ornate and intricate. Highly decorated with all kinds of engravings and etchings, the helmet looked more like a beautiful piece of artwork than a simple piece of metal formed to fit the head of a soldier.

It was not uncommon for a Roman helmet to be decorated with depictions of pastoral farm scenes, complete with all kinds of animals. Frequently the entire helmet was fashioned to look like an animal, such as an elephant or a horse. Some of the helmets had intricate engravings and etchings depicting fruit.

Furthermore, as if these fabulous engravings and etchings were not enough, a huge plume of brightly colored feathers or horse hair stood straight up from the top of the helmet. If the helmet was designed to be used in a public ceremony or parade, this brightly colored plume could be very long — long enough to hang all the way down the soldier's back!

The helmet was made of bronze and was equipped with pieces of armor that were specifically designed to protect the cheeks and jaws. It was extremely heavy; therefore, the interior of the helmet was lined with sponge in order to soften its weight on the soldier's head. This piece of armor was so strong, so massive, and so heavy that nothing could pierce it — not even a hammer or a battle-ax.

It would be very hard to walk past one of these soldiers without taking note of him. It would be hard *not* to notice a man who had a piece of sculpture on his head or who wore a helmet with a brightly colored plume standing straight up on top of it! *Yes, these helmets made the Roman soldier noticeable!*

Why would the Holy Spirit compare a piece of weaponry like this to salvation? *Because your salvation is the most gorgeous, most intricate, most elaborate, most ornate gift God ever gave to you!*

Paul calls this marvelous gift "the helmet of salvation." He likened salvation to these flamboyant helmets that were worn on the head where everyone would notice. By using this example, Paul is telling us something very important. When a person is confident of his salvation — and when he walks confidently in the powerful reality of all that salvation means for him — he is a *noticeable individual*!

But why did a Roman soldier need a helmet that was so tightly wrapped about his head, as the Greek word *perkephalaia* implies? This kind of helmet was essential because the Roman soldier's opponent carried a short-handled ax called a battle-ax — and when battle-axes were used, heads rolled!

If the Roman soldier didn't have a helmet on when he went out to fight, he could be absolutely sure that he would lose his head. Thus, the Roman helmet was not merely a beautiful piece of weaponry but a defensive weapon designed to save a man's head.

That's exactly what salvation will do for you when you wear it like a helmet on your head! But if you *don't* walk in all that your salvation entails, you may feel the brunt of the enemy's battle-ax as he comes to attack your mind and steal your victory.

If your salvation is not worn tightly around your mind like a helmet, the enemy will come to chop the multiple blessings of your salvation right out of your theology. He will try to hack away at your foundation, telling you that healing, deliverance, preservation, and soundness of mind were not really a part of Jesus' redemptive work on the Cross. By the time the enemy is finished with your mind, the only blessing he will leave you with is Heaven!

Many believers try to do the work of God without making it a personal goal to walk in the full knowledge of their salvation, and they are spiritually slaughtered as a result. By exposing their unprotected minds to the devil's insinuations, they place themselves in a position to be severely attacked and possibly deceived.

Facing the adversary without your "helmet of salvation" is foolish! *You must have this helmet if you are going to be useful and successful in the Kingdom of God!*

You see, the devil knows that if he can seize your mind and fill it with lies, he can then begin to operate from this lofty position in your life. He can try to manipulate your emotions, send signals of sickness and disease into your body, and so on. To protect you from such attacks is the very reason God has given you the "helmet of salvation."

The fact that Paul likens our salvation to a helmet means that we must know all that our salvation includes inside and out. We must spend time studying what the Bible has to say about healing, about our deliverance from evil powers, about God's desire to bless and prosper us, and about the benefits of our redemption in our everyday lives.

Our intellectual comprehension of all that salvation encompasses must be ingrained in our minds. When our minds are convinced of these realities — in other words, when our minds are trained and taught to think correctly in terms of our salvation — that solid knowledge becomes a helmet in our lives!

At that point, it doesn't matter how hard the devil tries to hack away at our spiritual foundation; we *know* beyond a shadow of doubt what Jesus' death and resurrection purchased for us. This knowledge has become a part of us, preventing the enemy from attacking our minds as he did in the past. *That's how the full knowledge of our salvation puts a helmet on our heads!*

MY PRAYER FOR TODAY

Lord, I am so grateful for my salvation! It is the most wonderful gift You have ever given me. It changed my life and set me free; it brought healing to my body and deliverance to my mind. I want to wrap the knowledge of all that my salvation includes around my mind so tightly that the devil can never steal these benefits from my life. Holy Spirit, I ask You to help me study and to understand everything Jesus purchased for me at the Cross. Reveal it to me; convince me of its truth; and help me to wear that revelation knowledge on my head like a mighty, fortified, spiritual helmet!

I pray this in Jesus' name!

MY CONFESSION FOR TODAY

I confess that I wear my salvation tightly around my mind like a helmet. When the enemy tries to attack my mind and to chop away at the benefits of my salvation, his attacks are completely ineffective! My mind is convinced of all that salvation means for me, and my mind is trained and taught to think correctly according to that knowledge. Therefore, the knowledge of my salvation becomes a helmet in my life. It doesn't matter how hard the devil tries to hack away at my mind, I still stand strong because I know what Jesus' death and resurrection purchased for me!

I declare this by faith in Jesus' name!

QUESTIONS FOR YOU TO CONSIDER

1. Do you wear the knowledge of your salvation tightly around your head like a mighty helmet to protect you against the mental assaults of the devil?
2. Do you spend time studying what the Bible has to say about your healing, about your deliverance from evil powers, or about God's desire to bless and prosper you? The only way you'll know these truths is by studying them, so how much time do you spend learning about the consequences of your redemption in your everyday life?
3. Are there any truths from God's Word that you are certain the devil has already stolen from you? What has he taken from you that was once a major part of what you believed? Why don't you start renewing your mind to that truth today so you can see its results restored to your life?

AUGUST 5

*A Partner To Help You
When You Don't Know How To Pray!*

Likewise the Spirit also helpeth our infirmities:
for we know not what we should pray for
as we ought: but the Spirit itself maketh intercession
for us with groanings which cannot be uttered.
— Romans 8:26

Have you ever experienced a time when you didn't know what to pray for yourself or for someone else? Have you ever been in a dilemma, and you didn't know how to get out of it? Have you ever felt stuck in a predicament where you were required to make a decision, but you didn't know what to do? Or have you ever said, "Lord, I'm so confused that I don't even know how to pray! Lord, please help me"? If you have felt this way before, or perhaps even now, then I have great news for you today! *The Holy Spirit wants to help you pray!*

Romans 8:26 says, "Likewise the Spirit also helpeth our infirmities: for we know not what we should pray for as we ought: but the Spirit itself maketh intercession for us with groanings which cannot be uttered."

This verse is packed with gems from the Greek that let us know the Holy Spirit wants to help us when we don't know how to pray! The word "helpeth" comes from the Greek word *sunantilambetai*, which is a very complex triple compound word. But the first part of the word is the Greek prefix *sun*, and this is what I want to draw your attention to right now because it's so important for you to understand.

The little Greek word *sun* is a very important word. It *connects* you to someone else. It carries the idea of *partnership* and *cooperation*. For instance, in Second Corinthians 6:1, when Paul writes, "We then, as workers together with him...," he uses the word *sunergos* to depict our *partnership with God*. If Paul had wanted to depict a person who was working alone, he could have used only the word *ergos*, for by itself, this word would picture *a single, solitary worker*. But when the word *sun* is attached to the front of *ergos*, it is transformed into the word *sunergos* and pictures *two or more people who are working together like partners on the same job*. This is no longer the picture of a lonely, solitary worker; now there is *an entire team working together to get a job accomplished*. Because of this, some newer translations render Second Corinthians 6:1 this way: "We then, as *co-laborers* together with him...."

There are literally scores of places where the word *sun* is used this way in the New Testament; however, this one sample from Second Corinthians 6:1 is sufficient to express the impact of the word, which conveys the ideas of *partnership, cooperation, collaboration, teamwork,* or *a joint effort.*

As Paul continues in Romans 8:26, he uses the word "infirmities" to depict our spiritual predicament. The word "infirmities" is the Greek word *astheneia*, which really should be translated *weaknesses*. This word describes *people who are weak, sick, or broken in their bodies, minds, or emotions*. But Paul is not writing about a physical problem; he's writing about a spiritual one. He identifies this problem when he says, "...for we know not what we should pray for as we ought...."

The word "what" is the Greek word *ti*, which means *the very little thing*. It underscores our total ignorance about how to pray — demonstrating that we don't even know how to pray about *the little things*, not to mention the larger issues in life. Because we are limited in our view, we are simply unable to see all the facts and details that are required to pray effectively. This is why we need divine guidance and help. Praise God, we are not left to try to figure it all out on our own! Remember, the Greek word *sun* in the word "helpeth" lets us know that the Holy Spirit comes to *partner, cooperate, collaborate, and join efforts* with us in moments when we feel weak and helpless and don't know how to pray!

Paul describes this supernatural assistance of the Holy Spirit when he writes, "...but the Spirit itself maketh intercession for us...." Do you see the word "intercession"? It is the Greek word *huperentugchano*, and it is only used in this one place in the New Testament to describe the unique, powerful, and wonderful intercessory ministry of the Holy Spirit!

The word *huperentugchano* is an old word that means *to fall in on behalf of someone else*. It is what we might call a *rescue*. For instance, if someone fell into a deep cavern, you would have to descend down into that cavern to where that person is in order to rescue him and get him out.

This is precisely the idea of this word *huperentugchano*. By using this word, Paul tells you that the Holy Spirit performs this special work of intercession when you are at a loss for words and don't know how to pray, or when you feel trapped and you don't know what to say. Suddenly and supernaturally, the Holy Spirit falls into that place of helplessness with you to join you as a Partner in prayer in the midst of your circumstances.

Are you one of those people who has experienced moments when you didn't know how to pray? Have you been in a tight spot you didn't know how to get out of? Have you prayed, "Lord, I'm so confused, I don't even know what to say! Please help me"? If your answer is yes, you are a perfect candidate for the help of the Holy Spirit! He is your divine Partner — standing by, ready at any moment to come to your rescue! *Just cry out today and say, "Help me, Holy Spirit!"*

MY PRAYER FOR TODAY

Lord, I need Your help! I am so frequently at a loss for words and don't seem to know what to say when I pray. Since You sent the Holy Spirit to help me, I am asking the Spirit of God to fall into my situation with me; to join me as my Partner; to collaborate with me in prayer; to become a part of my team; and to get me out of this mess I'm in, putting me on a right and stable path. I am obviously never going to get there without special assistance, so today I'm asking for HELP!

I pray this in Jesus' name!

MY CONFESSION FOR TODAY

I confess that the Holy Spirit is my Partner! I call out to Him in my moment of need, and He quickly comes to my rescue. He enlightens my eyes; He shows me what I cannot see by myself; and He gives me the right words to say when I pray. Because I have the Holy Spirit, I am no longer speechless or helpless to know how I should pray. With Him as my Helper, I am getting better and better in prayer every day!

I declare this by faith in Jesus' name!

QUESTIONS FOR YOU TO CONSIDER

1. Have you ever experienced a moment when you didn't know how to pray? What did you do in that moment? Did you walk away in defeat, or did you call out and ask the Holy Spirit to help you pray?

2. Have you ever experienced one of those supernatural moments when you were suddenly aware that the Holy Spirit had come to your rescue? After feeling powerless and tongue-tied minutes earlier, did you unexpectedly become supercharged with power and authority and immediately start taking command of the situation in the power of the Spirit?

3. Is there presently any area of your life in which you need to invite the Holy Spirit to enter and rescue you, putting you back on a path that is more pleasing to God and to you?

AUGUST 6

Pray That the Word of the Lord May Have Free Course!

Finally, brethren, pray for us, that the word of the Lord may have free course, and be glorified, even as it is with you.
— 2 Thessalonians 3:1

*H*ave you ever wondered how you should pray for missionaries or for people who are preaching the Word on the front lines where it is more difficult? Well, today I'm going to give you the answer. And please — while you're praying for people on the front lines, be sure to remember to pray for me too!

The apostle Paul did what I call "front-line ministry work." As noted earlier (*see* August 3), Paul's ministry took him places where the Church was non-existent. He dealt with hostile governments; he faced opposition from false religions; he pushed the evil forces of the demonic realm out of the way; he brought converts from the bleakness of paganism and turned them into living, breathing members of the Body of Christ. This task is never for the light-hearted, but only for the extremely committed.

As Paul makes his final remarks to the Thessalonians in Second Thessalonians 3, he says, "Finally, brethren, pray for us...." The word "finally" comes from the Greek words *to loipon*, which mean *for the rest of the matter* or *to the last issue at hand*. Paul has saved some very vital information for the end of his letter; therefore, he uses the words *to loipon* to let us know that although his letter is concluding, he still has something of high importance to say to the Thessalonian church.

Then Paul makes his request: "Finally, brethren, pray for us...." The Greek word translated "pray" is from the word *proseuchomai*. As it is used in this verse, this word means to *pray continually* or *to pray without stopping*. Paul is sincerely asking for committed prayer partners who will pray nonstop for his team, his ministry, and for himself. When he says, "Pray for us," the word "for" is the Greek word *peri*, which means *around* or *about*. Paul is specifically requesting prayer for those things that are *around* or *about* them — hence, the things that *concern* them and their ministry.

Next, Paul gets more specific about *how* to pray. He says, *"Pray for us, that the word of the Lord may have free course...."* The Greek could be better translated, "Pray for us, that the Lord's word may have free course...." The Greek actually means *the word that originates from the Lord.*

This tells us that Paul was very conscious of the fact that he was not preaching his own man-made message or a message that belonged to him (*see* Galatians 1:11,12). He was carrying a divinely revealed message that originated with and belonged to the Lord. In all his years of ministry, Paul was always mindful that the message he carried was given to him by the Lord.

Furthermore, Paul knew that his responsibility was to preach that message. Therefore, he asked the Thessalonians to join him in praying that the Lord's message might have "free course." These words "free course" come from the Greek word *trecho*, which means *to run.*

Before we go any further, let's stop and look deeper into the meaning of the word *trecho*. This word often referred to *runners who ran a foot race in a huge stadium before adoring crowds of fans.* In order for the runner to run successfully and finish triumphantly, every ounce of his strength and his complete attention was required.

There is no doubt that Paul had this picture in his mind as he wrote this verse, for he was in a race to preach the Gospel to as many souls as possible before he came to the end of his life. He was in a spiritual race, a real competition. Racing urgently and with all his might against the enemy who wants to eternally destroy and damn souls, Paul put forth his best efforts to save as many souls as possible.

However, there is another powerful image in the word *trecho* that applies to this verse. This word was also used to describe the swift-running messengers who dashed between enemy lines to carry vital messages of instruction to those who waited on the other side of the battle. These especially brave and courageous messengers were essential if battles were to be won.

You can clearly see why Paul would have chosen to use this illustration, for he was indeed a God-sent messenger running back and forth through enemy territory, delivering the message of the Cross, as well as instructions to the churches that looked to him for apostolic leadership. Paul was God's special, swift-running messenger!

There is no doubt in my mind that Paul used the Greek word *trecho* to convey both of these ideas to his readers. Paul saw himself as one who was running in a race, competing for the souls of men. He also saw himself as God's messenger, whose principal goal was to run back and forth through enemy territory, delivering vital information to the people who awaited it. Paul's intention was that both of these ideas would convey the challenge that lay before him — as well as the reason he needed people to regularly pray for him.

One more important fact must be pointed out. The tense Paul uses when he requests prayer that the word of the Lord may have "free course" indicates a constant and continuous pace. Thus, it is possible to translate this phrase, *"Pray that we will be able to keep up the pace that is required for us to get this message out!"*

You see, Paul and his associates were already running very hard. If they were going to keep up with God's pace — if the Gospel message was going to keep spreading at such a miraculous rate of speed — they would need supernatural assistance and empowerment from above!

Finally, Paul makes one last prayer request. He asks for prayer that the word of the Lord may "...be glorified, even as it is with you." The word "glorified" is the Greek word *doxadzo*, which paints the picture of *the triumphant arrival of God's glory, ushering in a new and glorious day in the lives and the territories where the word of the Lord is heard and received.*

Dr. John Catlin, Professor of Classical Greek and Chairman of the Classics Department at a leading university, once wrote this to me:

> At first glance, the language of the New Testament appears to be disarmingly simple, but a deeper look gives us an appreciation of the difficulties facing translators of that work. *It is clear that whereas no translation can exactly reproduce the original meaning, nevertheless, through an understanding of the original language, or at least the broad range of meaning that many of the words in that language have, it is more readily possible to penetrate and comprehend the meaning of that original language.* It's all too easy for those who are fluent in only one language to assume that there are exact equivalents between languages.

One of the greatest challenges of Bible translators is to translate into English the many ideas and images that are in Greek words. Perhaps no example makes this clearer than Paul's prayer request in this verse, which in English is a mere twenty-four words in length. But those twenty-four words are packed with power and meaning!

These powerful words used by Paul in Second Thessalonians 3:1 convey the following ideas:

"Finally, brothers, pray for us and for those things that concern us. Pray that the word of the Lord will spread quickly and without resistance. Pray that we will be able to keep up the pace that is required for us to get this message out!

"To fulfill this task, we have to be like runners whose eyes are fixed on the goal before us! We must be like brave, bold, daring, and courageous messengers, whose job is to carry vital information across enemy lines. We have to move promptly and swiftly to get the message of the Gospel to the other side where people are desperately waiting.

"Since the Lord has dispatched us to carry this message, and since this task requires us to run speedily through dangerous territory, we request prayer that we will be able to make it through every skirmish, clash, confrontation, and struggle that we might come across as we run to the other side to deliver the word of the Lord. I request that your prayers be unbroken, uninterrupted, and never-ending. As you pray, remember to specifically stipulate that the word of the Lord would usher in a triumphant and glorious new day in the lives of those who hear it, as it has done among you."

So now you have an idea of how to pray for missionaries, preachers, or people who are ministering the Word and planting churches in new, unreached regions — the difficult front lines where the Word has never or rarely been preached. Here is a wrap-up of Paul's prayer request for you to use as you pray for people you know who are working in difficult parts of the world:

- ✦ Pray for the missionaries and preachers themselves.
- ✦ Pray for the things that concern them, i.e., their families, their finances, their health, etc.
- ✦ Pray for the Lord's message to spread without hindrance from hostile forces.
- ✦ Pray for the missionaries and preachers to win the race for souls.
- ✦ Pray for them to be protected as they dash through enemy territory.
- ✦ Pray constantly, around the clock, for those who are laboring on the front lines!

Now that you know how the apostle Paul wanted people to pray for him, you can use this as a guide to pray for *missionaries and preachers in other parts of the world. Why don't you take a few minutes to start praying for them today?*

MY PRAYER FOR TODAY

Lord, I ask You today to bless missionaries who are living and working in other parts of the world. Bless their families, their health, their finances, and everything that concerns them. Help them preach with little or no resistance. Empower them to run fiercely as they race to reach souls from being eternally lost. Protect them as they live, work, and dash back and forth through dangerous territory. I pray that the entrance of God's Word in their communities will break the powers of darkness and usher in a new triumphant day! Help me to remember to pray for them every day!

I pray this in Jesus' name!

MY CONFESSION FOR TODAY

I confess that I love missionaries and support them with my prayers and finances. I appreciate them for leaving their homes, their families, and their natural surroundings, and for uprooting their wives and children and moving to the other side of the world to take the Good News to those who do not have it. I will be faithful to remember them, to honor them, to pray for them, and to support them with my substance. The role I play to support them in prayer and with my finances is essential for their success, so I will fulfill my role faithfully!

I declare this by faith in Jesus' name!

QUESTIONS FOR YOU TO CONSIDER

1. How often do you think of missionaries and preachers who live on foreign soil and who are giving their lives to reach people in other parts of the world?
2. Do you financially support any missionaries? If not, is there a reason you've never made this a priority in your life? Don't you think you have a responsibility to make sure the same message that changed your life reaches people who have never heard it before?
3. How long has it been since you took the time to sit down and write a missionary to thank him for uprooting his family and moving them to the other side of the world? Even though that missionary family may be a long way from you, a note from you might be the very word of encouragement they need right now. Would you please consider taking a few minutes of your time to show them love and encouragement today?

Paul saw himself as God's messenger, whose principal goal was to run back and forth through enemy territory, delivering vital information to the people who awaited it.

AUGUST 7

❧

Developing the Divine Romance

But thou, when thou prayest, enter into thy closet,
and when thou hast shut thy door, pray to thy Father
which is in secret; and thy Father which seeth
in secret shall reward thee openly.
— Matthew 6:6

*I*f you would like to know the Holy Spirit more intimately, it is important for you to understand what Jesus said in Matthew 6:6. He said, "But thou, when thou prayest, enter into thy closet, and when thou hast shut thy door, pray to thy Father which is in secret; and thy Father which seeth in secret shall reward thee openly."

When Jesus said that you are to "enter into thy closet," was He actually telling you to get up every morning, open the closet door, shove all your shoes and clothes to the side, crawl inside that dark room, shut the door, and pray? *Of course not!*

The word "closet" is taken from the Greek word *tameion*, an old word that has an interesting progression in history. At first, the word *tameion* was used to depict *a secret place where one would hide his or her most valuable possessions*. But as time progressed, the word *tameion* came to describe *a secure place where a person could put money or treasure*, such as *a safety deposit box* or *a vault at the bank*. It represented a place so secure that no one would be able to break in to disrupt or steal these valuable possessions.

But by New Testament times, the word *tameion* had evolved even further. First, it depicted *a secret place* where one hid his prized possessions. Then it referred to *a secure place* such as a safety deposit box or a vault at the bank. Finally, *tameion* came to describe *a bedroom*.

Because a bedroom is a secret place where a treasured relationship takes place between a husband and a wife, it makes perfect sense that the word *tameion* would eventually describe this most private place. Intimate moments shared between a husband and wife occur in the bedroom. Although the husband and wife love their children in nearly every other sphere of their lives, this is one sphere that isn't available to anyone else. It is a private place and experience to be shared only between husband and wife.

Thus, this verse could actually be translated:

"When it's time for you to pray, enter into your bedchamber, and when you have shut the door behind you and secured a place of privacy, then pray…."

The word *tameion* is used in this verse to convey the idea of *intimacy with God* in prayer. Jesus was figuratively saying, "Just as a husband and wife enter into their bedroom and shut the door so they can bare their hearts and souls to each other in intimacy, so also you should have a relationship with God that is so tender, so special, and so intimate that it is shared only between you and Him and no one else. Therefore, find a secure place where you can go to share your heart and soul with God in prayer."

Jesus portrays prayer as something so precious that it should occur in a bedroom with the door shut. This does not literally mean you must pray in the bedroom any more than it means you must pray in a closet. The concept of a bedroom is only used to convey the idea of an isolated and solitary place where you can be alone with the Lord.

When we enter into a time of prayer, it should be done at a place and time when we are not interrupted so the Holy Spirit can speak to our hearts and we can bare our hearts to Him. It should be a time of a sweet mingling together of human spirit with the divine Spirit. Each of us should make it a daily priority to have this special time of communion with the Father through the Holy Spirit. It doesn't matter *where* you and I spend this private time with God; it just matters that we actually do it. Of course, it is best to find a time of the day when we can put everything else aside and concentrate only on Him, for the time we give to seeking God is a sacred time.

When we read the Gospels, we find that Jesus often arose early in the morning to pray when the other disciples were still sleeping. He often prayed on a mountaintop or out in the wilderness, far from the hustle and bustle of the city. There is nothing in the Bible that says the early morning hours are more holy than other hours of the day, and nowhere does the Bible teach that praying on a mountaintop is somehow better than other places. Jesus chose those early morning hours because it was a moment when He could find solitude and quietness with God. He prayed on those mountaintops and in the wilderness because He could pray in those isolated places without the interference of others.

Your place of prayer — your quiet place — may be in your car when you are driving to work alone every morning because that's the only time and place you can find to be alone. It may be in the shower as you prepare for the day. It may be early in the morning when everyone else in the house is still sleeping. Or perhaps you are like me in that you find it better to pray late at night after others have gone to bed and you are finally alone. The point is this: Each of us must have a quiet place and a sacred time when we can give ourselves fully to God in prayer.

You may say, "I know I need to spend quality time with the Lord, but my schedule is so busy that it's hard for me to find a time to do it." But the truth is, you find time for everything else that is important to you. So if you really want to be with the Lord, you will find time for that as well. Think about it. Don't you have time to read the newspaper? Do you watch the morning and evening news? Do you watch television programs or find time to go to the theater or movies? Do you make time in your schedule for recreation?

You see, you always make time for whatever is important to you. If you really wish to have an intimate, personal relationship with the Holy Spirit, you will make time for it.

So select a quiet place where you won't be disturbed. Once you go to that place, shut the door to outside interference and to the voices that are constantly calling out for your attention. Focus on only one thing: this very intimate and private time with the Father. *This is so important that you shouldn't delay in acting on it! You need to start enjoying times of intimate fellowship with the Lord today!*

MY PRAYER FOR TODAY

Lord, I ask You to forgive me for making time for everything except You. The truth is, I haven't made my prayer time a priority in my life; therefore, I haven't been consistent in prayer. So often when I do start to pray, other things scream for my attention and distract me. So I am asking You to help me locate a time and place where I can be alone and uninterrupted with You. I know that this is essential for my spiritual life, so starting today, I am making this the highest priority in my life.

I pray this in Jesus' name!

MY CONFESSION FOR TODAY

I confess that my daily time with God is the highest priority in my life. I treat my time with the Lord like it is the most important moment of my day and week. I am faithful to pray, to fellowship with the Father, to bare my heart before Him, and to listen to what His Spirit has to say to me. Because I make this time a priority in my life, I walk away from my prayer time energized and revitalized with the strength I need to face any situation that might come my way.

I declare this by faith in Jesus' name!

QUESTIONS FOR YOU TO CONSIDER

1. Where do you go to spend quality time with the Lord? What time of the day have you found to be best for you to really pray without being interrupted by other people or business?
2. When you do spend time in prayer, what is the average amount of time you stay in the Presence of God? Can you honestly say you linger in His Presence, or do you have a "rush-in, rush-out" experience with the Lord?
3. If you examine your prayer time, what do you find that you pray about more than anything else? What does this reveal about you and your station in life?

AUGUST 8

❧

Have You Ever Wondered What Songs They Sang in New Testament Times?

It is a faithful saying: For if we be dead with him,
we shall also live with him:
If we suffer, we shall also reign with him:
if we deny him, he also will deny us:
If we believe not, yet he abideth faithful:
he cannot deny himself.
— 2 Timothy 2:11-13

Have you ever wondered what kind of worship services took place in the first-century Church? What did the early believers do during their praise and worship? How did they take their offerings? How did they pray for the sick? How loud did they pray in the Spirit? Or how did they flow in the anointing and gifts of the Holy Spirit? Imagine the kind of vitality that must have filled their church services!

In Second Timothy 2:11-13, Paul gives us a glimpse into one of those Early Church meetings. As he writes to Timothy, Paul actually quotes a literal song or hymn that the early believers sang when they met together to worship. "Hymnic literature" is what scholars call Second Timothy 2:11-13. In other words, these verses are *an actual quote* of a real New Testament hymn. This song was so well known that Paul included its lyrics in this epistle. It was most likely sung by Paul, Timothy, the apostle John, as well as thousands of others.

In addition to this hymn in Second Timothy 2:11-13, a second hymn is found in Colossians 1:15-19 that proclaims the Lordship of Jesus Christ and His dominion over all the universe. In both of these instances in the New Testament when "hymnic literature" is used, the quote is from a "hymn" that was well known throughout the Church. These hymns were intended to be more than mere music; they were tools of instruction that chronicled the *true thinking* of the Early Church.

But when Paul was writing Second Timothy, he was trying to encourage Timothy to bravely face the challenges that were before him. By using this hymn, it is almost as if Paul is saying, *"Timothy, I know how to get you to understand the point I am trying to make to you! Do you remember that powerful song your congregation sings every week? You surely know the one I'm talking about. You know, the one that goes like this...."* Then Paul quotes the familiar hymn from Second Timothy 2:11-13, which says:

> It is a faithful saying: For if we be dead with him, we shall also live with him:
> If we suffer, we shall also reign with him: if we deny him, he will also deny us:
> If we believe not, yet he abideth faithful: he cannot deny himself.

Look at the first line of the song, "It is a faithful saying: For if we be dead with him, we shall also live with him...." Can you imagine getting together in church to sing about *martyrdom*? This was not an allegorical speech; this was reality for these early believers! Persecution and death were so imminent that Christians actually included these subjects in their worship services!

One great historian said, "Let me write the songs for a nation, and I can determine the history of that nation." In like manner, the leaders of the Early Church understood that to prepare themselves and the people to live bravely for the Lord, they had to use every available tool to instill *bravery* in the ranks.

One tool these early believers used was *hymns*. Just as we leave church each week with a song in our hearts and minds, these early believers left their church services with songs of bravery echoing in their souls — and they would sing those songs all week long to encourage themselves!

The first line of the song in verse 11 says, "...If we be dead with him...." This phrase comes from the Greek word *sunapothnesko*, which refers to *a literal partnership in death with someone else*. This means the first line of this hymn could be rendered, "...*If we join Him as a full-fledged partner in death....*" Imagine trying to put that to music! Even more, imagine trying to teach your congregation to sing those words with conviction!

The song goes on, "...we shall also live with him." This phrase is based on the Greek word *sudzao*, which conveys again the idea of *partnership*. However, this time it means *to join someone else in life*, not in death. This line of the song could be taken as a kind of faith declaration that proclaims, "...*We will join Him in the same kind of life that He now lives.*" Singing this kind of song over and over again worked bravery into the fiber of the Early Church.

Today we still need songs that produce brave warriors. Oh, that the Church today was committed enough to sing this type of song *and mean it*! Instead, most people would be offended by such lyrics and would refuse to even participate in singing them. Others would claim that these lyrics were filled with doubt and unbelief. But these lines represent *powerful faith*, not unbelief! They basically declare, "Come hell or high water, we're in this to stay! If they kill us, that's all right, because we will soon join Jesus in His glorious, new, resurrected life!"

The next line of the song says, "If we suffer, we shall also reign with him…" (v. 12). The phrase "if we suffer" once again conveys the idea of *partnership*. Literally translated, it means, "*If we join Him in His suffering and suffer the same way He did.…*"

Notice that this line has no note of sorrow or pain about these Christians' suffering. They knew that feeling sorry for themselves wouldn't help the situation, so they faced it bravely in the power of the Spirit. Although they didn't seek to suffer, they weren't afraid to suffer *if* it was forced upon them because of their faith.

These were the lyrics of *a fearless people.* They were determined to win the victory, regardless of the price they had to pay. Therefore, the song continues, "…we shall also reign with him.…" The phrase "reign with him" is the Greek word *sumbasileuo*, which can be translated "…*we will reign and rule like nobility with Him.…*" These believers had their sights fixed on ruling with Jesus! To reach that goal, they were willing to face and fight any foe!

Now comes the hard part of the song — the part that carries consequences. It says, "…If we deny him, he also will deny us." Can you imagine looking someone straight in the eyes to sing to him, "If you deny the Lord, the Lord will deny you too"?

These early believers saw no room for the excuses of defectors in the army of the Lord. Either a person was with Jesus, or he was against Him. Furthermore, when a brother in the Lord defected, the early believers didn't sweep it under the carpet. Neither did they simply pat the errant brother on the back and say, "Well, now, come back and visit us again some time." They saw themselves as a mighty army, and those who deserted the ranks were not worthy of honor *or* privileges.

This militant lack of tolerance couldn't be any plainer than in this line of the hymn they sang. It was a reflection of who they were and how they thought. They had no tolerance for defectors!

From the content of this hymn, it is quite clear that these early saints were extremely serious about what they believed and about the Kingdom of God. Their Christian walk wasn't just "another thing" for them to do in life. Christianity was their "all in all," for they had given their lives — lock, stock, and barrel — over to this cause.

Please understand that this hymn was not a theological statement; rather, it was a reflection of the hour in which these believers lived and the attitude that they possessed. Church songs are always indicative of the specific period in which they were written. The hymn writer, whoever he or she was, chronicled the messages preached to the congregation and put them to music so the saints could sing them at home, at work, in their leisure time, or at church gatherings.

I can almost hear the first-century saints singing the lines of this hymn now! Can you can hear them raising their voices and bravely singing?

> *If we are killed like He was killed,*
> *Then we shall live again as He now lives;*
> *If suffering is forced upon us,*
> *Then we'll reign with Him like nobility;*
> *If we deny or forsake Him,*
> *He will deny us of our rewards;*
> *If we believe not or grow faint-hearted,*
> *Still He abideth faithful.*
> *He cannot, cannot, cannot deny — Himself!*

As time moves on and the coming of the Lord draws nearer, God expects you to step forward and take your place in His modern-day army. It is very possible that in the days and decades to come, there will be clashes between the kingdoms of this world and the Kingdom of God. Are you ready for this? Are you ready to follow the voice of our Commander-in-Chief? Are you committed to getting in the fight and staying in it until the victory is won? *Are you a true soldier in the army of the Lord?*

Take advantage of the time you have right now to strengthen yourself spiritually, to become dressed in the whole armor of God, and to develop a winning attitude. It is a fact that attitude is 99 percent of every fight; therefore, being mentally equipped is very important for your survival and victory.

The believers in the Early Church maintained the attitude to never give in, give up, or surrender to defeat. As a result, they conquered the world in which they lived.

Do you have the same kind of attitude that will assure your victory in life? If not, you need to start developing that attitude in your life immediately! *There is too much at stake for you to allow yourself to be defeated because you didn't possess a right attitude!*

MY PRAYER FOR TODAY

Lord, help me have an attitude that is determined to win every struggle and fight that I face in life! You have given me spiritual power, spiritual weapons, and the wonderful Word of God. It is a fact that You have equipped me with everything I need to win. Now the victory depends on me and my attitude. Help me maintain the attitude that never gives in, never gives up, and never surrenders to defeat. As I make up my mind to take hold of Your power, Your spiritual weapons, and Your Word, it is guaranteed that I will push the devil clear out of my life. So please help me to make this decision and to do it quickly!

I pray this in Jesus' name!

MY CONFESSION FOR TODAY

I confess that I am following the voice of my Commander-in-Chief. I will go where Jesus says to go, and I will do exactly what He tells me to do. I am committed to get in the fight and stay in it until the victory is won! I have an attitude that never gives in, never gives up, and never surrenders to defeat. God has given me spiritual power, spiritual weapons, and the promises of His Word on which I can stand. He has equipped me with everything I need to win — and now the victory depends on me!

I declare this by faith in Jesus' name!

QUESTIONS FOR YOU TO CONSIDER

1. What do you think about this song that the believers sang in the first century? What do the lyrics of this song tell you about the early believers and their attitude about life and about living in victory?
2. Do you have the necessary attitude for winning the victory in your life and circumstances? Can you say with confidence that you are committed to staying in the fight until the victory is yours and the long-awaited prize is finally in your hands?
3. Is your Christian walk just "another thing" for you to do in life, or is it your "all in all," as it was in the lives of these early believers? Are you giving your life — lock, stock, and barrel — to the pursuit of your walk with God?

AUGUST 9

❧❧❧

What Lies in Your Future
If You Choose To Give Up and Quit?

Now the just shall live by faith: but if any man draw back,
my soul shall have no pleasure in him.
But we are not of them who draw back unto perdition....
— Hebrews 10:38,39

One day as I was ministering in a certain church, the pastor of the church asked me if I would take the time to have lunch with a minister who had previously been associated with many great men and women of faith. The pastor told me that this minister had worked at one time on the staff of a very large and successful ministry. However, after deciding that his assignment there was finished, the man had left to start his own ministry.

Several years had passed since this particular minister had taken the step of faith to start his own organization. But because his new organization hadn't grown as quickly as he had wished, he had become very discouraged and depressed. As a result of these disappointments, he had begun to question everything he believed about walking by faith. He had even become very bitter and sour toward anyone who claimed to walk in faith. Unfortunately, this minister made the mistake of starting to measure what he *believed* by what he was *experiencing.*

That day when I went to lunch with this man, I was shocked that anyone who had known such a high level of faith could slip into such a miserable state. He wasn't just negative; he was extremely critical and cynical of anything that had to do with faith. As I tried to encourage this man, he said, "Yeah, I know all about you faith guys! Name it and claim it; that's who you guys are! But you're all so shallow. You guys don't know anything about hardships or suffering. You just live in a fairy-tale world that doesn't touch anyone's real existence."

As this man alleged that I and my other faith friends didn't know anything about hardships, I thought of all the personal challenges I had been through — the many assaults the devil had made against my life and my ministry. I also thought about how the very ministries he was specifically accusing of being shallow had stood so steadfastly against problems of which he was obviously unaware.

I felt a need to speak up and tell the man about some of these challenges and how I and my fellow ministers had won the victory by standing steadfastly in faith. But when I tried to speak to him, it was like talking to a concrete wall. He had already made up his mind that God had no plan of victory for his life — and that anyone who believed it was God's will for people to be victorious was a charlatan!

After two hours of this man's verbal abuse, I told the pastor who brought me to the lunch, "Excuse me, but I am not going to sit here and be verbally abused by this man anymore. I don't even know him, yet he is viciously attacking me and my friends. I'm sorry he wouldn't listen to me today, because I believe I could have helped him."

With that, I pushed away from the table, stood up, put on my jacket, and left the restaurant. There was no reason for me to stay there any longer, because the bitterness in this man had defiled him so completely that he wasn't willing to hear anything from me or from my friends who also believe in the walk of faith. In the end, I discovered the only reason he wanted to meet me for lunch was to have the opportunity to berate me for what I believed.

That experience made me think of Hebrews 10:38 and 39, which says, "Now the just shall live by faith: but if any man draw back, my soul shall have no pleasure in him. But we are not of them who draw back unto perdition...." This verse tells us *explicitly* what happens to people who walk away from the life of faith. According to this verse, the ramifications of this departure from faith are grim and ghastly. The man who berated me that day at lunch was a perfect example of what this verse communicates to you and me.

The words "draw back" are from the Greek word *hupostello*, which is a compound of the words *hupo* and *stello*. The word *hupo* in this case means *back*, and the word *stello* means *to send*. But when these two words become the word *hupostello*, it depicts *someone who is shrinking back, withdrawing, retreating, regressing, receding, backing away, backsliding,* or *someone who is recoiling from something.* This is a person who started on a journey but then abruptly reversed his direction. He is now moving *backward* instead of forward. For some reason, this person is *backing out* of a position or belief that he once strongly held.

The word "perdition" is the Greek word *apoleia*, which describes *something so ruined and rotten that it is decomposing,* such as rotten potatoes that have sat too long and are now spoiled and ruined. Frequently this word was used to describe *the stench of a decaying animal or a dead human body* — a loathsome, putrid, vulgar, disgusting, *nauseating* scent. One whiff leaves you with a sick feeling in the pit of your stomach. The smell is so repulsive that you feel like running to the bathroom to vomit. This is exactly the image that Hebrews 10:39 gives us of what happens when a person turns and walks away from the call of God or a life of faith. It results in *a sickening, stinking situation.*

Don't be like the man given in this example above. If God has spoken to you, stand fast and refuse to budge until you receive the manifestation of the promise God made to you!

I am amazed at the short-lived nature of some people's faith. For example, if their prayers for healing aren't answered as quickly as they wish, they permit their flesh to lead them to the conclusion that it must be God's will for them to be sick! Or if they sow their finances believing for a financial harvest but don't see that harvest after a few months, they conclude that what they were taught about prosperity must be wrong.

But you have to give faith time to work! Faith and patience are partners. That is why Hebrews 10:36 says, "For ye have need of patience, that, after ye have done the will of God, ye might receive the promise." The word "patience" comes from the word *hupomene*, a compound of the words *hupo* and *meno*. The word *meno* is the primary root of the word, and it means *to stay, to remain, to continue,* or *to permanently abide in one place.* It is the very word that Jesus used in John 15:7, when he said, "If ye abide in me, and my words abide in you, ye shall ask what ye will, and it shall be done unto you." A literal translation of John 15:7 could be, "If you *steadfastly and continuously abide* in Me, and if My words *steadfastly and continuously abide* in you, you may ask what you will, and it shall be done for you." The word *meno* gives the idea of something that is *rooted, unmoving,* and *stable.*

But when you add the prefix *hupo* to the front of *meno*, thus forming *hupomene*, the picture changes radically! In this situation, the word *hupo* means *under*, as *to be underneath something that is very heavy.* But when it is connected to the word *meno* — becoming the word *hupomene* — it pictures *a person who is under a very heavy load but who has resolved that he isn't moving; he is going to stay in that one spot.* Regardless of how heavy the load or how long it takes, he refuses to move from his position because he knows that it is where he is supposed to be!

The word *hupomene* pictures a person who is completely committed to maintaining his position. He will stay under that heavy load as long as it is necessary for him to achieve his victory. He is intent on standing by his commitment, regardless of the cost he must pay. Nothing can sway or move him to change his mind. He is not going to relinquish his territory! One scholar says *hupomene* would be better translated "endurance" because it portrays an attitude that never gives up. It is a faith that manifests as a tough, resistant, persistent, obstinate, stubborn, tenacious spirit that refuses to let go of what it wants or believes. I personally translate the word *hupomene* as *hang-in-there-power*!

You must have *hupomene* if you intend to beat the devil at his game and successfully do what God has called you to do. If *hupomene* is working in your life, it's just a matter of time until your victory comes to you. It's not a question of *if* your victory will come — it's only a question of *when* it will come. But for you to reach that glorious and long-awaited place of victory, it is essential that you have *hupomene* in your life!

So don't let loose of your faith! The day your vision dies is the day your joy will disappear, your life will be depressing, and you will turn bitter. You'll end up in "perdition" if you let go of the word of truth God gave you. You'll start putting out the putrid stench of a faith turned sour — just like that minister who backed away from his once-strong position of faith and became bitter and cynical about anyone who walked in faith. Instead of resisting the lies the devil was speaking to him and maintaining his rock-solid stance on the Word of God, he relinquished his position of faith and gave place to doubt and unbelief.

Seated before me that day was a man who had turned around and backed out of the life of faith he had once embraced. His whole mind was doused in defeat. He had even rationalized his defeat by immersing himself in a doctrinal system designed to support his depressing existence. The entire conversation with him just made me feel ill. It was sickening to see someone who once walked in victory now walking in such a terrible low-level existence.

That's why Hebrews 10:38 says, "...if any man draw back, my soul shall have no pleasure in him." It isn't a pleasurable experience to see someone who once made such advances later take a turn for the worse. In fact, it's heartbreaking.

Perhaps you know people who once intensely longed to do the will of God and who firmly believed in what God had called them to do. But when it didn't turn out the way they expected or when they hit a few unexpected bumps along the way, they said, "Forget this faith thing! It doesn't work!" Did those same people then turn around and back away from what God had called them to do or from what He had revealed to them? Isn't it sad to see what happens to people like this — people who had so much potential and who could have achieved so much if they had just held on a little longer?

Perhaps you are the one who once tried to do God's will but then allowed yourself to become discouraged and defeated. Did you throw in the towel and let the devil have his way in ruining your dream? Did you give up, turn back, and withdraw from doing what you were called to be or to do? If the answer is yes, you're probably disgusted with yourself and you feel unhappy and unfulfilled. *Right?*

Well, there's no reason for you to remain in this miserable condition for the rest of your life. The table is prepared, and the meal is cooked. God is waiting for you to pull up your chair to the table, pick up your knife and fork, and begin again to dig into the awesome plan He has for your life. Don't let discouragement keep you from being who God wants you to be. Just hold fast, hold tight, and determine that you're not going to stop until you see your dream come to pass!

Aches and pains will soon be forgotten when the powers of hell move out of the way and your dream becomes a reality. *When that happens, you'll be so glad you didn't take the low road and join the club of quitters!*

MY PRAYER FOR TODAY

Lord, I am asking You to help me stay focused and to remain determined to stay in my race of faith until I reach the finish line and receive my long-awaited prize! When the devil tries to dissuade me from holding on to my faith, help me to rebuke him, to command him to be silent, and to order him to leave! With Your Spirit empowering me, I know I will be able to keep believing and walking by faith until I finally see the manifestation of my dreams!

I pray this in Jesus' name!

MY CONFESSION FOR TODAY

I confess that regardless of how heavy the load or how long it takes, I am going to refuse to move from my faith position until I achieve the victory Jesus promises to me. I will remain steadfast in my commitment, and nothing can sway or move me to change my mind. I refuse to relinquish any of my God-promised territory! My faith is tough, resistant, persistent, obstinate, and stubborn. My spirit is so tenacious that it refuses to let go! It isn't a question of IF my victory will come — it's only a question of WHEN it will come!

I declare this by faith in Jesus' name!

QUESTIONS FOR YOU TO CONSIDER

1. Have you ever known people who once walked in faith but then let discouragement turn them sour? Are those individuals now bitter, hardhearted, and cynical toward anyone or anything that symbolizes the faith they once possessed?
2. How would you describe the current status in life of these individuals after having left behind their faith and their dreams? Have their lives become better, or have they deteriorated into a sad shadow of the faith-filled lives they once lived?
3. If you have been feeling tempted to get discouraged and to give up on the dream God has given you, what steps can you take to begin to renew your hope and strengthen your resolve to hold on to the end?

AUGUST 10

Lay Hands Suddenly on No Man!

Lay hands suddenly on no man,
neither be partaker of other men's sins: keep thyself pure.
— 1 Timothy 5:22

No car manufacturer would release a new model car to the public without first testing the weaknesses and strengths of that automobile. To test the new model, the manufacturer will order it to be driven as fast as it can be driven. It will be crashed into a wall. It will be driven on nails to test the strength of the tires. It will be driven over every conceivable kind of pavement and in all kinds of temperatures. Only after the car passes the final inspection will it be deemed "fit" for public usage.

To release a car without these kinds of tests would be considered irresponsible. If the manufacturer doesn't test a new model, how can he know whether or not it will perform well? How can he know whether or not it has fatal mistakes in its structure? How can he know for sure that it won't kill someone? The manufacturer is well aware that if he releases the car to the public and it falls apart or kills someone, he is the one who will be held responsible for that failure.

New automobiles are tested to protect people from being physically hurt in automobile accidents. But what about testing potential leaders before giving them highly visible places of power and authority in a church, business, or organization?

People are precious to God, and they should be precious to us as well. But before we give people great power and authority in a church or an organization, they first need to be tested and proven. It is essential that those of us who are in leadership positions know who these individuals *really* are and how they will perform in various situations.

The apostle Paul referred to this testing process when he wrote, "Lay hands suddenly on no man, neither be partaker of other men's sins: keep thyself pure" (1 Timothy 5:22). The word "suddenly" is the Greek word *tachus*, and in this verse it carries the idea of doing something *quickly* or *hastily*. The words "lay hands" are from the Greek word *epitithimi*, which means *to place hands upon*. In both Old Testament and New Testament times, a "laying on of hands" ceremony was the equivalent of *stamping that individual with one's personal seal of approval*. When those in leadership positions laid hands on a person, they were signifying that they believed in him, supported him, and desired to empower him to perform some task or duty. Hence, the laying on of hands was an act that was carried out very cautiously, since it gave the recipient such a high status in the eyes of the beholders.

Paul tells us, "Lay hands suddenly on no man...." A better translation would be, "*Don't give your seal of approval to people too hastily....*" You see, it's very possible to lay hands on people too quickly — to give them the seal of our approval before we really know them and to impart authority to them before they are ready. This is a foolish mistake that produces painful consequences.

If you feel God has chosen you, don't get frustrated if you are held back for a while by those who are in authority over you. It is wise and right for them to know you, to test you, and to be sure you are the right candidate for the job. If God has really chosen you, it won't hurt you or the call He has placed on your life to wait just a little longer. If anything, your divine call will be confirmed and reconfirmed again and again as you patiently wait for God's timing to be manifested.

When I was a young man, I had desire; I had ambition; and I had the necessary "get up and go" to do what God had placed in my heart. But there were characteristics in me that needed to be corrected before God could use me. If I'd gotten started before God uprooted those undesirable traits, they would have later overgrown my ministry and destroyed any fruitfulness God wanted to produce through me. This is why it is an aspect of immaturity to want to do everything *right now*.

If *you* are the one who chooses the leadership for your church, ministry, or organization, don't move hastily! Nothing is more important in your organization than the people you choose for its leadership. If you choose people who share your heart and are submitted to you and your vision, they will be a blessing. But if you choose people who have a different vision and are not in agreement with what God has put in your heart, you have invited a spiritual hurricane into your midst that has the power to destroy everything you have built. So take the time to be sure you're making the right decision!

We *all* have glitches and flaws in our character. Not one of us is perfect. Fortunately, small flaws are correctable as long we have receptive and teachable hearts. But if a person refuses to see his need for change and is closed-hearted to suggestions made by those who love him, this is evidence of *the most serious* character flaw. From the outside, this person may look like he's just what we're looking for, but we must not forget to consider the *deeper issues* of the heart.

Pastors and leaders of ministries and organizations can attest to the dreadful mistake of "laying hands on" people before they were ready. Most leaders could tell you about people they promoted into leadership too quickly — *before they really knew them*. These are the people who often betrayed their leaders, split their churches, divided their organizations, and wounded those leaders' spirits so deeply that it took a long time for them to recuperate and return to a state of normalcy again in their lives and ministries.

Often the hurt a person causes in such a case is unintentional. He or she was simply not ready for that much power and authority. And to think that the whole mess could have been avoided if more time had been taken before the person was elevated to a leadership position!

Many dreadful mistakes have been made through two thousand years of Church history simply because people were placed into leadership positions too quickly. Had time been taken and had those people really been tested, it would have been clear that they were not spiritually prepared to lead. But as a result of hasty decisions and quick actions, multitudes of people have been mishandled and hurt by immature leadership.

Don't make that same mistake! Before someone is invited to be a permanent part of any leadership team, it is right to make sure that there is nothing in his character, attitude, or actions that could spiritually hurt others or the organization along the way. Remember, you are putting this potential leader over *people*, and nothing in the world is more valuable or precious than the people of God. You don't want to make a hasty decision that reaps terrible consequences for your church, ministry, or organization.

Paul told Timothy that by not laying hands on people too quickly, he could avoid being a "...partaker of other men's sins...." The word "partaker" is the Greek word *koinonia*, which conveys the ideas of *fellowship, interaction,* or *mutual participation.*

You see, when those in leadership discover that a person has a serious character flaw *after* they have put that person into a high position too quickly, they are now involved in a mess, whether they like it or not! They have someone on their team who isn't a right "fit" for them, who has a different standard of excellence, or who has some problem. But because they moved too quickly and publicly promoted that person, they are stuck with having to make a difficult decision. They have become locked in a mess that they could have avoided simply by moving a little slower!

So if you are in a leadership position, take the time to know someone before you give that person new power and authority. And if you are wanting to be chosen for a higher position yourself, be patient with those who are waiting and watching you. They have a God-given responsibility to know you and to feel confident about you before they lay their hands on you!

Finally, pray for your pastor or employer to make right decisions about people they promote into leadership positions in their church, business, or organization. *They need your prayer support, so get behind them with your prayers today!*

MY PRAYER FOR TODAY

Lord, You know me better than anyone in the world, so I trust You to know exactly when I am ready for the next big promotion that You have designed for my life. Help me to quit being frustrated with my superiors for not promoting me more quickly, and help me instead to take a look at the deeper issues of my life that hold me back from being elevated. Holy Spirit, help me use this time in my life to clean up my act and to get my heart ready for the next upward step that Jesus has waiting for me!

I pray this in Jesus' name!

MY CONFESSION FOR TODAY

I confess that my character, attitude, and actions are being refined by the fire of God in my life. The Holy Spirit is helping me discover any serious character flaws that would negatively affect my future. God is changing me, teaching me, and preparing me for greater responsibility. I am serious about my walk with God and about being greatly used by Him in this life. Therefore, I want Him to identify every part of my life that is out of order or that needs to be fixed. So today I yield to the Holy Spirit so He can delve deep into my soul and extract those traits that would keep me from the blessings and positions God would love to give me!

I declare this by faith in Jesus' name!

QUESTIONS FOR YOU TO CONSIDER

1. Can you think of someone who was promoted too hastily into a position of leadership and, as a result, caused damage to a church, business, or organization?
2. Have there been times when your desire to be promoted was delayed? In retrospect, can you now see that you wouldn't have been ready for the job if you had been promoted at that exact time? Does it make you thankful that you were put "on hold" just a little bit longer?
3. What do you need to be dealing with in your personal character right now to better prepare you for the next promotion that God has designed for your life?

Pastors and leaders of ministries and organizations can attest to the dreadful mistake of "laying hands on" people before they were ready. Most leaders could tell you about people they promoted into leadership too quickly — *before they really knew them.* These are the people who often betrayed their leaders, split their churches, divided their organizations, and wounded those leaders' spirits so deeply that it took a long time for them to recuperate and return to a state of normalcy again in their lives and ministries.

AUGUST 11

༺᠁༻

Be Sure To Go
To Sword Practice!

And take...the sword of the Spirit,
which is the word of God.
— Ephesians 6:17

*H*ave you ever been confronted with a situation where you felt you needed a word from the Lord, but you didn't know which word you needed? Did you run to your Bible and start flipping through the pages, searching for that perfect word you needed — but it seemed like you just couldn't quite find the right word to fit your situation?

Well, today I want to talk to you about the sword of the Spirit. You will find that when the Holy Spirit drops a word into your heart for your exact situation, that *rhema* word will have incredible power to drive back the enemy from his attack!

Let me begin by telling you a little bit about how Roman soldiers went to sword practice, because it will help you understand the difference between a *rhema*, or *a quickened, specific word from the Spirit*, and the *logos*, which is *the written Word of God*.

Because the Roman army was so committed to warfare, its soldiers practiced the arts of warfare *continually*. One of the primary exercises was daily sword practice. The soldiers exercised themselves in this skill morning and afternoon. The ancients gave their recruits bucklers that were woven with willow branches and were *two times heavier* than the ones used in actual battle.

In addition to these heavy bucklers, the swords that Roman soldiers used in practice were made of heavy wood and were *twice the weight* of the real swords used in battle. Every soldier practiced combat with a wooden post about six feet high, which was firmly fixed in the ground. This six-foot post became his "enemy" during practice. Just as with a real enemy, he would advance upon his target, strike hard with his sword, and then retreat.

The soldier's job in practice was to learn how to take advantage of his enemy; how to hit him at his weakest point; and how to strike him so he could not respond. The aim of the man wielding the sword was nearly always pointed toward the head or face, toward the thighs or legs, or occasionally toward the sides of the target.

Flavius Vegetius Renatus, who lived around 380 AD and who documented the affairs of the Roman military, wrote: "They [the military recruits] were likewise taught not to cut, but to thrust their swords. For the Romans not only made jest of those who fought with the edge of that weapon, but always found them an easy conquest. A stroke with the edges, though made with ever so much force, seldom kills, as the vital parts of the body are defended by both the bones and armor. On the contrary, a stab, although it penetrates but two inches, is generally fatal."[1]

It was from this background that Paul said, "And take...the sword of the Spirit, which is the word of God" (Ephesians 6:17). Notice particularly that Paul says, "...the sword of the Spirit, which is the word of God." The word translated "word" is not the Greek word *logos*, which would refer to *the written Word*. Instead, Paul employs the use of the Greek word *rhema*. This is so powerful — and I want to tell you why!

---

[1] Flavius Vegetius Renatus, *The Military Institutions of the Romans*, trans. Lt. John Clark (Westport, Connecticut: Greenwood Press, 1944), pp. 20-21.

Had Paul used the word *logos* in this verse, he would have implied a "sweeping stroke" against the enemy, and this would never do. You see, the *logos* — although broad, heavy, wonderful, and full of general direction for our lives — is not sufficient to deal the enemy a fatal blow. *We need to stab the enemy!* This will require a *rhema* — *a specific, quickened word from the Scriptures, placed into our hearts and hands by the Holy Spirit.* With a *rhema* from God placed in our hearts and hands, we have real *sword power* to use against the enemy!

A genuine *rhema* doesn't have to be six pages long to be effective against the work of the devil. As Vegetius recorded in his history of the Roman army, all that was needed to kill an enemy was a mere two-inch penetration. Likewise, one very small *rhema* from the Lord has the power to do the adversary in!

The best example of this *sword power of the Spirit* is found in Luke 4:3-13. In this passage, Satan is the aggressor who is found attacking Jesus on repeated occasions. But Jesus doesn't simply say, "Satan, get out of here." *Instead, Jesus stabs the devil repeatedly with direct blows!* Jesus had a specific, quickened *rhema* from the Holy Spirit!

After the devil tempted Jesus with food, Jesus drew the sword that the Holy Spirit put in His hand (*a rhema*) and said, "…It is written, That man shall not live by bread alone, but by every word of God" (v. 4). *To this stabbing sword of the Spirit, the enemy had no response.*

After offering Jesus all the kingdoms of the world in exchange for worship, Satan was wounded deeply by one *rhema* from the Master's mouth. Jesus told him, "…It is written, Thou shalt worship the Lord thy God, and him only shalt thou serve" (v. 8). *To this sword of the Spirit, Satan had no answer.*

Then Satan tried to tempt Jesus to prove His deity. But Jesus answered His adversary with *a sword,* saying, "…It is said, Thou shalt not tempt the Lord thy God" (v. 12). *With one final stab, Jesus penetrated Satan's armor and delivered an almost fatal wound* — and at that point, Satan fled from the scene!

Like the Lord Jesus, you are equipped with all the armor of God, and this includes the sword of the Spirit. As long as you have this spiritual equipment, no battle is a real threat to you! Today if you will open your heart and listen, the Holy Spirit will place in your heart and hands the exact *rhema* you need to put the devil on the run!

MY PRAYER FOR TODAY

Lord, thank You for giving me the sword of the Spirit as part of my spiritual weaponry. When the devil attempts to attack me, please help me be sensitive to hear the exact rhema that the Holy Spirit desires to drop into my heart with which I can then deal the enemy a fatal blow. Starting right now, I open my heart and soul to listen so I can hear any scripture or word the Holy Spirit wishes to give me to use against the works of the devil in my life.

I pray this in Jesus' name!

MY CONFESSION FOR TODAY

I confess that I have the sword of the Spirit, which is the word of God, and that this spiritual weapon is working in my life! I have the exact word I need for every situation — a specific, quickened word from the Scriptures, placed in my heart by the Holy Spirit. Because this rhema from God is in my heart, I have real sword power to use against the enemy!

I declare this by faith in Jesus' name!

QUESTIONS FOR YOU TO CONSIDER

1. Can you think of a time when you were facing a difficult situation — and suddenly it was as if God dropped a verse into your heart that had the very answer you needed? Did it equip you to deal with the challenge you were facing and cause the situation to turn around?

2. Why don't you think of three times in your life when you emphatically knew that God gave you a *rhema* for the particular situation you were facing? What were those times, and how did that *rhema* make a difference?

3. Are there any areas in your life right now where you could use a *rhema* from the Holy Spirit to help you know how to overcome a problem or a challenge?

AUGUST 12

Being Led by the Holy Spirit

And when Jesus departed thence, two blind men followed him,
crying, and saying, Thou son of David, have mercy on us.
And when he was come into the house, the blind men came to him:
and Jesus saith unto them, Believe ye that I am able to do this?
They said unto him, Yea, Lord. Then touched He their eyes,
saying, According to your faith be it unto you.
And their eyes were opened....
— Matthew 9:27-30

*I*t may be hard for you to believe, but most of what we have done in life has been initiated by us, not by the Spirit of God. After the ball is rolling and we've already started "doing our thing," that's usually when we pray and ask God to bless what we have initiated. We just assume that it is His will because it seems like such a good idea. No wonder we have such poor results!

We must learn to put on the brakes, stop ourselves for a while, and learn to wait until the Holy Spirit speaks clearly to our hearts. It may seem as if this way of doing things takes longer; but when He does speak, the results will be more rewarding and longer lasting. Furthermore, we can avoid pitfalls that would have cost us a lot of time and effort in the long run.

Believers must learn to let the Holy Spirit lead them. Take healing as an example. How many ministers have thought, *I'm going to empty all those wheelchairs by praying for those sick people!* But after they finished praying, most of the people were still in their wheelchairs and those ministers left feeling embarrassed, defeated, and powerless. Didn't God want to heal those people? Of course He did, but the anointing may not have been present at that exact moment to heal in that particular way.

Being sensitive to the Holy Spirit is important if we want to see successful results in any sphere of life, including healing, family, business, and leading a church congregation. Only the Holy Spirit sees and knows everything that should be done; that's why it is so imperative to learn how to follow His leadership if we want to be successful in life.

I think a classic example of being led by the Spirit can be seen in the account of the two blind beggars in Matthew 9:27-31. These two blind beggars heard that Jesus was walking by, so they waited for Him to heal them. However, Jesus walked right past, never stopping to heal them. The two blind beggars were so upset that Matthew 9:27 tells us, "And when Jesus departed thence, two blind men followed him, crying, and saying, Thou son of David, have mercy on us."

The word "followed" is the Greek word *akoloutheo*, which means *to follow after someone or something in a very determined and purposeful manner.* Even though these two men were blind and couldn't see where they were going, they were determined to follow Jesus until they got His attention! The verse continues to tell us that they were "crying" out. The word "crying" is the Greek word *kradzo*, and it means *to scream, yell, exclaim,* or *cry out at the top of one's voice.* In other words, they were screaming as loudly as possible to get Jesus' attention! What a dramatic picture! Think about it — here were two blind men, desperately wanting to be healed, who were screaming, shouting, and yelling, trying to get Jesus to notice them. But He just continued walking on as though they weren't even there. Pursuing Jesus relentlessly, they groped along in their darkness, still screaming, yelling, and crying out for Him to heal them.

Jesus couldn't have missed these two blind beggars because they were yelling so loudly; yet still He didn't stop. So they just kept screaming at the top of their lungs, over and over again, "Have mercy on us! Have mercy on us! Have mercy on us! Jesus, thou Son of David, have mercy on us!"

For years this section of Scripture perplexed me because I couldn't imagine why Jesus wouldn't acknowledge the two blind men. I wanted to know why He didn't immediately turn around and heal them. They were so determined to get His attention that they followed Him all the way to the house where He was staying, crying, "Son of David, have mercy on us!"

Finally, Jesus came to the two blind beggars and asked, "Do you believe that I am able to do this?" They answered, "Yea, Lord." Matthew 9:29 says, "Then touched he their eyes, saying, According to your faith be it unto you." But why didn't Jesus stop and heal the blind men when He first saw them? Why didn't He immediately turn to heal them when He recognized their blind condition? And why did He answer them, "...According to your faith be it unto you"?

Jesus evidently did not sense the anointing to heal at that moment; otherwise, He would have stopped to lay His hands on those men. However, this didn't stop the two blind men from receiving. It was as though Jesus said, "I don't sense the anointing to heal right now, so you're going to have to receive this on your own! Be it unto you according to your faith!"

So the only explanation for the fact that Jesus didn't stop to heal the two blind beggars is that the Holy Spirit wasn't leading Him to heal at that exact moment. The good news is that the two blind men could use their own faith to be healed anyway — and they *were* healed!

As for those whom the Holy Spirit led Jesus to heal, He healed them with a perfect, 100-percent success rate. The Bible describes His healing ministry this way: "And the whole multitude sought to touch him: for there went virtue out of him and, healed them all" (Luke 6:19).

You see, when that healing virtue was flowing, everyone got healed. But when it *wasn't* flowing, Jesus didn't attempt to heal. There are other instances like Luke 5:17 where Jesus was busy teaching the Word of God. Suddenly He sensed that "...the power of the Lord was present to heal them."

When Jesus sensed the anointing to heal, He put aside His teaching and followed the leading of the Spirit. As a result, multitudes were healed that day, including the paralytic whom a group of friends lowered down into the room through an opening in the roof of the house.

I love this example in Luke 5:17, for it shows Jesus' pliability in the hands of the Holy Spirit. Although He was busy teaching at the moment, suddenly He felt the anointing shift. The power of God was suddenly present to heal the sick, and Jesus knew it was time to set aside the preplanned program and go with the flow of the Holy Spirit. He faithfully followed wherever the Holy Spirit led, and He did what the Holy Spirit told Him to do. If the Spirit told Him nothing, then nothing was the right thing for Him to do.

In John 5:30, Jesus told of His complete dependency upon the Holy Spirit. He told the disciples, "I can of mine own self do nothing: as I hear, I judge: and my judgment is just...." Notice that Jesus said, "...As I hear, I judge...." You see, Jesus was constantly listening to the voice of the Spirit, waiting for that divine signal to act, to heal, to deliver, or to cleanse someone who was sick.

Then Jesus said what He did as soon as He was confident of the Spirit's direction to act: "...I judge: and my judgment is just...." The word "judge" and "judgment" are both from the Greek word *krino*, a legal term meaning *to make a decision on the basis of information*, like a jury who has heard all the evidence in a trial and now possesses all the information needed to take action.

This word is used in John 5:30 to let us know that Jesus never acted until He had all the direction He needed from the Spirit. Once that direction was given and Jesus had all the information He needed, *He acted.* Because He acted on directions given by the Spirit of God, He was able to say that His actions were always right. In other words, Jesus had a 100-percent success rate because He followed the Spirit's leading!

Jesus didn't go with a preplanned program or act mechanically every time He was confronted with a need. Therefore, we need to learn from His example and depend on the leading of the Holy Spirit just as He did. If we will listen to the Spirit and do what He tells us to do — if we will learn to wait until we hear Him speak — we will have powerful results just like Jesus had in His earthly ministry.

So what about you, friend? Are you ready to let the Holy Spirit become the Leader in your life today?

MY PRAYER FOR TODAY

Lord, I want to learn how to follow You more closely! I want to learn the sound of Your voice, to sense when You are speaking to me and trying to lead me, and to become so sensitive to You that I know when to act and when to wait. I am sorry for all the times I've acted before praying — and then assumed that You would bless what I was doing. I don't want to function this way anymore. I only want to initiate what I know You are leading me to do. So please help me become more sensitive. Give me the boldness to do what You say to do and to wait when I hear You tell me to wait.

I pray this in Jesus' name!

MY CONFESSION FOR TODAY

I confess that I am completely dependent upon the Holy Spirit. Just as Jesus was constantly listening to the voice of the Spirit, waiting for that divine signal to act, to heal, to deliver, or to cleanse someone who was sick, I am also sensitive to the Holy Spirit's voice and wait for Him to speak to my heart. When He speaks, I hear; then I do exactly what He instructs me to do. Because I follow His voice, I make few mistakes and I see great results!

I declare this by faith in Jesus' name!

1. Has there ever been a time when you suddenly sensed the Holy Spirit leading you to stop what you were doing so He could use you to do something different than you had previously planned?
2. Did you follow the leading of the Holy Spirit, or did you stick with the pre-planned program because you didn't want to interrupt your schedule?
3. Is there a reason you resist when you sense that the Holy Spirit is trying to redirect your steps? What are those reasons?

AUGUST 13

Have You Noticed the People Whom God Has Called To Help You?

Let a man so account of us, as of the ministers of Christ,
and stewards of the mysteries of God.
— 1 Corinthians 4:1

When I was first starting to study New Testament Greek many years ago, I pulled out my Greek New Testament one day and flipped it over to First Corinthians 4:1. There I discovered that the Greek word for "ministers" was the word *huperetas* — the Greek word that was used to depict *the very lowest class of criminals.* I knew Paul must have had a reason for selecting this word to describe "ministers," but it made me wonder.

The *huperetas* of ancient times were the criminals assigned to live the rest of their lives in the bottom galleys of huge ships. In those galleys, they became the engines that moved the ships through the seas. As I pondered this, I could see so many reasons why Paul used this word to describe those of us who are serving in the Kingdom of God!

For instance, a great number of these criminals were held in the bottom galleys of ships. They were seated and chained to a bench along with other criminals — and together they shared common chains, held a common oar, and worked the same number of hours. They all had to provide equal labor to the task. Their entire lives became a group effort. *They became inseparable from the other men who were on the bench with them.* As I reflected on this, I thought of how God never calls you to do a big job all by yourself. He will call others at the same time to assist you. When you say yes to the will of God — when you jump into the middle of your assigned task and surrender your time, money, talents, and ideas to the Lord — you will discover that others will be right there by your side to help you with the task. *You're not the only one God has been speaking to!*

The ships on which the *huperetas* served were so huge that it would have been impossible for one servant to move an entire ship by himself. It required the strength and effort of many servants working together in order to move those huge ships.

In the same way, you cannot accomplish what God has called you to do all alone! *Look around you!* Look at the people God has placed around you to help you fulfill your dream. Don't ignore them, thinking you can do it alone. If your vision from the Lord is big, it will require others to become involved in what you are doing.

I wouldn't be able to do what God has told me to do if I had to do it by myself. The vision is too big and demanding. That's why God didn't stop after He called me. He also called others to stand with me, pray with me, and stay for the long haul, working beside me "on the under-rowers' bench." Their call is just as real as my call. They will answer for their part just as I will answer for mine. And when rewards are given, they will be rewarded for how they helped "row the boat" and keep this ministry moving forward to reach millions of souls.

For example, the Lord has called me to take the teaching of the Bible to spiritually hungry people in the former USSR every day through the vehicle of television. But at the same time He placed this vision in my heart, He also called partners to pray for the program, pay for television time, and support our ministry in the United States. Without our partners, I could not do my part in the territory of the former USSR. They are equally as important as Denise and me and our ministry team.

How about the staff members of our television ministry outreach, such as our television producers, editors, and secretaries? How about the dedicated work force who answer letters from our television viewers? Since 1992, this television staff has answered millions of letters from those who have written to Denise and me as a result of watching our television program. Our television department has also edited thousands of television programs and distributed several hundred thousand separate showings to eleven time zones of the former Soviet Union.

These precious staff members are the ones who do the work behind the scenes so that these programs can go into millions of homes every day of the week. If I didn't have them, I wouldn't be able to minister to the masses of people God has entrusted to me or help the hundreds of churches and pastors located all over the former USSR who look to me for apostolic guidance. I am so thankful for the others on my team whom God called to help me with this awesome task, because this job is too big for me to do alone!

Likewise, if you are going to fulfill the dream God has given *you*, you will have to learn how to cooperate with other key people — *your partners in life* — who can assist you in fulfilling that dream.

The *huperetas* in Paul's illustration lived together and worked together. And when rewards were given for their extremely hard work, every man in the group was rewarded. Since they labored at the same task, shared the same oar, and sweated the same amount of sweat, the entire bench of workers was equally rewarded. On the other hand, if one rower on a bench was lazy and kept the whole bench of rowers from carrying their share of the load on the ship, every rower on that bench was punished.

In other words, the difference in one coworker's attitude was so powerful that it had the ability to bring about victory or defeat for all of them. Since each member of the team was vital to success, their entire existence became a group effort. *Therefore, they had to learn how to function as a team.*

When these men rowed, the boat moved. When they stopped rowing, the boat stopped. These servants were the driving force behind the speed of the ship. If they ever stopped working hard at rowing, the ship stayed motionless in the water. It was totally dependent on the rowers in the bottom of the boat, which was powerless to travel anywhere without them.

Similarly, if you are going to move ahead with what God has called you to do — *whether it is your ministry, your family, or your business* — you must learn how to be a faithful servant, working together with others as a team "in the bottom of the boat."

The bottom of the boat may not be the most pleasurable place to be. Serving day in and day out may seem monotonous and almost boring at times. But sticking with the vision and continuing to row will eventually produce eternal results for the Kingdom of God! So surrender to the plan of God, take your place in the ship, grab an oar, and start rowing! *If you want to get to your destination more quickly, put your whole heart and soul into rowing that boat!*

MY PRAYER FOR TODAY

Lord, I thank You for the life-changing truths I just read! I want to take my place in Your plan for my life — and I want to give 100 percent of my attention and strength to see it come to pass in my life. With all my heart, I tell You that I want to follow You and to do whatever is required to see that vision come to pass in my life. And thank You for calling others to come alongside to help me move this vision along a little faster!

I pray this in Jesus' name!

MY CONFESSION FOR TODAY

I confess that I have taken my place in God's plan. I have grabbed hold of an oar, and I am rowing and rowing with all my strength and energy. The assignment God has given me probably won't be achieved quickly, so I have mentally prepared myself for a long-term stint at doing what God is calling me to do. It will take unbelievable strength and energy to move that vision from the realm of dreams to the realm of reality. But because of the power of the Holy Spirit in me, I have all the strength I need for this wonderful and awesome task!

I declare this by faith in Jesus' name!

QUESTIONS FOR YOU TO CONSIDER

1. Do you know what boat God has called you to jump into and start rowing? What church, organization, ministry, or mission are you supposed to be helping?
2. When you look at your own life, can you see that it has taken the combined efforts of many faithful people to get you where you are today? Have you ever made a list of the people who helped you get where you are — and have you taken the time to write them a note to say thank you for what they have done for you?
3. If your answer to the above question is no, then why don't you take a few minutes today to make that list and to write a few notes to people who have made a difference in your life?

If you are going to fulfill the dream God has given you, you will have to learn how to cooperate with other key people who will assist you in fulfilling that dream.

AUGUST 14

A Celebration Like No Other!

And having spoiled principalities and powers,
he made a shew of them openly, triumphing over them in it.
— Colossians 2:15

Have you ever wondered what kind of celebration took place in Heaven after Jesus' defeat of the devil? Well, it is possible for us to know exactly how Heaven celebrated because Paul gives us a glimpse into that heavenly gala event in Colossians 2:15. It says, "And having spoiled principalities and powers, he made a shew of them openly, triumphing over them in it."

This is an extremely *graphic* verse! It is a *picture* painted for us by the Holy Spirit — a glorious, *vivid* illustration of what happened the day Jesus defeated death, hell, and the grave!

The word "spoiled" is the Greek word *apekduomai*, which means *to strip off* or *to put off as one would put off his garments*. This word could depict *the disarming of an enemy — literally stripping his weaponry and artillery from him and leaving him without any weapons with which to respond*. One scholar has noted that it refers to *stripping one to the point of complete nakedness*. By using this word, the Holy Spirit tells us that when Jesus arose from the dead, He *thoroughly* plundered the enemy!

Furthermore, when Jesus' sacking and plundering of hell's powers was complete and His mission was accomplished, Paul tells us that He rubbed this defeat in the devil's face by throwing the biggest party the universe had ever seen! Colossians 2:15 says, "And having spoiled principalities and powers, he made a shew of them openly, triumphing over them in it."

The word "shew" is taken from the word *deigmatidzo*, and it literally means *to display* or *to expose something*. It was used in classical Greek writing to denote *the display of captives, weaponry, and trophies that were seized during war on foreign soil*. Once the war was finished and the battle was won, the reigning emperor would return home and victoriously *display* and *expose* the treasures, trophies, weaponry, and captives that he had seized during his military conquest. This was a grand moment of celebration for the victor — but it was a humiliating experience for the defunct foe.

But wait — there is still more to Colossians 2:15 that you must understand. Paul goes on to tell us that "...he made a shew of them *openly*...." The word "openly" is taken from the Greek word *parresia*, which is used throughout the books of the New Testament to denote *boldness, confidence,* or *something that is done blatantly or even publicly*. By using the word *parresia*, Paul declares that when this heavenly party and celebration of Jesus' victory commenced, it was no quiet affair! On the contrary — He *boldly, confidently, loudly, blatantly,* and *publicly exposed and displayed* this now-defunct foe to the heavenly hosts! It was the greatest celebration in history!

In fact, Paul goes on to say, "...he made a shew of them openly, triumphing over them in it." The phrase "triumphing over them in it" is a major key to this verse. This phrase comes from the Greek word *triambeuo*, which is a technical word used to describe the general or emperor who was returning home from a grand victory in the enemy's territory. The word "triumph" (*triambeuo*) was a specific word used to describe *a glorious triumphal parade*!

When news reached the city that the enemy had been defeated, plans for a triumphal parade went into action. By the time the gates of the city were opened wide to receive this emperor who was now returning home in triumph, his people were ready to celebrate his victory! As the gates swung open and this mighty warrior rode through, *the celebration began*!

Sitting astride a large, beautiful, white stallion; draped in his kingly, regal garments; and wearing his bright, shining crown upon his head, the returning emperor would lead the entire city in a procession of celebration and victory. It was called his "triumphal parade." As he rode down the main avenue of the city with his head held high and a look of elation on his face, the city would begin rejoicing. "He's back! He's back! Our king has won a massive victory!" the people would cry as they broke into jubilant dancing and singing, joyously twirling around in circles. This was indeed a time to rejoice!

In order to flaunt his great victory, the returning victor would parade behind him the foreign king — the defeated foe, taken in captivity and bound in heavy chains of bondage. Behind this now-defunct enemy would walk the defeated ruling men and leaders, bound and chained along with their ruined king. Further back in the procession were oxcarts loaded to overflowing with booty taken *by force* from the enemy's homeland. Once these goods had belonged to the enemy, but now they belonged to the conquering king!

As the returning, victorious emperor rode down the avenue, he'd strut with pride, flaunting his defeated foes. In other words, he'd "make a shew of them openly." He wanted everyone to see the fabulous goods he had stolen from his enemy's hand — proof that the conquered foe had been completely "spoiled."

But the most exciting moment of the entire celebration occurred when the emperor sang a song of victory. As he rode that horse through the gate, leading his triumphal parade, he would open his mouth and begin to sing as loudly as he could sing! With all his might, he would sing something like this: "The enemy is defeated; the foe is conquered; let it be known that I am still the king!" This song would throw the crowd into a frenzy. This was the voice and the song they had been waiting for! The king had returned, and he was *still king*!

Then, after riding down the main avenue, revealing his booty, and singing his song of victory, the victor would stop in front of a large set of stairs that led upward to a huge, ornate throne. His military conquest had proven that he was still the holder of authority. Therefore, he proudly walked up those steps, turned toward the great crowd who was watching, and lowered himself down to sit in his rightful place — *the throne*.

Since all this is the background to Colossians 2:15, the verse could be interpreted to read:

"He completely stripped principalities and powers and left them utterly naked; nothing was left at their disposal with which to retaliate. He boldly, confidently, loudly, blatantly, and publicly exposed and displayed this now-defunct foe, leading a gallant triumphal parade in celebration of the enemy's defeat and His victory!"

Does all this mean that this actual type of celebration took place in Heaven after Jesus' defeat of the devil? There is no explicit biblical account that records the type of celebration that occurred the day Jesus was raised from the dead, but Paul's words in Colossians 2:15 certainly indicate that Heaven threw quite a party that day. Jesus' victory over the devil was the greatest victory ever known! It would be entirely expected that Heaven would celebrate that victory with the Son of God.

So if you feel like shouting when you think about what Jesus did to the devil, go ahead and shout! If thinking of Jesus' victory makes you want to jump up and down, dance, or twirl around in circles, then go for it! There's nothing strange about this behavior at all — you have something to rejoice about! *When you start rejoicing about Jesus' victory over the devil, you join the throngs of Heaven who also wildly celebrate Jesus' victory and Satan's defeat!*

MY PRAYER FOR TODAY

Lord, I am stopping everything I'm doing right now to praise You for Your victory over Satan! Thank You for stripping him bare and for leaving him with nothing in his hands with which to retaliate. Thinking of what You did makes me want to shout — so right now I'm going to shout! Realizing what You did makes me want to jump with joy — so right now I'm going to leap up and down in praise to You! I'm excited about what You did, and I'm not ashamed to show how I feel about it. I praise and worship You for the great victory You gained!

I pray this in Jesus' name!

MY CONFESSION FOR TODAY

I confess that I am free from Satan's grip on my life because Jesus stripped him bare and left nothing in his hands that he could use against me! Jesus defeated and disarmed Satan; then He gave me authority over the devil and all his works. Greater is He who is in me than he who is in the world. That means in Jesus Christ I am fully empowered to enforce Satan's defeat!

I declare this by faith in Jesus' name!

QUESTIONS FOR YOU TO CONSIDER

1. What did you learn from today's *Sparkling Gem* that you never knew before?
2. How does this new insight into Jesus' victory over the devil shape your view of your own ability to walk in victory through every situation of life?
3. How long has it been since you spent some time thanking Jesus for what He did for you through His death and resurrection? After reading this today, don't you think you ought to take a few minutes to really praise Him for His glorious victory and Satan's defeat?

The word "openly" is taken from the Greek word *parresia*, which denotes *boldness, confidence,* or *something that is done blatantly or even publicly.* By using this word, Paul declares that when this heavenly celebration of Jesus' victory commenced, it was no quiet affair! Jesus *boldly, confidently, loudly, blatantly,* and *publicly exposed and displayed* this now-defunct foe to the heavenly hosts! It was the greatest celebration in history!

AUGUST 15

❧❧❧

Where Does the Bible Ever Say God Is Looking for Brains?

For ye see your calling, brethren, how that not many wise men
after the flesh, not many mighty, not many noble, are called:
But God hath chosen the foolish things of the world
to confound the wise; and God hath chosen the weak things of the world
to confound the things which are mighty;
And base things of the world, and things which are despised, hath God chosen....
— 1 Corinthians 1:26-28

If you see yourself as weak, feeble, or unskilled, don't let that bother you too much. God has been calling feeble and unskilled people from the beginning of time. Few of those whom God has called have been the "cream of the crop" according to the flesh. Again and again, God has chosen people who were ill-esteemed in the eyes of the world when He needed a candidate or a group of people to do a job.

God has always used common people to build His Kingdom. He doesn't primarily choose famous movie stars or the royalty and nobility of the world to fulfill His plans and purposes on this earth. God's criteria are different from the criteria of the world. As Isaiah 55:8 says, "For my thoughts are not your thoughts, neither are your ways my ways, saith the Lord."

When God chose Samuel to lead the nation, Samuel was just a young boy. When God looked for someone to kill a giant, He chose a young shepherd boy named David. When the fullness of time came and it was time to send His Son to this earth, God chose a young girl named Mary to give birth to the Savior of the world.

When it was time for Jesus to choose disciples, He didn't go to the theological institutes or seminaries of the day. Rather, Jesus chose disciples who knew more about fishing and tax-collecting than about the Scriptures. And when God searched for someone He could use to write the majority of the New Testament, He chose the apostle Paul, who was once one of the meanest Christian killers of all time!

God has always shown up in places where He wasn't expected. Just consider the location where Jesus was born — *in a lowly shepherd's stall.* This was certainly not the place anyone would have expected the King of kings to be born. Wouldn't it have been better for the King of kings to be born in a gold-gilded hall with trumpets blasting to announce His birth?

So if you have ever thought you weren't good enough for God to use, it's time for you to renew your thinking! God is looking for people no one else wants or deems valuable. When great victories are won through ordinary folks, there's no question as to who should receive the glory! As First Corinthians 1:29 says, "That no flesh should glory in his presence."

The Old and New Testaments are filled with illustrations of people whom *God wanted,* but whom *the world rejected.* God's choice is not based on beauty or ugliness, talent or lack of talent, education or lack of education, a diploma or lack of a diploma. If a person has a *right heart* toward God, he is qualified to be used by God.

In First Corinthians 1:26-28, Paul wrote, "For ye see your calling, brethren, how that not many wise men after the flesh, not many mighty, not many noble, are called: but God hath chosen the foolish things of the world to confound the wise; and God hath chosen the weak things of the world to confound the things which are mighty; and base things of the world, and things which are despised, hath God chosen...."

As Paul writes his list of those whom God *does* and *doesn't* call, he begins by stating that God doesn't call many who are considered "wise" by the world. The word "wise" is from the Greek word *sophos*. It refers to a person who possesses *special enlightenment or special insight*.

The word *sophos* was usually used to portray highly educated people, such as scientists, philosophers, doctors, teachers, and others who were considered to be the *super-intelligentsia* of the world. These belong to a class of individuals whom the world would call *clever, astute, smart,* or *intellectually brilliant*. This term was reserved only for those considered to be *super-impressive* or a *cut above* the rest of society.

But Paul says, "For ye see your calling, brethren, how that not many *wise* men after the flesh...." Paul informs us that most of the folks God calls don't fit into this category of the *super-intelligentsia*. In other words, God doesn't specialize in calling people who are *especially bright, educated, astute, smart, or eminently enlightened*.

I would be foolish to overlook the fact that over the years, many intelligent men and women who loved God have made a great impact on the world. Paul himself was a part of this elite group before he came to Christ. Apollos, Paul's friend who later pastored the church of Corinth, also came from this intellectual "upper echelon" of society. But Paul and Apollos were not typical of the first-century Church.

It was the *sophos* who scorned and ridiculed Paul when he preached in Athens. The philosophers of Athens, the Epicureans, and the Stoics derided him and made him a laughingstock. Paul said that "not many" are called who fit into this *sophos* category. Of course, God's call is to all men; nevertheless, "not many" from this category *respond* to God's call.

Take a close look at the Early Church, and you'll see that it was primarily composed of servants, slaves, and poorer people who heard the Good News of the Gospel and believed. *It was an army of common people.* Although there were a few elite in the Church, these were the exception rather than the rule. In fact, as you study Church history, you will see that God specializes in calling people from a much lower class. And if you take a close look at the Church today, you'll see that God still specializes in calling common people.

Now, I'm not debasing education. People should get as much education as possible. But school-issued pieces of paper are not the criteria that impresses God and gets His attention. There have been many educated people whom God could not use. Even though they were brilliant according to the flesh, they were not worthy of being chosen because their hearts weren't right.

Educational degrees may help you get a good job and positively sway the opinion of men in your favor, but Paul makes it very clear that God is not bent on using people who are *especially bright according to the standards of the flesh*.

In fact, the Bible shows that when God does call people who are intellectually impressive, such as Moses or the apostle Paul, He usually has to empty them *of themselves* before He can use them! When they lean on their own understanding, they are unable to accomplish what God wants. But when they lean wholly upon *Him*, He is able to perform miracles through their lives.

Proverbs 3:5 says, "Trust in the Lord with all thine heart; and lean not unto thine own understanding." Certainly natural knowledge and understanding are needful in the world we live in today.

But if our natural understanding rather than our trust in God becomes the basis for our confidence, we put ourselves at a disadvantage. *We have to learn to use what we know while leaning only on the Lord and His might.*

David wrote, "Some trust in chariots, and some in horses: but we will remember the name of the Lord our God" (Psalm 20:7). The best technology of David's time was used to develop chariots. Man's greatest intellectual powers were employed to make chariots faster, stronger, and safer. In addition, horses represented natural power, strength, and might. Therefore, David was saying, *"Some trust in man's mind and his great achievements; others rely on their own natural power and might; but we will rely upon the name of the Lord."*

Perhaps you're one of those people who says, "God can't use me because I don't have enough gifts or talents. I haven't even been to college. I don't even have a Bible school degree." If you are, it's time for you to change the way you're thinking and talking. It's time for you to start seeing yourself the way God does!

In fact, if you feel *inferior* to others, remember that God regularly calls unskilled and uneducated people. Just think of the majority of the apostles whom Jesus hand-picked to serve at His side and to lay the foundation of the Church. Those apostles were fishermen, tax collectors, common people — *not* theologians.

God is looking to build a strong, powerful army. The soldiers of an army are rarely composed of the intellectually astute. Flavius Vegetius Renatus, who lived around 380 AD, was the author of the most influential military book ever written for the Roman Empire. Look at the type of person he says makes the best soldier: "Peasants are the most fit to carry arms.… They are simple, content with little, inured to fatigue, and prepared in some measure for military life by their continual employment in farm work, in handling the spade, digging trenches and carrying burdens."[1]

The truth is, God is looking for people who know how and are willing to pay a price — to undergo any hardship needed, to confront the power of hell, and to "dig trenches and carry burdens" until their assignment is completed just as God ordered it. God doesn't necessarily need the super-intelligentsia of the world to get these jobs done. In fact, common people are often God's *first* choice because they are already equipped to a certain degree to face the challenges and difficulties of life.

So if you want to be used by God and serve in His army, quit complaining that you're not as smart or sharp as someone else. Where does the Bible ever say God is looking for brains? He's looking for hearts that are willing to follow Him. *If you have that kind of heart, you are exactly the kind of person God wants to use!*

MY PRAYER FOR TODAY

Lord, I am so glad You don't choose only the intellectually brilliant. You are looking for anyone who has a heart to be used by You. Well, that's me, Lord. I want You to use me. I offer You everything I have — my good points, my weak points, my gifts, my talents, and everything else that I am. I want You to use me for Your glory! I've told You before, but today I'm telling You again that I want You to take my life and do something wonderful with me!

I pray this in Jesus' name!

---

[2]Flavius Vegetius Renatus, *The Military Institutions of the Romans*, trans. Lt. John Clark (Westport, Connecticut: Greenwood Press, 1944), p. 14.

MY CONFESSION FOR TODAY

I confess that I am exactly the kind of person God can use! God is looking to carry out great victories through my life! His choice is not based on beauty or a lack of beauty, talent or lack of talent, education or lack of education, a diploma or lack of a diploma. No, God has chosen me because I have a heart that is right before Him!

I declare this in Jesus' name!

QUESTIONS FOR YOU TO CONSIDER

1. Can you recall concrete examples of people in the Bible whom the world thought to be worth nothing — yet God called them, changed them, and then used them to change world history? Try to name five people who fit into this category.
2. Can you think of specific people outside the Bible whom the world thought to be worth nothing, yet God used them to change society? Try to name five people who fit into this category as well.
3. If God specializes in calling people who come from common backgrounds, what does this mean for you?

AUGUST 16

Look at What You've Been Given In Jesus Christ!

But as many as received him, to them gave he power
to become the sons of God,
even to them that believe on his name.
— John 1:12

Y ou have been given so much in Jesus Christ! You have no legitimate reason for failing to be an awesome success in life, because you have so much going for you! In fact, you have much more going for you than you could possibly imagine. Today let me encourage you with just a few of the things you've been given in Jesus Christ!

John 1:12 says, "But as many as received him, to them gave he power to become the sons of God, even to them that believe on his name." This verse reveals that you received divine power the day you became a child of God. The word "power" is the Greek word *exousia*. It describes *delegated authority or influence.* The day you chose to make Jesus your Lord and Savior is the day He delegated to you the power and authority to become a child of God. Think of it — at that moment of decision, all the power, authority, and divine influence that is resident within the mighty name of Jesus Christ came to live on the inside of you!

So rather than complain that you're weak and nothing special, it's time to start laying claim to what is stored up inside you! The same explosive, dynamic, phenomenal authority and power that resides within Jesus has now been delegated to reside in *you*!

As if that wasn't already enough, Second Corinthians 5:17 declares, "Therefore if any man be in Christ, he is a new creature: old things are passed away; behold, all things are become new." This verse says you're a brand-new creature if you are in Christ Jesus. The word "new" is from the Greek word *kainos*, and it describes *something that is brand new or recently made*. It also carries the idea of *something that is superior*. This means when Jesus Christ came into your life, you were made *brand, spanking new*! The new you is *superior* to the old you! In fact, you are so new that this verse calls you a new "creature."

The word "creature" is the Greek word *ktisis*. It is the same word used to describe *the creation of the world*. When God created the universe, he used no existing materials or old elements to make it. Everything in creation was newly made. Now that same word is used to describe what happened to you the day you got saved. *Everything about you is new!* You're not an amended, corrected, improved version of what you used to be. You are an absolutely brand-new creation! You are completely detached from the person you once were before Christ.

Psalm 103:12 tells you how far your old ways have been removed from you: "As far as the east is from the west, so far hath he removed our transgressions from us." When Jesus Christ came into your life, He created you to be free from the past, free from the negative effects of your family, and liberated from all former hang-ups — in short, *a brand-new creature*!

So stop laying claim to your family's genetic problems, inheritable sicknesses, dysfunctional behavior, disorders, hang-ups, curses, or any other negative thing that was a part of your life before Christ. That old person no longer exists. He is *dead*. You are *brand new*.

But wait — there's so much more that you've been given in Jesus Christ! For instance, Ephesians 2:10 says, "For we are his workmanship, created in Christ Jesus unto good works, which God hath before ordained that we should walk in them."

The first part of this verse says that you and I are God's "workmanship." This comes from the Greek word *poiema*. The word *poiema* carries the idea of something that is *artfully created*. The Greek word for a poet, *poietes*, comes from this same word. In reference to a poet, this Greek word would denote *one who has the extraordinary ability to write or create a literary masterpiece*.

Because Paul uses the word *poiema* to explain what happened when you became a child of God, it emphatically means that on the day you got saved, God put forth His most powerful and creative effort to make you new. Once God was finished making you new, you became *a masterpiece, skillfully and artfully created in Christ Jesus*. There's nothing *cheap* about you at all! *God's creative, artistic, intelligent genius went into your making*.

Look how much you've been given in Jesus Christ! Don't you think it's time to stop moaning about how dumb, stupid, ugly, or untalented you "feel" compared to others? Those "feelings" are all lies. Some of that may have been true before you were born again, but none of it is true of you now that you are in Christ. God turned you into something spectacular. That's who you are now! *So lay claim to your new identity. Adjust your thinking and talking to reflect who you really are!*

MY PRAYER FOR TODAY

Lord, forgive me for being so negative and for talking so badly about myself after You have given me so much! I have no excuse for accepting defeat or low self-esteem as a way of life, because You have made me totally new! Help me renew my mind to the truth about who You have made me to be, and help me guard the words of my mouth so that instead of speaking evil of myself, I affirm the truth about who I am in Christ.

I pray this in Jesus' name!

MY CONFESSION FOR TODAY

I confess that the day I was born again, I received the dynamic, explosive power of God into my life. That power removed my old nature and made me a brand-new creature! Nothing from the old me continues to exist, for I am completely brand new. When God made me, He put forth His finest creative powers, and I now live on this earth as a masterpiece of His grace. God has made me into something quite spectacular!

I declare this by faith in Jesus' name!

QUESTIONS FOR YOU TO CONSIDER

1. In what ways did you notice that you immediately changed after you invited Jesus Christ to be the Lord of your life?
2. Do you regularly meditate on who you now are in Jesus Christ, or do you still look at yourself through the eyes of the person you used to be? Do you affirm what Jesus has done in you, or do you "nit-pick" yourself to pieces?
3. How long has it been since you regularly confessed scriptures about your new nature? It's always healthy to speak the truth to yourself, so why don't you make the decision that for the next couple of weeks, you are going to confess the truth about who you are in Jesus Christ every morning before your day gets started?

AUGUST 17

What Triggers a Demonic Attack?

Whereunto I am appointed a preacher, and an apostle,
and a teacher of the Gentiles.
For the which cause I also suffer these things....
— 2 Timothy 1:11,12

What triggers demonic attacks against you, your dream, your vision, your calling, your business, your family, your church, or your ministry? What makes the devil so upset that he rises up to resist you and your efforts? If God chose you, why are you experiencing so many hassles and difficulties along the way to your goal of fulfilling all He has called you to do?

In Second Timothy 1:11 and 12, Paul gives us incredible insight into what triggers a demonic attack. He says, "Whereunto I am appointed a preacher, and an apostle, and a teacher of the Gentiles.

For the which cause I also suffer these things...." In this verse, Paul writes about his specific calling in the Body of Christ. He affirms to us that he is called and appointed to be a preacher, an apostle, and a teacher of the Gentiles. Then notice that he immediately follows by saying, "For the which cause I also suffer these things..." (2 Timothy 1:12).

The word "suffer" is the Greek word *pascho*, and first and foremost it means *to suffer as a result of outside forces or outside circumstances*. It could include *physical suffering* due to persecution; *mental suffering* due to outside pressures; *financial suffering* due to monetary hardships; or *any inconvenience that stems from something outside of oneself or outside of one's control*. Thus, the word *pascho* would depict any *suffering* or *inconvenience* due to forces beyond oneself.

When Paul wrote this verse, he used a tense in the Greek that lets us know he was experiencing these inconveniences at the very moment he was writing this epistle. At that time, Paul was in Rome, sitting in a prison cell, awaiting his own execution, and being accused of crimes that he had not committed. Because Satan couldn't find a way to personally destroy Paul, the enemy was manipulating outside forces against Paul and his ministry. The apostle's situation had been created by outside pressures that had nothing to do with himself but that the devil had orchestrated to use against him.

Satan was terrified of Paul's calling! The reason Paul was recurrently attacked is that the devil was fearful of the enormous progress Paul would make if he didn't face opposition. Paul let us know that his anointing, his calling, and his potential were the factors that triggered these demonic attacks. It's almost as though Paul was saying, *"Do you want to know why I've suffered so many crazy things during the course of my ministry? Because I am appointed a preacher, an apostle, and a teacher of the Gentiles."*

You see, Satan was scared stiff of what would happen if Paul operated 100 percent in his call. How much would he be able to accomplish if he had no resistance? If Paul was able to do the incredible things he did for God's Kingdom in the face of such opposition, what kind of Gospel advancements would he make if there was no opposition? This thought was so chilling to the devil that he threw every possible obstacle in Paul's path to slow him down, to discredit him, to destroy his friendships, and, if possible, to even kill him. *Satan hated the call on Paul's life.*

The reason Paul was never defeated by these attacks is that *he had made a decision*. He decided he would not stop or give up until he had apprehended that for which Christ Jesus had apprehended him (Philippians 3:12). Likewise, the only way you'll be able to resist the devil's attacks and successfully achieve all God has called *you* to do is by determining *never* to stop until you have accomplished your divine assignment. Jesus taught that those who "endure to the end" are the ones who will receive the prize (Matthew 24:13).

If you want to overcome all the attacks the devil tries to wage against you through outside forces, you will have to be determined to outlast every attack! *Determination is a key factor in finishing one's race of faith.*

Of course, no one can successfully resist the devil's attacks without the power of the Holy Spirit, but neither is the power of the Holy Spirit enough by itself. For that power to be effective, it must work in a committed person. God's power works in people who have resolve. It works proficiently through people who have decided they will never turn back until the assignment is finished. God delights in using people who are steadfast and unmoving in their conviction, tenacious and diehard in their commitment. He takes pleasure in those who have stamina, spunk, and a dogged determination to hold on to the vision He put in their hearts.

The most common reason people don't make it all the way to the end is that they weren't *totally committed* to completing the task assigned to them. Maybe they tried it or gave it a shot, but their commitment wasn't strong enough, and that's why they didn't make it.

There are many things Satan can do to try to elbow us out of the race, but the only one who can decide to *quit* is you or me. *Satan can't make us quit.* That choice lies in our hands alone.

If you make the decision to stay in faith and "slug it out" with the power of God at your side, you can do exactly what God called you to do. But you must begin with a rock-solid, hard-core decision to do it, do it, and keep doing it until it's done. *Make any lesser choice, and you will never fulfill your God-given purpose.*

MY PRAYER FOR TODAY

Lord, help me stay focused on my calling and remain determined to do what You've told me to do, even if I am assaulted by outside forces that seem to be beyond my control. I know the devil hopes to slow me down or even to stop me by orchestrating outside pressures to come against me. But I also know that Your Spirit works mightily in me, giving me all the power I need to resist every assault the devil tries to bring against me. Help me to be completely determined and committed to keep pushing ahead and to never let go until I've accomplished my God-given mission!

I pray this in Jesus' name!

MY CONFESSION FOR TODAY

I boldly confess that I will not stop or give up until I have apprehended that for which Christ Jesus apprehended me! I will resist the devil's attacks and successfully achieve all God has called me to do, for I have determined that I will never stop until I have finished the task. I have the stamina, spunk, and doggedness it takes to get the job done. I have made the decision to stay in faith and slug it out with the power of God at my side. I can and will do exactly what God called me to do!

I declare this by faith in Jesus' name!

QUESTIONS FOR YOU TO CONSIDER

1. What are the outside forces that Satan has tried to use to hinder you? Has it been your health, your job, your children, your family, your finances? What is the one thing Satan seems to use repeatedly as he tries to resist you?
2. When you are aware that the devil is trying to use events, circumstances, or people to slow you down or to distract you from your calling, how do you respond to these attacks? What steps do you take to overcome them and to stay on track?
3. Do you seek the strength and counsel of other believers when these attacks occur, or do you usually slug it out silently on your own? Judging by the outcome when you go through these difficult times alone, do you think you need to seek the strength and counsel of others more often?

AUGUST 18

❧❧❧

Don't Give Place to the Devil!

Neither give place to the devil.
— Ephesians 4:27

Y ou and I never have to fall prey to the devil! If we can shut every door, close every window, and seal every place in our lives through which the enemy would try to access us, we can prevent him from getting into the middle of our affairs.

One of the "entry points" the devil tries to use to enter our lives is relationships. If there is an unresolved issue or an ugly conflict with a loved one or friend, these *conflict points* often become *entry points* through which the devil tries to get a foothold in our relationships with those we love. Once the enemy is able to slip in through one of these "cracks" and build an offended place in our minds, then a wall has already begun to be constructed that will eventually separate us from the people we need and love the most.

In Ephesians 4:27, the apostle Paul writes, "Neither give place to the devil." The word "place" is the Greek word *topos*. It refers to *a specific, marked-off, geographical location*. It carries the idea of a *territory, province, region, zone,* or *geographical position*. It is from this word that we get the word for a *topographical* map. Because the word *topos* depicts a geographical location, this lets us know that the devil is after every region and zone of our lives — *money, health, marriage, relationships, employment, business, and ministry*. He is so territorial that he wants it *all*. But to start his campaign to conquer all those areas of our lives, he must first find an *entry point* from which he can begin his campaign of unleashing his devilish destruction in our lives.

We often throw open the door to the devil when we:

✦ Refuse to let go of old hurts and wounds.
✦ Refuse to acknowledge what we did wrong.
✦ Refuse to forgive others for what they did.
✦ Refuse to stop judging others for their grievances.
✦ Refuse to admit we were wrong too.
✦ Refuse to say, "I'm sorry" when we're wrong.
✦ Refuse to lay down our "rights" for others.

If you and I do any of these things, we leave a "marked-off place" through which the devil can enter to accuse others in our minds. But we don't have to fall victim to the enemy's tactics. We can say, "No, you're not going to do this!"

We are more than conquerors through Jesus Christ, so we don't have to let the devil run all over us. The Bible boldly declares, "…Greater is he that is in you, than he that is in the world" (1 John 4:4).

The apostle Paul told us, "Neither give place to the devil." The Greek makes it clear that we must *choose* to give the devil no territory. You see, we have a choice: We can *choose* to "give the enemy place" in our minds and emotions, or we can *choose* to walk in the Spirit. If we choose the lower road, we will end up doing and saying things we later regret. Those regretful things are usually what opens the door for the devil to wreak havoc in our relationships.

I'm thinking specifically of a day I got very upset with one of our employees. I received information about one department of our ministry that really upset me. What upset me even more was that I believed one of our employees had known about this problem but hadn't conveyed the full truth to me about it. I scheduled a meeting to talk to that person the next morning to discuss this situation. That night as I lay in bed, I began to think about the problem we were facing. The longer I thought about it, the more angry I became that I hadn't been fully informed about the details as I should have been. I could feel a flash of heat pass through me as I kept pondering what to do next.

As I lay there in that bed, I began to take up an offense with this leader in our ministry. Once the devil got that foothold in my mind and emotions, it was as if a door had suddenly swung wide open for the devil to come in and begin accusing and slandering that precious employee to me. I tossed and turned all night long. I knew I could lay this issue down and walk in peace, or I could let it build in my mind until I became a walking time bomb. I chose to hold on to it and let it fester throughout the night.

The next morning when our meeting began, *I exploded*! My thinking was so distorted by the devil's ravings in my mind all night that I couldn't hear anything being said. I was *livid* with this employee. This employee couldn't even say anything, as I never even gave her ten seconds to respond to my accusations.

Later when the whole ordeal was over, I discovered that every detail of the problem had already been fully communicated to me. But I had been so busy at the time that I didn't even remember the conversation. Others on the staff remembered it very well. It was *my fault* that I didn't know and *not* hers.

I was so embarrassed that I had lost my temper. I asked my staff members for forgiveness, and they were spiritual enough to forgive me and allow me to be a man with real human frailties. *Thank God, our long-term relationship and commitment to work as a team overrides moments of human weakness that all of us display at one time or another.*

But there are *many* people who don't know how to recover from conflicts such as this one. Rather than face the situation head-on and either apologize or openly forgive, they hold their failure or their offense in their hearts, never forgetting it and never getting beyond it.

On the particular day that I exploded in anger, it was I who "gave place to the devil." As I tossed and turned in that bed the night before, I knew I was making a choice. I pondered the problem so long that I let anger well up inside of me and make my decision for me.

What about you? Have you ever given place to the devil by allowing anger, resentment, bitterness, or unforgiveness to have a "place" in you?

But let's look at the word "devil" for a moment. The word "devil" comes from the Greek word *diabolos*, an old compound word that is made from the words *dia* and *ballo*. This name is used sixty-one times in the New Testament. The first part of the word is the prefix *dia*, which means *through* and often carries the idea of *penetration*. Because *dia* is used at the first of this word, it tells us that the devil wants to make some kind of *penetration*.

We've already seen that the devil is looking for an *entry point*. Once a point has been located through which he can secretly slip into people's lives, he begins penetrating the mind and emotions to drive a wedge between those individuals and the other people in their lives. *The enemy's objective is to separate them from each other with his railing, accusing, slanderous accusations.*

You'll know when the accuser has gone to work in your mind because your whole perspective about the person you are upset with suddenly changes. *You become nit-picky, negative, and fault-finding.* You used to have high regard for that person, but now you can't see anything good about him at all.

It's as if you've put on a special set of eyeglasses that are specially designed to reveal all his wicked, ugly, horrid details. Even if you do see something good in him, all the bad you see outweighs the good.

This is clear evidence that the work of the "accuser" has found an entry point to penetrate your relationship with that other person. He is trying to disrupt what has been a pleasant and gratifying relationship in your life. Don't allow that conflict, disagreement, or disappointment to cause you to pick up a wrong attitude that will ruin your relationship. That's exactly what the devil wants you to do!

Rather than allow this to happen, stop and tell yourself, *Okay, this isn't as big of a deal as I'm making it out to be. The devil is trying to find a place in my mind to get me to start mentally accusing that person, and I'm not going to let him do it.*

Instead of meditating on all the bad points of that person, *look in the mirror yourself*! Consider how many times you've let down other people; how many mistakes you've made in your relationships; the times you should have been held accountable but instead were shown unbelievable mercy. Remembering these things has a way of making you look at an offensive situation a little more mercifully.

Ask the Holy Spirit to take the criticism out of your heart and to cause the love of God in you to flow toward that other person or group of people. Pray for an opportunity to strengthen that relationship so all the entry places to your life and to that relationship remain sealed. Stop the devil from worming his way into the middle of your relationships with people you need and love!

MY PRAYER FOR TODAY

Lord, I ask You to help me keep the doors to my heart and soul closed to the devil! I know he would like to slip into my relationships and ruin them, so I am asking You to help me stay free of offense, free of unforgiveness, and free of bitterness. I realize these wrong attitudes create "entry points" through which the devil tries to gain territory in my relationships. I don't want to give the devil a foothold in my affairs through a wrong attitude. So I'm asking You, Lord, to help me identify every wrong feeling or attitude in my life that the devil could use to ruin relationships with people I need and love.

I pray this in Jesus' name!

MY CONFESSION FOR TODAY

I confess that I walk in forgiveness! Offense, bitterness, strife, and unforgiveness have no place in my life. The Spirit of God dwells in me, and He always convicts me of wrong attitudes that the devil could potentially use to bind me. I love Jesus, and I want to please Him; therefore, I refuse to allow these destructive attitudes to remain in me. I am full of mercy, longsuffering, and slow to anger. All of these qualities keep me safe and secure from the devil's attempts to invade me.

I declare this by faith in Jesus' name!

QUESTIONS FOR YOU TO CONSIDER

1. Can you recall a time when the devil got you all upset over something that wasn't really such a big deal? Did he stir you up so much that you couldn't sleep; you couldn't think straight; and you said or did things that you later regretted?

2. What did you learn from that experience? Did you see how the devil operates to toss you into a tizzy, steal your peace, and harm your relationships? If yes, how have you learned to keep the door closed so He can't access you this way again?
3. If you were counseling someone else who was struggling with a similar problem, how would you counsel that person to keep his heart free of bitterness, anger, or strife?

AUGUST 19

Recognize and Respect Your Limitations!

For I say, through the grace given unto me,
to every man that is among you,
not to think of himself more highly than he ought to think;
but to think soberly, according as God hath dealt
to every man the measure of faith.
— Romans 12:3

Have you ever been so anxious to do something big and powerful that you rashly offered to do a job you later discovered was way above and beyond your abilities?

One summer when I was a university student, I was hired by a man who had a lot of confidence in my writing abilities. His firm was creating highly specialized computer programs for a steel corporation. They needed a good writer to document all the steps they were taking, so he hired me to write these reports. At that time I had *never* worked on a computer, nor did I know anything about computers. Therefore, I obviously didn't have a clue about what I was getting into when I agreed to take that job!

Soon I found myself seated in an executive office filled with computer programmers who spoke computer jargon that I had never heard in my life! This was a long time before people owned personal computers. Most common people had never placed their fingers on a computer — including me! And here I was, assigned to write a lengthy report about these extremely specialized computer programs. It only took a couple of hours for me to figure out I was the wrong person in the wrong place!

Finally, I had to say, "Hey, could someone please help me? I don't mind doing the job, but I can't do it without help." As it turned out, I asked them to reposition me in another job where I felt more qualified. I simply wasn't able to do the job because I wasn't equipped for the task. In the second position, I worked very well and was very successful. Had I refused to admit that the first assignment was too much for me, it would have been a very long summer of frustration for both me and my employers.

If you've ever found yourself in a similar place, you know it's overwhelming to be in so far over your head. There is nothing worse than feeling like you've been put in a position you aren't qualified to take. It can be so difficult for the flesh to admit that it can't do a job. Yet there is such great wisdom and peace in learning to recognize and respect your limitations!

This is why the apostle Paul told the Romans, "For I say, through the grace given unto me, to every man that is among you, not to think of himself more highly than he ought to think; but to think soberly, according as God hath dealt to every man the measure of faith" (Romans 12:3).

If anyone could have thought highly of himself, it would have been Paul, yet he admonishes believers that a person should not "…think of himself more highly than he ought to think…." This phrase comes from the Greek word *huperphroneo*, which is a compound of the words *huper* and *phroneo*. The word *huper* means *above, beyond,* or *way over the top,* and the word *phroneo* means *to think* or *to consider.*

When these two words are compounded into one word, it means that Paul is urging us not *to over-think* about ourselves, or not *to think over-confidently* about our abilities. Instead, he commands us to think "soberly." The word "soberly" is the Greek word *sophroneo,* which means *to think sensibly; to think reasonably; to think realistically; to think rationally; to think practically; to keep in proper measure;* or *not to think beyond the set boundaries.*

One Greek expositor says this word means *to recognize your limits and respect them.* In other words, don't pretend to be more than you are! Recognize your God-given abilities and use them. But when you come to the edge of your limitations, be willing to say, "This is too much for me."

If you act like you can do everything, you're going to find it quite humiliating when you fail miserably in front of everyone. So instead of thinking too highly of yourself and attempting to take on tasks and projects that are too daunting for you, realize that some jobs are meant to be assigned to someone else. You need to be very realistic about your limitations. If you have tackled a job that is too big for you, there is nothing wrong with admitting that someone else should take over the project.

If you refuse to admit you're over your head because you don't want to be embarrassed, you'll probably end up a whole lot more embarrassed later on when everyone else has to tell you that you can't do the job! When you fail and fall flat on your face, you'll regret that you didn't say, "I think someone else can do this job better than I can. This is simply not where I'm most gifted. Does anyone else on this team want to help me out with this project?"

When Paul said we were "…to think soberly, according as God hath dealt to every man the measure of faith," he was reminding us that there are other gifted members of the Body of Christ, and we must make room for their gifts as much as ours. God has gifted His entire Body with faith, spiritual gifts, talents, and abilities. Therefore, rather than try to do it all, which we can't do anyway, we need to learn to think "soberly." *In other words, we're to recognize our limitations and allow other people to be used by God too!*

This principle applies to the church, to the workplace, to school, and to every other sphere of life. Yes, we should respect our own gifts, talents, and callings from God, but we should also respect the fact that it takes all of us to get a job done! *So learn to recognize and respect your limitations — and learn to embrace others who are just as needed as you are!*

MY PRAYER FOR TODAY

Lord, help me recognize and respect my gifts and limitations. Forgive me for the times I've been too prideful to admit I was in over my head and as a result did an inferior job. I'm so sorry I didn't step out of the way so someone else who was gifted for the job could take my place. Help me specialize in those areas where I feel confident that I will be a blessing. Teach me to embrace and appreciate those who are more gifted than I am in other areas.

I pray this in Jesus' name!

MY CONFESSION FOR TODAY

I confess that I think soberly about myself and about my gifts and abilities. I thank God for the gifts and talents He has placed in my life, but I also recognize and respect my limitations. Just as I appreciate my own gifts and abilities, I am also grateful for those who are more gifted than I am in other areas. I need them; I embrace them; and I appreciate what they have to contribute. I can't achieve alone what can be accomplished in partnership with others. Therefore, I choose to partner my gifts and talents with the God-given gifts and talents in other people.

I declare this by faith in Jesus' name!

QUESTIONS FOR YOU TO CONSIDER

1. Have you ever found yourself in a job or position that was way over your head? Did you feel like you were drowning, desperate to find a way out of your commitment without being embarrassed? If your answer is yes, what did you do to remedy the situation?
2. Have you ever seen someone in leadership whom everyone else on the team knew was in a position that was way too high for him? Did that person struggle, make mistakes, or constantly try to cover up his lack of ability?
3. If the team members recognized the source of the problem with their struggling leader, how did that knowledge affect their attitude toward him?

AUGUST 20

When Mary Brought Jesus A Lavishly Expensive Gift

Then took Mary a pound of ointment of spikenard,
very costly, and anointed the feet of Jesus,
and wiped his feet with her hair:
and the house was filled with the odour of the ointment.
— John 12:3

*H*ow a person spends his money tells a lot about his priorities in life. Jesus said, "For where your treasure is, there will your heart be also" (Matthew 6:21).

Jesus' teaching is very clear: *What a person does with his money reveals what is inside his heart.* For example, someone may say he loves the local church. But if he never gives one cent to the church, the principle stated in Matthew 6:21 says his heart is *not* in the church, no matter *what* he says. *Where is his treasure?* If his *treasure* isn't in the church, his *heart* isn't in the church either.

I may say I love the Lord, but if I don't tithe as the Lord commands, what does it say about me? I'm either ignorant about tithing, or my words are cheap. *If I really loved the Lord, my money would reflect that I love Him.* I would *tithe*.

Words are cheap and easily spoken. Anyone can say he loves his church. But when a person sacrifices and gives to the church, he is demonstrating that his words are *real*. His heart really is *in* the church.

If a person *never* gives to the church, it reveals that he either has no money or that he's a liar. Of course, a person who has no money will find it difficult to give. But if he *does* have money and *doesn't* give, his words and actions don't match. When he spends his extra money on all kinds of material junk and then drops a few dollars into the offering, he's telling the *true* story! He loves his junk more than he loves the church.

Or consider a man who says he loves his wife but never gives her any money or special gifts to demonstrate that love. Yet somehow that same man is able to find the money to go fishing, buy a fishing boat, go work out at the gym with the guys, and so on. What has he demonstrated? *He loves himself more than he loves his wife.* That's why he's spending his treasure on himself.

How many men have told their wives, "I love you, Sweetheart" and then spent all their extra money on themselves? Then the wife is told that there just isn't any money available to do what *she* wants to do. How does it make the wife feel when her husband does this to her time after time? He can say, "I love you" all he wants, but she knows he really loves *himself*. What he does with his money tells the *real* story.

Jesus made it very clear that where a person's treasure is — where his *money* is — that's where his heart will be also. So if you really want to know where a person's heart is, *follow his money* and you'll find out. Again I say, *money tells the truth*!

In John 12, Jesus and His disciples were having dinner in the home of Mary, Martha, and their brother Lazarus, whom Jesus had raised from the dead. This family was very close to Jesus during His earthly ministry. At that dinner, Mary showed her love by bringing Jesus an extremely expensive gift. The Bible tells us that Mary brought Jesus a gift of ointment of spikenard — in fact, she brought Him an entire pound of it!

The word "spikenard" comes from the Greek word *nardos*, which describes one of the most expensive perfumes that existed at that time. Let me tell you a little about spikenard so you can appreciate what Mary did for Jesus that day.

Spikenard was an uncommon perfume extracted from grasses that grew in the country of India. Once the juices were squeezed out of the grass, they were dried into a hard, lardlike substance. Turning that lardlike substance into perfume was a very lengthy and costly process. If you add to this the cost of transporting spikenard from India to other parts of the world, you can see why this particular perfume cost so much money.

Spikenard was so expensive that few people could buy it; most had to buy one of the many cheap imitations available. But the word used in John 12:3 tells us that Mary didn't bring Jesus a cheap imitation; she brought Jesus *the real thing* — an ointment so valuable that it was normally reserved and used only as gifts for kings and nobility. *This was the gift Mary brought to Jesus.*

We can learn more about the value of Mary's gift in John 12:3, where it says the ointment was "very costly." This phrase "very costly" is from the Greek word *polutimos*, a compound of the words *polus* and *timios*. The word *polus* means *much* or *great*. The word *timios* means *to honor; to respect; or worth*. Together these words describe *something that is of great worth* or *something that is of considerable financial value*.

We'd call this "top-of-the-line giving"! As remarkable as it is that Mary even possessed a gift this valuable, what she did with this perfume once she brought it is even more phenomenal! John 12:3 says, "Mary took a pound of ointment of spikenard, very costly, and anointed the feet of Jesus...."

When Mary took the lid off that expensive bottle, tipped it downward, and began to pour that precious ointment onto Jesus' feet, everyone in the room must have gasped! This kind of perfume was not normally used for feet! Rather, it was the kind of ointment used to anoint the heads of kings and dignitaries. Mary's actions would have been considered a horrible *waste* in most people's minds, but that wasn't how she saw it. Mary *loved, appreciated,* and *valued* the feet of the Master!

Isaiah 52:7 describes why Mary felt this way: "How beautiful upon the mountains are the feet of him that bringeth good tidings, that publisheth peace; that bringeth good tidings of good, that publisheth salvation; that saith unto Zion, Thy God reigneth!"

You see, no other feet in the entire world were more beautiful to Mary than the feet of Jesus. Jesus had changed her life. Jesus had brought her brother back from the dead (*see* John 11:32-44). Jesus had brought new meaning into her family. To Mary, every step Jesus took was *precious, honored,* and *greatly valued.*

Remember, Jesus taught, "...Where your treasure is, there will your heart be also" (Matthew 6:21; Luke 12:34). Mary's actions revealed her heart as she poured her *most valuable treasure* onto the feet of Jesus. She deeply loved Jesus, and she showed it with the gift that she brought to Him.

John 12:3 continues to tell us that she "...wiped his feet with her hair...." After she poured the spikenard onto Jesus' feet, Mary reached up to her head and untied her long, beautiful hair, gathering it in her hands. Then she leaned down and began to wipe Jesus' feet dry with her hair.

In the days of the New Testament, a woman's hair represented her *glory* and *honor.* The apostle Paul referred to this in First Corinthians 11:15 when he wrote that a woman's hair was a "glory" to her. For Mary to undo her hair and use it as a towel to wipe Jesus' feet was probably the greatest act of humility she could have shown. She was demonstrating how deeply she loved and how greatly she valued Jesus. She didn't throw a financial offering at His feet, but she possessed an attitude of worship as she gave Jesus the best gift she had to offer.

I can imagine the tears that streamed down Mary's cheeks as she touched those precious feet. In total humility, she dried Jesus' feet with the glory and honor of her hair. John 12:3 tells us that "...the house was filled with the odour of the ointment." Certainly the house *would* be filled with the odor of spikenard once Mary poured an entire pound of that expensive perfume on Jesus' feet!

Considering how much spikenard cost, this was an enormous amount for Mary to use to anoint Jesus' feet. In fact, Judas Iscariot indignantly asked Jesus, "Why was not this ointment sold for three hundred pence, and given to the poor?" (John 12:5). The Greek word for a "pence" is *denarius*. In that day, a Roman *denarius* was *one day's salary*. So when Judas announced that the spikenard could have been sold for three hundred pence, he was saying that Mary's perfume was worth *three hundred days of salary*. That is why I say it was an *extremely expensive gift*! It was worth almost an entire year's income!

If it's true that what a person does with his money tells a lot about his priorities in life, Mary's gift that day revealed that Jesus was her highest priority. What does your giving reveal about how much *you* love Jesus?

You see, it may sound very simple, but it is a fact that if you follow a person's money, you'll discover what is or isn't important to that person's life. Look at a person's finances, and in just a matter of minutes you can tell what he values most in life. *The way he spends his money will tell the whole story of what he prizes, cherishes, loves, and adores.*

Of course, everyone has basic needs of life that require money, such as food, electricity, gas for the car, and so on. But once these things are paid, what a person does with the money that's left over will tell you what he esteems more highly than anything else. This may sound like a very narrow teaching about money, but this is exactly what Jesus meant when He said, "For where your treasure is, there will your heart be also." *Since this is the case, what does the way you spend your money reveal about you?*

MY PRAYER FOR TODAY

Lord, I ask You to help me be honest about what my finances reveal about me. I don't want anything else in my life to have a higher priority than You, so please teach me how to demonstrate my love for You with my finances. Help me to really worship You with my financial gifts and not to just casually throw them into an offering plate. Forgive me for the times I've said I didn't have enough money to give to the church or to missions, yet somehow I found a way to spend money on all kinds of material things. My priorities have obviously been wrong, so today I repent. I have made up my mind that I am going to honor You with my finances as I ought to do.

I pray this in Jesus' name!

MY CONFESSION FOR TODAY

I confess that I am growing more and more faithful in the giving of my tithes and offerings. Jesus Christ and the preaching of the Gospel are the greatest priorities in my life. Therefore, when I get paid, the first thing I do is set aside my tithe for the church and my offering for world missions and other worthy ministries. As I learn to love Jesus even more, my financial gifts are increasing as well. My treasure is in Jesus and the Gospel, because that is exactly where my heart is fixed.

I declare this by faith in Jesus' name!

QUESTIONS FOR YOU TO CONSIDER

1. What does your monthly expenditure of money tell you about what you value most highly in life?
2. If Jesus looked at your finances to make an analysis of what you prized most highly, what would He find? You might as well be honest about it, because He already knows!
3. What changes do you need to make in your heart and expenditures to reflect that your heart is first and foremost in the Kingdom of God?

Look at a person's finances, and in just a matter of minutes you can tell what he values most in life. The way he spends his money will tell the whole story of what he prizes, cherishes, loves, and adores.

AUGUST 21

High-Class Service
With Distinction and Style

And whosoever of you will be the chiefest, shall be servant of all.
For even the Son of Man came not to be ministered unto,
but to minister, and to give his life a ransom for many.
— Mark 10:44,45

*I*n the city of Moscow is a restaurant that is indisputably one of the most elegant place of fine dining in the entire world. The setting of this magnificent restaurant is a fabulou old Moscow palace that was built in the year 1889 as the personal residence for the Count Altuphev who was a general of the Russian army during the reign of the Russian Czar, Alexander III.

As one enters the Great Hall of the palace, he is instantly overwhelmed by the great vaulted ceiling, the massive hand-carved wooden staircase, the gorgeous stain-glassed windows, and the imposing and awe-inspiring chandelier that was bequeathed to this building many years later by the dictator Joseph Stalin. All of this adds to the opulence and magnificence of this historical place — which makes an evening spent in fine dining here nearly overwhelming.

When guests from the West come to visit, my wife and I enjoy taking them to this restauran because it is such a unique experience to have dinner in an actual Russian palace. However, wha makes the occasion even more impressive is the level of service provided to each customer. A clien can hardly breathe before an attendant shows up to courteously ask how he can serve you better o provide anything that is needed.

When dinner finally arrives, it is carried to the table by servers dressed in tuxedos and whit gloves. One by one, the servers set the plates on the table. Each plate is covered by a glistening, pur silver dome that conceals the entree until the appropriate moment. Once all the plates are set in place the servers stand to the side of each person at the table. All at once, in perfect unison, they lift the pur silver domes from the plates to reveal food that has been meticulously prepared for each diner. By th time the dinner is finished, all those at the table feel like they have been treated as royalty.

Once when I was dining at this Russian palace, I carefully watched the attentiveness shown by the servers to each customer. As I watched how excellently they served, I thought of Jesus' words "And whosoever of you will be the chiefest, shall be servant of all" (Mark 10:44).

The word "servant" in this verse comes from the Greek word *diakonos*, the Greek word for *servant* whose primarily responsibility was *to serve food* and *to wait on tables*. It presents a picture o a waiter or waitress who painstakingly attends to the needs, wishes, and wants of his or her client Professionally pleasing clients was these servants' supreme task, so they served honorably, pleasura bly, and in a fashion that made every man feel as if he were nobility.

Restaurants in the first century were very rare, so most servers worked in the very exclusiv homes and palaces of the elite, rich, and famous. Hence, these were well-trained, highly refined, cul tured, high-class servants who served with sophistication and finesse. Jesus used this word *diakono* in a parable to describe exactly these kinds of servants assisting a wealthy king (Matthew 22:13).

This high standard and attitude of excellence is what God expects from every believer who serves" in the Kingdom of God. Think about it — why would this level of excellence be expected in a high-class restaurant but not in God's Kingdom?

As God's servants, we should be well-trained, highly refined, cultured, and equipped to minister to any need with which we are confronted. Serving with an excellent standard should be our goal. There is nothing more important than what we do for the Lord, so God expects us to serve with the best attitude, the finest appearance, and the highest form of service and professionalism we can render in His name.

It must be distressing to God when He sees believers tolerate a standard in the Church that is lower than the one found in the world. Why should our standard be lower? Aren't we serving the King of kings? Aren't we working at His table? Therefore, shouldn't our standard be the highest, the one by which all other standards are measured? When people come to the Kingdom of God for the first time, shouldn't they be shocked to see a higher level of excellence than they have ever beheld before?

As God's "servants," we should set the example of excellence in every sphere. Here are just a few examples where the word *diakonos* in the New Testament lets us know that an excellent attitude and a high level of professionalism was expected by the Early Church leadership. If it was expected then, why would we settle for anything less now?

The Ministry of Tithes and Offerings:

In Acts 11:29, the word *diakonos* described the financial "relief" that was received and sent to believers in Judea. Because the word *diakonos* was used to describe the receiving and sending of this offering, it shows the professional manner in which the Early Church received and administrated these funds. They did it with *excellence*.

In Second Corinthians 8:4, Paul used *diakonos* to describe another special offering. The phrase "ministering to the saints" referred to the giving of that offering, but the word "ministering" is the word *diakonos*. This categorically makes us aware that these offerings were no sloppy event. It was a *serious matter* that was handled in the *most professional* and *excellent manner*.

The Ministry of Preaching the Gospel:

In Acts 20:24, Paul used the word *diakonos* to describe his "ministry." Those who preach the Gospel literally "serve" the bread of life to hungry souls, so the word *diakonos* is well suited for picturing the proclamation of the truth. Paul saw the handling of God's Word as such a high responsibility that he ministered the Word with the *greatest seriousness* and *professionalism*. When he stood to preach, it was no last-minute, thrown-together sermon. Paul prepared and served his messages with painstaking care.

The occurrences of the word *diakonos* depicting the ministry and the preaching of the Gospel are numerous throughout the New Testament. This suggests that our ministry should always be done with *excellence*.

The Ministry in General:

In Second Corinthians 6:3, Paul used the word *diakonos* to embrace all the wider aspects of "ministry." Whether "ministry" is done publicly, as when preaching, or in a less visible area of the church, it should be done with *excellence*. This is the reason Paul said, "Giving no offence in any thing, that the ministry be not blamed." Ministry demands excellence of testimony, conduct, and deed in the lives of those who are involved in it. We are never to forget that we are *God's servers*!

In Colossians 4:17, Paul told Archippus to take heed to the "ministry" he had received from the Lord. This word "ministry" is the word *diakonos*. For Archippus, taking heed to his ministry meant being the best he could be, serving in the most professional manner possible, conscientiously fulfilling every wish God had made known to him, and doing his work with an *excellence* that would honor Jesus.

In Second Timothy 4:5, Paul tells Timothy to "...make full proof of thy ministry." The word "ministry" is the word *diakonos*. Paul was urging Timothy to bring the level of his ministry to the highest level — to show *commitment* and *excellence* in everything he did in the name of ministry.

The Ministry of the Saints:

In First Corinthians 16:15, Paul uses the word *diakonos* when he refers to the household of Stephanas having "...addicted themselves to the ministry of the saints." Although the word *diakonos* emphatically speaks of their *servant attitude*, it also shows us that they were addicted to serving others with the highest possible standard of *excellence*.

In Revelation 2:19, the word *diakonos* is used when Jesus speaks to the leadership of the church of Thyatira. Although this church had many problems, one of the things for which Jesus commended them was their "service." This is the Greek word *diakonos*, letting us know that *serving with a high standard* is commendable in God's sight.

The Ministry of Angels:

In Matthew 4:11, the word *diakonos* is used when the Bible says, "Then the devil leaveth him, and, behold, angels came and ministered unto him." These angels came to "minister" to Jesus and to meet His needs. They served Him like *deacons*, or like *waiters* whose supreme pleasure was knowing they had attended well to the needs of their Master. They "served" Jesus with the greatest attention, care, excellence, and professionalism.

In Hebrews 1:14, the word *diakonos* is used again to describe the ministry of angels. It says, "Are they not all ministering spirits, sent forth to minister for them who shall be heirs of salvation?" When this verse says the angels are sent forth "to minister" for them who shall be heirs of salvation, the words "to minister" comes from the word *diakonos*. This clearly means angels have a God-given assignment to "serve" believers with meticulous, detailed attention. Angels are *God's supernatural servers* who have been dispatched to attend to the needs, wants, and wishes of the saints.

The Ministry of Jesus:

In Mark 10:45, the word *diakonos* is used to depict Jesus and His own ministry. The verse says, "For even the Son of man came not to be ministered unto, but to minister, and to give his life a ransom for many." When this verse says Jesus came "to minister," it is the word *diakonos*. Jesus was the supreme Example of serving the needs of people with excellence. He was so committed to fulfilling the assignment given to Him that He was even willing to "serve" to the point of sacrifice. His "service" would demand *the highest level of commitment, dedication, attention*, and *excellence*.

Think of it! Jesus is the Lord of all, the Creator of the universe, the only begotten Son of God. Yet when He came, His purpose was not "...to be ministered unto, but to minister...." Jesus' entire purpose was to serve and to give His life away, not to be served or to demand the respect, approval, or adoration of men.

In all the above examples, the word *diakonos* describes those who are excellently serving someone and who are profoundly committed to fulfilling a specific task with the highest standard and level of professionalism. This is excellent, high-level servanthood, not sloppy service as is found in so many places today.

If you possess this right attitude about doing God's work, it won't be too long until Jesus promotes you to a higher position. However, don't think that a higher position will alleviate your need to keep serving, for we're all called to serve, regardless of our status, rank, or position.

So keep in mind that God is watching you today. Are you:

✦ Serving with excellence?
✦ Genuinely concerned about the welfare of those whom you serve?
✦ Sincerely wanting to serve them in the best way you can?
✦ Honestly thinking of how to help those who have been assigned to your care?
✦ Truthfully wanting to serve in a professional and timely manner?
✦ Faithfully doing your job from the depths of your heart?

If these are the qualities that God sees in you, it probably won't be long until He makes sure you are rewarded with a greater level of responsibility. Why? Because He'll know you are trustworthy and ready to handle the promotion. In fact, the word *diakonos* later came to represent a person found so extremely trustworthy and reliable that he was placed in charge of managing a palace!

How about you, friend? Are you faithfully "serving" at God's table? Does your service demonstrate the excellent standard that God expects in His Kingdom? Have you been satisfied with a low level of professionalism in your life? If you want God to entrust you with greater responsibility, you must start looking at your assignment and place of service as the most important job in the whole world. *Fulfill your task with a high standard of excellence — and God will see to it that you are richly rewarded!*

MY PRAYER FOR TODAY

Lord, I want to serve You with the highest level of excellence! Forgive me for times when I have tolerated a low standard in my life, my business, my ethics, my church, or my ministry. Nothing in the world is more serious than the services I render in Your name, so help me do it in a way that glorifies You.

I pray this in Jesus' name!

MY CONFESSION FOR TODAY

I confess that I have a high standard of excellence in my life and that I am growing daily in my level of professionalism. As I serve God at work and at church, I demonstrate the excellence of Jesus' name! When people see me, they see the Kingdom of God. In fact, God is happy that I am His representative because my life shows forth an excellent image of who Jesus is and what He stands for in this world. I am His representative, and therefore I do everything with the highest level of excellence!

I declare this by faith in Jesus' name!

1. Can you honestly say that you are serving in your business or church with a high level of excellence, or have you permitted your performance to slip to a mediocre standard that is unacceptable for a child of God?
2. Would Jesus say your work and attitude glorifies Him? Does your work and attitude make Him glad that you are known as one of His servers?
3. If you were the boss, would you be pleased with someone who works like you do at your job — or would you expect your employees to give a much better effort?

AUGUST 22

You Can Beat Any Temptation!

There hath no temptation taken you
but such as is common to man:
but God is faithful, who will not suffer you
to be tempted above that ye are able;
but will with the temptation also make a way to escape,
that ye may be able to bear it.
— 1 Corinthians 10:13

*E*veryone has to deal with temptations at one time or another, so you don't need to feel embarrassed if you're facing a particular temptation right now. But at the same time, you don't have to succumb to temptation, because it is something you can overcome! *All temptations can be beaten!* You just have to make up your mind that you're going to be the *conqueror* and not the *conquered!*

You may not have thought of it before, but the devil tries to lure you into sin by using your mind and emotions. He injects thoughts into your mind and emotions that act as stimulants to get you all stirred up in a certain area of your life. At that moment, you are consciously aware that you can let the temptation pass you by — or you can allow those thoughts to fester in your mind and take root in your emotions until they become a major stronghold in your mind to battle and conquer. By refusing to accept the thoughts in the first place, you can avoid the whole struggle!

It's similar to a sexual temptation. You can choose to turn and look the other way, or you can dwell on that temptation until it fills your mind and imagination. If you choose to meditate on the thought that the devil is trying to put into your head, it won't be too long until the devil is waging a full-scale battle in your mind! If you don't put on the brakes and stop those thoughts, the devil will conquer you. That's why it's so important that you learn how to control your thinking. If you can keep your mind under the control of the Holy Spirit, you will make it almost impossible for the devil to defeat you in any realm of your life.

The devil is a master when it comes to mind manipulation. He knows that if he can get you to spend a little time meditating on something wrong, he can eventually entice you to do it! If the devil was persuasive enough to deceive brilliant, mighty, powerful angels, how much more easily can he deceive people who live in a far-from-perfect environment and wrestle daily with their own imperfections! The emotional makeup of human beings makes them even more susceptible to the devil's masterful skills of lying, deception, and manipulation.

Satan watches for the right timing. He comes along at an opportune moment. He waits until you're *tired, weary,* or *exasperated.* Perhaps you woke up in a bad mood; someone gave you a "look" you didn't like; or you just started off your day on the wrong foot. Then suddenly he strikes you with a thought — something that takes you totally by surprise when your guard is down!

When negative thoughts begin to deluge your mind, you need to know that it is Satan setting a trap in front of you. He is trying to ensnare you so he can cripple and devastate both you and the people you love. He's trying to get you to bite the bait *so he can set the hook!* But you don't have to fall into this trap anymore! If you really want out of this type of emotional quandary, there *is* a way out.

First Corinthians 10:13 promises, "There hath no temptation taken you but such as is common to man: but God is faithful, who will not suffer you to be tempted above that ye are able; but will with the temptation also make a way to escape, that ye may be able to bear it."

The word "temptation" is the Greek word *peirasmos,* and it may refer to *any outside source that appeals to a weakness in your flesh.* That appeal pulls you like a magnet; it lures you mentally, emotionally, and sensually; it fascinates the imagination; it entices the flesh to take a closer peek. If you don't stop this process, it will set its hook in your soul and haul you right smack dab into the middle of some kind of sin!

Because the word *peirasmos* ("temptation") can describe any weakness of the flesh, this scripture could apply to any fleshly weakness you might struggle with — from being lazy or easily offended; to thinking too lowly or too highly of yourself; to having a problem with anger or sexual temptation. Whatever your flesh responds to is what this word *peirasmos* refers to!

But this verse promises that God will make a way for you to escape temptation — *if* you really want to escape it! The Greek word for "escape" is the word *ekbasis.* This word is a compound of the word *ek,* meaning *out,* and the word *basin,* meaning *to walk.* When they are compounded together, it means *to walk out,* as *to walk out of a difficult place; to walk out of a trap;* or *to walk out of a place that isn't good for you.*

This makes me think of the time Joseph fled from Potiphar's wife when she tried to seduce him. Rather than stay there and try to negotiate in the midst of the situation, Genesis 39:12 says Joseph "...fled, and got him out." In other words, he got out of there as quickly as he could!

Negotiating with sin usually leads to falling into it rather than conquering it, so it's better for a person to just get up and get away from the situation as quickly as he can! This is why Paul was constantly telling the early believers to "flee" evil influences (*see* 1 Corinthians 6:18; 1 Corinthians 10:14, 1 Timothy 6:11; 2 Timothy 2:22).

The word "flee" is the Greek word *pheugo,* which means *to flee, to take flight, to run away, to run as fast as possible,* or *to escape.* This means you don't want to succumb to those temptations that are surrounding you. You just need to get up, put on your jacket, pick up your things, and get out of that place of temptation as fast as you can! Let your feet fly as you flee that situation! *You're not stuck there!* You can get out! You can walk out of that place just as easily as you walked in there! *Your feet work in both directions!* God will make a way for you to escape those negative emotions *if* you really want to escape them. But you are the only one who can make the choice to jump through that escape hatch!

- ✦ If you know you're being tempted to angrily explode, *walk out before it happens!*
- ✦ If you know you're being tempted to get your feelings hurt, *go somewhere else to avoid the offense!*

✦ If you know you're being tempted to slip into a state of laziness, *then get up and get busy*!

✦ If you know you're being tempted to steal, *get as far away as you can from the money or the coveted object*!

✦ If you know you're being tempted to sexually sin, *get out of that situation immediately*!

✦ *If you know you're being tempted to do anything wrong, it's time for you to flee from the temptation!*

Millions of Christians are held captive because they will *not* take the leap through that escape hatch. As a result, they have no joy, no peace, and no victory in their lives. They may be Christians, but they're miserable because they haven't made the choice to jump through the escape hatch God has provided for them and leave all those negative temptations and garbage behind.

If you'll say yes to the Lord, He will show you how to walk out of this mess! *You can avoid, evade, dodge, elude, shake off, get out of, and break away from every temptation!* You are *the only one* who can choose to walk out of those killer mental attacks or negative situations. The moment you make that decision, your journey to freedom has begun!

So today the Lord is asking you: *"Are you going to stay the way you are right now, or are you willing to take the proper steps to escape from this emotional temptation and demonic trap?"* What is your answer? What are you going to do? God is waiting for you to decide if you will receive the freedom He is offering you or remain a hostage for the rest of your life. *The choice is yours to make.*

MY PRAYER FOR TODAY

Lord, help me find the strength to say no to my flesh and to flee from temptation when it tries to wrap its long tentacles around my soul and drag me into some kind of sin. I know what it's like when sin calls out to my flesh, beckoning it to do something that is forbidden or wrong, but I don't want to cooperate with it anymore. I want to walk free — to flee from sin and break free of its vicious grip. Help me bring my mind under the control of the Holy Spirit so I can think rationally when Satan tries to attack me through my mind, my emotions, or my senses.

I pray this in Jesus' name!

MY CONFESSION FOR TODAY

I confess that God makes a way for me to escape temptation. I do not negotiate with sin! When it tries to call out to me, I get up and get out as quickly as I can. I flee, take flight, run away from, and escape as quickly as I can when I know the devil is attempting to lure me into his trap. That's when I put on my jacket, pick up my things, and let my feet fly! God always makes a way for me to escape — and I always make the right choice to jump through that escape hatch!

I declare this by faith in Jesus' name!

QUESTIONS FOR YOU TO CONSIDER

1. Can you think of times when you were tempted to yield to sin? Knowing that you needed to get up and get out of that place of temptation, did you stay and fall into some kind of sin? Were you sorry later that you didn't flee when you had the chance?

2. What is the chief area of temptation that you struggle with more than any other right now?

3. In order for you to walk free from the struggle of that temptation, what changes do you need to make in your life?

AUGUST 23

Whatever Happens in a Person's Private Life
Affects His Public Life!

Let a man so account of us, as of the ministers of Christ,
and stewards of the mysteries of God.
— 1 Corinthians 4:1

I want to devote today's *Sparkling Gem* to the private lives of potential leaders. In particular, I want to talk about their marriages, their children, the physical condition of the houses where they live, and the manner in which they manage their personal finances. These four points are *extremely important* when you're considering someone to be a leader.

What happens in a person's private life affects his job or his public ministry. Someone may argue, "But my private life and my home life don't have anything to do with my ministry at the church, my ability to serve, or how I perform at work. You have no right to dig into my personal life."

This way of thinking is wrong. *What happens in a person's private life spills over into his public life.* What goes on behind closed doors in a leader's home will tell you *exactly* what kind of blessings or problems he will bring to his public ministry or job. This is precisely why the apostle Paul *urged* Timothy to take a deeper look at the personal life of a potential leader before inviting him to be a part of his leadership team (*see* 1 Timothy 3:4,5). You see, God designed the home as a honing instrument for many of the qualities required to be a leader in the Kingdom of God.

Paul told Timothy that a leader must be "one that ruleth well his own house, having his children in subjection with all gravity; (For if a man know not how to rule his own house, how shall he take care of the church of God?)" (1 Timothy 3:4,5).

The Greek word for "ruleth" is the word *proistimi*, a compound of *pro* and *istimi*. The word *pro* means *before* or *in front of,* and the word *istimi* means *to stand.* When compounded together, the new word depicts *someone who is standing up front before others in order to lead, guide, direct, or manage a situation.* It conveys the meaning of *a leader who is responsibly giving oversight and direction to a group of people or to a project.* Paul uses the word "well" to describe the way this person rules. It is the Greek word *kalos,* which means *good, well,* or *skilled.* Thus, it pictures an individual who has shown that he is able *to successfully give oversight* to a group of people or to a specific project.

Paul says it is required that a spiritual leader rule well his own "house." The word "house" is the Greek word *oikos,* which is the word for *a physical house.* However, as it is used here, it includes *the management of the house and everything that happens in that house.* Thus, "ruling" one's household would include how a leader manages his home life, his children, the upkeep of the physical house or apartment where he lives, and his personal finances. All of this would be part of his *oikos* — *his house.*

Important information about how well potential leaders will serve at church or at work can be ascertained by delving into these four points. So let's briefly review these four critical areas of concern.

Their Home Life:

Paul said a leader must be "one that ruleth well his own house...." As noted, the word "house" is the word *oikos* and includes everything about a person's home life. One of the most strategic factors to consider when selecting new married leaders is the condition of their marriage. What kind of relationship do they have with their spouse? Is it a supportive, healthy marriage, or one that is full of problems? Does the relationship reveal good communication between the husband and wife? If that potential leader cannot successfully communicate with the most important person in his life, how do you know he will be able to properly communicate with others at church or at work? These questions may give you great insight into the pluses and minuses that come with new potential leaders.

Their Children:

Paul said a leader must be one who has his "...children in subjection with all gravity." If potential candidates have children, perhaps nothing gives you clearer insight into what kind of leaders they will be than the example of their own children. Although you can't make this a hard and fast rule, most often the children of potential leaders are a reflection of the kind of leadership those candidates are currently exercising in their own home.

Since people can impart only what they have in their private lives, it is good to observe what potential leaders have imparted within their own homes. What is the visible fruit of their influence and leadership in their children's lives?

✦ *Do the children speak respectfully to elders?*
✦ *Do they speak respectfully to each other?*
✦ *Do they understand authority and submission?*
✦ *Do the children do what they are told, or do they ignore their parents' instructions?*

The answers to these simple, basic questions are important indicators to let you know how potential candidates are leading their own homes. If they're not leading their own homes with excellence, why would you imagine they could lead an entire division of the ministry with excellence? That's why it's important to never overlook a potential leader's children. They will always be one of the clearest signals to alert you to the kind of leader this person will be.

Their House or Apartment:

Paul wrote that a leader must be one that "...ruleth well his own house...." As already stated above, the word "house" refers to everything connected to home life. Part of home life is the physical house where the family lives. Therefore, it's valid to ask:

✦ *What kind of home does this potential leader have? Is it well-kept and maintained?*
✦ *Is it needlessly neglected? Does it look like it's falling apart?*
✦ *Is the yard mowed so this candidate has a good testimony with his or her neighborhood?*

What exactly did Paul mean when he said leaders must *rule well* their own homes? One thing is for sure: If a potential leader can't decently take care of his own domain, you don't want to put him in charge of *your* domain. That's why this is such a serious question to consider when selecting someone for a prominent place of leadership in your church, ministry, or organization.

Their Finances:

In regard to finances, the phrase "ruleth well his own house" leads me to ask, "How does this potential leader handle his money and the payment of monthly bills?"

How a person handles money is very revealing. It tells a lot about his personal integrity, his character, and how he respects the rights of others. When a person doesn't regularly pay his bills on time, he inconveniences and upsets other people's financial plans. This failure to keep financial commitments often reflects a lack of respect for others' needs and rights.

It also may simply be a sign that this person is immature in his understanding of money management and responsibility. Or he may not do well at saying no to his fleshly lust for material things. A person's financial problems may also be an indicator that he's experiencing problems in his marriage as well. Or perhaps his life is unstable due to irregular work conditions.

No matter which of these factors may be the cause for a candidate's financial problems, they are all serious enough to require thoughtful consideration on your part. Does this person have the time, energy, or maturity to handle a position of greater responsibility in your church, ministry, or organization?

Never forget that it is impossible to separate a person's public life from his private life. What happens in one area spills over into the other. *What is in a potential leader's personal life is exactly what he will bring into his public life.* If he has order and peace in his private life, it will give him a solid foundation for public ministry. But if he struggles with disorder, chaos, turmoil, confusion, upheaval, and anarchy in his private life, it will obviously affect his ability to carry on publicly as a leader.

What happens at home really *does* affect one's ability to work, serve, and follow God's will for his life. If this is the case, what do these things reveal about those people who are being considered for leadership at church, business, or organization? Does their home life show that they are ready for larger areas of responsibility?

And by the way — while you're thinking about the home life of these leadership candidates, it would be good for you to turn these questions around and apply them to yourself. *What does your home life reveal about YOU?*

MY PRAYER FOR TODAY

Lord, help me bring order into my own personal life! Since what is happening in my private life is exactly what I will bring into my public life, I want to bring more order into my own personal affairs. Help me take an honest look at my life so I can see those areas that desperately need my attention. Once I acknowledge the areas that need fixing, please give me the courage to delve into those areas and to get things right. I want every area of my life to glorify You, so if there is a secret part of my life that doesn't bring honor to You, I'm looking to You to help me make the needed changes.

I pray this in Jesus' name!

MY CONFESSION FOR TODAY

I confess that with God's help, I am putting my house in order! The way I handle my family life, my children, my physical home, and my finances brings glory to Jesus Christ. I am serious about my walk with God, and I therefore invite Him to invade every sphere of my life and to bring it under His Lordship. Jesus is Lord of my marriage, my children, my home, and my money. It all belongs to Him; therefore, I want to be a wise steward for His sake — and I will!

I declare this by faith in Jesus' name!

QUESTIONS FOR YOU TO CONSIDER

1. If you are seeking new leadership for the church, business, or organization, have you considered these deeper issues? If you had considered this before selecting leaders in the past, do you think it would have helped you make better leadership choices?

2. Have you seen glaring problems in a potential leader's home that you overlooked because his gifts and talents were needed? Did you later regret your choice because he brought many of those same problems to his job?

3. After reading today's *Sparkling Gem*, do you see areas in your own life that need attention? If your answer is yes, what are you going to do to start bringing order into those areas of your home life?

AUGUST 24

Make Up Your Mind To Live Fearlessly And Peacefully in These Last Days!

That ye be not soon shaken in mind, or be troubled,
neither by spirit, nor by word, nor by letter as from us,
as that the day of Christ is at hand.
— 2 Thessalonians 2:2

*I*n Second Thessalonians 2:2, the apostle Paul wrote to the Thessalonian believers and warned them about events that would occur right before the coming of the Lord. He wanted to prepare them so these major world events wouldn't take them off guard and throw them into a state of panic. Therefore, Paul told them, "That ye be not soon shaken in mind, or be troubled, neither by spirit, nor by word, nor by letter as from us, as that the day of Christ is at hand" (2 Thessalonians 2:2).

Notice that Paul told the Thessalonian believers not to be "soon shaken." The word "soon" is the Greek word *tachus*, which means *quickly, suddenly,* or *hastily.* The word "shaken" is the Greek word *saleuo*, which means *to shake, to waver, to totter,* or *to be moved.* The tense used in the Greek points to events so dramatic that they could result in *shock* or *alarm*. In fact, the Greek tense strongly suggests a devastating occurrence or a sequence of devastating occurrences so dramatic that they will throw the world into a state of *shock* or *distress*.

By using the words "soon shaken," Paul was urging his readers (and us!) to resist being easily shaken up by events that will occur just before the coming of Jesus. He was particularly careful to mention that we must not be "soon shaken in mind." The Greek word for the "mind" is *nous*, which describes *everything in the realm of the intellect, including one's will, emotions, and ability to think, reason, and decide.*

Whoever or whatever controls a person's mind ultimately has the power to dictate the affairs and outcome of that person's life. Thus, if a person allows his mind to be doused with panic or fear, he is putting fear in charge of his life. Because Paul wanted his readers to remain in peace regardless of the tumultuous events that transpired around them, he urged them not to allow fear from these shocking and distressful events to penetrate their minds, will, and emotions.

Then to make certain we comprehend the magnitude of these last-day events, Paul went on to say, "That ye be not soon shaken in mind, or be *troubled*...." The word "troubled" is the Greek word *throeo*, which indicates an *inward fright* that results from the shocking occurrence described above. The shock resulting from these nerve-racking events could be so severe that it could cause a person to be devoured with *worry*, *anxiety*, or *fear*.

Paul is confident these events will not be only a one-time occurrence; thus, he uses a Greek tense that points to an *ongoing state of worry and inward anxiety* resulting from these outward events that keep occurring again and again. It is as if he prophesies that there is no pause between these shocking, debilitating, and nerve-racking happenings. One scholar therefore translates the word "troubled" as *being jumpy or nervous*.

These words are so jammed-packed with meaning that it is almost impossible to directly translate them. To help you see exactly what Paul was communicating to his readers, I have translated and paraphrased the original Greek words, pulling the full meaning out of each word and then transferring those meanings into the interpretive translation below.

All the words Paul used
in Second Thessalonians 2:2 convey this idea:

"Some things will be happening right before His coming that could shake you up quite a bit. I'm referring to events that will be so dramatic that they could really leave your head spinning — occurrences of such a serious nature that many people will end up feeling alarmed, panicked, intimidated, and even unnerved! Naturally speaking, these events could nearly drive you over the brink emotionally, putting your nerves on edge and making you feel apprehensive and insecure about life. I wish I could tell you these incidents were going to be just a one-shot deal, but when they finally get rolling, they're going to keep coming and coming, one after another. That's why you have to determine not to be shaken or moved by anything you see or hear. You need to get a grip on your mind and refuse to allow yourselves to be traumatized by these events. If you let these things get to you, it won't be too long until you're a nervous wreck! So decide beforehand that you are not going to give in and allow 'fright' to worm its way into your mind and emotions until it runs your whole life."

Paul strongly urges us *not* to allow ourselves to be shaken or moved by anything we see or hear. He tells us that we must get a grip on our minds and refuse to allow ourselves to be traumatized by the events that occur in the world around us or to allow fear to control our whole lives. Instead of letting these things "get to us" and rob us of our joy, peace, and victory, we need to be deeply rooted in the confidence of God's promises!

If you take a look at the world around us today, it is clear that Paul's prophecy about the last days is unfolding before our very eyes. Because of the many different situations that our generation is facing, we must take a stand against fear and determine to stay in faith! But in order for us to stay in faith, it is imperative that we keep our minds focused on the Word of God.

Colossians 3:15 says, "And let the peace of God rule in your hearts...." Verse 16 goes on to say, "Let the word of Christ dwell in you richly...." When the Word of God *dwells richly* in our lives, it produces *peace* — so much supernatural peace that it actually *rules* our hearts!

The word "rule" that is used in this verse is the Greek word *brabeuo*, which describes *an umpire who calls all the shots and makes all the decisions.* You see, when God's Word is dwelling richly in your heart, suddenly the *peace of God* makes all the big decisions, calls all the shots, and umpires your emotions. Rather than being led by the ups and downs of the day or by what you read in the newspaper, you will be ruled by the wonderful peace of God!

But to receive this benefit of God's Word, you must let it dwell in you *richly*. This word *richly* is the Greek word *plousios*, and it can be translated *lavishly*. This presents the picture of you giving the Word of God a wonderful reception as you roll out the red carpet so you can *richly* and *lavishly* welcome the Word into your heart. When you let God's Word have this place of honor inside your heart, mind, and emotions, it releases its power to stabilize you and keep you in peace, even in the most difficult times.

There is no doubt that we are living in the very end of the last days. We are a chosen generation — and we will observe events that no other generation has ever seen.

If you are going to keep your heart fear-free so you can live in continual peace, you *must* make a firm commitment to let God's Word rule in your heart! God's Word will protect your mind and prohibit fear from worming its way into your emotions and turning you into an emotional mess. *Is God's Word the foundation of your life today?*

MY PRAYER FOR TODAY

Lord, I am so thankful that Your Word prepares us for every event that comes along in this life! I know I am living in the last days and that these challenging times require a higher level of commitment from me if I am going to live free from fear. This is such a critical moment for me to be strong, free, and secure. When I am strong, I can be a tower of strength to others who are drowning in the world around me. Help me be that source of strength and power to the people who surround me, Lord. I want to be all that I need to be in this hour.

I pray this in Jesus' name!

MY CONFESSION FOR TODAY

I confess that God's Word dominates my mind, my will, and my emotions! Because I have put God's Word into my heart, I am not shaken or easily moved by the things that occur in the world around me. I know who I am; I am secure in my Father's love; and I recognize that He destined me to live in these last days because He has a special plan for me. Regardless of what I see or hear, I take my stand on the promises of God's Word, and it provides me with safety and security!

I declare this by faith in Jesus' name!

QUESTIONS FOR YOU TO CONSIDER

1. In light of the world events that have occurred in recent years, how pertinent for you are Paul's words in Second Thessalonians 2:2? Does it sound like Paul is writing about the nonstop traumatic events that have shaken the world over the past several years?

2. If it is true that we are living in the last days just before the coming of Jesus Christ, how should this affect the manner in which you are living your life?

3. Do you spend more time reading your Bible, reading the newspaper, or watching the news? Whatever you dwell on the most is what will dominate you, so isn't it time that you make God's Word the primary focus of your attention?

AUGUST 25

Truthfully Assessing Your Situation

Brethren, I count not myself to have apprehended:
but this one thing I do, forgetting those things which are behind,
and reaching forth unto those things which are before,
I press toward the mark for the prize
of the high calling of God in Christ Jesus.
— Philippians 3:13,14

*E*very once in a while, my wife and I take time to seriously and thoughtfully review what we are accomplishing and what we are not accomplishing in our lives and our ministry. We do our best to be very honest with ourselves and each other about these questions.

Taking this kind of look at ourselves and our work is not always pleasant. Sometimes we find areas of glaring failure or areas where we know the Lord expected more of us. But in order for us to see the truth about our lives the way God sees it, He requires us to lay down our pride and be honest with ourselves. In the end, we're always glad we did the review because it helps us repent for the times we failed, rejoice over what God helped us to accomplish, and make sure we're on the right course where we will be the most focused and effective.

When other people say, *"Wow, you accomplish so much!"* we are always glad that they can see fruit in our lives. However, the most important question to us is not what other people think, but what *the Lord* thinks of us and our accomplishments. Maybe it's true that we accomplished a lot compared to what others have done. But how we compare to other people and ministries is *not* the measuring stick we are to use to determine how we are doing.

In Second Corinthians 10:12 (*AMP*), the apostle Paul wrote that when people "…measure themselves with themselves and compare themselves with one another, they…behave unwisely." This means our measuring stick should never be how we measure up to other human beings. Compared to them, we may have done well, but the real issue is how we "measure up" to the goals the Lord gave *us*. When we stand before Jesus, He isn't going to judge us by how we did in comparison to others. He will judge us for how we did with the assignments He gave *us* to do.

Therefore, you should ask yourself on a regular basis:

+ *Am I accomplishing the goals the Lord has given me?*
+ *Can I stand before Him with a heart free of condemnation, knowing that I gave my very best effort, work, and faith to achieve His will?*
+ *What, if any, changes do I need to make in my life, schedule, commitment, and financial resources to do what the Lord has told me to do?*

Learning to be honest about ourselves, our work, our successes, and our failures is vitally important. We learn from our past mistakes. We ask the Lord to forgive us for our failures. Then we turn our eyes to the present — and we begin to make the necessary corrections in order to start doing better!

When Paul was imprisoned in Rome, he had a lot of time to think, so he sat in that prison and reflected on his life and achievements. He thought about what he had done, what he hadn't done, and what he still needed to do. I'm sure that, like all of us, Paul was tempted to look at his life in comparison to others. And compared to others, he had done a great deal!

+ He had preached all around the Mediterranean Sea.
+ He had preached in the imperial palace.
+ He had started churches all over Asia Minor.
+ He had written most of the New Testament.
+ He was one of the greatest apostles of his generation.

Paul could have rightfully told himself, *I've done more than most men will ever dream of doing! I've done more than anyone else I know!* But rather than revel in his own accomplishments, Paul used that time in prison to truthfully assess his life. Then he wrote these famous words: "Brethren, I count not myself to have apprehended: but this one thing I do, forgetting those things which are behind, and reaching forth unto those things which are before, I press toward the mark for the prize of the high calling of God in Christ Jesus" (Philippians 3:13,14).

Notice that Paul said, "I count not myself to have apprehended...." The words "count not" give us insight into the way Paul looked at his life. Paul borrowed these words from the bookkeeping profession. It is the Greek word *logidzomai*, which originally meant *to mathematically count, calculate, or tabulate* or *to make a conclusion*. This word was primarily used in the bookkeeping world to portray the idea of *a balance sheet* or *a profit-and-loss statement that a bookkeeper prepared at the end of the month or year*.

You might "think" your business is doing quite well, but when the bookkeeper adds up all the numbers and hands you the profit-and-loss statement to read, that's the moment you find out how well your business is really doing. You don't have to guess anymore about your situation, because "the numbers" tell the real story.

Why did Paul use this word as he wrote verse 13? It is obvious that Paul had been seriously reviewing his life. Rather than "guess" about how well he had done, Paul carefully reviewed the original goals God had given him. It is almost as if Paul had written God's plan for his life on one side of the page and what he had actually accomplished on the other side of the page. After looking at the original goal and truthfully assessing how much of that goal he had accomplished, he wrote, "I count not myself to have apprehended...."

Although Paul had accomplished a great deal in his ministry, he knew he hadn't done everything he was supposed to do. That is one reason he knew it was *not* time for him to die. His prison situation was dreadful, and the legal prognosis didn't look good. But Paul knew it wasn't time for him to leave yet because he still had so much work to do. (He referred to this work in Philippians 1:22-26.)

I'm sure Paul was thankful for everything he had seen and all that God had already accomplished through him. This is why Paul went on to say, "...but this one thing I do, forgetting the things which are behind, and reaching forth unto those things which are before" (Philippians 3:13). But I want you to stop and think about what Paul was choosing to forget and put behind him!

Some say Paul was forgetting his past life of sin, but he had put that behind him long ago. Now he was putting *his past successes and accomplishments* behind him. Do you know why he had to do this? Because stopping at *past* victories is what keeps most people from moving into *future* victories. They become so fixated on what they have done that they lose sight of what they need to do — and that keeps them from moving forward to possess new territory in God's plan for their lives!

Think of it like this: Many big corporations lost the cutting edge they once held because they spent most of their energy gloating about how big and how good they were. While they were gloating, some smaller company with dedicated people and a huge vision snuck up from behind and surpassed that larger corporation! Before the larger company knew what was happening, they had lost the leading edge they once held and were no longer the leader. They had spent so much time focusing on the past that someone else passed them by!

Paul knew he had done more than most men, and it was all right for him to cherish those memories. But dwelling on his past accomplishments wasn't going to get him out of jail or back in the swing of what he needed to be doing. There were still huge parts of his vision that were unfinished. Even though the past had been great and he was thankful to God for every victory he had experienced, it was now time for him to begin reaching forth unto those things which were before him (Philippians 3:13).

You need to rejoice over all that God has already done in your life; however, you must still focus on what you *haven't* seen yet! Thinking of the past victories will encourage and remind you of God's faithfulness, but eventually you have to leave the past behind and turn your eyes to the present and the future. *You can't go forward while constantly looking backward.*

+ Yesterday's victories were for yesterday.
+ Yesterday's good reports were for yesterday.
+ Yesterday's accomplishments were for yesterday.

Your future is *important*, so treat it that way. Look at your life, and seriously appraise your status. Let the Holy Spirit speak to your heart, and be willing to accept what He says to you. *Thank God for every victory, but keep your eyes fixed on the future so you can keep marching forward to fulfill every detail of the vision God has put into your heart!*

MY PRAYER FOR TODAY

Lord, I am so very thankful to You for all the progress I've already seen in my life. But today I am turning my eyes to the future because I know You have so much for me to do. I don't want to miss anything You have designed for me, so I am choosing to turn my attention to the vision and to run my race with all my might! Help me remove anything that would hinder my race so I can press forward toward the prize of the high calling of God for my life!

I pray this in Jesus' name!

MY CONFESSION FOR TODAY

I boldly confess that I am focused, concentrated, and determined to run my race! God has called me and anointed me; therefore, I can do exactly what He has asked me to do. I have no excuse for failure or any reason to slow down or quit, for God's Spirit in me is ready to empower me to run this race all the way to the finish. Doing it halfway will never do, so I am committed to seeing this all the way through!

I declare this by faith in Jesus' name!

QUESTIONS FOR YOU TO CONSIDER

1. How long has it been since you assessed your situation to determine the progress you are making in your life, church, or business? How frequently do you take time to review your situation so you can gauge your progress?
2. Are you stuck in a rut, or are you still moving forward with the same speed and the same passion that once possessed you? Does the vision still burn in your heart?
3. What alterations do you need to make in your church, business, organization, or ministry in order to get back on track and to start moving forward again?

AUGUST 26

The Devil's Destination

Put on the whole armour of God, that ye may be able
to stand against the wiles of the devil.
— Ephesians 6:11

What I am about to tell you is so simple — yet it is also life-changing and revolutionary. I want to help you understand how the devil tries to work in the realm of the mind and emotions. If you grab hold of these truths, they can set you free from the devil's lies forever!

In Ephesians 6:11, Paul explicitly tells us how the devil operates. He writes, "Put on the whole armour of God, that ye may be able to stand against the wiles of the devil." I want you to especially pay attention to the phrase "the wiles of the devil."

The word "wiles" is taken from the word *methodos*. It is a compound of the words *meta* and *odos*. The word *meta* is a preposition that means *with*. The word *odos* is the word for *a road*. When the words *meta* and *odos* are compounded into one word, as in Ephesians 6:11, it literally means *with a road*. You've probably already figured out that the word *methodos* is where we get the word "method." Some translations actually translate the word *methodos* as the word "method," but the word "method" is *not* strong enough to convey the full meaning of the Greek word *methodos*.

Let me make the meaning of this word real simple for you. As I said, the most literal meaning of the word "wiles" (*methodos*) is *with a road*. I realize this seems strange, but when you connect this to the devil as Paul does in Ephesians 6:11, it means that the devil is like *a traveler who travels on a road*. He is headed in one direction and has one destination.

Let me give you an example of what I mean. If you're going to take a trip, the logical thing for you to do is get a map and chart your journey to your destination. You don't take just any road; rather, you strategize to find the best and fastest way to get where you're going. *Right?* It would be pretty foolish for you to jump in the car and take off with no sense of direction. Taking any road could lead you in a multitude of wrong directions. It's just better to use a map and stay on track. *Correct?*

This is precisely the idea of the word *methodos*. The devil isn't wasting any time. He knows where he wants to go. He has chosen his destination. Rather than mess around on a bunch of different routes, he has mastered the best way to get where he wants to go. He is *not* a mindless traveler. And when he arrives at his place of destination, he has one main goal he wants to accomplish: He wants to wreak havoc and bring destruction. Therefore, we must ask: *"Where is the devil traveling, and what does he want to do once he gets there?"*

Paul answers the question about Satan's destination in Second Corinthians 2:11 when he says, "…we are not ignorant of his [Satan's] *devices*." Pay careful attention to the word "devices" in this verse. It is the Greek word *noemata*, a form of the word *nous*. The Greek word *nous* describes the *mind* or the *intellect*. Thus, in one sense Paul is saying, *"…we are not ignorant of the way Satan schemes and thinks."*

But the word *noemata* also denotes Satan's insidious plot to fill the human mind with *confusion*. There is no doubt that the mind is the arena where Satan feels most comfortable. He knows if he can access a person's mind and emotions, he will very likely be able to ensnare that individual in a trap. One writer says that the word *noemata* not only depicts Satan's scheming mind but also his crafty, subtle way of attacking and victimizing *others'* minds.

I personally like this because it identifies the primary destination of the devil — *to get into a person's mind and fill it with lying emotions, false perceptions, and confusion*. It was for this reason that Paul urged us, "Casting down imaginations, and every high thing that exalteth itself against the knowledge of God, and bringing into captivity every thought to the obedience of Christ" (2 Corinthians 10:5).

The words "bringing into captivity" are from the Greek word *aichmalotidzo*, which pictured *a soldier who has captured an enemy and now leads him into captivity with the point of a sharpened spear thrust into the flesh in his back*. The captured enemy knows that if he tries to move or get away, the Roman soldier will shove that spear clear through his torso and kill him. Therefore, this captive doesn't dare move but remains silent, submissive, and non-resistant.

However, when Paul uses the word *aichmalotidzo* in this verse, he writes in a tense that describes the continuous action of taking such an enemy captive. This is not a one-time affair; it is the lifelong occupation of this soldier. He constantly has a spear in his hand, and he is always pushing it against the flesh of an enemy's backside as he leads him away to permanent captivity.

Because the devil loves to make a playground out of your mind and emotions, you must deal with him like a real enemy. Rather than fall victim to the devil's attacks, you must make a mental decision to seize every thought he tries to use to penetrate your mind and emotions. Rather than let those thoughts take you captive, you have to reach up and grab them and *force* them into submission! You must take *every* thought captive to the obedience of Christ!

But if you're going to beat the devil at his game, you have to put *all* your energy into taking every thought captive. If you're not really committed to seizing *every* thought the devil tries to inject into your mind and emotions, he'll strike you again! So once you make the decision to do it, stick with it. *It's time for you to take charge of your thoughts and drive his lying insinuations right out of your brain!*

MY PRAYER FOR TODAY

Lord, I don't want the devil to fill my mind with insinuations and lies. My mind belongs to You, and the devil has no right to flood me with false perceptions, vain imaginations, or lies about who I am or what I will never be. I refuse to let him operate in me any longer! You have provided me with the helmet of salvation, and by faith I put it on to protect my mind against the devil's assaults. He can strike as hard as he wishes, but Your Spirit and Word protect me!

I pray this in Jesus' name!

MY CONFESSION FOR TODAY

I confess that I bring every thought into the captivity of Christ! When the devil tries to invade my mind with lies, I capture those lies and drive them clear out of my brain! Rather than fall victim to the devil's attacks, I seize every thought that he tries to use to penetrate my mind and emotions. I grab each lie and force it into submission! Because I stand firm on the Word, the enemy's lies are not able to exert any power against me.

I declare this by faith in Jesus' name!

QUESTIONS FOR YOU TO CONSIDER

1. Can you think of one area in your mind where Satan repeatedly tries to attack you? What is that area, and how long has he been attacking you in this area of your thought life? Has it gone on for a day, a week, a month, a year, or for many years?
2. When you feel heavily assaulted in your mind and emotions and you need someone to pray with you, is there someone you know you can go to for prayer and support? If so, who is that person? If not, don't you think it would encourage you to find a friend to whom you could talk and who could help you resist the lies of the devil?
3. What is the most successful tactic you've learned to shut the devil up when he's trying to roar loudly inside your head?

Rather than fall victim to the devil's attacks, you must make a mental decision to seize every thought he tries to use to penetrate your mind and emotions. You have to reach up and grab those thoughts and *force* them into submission! You must take *every* thought captive to the obedience of Christ!

AUGUST 27

❦

Who Were the Nicolaitans, And What Was Their Doctrine and Deeds?

But this thou hast, that thou hatest the deeds
of the Nicolaitans, which I also hate.
— Revelation 2:6

*H*ave you ever wondered who the "Nicolaitans" were, mentioned in the book of Revelation? Whoever they were, Jesus loathed their doctrine and hated their deeds. Let's delve into this subject today to see if we can ascertain the identity of this group. What was their damnable doctrine? What deeds were they committing that elicited such a strong reaction from Jesus?

Let's begin in Revelation 2:6, where Jesus told the church of Ephesus, "But this thou hast [in your favor], that thou hatest the deeds of the Nicolaitans, which I also hate."

Jesus was proud of the church of Ephesus for their "hatred" of the deeds of the Nicolaitans, which He also "hated." The word "hate" is a strong word, so let's see exactly what it means. It comes from the Greek word *miseo*, which means *to hate, to abhor,* or *to find utterly repulsive.* It describes a person who has *a deep-seated animosity,* who is *antagonistic* to something he finds to be *completely objectionable.* He not only *loathes* that object, but *rejects it* entirely. This is not just a case of dislike; it is a case of *actual hatred.*

The thing Jesus hated about them was their "deeds." The word "deeds" is the Greek word *erga,* which means *works.* However, this word is so all-encompassing that it pictures all the deeds and behavior of the Nicolaitans — including their actions, beliefs, conduct, and *everything else* connected to them.

The name "Nicolaitans" is derived from the Greek word *nikolaos,* a compound of the words *nikos* and *laos.* The word *nikos* is the Greek word that means *to conquer* or *to subdue.* The word *laos* is the Greek word for *the people.* It is also where we get the word *laity.* When these two words are compounded into one, they form the name *Nicolas,* which literally means *one who conquers and subdues the people.* It seems to suggest that the Nicolaitans were somehow conquering and subduing the people.

Ireneus and Hippolytus, two leaders in the Early Church who recorded many of the events that occurred in the earliest recorded days of Church history, said the Nicolaitans were the spiritual descendants of Nicolas of Antioch, who had been ordained as a deacon in Acts 6:5. That verse says, "And the saying pleased the whole multitude: and they chose Stephen, a man full of faith and of the Holy Ghost, and Philip, and Prochorus, and Nicanor, and Timon, and Parmenas, and Nicolas a proselyte of Antioch."

We know quite a lot of information about some of these men who were chosen to be the first deacons, whereas little is known of others. For instance, we know that the chief criteria for their selection was that they were men "...of honest report, full of the Holy Spirit and wisdom..."(v. 3). Once they had been chosen, they were presented by the people to the apostles, who laid hands on them, installing and officially ordaining them into the deaconate.

Stephen

Like the other men, Stephen was of good report, filled with the Holy Spirit and wisdom. However, Acts 6:5 makes a remark about Stephen that is unique only to him. It says that he was "...a man full of faith and of the Holy Ghost...." This stronger level of faith may have been a contributing factor to the development recorded in Acts 6:8: "And Stephen, full of faith and power, did great wonders and miracles among the people."

Stephen was a God-called evangelist, and he was later privileged to be the first martyr in the history of the Church — killed at the order of Saul of Tarsus, who later became known as the apostle Paul (*see* Acts 7:58-8:1). The deaconate ministry was vital proving ground to prepare Stephen for the fivefold office of the evangelist. The name Stephen is from the Greek word *stephanos*, and it means *crown*. This is worth noting, for he was the first to receive a martyr's crown.

Philip

Philip was ordained with the other six original deacons. However, Acts 21:8 informs us that Philip later stepped in the ministry of the evangelist. He had four daughters who prophesied (v. 9). Just as the deaconate was training and proving ground for Stephen to step into the office of the evangelist, it was also Philip's school of ministry to prepare him for evangelistic ministry. The name Philip means *lover of horses*. This name often symbolized a person who ran with swiftness, as does a horse — a fitting name for a New Testament evangelist who ran swiftly to carry the Gospel message.

Prochorus

Very little is known about this member of the original deaconate. His name, Prochorus, is a compound of the Greek words *pro* and *chorus*. The word *pro* means *before* or *in front of*, as with the position of *a leader*. The word "chorus" is the old Greek word for *the dance* and is where we get the word *choreography*. There is a strong implication that this was a nickname, given to this man because he had been the foremost leader of dance in some school, theater, or musical performance. There is no substantiation for this idea, but his name seems to give credence to the possibility.

Nicanor

This unknown brother was found to be of good report, filled with the Holy Spirit and wisdom. Other than this, nothing is known of him. He is never mentioned again in the New Testament after Acts chapter 6. His name, Nicanor, means *conqueror*.

Timon

Like Nicanor mentioned above, Timon was known to be of good report, filled with the Holy Spirit and wisdom. Nothing more is known of him outside of Acts chapter 6. His name means *honorable* or *of great value*.

Parmenas

We know nothing more of Parmenas other than what is mentioned here in Acts chapter 6. His name is a compound of the words *para* and *meno* — the word *para* meaning *alongside* and *meno* meaning *to remain* or *to abide*. Compounded together, his name came to mean *one who sticks alongside* and conveyed the idea of *one who is devoted, loyal, and faithful*.

Nicolas

Acts 6:5 tells us that this Nicolas was "a proselyte of Antioch." The fact that he was a proselyte tells us that he was not born a Jew but had converted from paganism to Judaism. Then he experienced a second conversion, this time turning from Judaism to Christianity. From this information, we know these facts about Nicolas of Antioch:

✦ He came from paganism and had deep pagan roots, very much unlike the other six deacons who came from a pure Hebrew line. Nicolas' pagan background meant that he had previously been immersed in the activities of the occult.

✦ He was not afraid of taking an opposing position, evidenced by his ability to change religions twice. Converting to Judaism would have estranged him from his pagan family and friends. It would seem to indicate that he was not impressed or concerned about the opinions of other people.

✦ He was a free thinker and very open to embracing new ideas and concepts. Judaism was very different from the pagan and occult world in which he had been raised. For him to shift from paganism to Judaism reveals that he was very liberal in his thinking, for most pagans were offended by Judaism. He was obviously not afraid to entertain or embrace new ways of thinking.

✦ When he converted to Christ, it was *at least* the second time he had converted from one religion to another. We don't know if, or how many times, he shifted from one form of paganism to another before he became a Jewish proselyte. His ability to easily change religious "hats" implies that he was not afraid to switch direction in midstream and go a totally different direction.

According to the writings of the Early Church leaders, Nicolas taught a doctrine of compromise, implying that total separation between Christianity and the practice of occult paganism was not essential. From Early Church records, it seems apparent that this Nicolas of Antioch was so immersed in occultism, Judaism, and Christianity that he had a stomach for all of it. He had no problem intermingling these belief systems in various concoctions and saw no reason why believers couldn't continue to fellowship with those still immersed in the black magic of the Roman empire and its countless mystery cults.

Occultism was a major force that warred against the Early Church. In Ephesus, the primary pagan religion was the worship of Diana (Artemis). There were many other forms of idolatry in Ephesus, but this was the primary object of occult worship in that city. In the city of Pergamos, there were numerous dark and sinister forms of occultism, causing Pergamos to be one of the most wicked cities in the history of the ancient world. In both of these cities, believers were lambasted and persecuted fiercely by adherents of pagan religions, forced to contend with paganism on a level far beyond all other cities.

It was very hard for believers to live separately from all the activities of paganism because paganism and its religions were the center of life in these cities. Slipping in and out of paganism would have been very easy for young or weak believers to do since most of their families and friends were still pagans. A converted Gentile would have found it very difficult to stay away from all pagan influence.

It is significant that the "deeds" and "doctrines" of the Nicolaitans are *only* mentioned in connection with the churches in these two occultic and pagan cities. It seems that the "doctrine" of the Nicolaitans was that it was all right to have one foot in both worlds and that one needn't be so strict about separation from the world in order to be a Christian. This, in fact, was the "doctrine" of the

Nicolaitans that Jesus "hated." It led to a weak version of Christianity that was without power and without conviction — a defeated, worldly type of Christianity.

Nicolas' deep roots in paganism may have produced in him a tolerance for occultism and paganism. Growing up in this perverted spiritual environment may have caused him to view these belief systems as not so damaging or dangerous. This wrong perception would have resulted in a very liberal viewpoint that encouraged people to stay connected to the world. This is what numerous Bible scholars believe about the Nicolaitans.

This kind of teaching would result in nothing but total defeat for its followers. When believers allow sin and compromise to be in their lives, it drains away the power in the work of the Cross and the power of the Spirit that is resident in a believer's life. This is the reason the name *Nicolas* is so vital to this discussion. The evil fruit of Nicolas' "doctrine" encouraged worldly participation, leading people to indulge in sin and a lowered godly standard. In this way he literally *conquered the people*.

God wants to make sure we understand the doctrine the Nicolaitans taught, so Balaam's actions are given as an example of their doctrine and actions. Revelation 2:14,15 says, "But I have a few things against thee, because thou hast there them that hold the doctrine of Balaam, who taught Balac to cast a stumblingblock before the children of Israel, to eat things sacrificed unto idols, and to commit fornication. So hast thou also them that hold the doctrine of the Nicolaitans, which thing I hate."

When Balaam could not successfully cure the people of God, he used another method to destroy them. He seduced them into unbridled, sensual living by dangling the prostitutes of Moab before the men of Israel. Numbers 25:1-3 tells us, "And Israel abode in Shittim, and the people began to commit whoredom with the daughters of Moab. And they [the daughters of Moab] called the people [the men of Israel] unto the sacrifices of their gods: and the people [the men of Israel] did eat, and bowed down to their gods. And Israel joined himself unto Baal-peor...."

Just as the men of Israel compromised themselves with the world and false religions, now the "doctrine" of the Nicolaitans was encouraging *compromise*. As you are well aware, compromise with the world always results in a weakened and powerless form of Christianity. *This was the reason Jesus "hated" the "doctrine" and the "deeds" of the Nicolaitans.*

MY PRAYER FOR TODAY

Lord, after what I've read today, I don't want to allow any spirit of compromise in my life! I now understand that the doctrine of the Nicolaitans is compromise with the world. Lord, I don't want to live with one foot in the church and another foot in the world. I want to break free completely from the world and its influence so I can give myself completely to Your cause! I want to be holy, to live in a way that pleases You, and to experience Your power in my life. Today I am renewing my commitment to You all over again! I turn from the world, and I am running to You!

I pray this in Jesus' name!

MY CONFESSION FOR TODAY

I confess that I am free from the world! I do not walk in compromise! I am determined to live a committed and holy life before the Lord. As a result of my firm determination to walk with God, I have power over sin, power over Satan, and power when I pray. God's Word promises that if I draw near to Him, He will draw near to me. I am drawing nearer and nearer to God every day, so I am confident that His Presence in my life is getting stronger too!

I declare this by faith in Jesus' name!

QUESTIONS FOR YOU TO CONSIDER

1. Can you think of any area of your life where you have allowed yourself to be compromised by the world? If so, has that compromise hindered the power of God from operating in your life?
2. Do you know any other believers who thought they could live with one foot in the church and another foot in the world — but in the end, the world ensnared them and they backslid into a life of sin?
3. If you know someone who is on the verge of backsliding, what do you think the Lord would have you do to help bring that person back to where he or she ought to be?

AUGUST 28

Don't Jump Ship!

Let a man so account of us, as of the ministers of Christ,
and stewards of the mysteries of God.
— 1 Corinthians 4:1

When you are serving faithfully and trying to obediently do what God has asked you to do, the devil hates it! He'll do everything he can to dissuade you to stop. Often he attacks your mind with allegations, such as, *"Why are you doing this? No one appreciates you anyway! Here you are, working, striving, sweating, and slugging it out while other people are having a good time. If no one else cares, why should you care? Come on — you've done enough!"*

If you're not really committed to staying in place and doing what God asked you to do, those allegations from the devil may pull you off the bench where God called you to serve. This makes me think again of First Corinthians 4:1, where Paul says, "Let a man so account of us, as of the ministers of Christ, and stewards of the mysteries of God."

As noted earlier (*see* August 13), the word "ministers" in this verse is the Greek word *huperetas* and referred to *the slaves or servants who were placed into the bottom galleys of huge ships*. A huge oar was placed in the hands of these slaves, and they began to row and row and row — literally becoming the engines that moved those ships through the sea.

If you had been allowed to peek into the bottom galley of those huge ships of New Testament times, you'd have seen that these prisoners were all chained to a post near their respective benches. *There was a good reason for this heavy chain.*

Because their work was so difficult and their destiny was sealed in the bottom of that ship, these men's minds would wander to more beautiful, restful places where palm trees overlooked sandy seashores or tall pines swayed in refreshing mountain breezes. Had the "under-rowers" not been chained to their posts, they may have attempted to escape from their bench to find a more restful lifestyle somewhere else. Therefore, chains kept the men where they belonged — *right in the bottom of the boat, tied to their post with oar in hand, compelled to effectively do their job.*

Likewise, you must know that as you seek to do God's will for your life, you'll have to take on all kinds of assaults and challenges that inevitably accompany obedience. And let me warn you, there will be times when your flesh tries to find a way to jump ship and get out from underneath the pressure of obeying God! Your flesh would love to be "led" somewhere else where faith isn't required and the crucifixion of flesh doesn't seem so necessary.

You see, it's easy to start obeying God. Initiating a project is fun and exciting, and it's always the easiest part. The difficult part is sticking with that project and seeing it through all the way to the end. *The real test comes when the excitement is gone and the reality of hard work and commitment begins to dawn on you.* That's always the golden moment when the flesh is tempted to forget you ever heard from God and to start looking for a way out!

If you are not really committed to go all the way in fulfilling your God-assigned task, you probably won't do it. Therefore, you must be absolutely committed to do what God has called you to do, "chaining yourself" to your decision to obey so you cannot flee in hard times. If God has called you, *don't jump ship*! He needs you in the bottom of the boat in order to keep the Body of Christ moving forward toward maturity. *You* are very important!

I'm sure there were times when the under-rowers said, *"I'm tired of rowing! Get me off this boat!"* They probably had to be reminded, "You are the engines of the ship. If you get off the boat, the boat will stop moving. You are too vital to jump ship now. We can't go on without you!"

There were also probably times when these men in the bottom of the ship said, "No one appreciates us or says thank you for what we do! We work, work, work, and *work*, and yet we are treated like slaves! I just wish someone would occasionally show some appreciation."

We all want to be appreciated. I like to be thanked when I work hard, just as we all do. This is a natural, normal desire. If we'd all just treat each other with good manners in the Body of Christ, it would solve a world of problems and remedy a lot of hurt feelings. But people are people, and sometimes they forget to say thank you. It's absolutely true that people should be more thoughtful and appreciative. But the bottom line is this: Ultimately, it doesn't matter whether or not those around us ever show us appreciation for what we do. *If the boat is going to move, we must row the boat!*

Just like these "under-rowers," if you stop rowing — if you stop doing your job — it could possibly jeopardize the destiny God has called you to fulfill. If the boat is going to move, you *must* row, whether or not you ever hear the words "thank you" from anyone.

That is the hard reality of life for all of us as servants of God. Yes, it would be nice to hear "thank you" from time to time. But lack of appreciation must not affect our determination to row our boat and do what God has called us to do.

When you said yes to the will of God, you surrendered to Him, agreeing to pick up the "oar" He has placed before you. For you, that oar may be a ministry God has given you or a position serving in the local church or a certain business. Perhaps God has instructed you to give money regularly to a ministry. Whatever responsibility God has set before you, it's time for you to grab hold of that oar! Like the under-rowers who rowed in order to move those big ships, you must begin a lifelong occupation of "rowing" to advance the cause God has put on your heart. From now on, your lifelong slogan needs to be *"Row, row, row your boat!"*

Lord, help me today to keep a right perspective of what You have called me to do. When I get tired and the devil tries to convince me to quit, please help me remember that if everyone stops rowing the boat, it won't go anywhere. Even if no one else notices what I am doing, I know that You see every move I make. Whatever I do, Lord, I do for You!

I pray this in Jesus' name!

I confess that I have a job to do and that I'm going to do it! I will not jeopardize my destiny by succumbing to the discouraging voice of the enemy. If the boat is going to move, I must do my part to move it. Whether or not I ever hear the words "thank you" from anyone, I am the servant of God and I will do my service as unto Him!

I declare this by faith in Jesus' name!

QUESTIONS FOR YOU TO CONSIDER

1. When do you most easily get discouraged? For instance, does discouragement strike when you are physically weary? Have you found that if you stay in prayer, you stay stronger and more encouraged?
2. When you're slugging it out and pushing forward with every ounce of your might, what helps you more than anything else to keep pushing ahead?
3. Does the knowledge that you are willing to do something no one else is willing to do motivate you? Do you get satisfaction when you know you're being obedient to God, even if no one else is willing to stick in there and be obedient with you?

AUGUST 29

You Are the Bishop Of Your Own Heart!

Looking diligently lest any man fail of the grace of God;
lest any root of bitterness springing up trouble you,
and thereby many be defiled.
— Hebrews 12:15

One of the most powerful verses in the New Testament is Hebrews 12:15. It says, "Looking diligently, lest any man fail of the grace of God; lest any root of bitterness springing up trouble you, and thereby many be defiled." I want you to especially notice the words "looking diligently" in this verse. This phrase comes from the Greek word *episkopos*, taken from the two words *epi* and *skopos*. The word *epi* means *over*, and the word *skopos* means *to look*. When these two words are compounded into one word as in Hebrews 12:15, the word means *to look over* or *to take supervisory oversight*.

The word *episkopos* is the same Greek word translated "bishop" in First Timothy 3:1. As you know, a bishop has *oversight* or *responsibility* for a group of churches. As the chief overseer for those churches, it is the bishop's responsibility to *watch, direct, guide, correct,* and *give oversight* to the churches under his care. As long as he serves as bishop, he will be held responsible for the *good* and the *bad* that occurs under his ministry.

Hebrews 12:15 uses the word *episkopos* to alert you and me to the fact that *we are the bishops of our own hearts.* The use of this word in this verse means it is our responsibility to *watch, direct, guide, correct,* and *give oversight* to what goes on inside us.

As the bishop of your own heart, it is your responsibility to guide, direct, and give oversight to what goes on inside your emotions and thinking. You alone are responsible for what you allow to develop inside your head and heart. Like a bishop, you are personally responsible for both the good and the bad that occurs within your thought life.

Why do I make this point? Because we are often tempted to blame our *bad attitudes, bitterness, resentments, or feelings of unforgiveness* on other people. But the truth is, we are responsible for our own emotions and reactions! If a person does something that has the potential to offend us, God holds *us* responsible for whether or not that offense takes root in our minds. We can choose to let it sink into our souls and take root, or we can opt to let it bypass us. We are not able to control what others do or say to us, but we *are* able to control what goes on *inside* of us.

It is that "inside" part — *the part you control* — that God will hold you responsible for. Why? Because you are charged with a personal responsibility to *oversee* what goes on inside your soul. That means *you* have the last word. You are the one who decides whether or not that wrong settles down into your soul and starts to take root in your emotions.

Anger is an emotion that comes and goes. You *choose* whether or not irritation turns into *anger*, anger into *wrath*, wrath into *bitterness*, bitterness into *resentment*, and resentment into *unforgiveness*. You *choose* whether these foul attitudes and emotions take up residency in your heart or are booted out the door!

When the devil comes to tempt you with an annoying, hounding thought about the person who offended you, at that moment you have a choice whether or not to let it sink in. You are the *only* one who can give permission for these attitudes to make their habitation in your mind and emotions. If you're filled with *bitterness, resentment,* and *unforgiveness,* you *permitted* the devil to sow that destructive seed in your heart and then you *permitted* it to grow. Remember, you're the bishop of your own heart!

There is only one reason weeds grow out of control in a garden — because no one took the proper time and care to uproot and remove them. When the garden is choked by weeds, the gardener can't complain, "I just don't know how this happened! How did this occur right under my nose?" It occurred because he was being irresponsible with his garden. If he'd been exercising the proper amount of diligence, he would have known that weeds were about to get the best of him. His *lack of diligence* is the reason his garden got into this mess!

Hebrews 12:15 says, "Looking *diligently....*" It takes *diligence* to keep your heart in good shape. The only way you can stay free of the weeds the devil wants to sow in your "garden" is to be attentive, careful, thorough, and meticulous about the condition of your own heart. Don't expect others to take care of your heart for you either. It's *your* heart!

Also, don't make excuses for the rotten attitudes that fill your thoughts about people who supposedly did you wrong. Even if they really did commit a wrong against you, was it necessary or beneficial to permit the devil to fill you with putrid feelings of bitterness, resentment, and unforgiveness? Get over it! What good does it do to let the offense fester inside you until you are inwardly eaten up by its bad memory?

As long as you blame everyone else for the bitterness that rages inside, you'll never walk free. The only way you can get over the offense and walk free of your emotional prison is by accepting responsibility for your own heart.

If someone deliberately sows bad seeds in our "garden" in an effort to hurt or destroy us, *God will deal with them.* But if we know bad seed has been sown in our hearts and we just ignore it, allowing it to take root and grow unchecked, *God will deal with us.*

◆ *God will hold others responsible for what they do to us.*
◆ *God will hold US responsible for what we allow to go on inside our minds and hearts.*
◆ *We cannot answer for the actions of other people.*
◆ *We will answer for our inward responses to what others have done to us.*

Since the phrase "looking diligently" is from the Greek word *episkopos*, implying that you are the bishop of your own heart, what are you going to do about the negative and wrong attitudes that are trying to take root in your soul right now? Are you going to let them fester, take root, and begin to produce bad fruit in your life? Or are you going to take the initiative to rip out those attitudes by the roots so your heart can stay free?

Never forget that you are the bishop of your heart. It is *your* heart, and you are the only one with the authority to decide what does and doesn't go on inside of you. In light of this truth, what are you going to do about the situation you are facing right now? Forgive and let it go, or hang on to that grievance and let it grow? *The choice is yours!*

MY PRAYER FOR TODAY

Lord, help me keep my heart free of offense! You have given me authority over my own will, mind, and emotions, so I know I have the authority to tell offense that it has no right to dwell inside me. I refuse to blame everyone else for the mess I've allowed to grow inside my heart — and today I am asking You to help me, Holy Spirit, to quit making excuses for the wrong attitudes I've permitted to grow in my life. With Your supernatural help, I am making the choice to repent, to turn from these destructive thoughts, and to replace them with thoughts and words of kindness for those who have caused me hurt or grief in the past.

I pray this in Jesus' name!

MY CONFESSION FOR TODAY

I confess that I deal diligently with my heart to keep it in good shape. I don't make excuses for rotten attitudes that try to fill my thoughts about people who have wronged me. Even if they really did commit a wrong, I refuse to let the devil use it to eat me up and ruin me. I am the bishop of my own heart, so I refuse to let wrong attitudes fester, take root, and begin to produce bad fruit in me!

I declare this by faith in Jesus' name!

1. Is there any feeling of bitterness, resentment, or unforgiveness that you have held on to and allowed to grow in the soil of your heart? Has the Holy Spirit been trying to convince you to forgive and to let it go?

2. If the Holy Spirit is dealing with you about forgiving someone, what are you going to do about it? Will you resist the Spirit's dealings and develop a hard heart, or are you willing to forget it and go on with your life?

3. When you hear that a person who hurt or wronged you is being blessed in his job or in some other way, can you rejoice with that person — or do you find yourself inwardly seething that he isn't being punished because of what he did to you? If you can't rejoice with him, it's probably a good indicator that you have some unresolved issues festering on the inside that you need to take to the Lord!

AUGUST 30

Be Proud of the Fruit Produced By Your Personal Investments!

So that we ourselves glory in you in the churches of God
for your patience and faith in all your persecutions
and tribulations that ye endure.
— 2 Thessalonians 1:4

*H*ave you ever been so proud of someone that you just wanted to brag and boast about him or her for a few minutes? When you've invested a lot of your own time, talents, and energy into people you love and then you see them prospering and growing strong in the Lord, it's normal for you to want to shout and rejoice about it!

This is how my wife and I feel when we see our own sons. They are strong in the Lord, active in His service, and committed to do what He wants them to do. As parents, it simply thrills our hearts — and we have every God-given right to be proud of them and thankful for what is happening in their lives! They are diligent, serious, and unwilling to give in to fatigue or discouragement; they just keep marching forward like soldiers. Of course we are proud of our sons and have every right to feel that way!

We feel the same way about the men and women we have discipled and poured our lives into over the years. When they came to us, many of them were young and inexperienced, but so hungry to grow and to learn. They were willing to be taught, to be corrected, to be instructed, and to pay the heavy price we demanded of them. We weren't interested in developing only believers — we were working to produce real disciples. So when we see them standing strong in their own ministries, firm in faith and growing in grace, wisdom, and mercy, it simply thrills our hearts!

When Paul wrote to the Thessalonians, he was so proud of them and the way they walked in faith and patience that he said: "So that we ourselves glory in you in the churches of God for your patience and faith in all your persecutions and tribulations that ye endure."

I want you to notice that Paul declared how proud he was of the Thessalonians. He said, "...We ourselves glory in [or about] you in the churches of God...." In this phrase, Paul used the word Greek word *egkauchaomai*. This is the only time this word is found in the New Testament, although it was frequently used in the secular literature of New Testament times. It means *to brag, to boast, to give praise,* or *to speak laudatory words.*

Paul was proud of the Thessalonians. As a spiritual father to them, he was thrilled with the growth they were experiencing. This is a healthy type of pride — the same kind of pride a father feels for his children when they do well. He went on to list the reasons he was so proud of them: "...for your *patience* and *faith* in all your *persecutions* and *tribulations* that ye *endure.*" Let's look at each of these words one by one.

The word "patience" is a favorite word in Paul's epistles. It is the compound Greek word *hupomene,* and it paints the picture of *one who is under a heavy load but refuses to bend, break, or surrender because he is convinced that the territory, promise, or principle under assault rightfully belongs to him.* This word denotes *a refusal to give up* and *an attitude that is determined to receive what is promised or hoped for.* The *King James Version* translates it "patience," but a better rendering would be *endurance.*

This word tells us, first of all, that the Thessalonians were under severe pressure. They lived in an environment that was aggressively anti-Christian. Every day of their lives, they were affronted and assaulted for their faith. Yet regardless of how severe the pressure became, they refused to surrender to these attacks or to throw in the towel of defeat. Paul was proud of them for their conviction to stand tall and steadfast in spite of what they were facing!

Then Paul said he was proud of them because of their "faith." The Greek word for faith is *pistis.* The very nature of the Greek word *pistis,* translated *faith,* denotes *a force that is forward-directed and aggressive — never passive or backward-reaching, but always reaching forward to obtain or achieve a specific target or goal.*

This means that the Thessalonians *never drew back or retreated* simply because they ran into difficult or hard times. Instead, their faith was like an arrow that had been shot and could not be retracted, constantly reaching forward to grab hold of God's promises. Paul recognized that this was *real* faith, and he was proud of the Thessalonian believers for never backing up on the promises of God!

Paul went on to describe the intensity of problems the Thessalonians were encountering. He mentions this because their problems were not normal, but problems of the most severe and difficult kind. Paul used the word "persecution" to describe the events that were coming against them. This is the Greek word *dioko,* a commonly used word in Paul's epistles, meaning *to pursue, to follow after,* or *to aggressively seek after.*

This word was first used as a *hunting term* to denote *the actions of a hunter who strives to follow after, to apprehend, to capture, or to kill an animal.* Thus, the word can be translated "to hunt." This same word is also translated "to persecute" throughout the New Testament, indicating *the brutal nature of persecution* that was experienced by the Thessalonian church. *They were viciously and relentlessly pursued.*

As if this is not enough, Paul informs us that the Thessalonians had experienced some kind of life-threatening "tribulation." The word "tribulation" comes from the Greek word *thlipsis,* a favorite with Paul when he described the difficult events he and his team encountered in ministry. This Greek word *thlipsis* is so *strong* that it leaves no room to misunderstand the *intensity* of these persecutions. It conveys the idea of a *heavy-pressure situation*.

One scholar says the word *thlipsis* was first used to describe *the specific act of tying a victim with a rope, laying him on his back, and then placing a huge boulder on top of him until his body was crushed.* Paul used this word to alert us to moments when he or others went through *grueling, crushing situations* that would have been *unbearable, intolerable,* and *impossible to survive* if it had not been for the help of the Holy Spirit.

But in this scripture, Paul used this same word to tell us what the Thessalonian believers had undergone. As noted above, their problems were not normal but of the most serious nature. Without the help of the Holy Spirit, it would have been enough to crush them — but they *weren't* crushed. They were still walking in faith; they were pushing forward to obtain the promises of God; and they were believing for victory!

Then Paul used the word "endure" to denote the attitude with which they had faced these obstacles and moments of opposition. The word "endure" is from the Greek word *anechomai*, which means *to put up with, to endure,* or *to bear up under.* Yet this word doesn't portray the sufferer as one who simply surrenders to defeat, but rather as one who exhibits an attitude of *fortitude* and *resistance* to such negative forces.

**When you put all this together,
Second Thessalonians 1:4 could be translated:**

"We are so impressed with what God has done among you that, when we tell all of God's churches about you, we're outright braggadocios! We proudly tell them about your refusal to bend to pressure; your resolve to never abandon or give up what belongs to you; your commitment to hang in there, no matter how heavy the load; and your determination to 'stay put' until your hopes are realized. We've also told them how your faith has remained aggressive and forward-directed, regardless of the ordeals you've been through — such as those times when you've been hunted down like animals and relentlessly pursued. Your faith has stayed out front, despite the horribly tight, life-threatening, terrifically stressful situations you have undergone but steadfastly resisted."

I don't know about you, but when I read all of this, it makes me want to be sure that I belong to the ranks of the Thessalonians! We have the same Holy Spirit living in us who lived inside the Thessalonian believers. If they could live so triumphantly for the Lord in their difficult position, you and I can make the decision to live *victoriously* for Jesus Christ in our situations too. *Amen?*

MY PRAYER FOR TODAY

Lord, help me invest my life in people who will grow strong and who will bring forth good fruit! I want to give my life to people who are going to do something in this world. I want to know that I have made a difference in the life of someone who is going to make a difference in the lives of others. The last thing I want is to have lived this life without ever making a personal investment in anyone else, so please help me recognize those people You want me to pour myself into. Then give me the wisdom and grace to pull up alongside and share with them the treasure You have placed in me!

I pray this in Jesus' name!

MY CONFESSION FOR TODAY

I confess that I bear good fruit in the lives of people whom God has called me to help! They are growing! They are prospering! They are learning to overcome the evil one! They are strong, stable, resilient, reliable, faithful, and committed to do whatever it takes for them to fulfill the assignment Jesus Christ has given them. My fruit is good fruit — fruit that remains! In this I know that my Father is glorified, because I am producing the kind of fruit that brings glory to His name!

I declare this by faith in Jesus' name!

QUESTIONS FOR YOU TO CONSIDER

1. Who is that person or group of people God has called you to disciple? If you are not actively discipling someone right now, why aren't you?
2. How does it affect you when you see that those you've poured your life into are doing well and growing strong in the Spirit? Does it make you want to stand tall, throw back your shoulders, and rejoice in the Lord that good fruit is being produced in them?
3. Do you take the time to let these individuals know how proud you are of them? How long has it been since you've put your arm around someone's shoulder and let him know how pleased you are about what is happening in his life?

AUGUST 31

Are You Going From Glory to Glory Or From Mess to Mess?

> But we all, with open face
> beholding as in a glass the glory of the Lord,
> are changed into the same image
> from glory to glory, even as by the Spirit of the Lord.
> — 2 Corinthians 3:18

Most believers quote the verse above when they are facing a difficult challenge. I did the same thing for many years. I often told myself, "Soon this mess will be over, and when it is, we're headed to the next level of glory that God has for us! This won't last long. We're going from glory to glory!"

But one day I was pondering this verse and thinking deeply about what it meant to go from glory to glory. Suddenly it struck me that it doesn't say we are going from a *mess* to *glory*. It says we are going from *glory* to *glory* — in other words, from *a current glorious place* to *another higher glorious place*.

This clearly means that you and I won't be promoted to the next realm of glory until the realm where we presently live is glorious. So if we want to go upward into a greater glory, we have to first make *glorious* the place where we are living and functioning right now.

When I saw this, it made me want to take a good, hard look at my life and ministry. I asked myself: *Am I living in a glorious stage, or am I stuck in an ugly, messy stage of my life?* I realized that according to this verse, I wouldn't be moving upward into the next great and glorious phase God had for me until the situation I currently found myself in became glorious! Only then would God promote me to the next level of glory He had planned for my life.

So I began to ask myself:

✦ *Have I done all the Lord has told me to do right now?*
✦ *Have I really completed the assignment as God instructed me to do?*
✦ *Have I done it professionally and on time?*
✦ *Have I made my present financial situation glorious, or am I living in financial shambles?*
✦ *Have I done everything I can to make this present stage of my life a bright and shining example to others, or is this part of my life a dismal failure of which I'm embarrassed?*
✦ *Have I brought this part of my life to a glorious finish?*

Second Corinthians 3:18 says, "But we all, with open face, beholding as in a glass the glory of the Lord, are changed into the same image from glory to glory, even as by the Spirit of the Lord." I find it very interesting that the first part of this verse talks about us having "open faces." The word "open" is the Greek word *anakalupto,* which means *to unveil, to uncover,* or *to disclose.* However, the Greek tense doesn't refer to a one-time unveiling, but to *a veil that, once lifted, remains lifted forever.*

When I saw this, I immediately understood another very vital truth: We must be willing to permanently remove the veil from our eyes and to take an honest look in the mirror in order to truthfully acknowledge the condition of our present stage. Only after we have truthfully seen and acknowledged what we are can we make a sincere decision to change. A truthful recognition of the facts is part of the process that removes the veil from our eyes so the Lord can correct us, change us, transform us, and prepare us to move upward into the next glorious phase for our lives. That is precisely why the apostle Paul went on to say that we are "changed" after the veil is removed from our eyes.

The word "changed" is the Greek word *metamorpho.* It is a compound of the words *meta* and *morphoo.* The word *meta* carries the idea of an *exchange,* while the word *morphoo* is the Greek word for a person's *outward form.* Together, the compound word means *to transfigure or transform one's appearance.* The word *metamorphoo* is never used in the Old Testament Septuagint, and it appears only four times in the New Testament. It is used in Matthew 17:2 and Mark 9:2 to describe the *transfiguration* of Jesus. Paul also uses it in Romans 12:3 to tell us that we are to be *transformed* by the renewing of our minds. And finally, Paul again uses the word *metamorphoo* here in Second Corinthians 3:18.

There is no doubt that the word "changed" speaks of an actual, real transformation of our minds and even our outward appearance. The Holy Spirit lets us know through Paul that we can actually *exchange* our present appearance, our current status, for one that is more glorious. If we sincerely desire it, we can move upward and into the glory that God has prepared for us!

Now, we can try to hide our heads in the sand and pretend that everything in our lives is glorious when it is not, but that does *not* make everything glorious. In fact, denial of the truth will just keep s stuck in the same hard place for a longer period of time. To move into the next phase of our life in God, we must be willing to lift the veil from our eyes and acknowledge that we need to be *transformed*!

If may be difficult on your flesh and pride, but eventually a time comes when you must look in the mirror to see what is really there! Self-deception is very costly. Telling yourself that everything is all right when it isn't may temporarily relieve you from the pain of having to look at the facts head-on. But in the end, ignoring the facts will cost you so much more in terms of time, heartbreak, and defeat.

Truthfulness can be painful, but the pain is short-lived and in the end produces tremendous change. But the kind of change I am describing to you today is only initiated when you are willing to get honest with yourself and with God about your behavior, your attitudes, and the condition of every area of your life at this present moment. If you're willing to remove the veil from your eyes and let the Holy Spirit really show you the areas where you need to be transformed, He *will* change you. And as this kind of transformation begins to work in you, you will become more and more prepared for upward movement and promotion in your life.

So establish this truth in your heart today: If the stage of life you are in right now is not glorious, you will be stuck in the current mess until you become willing to take off the veil, look honestly at your situation, and begin to make the changes that are required to make your present status more glorious! Once you've done that, God will be ready to move you upward and onward to the next more glorious place you are longing to experience!

Yes, it's true that God wants to take you from glory to glory. However, He isn't bothered if He has to wait until you correctly finish your current task. God has lots of time. *But when you get serious about doing what is necessary to make your present situation glorious, you signal to the Holy Spirit that it's time to open the way to the next glorious phase God has planned for your life!*

MY PRAYER FOR TODAY

Lord, I want to take the veil off my eyes and get honest about my situation. I can see that much of my present life is not glorious. I have wanted You to promote me from my mess to a new level of glory, but I see now that Your promotions always move from one level of glory to a higher level of glory. Show me every area in my life that needs to be changed, and help me give You complete liberty to transform those parts of my life. I want to go to a higher level of glory, Lord, so I am asking You to help me first make my present situation a glorious testimony of Your grace!

I pray this in Jesus' name!

MY CONFESSION FOR TODAY

I confess that by God's grace, I am making my present situation more and more glorious! I have asked the Holy Spirit to open my eyes and to help me see those parts of my life that need to be transformed. As He shows me these areas, I will diligently pray about them and do everything I can to allow God to change me so this present season of my life can become glorious. Because the Holy Spirit sees my willingness to go through the necessary transformation process, He is preparing to move me upward into a more glorious phase in my life. I am going from glory to glory!

I declare this by faith in Jesus' name!

QUESTIONS FOR YOU TO CONSIDER

1. What are the areas of your life that are *not* glorious — the areas you most need to work on?
2. Now that you know God will not promote you higher until you have made your current status glorious, what changes do you need to make in your life right now to get ready for the next step upward?
3. Write down the steps you are going to take to turn your messes into shining examples that will open the way for God to start the promotion process in your life.

SEPTEMBER 1

༺༻

The Holy Spirit Knows How To Get You There Faster and Safer!

Howbeit when he, the Spirit of truth,
is come, he will guide you....
— John 16:13

Occasionally when people visit Moscow, my wife and I give them a tour of the Kremlin. Because people usually want to see the Kremlin, we have been there hundreds of times and we know all the routes and shortcuts. Often as we visit this historic complex of buildings with our guests, I am amazed to see people in other groups taking the longest, most difficult route on that extensive tour. I always think, *They are taking the longest and hardest route possible! If I were leading them, I could save them a lot of time and energy.* These people ultimately get the same tour as they keep exploring on their own, but the route they take requires twice the time and energy as the tour I could give them.

As I was pondering this one day, I started thinking of all the times each of us could have avoided wasting precious time and energy if we had only allowed the Holy Spirit to lead us. We may eventually get to the same point, but if we try to go it alone, that usually means we will take twice as long to get there and the journey will be much harder. The Holy Spirit sees everything. He knows every nook, corner, and bend on the road of life. If we reach out and take His hand, He will lead us on shortcuts that will save time, energy, and many tears.

The Holy Spirit wants to *guide* us through life. He wants to *guide* us as we walk into the future. In John 16:13, Jesus used this illustration of a guide to describe the ministry of the Holy Spirit. He said when the Spirit came, "...he will shew you things to come" (John 16:13).

The word "show" is the Greek word *odegeo*, and it is the word for *a guide who shows a traveler the safest course through an unknown country*. This means Jesus sent the Holy Spirit to be our Guide! The Holy Spirit knows the way we should go. He knows how to avoid every trap and every attack; He knows the safest and fastest route for us to take. When we are stepping into territory that is new o us, it is imperative that we let the Holy Spirit lead us, for He wants to show us the precise route o take so we can successfully reach that place God has put in our hearts. This is part of the Holy pirit's ministry in our lives — to get us safely to our God-ordained point of destination.

In the life of Jesus, we see this *guiding* work of the Holy Spirit very clearly.

✦ Jesus was led by the Spirit *not* to go to Bethany to see Lazarus when His friend was sick unto death. Hostile Jewish leaders expected Jesus to come to Lazarus' aid and were waiting there to trap him. Jesus waited two days after hearing of Lazarus' sickness; in fact, He didn't go until He knew Lazarus was dead. It must have been difficult for Jesus to refrain from rushing to Lazarus' side, but the Holy Spirit guided Him to stay away from that place because there were people there who wanted to stone Him (*see* John 11:1-11).

✦ Jesus was led by the Holy Spirit to go to Bethany the moment the Jewish leaders left. When Jesus didn't appear after Lazarus had died, the religious leaders concluded He wasn't coming, so they left the graveside. As soon as these evil leaders had abandoned Bethany and this treacherous situation had passed, the Holy Spirit gave Jesus the go-ahead to travel to Bethany, where He raised Lazarus from the dead. Thus, because Jesus allowed the Holy Spirit to guide Him and only left for Bethany after He sensed a release to go, He avoided an ugly confrontation with angry religious leaders (*see* John 11:11-45).

✦ Jesus was led by the Spirit through dangerous situations on many occasions. When religious leaders with evil intentions wanted to capture and kill Jesus, He was supernaturally guided by the Spirit right through the midst of the crowd, escaping injury and harm (*see* Luke 4:29,30; John 8:59; John 10:39).

When you study the book of Acts, you will find that the Holy Spirit constantly *guided* people hrough hard and difficult territory. In each case, He would protect people from danger or from naking mistakes; He would help them avoid those who wished to hurt them; or He would lead them way from a fruitless situation to a place of blessing. Here are some instances where the Holy Spirit varned the Early Church *in advance* about persecutions, famines, and other trials, guiding them safely hrough and around many treacherous moments.

✦ The Holy Spirit led the Early Church to prepare for a soon-coming famine. Because the early believers responded to this word from the Spirit that was delivered through the prophet Agabus, they were *guided safely* through this hardship (*see* Acts 11:27-29).

✦ The Holy Spirit led the apostle Paul and his team to stay away from Bithynia. The Bible doesn't tell us why the Spirit forbade them to go to this destination. Perhaps there were unknown dangers awaiting them of which they were unaware. The Holy Spirit was guiding them away from danger as He directed them to take another, more important route (*see* Acts 16:7).

✦ The Holy Spirit led the apostle Paul to the region of Macedonia to preach the Gospel by speaking to him in a dream. Paul was so convinced that the Spirit was guiding him that he and his team immediately changed plans and followed the Holy Spirit's leading to Macedonia, where they reaped great fruit for the Kingdom of God (*see* Acts 16:9).

Being led by the Spirit is one of the privileges we receive as children of God. Romans 8:14 says, "For as many as are led by the Spirit of God, they are the sons of God." As noted earlier (*see* July 3), he word "led" is the Greek word *ago*, which is the picture of *someone gently leading someone else*. This neans the Spirit will lead us, but we must extend our hearts and hands to Him first, for without our cooperation, He cannot guide us anywhere.

Without the Holy Spirit's guidance, we are left to find our way on our own. This no doubt means we will waste valuable time, energy, and money, not to mention shed a lot of unnecessary tears along the way! The Holy Spirit sees what we can't see; knows what we don't know; and understands the best routes, the most efficient shortcuts, and the safest paths to take. Since this is the kind of Leader the Holy Spirit is, we would be wise to let Him lead us!

Oh, if you only knew how many times the Spirit of God has wanted to be your Leader in the situations of life! He knew exactly how to lead you past every attack. He knew how to avoid each strategy that the devil arrayed against you. But even if you didn't accept His guidance in the past, you don't have to continue making that same mistake, trying to forge your way through life by yourself. You can extend your heart to the Holy Spirit today. Let Him take you by the hand — and He will safely guide you to the place where God wants you to go!

MY PRAYER FOR TODAY

Lord, I thank You for the leadership of the Holy Spirit. I am so sorry that I've wasted time, energy, and money trying to find my way on my own when You have already sent me the Holy Spirit to be my Guide. Holy Spirit, please step into my life and take Your place as my Teacher, my Leader, and my Guide. I extend my heart and my hand to You today so You can begin to guide me through life. I thank You, Father, for providing the most wonderful Guide in the whole universe to help me make it successfully through life!

I pray this in Jesus' name!

MY CONFESSION FOR TODAY

I confess that I am led by the Spirit of God! Because I cooperate with Him, I don't waste valuable time, energy, or money, and I don't shed a lot of unnecessary tears. I gladly let the Holy Spirit lead me, since He sees what I can't see; knows what I don't know; and understands the best routes, the most efficient shortcuts, and the safest paths to take. As a result, He leads me past every attack; He helps me avoid each strategy of the devil; and He safely guides me to the place where God wants me to be!

I declare this by faith in Jesus' name!

QUESTIONS FOR YOU TO CONSIDER

1. Can you think of a time when the Holy Spirit stopped you from doing something that you thought was the correct thing to do? What was the result of following the Spirit's leadership?
2. Has there ever been a moment when the Holy Spirit guided you to do something that made no sense to you naturally, but after you did exactly what He told you to do, you could see why He had led you in this way? If so, what was that occasion, and what was the fruit of your being guided by the Spirit to do things differently?
3. Is the Holy Spirit trying to lead you to do something right now that is different from what you had planned or thought? Have you been arguing with Him in your mind, thinking that His instructions make no sense? What are you going to do — stick with your original plan, or let the Holy Spirit be your Guide?

September 2

✾

Are You Guilty of Exaggerating the Facts Or Embellishing the Truth?

Lie not one to another, seeing that ye have put off
the old man with his deeds.
— Colossians 3:9

*T*he Bible has much to say about liars. If you have a tendency to lie, it is essential that you bring correction to this part of your life as soon as possible. But you may ask, "How do we define a lie? What exactly does the Bible mean when it says we need to stop lying?"

In Colossians 3:9, the apostle Paul said, "Lie not one to another, seeing that ye have put off the old man with his deeds." The word "lie" is the Greek word *pseudomai*, which carries the idea of *any type of falsehood*. It can picture *a person who projects a false image of himself; someone who deliberately walks in a pretense that is untrue;* or *someone who intentionally misrepresents facts or truths.*

In Greek, the word *pseudomai* is used in a variety of ways:

✦ *pseudapostolos:* describes *false apostles* (2 Corinthians 11:13).
✦ *pseudoprophetes:* paints a portrait of *false prophets* (Matthew 7:15).
✦ *pseudodidaskalos:* pictures those who are *false teachers* (2 Peter 2:1).
✦ *pseudochristos:* denotes those who are *false Christs* (Matthew 24:24).
✦ *pseudoadelphos:* plainly depicts a *false brother* (2 Corinthians 11:26).
✦ *pseudomartureo:* conveys the idea of a *false witness* (Matthew 19:18).
✦ *pseudologos:* denotes a *false word* or *one who speak falsehoods* (1 Timothy 4:2).

In every instance where the word *pseudomai* ("lying") is used in the New Testament, it portrays *someone who misrepresents who he is by what he does, by what he says, or by the fact or truth he purports to be true.* It was in regard to this wrong behavior that Paul said, "Lie not one to another...." It is very important to point out that in Greek, the grammar conveys the idea of *a strong prohibition,* meaning this verse should be translated, *"Stop lying to one another...."* It implies that the believers to whom Paul was writing struggled with the issue of honesty in their lives.

Paul's words to the Colossians could be interpreted like this:

"I command you to stop the practice of misrepresenting the truth, twisting the facts, projecting untrue images, or deliberately misleading others by giving them false information...."

Lying is a temptation that all of us have to deal with in our lives. Apparently even the Colossian church struggled so strongly with this problem two thousands years ago that Paul had to write and tell them to stop lying.

You may not deliberately set out to lie, but anytime you misrepresent the truth about your abilities; say something about another person that you don't know to be true; slightly twist the facts to your advantage; or trump up a story about yourself or your past deeds to make yourself look better in the sight of others — you have fully entered into what the Bible views as "lies."

All this behavior was forbidden by Paul when he wrote, "Lie not to one another...." Paul's words cannot be misunderstood or misinterpreted. This is a clear mandate to stop the habit of lying and to no longer give your consent to participate in any type of falsehood, dishonesty, deceit, fabrication, or misrepresentation of the truth in your life or in your conversation.

If you are the head of your household, church, ministry, or business, you have *every right* to demand that people stop being untruthful with you and each other. Let it be known that truthfulness is important — so important, in fact, that it is the foundation of all successful relationships at home, at church, and at work. It is impossible to build trust in a relationship if you suspect that the other person is being dishonest with you.

If you are the one in charge, set the example by always being truthful with the people under you. When people know that you are being straight with them, at least they'll know they can always depend on you to tell the truth, even if they don't like what you're telling them. In this way you can set the standard for integrity and truthfulness between all the members of your family, your church, or your business.

But what if you are the one who dresses up or slightly misconstrues the facts to your advantage or to the disadvantage of others? If that is the case, it's time for you to get honest about this sin in your life! And that's exactly what it is — *sin*! Quit telling yourself that you're just exaggerating a little or being dramatic. Maybe that's how you try to rationalize your behavior, but God views it as telling falsehoods and says it should not be tolerated in your life!

Are there any areas in your life where you have permitted a little exaggeration? Have you ever misrepresented the truth about who you are, what you can do, what you have done, or what you have heard or think of others? Can you honestly say that the words you speak are accurate, or would you have to admit that you have been a little dishonest in how you report certain matters? *If you know in your heart that you haven't been totally truthful, what are you going to do about it now?*

Or perhaps you are a leader in your family, church, or business, and you know that people under your authority are regularly misrepresenting the truth to you. If so, will you continue to tolerate this seriously wrong behavior and thus allow a lack of confidence and suspicion to prevail? Or are you going to put an end to all lies and deception? *What are you going to do about this situation?*

The Holy Spirit is available to help both the liar and the one who must bring correction to the liar. So if you have misrepresented the facts in the past but are willing to repent and change, God's Spirit will enable you to stop lying and to learn how to be more truthful. And if you are the one who must bring correction to the dishonest person, just turn to the Holy Spirit for help. He will show you exactly what to say and how to say it so truth can prevail in that particular situation.

MY PRAYER FOR TODAY

Lord, I admit that I've exaggerated the facts and embellished the truth on many occasions. I'm so sorry for doing this. I blamed it on my personality, but now I understand that You view this as dishonesty. I ask You to help me stop making excuses for this behavior and to accept responsibility for the words and messages I project to others. When I stand before You, I want a clear conscience that I have been honest, forthright, and balanced in the things I've said about myself or about others. Holy Spirit, I need Your help to bring correction to this part of my life, so today I yield myself to You.

I pray this in Jesus' name!

I confess that I speak the truth and that I don't exaggerate the facts or speak lies! When people talk to me, they can count on the fact that I don't embellish the truth or twist the facts to my advantage. They can rest assured that I'm honest about myself and the situations in which I find myself. I keep my nose out of other people's business and concern myself instead with those issues that have to do with me and my areas of responsibility. Because God is my Helper and His grace is working mightily in me, I am becoming more and more honest every day!

I declare this by faith in Jesus' name!

QUESTIONS FOR YOU TO CONSIDER

1. Are there any areas in your life where you know you've been dishonest about who you are, what you've done, or what you can do? Or have you ever been dishonest in regard to what you've said about other people?
2. If your answer is yes to these questions, what steps are you going to take to bring correction to the times you have lied in the past? Are you going to let the lie continue to be repeated as though it were a fact, or will you go to those who heard your dishonest words and tell them the truth?
3. What do you think God is telling you to do about the falsehoods and dishonest issues you have allowed in your life?

SEPTEMBER 3

Here's What To Do if the Devil Is Trying To Devour You!

Be sober, be vigilant; because your adversary
the devil, as a roaring lion, walketh about,
seeking whom he may devour.
— 1 Peter 5:8

Has the devil ever tried to use your past against you? Maybe he's told you, "You're in this mess because of your own actions! Don't even try to ask God to help you because you got into this mess by yourself, and now you're going to have to get out of it by yourself! God won't help you, because you're reaping exactly what you've sown!"

If you've ever heard these kinds of accusations from the devil, then First Peter 5:8 is just for you! It says, "Be sober, be vigilant; because your adversary the devil, as a roaring lion, walketh about, seeking whom he may devour."

The word "vigilant" comes from the Greek word *gregoreo*, which means *to be on your guard, to be watchful,* or *to be attentive.* This word primarily denotes *the watchful attitude of one who is on the lookout to make certain no enemy or aggressor can successfully gain entry into his life or place of residence.*

This tells us that we must be on high alert against an enemy who is seeking to gain access to our lives. The Greek tense for the word "vigilant" means *to be continually, perpetually vigilant.* That means this is not a one-time act of vigilance, but the attitude of a person who is unwavering in his commitment. This person has resolved that he will never let up in his pledge to be *watchful, wide awake, and on the lookout* to make sure some sinister force doesn't successfully sneak up to attack and overtake him.

The fact that Peter uses the word *gregoreo* lets us know that the devil can be pretty sneaky in the way he attacks. Therefore, we must be *constantly observant* to keep the devil out of our affairs.

Peter goes on to say, "Be sober, be vigilant; because your *adversary....*" That word "adversary" is from the Greek word *antidikos.* This word was used in New Testament times for *a lawyer who argued in a court of law.* This was the picture of a *prosecutor* who brought offenders to court, argued vehemently against them, and then sent them off to prison. Now Peter uses this word to depict the way the devil may try to overtake us!

Peter is telling us that when the devil strikes, he often acts like a lawyer who tries to bring us down by prosecuting us with the facts of our past sins and mistakes. The enemy drags up facts from the past and reminds us of our former failures; then he vigorously tries to convince us that we deserve to be in the mess we are in. If the devil is successful in his prosecution, he will persuade us to believe that we are unrighteous and unworthy and that we deserve as just punishment whatever difficulties he is throwing our way.

It is unfortunate that many believers assist the devil in his efforts to prosecute them by being irresponsible or negligent in key areas of their lives. For instance, many people have money problems because they have spent too much money or used their credit cards way beyond the limit of what they could afford. Others get sick in the wintertime because they go outside without proper clothing. Marriages get into trouble because the spouses never spend time together or do anything to nurture their relationships. Christians like to blame the devil for everything that happens, but the truth is, people usually help out the enemy a little along the way!

Praise God, when we sin and do wrong, His grace is there to forgive and to restore us! But the devil is also there. The enemy remembers every innocent mistake made along the way, and like a *prosecutor* or "adversary" (the Greek word *antidikos*), he comes to accuse you. Like a lawyer, he argues his points in your mind, saying:

- ✦ *You're in this mess because of your own dumb mistakes!*
- ✦ *You're reaping what you sowed, and there's no way for you to get out of this mess!*
- ✦ *You're paying for your past!*
- ✦ *Your kids are a mess because you failed as a parent!*
- ✦ *You're going to go bankrupt because you spent too much money on worthless things!*
- ✦ *You've destroyed all your friendships because you weren't a faithful friend!*

Sometimes the devil is accurate in what he tells you. *It may be true that you created this mess!* You really may have messed up your friendships by not being a faithful friend. You may have spent too much money, and the financial trouble you're in now may very well be your own fault! *All* the devil's accusations may be true. Believe me, he isn't going to make up some absurd fantasy that won't affect you. *The devil is going to try to use facts and arguments that make sense to you so you'll agree with him!*

But you must never forget what David told us: The Lord is the One who redeems our lives from destruction (Psalm 103:4). He is a restoring, delivering, redeeming God! He wants to snatch you out of the power of darkness and get you over into His realm of life and light where past sin won't continue to exert its influences upon you (Colossians 1:13)! You just need to genuinely repent of past mistakes, get your heart right with God, and then tell the devil to flee!

If you keep dwelling on the accusations that the enemy is speaking against you in your mind, you'll find yourself in trouble pretty quickly. Peter goes on to tell you why this is so: "…The devil, as a roaring lion, walketh about, seeking whom he may devour."

Have you ever heard lions when they are hungry? They roar so loudly that the sound is nearly deafening. Peter says that this is what it's like when the devil starts attacking your mind. Your mind is so filled with the roars of the enemy's accusations that you can't hear anything else *but* those lies. He tells you over and over, *"You're going to fail…fail…fail…fail…FAIL!!!"* Even when people try to tell you the truth, it's hard to hear what they're saying because those lies are roaring so loudly in your mind and ears!

If you keep giving ear to the devil's accusations, he will keep you all torn up inside and in a constant state of turmoil. In fact, Peter says he will "devour" you. The word "devour" is the Greek word *pino*, which means *to drink, to lick,* or *to slurp up, as a lion might lick the blood of his prey off the ground.* The devil wants to turn you into a mess of liquid emotions and then lick you up until there's nothing left of your life. That's what he *wants* to do with you — but you don't have to let him do it!

When you put all these words together,
First Peter 5:8 could be interpreted:

"You must be constantly alert and on your guard! The devil, like an accusing lawyer, will try to charge you with all kinds of arguments and accusations. You need to know that he is like a lion on the prowl — constantly walking around, roaring with a deafening sound, earnestly seeking the kind of person he can completely consume and slurp up!"

You don't have to fall victim to the devil's attacks! Peter tells us, "Whom resist stedfast in the faith…" (1 Peter 5:9). If you'll resist the devil, you can run him clear out of your mind and your life. He doesn't know how to deal with those who stand up to him, so he runs in fear when a believer challenges him! And if you feel too weak to resist the devil by yourself, I would advise you to find people who know how to pray and let them help you!

Has the devil been harassing you about anything in particular? Are you tired of this constant harassment? If so, it's time for you to stand up, throw back your shoulders, and command him to leave in Jesus' name! Then determine to stay alert and watchful, constantly on your guard. You can be sure that the enemy will try to come back to accuse you again — but next time, you'll be ready for him!

MY PRAYER FOR TODAY

Lord, I am asking You to help me take authority over the accusations that the devil has been speaking in my mind. He's been telling me all the reasons that I shouldn't have any hope and that I deserve to be in this mess. But Your grace is greater than any mistake I've made or sin I've committed in the past! I know that You have forgiven me and redeemed me from any mess I've created by my own actions. I thank You now for Your forgiveness and mercy, and today I lay claim to the power of restoration! Devil, right now I command you to leave me in Jesus' name! I refuse to listen to your accusations any longer!

I pray this in Jesus' name!

MY CONFESSION FOR TODAY

I declare that I have confessed all my past sins and mistakes. Therefore, I am forgiven; I am clean; and I am free in the sight of the Lord. He does not hold my past against me. He is my Redeemer, my Restorer, my Deliverer, and my Salvation. His Spirit is operating in me right now to get me out of every mess I have created, both intentionally and unintentionally. My heart is repentant, and my desire is to do what is right. Therefore, God is helping me walk out of the problems that have tried to grip my mind and my life!

I declare this by faith in Jesus' name!

QUESTIONS FOR YOU TO CONSIDER

1. Are there areas in your life in which the devil is trying to drag up the past so he can accuse you and convince you that you deserve the attacks that are coming against you right now?
2. Have you taken the time to sincerely repent for those past sins and mistakes before the Lord? Or did you just quickly admit you sinned, never allowing the Holy Spirit to deal with you deeply about these matters?
3. If the devil has been roaring in your mind, consider what steps you can take to stop those roaring accusations, such as listening to praise and worship music or teaching tapes, meditating on the Word, etc. What other steps can you take to silence the enemy's accusations?

SEPTEMBER 4

Tell-Tale Signs That Bitterness Is Growing in Your Life

Looking diligently lest any man fail of the grace of God;
lest any root of bitterness springing up trouble you,
and thereby many be defiled.
— Hebrews 12:15

When you find yourself constantly saying something derogatory about someone else, pay attention to what's happening! What you're saying about that person is a *tell-tale sign* that some bad seed is trying to take root in your heart.

Hebrews 12:15 tells us how to recognize bad seed when it begins to produce destructive fruit in our lives. It says, "...lest any root of bitterness *springing up* trouble you...." The words "springing up" are from the Greek word *phuoo*. This word depicts *a little plant that is just starting to sprout and grow*. It isn't a large plant yet; rather, it's a small seedling that is just breaking through the soil and starting to peek out at the world. However, the very fact that it's peeking through the soil means there is a seed hidden in the soil producing this new life.

This is a very significant picture. It tells us that bitterness doesn't overwhelm us all at once. Instead, it grows a little here and a little there until it finally becomes a huge, ugly growth that defiles our entire lives. Bitterness usually starts peeking up out of the depths of our souls in the form of negative thoughts about another person or a sour, sharp, distrusting, cynical attitude toward someone who has offended us. If the root is not quickly uprooted and removed, that bitterness will eventually become a full-blown tree that produces *bitter, wounding, hurtful,* and *scornful* fruit for everyone who eats of it.

Hebrews 12:15 shouts its warning: If you don't stop these attitudes, they will eventually "trouble you." The words "trouble you" are from the Greek word *enochleo,* which means *to trouble, to harass,* or *to annoy.* It refers to something inside that *bothers* and *upsets* you so much, you are constantly *pestered* by thoughts about it. In fact, your whole life is *stalked* by these hassling, troubling thoughts. What you allowed to take root and to fester inside your soul has now become a major nuisance to your peace, keeping you upset and emotionally torn up all the time.

✦ Do you have a grudge against someone that just gnaws away at you all the time?
✦ Every time you see that person, do you feel something sharp and ugly inside?
✦ When you hear about that person being blessed, do you wonder how God could possibly bless him when he did such an ugly thing to you?
✦ Do negative thoughts like these pester and bother you all the time?

If you relate to the questions I just asked you, then *watch out!* It may mean that a root of bitterness is growing inside you and that bitterness, resentment, and unforgiveness are starting to *hound* and *stalk* you wherever you go!

You need to get a grip on yourself and let the Holy Spirit help you permanently rid yourself of these feelings; otherwise, you'll end up troubled, annoyed, and terribly upset. You'll lose your peace, forfeit your joy, and toss aside your victory. Friend, you *don't* want to take this path! It's too painful, too hurtful, and costs you too much in your walk with God.

So if you find yourself constantly saying something derogatory about someone else, pay attention to what's happening! That is a *tell-tale sign* that some bad seed is trying to take root in your heart that could potentially grow into a major issue that hassles your whole life. Don't let it happen! Ask the Holy Spirit to help you jerk out those roots from the soil of your heart so you can stay free!

The Holy Spirit is willing, ready, and waiting to help you grab hold of those roots of bitterness and pull them clear out of your life. All He needs is your invitation, so why don't you go ahead and ask Him to assist you right now?

MY PRAYER FOR TODAY

Lord, I ask You to please forgive me for allowing negative thoughts about others to consume me. Even though I don't like what they did to me, I have no right to be bitter and resentful. I realize now that I am acting just as ugly inwardly as they acted outwardly. In Your eyes, my sin is just as bad as theirs. I am truly sorry for allowing these attitudes to grow inside me, Lord. To the best of my ability, I turn right now from the wrong thoughts that have been consuming me, and I choose instead to speak well of those who have offended or hurt me. Holy Spirit, help me uproot those wrong feelings from my heart and replace them with love and forgiveness.

I pray this in Jesus' name!

MY CONFESSION FOR TODAY

I confess that my heart is free of bitterness, resentment, strife, and unforgiveness. God's Spirit lives in me, and He doesn't allow me to keep living with wrong attitudes in my life. He speaks to me when I begin to think poorly of others; He convicts me of every wrong attitude; and He helps me bring my thoughts under His control. Because my mind and emotions are controlled by the Spirit of God, I think only positive thoughts about those who are near or around me. If any negative thoughts about someone else try to enter my mind, the Holy Spirit quickly helps me recognize them and bring correction to the way I am thinking!

I declare this by faith in Jesus' name!

QUESTIONS FOR YOU TO CONSIDER

1. Is there one particular person or group of people you find yourself constantly speaking badly about? Why do you feel the need to speak so derogatorily about that person or group? What does this reveal about the condition of your own heart?

2. Has God been trying to deal with you about your attitude toward that person or group of people? *Be honest!*

3. Would you have to honestly admit this bitterness or unforgiveness has affected the level of joy you once experienced in the Lord? It's difficult to be filled with joy when you are "eaten up" on the inside with negative thoughts about someone else. If you are being hounded by hassling thoughts, what do you plan to do about your condition?

SEPTEMBER 5

Thoroughly Furnished Unto All Good Works!

That the man of God may be perfect,
throughly furnished unto all good works.
— 2 Timothy 3:17

When I was growing up, my father loved to go fishing. As the years passed and his love for fishing grew more intense, he purchased himself a boat so he could go to the lake and fish at any location he wished. I remember his first boat well. It was just a plain, simple, ordinary boat with nothing but a very small motor and two wooden oars for rowing just in case the motor stopped working.

Like most serious fishermen, my dad wasn't content with that beginner's boat very long! He had to have something better, nicer, and more seriously equipped. Soon he swapped his simple boat for a rig that was completely decked out with every imaginable device. It had a huge motor, a trolling motor, a depth-finder, a computerized temperature gauge, and a sophisticated fish locator. Even the anchor was operated by a special electric motor. He finally had the boat of his dreams, loaded with everything he ever could have imagined having on his fishing boat. What an improvement this was from that first very simple, basic boat he had started out with when he first took up fishing as a sport!

Well, believe it or not, when the apostle Paul describes what the Word of God does in our lives in Second Timothy 3:16 and 17, he uses a Greek word that describes a well-decked boat like Dad's boat. These verses say, "All scripture is given by inspiration of God, and is profitable for doctrine, for reproof, for correction, for instruction in righteousness: that the man of God may be perfect, throughly furnished unto all good works."

I want you to notice the phrase "thoroughly furnished" in verse 17. This phrase contains a "gem" that reveals what God's Word can do if you give it top priority in your life. You're about to discover that there is no replacement for what God's Word can do in you and for you!

The phrase "thoroughly furnished" is from the Greek word *exartidzo*, which means *to completely deck out* or *to fully supply*. It was used to depict *a ship that had previously been ill-equipped for traveling; but because its owner had decked it out with new equipment and gear, this ship had become thoroughly furnished to sail anywhere in the world.* This boat was *fully supplied, completely equipped,* or *thoroughly furnished.*

Paul uses this word to tell us that we are not prepared to set sail in life until the Word of God has done its work in our hearts and souls. When we first come to Jesus, we are like the first boat — just beginners who hardly know enough to get by in life. Yes, we're saved and on the way to Heaven, but we haven't had enough of the Word placed into us to fully equip us for sailing through all kinds of weather.

You can be sure that you will encounter all kinds of weather in your journey through life — including strong storms. Therefore, if you're going to make it all the way to your destination, you will need all the equipment and gear you can get!

Paul's words in Second Timothy 3:17 could be interpreted to mean:

"That the man of God may be perfect — completely outfitted and fully supplied, decked out, furnished, and equipped unto all good works."

You see, when a believer never reads the Word of God, never meditates on the truths of the Word, and doesn't regularly renew his mind with the Word of God, he is like a simple boat that isn't equipped for long-distance sailing. He might be able to make it across a little lake; however, in order to victoriously make it across the sea of life and through all the storms he will encounter along the way, he will need major equipment!

That equipment is imparted to a believer when the Word becomes an integral part of his life. God's Word working inside his heart and mind actually outfits him, decks him out, equips him, or furnishes him with all the spiritual gear he needs to take the adventurous trip God has planned for his life. With God's Word fitted tightly in place, that believer is ready to set sail and follow wherever the Holy Spirit leads!

So we have a choice. If we choose to not make God's Word a priority in our lives, we are still headed to Heaven, but we're like that first simple, plain, basic boat. In other words, we're just believers who have only enough spiritual equipment to make it across the little lakes of life. On the other hand, if we choose to take God's Word deeply into our minds and hearts and then apply it to our lives, that Word will release its supernatural power to transform us from simple, basic believers to super-believers — endowed with everything needed to successfully make the long-distance journey the Holy Spirit has planned for our lives!

So how far do you want to go in life? Your answer will determine how deeply you need to take God's Word into your heart and mind. If you're just in this for a little jaunt across a lake, you will be satisfied with a low level of God's Word in your life. But if you're planning to take a long, adventurous, exciting faith journey, you better *dive* into the Word of God. *As you do, that anointed Word will deck you out with all the provisions you need to make it all the way to your destination!*

MY PRAYER FOR TODAY

Lord, I thank You for loving me so much that You would give Your Word to equip me for life. I realize that all the answers I need are found in Your Word. I have often complained that I needed more power and wisdom. But the truth is, everything I need is in Your Word. Help me to diligently read my Bible, take it deeply into my heart and soul, and apply it to my life. As I do so, I ask that it would supernaturally release its divine power to transform me from being a simple, basic believer to becoming one who is super-equipped for life!

I pray this in Jesus' name!

MY CONFESSION FOR TODAY

I confess that God's Word has a central place in my life. I regularly read God's Word and meditate on its truths; therefore, my mind is being renewed with the Word day by day. As a result, that Word decks me out — equipping, outfitting, and furnishing me with all the spiritual gear I need to take the adventurous trip God has planned for my life. With God's Word fitted tightly in place, I am ready to set sail and follow wherever the Holy Spirit leads!

I declare this by faith in Jesus' name!

QUESTIONS FOR YOU TO CONSIDER

1. If you were to appraise your spiritual condition today, would you say you are a simple, basic, unequipped believer, or would you deem yourself well-furnished and excellently equipped in a spiritual sense?
2. In order for you to become spiritually well-equipped, what do you need to start doing that you are not doing right now?
3. If you continue to do exactly what you are doing right now in your spiritual life, how far do you think you are prepared to sail? Are you sufficiently supplied to do anything God asks you to do or to go anywhere He wants to send you?

You will encounter all kinds of weather in your journey through life, so if you're going to make it to your ultimate destination, you will need all the equipment and gear you can get!

SEPTEMBER 6

❧✦❧

Here's How To Extinguish The Fiery Darts of the Wicked!

Above all, taking the shield of faith,
wherewith ye shall be able to quench
all the fiery darts of the wicked.
— Ephesians 6:16

Would you like to extinguish every flaming dart the devil ever tries to shoot in your direction? Does that proposal sound too good to be true? Well, Ephesians 6:16 assures you that if you have your shield of faith lifted high in front of you, you will be supernaturally empowered to defend yourself against the fiery darts of the enemy. But more than that, you will be able to literally *extinguish* every single fiery dart the devil will ever try to send your way!

This makes our shield of faith very important! Therefore, let's look at Ephesians 6:16 to see exactly what it says about us being able to extinguish all the flaming arrows of the enemy. It says, "Above all, taking the shield of faith, wherewith ye shall be able to quench all the fiery darts of the wicked."

Today I would like to draw your attention to several very important points in this verse. First, I want you to notice the phrase "...wherewith ye shall be able...." The first part of this Greek phrase would be better translated *by which*. For the words "ye shall be able," the Greek word used here is the word *dunamis*, which denotes *explosive power* or *dynamic power* and is where we get the word "dynamite." When these Greek words and phrases are used together as they are in Ephesians 6:16, it could actually be translated, *"Above all, taking the shield of faith, by which you will be dynamically empowered...."*

Paul uses these Greek words to explain the supernatural empowerment that occurs when a believer uses his shield of faith. When a believer lifts his shield high and holds it out in front of him where it belongs, that shield divinely energizes the believer to stand bravely against every assault of the devil. That shield of faith becomes dynamically and supernaturally empowered to act as an impenetrable wall of defense against the enemy's tactics. *In other words, faith is a shield to the believer!*

The shield of faith is so powerful that it makes you fortified, invulnerable, and armed to the teeth! It equips you to hold an ironclad position. It turns you into a spiritual tank so you have the ability to move your position forward without taking any losses yourself. This doesn't mean the devil won't try to stop you, but when the shield of faith is held out in front of you as it ought to be, you become divinely empowered "...to quench all the fiery darts of the wicked."

The word "quench" in this verse is the Greek word *sbennumi*, which means *to quench by dousing* or *to extinguish by drowning in water*. It refers to the water-soaked shield of Roman soldiers. You see, before Roman soldiers went out to battle, they purposely soaked their shields in water until they were completely water-saturated. The soldiers did this because they knew the enemy would be shooting fire-bearing arrows in their direction. If a shield was dry, it was possible for it to be set on fire when struck. But if this vital piece of armor was water-soaked, the flames would be extinguished even if an arrow penetrated its heavily saturated surface.

How does this apply to us as believers? Well, Romans 10:17 says that our faith is increased by hearing the Word of God. In Ephesians 5:26, the Word of God is likened to water. So as we regularly submit ourselves to the Word of God, we soak our faith with the Word just as a Roman soldier soaked his shield with water. And when our faith becomes Word-saturated or Word-soaked, it becomes just like the soldier's water-saturated shield. In other words, it will be so heavily inundated with the water of God's Word that even if a fiery dart pierces our shield, the huge amount of Word in us will extinguish the flames and put out a potentially damaging situation!

The words "fiery darts" are from the Greek word *belos*. It referred to *an arrow with its tip wrapped with fabric soaked in flammable fluids so it would burn with hot and angry flames.* The famous Greek writer Thycidides used this Greek word *belos* to depict specially-made, long, slender arrows that outwardly looked harmless; however, the hollow interior of the arrow was filled with flammable fluids that, upon impact, exploded into a raging fire. This last arrow is most likely the picture that Paul had in his mind when he wrote about the "...fiery darts of the wicked."

Often when the devil strikes, his attack looks inconsequential at first, like harmless little arrows that can do little damage. But when those arrows strike into the heart or emotions, they often explode and set human passions aflame, causing a minor issue to develop into a fierce, flaming situation. The damage done in such a moment is very serious — and all of it could have been avoided if the shield of faith had been held high and regularly doused in the water of the Word!

There is no doubt that the devil will try to shoot his arrows in your direction. But having a shield of faith that is soaked in the Word of God gives you double protection against these attacks. It guarantees that the enemy's fiery darts will have little or no effect, even if they get close enough to strike your heart, mind, or emotions in the midst of the situations you find yourself facing today.

So I urge you today to take the time to soak your faith in the Word of God. Let the water of the Word so saturate your faith that if the enemy tries to launch a surprise attack on you — your health, your finances, your marriage, your children, your family, your church, your business, or your job — he will find that his fiery darts have no impact on your Word-soaked faith shield!

Refuse to let yourself become the devil's victim! Hold your Word-doused shield of faith high in front of you so it completely covers your life. Then rest assured that no fiery dart of the enemy will make any serious impact on you. *That faith shield will protect you from anything the enemy throws at you through the dynamic, explosive power of God!*

MY PRAYER FOR TODAY

Lord, thank You for giving me the shield of faith. Help me to be brave and bold and to hold my shield high in front of me to stop every attack of the enemy. After reading today's Sparkling Gem, I understand that I have a responsibility to soak my faith in Your Word so it can extinguish each and every flaming arrow the devil tries to shoot into my life. I ask You to help me be sincerely committed to making Your Word the top priority in my life — soaking my faith with that Word until it becomes an impenetrable wall of defense against the enemy's attacks!

I pray this in Jesus' name!

MY CONFESSION FOR TODAY

I confess that my faith is saturated with the Word of God! The devil may try to attack me, but my faith is held out high in front of me, covering my life completely and extinguishing every flaming arrow the devil attempts to shoot in my direction. My faith is supernaturally energized, and I am empowered to stand against every assault the devil tries to make on my life!

I declare this by faith in Jesus' name!

QUESTIONS FOR YOU TO CONSIDER

1. Are you spending enough time in the Word to see that your shield of faith is soaked and saturated with the water of God's Word? Or is your faith so parched from a lack of the Word that your shield isn't working anymore?
2. Can you remember a time when a fiery dart struck that would have normally set everything ablaze with negative emotions and destruction — but because your faith was Word-soaked and in place, that attack had very little impact in your life? What was that situation?
3. Have you ever seen a fiery dart from the enemy that released a blaze of destruction when it struck? When you saw it happen, did you realize that the success of the devil's attack was due to a lack of time in God's Word?

SEPTEMBER 7

Learn To Think Like a Snake!

Behold, I send you forth as sheep in the midst of wolves:
be ye therefore wise as serpents,
and harmless as doves.
— Matthew 10:16

When I was growing up, we had a lot of snakes in the countryside where we lived, and many of my young friends thought it was fun to search for and collect snakes. Because I was a typical little boy, I joined the rest of my friends in their pursuit of snakes. This first-hand experience taught me quite a lot about the behavior of snakes and later enabled me to have a deeper appreciation for what Jesus meant when He said, "Behold, I send you forth as sheep in the midst of wolves: be ye therefore wise as serpents, and harmless as doves" (Matthew 10:16).

In this verse, Jesus commanded His disciples (and us) to be "wise as serpents." The word "wise" is the Greek word *pronimos*, which means *prudent, careful, cunning, discerning, thoughtful, intelligent,* or *sensible*. This word perfectly depicts the behavior and actions of snakes. They are very *careful, discerning, intelligent,* and *prudent* in how they act. The Greek word for "serpent" is the word *ophis,* which is the normal Greek word that refers to *a snake.*

It is a fact that Jesus told us that we need to be "wise as serpents"! The Greek literally means we need to be as prudent, discerning, intelligent, thoughtful, and careful as snakes! There is obviously something Jesus wanted us to learn from the behavior of snakes, so I took the time to ponder this subject. Finally, I understood exactly why Jesus used this example and how it applies to all of us regarding our families, businesses, ministries, or *any* opportunity God places before us in life.

If you are squeamish about serpents and snakes, stay with me for the next few moments so you can get the full impact of what Jesus was telling us. *Remember, Jesus is the One who chose to use a serpent to make this point.* So let's consider the behavior of serpents for a moment and see how this relates to us being "wise" in the way we live our lives and conduct our ministry or business.

First, when serpents first move into a new territory, they don't announce their presence. Instead, they lay low, stay quiet, and blend into the environment. In fact, you can walk right past a snake and not even realize it! Snakes have the ability to be nearly invisible. They are designed to be camouflaged.

This camouflage serves as a protective covering. The vilest aggressor can walk right past, but the serpent is not noticed because it has blended so well into the landscape. That camouflage gives the serpent latitude to move about freely as it finds its way around new territory.

As snakes evaluate a new situation, they see what kind of opportunities are in the area. They identify places of shelter. They find "hiding places" to protect themselves from attack. They observe to see where they can find the easiest prey. When all these facts are assimilated, the serpent is ready to act. But this "settling-in" period is a key time for a serpent. *And Jesus said there is wisdom in a serpent's behavior from which we need to learn!*

When God calls you or me to do something new — to move to new territory or to seize a divine opportunity — it is wisdom for us to move carefully and slowly into that new phase of our lives. A common mistake is to act too fast. Acting hastily before all the facts are gathered and assimilated can lead us to make erroneous decisions. In fact, one serious mistake can cause us to lose an opportunity altogether. It is better to lay low, stay quiet, and blend into the environment for a while, learning from the sights and the facts we observe.

Let me give you an example. When Denise and I first moved to the former USSR, we took time to learn the customs and culture of the new territory. We knew it would take time to understand everything we would see and experience, so we moved very slowly and carefully. Although we immediately saw opportunities, we decided to first watch and gain as much knowledge as possible about the circumstances we found ourselves in at that moment. *Acting too quickly would have certainly meant making some bad and regrettable decisions.*

In the first few months we lived there, we made little noise and our presence was hardly noticed. This allowed us the ability to move about freely and without disruption. We visited churches unannounced. We wandered in and out of different parts of the city to observe and ascertain the spiritual condition of our new environment.

Also, before I made any grand announcement that we were going to go on television, I first wanted to know something about television, and I felt that the best way to learn was to do it covertly. I had observed too many American missionaries who announced great plans that unfortunately never developed. Their ideas were great, perhaps even from God; but because these missionaries had acted before they understood the full picture, they ruined their testimony and lost a glorious opportunity.

Many missionaries were hurt because they acted too fast and got in a hurry. They were trying to take ground for the Kingdom of God in a land they knew nothing about. In reality, it was utter foolishness to start such fantastic projects without first understanding the challenges, risks, and dangers.

My wife and I knew that moving slower might take more time, but in the end such a strategy would produce more stable and serious results. We therefore made the choice to move slowly and steadily, gathering all the facts we could, analyzing the information, and then listening to what the

Lord might say to us about the facts we had learned. Then and only then would we make an announcement about our plans. *To make such an announcement without first taking the previous steps would have been a mistake.*

Most serious mistakes are avoidable when moving to a new situation or environment. I strongly advise you to take your time and be sure of the actions you take before you ever act. I would suggest that you first:

+ Learn the landscape of your new environment.
+ Locate places of spiritual shelter for you and your family.
+ See what kind of attacks could potentially come against you.
+ Take time to really understand the opportunities around you.
+ Take advantage of your preparation time before you announce great and glorious plans, making sure that you are completely informed of all the facts.

Second, serpents are wise enough to know when to seize the moment and strike! *Knowing when to act is as important as knowing when to lay low.* When prey passes before a serpent, that serpent knows it's time to *strike*! If the snake waits too long, the opportunity will pass by and the prey will reach an irretrievable position.

So when it's time to act, put your fears and emotions aside *and seize the moment*!

I have seen so many ministers and businessmen pray and pray for divine opportunities to come to them. They fast, pray, and wait for that golden moment to come — and at last, it does! A great door of opportunity stands directly in front of them. It's time to act. But rather than seize the moment and walk through that door, they pause to pray just a little bit longer. God brought them *exactly* what they had been praying for, but because they paused, they lost the opportunity. When they finally got around to saying yes, it was too late.

Let me give you another personal example. In 1993, I earnestly prayed and sought God to open a way for us to start a Christian television network in the former Soviet Union. One day I received a phone call from the top directors of a national television station. They asked me to fly to their city to meet with them and talk about broadcasting our television program every week on national television. My associate and I jumped on the next available plane and went to meet this powerful group of people who were making such an exciting offer to us.

My heart was filled with anticipation. I wondered, *Is this the opportunity I've been praying would happen? Is it really occurring? Is God answering my prayer?* I had a sense that something great and awesome was about to transpire, and I could hardly wait to arrive at the meeting to hear this group's proposal.

I had already done my homework. I had studied the statistics regarding the full reach of the television channel about to be offered. I had spoken with pastors and churches all over that nation to see what they thought of that channel. My time of "laying low and blending into the environment" had given me the knowledge I needed for the moment I stepped into that meeting with those television directors. I was equipped for this long-awaited conversation, armed with information and supported by the prayers of our partners.

As the meeting began, the directors asked me, "Would you like to broadcast your television program on the national channel and penetrate every single home in this nation?" This is exactly what I had long been praying and waiting for! The opportunity of a lifetime was sitting on the table in front of me in the form of a television contract. But I held my composure, not wanting them to know how excited I was at this chance to reach every home in the nation. I wanted to hear how much this divine door of opportunity was going to cost our ministry each month.

The cost was much more than we had imagined. But I knew it was worth the money, considering the fact that our program would be broadcast into every single home in the entire nation. When I heard the price of the broadcast time, I felt a hesitation at first, a fear that we wouldn't be able to come up with the cash each month. Yet I knew a door had been opened before me that had *never* been offered to anyone else before. Only God could open such an incredible door for the Gospel. There was no doubt that He was orchestrating the entire event.

I asked for a few minutes to be alone. When the television directors stepped out of the room, I told my associate, "I don't know where the money is going to come from to pay for this, but only God could have opened this door of opportunity. It's going to be a miracle payment each month, but I am going to sign this contract right now before we lose this opportunity for the Gospel."

My head and logic said, *Don't do it*, but my spirit said, *DO IT NOW!* In my heart, I knew it was the moment to strike and seize this incredible opportunity. So a few minutes later, I picked up an ink pen and signed my name on the dotted line. National television had fallen into my hands! Our programs would now be broadcast into the homes of more than fifty million people each week!

Within days of signing that contract, politics radically changed in the nation. If I hadn't seized the opportunity at that exact moment, I would have lost it. If I had even hesitated one week, the door would have been closed. Because we seized it at the *right time*, our television program was locked into a contract that the government had to honor. As a result of acting at the *right time*, our ministry and television program became one of the most powerful spiritual forces in that nation. Since 1993 when we first walked through that door, we have been impacting that nation with the apostolic and teaching ministry God has given us, and countless lives have been changed forever.

I thank God that I had the spiritual guts and gumption to act at the *right moment*. I had already prayed and prayed. But as I sat with those directors that day, I sensed that I had to seize the moment and act. It was time to *strike!* Through experiences like this one, the Lord has taught me that there are moments to "lay low" and there are moments "to strike fast!" Surely this is one of the points Jesus was making to us when He told us to "…be ye therefore wise as serpents…" (Matthew 10:16).

You may be asking, "But how do I know when it's time to lay low or time to take action and seize the moment?" The Holy Spirit will lead you in these areas if you will be sensitive enough in your spirit to follow His leading. If you will take the time to get quiet and listen for His voice, He will guide you past every obstacle, camouflage you from every attack, and show you exactly when to take action in your family, your business, your church, and the ministry God has given you.

Many people are afraid to obey what the Spirit puts in their hearts to do. Fearful that they will be led astray or that they will make a mistake, they sit on the sidelines and watch other people achieve success, while they remain right where they've always been. Let me tell you something, friend — you can trust the leading of the Holy Spirit! *If you will let the Holy Spirit become your eyes and ears, you will never fail to recognize key moments and divine opportunities for your life, family, business, or ministry.*

You and I are not brilliant enough to figure out the right timing for everything by our own logic. The *timing* for our actions must be directed by the Holy Spirit, not by us. If we learn to depend on the Spirit's leading, we will walk through many strategic doors at key moments. But it is imperative that we understand this: When He says *"NOW!"* it really means *"NOW!"*

I pray that you have fresh insight into what Jesus meant when He commanded us to "…be ye therefore wise as serpents…." He was giving us a *powerful* message, wasn't He? So be very careful not to move too fast, and be careful also not to delay when the time is right to act. *Open your heart to the Spirit of God today, and let Him begin to teach you when to lay low and when to strike!*

MY PRAYER FOR TODAY

Lord, I ask You to help me be wise, prudent, intelligent, discerning, and sensible in the way I think and act. You see everything and know exactly what is really happening, so I am leaning on You to lead me in every situation. Teach me when to sit still and when to act. You are my Leader, so I look to You to lead me and to help me do exactly what is right in each situation.

I pray this in Jesus' name!

MY CONFESSION FOR TODAY

I confess that I have the mind of Jesus Christ! His mind makes me sensible, intelligent, prudent, discerning, and accurate in the way I think and behave. Because the Holy Spirit is producing the mind of Christ in my life, I make very few mistakes. In fact, I am getting better and better all the time at seeing things accurately and knowing what to do in different situations. I am careful to lay low when the Spirit says to wait, and I am bold to obey when the Spirit says to act!

I declare this by faith in Jesus' name!

QUESTIONS FOR YOU TO CONSIDER

1. Have you had a moment in the past when you knew an opportunity was passing before you — and you had to strike right at that moment or you'd lose the opportunity God was giving you?

2. In that instance, what did you do? Did you hesitate and lose the golden moment God was trying to drop into your hands, or did you seize the opportunity and *strike*? If you hesitated and lost the opportunity, have you asked the Lord to forgive you for letting fear defeat you? Have you asked Him to give you another chance?

3. Do you recognize the opportunities the Holy Spirit brings before you? What opportunity is passing in front of you right now? How are you going to respond differently now than you did before to assure that you don't lose another God-given chance to do or to achieve something great?

Many people are afraid to obey what the Spirit puts in their hearts to do. Fearful that they will be led astray or that they will make a mistake, they sit on the sidelines and watch other people achieve success, while they remain right where they've always been. Let me tell you something, friend — you can trust the leading of the Holy Spirit! If you will let the Holy Spirit become your eyes and ears, you will never fail to recognize key moments and divine opportunities for your life, family, business, or ministry.

SEPTEMBER 8

The 'Morons' of the World Are God's Kind of People!

For ye see your calling, brethren,
how that not many wise men after the flesh,
not many mighty, not many noble, are called:
But God hath chosen the foolish things
of the world to confound the wise....
— 1 Corinthians 1:26,27

*I*f you feel that you just aren't smart enough to be used by God, then today's *Sparkling Gem* is written just for you! Get ready, because you're about to be abundantly blessed when you see exactly whom God delights in choosing and using to do mighty things in His name! In First Corinthians 1:27, the apostle Paul writes, "But God hath chosen the *foolish things* of the world to confound the wise...."

The word "foolish" is from the Greek word *moraino*. It depicts someone who is *dull, dense,* or *slow*. It was used in New Testament times to portray a person who was *stupid* or *foolish* — hence, *a fool*. It could also picture a person who is *mentally ill* or *mentally deranged*. The word *moraino* was used derogatorily *to make fun of people* or *to put them down for being intellectually inferior*. It comes from the same word from which we get the word *moron*. My thesaurus gives these other synonyms for a "moron": *idiot, imbecile, halfwit, numskull, dimwit, dunce, blockhead, dope, ignoramus, lamebrain, jerk,* or *twerp*!

The truth is, no one is an idiot in God's view. But the world often has a scathing opinion and view of people whom God chooses. It is simply a fact that the world regularly ridicules us as being *nitwits, lamebrains, and idiots*. This is precisely the way the word *moraino* was used in Paul's time, depicting people whom the world *scorned, made fun of, and treated with contempt*.

Because much of the Early Church was comprised of servants and slaves, most of the people in the local congregations were very uneducated, uncultured, clumsy, crude, awkward, and unpolished. It wasn't that they were stupid. They had simply never been exposed to or taught about manners, culture, and refined behavior. Reared and treated as servants since birth, they'd never had a need to know these skills. As a result, it is a historical fact that the vast majority of the Early Church was uncultured.

Although there was a logical reason why many of the early believers were so uncultured, this lack of polish made them look stupid in the world's eyes. In fact, at first the Roman Empire looked upon Christianity as the religion of stupid, poor people because it grew so rapidly among the lower slave classes.

Yet Paul says, "...God hath chosen the foolish things of the world to confound the wise..." (1 Corinthians 1:27). The word "confound" is the Greek word *kataishuno*. It means *to put to shame, to embarrass, to confuse, to frustrate,* or *to baffle*. The word "wise" is the word *sophos*, referring to *those who are naturally brilliant, intellectually sharp,* or *especially enlightened*. Paul is saying that God calls people whom the world considers *morons* in order to put to shame, embarrass, confuse, frustrate, and baffle those who think they're so smart!

**Taking all these Greek words into consideration,
an interpretive translation of First Corinthians 1:26,27 could read:**

"God selected people who are idiots in the world's view; the world sees them as imbeciles, jerks, real twerps. Yet God is using them to utterly confound those who seem smart in the world's eyes."

If anyone has ever called you an idiot — if you've ever been called a stupid imbecile, a jerk, or a twerp — it's time for you to rejoice! This makes you a candidate! *You are exactly the kind of person God wants to use!*

So don't let *anyone* put you down or make you feel badly about yourself. A lack of education, culture, or polish has never stopped God from using people who have a willing heart. If your heart is right and you are willing for God to use you, you are the very one He is seeking right now! *Just say,* "Lord, here I am! I'm ready to be used!"

MY PRAYER FOR TODAY

Lord, I thank You for choosing to use people like me! I realize that I may not have the education, skills, culture, or high-level training that others may possess, but I do have a heart to be used by You. I want You to take me and use me for Your work in this earth. Today I surrender to You anew, asking You to take me and to use me mightily in this life!

I pray this in Jesus' name!

MY CONFESSION FOR TODAY

I confess that I am exactly the kind of person God wants to use! My heart is right; my attitude is willing; and I deeply desire for God to use me in a special way in this life. I am willing to learn and ready to be corrected. I want God to shape me to become a mighty instrument in His hands. Because of my attitude and willing heart, God is going to use me mightily to further His Kingdom on this earth!

I declare this by faith in Jesus' name!

QUESTIONS FOR YOU TO CONSIDER

1. Have you accepted God's call on your life?
2. If yes, what do you believe He has called you to do? What do you know about the special, unique plan He has for you that He doesn't have for anyone else?
3. If you haven't accepted your unique calling yet, what is stopping you today from saying yes to the Lord and stepping into the glorious future He has planned for your life?

If anyone has ever called you an idiot — if you've ever been called a stupid imbecile, a jerk, or a twerp — it's time for you to rejoice! This makes you a candidate! *You are exactly the kind of person God wants to use!*

SEPTEMBER 9

❧❧❧

Do You Sound Like a Sounding Brass Or a Tinkling Cymbal?

Though I speak with the tongues of men and of angels,
and have not charity [*agape* love], I am become
as sounding brass, or a tinkling cymbal.
— 1 Corinthians 13:1

It seems that the apostle Paul encountered a group of people who were extremely "super-spiritual" in the city of Corinth. However, Paul was unimpressed with these people and their level of spirituality because they had an obvious lack of love. Their deficit of love bothered him so deeply that he alluded to it when he wrote First Corinthians 13:1: "Though I speak with the tongues of men and of angels, and have not charity, I am become as sounding brass, or a tinkling cymbal."

The words "sounding brass" are very important in this verse. Let's begin our study today with the word "brass." It comes from the Greek word *chalkos*, an old word that referred to *metal*. However, it wasn't just any metal; it was bronze or copper to which a small amount of tin had been added. This tin caused the metal to have a hollow, empty sound when it was beaten. That is why Paul also used the word "sounding" — the Greek word *echo*, which described *a noise that reverberates or echoes*. When these two words were used together, they portrayed *the endless beating of metal that produces a hollow, annoying, irritating echo that seems to eternally reverberate.*

So when Paul wrote about a "sounding brass," he borrowed an illustration from the pagan world of Corinth to make his point about super-spiritual people who demonstrate no love. The illustration he chose to use was the endless, nonstop, annoying, aggravating, irritating, frenzied beating and clanging of brass that was performed in pagan worship and that echoed ceaselessly throughout the city of Corinth. The citizens of Corinth could never escape the endless banging of this metal, so this was an illustration everyone in the Corinthian church could readily comprehend.

The unsaved citizens of Corinth were deeply devoted to pagan religions. In terms of paganism and idolatry, Corinth stands out as one of the most wicked, idolatrous cities in world history. The pagan temples of the city were filled with worshipers who danced wildly under the influence of wine and drugs. In order to drive the people over the edge and into an emotionally frenzied state of spiritual ecstasy, the pagan priests would wildly beat the metal drums faster and faster and louder and louder.

The citizens believed the piercing, deafening banging and clanging of the drums was essential for achieving a state of spiritual ecstasy. Nevertheless, it was a constant nuisance to them, for they could never escape the constant, rhythmic pounding of metal that produced this clamoring noise.

As time passed, this well-known and commonly loathed, nonstop clanging noise became the very word people used to describe *a person who talked incessantly.*

Have you ever been around a person who talked so much that you didn't even listen to him anymore? After a while did you just look at the person without listening because words never seemed to stop pouring from his mouth? Did his words eventually just sound like noise to you? Well, that is exactly what Paul is talking about here in First Corinthians 13:1 — people who say a lot and claim a lot, but who don't have a life to match their many words. Paul says people like this are just a lot of empty, shallow, clanging, banging *noises* that eventually become an irritant to all who are near enough to hear them.

But wait — Paul also likened these super-spiritual people who lacked love to "a tinkling cymbal." The word "tinkling" is a very poor translation, for the Greek word *alalazon* means *to clash* or *to crash loudly*. The word "cymbal" comes from the Greek word *kumbalon*, which is the Greek word for *cymbals*. But when these two words are compounded together, it describes *a constant, loud clashing of cymbals*, much like the clashing cymbals played by the Jewish people just before they went to war! The clashing of those cymbals was a call to arms! It sounded the signal that it was time *to fight*!

I find it interesting that Paul would use the phrases "sounding brass" and a "tinkling cymbal" to describe these people. Just as a "sounding brass" was irritating and nerve-racking to all who heard it, and just as the "tinkling cymbal" aroused the mind and emotions for war — a person who claims great spirituality but doesn't demonstrate love can be just that much of an irritant!

As this type of person goes on endlessly in a perpetual, nonstop, shallow, boastful, self-glorification of himself, he almost makes you want to stand up and fight. But don't do it! You need to pray for patience when you're dealing with a person like that. If he isn't willing to listen and be changed, you need to ask God to show you a way to graciously remove yourself from the difficult encounter. But if a door opens and an opportunity arises for you to speak the truth in love, tell that person how he is coming across to others. If you were in that person's shoes, wouldn't you want someone to tell you the truth, even if you didn't like what he was telling you?

You might as well learn how to deal with this situation, because people who fit this description are not going away. Instead of focusing all your prayers on how these selfish people need to change, maybe it's time for you to start asking God to change *you* so you can deal with them in a spirit of love. Maybe they've never seen real spirituality, so they don't know what it looks like or how it sounds. If so, this is your opportunity to show them the real thing!

Don't wait until this person's nonstop talking drives you to the point of wanting to rise up and slap him and tell him to shut up. Before that ever happens, go to the Lord and ask Him to give you His heart for that person. *When you have God's heart and mind about the situation, you'll be able to deal with it in the spirit of Jesus.*

But what should you do if *you* are the one who talks nonstop? You need to pay attention to what you've read today. Do your words act like a repellant that drives people away from you? If you've noticed that people are avoiding you, maybe you need to find out the reason why! Go to someone and ask, "Would you please tell me what I am doing that is driving people away from me?" However, if you're going to ask this question, be prepared to receive the answer. You must be willing to make corrections in your character, your words, and your life.

The last thing you or I want to be is a sounding brass or a tinkling cymbal. Therefore, it would be good for all of us to go to the Lord and ask Him to reveal anything in our words or actions that needs to be changed. *And if the Holy Spirit does reveal something to us, we need to give all our effort to bringing correction to our lives!*

MY PRAYER FOR TODAY

Lord, please help me be patient with people who are inconsiderate of others and won't stop talking about themselves. When I am tempted to lose my patience and to become angry with them, give me the grace to moderate my emotions so that I can respond to them in the spirit of Jesus. I know that You have been patient with me so often, and now it is my turn to be patient with others. Help me to show them the same kindness You have shown me and to avoid falling into the trap of being judgmental and impatient.

I pray this in Jesus' name!

MY CONFESSION FOR TODAY

I confess that I am loving, patient, and kind, and I do not quickly lose my temper with people who are self-consumed. These "motormouths" are not my enemies. I am their friend. As God enables me, I will speak the truth to them in the spirit of Jesus Christ. I believe that in their hearts, they want to change. Therefore, I overlook their weaknesses and am patient with them as God works on transforming them day by day!

I declare this by faith in Jesus' name!

QUESTIONS FOR YOU TO CONSIDER

1. Who is the motormouth you've been trying to deal with in your life? Has that person's perpetual talking about himself revealed impatience in your own character?
2. If you encounter a person who boasts of great spirituality but demonstrates none of it in his or her personal behavior, how do you respond to this situation?
3. If you were the motormouth who negatively affected other people, would you want someone to speak the truth to you in love so you could bring correction to your life? If so, how would you want that person to approach you about the matter?

SEPTEMBER 10

Love Is Patient and Kind

Charity [*agape* love] suffereth long,
and is kind; charity envieth not....
— 1 Corinthians 13:4

During the next six *Sparkling Gems*, I want to speak to you about Paul's words in First Corinthians 13:4-8, where he speaks of *love*. These powerful verses are like a mirror. If you will be brave enough to look honestly into that mirror, you will find that Paul lists fifteen powerful points about the love of God and how it behaves. By peering into these verses, you will be able to determine if your life is a reflection of the high-level kind of love God wants you to exhibit toward others.

If you discover that your life is a reflection of this love, you can praise God for the great growth and maturity you have attained in your life. But if you find that your life does *not* reflect the kind of love God wants you to possess, take it as a signal from Heaven that you need to change and become more like Jesus!

Paul wrote, "Charity [God's high-level *agape* love] suffereth long, and is kind; charity envieth not; charity vaunteth not itself, is not puffed up, doth not behave itself unseemly, seeketh not her own, is not easily provoked, thinketh no evil; rejoiceth not in iniquity, but rejoiceth in the truth; beareth all things, believeth all things, hopeth all things, endureth all things. Charity never faileth…" (1 Corinthians 13:4-8).

In these verses, the apostle Paul tells us fifteen primary marks or characteristics of *agape* love. We are going to be looking at all fifteen of these points; however, before we get into the specific manifestations of *agape* love, let's first look at the word *agape* itself, for this is a very special kind of love, unlike any other in the world.

In First Corinthians 13:4-8, Paul uses the word *agape* to describe the highest level of love in this world, which is also the kind of love God expects every believer to demonstrate in his or her life. This word *agape* describes a love so completely different from what the world offers that it is only used in the New Testament to describe God's love and the love that *should* flow from the hearts of believers.

Agape is a divine love that gives and gives and gives, even if it's never responded to, thanked, or acknowledged. You could say that *agape* is a love that isn't based on response but on a decision to keep on loving, regardless of a recipient's response or lack of response. Because *agape* is such an unconditional love, I call it *high-level love*. It is the highest, most noble, purest form of love that exists.

◆ *What are the marks of this kind of love?*
◆ *How does agape love behave?*
◆ *How can you recognize it?*
◆ *What is the evidence that a person is moving in this kind of high-level love?*

In First Corinthians 13:4-8, Paul describes the characteristics of *agape* love. God designed these verses to help you determine whether or not you are walking in this kind of high-level love in your own life.

As Paul begins his description of the conduct of *agape*, he first writes, "Charity [*agape* love] suffereth long.…" The words "suffereth long" are taken from the Greek word *makrothumia*, a compound of the words *makros* and *thumos*. As noted earlier (*see* July 25), the word *makros* means *long*. The word *makros* may indicate *something that is long, distant, far, remote, or of long duration*. The word *thumos* means *anger*, but it also embodies the idea of *swelling emotions* or *a strong and growing passion about something*.

When these two words are compounded into one, it forms the word *makrothumia*, which pictures *the patient restraint of anger* and therefore *longsuffering*. It can be translated as the words *forbearance* and *patience*.

The word *makrothumia* ("longsuffering") is like a candle that has a very long wick. Because its wick is long, it is prepared to burn a long time. It is ready *to forbear* and *patiently wait* until a certain person finally comes around, makes progress, changes, or hears what you are trying to communicate or teach him. This is the picture of a person whose feelings for someone else are so passionate that he doesn't easily give up or bow out; instead, he keeps on going and going and going, even though the other person doesn't quickly respond to him.

So when Paul says, "charity suffereth long," his words could be rendered:

"Love patiently and passionately bears with others for as long as patience is needed...."

Dear friend, this means *agape* love doesn't throw in the towel and quit. In fact, the harder the fight and the longer the struggle, the more committed *agape* love becomes. Like a candle with an endless wick, it just keeps burning and burning and burning, for it never knows how to quit. This, of course, is contrary to human nature, which says, "I'm sick and tired of waiting and believing. If that person doesn't come around pretty soon, I'm finished with this relationship."

Are you in a relationship that tests your patience? Are you tempted to throw up your arms in exasperation? If so, you need a good dose of *agape* love to be released in you!

According to Romans 5:5, the *agape* love of God has already been "shed abroad" in your heart by the Holy Spirit. This means you don't have to come up with this supernatural love by yourself. The words "shed abroad" are from the Greek word *ekcheo*, which denotes *a pouring forth, a discharge, a spilling out,* or *something that is dispersed in abundance*. In other words, God has magnificently bestowed on you sufficient love to be longsuffering in any relationship or situation.

God's love has literally been poured forth, dispensed, and shed abroad in your heart. So when you ask the Holy Spirit to help you, He will release a river of this divine love to flow forth from within you and cause you to be supernaturally longsuffering toward that person who has frustrated you so much.

It's just a fact that human nature is short-tempered and intolerant, but *agape* is slow to anger, slow to wrath, and doesn't know how to quit! It supernaturally becomes stronger and more committed the longer it takes to get through to the heart of the one who is loved. This is a miraculous love — a love that transforms and changes people's lives.

Second, Paul tells us that love is "kind." The word "kind" is the Greek word *chresteuomai*, which means *to be adaptable or compliant to the needs of others*. When *agape* is working in your life, you don't demand that others be like you. Instead, *agape* makes you want to bend over backwards to become what others need you to be for them! Thus, the word "kind" portrays *a willingness to serve and to change in order to meet the needs of others*. This is completely opposite of selfishness and self-centeredness.

So when Paul writes that love is "kind," an expanded interpretation of this phrase would mean:

"...Love doesn't demand others to be like itself; rather, it is so focused on the needs of others that it bends over backwards to become what others need it to be...."

If this is what Paul means when he says that love is kind, we must look into the mirror and ask ourselves: *Do I become what others need me to be, or do I demand that others be like me?* Real *agape* love doesn't think of itself first. Instead, it is always reaching out, thinking and focusing primarily on the needs of others. The person walking in *agape* love adapts to those around him in order to touch them, help them, and impact them in a meaningful way.

Third, Paul tells us that "...charity [*agape* love] envieth not...." The word "envy" is the Greek word *zelos*, which portrays *a person who is radically consumed with his own desires and plans*. This is a person so bent on getting his own way that he is willing to sacrifice anything or anyone to get it. You might describe this person as being ambitious and self-centered. He is so consumed with himself that he doesn't ever think of the needs or desires of others. His own plans are paramount in his mind, and everyone else come after him.

**Therefore, when Paul says, "charity envieth not,"
his words could actually be rendered:**

"...Love is not ambitious, self-centered, or so consumed with itself that it never thinks of the needs or desires that others possess...."

I long so much to see this terrible flaw uprooted from all our lives! You see, real *agape* love doesn't think of itself first but is always looking outward, thinking of the other person rather than itself. So examine your relationships at home, at church, and at work, and ask yourself: *Am I committed to seeing others blessed and successful, or am I more committed to my own cause than anyone else's?* If you're walking in *agape* love, your greatest concern is that *others* succeed!

**When all these Greek words and phrases are translated together,
this could be an expanded interpretive translation:**

"Love passionately bears with others for as long as patience is needed; love doesn't demand others to be like itself, but is so focused on the needs of others that it bends over backwards to become what others need it to be; love is not ambitious, self-centered, or so consumed with itself that it never thinks of the needs or desires that others possess...."

This is what it means when the Bible says love is patient; love is kind; and love is not envious. Now you must look into God's "mirror" and see what it tells you about your own life today. Do you demonstrate these characteristics of divine love in your life? Are you passionately patient with others? Do you bend over backwards to be what other people need you to be? Are you more focused on people around you than on yourself?

If your answer is yes to these questions, then praise God for the great growth and spiritual maturity you have gained in your life. But if you see that your life is *not* reflecting these attributes of God's love, you still have something to rejoice about — you can be thankful that God has revealed this deficiency to you. *Now you can ask Him to help change you and make you more like Jesus!*

MY PRAYER FOR TODAY

Lord, I ask You to help me open my heart so that agape love can flow up from within me. I realize that I've allowed myself to get clogged up with my own self-interests far too often. I need to be more focused on the needs of others than I am on myself. I realize that the only way I can become this selfless is to yield to the Holy Spirit so He can do a deep work in my life. Holy Spirit, I am asking You today to do whatever is necessary to teach me how to regularly walk in this high-level, agape love of God.

I pray this in Jesus' name!

MY CONFESSION FOR TODAY

I confess that I walk in the agape love of God. I am patient with other people. I am also very slow to anger or to get upset. I am so concerned about the welfare of others that one of my chief priorities in life is to become everything I need to be to meet their needs. Other people see me as a friend who wants to help them succeed. Although God has given me my own dreams and desires, I never neglect to help others achieve their dreams and aspirations as well. Because high-level love works in me, I am becoming more and more like Jesus Christ!

I declare this by faith in Jesus' name!

QUESTIONS FOR YOU TO CONSIDER

1. Can you say that you are longsuffering and patient with others, or would you have to admit that you tend to be short-tempered and quick to "blow your top" when other people don't do exactly what you expected them to do?
2. Can you say that you are compliant to the needs of those around you, or would you have to say you are continually demanding that others meet *your* needs? If we asked people who know you this question, how do you think they would answer? What would their answer reveal about you?
3. Can you say that you are more focused on other people's needs and successes than on your own, or are you so totally consumed with yourself that it's been a very long time since you've done something sacrificial to help someone else?

SEPTEMBER 11

Love Vaunts Not Itself, Is Not Puffed Up, And Does Not Behave Itself Unseemly

Charity [*agape* love] suffereth long,
and is kind; charity envieth not;
charity vaunteth not itself, is not puffed up,
Doth not behave itself unseemly....
— 1 Corinthians 13:4,5

When Paul wrote First Corinthians 13:1, he alluded to "super-spiritual" people in Corinth who boasted of great spirituality but who exhibited very little love in their lives. He said they were like a "sounding brass" and a "tinkling cymbal."

As noted earlier (*see* September 9), these particular phrases indicate that these people talked incessantly, annoying and aggravating others with their never-ending, self-consumed chatter. In fact, the words "tinkling cymbal" were the very Greek words used to depict *the clashing of cymbals that announced the onset of a war*. This gives us the impression that the ceaseless talking and bragging of these "super-spirituals" often made their listeners fighting mad!

Could this be the reason Paul makes his fourth point on the characteristics of *agape* by saying that love "...vaunteth not itself..."? The word "vaunteth" has lost its meaning in today's vernacular, but in Greek it is very powerful! This word comes from the Greek word *perpereuomai*, which means *a lot of self-talk*. In other words, it describes *a person who endlessly promotes himself and exaggerates his own virtues*. His self-promotion is so outrageous that he is usually prone to exaggeration that borders on lying. One Greek scholar has said that the word *perpereuomai* pictures *a person who is full of hot air*. Another expositor has said this word refers to a *windbag*!

The word "vaunteth"
is Paul's strong warning to let us know:

"...Love doesn't go around talking about itself all the time, constantly exaggerating and embellishing the facts to make it look more important in the sight of others...."

Even as I write, my thoughts have turned to an individual who fits this description perfectly! f you know anyone like this, you're probably thinking of that person as well, because people like this re such an annoyance that it's hard to ignore or forget them.

Regarding the man I'm thinking of, people who see him coming in their direction immedi-tely begin to look for a way to escape. They know that once this man gets hold of them, he's going o start talking endlessly about himself, his projects, his ideas, and his accomplishments. He boasts o such an extreme degree that it is outright obnoxious. The problem is, he doesn't seem to be aware 1ow full of his "self" he is!

Once a mutual friend asked him, "Why don't you ever ask about anyone else? All you ever talk about is yourself and your own feats. Don't you think it would be good to show at least some inter-st in what others are doing? Do you know how selfish you seem to be to other people?"

The man answered, "Is anyone else besides myself doing anything that is worth talking about? 'm the only one doing anything significant." He was so self-consumed that he couldn't even recog-1ize the fact that there are other hard-working high achievers in the Kingdom of God!

Coming from a terrible, insecure foundation in his own life, this man somehow feels that he must stretch the truth to a ridiculous extreme and brag about his own accomplishments. He has sung his own praises so long that no one close to him wants to hear those songs anymore! His total lack of concern for others and his complete preoccupation with himself have become offensive and dis-gusting to nearly everyone who knows him.

Often people exaggerate and boast endlessly because they have a hidden agenda they want to pro-mote or because they want to gain some higher position or place of authority. Other times they are hop-ing to make the kind of impression that might give them special status or recognition in the eyes of others. Finally, they may just feel driven to prove their worth. Regardless of the reason that people boast about themselves, this kind of behavior does *not* demonstrate the way that *agape* love behaves!

Agape love is so strong, so sure, and so confident that it doesn't need to speak of itself or its accomplishments, even if those accomplishments are greater than anyone else's. Real *agape* love would never flaunt itself in this way; instead, *agape* love wants to focus on the accomplishments of others in order to build them up and make them feel more valuable and secure. Remember, *agape* isn't a self-focused love — it is focused on giving of itself in order to meet other people's needs.

Paul gives the fifth characteristic of *agape* love when he tells us that love "...is not puffed up." These words are based on the Greek word *phusio*, which means *to be proud, to be swollen,* or *to be inflated.* Thus, this word vividly paints the picture of *a person who is filled with pride.*

Paul warns that *agape* is never *phusio.* This means *agape* love is never *deceived into thinking too highly of itself,* nor does it *arrogantly claim that it is better than others.* Making this word even more significant is the fact that the word *phusio* also carries the notion of *a person who has an air of supe-riority and haughtiness* or *a person who is snooty or snobbish in his dealings with other people.*

Paul uses the word *phusio* in First Corinthians 4:6 to denote the *pride* and *arrogance* that was developing between wrangling members of the Corinthian church, each of whom believed that his or her particular leader was more important than other leaders. In First Corinthians 4:19, Paul uses *phusio* again as he warns these believers to change their behavior; otherwise, he will come to rebuke those who are "puffed up." This arrogance involving leadership was the primary source of division, contention, and rivalry in the Corinthian church.

In First Corinthians 5:2, Paul uses the word *phusio* yet again. After boldly confronting the Corinthian church for tolerating a grossly immoral situation among its members, Paul expresses his amazement that they could be "puffed up" in light of the ungodly relationship that was thriving right before their eyes. Then in First Corinthians 8:1 (*NKJV*), Paul uses the word *phusio* when he tells the Corinthians, "...Knowledge puffs up, but love edifies."

**When you consider the Greek meaning
of the words "puffed up," it becomes evident
that Paul was letting us know:**

"...Love does not behave in a prideful, arrogant, haughty, superior, snooty, snobbish, or clannish manner."

After Paul tells us that love is not puffed up, he proceeds to give us his sixth point. He writes that love "doth not behave itself unseemly...."

The Greek word for "unseemly" is *aschemoneo*, an old word that means *to act in an unbecoming manner*. It suggests *a person who is tactless or thoughtless*. It also expresses the notion of *a person who is careless and inconsiderate of others*. Both his actions and words tend to be *rude* and *discourteous*, and he exhibits *bad manners* in the way he deals with people. His language is *harsh* and *brutal*, revealing that this person is *uncaring, insensitive,* and *unkind*. In short, we would say that this is a person who "acts *ugly*."

**Because of the word "unseemly"
in First Corinthians 13:5,
it explicitly means that the Holy Spirit is telling us:**

"Love is not rude and discourteous — it is not careless or thoughtless, nor does it carry on in a fashion that would be considered insensitive to others...."

So how do you fare when you look into the mirror of God's Word today? Do you pass the love test, or have you come up short again? If you see that you have fallen short of the high-level love God wants you to possess and exhibit in your life, it's time for you to go back to the Lord and talk to Him about it again! Never stop going to Him until you know that you are walking continually in the high-level love He wants you to demonstrate in your life!

**When all these Greek words and phrases
are translated together,
an expanded interpretive translation could be as follows:**

"...Love doesn't go around talking about itself all the time, constantly exaggerating and embellishing the facts to make it look more important in the sight of others; love does not behave in a prideful, arrogant, haughty, superior, snooty, snobbish, or clannish manner; love is not rude and discourteous — it is not careless or thoughtless, nor does it carry on in a fashion that would be considered insensitive to others...."

Is the Holy Spirit speaking to your heart? Is He showing you areas where you have:

✦ Exaggerated the truth to make yourself look better to others?
✦ Acted in a prideful, haughty, snooty, snobbish, or clannish manner?
✦ Permitted yourself to act in a way that is not acceptable for someone who is striving toward excellence in God?

If the answer is yes to any of these questions, it's time for you to take immediate action! You need to spend some quality time with Jesus. Ask Him to forgive you, and let His blood cleanse you; then ask the Holy Spirit to start the process of transforming you into the image of Jesus. *Don't stop until you think, see, and act like Jesus Christ — every moment of every day!*

MY PRAYER FOR TODAY

Lord, I ask You to help me live my life in a way that glorifies You. You are my Lord, and I am Your servant and child. I don't want to do anything with my life that brings disrespect or dishonor to Your precious name! Help me to not exaggerate or embellish the truth. I ask You to correct me when I am lured into snobbery or pride and to lovingly rebuke me when I "act ugly" toward others. I want to be like You, Jesus, and I'm not going to stop pressing ahead until I demonstrate Your life and Your nature in my life!

I pray this in Jesus' name!

MY CONFESSION FOR TODAY

I confess that I am never going to stop until I have attained the high level of love Jesus wants me to have in my life! I don't go around talking about myself all the time, constantly exaggerating and embellishing the facts. I don't behave in a prideful, arrogant, haughty, superior, snooty, snobbish, or clannish manner. I'm not rude and discourteous. I'm not careless or thoughtless. As I spend time with Jesus, I am being changed into His image — and I demonstrate His life and His nature to other people!

I declare this by faith in Jesus' name!

QUESTIONS FOR YOU TO CONSIDER

1. Have you been guilty of exaggerating or embellishing the truth to make yourself look better in front of other people? Would you feel comfortable telling those same stories if you were face-to-face with Jesus?
2. Have you ever been guilty of acting in a snobbish or clannish manner? Are you and your friends so tight that others might view your group as an exclusive little clique?
3. Have you been acting in a fashion that glorifies the name of Jesus? Or are there certain ways you behave that are too "ugly" to be representative of Jesus?

Agape love is so strong, so sure, and so confident that it doesn't need to speak of itself or its accomplishments, even if those accomplishments are greater than anyone else's. Real *agape* love would never flaunt itself in this way; instead, *agape* love wants to focus on the accomplishments of others in order to build them up and make them feel more valuable and secure.

SEPTEMBER 12

Love Seeks Not Its Own,
Is Not Easily Provoked, Thinks No Evil

Charity [*agape* love] suffereth long, and is kind;
charity envieth not; charity vaunteth not itself, is not puffed up,
Doth not behave itself unseemly, seeketh not her own,
is not easily provoked, thinketh no evil.
— 1 Corinthians 13:4,5

*I*n First Corinthians 13:5, Paul continues his message about the *agape* love of God. The seventh characteristic he gives us is that this high-level love "…seeketh not her own…."

The word "seeketh" is the Greek word *zeteo*, which means *to seek*. However, it was also used to depict *a person who is so upset about not getting what he wanted that he turns to the court system to sue or to demand what he is striving to obtain*. Instead of taking no for an answer, this person is so intent on getting his own way that he will search, seek, and investigate, never giving up in his pursuit to get what he wants. In fact, he's so bent on getting his way that he'll twist the facts; look for loopholes; put words in other people's mouths; try to hold others accountable for promises they never made; leap on administrative mistakes as opportunities to twist someone's arm; or seek various other methods to turn situations to his benefit. This is *manipulation*!

There is no doubt that Paul had the image of a manipulating, scheming person in his mind when he wrote this verse. Have you ever met such a person? Have you ever encountered a man or woman who schemed and manipulated all the time to get what he or she wanted?

The point Paul makes here is that love is not scheming or manipulating, for this kind of behavior is dishonest and untruthful. Scheming and manipulating to get your own way is simply wrong! If you can't honestly state what you think or what you want, then don't say or do anything. Speaking half-truths and white lies or operating according to a secret agenda is not the way that *agape* love behaves.

The Greek words in this text
could be understood to mean:

"…Love does not manipulate situations or scheme and devise methods that will twist situations to its own advantage…."

After making this point, Paul then lists the eighth characteristic of *agape* love. He tells us that love "…is not easily provoked…."

The word "easily" does not appear in the original Greek, but it was later supplied by the King James translators. Some scholars have asserted it was injected into the *King James Version* because the translators of the day wanted to make a certain point to King James, who was famous for losing his temper and flying off the handle!

The Greek text has the word *paroxsuno* for the word "provoked." It is a compound of *para*, meaning *alongside*, and *oxsus*, which means *to poke, to prick, or to stick, as with a sharpened instrument*. When compounded together, the new word portrays *someone who comes alongside another and then begins to poke, prick, or stick that other person with some type of sharpened instrument.* He continues to pick, poke, and stick until the victim becomes *provoked.* He's finally had enough of this person's relentless actions of picking, poking, and sticking, so he responds by violently and aggressively assaulting the offender. *The result is a fight — a conflict of the most serious order.*

We find the word *paroxsunos* used in this way in Acts 15:39, where Luke records information about a conflict that transpired between Paul and Barnabas. Barnabas wanted to take John Mark on the next journey, but Paul was against it because John Mark had already proven himself unfaithful on an earlier trip. As they debated the issue, the words they exchanged must have been very sharp. This is why Luke wrote, "And the contention was so sharp between them...."

This is a translation of the word *paroxsuno,* letting us know that Paul and Barnabas came alongside each other in close debate and then began to poke, stick, prick, and jab each other with their words. The Greek language leaves no doubt that the conversation that ensued was *extremely hot.* In fact, this *provocation* was so severe that it disrupted their friendship and destroyed their partnership in ministry.

The word *oxsus* is also the Greek word for *vinegar.* I especially find this interesting because the word *oxsus* is the exact word for "vinegar" in the Russian language. The fact that this is the word for *vinegar* lets us know that the words Paul and Barnabas spoke to each other were *stringent, sharp, severe, sour, tart, bitter,* and *acidy.* These words were so bitter that it left a sour taste in their mouths and their memories. As a result of these harsh words, these two men who had served God together in the ministry separated: "...Barnabas took Mark, and sailed unto Cyprus; and Paul chose Silas, and departed..." (Acts 15:39,40).

I'm sure Paul remembers this experience very well as he warns believers everywhere that love is "...not easily provoked...." He speaks by experience when he tells us that this is not the behavior of love. Having reaped the consequences of losing his temper and saying regrettable, acidy words in a moment of conflict, Paul warns us that *agape* love does not behave in this fashion.

An interpretive translation of Paul's words
in First Corinthians 13:5 could read this way:

"...Love does not deliberately engage in actions or speak words that are so sharp, they cause an ugly or violent response...."

Then Paul lists his ninth point about love, telling us that *agape* love "...thinketh no evil." The Greek word for "thinketh" is *logidzomai,* which was an accounting term that would be better translated *to count* or *to reckon.* It literally meant *to credit to someone's account.*

Before us is the image of a bookkeeper who meticulously keeps accurate financial records. But in this case, the bookkeeper is an offended person who keeps detailed records of every wrong that was ever done to him. Just as a bookkeeper has an entry for every debit and credit on the books, this person painstakingly stores in his memory all the mistakes, faults, grievances, disappointments, failures, or perceived wrongdoings that someone has made against him. Rather than forgive and let it go, the offended person has carefully maintained records of each action done to him that he deemed unjust or unfair.

This is certainly not the way love behaves! If you want to know how love behaves, look at the behavior of God toward you. Although God could drag up your past before you all the time, He doesn't do that! In fact, after He forgave you (Psalm 103:3), God decided He wouldn't deal with you according to your sins or reward you according to your iniquities (Psalm 103:10). Although He *could* remember your past mistakes if He chose to do so, God *doesn't* and *never will* choose to remember them.

Psalm 103:12 says, "As far as the east is from the west, so far hath he removed our transgressions from us." This means that God doesn't keep records of your past forgiven sins! Once they are under the blood of Jesus, God separates them from you forever.

You see, that is how real *agape* love behaves. So if you are ever tempted to keep mental records of wrongs someone has done to you, be aware that you're not giving to that person the same mercy God has given to you. Someone who has been forgiven as much as you have been forgiven has no right to keep a record of someone else's mistakes!

Paul's words "thinketh no evil" should actually be translated:

"…Love does not deliberately keep records of wrongs or past mistakes."

Is there anyone you are holding hostage in your mind because of what you deemed to be an inappropriate action taken against you? If that person did wrong, it's right for you to confront him in love. But once you have dealt with the matter, you need to release the offense and let it go — just as Jesus has released you from your past and is believing that you are now on the right track!

If you have a hard time releasing people from their past wrongs, it's a sign that you need *agape* to be released in your life. The fact that you're flipping back to that old record of wrongs again and again — bringing up past grievances that should have been forgiven and forgotten — means you are not perfected in love! Throw that diary away! *Didn't God throw away His diary about YOUR past?*

When all these Greek words and phrases are translated together, an expanded interpretive translation could read:

"…Love doesn't manipulate situations or scheme and devise methods that will twist situations to its own advantage; love does not deliberately engage in actions or speak words that are so sharp, they cause an ugly or violent response; love doesn't deliberately keep records of wrongs or past mistakes."

Well, how do you feel after looking into the mirror of First Corinthians 13:4-8 today? There are three more days to go as we delve deeply into the precious, Spirit-anointed words in this passage of Scripture. Don't rush through these particular *Sparkling Gems*. As you read them, take the time to carefully digest them; take them deep into your heart and soul. God wants to change you, but before you can change, you must first recognize what needs to be fixed!

If God is speaking to your heart, don't rush from this quiet time with Him too quickly. *Stop everything you are doing, and make it your most important matter of business to get your heart right first with the Lord and then with others!*

MY PRAYER FOR TODAY

Lord, I ask You to help me put an end to any scheming or manipulating tendencies that still reside in my soul. I know that this is very grievous to You and damaging to my relationships. I repent for participating in this evil behavior, and I ask You to help me be honest in all my dealings with other people. Help me to curb my anger, hold my tongue, and refrain from speaking words that bring harm. Thank You for forgiving me for past sins. Today I am making a decision to wipe the slate clean regarding anyone who has ever acted unjustly or unfairly with me.

I pray this in Jesus' name!

QUESTIONS FOR YOU TO CONSIDER

1. Have you ever been guilty of manipulating situations or scheming behind the scenes to get what you wanted? When you were doing it, was your heart grieved because you knew what you were doing was displeasing to the Lord?
2. Have you ever spoken words that were so ugly, they resulted in harming a precious relationship? Were you afterward sorry that you didn't control your temper? If you have damaged a relationship due to bad words, why don't you lay down your pride and go ask that person to forgive you?
3. Have you forgiven those who have done wrong to you in the past, or do you still hold them hostage in your mind? Have you kept a record of their offenses so you can replay them over and over again in your mind, or can you honestly say that you have forgiven them and have no ill feelings toward them?

SEPTEMBER 13

Love Rejoices Not With Iniquity, But Rejoices With the Truth

Charity [*agape* love] suffereth long, and is kind;
charity envieth not; charity vaunteth not itself, is not puffed up,
Doth not behave itself unseemly, seeketh not her own,
is not easily provoked, thinketh no evil;
Rejoiceth not in iniquity, but rejoiceth in the truth.
— 1 Corinthians 13:4-6

*H*ave you ever secretly rejoiced when you heard that someone you didn't like or someone you disapproved of had gotten into some kind of trouble? Upon hearing of that person's difficulty or hardship, perhaps you were tempted to think, *Serves him right! He deserves what he's getting! After what he did to me and to so many others, he deserves a little punishment!* If this describes you, let me tell you — this is *not* the way God's love reacts to such situations!

There was once a man who seriously wronged our organization. What he did was so wrong that if the events concerning him had occurred in a Western nation, he would have been judged in a court of law and sentenced to prison for his actions. But because it was not in a Western nation and many complications existed in this case, all my wife and I could do was let it go and pray for God to deal with this individual. We knew if he didn't repent, he would come under severe judgment.

In the years since that event occurred, this man has come into many miserable hardships in his life. His children fell into terrible sin; he lost everything financially; and his reputation became stained because of the many things he had done to a whole host of people. When I first met this man, he went to church and had a ministry; the touch of God was on his life. But he became a mess of a man — one of the saddest stories I have ever personally known.

When this individual first began to fall into trouble, I found myself privately wanting to rejoice that judgment had finally come his way. Then the Holy Spirit convicted my heart, and I realized that rejoicing in this man's trouble was not the way the love of God behaves. After allowing the Spirit of God to deal with my heart, I began to inwardly mourn over the condition of this man who had once been so mightily used by God.

In First Corinthians 13:6, Paul wrote that love "...rejoiceth not in iniquity, but rejoiceth in the truth." The phrase "rejoiceth not" comes from the Greek phrase *ou chairei*. The word *ou* means *no* or *not*, and the word *chairei* is from the word *chairo*, which is the Greek word for *joy*. It carries the idea of *being glad about something*. It is the picture of a person who is *euphoric* over something that has happened. Other words to describe *chairo* would be *overjoyed, elated, ecstatic, exhilarated, thrilled, jubilant,* or even *rapturous*. The word "iniquity" is the Greek word *adikos*, which conveys the idea of an *injustice* or *something that is wrong or bad*.

**The entire phrase *ou chairei*
could be translated in the following way:**

"Love does not feel overjoyed when it sees an injustice done to someone else...."

My secret desire to rejoice at this other individual's hardships was completely contrary to the love nature of God. Even though this man had done wrong to me and to many others in the Christian community, the right response was to pray for his restoration. Real love simply doesn't rejoice at someone else's misfortunes.

Then Paul goes on to tell us that when someone else gains some kind of advantage in life that we have been desiring, love isn't threatened by that person's success but rather rejoices with his victory! The word "rejoice" is again the Greek word *chairo*, the same word used above.

**This means the second part of this verse
could be translated:**

"...Love is elated, thrilled, ecstatic, and overjoyed with the truth."

When you see other people blessed — perhaps receiving a blessing or special attention that you have longed to receive yourself — are you able to truly rejoice with them? Does it thrill you to know that other people are moving upward in life? Or does it threaten you and make you sad when you see someone else receiving a blessing you wished was yours?

How you respond to other people's troubles and blessings reveals a great deal about your true level of spiritual maturity. So ask yourself:

✦ *Do I rejoice when I hear bad news about someone who did me wrong in the past? Or does it break my heart to hear about the problems that person is facing?*

✦ *When someone steps into the blessing I've been believing for in my own life, am I elated for that person, or does it make me turn green with envy?*

It's good to ask yourself these questions and to let the Holy Spirit deal with your heart about these issues. *Why don't you take a little time today to let God's Spirit search your heart and show you if you can improve in these areas of love in your life?*

MY PRAYER FOR TODAY

Lord, I ask You to help me overcome those fleshy moments when I am tempted to rejoice at someone else's hardships. I must admit that when I hear something has happened to a person who wronged me, something inside me secretly rejoices. I know that this is wrong and that it is not the way You behave. Please forgive me for responding in a way that is contrary to love. Help me to be concerned and prayerful for every person who is undergoing any kind of hardship in life — even those who have acted like they are my enemies.

I pray this in Jesus' name!

MY CONFESSION FOR TODAY

I confess that I am blessed when I see someone else receiving a blessing or special attention. It thrills me when I see other people moving upward in life. Even when someone steps into the blessing I've been believing for in my own life, I am elated for them!

I declare this by faith in Jesus' name!

QUESTIONS FOR YOU TO CONSIDER

1. When you see other people receiving a blessing or special attention that you long for yourself, are you able to really rejoice with them? Does it thrill you to know that other people are moving upward in life?
2. Would you have to honestly say that it upsets you and makes you sad when you see someone else receiving a blessing that you wished was yours?
3. Do you rejoice when you hear bad news about someone who did you wrong in the past, or does it break your heart to hear about the problems he or she is facing?

Have you ever secretly rejoiced when you heard that someone you didn't like or someone you disapproved of had gotten into some kind of trouble? Upon hearing of that person's hardship, perhaps you were tempted to think, *Serves him right! He deserves what he's getting! After what he did to me and to so many others, he deserves a little punishment!* If this describes you, let me tell you — this is *not* the way God's love reacts to such situations!

SEPTEMBER 14

Love Bears All Things, Believes All Things, Hopes All Things, Endures All Things

Charity [*agape* love] suffereth long, and is kind;
charity envieth not; charity vaunteth not itself, is not puffed up,
Doth not behave itself unseemly, seeketh not her own,
is not easily provoked, thinketh no evil;
Rejoiceth not in iniquity, but rejoiceth in the truth;
Beareth all things, believeth all things,
hopeth all things, endureth all things.
— 1 Corinthians 13:4-7

*A*s Paul continues giving us the characteristics of *agape* love in First Corinthians 13, he move to the next four points in his message. He explains to the Corinthians (and to us) that gen uine *agape* love "beareth all things, believeth all things, hopeth all things, endureth all things" (v. 7).

The eleventh point that Paul makes in this wonderful text is that love "beareth all things...." The word "beareth" is the Greek word *stego*, which means *to cover*, as a roof covers a house. Buil within the word *stego* is the concept of *protection*, exactly as a roof *protects, shields,* and *guards* the inhabitants of a house from exposure to the outside influences of weather. The roof of a house i designed to shield people from storms, hurricanes, tornadoes, rain, hail, snow, wind, blistering ho temperatures, and so on. This protection is vital for survival in most climates, preventing peopl from either freezing to death or burning as a result of continual exposure to sunlight.

By using this word *stego* ("bear"), the apostle Paul is giving us a powerful illustration. First, w must understand that there are many different seasons to life, and not all seasons are pleasurable. I fact, some seasons of life are very stormy and difficult. There are moments when external circum stances assail us from without. If we have no shield to guard us during these stormy times, it become much more difficult for us to survive spiritually.

Paul lets you know that *agape* serves like a protection for you. Like the roof of a house, a frienc who moves in the *agape* love of God will stay near in times of trouble. That friend will hover ove you to protect you from the storms of life. Rather than expose you and your flaws to the view of oth ers, a person who operates in this kind of love will *conceal, cover,* and *protect* you, for real *agape* love is always there in times of trouble to lend support.

The phrase "beareth all things" could be translated:

"Love protects, shields, guards, covers, conceals, and safeguards people from exposure...."

Paul goes on to mention the twelfth characteristic of *agape* love, saying that love "...believeth all things...." The word "believeth" is actually the word *pisteuei*, which is the Greek word meaning *to put one's faith or trust in something or someone.* The tense used in the Greek text lets us know tha this is a constant, continuous entrusting of one's faith in something or someone — involving "never-give-up" kind of belief that something will turn out the very best. In light of this, the Gree phrase could actually be taken to mean that love "believes the best in every situation."

Don't misunderstand; *agape* love isn't stupid, nor is it blind. It sees everything — the good, the bad, and the ugly. But because *agape* is so filled with faith, it pushes the disconcerting, disturbing, negative realities out of the way. This doesn't mean *agape* ignores problems or challenges. It just makes a choice to see beyond the problems and conflicts, to strain forward to see the highest potential that resides in every person.

Let's apply this to your children. Perhaps it is true that they are having problems right now or that they have done some things in the past they shouldn't have done. But there is still hope! Today is a new day, and *agape* simply cannot give up believing that they will turn around! Although the past may have been filled with troubled times, the future is bright for those who believe God! Therefore, *agape* continually presses ahead full of faith — reaching forward by faith to see the other person whole, sound, healed, saved, redeemed, and right in the middle of God's will for his or her life.

You see, the *agape* love of God just doesn't know how to quit! It hangs on even when the going gets tough! It just keeps believing the very best, no matter what.

So I urge you to take a good, honest look at yourself to see if you are operating in this kind of high-level love. Do you strain forward to believe the best, or do you pick people apart and point out all their flaws and weaknesses? Do you see their potential through the eyes of love, or do you look on them through eyes of criticism? *Never forget that love believes the best!*

The phrase "believeth all things" could be translated:

"…Love strains forward with all its might to believe the very best in every situation…."

Paul gives us his thirteenth point about love when he says that love "…hopeth all things…." The Greek word for "hopeth" is the word *elpidzo*, which depicts not only *a hope*, but *an expectation of good things*. This means that rather than assuming failure or a bad result in someone's life, the *agape* love of God always expects the best in someone else. It not only expects it, but it is filled with an *anticipation* to see the manifestation of the thing hoped for.

The phrase "hopeth all things" could be taken to mean:

"…Love always expects and anticipates the best in others and the best for others…."

Next, Paul mentions the fourteenth characteristic of *agape* love, telling us that love "…endureth all things." The word "endureth" is the Greek word *hupomeno*, which we have discussed several times before. It is the word *hupo*, which means *under*, and the word *meno*, which *means to stay* or *to abide*. Compounded together, it depicts the attitude of *a person who is under a heavy load but refuses to surrender to defeat because he knows he is in his place*. Because this person knows he is where he's supposed to be, he has therefore decided that regardless of what tries to come against him, he is going to *stay put* and *refuse to move*!

This means *agape* never quits or throws in the towel. It simply doesn't know how to quit. Real *agape* says, "I'm committed to be here — to stay with you and to work it out, regardless of the cost or the time involved. I am not quitting. I am here to stay!"

You see, that is what the Bible means when it says love "…endureth all things." This kind of love is completely contrary to the flesh, which says, "I've done all I'm going to do. I'm not wasting any more of my life. I'm finished, and I'm leaving!"

A contemporary translation of the phrase "endureth all things" could be the following:

"…Love never quits, never surrenders, and never gives up."

As you look into the mirror of God's Word and examine the characteristics of *agape* love, can you say that this kind of love is operating in your life? Would others say that you have been a "roof" for them — protecting, covering, concealing, and guarding them during the hard and difficult seasons of life? Would others say you believe the best about people, or that you tend to be nit-picky and critical of others? Have you made the decision to "stick it out," regardless of how long it takes?

When all of these Greek words and phrases
are translated together,
an expanded interpretive translation could read:

"Love protects, shields, guards, covers, conceals, and safeguards people from exposure; love strains forward with all its might to believe the very best in every situation; love always expects and anticipates the best in others and the best for others; love never quits, never surrenders, and never gives up."

Today I want to encourage you to do the right thing by determining to learn to operate in this high-level *agape* love of God. This divine love is already shed abroad in your heart by the Holy Spirit, so now it's up to you to open up your heart and let this divine river of love flow forth from you to others.

Are you going to open your heart and let God's love spill out to those around you? *The choice is now before you!*

MY PRAYER FOR TODAY

Lord, I ask You to help me learn to operate in this supernatural, life-changing, high-level love. Please help me to quit judging others for the problems in their lives and to start thinking about how I can protect and cover them in times of difficulty. Holy Spirit, please help me believe the best about them. I also ask You for the strength to remain committed — to stick by their side until the victory has been won and they have become everything You intended for them to be! I am anticipating a new surge of Your power and strength right now to help me get started on this path, and I'll keep believing and confidently expecting until I see the results in my life that I know You want!

I pray this in Jesus' name!

MY CONFESSION FOR TODAY

I confess that God's love operates mightily in my life! Because I walk in agape love, I protect, shield, guard, cover, conceal, and safeguard people from exposure. The love of God in my heart compels me to strain forward with all my might to believe the very best in every situation and the best about every person. This love of God that has been shed abroad in my heart never quits, never surrenders, and never gives up on other people. I bear all things, believe all things, hope all things, and endure all things!

I declare this by faith in Jesus' name!

QUESTIONS FOR YOU TO CONSIDER

1. Have others believed the best about you in the past, even though you didn't give them much reason to hope for a turn around in your life?

2. Has anyone ever been a "roof" to you — protecting, concealing, and covering you in a time of weakness? What did this mean to you? Have you ever gone to that person and thanked him or her for being such a help in your time of need?

3. Who is the one person in your life right now whom you are believing will make a big change in his or her life? How much time do you spend praying for this person every day?

SEPTEMBER 15

Love Never Fails!

Charity [*agape* love] suffereth long, and is kind;
charity envieth not; charity vaunteth not itself, is not puffed up,
Doth not behave itself unseemly, seeketh not her own,
is not easily provoked, thinketh no evil;
Rejoiceth not in iniquity, but rejoiceth in the truth;
Beareth all things, believeth all things,
hopeth all things, endureth all things.
Charity never faileth....
— 1 Corinthians 13:4-8

*I*n today's *Sparkling Gem*, we come to the end of our study of First Corinthians 13:4-8, where Paul describes the behavior of the love of God. As Paul comes to the conclusion of his fabulous text about the *agape* love of God, he concludes powerfully in verse 8 by affirming that love "...never faileth...."

The word "faileth" is the Greek word *pipto*, a word that dates back to classical Greece and generally means *to fall from a high position*. It was also used on rare occasions to depict *a warrior who fell in battle*. In many places the word *pipto* is used to depict *falling into ruin, into destruction, into some kind of misfortune, or into disappointment*. In First Corinthians 13:8, Paul uses this word to affirm the eternal truth that love never *disappoints* or *fails*.

It is simply the truth that human beings often fail each other. I'm sure you have felt let down by someone else at some point along the way. And if you're honest about your own dealings with others, you'll have to admit that you have been guilty of letting others down as well. But *agape* love — God's love — never disappoints, never fails, and never lets anyone down. It is a love that can always be depended on and is always reliable.

People you know and respect may occasionally fall from the high position they hold in life — and that can be an emotionally difficult experience for you when you see it happen. Other times, fellow warriors may fall in battle or stumble into some kind of misfortune that disappoints you, and that is painful as well.

But you can be sure that the *agape* love of God will never fail you or let you down. This love is constant, unchanging, and unbendable. It is a love you will always find to be reliable and true — a love on which you can depend.

God wants you to learn to function in His high-level *agape* love, which is why the Holy Spirit so carefully inspired the apostle Paul to write these famous words in First Corinthians 13:4-8. This passage of Scripture is God's mirror, designed for us to look into so we can see how well we fare at walking in the *agape* love of God.

I have compiled all the words, phrases, and translations we have been studying and placed them here as one complete text for you to read. Take a few minutes to read this text slowly; then ask yourself, *Do I pass the love test? Or does this reveal that I need to mature more in this part of my life?*

The following is an expanded interpretive translation of First Corinthians 13:4-8:

"Love patiently and passionately bears with others for as long as patience is needed;
Love doesn't demand others to be like itself; rather, it is so focused on the needs of others that it bends over backwards to become what others need it to be;
Love is not ambitious, self-centered, or so consumed with itself that it never thinks of the needs or desires that others possess;
Love doesn't go around talking about itself all the time, constantly exaggerating and embellishing the facts to make it look more important in the sight of others;
Love does not behave in a prideful, arrogant, haughty, superior, snooty, snobbish, or clannish manner;
Love is not rude and discourteous — it is not careless or thoughtless, nor does it carry on in a fashion that would be considered insensitive to others;
Love does not manipulate situations or scheme and devise methods that will twist situations to its own advantage;
Love does not deliberately engage in actions or speak words that are so sharp, they cause an ugly or violent response;
Love does not deliberately keep records of wrongs or past mistakes;
Love does not feel overjoyed when it sees an injustice done to someone else but is elated, thrilled, ecstatic, and overjoyed with the truth;
Love protects, shields, guards, covers, conceals, and safeguards people from exposure;
Love strains forward with all its might to believe the very best in every situation;
Love always expects and anticipates the best in others and the best for others;
Love never quits, never surrenders, and never gives up;
Love never disappoints, never fails, and never lets anyone down."

So after pondering these verses, what is your answer? Are you walking in this kind of love? Have you achieved the level of love that God wants you to have in your life? Do you manifest this type of love to others who are around you? Or do you now see that you still have areas in your life where you need to grow, develop, and change in regard to walking in love?

I plead with you to spend time in prayer about this issue of God's love in your life. How you relate to others, love others, and impact others is the most important question in your life. Since this is such a vital issue, don't you think it's worth your time to get into the Presence of the Lord and ask Him to reveal those areas in your love walk that need to be improved?

MY PRAYER FOR TODAY

Lord, I want to be the embodiment of Your love. I know that I fall very short of the agape love that You desire to see operating in my life. Therefore, I am asking You to help me move upward to the highest level of love so I can be a channel through which this love can be poured out to others whom I know and meet. Just as You have loved me, help me become a life-changing source of divine love to other people.

I pray this in Jesus' name!

MY CONFESSION FOR TODAY

I confess that God's love dwells in me. It flows from my heart to all those around me. People who are close to me are changed and transformed by this love that operates so mightily in me. When others see me, they think of the love of God, for it is demonstrated continually in my life.

I declare this by faith in Jesus' name!

QUESTIONS FOR YOU TO CONSIDER

1. After studying First Corinthians 13:4-8, what have you learned about yourself and the areas where you need to improve in regard to walking in love?
2. Which characteristics of *agape* love do you feel you are growing in and gaining territory? What is the proof on which you base your belief that you have achieved maturity in these areas of your love walk?
3. If Jesus were standing before you right now to examine your life, what would He say about how you walk in love toward others? What would other people in your life say about how well you walk in love toward them?

SEPTEMBER 16

I Am in a Strait Betwixt Two

For I am in a strait betwixt two, having a desire to depart,
and to be with Christ; which is far better:
Nevertheless to abide in the flesh
is more needful for you.
And having this confidence,
I know that I shall abide and continue with you
all for your furtherance and joy of faith.
— Philippians 1:23-25

Have you ever been so exhausted from the never-ending problems of life that the thought of dying and going to Heaven sounded like a wonderful dream? Maybe you imagined what it would be like to close your eyes, fall asleep, and wake up in the Presence of the Lord, never to awake again in this world. Have you ever had a moment when such thoughts seemed so wonderful that you wished the Lord would immediately call you home to Heaven?

Judging from Paul's letter to the Philippians, we can see that his heart was being heavily tugged toward Heaven while he was a prisoner in Rome. Paul was tired. He had already done more than anyone else could claim to have accomplished. He had suffered endlessly for his ministry. It would have been very easy for Paul to say, "Lord, I'm tired. I've done enough. I'm ready to go to Heaven. Please take me home!"

When Paul wrote to the Philippians, he made it very clear that the temptation to leave life and to join the Lord was before him. His choice of words in Philippians 1:23-25 make it very evident that a choice was before him: to continue in the flesh so he could completely fulfill his ministry to the saints, or to depart this life and to be with the Lord. After thinking through these options, Paul made the choice to abide in the flesh and to continue his ministry a little longer.

Paul tells us about the inward struggle he felt as he decided whether to keep living or to die and join the Lord in Philippians 1:23. He writes, "For I am in a strait betwixt two, having a desire to depart, and to be with Christ; which is far better."

When Paul writes that he is in a "strait betwixt two," he uses the Greek word *sunecho*, which expresses the idea of *a pressure being applied to a person from two different directions*. This is a force that pulls a person first one way and then another, as if his arms are being pulled in two different directions by opponents in a fierce tug-of-war contest. However, the Greek word indicates that the person in the middle is the one who has the deciding vote as to who will win this tug-of-war.

Paul felt two different forces pulling at his heart. On the one side, he was pulled "...to depart, and to be with Christ...." On the other side, he was pulled "...to abide in the flesh..." a little longer in order to help other people and to totally fulfill the part of his calling that remained undone.

The strength of the pull toward Heaven is evident in Paul's words in verse 23, where he writes that he has a "desire to depart." The word "desire" is the Greek word *epithumia*, which is a compound of the words *epi* and *thumos*. The word *epi* means *for* or *over*, and *thumos* is the Greek word for a *strong passion* or *urge*. It usually denotes a *swelling or growing emotion*. But when the word *thumos* is compounded together with the word *epi*, forming the word *epithumia*, it depicts *a person who is excited about something*. This person is *passionate* about this idea; he is *consumed* with this thought! Because Paul uses this word, it emphatically lets us know that the prospect of departing from this world and going to Heaven to be with the Lord was a *thrilling* and *exciting* thought to Paul!

When Paul thought of death, he didn't even think of *dying* as we think of it. Instead of thinking of the cessation of life, he looked upon death as nothing more than a *departure* that signaled the beginning of the next part of his journey in eternity. The word "depart" is the Greek word *analusai*, a Greek word which pictures *a ship that is being loosed from its moorings so it can finally be free to sail*.

No wonder Paul was excited! When he thought of death, to him it meant being set free from the human limitations and physical restrictions that had been imposed on him in this earthly life. The prospect of being set free was a glorious thought to Paul. Once liberated from this realm, he knew he would really be able to set sail in the Spirit and soar to spiritual heights he had never before attained. To Paul, death was not the end. It was an exciting beginning, the next leg of his journey — a phase of his walk with God that he was excited and enthusiastic to experience!

But wait — there's more to this word *analusai* ("to depart") that is very important to this text. The word *analusai* was also a military word, used when *a decision was made that it was time for an army to break camp, pack up their tents, pick up their gear, gather up all their other belongings, and move onward to conquer new territory*. This gives us another view of the way Paul viewed the prospect of death.

As a soldier who had fought many battles on earth, Paul was ready to break camp and to move upward into new spiritual territory. He had fought long and hard, and the expectation of moving onward to heavenly territory was a thought that captured his heart, his mind, and his imagination. Paul's "desire to depart" and to be with Christ was so strong that he felt as if he were in a "strait betwixt two." He was pulled on one side to depart from this earthly realm and to be with Christ. But he was also pulled from the other side to abide in the flesh a little longer.

You see, Paul knew that part of his ministry remained unfinished. If he left at this time, the entirety of his vision would not be fulfilled. So although he was "pulled" to set sail, to break camp, and to move onward to be with the Lord, he could not allow himself to do that yet, because he knew there was still work for him to do for the Kingdom. That is why he wrote in verse 24, "Nevertheless to abide in the flesh is more needful for you."

Although Paul would have loved to enter the heavenly realm, it wasn't yet time, for he had more to accomplish before he finished his race. Therefore, he wrote that he had made a decision to continue a little longer in the flesh. Although it seems Paul actually could have chosen to let his life slip away, he chose instead to press onward to fulfill his call and to take others higher with him.

In Philippians 3:14, he wrote, "I press toward the mark for the prize of the high calling of God in Christ Jesus." The words "press toward" are from the Greek word *epekteinomai*, a word that pictures *a foot racer*. It is the image of a racer who is pressing forward so hard and is so stretched out that his entire body is arching forward as his arms reach ahead to grasp the goal before him.

The word "mark" is the Greek word *skopos*, which describes the *finish line* for a runner. Like a runner, Paul was straining toward the finish line. At that time in his life, he was on his last run around the track before the race concluded. Rather than slowing down, taking it easy, or resting, he had chosen to put forth all his efforts and push harder than ever before so he could finish *first*, knowing that he had given his very best to the very end of his life.

Paul then wrote that he was pressing toward the "prize." The word "prize" is the Greek word *brabeion*, describing the *rewards given to those who won their competitions in the public games*. This means Paul had his reward on his mind. When it was finally time for him to depart to be with Christ, there would be a reward waiting for him. With this in mind, Paul chose to shove all obstacles and hindrances out of the way and to strain forward as he ran around the track for the final period of time in his life!

How does all of this apply to you today? When you are exhausted from the never-ending problems of life and the thought of dying or going to Heaven sounds like a welcome relief, stop to ask yourself:

✦ *Have I done everything God has asked me to do?*
✦ *Can I say that I have run my race and finished it all the way to the finish line?*
✦ *Are there others who are depending on me and who still need me?*

If your answers to these questions reveal that your job is undone and that others are still depending on you, then it's not time for you to go! One day you can set sail and soar out into eternity. There is a day coming in your life when you will break camp from this earthly realm and move onward to heavenly territory. But that day isn't now. Instead, you need to grab hold of the power of God and run fiercely to finish the race that is still left undone and that is before you. *Don't stop running your race until you know you have done EVERYTHING Jesus has asked you to do.*

So pull yourself together. Muster your strength. Draw upon the power of the Holy Spirit. Get ready, get set, and start running your race — and keep running until you can say without any doubt that you have finished your course! *Until you can say that with confidence, you need to quit thinking about Heaven and start thinking about how to run your race to the end!*

When Paul thought of death, he didn't even think of *dying* as we think of it. Instead of thinking of the cessation of life, he looked upon death as nothing more than a *departure* that signaled the beginning of the next part of his journey in eternity.

SEPTEMBER 17

꧁꧂

Do You Know People Who Talk Out of Both Sides of Their Mouths?

Likewise must the deacons be grave, not doubletongued,
not given to much wine, not greedy of filthy lucre.
— 1 Timothy 3:8

*H*ave you ever known a person who agreed with whomever he was talking to at the moment? When he was with you, he agreed with you. But when he was with someone else who had a different opinion, he agreed with that person. Did that person's opinion fluctuate so quickly that it nearly shocked you?

It is very difficult to build trust with a person like this because you never know if he is really with you, or if he's just agreeing with you to your face until he can turn around and disagree with you behind your back. This type of person's lack of integrity makes it difficult to build a significant relationship with him.

Even if I don't always like what the members of my ministry team say or think, their honesty is very important to me, for it guarantees truthful relationships. The day a staff member tells me one thing but then turns around and tells a fellow employee something else is the day my trust in that person is disrupted. The apostle Paul called this kind of person "double-tongued" (1 Timothy 3:8).

The Greek word for "double-tongued" is the word *dilogos*, which is a compound of the words *di* and *logos*. The word *di* means *two*, and the word *logos* means *words*. When compounded together, these two words form the word *dilogos*, which could be literally translated *two-worded*. It is the picture of *a man or woman who says one thing to one person but a different thing to the next*. In other words, people like this are *inconsistent* in what they tell others. They are so wishy-washy that their opinion is constantly fluctuating, depending on whom they are speaking to at the moment.

This is usually an indication that this person is a people-pleaser. Because he wants everyone to like him, he agrees with whomever he is with at the moment. This is a serious character flaw. In fact, First Timothy 3:8 forbids us from giving this kind of person any prominent place of leadership in the ministry. It is also a principle that should be taken into consideration when looking for a prospective leader in any church, business, or organization.

Truthfulness is necessary so trust can be built between leaders and followers. It is compulsory in marriages, in friendships, and in relationships between employers and employees or between a pastor and his leaders. If a long-term relationship is to be built, trust is not optional — it is *essential*.

If there is a person in your church, business, or organization who is constantly changing what he says depending on who he is with at the moment, I urge you not to elevate this person into a leadership role. That person doesn't demonstrate the character that is required in leaders.

Being honest isn't always easy. Often it is *very* difficult. But truthfulness is the clearest and most noble path. The challenge we face is learning how to "speak the truth in love" as Ephesians 4:15 commands us.

I've learned that the truth isn't so difficult to hear; it is the *way* truth is sometimes spoken that can be difficult to hear. It is much easier to hear the truth if it is mixed with love, patience, and understanding. I think you know that cold water thrown in your face is not very enjoyable. In fact, it can be such a chilling experience that you may be tempted to throw it right back! So when *you* are the one speaking the truth to someone else, ask the Holy Spirit to help you know how to speak your opinion in a non-threatening and respectful manner.

In Ephesians 4:25, the apostle Paul commanded us, "Wherefore putting away lying, speak every man truth with his neighbour...." In Greek, the tense of the word "speak" points to habitual action. In other words, God wants you to develop the *habit* of always telling *the truth, the whole truth, and nothing but the truth, so help you God*! If you are guilty of agreeing with whomever you are talking to at the moment, it's time for you to ask the Holy Spirit to help you overcome this weakness.

If your opinion is required, be sure to speak exactly what you think and believe. And before you speak, pray for grace to speak the truth kindly. Once you have said what you believe, stick to what you said. If you later decide you were wrong, go back to the person you talked to — your pastor, boss, friend, or so forth — and tell him that you've changed your position. That person will appreciate your honesty. On the other hand, if you tell one person one thing and then turn around and say something different to someone else, the first person you spoke with will not understand your behavior. He will view you as a hypocrite who cannot be trusted, as someone who is *double-tongued*.

But what if you are the leader, pastor, or employer, and you have someone working under your authority who is constantly switching what he says, depending on whom he is talking to? In that case, take Paul's words to heart. Don't promote that person to a higher level of responsibility until this habit has been broken. *Don't lay hands on a person who is double-tongued!*

MY PRAYER FOR TODAY

Lord, please forgive me for the times I have been two-faced and double-tongued, speaking different things to different people. After reading today's Sparkling Gem, I realize it is wrong to act this way with those who are over me in authority. They need to be able to rest assured that I am being truthful with them, and now I see that I have given them a cause to doubt my word. Forgive me, and please help me conquer this serious character flaw in my life. Holy Spirit, help me today to uproot this double-tongued tendency from my life. Teach me how to habitually speak the truth!

I pray this in Jesus' name!

MY CONFESSION FOR TODAY

I confess that I am not two-faced or double-tongued. When I speak, people know that my word is as good as gold. I do not change my opinion based on the person I am with or what others think of me. What I say I mean, and I am faithful to keep my word. Every day I am growing in grace — and God is making me stronger, better, more dependable, and more truthful every day. I am exactly the kind of person my authorities can rely on!

I declare this by faith in Jesus' name!

1. Do you know a person who is two-faced and double-tongued? Have you seen him sway back and forth in his opinions, depending on whom he is with at the time? How does this fluctuating behavior affect your opinion of that person?
2. Are you guilty of being double-tongued? Have you told your leader one thing and then said something different behind his back to people in the church, business, or organization? If your answer is yes, what does this reveal about your own character?
3. How should you help correct a person who is double-tongued? Do you think you should ignore that person's dishonesty, or should you confront him in love and try to help him correct this character flaw in his life?

SEPTEMBER 18

Never Forget How Good God Has Been to You!

When your fathers tempted me, proved me,
and saw my works forty years.
— Hebrews 3:9

What kind of impact do you think it would have on your life if you personally witnessed a continuous stream of nonstop miracles in your life? Would you like to have that kind of experience?

Well, that is exactly what happened to the children of Israel when they left Egypt and wandered in the wilderness for forty years. This is what Hebrews 3:9 is referring to when it says, "When your fathers tempted me, proved me, and saw my works forty years."

Let's see what the Bible means when it says the children of Israel "tempted" God. The word "tempted" comes from the Greek word *peiradzo*, an old Greek word that means *to put to the test*. It means *to test an object to see if its quality is as good as others have claimed, boasted, or advertised*. For instance, if you hear that a certain product is the finest of its kind in the world, it would be natural for you to want to check out and test the product to verify whether or not it really lives up to its claims. That is exactly the idea of the word *peiradzo* in Hebrews 3:9.

The children of Israel were in a situation that demanded miraculous intervention. If they hadn't had the divine intervention of God, they would never have survived their flight from Egypt or their years in the wilderness. Their circumstances alone gave rise to a situation that allowed God to be tested — in other words, a situation that allowed God to demonstrate who He is and how faithful He is to His people. God had told the Israelites that He is good, so they "tested" Him, giving Him an opportunity to show that He is everything He declared Himself to be!

You can apply this same principle to your life. For instance, suppose you were in a tight financial jam. Although you didn't intend to get into that financial mess, you found yourself in a situation where you needed to see the goodness of God! You had heard and believed that God is a supernatural Provider; therefore, in a certain sense, your situation created a moment when God's goodness and delivering power could be tested. This situation would be the equivalent of you saying, "Lord, You say that You are a great Provider, so I need You to show me who You are! Please provide for me now in this situation!"

The many challenges the Israelites faced put them in a position in which they *had* to see the deliverance of God — and each situation put God in a position to prove who He was to them. That is why the verse goes on to say that the children of Israel "proved" God. The word "proved" is taken from the Greek word *dokimadzo*, which describes *something that has been tested and found to be true and genuine*. It can be also translated as *something that is authentic, reliable, approved, trustworthy, and real*.

Moses had declared the goodness of God to the children of Israel, but each challenge they faced gave God an opportunity to prove that He is exactly as Moses had declared Him to be. In each predicament, they found God to be faithful, true, and steadfast. Never once did God fail them or fail to live up to the reputation of His name. They personally witnessed His goodness and the undeniable fact that He is trustworthy, reliable, and true.

In fact, Hebrews 3:9 says the Israelites "saw" God's works for forty years. The word "saw" is the Greek word *horao*, which means *to see*. But in a broader sense, *horao* carries the idea of *seeing, perceiving, understanding, experiencing, and assimilating into one's self*. This tells us that the children of Israel saw and experienced enough of God's power to fully understand and assimilate it into their consciousness. Furthermore, the Greek grammar describes *a constant, continual, nonstop seeing and experiencing of God's works* during those forty years. They experienced this high-level power on a continuous basis — perhaps like no other generation before or after them.

We could discuss the supernatural provision and protection the Israelites experienced for many pages, but let's just consider a sample of what they saw and experienced:

1. The manna God provided to them for forty years.
2. The quail that supernaturally came to them in the wilderness.
3. The rock from which flowed enough water to nourish all of them.

Let's assume that the Israelites numbered about 3,000,000 people, which is what many Bible scholars estimate. *In that case, do you know how much manna was needed to feed the children of Israel in the wilderness?* One scholar has estimated that they needed *4,500 tons* of manna every day! If this is true, and if you take into account that God fed His people every day for 40 years, this means *65,700,000 tons* of manna supernaturally appeared on the ground over a period of forty years!

This manna appeared so regularly, so faithfully, so "day in and day out," that after a while, the children of Israel didn't even think too much of it anymore. Supernatural provision became so commonplace among them that they forgot how supernatural it was and began to accept it as a normal, regular occurrence. During those forty years, young children were born and grew up thinking it was *normal* for 4,500 tons of manna to appear each morning out of thin air (*see* Exodus 16)!

What do you think would happen if your city woke up tomorrow to find 4,500 tons of beautiful, freshly baked, nourishing manna lying on the ground all over the city, free to anyone who wanted to go out, pick it up, and take it home? *It would be huge news!* Scientists would fly from around the world to see it, study it, and taste it. Journalists would write about it, and major news programs would cover the story. It would be a worldwide sensation. *But for the children of Israel, this was an event that occurred every morning!*

Do you remember when God sent the quail to feed the children of Israel? How many quail do you think it would take to feed that massive group of Israelites for thirty days a month? Let me tell you how many: It would take at least *90,000,000 quail.* That's right — if each Israelite ate only one quail a day, in one month it would amount to 90,000,000 quail. If they ate two quail a day, the total number needed to feed them all for thirty days would rise to *180,000,000 quail.* That's how many quail it took to feed that crowd of three million Israelites in a thirty-day period. Needless to say, this was an incredible supernatural provision of God!

Remember, the Israelites were in the middle of the wilderness. It was *not* a natural place for quail to show up! But suddenly, they heard a noise in the distance and looked up. There in the sky overhead they saw millions of quail flying in from out of nowhere and landing in their camp. *What would be the odds of such a thing happening in the natural?*

Try to imagine what that many millions of quail flying right over your head would look like. The thick clouds of quail must have been dense enough to nearly block the people's view of the sun! Or try to imagine millions of quail flying right into the camp where you are living for thirty days, landing conveniently at your feet as if to say, *"Please eat me!"*

Where did all these quail come from? They certainly didn't fly in from the wilderness. How far did these birds have to travel to reach the children of Israel? From what distance did God supernaturally call in the quail to feed the children of Israel?

This phenomenon simply could not be naturally explained. It was *a supernatural provision.* It was just as miraculous as the 4,500 tons of manna that miraculously appeared on the ground every morning for forty years.

How about the water that came out of the rock to meet the Israelites' need for water in the wilderness? Do you have any idea how much water it would take to support three million Israelites in the blistering hot temperatures of the wilderness? You also have to take into account all the animals that needed to be nourished with water.

Keep in mind that God's people were in a dry, arid wilderness. It was a barren place — *a desert*! The only available source of water was bitter and undrinkable; there was *no* natural source of water to nourish that huge crowd of people. And consider the amount of water it would have taken to adequately nourish 3,000,000 people and all the animals in the hot temperatures of the wilderness. It would have required up to 15,000,000 gallons of water every day just to meet their basic needs for existence!

Water was especially crucial in that extremely hot climate. Both people and animals needed much more water than they normally would. Without water, they would have dried up and died in the wilderness. But because there was no natural source of water, it had to be provided for them *supernaturally.*

So God told Moses to strike the rock (*see* Exodus 17). When Moses obeyed, water began to supernaturally flow from the midst of that rock. And once water started to flow, it continued to flow and flow and flow, providing all the water needed by the people of God. One week's supply would equal approximately 100,000,000 gallons of water!

You would think that after living in this kind of supernatural provision day in and day out for more than forty years, the children of Israel would be *alive* to the things of God. After experiencing this kind of miraculous supply on such a continual basis, they should have trusted the Lord and found it easy to follow Him. Hadn't He always proven Himself faithful to them? Hadn't He always supernaturally provided what they needed when there was no natural provision to be found? What a privileged generation they were to see such marvelous acts of God!

But in spite of all the Israelites had seen, experienced, and assimilated about God's goodness, they became hardhearted. Hebrews 3:8 therefore warns us not to be like them, saying, "Harden not your hearts, as in the provocation, in the day of temptation in the wilderness."

The word "harden" is the Greek word *skleruno*, a medical term that described *something hard, such as a callus*. It could also denote *a limb that is so stiff, it is difficult to move*. Thus, this word is often translated *stiff-necked*. It was also used to describe the *hardened soil of the desert* — soil that was so hardened that water was unable to penetrate it and instead rolled right off. As time progressed, the word *skleruno* came to depict a person who was *thick-skinned, indifferent*, or *insensitive*.

Could it be that after seeing God perform so many wonderful works, the people became numb to and unappreciative of demonstrations of His power? Is it possible that they became calloused to the goodness of God because He had showered them with so much goodness? Did the supernatural demonstrations that were once considered wonders become such common occurrences that such miracles didn't even make an impression on God's people anymore?

It seems that the Israelites became like spoiled children, not even acknowledging how gracious God was to them or how miraculous their supply had been. The word "harden" seems to imply they became so calloused that nothing impressed them anymore. They became so stiff that even God couldn't move them to obedience. No matter how much of God's Spirit was poured out on them, His Presence just rolled off them, unable to penetrate their hard hearts. They became indifferent, insensitive, and unthankful, constantly complaining and bickering among themselves and with Moses about God's provision.

You may ask, "How could they become so hardhearted after all that God had done for them?" But take a moment to apply this same question to yourself. Let me tell you, it doesn't take forty years for any of us to become hardhearted and ungrateful!

If you honestly evaluate your own life, you may find yourself in this same sad condition. Consider how God has blessed you. He changed you, healed you, delivered you, rescued your family, gave you a new job, answered your prayers, and provided for you financially time and time again, showering you with blessing upon blessing over the years. In fact, you have probably lived in God's constant, nonstop, miraculous provision much of your life.

Hasn't your life been miraculously marked with the supernatural goodness, mercy, and provision of God? Yet are you still tempted to worry, fret, and doubt His faithfulness? How could it be possible that you would ever doubt God after all He has already proven to you?

Just as the children of Israel faced situations that gave rise to moments when God was put to the test, so do you. And every time, God passed the test! He proved Himself again and again, repeatedly demonstrating that He is reliable, trustworthy, and true. You have seen demonstrations of God's goodness throughout your entire life. So raise your arms toward Heaven, open your mouth, and begin to acknowledge that it's true!

Don't you think it would be good for you to stop what you are doing and recount the blessings of God and express your eternal gratefulness to Him today? As you continually remind yourself of God's goodness and do whatever else is necessary to maintain a thankful heart, you will avoid falling into the trap of becoming hardhearted and stiff-necked like the children of Israel.

Don't be classified with those who murmured, complained, and didn't trust God. Be counted among those who are grateful and thankful, who trust God to be exactly who He has declared Himself to be. *God is good to you — and don't ever let yourself forget it!*

MY PRAYER FOR TODAY

Lord, I am thankful for Your goodness in my life. You have saved me, delivered me, redeemed me, and changed me. My entire life is marked by Your supernatural goodness and mercy! It is true that You have showered me with nonstop blessings — and today I want to take this opportunity to thank You for every good thing You've done in my life. The situations I have faced in my life have put You to the test, and You have jumped at every chance to prove how good You are. In fact, Your goodness to me has been constant and never-ending. I praise You and thank You for loving me so much!

I pray this in Jesus' name!

MY CONFESSION FOR TODAY

I confess that I am grateful for and constantly aware of God's goodness in my life. I have every reason to trust Him, for He has proven Himself to me again and again and I know He will never let me down. He has shown His goodness and mercy to me, and I am a recipient of His grace. I choose to lift up my hands, open my mouth, and declare the goodness of the Lord. The Bible says, "Let the redeemed of the Lord say so," so I am saying so right now! Jesus, You are good, and Your mercy endures forever! Thank You for showering me with Your mercy and Your might!

I declare this by faith in Jesus' name!

QUESTIONS FOR YOU TO CONSIDER

1. As you read today's *Sparkling Gem*, did you begin to think of all the times God has supernaturally provided for your own life? It would be very beneficial for you to take a few minutes to reflect on all the times God has miraculously supplied what you needed.
2. Are you facing a challenge right now in your life? If so, do you find yourself rushing forward to believe and trust the Lord, or do you have to fight off fearful thoughts that God might not prove Himself faithful to you?
3. Is it possible that you have fallen into the same trap the children of Israel fell into? Have you had so many miraculous provisions in your life that you've begun to lose your appreciation for all that God has done for you? If the answer is yes, I advise you to take some time today to get into the Presence of God and make your heart right with Him.

Don't you think it would be good for you to stop what you are doing and recount the blessings of God and express your eternal gratefulness to Him today? As you continually remind yourself of God's goodness and do whatever else is necessary to maintain a thankful heart, you will avoid falling into the trap of becoming hardhearted and stiff-necked like the children of Israel.

SEPTEMBER 19

❧❧❧

Location, Location, Location!

But without faith it is impossible to please him:
for he that cometh to God must believe that he is,
and that he is a rewarder of them that diligently seek him.
— Hebrews 11:6

*A*ll over the world, the golden rule of real estate is *location, location, location*. Property situated in the best areas is most desirable because it has the greatest value and demands the highest prices. Even though residences in other areas may be more beautiful and even have larger yards, they simply can't demand the same high prices as residences situated in better locations.

My family and I live minutes from the Moscow Kremlin where the seat of government resides and where the beautiful Red Square and St. Basil's Cathedral are located. Apartments here are older and smaller, but this area is in the very center of Moscow and is considered prestigious because it is so close to the seat of power. Therefore, property and rental values in this area are much higher.

I recently drove outside the city limits to see the fabulous new homes being built by Russia's brand-new, emerging middle class. When I asked how much these homes could be purchased for, I was stunned to discover that their selling price is a fraction of what smaller apartments cost in the neighborhood where we live. However, if we lived outside the city, we would have to fight traffic for an hour and a half every morning on the way to the office; then we'd have to do it all over again every night on the way home! That's another reason why the homes located outside the city are cheaper. Living near the center of the city is much easier, more convenient, and more productive.

As I drove back into the city after looking at these country homes, I started thinking about the contrast between living *inside* and *outside* of the city. As I pondered this subject, I found my mind going to Hebrews 11:6, which says, "But without faith it is impossible to please him...."

The word "without" comes from the Greek word *choris*, which means *to be outside of something, such as someone who lives outside the perimeters of a city*. It is a comparison between being *outside* or *inside* something — for example, *in* the house or *out* of the house; *in* the yard or *out* of the yard; or *in* the car or *out* of the car. The word *choris* depicts someone who is *out of*, not *in*, a specific location.

Because this word is used in connection with faith, the writer of Hebrews is letting us know that we can live *in* faith or *out* of faith. This means faith must be *a real place* that has borders, perimeters, and boundaries. Just as you can live *in* the city or *out* of the city, you can live *in* faith or *outside* of faith. The determining factor is *your obedience to the assignment God has given you*. God wants you to be located at the address of faith — for this is the location He deems the most valuable and profitable for your life.

Hebrews 11:6 could be accurately rendered:

"When you live outside of faith — living beyond its boundaries and perimeters — you make it impossible to please Him...."

To determine if you are *in* or *out* of faith, you must ask yourself these questions:

✦ *Am I doing what God told me to do?*
✦ *Am I fulfilling the assignment He gave for my life?*
✦ *Am I living in obedience to His Word and to the revelation He has given me?*
✦ *Am I sticking with the plan Jesus asked me to execute?*

That place where God called you; that place requiring your obedience, faith, and patience; that place where you are confident God wants you to be working and functioning — *that* is the address of faith where God wants you to live. As long as you stay "in" that place where God told you to be, you are "in" faith and you therefore please God. But the day you give up and move "out" of that place of faith, you are moving to cheaper territory that God doesn't value as highly — a location where you will experience the hardships and inconveniences of poor choices and defeat.

The entire eleventh chapter of Hebrews is about men and women who lived "in" faith. They each received a word from God for their lives or for their generation. Although it was difficult to do, they held tightly to their mandate from Heaven. As a result, they changed their generations and pleased God. Faith was the location where they lived — and because they stayed in that place where God had called them to be, they brought great pleasure to Him.

But the only way to stay "in" faith is to keep your eyes fixed on Jesus! The devil will try to discourage you from being steadfast and faithful. He'll orchestrate situations to make you take your eyes off Jesus and to fill you with worry and fear. If you let the enemy's plan work, it won't be long before your bags will be packed and you'll be changing locations — moving "out" of faith to low-level areas of defeat where you will not please God.

But you don't have to let that plan work! You never have to leave the address of faith where God wants you to live! Just refuse to allow the devil to persuade you to fix your eyes on the circumstances. Don't take the enemy's path that leads straight "out" of faith.

For those who stay in faith, there is a reward. That is why Hebrews 11:6 says that God is a "rewarder." For those who continually live at the address of faith — who refuse to be moved by circumstances; who adamantly reject any inclination to throw in the towel and to give up; who rebuff any temptation or pull to let go of the word God gave them — it is just a matter of time until their faith is rewarded. *They will receive the full manifestation of what they believe!*

Hebrews 11:6 goes on to say that God "…is a rewarder of them that *diligently* seek him." You see, it takes diligence to stay in faith! It will require you to be focused, concentrated, and committed to the end. When circumstances try to knock you "out" of faith, you must have a fierce, unwavering commitment that you are not going to leave where God called you.

The reason most people fail is that they weren't really committed from the very beginning. That's why the devil eventually found a way to move them "out" of that place of faith. One great man of God said, *"Anything that ends in a fizzle had a flaw in it from the beginning."* So make sure there are no fatal flaws in you that will knock you out down the road!

I assure you that if you see anyone consistently living at the address of faith, that person has persistently pursued that goal. You see, living "in" faith cannot be a sideline issue in your life. It must have your complete, undivided attention. For you to stay "in" faith, you must be constant. You definitely must be persistent. Your commitment to live and walk in faith must be unbending and immovable.

✦ So what has God asked you to do?
✦ What is that place of faith where you are supposed to be living right now?

✦ Are you staying in that place of faith, or have you been vacillating back and forth and "in" and "out" of the place where God called you to be?

Make the decision that there is no turning back from where God has called you. God promises that if you stay "in" faith, there is a glorious reward awaiting you in the near future. It's only a matter of time until the full manifestation of what you believe will come into view!

So make every effort to stay at your address of faith. You are living in the most valuable, beneficial place for your life. You are living where God can bless you!

Since location determines everything else, why don't you take a few minutes today to assess your life? See if you are properly located "in" or "out" of faith. If you find that you are "out" of faith, make the goal of getting "in" faith your most important priority. *The outcome of every other area of your life will be determined by this one decision!*

MY PRAYER FOR TODAY

Lord, help me stick with the assignment You have given me for my life. I know that is where I am supposed to be — and I know that is what I am supposed to be doing. Forgive me for vacillating back and forth, in and out, backward and forward. I am asking You to help me become single-minded, concentrated, and focused in my determination never to move out of faith again. I want to live at the address of faith, for I know that is where I will please You the most. Holy Spirit, empower me to push aside every distraction of the devil and to remain fixed and focused on doing exactly what God has instructed me to do.

I pray this in Jesus' name!

MY CONFESSION FOR TODAY

I confess that I live "in" faith. Although Satan tries to use situations to distract me and dissuade me from staying in faith, I have resolved that I am never moving from the place where God has called me to be. I will never relinquish the dream He has put in my heart. I will stay in this place; I will use my faith; I will be steadfast, unwavering, and committed to seeing His promises come to pass in my life. Because I have made this decision, I am a person who pleases God!

I declare this by faith in Jesus' name!

QUESTIONS FOR YOU TO CONSIDER

1. Are you living at the address of faith? Or have you moved out of faith and into the neighborhood of doubt and unbelief, where you know that you are no longer pleasing God?
2. How has the devil tried to distract and dissuade you from staying "in" faith? What people or situations has he used to try to pull you out of faith and into the territory of disobedience and unbelief?
3. What are you going to do to reinforce yourself spiritually so you can remain "in" faith until you see the full manifestation of what God has promised to you?

SEPTEMBER 20

ಲ⁂ಲ

Taken Captive by the Devil To Do the Devil's Will!

And that they may recover themselves
out of the snare of the devil,
who are taken captive by him at his will.
— 2 Timothy 2:26

*E*very once and a while in the local church, someone gets so bent out of shape and upset with the church leadership that he behaves in a way that is shocking to everyone. Often this person has served faithfully in the past; yet suddenly he becomes a raging torrent — accusing the pastor, getting upset with the pastoral staff, and trying to stir up as much trouble as possible. The amazing thing is that this person is usually blind to how ugly and ungodly his behavior really is. Often the person even thinks he's doing the will of God by pointing out the flaws of the church leadership!

Timothy was having similar troubles with several people in his own congregation. Paul referred to this predicament when he wrote that some people in his church were "…taken captive by him [the devil] at his will" (2 Timothy 2:26).

The words "taken captive" are from the Greek word *zoogreo*, which means *to take an animal alive*. It is the picture of *putting an animal in a cage or behind bars at the zoo*. This means people who are behaving this way are themselves victims — somehow caught and trapped by the devil, caged in resentment or bitterness that drives them to act in a fashion that is inconsistent with who they really are!

**When Paul says "taken captive by him [the devil] at his will,"
it could be better rendered:**

"…who are taken captive by him [the devil] to carry out the devil's will."

Here we see a picture of a believer whose emotions the devil has manipulated until the person himself becomes the source of strife, discord, and subversion in the church, all the while thinking that he is doing the will of God. This is a deceived believer, captured by the enemy and now working for the devil to disrupt the local church!

Offense is usually the entry point the devil uses to seduce a believer into this behavior. And it's amazing just how quickly a dart of offense from the enemy can be thrown into a person's heart. Equally amazing is the speed in which just one of his evil darts can change that person's perspective of someone he used to honor and respect! In a matter of *seconds*, his entire view of that other person can become adversely affected.

Like the dripping of water, the devil begins to repeatedly strike a person's mind with accusations against the one who was once so revered. Let's say the one accused is the person's pastor. The enemy might pound that person's mind with false allegations such as these:

◆ *He is so arrogant and proud!*
◆ *If other people saw what you see, no one would attend this church.*

✦ *He doesn't appreciate you.*
✦ *He doesn't deserve to have you serve on his staff. Leave him!*
✦ *The people in this city need a pastor who really loves them.*
✦ *It's time for you to leave him and go start your own church!*

When the enemy is attacking the mind and emotions in this way, the victim often doesn't realize that deception is trying to creep into his heart. He is falling into the devil's trap and doesn't even know it! At the moment it is happening, the person *really* believes that what he is thinking and doing is right. This is a classic example of a believer taken captive by the devil to do the devil's will. This believer truthfully believes he is acting in a right spirit and executing the will of God as he rebels against his God-ordained authority.

Thankfully, God can deal with that person's heart and reveal how wrong he is, and his relationship with his authority can be completely restored. However, restoration in these kinds of cases is a rare occurrence. The damage is usually so severe that people are left deeply wounded — which is precisely the objective the devil wants to accomplish!

Let me give you this advice to help you avoid ever being caught in this devilish deception. Whenever something becomes *a major issue* between you and someone else, you would be wise to back up and reexamine what you are upset about. So often the person you are upset with is someone you love and need in your life. Therefore, ask yourself these questions:

✦ *Do I want to let the devil build a wall between me and that other person over something that won't even matter one or two years from now?*
✦ *Do I really think that person intended to hurt me?*
✦ *Wouldn't it be better to forgive that person and preserve our relationship that has taken so long to build?*
✦ *Is what happened really so serious, or am I blowing the whole incident out of proportion?*
✦ *Have I ever been guilty of doing the same thing to someone else?*

I have discovered from my own experience through the years that the devil is constantly seeking opportune moments to wedge bad feelings between people. He is a master at embellishing real or imagined offenses until they become inflated and larger than life. And he knows just when to "sock it to you"!

So slow down, calm down, and give yourself a little time to think and pray before you start accusing someone. It would be a good idea to find a friend who will be honest with you. Ask that friend to tell you the truth about what you are feeling and about how you are behaving. *A good dose of honesty from a truthful friend might be exactly what you need to wake you up to what the devil is trying to do in you and through you!*

MY PRAYER FOR TODAY

Lord, I never want the devil to take me captive to do his will in my church or place of employment. He is an accuser, so if I am tempted to accuse and slander, it means that the devil is trying to work through me. Give me the ability to recognize this strategy of the enemy as soon as it starts, and to put on the brakes before I get so embroiled in a conflict that I can't see or think correctly. Holy Spirit, You are the Spirit of Truth, so please enable me to both see and to hear the truth about myself, because I want to stay free!

I pray this in Jesus' name!

MY CONFESSION FOR TODAY

I confess that I am free from the deception of the devil! My mind is renewed to the truth of God's Word. My mind thinks straight and clearly, and I am sound and balanced in my perspective of the situations I face in life. I am teachable when my friends tell me the truth, helping me see when I am getting too upset about things that aren't so important. Therefore, I'm able to walk free of the devil's snare and stay balanced in my emotions because of the Word that works mightily in me!

I declare this by faith in Jesus' name!

QUESTIONS FOR YOU TO CONSIDER

1. Has there ever been a moment in your life when the devil trapped you emotionally and used you to stir up trouble? Were you later very regretful for your negative role in that situation? Did you ever go back and apologize for what you did?
2. Have you ever seen someone else fall in this trap at your church or place of employment? At the time this incident occurred, did you recognize that the person acting so destructively was literally captured in his mind and emotions?
3. If the person being used by the devil won't listen to those who are over him, what actions do you think his authorities should take in response to his or her behavior?

SEPTEMBER 21

Are Worry and Anxiety Trying To Seize or Control You?

Be careful for nothing; but in every thing by prayer
and supplication with thanksgiving
let your requests be made known unto God.
— Philippians 4:6

Do you ever have moments when anxiety tries to creep up on you and seize your heart? I'm talking about those times when you are thrown into a state of panic about things that concern you — such as your family, your friendships, your business, or your finances. Very often this state of panic is caused by the mere thought of a problem that doesn't even exist and is unlikely ever to come to pass. Nevertheless, the mere thought of this non-existent problem troubles you deeply. Soon you find yourself sinking into such a strong state of worry and anxiety that it literally takes you emotionally hostage!

An example would be a wife or mother who worries endlessly about the health of her husband or children. Although in reality they are as healthy as can be, the devil constantly pounds the woman's mind with fear-filled thoughts about her loved ones getting sick or dying prematurely. This fear acts like a stranglehold that gradually chokes off her life, paralyzing her until she can no longer function normally in her daily responsibilities.

Or have you ever known a successful businessman who lives in constant terror that he is going to lose his money? I've known many such men. Their businesses were blessed, stable, and even expanding. But because the devil struck their minds with worry and anxiety about losing it all, they weren't able to enjoy the success God had given them. Instead of enjoying God's goodness and His many blessings in their lives, they often lived like beggars, afraid that if they used what they had, they might lose it. This is a strangling, choking fear that steals people's ability to enjoy what they possess.

Some people are so controlled by fear that they pray *fretful* prayers instead of *faith-filled* prayers. I must admit that I've had moments in my own life when I've prayed more out of fretfulness than out of faith. Have you ever had one of those times? Praying fretful prayers doesn't get you anything. It is non-productive praying. God does not respond to fretfulness; He responds to *faith*.

In Philippians 4:6, Paul says, "Be careful for nothing; but in every thing by prayer and supplication with thanksgiving let your requests be made known unto God." Do you see the word "careful" in this verse? It is the Greek word *merimnao*, which means *to be troubled; to be anxious; to be fretful; or to be worried about something*.

In New Testament times, this word was primarily used in connection with *worry about finances, hunger, or some other basic provision of life*. It pictured a person who is fretful about paying his bills; a person who is worried he won't have the money to purchase food and clothes for his family's needs or pay his house payment or apartment rent on time; or a person who is anxious about his ability to cope with the daily necessities of life.

This is the same word used in Matthew 6:25, when Jesus says, "Therefore I say unto you, Take no thought for your life, what ye shall eat, or what ye shall drink…." The word "thought" is also the Greek word *merimnao*. But in this particular verse, the Greek New Testament also has the word *me*, which is *a strong prohibition to stop something that is already in progress*.

This strongly suggests that Jesus was speaking to worriers who were *already* filled with fret and anxiety. He was urging these people *to stop worrying*. The verse could be translated, "*Stop worrying about your life….*" Then Jesus specifies that they were to stop worrying about "…what ye shall eat, or what ye shall drink…." So again we see the word *merimnao* used to describe *worry, fretfulness, and anxiety about obtaining the basic necessities of life*.

We also find the word *merimnao* used in the parable of the sower and the seed. Matthew 13:22 says, "He also that received seed among the thorns is he that heareth the word; and the care of this world, and the deceitfulness of riches, choke the word, and he becometh unfruitful." The word "care" is the Greek word *merimnao*, again connected to *material worries and concerns*.

Jesus says such worry "chokes" the Word. The word "choke" is the Greek word *sumpnigo*, which means *to suffocate, to smother, to asphyxiate, to choke*, or *to throttle*. You see, worry is so all-consuming in an individual's mind that it literally chokes him. It is a suffocating, smothering force that throttles his whole life to a standstill.

In Luke 21:34, Jesus gives a special warning to people who live in the last days. He said, "And take heed to yourselves, lest at any time your hearts be overcharged with surfeiting, and drunkenness, and cares of this life, so that day come upon you unawares."

When Jesus mentions the "cares of this life," the word "cares" is the Greek word *merimna*. This time, however, it is used in connection with the word "life," which is the Greek word *biotikos*. This comes from the root word *bios*, the Greek word for *life*. It is where we get the word *biology*. But when it becomes the word *biotikos*, it describes *the things of life* — pertaining primarily to the events, incidents, and episodes that occur in one's life.

Thus, this phrase could be understood to mean that we should not allow ourselves to worry and fret about the events, incidents, or episodes that occur in life. This is a particularly fitting message for people who live in the last days and who are confronted by the incidents and episodes that occur during this difficult time.

So when the apostle Paul writes in Philippians 4:6, "Be careful for nothing…," he is pleading with us not to be worried about the basic needs and provisions required for life. Paul is also telling us not to let the events of life get to us and throw us into a state of anxiety or panic. To let us know how free of all worry we should be, Paul says we are to be "careful for nothing." The word "nothing" is the Greek word *meden*, and it means *absolutely nothing*!

So this phrase in Philippians 4:6 could be translated:

"Don't be worried about anything — and that means nothing at all!"

So what is bothering you today, friend? What is stealing your peace and joy? Is there one particular thing Satan keeps using to strike your mind with fear? Can you think of a single time when worry and fretfulness ever helped make a situation better? Doesn't worry serve only to keep you emotionally torn up and in a state of panic?

I urge you to put an end to worry today, once and for all. If you let worry start operating in you even for a moment, it will try to become a habitual part of your thought life, turning you into a "worrier" who never knows a moment of peace.

Jesus is sitting at the right hand of the Father right now, interceding for you continually. Jesus understands every emotion, every frustration, and every temptation you could ever face (*see* Hebrews 2:18). So why not make a deliberate decision to turn over all your worries to Jesus today? Rather than try to manage those anxieties and needs all by yourself, go to Him and surrender everything into His loving, capable hands. Walk free of all those choking, paralyzing fears once and for all.

Jesus is waiting for you to cast *all* your cares upon Him, because He really does care for you (*see* 1 Peter 5:7). *Then once you throw your worries and concerns on Him, He will help you experience the joy and peace He has designed for you to enjoy in life all along!*

MY PRAYER FOR TODAY

Lord, I admit that I've allowed fear, worry, fretfulness, and anxiety to play a role in my life. When these negative emotions operate in me, I lose my peace and my joy. I am tired of living in this continual state of worry and fear about bad things that might happen. Jesus, today I am making the choice to turn all these destructive thoughts over to You. I don't want to live this way anymore. I know this isn't Your plan for my life, so by faith, I cast all my concerns on You. I release them into Your hands, Lord, and ask You to take them right now!

I pray this in Jesus' name!

MY CONFESSION FOR TODAY

I confess that I am free from worry, fretfulness, and anxiety. These forces have no place in me. I have surrendered every care and concern to Jesus, and He has taken them from me. As a result, I am free of every burden, every weight, and every problem. Jesus is my great High Priest, and He is interceding for me right now. With God on my side, I can enjoy life as He intended for me to enjoy it. I boldly confess that I am fear-free and worry-free and that anxiety has no place in me!

I declare this by faith in Jesus' name!

QUESTIONS FOR YOU TO CONSIDER

1. What is the one area in your life where Satan most often strikes your mind and emotions with fear, fretfulness, and anxiety? Do you know what triggers this attack of fear and worry?
2. For you to get out of fear and to walk in peace, what steps do you need to take in your life? In other words, what do you need to do differently than you are doing right now in order for you to move into a place of constant peace?
3. If you were going to counsel someone else who was being held hostage by worry, fretfulness, and anxiety, what would you tell that person to do to get free and to stay free?

SEPTEMBER 22

Five Important Steps To Move From Fear to Faith, From Turmoil to Peace, And From Defeat to Victory!

Be careful for nothing; but in every thing by prayer
and supplication with thanksgiving
let your requests be made known unto God.
— Philippians 4:6

I vividly remember a time in my life when I was very concerned about something that was about to occur. Although the challenge before me really wasn't so life-shattering, at the moment it seemed huge and mountainous. Therefore, I was *extremely* concerned.

I'm sure you know what it's like when worry tries to flood your mind. It has a way of magnifying issues to the point of being ridiculous, but when you're in the midst of the situation, it seems so real. Only after the event has passed do you realize how silly it was to be so worried about something that was so non-eventful.

But at the time I'm telling you about right now, I was consumed with worry. I paced back and forth, fretting, thinking, and pondering, making myself even more nervous by my anxious behavior. I was nothing but a bag of nerves. Realizing how deeply I was sinking into worry, I reached for my Bible to try to find peace for my troubled soul. I opened it to Philippians 4:6, which says, "Be careful for nothing; but in every thing by prayer and supplication with thanksgiving let your requests be made known unto God."

I tried to push everything else out of my mind so I could concentrate on God's words in this verse. Through Philippians 4:6, I could see that God was calling out to me and urging me to lay down my worries and come boldly before Him to make my requests known. As I focused on this verse, I suddenly saw something I had never seen before. I realized that this verse showed me step by step how to lay down my worries and boldly make my requests known to God. If I followed the steps laid out in this verse exactly as I understood them, I would be set free from worry and fear! I promptly followed these steps, and in a matter of minutes my worry was replaced with a thankful, praising, and peaceful heart!

As the years have passed, I have had many occasions when worry and fear have tried to plague my mind. It would be impossible to exaggerate the challenges my wife and I have faced as we've fulfilled our apostolic ministry overseas. At times, these challenges have simply been enormous.

This is the reason I so entirely identify with the apostle Paul as he describes the difficulties he encountered in his ministry. Just as Satan regularly tried to disrupt Paul's ministry, the enemy has also attempted on many occasions to hinder our work and thwart the advancement of the Gospel. However, none of his attacks have ever succeeded, and the Gospel has gone forth in mighty power!

In moments when worry or fear is trying to wrap its life-draining tentacles around me, I rush back to the truths found in Philippians 4:6. Just as I followed the steps found in this verse so many years ago, I still carefully follow them whenever I start getting anxious. Every time I do, these steps lead me from worry and fear to a thankful, praising, and peaceful heart. In fact, I have learned that if I faithfully follow these steps, fear will *always* be eradicated and replaced with the wonderful, dominating peace of God (*see* January 1).

So don't let worry wrap its tentacles around *you*. Instead, listen to Paul's advice about how to deal with the problems and concerns that try to assail your mind. Let's look once again at what he says in Philippians 4:6: "Be careful for nothing; but in every thing by prayer and supplication with thanksgiving let your requests be made known unto God."

In this verse, Paul lays out five very important steps to move from fear to faith, from turmoil to peace, and from defeat to victory. We'll look at five key words that tell us exactly what we must do when worry and concerns are trying to assail our minds: 1) *prayer;* 2) *supplication;* 3) *thanksgiving;* 4) *requests;* and 5) *known.*

When Paul uses the word "prayer" in this verse, it is the Greek word *proseuche*, which is the most commonly used word for prayer in the New Testament. This particular word and its various forms is used approximately 127 times in the New Testament. It is a compound of the words *pros* and *euche*. The word *pros* is a preposition that means *toward*, which can denote a sense of *closeness*. Nearly everywhere it is used in the New Testament, the word *pros* carries the meaning of *close, up-front, intimate contact with someone else.*

One scholar has noted that the word *pros* is used to portray the intimate relationship that exists between the members of the Godhead. John 1:1 says, "In the beginning was the Word, and the Word was with God...." The word "with" is taken from the word *pros*. By using this word to describe the relationship between the Father and the Son, the Holy Spirit is telling us that theirs is an intimate relationship. One expositor has translated the verse, "In the beginning was the Word, and the Word was *face-to-face* with God...."

The second part of the word *proseuche* is taken from the word *euche*. The word *euche* is an old Greek word that describes a *wish, desire, prayer,* or *vow*. It was originally used to depict a person who made some kind of vow to God because of a need or desire in his or her life. This individual would vow to give something of great value to God in exchange for a favorable answer to prayer. Thus, inherent in this word is the idea of an *exchange* — giving something to God in exchange for something wanted or desired.

So instead of carrying your worries and burdens, you are to take the first step Paul gives you in moving from a place of turmoil to peace: *Come close to the Lord in prayer.* Once you are in that intimate, face-to-face place with God, take that opportunity to give Him your worries, fears, and concerns. Then ask the Lord to give you something back in exchange for the worries you have given Him — ask Him for peace! You see, this is a part of the great exchange found in the Greek word *proseuche*. When you give God *your problems*, in return He gives you *His peace*.

Perhaps you've experienced this great exchange at some previous moment in your life. Can you think of a time when your mind was hassled with fears? Once you truly committed your problem to the Lord, did a supernatural peace flood your soul and relieve you from your anxieties? This is the first step that Paul urges you to take when worry, fear, and concerns are trying to take over your mind or emotions.

The second step Paul tells us to take is found in the word "supplication." The word "supplication" in Greek is the word *deisis*, which depicts *a person who has some type of lack in his life and therefore pleads strongly for his lack to be met.* The word *deisis* is translated several ways in the *King James Version*, including *to beseech, to beg,* or *to earnestly appeal.* This word pictures a person in such great need that he feels compelled to push his pride out of the way so he can boldly, earnestly, strongly, and passionately cry out for someone to help or assist him.

One of the most powerful examples of the word *deisis* is found in James 5:16. In this famous verse of Scripture, the Bible says, "...The effectual fervent prayer of a righteous man availeth much." Here the word *deisis* is translated as "fervent prayer." You see, *deisis* is a *passionate, earnest, heartfelt, sincere prayer.* It comes to God on the most serious terms, strongly beseeching Him to move and to meet a specific need that the person praying is facing in his life.

So when you are facing a problem that deeply concerns you, don't be afraid to go to the Lord and *earnestly beseech* Him to meet your need. Paul's use of this word means you can get *very bold* when you ask God to move on your behalf. There is no reason for you to be timid or mealy-mouthed when you pray. You can tell God *exactly* what you feel, what you're facing, and what you want Him to do for you. This is what "supplication" is all about!

After mentioning "supplication," Paul then gives us the third important step to take when giving our worries and concerns to the Lord. Paul tells us to make our requests known to God "...by prayer and supplication with thanksgiving...."

God not only expects you to be bold; He also expects you to thank Him for being good to you! It simply isn't right to ask boldly without expressing thanksgiving. If you've ever generously given to someone who never took the time to thank you for the sacrifice you made for him or her, you know how shocking ingratitude can be. In a similar way, you must be careful to thank God for being so good to you!

The word "thanksgiving" that Paul uses in this verse is the Greek word *eucharistia*, which is a compound of the words *eu* and *charis*. The word *eu* means *good* or *well*. It denotes *a general good disposition* or *an overwhelmingly good feeling about something*. The word *charis* is the Greek word for *grace*. When these two words are compounded into one, they form the word *eucharistia*. This compound word describes *an outpouring of grace and of wonderful feelings that freely flow from the heart in response to someone or something.*

By using this word, Paul teaches us that when we *earnestly ask* God to do something special for us, we must match it with *an earnest outpouring of thanks*. Although the request has only just been made and the manifestation isn't evident yet, it is appropriate to thank God for doing what we have requested. Thanking Him in advance demonstrates faith.

So always make sure to follow up your *earnest asking* with *earnest thanksgiving*! Make it a goal to be just as passionate in your thanksgiving as you were when you made your request.

Paul then gives you the fourth step out of worry and anxiety when he tells you, "...Let your *requests* be made known unto God." The word "requests" is the Greek word *aitima*, from the word *aiteo*. The Greek word "ask" destroys any religious suggestion that you are a lowly worm who has no right to come into the Presence of God. You see, the Greek word *aiteo* means *to be adamant in requesting and demanding assistance to meet tangible needs, such as food, shelter, money, and so forth*.

In fact, in the New Testament, the word *aiteo* is used to portray *a person who insists or demands that a specific need be met after approaching and speaking to his superior with respect and honor*. Additionally, it expresses the idea that *one possesses a full expectation to receive what was firmly requested*.

There is no doubt that this word describes someone who prays authoritatively, in a sense *demanding* something from God. This person knows what he needs and is so filled with faith that he isn't afraid to boldly come into God's Presence to ask and expect to receive what he has requested. (*See* March 23 for a fuller study of the Greek word *aiteo*.)

This means when you pray about a need that concerns you, it is right for you to pray authoritatively. *As long as your prayer is based on the Word of God, you can have the assurance of God's promise regarding the issue you are most concerned about.* Furthermore, when you pray, it is spiritually appropriate for you to fully expect God to honor His Word and do what you have requested.

As a final, fifth point, Paul says "...let your requests be *made known* unto God." The word "known" comes from the word *gnoridzo*, and it means *to make a thing known; to declare something; to broadcast something;* or *to make something very evident*. This plainly means that your asking can be extremely bold! Declare to God what you need; broadcast it so loudly that all of Heaven hears you when you pray. You can be exceptionally bold when you come before Jesus to make your requests known!

An expanded, interpretive translation
of Philippians 4:6 could be rendered:

"Don't worry about anything — and that means nothing at all! Instead, come before God and give Him the things that concern you so He can in exchange give you what you need or desire. Be bold to strongly, passionately, and fervently make your request known to God, making certain that an equal measure of thanksgiving goes along with your strong asking. You have every right to ask boldly, so go ahead and insist that God meet your need. When you pray, be so bold that there is no doubt your prayer was heard. Broadcast it! Declare it! Pray boldly until you have the assurance that God has heard your request!"

So in moments when worry or fear is trying to wrap its life-draining tentacles around you, rush to the truths found in Philippians 4:6. You don't have to live subject to worry, concerns, and fears the rest of your life. If you follow these steps, worry and fear will always be replaced with a peaceful and praising heart!

Why don't you take the time today to enter God's Presence and walk through these five important steps? It's time to move from fear to faith, from turmoil to peace, and from defeat to victory!

MY PRAYER FOR TODAY

Lord, I thank You for allowing me to come boldly before You in prayer. I know that You love me and want to richly meet the needs I am facing in my life today. My temptation is to worry and fear, but I know that if I will trust You, everything I am concerned about will turn out all right. Right now I reject the temptation to worry, and I choose to come before You to boldly make my requests known. By faith I thank You in advance for acting to answer my requests!

I pray this in Jesus' name!

MY CONFESSION FOR TODAY

I confess that I am not ruled by worry, fear, or concerns. I go to God with those things that are on my heart, and I clearly articulate what I feel, what I need, and what I expect Heaven to do on my behalf. Because of the promises in God's Word, I know exactly how to boldly make my requests. I always match my requests with thanksgiving, letting God know how grateful I am for everything He does in my life. Heaven is on my side; therefore, I know I will survive and victoriously overcome each and every attack that ever tries to come against my family, my relationships, my business, my finances, and my life.

I declare this by faith in Jesus' name!

QUESTIONS FOR YOU TO CONSIDER

1. When worry, fears, and concerns try to overwhelm you, what do you do in response? Do you give in and allow worry and fretfulness to fill your mind, or do you run to the Lord and commit your problems to Him?
2. Can you recall times in your life when you gave an all-consuming worry to the Lord? In return, did He fill you with supernatural peace, enabling you to overcome the worries that were trying to devour you?
3. What new truth did you learn from today's *Sparkling Gem*? If these truths were helpful to you, can you think of someone else you know who needs this same encouragement? If so, why don't you contact that friend today to encourage him or her from the Word of God?

It simply isn't right to constantly ask God to do things for you and never take the time to express thanksgiving to Him. If you've ever generously given to someone who never took the time to thank you for the sacrifice you made for him or her, you know how shocking ingratitude can be. Don't you think it is right for you to take the time to thank God for being so good to you?

September 23

*It's Time for You To Start
Confessing 'Good Things' About Yourself!*

That the communication of thy faith
may become effectual by the acknowledging
of every good thing which is in you in Christ Jesus.
— Philemon 1:6

W hat kind of things do you say about yourself? Do you speak well of yourself, or are you hyper-critical of your appearance, your weight, your intelligence, your talents, your skills, and every other aspect of who you are as a person?

I used to be so hyper-critical of myself that one day the Holy Spirit spoke to me and said, "How dare you continually talk so badly about yourself after the good work I've done inside you. Don't you know how marvelously I created you to be in Jesus Christ? Quit speaking so negatively of yourself, and start acknowledging every good thing that is in you."

I didn't realize how badly I was speaking of myself until the Holy Spirit brought it to my attention. But after He spoke to me, I started noticing every time something evil slipped out of my mouth about myself. I was stunned to see how many times I did it! I became painfully aware that my own mouth had become one of my greatest enemies. With the help of the Holy Spirit, I made a decision to quit speaking such foul things and to start aligning my mouth with what God's Word declared me to be.

Paul said we need to speak good things about ourselves! In Philemon 1:6, he said, "That the communication of thy faith may become effectual by the acknowledging of every good thing which is in you in Christ Jesus." Today I want to especially draw your attention to the part of the verse that says, "…May become effectual by the acknowledging of every good thing which is in you in Christ Jesus."

Even though God has done great things in you and has planned a powerful future for you, it is up to you to *activate* His blessings in your life! This is why Paul says, "That the communication of thy faith may become effectual.…"

The word "effectual" is the Greek word *energeo*. It is where we get the word *energy*. However, in this verse, the word *energeo* carries the idea of something that has suddenly become *energized* or *activated*. Paul's words could actually be rendered, "*That the communication of your faith may become energized and activated.…*"

Let me give you an example to help you understand what this word *energeo* means in the context of this verse. An automobile may be filled with enough fuel to drive a long distance, but it won't go anywhere until someone puts the key into the ignition and then turns the key. The moment that key is turned, the spark plugs are sparked, which fires up the engine. Once the engine has been activated, the potential in that car is ready to be unleashed.

The car always has the capability of moving, but if it is never activated, it sits silently in the driveway. No matter how much fuel is in the tank or how much horsepower that car possesses, its power and potential will never be realized until someone turns the key in the ignition.

Now let's apply this to you. In Philemon 1:6, the apostle Paul writes that "every good thing" has been placed in you by Jesus Christ. Think of it — He saved you, healed you, redeemed you, and protected you. He has given you a sound mind; He has given you the mind of Christ; He has imparted gifts and talents to you; and He has planned a future for your life that is simply glorious. You are loaded with phenomenal potential that is just waiting to be activated!

You may say, "Yes, well, I know that the Bible says I've been given all those good things, but I don't *feel* like any of that is true about me! I feel so defeated. Even though the Word says I'm healed, the reality is that I feel sick. Even though God's Word says I have a sound mind, I continually feel like I don't have control of my thought life. And in spite of the fact the Bible says God has blessed me with gifts and talents, I feel like a dope who has nothing to offer to this world. There is a big gap between what the Bible says about me and what I *feel* about me!"

My friend, you are like a car that is loaded with enough fuel and horsepower to get anywhere you need to go. But for that potential in you to be released, you have to hold the right key in your hand.

Furthermore, it isn't enough for you to just possess the key. You have to put that key into the "ignition" and turn it so the latent potential that resides inside you will be ignited. When you turn the key in the ignition, suddenly the potential you possess in Jesus Christ is supernaturally ignited, activated, energized, and released inside you!

+ So what is the key that sparks all the good things God has placed inside you into becoming an outward reality?
+ What is the key that causes all that God declares about you to become manifested in your life?
+ How do you "turn the key in the ignition" so that the great work God has done inside you is activated and released?

Paul says, "That the communication of thy faith may become effectual by the acknowledging of every good thing which is in you in Christ Jesus." The word "acknowledging" in this verse holds the answer to the questions above. This word is from the Greek word *epignosis*, which describes *a well-instructed, intensive, deep knowledge of the facts.*

The word *epignosis* pictures a person who knows his facts like a professional. This is a person so sure of his information that when he speaks, he does so with confidence and boldness. He has no reason to be ashamed or to fear that others may accuse him of being incorrect because he is well instructed and has an intensive, deep knowledge of the facts.

But how did he obtain such knowledge of the facts? No one becomes this knowledgeable accidentally.

For example, consider the book you hold in your hands. The information contained in this book didn't come to me while I was sleeping. It is the result of many years of study and very hard work. I have passionately applied myself to understanding the Greek New Testament so I could share these truths confidently and boldly with others.

To become astute requires study, meditation, digging deep into truth, and applying oneself to know the facts inside and out. The result of this hard work is such a thorough knowledge of the facts that a person has a strong confidence regarding what he says or writes.

In my case, I am confident of what I have written in this book because I have put so much study into it. You could say that I have an *epignosis* of this information.

Now Paul uses this same idea when he says we are to "acknowledge" every good thing that has been placed in us by Christ Jesus. Of course, this means we are to confess the truth about ourselves — but before we can confess the truth, we must first *know* the truth!

Because the word *epignosis* depicts a well-instructed, intensive, deep knowledge of the facts, Paul is letting you know that it is essential for you to possess:

✦ a knowledge of exactly who you are in Jesus Christ.
✦ a knowledge of what Jesus has purchased in your redemption.
✦ a knowledge of every good thing that God has placed in you by Jesus Christ.
✦ a knowledge of all these truths that is so concrete and so unshakable that you are immovable in what you think and believe.

If you don't know the facts of who you are in Jesus Christ, it's time for you to get serious about digging into the Bible until you know these truths like a professional. The truth about who you are in Jesus Christ is the key to your victory. You should study, read, listen to teaching material — in other words, you should use every available resource to discover what God's Word says you've been given in Jesus Christ. This knowledge is the key that will set you free. However, merely possessing the key won't activate these realities in your life. You must put the key into the ignition and turn it, sparking these truths into manifestation in your life!

A key in the ignition switch does no good unless it is turned. Likewise, the truth in your life does no good until it is spoken! The moment you open your mouth and start confessing the good things that are in you by Jesus Christ, a supernatural connection is made between your faith and all that Jesus has deposited inside you. At that moment, the gifts and treasures God has placed inside you become supernaturally activated. The confession of your mouth — your acknowledgement of the truth — is what sparks these spiritual blessings and causes them to become operative, activated, and manifested realities.

Sadly, many people who know the truth remain in bondage because they never align their mouths *with* the truth. Instead of speaking what God says about them, they ridicule themselves, put themselves down, and speak badly of themselves. They possess all the potential that God has placed inside them, but they never experience that potential because their mouths have never sparked and activated those spiritual blessings into becoming manifested realities.

To make these truths real in *your* life, you have to put the key in the ignition switch.

✦ The key is the Word of God.
✦ The ignition is your mouth.
✦ The key is turned in the ignition when you open your mouth and start to speak the truth.
✦ The good things in you are *activated* the moment you start confessing the truth.
✦ The way to make these blessings real in your life is to: 1) thoroughly know them through diligent study; 2) put these truths into your mouth; and 3) speak them out loud!
✦ *That is how you turn the key in your ignition and energize these truths until they begin to manifest in you!*

You see, it's time for you to stop speaking so badly about yourself. Instead, you need to open your mouth and start acknowledging who you are in Jesus Christ! By acknowledging the basic truths of what you have been given in Jesus, you will release so much divine energy that it will radically transform your life. The recognition of these spiritual treasures that reside within you will pick you up, lift you high, and carry you right over into the realm of victory you desire!

So quit talking negatively about yourself, and begin to bring the words of your mouth into agreement with the truths God has deposited in your life.

✦ God's Word says you're healed, so begin to say you're healed.
✦ God's Word says you have the mind of Christ, so begin to say you have the mind of Christ.
✦ God's Word says you're blessed, so begin to say you're blessed.

You turn the key in the ignition by getting your mouth in agreement with God's Word. *And as you start speaking what God says about you, all your potential will start becoming a manifested reality!*

MY PRAYER FOR TODAY

Lord, I know I have been speaking badly about myself. When I hear my own words, even I can tell it's wrong for me to speak so lowly about myself. You have done a great work in me, and I have kept myself bound by the words of my mouth. Forgive me for speaking so wrongly and for allowing myself to remain imprisoned in self-defeat. I am truly repentant for these actions, and I ask You to forgive me and to give me the power to change my behavior. Holy Spirit, I can only do this by Your power, so I am asking and expecting You to empower me to make these changes in my life and in my mouth!

I pray this in Jesus' name!

MY CONFESSION FOR TODAY

I confess that I speak well of myself. I don't batter myself with wrong or negative words. I agree with all that God's Word declares me to be, and I speak these truths about myself. Every day I am getting more positive and more faith-filled, and my mouth is speaking what God says about me. As a result, I am getting better, freer, and I am stepping upward more boldly into the plan God has for me!

I declare this by faith in Jesus' name!

QUESTIONS FOR YOU TO CONSIDER

1. Do you speak well of yourself, or do you find that you constantly criticize yourself and continually point out all your flaws? If you were to ask your friends what they hear you saying about yourself, would they say you speak positively or negatively?
2. How much time do you spend meditating on truths about who you are in Jesus Christ? Do you regularly read and confess what the Word of God says about you?
3. What changes do you need to make in your life in order to change your confessions about yourself? For those changes to happen, what do you need to do differently in your life and your daily routine?

It's time for you to stop speaking so badly about yourself. Instead, you need to open your mouth and start acknowledging who you are in Jesus Christ!

SEPTEMBER 24

How To Respond To a Financial Attack

And let us not be weary in well doing:
for in due season we shall reap, if we faint not.
— Galatians 6:9

One area where many people struggle is in the realm of finances. Financial stress is one of the most difficult pressures that can be experienced in life. If you've ever experienced the stress that comes from financial pressure, you *know* how difficult it is when you are so strapped that you don't have enough money to pay your bills.

But I want to tell you that God is always faithful! If you are living for God, walking in holiness, doing what the Holy Spirit has told you to do with your life, and sowing your financial seed into the soil of God's Kingdom, then you are *promised* a harvest to meet the needs in your own life. Sowing and reaping is not a fantasy or a fairy tale. This is God's promise to you, and it *always* works.

But what should you do when the devil is assailing your finances? I'm talking about those times when you've done everything you know to do, but you are still being financially hassled.

During those times when my family or our ministry experiences a financial shortage, we always evaluate several areas to see if we are doing anything that would hinder us from receiving the resources God wants to give us. In such moments, I always carefully examine my own heart, and I ask myself:

◆ *Am I harboring any unforgiveness that would block me from receiving God's blessings in my life?*

◆ *Am I walking in holiness before the Lord, or am I allowing any sinful thoughts or actions to have a place in me that would block me from receiving from the Lord?*

◆ *Am I doing what God has told me to do with my life, or am I disregarding His instructions and going my own way instead?*

◆ *Am I being faithful to sow my tithes and offerings into the Kingdom of God, or have I gotten behind in my giving or forgotten to sow a seed that the Spirit of God told me to sow?*

◆ *Am I under attack because the devil is against my dream or my mission and is therefore trying to turn off the valve of blessing so I become drained of what I need to fulfill the assignment God gave me?*

If I am at peace and sure that I have done nothing to hinder God's blessings from flowing into my life or ministry, I then proceed to deal with these shortfalls as devilish attacks. I take authority over the devil and tell him to take his hands off my finances. I press deep in prayer until I know inwardly that the blockage has been removed. Often I literally feel that barrier move out of the way as the Spirit of God shoves it aside and makes an avenue for His blessings to flow into my life and ministry. When this occurs, it is never long before my wife and I see a manifestation of God's blessings.

As we are commanding the devil to move out of the way, God's Spirit often speaks to our heart and tells us that we need to sow an extra, sacrificial financial seed into someone else's ministry in order to break the stranglehold the devil is trying to put on us. For instance, once when we needed a new building and were desperate to find the money to pay for it, the Holy Spirit instructed us to sow a seed into someone else's building project. "If you have a need, sow a seed" is the message always share with our congregation and partners.

Therefore, at the time of our own need, we knew it was time for us to sow an extra large gift into someone else's building program. Although the amount of money was huge to us at the moment, we knew that sowing that seed was *essential* if we were going to experience the financial breakthrough we needed for our own building. After we sowed that seed, it wasn't long before doors began to supernaturally open and the next facility we needed became available to us.

You see, sometimes you have to do something that requires extra faith in order to break the vice-like grip that the devil is trying to put on you. That extra sacrificial gift the Holy Spirit tells you to give may be the very act of faith that releases the power needed to rip the devil's hands off your situation. *Could it be that this is what you need to do right now in order to make a bold stand of faith?*

In Galatians 6:9, the apostle Paul told us, "And let us not be weary in well doing: for in due season we shall reap, if we faint not." Do you see the word "weary" in this verse? It comes from the Greek work *egkakao*, which is a compound of the words *en* and *kakos*. The word *en* means *in*, and the word *kakos* describes something that is *evil* or *bad*. When these two words are used together, as in this verse, the new word means *to grow weary; to give in to evil;* or *to let something bad defeat you.* It gives the idea of *surrendering* or *giving in to bad circumstances.*

This means the apostle Paul was telling the Galatians:

"Don't let evil get the best of you...."
"Don't let the bad circumstances wear you down and wear you out...."
"Don't give in to the evil that intends to defeat you...."

When hard financial times come, that isn't the time for you to surrender to circumstances — it's the time for you to put up a fight! Instead of giving in and surrendering to the attacks that are assailing you, you have to "put up your dukes," heave backward with all your spiritual might, and throw a knockout punch at the face of the devil! Don't shrink back in fear or worry; instead, make this a critical moment when you sow an extra financial seed! Do something bold that will break that stranglehold the devil has tried to put on you.

Could it be that this is one of those moments when you need to throw all your spiritual weight against the devil and show him that you're not going to take any more flak from him by sowing an extra seed?

Do exactly what the Holy Spirit impresses you to do. Once you obey His leading, you must then use your God-given authority and command the devil to take his foul hands off your finances! Boldly declare by faith that God's blessings are yours. *You have every right to expect God's blessings to come pouring into your life!*

MY PRAYER FOR TODAY

Lord, thank You for showing me today how to respond to the financial attacks I am experiencing in my life. Please help me know where to sow an extra financial seed right now. Help me to sow it by faith, confidently expecting it to break the stranglehold that has been on my financial situation. Satan, I command you to take your hands off my finances! I am a giver and therefore a receiver of God's promised blessings. You have no right to exercise any control over my money and possessions! I tell you to go in Jesus' name! Father, I thank You for honoring Your Word and causing my situation to turn around. I thank You in advance for the abundance that is going to start flowing into my life!

I pray this in Jesus' name!

MY CONFESSION FOR TODAY

I confess that I am an overcomer! Difficult circumstances do not control my life or my obedience. Instead of surrendering to the attacks that are assailing my finances, I am going to throw a knockout punch at the face of the devil! At this critical moment, I am going to sow an extra financial seed that will break the devil's stranglehold on my life. Once I obey what the Holy Spirit is telling me to do, I will boldly command the devil to take his foul hands off my finances! It won't be long before the seed I sow is multiplied back into my life. Then I'll stand in the manifestation of God's blessings!

I declare this by faith in Jesus' name!

QUESTIONS FOR YOU TO CONSIDER

1. Can you think of a specific time in your life when you were under great financial stress and the Holy Spirit instructed you to sow an extra large, extra sacrificial gift into your church or into someone's ministry?
2. What happened to your situation after you sowed that gift? Did you ultimately experience a turnaround in your situation? Did you attribute your financial breakthrough to your bold act of giving in a difficult moment?
3. If you are facing financial stress right now, could it be that you need to sow a special seed to break the stranglehold the devil is trying to force upon you?

SEPTEMBER 25

If You Give Mercy, You'll Be Shown Mercy!

Wherefore receive ye one another,
as Christ also received us to the glory of God.
— Romans 15:7

Have you ever been taken totally off-guard by someone who behaved in a way that was far different from what you expected from him? When this occurred, did you walk in love and forgive that person for what he did?

I've learned through the years that most people who act offensively don't do it on purpose. Sometimes they just inadvertently act in a way that gives a wrong impression to others. Often people who have done something offensive or hurtful to others aren't even aware of how they are being perceived by others.

Think about it. Haven't you had times when your actions were perceived differently than how you meant them to be perceived? *Have you ever been misunderstood?* Has anyone ever called your motives into question? Did it shock you to hear what others thought about you, especially when you knew your intentions were right? You may have meant one thing, but everyone seemed to perceive something totally different from what you intended. When you learn that others have misunderstood you, don't you wish they would believe the best about you rather than rush to judgment and condemn you for something you never intended to project?

Just as you want others to believe the best about you, you also need to reverse that grace and believe the best about others. So consider this question: If someone does something offensive, do you rush to judgment, or do you assume that the other person would never deliberately intend to be offensive?

A good rule to live by is to give the same grace to others that you want them to extend to you. You'll never go wrong by extending mercy to people. In fact, according to the law of sowing and reaping, if you give mercy to others, you are guaranteed to reap mercy from others when you need it the most.

So before your flesh becomes stirred up and upset the next time someone offends you, remember this: The chances are very good that you've done the very same thing to others that this person has done to you! That's why you need to speak to your emotions when you are tempted to get offended or to get into strife. Remind yourself of the many times you've been loved, forgiven, and freely accepted in spite of something you've done.

In Romans 15:7, the apostle Paul gave us a helpful word to assist us in our endeavor to walk in harmony and peace with other people. He said, "Wherefore receive ye one another, as Christ also received us to the glory of God." Do you see the word "receive" in this verse? It comes from the Greek word *proslambano*, a compound of the words *pros* and *lambano*. The word *pros* means *toward* and carries the idea of *being close to something*. The word *lambano* is the Greek word that means *to take* or *to receive*. When the two words are used together, the compound word means *to receive closely*. An even better rendering would be *to receive with a welcoming attitude*.

✦ Isn't this how Jesus received you?
✦ Didn't He take you just as you were at the time you came to Him?
✦ Didn't He take you with all your attitude problems, defects, inconsistencies, and blemishes?

According to the meaning of the Greek word *proslambano* that is used in Romans 15:7, we are to receive each other with wide-open arms, just as Jesus Christ received us when we first came to Him. But for us to obey this divine command, we'll have to do a lot of forgiving and overlooking in this life!

I strongly advise you to quit concentrating so fiercely on the faults and flaws of others and to start concentrating on how to be more forgiving and merciful. *If you give mercy, you'll be shown mercy.* Take the route of mercy, and you'll never be sorry. Believe it or not, there are times when you're supposed to shut your eyes to what you see other people do and just let it go!

If you'll take this approach to life, you'll have far less emotional disappointments and problems with your nerves. So determine today to give people the same forgiveness and mercy you want others to extend to you!

MY PRAYER FOR TODAY

Lord, please forgive me for being so harsh and judgmental of other people when they make mistakes or behave in ways that shock me. I know I become judgmental when I forget the mercy and grace that has been extended to me through the years. Therefore, I ask You to help me walk in a constant awareness of all the times I've been loved, forgiven, and accepted in spite of my behavior. Holy Spirit, help me now to be an extension of this same mercy and grace to others who need it from me.

I pray this in Jesus' name!

MY CONFESSION FOR TODAY

I confess that I walk in mercy and grace! I don't rush to judgment when others do things that are less than what I expected of them. I realize that everyone makes mistakes and that no one who truly loves Jesus would intentionally do the offensive and hurtful things I've seen some people do. These people don't realize how they are being perceived. I know they're making these mistakes because they need to grow and mature. So rather than judge others for what they have said, done, or failed to do, I will walk in mercy, grace, and forgiveness toward them just as I would want others to do for me.

I declare this by faith in Jesus' name!

QUESTIONS FOR YOU TO CONSIDER

1. How did Jesus receive you? Did He require perfection of you before He would accept you, or did He take you just as you were at the time you came to Him?
2. Since you started walking with the Lord, have you ever done anything to cause Jesus to turn His back on you? Or have you found Him to be completely committed to you regardless of your behavior?
3. Since this is how Jesus has accepted you, how should you respond to other people in your life who make mistakes and are less than perfect?

I strongly advise you to quit concentrating so fiercely on the faults and flaws of others and to start concentrating on how to be more forgiving and merciful. *If you give mercy, you'll be shown mercy.* Take the route of mercy, and you'll never be sorry. Believe it or not, there are times when you're supposed to shut your eyes to what you see other people do and just let it go!

SEPTEMBER 26

❧

*Do You Esteem Others
Better Than Yourself?*

Let nothing be done through strife or vainglory;
but in lowliness of mind let each esteem other
better than themselves.
— Philippians 2:3

When I was a young university student, I attended a small church where many college students worshiped. One day while attending a leaders' meeting where several issues were being discussed, I began to express my views about the subject under discussion. I didn't realize how long I had been talking until a fellow leader, who was older than I was, stopped me and said, "Rick, would you please be quiet? No one else can get a word into this conversation because you have been talking nonstop. It may be hard for you to believe, but you are not the only person who has an opinion and who knows something. We all have ideas and opinions that are just as valuable as yours, and we'd like to express them."

In my eagerness to provide input in the conversation, I didn't realize that I had inadvertently dominated the entire meeting. Finally, this leader had heard enough of me and kindly spoke up, telling me to be quiet so other people could express themselves. When I looked around the room at the other leaders, I realized they were all breathing a sigh of relief that someone had finally told me to be quiet. I was so embarrassed!

In retrospect, I realize that because I was the youngest in the group, I was unconsciously trying to prove I had something to contribute that was as important as what everyone else had to say. But in my efforts to prove my worth in the sight of those other leaders, I nearly took over the discussion, making it appear as if I wanted to "hog" the whole conversation. Of course, this was *not* the greatest way to show that I had respect for other people! I didn't intend to give this impression, but that was the impression I gave to the others in that group.

After that incident, I remember turning to Philippians 2:3 and reading the words of the apostle Paul. It says, "Let nothing be done through strife or vainglory; but in lowliness of mind let each esteem other better than themselves."

When I saw this verse in light of the stern rebuke I had just received, I decided I wanted to understand clearly what it meant to "esteem" others better than myself. But first I decided to study those words "strife" and "vainglory" so I could completely comprehend what Paul was referring to in this verse.

When Paul writes about "strife" and "vainglory," he uses two very strategic Greek words. The word "strife" is the Greek word *eritheia*, which is the picture of *a person who is jockeying for some kind of position*. This is a person who is trying to make himself look powerful, insightful, or significant in the sight of other people. But Paul then mentions "vainglory," which is the Greek word *kenodoxia*. This is an interesting Greek mixture of concepts that describes the utter futility of such jockeying and positioning. The word *kenodoxia* is a compound of the words *kenos* and *doxas*. *Kenos* describes something that is *hollow* or *empty*, and the word *doxas* is the word for *glory*. But when these two words are compounded together into one word as in this verse, it portrays *a hollow or empty boasting* — a kind of *self-glory* that echoes of *self-promotion*.

These words could thus be interpreted to mean:

"Do not jockey for position or try to prove your importance to others with a lot of hollow, empty boasting and self-promotion...."

Paul says that instead of acting in this manner that is so wrong in God's sight, we are to act in "lowliness of mind." This phrase comes from the Greek word *tapeinoprosune*. The first part of the word is the Greek word *tapeinos*, which describes *something that is lowly, humble, or base*. It pictures the attitude of someone who is unassuming and not self-promoting. It suggests a person who is modest, unpretentious, and "without airs" about himself, even if he knows that he is more intelligent, gifted, or talented than others. The second part of the word is *phronos*, which means *to think*. When these two words are compounded together, the new word means *to think lowly; to think in an unpretentious way about oneself;* or *to think modestly of oneself*.

A person who fits this description doesn't jockey for a position of importance, "hogging" every conversation and trying to prove how great he is. Instead, he has learned to "esteem others better than himself." The word "esteem" comes from the Greek word *hegeomai*, which means *to lead* or *to consider*. This word and its related forms referred to *outstanding and resplendent leaders who were worthy to be recognized and honored*. These leaders held a noteworthy and superior position in the eyes of others, commanding people's respect, honor, and silence when in their presence.

If you add these Greek word meanings to the interpretive translation above, the entire verse could be interpreted to mean:

"Do not jockey for position or try to prove your importance to others with a lot of hollow, empty boasting and self-promotion. Instead, have a modest opinion of yourself, and learn to recognize the outstanding contributions that others have to impart."

By using this word, Paul is telling us that we must learn to quit promoting ourselves and learn to respect the outstanding, resplendent gifts and ideas God has given to others. Rather than incessantly talk and "hog" every conversation, we must learn to make room for the gifts that lie resident in other people. Their talents and ideas are just as important as ours are. However, if we constantly demand everyone's attention and never allow others to have an opportunity to express themselves or to use their gifts, we create a situation in which others go *unrecognized* and are thus *dishonored*.

When I was a university student, on fire for God and eager to fulfill God's call on my life, I didn't realize how self-consumed I was with my own vision and calling — so consumed that I ignored the outstanding gifts God had placed in the people around me. Although it was right for me to be completely committed to my calling, I had to be taught that it was wrong to be so self-projecting and negligent to recognize the gifts, callings, and dreams of others. In my youthful attempts to prove I had something valuable to contribute, I dishonored those who also had insights just as worthy as my own. I had to learn to think lowly of myself, to keep my mouth shut, and to recognize that I wasn't the only one in any given setting who had something to say.

If you've inadvertently fallen into the habit of constantly talking and promoting yourself with a lot of vainglorious self-talk, it's time for you to let the Holy Spirit teach you to respect and make room for the contributions of others in the group. *If you'll sincerely ask the Holy Spirit to help you, He will begin to teach you how to esteem others better than yourself!*

MY PRAYER FOR TODAY

Lord, forgive me for the times I was so engrossed in my own ideas and convictions that I "hogged" entire conversations and didn't give others an opportunity to express what was on their hearts. I am truly repentant for giving people the impression that I thought I was the only one in the group with something worthy to say. Forgive me for being so self-absorbed and for not recognizing the other outstanding people with gifts, talents, and ideas that were just as valuable as my own. Please help me learn to think more highly of others, to keep my mouth shut more often, and to genuinely appreciate the gifts, talents, and ideas You have placed in other people.

I pray this in Jesus' name!

MY CONFESSION FOR TODAY

I confess that I am very respectful of other people and that I recognize the gifts, talents, and ideas God has given them. I need the insights and gifts that God has put in other people. Because they are just as important as I am, I always give them time to express themselves and to let their gifts function as God intends. I am a part of a God-gifted group, and every member is filled with gifts and ideas that I need. Therefore, I make room for them to let those gifts and ideas flow!

I declare this by faith in Jesus' name!

QUESTIONS FOR YOU TO CONSIDER

1. Do you esteem others better than yourself? Do you treat people like they are valuable, unique creations of God who deserve the highest respect? Or have you inadvertently focused only on yourself, giving others the impression that you think you are the only one who has something to contribute?
2. Have you ever had to work with someone who "hogged" every conversation and didn't give anyone else an opportunity to express himself? How did it make you feel toward that person?
3. What can you do to show others that you value them and their opinions? What visible actions can you take to demonstrate your appreciation for others in the group you belong to?

Do not jockey for position or try to prove your importance to others with a lot of hollow, empty boasting and self-promotion. Instead, have a modest opinion of yourself, and learn to recognize the outstanding contributions that others have to impart.

SEPTEMBER 27

❦

Confess Your Faults One to Another

Confess your faults one to another,
and pray one for another, that ye may be healed....
— James 5:16

I remember how glad I was when I finally admitted that Satan was trying to drive a lie into my head! Even though I knew that the lie I was hearing was untrue, the devil wouldn't let up. He just kept pounding my mind hard and fast, one blow after another, as he tried to batter his way into my head and take my thinking captive.

I was too embarrassed to share with anyone else the stupid thought that was trying to take me hostage, so I tried to handle it on my own for a long time. Finally, I thought I would break under the assault that was bombarding my mind and emotions. The lie was beginning to affect how I viewed myself, penetrating and manipulating my mind to think poorly of myself. So in obedience to James 5:16, I went to a friend and told him what the devil was trying to make me believe. The moment I confessed the lie, it was as if an over-inflated balloon had just popped. The power that lie had held in my mind simply dissipated once I admitted to a friend what I was hearing!

I'm not recommending that you go from person to person, blabbing about all your faults. But if you experience a time of real need in your life when the devil is assaulting your mind and emotions, you might need to go to your spouse, a good friend, a brother or sister in the Lord, your pastor, or your parent and confess: "I need someone to help me! I'm being attacked in my mind, and I need someone to speak to me and to tell me the truth!"

In James 5:16, the Bible commands us, "Confess your faults one to another, and pray one for another, that ye may be healed...." The word "confess" is the Greek word *ekzomologeo*, a word that means *to declare, to say out loud, to exclaim, to divulge*, or *to blurt*. I particularly like the last meaning — *to blurt*.

You see, sometimes it's hard to confess the wrong thoughts that are rolling through your mind. Even though you know you need to confess and thus destroy what the devil is trying to tell you, it can be embarrassing and humiliating to be so honest. Perhaps you've tried to admit these things before to someone, but each time you retreat back into silence because you can't bear the idea of anyone knowing that you ever entertained such foolish thoughts!

It's time for you to get bold! Go find a friend in whom you can confide — one who will not repeat what you tell him or her. Tell that person you have something you need to confess. If you feel yourself pulling back, just go ahead and *blurt it out*! Once you say it, you'll be done with it. Then the agony of telling someone will be over, and you'll be on the road to freedom!

But what are the parameters of what we are to confess to each others? James 5:16 goes on to define what we are to confess. It says, "Confess your faults...." The word "faults" is the Greek word *paraptoma*, which describes *a falling in some area of one's life*. That "falling" may be an actual falling into sin, or it may be a tripping up in the way one thinks. Either way, this word refers to *a person who has fallen, failed, erred, or made some kind of mistake*. One Greek translator says it can also denote *a person who has accidentally bumped into something* or *one who has accidentally swerved or turned amiss and has thus thought something or done something that is erroneous*.

This perfectly describes what had happened to me that time when my mind was being harassed with those distracting thoughts. The devil was pounding away at my head, and I was starting to believe the lie! As a result, it was affecting me; I was even starting to produce failure in that part of my life. I had bumped into a mental lie that was about to knock me off my feet and cause me to make some very erroneous decisions in my life!

I think of others who were harassed in their minds and never confessed it to anyone. Because they were not able to conquer those lies by themselves and yet were too proud to confess it to anyone else, these people eventually became enslaved by the lie and ended up doing some very regrettable things. If only they had confessed their faults to a godly friend who loved them, they could have been liberated from the lie and the actions that followed.

When you blurt out those destructive lies to a trustworthy friend, your confession is often the very thing that throws that lying spirit off you. As long as you keep those lies secretly hidden away in your mind and soul, they will continue to have the power to hold you hostage. But the day you expose them to the light of day, those lies will begin to lose their power over you!

You may be afraid to confess what you've been experiencing because in the past, something you shared privately wasn't held in confidence. That memory is Satan's ploy to keep you all tied up. But you must forgive those who betrayed your confidence and go get the help you need right now. *Get that lie out of the darkness! Bring it into the light so it can dissipate and lose its power over your mind and emotions.*

MY PRAYER FOR TODAY

Lord, I thank You for speaking to my heart today about confessing the things that are secretly bothering me. It is no secret to You that I have been struggling with fear, insecurity, and temptation. You know that I desperately need someone to stand with me in faith and to assure me that everything is going to be all right. Help me to know exactly to whom I should go to discuss what is disturbing me — someone who will be faithful to hold what I say in confidence. Once I confess this burden and get it off my heart, please let this be the very act that sets in motion the power to liberate me!

I pray this in Jesus' name!

MY CONFESSION FOR TODAY

I confess that I have friends who are trustworthy and in whom I can confide when Satan is trying to pound my mind with his lies. I do not fear that friends will laugh at me or repeat what I tell them. They will stand with me, speak the truth to me, and help me step out of the darkness and into the light. My confession will break Satan's vice grip on my mind and bring wholeness and soundness of thinking to my soul!

I declare this by faith in Jesus' name!

QUESTIONS FOR YOU TO CONSIDER

1. Have you ever gone to someone and confessed something that was secretly bothering you? Once you finally blurted out to someone what you'd been struggling with, what effect did it have on you?

2. Are you the kind of person that people can confide in when they are being inwardly harassed? Do they consider you to be faithful and confidential, or would they be concerned that you might repeat what they told you?

3. Has the enemy been bombarding your mind with his lies lately? If so, who is the one person to whom you'd most like to confess this inward harassment?

SEPTEMBER 28

A Hard Lesson
About Paying Attention!

After they were come to Mysia, they assayed to go into Bithynia:
but the Spirit suffered them not.
— Acts 16:7

*A*s I lay down on the hotel bed to take a one-hour nap before we left for a church service in a large Midwestern city, I kept feeling a "tug" in my heart to stay home from the meeting that night. But I wanted to go hear the special speaker that evening. Besides, many of our ministry friends were going to be there, and I wanted to tell them goodbye since this was to be our last night in the area.

As we walked out the door of the hotel room, I turned to Denise and said, "I don't know why, Denise, but I think I'm going to let you go tonight, and I'm going to stay here." As she walked out the door, however, I couldn't bear the thought of missing a fantastic night at the meeting, so I headed downstairs to the car that waited to take us. I couldn't figure out why I seemed impressed to stay in the room that night, so I overruled what my spirit was telling me and went on to church.

When the car pulled up to the church, I was overwhelmed with a "knowing" that I had to go back to the room. Once again, I told Denise, "I'm going to tell everyone goodbye right now before the meeting begins; then I'm going back to the room. I'll see you when you get home from church tonight." But as I went around telling people goodbye, I got involved in first one conversation, then another, and then another, until time began to slip away. Finally, the turmoil in my spirit became so strong that I asked the driver to take me right back to the hotel.

As I drove to the hotel, I kept thinking how irrational it was for me to feel like I needed to be at the hotel that night. Why would I need to be there? There was nothing urgent to do and no calls to make, so why did I have this incredible "urge" to get back to the hotel room? *But when I opened the door to our room, I was stunned to see that the entire room had been ransacked.*

✦ Suitcases were sprawled across the room.
✦ Clothes were hurled all over the place.
✦ Denise's jewelry boxes were opened, empty, and scattered on the floor.
✦ My computer had been taken from the desk where it had been sitting.
✦ My briefcase that contained my tickets, my passport, and my visas was gone.

When I saw that my computer and briefcase were gone, I realized that whoever had done this hadn't just stolen those two items. The information on my computer and in my briefcase included:

✦ Nine years of important study notes.
✦ My American passport.
✦ My Latvian residence visa.
✦ My brand-new Russian visa.
✦ All my international travel documents.
✦ All my credit cards.
✦ My birth certificate.
✦ My Daytimer that was filled with vital addresses and phone numbers.

I went straight to the hotel desk to inform them that we had been robbed. I called Denise home from the church meeting, and we spent the rest of the evening with a group of police, who searched for clues as to who might have done this to us. When Denise looked through those empty, scattered jewelry boxes, she discovered that many pieces of jewelry recently given to her by a relative were gone. These pieces weren't worth a great deal monetarily, but they had great sentimental value.

I looked at Denise and said, "Now I know why I kept feeling a tug in my spirit to stay home from the meeting tonight. The Holy Spirit was trying to prevent this from happening. If I had obeyed that still, small voice in my heart and stayed home, that thief would have never entered this room."

What was so maddening about this was that I had been *diligently* paying attention to even the most gentle leadings in my spirit for a solid month. In fact, I had ardently *focused* and *concentrated* on being "in tune" with the still, small voice of the Holy Spirit in my own heart during that month. Because of my sensitivity to the Spirit of God, it had been a month of supernatural intervention and intimate fellowship with Him.

But that night, I simply overruled that still, small voice I heard in my heart because I wanted to be in that meeting so much. After listening so carefully for the Holy Spirit's leading for a full month, I didn't pay attention to Him. The Spirit of God was *blaring* His warning in my heart, trying to keep us from being taken advantage of — but I missed it. Later as I looked around at our ransacked room, I was more upset with myself than I was with the thief who took our belongings!

We must all learn to put on the brakes, stop ourselves for a while, and listen carefully to what the Holy Spirit is speaking to our hearts. Although we may not immediately understand what He is telling us to do or why we should do it exactly the way He is leading us, the results of our obedience will be powerful and we will experience less defeat and fewer mishaps in our lives.

In Acts 16:7, Paul and his apostolic team were headed to Bithynia when suddenly, the Spirit of God impressed them to stay away from that region. The verse says, "After they were come to Mysia, they assayed to go into Bithynia: but the Spirit suffered them not."

The word "assayed" tells us how badly Paul and his team wanted to go to Bithynia. The word "assayed" is the Greek word *peiradzo*, which means *to attempt* or *to try*. The Greek tense used in this particular verse indicates *an incomplete action*, which alerts us to the fact that Paul and his team actually tried to go to Bithynia but were unsuccessful in their attempt. How hard they tried is not clear, but the Greek word *peiradzo* implies that they tried very hard to go there.

Paul suffered many difficulties as he traveled to different regions, but it rarely stopped him from going where he had intended to go. The reason he and his ministry team didn't press on in their efforts this time is that the Holy Spirit "suffered them not" to go to Bithynia. The phrase "suffered them not" comes from the Greek words *ouk eiasen*. The word *ouk* is a strong *"No!"* The word *eiasen* is from the Greek word *eao*, which means *to allow* or *to permit*. When these words become the phrase *ouk eiasen*, the new word means *to not permit* or *to forbid*.

That day, the apostle Paul and his team listened to the leading of the Spirit to stay out of the region of Bithynia. By staying away from Bithynia, they apparently circumvented some kind of disaster that awaited them there. We don't know what devilish trap had been set for Paul if he had gone to that region, but we do know he avoided it by obeying the Holy Spirit's instructions.

As children of God, we must learn to follow the Holy Spirit's leadership, direction, and guidance. The vandalizing of our hotel room is a good reminder to all of us to stay sensitive to what the Holy Spirit is telling us to do, even if we can't rationalize or figure out why He is telling us to do it.

If the Holy Spirit impresses you to stay home, then stay home. If He impresses you not to get on an airplane, then don't get on that airplane. If He impresses you to give a special offering, then you need to sow that offering. Don't learn the hard way how important it is to pay attention to the Holy Spirit. *Whatever He impresses you to do is exactly what you need to do!*

MY PRAYER FOR TODAY

Lord, help me follow the Holy Spirit's leading whenever He impresses me to do something. I know there have been moments in my life when the Spirit was leading me to do something. But because I didn't understand it, I didn't obey — and later I was always sorry. Please help me become more sensitive to the Holy Spirit and to trust Him when He speaks to my heart. I want to be obedient and to experience the supernatural life that He wants to give me!

I pray this in Jesus' name!

MY CONFESSION FOR TODAY

I confess that I listen to the leading of the Holy Spirit. Because I follow His leading, I am able to circumvent traps that the devil tries to set for me. If the Holy Spirit impresses me to stay home, I stay home. If He tells me not to get on an airplane, I don't get on that airplane. If He nudges me to give a special offering, I sow that offering. Whatever the Spirit impresses me to do is exactly what I do!

I declare this by faith in Jesus' name!

QUESTIONS FOR YOU TO CONSIDER

1. Can you think of some instances in your life when the Holy Spirit tried to stop you from doing something, but because you didn't understand or want to obey what He was saying, you ignored His leadership and did something you later regretted?
2. Can you think of several instances when the Holy Spirit told you to do something and you obeyed Him? What happened as a result of your doing exactly what the Spirit was telling you to do?
3. Is there anything the Spirit is leading you to do right now that you have been hesitant to do? What's stopping you from obeying the Holy Spirit in this matter?

SEPTEMBER 29

❧❧❧

Do You Know
What You Are Called To Do?

Not as though I had already attained, either were already perfect…
— Philippians 3:12

I have no doubt as to what God has called me to do with my life. He has called me to preach the Gospel and to help establish the Church in regions of the world that are unstable, difficult, and unchurched. That is my calling, and I am very confident of this fact. But for me to fulfill this divine call on my life requires hard work, attention, and a determination to *never* stop until I have achieved exactly what Jesus intended for me to achieve with my life.

When you look at the life of the apostle Paul, you'll find it very evident that he emphatically *knew* his calling. Furthermore, he was able to concretely express it and often wrote of it in his epistles. Over and over again, he wrote that he was an apostle to the Gentiles (Galatians 2:8). Paul lived, breathed, ate, and slept and awoke every day to the call of God that was on his life.

When Paul was in a Roman prison with the prospect of death staring him in the face, he never gave up because he knew he hadn't yet fulfilled the entire plan God had revealed to him. I personally believe that reaching his God-given goal was in Paul's mind when he wrote, "Not as though I had already attained, either were already perfect…" (Philippians 3:12).

The word "perfect" is the Greek word *teleo*. It refers to *something that is ripe, mature, perfect, or complete*. It suggests that Paul meant, "I have done a lot and accomplished much in comparison to others, but I haven't yet brought my assignment to completion. The job is not finished. I have not yet completed what God has called me to do."

During his multiple years of serving the Lord, Paul had achieved more than any other Christian leader of his time. He had preached on different continents, traveled to the countries of the Mediterranean Sea, and preached to governors and kings. Besides all these notable accomplishments, Paul had written the majority of the New Testament text! But none of this mattered to him because he knew he hadn't yet "attained" that for which Jesus Christ had apprehended him.

Instead of relaxing and taking it easy at the end of his life, Paul therefore turned his attention to the dream — to the unfulfilled vision or assignment that was still before him. Because there was still so much left to do, he went on to say, "…I follow after…." This phrase comes from the Greek word *dioko*, which is the word that is usually translated *to persecute*. Let's stop and talk about this for a moment so we can understand the full force of what Paul was writing in this verse.

The word *dioko*, translated as "I follow after," is a fiercely aggressive word. In historic Greek literature, it means *to hunt; to pursue; to chase; to track down and kill*. It is the picture of an outdoorsman who is so determined to hunt down an animal that he will stop at nothing to pursue, chase, track down, and ultimately get his game!

Do hunters accidentally bag their game, or do they strategize in their plans to get a good one each hunting season? *Hunters strategize!* They dream! They talk to other hunters about the best places to hunt! They dress in camouflaged clothes; then they perch themselves high up on tree branches and wait for hours upon hours for an unlucky deer to walk into their trap. Once the deer comes in range, *they shoot to kill*! They hunt, hound, and stalk that animal until they finally kill it. Then they throw the big catch in the back of their truck and head home with their trophy — and the prospect of many good venison meals in their future! That is exactly what Paul means when he says, "I follow after."

The apostle Paul strategized, planned, studied, and ardently followed after the call of God on his life. You could say that he hunted, hounded, and stalked the call of God with all his heart, never stopping until he could say, "I got my game!" When Paul's job was finished, he gladly said, "...I have finished my course..." (2 Timothy 4:7). That's when he packed it all up and went home to Heaven with his trophy — a crown of reward.

For you to achieve what God has planned for your life, it will likewise require a fierce determination to keep pressing ahead. You can never stop until every part of your God-given assignment has been fulfilled. Jogging along at a comfortable pace will never get you where you need to go. You must focus your attention on the goal and then strategize, plan, and work until you can confidently say, "I've done exactly what Jesus wanted me to do!" But be forewarned: Achieving this goal will demand your utmost concentration and undivided attention and the empowerment of the Holy Spirit.

Do you know God's plan for your life? Do you know the assignment He has designed just for you? Are you following after that divine call with all your heart? *If not, today is the perfect time to start discovering and then following after God's call on your life!*

MY PRAYER FOR TODAY

Lord, I am asking You to help me to really know my calling so I can ardently follow after it with all my might. Help me push all distractions out of my way and to put my sights on fulfilling the assignment You have designed for me. I know this is going to take the greatest concentration, so please help me to focus on Your plan and to refuse to allow anything to pull me away from reaching Your goal for my life!

I pray this in Jesus' name!

MY CONFESSION FOR TODAY

I confess that I will achieve what God has planned for my life. I am fiercely determined to keep pressing ahead, and I will never stop until every part of my God-given assignment has been fulfilled. I have set my sights on reaching God's plan — and I will not stop until I can confidently say, "I've done exactly what Jesus wanted me to do!"

I declare this by faith in Jesus' name!

QUESTIONS FOR YOU TO CONSIDER

1. Do you know what God has called you to do with your life? Are you really confident of your calling, or are you just taking a stab in the dark, hoping you are headed in the right direction?
2. If you keep pursuing God's plan at the rate you are moving at right now, will you reach your God-ordained destination?

3. What changes do you need to make in order for you to reach the goal God has planned for your life? Why not make a list of ten things you need to do to streamline your life and help you stay more focused so you can successfully do what God has called you to do?

SEPTEMBER 30

A Bitter Root Produces Sour Fruit!

Looking diligently lest any man fail of the grace of God;
lest any root of bitterness springing up trouble you,
and thereby many be defiled.
— Hebrews 12:15

When a person becomes offended and doesn't deal with that offense correctly, that bitterness often churns so long in a person's soul that it turns into a root of bitterness. This is exactly what Hebrews 12:15 is talking about when it says, "Looking diligently lest any man fail of the grace of God; lest any root of bitterness springing up trouble you, and thereby many be defiled."

The word "root" is the Greek word *ridzo*. It refers to *a root, such as the root of a tree*. These are *roots that have gone down deep and are now deeply embedded*. Therefore, the word *ridzo* often denotes *something that is established or firmly fixed*.

By using the word *ridzo* ("root"), God is telling you that if you don't repent of bitterness and remove it from your life, it becomes *deeply embedded* in your soul. Once it becomes this deeply rooted in your soul, your negative opinion of the offender will become *firmly fixed*. As time passes, your thoughts of judgment against him will become more developed, rationalized, and established. That root of bitterness will become so firmly fixed inside you that your angry, judgmental thoughts about the person will actually begin to make sense to you.

When a "root of bitterness" gets this *deeply embedded* in your mind and emotions, it's no longer just a "root" you're dealing with; now you have *a mental stronghold*. That stronghold of bitterness will take a lofty position in your mind and emotions. From that position, it will then present a myriad of logical reasons to explain why you shouldn't have anything else to do with that person and why you should keep your distance from him.

The word "bitterness" comes from the Greek word *pikria*. It refers to *an inward attitude that is so bitter, it produces a scowl on one's face*. In other words, you become so inwardly *infected* with bitterness that you are outwardly *affected* in your appearance and disposition.

This "bitterness" is acid to one's soul, and eventually it begins to surface. When it does, the fruit it produces is *unkind, sour, sharp, sarcastic, scornful, cynical, mocking, contemptuous,* and *wounding*. Bitterness has nothing good to say about the other person. In fact, it looks for negative things to say about that person in order to affect others' opinions about him as well.

If you find yourself constantly saying negative things about someone who has offended you or upset you in the past, it may be that a root of bitterness is trying to grow inside your heart. If this describes you, it is essential that you grab hold of that root of bitterness through the act of repentance and *rip* those destructive roots clear out of your soul! If you don't, the roots of bitterness will go down deep into the soil of your soul, and eventually you'll be filled with the bitter fruit that bitterness produces.

If God's Spirit has been trying to deal with you about a negative attitude you have toward someone else, pay attention to what the Holy Spirit is saying to you. Go get alone with God. Ask Him to put His divine hand into your soul and to extract that ugly growth that is trying to grow inside of you. *God wants to liberate you, but it must begin with your invitation!*

MY PRAYER FOR TODAY

Lord, I don't want any bitterness to sprout inside me, so I am asking You to turn on the spotlight of the Holy Spirit and reveal any unforgiveness or resentment that might be lurking inside my heart. I know that the fruit of bitterness is very sour, and I don't want that fruit to be a part of my life. So, Holy Spirit, I ask You to please show me every root of bitterness, and then help me rip it clear out of my soul!

I pray this in Jesus' name!

MY CONFESSION FOR TODAY

I confess that I refuse to allow a root of bitterness to grow deep into the soil of my heart. The instant I recognize that a seed of bitterness is trying to sprout in me, I will grab hold of that root, and through the act of repentance, rip those destructive roots out of my soul. I choose to walk in forgiveness and to stay free!

I declare this by faith in Jesus' name!

QUESTIONS FOR YOU TO CONSIDER

1. Is there anyone against whom you have a root of bitterness right now? If so, who is that person? Is there a reason you've allowed bitterness to fester inside your soul? Don't you see that it would be more healthy for you to forgive your offender and to walk free of those detrimental attitudes?
2. Is there anyone whom you have wronged and who now has a root of bitterness because of you? If yes, who is that person? What is stopping you from going to that person to ask him or her for forgiveness?
3. Which person comes to your mind as an example of someone who has been controlled by bitterness? When you think of that person and the bitterness that has dominated his or her life, doesn't it make you want to be sure that bitterness never controls you?

If you find yourself constantly saying negative things about someone who has offended you or upset you in the past, could it be possible that a root of bitterness is trying to grow inside your heart?

OCTOBER 1

If You Lack Wisdom

If any of you lack wisdom, let him ask of God,
that giveth to all men liberally, and upbraideth not;
and it shall be given him.
— James 1:5

*H*ave you ever had a time in your life when you needed answers for a problem you were facing, but it seemed that you just couldn't come up with the right solution? Even though you tried hard to figure things out, did it seem like the right answer to your problem kept eluding you?

In our own ministry, I have found myself baffled in this way on several occasions. When I face one of those moments, I claim James 1:5 and go to God for wisdom. I have even brought our top leadership together so we could corporately pray to get God's wisdom on how best to confront and conquer the challenge we were facing.

James 1:5 promises that if we will go to Him when we need wisdom, He will give us the answers we need! This verse says, "If any man lack wisdom, let him ask of God, that giveth to all men liberally, and upbraideth not; and it shall be given him."

If you've ever faced a time when you lacked:

✦ Wisdom about how to pay your bills;
✦ Wisdom about how to deal with debt;
✦ Wisdom about how to reverse a decline you were experiencing in your business;
✦ Wisdom about how to resolve challenges with your children;
✦ Wisdom about how to fix things between you and your spouse;
✦ Wisdom about how to get along with your boss or fellow employees;
✦ Wisdom about how to make key decisions that affect your future — then the word "lack" in James 1:5 perfectly describes you!

You see, the word "lack" is the Greek word *leipo*, a Greek word that pictures *a deficit* of some kind. In our modern-day language, we might call this *a shortfall, a shortage, a scarcity,* or *a deficiency.* For instance, people often speak of a "shortfall" of finances. When they experience such a financial shortfall, it greatly impairs their ability to do business as necessary. Or when a city experiences an electrical blackout, they experience a "shortage" of electrical power. This kind of shortage paralyzes the whole city and has a powerfully negative effect on people's lives.

For example, when my family first moved to the Soviet Union at the end of the Soviet period of Perestroika, there was a scarcity or deficit of almost every kind of product. For instance, it was very problematic to find sugar, flour, eggs, milk, butter, meat, and gasoline to purchase. We would search store after store, trying to find these nearly non-existent products. If items did suddenly become available, the news raced across the city so fast that long lines of people almost instantaneously formed around the store and down the street. Citizens would stand in those lines for hours at a time, clinging to the hope that there would be enough of these products to last until they reached the front of the line. However, those at the end of the lines usually went home disappointed, for whenever a product did suddenly become available, it usually arrived in very small quantities.

In fact, if a person didn't have in his possession the government-issued "ration coupons" necessary to obtain these basic products, he couldn't purchase them at all. Once a person's monthly supply of those coupons were used up, it was impossible for him to go back to the store to get more until the next month. Thus, when a person's coupons ran out, so did his ability to get any of these basic essentials. This meant that people were very careful about how they used sugar, flour, eggs, milk, butter, meat, and gasoline.

This was life when I first moved my family to the USSR. The system was economically broken, and the scarcity or deficit that existed was so far-reaching, it affected the entire nation. I can tell you from personal experience that when this kind of scarcity exists, it has a great effect on one's ability to live and to function normally.

These kinds of scarcities and deficits could be described by the Greek word *leipo*, which is translated "lack" in the *King James Version* of James 1:5. But the "lack" James is referring to is not sugar, flour, eggs, milk, butter, meat, or gasoline. James says, "If any of you lack *wisdom*...."

A lack of "wisdom" is the most devastating kind of deficit a person or nation can face, for wisdom has the answers, the solutions, and the principles that are needed to reverse any situation and turn it around for the better. A person is at a great disadvantage when he is void of wisdom about how to pay his bills and conquer debt; how to reverse a decline in his business; how to resolve challenges with his children, his spouse, his boss, or his coworkers; or how to make key decisions that will affect his future. When a person lacks this kind of wisdom, it nearly paralyzes him, because he doesn't know what to do!

When James says, "If any of you lack wisdom," the word "wisdom" is the Greek word *sophias*. This word *sophias* could describe *enlightenment*, *insight*, or even *special insight*.

Just because someone has a university degree doesn't mean he possesses wisdom. I assure you that there are many stupid university graduates in the world. Although they are intellectually bright and have diplomas hanging all over the walls of their homes and offices, many of them have an approach to life that is totally impractical and fruitless. They theorize all day long but never get anything done. On the other hand, there are many down-to-earth people who never had the privilege of going to college but possess so much wisdom that they've become very successful in life.

You need to treat education like it is important, for it definitely is. However, you also need to understand that having an education is *not* the equivalent of having wisdom. Education gives you information and facts; but wisdom gives you principles, solutions, and answers. Wisdom gives you special insight that helps you know what to do. Wisdom contains the principles that will lead you out of that baffling situation and into a place where things begin to work again! Wisdom guides you to do what is right. Man has education; but God has wisdom.

Are you experiencing a time in your life right now when you need wisdom about a particular situation? Even though you've studied and tried to find solutions on your own, have those solutions been evading you? If so, it's time for you to get a good dose of wisdom from on High! That's why James says, "If any of you lack wisdom, let him ask of God...."

The word "ask" is the Greek word *aiteo*. As noted earlier (*see* March 23), the word *aiteo* means *to be adamant in requesting and demanding assistance to meet tangible needs*, such as food, shelter, money, and so forth. This person may *insist* or *demand* that a certain need be met, but he approaches his superior with respect and honor as he makes his very strong request. The word *aiteo* also expresses the idea that *the one asking has a full expectation to receive what has been firmly requested.*

When James tells us to "ask" God for the wisdom we need, the Greek tense used is a command. This plainly means God isn't suggesting that we come to Him for wisdom; He is commanding us to do so!

**When these words are used together
in one phrase, it could be translated:**

"If anyone lacks insight, let him firmly request it...."
"If anyone has a shortage of wisdom, he should demand it...."
"If anyone is baffled and doesn't know what to do, he should be bold to ask...."

You see, God wants you to come to Him for wisdom first instead of trying to figure things out on your own. Instead of relying on your education and the books on your shelf to give you the answers you need, go to God first and firmly ask Him for wisdom. Approach Him with respect and honor, but also be bold. As a child of God, you have a right to request wisdom from God when you need it!

When your mind is suddenly enlightened and you miraculously see exactly what you need to do or what steps you need to take, those problems that have seemed so mountainous will melt before you. You see, your biggest problem is not the one that is staring you right in the face. Your biggest problem is your lack of wisdom about how to deal with that situation.

So rather than continue to struggle in your own strength, why don't you go to God and *ask* Him to give you the necessary wisdom to conquer the situation you are facing in your life right now? As a child of God, you have every right to ask Him. In fact, God *commands* you to come to Him when you lack wisdom! *So take a few minutes today to obey that command. Ask God to give you the wisdom you need!*

MY PRAYER FOR TODAY

Lord, help me to come to You when I find myself lacking answers about situations that need to be changed in my life. When I have done all I know to do and don't know what else to do, remind me that every answer I need resides with You. Your wisdom holds the answers I am looking for; therefore, I am making the decision to come to You now so You can start speaking to me!

I pray this in Jesus' name!

MY CONFESSION FOR TODAY

I boldly confess that I go to the Father when I need wisdom from above. He has the answers to all my problems, and He is standing before me, ready to help. God is on my side. He wants to help me. He is waiting for me to come into His Presence so He can give me the wisdom I need to confront and overcome every situation I am facing right now. God wants me to succeed, and His wisdom is what I need to achieve what is in my heart. So rather than try to figure it all out on my own, I run to the Father and ask Him for wisdom — and He is swift to give me the wisdom I need!

I declare this by faith in Jesus' name!

QUESTIONS FOR YOU TO CONSIDER

1. When was the last time you drew near to the Lord and asked Him to give you the wisdom you need for the situations you were facing at that moment?

2. Have you gotten so busy that you often forget to seek God in your affairs?

3. If you suddenly received the answers and the wisdom you need for the situations you are facing right now, what kind of change would this bring to your life?

OCTOBER 2

Wisdom — God's Guarantee!

If any of you lack wisdom, let him ask of God,
that giveth to all men liberally, and upbraideth not;
and it shall be given him.
— James 1:5

Yesterday we learned from James 1:5 that if you and I lack wisdom, we have the right to go to God and insist that He give us the answers we need. In fact, the Greek tense used in that verse tells us that God actually *commands* us to come to Him when we need wisdom. Furthermore, the Greek word used to describe us asking God for wisdom indicates that God wants us to be firm and resolute when we request wisdom from Him.

But before God will open His hand and give us the wisdom we need, there is a condition we must meet. That condition is spelled out very clearly in James 1:5, where the Bible says, "If any of you lack wisdom, let him ask of God...."

The condition we must meet to receive wisdom from God is found in the phrase "of God." In Greek, these are the words *para theou*. The word *para* means *alongside of*, and it depicts *a very close, side-by-side, intimate position next to someone else*. The word *theou* is the Greek word for *God*. When these words are placed together in a phrase, as in this verse, it pictures *a person who comes right alongside of God, who comes as close to God as possible, who stands side-by-side with Him*. In this statement, we discover God's requirement of us before He will give us the wisdom we need. If we want wisdom, we must come right up alongside of God in order to obtain it.

You see, God wants a relationship with us. He doesn't want to just freely hand out answers to our problems. He wants us to come to Him. And the moment we get side-by-side with God, He opens His hand and reveals everything we need to know and understand about the situations we are facing.

So often, however, believers allow themselves to become too busy with the affairs of life, and they fail to take time out of their hectic schedules to get into the intimate Presence of God. They want God to meet their need "on demand," but they don't want to fulfill God's need to be close to His people.

Rushing into the Presence of the Lord, these believers stay only long enough to make their requests known to Him before they rush out again to resume their busy schedules. They don't stay long enough for God to enjoy them and to speak to their hearts about the deeper subjects of life that may be the real root of their problems and shortfalls.

When James tells us to "ask" God for the wisdom we need, the word "ask" means we can be very bold and insistent. But for us to get what we request, we must ask "of God." In other words, we must come right up alongside of God, getting as close to Him as possible, and then make our request. If we will fulfill this requirement of coming close to God and opening our hearts to Him and to His touch, He will then gladly open His hand and show us every answer we need.

But be prepared for God to show you additional things you weren't expecting to see! When you come into His glorious light, that light penetrates you and reveals defects and dark places in your soul and behavior patterns that need to be changed. But if you stay out of God's Presence, it is very possible that these defects may never become apparent to your own eyes, for many things can only be revealed by getting into His Presence. *Could it be that you have avoided the Presence of God because you are afraid of what you might see in yourself if you came into His glorious light?*

Once you fulfill this requirement of getting right alongside of God, He is obligated to give you the wisdom you seek from Him. That is why James says that God "…giveth to all men liberally, and upbraideth not…." The word "giveth" is the Greek word *didontos*, which comes from the word *didomi*. The word *didomi* means *to give*, but the form used here is *didontos*, which describes *one who is in the habit of constantly giving*. This assuredly tells us that God is not one who holds out on His people or who refrains from giving them wisdom when they need it. Instead, James tells us that God is in the habit of giving wisdom to His people when they need it. He is "the giving God."

Not only does God give us the wisdom we need when we meet His requirement to come close to Him, but James 1:5 promises that He gives it "…liberally, and upbraideth not…." The word "liberally" is the Greek word *haploos*. It depicts something that is given *generously, abundantly, plentifully, bountifully,* and *open-handedly*. You see, if we'll meet God's requirement to come close to Him, He will profusely answer the questions we have and impart the wisdom we need.

The words "upbraideth not" are from the Greek word *oneididzo*, which means *to rebuke* or *to reprove*. However, in this case, the word *me* is used in front of this word, making the entire Greek phrase *me oneididzontes*, which means *to not rebuke* or *to not reprove*.

In other words, God will *not* rebuke you or reprove you for asking anything of Him. You are His child, and He wants you to have the wisdom you need for life. You'll find God to be open-hearted and ready to answer any question you ever put to Him. But before He gives you those answers, He first wants you to fulfill His requirement of coming alongside of Him, where He can love you and fellowship with you and where you can feel and experience His love.

In that up-close, side-by-side encounter with God, you will also become aware of all the other areas of your life that need attention. And here's the good news: In His glorious Presence, God will not only make you aware of these areas that need adjustment, He will also give you the power and ability to change!

James 1:5 says that if you will meet God's requirement to come close to Him, "the giving God" will give you the wisdom and answers you need. So don't let yourself rush in and out of the Presence of God too quickly any longer. It's time for you to learn how to spend time in the Presence of the Lord so He can shine His glorious light upon your life! Let Him bathe you in His glory. Let His glory shine on you and reveal the dark areas in your life that need to be changed. Stay in His Presence long enough to let the wisdom you are seeking sink into your spirit and soul.

Never forget that God is "the giving God" who wants to meet your need. But for that need to be met, you have to come right up alongside Him — and you can only do that by making room in your daily schedule for spending time in His Presence. *Are you ready to include God in your schedule today?*

MY PRAYER FOR TODAY

Lord, I know that You are a giving God who wants to meet my needs and answer my questions. But I understand now that I have a condition to meet first: You require me to come close to You so You can reveal to me those things I need to know. Please forgive me for rushing in and out of your Presence so quickly in the past — making my demands and insisting on those things I need, but not taking enough time to fellowship with You and meet Your need to be with me. I am so sorry for the times I've been in such a hurry that I neglected spending time with You. Starting today, I want to change my daily schedule so I can spend time in Your Presence and come closer to You than ever before!

I pray this in Jesus' name!

MY CONFESSION FOR TODAY

I confess that spending time with God is the highest priority in my life. This time with Him is not an option in my life. He wants to give me all the wisdom and answers I need, but first I must meet His requirement to come close to Him. When I get right next to God, He is obliged to open His hand and show me everything I need to see. I live continually in His Presence; therefore, no form of darkness or ignorance nor any defect in my character can remain in my life!

I declare this by faith in Jesus' name!

QUESTIONS FOR YOU TO CONSIDER

1. Do you spend time in the Presence of God each day? If a friend asked you to describe the quiet time you spend with the Lord every day, how would you go about describing it?
2. How much time do you spend alone with God each day? What do you do during this time? What results have you experienced in your life because of the daily quiet time you spend with the Lord?
3. What is the best time of the day for you to spend with God in order to avoid being interrupted by other people or by the constant ringing of the telephone?

God will *not* rebuke you or reprove you for asking for wisdom. You are His child, and He wants you to have the wisdom you need for life. You'll find God to be open-hearted and ready to answer any question you ever put to Him. But before He gives you those answers, He first wants you to fulfill His requirement of coming alongside of Him, where He can love you and fellowship with you and where you can feel and experience His love.

OCTOBER 3

Wives, Be Supportive
Of Your Husbands

Likewise, ye wives, be in subjection to your own husbands;
that, if any obey not the word, they also may without the word
be won by the conversation of the wives.
— 1 Peter 3:1

When the apostle Peter wrote about the needs of husbands and wives in First Peter 3, he knew *exactly* what he was writing about. Peter had been married for a very long time when he wrote these famous words about marriage. That means Peter was speaking from many years of being successfully married to a wife who traveled with him in the ministry (*see* 1 Corinthians 9:5).

As Peter addresses wives about how to be a blessing to their husbands, he begins by telling them, "Likewise, ye wives, be in subjection to your own husbands...." The word "subjection" is the Greek word *hupotasso*, a compound of the words *hupo* and *tasso*. The word *hupo* means *under*, and the word *tasso* means *to arrange* or *to put something in order*. It was often used in a military sense to describe *soldiers who were expected to fall in line and submit to their commanding officers*. Every time the word *hupotasso* is used, it describes *the relationship of someone who is submitted to some type of authority and who is expected to act according to that order of authority*.

There are many other examples where the word *hupotasso* is used in the New Testament. For instance, Paul uses this word in First Timothy 3:4, where he gives the instruction that children are to be "in subjection" to their parents. The word "subjection" in this verse is also the word *hupotasso*, which emphatically means that God has given parents the authority to lead their children and that children are to respectfully submit to their parents' authority.

When Luke writes of Jesus' relationship to Joseph and Mary in Luke 2:51, he uses the word *hupotasso* to describe this parent-child relationship. You see, Jesus was the Son of God and Creator of the universe. But while He was in the flesh, He followed God's pattern, respectfully submitting to and following His parents' God-given authority.

This example in Jesus' life shows the extent to which God respects the order He has set in the home. Although Jesus is God and could have done what He wished while He walked on this earth, He voluntarily submitted to the authority God had entrusted to His parents, thus setting an example for all children to follow.

The word *hupotasso* was most frequently used in a military sense to describe *a soldier's submission to military authority*. This tells us that just as the army has a specific order of authority, so has God designed a certain order for the home that He expects to be followed. Because Peter uses the word *hupotasso* when writing to wives, he leaves no doubt from a linguistic point of view that God has set the husband as the head of the home and the wife is *to respectfully fall in line* and *submit* to his authority.

**Because Peter uses the Greek word *hupotasso* in this verse,
it means he is encouraging wives in this way:**

*"Likewise, wives, you need to position yourself under your husband's authority. This is God's
order for your home, so do all you can to become supportive of your husband...."*

Peter knew that one of the greatest needs of a husband is to have a wife with a supportive attitude. You see, a man fights at his job all day long, struggling to pay the bills and trying to overcome his own insecurities and self-image problems. If he then comes home to a wife who nags, complains, and gripes about everything he doesn't do right, her behavior has a very negative effect on him. He's already fought the devil all day long; he certainly doesn't need to come home to a wife who is ready to fight with him!

As a result, the husband often responds to a nagging and critical wife by hardening and insulating his heart against her. Instead of drawing closer to his wife, he withdraws from her emotionally.

Now, it's important to understand that when Peter commands a woman to be in subjection to her own husband, he is not recommending that she become a "doormat" whom the husband takes advantage of. Rather, Peter is urging each wife to take her place as her husband's chief supporter and helper.

When a husband comes home from a hard day at work, he needs to be greeted by a loving, caring, kind, understanding, and supportive wife. This kind of wife makes a husband feel as if he's found a place where he can find rest and solace for his soul. Her supportive attitude makes him want to run to her, for she has fulfilled her role as his best friend and partner.

Although we do find one New Testament scripture where the older women are told to teach the younger women how to love their husbands (Titus 2:4), it is very interesting to note that nowhere in the New Testament are women directly commanded to love their husbands. Instead, wives are told to be "in subjection" to their husbands. Why is this? *Because a husband perceives his wife's love when he senses her support.*

Nothing communicates a wife's love to her husband better than a supportive attitude. It is when a wife gets out of that supportive role and attempts to become the husband's authority and head, constantly rebuking and correcting him for what he isn't doing right, that her actions cause him to emotionally push away from her.

Wife, God never designed you to assume authority over your husband. It will therefore bring disruption to your marital relationship whenever you attempt to do so. So if you want your husband to know how much you love him, look for ways to show him your support. In this case, your attitude and actions really do speak louder than words.

Writing by the inspiration of the Holy Spirit and from many years of personal experience, Peter urges wives to be submissive to their husbands and thus demonstrate their love and respect to them. Now, it is important to understand that submission is not just an outward action; it is a condition of the heart. It is possible for a wife to outwardly comply but still be inwardly unsubmissive and resentful.

Thus, there are two ways a wife can respond to her husband's authority:

1. She can follow his leadership angrily and resentfully, kicking and screaming all the way.
2. She can submit voluntarily with a joyful and supportive attitude.

If a wife follows her husband with resentment in her heart, he will feel this resentment. A man can sense whether his wife is complying because she *must* or submitting with a joyful and supportive heart.

When the wife takes the second approach and follows him with a thankful and happy heart — even if she has to deny her own desires or pleasures to do so — she sends a loud signal to the husband that causes him to want to love her. This is an important result of willing submission, for being loved is the primary thing every wife needs to receive from her husband. This is also the reason God commands men to love their wives (*see* Ephesians 5:25).

Wife, have you been assuming a corrective role toward your husband? Does it seem like he is becoming more and more distant from you? If so, I urge you to take a new approach in your relationship with your husband on the basis of Peter's instruction in First Peter 3:1. Rather than constantly correcting him and pointing out all his flaws, go to God with the things that disturb you about him. Meanwhile, work on becoming the most significant supporter and friend your husband has ever known.

If you respond correctly to your husband's God-given authority in the home, God will work on his heart. The end result will be a growing desire in your husband to shower you with all the love, tenderness, and affection that you need!

MY PRAYER FOR TODAY

Lord, I ask You to please forgive me for complaining to my husband about everything he does that I don't like. He needs me to be his friend and supporter, and I now realize how often he must perceive me as another enemy he has to fight. Please help me to come to You with all my complaints while maintaining a helpful and supportive attitude toward my husband. I am sorry for the damage I've done, and I now ask You to help me turn things around in my marriage relationship. Teach me how to respond in every situation with a respectful and supportive attitude toward my husband. I know I need Your help, Lord, so I am looking to You for the grace and the strength I need to do this right.

I pray this in Jesus' name!

MY CONFESSION FOR TODAY

I confess that I am a supportive wife who demonstrates love in the way I approach my husband. He doesn't see me as a nagging and complaining wife but as a friend to confide in and to look to for strength. God is able to speak to my husband without my interference. I trust God to speak to him, and I trust God to deal with my heart and to help me take on a supportive role in our home.

I declare this by faith in Jesus' name!

QUESTIONS FOR YOU TO CONSIDER

1. Are you a support to your husband, or does he feel like you are attacking him most of the time? Does he draw near to you, or does he shut up and emotionally protect himself when the two of you are together?
2. Judging from your husband's response to you, what do you need to change in the way you are approaching him?
3. Why don't you ask the Holy Spirit to give you ten new ways you can demonstrate your support for your husband and show him that you are behind him? Write down these ten ways to be supportive, and then begin to do them today.

OCTOBER 4

᠃᠃᠃

Wives, Don't Be 'Preachy'
With Your Husbands

Likewise, ye wives, be in subjection to your own husbands;
that, if any obey not the word, they also may without the word
be won by the conversation of the wives;
While they behold your chaste conversation coupled with fear.
— 1 Peter 3:1,2

Many years ago we had a young couple in our church who were madly in love with each other. Every time I saw them, they were holding hands and looking blissfully into each other's eyes. We all got such a kick out of watching them and were excited about their upcoming wedding.

Several months after they were married, I noticed that this young husband looked downcast and depressed. I went to him privately and asked, "How is marriage?"

He replied, "Why didn't someone warn me about how terrible this was going to be?"

I was shocked by his response, so I asked him, "Please tell me what is happening to give you such a bad impression of marriage."

The husband proceeded to tell me about all the rules his wife had made for him and their household. For instance, if he didn't read his Bible when he woke up in the morning, she refused to make his breakfast. Her rule was "No Bible, no breakfast!" He told me that many mornings he would go to the kitchen to get his sack lunch for the day, and his new bride would tell him, "Today the Lord has told me that you need to fast, so there won't be any lunch for you today. You need to spend time in prayer."

The young man continued to tell me that many evenings when he came home from work exhausted, his wife would order him, "Tonight we are going to sit on the couch and read the Bible together for two hours —you, me, and my mother. Then we're going to spend an hour in prayer."

When I heard what was happening, I chuckled inside. I knew this sweet little new bride was trying to encourage her husband to be the spiritual leader of their new home, but her approach wasn't effective. In fact, it was having just the opposite effect she desired.

Instead of causing her husband to feel closer to her, this young wife was pushing him far away by constantly preaching at him and demanding that he become the spiritual leader she expected him to be. But after the couple attended a few counseling sessions with me, the wife backed off and let her husband assume his leadership role on his own terms. When she relaxed and let him lead in a way that was more natural to him, the tension left their marriage and they reentered marital bliss!

A wife who takes on the role of preaching at her husband will never find this method very effective. It is usually a huge turn-off for a husband because it makes him feel like his wife, who is supposed to be his greatest supporter, has instead become his corrector and boss. Men resent this behavior. This is why Peter told the wives, "Likewise, ye wives, be in subjection to your own husbands;

that, if any obey not the word, they also may without the word be won by the conversation of the wives" (1 Peter 3:1).

In the first century, women came to Christ more readily than men — a situation that has always seemed to exist in the Church. This meant that a huge portion of the Early Church was comprised of women who had come to Jesus Christ but whose husbands remained unsaved. Of course, these women wanted their husbands to be saved, so after a church service, they would often run home and begin to preach to their husbands. They saw themselves as God's anointed evangelists to bring their husbands into the fold.

But those unsaved husbands didn't perceive this to be a blessing! From the husbands' perspective, their wives' preaching sounded like nagging and complaining. This approach produced such negative results that Peter told wives to stop preaching to their husbands and to instead live godly lives before them as their method of evangelizing. Peter wrote, "...If any [husbands] obey not the word, they also may without the word be won by the conversation of the wives" (1 Peter 3:1).

The phrase "...if any obey not the word..." alludes to unsaved husbands, but it could also refer to saved husbands who are not living in obedience to God's Word. The words "obey not" are from the Greek word *apeitho*, which emphatically refers to *someone who refuses to be persuaded*. This person isn't just ignorant of the truth; he is *defiant* and *rejecting* of it. Therefore, besides referring to unsaved husbands who hear the message and reject it, as Peter was most likely writing about, this phrase could also refer to saved husbands who refuse to do what they know God wants them to do.

I can think of so many Christian wives who want their husbands to change. These wives beg, plead, nag, and pester their husbands all the time to do this different or to do that different. But no matter how hard a wife pressures her husband, he will remain stubborn, obstinate, and unmoved. If God doesn't touch his heart and cause him to respond on his own, all the begging and nagging in the world won't change his heart.

Wife, whether your husband is saved or unsaved, the method of impacting him is the same. Peter says you can win your husband without ever uttering a single word!

Now look at the phrase "...they also may without the word be won...." The word "won" is the Greek word *kerdeo*, an old Greek word which means *to act cleverly*. It was often used in secular literature to depict *someone who won a game*, such as the game of casting lots. In today's world, it could depict a person who plays his cards right and therefore walks off with the booty!

Therefore, the word *kerdeo* ("won") means *to wise up; to act cleverly; to play the game correctly*; or in today's vernacular, *to play your cards right*. Peter is telling wives how to win the game of positively influencing their husbands without ever saying a word! He tells them that the most influential thing wives can do is to let their husbands see their "conversation."

The word "conversation" is the Greek word *anastrophe*, a Greek word that refers to *how a person rises up and sits down; goes in and goes out; and turns this way or that way*. In other words, the word *anastrophe* gives a picture of *how a person conducts his life* and *how he or she behaves in every situation*. By using this word, we are told that there is no message more powerful than a godly life — and that a wife who lives a godly life before her husband greatly impacts his decisions and the way he lives.

The Greek words used in this text
present the following idea:

"...If any refuse to comply with the Word and do what it says, you can still win the game without ever uttering a single word by simply letting your husband take note of and observe the way you live your life before him."

I am married to a very godly woman. Denise has great influence in my life, not because of what he says but because of how she lives. I see her pray every morning. I watch as she sacrifices to follow me and how she has always done it with a willing and joyful heart. I have watched her forgive those who wronged us and our ministry. I see how attentively she takes care of our sons and how she loves our son's wife. She stands by me, supports me, helps me, encourages me, and is indeed my closest friend.

Denise's godly life is her greatest pulpit. I see her rising up, her sitting down, her going in, her going out, her turning this way and that way. Because I know her life and her outstanding attitude, I have great respect for her, and I listen when she speaks to me about things that concern her. In fact, of all the people in my life, my wife has the single greatest impact on me and my decisions. Her godly life has empowered her to have this authority with me. You could say that she won me and my respect because she showed me her life instead of just preaching sermons at me.

This is a good example of Peter's statement to wives in verse 2 that husbands will "…behold your chaste conversation…." The word "behold" is the Greek word *epopteuo*, which in Greek means *to observe, to watch, to monitor, to scrutinize,* or *to keep under observation.* The tense used in the Greek indicates a continual observation. This means a husband doesn't just notice his wife's behavior once; rather, he keeps a watch on her behavior and attitude all the time.

Wife, let me tell you a secret. Your husband may not tell you, but he is watching you. He sees and is amazed when you remain happy and content in very unhappy circumstances. He notices when you have an opportunity to be angry but choose instead to be silent and to take that anger to the Lord. Your husband observes your uncomplaining attitude when financial sacrifice is required. On the other hand, he also takes note when you blow your top and say ugly things. You can be sure that even though your husband may not tell you, he is constantly monitoring your attitude and responses to the situations of life.

This is why Peter says that you should let your husband "…behold your chaste conversation…." The word "chaste" is the word *agnos*. It refers to *holiness, purity,* or *irreproachable conduct*. In other words, men notice it when their wives are awesome! A wife's godly conduct is the most influential, powerful sermon she could ever preach to her husband.

Peter goes on to say, "While they behold your chaste conversation *coupled with fear.*" This word "fear" does not refer to the kind of fear that makes a person shake and tremble because he is terrified. In this context, it carries the idea of *respect*. Knowing that a husband feels valued when he senses his wife's respect, Peter urges women to live holy lives before their husbands and to do everything they can to demonstrate respect to them.

The words in First Peter 3:2 could be paraphrased to carry this meaning:

"Wives, your husbands are watching you constantly. They see you rising up; they see you sitting down; they see you going in; and they see you going out. They are constantly observing you, so make sure they are seeing you live a pure and holy life, and give them honor and respect as you do it."

If you've been preaching at your husband to no effect, perhaps it's time for you to change your method. Make the quality decision to stop talking to him about the things you've been wanting him to change in his life. Instead, take your concerns to God in prayer. Leave your husband alone, and let God deal with him.

When you suddenly fall silent and cease to preach at your husband, I guarantee you that he will notice a change has taken place in your approach toward him. He will "behold" this change in your attitude. He will "behold" that you aren't correcting him anymore. He will "behold" that you are leaving him alone and that you have chosen to take a different route.

As you learn to stay silent rather than preach at your husband, he will probably begin to hear the Holy Spirit speaking to his heart. And when your husband sees you maintain an excellent attitude in the midst of circumstances that aren't going your way, his heart will be drawn to you. He'll begin to get convicted, and his desire to do more to please you will start to grow.

You see, wife, Peter knew exactly what he was talking about when he wrote that you could win your husband without a word. Therefore, it's time for you to get before God and ask Him to change your heart and your attitude about your husband. *Learn to be clever by keeping your mouth closed and letting your godly life and good attitude do the preaching for you!*

MY PRAYER FOR TODAY

Lord, I ask You to help me learn when to speak and when to be silent. I don't want my husband to perceive me as a nagging wife. Please forgive me for preaching at him when I should have been praying for him. Help me to stop focusing on all the things I don't like about him and to start working on all the things that need to change inside me. I want to be a blessing to my husband. Please help me live a life so godly and powerful that it becomes my pulpit in our marriage.

I pray this in Jesus' name!

MY CONFESSION FOR TODAY

I confess that I live a powerful, godly, and chaste life before my husband and am therefore a constant encouragement to him. He seeks my advice; he wants my help; and he desires to know what I believe is right regarding decisions that affect our family and relationship. God's Spirit is changing me and making me to be the kind of wife He wants me to be!

I declare this by faith in Jesus' name!

QUESTIONS FOR YOU TO CONSIDER

1. Can you think of a time when your husband resisted your continual requests for him to do something — but then suddenly changed his mind after you backed off and left him alone?
2. Have you had moments when you've heard the Holy Spirit say, "Leave your husband alone, and I'll deal with him"? Did you leave your husband alone as the Spirit instructed you, or did you keep hammering at him to do what you wanted?
3. What is the most important thing you have learned from today's *Sparkling Gem*?

If you've been preaching at your husband to no effect, perhaps it's time for you to take your concerns to God in prayer and leave your husband alone so God can deal with him.

OCTOBER 5

❦

Is God Against Cosmetics?

> Whose adorning let it not be that outward adorning
> of plaiting the hair, and of wearing of gold, or of putting on of apparel;
> But let it be the hidden man of the heart,
> in that which is not corruptible, even the ornament
> of a meek and quiet spirit, which is in the sight of God of great price.
> — 1 Peter 3:3,4

*M*any years ago, my wife and I were invited to minister in a church that believed it was a sin for women to wear jewelry or cosmetics. We only discovered it was this kind of church when we arrived that evening.

As is our custom in our ministry before I preach the Word, Denise stood to sing. Her song was exceptionally beautiful and anointed that night. However, I noticed that while she sang, the people kept pointing to her lips and to her earrings. They were obviously distraught about Denise's jewelry and cosmetics — and as a result, they missed the entire song!

It is on the basis of First Peter 3:3,4 that some religious groups believe the use of jewelry and cosmetics is a sin. Those verses say, "Whose adorning let is not be that outward adorning of plaiting the hair, and of wearing of gold, or of putting on of apparel; but let it be the hidden man of the heart, in that which is not corruptible, even the ornament of a meek and quiet spirit, which is in the sight of God of great price."

Was Peter really saying that it was a sin for a wife or a woman to wear jewelry or cosmetics? Let's look at these verses to see *exactly* what Peter was communicating when he wrote them. You will see that Peter was not bothered by wives or women wearing jewelry or cosmetics. Instead, he was telling them not to invest all their time in their faces and their outward appearance while forgetting to invest time in developing their hearts.

You see, women in the first century, especially upper-class Greek and Roman women, were obsessed with their outward appearance. They were flamboyant in their hairstyles, spent vast amounts of money on cosmetics, arrayed themselves in luxurious jewelry, and prided themselves in the lavish clothing they wore. Nothing was wrong with their desire to look nice — except they were so consumed with adorning their bodies that they forgot to adorn their hearts!

The word "adorning" in First Peter 3:3 is the Greek word *kosmos*, which is used 187 times in the New Testament. As noted earlier, the word *kosmos* carries the idea of *something that is ordered* or *something that is set in a certain arrangement*. This word *kosmos* is where we get the word *cosmetics*. This tells us that when a woman applies makeup to her face, she is trying to add *order* to her face. The *King James Version* translates it *adorning* because the application of cosmetics not only beautifies a woman's appearance, but also gives it a greater sense of *order*. I assure you that husbands appreciate this "adorning" very much!

Contrary to what some religious groups assert, there is no implication in this verse that cosmetics are a sin. Peter simply never says that! As noted above, Peter's point is that women shouldn't put all their efforts into adorning their faces; they need to remember to adorn their hearts as well.

Then Peter goes on to mention the "plaiting of hair." By using this phrase, he is referring to a practice that was very common among Greek and Roman women in the first century. These women didn't just pull out the blow dryer and spend twenty minutes preparing their hair for the day. Rather, they literally spent multiplied hours toiling with their hair! I say women "toiled" with their hair because it took a great deal of work and time to produce the fashionable hairstyles of that time. In fact, the word "plaiting" used by Peter is the Greek word *emploke*, which describes *the intricate, complex, and outrageously elaborate braiding of a woman's hair.*

You see, the Greek and Roman women were obsessed with turning their hair into towers of intricate curls and braids. If you visit a museum of antiquities and look at the statues of first-century women, it will amaze you to see the thousands of little curls that were woven into women's hair.

This hairstyle was considered beautiful, elegant, and fashionable in the first century. Husbands must have thought this style was beautiful on their wives because the fashion trend was imitated all over the Roman Empire. As a result of this popular rage, women invested huge amounts of time and great sums of money to produce the desired effect.

As you will see, Peter was not against woman making their hair more beautiful. He simply didn't want believing women to focus all their attention on their hair and forget to improve the condition of their hearts.

Next, Peter mentions the "wearing of gold." This was another common practice that was considered very fashionable. The word "wearing" is from the Greek word *perithesis*, and it describes *placing an object, such as a piece of jewelry, around oneself.* You see, the Greek and Roman women loved to drape many chains of gold around their necks, affix multiple solid gold bands around their upper arms, and wear many golden rings on each finger. They considered their appearance to be more impressive and beautiful when they were elaborately decked out in layers of gold.

Peter then discusses the "putting on of apparel." The word "apparel" is the Greek word *himation*. It pictures *the brightly colored, richly beaded, posh clothing* that was popular among Greek and Roman women in the first century. Women were so fashion-conscious that they frequently changed their clothes during the course of the day. This means they were constantly running in and out of the closet and looking at themselves in the mirror as they fine-tuned their outward appearance for the day's different events.

Consider the many hours women spent applying their cosmetics, fixing their hair, and draping themselves in gold. Now add the multiple times they changed clothes in a day and all the time spent adjusting their clothes in front of a mirror after each change. When you take all this into account, you realize that these women used a very significant portion of their time — not to mention investing a large amount of their money — in maintaining their outward appearance.

When Peter wrote about all these things, he began by saying, "Whose adorning let it *not* be...." Many have understood this statement to be a prohibition against wearing cosmetics, gold, or expensive clothing and against fixing one's hair. But in reality, Peter was simply urging wives not to make the mistake of putting so much time and attention into improving their outward appearance that they failed to invest time in the maintenance and beautifying of their inner man.

This is why Peter goes on to say, "But let it be the hidden man of the heart, in that which is not corruptible, even the ornament of a meek and quiet spirit, which is in the sight of God of great price." In essence, he was saying, "Ladies, it's all right to do what you can to look outwardly beautiful. However, don't forget that the most important emphasis and the place to invest most of your time should be in the beautifying of the hidden man of the heart."

Dear wife, it is all right for you to look beautiful. In fact, your husband appreciates it when you make yourself look beautiful for him. Demonstrating to your husband that you want to look pretty for him is one way you can show honor to him. Therefore, Peter's words are *not* a prohibition against trying to look the best you can in your outward appearance!

Then what *is* Peter saying to wives and women? He is simply stating that it is a mistake for women to put so much time and effort into their outward appearance that they ignore their inner man — the true source of their beauty. Peter knew it was the custom of first-century wives and women in general to spend countless hours working on their face and hair, so he wanted to encourage them to work on their hearts as much as they worked on their outward appearance!

So do all you can to look beautiful, wife, and don't feel guilty because you wear beautiful jewelry or nice clothes. But at the same time, don't forget that your spirit is the real you and the most beautiful part of you. God isn't against your desire to work on your outward appearance; however, He wants you to spend at least an equal amount of time developing and beautifying your spirit.

Are you spending enough time "adorning" your spirit the way God wants you to? The answer to that question will largely determine the quality not only of your marriage, but of your life!

MY PRAYER FOR TODAY

Lord, thank You for wanting me to look beautiful, both inside and outside, both for myself and for my spouse. I take this word to my heart today, and I make the decision that from this day forward, I will spend at least the same amount of time beautifying my spirit as I spend looking nice in my outward appearance. Forgive me, Lord, for those days when I have found time to dress properly and look outwardly attractive, but I didn't take the time to pray or read my Bible. Help me get my priorities in order as I make the development of my spirit a higher priority than fixing my hair or putting on makeup.

I pray this in Jesus' name!

MY CONFESSION FOR TODAY

I confess that the beautifying of my spirit is a high priority in my life. I don't make the mistake of putting all my time and effort into improving my outward appearance while forgetting to invest time in the development of my spirit. I read my Bible; I pray; and I let God deal with my heart. Because I have made the choice to make my spirit beautiful, I am becoming more godly and beautiful all the time. I have an inward beauty that far outshines anything I could ever do to improve the appearance of my outward man!

I declare this by faith in Jesus' name!

QUESTIONS FOR YOU TO CONSIDER

1. How much time do you spend on your outward appearance every day? How does that compare to the amount of time you daily spend with God?
2. How much time do you think you should be spending alone with God every day in order to develop and beautify your spirit the way God wants you to?

3. What is one area in your inner thoughts and attitudes that you know needs to be changed? What steps are you taking to remove the ugliness that keeps springing from that part of your life and to replace it with the godly fragrance of Jesus Christ?

OCTOBER 6

ॐ

What Will You Do
When the Effects of Gravity
Start To Show Up?

Whose adorning let it not be that outward adorning
of plaiting the hair, and of wearing of gold,
or of putting on of apparel; But let it be
the hidden man of the heart, in that which is not corruptible,
even the ornament of a meek and quiet spirit,
which is in the sight of God of great price.
— 1 Peter 3:3,4

When a young bride prepares for her wedding, she wants to be beautiful for the man she is about to marry. She goes to the salon to have her hair fixed and her nails manicured. Everything has to look as perfect as possible for that moment when she says "I do" to her husband at the church altar.

It is right and normal for a woman to desire to look gorgeous for this long-awaited moment in her life. But when I am the one performing the wedding ceremony, there always comes a point in the ceremony when I peer into the eyes of the beautiful young bride and tell her:

"Today you look so beautiful in your white wedding gown. You are the perfect picture of a gorgeous bride. But a day will come when your body will begin to change, when wrinkles will start to appear, and gravity will begin to move things from where they used to be! When that day comes — and it will come — the most beautiful thing you'll have to offer your husband will not be your body but a godly, beautiful, unfading spirit. Never forget that your spirit is what will make your husband think you are beautiful to the very last day of your life!"

People in the audience always giggle when I say these words. Most of these giggles come from people who are middle-aged and who see wrinkles when they look in the mirror. They are beginning to experience the middle-aged effects of gravity! Parts of their bodies that used to be strong and firm are starting to droop, and they feel tempted to lament when they look in the mirror.

That's why it's important to remember that the most beautiful thing a wife has to offer her husband is not her body but her spirit. The good news is that when the body begins to show signs of age, the human spirit remains remarkably free from its effects. This is why Paul said, "…Though our outward man perish, yet the inward man is renewed day by day" (2 Corinthians 4:16).

Perhaps you can think of a time when you met an elderly man or woman who was so young at heart that it simply amazed you. Now you know why! The process of aging affects the human body, but it has no effect on the spirit.

When Peter wrote to wives in First Peter 3, he instructed them to give attention to the "hidden man of the heart." These words are very significant, for they refer here to the spirit of a godly woman. The word "hidden" is the word *kruptos*, which describes *something that is hidden or veiled from the eyes*. The word "heart" is the Greek word *kardia*, which is the Greek word for *the physical organ of the heart*. Just as the physical organ of the heart is hidden from human sight, so the inner man is not visible to the natural eye.

By using the word *kardia* (the Greek word for the "heart"), Peter is giving us a powerful insight regarding the human spirit. The heart is the central vital organ of the body. Although the heart is invisible to natural sight, the human body cannot live without it. The heart has a direct impact on every single part of the body as it pumps blood through arteries and many miles of blood vessels.

Paul uses the word *kardia* ("heart") to let us know that the human spirit is very similar to the natural heart. For instance, although the human spirit is invisible to the eyes, it is vital to life. According to James 2:26, where there is no spirit, the physical body dies. Thus, the spirit is the life-giving force within a human being.

The natural heart pumps blood into every part of the body and thereby influences a person's ability to live and function. Similarly, whatever is produced in the human spirit determines the ultimate outcome of a person's life. If a person's spirit is filled with darkness, it will pump darkness into every part of that person's life. On the other hand, if a person's spirit is filled with the life of God, it will pump life into every part of that person's being. *Whatever is in the spirit is exactly what will be reproduced in a person's life and conduct.*

This is precisely why Peter urges wives to take time and care to develop their spirits, which he calls "the hidden man of the heart." A woman who wants to be truly beautiful, even after her body begins to age, must put time and effort into the development of her spirit.

You see, there are many outwardly beautiful people who are inwardly wicked; therefore, their beauty is only skin deep — neither long-lasting nor impressive. Although these people spend hours adorning and grooming themselves, what is inside them is projected clear through their outer adornment. Since they are actually unkind and inwardly ugly people, their inner ugliness ruins the effect of their physical beauty and causes them to be perceived as unattractive people. The truth is, some of the meanest and most wicked, vile people in the world are physically beautiful, yet their inner attitudes cause them to be very repulsive to those around them.

Peter is addressing this exact issue in First Peter 3:3,4. Because the human spirit is the life-force of an individual, he encourages women to not only fix their faces and their hair, but to also beautify their spirits, even though the spirit man is invisible to the natural eye.

Peter also declares that the hidden man of the heart is that part of the human being that is "incorruptible." The word "incorruptible" is the Greek word *aphthartos*, which refers to *something that is incapable of decay* or *something that is incapable of suffering the effects of wear, tear, and age*. This word clearly describes the hidden part of the human being that never grows old or experiences the effects of aging.

As my wife grows older, I look upon her with greater respect than ever before. Honestly, I think she is physically beautiful and I am honored to be married to such an attractive woman. But what makes her most beautiful to me is not her hair, her face, her figure, or her clothing. The most beautiful part of my wife is her heart. The sweet fragrance of Jesus Christ emanates from her heart, through her attitudes, and into her words and actions, making her one of the loveliest people I've ever known.

Of course, I appreciate the fact that Denise works hard to stay in shape, to eat right, and to look so striking every day. The way she dresses reveals her character and desire to be excellent in everything she does. I am very aware that another reason she diligently works to look beautiful is that she wants to honor me by looking nice.

As a husband, I have a responsibility, as every husband does, to acknowledge when my wife looks beautiful. She needs that acknowledgement from me. But the part of Denise that first captured my heart and continues to do so today is not her body; it is her *heart*. Her heart is so beautiful that it makes me stand back and watch her with great admiration!

I regularly observe and take note of what Denise does to keep her heart in this godly shape. She rises early to read her Bible and to seek the face of God. When the rest of us are still sleeping, she kneels on the floor in her prayer room to pray and to worship. She weeps before the Lord as He deals with her about the attitudes He wants to change in her. She spends hours asking Him to change her and to make her more like Him.

Because my wife has made the development and maturity of her spirit such a central focus in her life, I can tell you that she continually captures my heart. Although we are getting older and our bodies are beginning to change, she is more gorgeous to me today than ever before. I know that as we grow older and older, she will only become more beautiful, because as the flesh wanes, it will only make it more possible for her dynamic heart to shine brighter!

As noted in yesterday's *Sparkling Gem*, God is not against women using cosmetics, wearing jewelry, or arraying themselves in fine clothing. But all the world's finest jewelry and most expensive makeup and clothing cannot make a person with an ugly heart look beautiful. *Whatever is in the spirit is exactly what will be reproduced in a person's life.*

Wife, I urge you to take heed to Peter's plea in these verses. For the sake of both your marriage and your personal walk with God, make the decision to not only adorn your outward appearance, but also to turn your attention to the hidden man of the heart.

MY PRAYER FOR TODAY

Lord, help me give adequate attention to my heart so I can develop my spirit and become more godly in how I live my life. I pray that the strength and godliness that resides in my spirit will manifest in my life, emanating from within me and making me more gracious and more beautiful the older I get. I look to You, Lord, for help in growing old gracefully and emanating power in my older years.

I pray this in Jesus' name!

MY CONFESSION FOR TODAY

I confess that my spirit is getting stronger and stronger as I get older. My inner man is adorned with godliness and grace. The older I get, the more visible my inward man becomes — and what is seen coming from within me makes me attractive, even though I am getting a little wrinkled and gravity is having its effects on my physical form. I am inwardly strong and beautiful, and this inner beauty is what attracts people to me.

I declare this by faith in Jesus' name!

1. What are you doing on a daily basis to develop the inner beauty within you?
2. Can you name some individuals who grew more powerful and more beautiful the older they became? What is it that strikes you most about these individuals?
3. Why don't you take the time to ask a few of these individuals to tell you the secret of their beauty in their latter years?

OCTOBER 7

What Is a Meek and Quiet Spirit?

Whose adorning let it not be that outward adorning
of plaiting the hair, and of wearing of gold, or of putting on of apparel;
But let it be the hidden man of the heart,
in that which is not corruptible, even the ornament
of a meek and quiet spirit,
which is in the sight of God of great price.
— 1 Peter 3:3,4

One day I was invited to speak at a church in the city of Kiev in the country of Ukraine. Ministers had gathered from all over to meet me that day and to attend our morning teaching session. After that morning meeting, a large table was set outside on the driveway where all the special guests were seated so they could be served Ukrainian borsch for lunch.

I noticed that an elderly woman, approximately seventy-five years old, was the primary person serving lunch to us that day. As she passed by me, I looked into her face and saw the deep wrinkles that testified to a very hard life. This was a woman who had faced many intense challenges in the course of her life.

Yet when I looked into her eyes, I could see that this was a woman who was very strong in spirit. Although it was evident that she had lived a hard and difficult life, it was also evident that she had never been broken by hardship. The look in her faded blue eyes gripped me, for those eyes seemed to literally radiate life from within her.

I watched with amazement at the way this elderly woman carried bowls of borsch to this person, then to that person, and then to the next. It was obvious that she was delighted to serve the pastors who sat around the table. The tender smile that graced her face and the sweet spirit with which she served captivated my attention. As I kept watching her, I thought to myself, *This woman must be one of the most beautiful and graceful women I've ever met in my life.*

Finally, I turned to the elderly pastor sitting next to me, and I asked, "Who is that woman?"

He looked at me with a sparkle in his eyes and glowingly answered, "That's my wife."

During the Soviet years, this pastor had been arrested and sentenced to fifteen years of prison because of his faith. While he was in prison, his wife had been completely responsible for rearing and providing for their fifteen children. As he told me their story, I began to understand why she had such deep wrinkles — a sign of the many hardships she had faced while her husband had been in prison.

Despite her wrinkles and gray hair, this woman's indomitable spirit shone through and was evident for all to see. This was a woman who had lived a godly life. This was no weak woman, but a very strong and very capable woman.

I continued to watch the pastor's wife as she kept serving the men around the table, smiling graciously as she refilled empty bowls with more borsch. As I observed her strong but gentle spirit, I thought of Peter's words to women in First Peter 3:3,4. In those verses, Peter wrote, "Whose adorning let it not be that outward adorning of plaiting the hair, and of wearing of gold, or of putting on of apparel; but let it be the hidden man of the heart, in that which is not corruptible, even the ornament of a meek and quiet spirit, which is in the sight of God of great price."

Today I want to speak to you about the phrase "meek and quiet spirit." Contrary to what most people think, these words do not picture a woman who is weak, timid, or soft-spoken. The word "meek" is the Greek word *praus*, a word that describes *the attitude of one who is friendly, warm, forbearing, patient, kind, and gentle.* This would picture someone who is just the opposite of a person who is angry, temperamental, or given to outbursts of anger. Although a meek person faces opportunities to react in anger or to get upset, he or she has chosen to be controlled, forgiving, and gentle. Thus, "meek" people are individuals who have become skilled at controlling themselves and their temperament. You might say that meekness is *power under control.*

When Peter goes on to use the word "quiet" in this verse, he employs the use of the Greek word *hisuchios*, which depicts *a person who knows how to calm himself and to maintain a state of peace and tranquility.* Rather than speak up and utter words that are later regretted, this individual stays quiet and refrains from angry responses. He or she deliberately decides not to be a contributor to conflicts, but to be a peacemaker instead.

So when Peter writes about a "meek and quiet spirit," he is paying the highest compliment to wives who fit this description. These wives are so strong in spirit that they are able to refrain from outbursts of anger and thus are able to become a calming force in a variety of difficult situations. Considering the many opportunities wives have to get shaken or upset by the affairs of life, it is very commendable when a wife is so strong, so consistent, and so stable in the home that she consistently "steadies the ship" and helps keep peace in every situation.

Once again let me stress that Peter is not referring to women who are timid, shy, or weak. It takes great strength to be the kind of woman he is describing. A woman who continually controls herself — holding her temper, keeping a lid on her emotions, and remaining a stable, tranquil force in every situation — is demonstrating evidence of great maturity.

This quality of a meek and quiet spirit is quite a treasure — so much so that God says a woman who has achieved this state of maturity possesses something of "great price." The words "great price" are from the Greek word *poluteles*, which conveys the idea of *something that is very valuable; something of great cost or great worth;* or *something that is precious and dear.*

God highly values a woman who becomes this kind of strong, steady force in the home. He knows how many times a wife has an opportunity to get upset about something that has happened. So when she chooses to control herself and be a contributor to peace instead of strife, God sees this kind of woman as rare, precious, dear, and to be valued. He appreciates it when she puts aside her own anger or emotions and instead helps peace reign in the situation. God thinks very highly of such a woman!

When I looked into the face of that elderly Ukrainian woman, I could see the strength she possessed, for it was a strength that literally emanated from her. Seeing those deep wrinkles in her face, I could tell she had faced many hardships in life that could have upset her, hurt her, or made her want to take matters into her own hands.

But this was a woman who had allowed God to teach her how to look to Him rather than be swayed by the circumstances of life. Far from being weak and wimpy, she was a tower of strength. Her spirit was both gracious and indomitable. It was obvious that she was godly, pure, and powerful — someone who had made an eternal impact on many lives because of the life she had led.

How about you, my friend?

- ✦ Can you say that you are a contributor to peace in your home?
- ✦ Can you testify that you are a steady force in rough and upsetting situations?
- ✦ Can you really say that you have learned to control your emotions and to be a peacemaker?
- ✦ Would you have to admit that you contribute to strife and often make matters worse by giving in to your emotions and speaking things that you later regret?
- ✦ Does God see you as a rare and special treasure who brings a sense of peace and stability to your family, or does He see you as a frequent cause of conflict, strife, and a lack of peace in your home?

You may not have experienced the same kind of hardships as the elderly woman in my story today, but you still face many potential conflicts in your own life every day. You have a choice to react either in anger or in meekness. Every time you have an opportunity to react in the flesh or be angry and upset, you can choose instead to be controlled, forgiving, and gentle. Rather than speak up and utter words that will later be regretted, you can choose to be a peacemaker.

In view of what you have read today, can you say that you demonstrate a "meek and quiet spirit," or do you give evidence of a different kind of attitude? *What is God saying to you about your heart and actions, and what are you going to do in light of what you have learned from today's Sparkling Gem?*

MY PRAYER FOR TODAY

Lord, I am so thankful for what I read today. Please help me learn how to keep a rein on my tongue and how to submit my attitude to the Cross of Jesus Christ. Help me also to perceive how I can become a contributor to peace and tranquility instead of strife and conflict. I want to be one of those rare and special women You consider of such great value and worth. Holy Spirit, it's going to take a deep work of Your grace in my life for me to become this kind of person. So today I ask You to initiate this vital work deep inside my soul. Please transform me and make me into the person You want me to be.

I pray this in Jesus' name!

MY CONFESSION FOR TODAY

I confess that I am a source of stability and peace in my home. I don't give in to anger or fly into a rage and say things I later regret. My husband and my children can depend on me to be a tower of strength even in the midst of turmoil and difficult situations. Because I am so stable, I help bring stability to my husband, to my children, and to the general atmosphere in my home. Instead of being a contributor to strife, conflict, and turmoil, God uses me to bring peace and tranquility to all those who are near me.

I declare this by faith in Jesus' name!

QUESTIONS FOR YOU TO CONSIDER

1. Are you a source of stability in your home? Or are you a constant contributor to strife, turmoil, and a lack of peace?
2. If your husband felt the freedom to say what he really thought, would he say you are a help or a hindrance to the peace and tranquility of the home? What do you think your children would say if they were asked this question?
3. In light of what you have read today, what do you sense God is telling you about needed changes in your life, attitude, and actions?

OCTOBER 8

Husband, You Need To 'Dwell' With Your Wife!

Likewise, ye husbands, dwell with them according to knowledge,
giving honour unto the wife, as unto the weaker vessel,
and as being heirs together of the grace of life....
— 1 Peter 3:7

*O*ne of the meanest tricks in the world occurs when a man romances his future bride and treats her like a princess as they are courting — but then once they get married, everything suddenly changes! Before the marriage, the man held her hand, walked with her, opened the door for her, called her on the telephone, wrote her romantic notes, sent her flowers, and took her to dinner. He treated her so royally that she viewed him as her "Prince Charming" and felt like she was his queen!

Unfortunately, upon returning from the honeymoon, many new husbands suspend all those romantic gestures that made their future brides feel so special. These men begin to act as if they have forgotten how to show their brides the tenderness to which they had grown accustomed. As a result of this change in behavior in their new husbands, young brides often feel disappointed, let down, and deceived. They inwardly ask themselves:

✦ *Where is the Prince Charming I fell in love with before I got married?*
✦ *Was that all an act?*
✦ *Who is this man I have married?*
✦ *Who is this man who rarely calls me, who rarely treats me to a date, who seems to have*

time for everyone except me, and who shows very little tenderness in our relationship?

✦ *Where did the man go who once treated me so nicely?*

Men are often unaware that they are becoming insensitive and neglectful of their wives. Perhaps they get busy at work, or their minds are heavy with details, or they are mentally and physically exhausted. These may be some of the contributing factors that explain why men do the things they do. But regardless of what a husband is feeling or going through at work or in his financial affairs, his wife needs his attention and affection. She married him because she wants to be a part of his life. She has a need to feel cherished by him and to know that he wants to include her in his life.

This is precisely why Peter in First Peter 3:7 told husbands that they are to "dwell" with their wives. The word "dwell" is the Greek word *sunoikeo*, a compound of the word *sun* and *oikos*. The word *sun* always carries the idea of *partnership* and *cooperation*. When the word *sun* is used in the New Testament, it always *connects two or more people into a very vital union*. The second part of the word, *oikos*, is the Greek word for *a house*. When these words are linked together as they are in First Peter 3:7, it means *to share a house together* or *to dwell together in one residence*.

But there's more to this than simply sharing a house together. The fact is, there are many husbands and wives who live in the same house, who eat at the same table, and who share the same bed, yet who don't really "dwell" together. They are like two ships that occasionally pass each other. Although they share the same residence, they live separate lives, never really connecting with each other.

Because the first part of the word *sunoikos* ("dwell") is the word *sun*, which always conveys the idea of *partnership* and *cooperation*, this lets us know that Peter is urging husbands to *share* their lives with their wives. This is a great challenge to men, who often want to be quiet when they come home after a busy day at work. Many men would rather sit down in front of the television and flip the channels all evening rather than communicate with their wives.

Husband, learning to share your life with your wife is a skill that must be developed. This is why Peter goes on to say that husbands are to "dwell with them *according to knowledge.*" The phrase "according to knowledge" implies that you must gain understanding of what blesses and distresses your wife. First, you must seek to obtain that knowledge by reading the Word, by reading a good book on marriage, by attending a seminar on how to be a better husband, by listening to a teaching tape on the subject, and so on. Then you must apply what you learn to your marriage if you want to have a happy wife.

For instance, what do you do, husband, when you come home from work in the evening? Perhaps you're one of those husbands who walks in the door, plops down on the couch, turns on the television, and begins to flip mindlessly through so many channels that it is impossible to focus on any single program. Meanwhile, your wife has been waiting to talk to you all day long, so she sits next to you as you flip from one channel to the next and wonders, *Why doesn't he turn off the television and talk to me instead?*

The truth is, you've talked to people all day long, and you probably don't want to talk anymore. But you have a precious wife who needs you at that moment. She has cleaned the house, taken care of the children, cooked your evening meal, and faced her own challenges throughout the day. After an entire day of caring for the children, she needs some adult fellowship. Even more importantly, she wants fellowship with *you* because you are the one she loves and needs the most.

Why not turn off the television, take your wife by the hand, and ask her to take a walk with you? Or why don't you sit at the kitchen table with your wife and let her tell you all about her day over a cup of coffee or tea? And after she is finished telling you every nitty-gritty detail of her day, take the time to tell her about *your* day! She wants to know what you did, whom you talked to, what they said, what happened next, and so on. She wants to know all about *you* and *your day*.

Also, instead of spending most evenings and Saturday with the guys or with other people, send a powerful signal to your wife that she is important by scheduling time to be only with her. That's right, husband — spend quality time with your wife! Take her out to dinner or a movie. Do things together that you both enjoy so you can keep your relationship fresh and alive.

You need to treat your wife like she is the most central, significant, and important partner in your life. This doesn't mean you can't spend time with the guys. Certainly you need fellowship with Christian brothers. However, if you spend every free minute with them and never schedule any time with your wife, you are communicating that your male friends are much more important than she is. *Is this the message you want to send to your wife?*

As you learn to treat your wife with tender care, it will pay off big dividends in your life. If she is assured that she is a top priority in your life and feels secure in her relationship with you, she will gladly follow you and help you wherever God leads. But if she *doesn't* feel valued or secure in her position as your wife, she will find it much harder to follow you with a sweet and submissive heart. She may be afraid that if she follows you, she will ultimately find herself abandoned and uncared for. Thus, how you care for your wife greatly determines how easy or difficult it is for her to follow you.

In my own life, my wife and I actually schedule our times to be together. We plan those moments when we will go for a walk together, go shopping, go to a café to have a cup of coffee or tea, or share a special meal with each other. Like most people, our schedules are very busy. We have found that if we don't plan these times together, all the other responsibilities of our lives and ministry consume us, and in the end, we don't spend enough quality time together. But because we both consider our marriage relationship to be the most important relationship in our lives, we treat it like it *is* important and make certain that we spend quality time together on a regular basis.

Husband, I urge you to make the decision that you are going to do more than just share the couch, share the table, and share the bed with your wife. Share your *life* with her. Open your heart to her; talk to her like she is your best friend and most important confidant. "Dwell" with her and do everything you can to let her know that no one else is as important to you as she is.

If you're wondering what your marriage will be like if you fail to treat your wife with this kind of tender care, just ask those husbands who have made the mistake of ignoring their wives. They will testify how they hurt their wives, and many husbands will have to admit that they were a big factor in their wives becoming bitter and hardhearted.

When you invest in your wife, you are investing into your own life. You see, if you have a happy wife, you can be sure that you'll have a partner who is with you all the way. So I urge you today to learn how to dwell with your wife according to knowledge. *Make sure that from this day forward, you treat your wife like she is a top priority in your life!*

MY PRAYER FOR TODAY

Lord, I ask You to forgive me for not spending enough time with my wife. I know that she needs me and that I haven't done what I should do to show her the love and attention she deserves. She does so much for me. She loves me and our children and serves us with her whole heart. I am so sorry I've been so selfish and haven't been the husband I need to be for my wife. I repent for my self-centeredness, and I make the decision today to reverse my actions. I want to love her as I should and to do everything I can to communicate that love. Please help me, Lord, to become all I need to be for my wife!

I pray this in Jesus' name!

MY CONFESSION FOR TODAY

I boldly confess that I am a loving, caring, attentive husband. As God's Spirit works in me and transforms me more and more into the image of Jesus Christ, I am becoming a better husband to my wife. Because I love her deeply and regularly show my love to her, she feels secure and confident in our relationship. As a result, she is willing to follow me wherever God leads and is supportive of my decisions. Investing in my life partner is the best invest-ment I can make in my own life. Therefore, I choose this day to invest love and attentive care into my wife — the most important person in my life!

I declare this by faith in Jesus' name!

QUESTIONS FOR YOU TO CONSIDER

1. Husband, how much time in a week do you think you spend using your remote control to mindlessly flip through the television channels?
2. How much time do you spend talking to your wife and letting her talk to you? Do you have scheduled times when the two of you sit down together to discuss what is happening in your lives so you can stay vitally connected to each other?
3. Husband, what can you eliminate from your schedule so you can spend more time with your wife? Are you sending her the right message when you never have time for her, but you somehow have time for everyone else? Don't you think it's time for you to reevaluate your list of activities and make schedule changes to reflect the fact that your wife is more precious to you than anyone else?

OCTOBER 9

Planning Premeditated Acts Of Kindness Toward Your Wife

Likewise, ye husbands, dwell with them according to knowledge,
giving honour unto the wife, as unto the weaker vessel,
and as being heirs together of the grace of life….
— 1 Peter 3:7

Husband, absolutely no one in your life is more precious or important to you than your wife. One day when you are older and your children have started their own families and have moved to another city or state, or when your friends become elderly and pass away, your wife is the one who will still be right at your side. She started with you; she stayed with you; she will be with you through many years yet to come. And at the end of your life, she is the one who will still be right there at your side. Of all the relationships you have in this life, none compare in importance to your relationship with your wife.

This is exactly why the apostle Peter wrote to husbands in First Peter 3:7, "Likewise, ye husbands, dwell with them according to knowledge, giving honour unto the wife, as unto the weaker vessel, and as being heirs together of the grace of life...."

Peter had been married many years when he wrote this verse. He had a godly marriage that was an example to the Early Church. So when Peter spoke about marriage, he had a platform from which to speak. He had done well as a husband. Peter knew what God expects from husbands and therefore spoke strongly to husbands regarding how they should treat their wives.

In First Peter 3:7, Peter commanded husbands to "give honor" to their wives. What does this mean? The Greek word for "give" is *aponemo*. This word means *to assign, to designate, to allocate,* or *to intentionally give something to someone.* It refers to *a calculated decision to show attention, awareness, or consideration to someone else.* In this case, it refers to a man purposefully showing attention to consideration for his wife. Because Peter uses the Greek word *aponemo* ("giving"), this strongly suggests that the husband's attention, awareness, and consideration don't occur accidentally. Rather, this word pictures *a purposeful and premeditated action by a husband to intentionally demonstrate consideration for his wife.*

The word "honour" is from the Greek word *timao*, a word that carries the idea of *something so valuable that it is held as precious, prized, cherished, treasured, valuable, and very dear.* Peter uses the word in this verse to speak of a husband who *values his wife highly; holds her in honor; treats her graciously; esteems her; handles her respectfully; and treats her like a prized treasure that is very precious to him.*

As Peter continues exhorting husbands to treat their wives with special care, he makes one statement that unfortunately is often misunderstood. He tells husbands that they are to give honor unto the wife as unto the "weaker vessel."

The word "weaker" does not mean *inferior* or *substandard.* This is the Greek word *asthenes*, which actually carries the idea of *something that is fragile and of great value,* like a priceless, beautiful, hand-painted porcelain vase that must be treated with supreme care. Furthermore, the word "vessel" is from the Greek *skeuos*, which presents the idea of *a vase or treasure so rare and valuable that it should be treasured, cherished, highly prized, and handled with special care.*

Unfortunately, many men treat their wives like a bucket that is to be thrown under the kitchen sink or used in the barn to milk the cows! They don't comprehend that their relationship with their wife is the most precious relationship that exists in their lives.

Because a wife is so vital to the life of the husband, he should treat her like she *is* important. She is to be given a place of high honor in his life, as if she were a fragile and priceless vessel. She deserves a place of distinction and should know without a doubt that her husband views her as precious, valuable, and special in his life.

Husband, I want to give you some practical suggestions for expressing appreciation to your wife. These ten suggestions may sound very simple, but they are the kinds of actions that communicate to your wife how valuable she is to you. As you look at these ten suggestions, you will see that they are small, almost effortless acts of kindness; nevertheless, your wife will deeply appreciate them.

Certainly these acts of love and consideration are the least you can do for a wife whom you expect to faithfully follow you through life! Therefore, pay close attention to the following ten easy-to-follow suggestions:

1. When you and your wife approach a door, open the door for her and let her go through the door first. If you step through the door first and then let the door slam in your wife's face as she follows behind you, you give her the impression that she is of little value to you. So quit thinking only of yourself, and be a gentleman! Hold the door open for your wife!

2. When your wife walks up or down the stairs or when she gets in or out of the car, show enough consideration for her to reach out and take her by the hand and help her. This little tender touch communicates that you want to treat her with care. It makes her feel very special.

3. Instead of spending all the extra money on yourself, on your fishing trip, or on your personal pleasures, why not sacrifice a few of your own desires and give her that extra money to go do something for herself? When you give her a check or cash and tell her to go buy something for herself, it will probably shock her! But as she realizes that you are making a sacrifice of your own desires to bless her, it will send a gigantic signal that you love her and want to bless her.

4. Tell your wife often how beautiful she is to you. This makes her feel cherished. She works hard to be beautiful for you, and it is only right that you acknowledge it when she looks pretty.

5. Speak honorably of your wife in front of your children. If you treat her with honor, your children will treat her with honor as well. If you have sons, you are also providing a good example to them of the way they should honor their own future wives.

6. Take your wife to dinner and let her talk, talk, and talk. The one thing she wants more than anything else is time with you. When you give her time that is completely undistracted, it lets her know that you want to be with her. By the way, in those special times set aside for your wife, it would be a good idea to leave the mobile phone at home!

7. When you are at work, remember to pick up the telephone to call her during the day, just to let her know you are thinking about her. It doesn't take long for you to make a quick phone call, but that moment of consideration means a lot to your wife because it communicates to her how much you value her. If you tend to be forgetful about calling your wife during your busy workday, write a note to remind yourself.

8. Make time in your schedule to be only with your wife. This communicates that she is a high priority in your life. If you always have time to be with everyone else but never have time with her, you are sending her the message that she is the lowest priority in your life. Put yourself in her place, and you'll realize that if she had time for everyone but you, it would probably make you feel pretty insignificant as well. So make time for your wife, and she will feel valued by you.

9. Men don't like to write notes, but women love to receive them. So take a few minutes every so often to write a little note or card and leave it for your wife to find. How much time and effort does it take for you to pick up an ink pen and a piece of paper and write two or three sentences of appreciation to your wife? It's a small investment of time and creativity that speaks volumes to your wife about your love for her.

10. Always remember special dates, such as your wife's birthday or your wedding anniversary. Men tend to forget these things, but these are special memories to a

wife and it means so much to her when these times are celebrated with her husband. Also, don't forget to buy her a gift for these occasions. After all, wouldn't you be shocked and disappointed if she forgot *your* birthday?

Now let me take this one step further and suggest ten things a husband should never do to his wife! If you do any of these ten things, you are sending a wrong signal to your wife, for none of these actions will make her feel cherished and treasured by you. In fact, they will have the opposite effect!

Husband, listen carefully:

1. Never put your wife down in front of others. She didn't marry you to be the brunt of your jokes. Even if she smiles and laughs, trying to shrug off your verbal jabs, this kind of behavior on your part is deeply hurtful to your wife. She needs your honor, not your sarcasm. If there is a conflict between you, wait until you get home where you can talk about it privately, but never make fun of her or put her down in front of others. You certainly wouldn't want her to do this to you!

2. Never point out your wife's weaknesses to others. Husbands often do this, not realizing how disrespectful they are being to their wives. Talking in public about your wife's weaknesses will embarrass her. And I must ask you again, do you want her to point out all your flaws in front of other people? You would prefer that she speak to you privately about such matters, so show her the same courtesy.

3. Never tell your wife there isn't enough money in the budget for her to buy a new outfit — and then turn right around and spend a lot of money on yourself, your fishing trip, your hobbies, etc. When she sees you do this, it communicates to her that you love yourself more than you love her. Do you want your wife to perceive you as a selfish person who is more in love with yourself than concerned about blessing her?

4. Never tell your wife that you don't have time for her. Even if your schedule is packed, look for time to be with her. She married you because she loves you and wants to be with you. When you consistently make time for everyone in your life except your wife, you are making a very big mistake. If needed, cancel something in your schedule so you can give attention to this most important relationship in your life.

5. Never walk in front of your wife. Husbands are notorious for walking in front of their wives, and wives detest it. Too often men act as if they are racing when they walk, usually leaving their wives to walk five to fifteen feet behind them. Now, I understand that you may think your wife walks too slowly, but what is the use of racing in front of her if you must then stop, turn around, and wait for her to catch up with you? It takes the same amount of time to get to your destination, whether you walk alongside your wife or you walk ahead and then wait for her. So take your wife's hand, and discipline yourself to walk by her side. You'll shock her by doing this!

6. Never compare your wife to another woman. She wants to be the one and only woman in your life, so comparing her to other women is not wise and shows great disrespect. Do you want her to compare you to other men? I don't think so.

7. Never make sexual innuendoes about your wife in front of others. This is not only disrespectful; it is deeply offensive to a wife. Your sexual relationship is a time of intimacy that is to be shared only between the two of you. Therefore, when you make jokes about it or talk about it in front of others, you are humiliating your wife and making her feel cheap. This is certainly not a way to cherish her or to treat her like a treasure!

8. Never lie to your wife or tell a half-truth to cover your tracks. Honesty must be the foundation of your relationship. If you violate her trust by lying to her and she discovers it,

your act of deception will affect her ability to trust you in the future. Therefore, if you really love your wife, always level with her and be honest. It may be difficult for her to hear what you have to say, but at least she will know you are being honest with her. If she discovers you have been lying to her, this will result in a far greater hurt than if you honestly admit to her what you have done wrong.

9. Never dishonor your wife in front of your children. She is their mother, and they need to be taught to respect and honor her. If you treat her like a joke in front of the kids, they will treat her the same way. Dishonoring her and arguing with her before the children discredits her in their eyes. Do you want her to scold you or rebuke you in front of your children? Wouldn't you prefer that she express her disagreements with you in private? Then show her the same consideration that you want her to show you.

10. Never forget your wife's birthday or your wedding anniversary! Excuse me for repeating this point, but it's important. Men who consistently forget these two important dates and yet expect their marriage relationship to stay healthy are either ignorant or stupid. These are special dates in your wife's mind. Remembering her birthday tells her that you are thinking of her. Remembering your wedding anniversary tells her that you deeply care about your relationship with her.

Remember, Peter commands husbands in First Peter 3:7 to "give honor" to their wives. As noted earlier, the word "give" describes *a calculated decision to show attention, awareness, or consideration to someone else*. This pictures a *purposeful* and *premeditated* action by a husband to intentionally show attention and demonstrate consideration for his wife.

If these kinds of thoughtful acts don't come naturally to you, it's time for you to learn how to do them. Quit saying, "I just don't think that way," and learn to think that way! The truth is that you show kindness and consideration to other people, so you *can* do the same for your wife as well. Peter tells you what your responsibility is as a husband: "...giving honour unto the wife, as unto the weaker vessel...." If you intend to be an obedient son of God, you have no choice but to learn how to develop these skills in your life, because God commands that you show this kind of consideration to your wife.

If you sincerely want to please the Lord and to be a blessing to your wife, why don't you go before the Lord today and ask Him to forgive you for being insensitive to her needs? After you talk to the Lord, it is also important that you humble yourself and ask your wife to forgive you as well. Then follow up your repentance with actions. Let the Holy Spirit teach you, correct you, and show you how to become more sensitive to the woman you have chosen to spend the rest of your life with. Never forget — there is no relationship in your life more important than the one you have with your wife!

MY PRAYER FOR TODAY

Lord, I am asking You to please forgive me for being so selfish, self-centered, and neglectful of my wife and her needs. I expect her to faithfully serve me, but I have given her so little in return. I am truly sorry that I've ignored her and, as a result, hurt her. I accept responsibility for the role I have played in wounding her and making her feel unimportant. Please help me become more sensitive to my wife. Teach me to speak words that build her up, not words that put her down. As I follow Your leading in this area, please heal my wife's heart and bring tenderness back into our relationship once more. I accept Your challenge to purposefully show the honor, attention, respect, and tenderness she deserves. Thank You for helping me change in this vital area of my life!

I pray this in Jesus' name!

MY CONFESSION FOR TODAY

I confess that I am a loving and caring husband. My wife feels loved, respected, esteemed, and special because I do the things that communicate value to her. The Holy Spirit is helping me become more considerate, more tender, and more thoughtful. Every day I am dying to the flesh and becoming less selfish and self-centered. I am a godly example of what a husband ought to be, and my actions give a great sense of worth to the wife whom Jesus has given to me.

I declare this by faith in Jesus' name!

QUESTIONS FOR YOU TO CONSIDER

1. When is the last time you did something really extra special for your wife to show her how much you love and care for her?
2. Have you been guilty of jesting about your wife in front of others or of putting her down in front of the children? Would you want her to do this to you?
3. Is it time for you to humble yourself and to ask your wife to forgive you for the times you have been insensitive and uncaring of her needs?

OCTOBER 10

೭⊚⊚ຄ

Husband, You Are A Co-Ruler With Your Wife!

Likewise, ye husbands, dwell with them according to knowledge,
giving honour unto the wife, as unto the weaker vessel,
and as being heirs together of the grace of life;
that your prayers be not hindered.
— 1 Peter 3:7

Husband, it is simply a fact that you married a woman who loves you and needs you. Your wife is your partner, and she wants to be treated like she is a partner.

That is exactly the way God designed marriage in the first place. God intended for your wife to be more than your housekeeper, your bookkeeper, your personal slave, or the babysitter for the children you bore together. God desires that she be your partner in life. Literally, she is to be a co-ruler in the partnership of life.

This is why Peter told husbands in First Peter 3:7 to view their wives as "…being heirs together of the grace of life…." I want you to especially notice the phrase "heirs together." This phrase is taken from the Greek word *sunekleronomos*, a compound of the words *sun* and *kleros*. As noted earlier (*see* October 8), the word *sun* always carries the idea of *partnership* and *cooperation*. When the word *sun* is used in the New Testament, *it always connects two or more people into a very vital union*.

The second part of the word, *kleros*, describes *a portion, an allotment,* or *a part of something that belongs to a person or to a specific thing for which the person is responsible.* As time passed, the word *kleros* later came to denote *a parcel or portion of land that was inherited and thus became one's possession and responsibility.*

When the words *sun* and *kleros* are compounded as in First Peter 3:7, it carries the idea of *two people, a husband and wife, who are joined together in vital union to share life together.* They are literally joined to become *co-inheritors.* The word *sunkleromenos* means they are *partners,* not only in marriage but in all the affairs of life. This is a *joint venture,* a *joint partnership,* a *co-joining* of two people into a shared adventure of life.

You see, God intended for marriage to be a joint venture. Whenever a spouse is treated as less than an equal partner, that spouse can become deeply discouraged regarding the marriage relationship. This discouragement, if not corrected, leads to bitterness, hurt, and hardness of heart. This is why it is so essential that a husband learn to esteem his wife as his partner in life, which is precisely who God called her to be. If the husband's perception of her is anything other than this, he must renew his mind to the truth of God's Word and learn to value and appreciate her. He also needs to find ways to show his wife that he counts her as his most valued partner and friend.

When a husband and wife treat each other as equal and valued partners in life, they become a powerful team. On the other hand, if a marital relationship is out of order and one or both of the spouses do *not* value or appreciate each other, First Peter 3:7 says that this out-of-sync condition will "hinder" them when they pray together.

The word "hinder" is the word *egkopto,* a word used in Greek times to portray *the moment when a runner comes alongside another runner and literally elbows him out of the race.* Although the runner was previously running a good race, the aggression of a competitor literally breaks in on his race and destroys his effectiveness.

This categorically means that when disruption comes between a husband and wife or when spouses don't hold each other in esteem, the enemy is able to *elbow* into their relationship and invalidate the power of their prayers. That is why it is so important that husbands and wives view and receive each other as co-partners and co-inheritors in life. When a married couple see themselves as a unified team, their prayer life becomes powerful and effective. But if they allow their relationship to remain disjointed and disrupted, their prayers will be powerless and ineffective.

Therefore, husband, adjust your thinking to see your wife as your co-partner, co-inheritor, and co-ruler in life. If you are married, you are no longer just one; you have now become inseparably joined to your wife. Isn't it time for you to start treating her like she is your princess?

Before you got married, you treated her with respect, and that's the way God expects you to treat her after the wedding as well. So if you have become insensitive or have failed to treat your wife like the equal partner God intends for her to be, don't you think it's time for you to ask her forgiveness and then start treating her with the same courtesy and respect you expect her to show toward you?

Never forget — God intended for your marriage to be a powerful partnership. So make the decision today to treat your wife as though she is just as important and significant as yourself!

MY PRAYER FOR TODAY

Lord, help me treat my wife like the partner You intended for her to be in my life. You gave her to me to be a co-ruler and co-inheritor of the grace of life. You placed her at my side to be my helper, my companion, and my partner. You called us together to achieve Your will for our family. I am sorry for the times I have ignored her or unintentionally forgotten to treat her like the partner she is in my life. Starting today, please help me reverse any of my behavior patterns that my wife perceives to be unkind or insensitive. Show me ways to demonstrate to her that she is truly my partner and my co-ruler in this life!

I pray this in Jesus' name!

MY CONFESSION FOR TODAY

I confess that my wife is my co-ruler in life. She is my helper, my companion, and my partner. God called us together to make an impact in this world. Without her, I am incomplete, lacking all that is necessary to do this job. I acknowledge that I need my wife. I treat her as my equal partner whom God has joined to my life. She and I together make a powerful team, and together we are achieving great things!

I declare this by faith in Jesus' name!

QUESTIONS FOR YOU TO CONSIDER

1. Do you treat your wife like your partner in life, or do you treat her like she is your maid, your housekeeper, or your lifelong professional babysitter?
2. How often do you sit down to discuss your plans, your dreams, your future, or your daily schedule with your wife? Does she feel like she is a central part of your life, or does she feel like she is always the last one to be considered and the last one to find out what is happening?
3. If you were really honest with yourself about the way you treat your wife, what changes would you have to make in order to get your marriage in God's order and make your wife feel like she is a vital part of your life?

OCTOBER 11

Becoming of One Mind And Having Compassion One of Another

Finally, be ye all of one mind, having compassion one of another,
love as brethren, be pitiful, be courteous.
— 1 Peter 3:8

*I*t doesn't take too long for a newly married couple to start discovering the differences between the way a man and a woman think and feel. But the husband and wife just need to stay committed to their marriage and seriously work at learning to understand one another. Then as they grow together through the years, they will eventually start to think the same and see things from the same perspective.

When this level of unity is finally achieved, it brings power to a marriage. This is exactly the reason Peter exhorted husbands and wives, telling them, "Finally, be ye all of one mind...."

Notice Peter begins by saying, "Finally...." In Greek, this is the phrase *to telos*, which lets us know that he is coming to the final conclusion of what he has been saying to husbands and wives. The words *to telos* serve as an exclamation mark, letting the reader know that Peter is wrapping up and concluding this subject with some very important final remarks.

Then Peter tells the husbands and wives to be of "one mind." This is the challenge that has been set before husbands and wives since the beginning of time! The words "one mind" come from the Greek word *homophron*. The first part of the word is the Greek word *homos*, which means *one of the very same kind*. The second part of the word comes from the Greek word *phren*, which refers to *the mind* or *the intelligence*.

When these two words are compounded into one, forming the word *homophron*, it means *to be similarly minded*. It could be translated *of the same mind*. It is the idea of two people who think the same, feel the same, and view things in life the same way. They are similar in their thinking, reasoning, and conclusions.

Commitment is required in order for two people to become of one mind. These two people must *want* to understand each other, *want* to see things the same way, *want* to think the same way, and *want* to have the same vision, goal, and purpose in life.

Because my wife and I love each other, we work very hard to understand one another. When we don't understand what the other is projecting or saying, we stop and work on it until we do understand.

Misunderstanding through miscommunication is the door the devil likes to use to get in between spouses and divide them. But if a husband and wife will commit themselves to keeping the door shut to misunderstanding and miscommunication, this one factor alone can keep the devil from finding access into their relationship.

What are you doing to become of one mind with your spouse? Do you talk at length with each other? Do you pray and worship together? How often do you read the Bible together? Do you regularly devote time to one another that is free of the mobile telephone and the children crying out for your attention? Becoming of one mind takes focus and concentration. It doesn't happen by accident. If you and your spouse are going to achieve this blessed state God wants you to have, it will take a deliberate decision and action on your part.

Then Peter says that husbands and wives are to have "...compassion one of another...." I think it is very significant that he placed this command right after telling us to be of one mind, because our attempts to understand each other can cause some definite moments of frustration! Nevertheless, instead of giving in to those feelings of exasperation, we are to put aside our frustration and let compassion start to operate.

Sometimes you may not understand a single thing your spouse is trying to say. Other times you may express yourself over and over again, and your spouse still won't get it. But rather than get angry or frustrated when that happens, you can choose to let compassion flow!

What do I mean by "compassion"? The word "compassion" is the Greek word *sumpathos*, a compound of *sun*, describing *something that is equally shared*, and the Greek word *pathos*, meaning *feelings, affection*, or *passion*. When these two words are compounded together, they literally mean *to share feelings and emotions*. This refers to one who enters into someone else's experience to share that experience and to be a partner who understands what that person is going through. The word *sumpathos* is where we get the English word *sympathy*. It means *to be empathetic, kind, considerate, caring, and full of mercy.*

**When you take the meaning of these Greek words
into consideration, the verse conveys the following idea:**

"In conclusion, do everything you can to see and understand things the same way and to be sympathetic, kind, considerate, and caring of each other...."

By using the word *sumpathos* ("compassion"), Peter urges all of us to try to be *sympathetic* with each other. Rather than rush to judgment and get upset when we don't understand what someone else is saying or doing, we need to reach out to that person and *try* to understand. This principle is especially true in marriage. It is absolutely essential that we learn to be sympathetic with our spouses.

When an opportunity arises that would normally cause us to get upset with our spouses, we need to instead reach out to them and ask how we can help. And when we see our spouses struggling in some area, that isn't the time to preach at them or judge them for it. They need us to be their closest, most sympathetic friend.

So the next time you want to get upset with your mate, determine to have compassion instead. Reach out to him or her in love and say, *"I see that you are struggling. Is there anything I can do to help?"*

MY PRAYER FOR TODAY

Lord, help me to put aside my fleshly pride and to do everything I can to understand my precious spouse. I confess that there are times when I just don't understand what my spouse is trying to say or do. I often get frustrated and allow myself to get upset. Therefore, Holy Spirit, I am telling You right now that I need Your assistance to remain calm, to be at peace, and to let sympathy flow from my heart in place of the aggravation I have allowed to pester me. Today I want to turn a new page in my life. I want to be the best friend my spouse has ever had. Help me recognize where I need to change in order to be what I need to be in this marriage relationship.

I pray this in Jesus' name!

MY CONFESSION FOR TODAY

I confess that I am an understanding and compassionate spouse. My mate feels no judgment or rejection from me. We are working on our relationship. We are becoming more understanding of one another. We are achieving more unity than we've ever known in our relationship. As a result, we are on our way to being happier than we've ever been at any other time in our marriage. The worst days are behind us, and the best days are before us. Because the Holy Spirit is helping us, we are overcoming every struggle and experiencing new realms of victory in our lives!

I declare this by faith in Jesus' name!

QUESTIONS FOR YOU TO CONSIDER

1. Would your spouse say that you are the kind and compassionate friend he or she needs or that you tend to be preachy and judgmental?

2. Does your spouse feel "safe" with you? Is it easy for your spouse to open his or her heart and be totally honest in front of you? Or does your mate dread facing your judgmental attitude or your reprimand for his or her perceived weaknesses or shortcomings?

3. What do your answers to the two questions above indicate about the changes you need to make in your words and actions so your spouse can feel more comfortable with you? What steps can you take to foster a closer friendship and partnership with your spouse?

OCTOBER 12

Love as Brethren

Finally, be ye all of one mind, having compassion one of another,
love as brethren, be pitiful, be courteous.
— 1 Peter 3:8

When Denise and I first got married, I got upset with her one day over something very silly. Such a small issue shouldn't have upset me, but I was just beginning to learn how to be a husband, and Denise was learning to be a wife. As often happens when a couple first gets married, we got our wires crossed and misunderstanding resulted. And on this particular occasion, I allowed myself to get all worked up over nothing!

That day I sternly reprimanded Denise for what had transpired. Even though I knew I was raising my voice and speaking in a tone that wasn't exactly kind, it was almost as if I had tapped into a volcano on the inside of me. I felt like I was about to explode. I knew that if I didn't get a grip on myself, I would soon be saying overblown, angry words that I would later regret. It was suddenly clear to me that I was allowing the devil to blow this thing all out of proportion in my mind. So in order to get control of my emotions, I walked away and found a place where I could pray.

When I got alone with the Lord, the Holy Spirit spoke to me and said, "Would you speak with that tone of voice to any other woman at the church?"

I said, "No, I would never speak to any of the other women in the church the way I just spoke to my wife. Even if they did something very wrong and made me angry, I would treat them with courtesy simply because they are my sisters in Christ."

The Holy Spirit answered, "Well, not only is Denise your wife, she is your sister in Christ. From this moment forward, even if you are upset with her, show her the same respect you would show any other sister."

That word from the Holy Spirit changed my life. Denise was my sister in Christ before we got married, and the fact is, she is still my sister in Christ even though we are now joined together as husband and wife. If for no other reason, I should speak to her graciously and with dignity simply out of respect for her as my sister in the Lord. This shed new light for me on Peter's words in First Peter 3:8, where he said that husbands and wives are to "love as brethren."

The words "love as brethren" are from the Greek word *philadelphia*, a compound of the words *philos* and *adelphos* or *adelphia*. The word *philos* describes *friendship* and carries the idea of *affection* and *a profound love for someone who is dear*. The words *adelphos* and *adelphia* are the Greek words for *a brother* and *a sister*, respectively. When *philos* is compounded with one of these two words, the compound word means *to love as a brother* or *to love as a sister*.

It may seem strange to some that Peter tells husbands and wives to love as brethren. But the fact is, this is the most eternal part of the marriage relationship.

For instance, when Denise and I eventually go to Heaven, we will no longer be husband and wife, but we *will* be brother and sister in Christ. During our journey here on earth, we have partnered together as a marital team. I thank God that He joined me to Denise in this life in this particular relationship. But our long-term status and our most vital relationship is as a brother and sister in Christ. That aspect of our relationship will last throughout eternity.

So if you are ever tempted to get upset with your believing spouse, remember that he or she is *first* your brother or sister in the Lord. Then give your mate the same courtesy you would give any other brother or sister in the Christian community!

MY PRAYER FOR TODAY

Lord, please forgive me for the times I have spoken wrongly to my spouse. Help me to never take my spouse for granted again, but to always remember that if for no other reason, I should speak kindly to my mate out of respect for his (or her) position in Christ. I admit I've done wrong in the way I've spoken to my mate in the past. I know I wouldn't speak that way to anyone else in the church. Please help me to love my spouse as one of my brethren in the Lord and to reverence the Holy Spirit who lives in him (or her).

I pray this in Jesus' name!

MY CONFESSION FOR TODAY

I confess that I treat my spouse as a brother (or sister) in Christ. I speak to my spouse with respect; I reverence the Spirit of God who lives inside him (or her); and I honor my mate as a part of the Body of Christ. As God works in me and transforms me day by day, I am becoming more controlled and more temperate in the way I relate to my spouse. I don't fly off the handle with him (or her) and say things that are unacceptable to say to a brother or sister in Christ.

I declare this by faith in Jesus' name!

QUESTIONS FOR YOU TO CONSIDER

1. Can you honestly say that you treat your spouse with the same respect you show to other brothers or sisters in your local church?
2. Would you ever allow yourself to fly off the handle and indulge in an outburst of anger with brothers and sisters at church as you do with your spouse?
3. If you have treated your spouse with less respect than you show toward other people, don't you think it's time for you to first repent before God and then to ask your spouse for forgiveness and ask him (or her) to pray with you about this problem?

OCTOBER 13

༄༅༖

Be Pitiful, Be Courteous!

Finally, be ye all of one mind, having compassion one of another,
love as brethren, be pitiful, be courteous.
— 1 Peter 3:8

*A*s Peter continues to make his concluding remarks to husbands and wives, he urges them to "...be pitiful, be courteous." Today I want us to delve into the meanings of these Greek words to see what Peter means when he commands husbands and wives to be "pitiful" and "courteous" with one another.

The word "pitiful" is the Greek word *eusplagchnos*. It is a very strange combination of the words *eu* and *splagchnos*. The word *eu* means *well* or *good*. It describes a person who feels *swell* or *pleased* about something. It depicts *a positive emotional response to someone or to something that has been done.*

One of the best examples of the word *eu* in the New Testament is found in Matthew 3:17. When Jesus came up from the baptismal waters of the Jordan, a voice spoke from Heaven, saying, "...This is my beloved Son, in whom I am well pleased." The words "well pleased" are from the word *eudokeo* — which is the word *eu,* meaning *great pleasure,* connected to the Greek word *dokeo,* meaning *to think* or *to imagine.* But when these words are compounded to form the word *eudokeo,* it means, "I am more pleased than you could possibly imagine! I am *supremely* pleased!"

Now that we have looked at the word *eu,* the first part of the word *eusplagchnos,* let's now move to the second part of the word to see what the word *splagchnos* means. The word *splagchnos* is the Greek word for the *intestines* or *bowels.* Paul uses the word *splagchnos* in Second Corinthians 6:12 to describe his *deeply felt affection* for the Corinthian believers. He uses the word *splagchnos* in Philippians 1:8 to describe the *deeply felt affections* of Jesus Christ. In Philemon 1:12, we find Paul using the word *splagchnos* when he says to Philemon concerning Onesimus, "Whom I have sent again: thou therefore receive him, that is, mine own bowels." The use of the word *splagchnos* ("bowels") in this verse tells us that Paul *felt very deeply* about Onesimus.

From the examples in the paragraph above, we see that the word *splagchnos* can describe *tender emotions,* or it may picture *deeply felt feelings for someone else.* But we also find that the word *splagchnos* ("bowels") is used throughout the Gospels to express those moments when Jesus was "moved with compassion." There are many examples of the word *splagchnos* being used exactly in this way. For example:

+ Matthew 14:14 says, "And Jesus went forth, and saw a great multitude, and was *moved with compassion* toward them, and he healed their sick."
+ Matthew 15:32 says, "Then Jesus called his disciples unto him, and said, I have *compassion* on the multitude...." As a result of this deeply felt compassion, Jesus fed the multitude of people who were following Him that day.
+ Matthews 20:34 says, "So Jesus had *compassion* on them, and touched their eyes: and immediately their eyes received sight, and they followed him."
+ Mark 1:41 says, "And Jesus, *moved with compassion,* put forth his hand, and touched him, and saith unto him, I will; be thou clean."

✦ Mark 6:34 says, "And Jesus, when he came out, saw much people, and was *moved with compassion* toward them, because they were as sheep not having a shepherd: and he began to teach them many things."

✦ Mark 8:2 says, "I have *compassion* on the multitude, because they have now been with me three days, and have nothing to eat." Just as Matthew recorded in Matthew 15:32, Mark tells the same story in this text about how *compassion* moved Jesus to supernaturally provide food for His followers.

✦ Luke 7:13-15 says, "And when the Lord saw her, he had *compassion* on her, and said unto her, Weep not. And he came and touched the bier: and they that bare him stood still. And he said, Young man, I say unto thee, Arise. And he that was dead sat up, and began to speak. And he delivered him to his mother."

In every example where Jesus felt *compassion* for someone or for a mass of people, there was such a *movement of compassion* from within Him that it surged out of Him to meet the needs of people. In some cases, that *movement of compassion* caused Him to provide food, to raise the dead, to deliver the demon-possessed, to heal the sick, and to provide teaching for those who were like sheep without a shepherd.

Forgive me for being so straightforward, but I want to tell you exactly why the Holy Spirit chose the word *splagchnos* ("bowels") to describe compassion. Let me get very biological for a moment. What happens when a person's bowels move? The movement of the bowels produces action, doesn't it? Likewise, when the human spirit is deeply touched and moved by the need of another person, it causes a movement or a release of divine power to surge from deep within that person to reach out and meet the needs of that other individual.

This is the reason that every time Jesus was *moved with compassion,* it always resulted in a healing, deliverance, resurrection, supernatural provision, or some other action that changed someone's life. *You see, compassion always produces action.* The force of compassion cannot leave a person in the sad condition in which he was found; it moves one to do something to change that other person's situation.

We find the word *splagchnos* ("bowels") in First John 3:17, where John writes, "But whoso hath this world's good, and seeth his brother hath need, and shutteth up his *bowels of compassion* from him, how dwelleth the love of God in him?" The word "shutteth" is the Greek word *kleio,* which means *to lock up* or *to tightly shut up.* It pictures a believer who is *deeply moved* by someone else's need. But instead of letting that compassion move him to action, this believer deliberately puts up a barrier and shuts off the flow of compassion.

The urge to be compassionate is so strong that this believer must deliberately harden his heart in order to shut off that force of compassion and hinder it from flowing forth from him to meet that human need. John describes this urge to meet someone else's need as "bowels of compassion."

But when these two words — *eu* and *splagchnos* — are compounded together, it means *to be tender-hearted or affectionate.* The second part of the word, *splaghnos,* pictures *a person who is deeply moved.* However the word *eu,* the first part of the word *eusplagchnos,* pictures *a person who feels very positive about someone or something else.* When compounded together, the new word means *an inward feeling of delight and a deep desire that moves someone to do something for someone else.*

Peter uses this same word in First Peter 3:8 when he tells husbands and wives to be "pitiful." Peter is actually exhorting them to *feel deeply* for each other and to put actions to those emotions. *Compassion always produces action.*

If you deeply love your spouse, that love will *move you* to do things to help him or her in life, for real love cannot just sit idly by and watch the loved one struggle. Your deeply felt love for your mate will motivate you to get up and do something to help!

But then Peter follows this up by telling husband and wives to be "courteous." The word "courteous" is an unfortunate translation of the Greek word *tapeinophron*. It is a compound of the words *tapeinos* and *phren*. The word *tapienos* means *to be lowly, to be humble,* or *to exhibit humility and modesty.* The word *phren* is the Greek word for *the intellect* or *the mind.* When these two words are used together, it means *to be humble-minded* or *to be lowly-minded* — a concept that goes beyond merely being courteous or polite.

It is just a fact that when we see someone else with a need, our flesh wants to rise up and say, "I'm going to quit being so merciful and compassionate! That person can just grow up! I am finished intervening to help every time he struggles!"

In moments when our flesh is tempted to be judgmental toward our spouses, we must resist the temptation to act high and mighty and condescending. Instead, we must choose to be humble-minded, to come down to a level where we can be understanding and release a flow of compassion to help instead of becoming our spouses' judge!

This is what Peter means when he tells husbands and wives to be "pitiful" and to be "courteous." *Now that you know the way you are supposed to relate to your spouse, what are you going to do?*

MY PRAYER FOR TODAY

Lord, I want to be moved with compassion toward my spouse! Help me to truly feel compassion for what my spouse is going through, and teach me how to let mercy flow from my spirit to strengthen him (or her). I know that my spirit is filled with everything my spouse needs in moments of difficulty, so I want to know how to release those good things from my spirit to strengthen and edify him (or her). Holy Spirit, please help me be moved with compassion toward my spouse. Teach me how to esteem and to treat him (or her) as more important than myself.

I pray this in Jesus' name!

MY CONFESSION FOR TODAY

I confess that I am filled with compassion and that I let that force of compassion flow from my heart to my spouse. I am the strongest source of blessing and encouragement in my spouse's life. I deliberately think of ways I can be a blessing to him (or her), and I speak words of blessing that will bring the strength and encouragement my spouse needs from me.

I declare this by faith in Jesus' name!

QUESTIONS FOR YOU TO CONSIDER

1. Can you remember times when you felt a surge of compassion flow from your heart toward your spouse? When you released that compassion and let it flow from your heart, did you become a source of great strength and encouragement to your mate?
2. Have there been moments in your marriage when that flow of compassion wanted to operate through you, but you refused to allow it to flow toward your spouse? *Be honest.*

3. Can you recall a time when you were the recipient of divine compassion flowing from another person? What effect did this flow of compassion have on you and your situation?

OCTOBER 14

Do Not Render Evil for Evil Or Railing for Railing

Not rendering evil for evil, or railing for railing:
but contrariwise blessing; knowing that ye are thereunto called,
that ye should inherit a blessing.
— 1 Peter 3:9

One day when I was flying on a plane, I noticed that the woman next to me seemed to be seething about something. I asked her if everything was all right, and she erupted in anger about something her husband had done to her. She angrily said, "I am furious at my husband. I'm so mad at him that I am determined to find a way to pay him back for what he did to me! You just watch! I'm going to get him so badly that he'll be sorry for the rest of his life for his actions! By the time I'm finished, he'll be sorry he messed with me!"

As I listened to this woman vent these very angry emotions, I thought of how many husbands and wives in the world would probably say these same words about one another from time to time. Her words grieved me deeply, for I knew the raging conflict between this woman and her husband, if not properly resolved and reconciled, would be the key that unlatched the door to their marriage, enabling the devil to come inside and inflict serious harm to their relationship.

The way a husband and wife respond to conflict and disappointment is very important. They can choose to be forgiving and merciful, allowing the conflict and the improper attitudes and behavior to be covered by the blood of Jesus. If they make this choice, the two of them will be empowered to walk in peace, to experience uninterrupted unity, and to remain the powerful team God intended them to be as husband and wife.

However, a married couple can also choose to constantly remind one another of their past wrongs and failures, holding each other hostage by laying the blame and guilt for every problem at one another's feet. If the couple chooses this latter course, they will open the door for the devil to get into their relationship and make a mess of their marriage.

When Peter writes to husbands and wives in First Peter 3, he urges them not to let this kind of wicked behavior be a part of their married lives. He says, "Not rendering evil for evil, or railing for railing: but contrariwise blessing; knowing that ye are thereunto called, that ye should inherit a blessing" (1 Peter 3:9).

Notice that Peter says, "Not rendering evil for evil...." The *King James Version* I am quoting begins with the word "not" because the Greek denotes *a strong prohibition to stop something that is already in progress.* The implication is that the husbands and wives to whom Peter was writing were already carrying out these improper and destructive actions; therefore, he was strongly warning and forbidding them to stop this wrong behavior. The Greek actually means, *"Stop it! Don't do it anymore! You should never do this!"*

Then he used the word "rendering" to describe the attitude that many of them seemed to be demonstrating to each other and that he was forbidding them to continue. The word "rendering" is the Greek word *apodidomi*, which actually means *to pay back*. It is the idea of *getting back at someone for what that person did to you*. It refers to *sending back exactly what was sent to you*. You could say that this word pictures a person who is determined to do to someone else exactly what the offender did to him. In other words, this is *payback* time!

How many times have you heard husbands and wives say they are going to "get back" at their spouse for what he or she did to them? I'm telling you, friend, this is the wrong route to take!

What you sow is exactly what you reap. It is far better for you to sow mercy and forgiveness than to get into the business of sowing bitterness. Even though it may seem very difficult to forgive and to let go of the offense, it is far easier to take this route than to sow wrong seed and thus get trapped in a destructive cycle of sowing and reaping bitterness and strife that will ultimately hurt you, your marriage, and your children.

Peter tells us, "Not rendering evil for evil...." The word "evil" is the Greek word *loidoria*. This Greek word tells us exactly what the husbands and wives to whom Peter was writing must have been feeling. This word *loidoria* pictures a person who feels (whether or not those feelings are based on actual truth) that he or she has been *ill-treated, misused, berated,* and *abused.* This person considers himself *victimized, oppressed, mishandled, harassed, manhandled, violated, defiled, imposed upon wrongly, debased,* and *humiliated.* The Greek word *loidoria* ("evil") thus projects the ideas of *insult, injury, hurt,* and *damage.*

Peter's words in this verse
could accurately be taken to mean:

"Do not pay back one insult with another insult...."
"Do not get back at your spouse by injuring him or her the same way you were injured...."
"Do not retaliate against your spouse by abusing him or her
in the same way you have felt abused...."
"Do not pay your spouse back with the same treatment he or she has given to you...."

Before you rush into "railing" at your spouse for the injustice that you perceive has been done to you, let God first speak to your heart about your own role in the matter. "Railing" at one another is not God's way for you or your spouse to respond to disappointment. That is the way the flesh responds, but it is *not* God's way in a marital relationship. He has a far better way for you to respond that will release power and bring blessing to your marriage!

Peter says you and your spouse are called that you should inherit a "blessing." Do you see the word "blessing"? It is the Greek word *eulogia*, a compound of *eu* and *logos*. The word *eu* means *good* or *swell*, and it describes *something wonderful or pleasurable.* The word *logos* is the Greek word for *words*. When compounded together, the word *eulogia* means *good, swell, wonderful, and pleasurable words.*

You can be sure that at some point along the way, your spouse will disappoint you and let you down. Even if he or she doesn't mean to do it, it will happen simply because your mate is human or because you have expectations that are impossible for anyone to meet 100 percent of the time.

So when your flesh gets riled up and feels like it has been violated or mistreated, don't immediately blow your top and start acting ugly in response. Instead, run to the Lord and ask Him to help you perceive this situation correctly. If you'll let the Holy Spirit work in you, He will show you how to return kindness for every injustice you perceive has been done to you. A right response from you can change the entire situation. A wrong response from you will only aggravate the situation and make it worse.

Instead of paying back acts of unkindness with harsh, retaliatory remarks or calculated acts of revenge, make the decision that you are going to respond to every incident by speaking a blessing over your spouse! In other words, when you think of something negative that your spouse has done, determine not to give in to the urges of your flesh to retaliate. Choose instead to return those inconsiderate acts with words of love.

If something has happened that tempts you to be bitter, refuse to take offense. Instead of responding with words that attack and tear down your spouse, decide that you're going to speak words that build him or her up. Instead of paying back an insult with an insult, make the decision to speak a blessing!

That day when the woman sitting next to me on the airplane talked about how she was going to pay her husband back for the things he had done to her, I could see that she was headed down a road of revenge that would only aggravate her situation. The same is true in your marriage. It's all right to talk about things that disappoint you, but that kind of discussion needs to take place in a healthy, productive way. Make sure your mouth is filled with sweet words instead of harsh words — and *never* let yourself get into the retaliation business, for that will only make your situation worse.

The Holy Spirit will show both you and your spouse how to respond in every situation with words of kindness. He'll fill your mouth with good things if you'll allow Him to work in you this way. *In fact, as you speak the blessings the Holy Spirit wants you to speak instead of making argumentative, insulting remarks to your spouse, your words will become the very force that turns the situation around in your marriage!*

MY PRAYER FOR TODAY

Lord, forgive me for allowing myself to get so upset in the past that I have acted unkindly toward my mate and made ugly remarks in moments of rage. I'm wrong for permitting my flesh to control me in such an ungodly way. Even though my spouse has been wrong as well, he (or she) couldn't have been any uglier or more hurtful than I was when I spoke those harsh, retaliatory words. Please help me to become more like Jesus — to release blessing after blessing as I speak only words of kindness to my spouse. I know that my words have the power of life and death, so help me turn around every difficult situation as I start speaking blessings into my marital relationship!

I pray this in Jesus' name!

MY CONFESSION FOR TODAY

I confess that I speak blessings into my relationship with my spouse. I don't speak curses, nor do I pay back abuse with abuse or insult with insult. I am called to be a blessing; therefore, I AM a blessing, and my mouth speaks good things even when I am tempted to say words that are not so edifying. I refuse to get into the retaliation business, for I am called to be in the blessing business! I take every opportunity — both pleasurable times as well as moments of conflict — to speak blessings over myself, over my spouse, and over our relationship together!

I declare this by faith in Jesus' name!

QUESTIONS FOR YOU TO CONSIDER

1. Have there been times when the Holy Spirit told you to keep a tight rein on your tongue and to respond to a situation with positive words instead of ugly words? Did you obey what the Spirit prompted you to do, or did you go ahead and verbalize the anger you felt?
2. What happened when you responded to a bad situation with words of kindness instead of with retaliatory remarks? Or what happened when you returned insult for insult in an argument with your spouse?
3. Are you willing to ask the Holy Spirit to prepare you for the next time you face a potentially explosive situation in your marriage? Will you make a firm decision beforehand to respond with great patience and kindness so your response can disarm all potential for strife in the situation?

OCTOBER 15

If You Love Life And Want To See Good Days

For he that will love life, and see good days, let him
refrain his tongue from evil, and his lips that they speak no guile:
Let him eschew evil, and do good; let him seek peace, and ensue it.
— 1 Peter 3:10,11

Do you want a good marriage? Do you want to live a long and happy life with your spouse? If your answer is "Yes, that's exactly what I want," you need to pay close attention to the words of Peter recorded in First Peter 3:10,11. It says, "For he that will love life, and see good days, let him refrain his tongue from evil, and his lips that they speak no guile: let him eschew evil, and do good; let him seek peace, and ensue it."

Peter tells us that if a spouse wants to experience a full life and see good days together with his or her mate, that spouse must learn to "…refrain his tongue from evil, and his lips that they speak no guile." The word "refrain" is the word *pauo*, which means *to pause*. It means *to take a break; to take a rest;* or *to cease from what one is doing*. The word "evil" is the Greek word *kakos*, the word for *something that is evil, vile, foul, or destructive*. In this context, it implies *ugly words that, when spoken, bring destruction and harm*.

Can you think of a time when you got so angry that you exploded and spewed destructive words? Were you sorry later that you said those words? That is what Peter is talking about here. He is basically saying, "If you want to have a long and happy life together, you have to learn how to refrain from saying ugly, hurtful, and destructive things to each other. It's time for you to cease from this behavior!"

Then Peter urges husbands and wives to make sure their lips "speak no guile." The word "guile" is the word *dolos*, an old Greek word that carries the idea of *trickery and manipulation*.

Manipulation and dishonesty are destructive to a marital relationship. When a husband and wife manipulate, deceive, or lie to each other, they create an atmosphere of distrust that disrupts their ability to maintain a peaceful, harmonious home. Talk to any marital counselor, and he or she will tell you that deception and manipulation in a marriage is very destructive to the trust that is required to keep the marriage relationship strong. That's why Peter urges spouses to stay out of the deception and manipulation business!

So if you want to have a good life and a happy marriage, you must learn to take a lifelong break from speaking evil. You must also determine in your heart that you will no longer play the manipulation game with your spouse! Peter says that instead of taking that wrong route, you must "eschew evil."

The word "eschew" is the Greek word *ekklino*, from the word *ek* and *klino*. The word *ek* means *out*, and the word *klino* means *to turn*. When they are used as one word, it means *to turn aside* or *to intentionally turn away from something*.

This means that instead of following the volatile and destructive patterns that have been a part of the marriage for so long, a spouse who wants to change must determine to put aside these negative practices. There must be an intentional turning away from every destructive behavior pattern and an intentional turning *toward* those actions that build trust and make a relationship strong and healthy. This is why Peter goes on to say that spouses must "do good."

The word "do" is the word *poieo*, the Greek word that means *to do something*. But as noted earlier (*see* January 15), the word *poieo* also carries with it the idea of *creativity*. In other words, if we can't easily think of a way to do good to our spouses, we need to get creative and put some effort into thinking of ways to bless and to be a blessing to them!

The word "good" is the word *agathos*, a word that suggests *actions that are good, profitable, beneficial, and virtuous*. So if you want your marriage to be blessed, strong, long-lasting, and healthy, you must deliberately look for ways to be a blessing. Find ways to become a benefit to your spouse!

Peter tells husbands and wives to "seek peace" instead of constantly getting into conflicts with each other. The word "seek" is the Greek word *zelos*. It describes *a fierce determination to have something or to become something*. The Greek tense Peter uses when he writes the word *zelos* implies *a constant and arduous seeking to obtain something*, not just an occasional attempt. This person is straining forward with all his might. He is committed; he has a never-give-up attitude; and he will not stop until he finally obtains that which he deeply desires!

What is the treasure that Peter tells spouses to seek after? *Peace!* Anyone who has been successfully married for a long period of time will tell you that "peace" in a marriage doesn't happen accidentally. If a husband and wife are able to live together in peace and harmony, they have achieved that goal through hard work, patience, understanding, and a never-give-up desire to have peace in their relationship.

Many events and misunderstandings can occur to disrupt peace in a relationship, so your desire for marital peace must be stronger than any of these other forces. If you're not totally fixed on having peace with your spouse, the devil will find a way to constantly get in between the two of you.

Peter says that if you're going to have this kind of peace between you and your spouse, you must "ensue" it. The word "ensue" is the Greek word *dioko*, an old Greek word that means *to hunt, to chase,* or *to pursue.* It was a hunting term used to illustrate a hunter who is so committed to getting his trophy that he goes out into the forest and begins to literally stalk that animal. He follows the tracks and the scent of the animal; he watches, waits, and strategizes. And because of the hunter's careful planning and determined following of that animal, eventually he gets his game!

Isn't it interesting that Peter would use this word to tell us how we should seek after peace? This means peace won't come to us by accident. If we are going to have peace in our relationships — especially our marital relationship — we must put on our hunting clothes and develop a plan for peace! If necessary, we must be willing to *stalk* peace — following its tracks and its scent and, with the help of the Holy Spirit, strategizing on how to finally obtain peace in our marriage relationship!

Remember, we live in a day when marriages are quickly made and quickly dissolved. Therefore, if you see a healthy marriage that has lasted through many years, realize that this couple has worked very hard to have such a good relationship.

I urge you to take Peter's words deep into your heart. Determine to do everything you can to make your marriage strong and healthy. It's going to take hard work and commitment to make it happen. But if you want to experience a happy, fulfilling life with your spouse, every bit of that hard work will be well worth it in the long run!

MY PRAYER FOR TODAY

Lord, help me to become more committed to my marriage. Forgive me for being a contributor to strife and conflict, and teach me how to refrain my tongue from speaking evil so I can bring benefit and blessing to my spouse. Open my heart and my eyes, Lord. Show me things I can do to encourage my mate. No one has more influence in my spouse's life than I do, so I am asking You to help me to be the right kind of influence he (or she) needs!

I pray this in Jesus' name!

MY CONFESSION FOR TODAY

I confess that I am a great encouragement to my spouse! I work hard on my marriage. I find ways to be a blessing. The Spirit of God is showing me the steps I need to take to obtain peace with my spouse. I am not a source of conflict, and I refuse to let the devil use me any longer. From this day forward, the enemy will not use my lips as his entryway into my marriage. I will do everything needed to make my marriage strong and healthy, just the way Jesus wants it to be!

I declare this by faith in Jesus' name!

QUESTIONS FOR YOU TO CONSIDER

1. Can you think of a time when you got so angry at your spouse that you said a lot of ugly, destructive words to him or her? How did your poisonous words affect the outcome of that particular conflict? Did you ever allow God's peace to resolve that situation by humbly asking your spouse for forgiveness?

2. What can you do to make sure you don't make the same mistake the next time you are dealing with an emotionally charged situation in your marriage?

3. Can you think of some good things you can do to bless your spouse in the days ahead as you seek to establish God's peace as the abiding force in your marriage? *Get creative!*

OCTOBER 16

❧

You Will Receive Exactly What You Believe!

...If thou canst believe,
all things are possible to him that believeth.
— Mark 9:23

I cannot begin to count the times people have told me, "Rick, no one has ever been able to do what you're attempting to do in your part of the world. We know several who tried to do it in the past, but they failed and ended up in a mess. So be careful, because it is highly unlikely that you'll be able to achieve what you are attempting to do!"

This kind of "doom-and-gloom" prediction has been made to us over the years more times than we can number. People have told us that nearly everything we have ever done is impossible.

For instance, people said it was impossible to broadcast God's Word on television in our part of the world, but we did it anyway. We were told it was impossible for a foreigner to have a great impact on national pastors and churches, but we're having an amazing impact that is affecting thousands of pastors and churches. When we started churches in several key cities, we were warned, "No one has ever been able to establish a big church in those cities, and you won't be able to do it either." But with God's help, we did it, and today those cities have large, powerful churches that are flourishing!

When God called us to start our church in the heart of Moscow, people came crawling out of the woodwork to tell us, "Moscow is the seat of demonic principalities and powers. This heavily concentrated demonic influence is so strong that no one has been able to break through and establish a powerful church in the heart of Moscow. We want to prepare you so you won't be too disappointed, because you probably won't be able to do it either!"

When I heard that, I laughed out loud! Jesus said, "...If thou canst believe, all things are possible to him that believeth" (Mark 9:23). Jesus made it plain — if we will believe, all things will be possible to us!

The word "possible" is the Greek word *dunata*, which comes from the word *dunatos*. It expresses the idea of *ability; power; one who is able and capable;* or *one who is competent.* The word *dunatos* shares the same root with the word *dunamis*, which is the Greek word for *power.* This emphatically tells us that there is a power that causes one to become able, capable, or competent for any task.

When this explosive power comes on the scene and begins to operate in an individual's life, it doesn't matter how unfit or unqualified he was before; this power energizes him and makes him capable for the task before him.

But who is this person who can accomplish impossible feats? Jesus said that all things are possible to him "that believeth." The word "believeth" is the Greek word *pisteuonti*, from the word *pistis*, the Greek word for *faith*. However, when *pistis* becomes *pisteuonti*, as in this verse, it pictures a person who is *believing*. This is not someone who once had an experience of faith in the past; rather, this is a person who is *presently believing* right now. He didn't just believe in the past; he is *a believer*. His faith is actively reaching forward right now to grab hold of what God has promised. His faith is habitually, constantly, consistently, unwaveringly straining forward to take hold of that desired goal he sees before him!

You see, faith is the spark that ignites the impossible and causes it to become possible. When a person's faith is activated, it sets in motion supernatural power that enables that person to do what he normally would never be able to do! This is why Jesus said, "…If thou canst believe, all things are possible to him that believeth." Once faith has been activated and remains activated, a person becomes enabled and empowered so that he is capable and competent to do whatever it is God has told him to do. That person can even do the impossible!

When I receive a new mandate from God to push forward into new and uncharted territory, I don't let fear and doubt flood my mind. Instead, I immediately begin renewing my mind to believe that I can do anything God has asked me to do. If He has told me to do something — regardless of how big or how impossible it seems to the natural mind — then I tell myself that I can do it. After all, if it couldn't be done, why would He tell me and our team to do it?

The fact is, in God *all* things are possible, so it's up to me and the others on my team to get our thinking in line with God's Word. And as I build up my faith to the level it needs to be for the new challenge, I experience an explosion of supernatural power in me that literally carries me over into the realm where impossible things becomes possible!

Jesus made it very clear that we receive exactly what we believe. If I believe I can do the impossible, I will do it. But if I believe I cannot do the impossible, I will *not* do it. When I look at those who have warned me about all the things they thought couldn't be done, most of those people have done *nothing*. In other words, they have gotten exactly what they have believed for! But because we dared to believe, today we are standing in the middle of many accomplished "impossible" assignments that others said could never happen. They were wrong!

Never underestimate the power of faith! Make sure you are thinking and believing correctly — because what you believe is *exactly* what you will receive!

MY PRAYER FOR TODAY

Lord, since Your Word says all things are possible to the one who believes, I am asking You to help me renew my mind to believe I can do anything You ever ask me to do with my life. Help me to truly understand that there is absolutely nothing impossible to me when I believe. I so regret the times I've listened to voices of doubt and unbelief who talked me out of the great victories You had in store for me. With the assistance of the Holy Spirit, I will shut my ears to the voices of unbelief from this moment forward. I release my faith today to believe that ANYTHING is possible for me to do, as long as You are the One asking me to do it!

I pray this in Jesus' name!

MY CONFESSION FOR TODAY

I confess that I can do anything God puts in my heart to do. Nothing is impossible to me, because everything is possible to him who believes! I believe God's Word. I believe I can do what He tells me to do. I believe the vision He put in my heart is achievable. Because I believe, I will receive the impossible!

I declare this by faith in Jesus' name!

QUESTIONS FOR YOU TO CONSIDER

1. Can you think of instances in your life when the Lord put a dream in your heart that others thought was impossible, but you stood strong in your faith and refused to let those voices of unbelief affect you? In time did you see that dream come to pass?
2. How would you be different today if you hadn't believed and held fast to what God had told you until you saw the manifestation of that promise?
3. Is there a specific dream that God's Spirit has put in your heart during this present season of your life? Does it seem too big for you? Since everything is possible to him who believes, are you willing to release your faith today and start believing for the impossible to come to pass in your life?

OCTOBER 17

Why Should We Stop Just Because the Devil Gets in the Way?

Wherefore we would have come unto you,
even I Paul, once and again; but Satan hindered us.
— 1 Thessalonians 2:18

*I*f you are going to do anything significant for the Kingdom of God, you must know in advance that Satan will not be delighted about it. He will try to stop you, thwart you, and dissuade you from staying on track. The last thing he wants is for you to step into the middle of God's will for your life, because he knows the moment you do, mighty and powerful things will begin to happen that negatively affect his dark kingdom. Therefore, Satan will most definitely do all he can to keep you from getting where God wants you to be!

In the January 17 *Sparkling Gem*, we looked at a key word in First Thessalonians 2:18. Today I want us to look at this scripture again, for in this verse, Paul gives his own testimony of how Satan tried to hinder him from doing what God put in his heart. He wrote, "Wherefore we would have come unto you, even I Paul, once and again; but Satan hindered us."

The word "hindered" is the Greek word *egkopto*. As noted earlier, this word was used to depict *a runner who was elbowed out of the race by a fellow runner*. However, it was also used to picture *the breaking up of a road to make it impassable for travelers*. This kind of *impasse* made it impossible for a traveler to get where he needed to go. As a result, the traveler's trip was *hindered, delayed, postponed, or temporarily put off*. The traveler could still take another route to get to the same destination, but the alternate route was inconvenient, cost a lot of extra money, and took precious time that could have been used another way.

By using this word, Paul informs us that demonic attacks inconvenienced him on occasion. Satan craftily sought to abort advances of the Gospel by arranging unexpected problems that delayed, postponed, and hindered the missions God had placed on Paul's heart. But did Paul sit down and cry because plans didn't work out as he intended? Did he throw in the towel and quit? *No!*

The apostle Paul never stopped just because the devil tried to get in his way! No impasse or roadblock was going to stop him! He refused to take no for an answer! He was going to get the job done, regardless of the inconvenience, money, time, or effort involved. He was so stubborn about doing what he was called to do that he always found a way to do it.

An example of this is the time Paul left the city of Ephesus because his life was in danger (*see* Acts 19 and 20). Paul had given three years of his life to the believers in Ephesus. When he left, he could have cried, "Oh, I don't understand why the Lord let this happen! He knows how much I love the leadership of Ephesus!" Paul could have bemoaned, "Now I'll never see the Ephesian believers again. The devil has attacked me, and the door to Ephesus is permanently closed for me!"

But Paul understood that crying and lamenting don't change a thing. So instead, he went down the road to the seaside town of Miletus and secured a facility for a meeting. Then he called for the elders of Ephesus to meet him there! Paul figured if he couldn't go to Ephesus, why not invite the leadership to come see him? Why resign himself to defeat just because he had hit an impasse in the road? Paul knew that there is more than one way to accomplish a goal. So he put his brain to work and found a way to do what God wanted him to do.

Why should we stop just because the devil gets in the way? If that were the case, we might as well stop everything we're doing for the Lord right now! There will never be a time that the devil just lets us do what is in our hearts. We must be determined to keep doing what we're called to do even if the devil tries to slam the door shut in our faces.

So what if Satan shut the door to Ephesus? That was a good time for Paul to look for a open window! If he couldn't go to the elders, why not call them to him? Paul discovered an open window in Miletus. He called for the leaders, met with them, and finished his assignment, exactly as God had ordered him to do. *Mission accomplished!*

You see, Paul had an attitude that would not give up. It didn't matter how much opposition was leveled against him, he had already decided he would outlive the opposition. Somehow he'd find a way to do what God had called him to do.

You can do anything God calls you to do too! Determine in your heart that you will not allow Satan to do anything to stop you, thwart you, or dissuade you from staying on track with the assignment God has given you. God's will for your life is where mighty and powerful things are going to happen! That is why the devil is putting up such a fuss to try to keep you from getting there. He's afraid of what will happen if you actually do what God has put in your heart to do.

So dig in your heels, and determine that you are *not* giving in or giving up. Refuse to back up or relent, and keep on pressing ahead. The devil may have put an impasse in the road before you, but that doesn't mean the show is over! If you'll listen to the Holy Spirit, He'll show you another route to get you where you need to be.

The Holy Spirit needs a partner who is committed. So just commit yourself to pressing ahead, regardless of the opposition. As you do, the Spirit of God will empower you to conquer every attack that comes against you. Then He will masterfully show you another and more effective way to fulfill your divine assignment. *In the end, the devil will be sorry he messed with you!*

MY PRAYER FOR TODAY

Lord, I ask You to help me stay fiercely committed to fulfilling the assignment You have given to me. Forgive me for the times I've given in to weakness and allowed myself to complain when I should have grabbed hold of Your strength and pressed full steam ahead. I repent for allowing my flesh to talk me into moments of defeat. Today I choose to push forward to do exactly what You've told me to do. Holy Spirit, if the devil creates an impasse for me, please show me a better route to take so I can fulfill my divine assignment!

I pray this in Jesus' name!

MY CONFESSION FOR TODAY

I confess that I am led by the Holy Spirit and that He shows me how to get around every obstacle the devil tries to put in my path. No impasse the devil puts before me is sufficient to prevent me from achieving what Jesus has asked me to do and to be. I refuse to accept no for an answer, and I reject any temptation to quit. I am empowered by the Spirit of the Almighty God, and I can do anything He will ever ask me to do!

I declare this by faith in Jesus' name!

QUESTIONS FOR YOU TO CONSIDER

1. Has there been a time in your life when it seemed like an impasse stood between you and what God wanted you to do? How did you respond to that impasse?
2. If you listened to the Holy Spirit and found another, better route to finish the task before you, did it thrill your heart to realize that He knows how to get around every attack of the enemy? What did you learn by following the Holy Spirit rather than allowing discouragement to hold you back from fulfilling your divine assignment?
3. Who are the people in your life who seem blocked from doing what God wants them to do? Could you be an encouragement to these individuals by contacting them and sharing how God supernaturally led you around impasses in the past?

Determine in your heart that you will not allow the devil to do anything to stop you, thwart you, or dissuade you from staying on track with the assignment God has given you. Isn't it time for you to start declaring that you can do anything God calls you to do?

OCTOBER 18

༻✿༺

How Is Your Work Ethic?

Are they ministers of Christ? (I speak as a fool) I am more;
in labours more abundant....
— 2 Corinthians 11:23

I personally gain strength when I consider the many victories the Lord gave the apostle Paul. He had multiple challenges that came against him and his ministry, but none of them ever stopped him from his task. As noted earlier (*see* August 3), it is simply a fact that those who preach the Gospel in difficult parts of the world often encounter extremely hostile situations. In order to overcome these situations, a person has to possess a strong, internal resolution that no devil, no person, no government, and no force is going to stop him from executing the assignment God has given to him.

But this isn't true only of people who serve on the front lines of the Gospel. It is also true for you. God has a plan for your life. He has a specific vision He wants you to discover and achieve. On the other hand, you have an enemy who doesn't want you to find that vision. And I want to warn you — from the moment you do discover God's plan for your life, that enemy will try to stop you from achieving it.

But don't worry, friend — God has given you all the promises you need to overcome every attack Satan arrays against you. However, in order for those promises to be effective, you have to decide that you are going to stand in faith and resist each attack!

Because of the challenges my wife and I have encountered in our own ministry, I find great strength when I study about the attacks that came against the ministry of the apostle Paul. I like to read about how he persisted and overcame these attacks. The events Paul encountered would have shattered a normal man. But because he used his faith and kept his focus on the prize before him, Paul was able to *override* and *supercede* each act of aggression that Satan perpetrated against him. There is no doubt that Paul was hindered by these devilish attacks, but they never stopped him. The devil wasn't able to stop Paul because the apostle had made a commitment to be *unstoppable*.

In Second Corinthians 11:23-27, Paul describes some of the difficulties and hassles he encountered in the ministry:

Are they ministers of Christ? (I speak as a fool) I am more; in labours more abundant, in stripes above measure, in prisons more frequent, in deaths oft.
Of the Jews five times received I forty stripes save one.
Thrice was I beaten with rods, once was I stoned, thrice I suffered shipwreck, a night and a day I have been in the deep;
In journeyings often, in perils of waters, in perils of robbers, in perils by mine own countrymen, in perils by the heathen, in perils in the city, in perils in the wilderness, in perils in the sea, in perils among false brethren;
In weariness and painfulness, in watchings often, in hunger and thirst, in fastings often, in cold and nakedness.

Let's look more closely at this list of difficulties so you can see what Paul faced as he carried out God's will for his life. Keep in mind that regardless of the cost or the roadblocks Satan tried to set before him, none of these difficulties ever knocked Paul out of his spiritual race. When you see the hardships Paul faced in the fulfillment of his life assignment, your hardships will pale by comparison! Here's what Paul tells us that he experienced:

Labors More Abundant

Paul says that in the course of his ministry, he worked "…in labours more abundant…." He uses the Greek word *kopos* to describe the kind of "labor" he put forth in the fulfillment of his apostolic call. This word *kopos* represents the *hardest, most physical kind of labor*. It is often used to picture a farmer who works in the field, enduring the extreme temperatures of the afternoon sunshine. The farmer strains, struggles, and toils to push that plow through that hardened ground. This effort requires his total concentration and devotion. No laziness can be allowed if that field is going to be plowed. The farmer must travail if he wants to get that job done.

This word *kopos* is the same word Paul uses to describe the kind of worker he is! He's perhaps the hardest worker he knows! In fact, he goes on to say, "…In labours more *abundant*…." The word "abundant" is the Greek word *perissos*. It is used here in the superlative sense, meaning *very abundantly*. It would be best translated, *"I worked more abundantly than most men"* or *"I worked more than you could even begin to comprehend."*

By making this statement, Paul emphatically declares, *"When it comes to hard work, no one is a harder worker than I am!"* He has personally put out incredible energy to apprehend what Jesus apprehended him to do (*see* Philippians 3:12).

I personally like this scripture because I believe in doing hard work. We live in a day when the work ethic is not what it once was. People are much "softer" than they used to be. The older generation who lived through World War I, World War II, and the hard economic times of the 1930s have a totally different mindset about work than the present generation. These older people lived through hard times and had no choice but to work hard to build their lives. They worked and worked and *worked*, and as a result, they achieved much and built great nations.

Today's generation knows little of hardship. I thank God for the great blessings that have come on the nations during these last days. However, much of it has come so easily for the younger generation that they don't comprehend the great price the older generation paid to build this easy success for them. When members of the younger generation are asked to do something extra or sacrificial, many of them resent the request or consider it to be almost abusive. Rather than focus on how they can do something extra to contribute to the health and success of the business, organization, or church, they just want to know if they are going to be paid for their efforts.

Paul was not a clock-watcher. He worked harder than anyone else he knew. Although we like to think of the mighty anointing that was on his life, a key factor to his amazing success as an apostle was that he worked at it harder than anyone else. Hard work always produces the best results.

Friend, if you want to be successful or to achieve more than others, you have to develop the mentality that you are going to do more than anyone else is doing. If you only do what everyone else is doing, you will produce nothing better than anyone else.

Align yourself with the apostle Paul. Determine to follow his example so that one day you'll be able to say, *"When it comes to hard work, no one is a harder worker than I am!"*

MY PRAYER FOR TODAY

Lord, I want You to help me become a worker who pleases You. Help me also to please my employer and direct supervisor with the quality of my work. Forgive me for wanting to take it easy and for complaining when I am asked to do something extra or to fulfill a task that isn't in my job description. I want to be the kind of Christian worker who brings joy and pleasure to those who are over me and who presents a good testimony to the name of Jesus. This is really my desire, so I am asking You to help me to do more, to be more, and to demonstrate an attitude of excellence regarding my work!

I pray this in Jesus' name!

MY CONFESSION FOR TODAY

I confess that I am a Christian who brings glory to the name of Jesus by the way I work and the attitude I demonstrate on the job. When people think of me, they think of how willing and cooperative I am to do anything that needs to be done and what a pleasure it is to work with me. When my attitude is wrong, I quickly repent and let the Holy Spirit make me what I should be. My supreme desire is to please God and to do a good job for those who pay me!

I declare this by faith in Jesus' name!

QUESTIONS FOR YOU TO CONSIDER

1. If it were time for your boss to review your work habits and attitudes, would he find you to be a hard worker or one who just does the minimum on the job? If you were the boss, would you be satisfied with an employee who demonstrates the attitudes you do at the workplace?
2. How does the quality of your work reflect on the name of Jesus Christ? Do you believe that your work habits and attitudes give others a good impression of Jesus, or does working with you leave people with a bad impression about Christians?
3. What are the specific areas in your work habits or attitudes that need to be improved? Why don't you write these areas down so you can pray about them as a part of your daily prayer regimen?

Thank God for the great blessings that have come on the nations during these last days. However, much of it has come so easily for the younger generation that they don't comprehend the price the older generation paid to build this easy success for them. When members of the younger generation are asked to do something extra or sacrificial, many of them resent the request or consider it almost abusive. Rather than focus on how they can do something extra to contribute to the health and success of the business, organization, or church, they just want to know if they are going to be paid for their efforts.

OCTOBER 19

Become More Determined Than Hell Itself!

Are they ministers of Christ?
(I speak as a fool) I am more; in labours more abundant,
in stripes above measure, in prisons more frequent, in deaths oft.
— 2 Corinthians 11:23

I am often amazed by people who say they want to be mightily used by God but yet are so "soft"! It doesn't take much at all to ruffle these people's feathers. A little inconvenience or discomfort is enough to upset them and start them complaining. And if they are asked to do a little extra work for free, they act like martyrs who are doing something extremely sacrificial!

If you're going to do something mighty for God, you have to throw yourself into the call of God and do what is needed, regardless of whether or not it is convenient to you. The fact is, doing what God has called us to do must be paramount in our lives — more important than any comfort or pleasure. Like the examples we see in the lives of Jesus and the apostle Paul, we must be willing to do anything required or go to any length to do exactly what God has assigned to us.

Of course God wants His people to be blessed! But a believer shouldn't start whining and complaining just because he runs into an attack of the devil that affects the level of comfort he is accustomed to. And if he's asked to do a little more than what is usually asked of him, he shouldn't start griping that the extra task is not a part of his job description. When a person does that, we can know that this is someone who will *not* do something mighty for God — at least not until he makes an adjustment in his attitude!

To push the forces of hell out of the way, you have to be more determined than hell itself. You have to be willing to do *anything* necessary to get the job done. The vision before you must be more important than your own personal pleasure. When you adopt this mentality for your life, you will always push through hard times and take significant territory for the Kingdom of God.

Paul then goes on to tell us more about his determined attitude to finish God's call, regardless of what he has to do to finish it and the challenges he has to face on his way to victory.

Stripes Above Measure

In addition to working hard, Paul tells us what he has physically endured in order to fulfill his heavenly assignment. He tells us that he has been physically beaten as he pursued the fulfillment of his God-given task, experiencing "...stripes above measure...."

The word "stripes" is the Greek word *plege*. It means *to smite, to hit, to wound,* or *to violently strike*. There are many examples of this word in the New Testament. In Luke 10:30, Jesus tells us, "And Jesus answering said, A certain man went down from Jerusalem to Jericho, and fell among thieves, which stripped him of his raiment, and *wounded* him, and departed, leaving him half dead." The word "wounded" is this Greek word *plege*.

Notice that the man's wounds were so devastating that when the thieves departed, they assumed he was dead. These were *mortal wounds*. Now Paul uses this same word to describe the kinds of beatings he received as he sought to fulfill his God-given assignment in life.

This word is also used in Acts 16:33 to describe the kind of beating Paul and Silas received in Philippi. After God's power shook the prison walls and set Paul and Silas free, the keeper of the prison came to them to ask how to be saved. Acts 16:33 tells us that once the prison guard was saved, he "…took them the same hour of the night, and washed their *stripes*…" This word "stripes" is the same Greek word *plege*. Here we see an example of the physical beatings Paul endured.

But this incident in Philippi was just one example of Paul being physically knocked around by opponents to the Gospel. In Second Corinthians 11:23, he goes on to say that he experienced these stripes "above measure."

The words "above measure" are from the Greek word *huperballo*. It is a compound of the words *huper* and *ballo*. The word *huper* means *above and beyond what is normal*. The word *ballo* means *to throw*. And when these two words are joined together, they depict a very powerful picture!

Imagine an archer who takes his bow and arrows to the field for target practice. He aims his arrow at the bull's-eye, pulls back on his bow, and shoots the arrow. But he misses his target and shoots *way over the top* or *exceedingly out of range*. The arrow flies *way beyond the range of anything considered normal*. This pictures the meaning of the Greek word *huperballo*.

Paul's use of this word tells us that he was beaten way beyond the range of what we could even begin to imagine. The word *huperballo* describes both the *frequency* and the *intensity* of his beatings. The beatings Paul received occurred frequently. They were cruel, severe, merciless acts of brutality. What Paul's enemies did to his body was *way over the top*! But Paul never allowed even these acts of physical brutality to affect his commitment to the task God had given him.

You *must* be more determined than the forces that will try to come against you. Otherwise, it won't take much pressure to make you say, "This is too hard" or "I didn't understand how difficult this was going to be." You'll mentally start packing your bags so you can transfer back to more comfortable territory where less is expected of you.

By no means am I wishing hardships or hard times on you. But I do pray that you make up your mind to be tougher than anything the devil ever tries to throw in your direction. In your flesh alone, you are not strong enough to withstand the devil's assaults. But with the power of the Holy Spirit, you can resist, stand against, and drive back everything the devil will attempt to do to you, to your family, to your business, or to your church or ministry. *Isn't it time for you to make up your mind to stick with God's call on your life and press ahead in the power of the Holy Spirit?*

Prisons More Frequent

Paul goes on to tell us that he has been "…in prisons more frequent…." The word "prison" is the Greek word *plulake*. It describes *a place of custody, a prison ward,* or *a place heavily guarded by keepers and watchmen*. Such a prison was usually a small, dark chamber in which the most hardened, dangerous, and menacing prisoners were confined. The prisoners who were put into this particular kind of chamber were considered so risky that they were usually accompanied by a host of prison guards who guarded them twenty-four hours a day.

This word *plulake* ("prison") is used in Acts 12:4 for Peter's imprisonment in Jerusalem. Acts 12:4 tells us, "And when he had apprehended him, he put him in prison, and delivered him to four quaternions of soldiers to keep him; intending after Easter to bring him forth to the people." Peter must have been viewed as especially risky to have four quaternions of soldiers assigned to keep watch over him!

Paul was also kept in this kind of extreme confinement many times during his ministry; this is what he means when he says here that he has been in "prisons more frequent." In fact, Paul became so familiar with this type of confinement that he even spent his final days under similar circumstances: "And when we came to Rome, the centurion delivered the prisoners to the captain of the guard: but Paul was suffered to dwell by himself with a soldier that kept him" (Acts 28:16).

No one wants to go to jail! But if going to jail meant that Paul would accomplish his apostolic calling along the way, that was what he was willing to do. Paul was ready to undergo any inconvenience, pay any price, and go to all lengths to do what God had commissioned him to do. Even jail would not stop him.

Deaths Oft

In addition to the beatings and imprisonments he endured, Paul also says he was "…in deaths oft." The word "deaths" is from the Greek word *thanatos*. Here, however, Paul uses the plural form, *thanatoi*, which is literally translated "deaths."

We know that Paul wrote in First Corinthians 15:31, "…I die daily." We tend to spiritualize this statement, but in reality, Paul faced actual physical death on a regular basis. When he wrote, "…I die daily," he actually meant, *"I am constantly confronted with the prospect of death."*

Paul faced death so often that he learned how to face it bravely. In Romans 14:8, he wrote, "…whether we die, we die unto the Lord…." In First Corinthians 15:55, we see that he learned to meditate on victory rather than on mortality and fatality: "O death, where is thy sting? O grave, where is thy victory?" These are not allegorical verses about death. They are the thoughts of a man who faced the prospect of death almost on a daily basis.

Paul never sought to live under this constant threat of murder or execution. It was just a part of the journey to get where he needed to go. But rather than run and hide from imminent danger, he faced it bravely and kept moving forward to do what he was called to do.

Had Paul been less committed, it would have taken only a few of these difficult experiences to knock him out of the race. But because he was totally focused on finishing the assignment Heaven had given him, he pushed beyond each of these attacks, and at the end of his life, he was able to say, "…I have finished my course…" (2 Timothy 4:7).

The Holy Spirit who empowered the apostle Paul to overcome each of these instances is the same Holy Spirit who is available to help *you*. You never have to be a defeated victim. If you choose to take advantage of the power that is available to you, the Spirit of God will energize and lift you to a place of victory over any obstacle the devil tries to throw in your way. Never forget that you have resurrection power residing inside you (*see* Romans 8:11). If you'll yield to that power, it will supernaturally quicken you to overcome every time!

So throw open your arms of faith and embrace the Spirit's power to overcome each attack the devil has tried to orchestrate against you. If you'll embrace that power, it will begin to flood you with everything you need to survive and to gloriously succeed in your task! *Make the decision to let it start flowing today!*

MY PRAYER FOR TODAY

Lord, I thank You that because Your Spirit lives in me, I have everything I need to overcome any attack the devil would try to orchestrate against me. Because Your resurrection power resides in me, I am stronger than the devil; I am tougher than any problem; and I can outlast any time of difficulty. It is not a question of IF I will win, but of WHEN I will win the victory! I thank You for giving me the power of the Holy Spirit to outlast every attack and to persist until I have accomplished what You have asked me to do!

I pray this in Jesus' name!

MY CONFESSION FOR TODAY

I confess that I am totally focused on finishing the assignment Heaven has given to me. I will successfully push beyond each attack of the enemy because the Holy Spirit is empowering me. I don't have to be a defeated victim. I choose to take advantage of the power that is available to me. Therefore, the Spirit of God will energize and lift me to a place of victory over any obstacle the devil tries to throw in my way. I have resurrection power residing inside me, and it supernaturally quickens me to overcome every demonic attack that tries to assault me and my purpose in life!

I declare this by faith in Jesus' name!

QUESTIONS FOR YOU TO CONSIDER

1. Was there a time in your past when you felt extremely weak, but then the Spirit of God suddenly quickened you with such divine energy that you became supernaturally strong to overcome a difficult challenge in your life? If yes, what was that occasion when divine power flooded you so strongly?
2. Can you verbalize the changes that occurred in you when God's power infused you with new strength? Were there immediate changes in your attitudes? Did it have an impact on your ability to endure?
3. How was that difficult situation resolved as a result of the supernatural empowerment you experienced?

OCTOBER 20

Jesus Has Overcome Everything!

Are they ministers of Christ? (I speak as a fool) I am more;
in labours more abundant, in stripes above measure,
in prisons more frequent, in deaths oft.
Of the Jews five times received I forty stripes save one.
— 2 Corinthians 11:23,24

*O*nce when I was teaching from Paul's words in Second Corinthians 11:23-25, I especially emphasized the afflictions Paul overcame by the power of the Spirit. Later a young man came up to me and said, "It's obvious to me that the apostle Paul had no faith!"

Shocked by his words, I asked him, "What do you mean when you say the apostle Paul had no faith?"

He answered, "If Paul had walked in faith, he wouldn't have gone through any of those ordeals."

The young man's words made me think about the great number of people who have the wrong impression about faith. They think that if a person walks in faith, that somehow means he will escape all adversities in life.

But when you read the New Testament, you find that the early believers and the apostles faced many adversities. Certainly it wasn't God who planned those hardships. The devil was the one who shrewdly planned those attacks in order to stop the preaching of the Gospel. And Satan is still working nonstop to prevent people from stepping into the glorious plan God has designed for their lives.

There is something very encouraging about studying the strategies the devil arrayed against the early believers. You see, regardless of what the enemy tried to do, he was unsuccessful in stopping them! Because they *did* have faith, they were unconquerable.

So I told the young man who talked to me that night, "Young man, the fact that Paul survived all those ordeals and continued his ministry to the end of his life is proof that he *did* possess faith. A man with no faith wouldn't have survived those attacks."

Don't get the impression that walking in faith removes you from all challenges. Faith just gives you the ability to *overcome* the challenges that will attempt to assail you. Even Jesus said, "…In the world ye shall have tribulation: but be of good cheer; I have overcome the world" (John 16:33).

The word "tribulation" is the Greek word *thlipsis*, which describes *a situation so difficult that it causes one to feel stressed, squeezed, pressured, or crushed.* It can be translated as *distress, affliction,* or *trouble,* always indicating a level of intensity that is almost unbearable in the natural.

But Jesus tells us to be of "good cheer." These two words are from the single Greek word *tharseo*, which literally means *to be courageous.* It is consistently translated, "Fear not," but a better rendering would be *"Take heart!"* It is a word that would be spoken to strengthen someone who is facing some kind of hardship or difficult ordeal. Jesus was literally saying, *"In this world you will go through some distressing times, but take heart and be courageous.…"*

Then Jesus tells us, "I have overcome the world." The word "overcome" is the Greek word *nikos*, which is also the word for *victory.* But the grammar used in this statement does not imply a single victory in the past, but *a continuous and abiding victory.* Therefore, the idea that this Greek word presents is this: "I have overcome the world; I am still overcoming the world; and I will always be in an overcoming position over the world!"

The word "world" in Greek is *kosmos*, the Greek word that is always used to depict *the arena where Satan attempts to wield his influence* and describes *all the human systems of the world.* It is the very word Paul uses in Second Corinthians 4:4 when he refers to Satan as the "god of the world." Satan is not god of the earth, but he operates through the human systems in the world — and these systems are what the enemy usually uses to attack the Church and God's people.

When we consider all the things that assailed the apostle Paul, we realize that most of the attacks came through the world systems of government or religion. These were the primary instruments Satan used in his efforts to curb Paul's activities. But Paul learned to take heart in such situations. He never gave up! Paul had obviously grabbed hold of Jesus' words in John 16:33, because he overcame everything Satan ever tried to use against him. The devil simply was unable to stop this man who was determined to finish the assignment Heaven had given him!

Five Times Received I Forty Stripes Save One

In Second Corinthians 11:24, Paul goes on to say, "Of the Jews five times received I forty stripes save one." This was a Jewish method of punishment, applied to Paul on five different occasions. Deuteronomy 25:2,3 refers to this method when it specifies how the wicked man should be punished: "And it shall be, if the wicked man be worthy to be beaten, that the judge shall cause him to lie down, and to be beaten before his face, according to his fault, by a certain number. Forty stripes he may give him, and not exceed...."

This was one of the most vicious treatments of the ancient world. The tortured person's clothing was completely removed so he appeared before his persecutors naked. His arms were tied so he could not defend himself. Then the torturer would begin to lash the prisoner's bare body with a whip made of three long cords, one from calf hide and the other two from donkey hide.

Pieces of glass, bone, and metal were often attached to the end of the cords to make the lashing more memorable. The torturer would hit so hard that the pieces of glass, bone, and metal would lodge into the victim's skin. Then as the cords were jerked backward for the next lash of the whip, those pieces of glass, bone, and metal would rip out significant amounts of flesh. This left horrid scars on the victim's body — *permanently*.

The first third of these lashes were given across the prisoner's upper chest and face, while the remaining two-thirds of lashes were applied to his back, buttocks, and legs; meanwhile, the victim was forced to bend over to make it easier for the torturer to hit his body. Blood flew everywhere as the cords whipped wildly through the air, making snapping noises as they struck the victim again and again.

But let's think a little deeper. If the whip was made of three cords and Paul received thirty-nine lashes each time, this means he received 117 lashes at each beating! And he went through this grueling exercise on five different occasions, which means 585 lashes were laid across Paul's upper chest, face, back, buttocks, and legs. There wasn't a place on his body that hadn't been beaten or had pieces of flesh ripped out of it!

Paul was so committed to fulfilling his God-given call that he wouldn't let anything stop him! After being repeatedly beaten in this terrible manner, he'd get up, put his clothes back on, and go right back to what he was doing before he was beaten. He had already made up his mind. *He would not stop until his mission was complete!*

Being beaten was an unpleasant experience. It was definitely a part of the journey that no one would relish. But Paul refused to let this experience become a permanent roadblock to his ministry. He pushed the opposition out of the way, got up, and went on. He overcame in the power of Jesus' name and in the power of the Holy Spirit!

What are you facing today? I'm sure it isn't a beating of thirty-nine lashes, yet it may still seem overpowering and overwhelming to you. How are you going to respond to these things? If you've been knocked down, are you going to stay there? Or are you going to get up, brush off the dirt, grab hold of the power of God, and start moving forward again?

Never forget that Jesus said, *"In this world you will go through some distressing times. But take heart and be courageous, for I have overcome the world; I am still overcoming the world; and I will always be in an overcoming position over the world!"*

If you'll make the choice today to get up, brush off the dirt, tell your mind and emotions to be silent, and submit yourself to these words of Jesus, the Holy Spirit will begin to fill you with new strength so you can come through the difficult situations you are facing victoriously. *And as you rely* on God's power to bring you to the place of victory you desire, you will learn how to overcome every challenge you will ever face in life!

Lord, I am so thankful that You have overcome the world and given me the power to overcome it! I am so sorry for the times I've allowed my flesh to whine and complain when I should have been digging in my heels and latching on to the power of the Holy Spirit. I know that even though victory is mine, I must take it and make it my own. Please help me take charge of my whining, complaining flesh so I can reach out by faith to seize the power of the Holy Spirit — the very thing I need to make me a winner in my situation today. I thank You in advance for this inflow of power!

I pray this in Jesus' name!

MY CONFESSION FOR TODAY

I confess that Jesus Christ has given me the power to be an overcomer in every situation in life! I am not a victim who has fallen to defeat. I don't have to take what the devil tries to send my way. In the power of the Spirit and in Jesus' name, I am well able to stand against each attack, to resist every devilish scheme that comes against me, and to maintain the victory of Jesus Christ in every part of my life. Jesus purchased victory for me, and I will not budge from my decision to have, to hold, to possess, and to enjoy His victory in my life!

I declare this by faith in Jesus' name!

QUESTIONS FOR YOU TO CONSIDER

1. Are you doing your best to walk in the victory of Jesus Christ? Or have you allowed your flesh to moan and groan and drag you down into the language of defeat?
2. What scriptures can you meditate on and confess daily that will take you to a higher place of victory? Why don't you write those verses down and put them in a visible place where you'll see them every day and be reminded to declare them over your life?
3. Can you think of any people in your life who are currently struggling with the temptation to give up in the midst of difficult circumstances? What are some things you could do to encourage these individuals to keep believing and to stand fast in faith for the victory they desire?

If you've been knocked down, are you going to stay there? Or are you going to get up, brush off the dirt, grab hold of the power of God, and start moving forward again?

October 21

❦

Even Beatings and Death Cannot Stop a Man Who Is Determined!

Thrice was I beaten with rods, once was I stoned....
— 2 Corinthians 11:25

I'll never forget the day one of our workers came to see me with deep gashes running across his cheekbones and nose. When I saw the condition of his face, I was completely taken aback. The sight simply broke my heart.

It was this young man's task to carry copies of our television programs to one of the most dangerous regions reached by our television broadcast. We all knew that this man was risking his life to travel every month to that region carrying the actual programs and the cash to pay for the broadcasting of the programs. However, we were all committed to the goal of reaching that region so the Word could be sent via television into the homes of millions who had never heard the Gospel before.

Because this man traveled extensively to a very hostile Muslim region of the world, he knew that each trip placed his life in jeopardy. Yet because he was so committed to getting the Word to the unreached people of that region, he was willing to even lay down his life if necessary as he continued to fulfill his assignment. His passion to see the lost saved had spilled over to his wife. She understood the seriousness of his job but rejoiced with him at the thought of people hearing the Good News of Jesus Christ.

As this young man stood before me that day with a battered face, a black-and-blue eye, and that ugly, deep gash that ran across his cheekbones and nose, I knew he had been attacked on one of his trips to that region to deliver our television programs. He was such a young, handsome man; it just broke my heart to see his face so marred.

When he saw that the gashes on his face deeply troubled me, the young man said, "Brother Rick, don't worry about me. I'll be all right. I'm so thankful they didn't get the television programs or the cash I was carrying to pay for the broadcasts. The Lord was with me, and I know that now He will heal me." Although he had obviously been severely beaten, he was still full of the joy of the Holy Spirit.

As I heard the whole story of what happened to him, I came to understand what a miracle it was that he was still alive. The trap these gospel-haters had set for him could have killed him. But instead of being afraid to go back to that region again, he had come to our office to pick up the next set of television programs and the cash to pay for them. As he walked out of my office, I wanted to salute him! In my mind, he was and continues to be a true hero of the faith!

Don't think that persecution is something that happened only in New Testament times. It is still happening today all over the world, and the believers who live and work in these dangerous regions need our prayers! Please remember to pray for them when you spend time with the Lord.

But just as the apostle Paul was energized to get up and get moving again, those who lay claim to God's power today are also energized to get past the times of intense persecution or opposition they endure. These believers know they're not destined to live in defeat or despair as long as they don't waste time bemoaning what happened to them. They also know that crying about the attacks of the enemy doesn't change the fact that they happened; therefore, they just grab hold of God's power and adamantly refuse to let the devil stop them or slow them down!

In Second Corinthians 11:25, Paul tells us about similar events that happened to him. Although these events could have been devastating to someone else, they had almost no effect on Paul. He was determined to do his job and not to let anything hinder him! In this verse, he says, "Thrice was I beaten with rods, once was I stoned...."

Thrice Was I Beaten With Rods

In the ancient world, a beating with rods was a horrible, ugly form of torture. A strong man would bind the victim's arms tightly around his body, incapacitating the victim's ability to move in much the same way as a straightjacket would do. Then while the victim's upper chest and head still lay on the ground, his legs would be pulled up into the air.

At this point, a man with a huge rod — normally made of metal — would begin whacking the bottom of the victim's feet. He would whack and whack and *whack* until the feet of the victim were bleeding, broken, and maimed. At times this beating was so severe that the victim would afterward never be able to walk again.

It's interesting that the book of Acts never gives us a specific example of Paul being beaten with rods in such a manner. However, as we continue to look at the entire list of what Paul encountered (2 Corinthians 11:23-27), we see that many events occurred during Paul's ministry that Luke never recorded in the book of Acts. But Paul never forgot any of them, and he tells us here about some of those events into which the book of Acts gives us no insight.

We don't know *when* Paul's feet-beating experiences occurred, but he tells us that he was beaten with rods three different times during the course of his ministry. It's obvious that the devil didn't want this Gospel preacher to take the Gospel anywhere else! Satan attempted to maim Paul's feet to permanently knock him out of the race.

You see, the feet of a Gospel preacher are threatening to the devil. Paul quoted Isaiah 52:7 when he wrote, "...How beautiful are the feet of them that preach the gospel of peace, and bring glad tidings of good things!" (Romans 10:15). This attack on Paul's feet was an attack against the Gospel.

It is evident that rather than throw in the towel and quit because of this experience, Paul grabbed hold of the power of God, put his shoes back on, got up, and went on his way to keep doing what God called him to do. This was a man the devil couldn't keep down!

No wonder Paul wrote about the resurrection power of God! He was writing from personal experience when he said, "But if the Spirit of him that raised up Jesus from the dead dwell in you, he that raised up Christ from the dead shall also quicken your mortal bodies by his Spirit that dwelleth in you" (Romans 8:11).

Once Was I Stoned

This event occurred in Acts 14:19. After a successful campaign among the Gentiles in Lystra, Jewish opposers came from Iconium to stir up trouble for Paul's ministry. They were so effective in distributing bad information about Paul that the entire city turned against him. In a moment of fury, the people of Lystra stoned him and "...drew him out of the city, supposing he had been dead" (Acts 14:19).

It may well be that Paul was dead. Stoning was a malicious act. The stoners aimed their sharp rocks at the victim's head in order to deal a fatal blow. To assure the victim's death, the people didn't usually stop the stoning until his head was crushed. When it was apparent that there was no possibility of survival, the remaining rocks were dumped and the victim's corpse was dragged out of the city and left for the dogs and wild beasts to eat. So when Acts 14:19 says the people of Lystra "supposed" Paul was dead, there is no reason to think he was *not* dead at that moment.

Acts 14:20 tells us that as the disciples came and stood near Paul's corpse, "he rose up." Is it possible that these disciples joined hands and prayed for Paul's resurrection? This is precisely my view.

Later Paul gave testimony of a visit he made to Heaven (*see* 2 Corinthians 12:1-4). He explained that he heard and saw things that he had never been given permission to speak. When did Paul make this visit to Heaven? Could it have been at the time he was stoned in Lystra? Yes, I personally think so.

No wonder Paul could write with such conviction: "For I am persuaded, that neither death, nor life...shall be able to separate us from the love of God, which is in Christ Jesus our Lord" (Romans 8:38,39). Even death cannot stop a man who is determined to keep on going!

Paul could have resigned himself to his fate as the people were stoning him and thought, *Well, I guess this is the end of the road. I guess I'll give up and die now.* If he had done that, I'm sure stoning would have been the end of him. But I'm just certain that as they stoned Paul, he thought, *I'm not dying now! My job isn't done! If they kill me, I'll just have to be resurrected!*

Being stoned was never a part of Paul's plan. It was an unexpected roadblock that the devil orchestrated to try to stop him from fulfilling his call. But although the experience stole time and delayed Paul's plans a little, it did not permanently hinder him from going on. God can join Himself to this kind of person! God knows this is the kind of person who is really going to get something done!

Are you this kind of person? Does God emphatically know that you will never surrender to any attack of the devil? Have you demonstrated that you are going to keep forging ahead to finish your assignment and that you will never quit until you can say the job is done?

Don't get too upset if troubles come against you. It doesn't mean you have a lack of faith; it just means you live in a world where the devil operates and hassles people. The fact that you *do* have faith means you never have to be overcome by these attacks of the enemy. If you'll grab hold of victory — the way Jesus did, Paul did, and so many others before you did — you can overcome the world and everything in it.

So take heart, and be courageous! As you determine to keep on walking in God's power, no matter WHAT comes against you, the victory really does belong to you!

MY PRAYER FOR TODAY

Lord, I want to be the kind of person who never allows the circumstances of life to stop me from accomplishing Your plan for my life. I am sorry for the times I've acted weak and complained that the circumstances I faced were too hard to deal with. The truth is, You have given me Your Spirit and Your power. That means there is no problem, no challenge, and no hardship I cannot conquer and overcome. If I take the power You make available to me, I can do anything You tell me to do. So today I am making my choice. I am reaching out by faith to grab hold of Your Spirit's power so I can be supernaturally quickened to complete every assignment Heaven ever asks me to do.

I pray this in Jesus' name!

MY CONFESSION FOR TODAY

I confess that I am the kind of person God can count on to get something done. God knows I will never surrender to any attack of the devil. I regularly demonstrate that I am going to keep forging ahead to finish my assignment and that I will never quit until I can say the job is done. Jesus overcame the world, and today He gives me the power to overcome it too. Like Jesus and other strong men and women of God before me, I will overcome the world and every form of opposition the devil puts in my way!

I declare this by faith in Jesus' name!

QUESTIONS FOR YOU TO CONSIDER

1. What is your initial reaction when you run into an especially difficult challenge? Do you immediately believe you can overcome it, or do you feel a stab of fear that you're going to fail or that you're not going to survive it?
2. What does your reaction to these challenges reveal about you and your level of faith?
3. When troublesome events occur to you, to your family, to your business, to your church, or to your ministry, what is the first action you take to repel Satan's attacks against you? If someone you knew was being attacked, what steps would you tell that person to take to overcome the enemy's strategies in his life?

OCTOBER 22

Turn Your Memories Around!

Thrice was I beaten with rods, once was I stoned,
thrice I suffered shipwreck,
a night and a day I have been in the deep.
— 2 Corinthians 11:25

Sometimes people get the impression that they have to be absolutely perfect before they can step out in faith to do something new and adventuresome. But there is rarely a perfect or easy environment in which a step of faith needs to be taken! The reason we call it a "step of faith" is that it requires us to move out of our comfort zone or to do something that is challenging!

So rather than wait for a perfect situation before you step out in faith, listen to the Holy Spirit for His timing. If the Holy Spirit says to do something now, you need to do it *now*, even if the surrounding environment seems difficult or unfavorable at the moment. And when you step out in faith, don't be surprised if you are met with obstacles and difficulties, at least at first.

Some people say, "I tried to step out in faith once, and I was met with all kinds of horrible circumstances! What happened to me is such a terrible memory that I don't know if I have the courage to ever step out in faith again!"

That's why I'm writing several *Sparkling Gems* to tell you about Paul's experiences. I want you to know that *everyone* runs into obstacles and difficulties — *even the apostle Paul with all his God-given revelation and anointing*!

You see, the devil will do his best to hinder what God puts in your heart because he doesn't want God's will to be accomplished through your life. The enemy is terrified at the thought of you actually doing what God has told you to do. But like the apostle Paul, you have to determine that *one way or another, you're going to get the job done.* Paul didn't throw in the towel and quit just because he ran into obstacles along the road to his goal. He just found ways to get around the obstacles and keep going until his divine assignment was fulfilled!

I guarantee you that if you freeze every time the devil throws a roadblock in your path, you'll spend most of your life frozen. Perfect circumstances are terrific if it's possible to line them up, but don't depend on it. Whether or not the circumstances are the way you'd like them to be, you have to decide to take hold of God's power and move ahead. God will show you how to get around that *impasse* so you can finish the job He's given you to do.

Thrice I Suffered Shipwreck

In Second Corinthians 11:25, Paul tells us about one roadblock the devil devised to hinder him. He writes, "…Thrice I suffered shipwreck, a night and a day I have been in the deep."

This verse is a bit of a mystery. The book of Acts only records one shipwreck. Yet as we have already seen from this list, too many significant events occurred during Paul's ministry for Luke to have included all of them in his written account in the book of Acts.

Traveling by sea was a perilous and risky undertaking. Ships were not always reliable. The routes often took them through waters cluttered with sharp rocks, reefs, and debris. Even if the vessel was guided by strong and skilled leadership, currents were so strong that even the best ships could be carried directly into rocks and other dangerous obstacles.

In Acts 27:14-44, we read that Paul was traveling aboard a ship that ran into rocks and broke into pieces in the midst of a great storm. In that moment of crisis, Paul became God's man on board ship! He spoke the word of faith to the crew and passengers, and soon he was in charge of the entire situation.

In addition to this shipwreck, Paul testifies that he has been shipwrecked on two other occasions as well. What are the odds that one person would be on three different ships that shipwrecked? This would be the equivalent of one person surviving three different plane crashes!

I think you can see that the attacks that assailed Paul's life were simply remarkable in their scope and nature. Satan tried to create all kinds of "impasses" to stop him and his work. These events were definitely inconvenient, but they were unable to permanently hinder him from getting to his destination.

A Night and a Day I Have Been in the Deep

The phrase "a night and a day" refers to a 24-hour time period. The word "deep" is the Greek word *bathus*, and it refers to the deepest parts of the sea. Because Paul mentions this event immediately following his recollection of shipwrecks, we may assume that this night and a day in the deep was the result of one of the other shipwrecks of which we have no knowledge.

It is impossible to make much comment on this, as we know only what Paul says in this verse. Whenever and however it occurred, it was a horrific event in Paul's life. The Greek tense shows that the experience is still fresh and vivid in Paul's mind as he writes about it. The language even suggests that this is a recent occurrence.

Paul spent a 24-hour period treading water in the deepest parts of the sea. Yet it didn't scare him away from getting on the very next ship to continue his trip and go where God ordered him to go. It was just another *impasse* on the journey, but it didn't stop his trip!

Likewise, you can't let past bad experiences determine your future actions. Consider what would have happened if Paul had said, "That's it! I'm never getting on another ship!" If he had taken this approach, the devil would have stopped Paul from traveling by sea to get to areas where he needed to go. But instead of letting fear grip his mind, Paul put away all thoughts of fear and boarded the next ship when that form of transportation was required in order to reach the destination where God was leading him to go.

Instead of thinking how horrific it was to go through that past experience, why don't you turn that memory around and reflect on how faithful God was to you in the midst of it? You didn't die! You survived! God's mercy intervened, and you came out all right! Even though the devil would love to paint a horrible memory for you about that event, the truth is, God was faithful to bring you through that ordeal, or you wouldn't be reading this *Sparkling Gem* today!

You're not defeated! Other people dropped out of sight or didn't survive after the devil assaulted them — but you are still here! So hold your head high, throw back your shoulders, and be proud of the fact that God's power enabled you to overcome in the past. *And He will continue enabling you to overcome in the future if you'll make the decision to keep moving forward by faith!*

MY PRAYER FOR TODAY

Lord, I admit that I've allowed some bad memories to paralyze me and keep me from taking the step of faith I need to be taking right now. I forgot to consider how You saved me, delivered me, and rescued me from the events that caused those painful memories. I only reflected on the bad part, failing to recognize how faithful You were to help me in that situation. Today I am making the choice to turn my memories around. Holy Spirit, help me see my past bad experiences in the light of God's goodness and faithfulness. Fill my mind with the good things God has done for me and the knowledge that He will continue to be faithful to deliver me, no matter what opposition comes my way!

I pray this in Jesus' name!

MY CONFESSION FOR TODAY

I confess that God is good! He has been faithful to me. He has never failed me. He will never fail me in the future. Even when bad things tried to come against me, God saved me, delivered me, and brought me out with no permanent harm. It is a miracle I survived everything that happened to me in the past. But from this moment on, I choose to turn my memories around and to reflect only on how good God has been to me through all of life's events. I will trust in Him to show me how to get around every impasse so I can finish the job He's given me to do!

I declare this by faith in Jesus' name!

QUESTIONS FOR YOU TO CONSIDER

1. When you reflect on the bad things that have happened to you in the past, can you see God's faithfulness to bring you through each difficult situation? Have you ever pondered those past events in your life from the perspective of how good God was to deliver you, or have you only meditated on how terrible those situations were to go through?

2. I want to encourage you to take a sheet of paper and to write down the times God has delivered and rescued you in the past. As you do, stop to meditate on each instance and to thank God for His goodness before proceeding to write down the next instance when He preserved your life or rescued you from a bad situation.

3. Do you know someone who has been paralyzed by some past event? Don't you think you could encourage that person and help him turn his memories around by sharing how God has intervened and rescued you so magnificently on many occasions?

OCTOBER 23

❧

Walking Thousands of Miles,
Crossing Wild and Dangerous Rivers

In journeyings often, in perils of waters....
— 2 Corinthians 11:26

When my family first moved to the territory of the former Soviet Union, it was at the worst economic time that part of the world had known since the events of the 1917 Bolshevik Revolution. It seemed there was a deficit of everything. Store shelves were empty. Pharmacies had no drugs to offer medical patients. There was little fuel available for automobiles or planes.

In those early days, I was traveling continuously across the eleven time zones of the USSR to obtain contracts for the television programs we broadcast on our television network. Often the pilot of the airplane would announce that the plane was landing because there wasn't enough fuel to reach our destination. Once we deboarded, we had to get very creative in order to figure out how we were going to get from where we were to the place where we were headed. It usually meant we had to travel by train or by car — and we often had very, very long distances still to go to reach our destination.

But even with all these inconveniences, our situation didn't begin to compare to what the first-century preachers had to do in order to get to hard-to-reach places and preach the Gospel. Cars and trains were slower than airplanes, but at least we weren't walking to get where we needed to go! In Second Corinthians 11:26, however, Paul tells us that he had no choice but to walk in order to reach many of his destinations. He said, "In journeyings often...."

In Journeyings Often

The word "journey" in Greek is *odoiporia*. This word describes a *walking journey*. The word "often" is the word *pollakis*, and it refers to *many times, often,* or *frequently*. Paul used this phrase to tell us that he had walked to most of the destinations where he had been called upon to preach.

For instance, he *walked* from Antioch Pisidia to Iconium (Acts 13:51); he *walked* from Iconium to Lystra (Acts 14:6); and he *walked* from Lystra to Derbe (Acts 14:20). From Derbe, he *walked* back to Lystra (Acts 14:21); and from Lystra he *walked* back to Iconium (Acts 14:21). From Iconium, he *walked* back to Antioch Pisidia (Acts 14:21); from Antioch Pisidia, he *walked* throughout the whole region of Pamphylia (Acts 14:24); and then he *walked* all the way to Perga (Acts 14:25).

For a brief period, Paul and his team traveled by ship to Antioch (Paul's home base). But then they *walked* to Phenice and Samaria (Acts 15:3). From there, they *walked* to Jerusalem (Acts 15:4); and from Jerusalem, they *walked* back to Antioch (Acts 15:22).

From Antioch, Paul *walked* throughout the regions of Syria and Cilicia (Acts 15:41). He *walked* back through the cities of Derbe (Acts 16:1) and Lystra (Acts 16:1). Then he *walked* to Phrygia (Acts 16:6) and *walked* throughout the regions of Galatia (Acts 16:6). After that, he *walked* to Mysia (Acts 16:8) and then *walked* all the way down to Troas (Acts 16:8).

After seeing a vision of a man in Macedonia calling to him for help (Acts 16:9), Paul took a ship from Troas (Acts 16:11). His ship ported in the city of Samothracia (Acts 16:11) but departed the next day to Neapolis (Acts 16:11). From there, Paul and his associates sailed to Philippi (Acts 16:12), a chief city in that part of Macedonia.

From Philippi, Paul *walked* through Amphipolis and Apollonia (Acts 17:1); then he *walked* to the city of Thessalonica (Acts 17:1). From Thessalonica, Paul *walked* to Berea (Acts 17:10).

Paul took a ship from Berea to Athens (Acts 17:14,15). From Athens, he *walked* to Corinth (Acts 18:1). He sailed from Corinth to Syria (Acts 18:18). Then from Syria, he *walked* to Ephesus (Acts 18:19). From Ephesus, he sailed to Caesarea (Acts 18:22); but from there, he *walked* to Antioch (Acts 18:22). From Antioch, he *walked* all over the regions of Galatia and Phrygia (Acts 18:23), and then he *walked* along the upper coastlines to Ephesus (Acts 19:1). The list of places where Paul traveled to fulfill his calling is amazing. Paul did a lot of *walking* during the course of his ministry!

If you add up all the miles/kilometers Paul walked, he probably spent more time *walking* than he did *preaching*. No wonder he could say, "I thank my God, I speak with tongues more than you all" (1 Corinthians 14:18). Paul had a lot of time to pray in tongues as he walked across the east and northeast side of the Mediterranean countries to preach the Gospel and to establish the Church.

This also gives us insight into the kind of relationships Paul had with his fellow travelers. It would have been impossible for him to travel so far, so regularly, and through such difficult circumstances without really getting to know his traveling companions. No wonder he could tell Timothy, "But thou hast fully known my doctrine, manner of life, purpose, faith, longsuffering, charity, patience, persecutions, afflictions..." (2 Timothy 3:10,11).

Keep in mind that the man who did all this walking was the same one whose feet had been beaten with rods three times (*see* October 21)! Paul could only have walked this extensively if he enjoyed a healthy body. A sick man could never have attempted this kind of physical exertion. Therefore, we know that although Paul's feet had been beaten with rods, he suffered no remaining effects from those hideous beatings. Here again, we see that Paul knew how to draw upon the resurrection power of God to quicken his mortal flesh.

In today's society, many people circle parking lots for twenty minutes just to look for a closer parking space. But the truth is, if they parked farther away, it still wouldn't take but five minutes to walk to their destination! People are often simply too lazy to walk unless they are forced to do it.

Paul had no car, train, or airplane to ride in order to get where he needed to go. Yes, traveling that far by foot meant he had to face incredible hardship and difficult circumstances. But nothing was so difficult to bear that it was going to stop Paul from fulfilling the call on his life. He had made up his mind. Even if it meant walking around the world by foot in order to fulfill his call, that is precisely what he would do.

If modern transportation had been available, Paul would have used it. Today cars, trains, and airplanes permit us to travel farther and faster and to take the Gospel to the ends of the earth. But the lack of these conveniences didn't stop Paul.

Yet how frequently does lack of convenience stop us today? If we allow lack of convenience to hinder us from doing the will of God, there is a serious flaw in our level of commitment.

I'm sure that as Paul traveled on these roads, he encountered literal *impasses* on roads that forced him to take unexpected, unplanned detours, costing him more time, effort, and money. Still he pressed onward to take the message of God's Kingdom to the Gentile world.

In Perils of Waters

After referring to these long walking journeys, Paul also says, "...In perils of waters..." (2 Corinthians 11:26). The word "perils" is the word *kindunos*. It is the Greek word for *an extremely dangerous or highly volatile situation*. Paul uses this word eight times in Second Corinthians 11 to tell us that much of his ministry required him to live in extremely dangerous situations. He basically lived in danger all the time. Danger wasn't something he sought. It simply went with the territory God gave him.

The word "waters" is the Greek word *potamos*, which is the Greek word for *a river*. By using these two words *kindunos* and *potamos*, Paul tells us that as he traveled, he was occasionally forced to cross extremely dangerous rivers to get to the places where the Holy Spirit sent him.

Crossing rivers was a very serious act in the ancient world. It's a vivid example of the hazards a traveler encountered in Paul's time. Bridges were few and far between, especially in remote areas. This presented awkward problems, especially during times of flash-flooding, which was a frequent occurrence. Although Paul does not mention the exact rivers he had to cross, we know that they would have included the *Jordan River* (Judea), the *Orontes River* (Syria), the *Cydnus River* (Cilicia), the *Meander River* and *Cayster River* (Asia), and the *Strimon River* and *Axios River* (Macedonia).

During Paul's journeys, he crossed "badlands," climbed cliffs, scaled bluffs, and passed through some of the most dangerous rivers of his time. We don't usually think of these kinds of hazards when remembering Paul's ministry. But these were daily risks Paul faced to do God's will.

How many people do you know who would put their lives at such risk to do God's will?

I am always amazed at the number of people who write to my family with concern when they hear of political unrest in our nation. They often tell me, "You and your family need to get out of there before it gets too tough! God doesn't want you to get caught in a difficult situation!" But if the Early Church and other God-called people through the last two millenia had taken that approach, none of us would know of the Gospel today!

Regardless of what you face or what you cross through to fulfill God's plan, nothing takes God by surprise. Certainly He didn't plan those problems. But when He called you, He equipped you with all the power, wisdom, and insight you would ever need to get across the hurdles Satan tries to put in your way. There is no *impasse* you cannot get through on your way to achieve God's will for your life!

MY PRAYER FOR TODAY

Lord, help me to stay absolutely committed to the assignment You've given me, ready to do whatever is necessary to finish the job. Forgive me for giving up so easily in the past when I ran into barriers. Help me to get more creative the next time I hit an impasse so I can find a way to do what You've called me to do. I know that by the power of Your Spirit, I can show much more fortitude in the face of obstacles than I've done in the past. Forgive me for being so easy on myself. I ask You now to teach me how to operate in Your strength and wisdom when I encounter impasses so that I can forge ahead to finish the job You've given me to do!

I pray this in Jesus' name!

MY CONFESSION FOR TODAY

I confess that regardless of what I face or what I cross through to fulfill God's plan, nothing takes God by surprise! When He called me, He equipped me with all the power, wisdom, and insight I will ever need to get across the hurdles Satan tries to put in my path. There is no impasse I cannot get through on my way to achieve God's will for my life!

I declare this by faith in Jesus' name!

QUESTIONS FOR YOU TO CONSIDER

1. Has there been a time in your life when it looked like there was no way to do what God wanted you to do, but you got creative and found another way to do it? What was that instance in your life?

2. Looking back on that situation now, what would your life be like today if you had taken no for an answer and walked away from that opportunity? What if you hadn't gotten creative but had instead given up, concluding that your situation was impossible?

3. If you are facing a roadblock in any area of your life now, have you taken the time to pray about it and to ask the Holy Spirit to show you a way around this hindrance? If not, don't you think it would be a good idea to take it to the Lord today and let Him speak to your heart about it?

When God called you, He also equipped you with all the power, wisdom, and insight you would ever need to get across the hurdles Satan tries to put in your way. There is no *impasse* you cannot get through or conquer if you are really determined to finish your God-given assignment.

OCTOBER 24

Highway Robbery!

In journeyings often, in perils of waters, in perils of robbers....
— 2 Corinthians 11:26

When you live and preach the Gospel in volatile regions of the world, you deal with issues that believers in more civilized nations never have to think about. Some of these challenges simply go with the territory of working on the front lines of the Gospel, and there is nothing that can be done to change it. This is why God gives special grace to people whom He sends to difficult parts of the world. His grace empowers them to successfully live, preach, and minister in environments that others would consider chaotic and even bordering on the insane.

On occasion, representatives of other very large ministries have come to the other side of the world to look at our work. After seeing what we have accomplished and obtaining a better understanding of the many problems we face in fulfilling our divine assignment, they leave amazed that we are able to do what we do. But we are able to do it only because we're recipients of God's *grace* and *anointing*. Without these two factors, it would be impossible to make such a major impact. *All the glory goes to Jesus!*

One of the issues we have faced is the criminal element that exists in the vast expanse of the former Soviet Union. Because the region is so huge, it is very difficult for the government to control the "mafia" that works in every area. Thus, many parts of this precious nation where God has called us is controlled by hoodlums and bandits. These criminals try to invade every sphere of life and get their hands into everyone's pockets.

Several times these very dangerous criminals have attempted to beset our own organization. But as we listened to the voice of the Holy Spirit and carefully obeyed His promptings, God enabled us to circumvent meticulously laid plans that the devil was inspiring these thieves to execute against us. Had these plans worked, it would have robbed us of ministry finances and seriously affected our ministry. But thanks be to God, we successfully survived each of these planned attempts to destroy our ministry!

The situation I just related to you is not something you probably have to think about in your city or town. You live in a civilized system where police are available to help and where the mafia doesn't hide in the shadows, devising sinister plans to take advantage of you. But for people who live in other, less civilized parts of the earth, such criminal activity is part of the norm of life that must be dealt with, considered, and taken into account when making plans.

When the apostle Paul wrote to us about the things he endured as he traveled to take the Gospel to new places, he let us know that thieves and bandits were also a constant concern to him and to his fellow travelers. He wrote that they were "...in perils of robbers...."

In Perils of Robbers

I want you to notice that the apostle Paul uses the Greek word *kindunos* for the second time in this text. As noted in yesterday's *Sparkling Gem*, it is the Greek word for *extremely dangerous*.

Paul faced many dangers as he went about fulfilling his ministry, but one danger he constantly faced as he traveled was the threat of robbers. The word "robbers" is the Greek word *lestes*. It refers to *a plunderer, robber, highwayman,* or *bandit.* This was a bad breed of bandits who were very cunning in their thievery of others and who used weapons and violence to achieve their wicked ends.

In the ancient world, robbers and thieves hid in the ditches and caves along roads that led from city to city — particularly along main routes of travel. This is why some Greek expositors translate the word "robbers" as "highwaymen." This term especially applied to bandits who ambushed those who traveled by roads. Considering how frequently Paul and his companions walked, we can easily see why Paul faced "perils of robbers." This gives a whole new idea to the phrase "highway robbery"!

Just imagine for a moment that you are traveling to the farthest ends of the earth by foot. You are physically carrying everything you need for that journey. The luggage piled on your back is filled with the clothing and cash you need for your journey. You know that pillaging, predatory plunderers are hidden in the ditches and caves along the roadside as you pass by, just waiting for the right prey to come by. You also know that these bandits are famous not only for stealing, but for wounding and killing their victims. Yet there is no other road for you to take if you are going to get where you need to go.

We can be sure that Paul and his traveling companions were alert the whole time they traveled on those roads. They most certainly took authority in the Spirit and bound the evil forces influencing the bandits who lay in the ditches and caves, waiting for them to come along. But because Paul uses the word *kindunos* ("perils"), we know this was an *extremely dangerous* predicament.

Yet even this danger was not strong enough to stop Paul from doing the will of God. He and his companions exercised authority in the Spirit and courageously walked on, traveling through regions so dangerous that others dared not even venture there.

You may not live in regions of the world where you have to think about highway robbers, members of the mafia, and other criminal elements, but God might be calling you to venture into new areas of ministry or business that seem to entail risks and dangers. You may feel like there are hidden dangers awaiting you at every turn. In these cases, don't allow yourself to retreat in fear! You must do your best to faithfully follow God's call. Use the common sense God has given you; gird yourself with the power of the Holy Spirit; and head in the direction where God is calling you.

It doesn't matter how difficult the task is that lies before you — if God is the One leading you, you can do it. God isn't going to give you an assignment you can't do. Remember, many others have had to fight the same fight of faith before you. They have faced the same questions you face. They have walked the same road you are walking. They followed the call of God, and they victoriously accomplished God's plan. If those believers could do it, so can you!

So put fear aside, and get ready for a journey of faith. Think soberly and stay alert as you let the Holy Spirit lead you down the path toward your destination, allowing nothing to deter you from your goal. As you do these things, the day will come when you produce more fruit for the Kingdom than ever before!

MY PRAYER FOR TODAY

Lord, I ask You to help me put aside fear and to believe that You will protect me as I follow Your call on my life. I know that You would never give me an assignment that You didn't think I could do. The fact that You've asked me to take this path means You are confident that I am capable of succeeding. Naturally speaking, I would feel fear at the prospect of taking such a step of faith. So please help me to permanently put away that fear and to trust that the Holy Spirit will carefully lead me past every danger and risk that lies along the way.

I pray this in Jesus' name!

QUESTIONS FOR YOU TO CONSIDER

1. Have you ever sensed the Lord leading you to take a step of faith that was risky?
2. When you knew that God was asking you to do something that moved you out of your comfort zone, were you excited to follow the Lord's leading, or were you fearful?
3. Did the Holy Spirit guide you past dangers that were secretly lying in wait for you? How did He safely lead you past those dangers so that you remained uninjured?

OCTOBER 25

Religious Hypocrites And Pagan Idol Worshippers!

In journeyings often, in perils of waters, in perils of robbers,
in perils by mine own countrymen, in perils by the heathen....
— 2 Corinthians 11:26

Often atheists say, "Religion is an evil force. It is the main source of hatred and war in the world." And if we carefully examine the regional conflicts in the world today, we would have to admit there is a certain degree of truth to that accusation. A large number of the wars that have been fought through the centuries were connected to differing religions, as is much of the hate that exists in the world today.

But the majority of what is done in the name of religion has nothing to do with God. First John 4:8 declares that "...God is love." As the Source of love, God would never initiate the wars, the hatred, the bloodshed, or the conflicts that are so often performed in the name of religion. These various conflicts may be done in the name of religion, but they have nothing to do with God, for God is a Restorer, Redeemer, Savior, and Deliverer, and there is no darkness in Him at all.

From the very beginning of time, religion without God has proved to be disastrous. That's why I say that to a certain degree, atheists are correct when they assert that religion is the source of mankind's problems. It was even the religious leaders of Jesus' day who failed to recognize that He was

God's Son and demanded that He be crucified on a Cross. By studying the Gospels, you will see that the religious leaders of Jesus' time were very mean, callous, cruel, malicious, spiteful, and malevolent.

The biggest enemies to the Gospel during the past two thousand years have been religious leaders. Acting in a spirit of fear, they attempt to stamp out any move of God that is not under their control. This has always been and is still the case. Religion will always be the biggest opponent to the declaration of the Gospel.

Certainly during Paul's ministry this was true. The greatest opponents to his ministry were the religious Jews who followed him, harassed him, stirred up trouble for him, and even tried to kill him. This is why Paul tells us that he was "…in perils by mine own countrymen…" (2 Corinthians 11:26).

In Perils by Mine Own Countrymen

Now for the third time in this chapter, the apostle Paul uses the word "perils" (from the Greek word *kindunos*, meaning *extremely dangerous*). The phrase "mine own countrymen" comes from the Greek word *genos*. The word *genos* is where we get the word "genes."

This word would *only* be used to denote someone with whom one shares a common ancestry. Paul is referring to the Jewish people who constantly opposed him everywhere he went. They opposed him in Salamis (Acts 13:8), Antioch Pisidia (Acts 13:45,50), Iconium (Acts 14:2), Lystra (Acts 14:19), Thessalonica (Acts 17:5-9), Berea (Acts 17:13), Corinth (Acts 18:12-16), and so on.

Paul tells us that what he faced from his own natural kinsmen was *extremely dangerous*. They persecuted and hunted him down everywhere he went. They were the primary tools Satan used to pester Paul. Angry, unbelieving Jews were *the thorn* in Paul's flesh that he later wrote about in Second Corinthians 12:7. These were the messengers of Satan who were sent to constantly buffet him.

But in spite of the endless persecution of these religious Jews, the apostle Paul pressed onward toward the high calling of God in Christ Jesus. He wasn't going to let any group of angry religious people keep him from doing what he was assigned to do. This particular *impasse* wouldn't stop him any more than the others had.

Let's pray that we never demonstrate the nasty attitude so many have paraded before the world in the name of religion. We must never forget that Jesus died for people — even for the religious leaders who hated Him and demanded His death. Like Jesus, we must make it our aim to walk in the love of God just as Jesus did.

If you are being harassed by religious people who don't understand your stance of faith, don't get too upset with them. They are operating in the same spirit of religion that has operated since the beginning of time. The devil wants to use them to upset you, steal your joy, make you angry, and get you into the flesh. However, you don't have to let the enemy get the best of you. Just make the decision to walk in love and to respond to them in the spirit of Jesus.

In Perils by the Heathen

The religious leaders weren't the only ones the apostle Paul had to face. He tells us that he was also "…in perils by the heathen…" (2 Corinthians 11:26).

The apostle Paul uses the word "perils" for a fourth time in this chapter. Again, it is the word *kindunos*, denoting *something that is extremely dangerous*. The word "heathen" is actually the Greek word *ethnos*. It specifically refers to *Gentiles* or *to anyone not Jewish*.

The Gentile world was a strange and curious world. It was filled with wild religious beliefs, customs, and a pagan culture opposed and adverse to the knowledge of a righteous and holy God.

The religion of the Gentile world promoted the grossest, most depraved, and most perverted sort of sexuality. Thousands of different gods were worshiped in pagan temples, each with its own particular style of worship. Most of these religious orders involved the use of wine and drugs to induce the worshiper into wild, mindless debauchery as a part of his or her act of "worship" to the gods.

These religions were filled with demons. As the wine, drugs, music, drum-beating, and sexual perversion of temple worship intoxicated those participating in the pagan ceremony, demonic activity became stronger and stronger in the temple. During a moment of such intensity, things could have easily gotten out of control.

At such moments, an act of aggression against Gospel preachers could have freely occurred. This environment was extremely dangerous, especially to Paul and his team as they confronted the powers of darkness and commanded these idol worshipers to repent.

The travels of the apostle Paul took him to some of the world's most pagan and demonic cities. In fact, Thessalonica, Athens, Corinth, and Ephesus are listed among some of the most pagan, demonic cities in the history of mankind! Yet these cities were the places where the Holy Spirit led Paul. They were also where he experienced his most successful periods of ministry.

Going where it is safe and secure is not always what God wants us to do. The Gospel must be taken into every country, every city, and every village in the world. If we go only where it's comfortable and safe, none of us will ever go very far from where we live right now. Thank God for those who went before us and who pushed the powers of darkness out of the way so we can now know the glorious light of the Gospel!

Paul faced extremely dangerous situations in both the Jewish and Gentile world, but it didn't stop him from going where God had called him. No danger was so terrifying that he couldn't conquer it with the power of God. Paul, whom history says was small in stature, was so mighty in the Spirit that he challenged and pushed his way through some of the most wicked, spiritually dark conditions known to man to do exactly what God had asked him to do.

When you allow God to infuse you with His power, you will also become a mighty force for God. The question is, will you determine to take the power and the love of God into every place He leads you to go so others can hear the Good News?

MY PRAYER FOR TODAY

Lord, help me to demonstrate the love of Jesus Christ and to never allow the unkind, cruel spirit of religion to operate in me. Help me also to love those who operate in this mean spirit and to counter their attitude with the love of Jesus Christ. And, Lord, when I am confronted by godless unbelievers, give me the wisdom to demonstrate the love of Jesus to them in a way that will touch their hearts. Both the religious and the irreligious need Jesus, so show me how to be an instrument of life to both types of people when I encounter them along the way.

I pray this in Jesus' name!

MY CONFESSION FOR TODAY

I confess that I will take the Gospel anywhere God tells me to take it! That means I am willing to go to every country, every city, and every village in the world. Nothing — no force, no group, no religion, and no godless, pagan influence — can stop me from going where God has called me. No danger is so terrifying that I can't conquer it by the power of God. I am mighty in the Spirit and can push my way through the most wicked, spiritually dark conditions using the power and the love of God.

I declare this by faith in Jesus' name!

QUESTIONS FOR YOU TO CONSIDER

1. Can you think of anyone you've met in the past who was very "religious" but who related to others with a cruel, mean spirit? When you encountered that spirit, were you able to love that person with Jesus' love, or did you allow him or her to make you angry and get you in the flesh?
2. Has there been a time in your life when you felt surrounded by godless unbelievers who laughed at you and made fun of you because of your faith? How did you respond to that situation? Were you able to love them with Jesus' love?
3. Have you ever witnessed a time when God's love melted the heart of such a godless person and that person's life was changed forever? How long did it take for the love of God to break through the hardness of that individual's heart?

OCTOBER 26

❧

Challenges in Town, Out of Town, and in the Sea!

In journeyings often, in perils of waters,
in perils of robbers, in perils by mine own countrymen,
in perils by the heathen, in perils in the city,
in perils in the wilderness, in perils in the sea....
— 2 Corinthians 11:26

*M*any years ago, I visited a city in the north of Russia where we were scheduled to hold a large evangelistic camapaign to reach the lost. We had been broadcasting our television programs in that region for many years; now we were coming to put the sickle into the harvest field and to reap souls for the Kingdom of God.

When our team arrived, we discovered that there was immense opposition to our arrival in that city. The religious leaders of the city were furious that we were coming to that region to preach. Their opposition was so hostile that they printed pamphlets and brochures filled with derogatory fabrications about us and then distributed them by the thousands throughout the city.

After arriving in the city, I could hardly believe my eyes when I saw the large billboard that had been erected to announce our upcoming campaign. The billboard had a picture of my face on it, and the religious leaders of that city had put ladders up to the billboard, crawled up the ladders, and painted horns on the top of my head to portray me as a devil!

The day our meeting was to begin, I looked out my hotel window and saw these religious leaders, dressed in their flowing gowns, standing on the steps of our rented facility. They were using a sound system to blare out the message that anyone who came to our meetings was in danger of eternal damnation. I'm telling you, the opposition to that campaign was *intense*.

Because those religious leaders had authority in that city, they were able to get negative articles printed about us in the newspaper and make sure the local city magistrates were also opposed to our message. Suddenly the prices for the auditorium changed as those who controlled the city turned against our meetings and decided to demand that we pay higher prices.

But when it was finally time for the meetings to begin, the religious leaders moved off the steps as we walked right past them into the auditorium. That evening we watched the auditorium fill up with the bold, the brave, and the spiritually hungry of the city who came despite all the attempts that had been made to keep them away. We saw many people come forward to give their lives to Jesus Christ.

When Paul was ministering in his day, he faced similar predicaments in his ministry. This is why he wrote that he and his team were "...in perils in the city..." (2 Corinthians 11:26).

In Perils in the City

Think about it for a moment. How many cities was Paul chased out of during his ministry? You would think a city would be a little more civilized, but some of Paul's worst confrontations occurred right in the heart of the world's most advanced and cultured cities.

Paul most often labored in larger metropolitan areas. As an apostle, his primary calling was to establish the Church in every place he went. Therefore, the Holy Spirit usually sent Paul into large population centers, where there were many people and the potential of a huge harvest.

As is true in large cities today, such as New York, London, Moscow and Chicago, there were dangers in the ancient cities that didn't exist in the smaller towns and villages. Paul faced these challenges courageously with the power of the Holy Spirit. I'm certain some of those challenges were in the financial, political, and religious realms, not to mention the normal stress a person faces when he attempts to do business in a big city.

However, none of these roadblocks ever kept Paul from doing what he was supposed to do. He pressed forward and completed his responsibility in every place to the best of his ability. He was a good soldier of Jesus Christ who kept marching forward, regardless of what the enemy tried to throw at him. But in addition to opposition in the city, Paul also said that he and his team experienced "...perils in the wilderness...."

In Perils in the Wilderness

When Paul writes about his experiences in the wilderness, he uses the word "perils" again (the Greek word *kindunos*, meaning *extremely dangerous*) to explain the events he faced in the wilderness. We don't have any information from the New Testament to alert us as to what Paul is talking about. We can only make assumptions. The word "wilderness" is the Greek word *eremia*. It describes *a remote, isolated location* in the middle of nowhere.

Paul's travels no doubt took him through remote areas where thieves and plunderers could have easily victimized him and his companions. It is very possible that wild beasts confronted them as they walked from place to place. The roads had deep ruts where deadly snakes and venomous scorpions hid.

Just as they faced certain dangers that were unique to the city, Paul and his team also faced dangers unique to the wilderness. Yet Paul faced these challenges with the assurance that God's power would enable them to conquer each peril successfully.

In Perils in the Sea

In addition to dangers in the city and in the wilderness, Paul tells us that he also faced "…perils in the sea…" (2 Corinthians 11:26).

For the seventh time in this chapter, Paul uses the word "perils" (the Greek word *kindunos*, meaning *extremely dangerous*), this time to describe his experiences of traveling by sea. As we've already seen, Paul survived three different shipwrecks. Only one of these is recorded in the book of Acts. In addition to the shipwreck Luke tells us about in his account in Acts, Paul encountered two other sea catastrophes during the course of his ministry.

Most people who have been in an airplane crash are hesitant to ever get back on another airplane. It leaves such a mark in one's mind that the traumatic impact of this memory is hard to overcome. Sea catastrophes in the ancient world were just as dramatic and memorable. It was surely a horrible experience for someone to be adrift at sea, not knowing whether or not he'd survive or be rescued. Paul went through this type of ordeal three separate times.

I'm sure these devilish attacks at sea were designed to put such a fear of sailing in Paul that he would never get back on another ship. But if Paul was going to get to the various places where God had called him to minister, he had no choice. Therefore, he didn't allow these occurrences to steal his joy or to determine whether or not he obeyed God. Even if it meant he had to get back on another ship and sail through dangerous waters again, he'd do it, if that was required of him in order to successfully fulfill his God-given assignment in life.

Do you understand that you have to be spiritually tough in order to do what God has asked you to do? It takes guts to do the will of God. You have to be totally convinced of what God has told you, or the devil will throw enough blockades in your way to make you turn around and permanently go back home.

Jesus showed this kind of spiritual fortitude. The religious leaders of His day were opposed to Him; the Cross and three days in the grave were before Him. Nevertheless, Jesus moved ahead in the power of the eternal Spirit and obtained our redemption for us (*see* Hebrews 9:14).

What has God called *you* to do? Are you committed enough to keep going, regardless of what the enemy throws at you? It's going to take a solid commitment on your part to do anything significant, so I want to encourage you to take a serious look at your commitment level and make sure you have what it takes to make it to the conclusion you desire.

If you don't establish a firm commitment in your heart to make it through to the end, then you won't. *So I urge you to take time before God today to thoughtfully examine your true level of commitment to God's call on your life. Make sure you are absolutely committed to do what God has told you to do!*

MY PRAYER FOR TODAY

Lord, I know I need to deepen the level of my commitment if I am going to accomplish the vision You have placed in my heart. To complete the task You've given me is going to require much of me, for I'm sure that Satan will try to resist Your plan for my life. I will have to stand strong and firm in order to obtain my goal; therefore, Holy Spirit, I am asking You today to show me every place in my spiritual foundation that needs to be fixed, strengthened, or repaired. I want to be completely fit and fully equipped to finish my race and win my prize!

I pray this in Jesus' name!

I confess that I am strong in the Lord. I am strong enough to do anything God will ever tell me to do. The Word of God abides in me, and the power of the Spirit works through me. Therefore, I am well able to overcome the strategies of the enemy. The future is mine because I have the promises of God's Word and the power of the Spirit on which I can rely.

I declare this by faith in Jesus' name!

| QUESTIONS FOR YOU TO CONSIDER |

1. Would you say that your level of commitment is strong enough to take you all the way to the goal that is in your heart?
2. If your answer to the above question is no, what do you need to do to upgrade your level of commitment? Would a more regular diet of the Word of God in your life make you stronger?
3. If you aren't spending time in the Word of God on a daily basis, is there a reason you haven't made this a priority? What does that reason reveal about your level of commitment?

OCTOBER 27

Dealing With False Brethren

In journeyings often, in perils of waters,
in perils of robbers, in perils by mine own countrymen,
in perils by the heathen, in perils in the city,
in perils in the wilderness, in perils in the sea,
in perils among false brethren.
— 2 Corinthians 11:26

Throughout the years I have lived and worked in the former Soviet Union, I've had numerous encounters with false brethren. When I say "false brethren," I am not only referring to unbelievers who pretend to be believers, but also to real brothers who are "false" in the way they have projected themselves. They portrayed one image when, in fact, they had ulterior motives behind the mask they wore so professionally.

As a result, I have often pondered Paul's words in Second Corinthians 11:26 when he wrote about "false brethren." Let's delve into the phrase "false brethren" today to see what it means.

In Perils Among False Brethren

For the eighth time in this chapter, the apostle Paul uses the word "perils" (the Greek word *kindunos*, meaning *extremely dangerous*). This time the danger he describes is connected with "false brethren."

The Greek word for "false brethren" is *pseudadelphos*. The first part of the word is *pseudes* and carries the idea of *something that is untrue*. It could be translated *pretend, phony, fake,* or *bogus*. The second part of the word, *adelphos*, is simply the word for *a brother*. Compound these two words together, and they describe *phony, fake, bogus, pretend brethren*.

Paul remarks about these bogus believers in Galatians 2:4,5: "And that because of false brethren unawares brought in, who came in privily to spy out our liberty which we have in Christ Jesus, that they might bring us into bondage: To whom we gave place by subjection, no, not for an hour; that the truth of the gospel might continue with you."

These "false brethren" in Jerusalem were in fact genuine brothers who had deceptive motives in their dealings with Paul. They projected one impression, but in reality, their intentions were very different from what they projected. They were "false" because they pretended to be in agreement with Paul's doctrine. In actuality, they wanted to take Paul's converts and revert them back to legalism. Paul's emphasis is not that they were unsaved, but that they were "false" with him.

It is heart-breaking to discover that someone you've trusted has been presenting a false image before you in order to gain some advantage over you. If this has happened to you, take heart, for it happened to Jesus too. Judas Iscariot claimed to be a disciple, but in reality, he had a secret agenda. Those who operate with secret agendas and undeclared motives are "false" in the sense that they are feigning to be something they are not. This would qualify them in a certain sense as "false brethren."

But I want you to also notice the phrase "came in privily" in Galatians 2:4, because it describes how these bogus believers behave. It comes from the Greek word *pareisago*. This word is a triple compound, comprised of the words *para, eis,* and *ago*.

The word *para* means *alongside*. It denotes *something that is very close*, such as in the word *parasite*. The second part of the word — the word *eis* — means *into* and conveys the idea of *penetration*. Finally, the third part of this compound is the word *ago*. It simply means *I lead*.

When all these words are compounded together, the word *pareisago* ("came in privily") conveys the idea of *smuggling something in undercover*. Literally, it is a picture of someone who is *leading* (*ago*) something into (*eis*) the Church *alongside* of themselves (*para*). It is the idea of *covert activity*.

The first part of this compound — the word *para* — indicates that the deceptive motives of these false brethren are held so secretly that they are able to sneak right into the midst of the Church undetected. By keeping their hidden agenda close to themselves, they are able to worm their way right into the Church leadership. Once they gain position inside a particular group, they start their destructive work from deep within the Church itself.

We know that Paul was constantly accosted by Judaizers, who came to spy out his light in Jesus Christ. It is also known that both the government and the religious leaders of the day would specially train and disguise agents to invade the Church. Using tactics similar to those used by the more recent Soviet KGB, these agents of biblical times would be so well camouflaged that they sounded like believers, looked like believers, and were often perceived to be true brethren in Christ. But in reality, these individuals were imposters who had been sent to discover the location of church meetings. They would inform the local authorities of the location; then the next time the church met, the police would arrest those who had gathered for worship.

Whoever these "false brethren" were, Paul said they were perilous to him. They created a situation that was *extremely dangerous* and *highly volatile*.

You can imagine how this situation could have driven Paul into a pattern of fear and suspicion. Paul knew that pretenders were out there, constantly trying to secretly hurt him and those he loved.

But instead of becoming suspicious of everyone he met, Paul relied on the Holy Spirit to give him clear discernment so he could recognize who was real and who was not. In the example given in Galatians 2:4 and 5, Paul was able to recognize the deceptive motives of the false brethren and therefore didn't even give them a single hour of his time.

Living in these types of stressful circumstances, Paul had a choice. He could either back up into insecurity, or he could take hold of the Holy Spirit's help and press forward toward his goal.

Paul chose the latter. He refused to let these "false brethren" become a stumbling block in his life and ministry. He didn't stop entering into new relationships just because some of the individuals he met might turn out to be "pretend brothers." Instead, he trusted the Holy Spirit to help him make right choices. This *impasse* didn't stop him from continuing to work closely with people, nor did it stop him from establishing the Church in various locations.

Likewise, you have to determine that regardless of whether people please you or disappoint you, they are not going to stop you from staying on track with the assignment God has given you. You are not going to allow Satan to knock you out of the race through the disappointments you experience with other people. If they prove to be false or you find that their motives were not what they portrayed them to be, you must learn to forgive them, let go of the offense, and turn your eyes to the future.

If you will listen to the Holy Spirit, He will help you develop a better sense of discernment about the people who are trying to get close to you. After all, there is nothing the Holy Spirit doesn't know. So if you'll allow Him to lead you in your relationships, you'll find that your discernment about people will become more and more accurate as you grow in your walk with God.

If you've been disappointed and hurt by false brethren in the past, ask the Lord today to help you stop dwelling on it. *Let the Lord heal your heart as you choose to forgive that person who deceived you and get back on the path toward God's destiny for your life!*

MY PRAYER FOR TODAY

Lord, I admit that I've been misled by certain people on several occasions. It has shown me that I need a better sense of discernment about those I allow to get close to me. Yet at the same time, I don't want to become hardhearted or callous because of what I've been through. So today I choose to turn from bitterness against those who have misled me. I make the decision to forgive them, to release them from the wrong they have done, and to turn my attention toward my future. Holy Spirit, I can only do this with Your help, so I am looking to You to empower me!

I pray this in Jesus' name!

MY CONFESSION FOR TODAY

I confess that the Holy Spirit is helping me to develop a keener discernment about people. I am able to recognize those who are genuine, and I can detect those who have ulterior, undeclared motives for getting close to me. Because the Holy Spirit sees and knows everything, I rely entirely on Him to lead and direct me in my relationships. As a result of being Spirit-led, I am making fewer mistakes in whom I choose to be my friends and close associates.

I declare this by faith in Jesus' name!

1. How many times have you been misled into thinking someone was a friend who turned out to be more of an enemy?
2. If this has happened to you on repeated occasions, what does this tell you about your sense of discernment about people? Do you think it may indicate that you need to go slower and be more careful about committing your heart to someone?
3. What steps can you take to improve your sense of discernment and to learn how to be more careful in giving your heart to others?

OCTOBER 28

A Hard Worker Who Experienced God's Sustaining Power!

In weariness and painfulness....
— 2 Corinthians 11:27

It takes hard work to get anything done in this world. If you want to do something significant, you must do significant work.

Those who do the minimum — who continually think of how to contribute as little as possible in any given situation — always remain minimal in their impact on the world around them. If a person wants to be successful or impacting in life, he must be willing to do whatever is necessary to accomplish the task that he has been asked to perform.

Are you the kind of worker who is willing to do whatever is necessary to finish a job the way it ought to be done? Do you see yourself as a vital member of the team whose maximum cooperation is needed and valued? Or do you just put in the minimum that is required for you to get your paycheck?

As Paul continues to tell us about his life experiences in Second Corinthians 11:27, he lets us know that he was willing to do very hard work. For him, there was no clock to punch with his time card, nor any employee's manual to specify how many days of vacation he got off each year. Paul's whole life was his calling. He couldn't separate who he was from what he was called to do. His identity and purpose for living was wrapped up in the life assignment God had given him. Because of this, every minute he lived and breathed was devoted to fulfilling his divine assignment. As you shall see, he was willing to do *anything* that was required to fulfill that call.

In Weariness

Paul uses the words "in weariness" to describe the incredible effort, toil, and physical exertion he put forth to fulfill God's calling on his life. The words "in weariness" are taken for the Greek word *kopos*. This word was also used in Second Corinthians 11:23, where Paul told us that he worked harder than anyone else he knew.

As noted earlier (*see* October 18), the word *kopos* represents the *hardest, most physical kind of labor*. It often pictured a farmer who works in the field, enduring the extreme temperatures of the afternoon sunshine. Although the temperatures are hard to endure, he strains, struggles, and toils to push that plow through the hardened ground. This effort requires his total concentration and devotion. No laziness can be allowed if that field is going to be plowed. The farmer must travail if he wants to get the job done.

Many people have the false idea that ministry is comprised primarily of sitting around praying and reading the Bible. The truth is, however, that ministry is very hard work. This is why Paul referred to it as "the work of the ministry" (Ephesians 4:12). To fulfill one's ministry effectively and responsibly, a great deal of hard work is required.

A minister must be willing to give his life to the task of pushing back the kingdom of darkness and establishing newly saved people into a stable and mature Christian walk. Effective ministry requires a person to work long hours, to be focused, to crucify his flesh, and to do whatever is necessary to see that God's Kingdom is furthered. The minister must fight off the devil's attacks, deal with people's instability, deliberately decide not to be hurt or wounded by those who disappoint him, and spend enough time with God to always have a fresh word from Heaven. Let me tell you from personal experience, friend — to do all this effectively demands a minister's entire life. This is why Paul called it the "work of the ministry."

Paul goes on to further elaborate about the way he had given himself so entirely and had so thoroughly devoted himself to the work of the ministry. He uses the phrase "in painfulness" to tell us the extent to which he had worked to achieve God's purposes.

In Painfulness

The words "in painfulness" come from the Greek word *mochthos*. This word has to do with the idea of *struggle*. The word *mochthos* is the picture of a person who has worked so hard that he is about to collapse. He is exhausted from physical labor.

You could say that this person is physically worn out because he has overdone it. His job demanded a level of physical commitment that was beyond what is considered normal. But the job needed to be done, so he kept pushing, pushing, and pushing himself further and further. Like it or not, it wasn't a time to rest. It was a time to *toil*.

Paul uses this word to amplify the message of how hard he worked in his ministry. You see, ministry wasn't a job that Paul worked from 8 a.m. to 5 p.m., Monday through Friday. Paul's entire life was consumed with and committed to fulfilling what God called him to do. It was the driving motivation of his life and the purpose for his existence.

The *King James Version* calls this type of hard work "painfulness," but that isn't the best translation. The only thing "painful" about Paul's consuming drive to obey God was what it doled out to the flesh, which always wants to take an easier, lazier course of action.

A better understanding of *mochthos* would be *to work yourself until you physically feel depleted of strength*. This is the picture of an individual who is dog-tired and drained and who feels like his physical strength is nearly used up. But by using this word, Paul isn't complaining! He's rejoicing that in his weakness, God's power has enabled him to push beyond the normal capacity of human strength.

Because Paul had a heart to never fail or give up, God's power came upon him and empowered him to do what other men and women could not physically do. Even physical weariness was not a strong enough impediment to stop this man of God.

It is just a fact that it takes hard work to do anything that is going to be successful. Those who try to avoid going the extra mile in doing their work with excellence will never reach the pinnacle of success.

Do you want to be super-successful in life? Then you must go above and beyond what everyone else is doing. If you continually put in only the minimum amount of work and effort that is necessary, you'll produce nothing more than the minimum with your life. In order to achieve something spectacular, you have to do something spectacular and unique to make it happen.

I urge you today to take a good look at your work habits and to evaluate what kind of worker you are. If you continue at the same pace and level of excellence you are working at today, where will you be in five years? *To get to a place of greater responsibility, authority, and blessing, what changes do you need to make in the way you work?*

MY PRAYER FOR TODAY

Lord, help me to be a good employee! I know I can do more than I've done and perform at a much higher level. And if I give 100 percent of myself to my place of employment, I know I can help my employer make a better profit and become more efficient. Please forgive me for taking a salary for work that hasn't been done with a full commitment to excellence. Jesus, I want to change in this area of my life. I ask You to help me become conscientious about the way I perform at my job.

I pray this in Jesus' name!

MY CONFESSION FOR TODAY

I confess that I am a good employee. I am so faithful at the tasks given to me that my employer or supervisor trusts me completely when I am assigned a new task. Because I work with all my heart, I bring blessing to my place of employment and to my employer. Every day the Spirit of God is showing me how I can improve in my work skills. Because I am a blessing at my place of employment, I give a good testimony of Jesus Christ to everyone I work with.

I declare this by faith in Jesus' name!

QUESTIONS FOR YOU TO CONSIDER

1. If you were the boss, would you be pleased with your work performance? Would you want to hire someone who has your work habits?
2. If your employer was specifically asked to describe your attitude and level of production as one of his employees, what do you truthfully think he would have to say about you?
3. If you were the boss, would you consider a worker like you to be an asset who can help take the company to a higher level of success? Or would you conclude that such a worker is just a low-level wage earner who will never add anything of much value to the company?

OCTOBER 29

A Leader Must Show Himself To Be a Team Player

In weariness and painfulness, in watchings often....
— 2 Corinthians 11:27

The phrase we are going to look at today is absolutely amazing to me. It reveals that the apostle Paul did not have a "movie star" mentality, thinking that he was too high and mighty to do a menial task. Even though he was a great apostle and was mightily anointed, he was also a real team member who was willing to pitch in and do what everyone else was required to do. If there was no one else to do a menial, mundane task, Paul would jump in to do whatever needed to be done.

The phrase "in watchings often" in Second Corinthians 11:27 reveals this phenomenal attitude in this great man of God. Today we will look at this phrase to discover the "team player" mentality that the apostle Paul possessed. I believe that you will be blessed to learn about Paul's attitude to work as a fellow team member. But even more importantly, I believe that God's Spirit will also speak to you about being a team player, no matter what position you hold in the organization where you work or at your church.

In Watchings Often

The word "watchings" is the Greek word *agrupvia*. It is most likely a reference to the long nights Paul lay awake to defend himself and his team against bandits and robbers who waited to attack them in roadside ditches and caves. The word "often" is the Greek word *pollakis*, which means *many times, often,* or *frequently*.

It was very common for a traveling group to take turns at "watching" during the night. If no one stayed awake and alert, plundering robbers would come and steal all the belongings of the traveling company while they slept. As noted earlier (*see* October 24), there were many highway robbers who lurked in the dark, waiting for travelers to pass their way so they could beat, rob, and plunder them.

This phrase "in watchings often" reinforces the fact that traveling was extremely dangerous back then, especially at night. And because Paul uses the word *pollakis* ("often"), we know there were times when he took a turn guarding the camp at night. In fact, Paul tells us that his turn to guard the camp happened "often" as his team traveled from place to place.

I think this little phrase "watchings often" gives us great insight into the willingness of the apostle Paul to act as a team player. Like everyone else on his team, he took his turn watching the camp while others slept. This may not sound like a spiritual part of ministry, but it was a necessary part of his job if he was going to get where he needed to go in order to preach the Gospel.

During the course of Paul's ministry, he had to do many tasks that seemed unspiritual and unconnected to ministry. These tasks were often mundane, boring, time-consuming, and uncomfortable. Nevertheless, these obligations had to be fulfilled, for without them, the true spiritual ministry could have never occurred.

When God has called you to do something important, you must be willing to do whatever is required to complete that task. This may mean that if there is no one else to do the job, you will have to sweep the floor, lick and seal envelopes, take out the trash, or answer the telephone. When someone else is raised up to do these smaller tasks, you will be freed to concentrate more fully on your larger vision. But until then, you must have a willing heart to do whatever is required to keep things functioning well on the road to fulfilling your assignment.

The fact that Paul sat "in watchings often" emphatically tells us that he was willing to do anything required to preach the Gospel message God had entrusted to him. So follow Paul's example. Don't be so high and mighty that you can't do a mundane, boring, time-consuming, or undesirable act along the way. It may not be something you relish doing. But if you don't do it, you might fail to achieve the real dream God has placed on your heart.

Make yourself valuable to your organization or church by demonstrating a willingness to do whatever is needed. And don't wait until someone has to ask you to do a job. If you see a need that no one else is meeting, show initiative by doing that job yourself. Demonstrate that you are willing to be a real team player.

Remember, whatever you sow is what you will reap. *So if you willingly give of yourself as a faithful team player in this present season, the day will come when you'll reap the team players you need to help you in fulfilling the vision God has given you!*

MY PRAYER FOR TODAY

Lord, help me to have the attitude of a team player! I want to be of benefit to my organization or place of employment and my church. I ask You to help me recognize opportunities where I can serve; then help me serve in these positions with all my heart. Help me to have the initiative to pitch in and become a helper to the rest of the team rather than to sit on the sidelines and watch everyone else work. I never want to think I'm so high and mighty that I can't do a menial, mundane task. Holy Spirit, help me to have the attitude of Jesus and to be willing to stoop low and do whatever is necessary in order to get the job done.

I pray this in Jesus' name!

MY CONFESSION FOR TODAY

I boldly confess that I am willing to do whatever is required to finish the task that has been assigned to me. If there is no one else to do a job, no matter how menial, I am willing to do it — and I'll do it with a happy heart. I don't think of myself as so high and mighty that I can't do a mundane, boring, time-consuming, or undesirable job along the way. I am valuable to my organization and church because I demonstrate a willingness to do whatever is needed. Since what I sow is what I will reap, I am going to give of myself and become a team player — and as a result, a day will come when I reap other team players to help me fulfill my own dream or vision.

I declare this by faith in Jesus' name!

QUESTIONS FOR YOU TO CONSIDER

1. If I asked you to think of one person who is a shining example of a team player in your organization, business, or church, who would that person be? What

qualities does this person possess that cause you to see him or her as a good team player?

2. Do you show initiative in your organization, place of employment, or church? Do you pitch in to do whatever needs to be done, or do you linger, waiting and hoping that someone else will do those menial tasks so you don't have to do them?

3. Would your coworkers agree that you show initiative, or would they say you're always looking for a way to get out of a job? How would they describe your attitude in the workplace?

OCTOBER 30

Is It Time for You To Make An Attitude Adjustment?

In weariness and painfulness, in watchings often,
in hunger and thirst, in fastings often, in cold and nakedness.
— 2 Corinthians 11:27

I remember an employee we once had in our ministry who got distressed because she was transferred to an area of the ministry that didn't have air control to suit her taste. Those in charge tried to adjust the thermostat to her liking, but they could never seem to please this individual. First it was too cold, and then it was too hot. And that was just the beginning. Next, this person complained because her office didn't have a window. Nothing we could do seemed to please this worker.

Because I believed this employee had great potential, I personally went to her to discuss her impossible-to-please attitude. If that employee was going to reach the level God desired for her, it would require a serious attitude change on her part. I wanted this unreasonable complaining to stop. When we hired this person, we had never agreed that she would be provided with a window or that we would meet the ideal atmospheric conditions she demanded.

I talked through these complaints one at a time with this employee. We had bent over backwards to make this person happy; now it was time for this employee to quit complaining and make an attitude adjustment in order to make *me* happy. Her constant complaining was bringing a spirit of discord into our organization that I didn't like. I decided I would not tolerate it any longer.

When I first spoke to this person, she showed thankfulness for the correction. But by the next week, she was back at it again — mumbling, murmuring, complaining, and sowing seeds of discord. The temperature wasn't right; the chair at the desk wasn't comfortable; the lunch hour wasn't the exact time she desired; there was no window in her office, and on and on and on. When I saw that this employee wasn't going to make the attitude adjustment I required, I decided to make an adjustment myself by removing her from our staff. That was that person's last week in our office.

It is unacceptable for us as Spirit-filled believers to be complaining people. After all, we are the ones who claim to possess the power of Almighty God!

To constantly complain about small annoyances such as those mentioned above is unacceptable. If it's possible to fix those little inconveniences, then fix them. But if the air can't be adjusted to your liking or if you can't have an office with a window, it's time for you to put a smile on your face and do a good job for your employer with a happy attitude. He didn't hire you to grumble and complain. He hired you to be a blessing!

The fact is, sometimes we don't get to have everything just the way we'd like to have it. Yet even in those moments, you and I should serve with all our might. If we are being paid to do a good job and to be cooperative with our employer and fellow employees, then we need to do what we are being paid to do! The day we give up that servant's attitude to become a source of constant complaining is the day we cease to be a blessing and become instead a hindrance that is no longer needed on the team.

If you're filled with the Holy Spirit and the power of God, it's time for you to get tough! You *can* do your job with joy, no matter what circumstances surround you! You can be victorious in any environment, even in working conditions that aren't exactly what you wish they could be. Besides, if you can't handle tiny inconveniences such as the ones we talked about earlier, how in the world do you ever think you'll be able to stand against the devil and the strategies he will try to use to assault you when you step out in faith?

As the apostle Paul continues telling us about his experiences in Second Corinthians 11, he lets us know that he has faced all kinds of inconveniences in order to obey the will of God. I'm sure he didn't enjoy those inconveniences, but he didn't allow them to affect his attitude or to keep him from fulfilling the task God had given him to do.

Let's look at a few of the inconveniences Paul endured as he marched forward to obey God.

In Hunger and Thirst

In Second Corinthians 11:27, he tells us that he endured "hunger" and "thirst." The word "hunger" is the Greek word *limos*. The word "thirst" is the Greek word *dipsos*. These words refer to *being hungry from a lack of food* or *thirsty from a lack of drink*.

This means there were times when Paul didn't have sufficient food to eat. This doesn't mean he was poor and therefore couldn't buy food. But in this verse, Paul is recalling times of inconvenience when food simply may not have been available to him and his fellow travelers.

Paul no doubt traveled through inhospitable, barren terrain where food was not abundant. Also, because of the great distances between some of the cities to which Paul and his team walked, it wasn't always possible for them to carry enough for their journey. In such times, they would simply run out of food and drink.

Yet this lack of food and drink didn't affect Paul's desire to go onward to the next town. Hunger and thirst was only an inconvenience — certainly not enough to hinder him from pressing on ahead.

To make sure we understand how serious this deficit of food was from time to time, Paul went on to say that he was "…in fastings often…."

In Fastings Often

The word "fastings" is the Greek word *nesteia*. It refers to *skipping or foregoing meals voluntarily*. In this case, Paul and his team probably skipped meals because there was no time to eat. The word "often" is *pollakis*, and it means *many times, often,* or *frequently*.

The apostle Paul and his team kept a rigid routine and a busy schedule. Eating food was obviously not a high priority on his list of things to do. First and foremost, he wanted to accomplish his

God-given objectives for each day and for each city where he labored. This doesn't mean Paul was against eating. It simply means his thoughts and focus were not on the comfort of food.

I know that when I travel to hold leadership meetings and crusades in the territory of the former Soviet Union, I am so focused on what I am called to do that personal comforts are always a last consideration. I frequently forget to eat because I am so consumed with the work before me. This is the kind of "fastings often" Paul makes reference to in this verse. Eating was not the highest priority on his mind.

I have personally known many people who took a missions trip and then swore they would never take another one because they didn't like the food they were given to eat on the trip. I am astonished when believers are so finicky about what they eat that they allow the issue to steal their joy and affect their obedience to God.

It perplexes me when people bewail that the food doesn't taste like food "back home." Of course it doesn't! They're not home! Then after grumbling about the food, they go to an evangelistic crusade where they expect to exercise spiritual authority to cast out demons. But how in the world do they ever think they'll have power over demons if they don't even have enough power to be thankful for a meal that is placed in front of them?

The phrase "in fastings often" tells us about Paul's priorities. He didn't take his trips to taste and experience the local menu. He went to get a job done. Good food or bad food, he went where the Lord told him to go. Time to eat or no time to eat, he was determined to succeed at the job he was given to do. Nothing as insignificant as food had the power to knock this man out of the race.

But how about the next inconvenience he lists? He went on to tell us that there were times when he and his team were also "…in cold and nakedness."

In Cold and Nakedness

This phrase could refer to many instances in Paul's life. For instance, he may be remembering the "cold" he felt as he treaded seawater after one of his three shipwrecks (*see* October 22 and October 26).

Paul may also be remembering the "cold" he felt during one of his many imprisonments. Ancient prisons were notorious for being damp and cold. Prisoners often contracted terrible cases of lung disease and died prematurely on account of these damp conditions. To make a captive's stay in prison even more miserable, the captor would often strip him almost naked before throwing him into the cave-like cell. It isn't possible to state definitely what Paul is referring to in his statement about "cold and nakedness," but whatever event he is remembering, it's obvious that it was *not* a pleasant experience.

In the former Soviet Union where we live, all public buildings and apartment complexes are centrally connected to a city-wide heating system. The heat is turned on for the entire city on a set day every fall, and the heat is turned off for the entire city on a set day every spring. Regardless of the temperature, the heat is not turned on or off until that date on the calendar. And once it is turned on, there is no thermostat in buildings, so the best way to control the temperature is either by opening the windows to let the cold air in or by closing the windows to retain the heat.

If it turns cold before that date in the fall when the heat is turned on, it means the entire city experiences the cold that permeates every apartment and office. Sometimes when the weather turns cold earlier than expected, the citizens may live in the cold for quite a lengthy period of time. When that happens, there is nothing people can do about it except dress in warmer clothes and try to keep themselves warm. Complaining won't change the situation, so people learn to work and function in the cold.

I admit that this isn't a pleasurable experience, but grumbling about the cold doesn't make the days pass any faster. Therefore, people mentally adjust to the inconvenience; then they live and work in the cold until the day finally comes when the city turns on the heat. Everyone survives the temperature because they have no choice. They make the mental adjustment to deal with the cold and are therefore able to live through the inconvenience.

Sometimes that is the way it is with life. We don't always get what we want or live in the style we prefer. But if we're not getting exactly what we want and we can't do anything to change the situation, we have a choice: 1) We can constantly complain and make it worse on ourselves and everyone else; or 2) we can make a mental adjustment and decide that we're tough enough to handle the situation until things change. The second choice is the one God wants us to make, for this is the one that demonstrates the attitude of Jesus Christ in our lives!

So if you've been grumbling or complaining about a situation that just can't be fixed to your liking, it's time for you to *quit grumbling* and to *start rejoicing*. Put praise in your mouth, and choose to be positive. As you do, you will find the strength to endure any hardship you are facing with joy.

As you make the choice to endure this hardship in the joy of the Lord, the Holy Spirit will fill you with a spirit of victory. And in the end, you will find that you came through the difficult situation you were facing much more quickly than you ever imagined you could!

MY PRAYER FOR TODAY

Lord, please forgive me for the times I've been a whiner and a complainer! I am so sorry that I've made life miserable for the people who work with me at my job or at church. I recognize that I complain more than I should, and I admit that I have been wrong. I repent for my wrong behavior, and I'm asking You today to help me make a mental adjustment. Help me learn to be thankful for the blessings I have and for the salary my employer pays me. Help me to serve with a happy heart and to be a continual source of blessing instead of a continual source of complaint.

I pray this in Jesus' name!

MY CONFESSION FOR TODAY

I confess that I am a blessing to my employer, my boss, my director, my supervisor, and to my pastor. They see me as a team player and a fine example of a Christian worker. My attitude is positive. I am willing to do what I am asked to do. I am never a source of contention; instead, I am a constant source of blessing to those who are over me. They are glad I work under them because I exhibit such a cooperative spirit of joy and thankfulness.

I declare this by faith in Jesus' name!

QUESTIONS FOR YOU TO CONSIDER

1. What are some of the inconveniences you face at your place of employment or where God has called you to serve? Are these annoyances really so terrible that you have a right to be upset about them? Or does God want you to deal with these inconveniences in the joy and the power of the Holy Spirit so you can gain the victory over them?

2. If your employer, supervisor, or pastor has tried to adjust things to your liking, have you expressed your thankfulness to that person for his or her attempts to please you? Remember — the person in authority over you didn't have to do anything at all to please you. So have you ever thanked that person for trying?

3. Is God telling you to make a mental adjustment so you can function victoriously where He has called you to live, to serve, and to work? What is that adjustment you need to make in your attitude?

OCTOBER 31

Don't Disqualify Yourself!

But I keep under my body, and bring it into subjection:
lest that by any means, when I have preached to others,
I myself should be a castaway.
— 1 Corinthians 9:27

*R*ecent years have been painful for the worldwide Christian community as they have witnessed famous Christian leaders fall into sin time and again. Not so long ago, I sat in a hotel room and watched with a broken heart as a famous evangelist, whose voice once touched the nations of the earth, preached with almost no effect on television. Because sin in his personal life had become public information years earlier, his words now seem empty, hollow, and irrelevant. Although he once preached to the nations of the world, now the world mocks him because they discovered the message he preached and the life he lived were not the same.

To me, one of the saddest things in the world is to see a man or woman whom God once powerfully used to preach the Gospel to millions of people around the world fall into sin. When that happens, it brings such shame to the name of Jesus Christ. These individuals may have once mightily impacted their nation or city for the Kingdom of God. But even if they are repentant and receive the forgiveness of God for the sin they committed, other people don't forget so easily. Like it or not, such sinful actions discredit them and ruin the effectiveness of their ministry. What they did or permitted themselves to get dragged into "disqualified" them from being as effective as they were before.

The apostle Paul wrote First Corinthians 9:27 to let us know that he never wanted to become discredited or disqualified. This is what he said: "But I keep under my body, and bring it into subjection: lest that by any means, when I have preached to others, I myself should be a castaway."

When the *King James Version* uses the word "castaway," it is actually the Greek word *adokimos,* which comes from the word *dokimos,* an old Greek word that means *approved.* But when an *a* is added to the front of the word, making it the word *adokimos,* it reverses the condition, which means this is no longer an approved person. Now this person has become *disapproved, discredited,* or *disqualified.*

This is a person who has lost a high position he once held. Although he was once honored and respected, he has now become a "castaway." He has lost his testimony and forfeited his reputation; as a result, he has become discredited, dishonored, and shamed.

I'm certain that Paul must have seen many people fall into sin during the course of his ministry. One example that comes to mind is Demas, a leader who was so beloved and respected by the Early Church that he is mentioned along with Luke in Colossians 4:14. But this same Demas who was once respected on the same level with Luke is mentioned again in Second Timothy 4:10, where we discover that Demas forsook the apostle Paul, abandoned his faith, and escaped into the world to spare himself from possible persecution.

People often make the tragic mistake of thinking that just because they have been successful in the past, they will continue to be successful in the future. But I have known many ministers of the Gospel who once experienced great success in the ministry and then slowly allowed their fire to go out. Whether they fell into sin or just became lethargic and complacent, the result was the same: They lost the cutting edge they once possessed in their ministries.

The primary reason people become discredited and shamed is that they don't control their flesh. Instead of crucifying the flesh and submitting it to the control of the Holy Spirit, they pander to the cravings of the flesh. As a result, they become dominated by the desires of the flesh, and those fleshly desires very deceptively lead them to fall into sin.

Paul was a great apostle who was filled with divine revelation and had preached to more people than anyone else in his day. Nevertheless, one of his greatest concerns was that after doing all he had done for the Kingdom, he might later become a "castaway" — the fate suffered by others whom he had known. Paul didn't consider himself so high and mighty that he couldn't imagine this happening to him.

Rather than make the mistake others had made by letting his flesh get the best of him, ultimately destroying both him and his reputation, Paul acted with great determination to keep his flesh under control. This is why he said, "...I keep under my body, and bring it into subjection...."

The word "subjection" is the word *doulagogeo*, a compound of the word *doulos* and *ago*. The word *doulos* is the word for *a slave*, and the word *ago* is the Greek word that means *to lead*. This means that Paul mastered his body and flesh rather than allowing his body and flesh to master *him*. He knew that many believers allow themselves to be led about by their fleshly desires. But Paul was determined that he would be the master of his own flesh. He was going to keep it in "subjection." In other words, he was going to lead his flesh about as his slave rather than be its slave and pander to its carnal desires.

By mastering his body and keeping it under his control, Paul made his flesh an instrument through which he preached the Gospel. His feet became his tool to take the Gospel to places that had never heard the Good News. His eyes became instruments through which he was able to identify needs that God's power could meet. His voice became the voice of salvation, healing, and deliverance to those who heard him preach. His hands became the hands of God that brought a healing and compassionate touch to those in need. Paul's body, which he determined to make his slave and his instrument, was never allowed to have its own way. Rather, Paul kept it under his command and made it his slave for the purpose of accomplishing his God-given dreams.

If you continue going the way you are going right now, is your physical body going to be a fine-tuned instrument that God can use, or is it going to be the very tool the devil uses to bring you into discredit and shame? Who is running your life today — you or your flesh?

If the apostle Paul was concerned that *he* could become discredited after all he had seen and done in the service of God's Kingdom, I think it would be wise for you to be concerned about who is running your life as well. Don't cut your flesh too much slack, friend, or it won't be long before it's running all over you and telling you what to do. You will reap the same result as others do when they refuse to discipline their flesh. In other words, you will eventually become broken by it.

Don't join the ranks of those who were once used by the Lord but are now set aside and ruined because they refused to bring their bodies into subjection. Your reputation, your influence, and the souls of unsaved men and women are at stake. *Make sure you don't become a castaway after all the good you have already done!*

MY PRAYER FOR TODAY

Lord, I never want to become a castaway who was once used mightily by You but who has now become disqualified for further use. I know of other people to whom this has happened. They were once mightily used, but they have since become discredited and disqualified because of their lack of passion or the immoral mistakes they have made in their lives. Help me to maintain Your fire in my soul and to walk a straight and narrow path that leads to life and abundance. I don't want to stray from the path You have set before me or to knock myself out of the race. Holy Spirit, I am asking You today to help me do everything I need to do to remain a viable, useful vessel in the hands of God.

I pray this in Jesus' name!

MY CONFESSION FOR TODAY

I confess that I walk with God and make it my aim to be an upright, moral, and godly example. I refuse to allow sin to have a place in my life. When evil thoughts try to invade my mind, I take those thoughts captive and command them to leave. I am the temple of the Holy Spirit, and these thoughts and ideas have no place inside me. I have invested too much of myself into the work of God to allow such low-level thoughts to pull me down and take me out. Because I am committed, determined, and serious about my walk with God, my future is bright and the anointing of God will grow ever stronger on my life!

I declare this by faith in Jesus' name!

QUESTIONS FOR YOU TO CONSIDER

1. Do you know ministers of the Gospel or well-known Christians who no longer have the powerful testimony and influence they once did in the Body of Christ because they allowed themselves to fall into immorality? Did those individuals lose their testimony to the extent that no one wants to hear what they have to say any longer?
2. As you ponder what happened to those individuals, what do you think was the primary mistake they made with their lives that allowed the devil to take them down and take them out?
3. As you look at what you are permitting in your own life, can you think of any destructive stronghold that could eventually grow into a problem serious enough to knock you out of the race of faith? If yes, what is that sin, and what are you going to do about it?

November 1

If You Want To Be a Leader

This is a true saying, If a man desire the office
of a bishop, he desireth a good work.
— 1 Timothy 3:1

When Denise and I were young in the ministry, we had a young man on our staff who was gifted in music and communication. This man had previously worked in the field of business, where he had done well until he was accused of taking funds from the cash register. A question had been raised about his integrity, and he was released from his job. However, I ignored every report about his lack of integrity because I was so impressed with his gifts and abilities.

I was most impressed by this man's ability to sing and write music, as well as his natural abilities to influence others. Soon I asked him to join our team. This turned out to be one of the most painful mistakes I had made in my life up to that time. Inviting this young man to come into our inner circle was like personally inviting Judas Iscariot to betray me! It didn't take too long until I began to see what kind of person he really was. The truth was far different from what I had first thought.

This young man talked only about himself. He looked for opportunities to put me down when others were present. He constantly exaggerated his importance in the eyes of others. I tried to overlook these faults, attributing them to his youthfulness. I hoped he would grow out of them. But as time passed, he didn't grow out of those troublesome traits; in fact, he became worse.

I met with the young man every morning and tried to teach him principles from God's Word. But he was a classic know-it-all! He acted as though he already knew everything, and it didn't take too long for me to realize that I had no real spiritual authority in his life. There was no foundation between us on which to build. Furthermore, he didn't seem to want a relationship; he was simply looking for a way to promote himself.

In terms of gifts and talents, this young man was everything a pastor could desire to have in an upcoming leader. But after a period of time, I found myself praying for a peaceable solution to our problem. I asked God to remove him and thus deliver us from a very uncomfortable situation, and eventually God did just that. Our dreadful experience with this young man was an important lesson in my early ministry of what *not* to do — a lesson I have not forgotten and have sought to never repeat!

As I have worked with pastors throughout the years, I have heard similar stories countless times — stories of pastors who were unwise in the way they chose leaders and eventually had to pray for a way to get a wrong person out of an important position. Just as I did when I was young in the ministry, these pastors also selected leaders according to the gifts and talents they saw rather than on the basis of the principles Paul so clearly laid out in First Timothy 3:1-7.

When Timothy's church was growing and he needed leaders to help him with his growing congregation, he asked Paul for advice about how to select leaders. Oddly enough, when the apostle Paul wrote Timothy back, he mentioned nothing about looking for people who were gifted or talented. Instead, Paul gave Timothy a list of what I call "character requirements" for those filling leadership positions in a local church. These "character requirements" were intended to be Timothy's guidelines for choosing the members of his leadership team.

However, don't think that these principles apply only to the church. When applied to the sphere of business, these principles will also safeguard any businessperson from making the critical mistake of choosing a wrong person for an important position.

Paul began this text on leadership selection by saying, "This is a true saying, If any man desire the office of a bishop...." Before we go any further, I want us to stop and look at the word "bishop" in this verse, for it is a word that has taken on an incorrect religious connotation that brings confusion to readers of the New Testament.

The word "bishop" is the Greek word *episkopos*. It is a compound of the words *epi* and *skopos*. The word *epi* means *over*, and the word *skopos* means *to look*. The word *skopos* by itself means *to watch, to look, to observe,* or *to survey*. But when the word *skopos* has the prefix *epi* added to the front of it, it becomes the word *episkopos*, which presents the idea of *a person who has oversight*. In other words, because this person has been placed in charge of a particular job or responsibility, it is his duty to supervise, manage, and provide oversight of it.

In secular Greek society, this word *episkopos* was used to picture *a ruler who was entrusted with the care of a city or country*. The task of that political leader was to provide oversight of an entire geographical area. That means he assumed management of the region and all the citizens who lived there and was personally held responsible for everything that happened under his care.

But the word *episkopos* was also used in the world of construction to depict *supervisors who had oversight of construction sites*. As the supervisor at such a site, an *episkopos* was required to ensure that funds were spent properly, that expenditures didn't exceed the budget, that people did their jobs correctly, and that the construction of a building was done according to code and in compliance with the desires of the architect. In other words, he was responsible for the entire project from beginning to end.

The word *episkopos* could be used to express the functions of:

- ✦ *an overseer*
- ✦ *a manager*
- ✦ *a director*
- ✦ *a supervisor*
- ✦ *a superintendent*
- ✦ *an administrator*

The reason it is so important to understand this is that when most people hear the word "bishop" (the Greek word *episkopos*), they think of a religious individual dressed in a long black gown, wearing a huge, heavy gold chain around his neck with a gold cross dangling at the end of it. This image is emphatically *not* what Paul had in mind when he used the word *episkopos* ("bishop"). Timothy didn't need religious leaders clad in black clothing and decorated with religious emblems; he needed *godly leaders* who could help him lead the flock!

You see, Timothy was building a huge congregation in Ephesus. In a sense, you could say he was in the "spiritual construction business." Because he was overseeing such a massive congregation as the church of Ephesus, Timothy needed people he could lean on to help him manage, direct, and supervise his growing congregation. He was looking for people who would take on the responsibility of entire areas of ministry, fulfilling their duties faithfully as they helped him supervise both people and projects within the church. These leaders had to be trustworthy individuals who would stick to the vision he gave them while making sure the people under their supervision properly performed their jobs and worked within the time frame and budget assigned to their project.

This is precisely what every pastor and business owner needs. As a church or business grows and expands, a pastor or business leader must have people he can rely on to do a good job and fulfill his desires. If he lacks such leaders, he will be limited in his ability to lead a large, growing organization. His arms only reach so far, and if he doesn't have good helpers to stand at his side and assist him, he'll never be able to oversee an organization that grows beyond his reach. He *must* have people who can help provide oversight, management, and supervision for the many tasks that must be performed within his church or business.

So I want to ask you today: Are you the kind of person that your pastor or employer can trust with bigger responsibilities? If he was looking for someone to step into a leadership position with greater responsibility, do you think he would think of you as a candidate for the job? What have you done to show yourself to be reliable? Why would your superior want to trust you to oversee a group of people, to manage a particular project, or to direct an entire department within the church or business?

It is just a fact that there are many gifted and talented people whom God will not use because they are not dependable. Gifts and talents are great, but they aren't everything. Throughout history, God has bypassed many people who were mightily gifted because He knew they couldn't be trusted with assignments given to them. Instead, He has chosen less gifted people He could count on to be faithful!

Are you a person God must bypass because you've been unfaithful, or does your record show that God can trust you to take on the responsibility of a leader?

MY PRAYER FOR TODAY

Lord, I ask You to help me become faithful and dependable. I want to be the kind of person others can rely on. I ask You to forgive me for those times when I got so lazy and complacent that I didn't follow through on commitments and, in the end, let other people down. I thank You for the gifts and talents You have placed in my life, but please help me bring my character to such a high level that You and others will know I can be trusted.

I pray this in Jesus' name!

MY CONFESSION FOR TODAY

I confess that God's Word and God's Spirit are turning me into a tower of strength! When people think of me, they think of reliability. I do what I'm asked to do, and I do it with excellence. People find me faithful and trustworthy, and they want me to be a part of their team. I am exactly the kind of person who helps bring success — and as a result, both God and man are excited to have me on their team!

I declare this by faith in Jesus' name!

QUESTIONS FOR YOU TO CONSIDER

1. Can you think of a person who is so reliable that everyone relies on him or her when there is a job that needs to be done? What can you learn from the way that person works and lives?
2. Can you think of a person who has failed people so many times that now no one wants to work with him or her any longer?
3. What part of you is the strongest — your gifts and talents, or your character?

November 2

❧❧❧

The First Requirement of a Leader

This is a true saying, If a man desire the office of a bishop,
he desireth a good work.
— 1 Timothy 3:1

One time many years ago, Denise and I were driving down the street, discussing our concern for certain church members who reflected *no* desire for excellence in the way they lived. As we discussed our desire to see the people in our church display a greater desire for excellence in their lives, we happened to look out the car window. There we saw one of our church members, an older woman, walking down the sidewalk. This elderly lady was extremely poor and had suffered miserable hardships in her life; yet every time we saw her, she always wore a beautiful smile on her face. My wife and I had commented to each other on many occasions about this woman's "never-give-up" attitude.

Like millions of other people living in the wreckage of the former Soviet Union, this woman had lost her money, her job, and even her national identity when the Soviet Union collapsed. As a pensioner, she existed on a salary so low that we didn't know how she even survived from day to day. Her monthly pension was barely enough to buy bread and milk. (This sad situation has happened to many people in the former Soviet Union. It's heartbreaking to see so many who live in despair, having lost all hope and sense of purpose in life.)

But on this particular day, this elderly lady's hair was beautifully combed and her face was prepared for the day. She had put on her best dress jacket, and she was holding her head high as she walked down the street. She looked as if she were a queen!

Then we noticed that the woman wobbled as she walked. Looking at her feet, we saw that her shoes were almost completely worn out and were surely causing her great pain as she slowly strolled along. When I saw how this little old woman hobbled along in old, worn-out shoes with her head held so high, it both blessed and saddened me. I felt sorry that her financial situation was so bleak and that she had to walk in such a decrepit pair of shoes. But her spirit and her mental attitude were so strong that she *refused* to let life get her down — and that blessed me!

I thought of all the people we knew who faced much less challenging situations, yet who sat around griping and complaining about everything. Because they didn't have the same *desire* this woman had to keep pressing toward excellence regardless of the obstacles, they were much more prone to give up and quit. But this little woman put on the best she had in an effort to look as excellent as possible in the midst of her very difficult circumstances.

It is sadly true that many believers live low-level lives simply because they have no ambition, passion, or desire to do anything to improve themselves. Their complacent attitude prevents them from ever doing anything better with their lives.

Considering the fact that the Spirit of God lives in believers and wants to take them higher, it is hard to understand any believer who:

✦ has the ability to improve himself *but doesn't.*
✦ has the money to buy better clothes *but doesn't.*

✦ has an iron to press his clothes *but doesn't use it.*
✦ has a comb to comb his hair *but doesn't care how his hair looks.*
✦ has the opportunity to study and increase his knowledge and skills *but never cares enough to do it.*
✦ has been reared in a good home with godly parental examples *but allows his living quarters to look like a pigpen.*

It is very important for you to understand that God doesn't choose passionless people to do mighty works. He carefully observes a person's *attitude* and *desire* before He lays His hand upon him and calls him to do something historic and monumental. Attitude and desire are very important to God; in fact, Paul wrote, "This is a true saying, If a man desire the office of a bishop, he *desireth* a good work."

As noted earlier (*see* May 25), the word "desire" is the Greek word *orego*. This word pictures *a person who wants something so badly that he stretches forward to obtain what he wants.* It literally means *to be outstretched* or *to stretch forward.* The idea is of *a fierce, unyielding desire to have or to be something.* It refers to a person's inward attitude and determination to always do the best he can with what he is and to become the best he can be.

You see, when a person has loads of talent and potential but never combs his hair, irons his clothes, makes his bed, washes his car, or cleans his pigpen of a home, it should *deeply* disturb us. It should especially concern us if that person has money to improve himself but never does it because he doesn't care.

A person who never attempts to make improvements in his living conditions is not someone I want to serve alongside me in my ministry. I know from the way he lives that he isn't a person with high standards of excellence. Likewise, an individual who is content to remain at his current level of proficiency at work, never striving for greater results, demonstrates a low level of desire to attain excellence.

This is probably *not* the kind of person God can trust to do great things for His Kingdom! A person's "take-it-easy, don't-rock-the-boat, never-achieve-anything-special" attitude reveals a lack of the passion and desire needed to be a mover and a shaker in life. This person could be developing his mind. He could be striving for excellence in his work. He could be reading books and developing skills of professionalism in his chosen field. Instead, he sits around in a puddle of mediocrity, satisfied with the status quo.

If you know someone who is called of God and loaded with gifts and talents but who is lazy in his approach to life, let me encourage you to speak correction to this person in love. God will never select that person to do anything great until he becomes willing to change. Why would God trust this kind of person with an important task when he can't even make his bed or comb his hair? Regardless of the talent or gifts this person possesses, he is eliminated by *his own lack of desire.*

This issue of *desire* is not a second-rate issue. *It is right at the top of the list of requirements for excellence!* It's so critical to advancement in life that when the apostle Paul gave Timothy his list of character requirements for Christian leaders, the first thing he put on the list was *desire* (1 Timothy 3:1).

When God observes your life, does He see the kind of desire that is essential for leaders? *If not, what are you going to do to change this in your life — starting today?*

MY PRAYER FOR TODAY

Lord, please help me stir up my desire to make significant changes in my life. I am so sorry for the times I've allowed complacency to keep me stuck in the same ol' place for such a long time. I want to change. I want to grow. I want to be different. I am asking You to super-naturally fill me with so much desire that no power on earth and no force in hell can stop me from becoming everything You want me to be!

I pray this in Jesus' name!

QUESTIONS FOR YOU TO CONSIDER

1. If you were to gauge the level of your desire for excellence, how would you rate yourself (with #1 designating the least desire and #10 the greatest desire)?
2. If you were to ask people who know you well to gauge your level of desire, how do you think they would rate you? Why don't you go ahead and ask them this question so you can find out what others see in you? You might learn something very valuable by allowing a dear friend to speak so honestly into your life.
3. In your opinion, what is the number-one area of your life that needs to change?

NOVEMBER 3

The Peaceable Fruit of Righteousness

Now no chastening for the present seemeth to be joyous,
but grievous: nevertheless afterward it yieldeth
the peaceable fruit of righteousness unto them
which are exercised thereby.
— Hebrews 12:11

*A*s you grow in your walk with God, you will discover that one of the strongest forces you'll have to face and overcome is your own flesh! Your flesh will try to oppose you, stand against you, and coax you into believing that you can do a little but still get a lot.

If you're going to be mightily used by God, your flesh must be disciplined so it can become an instrument through which the Holy Spirit can flow. You have to pay the price of crucifying the flesh in order to have the resurrection power of Jesus Christ expressed through your life.

If you look at a child with no parental guidance or discipline, you'll see exactly what the flesh does when it has its own way. The child will probably lie around, watch television, and eat junk food from morning till evening. And any person who lets his flesh do what it wants will most likely adopt the same lifestyle! That's why dealing with the flesh is almost like chastening a child. The flesh must be controlled, corrected, and made to obey even if it wants to do otherwise. The process is painful, but the rewards are eternal!

This is what Hebrews 12:11 is talking about when it says, "Now no chastening for the present seemeth to be joyous, but grievous: nevertheless afterward it yieldeth the peaceable fruit of righteousness unto them which are exercised thereby."

The word "chastening" in this verse is the Greek word *paideia*, an old Greek word for *the education or instruction of a child*. It comes from the word *pais*, the Greek word for *a boy*. However, as time passed, the word *paideia* came to signify *the education of all children*. By the time of Plato, the word *paideia* included not only the education of children, but also of adults. The concepts of discipline and regimen were so intrinsically interwoven in this word that in Luke 23:16 and 22, the verb form of the word *paideia* is translated as the word "chastise" and refers to Jesus being *whipped or scourged as punishment*.

So when this verse speaks of "chastening" in Hebrews 12:11, it refers to *disciplinary attitudes and actions that lead to one's betterment in life or to one's education*. The fact that this word can also be translated as *a whip, a scourge,* or *punishment* explicitly tells us that rigid discipline is required for the flesh to be chastened and changed so that fruit can be produced in one's life. The word *paideia* describes not only the *process* of education and change, but also the *attitude* required to bring about these benefits. An attitude of discipline is obligatory if the flesh is ever to make the needed changes.

Although the benefits of disciplining the flesh are too many to list, Hebrews 12:11 informs us that when this disciplinary process is in full force, it doesn't seem joyous but rather feels "grievous." The word "grievous" is the word *lupe*, the Greek word for *pain, distress, trouble, grief,* or *sorrow*. Although the discipline itself is good for us and provides us with the means to change, the flesh hates it when discipline is forced on it!

Haven't there been moments when your flesh screamed in disgust at the idea of discipline and commitment? It may be painful for the flesh to be crucified, but it is essential if you're going to render your flesh dead to sin and alive to God so He can transform it into an instrument through which His power and wisdom can flow!

Hebrews 12:11 says that this discipline will yield "...the peaceable fruit of righteousness unto them which are exercised thereby." The word "exercised" is the Greek word *gumnadzo*. This word *gumnadzo* depicts *radical discipline*! It was the word the ancient Greeks used to portray the athletes who *exercised, trained, and prepared for competition* in the often barbaric athletic games of the ancient world. It is where we get the word *gymnasium*.

This word *gumnadzo* ("exercise") portrays people who want to develop and change so much that they are willing to put themselves through vigorous, demanding, and strenuous discipline in order to bring about change and to achieve the results they desire. Now Hebrews 12:11 uses the word *gumnadzo* to tell us that if we will discipline the flesh, we will see great results in our lives, for we will begin to yield "...the peaceable fruit of righteousness...."

Let's face it — there is nothing more thrilling than to see progress in your life. But to get the kind of progress you desire, you will be required to do something more than you've been doing. You will have to say no to your flesh, denying its appetites and disciplining yourself to do what God says even if your flesh doesn't want to do it. This process often feels long and laborious, but afterward when you can *see* and *appreciate* the results, you'll be so glad you didn't quit!

So let the Holy Spirit exercise His discipline in your life. If you'll pay the price to crucify your flesh and to submit yourself to discipline, it will pay off with big dividends. You may not see immediate, tangible results while you are training and preparing. But eventually you will see the fruit of your labor, and you'll be so glad you took your flesh to school and taught it to obey!

MY PRAYER FOR TODAY

Lord, I admit that I need help in bringing discipline to my flesh and my emotions. Forgive me for being too easy on myself, and help me to be fiercely committed to bringing my body and my flesh under the control of the Holy Spirit. I want to be Your instrument so Your power can flow freely through me. So please help me today to submit to Your Word and to the control of Your Spirit. From this day forward, I purpose to no longer give my flesh the freedom to have its way in my life!

I pray this in Jesus' name!

MY CONFESSION FOR TODAY

I declare that the Word of God and the Spirit of God are working inside me! Every day my flesh is being rendered inoperative and my body is responding less and less to sin as I reckon myself alive unto God. I am God's instrument. His power flows through me. Because I am allowing God to bring discipline into my life on a daily basis, I have become a mighty weapon He can use to set people free and to make a significant difference in the world around me!

I declare this by faith in Jesus' name!

QUESTIONS FOR YOU TO CONSIDER

1. What is the number-one area in your life in which you know you need more discipline? What have you been doing to bring discipline to that part of your life?
2. If you haven't yet made any plans to change in this area of your life, what steps do you plan to take now that you've read today's *Sparkling Gem*? Do you want to stay the way you are, or do you want to bring that part of your life under the control of the Word and the Holy Spirit?
3. Name three areas of your life (such as diet, emotions, thought life, laziness, etc.) that used to be out of control but are now successfully crucified and brought under the control of the Holy Spirit.

It may be painful for the flesh to be crucified, but it is essential if you're going to render your flesh dead to sin and alive to God so He can transform it into an instrument through which His power and wisdom can flow!

November 4

Isn't It Time for You To Quit Daydreaming And Get To Work?

But refuse profane and old wives' fables,
and exercise thyself rather unto godliness.
— 1 Timothy 4:7

When the time came for our family to move to Moscow to start our next church, my wife and I knew that God wanted us to turn over the care of our large church in Riga, Latvia, to our associate pastor. After serving as a son in the Gospel for many years, he was as well-trained and prepared as anyone could be to step into the position of senior pastor of that church.

My associate was so excited. Just as we were certain he was the man to lead the church, he was convinced that God had chosen him. This was the day he had dreamed of for so long! After serving me for so many years as my associate, he would finally step into the senior pastor position and lead this great church. The vision of God was exploding in his heart as he dreamed of what would be accomplished in the ensuing years.

So with great reverence, my associate and his wife knelt on the platform of the large auditorium before the Riga congregation; then Denise and I laid our hands on him and installed him as the leading pastor of that congregation. After turning over the church to his care, my family and I turned our attention to the new work God had called us to establish in Moscow.

After the first year of leading that church by himself, my former associate told me, "Rick, I had no idea how much responsibility is placed on the senior pastor of a church. I thought I understood so much, but now I see that there was so much I never comprehended. It was only after you left and the whole weight of the church became my responsibility that I really began to realize the enormous responsibilities of a senior pastor."

I listened with great interest as he continued to give me his views about leading a large church. Then he said to me, "You know, it finally dawned on me that this was *my* responsibility and that I couldn't depend on anyone else to lead this church. As pastor, it's up to me to guide and to see that things are being done correctly. It's a huge responsibility to lead a church — much bigger than I ever realized!"

That conversation made me think of what Timothy went through after he became the pastor of the church of Ephesus — *the largest church in the world at that time*. Imagine how *extremely stretched* Timothy must have felt as he led the world's largest and most famous church! Yes, he had served at Paul's side for many years and was as prepared as anyone could possibly be for such a task. But now Paul was gone, and all eyes were on him!

The demands placed on the pastor of a large church are immense. His care for the church is nonstop. Twenty-four hours a day he must be available to the members of the congregation. Leaders must be trained; rebels must be corrected; and finances are needed to pay for the church as it grows. And in addition to church responsibilities, the pastor is most often a husband and a father as well. He has a massive church family to oversee and manage, and he also has his own personal family for which God will hold him responsible.

Timothy was just settling into the job of senior pastor when Paul wrote him the letter that became the book of First Timothy. At the time, Timothy's responsibilities were increasing daily. His massive church was becoming even more massive as it continued to grow. He was constantly training new leaders and replacing old, rebellious leaders who thought Timothy was too young to be pastor of such a prominent church. And in the midst of it all, Timothy was learning how to cope with being the most visible Christian leader in a large metropolitan city. It was in the midst of these developments that Paul wrote to him and said, "But refuse profane and old wives' fables, and exercise thyself rather unto godliness."

The Bible doesn't tell us exactly what these old wives' fables were. However, it seems that Timothy may have been so exhausted that he was starting to daydream about finding an easier and more trouble-free way to do his job (like all of us are tempted to do from time to time). I have personally wondered, *Was Timothy tempted to daydream about life in the ministry becoming simpler? Was he hoping that things would eventually become a lot less hectic, undemanding, and uncomplicated?* If Timothy *was* thinking along this line, his musings would definitely fall into the category of a fable!

When God trusts you enough to give you more and more responsibility, it always demands more of you, *not* less. I gave up the idea many years ago of thinking that life would eventually become less demanding. Ministry is *work*, and none of us should ever forget that fact!

If you are mightily anointed by God, it is just a fact that your schedule will get busier, your demands will increase, and your challenges will grow. But as long as you allow God to develop your character along the way, you will find that you're able to successfully manage anything He puts on your plate!

Paul ordered Timothy to quit fantasizing about things getting easier, telling the younger man to "…refuse profane and old wives' fables…." The word "refuse" tells us how strongly Paul felt about Timothy's frame of thinking. It comes from the Greek word *paraiteomai*, and it means *to reject, to refuse, to rebuff, to decline, to snub,* or *to decisively turn away from something*. It denotes the attitude of a person who is so disgusted with something that he has resolved he will have nothing to do with it. His feelings about this issue are so pungent that he sharply rejects what is being offered to him and vigorously declines any form of participation in it.

Whatever these "old wives' fables" were, Paul viewed them as extremely detrimental — so much so that he strictly ordered Timothy to reject these notions. To better understand what these "old wives' fables" might have been, let's see what the words "old wives" and "fables" mean in the original Greek.

The Greek word translated "old wives" is *grauodes*, which comes from the word *graus*, the word for an *old woman*. But when the word *graus* becomes *grauodes*, it denotes *anything that is old-womanish*. The word "fables" is the word *muthos*, which typically describes *fictitious stories* and is where we get the terms *myths* and *mythology*.

The word *muthos* describes *legends, folklore,* or *fairy tales* — the kind of stories an old woman would tell to entertain her grandchildren. One New Testament Greek scholar speculates that Paul was saying in effect, "*Timothy, it's time for you to quit fantasizing that you're going to escape hard work and find an easier way to do what God has called you to do. Why, this unrealistic kind of thinking is the stuff of fairy tales! You're thinking like an old woman who tells fairy tales to children.…*"

Instead, Paul challenges Timothy to adjust his thinking and to take a different approach to the challenges he faces. Rather than pray for these challenges to go away, Timothy should embrace those challenges and use this time to develop himself. This is Paul's message when he tells Timothy to

"…exercise thyself rather unto godliness." As noted earlier (*see* November 3), the word "exercise" is the Greek word *gumnadzo*, which describes *the strenuous physical exercise required to produce the finest athletes.*

When you are physically or mentally exhausted, your mind may be tempted to daydream or to wander to other places. It is amazing how the mind tries to escape from reality. But rather than let yourself float away on a cloud of fantasy that doesn't help you fulfill your God-given assignment, ask the Holy Spirit to help you see things realistically. That's the only way you'll be able to put your whole heart and soul into completing your task exactly as Jesus wants it done! You *can* do great things for God's Kingdom, but it will require both concentration and commitment!

MY PRAYER FOR TODAY

Lord, help me to stay focused on what You have called me to do and to embrace everything that comes with Your call on my life. Forgive me for the times I've tried to find a shortcut to avoid responsibility. I want to put my whole heart into the race You have set before me — to fulfill my assigned task fervently, passionately, and with the highest level of excellence.

I pray this in Jesus' name!

MY CONFESSION FOR TODAY

I confess that I am both faith-filled and realistic about what God has called me to do. I realize that it's going to take hard work and commitment to take this assignment to the high level that God expects of me. I refuse to shrink from my responsibilities, and I choose to put my whole heart and soul into the task Jesus has given to me.

I declare this by faith in Jesus' name!

QUESTIONS FOR YOU TO CONSIDER

1. Have you been trying to mentally escape from the responsibilities of your life? Have you been living in a fantasy that things are going to change without any effort?
2. What do you need to do to bring concrete change to the challenges you are facing in your life? What steps can you start taking today — right now — to start turning things around for the better?
3. Have you considered asking a close friend to help you focus on the things you need to be doing to get things moving in the right direction in your life? Who is a friend you could depend on to encourage you to take the right steps toward needed change?

If you are mightily anointed by God, it is simply a fact that your schedule will get busier, your demands will increase, and your challenges will grow. But as long as you allow God to develop your character along the way, you will find that you're able to successfully manage anything He puts on your plate!

NOVEMBER 5

❧❦❧

Never Go to Bed Angry!

...Let not the sun go down upon your wrath:
Neither give place to the devil.
— Ephesians 4:26,27

Have you ever gone to bed sizzling with anger about what someone did or didn't do or about what someone said or didn't say? If you think about it, you'll realize that this last phrase pretty well summarizes the primary reasons people get offended, insulted, irritated, or upset. Isn't it true that people's various responses or lack of responses in a given situation can send you to bed fuming if you allow yourself to take offense and get all worked up?

I have to admit that I've gone to bed angry on more than one occasion. *How about you?* Have you ever tossed and turned this way and that way, unable to sleep, because you were aggravated about something that happened? Did you become more and more angry the longer you thought about that issue?

Ephesians 4:26,27 warns us, "...Let not the sun go down upon your wrath: Neither give place to the devil." The word "wrath" is the Greek word *parorgismos*, a compound of the words *para* and *orgidzo*. The word *para* means *alongside*, as in something that is *very close* to you. The word *orgidzo* is the Greek word for *wrath*, which depicts *someone whose mood is so upset that he becomes completely bent out of shape over some issue*.

When *orgidzo* ("wrath") is operating in an individual, it often starts as silent resentment. That resentment slowly builds up inside the person, becoming stronger and stronger until one day, it finally explodes in rage! And because the resentment has simmered silently for so long, the outburst of explosive wrath is usually way out of proportion to the situation that caused the anger in the first place.

But when these two words are joined together, forming the word *parorgismos*, it presents the image of *a person who brings anger to his side and then embraces it*. Instead of rejecting anger or pushing it away when it shows up, this person draws anger to himself and then nurses it, nourishes it, feeds it, and holds it close. The aggravating issue gets "under his skin" and soon becomes so entrenched in him that it becomes his constant companion and partner. He takes the offense with him wherever he goes — and that includes taking it to bed with him!

When a person goes to bed sizzling over something that has inwardly angered him, the entire night becomes an opportunity for the devil to work inside his mind and emotions. As soon as the person's head hits the pillow, the devil begins to bombard his mind to prevent him from sleeping and to stir up his anger even more.

Remember, the name "devil" is the Greek word *diabalos*. This word *diabalos* is derived from two Greek words: *dia*, which means *through*, as when referring to *penetrating something all the way through*; and *balos*, which means *to throw*. When these words are put together to form the word *diabalos*, it paints a vivid picture of the devil as *one who repetitiously throws accusations at the mind — striking again and again until he ultimately penetrates the mind with his slanderous lies and relationship-destroying insinuations*.

But the devil likes to look for the most advantageous times to strike your mind with his lies — and one of his favorite times to do this is when you go to bed at night. That is why Paul urges you, "...Let not the sun go down upon your wrath: Neither give place to the devil."

The word "place" is the Greek word *topos*, a Greek word that describes *a specific place*, like a real geographical place on a map. The word *topos* is where we get the term for a *topographical map*. This is very important, for it tells us that the devil is seeking a specific place, an entry point, through which he can enter our minds and emotions to stir up trouble and affect our relationships.

So don't go to bed angry and let your mind become a movie screen on which the devil can portray every foul thing he wants you to meditate on all night long. That only allows the enemy to steal your peace and infuriate you even further. Why not instead deal with that anger or unforgiveness before your head ever hits the pillow? Do everything you can to stay free of anger, wrath, and strife, for these fleshly emotions are the entry points the devil uses to wage war in your mind.

If you find that you can't deal with this problem by yourself, talk to your spouse or call a friend and ask that person if you can talk and share something that has been weighing heavily on your heart. Ask him or her to listen to you and to help you see things in a better light. You may be surprised to find that a different set of eyes sees the situation very differently than you do. And as you listen to a different side of the story, it may even help you release the offense that angered you so you can put the entire issue to rest forever.

But whether or not you decide to talk to a friend about the matter, one thing is for sure: *If something or someone has upset or offended you, you will only make matters much worse if you let yourself go to bed angry!*

MY PRAYER FOR TODAY

Lord, I am sorry for the times I've allowed my anger to rise up and take control of me. I realize that I have no excuse, for the Spirit of God inside me is present to restrain me and to produce the fruit of the Spirit in me. I now see that I have opened the door to the devil in the past by allowing wrong attitudes to be pervasive in my life. I want to shut the door to the devil so he can no longer find access to me, to my family, to my business, to my church, or to any part of my life. To shut that door tight, I am asking You to help me remove uncontrolled anger from my life!

I pray this in Jesus' name!

MY CONFESSION FOR TODAY

I confess that the Holy Spirit is producing His fruit in me and my character. I am filled with the mind of Christ; therefore, anger and temperamental outbursts have no place in me. I am self-controlled, patient, and kind. When others do or say something to me that is wrong or unjust, I respond in the spirit of Jesus Christ. I refuse to allow offense to gain a foothold in my mind. I am determined to keep the door shut so the devil can no longer gain access to my life!

I declare this by faith in Jesus' name!

QUESTIONS FOR YOU TO CONSIDER

1. Have you ever noticed that bad things happen when you get upset or lose your temper? It would be worth your time to seriously ponder this question today.
2. Can you think of five times in your life when something bad happened as you were allowing anger and strife to get the best of you?

3. What steps should you take to make sure your anger doesn't continue opening a door for the devil to send his attacks into your life?

NOVEMBER 6

Confront, Forgive, and Forget

...If thy brother trespass against thee,
rebuke him; and if he repent, forgive him.
— Luke 17:3

*I*t is difficult for most people to confront someone else regarding an offense, but sometimes confrontation is necessary. Ignoring confrontation is often what causes bad feelings to turn inward and fester into something much worse. Those ugly feelings can sit in the pit of a person's stomach, churning away until he becomes so upset that he can hardly see straight.

Usually it's better to kindly say what you feel and get over it than to let those raw emotions turn into an ugly monster, just waiting to crawl out at an opportune moment and attack its victim. That is frequently what happens when you allow ugly emotions to go unchecked. Confrontation may be uncomfortable, but it's a lot less painful than having to apologize later for erupting in a fit of flesh like a volcano that spews destructive lava all over its surroundings.

This is exactly why Jesus said, "...If thy brother trespass against thee, rebuke him; and if he repent, forgive him" (Luke 17:3). The word "trespass" is the Greek word *hamartano*, which means *to violate a rule; to cross a line; to commit a grievance;* or *to miss the mark*. By using this word, the Bible teaches you what to do when someone has violated you, crossed a line he shouldn't have crossed, committed what you perceive to be a grievance against you, or seriously missed the mark of what you expected of that person: *You are to "rebuke" that person for what he did.*

The word "rebuke" is the Greek word *epitimao*, which in this case means *to speak frankly, honestly, and politely as you tell a person how you feel that he has wronged you.* This doesn't mean you have to speak to him like he's a devil; it just means you need to directly and honestly confront him.

This issue of honesty is a big one in the Body of Christ. Many believers are dishonest about what they really think and feel. Inside they seethe with anger toward someone about a perceived offense. Yet on the outside, they smile and pretend as if everything is all right. This dishonesty divides believers and keeps God's power from freely flowing between members of the Body of Christ.

Believers put themselves on dangerous territory when they harbor hidden disagreements or secret petty grievances against other people, yet go around smiling and acting as if everything is all right. They're not just being dishonest — they're engaging in outright lying and deception!

When you refuse to confront an offense, you are just as wrong as the one who violated your rights and stepped over the line. Jesus said, "...If thy brother trespass against thee, rebuke him..." (Luke 17:3). That means if you are going to be mature in your relationships, you must learn how to confront others when you feel they have wronged you. It may be difficult to do that, but it's a lot less painful and leaves less scars than does a soul that is filled with bitterness and resentment.

When you have to confront someone regarding an offense that you perceive he has committed against you, I recommend that you take the following three steps:

<u>STEP #1:</u>

Don't confront anyone until you've first made it a matter of prayer.

Prayer resolves a lot of problems by itself. There have been times in my own life when I've been upset with someone, only to discover after getting into the Presence of God and praying about the matter that my own attitude was uglier than the actions of the one who wronged me. Once I recognized my own sinful condition, I couldn't hold a thing against the other person anymore; I just wanted to get my own heart right before God.

Prayer will put you in a position where God can speak to your own heart. After praying, if you still sense that you are supposed to confront the other person, make sure you pray for that person first. The Spirit of God may give you a strategy regarding what to say, as well as when and how to say it.

Believe me, taking directions from the Holy Spirit about how to confront someone will only help you. Confrontation without prayer is like barging into the middle of the fray with no preparation. Therefore, let prayer be a time of spiritual fine-tuning as you prepare to do what you need to do.

As you pray, spend a few minutes thanking God for your offender. This will help bring you to a new level so you can deal with the issue at hand in the right spirit. Remember the good things that person has done. Take time to reflect on all the enjoyable moments you've had with him and all the benefits you've gained in life as a result of that relationship. It's difficult to remain angry at someone when you are thanking God for him at the same time!

<u>STEP #2:</u>

Don't confront anyone with a judgmental attitude.

We've all made mistakes — and that includes you! So assume that your offender would not deliberately hurt or offend you. Take a positive position about the other person.

When you do finally sit down to talk with the person who offended you, start the conversation by assuring him that you know he didn't intend to do what he did. Tell him that somehow the devil got into the middle of your relationship with him through his actions — and now you want to get the devil back out of the relationship as you get your heart right with him. This immediately removes any sense of an accusatory spirit and puts the spotlight on the devil instead of on that person. The issues will still be dealt with, but from a different perspective.

Starting from this approach is much more beneficial than taking a defensive approach that treats the other person as if he were your adversary. Remember, that person is not your enemy; he isn't on the other side of the line, fighting a battle against you. Your relationship may be going through some rough times right now, but you still need to view the two of you as being on the same side. The purpose of this time of confrontation is not to prove how wrong the other person is; it is to learn how to work together better and how to keep the channel of communication open and in the light.

<u>STEP #3:</u>

Remember that you, too, have been offensive in the past.

Never forget that you've probably offended people in the past. You didn't intend to do it. You didn't even know you did it until the person later told you. You were probably embarrassed or sad when you heard how the devil had used some statement you innocently made to leave a wrong impression.

When you were in this type of situation, didn't you want the person you had offended to tell you the truth rather than to walk around harboring bad feelings about you? Weren't you glad when that lie of the devil was exposed and your relationship was made right again? Weren't you thankful for the opportunity to make things right with that other person?

So when someone offends you, remember that you've stood in his shoes in the past. Were you forgiven at that time? Were you shown mercy? Now it's time for you to show the same forgiveness and mercy to someone else that has previously been shown to you.

If you still feel the need to confront the person who offended you after following these three steps, you should now be able to do it with the right attitude. You have prayed about the matter; you have been in the Presence of the Lord. Now your heart is free, liberated from negative feelings and attitudes toward that person. You are finally in a position to go to him or her in a spirit of love and reconciliation instead of in a spirit of accusation. As Jesus said, "...if he repent, forgive him" (Luke 17:3).

The word "forgive" is the Greek word *aphiemi*. It means *to set free; to let go; to release; to discharge;* or *to liberate completely.* It was used in a secular sense in New Testament times in reference to canceling a debt or releasing someone from the obligation of a contract, a commitment, or promise. Thus, it means *to forfeit any right to hold a person captive to a previous commitment or wrong he has committed.* In essence, the word "forgive" — the Greek word *aphiemi* — is the picture of totally freeing and releasing someone. A modern paraphrase of this Greek word would simply be *to let it go!*

This means you and I don't have the privilege of holding people hostage to their past actions if they repent and ask us to forgive them. If they sincerely seek forgiveness for offending us, we are obligated to "let it go." If your offender repents and sincerely asks for forgiveness, Jesus said you are to put away the offense and no longer hold on to it. You must release those ugly feelings you've held against that person. You have to let it go!

- ✦ *So are you able to let go of the offense that someone has committed against you?*
- ✦ *Are you able to put away that offense once and for all instead of dragging it up again and again?*

Just as God has removed your sin as far as the east is from the west (Psalm 103:12), you must now decide that this person is freed in regard to that past offense. Once you forgive him, you cannot drag up the offense again and again. You have released and liberated him completely from that sin. Therefore, you never have the right or privilege to pull out that offense later and use it against him. *It is gone!*

MY PRAYER FOR TODAY

Lord, please help me have the courage to lovingly speak to those who have sinned against me. Help me know how to tell them what they did wrong and kindly ask them not to do it again. If they repent and say they are sorry, please help me forgive them for what they did and then release them completely from that grievance, never to bring it up again. Help me put that offense out of my mind forever, just as You have done so many times for me!

I pray this in Jesus' name!

MY CONFESSION FOR TODAY

I confess that I am courageous, bold, and loving in the way I confront people who have sinned against me. I do not hold bitterness inside my heart; instead, I politely speak to those who have wronged me so my heart can stay free and they can learn from the experience. God's Spirit is changing me and helping me to speak to my offenders from a gracious, helpful spirit, rather than from a spirit that is bitter and critical. Therefore, the end result of each difficult situation is reconciliation and peace instead of division and discord!

I declare this by faith in Jesus' name!

QUESTIONS FOR YOU TO CONSIDER

1. Can you think of a time when someone truly forgave you for something wrong you did to him or her? When that person forgave you, what effect did this genuine forgiveness have on your life?
2. Are you able to forgive others as you have been forgiven, or do you find that you keep reaching into the past to try to drag up those past issues again and again?
3. Who is it that you need to confront and forgive right now? Why not spend some time in prayer and get the heart of God for this situation so you can go to that person in the spirit of Jesus and make things right in your relationship with him or her?

NOVEMBER 7

Partners in the Gospel Of Jesus Christ

Always in every prayer of mine for you all
making request with joy, for your fellowship in the gospel
from the first day until now.
— Philippians 1:4,5

When I think of all the people who have financially supported our ministry throughout these many years that we've been serving in the former Soviet Union, it fills my heart with gratitude to God for putting such wonderful and faithful people in our lives. Without them, we would not be able to do the front-line, cutting-edge, frontier-type work that God has assigned to us.

In fact, a day never passes that I don't dedicate time to pray for and to specially thank God for those who support us with their prayers and offerings. You see, they are our partners in this work of God. We don't use this term lightly; we truly mean it when we say that these friends and supporters of our work are our ministry *partners*.

You see, Denise and I are aware that:

✦ It is *our partners'* money that pays for the large evangelistic crusades we hold in various locations in this part of the world, where thousands of people come to Christ and the local churches grow and are strengthened.

✦ It is *our partners'* money that enables us to purchase television equipment and to pay for broadcast time on television — an outreach that sends the Good News into millions of homes in nations where the Gospel is only now beginning to penetrate.

✦ It is *our partners'* money that has enabled us to preach the Gospel through television to the several million people who have come to know Jesus Christ as a direct result of our television broadcasts. That means millions of people will go to Heaven because of broadcasts that our partners paid for with their gifts and offerings.

✦ It is *our partners'* contributions that consistently help us print massive quantities of books and literature, which we then distribute to people who respond to Christ through television, through crusades, and through our other various outreaches in this part of the world.

✦ It is *our partners'* gifts that assist us as we establish and strengthen churches in hundreds of locations across the eleven time zones of the former USSR. Without their gifts, we wouldn't be able to do this vital church-establishing work that is having such a great and eternal impact.

✦ It is *our partners'* faith-sown gifts that make it possible for us to help the poor, the needy, the homeless, and the orphans who live in this part of the world.

My wife and I understand that although we are the ones God has anointed to lead this work, we couldn't do any of it without the financial support our partners send to our ministry every month. It is *their* gifts that make it possible for us to accomplish all that God has called us to do.

Every time I pray for our partners, the law of sowing and reaping, found in Galatians 6:7, is the foundation of my petitions for them. I ask God to bring a rich harvest back into the lives of those who have sown financially by faith into this precious work of God. I desire and expect them to be blessed because of the acts of generosity they have shown toward the work of God.

This must be how the apostle Paul felt about those who financially supported his ministry. The church of Philippi was among his most faithful supporters. That is why he told them in Philippians 1:4 and 5, "Always in every prayer of mine for you all making request with joy, for your fellowship in the gospel from the first day until now."

By using the word "always," Paul lets us know how frequently he prayed for his partners. In Greek, it is the word *pantote*, which means *always, at all times,* or *constantly.* This lets us know that praying for his partners was a regular occurrence in Paul's daily life — something he did habitually. Paul understood what my wife and I are also well aware of — that his partners' role in his ministry was just as important as his role. Therefore, Paul made his responsibility to pray for them a very high priority in his life.

The word "prayer" is the Greek word *deisis.* This word describes *a heartfelt request for God to answer a concrete, specific need* — usually some type of physical or material need. The church of Philippi was suffering financially at this time. Considering how they gave of their finances despite their own financial struggles, it makes sense that Paul prayed earnestly for God to answer and meet the concrete, physical needs of this sacrificially giving church.

When Paul says he is "making request," the Greek tense carries the idea of Paul continuously making requests for the Philippian believers. This is definitely not a one-shot, occasional prayer; rather, Paul makes it very clear that praying for these believers is a part of his daily pattern. The word "request" is again the word *deisis,* now used twice in this verse, which categorically substantiates that Paul was asking God to answer and provide for the physical, tangible needs of this church. And notice that Paul said he made these requests "with joy." It was no burden for him to pray for his partners; he did it with pleasure and joy.

In Philippians 1:5, Paul explains the reason he feels so passionate about these believers who had so faithfully supported his ministry. He says, "For your fellowship in the gospel from the first day until now." The word "fellowship" is the Greek word *koinonia*, a word that depicted *partnership* or *a mutual participation in some project or event* and often referred to *a partner, a sharer,* or *a companion.*

Paul felt about his supporters the same way my wife and I feel about our supporters — that they are *partners.* By supporting the ministry with their finances and prayers, these partners actually enter into the work of the ministry and mutually work side-by-side with those on the front lines.

Paul had told the Corinthians, "Now he that planteth and he that watereth are one..." (1 Corinthians 3:8). The word "one" is the Greek word *hen,* which in this context means *one in purpose, one in aim,* or *one in terms of being on the same team and having the same goal.*

You see, Paul had a revelation that every person is essential in accomplishing the work of God. He knew that those who water the work with their prayers and finances are just as important as those who do the actual work of tilling the soil and planting the seeds. If the first group tries to do their job without the assistance of the other group, failure will be the inevitable result. On the other hand, if both work together as a team, appreciating and valuing each other's role in achieving their common purpose, the result will be a great harvest.

So when Paul wrote to the Philippians and spoke of their "partnership" in the Gospel, he truly did mean that they were his partners. He was doing his part and they were doing theirs — and together they made a great team that was having an eternal impact. One part of that team wasn't more worthy of honor than the other part. Everyone was on the same team, moving toward the same goal; they were simply fulfilling different roles to get the job done. Paul was a planter, and those who gave of their finances were the waterers. Both were essential to the success of the work.

And notice that the Philippians had been partners with Paul's ministry "...from the first day until now." They had been with him for a very long time. Through the years, people had come and people had gone in Paul's life; those who stayed with him through every circumstance and challenge were precious and rare. Paul was keenly aware of how special it was that the church of Philippi had not only supported him from the very beginning, but were also still standing with him as his partners in the work of the Lord!

Philippians 1:4,5 could be interpreted to read:

"I am always praying for you. In every one of my prayers, I am asking God to meet the tangible and physical needs in your lives. And I want you to know that praying for you is one of the greatest joys of my life. Why, you've been my partner in the work of the Gospel from the very start, and you're still with me now. Because of that, praying for you is a very special joy for me."

Never let the devil tell you that your partnership with a Gospel ministry isn't important. Think of what would happen if everyone simultaneously stopped giving! Preachers would be like automobiles with no gas in the tank. Although equipped to go with a vision burning in their hearts, they would be unable to do their work and fulfill that vision because of their "empty tanks."

The gifts you sow into a ministry "put gas in the tank" so the work of the ministry can go forward! Thus, it isn't just the minister's work but your work as well. One plants, another waters, and God gives the increase.

I want to thank you for what you do for God's work. Your partnership in the Gospel is not a light matter. It is one of the most significant things you can do in this life. When you stand before

Jesus and see all the people who are in Heaven because of the gifts you sowed, that is the golden moment when you'll *really* understand the power of every single gift you ever gave for the advancement of the Gospel of Jesus Christ!

MY PRAYER FOR TODAY

Lord, I thank You for allowing me to be a participant in the Gospel by sowing my finances every month into ministries that are touching the world. Help me to always be aware of the great impact my gifts have and to never let the devil make me think that what I do is unimportant. My gifts and prayers help "put gas in the tanks" of these ministries so they can take the Gospel forward. I want to give faithfully to these works, Lord. Therefore, I ask You to increase me financially so I can give even more! I want to partner with them to take the Gospel to the ends of the earth and to help fill Heaven with the souls of those for whom Jesus died.

I pray this in Jesus' name!

MY CONFESSION FOR TODAY

I confess that I am a faithful supporter of the work of God. I give regularly, consistently, and passionately to see the Gospel go forward around the world. My gifts are important. What I sow really does make a difference. Because of this, I am faithful to do my part, and God will reward me both here and in eternity for the financial seed I've sown to help further His Kingdom around the world.

I declare this by faith in Jesus' name!

QUESTIONS FOR YOU TO CONSIDER

1. What ministries or outreaches do you regularly and faithfully support with your finances?
2. How did the Holy Spirit lead you to support these particular works?
3. Do you pray for these ministries as well as give of your finances?

Never let the devil tell you that your partnership with a ministry isn't important. Think of what would happen if everyone simultaneously stopped giving! Preachers would be like automobiles with no gas in the tank. Although equipped to go with a vision burning in their hearts, they would be unable to do their work and fulfill that vision because of their "empty tanks." The gifts you sow into a ministry "put gas in the tank" so the work of the ministry can go forward!

NOVEMBER 8

❧❧❧

Grace, Mercy, and Peace

Unto Timothy, my own son in the faith:
Grace, mercy, and peace....
— 1 Timothy 1:2

*I*f you've ever felt like problems were mounting and growing all around you and you didn't have enough strength to make it another step, then I have some very good news for you! Today you're going to discover that God extends a very special measure of mercy to people who feel like they are being swamped by the affairs of life. Stay with me, because what you're about to read is exactly what you need to start your day!

In all of the apostle Paul's epistles, he begins by greeting his readers with "grace" and "peace." The exact wording from letter to letter may vary, but each of these epistles begin with some variation of a greeting that involves the words "grace" and "peace." (*See* Romans 1:7; 1 Corinthians 1:3; 2 Corinthians 1:2; Galatians 1:3; Ephesians 1:2; Philippians 1:2; Colossians 1:2; 1 Thessalonians 1:1; 2 Thessalonians 1:2; and Philemon 1:3).

Why did Paul so often use these two words in his greetings when he wrote his epistles? The answer is very simple. Because he was an apostle to the Gentiles or the Greek-speaking world, it was necessary for him to greet his foremost readers in a customary Greek manner. During New Testament times, the salutation of "grace" was the customary greeting exchanged between Greeks when they approached each other. Just as we would say, "Hello, how are you doing?" as a polite way of greeting someone we meet, the Greeks would say, "Grace!" when greeting one another.

This word "grace" is the Greek word *charis*, which means *grace* but also carries the idea of *favor*. So when a person greeted someone with this salutation, it was the equivalent of his saying, "I greet you with grace and favor."

But Paul wasn't only addressing the Greek world. As a Jew himself, he also wanted to greet the Jewish world that would be reading his epistles. When the Jews met each other, their customary way of greeting one another was to say, "Shalom!" In fact, this is still the customary greeting exchanged between Jews in Israel today. The Greek equivalent for the Hebrew word *shalom* is the word *eirene*, which is the word for *peace*.

By using both of these two greetings at the beginning of his epistles, Paul brilliantly reached out and embraced both the Greek and the Jewish world at the outset of his writings. One scholar has said that by using both the terms "grace" and "peace," the doors were thrown open for the whole world to read his letters. It is obvious that Paul deliberately addressed those letters to both the Gentile and Jewish world.

Because of the meaning of the words *charis* and *eirene*
and how these words were used as a form of greeting,
it is as though Paul was saying:

"To those of you who are Greeks, I greet you with grace and favor, and to those of you who are Jews, I greet you with peace and shalom."

When Paul wrote the books of First Timothy, Second Timothy, and Titus, he inserted the word "mercy" between the words "grace" and "peace" in his greeting, making the salutation read "grace, *mercy*, and peace from God our Father." In all three of these epistles, he was not writing to an entire congregation; rather, these letters were private letters intended to be read only by Timothy and Titus.

Why did Paul alter his traditional greeting to include the word "mercy" when he wrote these personal letters? Well, in all three of these letters, Paul was writing to someone in the ministry who felt overwhelmed by the affairs of life. For instance, when he wrote his first letter to Timothy (the book of First Timothy), Timothy was feeling overwhelmed by the phenomenal growth in the church under his care. Such growth is every pastor's dream; however, Timothy was young, and he was pastoring what had become the world's largest church. This was therefore a very challenging time in Timothy's life.

Timothy was feeling so challenged that he apparently wrote a letter to Paul, asking him for advice on how to choose leaders for his fast-growing congregation. As the young minister faced this daunting task, he needed to be reminded that there was special "mercy" available to help him in his time of need. Thus, when Paul wrote to Timothy, he inserted the word "mercy" between the traditional greeting of "grace" and "peace." He said, "Unto Timothy, my own son in the faith: Grace, *mercy*, and peace…" (1 Timothy 1:2).

Several years after Paul wrote that first letter to Timothy, the political environment in the Roman Empire radically changed and public opinion turned violently against believers. Just as the Church had grown quickly before this change occurred, it now began to quickly diminish as believers were captured, imprisoned, enslaved, and killed. Many believers also defected from the Christian faith and went back to their old pagan temples in order to comply with the wishes of the government and to save themselves from death.

The tragedy occurring inside Timothy's church was devastating. The size of his prized congregation was declining daily right before his eyes. His heart was broken as he watched leaders defecting and going back to their old ways in order to escape death — trusted team members who Timothy had thought would be faithful to the very end.

Apparently Timothy had written a letter to Paul, expressing his fears and hurts about the crisis he faced, so Paul wrote him back. That second letter to Timothy (the book of Second Timothy) is Paul's response to Timothy and to the predicament that surrounded the younger minister on every side. Writing Timothy to encourage him to be strong in the Lord, Paul began his second letter by once more inserting the word "mercy" between the words "grace" and peace." He said, "To Timothy, my dearly beloved son: Grace, *mercy*, and peace…" (2 Timothy 1:2).

The third time Paul inserted the word "mercy" between his traditional greetings of "grace" and "peace" was in his letter to Titus. As with Timothy, Titus found himself in a very difficult circumstance. After Paul started the church on the island of Crete, he left before the church was completely established and before leaders were firmly set in place. Paul left Titus to finish the job he didn't complete in Crete, instructing him to make the final selection of church leaders and then to establish them in their positions.

The people who lived on Crete at that time were famous for being lazy gluttons and liars. They were a devious, mischievous people who were very difficult to trust. Even more, Crete was known to be a repository for criminals and barbaric-like people. Paul wrote to Titus and told him, "For this cause left I thee in Crete, that thou shouldest set in order the things that are wanting…" (Titus 1:5). This would have been a monstrous task for even the most seasoned leader, and it loomed before Titus as a huge and daunting assignment.

The circumstances Titus faced were so immense that when Paul wrote to him, he said, "To Titus, mine own son after the common faith: Grace, *mercy*, and peace..."(Titus 1:4). It wasn't enough for Titus to hear about grace and peace — he also needed to be reminded that there was special mercy available to help him in his situation.

In all three of these cases, the readers were facing serious situations and needed to be reminded that God's mercy was extended to help them bravely face and overcome their challenges.

You may need to be reminded of the same thing today. If you are facing a situation that would normally be devastating or overwhelming to you, grab hold of this good news: God has made a special measure of His "mercy" available to you! Don't try to face the ordeal in your own strength until you end up feeling swamped and overwhelmed; instead, realize that God's mercy is available to meet you right where you are. If you'll open your heart to receive from God, He will tuck a special measure of mercy between the grace and peace He is offering you today. *So why don't you allow God's mercy to assist you with the challenges you are facing at this very moment?*

MY PRAYER FOR TODAY

Lord, I thank You for making special mercy available to help me in times of struggle and hardship. I admit that I often try to handle all my challenges on my own, but I know it is impossible for me to overcome my obstacles without the help of Your mercy. So today I am opening my heart and asking You to extend a special measure of mercy to assist me through this challenging time in my life. I thank You in advance for pouring this mercy upon me, and by faith, I receive it right now.

I pray this in Jesus' name!

MY CONFESSION FOR TODAY

I confess that God's mercy is working in me! God promises mercy to me, and I receive it by faith. That mercy empowers me to overcome my negative emotions, my struggles, and all the obstacles the devil has tried to set before me. Because God's mercy is working in me, I am well able to rise above the struggles I face and to overcome them victoriously!

I declare this by faith in Jesus' name!

QUESTIONS FOR YOU TO CONSIDER

1. Can you think of a time when you were suddenly invigorated by a supernatural flow of divine mercy that surged into you and gave you the strength and courage you needed to face and overcome a difficult situation?

2. When you became aware of that special mercy, how did it affect both your attitude and the situation you were facing?

3. If you are specially challenged by a situation in your life right now, why not take a few minutes today to ask God to give you a special measure of mercy to help?

God has made a special measure of His mercy available to you!

November 9

ଓଡ଼୧ଵ

What Was Paul's Thorn in the Flesh?

And lest I should be exalted above measure
through the abundance of the revelations, there was given to me a thorn
in the flesh, the messenger of Satan to buffet me,
lest I should be exalted above measure.
— 2 Corinthians 12:7

*I*n Second Corinthians 12:7, the apostle Paul writes that he had been given a "thorn in the flesh" because of "the abundance of the revelations" he had received. Today I want us to delve into this verse to discover the identity of this thorn in the flesh and where it came from. Did it come from God, as some assert, or was this thorn personally sent from Satan to impede Paul from making an even greater impact with his ministry?

Let's begin looking for the answer to this question by carefully examining Paul's words in Second Corinthians 12:7. He writes, "And lest I should be exalted above measure through the abundance of the revelations...."

The words "exalted above measure" are taken from the Greek word *huperairo*, a compound of the words *huper* and *airo*. The word *huper* means *over, above, and beyond*. It depicts *something that is way beyond measure* and conveys the idea of *something that is greater, superior, higher, better, more than a match for, utmost, paramount, or foremost*. It could also describe *something that is first-rate, first-class, top-notch, unsurpassed, unequaled, and unrivaled by any person or thing*. The second part of the word *huperairo* ("exalted above measure") means *to lift up, to raise*, or *to be exalted*.

When these two Greek words are compounded to form the word *huperairo*, it speaks of *a person who has been supremely exalted*. This is *a person who has been magnified, increased, and lifted up to a place of great prestige and influence*. Although *huperairo* could be used to express the idea of a person who has haughtily exalted himself, this is not the idea Paul has in mind when he writes this verse. Rather, this is a person who has been greatly honored and recognized due to something he has written, done, or achieved.

Notice that Paul refers to the "abundance of the revelations" that God had given to him. The word "abundance" is the Greek word *huperballo*, a compound of the word *huper*, described above, and the word *ballo*, which means *to cast* or *to throw*. But when these two words are compounded to form the word *huperballo*, it describes *something that is phenomenal, extraordinary, unparalleled, or unmatched*. It is the picture of an archer who aims for the bull's eye; but when he releases the string and shoots his arrow, he watches as his arrow flies way over the top of the target. Now Paul uses this word to explain that the revelations he had received were not only *unparalleled in quality*, but the vast number of them were *far beyond* what anyone else had ever received.

The word "revelations" is from the Greek word *apokalupsis*. It refers to *something that has been veiled or hidden for a long time and then suddenly, almost instantaneously, becomes clear and visible to the mind or eye*. It is like pulling the curtains out of the way so you can see what has always been just outside your window. The scene was always there for you to enjoy, but the curtains blocked your ability to see the real picture. But when the curtains are drawn apart, you can suddenly see what has been hidden from your view. The moment you see beyond the curtain for the first time and observe what has been there all along but not evident to you — *that* is what the Bible calls a "revelation."

From Paul's words in Second Corinthians 12:7, we know that the curtain had been pulled apart and Paul had seen into the spirit realm on many occasions. He'd had an "abundance" of these experiences. It was this "abundance of the revelations" that Paul was preaching as he traversed the regions surrounding the Mediterranean Sea. Everywhere he went, he preached what had been divinely revealed to him. As he preached, his power, authority, and fame grew greater and greater. As his authority grew, so did his ability to impact the world with the Gospel of Jesus Christ. Due to these revelations and his boldness to preach them, Paul was unquestionably becoming one of the most influential men of his day.

Now Paul lets us know that Satan was alarmed by the great progress the apostle was making with the Gospel; therefore, the enemy launched an full-scale attack to impede that progress. Satan didn't want Paul to be recognized or magnified to a greater extent than he already was. Instead, the devil wanted to pull down this man of God — to ruin him, to destroy him, and to discredit the message he preached. Since there was no moral flaw in Paul that Satan could use to destroy him, he inflicted Paul with a "thorn in the flesh."

The word "thorn" is the Greek word *skolops*, a word used to describe *a dangerously sharp, spiked instrument or tool*. However, this word was also used to describe *the stake on which an enemy's head was stuck after being decapitated*.

The word *skolops* gives the impression that this thorn was excruciatingly painful. Some have suggested that the words "in the flesh" refer to a physical sickness, but this is not affirmed by any scripture in the New Testament and should be taken as unsubstantiated conjecture. People have gone so far in their imaginations as to assert that Paul suffered from malaria, epilepsy, eye disease, club feet, or a hunched back. There is nothing in any New Testament scripture to back up such speculations!

One thing *is* clear, however: Satan wanted Paul's head on a stake! He wanted to eliminate this man of God and put him completely out of the picture. Instead of referring to sickness, the words "in the flesh" most likely describe a type of event that was a constant source of irritation to the apostle Paul. This event caused him personal distress and kept reoccurring over and over again. For this reason, he referred to it as a "thorn in the flesh."

Some argue that God sent this thorn in the flesh to keep Paul from being prideful about his many revelations. But there is no reason to debate this issue, for Paul plainly wrote that it was a "…messenger of *Satan* to buffet me…." The word "messenger" is the Greek word *angelos*, a word that can describe *an angel; one who is sent on a special mission;* or *a messenger who is dispatched to perform a specific assignment*. This "messenger of Satan," perhaps a demonic angel, was sent directly from Satan himself to buffet Paul and to restrict the progress of his ministry.

This thorn in the flesh categorically did *not* come from God; otherwise, Paul would have called it a "messenger of God." Paul himself plainly states that this thorn in the flesh was given to him by a "messenger of Satan" — a special force that had been dispatched to keep Paul from gaining additional status and prestige and to prevent him from taking the Gospel further and higher into the world scene.

Look at the facts: Paul was preaching to kings, governors, and world leaders. He was establishing churches, writing New Testament scriptures, and pushing back the forces of hell. His personal influence was growing, and his impact was increasing day by day. The revelations that God had given him were about to change the course of human history. Fearing that Paul's influence would grow too great, Satan strategically sent forces who had been instructed to create disturbances to "buffet" the apostle.

The word "buffet" is the Greek word *kolaphidzo*, a Greek word that comes from the word *kolaphos*, a word that describes *the fist* or *knuckles*. When it becomes the word *kolaphidzo*, as Paul uses it in Second Corinthians 12:7, it refers to *beatings with the fist*. The Greek tense describes *unending, unrelenting, continuous, repetitious beatings*. This means Paul is not telling us of a single event, but of a series of many events. This word *kolaphidzo* ("buffet") gives us our greatest insight into the "thorn in the flesh" Paul is writing about in this verse.

As noted earlier (*see* October 17-30), Paul endured many afflictions during his ministry. Many of the afflictions he faced were due to the religious leaders who so fiercely opposed him. These religious leaders included Jewish leaders who hated him and his message. They also included false brethren who were constantly trying to displace his position of authority in the local churches. Paul was resisted outside the church by leaders of the Jewish faith who hated him. He was also opposed from within the church by those who wanted him out of the picture so they could take his place of prominence.

Thus, the biggest "thorn" in Paul's life was the fact that he had to deal with these different groups of people who covertly planned the problems and hassles he frequently faced in the ministry. A special messenger from Satan, perhaps even a demonic angel, had been sent to incite these people against Paul.

If you survey the types of ordeals Paul endured, you will see that many of them were orchestrated by these people who wanted to get rid of him. They were so teeming with hatred toward Paul that they wanted to see his head on a stake! These people were the primary source of Paul's problems and distractions he faced in his life and ministry.

One type of attack Paul experienced at his opponents' hands were many physical "beatings," which explains his use of the word *kolaphidzo* ("buffet") in this verse. However, Paul was also constantly buffeted, harassed, hassled, and distracted by the negative activities of these people. As a result, he was hindered from focusing on what God had called him to do because of the great amount of time he had to spend defending his apostleship and answering the charges of those who were stirring up trouble against him. These opponents really were a thorn in the flesh for Paul. Their actions were a constant irritant that he had to deal with on an almost daily basis.

In light of these Greek words,
consider this fresh interpretation
of Paul's words in Second Corinthians 12:7:

"Because of the phenomenal revelations I have received and on account of the vast number of these revelations that God has entrusted to me — and to hinder the highly visible progress I am making in the Lord's cause — a special messenger has been sent from Satan to harass me with constant distractions and headaches. There's no doubt about it! Those whom Satan has stirred up against me want my head on a stake! Satan is using these people to constantly buffet and distract me in an attempt to keep me from reaching a higher level of visibility and recognition and to sidetrack me from preaching my revelations."

You see, Paul's thorn in the flesh wasn't sickness or epilepsy or any other physical malady; it was the *people* who opposed and irritated him and continually caused him problems! The devil used these people again and again, trying to keep Paul so distracted solving "people problems" that he wouldn't be able to make any more significant personal or Gospel advancements.

What about you, friend? What do you intend to do about the "thorns" that the devil is using to steal your joy and to sidetrack you from *your* mission? How do you intend to react to this ongoing disturbance? Paul never allowed people to keep him from fulfilling his divine call, so today I urge you to follow his example. Don't allow people to stop you! The devil is obviously afraid of you, your gifts, your potential, and your revelations; otherwise, he wouldn't need to incite people to stir up trouble for you.

More than likely, the opposition you're facing is a good indication that you're right on track. So just keep forging ahead toward your God-ordained goal, regardless of the distractions that try to steal your focus!

MY PRAYER FOR TODAY

Lord, I ask You to help me remain focused on my goals, even when the devil tries to use people to steal my focus and distract me. Knowing that the devil tries to use people, I ask You to help me equip myself spiritually and mentally so I will be able to keep my eyes on the goal You have given for my life. I choose to forgive those whom the devil uses. I will pray for them to change and to repent for their actions; I will keep my heart free of offense; and I will continue to march full-steam ahead to achieve what God has told me to do! Holy Spirit, please help me stay on track and keep my heart free from all strife!

I pray this in Jesus' name!

MY CONFESSION FOR TODAY

I confess that Satan is unable to distract me from what God has told me to do. Although the enemy tries very hard to knock me off track, I will not take my eyes off the goals God has given me, nor will I ever stop pursuing those goals until I know they have been achieved. The power of God resides in me. The power of Christ's resurrection operates in my life. I have all the power I need to shove aside every distraction and to keep pressing toward the mark for the prize of the high calling of God in Christ Jesus!

I declare this by faith in Jesus' name!

QUESTIONS FOR YOU TO CONSIDER

1. Are there any people that the devil regularly uses to inflict grief in your life? Do you find their behavior a distraction or an irritant — a "thorn" in your flesh that the devil uses to steal your joy and distract you from your God-given assignment?
2. Have you asked God to give you a strategy to turn these "enemies" in your favor? Have you prayed that they would have a change of heart and repent?
3. What can you do to undergird yourself in order to stay focused and undistracted and to successfully resist these types of assaults?

Paul's thorn in the flesh wasn't sickness or epilepsy or any other physical malady; it was the *people* who opposed and irritated him and continually caused him problems!

NOVEMBER 10

❧❦❧

A Prayer That God Cannot Answer

For this thing I besought the Lord thrice, that it might depart from me.
And he said unto me, My grace is sufficient for thee:
for my strength is made perfect in weakness….
— 2 Corinthians 12:8,9

Perhaps you've heard yourself praying this prayer in a moment of exasperation when dealing with people: "God, I can't deal with all these people anymore! Please remove all the people from my life who make me lose my peace and joy!"

As long as you live in this world, you will have challenges in your relationships with people. That's just a part of dealing with human beings. The only way you can be free of challenges with imperfect humans is to die prematurely and go directly to Heaven. But if you intend to live a full life here on planet earth, part of the package includes living with people who are far from perfect and who do things that occasionally surprise and disappoint you.

From Paul's words in Second Corinthians 12:8, it seems that he had prayed to be delivered of problem people on three different occasions during his ministry. He wanted to be free of these people so desperately that he said, "For this thing I besought the Lord thrice.…"

The word "besought" is the Greek word *parakaleo*, an intense word that is derived from the Greek words *para* and *kaleo*. The word *para* means *alongside*, and the word *kaleo* means *to call* or *to beckon*. When compounded together into the word *parakaleo*, the new word pictures *one who comes alongside someone else, as close as he can get, and then begins to passionately call out, plead, beckon, beg, and beseech that other person to do something on his behalf.*

In using the word *parakaleo* in this verse, Paul lets us know that he had passionately asked God to answer this prayer. Paul had drawn as near to God as he possibly could; then once he was in that close position, he earnestly pleaded with God, asking Him to deliver him from that thorn in his flesh and from the messenger of Satan that buffeted and constantly harassed him (*see* November 9 to learn more about Paul's thorn in the flesh).

Paul tells us that he asked God to cause this thorn in the flesh to "depart" from him. The word "depart" is the Greek word *aphistimi*, which means *to depart* or *to remove* and as a rule it is used to refer to people rather than things. The use of this Greek word amplifies the fact that Paul was praying to be freed of problem people! He was literally saying, "God, I don't want to deal with these people anymore. I earnestly ask You to please remove them from my life!"

But here is why God cannot fully answer this kind of prayer: Even if God did remove this particular group of people that caused Paul such trouble, it wouldn't be long until another group of problem people showed up!

As long as we live in this world, we will have to deal with people whom we don't enjoy or whom the devil tries to use to steal our joy and peace. If we constantly focus on getting rid of people we don't like or enjoy, we'll be praying to be delivered from people for the rest of our lives. As I said earlier, the only way for you to be permanently free of all imperfect-people problems is to go home to be with the Lord!

That's why the Lord told Paul, "...My grace is sufficient for thee: for my strength is made perfect in weakness..." (2 Corinthians 12:9). The word "sufficient" is the Greek word *arkeo*. This is an old Greek word that means *to be sufficient; to be satisfactory;* and *to give protection, power, and help.* In later Greek, it denoted *a man who possessed great financial means.* This type of person was sufficiently endowed with huge resources that were more than enough for him or for any endeavor he would ever attempt. Hence, he was *financially strong* or *financially sufficient.*

This is precisely the word the Lord used when He told Paul, "...My grace is sufficient for thee...." It was the equivalent of the Lord saying, *"My grace is more than enough to protect you, empower you, and help you deal with the problem people you encounter in life. You will find that My grace is completely satisfactory in meeting your need and that it will make you sufficiently strong to deal with these situations."*

Just like Paul, we may occasionally feel exasperated and incapable in our own strength to victoriously cope with troublesome people; nonetheless, the Lord gives us His promise: "...My strength is made perfect in weakness...." The word "strength" in this verse comes from the Greek word *dunamis,* the word for *dynamic power.* This is a strength that always releases sufficient *power* and possesses the *ability* to make needed changes. God knew that Paul needed a new surge of divine power that would change his perspective and empower him to successfully overcome his struggles with people.

The Lord continued to tell Paul (and us), "...My strength is made perfect in weakness...." The word "weakness" in Greek is the word *astheneo,* which describes *a person who feels weak, distressed, unsettled, or needy.* If Paul was referring to physical sickness, as some assert, he would have used the word *asthenes,* which actually describes *physical ailments.* However, because Paul used the word *astheneo* and not *asthenes* in this verse, he confirmed to us again that he was *not* talking about physical sickness; rather, he was referring to the *distressing, unsettling emotions* he experienced as a result of the people who were a constant source of conflict for him. The Lord knew that Paul felt insufficient in his own strength to successfully deal with these people.

But if Paul would open his heart to the Lord, God's promise was that His strength would be made "perfect" in his weakness. Here is the answer that Paul and you and I need when we feel exhausted in dealing with troublesome people and relationships. The word "perfect" is the word *teleo,* which means *perfection, completion,* or *something that is mature.* But the Greek tense used in this verse accentuates *continuing action,* which is a very important point! It means that this inflow of supernatural, strengthening power is not what God only does *sometimes;* it is power that God makes available at *all* times if we will only receive it. The verse could be translated, *"My power is constantly being perfected in you whenever you feel weak and needy...."*

This verse could be taken to mean:

"...My grace is more than enough for you. If you'll receive it, you'll find that it will sufficiently endow you with more than you need to deal with any situation. My power is always on hand, available to help you in moments when you are weak and needy...."

So the next time you feel exasperated with people and are tempted to pray to be delivered from them, remember that this is a prayer you really don't want God to answer exactly like you asked. If He were to permanently remove you from "problem people," He'd have to take you home early! That is the only way you could ever be permanently freed from people who cause challenges for you.

It's all right to pray for others to be changed, but never forget that God wants to do a work inside you as well! He wants to change you so that you can successfully live in the midst of imperfect people. If you'll open your heart to receive what God has for you, He will fill you with His dynamic, supernatural power — divine power that will transform your thinking and inwardly fortify you to live successfully in this world. You'll be able to cope with the problem people you have to deal with — and you'll do it all with joy, peace, and victory! God will strengthen you and help you overcome your own weaknesses, making you sufficiently strong to handle every people challenge that ever comes your way!

So instead of constantly asking God to remove all the problem people from your life, why don't you change the way you are praying? Start asking God to release His power to change *you* so you can walk in peace and victory even when people fail or disappoint you. If you can learn to appropriate the power of God to deal with people, the devil won't be able to use people to steal your joy and victory anymore!

MY PRAYER FOR TODAY

Lord, I realize today that I've been praying the wrong prayer! I've been asking You to remove all the problem people from my life; meanwhile, You've been wanting to reinforce me with sufficient strength to live with these people victoriously. Forgive me for wanting to run from my challenges. Help me face them bravely and confidently in the power of the Holy Spirit from this day forward. I know You want to give me this power, so I open my heart to receive it right now!

I pray this in Jesus' name!

MY CONFESSION FOR TODAY

I confess that God's grace is sufficient for me! When I feel distressed because of what people do to me, I turn to the grace of God and allow the Holy Spirit to fill me with sufficient power to love the unlovely, to be patient with those who act ugly, and to walk in kindness and long-suffering with everyone I encounter throughout the day. My weakness in dealing with people disappears when I yield to the power of the Holy Spirit that dwells inside me!

I declare this by faith in Jesus' name!

QUESTIONS FOR YOU TO CONSIDER

1. Have there been moments in your life when you were so exasperated with people that you were tempted to ask God to remove all problem people from your life?
2. Did you honestly think that was a prayer God could answer? Did it dawn on you that God might want to change *you* so you can live victoriously in the midst of imperfect people?
3. Do you know of anyone who never has problems with people? Since you will have to deal with imperfect people as long as you live on this earth, what kind of changes need to occur in you so you can live in peace with others and stop losing your joy all the time?

NOVEMBER 11

❧✦❧

Withdraw From Every Disorderly Brother

Now we command you, brethren, in the name of our Lord Jesus Christ,
that ye withdraw yourselves from every brother that walketh disorderly,
and not after the tradition which he received of us.
— 2 Thessalonians 3:6

Many years ago Denise and I worked with a young man who was very skilled in music and who had a stage presence that was simply electrifying. However, in his personal life, things were completely out of order. Not only did he make a constant string of unwise decisions for himself, but those horrendous decisions were detrimentally affecting many people's lives.

As pastors, we saw what this man did; we heard about the effect his behavior was having on other people; and we counseled people who had been abused by him. But because he was so talented and had such a strong stage presence, people ignored his chronic bad behavior, overlooking it as if it were just a minor flaw in his life and revering him as someone "great."

After many months of prayer, I had a strong "knowing" from the Holy Spirit that this young man was headed for serious trouble. I met with him to discuss his future, but he ignored my advice and pressed onward with his destructive behavior. I was left with no choice but to call my young leadership team together and tell them, "I know that you love this man. But because he lives such a rebellious life, refuses to listen to anyone in authority, and keeps making such bad choices in his life, I am asking that you withdraw from him and stop investing your time and energy in that friendship."

What my young team didn't know was that this young man had gone so far off track, he had begun committing criminal actions. As a pastor, I couldn't divulge everything I knew, so I asked my leadership team to trust me and submit to me in this matter by withdrawing from any further fellowship with him. As difficult as it may have been for them to obey me, I was *ordering* them to break off their relationship with this young man who was belligerently headed for a major catastrophe. I was sure that if they stayed close to him, he would try to drag them into the crisis with him.

As time passed, our young leaders became exceedingly grateful that I had ordered them to break off their relationship with the young man. Eventually he violated international trade laws and got into such a dangerous situation with the Russian mafia that he went into hiding to keep himself from being murdered. But although he tried to hide, members of the mafia found him, kidnapped him, and held him until they were confident he had the funds to pay the debt he owed them. When he was finally released, he was black and blue from the multiple beatings he had suffered at their hands.

You would think that after experiencing such brutality, this young man would have learned to change his ways. But instead, he persisted in his rebellion to authority and continued to commit grossly wrong actions in his life.

Although this young man was a brother in the Lord, he had never learned to submit to authority and refused to listen to those who could help him. Apparently, the apostle Paul was also aware of people who were unruly and insubordinate in the city of Thessalonica. It is evident that he was disturbed by this problem, for when he wrote his second letter to the Thessalonians, he gave them a stern order: "Now we command you, brethren, in the name of our Lord Jesus Christ, that ye withdraw yourselves from every brother that walketh disorderly, and not after the tradition which he received of us" (2 Thessalonians 3:6).

Notice that Paul says, "Now we command you...." The word "command" is so strong in the Greek that it leaves no room for misunderstanding. It is the Greek word *parangello*, which means *to order, to charge,* or *to give a command*. All of Paul's readers would have understood that this was not a suggestion — it was a *direct command*.

Paul went on to tell them, "Now we command you, brethren, in the name of our Lord Jesus Christ, that ye withdraw yourselves from every brother that walketh disorderly...." The word "withdraw" is the Greek word *stello*, which means *to gather up, to pull together, to move oneself,* or *to withdraw*. In some ancient texts, it meant *to shorten the sails* or *to pull in all the loose, flapping sails that would hinder a ship from moving forward at maximum speed*. In other places, the word *stello* was used to picture *a runner pulling up the long, dangling ends of his robe so the loose ends wouldn't hinder him in a foot race*.

When Paul used the word *stello*, the Thessalonians would have immediately understood that he was ordering them to make *an inward resolution*. He was ordering them to pull themselves together and get rid of all the loose ends that could hinder their spiritual walk, which would include withdrawing from any rebellious Christians who refused to get things right with the Lord. There is no doubt that Paul was explicitly ordering the Thessalonian believers to remove themselves from all such relationships that could adversely affect their own progress with the Lord.

In the next statement, Paul identified the exact group of rebellious believers he was talking about. He told them (and us), "...Withdraw from every brother that walketh disorderly...."

The words "walketh" is the Greek word *peripateo*. The word *peripateo* is very significant in this verse, for it means *to walk about* or *to walk around*, giving the impression of *one who habitually lives and functions in a certain way*. By employing the use of this word, Paul indicated that he wasn't writing about a believer who makes an occasional mistake in his life; rather, he was categorically referring to those believers who habitually live in a "disorderly" manner.

The word "disorderly" is taken from the Greek word *atakeo*. The word *atakeo* was a military term that described *a soldier who was out of rank* or *a soldier who was out of order*. It carries the idea of *one who is insubordinate* or *one who is disrespectful of those who have been placed in authority over him*.

The word *atakeo* was also used in Greek society to portray *individuals who refused to work and who lived off the goodwill of others*. Apparently some of the rebellious people in Thessalonica refused to listen to the church leadership's command to get a job. Instead, they took advantage of the goodwill of Christians, "sponging off them" whenever they needed some money.

This scenario is very clear as you continue to read Second Thessalonians 3. The word *atakeo* was also used to depict *people who meddled in other people's affairs*. As in the case of the Thessalonians, these loafers had no jobs and therefore had lots of time to interfere in other people's business. Paul was so against this behavior that he ordered the believers of Thessalonica to withdraw from these habitual loafers.

Paul finished this verse by reminding them that such a chronic loafer was not living "...after the tradition which he received of us." In the Greek text, the word "tradition" is the word *paradidomi*, a Greek word that means *to personally deliver* or *to personally transmit something to someone*. Paul had *personally delivered* instruction to the Thessalonians about living responsible lives. No one in Thessalonica could claim ignorance, for Paul had personally taught them. Those who continued to live in this fashion were simply ignoring his instructions. And rather than tolerate their behavior, Paul told them, "Enough is enough!"

When you take all these Greek word meanings into account, Second Thessalonians 3:6 could be interpreted to mean:

"Brothers, we give you this command in the name of the Lord Jesus Christ. Distance your-selves from every brother who routinely lives his life out of order — breaking ranks, violat-ing authority, living the life of a maverick, and perpetually refusing to submit to anyone's authority. If you're already entangled with a brother like this, do whatever you must to get free of that relationship. It's time to tie up all the loose ends with this brother and to inwardly resolve that you are not going to spend time with him any longer. Although he's a brother, his actions are not in agreement with the teachings you learned from us."

Paul's command is very clear: Even though such brothers or sisters are related to us in Christ, we are not to have close fellowship with those who show disrespect for authority and who routinely live their lives out of order. When a believer lives in defiance of God's Word and God-established authority, we must inwardly resolve to back away so we don't put our stamp of approval on them by affiliating ourselves with them. Yes, we must continue to love them; nevertheless, there comes a time when we must disassociate from unrepentant, erring believers. As we do, we will help them realize they are wrong and protect our own testimony from being negatively affected.

In light of Paul's message in Second Thessalonians 3:6, what is God saying to you about your current friendships? Do you closely associate with any individuals who have no regard for the Word of God or respect for God-established authority? If so, do you have a good reason why you maintain an intimate relationship with them? Are these the kind of close friends you need? Could it be that you need to back away from the people in your life who are living in rebellion? Is it time to invest yourself in someone else who loves God's Word, who is submitted to authority, and who has a heart to prosper under the blessing of the local church?

MY PRAYER FOR TODAY

Lord, I ask You to help me truthfully examine my relationships to determine which of them are helping me and which are hindering me. If any of my relationships are with people who are disorderly or rebellious and unwilling to change, please give me the courage to follow the instructions of Your Word. Holy Spirit, I am depending on You to lead and guide me and to help me do exactly what Jesus wants me to do.

I pray this in Jesus' name!

MY CONFESSION FOR TODAY

I confess that I carefully guard my life by closely affiliating with people who love God's Word, respect God-established authority, and act as positive influences in my life. I do not allow myself to be dragged into relationships with people who refuse to seriously walk with God. Those who could negatively influence me are not the people I choose to be my closest friends. Nothing in the world is more important than my walk with God. Since those who are close to me have a tremendous influence on my life, I choose friends who, like me, make their walk with God their greatest priority.

I declare this by faith in Jesus' name!

1. Have you ever maintained close relationships with people who you knew were not good for your spiritual life? Were you negatively affected by this close affiliation as a result?
2. Can you think of someone in your life who is associating too closely with people who have the potential of negatively influencing his or her life? Have you expressed your heartfelt concerns to this person?
3. Have you spent time in prayer, asking God to resolve this situation? If not, why don't you take a few minutes right now to ask the Lord to work in this situation as He protects your friend or relative from the potential harm you foresee?

NOVEMBER 12

A Great and Effectual Door

For a great door and effectual is opened unto me,
and there are many adversaries.
— 1 Corinthians 16:9

*J*ust after the collapse of the Soviet Union, through a series of very remarkable events, I found myself sitting in the central office for the national television station of a large country that had once been a part of the former Soviet Republic. A contract was laid on the table before me that gave me the privilege to broadcast the Gospel to that entire nation every day on prime-time television.

As the conversation with these national television leaders progressed, I learned that this was the first time such a door of opportunity had ever been opened to anyone since the fall of communism in the Soviet Union. As I sat and looked at the contract that lay on the table before me, I thought of Paul's words in First Corinthians 16:9, where he said, "For a great door and effectual is opened unto me...."

Just as Paul once stood before a great and effectual door, at that moment I was also standing before a great door of opportunity that God was entrusting into our hands. But let's talk for a moment about Paul's situation. Where was he when this great and effectual door opened to him?

After Paul had waited many years for the extremely pagan city of Ephesus to open up wide for the preaching of the Gospel, the atmosphere of Ephesus was finally starting to change. Previous resistance was crumbling, and Paul's prayers were finally being answered as the Gospel message began to conquer the city of Ephesus. First Corinthians 16:8 lets us know that Paul was in Ephesus at the time he wrote his first letter to the Corinthian church. He wrote, "But I will tarry at Ephesus until Pentecost."

Paul's accomplishment in Ephesus was no doubt one of his greatest works, if not *the* greatest. During the three years that he lived and worked in Ephesus, Paul established one of the greatest churches in world history. The revival that swept through the city was so massive that the church of Ephesus soon became the largest and most influential church in the first century.

Just as I have felt on so many occasions, Paul was keenly aware at this time that a door had opened to him that had never been opened to anyone else in human history. Notice that he wrote, "For a great door and effectual is opened *unto me*...." The words "unto me" come from the Greek word *moi*, which means *uniquely to me*. This was a moment when Paul was standing in the midst of an apostle's dreams. A city was falling to the Gospel; darkness was being driven out; and the church was being established.

Paul referred to this unique, unprecedented opportunity as "a great door and effectual." The word "great" is the Greek word *mega*, which always speaks of *something that is huge or massive*. The word "door" is the word *thura*. This is the Greek word for *a door*, but Paul uses it here as a metaphor to describe *a unique opportunity*.

Paul said that this huge door of opportunity "opened" to him. This word "opened" comes from the Greek word *anoigo*, which means *to open*. However, it must be noted that the tense Paul uses doesn't describe a door that is starting to open, but rather a door that is already standing wide open. This was the opportunity of a lifetime. *The doors were wide open.* Paul had complete and total access to the city of Ephesus.

Paul called this unique opportunity not only a "great" door, but also an "effectual" door. The word "effectual" is the Greek word *energes*, from which we get the word *energy*. But as used in New Testament Greek, the word *energes* describes *something that is forceful, effective, active, or powerful*. Paul declared that when this door opened to him and to the Gospel, it created a divine release of God's power that immediately began to engulf the city of Ephesus.

But notice what else often accompanies a great and effectual door of opportunity. Paul went on to say, "A great door and effectual is opened unto me, and there are many *adversaries*." The word "adversaries" comes from the word *antikeimai*, a compound of the words *anti* and *keimai*. The word *anti* means *against*, and the word *keimai* means *to lie*, as with *something that is lying around*.

When these two words are compounded together, they express the idea of *hostile forces that are standing in opposition to someone*. These forces are literally lying all around, pitted against a common foe and just waiting for the opportunity to strike! These sneaky, sinister powers lie in wait to deceive, attack, or pry away another's opportunity in order to steal it for themselves.

Anytime we find ourselves standing before a rare door of opportunity, people with impure motives and jealousy will appear on the scene to see how they can steal the victory we worked so hard to achieve. Paul was very aware (as I have been on many occasions in my own ministry) that there were deceptive people opposed to him who would have loved to remove him and steal the place God had given him in Ephesus.

Through the years that Denise and I have worked on the front lines of the Gospel, we've had a myriad of experiences with sinister people who saw our success as their opportunity. The television opportunity I mentioned earlier is just one of our many great and effectual doors for which we are so grateful. But like the apostle Paul, whenever we have stood before a great and effectual door that uniquely opened to us, the Spirit of God has made us very aware that our success was envied and coveted by others who wanted to steal it for themselves. Through these experiences, God has taught us to be wary of those who might want to take advantage of us.

You see, jealousy and covetousness in others is an unfortunate reality that often manifests when God opens a door of opportunity for you. That's why it is so imperative that you learn how to be discerning. Those with impure motives have a way of showing up wherever people are being blessed, so don't be surprised if it happens to you. If you're not careful, these individuals will try to steal the victory away from you after you have worked hard to achieve it.

So if you find that God has set a unique door of opportunity before you, walk through that door by faith, expecting the power of God to be mightily released. Meanwhile, however, don't forget to be sensitive to the Holy Spirit. He will warn you if someone tries to sneak up from behind to steal what God has dropped into your hands!

MY PRAYER FOR TODAY

Lord, I ask You to set a great and effectual door of opportunity before me. Please help me recognize when that door opens, for I desire to truly appreciate what You are doing in my life. At the same time, I need You to help me be spiritually discerning so I can differentiate my true friends from opportunists who might come to take advantage of me and steal this victory from my life. Give me spiritually discerning eyes to help me see who is and isn't with me whenever a great and effectual door is uniquely opened to me for Your purposes.

I pray this in Jesus' name!

MY CONFESSION FOR TODAY

I confess that God is setting a great and effectual door before me! I have prayed and waited for this day to come, and now is the time when God is opening that door to me. I don't take this unique time lightly. Rather, I am grateful to God for counting me faithful to receive such a rare and special opportunity. Because God's Spirit works in me, I am able to recognize those whom God has sent to help and those whom Satan has sent to hinder.

I declare this by faith in Jesus' name!

QUESTIONS FOR YOU TO CONSIDER

1. Have you ever had a moment in your life when you realized a great and effectual door of opportunity was being given to you that had never been given to any other person you knew?
2. How did it affect you when you realized that you were standing in the midst of such a God-ordained opportunity?
3. Have you ever been taken advantage of by opportunists with impure motives who showed up when you became successful? Did you listen when the Holy Spirit spoke to your heart and tried to warn you about these opportunists?

Jealousy and covetousness in others is an unfortunate reality that often manifests when God opens a door of opportunity for you. That's why it is so imperative that you learn how to be discerning. Those with impure motives have a way of showing up wherever people are being blessed, so don't be surprised if it happens to you. If you're not careful, these individuals will try to steal the victory away from you after you have worked hard to achieve it.

November 13

❦

Present Your Bodies a Living Sacrifice

I beseech you therefore, brethren, by the mercies of God,
that ye present your bodies a living sacrifice, holy, acceptable
unto God, which is your reasonable service.
— Romans 12:1

When Mary's days of purification were finished after the miraculous birth of Jesus, Luke 2:22 tells us that Mary and Joseph brought their son to Jerusalem to dedicate Him to the Lord. It says, "And when the days of her purification according to the law of Moses were accomplished, they brought him to Jerusalem, to present him to the Lord."

Mary and Joseph came to Jerusalem with the express purpose "to present" the young Jesus to God. To make such a journey to Jerusalem required finances to pay for the journey itself and to purchase the turtledoves and pigeons that would be offered to God at the time they presented Jesus. This was no casual, accidental, haphazard, unplanned event. Presenting Jesus to the Lord in the temple was a serious occasion, as it was for all males in Israel. Such an event was planned in advance and done with great reverence toward God. Thus, it was a very hallowed, consecrated, holy moment as Joseph and Mary approached the Temple at the time set for Jesus' dedication.

Luke 2:22 says that Joseph and Mary came "...to present him to the Lord." The word "present" comes from the Greek word *paristimi*, which is a compound of the words *para* and *istimi*. The prefix *para* means *alongside*, and the word *istimi* means *to place*. When these two words are compounded together, the new word means *to place beside; to place at one's disposal; to surrender; to offer, as to offer a sacrifice to God;* or *to present, as to present a special offering to God.* This word undoubtedly communicates the fact that Mary and Joseph were coming to the Temple on this day to intentionally place their newborn son into God's close care. They were dedicating and entrusting Him into God's protection. They were surrendering Him to God's supervision and making a pledge that this new baby boy was God's possession and that God could therefore use Him however He wished.

This Greek word *paristimi* ("present") is precisely the same word that Paul used in Romans 12:1, when he wrote, "I beseech you therefore, brethren, by the mercies of God, that ye present your bodies a living sacrifice, holy, acceptable unto God, which is your reasonable service." The fact that Paul used this same word sheds some very important light on Romans 12:1.

First, we know that Paul was very earnest when he wrote Romans 12:1 because he began by solemnly telling them, "I beseech you...." The word "beseech" comes from the Greek word *parakaleo*. As noted in other *Sparkling Gems*, the word *parakaleo* is a Greek compound of the words *para* and *kaleo*. The word *para* means *alongside*, and the word *kaleo* means *to call* or *to beckon*. When these two words are compounded together, the new word pictures *one who comes alongside someone else, as close as he can get, and then begins to passionately call out, plead, beckon, beg, and beseech that other person to do something on his behalf.*

In many places, the word *parakaleo* is used to depict *a person who is earnestly praying.* Therefore, the word *parakaleo* is also a word that can depict *a person who is sincerely expressing his heart to God in prayer.* In light of this fact, one Greek scholar says that it is almost as if the apostle Paul dropped to his knees in this verse and began to prayerfully plead for his Roman readers to hear his petition. His heartfelt request was that they would present their bodies a living sacrifice to God.

It must be noted that the word *parakaleo* also described what military commanders did before they sent their troops into battle. After summoning the troops together, their commander would *beseech* or *exhort* them as he warned them of the realities of warfare. The commander would describe in detail what they were going to face in their battle; then he'd urge them to keep on fighting bravely until the victory was won. All of this is included in the word *parakaleo*.

This is very significant in the context of Romans 12:1. Paul was urging believers to dedicate their bodies to God. However, Paul knew that when a believer makes the decision to dedicate his body to God, the carnal nature may respond by going to war against the spirit. The flesh just doesn't want to submit to the law of God or to do what God wishes. So when Paul besought his readers to yield their bodies to God, he was also warning them that such an action might stir up a battle in the flesh.

The carnal nature has long been the driving force for what is done with the body; therefore, it will most likely rebel when it is told to submit to God's control. This is why anyone who decides to present and dedicate his body to God must be ready and willing to fight the battle with the flesh until victory is achieved.

As mentioned earlier, Paul uses the Greek word *paristimi* when he says we are to "present" our bodies as a living sacrifice. This is exactly the same word used in Luke 2:22 to depict that moment when Jesus' parents presented baby Jesus to God in the Temple at Jerusalem. Just as Jesus' dedication was no casual, accidental, haphazard, unplanned event, now Paul is telling us that the presentation of our bodies to God is a serious occurrence in our lives. This is no light affair, but one that should be done in a very hallowed, consecrated, and serious manner. It is a crucial, historical moment in our lives when we intentionally place ourselves in God's close care. We surrender ourselves and all that we are to God's supervision, making a solemn pledge that we are His and that He can therefore use us in whatever way He wishes.

You may wrongly assume that because you are a believer, this act of surrender has already occurred. But just because you are a believer does not mean that you have completely surrendered your body to God. If becoming a believer automatically caused this act of surrender to take place, Paul wouldn't have found it necessary to earnestly urge the Roman believers to do it.

Notice that we are to present ourselves as a "living sacrifice." In the Old Testament, an animal sacrifice would be offered upon the altar. Because the animal was dead, it could only be presented to the Lord once as a sacrificial offering.

But in the New Testament, we are urged to present ourselves to God as a *living* sacrifice. This implies that we must live in a continual state of surrender and consecration. Our commitment may begin with a momentous, "once-and-for-all" decision, but it must be followed with a daily decision to keep on surrendering ourselves to the Lord. Thus, we must see every day of our lives as another day — another opportunity — to yield our lives to God.

Each new day necessitates new surrender and consecration. What you surrendered to God yesterday is already old. Today is a new day and demands a new and higher level of consecration.

Therefore, as you awake each morning, train yourself to begin your day with a prayer of consecration in which you solemnly and in holy reverence present yourself and all that you are to God's purposes. Don't assume that because you did it yesterday, you don't need to do it today. What you did yesterday remains in yesterday's sphere. Each new day beckons you to take a step closer to the Lord and to make a commitment more serious than the one you made before.

Have you willfully, deliberately, and intentionally presented your body to God? Just as Jesus' parents brought Him to the Temple to present Him to the Lord, God is asking you to reverently come into His Presence to offer yourself as a living sacrifice to be used for His purposes. If you haven't ever taken this step of faith, are you ready to take it now? The carnal nature may declare war when you make the decision to surrender completely to the Lord, so be prepared to deal with the flesh. Just determine that you *will not stop* until the victory has been won!

Today is the day to surrender yourself into the hands of God. Don't wait until tomorrow — and don't depend on what you did yesterday. This is a new day, and God is calling you to surrender yourself anew. *So don't let ANYTHING hold you back from taking this step of faith right now!*

MY PRAYER FOR TODAY

Lord, today I am surrendering myself as a living sacrifice to be used in whatever way You choose. I know You are beckoning me to come higher and closer than ever before, so right now I approach You with great reverence and surrender myself more fully to You. With all my heart I vow to give You my soul, my emotions, my spirit, my body, and everything else that I am and that I possess. I want to live for You and to serve You for the rest of my life. Starting today, I yield to You completely. When You speak, I will do exactly what You tell me to do.

I pray this in Jesus' name!

MY CONFESSION FOR TODAY

I confess that I am surrendered to the purposes of God. I daily consecrate myself to God — to do what He wants and to live a life that is pleasing to Him. My flesh may try to wage war against this consecration, but I take authority over my flesh and I tell it what to do. My body does not control me. Instead, I control it, using it as my instrument to do whatever God asks me to do. Every day when I awake, I renew my consecration and personal commitment to serve God with all my heart. I am His completely, and I will obey whatever His Spirit prompts me to do.

I declare this by faith in Jesus' name!

QUESTIONS FOR YOU TO CONSIDER

1. Has there been a moment in your life when you seriously consecrated yourself more fully to God's purposes? When was that moment? How did this deeper commitment affect your life?
2. Do you daily consecrate yourself to the Lord? If the answer is no, how long has it been since you dropped to your knees and reverently surrendered your life, your mind, your emotions, your talents, your money, your family, your job, your friends, your plans, and all that you are to the Lord?
3. Would God say that you live your life like a "living sacrifice"?

November 14

❧✦❧

Nothing Shall Separate You
From the Love of God

For I am persuaded, that neither death, nor life,
nor angels, nor principalities, nor powers,
nor things present, nor things to come,
Nor height, nor depth, nor any other creature,
shall be able to separate us from the love of God,
which is in Christ Jesus our Lord.
— Romans 8:38,39

When the apostle Paul wrote the above verses, he had been facing grueling times because he was a Christian. He had suffered rejection from friends, persecution from the government, and had spent many months of his life in an isolated prison cell. But regardless of what people or the circumstances of life did to him, Paul had discovered a vital truth: *Nothing that occurs in this life has the power to separate a believer from the love of God.*

That is why Paul said, "For I am persuaded, that neither death, nor life, nor angels, nor principalities, nor powers, nor things present, nor things to come, nor height, nor depth, nor any other creature, shall be able to separate us from the love of God, which is in Christ Jesus our Lord" (Romans 8:38,39).

Notice that Paul said, "For I am *persuaded....*" The word "persuaded" is the Greek word *peitho*. It means *to be persuaded, to be convinced,* or *to be swayed from one opinion to the opinion held by another.* This word describes a person who has been coaxed from a particular conviction to embrace a different one. Furthermore, the Greek tense implies that this was a persuasion that had occurred to Paul in the past but is still so strong that it continues to be his conviction in the present. He was persuaded, and he continues to be persuaded. It could therefore be translated, *"For I have been persuaded, and I remain convinced...."*

The word "death" is the Greek word *thanatos*, the Greek word for *physical death*, but it can also be used to depict *mortal danger* or *a dangerous circumstance.* In this case, Paul's primary meaning is that the love of God is so strong, even physical death cannot separate us from His divine love. Death may separate us from the earth and from people we love, but it is impossible for death to separate us from the love of God, for God's love doesn't stop with the cessation of life.

It is a fact that many believers feel overwhelmed by the situations they face in life. In fact, they often feel so confused and weighed down that they wonder if God is still near to them. This is precisely why Paul adds that even life cannot separate a believer from the love of Jesus Christ.

Just as the word *thanatos* describes *physical death*, this particular word for "life," the Greek word *zoe*, refers to *physical life.* Paul uses this word to let us know that neither the cessation of one's physical life nor the complex issues and events related to one's life on this earth are strong enough to separate a believer from the love of God.

Next, Paul lets us know that no spiritual being, good or bad, has enough power to separate us from God's love. The word "angels" is the Greek word *angelos*, which refers to *brilliant, spiritual, angelic beings.* Such angelic beings are extraordinarily strong, as is evidenced by hundreds of scriptures in both the Old and New Testament.

The word "principalities" is from the word *archai.* This is the same word that Paul uses in Ephesians 6:12, where he describes the rank and file of the devil's kingdom. The word *archai* is the plural for *archos,* the Greek word for *a ruler* or *one who has long held a lofty position of power.* The plural version of this word depicts *an entire group of high-ranking demon spirits that have held their positions of power since the most ancient times.* Although angels and demonic powers are indeed strong, they are not strong enough to disconnect a believer from God's love.

Paul also mentions "powers." This is taken from the word *dunamis,* which is the Greek word that sometimes depicted *the powerful governments of men.* Certainly Paul had been arrested, bound, and restricted by evil governments on many occasions, but none of these actions were ever sufficiently powerful to separate him from the love of God. A jail cell may have separated Paul from other believers. However, even in the deepest, darkest, most gruesome prison cell, Paul tangibly felt and personally experienced the love of God.

In addition to these points Paul has already mentioned, he uses the phrase "things present" to let us know that nothing that currently exists is able to prevent a person from experiencing God's love. The words "things present" are derived from the Greek word *enistemi,* a compound of the words *en* and *histemi.* The word *en* means *in,* and the word *histemi* means *to stand.* Thus, when these two words are joined to form the word *enistemi,* the new word describes *something that is presently standing in its place.* In this case, it means nothing *presently existing* or nothing that *currently stands* is sufficient to separate a believer from the all-powerful presence of God's love.

But Paul doesn't stop with the things that presently exist. He goes on to say that "things to come" are also not able to separate a believer from the love of God. The Greek word used here is from the word *mello,* and it describes *events that will occur in the future.* These are things that haven't happened yet, but will take place in the days and years to come. Paul has already said that nothing currently existing is strong enough to separate a believer from the love of God. Now he boldly declares that nothing will ever happen in the future that will contain enough power to hinder a believer from knowing and experiencing God's love.

As he continues, Paul also declares that neither "height, nor depth" shall be able to separate us from the love of God. The word "height" is the Greek word *hupsuma,* which expresses the notion of *something that is overhead.* It would include anything that is *lofty,* such as the sky and the heavens above. The word "depth" is the word *bathos,* the Greek word that expresses the notion of *something that is exceedingly deep,* like the deepest, darkest parts of the sea. Now Paul uses these illustrations to say that nothing in the sky or in the deepest parts of the earth has the power to keep one of God's children from knowing and experiencing His love.

To make sure absolutely everything is included in this comprehensive list, Paul adds "any other creature" to the list. The word "creature" is the Greek word *ktisis,* and it categorically refers to *all created things in both the physical and spiritual worlds.* Absolutely *nothing* in either of these spheres "…shall be able to separate us from the love of God, which is in Christ Jesus our Lord."

The words "shall be able" is from the word *dunamai,* which describes *strength, capacity,* or *ability.* The word "separate" is the Greek word *choridzo,* meaning *to sunder, to sever, to disunite, to tear apart, to disconnect, to cut off, to disengage,* or *to withdraw.* Notice that Paul says that nothing is capable of tearing a believer "from" the love of God. The word "from" is the Greek word *apo,* which means *away* and implies *distance.* This clearly means that there is *nothing* that can put distance between a believer and his Heavenly Father.

In light of the meanings of these Greek words in Romans 8:38 and 39, an interpretive translation of this verse could read:

"I have been persuaded, and I remain convinced, that neither death, nor the complications that often arise in life, nor powerful angelic beings, nor even an entire group of high-ranking demonic spirits, nor anything that currently exists, nor anything that could potentially happen in the future, nor any political power, nor anything in the highest heavens, nor anything that resides in the deepest depths, nor anything that has ever been created is capable of disconnecting us from the love of God or of putting any distance between us and the love of God, which is in Jesus Christ our Lord."

Never forget this message Paul proclaimed. *Nothing* in this world has enough power to disconnect you from the love of God. No angel, no demon, no government, no creature — and no mistake of your own making — will ever be capable of cutting you off from the love of God. God's love is greater than man will ever be able to comprehend. It reaches to the highest mountain, and it penetrates to the lowest parts of the earth. Regardless of what you are facing in your life today, God's love is with you — and nothing will ever be able to disconnect you from this awesome, powerful, all-consuming love!

MY PRAYER FOR TODAY

Lord, I am so thankful for Your love that never fails me and never deserts me. I am filled with gratitude that nothing in this world has the power to disconnect me from Your awesome, powerful, life-changing love. In moments when I feel overwhelmed by circumstances or problems, I ask that You give me a special awareness of Your unfailing love in my life.

I pray this in Jesus' name!

MY CONFESSION FOR TODAY

I confess that God's love is with me and never leaves me. There is nothing that can happen in this world or in my life to disconnect me from His awesome, powerful, wonder-working, life-transforming love. I walk through each day in peace because I know that the Lord loves me. I have been persuaded, and I remained absolutely convinced, that nothing can separate me from the love of God, which is in Jesus Christ my Lord!

I declare this by faith in Jesus' name!

QUESTIONS FOR YOU TO CONSIDER

1. Can you think of a time in your life when, in the midst of facing a seemingly hopeless situation, you were intensely aware that the love of God was with you? When was that time in your life?
2. Hasn't God always been faithful to you? Why don't you take a few minutes today to remember several times in your life when God's love brought you through a very difficult circumstance?
3. Can you think of some individuals who are currently facing hardships and need to be reminded that God's love will not fail them? Wouldn't it be a good idea to write them a note, call them, or stop by to personally see them and remind them of God's unfailing love?

NOVEMBER 15

❧❧❧

Be Careful of What You Dump On Those Who Are Listening to You!

Looking diligently lest any man fail of the grace of God;
lest any root of bitterness springing up trouble you,
and thereby many be defiled.
— Hebrews 12:15

My Grandfather Miller lived on a large parcel of land that was located just outside Tulsa. Right in the middle of his land was a small lake that the local people called "Dead Man's Lake," because a dead body had been found at the bottom of the lake many years earlier.

The water in that little lake was muddy red and terribly dirty because the entire lake bed was comprised of red clay. I can remember fishing with my grandfather on the banks of that lake, thinking with great distaste that we were actually going to eat the catfish we pulled out of that filthy water!

That little lake was fed by a notorious little river in Oklahoma called Bird Creek. Not only was Bird Creek known for being muddy, but it was also well-known for the oversized water moccasins that would slither over the branches and debris floating in its waters. This little river was so close to my grandfather's property that my family would cross over a Bird Creek bridge every time we drove to his house.

Nearly every spring during the Oklahoma tornado season, the waters of Bird Creek would rise during heavy rains. It would rise and rise until, finally, those filthy, stinking waters would spill out of the banks of the river and inundate the entire local area. Of course, whenever the waters of Bird Creek rose, they would also rush into Dead Man's Lake on my grandfather's property. The grimy waters would then flood out of the banks of that little lake and literally slime my grandfather's entire property with gunk and goo.

As a boy, I thought it was fun when my grandfather's property got flooded because it meant we had to get in our own boat, pull the motor, and ride across highways covered with water in order to reach Grandfather Miller's house. He and his wife would be standing on the porch, waiting and waving, as we pulled up to the house in our boat.

But when the waters finally receded, the fun was over. Now it was time to clean up the stinking mess left by the flood. Everything in sight was slimed with filth by those rising waters. Believe me, the mess left by a flood was always pretty nasty!

I always think of those messy floods of my boyhood when I read Hebrews 12:15, which says, "Looking diligently lest any man fail of the grace of God; lest any root of bitterness springing up trouble you, and thereby many be defiled." Earlier we looked at one part of this verse (*see* September 4), but today I want to take you further so you can see what eventually happens if a person doesn't surrender his hurts and grievances to the Lord.

As noted earlier, the words "trouble you" in this verse are from the Greek word *enochleo*, which means *to trouble, to harass,* or *to annoy*. It refers to something inside that bothers and upsets you so much that you are constantly pestered by thoughts about it.

The word *enochleo* pictures a person who is continually *troubled*, *harassed*, and *annoyed* by thoughts of how someone else wronged him. The offended person is now so troubled that he is almost emotionally immobilized. Instead of moving on in life, he gets stuck in the muck of that experience, where he wallows day after day in the memories of what happened to him. If that person doesn't quickly get a grip on himself, he will eventually fulfill the next part of the verse, which says, "…lest any root of bitterness springing up trouble you, and many be *defiled*."

The word "defiled" is the Greek word *miaini*. It means *to spill, to spot,* or *to stain*. Here is what Hebrews 12:15 is telling us: If you are inwardly upset with someone and don't get rid of those raw emotions, it won't be too long until you open your mouth and begin to verbalize those ugly inward emotions. As Jesus said, "…Out of the abundance of the heart the mouth speaketh" (Matthew 12:34).

According to Jesus, what you are full of is exactly what you will talk about! If you're filled with joy, then joy will come out of your mouth. But if you're filled with bitterness, anger, disappointment, frustration, or rage, then eventually those attitudes are going to show up in the words you speak! Like a rising river, what is inside you — if not corrected by the Spirit of God — will eventually flood out of the banks of your soul and spill out of your mouth, adversely affecting everyone around you.

This is what happens when we fail to deal with our hearts and instead allow wrong attitudes to fester inside us. Eventually we will begin to "run at the mouth" and say bad things about someone else, which has a devastating effect on those who hear us. As our negative attitudes rage out of control, our words *taint, spot, soil,* and *ruin* the way our listeners perceive the person we are speaking of. Thus, by permitting our mouths to be the spout for the mess that festers inside us, we end up sliming other people with our own stinking attitudes and destructive words.

Let me give you an example of how one person's root of bitterness can result in many being defiled. Suppose a father who has always loved his church becomes offended by something that happened in the church. Rather than go to the Lord, release the offense, and forgive, this father goes home and *fumes* about what happened. The longer he fumes about it, the more angry he becomes. As his anger grows, he starts venting and talking about how *upset* he is with that church!

Prior to this, this father's children loved their church. But day after day, they listen to their father rage about how bad the pastor is, how badly their father has been treated, and so on. The father doesn't realize it, but his words are having a profoundly negative effect on his children. Soon *the children* begin to feel what *their father* feels. They see what *he* sees and believe what *he* believes. Although no one in the church has ever wronged any of these children, it isn't long before they are carrying the same bitter feelings toward the church that their father carries.

In this case, the children have been *tainted, stained,* and *spotted* by a father who should have gone to the Cross and allowed the Spirit of God to liberate him from those bitter emotions. Instead, he opened his mouth and dumped his bitterness on his family. Now he's not the only one who has an attitude problem; he has imparted his bad attitude to his children as well. And the truth is, if his children have a negative attitude toward the church when they grow up, much of the blame will be laid at that father's feet because he didn't keep his mouth shut and act more mature.

What a pity to *dump* all your negative garbage on your friends and loved ones, defiling them with a spiritual problem that may hound them for years. How much better it would be for you to go to the Cross and deal with it rather than open the spout and let a flood of filth and slime defile those around you!

It may seem hard to keep your mouth shut and to go to the Lord when you're dealing with a difficult attitude challenge. But it is much easier to take this route than to spew a lot of garbage that you'll later have to clean up! *So I urge you today to let the Holy Spirit help you overcome your inward struggles. As you do, you will keep yourself free of bitterness and make sure others around you are not defiled by ugly words that you are tempted to speak!*

MY PRAYER FOR TODAY

Lord, please help me refrain from speaking words today that will negatively affect other people. I am so sorry for the times I've "run at the mouth" and said things I shouldn't have said. I realize how wrong this is and how I've stained other people's opinions because I didn't control my mouth and emotions. I am turning to You for help, and I'm asking You to help me control my tongue as I deal with these issues that have festered inside me. Holy Spirit, please help me to overcome the flesh and to allow You to have Your way in me!

I pray this in Jesus' name!

MY CONFESSION FOR TODAY

I confess that I carefully monitor the condition of my heart and regulate what comes out of my mouth. Because my words are seasoned with grace, those who are near me today will be positively impacted. I speak words of kindness, and I refrain from speaking ugly words that I would later regret. My heart is clean toward others, and my mouth speaks only words that build up and edify those who are listening.

I declare this by faith in Jesus' name!

QUESTIONS FOR YOU TO CONSIDER

1. Have you ever been guilty of "running at the mouth" — saying ugly things that negatively affected the people who were listening to you? Did you leave your listeners in better shape because of what you said, or did you "slime" them with your bad attitude?
2. Can you think of an example of parents who ruined their children's opinion of a pastor or church because the parents refused to keep their mouths shut and to control their tongues?
3. Is the Holy Spirit speaking to you today about certain attitudes in you that need to change? If so, what are those attitudes? Who are the individuals in your life whom you need to forgive?

If you're filled with joy, then joy will come out of your mouth. But if you're filled with bitterness, anger, disappointment, frustration, or rage, then eventually those attitudes are going to show up in the words you speak! Like a rising river, what is inside you — if not corrected by the Spirit of God — will eventually flood out of the banks of your soul and spill out of your mouth, adversely affecting everyone around you.

NOVEMBER 16

✦✦✦✦

Exercise Thyself Unto Godliness

...Exercise thyself rather unto godliness.
— 1 Timothy 4:7

*A*t the time I am writing this book, our apartment in Moscow frequently looks like an athletic club. Our three sons and their friends regularly fill our living room to do pushups, sit-ups, and weightlifting to develop their muscles and attain the form they desire. As a result of their hard work, commitment, and consistency, their muscles are getting bigger and bigger, and their bodies are nearly the ideal for young men their age.

Every morning, my wife gets up at the crack of dawn to walk up the seven flights of stairs in our Moscow apartment building a minimum of six times. Once she reaches the top, she takes the elevator back to the first floor and starts up the 210 steps to the seventh floor once more. Multiply that times six, and you'll find that Denise walks up 1,260 steps every morning of her life. When she finishes those 1,260 steps, she comes huffing and puffing into the apartment with a look of elation, thrilled that she accomplished her goal. Needless to say, she is in super shape!

We don't own an automobile in the city of Moscow where we live, so I walk many of the places I need to go. Because it's difficult to take care of an automobile in this massive city, most people in Moscow don't own automobiles, so I fit right into the crowd as I walk and walk. As a result of continual walking through the streets of this gigantic city, my lower legs are muscular and strong.

It takes hard work to get in good physical shape, and it takes a commitment to maintain a good physical condition. In the same way, it also takes hard work and commitment to maintain a good spiritual condition. Anyone who wants to get into good spiritual shape has to be diligent to exercise himself spiritually. This is why the apostle Paul told Timothy, "...Exercise thyself rather unto godliness" (1 Timothy 4:7).

The word "exercise" is the Greek word *gumnadzo*, and it literally meant *to exercise while stark naked* or *to exercise in the nude*. It is a word that was developed from the word *gumnos*, the Greek word that is literally translated *naked*. It is from these words that the English words *gym* or *gymnasium* are derived.

I realize that it may seem strange to our minds that Paul would use such a word, but to Timothy, this was a very powerful and graphic picture. You see, the word *gumnadzo* ("exercise") was only used to describe the professional athletes of that day. By using this word, Paul was conveying a message to Timothy that was absolutely clear to the younger man.

As noted earlier (*see* November 4), Timothy was the senior pastor of the world's largest church during the first century. As pastor of such a massive church, he was working very hard. Nevertheless, Paul urged Timothy not to fantasize about things ever getting easier but instead to joyfully dive into the work with all his strength and might.

This may not have been the message Timothy wanted to hear. But instead of falsely telling the younger man that a day would come when things got easier, Paul admonished him to "exercise unto godliness." And when Timothy saw the word "exercise," he knew *exactly* what Paul was telling him. Professional athletes and their activities were quite famous in Timothy's day.

The word "exercise" (*gumnadzo*) was only used to describe the professional combat sports of boxing, wrestling, and pankration (*see* June 9 to read more about these ancient athletic sports). These athletes wanted the freedom to move their muscles without hindrance, and they didn't want to wear any items of clothing that an opponent could grab hold of to take them down. For these reasons, they exercised and competed naked.

These combat sports were so ferocious that when each competition ended, one of the competitors was usually dead. Knowing that a stiff, life-or-death battle awaited them, these athletes exercised and exercised and *exercised* to get themselves into the best possible physical condition. This included submitting themselves to self-imposed hardships in order to make themselves tougher. For instance, because the actual games usually occurred during the blistering hot temperatures of summer, the athletes trained in extremely hot temperatures so they could become acclimated to intense heat. And in order to become hardened to brutality, they would deliberately ask other athletes and trainers to viciously beat them. In this way, they could learn to take as much abuse as possible without allowing it to affect their performance in case they were wounded during the actual games.

Rather than look for the easy way out, these combat-sport athletes stripped off all laziness, all comfort, and even all their clothes so they could energetically exercise and drive themselves nonstop toward physical perfection. Only those who were the most fit would survive and win the games, so they approached hardship as a positive occurrence — an opportunity to develop their mental resilience, their stamina, their courage, their physique, and their staying power. To these professional athletes, hardship was a good thing, for if they properly responded to it, it could only make them better and, in the end, help them live a longer life!

This was exactly the message Paul was giving to Timothy when he told him to "…exercise thyself rather unto godliness." Paul was telling the younger minister, "Don't run from the challenges before you or spend your time hoping to find an easier route for completing a very difficult task. Instead, strip yourself of all mentalities that would hinder your growth, and embrace this difficult time as an opportunity to spiritually exercise and to develop yourself in the Lord." Paul knew what would happen if Timothy stripped wrong attitudes from his life and approached these challenges with the right attitude: The hardships he faced wouldn't hurt him but rather would assist in developing him and making him stronger.

But notice that Paul said, "…exercise thyself rather unto *godliness*." The word "godliness" is the Greek word *eusebeia*, a Greek word that describes *piety, godliness,* or *a radical, fanatical devotion*. In other words, Paul was telling Timothy, "Don't do just the average that others would do and get an average result. Put your whole heart and soul into developing yourself to the maximum level."

Our commitment to spiritual development is to be so intense that we literally exercise and exercise and *exercise* ourselves to the point of a radical, fanatical devotion to God. We must be as committed to our spiritual development as those professional Greek athletes were to their *physical* development.

Just as physical muscles are developed only through exercise, hard work, training, and commitment, it takes exercise, hard work, training, and commitment to become fit spiritually as well. This is why Paul urged Timothy to take his moment of hardship as an opportunity to stretch, develop, exercise, and make himself stronger.

Do you hear the Spirit of God speaking to you today? Is He telling you to change the way you are looking at your current hardships? You don't ever have to be depressed and defeated by the affairs of life. Just change the way you're looking at the challenges you face. Determine that you are going to use this time in your life to exercise your faith and become stronger in the Lord!

MY PRAYER FOR TODAY

Lord, I ask You to help me change the way I've been looking at the hardships and challenges in my life. Yes, it's true that I don't enjoy them, but since I'm in this time of my life, help me use my time to the maximum by strengthening my faith and exercising myself spiritually. Rather than be broken by this difficult season, I want to come out of it stronger than ever. Holy Spirit, please help me today to change the way I am looking at life. I want to make a firm commitment to exercise myself unto godliness until I am so strong spiritually that nothing in life can stop me from fulfilling the dreams God has put in my heart.

I pray this in Jesus' name!

MY CONFESSION FOR TODAY

I confess that I am getting stronger and stronger in the Lord. I have made the choice to use everything that comes into my life as an opportunity to exercise my faith and develop myself spiritually. This is not a one-shot reaction, for I am making this my lifetime passion and devotion. I will exercise, train, and do everything I can to become stronger and stronger in the Lord.

I declare this by faith in Jesus' name!

QUESTIONS FOR YOU TO CONSIDER

1. What is the single most difficult issue you are facing in life right now? What is the second most difficult challenge you are facing on a regular basis?
2. How are you responding to the challenges in your life? Are you being paralyzed or broken by the hardships you face, or have you been using them as opportunities to learn, to spiritually exercise, and to develop yourself into a stronger, more resilient believer?
3. What thought processes do you need to change in order to receive great benefit from the hardships you face in life instead of being destroyed by them?

Do you hear the Spirit of God speaking to you today? Is He telling you to change the way you are looking at your current hardships? You don't ever have to be depressed and defeated by the affairs of life. Just change the way you're looking at the challenges you face. Determine that you are going to use this time in your life to exercise your faith and become stronger in the Lord!

NOVEMBER 17

The Fields Are White Unto Harvest

Say not ye, There are yet four months,
and then cometh harvest? behold, I say unto you,
Lift up your eyes, and look on the fields;
for they are white already to harvest.
— John 4:35

Once Denise and I and our team traveled by bus to conduct massive evangelistic campaigns in eight of the largest cities in the nation of Ukraine. Because we had been on television for many years in those particular eight cities, we were anticipating that thousands of people would attend these meetings.

As we drove through the vast wheat fields in eastern Ukraine, the golden wheat waved this way and that as the gentle, late-summer winds blew across the landscape. It was so beautiful that Denise and I asked the driver to stop so we could get out of the bus and walk through the beautiful golden fields. As we stood in the midst of those gorgeous shelves of golden grain, we thought of the vast, spiritual harvest fields of the former Soviet Union where God had called our family and ministry. Of course, we were especially thinking about the harvest of souls we were praying to see in those upcoming meetings.

As we stood in the middle of those beautiful fields of wheat, we looked at each other and quoted Jesus' words in John 4:35, which says, "Say not ye, There are yet four months, and then cometh harvest? Behold, I say unto you, Lift up your eyes, and look on the fields; for they are white already to harvest."

When Jesus spoke these words, He was just outside the city of Sychar in Samaria. His disciples had gone to the city to find food, and Jesus had just met the woman at the well (*see* John 4:1-27).

Jesus' encounter with this woman was life-transforming. He spent a significant amount of time talking to her about her personal life, answering her spiritual questions, and treating her with a level of dignity that had rarely been afforded to her. It was the first seed Jesus ever sowed into the heart of a Samaritan. The woman was so moved by His compassion that when she returned to her village, she told the people, "Come, see a man, which told me all things that ever I did: is not this the Christ?" (John 4:29).

This woman so enthusiastically shared her testimony of Jesus that the entire village of Sychar went out of the city to find Him (John 4:30). Thus, from the moment Jesus first sowed His seed into the heart of this Samaritan woman to the time He reaped His first major harvest among the Samaritans would only be a matter of hours. This was indeed quite remarkable. Certainly it often takes quite a period of time to reap a sizable harvest of souls in any new region of the world.

As the village of Sychar went out to meet Jesus, He and His disciples were on the outskirts of the city, where He was speaking to them about doing the work of God. From Jesus' words, it seems likely that He and His followers were standing near a wheat field at the time, similar to the one my wife and I stood in that day in the nation of Ukraine.

As Jesus was speaking to His disciples, He was apparently standing in a position that enabled Him to have a wide view of the nearby wheat fields. Meanwhile, His disciples were so focused on what He was telling them that they were unaware of the streams of people coming from the village and making their way through the fields to where they were located. It was at this moment that Jesus told the disciples, "Say not ye, There are yet four months, and then cometh harvest…."

Naturally speaking, it should take a minimum of four months for seed to be reaped as a full-grown harvest. But that time frame didn't apply in the case of the Samaritan woman. Seed had been sown into her heart just a short time earlier — yet it was already time to reap! That is why Jesus told his disciples, "…Behold, I say unto you, Lift up your eyes, and look on the fields; for they are white already to harvest."

When the disciples turned around and looked, they could see multitudes pushing through the vast wheat field as they made their way to Jesus. It must have been an amazing sight to the disciples. After all, this Samaritan woman had gone to her town only a few hours earlier, and already there was such a large response to her testimony! Jesus had only sown seed into one Samaritan woman's heart, but He was already reaping a massive harvest of souls.

I want you to notice that Jesus said that "…they are white already to harvest." Jesus was not referring to the unripe wheat fields, but to the people who were coming to see Him. One scholar has noted that workers in small villages were known to wear white workers' garments. This village of workers was so affected by the Samaritan woman's testimony that they dropped what they were doing and immediately went to see Jesus, still dressed in their white workers' garments. When the Lord saw a crowd of people coming toward Him dressed in white, He didn't see white garments; He saw a harvest that was white and ready to be reaped among the Samaritans.

As the crowd approached Jesus, He told the disciples, "And he that reapeth receiveth wages, and gathereth fruit unto life eternal: that both he that soweth and he that reapeth may rejoice together. And herein is that saying true, One soweth, and another reapeth" (John 4:36,37).

Jesus was the One who sowed the first seed into the heart of the Samaritan woman, but now it was time to reap — and it requires many more hands to reap than it does to sow. Jesus was the Sower, but the harvest could not be fully reaped and retained without the help of His disciples. Jesus felt great joy as He watched this harvest of souls coming in so quickly. However, now it would also be the disciples' great joy to help Jesus swing the sickle and bring these souls to God. Jesus sowed the seed, but it was essential for the disciples to help Him reap.

In John 4:38, Jesus said, "I sent you to reap that whereon ye bestowed no labour: other men laboured, and ye are entered into their labours." Jesus alone had sown the seed into the heart of the woman at the well. At the time He did this, His disciples were in the village looking for food. But now the disciples were privileged to participate in a huge reaping extravaganza for which they had done no work at all! They were literally entering into a harvest that was white and ready to be reaped because Jesus had taken the time to sow seed into a single person's heart.

Spiritual harvest often comes more quickly than natural harvests. It may take four months for wheat to be ready to be reaped. However, don't think that it will always take a long time before you see people respond to the Word you sow into their hearts. The souls of men are often ready to be reaped for the Kingdom of God very quickly after the initial sowing.

Also, please don't think that your role in sowing seed is small and insignificant. Remember, Jesus sowed a single seed into the heart of one person, yet that isolated, solitary event produced a harvest so huge that an entire village came to Jesus Christ. In the same way, the seed you sow into someone's heart today may be the very seed that produces the next massive harvest for the Kingdom of God!

So the next time you find yourself talking to someone about Jesus Christ or sharing the truths of God's Word with a stranger, don't allow the devil to tell you that you're wasting your time. You may be planting the very seed that will bring salvation to an entire group of people. And when the harvest is ready to be reaped, don't be threatened by people who join you in the reaping process of what you have sown. Harvests always require more reapers than sowers, so be thankful that one plants and others come alongside to help you reap!

As Denise and I finally stood on the stage to preach to the vast crowds that attended those meetings in Ukraine, I thanked God for giving us the awesome privilege of preaching to such huge numbers of people. But I also thanked Him for every single person who uses his or her own private life as a pulpit to share the seed of God's Word with people on the street and at work. Regardless of how or where the seed of God's Word is sown by believers, every seed sown is powerful and has an eternal effect. *Never forget that fact as you go through your day using YOUR life as a pulpit for sowing the life-changing seed of the Gospel!*

MY PRAYER FOR TODAY

Lord, I never realized the power that one single seed could make on such a large group of people. I have mistakenly thought that witnessing to one person was not as important as preaching to multitudes. Please forgive me for overlooking the power of a single seed sown into the human heart. Holy Spirit, I want to be ready when the harvest comes in — and that includes having enough friends and coworkers on hand to pitch in and help. So I ask You to dispatch a group of ready and willing workers who can step into the harvest field and assist me in bringing in the sheaves!

I pray this in Jesus' name!

MY CONFESSION FOR TODAY

I confess that the seed I sow into people's hearts has the power to bring great change to entire groups of people. Every time I share the Word of God with people who don't know the Lord, a seed is planted in their hearts and minds that has the power to revolutionize their lives, their families, their friends, and even their entire cities. Every person I touch has the potential of taking the Gospel message further, thus creating a larger harvest for the Kingdom of God. Therefore, I am bold to speak to anyone whenever I see an open door of opportunity to tell the Good News of Jesus Christ!

I declare this by faith in Jesus' name!

QUESTIONS FOR YOU TO CONSIDER

1. Can you think of a true-life story of how one person's testimony affected a nation or an entire group of people? Who was that person?
2. Can you recall a time when the words someone spoke to you brought tremendous change into your life? Who was that person? What did he or she tell you? What changes came about in your life as a result of those words?
3. Is that person aware of how God changed your life as a result of the seed he or she sowed into your heart? If you've never shared the impact that person's words had on you, don't you think it would be appropriate for you to do so?

November 18

Those Who Minister Out of Their Abundance

And certain women, which had been healed
of evil spirits and infirmities,
Mary called Magdalene, out of whom went seven devils,
And Joanna the wife of Chuza Herod's steward,
and Susanna, and many others,
which ministered unto him of their substance.
— Luke 8:2,3

When our ministry purchased a large facility in the city of Moscow, we had one year to pay off the entire building, or it would revert to the hands of the seller. We had paid a very large deposit, and by faith we were believing to completely pay off the balance on time so we wouldn't lose our total investment.

The deadline for paying off the balance approached. The Moscow church and our ministry partners had given generously, but we still lacked what we needed to finish retiring the debt on the building.

It was exactly at this time that God spoke to a pastor of a large church in the United States and told him, "You have a lot of money in your church bank account right now, and Rick Renner and his ministry are believing for the finances to pay off their building. What good is your money in this account when they need it in Moscow? If you'll give what I tell you to give, I'll multiply it to you more times than you can ever begin to imagine."

In obedience to the Lord, this pastor met with his board of directors, who unanimously voted to give a gift of $700,000 for the Moscow Good News Church building. They had no idea that this was the exact balance owed on the building. The pastor purchased a plane ticket and was soon on his way to Moscow. The following Sunday, he stood on the platform in our auditorium and said, "The Lord has sent me here to give you a $700,000 check for your new church facility!" Then he handed us the check, not knowing that he was handing the exact amount needed to completely pay off the balance on the building.

What words could ever be sufficient to express how grateful we were to this pastor and his church for this phenomenal act of generosity? And how can we ever appropriately thank all the partners who have sowed their finances for so many years into the work of our ministry?

My wife and I and our team may be the ones who are doing the actual work on the front lines of the ministry, but we can only do that work because of the resources entrusted to us by faithful partners. When we all stand before Jesus to be rewarded for what we have done for Him in this life, our partners will be as richly rewarded as those of us who worked on the front lines, for they financially empowered us to do the job!

You see, even though my wife and our team are anointed to lead this work, there would be no television outreach if we had no partners to pay for it. There would be no church-planting, church-strengthening organization if there was no financial support to underwrite the costs involved in this work. There would be no missions support for pastors and evangelists in these less fortunate nations if there were no people who designated monies for this special purpose. Although we are called and anointed to lead this thrilling work, others must be just as called and anointed to support it with their finances. That is why I say that all of us are truly working together to see God's purposes for this ministry accomplished.

I could write an entire book about the miraculous provision we have seen God supply for our ministry over the years. But when I stand back and review the times God has come through in miraculous ways to empower us financially, one thing is clear: His supernatural provision has primarily been delivered through the hands of men.

This is the principal way God provides financial support for the work of the ministry. He uses people — those who work very hard at their jobs, who earn a living at their profession, who believe Him for promotions and bonuses, and who love Him so much that they consecrate a certain portion of their income or assets for the advancement of God's Kingdom.

God also used people to supply money for the expenses of Jesus' ministry, although money to pay taxes was once miraculously provided through the mouth of a fish (*see* Matthew 17:27). In Luke 8:2 and 3, we find that Jesus had ministry partners who gave of their own substance to support His ministry while He was on the earth. Those verses say, "And certain women, which had been healed of evil spirits and infirmities, Mary called Magdalene, out of whom went seven devils, and Joanna the wife of Chuza Herod's steward, and Susanna, and many others, which ministered unto him of their substance."

Notice that Luke 8:3 says that these women "...ministered unto him of their substance." The word "ministered" is the Greek word *diakoneo*. As noted earlier (*see* August 21), the word *diakoneo* comes from the Greek word *diakonos*, the Greek word for *a servant whose primary responsibility is to serve food and wait on tables*. It presents a picture of a waiter or waitress who painstakingly attends to the needs, wishes, and desires of his or her client. It was these servants' supreme task to professionally please clients; therefore, the servants served honorably, pleasurably, and in a fashion that made the people they waited on feel as if they were nobility.

Luke uses this word to picture the attitude of the women who served Jesus by financially giving to Jesus' ministry. These women believed it was their God-given assignment to painstakingly attend to the needs, wishes, and desires of Jesus. Their supreme task was to provide what He and His disciples needed to fulfill their ministry without hindrance. Furthermore, the tense used in the original Greek indisputably means that these women did this task *consistently* and *regularly*; in other words, they *habitually* donated money to Jesus' ministry. They were faithful partners on whom Jesus could rely.

The verse goes on to say that these women ministered unto Him of their "substance." The word "substance" is the Greek word *huparchontos*, which is the word for *goods, possessions,* or *property*. The word *huparchontos* would only be used to describe *individuals of great wealth who possessed large fortunes or enormous assets*. This lets us know that these were wealthy women.

The *King James Version* says these women "...ministered unto him of their substance." But in Greek, it actually says *out* of their substance. This implies that these very wealthy women may have donated funds out of the income they earned on properties they owned.

But precisely *who* were these wealthy women who supported Jesus' ministry? Let's look very carefully at Luke 8:2,3 to see what we can find out about these women whom God used to financially support Jesus' ministry.

1. 'Certain women, which had been healed of evil spirits and infirmities'

First, Luke 8:2 tells us about "…certain women, which had been healed of evil spirits and infirmities.…" This was an unnamed group of women whom Jesus had healed from various sicknesses or delivered from demonic powers. Afterward, these women supported His ministry with their financial substance.

Notice that this verse says these women "…had been healed of evil spirits.…" The word "healed" is the Greek word *therapeuo*, an old Greek word from which we get the work *therapy*. This carries the idea of *repeated actions, such as a patient who visits a physician over and over until the desired cure is obtained*. This seems to suggest that these women had been so severely demonized that although they were helped when they first came to Jesus, they had to keep coming back again and again until, finally, they were completely freed. It may have been Jesus' constant, tender, compassionate attention that caused them to have such grateful hearts, producing in these women a firm commitment to support His ministry with their finances.

The verse also says that they were healed of "infirmities." The word "infirmities" is the Greek word *astheneia*, which emphatically depicts *physical frailties, weaknesses, sicknesses,* or *a state of ill health*. The word "healed" (*therapeuo*) is applied both to the women's deliverance from demonic spirits and to their freedom from illnesses. Just as the Greek suggests frequent visits were made to Jesus before they were finally and completely delivered from demon powers, it also implies that these women made recurring visits to Jesus before they found total relief from their physical maladies. The use of this word *therapeuo* lets us know, then, that it can sometimes take time before a healing is completely manifested in a person's life.

No wonder these women were such avid financial partners with Jesus' ministry! It was through His compassionate touch that they were set free from demons and restored to full health!

It is simply a fact that the best partners in the world are those whose lives have been changed by one's ministry. These women are vivid examples of people with grateful hearts who want to do what they can financially so the ministry that helped them can reach out and touch others' lives as well.

2. 'Mary called Magdalene, out of whom went seven devils'

After mentioning the first unnamed group of female supporters, Luke now gives the first recognizable name in this group of women. He says in verse 2, "…Mary called Magdalene, out of whom went seven devils."

Many tales have been told about Mary Magdalene working in the prostitution business before she met Jesus. However, there isn't a single New Testament source that records Mary Magdalene as a former prostitute. One thing *is* clear, though: She was possessed with an entire infestation of demons before Jesus touched her life. Both Luke 8:2 and Mark 16:9 affirm that she had been delivered of seven demons.

When Luke tells us of Mary, he identifies her as one "…out of whom went seven devils." The Greek word for the phrase "out of whom went" is *exerchomai*, a compound of the word *ex*, meaning *out*, as *to make an exit*, and the word *erchomai*, meaning *to go*. But when these are compounded together, forming the word *exerchomai*, it takes on the meaning *to go out, to drive out,* or even *to escape*.

The word *exerchomai* implies that these demons may have been so entrenched in Mary that Jesus had to literally drive them out of her. It is possible that when these seven spirits left her body, they literally *fled* in order to *escape* the fierce pressure Jesus was exercising on them. Once they were gone, Mary was freed.

The Bible has no concrete record of Mary's deliverance from these seven demons. However, it does let us know she was so thankful for what Jesus had done for her that she remained committed to Him to the very end of His ministry. Mary was present at the crucifixion (John 19:25). After the crucifixion when Jesus' body was being prepared for burial, Mary was among those who prepared His body for burial (Matthew 27:61; Mark 15:47; Luke 23:55). She was among the first to see the empty tomb (John 20:1), and she was the first to see Jesus after His resurrection (John 20:13-17). Finally, she was the first to preach that Jesus had been resurrected from the dead (John 20:18).

Evidently Mary Magdalene was also a wealthy woman who used her money to financially support Jesus' ministry, for she is listed in Luke 8:2,3 along with the other well-to-do women who gave out of their assets to support Jesus' ministry.

3. 'Joanna the wife of Chuza Herod's steward'

As Luke continues to name the affluent women who financially supported Jesus' ministry, he tells us next of "…Joanna, the wife of Chuza Herod's steward…" (v. 3).

Luke gives us very important insight into this Joanna by informing us that she was the wife of Chuza, who was the "steward" of Herod. The word "steward" is the Greek word *epitropos*. This word signifies *a person who has been entrusted with the guardianship or supervision of another person's belongings*. This was no low-level servant; rather, Chuza was a high-level dignitary who had authority to make decisions on behalf of Herod in regard to his personal fortunes. One of the rare uses of this word in the Greek Old Testament Septuagint is where it is used to describe Joseph's oversight of Potiphar's household.

The fact that Chuza held such a prominent position in Herod's household tells us that he was highly educated and was accustomed to managing massive sums of money. As the chief manager of Herod's personal fortune, Chuza served as the king's chief adviser regarding his personal financial matters. No doubt, a man in this position had many opportunities to increase his own personal wealth as well, for he lived in the atmosphere of affluence and had many high-ranking political connections as Herod's steward. Some have speculated that Chuza may have been the nobleman of John 4:46-53 whose son was healed by Jesus.

Chuza's wife was Joanna — a woman whose life had been dramatically touched, affected, and changed by Jesus. If Chuza was the nobleman of John 4:46-53, as some suggest, it is easy to imagine how grateful Joanna would have been to Jesus for saving her child from death. Certainly a person so impacted would want to use her fortune to make sure others could receive the same touch of God.

The Bible doesn't tell us how Joanna made her first connection with Jesus, but it apparently changed her life. After that encounter, she saw it as part of her responsibility to give of her personal substance to financially support Jesus' ministry. Joanna was also with Mary Magdalene and the other women who visited and discovered the empty tomb after Jesus' resurrection (*see* Luke 24:10), which lets us know that she was faithful to Jesus to the very end.

4. 'Susanna, and many others'

This is the only reference to Susanna in the New Testament, and we know nothing more of her, except that she ministered to Jesus out of her substance. This implies that she was another wealthy woman who used her personal resources to support Jesus' ministry.

Susanna is listed with "many others" who supported the ministry of Jesus. The word "many" is from the Greek word *polus*, which means *very many* and speaks of a *great quantity*. So in addition to these women whom Luke specifically names, there were also *many* others who supported Jesus faithfully with their personal finances. These were givers who considered it their responsibility, their service, and their assignment to make sure the needs of Jesus' growing ministry were financially supplied.

We rightly focus on Jesus and the great works He did while on earth. But think of the reward that is laid up in Heaven for Mary Magdalene, Joanna, Susanna, and all the others who gave of their substance so that those life-changing meetings could take place! Today these individuals are experiencing rich rewards because they gave of their personal income to help advance the ministry of Jesus. They were His ministry partners — and in Heaven, they share in the rewards for the results reaped by Jesus' ministry.

If your life has been touched and changed by a specific ministry, it is right for you to desire to give to that ministry to show your gratefulness and to make sure others receive the same touch you received. So when God calls you to be a ministry partner, never forget that what you do is vitally important. The gifts you give from your personal income and assets can make an eternal difference in other people's lives.

Please don't let it bother you if your name is never put on a building or if people never know that you were a big giver to a ministry. Instead, rejoice that you are among the "many others" who gave to Jesus' ministry but were not mentioned by name. *Most importantly, never forget that Jesus knows who you are and what you have done and that an eternal reward is awaiting you!*

MY PRAYER FOR TODAY

Lord, I am so grateful for the opportunity to serve You with my income and assets. I only want to give more and more with each passing year. Please give me wisdom to know how to increase my personal wealth so I can become an even bigger giver to the Kingdom of God. It isn't important to me that other people know what I've done, for I know that You see the seed I've sown and will reward me for what I have done. Help me to never use funds designated for Your work on anything else, Lord, but rather to make the advancement of Your Kingdom the highest priority in my life.

I pray this in Jesus' name!

MY CONFESSION FOR TODAY

I confess that I am a significant giver to the Kingdom of God. God's Word promises financial blessings to His children. Since I am God's child, I have a right to be financially blessed. From the financial resources that God entrusts to me, I purpose to be a major giver and a source of great blessing to the work of the ministry. Souls are waiting to hear the Gospel message, and I am going to use the resources God gives me to make sure the life-changing message of Jesus Christ reaches as many people as possible!

I declare this by faith in Jesus' name!

QUESTIONS FOR YOU TO CONSIDER

1. Is it a desire of your heart to be a big giver to the work of God? What ministry has God used to touch your life so dramatically that you want to serve that ministry with your finances?

2. What ministry or ministries do you support with your finances right now? Can you write down five reasons why you sow into these particular ministries?

3. Are you satisfied in your heart that you are giving to these ministries as often as God desires you to give? Or is it time for you to believe God for the financial ability to rise to a whole new level of giving?

NOVEMBER 19

Fight Like a Soldier!

Thou therefore endure hardness,
as a good soldier of Jesus Christ.
— 2 Timothy 2:3

In Second Timothy, Timothy was facing a horrible predicament. Thousands of his brothers and sisters in the Lord were being slain by a man on the Roman throne named Nero. Of course, Satan was behind this vicious persecution of believers. Infuriated that Jesus had been raised from the dead, the devil was releasing all the power and fury of hell in his fierce efforts to destroy the Church.

It is difficult for us to imagine the persecution and martyrdom the early believers experienced during this time period. However, an even greater crisis that Timothy faced was the mass defections that were taking place. Many people were fleeing the church and returning to the pagan temples in order to save their lives.

The fact is, crises only serve to reveal the genuineness of people's faith. The fires of persecution revealed that many in the Early Church were not as committed as they had pretended to be. Many forsook the Lord, deserted the faith, and went back to their old ways. Timothy was seeing this take place among the members of his congregation — and even among many of his leaders. Many of the men and women whom he thought he could depend on had left. They didn't want to be associated with Timothy and the church any longer. Hence, this was a very, very tough time for the Ephesian believers and their pastor.

It was in the midst of these catastrophic challenges that Paul wrote Timothy and said, "Thou therefore endure hardness, as a good soldier of Jesus Christ." The phrase "endure hardness" in Greek tells us something very important about doing the work of God. Please pay careful attention to this, because if you are going through a difficult ordeal as you obey God with your life, this also applies to you.

The phrase "endure hardness" comes from the Greek word *sunkakopatheo*, a compound of three Greek words. The first part of the word is the Greek word *sun*. This little word *sun* always connects you to someone else. It is a word that describes *partnership*. For example, in Second Corinthians 6:1, Paul says, "We then, as workers together with him...." The word *sun* is used in the phrase "workers together."

The word "workers" is from the word *ergos*, which simply means *work*, but when the words *sun* and *ergos* are compounded together as in Second Corinthians 6:1, the new word describes *coworkers* or *people who are partnered together as they work alongside each other on a common job*. These are workers who are *connected* and *joined* to each other in the pursuit of a shared goal.

You see, we are not working *for* the Lord *by ourselves*; rather, we are fellow workers with Him. Thus, Second Corinthians 6:1 is a description of *partnership* with God and carries the idea of *cooperating with Him* in our work. It also means that God is with us, working on the same task at the same time, cooperating with us as our Partner. This is exactly what Paul means when he writes that we are "…workers together with him…."

As we look at the phrase "endure hardness," it is imperative that you understand the use of the word *sun* in this Greek phrase. But you must also grasp the next two parts of this triple compound. The second word is the Greek word *kakos*. This is a very familiar Greek word that most often describes *something that is vile, foul, or wicked*. If all you had were these first two words, it would mean, *"become a partner with this vile, foul, horrible, wicked situation."* However, Paul goes further and uses a third Greek word, *pathos*.

The word *pathos* is another well-known Greek word. It normally describes *suffering*, but it has more to do with *mental suffering* than it does physical suffering. This was a word perfectly suited for Timothy at this time, for he was suffering great mental anguish as a result of the disturbing events occurring around him.

Have you ever been in such an intense situation that you thought your mind might "break"? Or have you ever felt like you might mentally collapse from being pushed hard up against the wall with no obvious way of escape? If the answer is yes, you may relate to what Timothy was going through at the time Paul wrote him.

Consider the thoughts that must have been racing through Timothy's mind. Nero was killing many of the young minister's friends and church members. As the most visible Christian leader, Timothy must have wondered if the emperor's men would kill him — and if they did, what kind of especially terrible death would be planned for him as the most famous Christian of the city? Add to all these concerns the great disappointment Timothy felt because of those who had abandoned him and the church, and it is clear that his mind could have felt very overwhelmed, subdued, and mentally affected. This is why Paul told him to "endure hardness," using the words *sun, kakos,* and *pathos* to make his point.

**Compounded together,
these words could be interpreted this way:**

"Join in as a partner with the rest of us (sun) and face this vile, horrible, ugly circumstance (kakos) that is all around you. And if you must undergo a little suffering (pathos) to do this job, then brace yourself and go for it!"

Several key messages to Timothy were included in this one word. First, Paul used the word *sun* to let the younger man know he wasn't the *only* soldier serving the Lord. Although Timothy may have emotionally perceived that everyone else was abandoning the Lord, this wasn't the truth of the matter. In reality, many believers were still faithfully fighting the fight of faith. This is why Paul told him, "Join in as a partner with the rest of us."

Second, by using the word *kakos*, it is almost as though Paul was saying, "Yes, you're right. It's pretty bad out there, and it seems like things are getting worse. There is no doubt that a terrible, ugly mess lies before us. It is the most wicked situation we've ever faced."

Third, by using the word *pathos*, Paul is telling Timothy to brace himself for a fight and to toughen himself. A job needed to be done, no matter what kind of atmosphere surrounded him.

Timothy's obedience couldn't depend on good or bad circumstances. If circumstances were turning against him and the other faithful Christians, it was time for them to make the quality decision to do whatever was necessary in order to complete their assignment. If suffering was required for Timothy to do his part in pushing the Kingdom of God forward, then he needed to be willing to undergo suffering. Every Christian soldier who is committed to taking new territory for the Kingdom of God must have this mentality.

The truth is, we all face hardships from time to time. And whether or not we want to admit it, we've all experienced times when fear has tried to wrap its tentacles around us and drain the victory of Jesus Christ from our lives.

But the next time fear tries to grab hold of *you*, just remember what Paul told Timothy. This is an opportunity for you to lay hold of God's power, rise up to meet the occasion, and overcome every challenge in the power of the Holy Spirit. *God is calling you to endure hardship as a good soldier of Jesus Christ!*

MY PRAYER FOR TODAY

Lord, please forgive me for being so soft and wimpy about my faith and my commitment to Your call on my life. Please help me to become tough in the Spirit so I can deal with any attack the devil might try to bring against my life. I am so sorry that I've bent under pressure, whining and complaining that things were too hard, despite the fact that the power of Your resurrection lives inside me. I don't want to waste one more minute feeling sorry for myself. Therefore, I ask You to help me brace myself, grab hold of Your power, and bravely overcome every situation in the power of the Holy Spirit!

I pray this in Jesus' name!

MY CONFESSION FOR TODAY

I boldly confess that I am filled with faith, courage, and confidence. I am able to face and overcome every situation in life with the promise of God's Word and the power of the Holy Spirit. I refuse to let fear rule me, and I choose to believe that I can do all things through Christ who strengthens me. With God's power working in me, I am more than enough for every challenge that will ever come up in my life!

I declare this by faith in Jesus' name!

QUESTIONS FOR YOU TO CONSIDER

1. What is the most difficult situation you have ever faced in life?
2. What is the primary challenge you are facing right now?
3. What are you doing to make yourself tougher in the Spirit so you can overcome this present challenge in your life and press onward to a time of victory?

The fires of persecution revealed that many in the Early Church were not as committed as they had pretended to be.

NOVEMBER 20

Prepare and Compete Like an Athlete!

And if a man also strive for masteries,
yet is he not crowned, except he strive lawfully.
— 2 Timothy 2:5

*A*fter telling Timothy to endure hardness as a good soldier of Jesus Christ, Paul then switches to a new illustration so he can make another important point. The purpose of the discussion is still the same: Paul is explaining to Timothy how he should face the difficulties that lie before him at the moment. With that purpose in mind, Paul says, "And if a man also strive for masteries, yet is he not crowned, except he strive lawfully."

The word "strive" is from the Greek word *athlesis*, which always described *a man involved in a tremendous athletic competition*. This kind of athlete was serious about his sport and totally committed to the goal of climbing to the top in his profession. He was willing to undergo any hardship, any training, any regimen, and any kind of discipline in order to reach that goal of becoming the very best in his field of sports. The word *athlesis* describes this type of *committed, full-time, professional, determined athlete*. This is the picture Paul now uses when he speaks to Timothy about overcoming the challenges he is facing.

Remember that Paul has already told Timothy to endure hardness as a good soldier of Jesus Christ (v. 3). Now by changing his illustration to that of a professional athlete, Paul is asking Timothy (and us) a very potent question: "Are you willing to be as committed to winning your fight as athletes are to winning in their sport? How committed are you? Is a little pressure going to elbow you out of the race, or are you more committed than the inconveniences you are experiencing along the way? *How badly do you want to win?*"

We must honestly ask ourselves these questions if we want to determine the true level of our commitment. You see, it is wonderful to serve the Lord and be a part of the local church when we aren't facing any big problems in life. It's easy to tithe, give offerings, attend meetings, pray, and sing with other believers when our level of service basically costs us nothing.

However, what are you going to do if things change and it starts to become more challenging to serve the Lord? What if it becomes difficult to hold fast to the vision He put in your heart or to the commitment you made to His call on your life? Will you still serve the Lord with joy? Will you still be faithful to your local church? Will you still give your tithes and offerings?

You see, it is the spiritual fights in life that always reveal the genuine level of our commitment. Look again at what Paul says in Second Timothy 2:5: "And if a man also strive for masteries...." Particularly notice the word "man," because this is the Greek word *tis*. This word *tis* would be better translated *anyone*. The idea this word presents is *anyone at all*.

This tells us two very important things. First, *anyone* can compete in the life of faith. This verse is for *tis* — for *anyone*. Second, it tells us that anyone who desires to be a successful competitor had better pay heed to the proper preparation and training required to make him a winner! Notice Paul says that a man will not be crowned "...except he strive lawfully."

The word "lawfully" doesn't refer to the rules of the game, but to the *training* and *preparation* that professional athletes went through before the game actually commenced. This tells us that we should never attempt to enter the real arenas of life until we have gone through the necessary preparation to win. If we enter an arena without preparation, we better be ready to spend some time recuperating, because we are headed for a beating!

Winners are those who have trained and prepared themselves. Then, as now, athletic "scouts" would go out into the communities to look over all the young athletes. After finding a promising athlete, the scout would issue him an invitation to the training camp. At camp, the athletes were introduced to bodybuilders, trainers, and others who were skilled at fighting and competition. The trainers would put the athletes through incredible routines to build both their bodies and their minds, for mental alertness was deemed to be equally important to physical fitness.

Timothy knew all about the manner in which professional athletes were trained. This was common knowledge during his day. Everyone was familiar with the strict, regimented training that athletes went through in order to compete. Therefore, Paul's statement on "striving for the masteries" didn't require a lot of deep contemplation in order for Timothy to know exactly what the apostle was telling him.

Rather than moan and complain about how hard it had become to serve God, it was time for Timothy to change his way of thinking. If he was to be a professional and not an amateur in the Kingdom of God, he needed to see all his challenges as opportunities to use his faith, exercising himself under the most strenuous circumstances and thus developing himself to handle the greater tasks that were still ahead of him.

Although Timothy was facing real hardships in the present, he would still have to face additional hardships in the future. Therefore, rather than let his current circumstances pass without benefiting from them, he needed to view his present challenge as an opportunity to train and prepare for the future. If he could pass this test, he could pass *any* test!

What test are *you* facing today, friend? What has this time of hardship revealed about your own level of commitment? Are you as committed as you thought you were, or have you discovered that you are much softer spiritually than you realized? Rather than go forward in life in that soft condition, don't you think it would be a good idea for you to look at this time in your life as an opportunity to get tougher and to grow stronger in the Lord?

I guarantee you — Satan hates every believer who dares to shine the light of God's Word into places previously held hostage in darkness. If you decide to be one of those committed believers and to endeavor to do exactly what God has told you to do, Satan will be very alarmed by your obedience. He may try to stop you, throwing obstacles in your path that you never dreamed could happen to you. If you haven't mentally and spiritually prepared yourself to be strong, these attacks of the enemy may overwhelm you.

Don't you think it's time for you to decide whether you are a professional or an amateur in God's Kingdom? If you are a professional, it's time for you to change your mental outlook on life and then get busy training and preparing so you can win every one of your future competitions!

MY PRAYER FOR TODAY

Lord, I want to be strong enough to overcome any situation I'll ever face in life. Forgive me for sitting around and wasting valuable time that I could have used to train and prepare myself to be spiritually fit. I'm sorry I've allowed myself to be lazy at times, and today I am making the decision to throw myself into spiritual preparation. I have decided to strive for the masteries and make my life count! Holy Spirit, please help me become everything Jesus intends for me to be and to make the changes in my mental outlook that are required for me to become a winner in life.

I pray this in Jesus' name!

MY CONFESSION FOR TODAY

I confess that I am serious about staying fit spiritually. I refuse to let laziness be a part of my life. I reject any temptation to moan, groan, and complain about how hard life is. I choose instead to see every event in life as an opportunity to flex my spiritual muscles and to become stronger in the Lord!

I declare this by faith in Jesus' name!

QUESTIONS FOR YOU TO CONSIDER

1. What situations are you facing right now that you could use to flex your spiritual muscles and grow stronger in your walk with the Lord?
2. Rather than moan and complain about how hard things have become in your life, is it time for you to change the way you are thinking? If you want to live like a professional and not an amateur in the Kingdom of God, isn't it time for you to see all your challenges as opportunities to exercise your faith?
3. Rather than let this present circumstance pass without providing you any benefit in life, don't you agree that you need to view it as an opportunity to train and prepare for the future? Remember, if you can pass this test, you can pass *any* test!

NOVEMBER 21

Work Like a Farmer

The husbandman that laboureth
must be first partaker of the fruits.
— 2 Timothy 2:6

When Paul wrote to Timothy to encourage him to bravely face his battles, he first told Timothy to endure hardness as a good soldier of Jesus Christ. Then Paul changed his illustration and exhorted Timothy to develop the mentality of a professional athlete. But suddenly the athletic talk stops, and Paul begins to instruct the younger minister to start thinking like a farmer! Second Timothy 2:6 says, "The husbandman that laboureth must be first partaker of the fruits."

Paul's abrupt changes in his illustrations must have left Timothy's mind whirling! Paul had already told him to endure and fight like a *soldier*, then to prepare and train like an *athlete*. But now he tells Timothy to work hard like a *farmer*!

It's almost as if Paul says, *"Timothy, you need to be a good soldier of Jesus Christ. Or let me give you another example: You need to train and prepare with the same determination and commitment an athlete possesses. Or here's another illustration to help you understand: You need to be hard-working like a farmer. I KNOW! You need to be all three of these things! You must fight like a soldier, prepare and compete like an athlete, and work like a farmer! You must begin to view yourself as all three — a soldier, an athlete, and a farmer!"*

When Paul writes Second Timothy 2:6, he uses words that convey images of farming life. For instance, the word "husbandman" is the Greek word *georgos*, the word for *a farmer who tills the soil*. Because Paul uses the word *georgos* ("husbandman"), there is no doubt that he has the varied activities of a farmer in his mind as he writes to Timothy.

As Paul begins to convey this idea to Timothy, he starts by talking about the hard work of a farmer. He says, "The husbandman that laboureth...." The word "laboureth" is the Greek word *kopos*, which always denotes *the hardest, toughest kind of work*. This presents the idea of *a person who works to the end of his strength or to the point of physical exhaustion*. This farmer is an individual who is giving every ounce of his strength to finish the task before him. Although he is weary, he keeps plodding on step after step, refusing to give up. Rejecting the temptation to throw in the towel, he keeps plowing the ground before him because the task *must* be done by someone.

The picture this word *kopos* suggests is of a farmer who labors in the heat of the afternoon sun during the hottest season of the year with sweat pouring down his face. Although the ground is like hard, dry clay and the work is strenuous, the farmer just keeps on *plowing and sowing, plowing and sowing*. After he finishes plowing one row of his garden, he turns at the end of the row and starts all over again on the next row. By the end of the day, the farmer is physically exhausted, mentally drained, drenched with perspiration, and covered with dirt. *He has done a hard day's work!*

By using this illustration, Paul tells us to face the facts: If you're going to reap a harvest, you have to get out in the field and do the job! If you will do your job faithfully like a hard-working farmer who wants to reap the benefits of a large crop, you will also reap an abundant crop of success and blessing.

Now we get to the rewarding part! The apostle Paul says, "The husbandman that laboureth must be first partaker of the fruits." This is God's personal promise to anyone who puts his hand to the plow and works hard — and it is His special promise to *you*!

Paul says that if you are faithful to work in His Kingdom, you "...*must be* first partaker of the fruits." The words "must be" in Greek is the word *dei*. It is always used to convey the idea of *a necessity, an obligation, a requirement, a demand*, or *a rule to which there is absolutely no exception and that can never be broken*. You could interpret the verse, *"The husbandman that laboureth absolutely must be..."* or *"The husbandman that laboureth is obligated and under command...."*

Paul tells what "must be" when he says, "The husbandman that laboureth must be first partaker of the fruits." In other words, God wants the committed, determined, hard-working believer to eat from the table of victory and to enjoy the sweet fruit of success *before* anyone else does!

When we look at the entire text of Second Timothy 2:3-6, we understand that God is telling us:

"If you will fight like a soldier; if you will prepare and compete like an athlete; and if you will put your heart and soul into working in your field the way a hard-working farmer does —

here is what I will do for you. I am establishing a permanent rule — one that can never be changed, altered, or modified — and I am making it a top priority and a necessity that when your battle is over and you've proven yourself to be a good soldier; when your spiritual opponents are defeated and you've won your competition; when you've plowed your fields and your crops begin to grow and mature before your eyes — you WILL eat before anyone else eats!"

You see, God wants you to eat and enjoy the fruit of your labors, just as a hard-working farmer does after giving his life to see his crops grow in his field. Your part is to work your land and labor strenuously to see your dream come to pass; then God promises that you will eventually eat the fruit of your hard work! As you focus on doing your job well, you can expect to be blessed, recognized, rewarded, and remunerated for your efforts, for God says that anyone who works hard and sticks with his project to the end deserves to eat the fruit!

Warriors *deserve* rewards. Good athletes *earn* recognition. Farmers have *every right* to eat their crops. And if *you* are living and fighting by faith to see a certain victory in your life, you can claim God's promise that a day is coming when you will eat the sweet fruit of victory!

This message must have been very encouraging for Timothy. At that moment, he was so immersed in the conflicts that swirled around him that his mind must have easily become swamped with fears and concerns about what was happening to his congregation. But Paul's encouraging message to Timothy is the same message God has for you today.

God is telling you, "If you will endure hardship as a good soldier; train and compete like a good athlete; plow your ground and work hard in the field where I have called you, no matter how hard or difficult it is — then I promise you that a day *will* come when things turn around. And on that day, you will be *richly* rewarded!"

MY PRAYER FOR TODAY

Lord, I am so blessed to know that You want me to eat the sweet fruit of victory. That knowledge makes me want to work my ground even harder to produce a great harvest for Your Kingdom. I know that in my own flesh, I will never be able to fulfill the dream You've given me. But by Your Spirit, I can do all things! So I ask You to fill me with so much strength and motivation that I'll never stop until I finally reap the harvest of my dreams!

I pray this in Jesus' name!

MY CONFESSION FOR TODAY

I confess that I will never stop until I see the harvest of my dream. It's going to take hard work and some time, but I am going to keep plowing and cultivating my ground until I see my crops mature. A day is coming in my future when I will pull up to the table, take out my knife and fork, and dive into the sweet victory for which I've worked so hard!

I declare this by faith in Jesus' name!

QUESTIONS FOR YOU TO CONSIDER

1. What is the dream crop you've been working for and waiting to reap in your life?
2. Are there changes you need to make in your work style if you are going to

achieve the great, super-abundant dreams God has put in your heart? If so, what are the changes you need to make to become a super-achiever?

3. Can you name five crops you've already reaped in life due to your hard work, consistency, and faithfulness?

NOVEMBER 22

A Message to the Rich

Charge them that are rich in this world,
that they be not highminded,
nor trust in uncertain riches, but in the living God,
who giveth us richly all things to enjoy.
— 1 Timothy 6:17

When the rule of communism began to dissipate in the Soviet Union, it left the economy in utter shambles. Nearly every basic commodity was unavailable, including basic items such as sugar, flour, cheese, milk, and eggs. There was a huge deficit of light bulbs, toilet paper, and most household products. Gasoline was so expensive that most people preferred to walk than to pay the kind of money needed to fill the gas tank.

This situation meant that whoever controlled the basic supplies of life had the ability to acquire incredible wealth. Because it was a time of great political and economic confusion, nearly anything was possible. As a result, a large number of scoundrels, bandits, thieves, criminals, lawyers, politicians, and especially bright common people began to think of ways to turn this great disadvantage into their own personal advantage.

Today's Russian society now includes a new class of super-rich. To say these people are fabulously wealthy is an understatement. They are what some might call filthy, stinking rich! It is difficult to imagine how this tiny part of Russia's population could have made this kind of money in such a brief period of time.

In this category are people who arrogantly drive their Rolls Royces, Bentleys, and Mercedes through the streets of Moscow, expecting the whole world to move out of their way as they drive past. As is often true with people who make a lot of money in a short period of time, they are usually very rude. Their newly made wealth goes to their heads, causing them to strut through the stores, restaurants, and shopping centers as if they were the owners of planet earth. Their snobbery is on a world-class level. They are completely consumed with how to frivolously spend the riches they have amassed. However, most of them end up losing their money just as quickly as they made it.

This type of person who makes loads of money quickly and then distastefully flaunts his wealth can be found in every nation of the world. There were even such people in the Roman world of the first century. Paul wrote Timothy and told him to tell the rich, "Charge them that are rich in this world, that they be not highminded, nor trust in uncertain riches, but in the living God, who giveth us richly all things to enjoy" (1 Timothy 6:17).

It is a fact that a small minority of "rich" people came to Christ in the first century and were members of the Church. It was in regard to this group of individuals that Paul told Timothy, "Charge them that are rich in this world...." The word "charge" is the Greek word *parangelo*, which means *to charge* or *to command*. It is such a strong command that it should actually be received as a *requirement* — *not* a negotiable option. Thus, when Timothy deals with the wealthy in his church, he is to give them the strong exhortation that Paul is about to give him with such firmness that they receive it as *an order* from the Lord!

When Paul calls these people "rich," he uses the word *plousios*, a very old Greek word that describes *someone who possesses incredible abundance, extreme wealth, and enormous affluence*. This word would not describe someone who is moderately wealthy but rather someone who is *extremely wealthy*. Just as there are people of great influence and enormous wealth who come to Christ today and learn to faithfully attend church, apparently this was also the case in the first century.

It is right that we should pray for the wealth of this world to pass into the hands of the godly who would use it for eternal purposes. God wants His people to be blessed. He wants them to have enough to meet their own needs and to abundantly meet the needs of others. He wants Christians to have enough to finance the preaching of the Gospel to the ends of the earth.

But so often when large sums of money pass into the hands of people for the first time, their wealth goes to their heads and creates in them the "high-minded" attitude I mentioned earlier and to which Paul now refers. This is not the attitude God wants from His people when money passes into their hands.

What exactly does the Greek word for "high-minded" mean? The word "high-minded" in Greek is *hupsilophroneo*. The first part of this word comes from the Greek word *hupslos*, meaning *exalted, elevated, high,* or *lofty*. The second part of this word is *phroneo*, which means *to think, to consider, to deem,* or *to be of a certain opinion*. When these two words are compounded together, the new word means *to think too highly of oneself*. It refers to *the opinion one has when he thinks he is better than others*.

Paul uses a negative in the Greek, which strongly alerts us that one shouldn't think of himself as better than others simply because he has more money than others. Even if a person is uncommonly financially blessed and operates in exceptional financial circles, he still shouldn't deem himself better than other people just because he has more money than they do.

Paul tells the wealthy people in the Church that they are not to "...trust in uncertain riches...." The word "uncertain" is the word *adelotes*. This is the only time that this exact word appears in the New Testament. It means *uncertain, inconsistent,* or *something so unstable that it can go as easily as it came*. The word "trust" is the Greek word *elpidzo*, the most common word for *hope* in the New Testament. As used in this verse, it means *not to place one's hope on one certain thing*. The particular Greek tense used here carries the idea of *one who places his hope in something and then keeps his hope there*.

Paul says the rich are not to set their hope "in" riches. The word "in" is the Greek word *epi*, which would be better translated *upon*. A more accurate rendering of this entire phrase would be that the rich are "*...not to fix their hope upon uncertain riches....*"

Riches are uncertain. Just ask those who thought they were financially set for life but then lost almost all their fortunes through a sudden change in the stock market. There are many people who wake up in the morning rich but go to bed that same night financially insolvent. Therefore, Paul tells the rich that instead of putting their hope in finances that are uncertain, they are to fix their hope "...in the living God, who giveth us richly all things to enjoy."

If your sense of security rests in your financial portfolio and then your portfolio diminishes or disappears, you could be thrown into an enormous identity crisis that results in great fear, anxiety, and insecurity. But when your trust is in the Lord, you are never shaken no matter what happens in the material realm. Why? Because your identity is not in what you possess but in who you are in Jesus Christ.

If you know others who are being financially blessed, rejoice with them. Pray for such people to have the necessary wisdom to use their finances the way God wishes them to use it.

And if you are financially blessed yourself, praise God for it! However, be careful to keep separate *who you are* from *what you own*. Don't let your identity get all wrapped up in what you own so that your sense of security becomes deeply shaken by any material loss. Never forget that who you are is much more important than what you own, and your relationships in this life are much more important than your possessions.

Financial prosperity is a blessing from Heaven and a great honor from the Lord. But if God has trusted you with riches, remember to keep your head on straight. Don't ever think you are better than others just because you possess a lot of wealth. God blessed you so that you could *be* a blessing. Therefore, learn to see yourself as a servant of God whose job is to manage and distribute the funds you have amassed as He desires!

Today I urge you not to fall into the category of those who think too highly of themselves just because they have more money than others. God certainly didn't give you wealth so that you could develop a pride problem!

Go to the Lord regularly and ask Him how He wants you to use those funds. As you keep your heart open to the Holy Spirit and stay willing to hear what He has to say, He will direct you on how to use the resources at your disposal. And if you ever get into pride, He will gently correct you and bring you back to the attitude He desires you to possess.

MY PRAYER FOR TODAY

Lord, thank You for the blessings You have given to my family and me. You have abundantly blessed me, and I am so grateful for everything You have done. I ask You to help me keep the right attitude toward others who have less than I do; to refrain from a false attitude of pride or haughtiness; and to see myself as the manager of divinely assigned funds. I want to trust in You, Lord — not in the things You have placed at my disposal. Possessions and material things are fleeting, but You are always the same. Therefore, I choose to fix my hope on You and not on the financial increase with which You have blessed me.

I pray this in Jesus' name!

MY CONFESSION FOR TODAY

I confess that because my trust is in the Lord, I am never shaken. My identity is not in what I own but in who I am in Jesus Christ! Even though I am financially blessed, I keep WHO I AM separate from WHAT I OWN. Who I am is much more important than what I own, and my relationships are much more important than the material things I possess! I will not let my prosperity go to my head and make me think that I am better than others. God has blessed me so I can be a blessing. Therefore, I see myself as the servant of God, called to manage and distribute the funds at my disposal as He desires!

I declare this by faith in Jesus' name!

QUESTIONS FOR YOU TO CONSIDER

1. What is the largest amount of money that God has ever entrusted to you? How was your attitude about yourself and others affected by your possessing such a large amount of resources?

2. Have you ever known someone whose attitude about others changed when money came into their hands? Did they flaunt their wealth and act so differently that it was obnoxious? After seeing how they acted, did their behavior make you inwardly decide how you will or will not act when money comes into *your* hands?

3. If God has found you faithful and has placed a large amount of financial resources at your disposal, are you regularly asking Him how He wants you to use that money? What is He telling you to do with that money right now?

NOVEMBER 23

If You're Financially Blessed, Don't Feel Guilty About It!

Charge them that are rich in this world,
that they be not highminded, nor trust in uncertain riches,
but in the living God, who giveth us richly all things to enjoy.
— 1 Timothy 6:17

Many years ago, my wife and I knew a family who was *extremely* wealthy. When I use the word "extremely" to describe their wealth, even this word inadequately expresses the immense reserves of worldly possessions they had accumulated. Due to their great-great-grandfather's wise planning two generations earlier, their family money had been invested in such a way that it couldn't be touched and therefore wouldn't be spent. As a result, the family investments had kept growing and accumulating for two generations.

Although vast sums of money were in the bank and belonged to these family members, they were not allowed to touch one cent of it until the date that had been set by their great-great-grandfather. They were enormously wealthy; yet they struggled financially to make ends meet because the treasure they had in the bank wasn't at their disposal.

When we first came to know this family, the time had finally arrived — their money became available for them to use and enjoy. But because they had lived for so long with so little, they didn't know how to enjoy the money. In fact, even though they could purchase anything they wished, they didn't. They felt guilty about owning so much money.

So instead of enjoying their wealth, these family members just let the money sit in the bank, where it continued to grow larger. Meanwhile, they lived like people who were financially strapped for cash. They wore old clothes; they balked at spending the money to purchase a new car; and they were very concerned about what people would think of them if word ever got out about how much money they had in the bank. When I saw these people, I'd try to encourage them to go buy some new clothes, but they didn't want to spend the money to do it. Even though they could purchase anything they wanted, they lived like poor people.

When Paul wrote to Timothy, he gave him instructions for the rich people who attended his church. He said, "Charge them that are rich in this world, that they be not highminded, nor trust in uncertain riches, but in the living God, who giveth us richly all things to enjoy" (1 Timothy 6:17).

I want you to notice that God's blessings are to be *enjoyed*. The word "enjoy" in this verse is from the Greek word *apolausis*, which describes *a person who gets the maximum benefit from something he owns*. Rather than feel guilty about what he owns, he derives great pleasure, gratification, and enjoyment from what he possesses. This means if God has entrusted abundant resources to you, you shouldn't feel guilty about your wealth or feel badly about enjoying it. God *wants* you to enjoy the blessings and resources He has entrusted to you!

Paul asked the Corinthians, "...Who planteth a vineyard, and eateth not of the fruit thereof? or who feedeth a flock, and eateth not of the milk of the flock?" (1 Corinthians 9:7). In other words, if you have worked hard to produce the success you are now experiencing, it is *right* and *normal* for you to personally enjoy a part of it!

Worldly wealth empowers you to get things done; it enables you to be a blessing to other people; and it gives you the ability to sow into the work and advancement of the Gospel. So stop feeling guilty if you are financially blessed. Stop feeling like it's wrong that you got a promotion when someone else didn't. You have worked hard for the harvest you are now reaping, and it's time to start enjoying what God has done for you!

Why don't you change the way you are thinking? Learn to see yourself as one who has been specially empowered in order to be a blessing to others and to give for the advancement of the Gospel. And if you want to enjoy some of your wealth along the way, there's nothing wrong with that either! *God has given you all things richly to enjoy!*

MY PRAYER FOR TODAY

Lord, I have asked You to bless me financially. So when increased finances begin to come, please help me have the grace both to enjoy them and to use them for the advancement of Your Kingdom. I don't want to flaunt the money I possess or to frivolously spend it. Instead, I want to use it to do something positive and eternal in this life. At the same time, please teach me how to enjoy the financial increase You have blessed me with and to know that it is all right for me to personally derive some benefit from it as well. Help me to truly understand that You give us ALL things richly to enjoy!

I pray this in Jesus' name!

MY CONFESSION FOR TODAY

I confess that I am blessed of the Lord. My personal finances are growing, and I am being positioned to become a source of huge financial blessing to other people. I have worked hard for the blessings that are coming my way, and I have every right to enjoy a part of them personally. The Holy Spirit is giving me wisdom to know how to administrate my finances — to whom I should give funds, as well as how I should spend and invest my money. I have the mind of Christ to deal appropriately with the financial blessings that God is sending into my life.

I declare this by faith in Jesus' name!

QUESTIONS FOR YOU TO CONSIDER

1. What would you do if a large sum of money was suddenly dropped into your hands today?
2. Are you sowing seed into the Gospel that will bring a harvest back into your life? Where are you sowing that seed? Why have you chosen to sow your seed into that particular ministry or organization?
3. Do you enjoy your possessions, or do you feel guilty about possessing them? To fully enjoy what God has given you, what changes do you need to make in the way you think about material possessions?

NOVEMBER 24

Do Good, Be Rich in Good Works, Be Ready To Distribute, Be Willing To Communicate

Charge them that are rich in this world,
that they be not highminded, nor trust in uncertain riches,
but in the living God, who giveth us richly all things to enjoy;
That they do good, that they be rich in good works,
ready to distribute, willing to communicate.
— 1 Timothy 6:17,18

I am so thankful that my wife and I personally know many godly wealthy people who are mission-minded and who generously give to see the Gospel go to the ends of the earth. Although they could selfishly use their money merely for the sake of self-embellishment, they have learned that God gave them money for a purpose: so they could empower preachers of the Gospel to take the message of Jesus Christ to people who need to hear it. Therefore, in addition to personally enjoying their wealth as they should, they have also learned to do a great deal of good with their finances.

I'll never forget the time we sat down with a particular family who fits this description. They invited us to dinner; then while we were at dinner with them, they told me and my wife that they had decided to invest into our ministry. We sat in shock as they told us how they had looked into our finances and checked us out as thoroughly as they possibly could. Then they said they were so blessed with what they had discovered, they decided to channel some of their money into our ministry for the advancement of the Gospel! After researching our ministry, they felt confident the finances would be used properly. So from that day onward, these precious people began to regularly sow into the work God has given us to do.

This wealthy family is diligent to fulfill God's command to the rich as presented in First Timothy 6:17,18. In these verses, Paul gives Timothy instructions for those who were rich in the younger minister's church. Paul tells Timothy to charge the rich that they "…do good, that they be rich in good works, ready to distribute, willing to communicate." Today I want us to delve deeply into this verse to see exactly what God's expectation is for those who are financially blessed in His Kingdom.

When Paul instructed the rich to "do good," he used the word *agathoergeo*, which is a compound of *agathos* and *ergos*. The word *agathos* means *good* or *beneficial*, and the word *ergos* is the most common word in the New Testament for *work*, presenting the idea of *someone who is very active*. When they are compounded together, the new word means *to do works that are good, beneficial, excellent, profitable, or helpful to others*.

These are deeds that leave people in a better condition than they were before the deeds were performed. But because the word *ergos* is used, it pictures *one who really works at doing good,* not one who lazily or thoughtlessly performs these actions. The rich are therefore instructed to be thoughtful, serious, and fervent about their giving, like the family I mentioned earlier who blessed our ministry. They should *work hard* at giving to the right people and to the right places.

Paul goes on to say that the rich are to "be rich in good works." The word "rich" is the word *plousios*, describing *incredible abundance, extreme wealth,* and *enormous affluence.* The word "works" is *ergos*, the Greek word for *work*. It tells the rich that they should be constantly *working* to use their wealth to benefit other people. Their giving should be something they do seriously and with focused attention.

To describe the level of works they are to perform, Paul uses the word "good." This is the word *kalos*, and it pictures *something that is sound, healthy, fine, or excellent*. These are *excellent* works. You could say that these are works that are done soundly and that leave the recipient in a healthy position.

Paul then tells the rich that they must be "ready to distribute." The words "ready to distribute" come from the Greek word *eumetadotos*. It is a triple compound word of the words *eu, meta,* and *didomi*. The word *eu* describes a feeling of *elation* and *ecstasy*. It is what a person feels when he is simply *thrilled* about something. It is where we get the word *euphoria*. The second part of the word is *meta*, and it can be translated a variety of ways, depending on the particular grammar being used in the sentence. In this verse, it means *with* or *about*. The third part of the word is from the word *didomi*, which simply means *to give*. Once these three words are compounded together, the new word literally means that those who possess a lot of material resources should be *elated, thrilled, and euphoric about every opportunity they have to give*.

Next, Paul tells the rich that they must be "willing to communicate." This phrase comes from the single Greek word *koinonikos*. This word is taken from the word *koinonia*, which expresses the idea of *anything that is shared in common*. But when the word *koinonia* becomes the word *koinonikos*, as it is in this verse, it pictures *a person who is a champion at sharing what he owns*. This person doesn't begrudgingly share what he owns; he liberally, generously, and joyfully shares it! He is big-hearted and open-handed — just the opposite of one who is tightfisted and stingy. This is a *heroic* giver. Therefore, when Paul tells the rich to be "willing to communicate," he is teaching them that they should be *champion givers*!

**When we put all these Greek words together,
we see that Paul is urging the rich to:**

"Work diligently at richly performing good deeds with the resources God has given you. Put your whole heart into using those resources to leave people in better shape then they were

before you acted on their behalf. You should be elated, thrilled, and euphoric about every opportunity you have to give. You should be excited about every chance that presents itself for you to be generous!"

God requires everyone to be a giver, but when a person is especially blessed financially more than others, God expects that richly blessed person to do more than others can do because he *has* more.

So if God has financially blessed *you*, He is calling you to use your wealth to become rich in good works! God expects you to go above and beyond what others do because you have the ability to do more. And God expects you to be *excited* about it!

So I want to ask you — when you are confronted with an opportunity to give of your finances, do you get excited about it, or do you begrudge every gift you give? Do you feel like you're losing something when you give of your finances, or do you see your gift as a welcome opportunity to help enrich someone else's life? Do you receive joy from giving, or does it break your heart when you see your money pass from your hands into someone else's hands?

Today I urge you to go before the Lord and allow His Spirit to speak to your heart about your giving. Rather than just thoughtlessly drop money into an offering plate or into some project, begin to give serious prayer and thought to the question of how and when you should give. Study those to whom you wish to give. Make sure you are giving to the right people and to the right places. And when you are confident that you've found a place that will handle your finances responsibly, begin to sow your finances with joy!

When you find good soil to sow your financial seed, you should be euphoric! And you should also rejoice in the fact that you have the ability to make a huge difference in other people's lives!

MY PRAYER FOR TODAY

Lord, I ask You to help me see exactly where I should sow my finances. Please help me to see those people and organizations that will wisely handle the money I sow; then give me the ability to sow into those places with elation and joy! I want to be excited about my giving! I want to give, knowing that my gift is truly going to make a huge difference. And as I give to benefit others, I ask You to honor Your Word and multiply it back to me again so I can continue to give and be a blessing to the Christian community.

I pray this in Jesus' name!

MY CONFESSION FOR TODAY

I confess that God's Spirit speaks to me and helps me know exactly where I am supposed to sow my finances. I am serious about my giving; therefore, I sow carefully and thoughtfully. My money is not to be spent selfishly only on myself, for God has richly blessed me so I can be a rich blessing to others for the sake of the Gospel. I therefore use my resources to do good works that will leave people in better condition than they were before I gave. I am excited about living my life as a liberal, generous, open-handed giver. Therefore, God continues to richly bless me, for He knows I will be a channel through which His blessings can keep flowing out to those who need it.

I declare this by faith in Jesus' name!

1. How should you respond to what you have read in today's *Sparkling Gem*? What new truths did you learn about the attitude you should have in your giving?
2. Would you describe yourself as a champion giver, or would you have to honestly say that you need to increase in your giving? Do you live to give, or do you give only when you feel like the Spirit of God is twisting your arm to do it?
3. When you do finally decide to give to a church, ministry, or organization, do you give regularly and faithfully so you can help make that organization more sound and healthy?

NOVEMBER 25

Investing in Your Eternity

Laying up in store for themselves
a good foundation against the time to come,
that they may lay hold on eternal life.
— 1 Timothy 6:19

When Russian Czar Peter the Great died, his daughter Elizabeta Petrovna came to the throne and became the Empress of Russia. She was perhaps the most flamboyant ruler ever to reign over Russia. The extravagance of her lifestyle was legendary. She owned more palaces than she could use, and the Cinderella-type carriages she owned were hand-carved and gold-leafed. In addition, the carriage doors and spikes of the wheels of each carriage were studded with dazzling diamonds to match the solid gold crowns that were laden with emeralds and rubies and affixed to the top.

The Empress Elizabeta also had an abnormal love of clothes. She completely changed her attire three times a day and never once wore the same article of clothing twice. This was no problem for her, given the fact that she owned 15,000 regal gowns, many of which were spun from pure silver and gold and encrusted with precious gems.

This ruler of Russia came to be known as the "party queen" because she threw hundreds of parties in her massive gold-gilded palaces. To make sure no royal woman ever wore the same gown to such an event twice, she established a new rule: Servants were to be stationed at all the doors; then as each woman left the palace parties, the servants were to stamp the back of these fabulous gowns with a huge black ink stamp. The ink stamp declared that the dress had already been worn to one party and could never be worn to another one. That stamp literally ruined the dress, ensuring that no one would ever dare attend one of the empress's celebrations in an already-used garment.

During the rule of Empress Elizabeta, she ordered the hundreds of massive columns and statues that adorned all her palaces to be covered with pure gold. However, when Catherine the Great came to power and became the Empress of Russia, she considered that much gold on the exterior of a palace to be garish and unfitting (although Catherine's lifestyle was actually no less ostentatious than Elizabeta's). Therefore, Catherine ordered her servants to scrape all the gold off the columns and statues and to throw it away, replacing it with white paint.

When the news of this disposal of gold reached the ears of the wealthy class in Saint Petersburg, a successful merchant came to Catherine the Great and asked if he could purchase the gold she was throwing away. Catherine sternly replied to him, "Excuse me, but who do you think I am? Do you think that I, the Empress of Russia, am so poor that I need to sell my rubbish?" With that, she ordered all the old, scraped-off gold to be thrown away.

Once when I was visiting Saint Petersburg and touring some of these vast historical palaces, I pondered the way these wealthy rulers spent such massive fortunes on themselves. I thought, *Today we visit the palaces of people who once lived luxuriously but whose bones now lie in their graves. Although these people lived in opulence during their lifetimes, what good does their wealth do for them now? Did they spend it all on themselves, only to spend an eternity in spiritual impoverishment? What is the eternal condition of these people?*

If we are to live wisely, we must invest not only in temporary moments of pleasure, but also in the eternity that lies before all of us. Moments of pleasure in this life are enjoyable but fleeting; however, what we invest in eternity never fades. This is why Paul told the rich in Timothy's church that they were to be "laying up in store for themselves a good foundation against the time to come, that they may lay hold on eternal life (1 Timothy 6:19). The same message applies to us today.

The words "laying up" are from the Greek word *apothesauridzo*. This Greek word is a compound of the word *apo*, which means *away*, and the word *thesaurus*, which is the Greek word for *a treasure*. The two words compounded together mean *to store away treasure* or *to amass a fortune*. The new word depicts *people putting their investments in a safe place where they cannot be stolen, ruined, or diminished*.

Most affluent and prosperous people work very hard to see that their money is invested in safe, profitable, money-making investments. This is why they put their money into stocks and bonds, property, art, or other investments that will eventually reap healthy dividends. They want to see their fortune grow. And if they are wise, they will not invest in ventures that are too risky because they don't want to see their fortunes stolen, ruined, or diminished.

Likewise, God expects you to be wise with the finances He has entrusted to you. This is made clear in the parable of the talents in Matthew 25, where Jesus commends the servants who caused their resources to grow and rebuked the servant who did nothing to increase his financial capacity.

Based on Jesus' teaching in Matthew 25, we know that each of us should do everything possible to increase the size of our wealth. However, this financial increase isn't to be gained so we can hoard it or spend it on ourselves! Paul says that if we've been blessed with wealth, we need to also think very seriously about how to "lay it up" where it will never be diminished. In fact, he goes on to say that we should use our money to amass "…a good foundation against the time to come…."

The word "good" in the phrase "a good foundation" is the word *kalos*. As noted in yesterday's *Sparkling Gem*, the word *kalos* pictures *something that is sound, healthy, fine, or excellent*. The word "foundation" is the Greek word *themelios*. This word is most likely an early combination of the Greek word *lithos*, which means *stone*, and the word *tithimi*, which means *to place*. It depicts *that which is set in stone; a foundation that cannot be easily moved or shaken;* or *something so solid that it will endure the test of time*. This is the reason it later came to be translated as the word *foundation*.

The words "time to come" are taken from the Greek word *mello* and describe *events that are coming in the future*. Later in the verse, Paul proceeds to talk about eternity, leaving no doubt that he is referring to eternity when he speaks of a "time to come." He wants to urge people to invest not only in the present, but also in the eternity that lies in all their futures.

You see, the money you spend on your own pleasures right now is gone once it is spent. As noted earlier (*see* November 23), it is normal for you to enjoy the finances you have worked so hard to attain. You *should* enjoy them. But to spend all of it on yourself here and invest none of it into your eternal future is simply stupidity. What you spend on yourself right now in this life is gone once you have died. On the other hand, what you sow into the Gospel reaches into the next life as an investment that keeps growing for all of eternity — an investment that amasses for yourself an enduring, never-ending reward in the life to come!

If you are a wise investor, you are already aware that you must think long-term when you make your investments. Likewise, as you sow your seed into the Gospel and into those who take it to the ends of the earth, you must remember that you may not see the tangible fruit of your investment in this life. But one day when you get to Heaven, you will at last see the phenomenal reward of your giving. Then you will reap the dividends of the finances you sowed into the Kingdom of God!

So don't spend all your money on your earthly existence and forget to lay up a good foundation for the eternity that lies in your future. *Give now, and by faith prepare for yourself a wealthy existence in the eternity that lies before you!*

MY PRAYER FOR TODAY

Lord, help me to always keep in mind that eternity lies before me. Too often I get so consumed in the affairs of this life that I forget to think about my eternal existence. I don't want to be so focused on making myself comfortable in this life that I forget to do what I must to make myself comfortable in the next life. Help me lay up a good foundation for the eternity that lies in my future. Holy Spirit, I ask You to teach me not only how to cause my personal wealth to grow here and now, but also how to sow financial seed into the Gospel that will benefit many and cause me to reap great rewards when I pass into the life yet to come!

I pray this in Jesus' name!

MY CONFESSION FOR TODAY

I boldly declare that I am investing in my future! All of eternity lies before me, so I am sowing seed into the Kingdom of God, believing that it will be multiplied back to me now as it is also laid up for me in my eternal future. I am a wise investor, so I sow regularly and faithfully into the work of God's Kingdom — and my faith investments are reaping for me a great harvest in the days to come!

I declare this by faith in Jesus' name!

QUESTIONS FOR YOU TO CONSIDER

1. Are you sowing for eternity, or are you investing only for the dividends you can reap in this life right now?
2. What can you do to make sure you are not spending all your money on your present pleasures, forgetting to lay up a good foundation for the eternity that lies in your future? When you evaluate what you sow into the Kingdom of God, can you conclude that you are serious about investing into eternity?
3. What changes do you need to make in your spending and investing habits in order to ensure that you will reap strong eternal dividends when you pass into eternity? Why don't you make a list of the ministries and organizations where

you sow your financial seed so you can reevaluate your giving and determine where you can give more?

NOVEMBER 26

⊱❧⊰

A Signal That Jesus' Return Is Near

Now we beseech you, brethren,
by the coming of our Lord Jesus Christ,
and by our gathering together unto him.
— 2 Thessalonians 2:1

W hen Paul wrote his second letter to the church of Thessalonica, he was exceedingly excited at the thought of Jesus' soon return. In fact, he was so thrilled about the prospect of Jesus' coming again that he devoted the entire second chapter of Second Thessalonians to the events that would occur in the last days. As Paul wrote this famous chapter about the events of the last days, he began by declaring, "Now we beseech you, brethren, by the coming of our Lord Jesus Christ, and by our gathering together unto him."

Notice that Paul uses the word "beseech" in this verse. Normally the word "beseech" would be the Greek word *parakaleo,* but in this verse, Paul uses the word *erotao* rather than the word *parakaleo.* The word *erotao* means *to ask* or *to make a strong request.* This word calls upon the listener to cautiously listen to what is being said and to respond in a fitting manner to what has been heard. Because Paul is speaking of the coming of the Lord and uses the word *erotao* to appeal to his listeners, he clearly means for them to take his words seriously and to let these words make a strong impact in their lives.

When we think about the coming of the Lord, it *should* make a strong impact in our lives. It should affect the way we live, the way we think, the way we carry on in our relationships, and the way we invest our money into the Kingdom of God. It is simply a fact that Jesus is coming for His Church, and we should constantly live in the light of His coming. When we live with the awareness that Jesus is coming again, it changes our conduct and behavior. By using the word *erotao* ("beseech"), Paul is communicating to his readers that they have a responsibility to respond to his message about Jesus' soon return. They are to live in a godly, upright, and holy manner as they wait for "the coming of our Lord."

Then he begins to speak to them about the "coming of our Lord." The word "coming" is from the Greek word *parousia.* This word always places special emphasis on the *Presence* of the Lord — especially the Presence of God that can be tangibly felt among His people. Here it is used to describe the strong Presence of God that will be felt when Jesus returns to gather His people to Himself. The word implies that the Church will feel a phenomenal divine Presence when it is time for Jesus to gather His people to Himself at the end of the age.

This means that as we come closer to the return of Jesus, the *parousia* — *the strong Presence of the Lord* — will be strongly sensed among believers. In fact, the ever-growing, strong Presence of the Lord in the midst of the Church will be one of the signals that Jesus' return is close at hand. As His Presence gets stronger and stronger, we will know it is time for Him to return to "gather" us to Himself.

When Paul speaks about "our gathering together unto Him," the phrase "gathering together" comes from the Greek word *episunagoge*. This word is used perfectly in the apocryphal book of Second Maccabees 2:7, where it refers to *that moment in the future when God will finally gather His people together to Himself*. This is exactly how Paul uses it in Second Thessalonians 2:1 as he talks about that moment when God will *finally gather His people together* to Himself at the coming of Jesus.

In Second Thessalonians 2:1, Paul uses the word *episunagoge* ("gathering together") to describe that future moment when the Lord will *quickly gather* or *collect* His people together to Himself at the end of the age. At that divine moment, all of God's people will be quickly gathered together and collected in a common assembly to meet the Lord in the air. *What a meeting that will be!*

**Considering the Greek words
that Paul used in Second Thessalonians 2:1,
this verse could be interpreted the following way:**

"Brothers, I make this urgent, heartfelt request to you today, earnestly and sincerely pleading with you from the bottom of my heart to hear what I'm telling you and to do exactly as I say. The appearance of the Lord Jesus Christ is very near. In fact, it is so close that we can almost feel His Presence as if He were already here among us. The moment we have all longed for and waited for is almost upon us! I'm talking about that moment when Jesus will finally gather us together to Himself."

The apostle Peter warned us that at the end of the age, many scoffers would mock at the promise of Jesus' return, asserting that if Jesus was going to come, surely He would have already come. Peter wrote, "Knowing this first, that there shall come in the last days scoffers, walking after their own lusts, and saying, Where is the promise of his coming?..." (2 Peter 3:3,4).

The word "scoffers" is from the Greek word *empaidzo*, and it described *one who makes fun of another through mockery*. It conveyed the idea of *disdain, scorn, derision*, and *ridicule*. The Greek word *empaidzo* also meant *to play a game*. It was often used for playing a game with children or for amusing a crowd by impersonating someone in a silly and exaggerated way. For instance, this word might be used in a game of charades when someone intends to comically portray someone or even make fun of someone.

We find this word used in Luke 22:63, where the Bible tells us, "And the men that held Jesus mocked him, and smote him." The Greek word *empaidzo* categorically lets us know that these men turned a few minutes of that nightmarish night before Jesus' crucifixion into a stage of comedy at His expense. They put on quite a show, hamming it up as they almost certainly pretended to be Jesus and the people He ministered to. Perhaps they laid hands on each other as if they were healing the sick; or lay on the floor and quivered, as if they were being liberated from devils; or wobbled around, acting as if they had been blind but now could suddenly see. Whatever these leaders did to mock Jesus, it was a game of charades to mimic and make fun of Him.

Now Peter uses this same word to depict mockers in the last days who would make fun of those who believe in Jesus' coming. I can almost hear them saying, "Come on, if Jesus was going to come, don't you think He would have been here by now? Quit hanging on to this false hope, you dreamers!"

But the grammar used in Second Peter 3:3,4 tells us that this mocking is the characteristic behavior of these scoffers. It could be more accurately translated, *"Mockers will come mocking."* In other words, they don't only mock on occasion; they are mockers *by habit*. They find great delight in regularly mocking and making fun of those who believe that Jesus is coming to gather His Church to Himself.

But regardless of what doubt-filled believers or antagonistic unbelievers say as they mock us, the truth is that Jesus *is* coming again soon! Second Thessalonians 2:1 gives us one of the signs that will occur to let us know His arrival is upon us: We will suddenly be aware of the supernatural Presence of Jesus in the Church like never before. The closer we come to the time of His return, the more strongly this phenomenal Presence of God will be felt in our midst. In fact, it will seem as if His coming is already upon us! That strong Presence of God will signal to us that it is just about time for Jesus to quickly gather us and collect us to Himself!

So in the days to come, close your ears to the mockers who make fun of you for believing in Jesus' soon return. Then open your heart to the Holy Spirit, and allow Him to make you sensitive to His voice inside your spirit. As you are faithful to do this, you will recognize that moment when the Presence of God becomes much stronger in the Church, and you'll know that moment for what it is — one of the greatest indications that Jesus' return is upon us!

MY PRAYER FOR TODAY

Lord, help me to be sensitive to Your Presence so I can be aware of that moment when Your coming is near to us. Help me close my ears to those mockers who say You will never come. By Your grace, I will hold tightly to Your promise that You will come one day to collect Your people to Yourself. Help me live a life that is holy — one that pleases You and for which I will not be ashamed when You suddenly appear to gather the Church to Yourself.

I pray this in Jesus' name!

MY CONFESSION FOR TODAY

I confess that I am living a holy life that pleases God, a life for which I am not ashamed. I say no to sin; I crucify my flesh; and I do my very best to yield to and walk in the Spirit. I am sensitive to the Presence of God. And when the moment draws near for Jesus to come and collect His people to Himself, I will sense the growing strength of His Presence in the Church and will recognize it as a signal that God's people will soon be leaving planet earth! I believe in Jesus' coming; I expect it in my lifetime; and I am doing all I can to preach the Gospel to the lost so they won't be left out when Jesus gathers the Church to Himself.

I declare this by faith in Jesus' name!

QUESTIONS FOR YOU TO CONSIDER

1. Are you living a life that makes you feel confident about seeing Jesus face to face when He returns for His people? Or are you allowing secret sins in your life that make you fearful about Jesus' soon return? If you answered yes to the second question, what are those secret sins, and what steps do you need to take to remove them from your life?

2. What can you do to increase your spiritual sensitivity so you will recognize the moment when the Presence of God suddenly and supernaturally energizes the Church, alerting God's people that the time for Jesus' arrival is upon them?

3. Write down two lists, answering the following two questions: What things do you need to remove from your life because they adversely affect your spiritual sensitivity? What do you need to add to your life to help you become more spiritually sensitive?

NOVEMBER 27

❧❧❧

The Appearance of the Antichrist

Let no man deceive you by any means:
for that day shall not come, except there come a falling away first,
and that man of sin be revealed, the son of perdition;
Who opposeth and exalteth himself above all that is called God,
or that is worshipped; so that he as God
sitteth in the temple of God, shewing himself that he is God.
— 2 Thessalonians 2:3,4

*F*rom my early childhood, I heard about the antichrist. In the many years that I've been a Christian, I've heard people speculate that this person or that person could potentially be the antichrist. However, although these individuals may have been forerunners to the antichrist, none of them turned out to be the long-anticipated Man of Lawlessness described in the Scriptures.

The Bible teaches us that at some point in the future, an evil ruler called the antichrist is going to step onto the platform of the world stage and take the leading role for a short time in the affairs of mankind. Many predecessors of the antichrist have already come and gone, but according to this scripture in Second Thessalonians 2, the real antichrist is still yet to be revealed in the last times.

Paul tells us about the supernatural appearance of the antichrist when he writes about the last days in Second Thessalonians 2:3,4. Paul writes, "Let no man deceive you by any means: for that day shall not come, except there come a falling away first, and that man of sin be revealed, the son of perdition; who opposeth and exalteth himself above all that is called God, or that is worshipped; so that he as God sitteth in the temple of God, shewing himself that he is God."

Paul says that before the antichrist can be revealed, first there must be a "falling away" that takes place in the world. The phrase "falling away" is taken from the Greek word *apostasia*, which describes *a falling away* or *a revolt*. The writer Plutarch used this word to describe *a political revolt*. In First Maccabees 2:15, the word *apostasia* is used to picture *people who are turning away from the Lord*. This word also occurs in the Septuagint version of Joshua 2:22, where it conveys the idea of *rebellion against God*. Thus, the word *apostasia* is a word that denotes *rebellion*, *mutiny*, and *defiance*.

Before the antichrist can be welcomed with wide-open arms by the world, a change in society's mentality must first take place. Paul uses this word to predict a *rebellion* or *mutiny* against God that will occur in the last days. The text does *not* imply that this mutiny will occur within the Church; rather, it seems to point to a change in *society's attitude* toward God.

Paul is describing a time when society's attitude toward God and holy things will become mutinous. Once this anti-God and anti-godliness mentality pervades society, the world will be primed and prepared to receive this man whom Paul calls "that man of sin."

The Greek word used here for "sin" is the word *anomia*. Translating the word *anomia* as "sin" is unfortunate, for the word *anomia* actually means *without law* and carries the idea of *a lawless attitude*. It has a definite article in Greek, which tells us emphatically that this individual is not just any person with a lawless attitude; rather, this is a reference to *the man of lawlessness* or *the antichrist*.

Paul points to a time when this evil leader will be "revealed." The word "revealed" is the Greek word *apokalupto*. It is a compound word, using the words *apo* and *kalupto*. The word *apo* means *away*, and the word *kalupto* is *something that is veiled, covered, concealed, or hidden*. When these two words are compounded, they form the word *apokalupto*, depicting *a veil that has been removed, exposing what is behind the veil that was formerly concealed or hidden from view*. Paul uses this word to inform us that a day is coming when the antichrist — who has been concealed and hidden from public view — will suddenly appear. In that moment when he suddenly emerges on the world scene, it will be as if a stage curtain has been pulled out of the way so that he can make his grand appearance.

Paul calls this wicked leader "the son of perdition." The word "perdition" is from the Greek word *apoleia*, which speaks of *something that is doomed, rotten, ruinous, or decaying*. Although this world leader may boast that he will lead the world to a higher and better day, what he will actually bring to the world is *doom, destruction, ruin, rot*, and *decay*. No redeeming value can be found in anything produced by the antichrist's rule. In the Greek text, Paul uses a definite article, loudly signaling that this evil world ruler is in a category like none other before him. He is not simply another evil person. *He is THE Son of Doom and Destruction.*

Next, Paul tells us that this wicked world leader will be one "who opposeth and exalteth himself above all that is called God, or that is worshipped; so that he as God sitteth in the temple of God, shewing himself that he is God." The Greek word for "opposeth" is *antikeimai*, which means *opposed to* or *against everything that is established*. There is no doubt that this is a clear reference to the *antichrist*.

The word "antichrist" means *against Christ*. Thus, the Greek word used in this verse tells us that this evil leader will be against *everything* having to do with God. It is important to note that the Greek grammar used in this verse paints the picture of *a continual, unending, and perpetual resistance against the things of God*. This is not just a one-time resistance against the things of God; rather, this poisonous quality will be deeply ingrained in the character of the antichrist. Everything in this evil ruler will be opposed to God and all that He represents.

Paul also warns that the antichrist "...exalteth himself above all that is called God, or that is worshipped...." The word "exalteth" is the Greek word *huperairo*, which means *to exceedingly exalt oneself* or *to be exalted highly*. In this case, it is the idea of *someone being exalted too highly*. According to Paul, the antichrist will go to all lengths to exceedingly exalt himself in the eyes of the world. As we continue to study this verse, we discover that this wicked ruler will even attempt to sit in God's rightful place in the temple and elevate himself higher than God Himself!

Paul says that the antichrist will oppose and exalt himself above all "that is worshipped." The word for "worship" is the Greek word *sebasma*, which refers to *anything that can be worshiped*, including God. Here we see that the antichrist will attempt to stop the practice of worshiping God and demand that he become the primary focus of human attention and worship.

Then Paul prophesies that the antichrist will sit in the very place of God in the temple. The word "temple" is the Greek word *naos*. It is sometimes used to refer to *the innermost part of the temple* and may be interpreted as *the Holy of Holies*. On the basis of this verse, many scholars assert that the antichrist will enter a rebuilt temple in Jerusalem, where he will go into the Holy of Holies and decree himself to be God incarnate.

Wasn't this exactly what Lucifer attempted to do when he declared that he would exalt himself above the very throne of God? Isaiah tells us of Lucifer in Isaiah 14:13,14: "For thou hast said in thine heart, I will ascend into heaven, I will exalt my throne above the stars of God: I will sit also upon the mount of the congregation, in the sides of the north: I will ascend above the heights of the clouds; I will be like the most High."

Following the long-held desire of Satan, the antichrist will again attempt to take the very place of God in the temple. Paul tells us that the antichrist will commit the ultimate offense of "…shewing himself that he is God." The Greek word for "shew" is the word *apodeiknumi*, which actually means *to vividly portray; to point out; to illustrate; to show off;* or *to make a vivid presentation*. This is the picture of the antichrist using all possible means to demonstrate that he holds a rank that is even higher than God Himself.

In Second Thessalonians 2:9, Paul warns that the antichrist will even employ supernatural signs and wonders to try to prove that he is God. He says, "Even him, whose coming is after the working of Satan with all power and signs and lying wonders."

The words "with all" are from the Greek words *en pase*, which emphatically declares that the antichrist will come with *all* power — implying that he will make his grand appearance with *all kinds* of power and supernatural displays. The Greek word for "power" is *dunamis*, which describes *something that is explosive or dynamic*. It is where we get the word *dynamite*. This means that when the antichrist appears, he will come with all kinds of powers that are truly *extraordinary* in the opinion of the lost world.

The Greek word for "sign" is *semeion*. This word denotes *an act that points the viewer in a certain direction* or *an action performed to prove a point*. It also means *a beacon, a signal,* or *a sign*. Just as a sign on the road gives directions to a driver, these supernatural feats are intended to point the attention and focus of the world to the antichrist.

The word "wonder" is the Greek word *teras*, and it is often translated *miracles*. This refers to *something that causes people to marvel or to be amazed*. The same word is used in Matthew 24:24, where Jesus warns that false prophets will perform *wonders* in the last days to deceive and to draw people away after themselves. Here it is used to say that when Satan finally has the opportunity to introduce his antichrist to the world, the evil ruler will energetically attempt to take the very place of God — even using lying signs and wonders to show that he is God.

When you put all these Greek words together, you discover
that Paul's words in Second Thessalonians 2:3,4,9 could be interpreted:

"In light of these things, I urge you to refuse to allow anyone to take advantage of you. For example, you won't need a letter to tell you when the day of the Lord has come. You ought to know by now that this day can't come until first a worldwide insurgency, rebellion, riot, and mutiny against God has come about in society.

"Once that occurs, the world will then be primed, prepared, and ready to embrace the Man of Lawlessness, the one who hates law and has rebellion running in his blood. This is the long-awaited and predicted Son of Doom and Destruction, the one who brings rot and ruin to everything he touches. When the time is just right, he will finally come out of hiding and go public!

"Do you understand whom I am talking about? I'm describing that person who will be so against God and everything connected with the worship of God that, if you can imagine it, he will even try to put himself on a pedestal above God Himself — sitting in God's rightful place in the temple and publicly proclaiming himself to be God!

"This evil one will be energized by Satan himself as he makes his arrival known to the world with all kinds of dynamic supernatural powers — powers that are truly extraordinary. These lying signs and wonders and supernatural feats have only one purpose: They are designed to draw attention to the Lawless One and to make the world stand in awe of him."

Any Christian who is sensitive to the Spirit of God is keenly aware that we are living in a time when society's attitude toward God is radically changing. The world is being primed and prepared to throw open its arms and receive this world ruler who will oppose God and bring rot, ruin, and destruction to mankind. Unfortunately, the lost world doesn't realize that it is being slowly seduced and trained for this moment the devil has long awaited.

As believers, we have no need to be afraid, for none of this will affect those who know Jesus Christ. However, it *will* affect those who are lost and without God. They will fall under the supernatural hypnotism of this devil-anointed leader. And if they don't come to know Jesus Christ before all of this occurs, they will be ensnared in the trap that the entire world is about to fall into in the days to come.

Please realize what a critical time you are living in right now. *Jesus is coming quickly.* Those who know Him will escape many of these trials and temptations, but those who don't know Him will be caught in the delusion and devastation. It's good to rejoice that you will escape, but what about those you love? *What are you going to do to ensure that they escape the evil days that are coming upon the earth?*

In light of this clear teaching of Scripture, don't you think it's time for you to reach out to your unsaved friends and family members and speak to them about the redeeming blood of Jesus Christ? Ask the Holy Spirit to give you an opportunity to speak to them; then let Him fill your mouth with the right words as you earnestly plead with them to make Jesus Christ the Lord of their lives.

MY PRAYER FOR TODAY

Lord, I ask You to give me the boldness I need to present the Gospel to my friends and family members who are unsaved. I know that if they don't receive Jesus, they will be lost in sin and caught in the delusion that is coming upon the world in the days to come. I don't want to stand before You knowing that they are lost because I was too afraid to open my mouth and tell them of Your saving blood. Holy Spirit, please give me the boldness I need and the right words to speak to those who are near and dear to my heart. When I stand before You, I want to be assured in my heart that I did everything I could to rescue those who are lost and perishing. Please help me to do this and to start today!

I pray this in Jesus' name!

MY CONFESSION FOR TODAY

I confess that I am not afraid to testify of Jesus Christ to others. In fact, the love of God compels me to reach out to those who are lost. I know I will give account for those I could have reached but didn't, so I will do everything I can to speak to them, to reach them, and to make sure they have an opportunity to hear the Good News of Jesus Christ. If they refuse to listen or to receive, I will be freed from my responsibility. My part is just to make sure they had a chance to hear and to believe. The Holy Spirit is empowering me to testify, so starting today, I will follow His leading and speak to unbelievers about Jesus as God provides opportunities for me to do so.

I declare this by faith in Jesus' name!

QUESTIONS FOR YOU TO CONSIDER

1. Do you have unsaved friends or relatives who need to know the Lord before all these terrible events begin to unfold on the world stage? Who are these loved ones? Do you regularly pray for their salvation?

2. How long has it been since you have personally presented the Gospel to those loved ones who are still unsaved? Is the Holy Spirit tugging at your heart, trying to prompt you to share Christ with them at this time?

3. Have you asked the Holy Spirit to give you an opportunity to present the Gospel to your friends and loved ones? When the Holy Spirit gave you an opportunity in the past, did you take advantage of it, or did you let it pass you by? If you let it pass you by, why don't you ask the Holy Spirit to give you another opportunity to present Jesus to those whom you love?

NOVEMBER 28

The Great Restrainer!

And now ye know what withholdeth that he might be revealed
in his time. For the mystery of iniquity doth already work:
only he who now letteth will let, until he be taken out of the way.
And then shall that Wicked be revealed....
— 2 Thessalonians 2:6-8

*I*f Satan has been waiting to introduce the antichrist to the world, what is stopping him from allowing this evil leader to step onto the platform of the world stage right now? Why is it taking so long for the devil to finally bring this man to public attention?

Paul answered this question when he wrote Second Thessalonians 2:6-8. He said, "And now ye know what withholdeth that he might be revealed in his time. For the mystery of iniquity doth already work: only he who now letteth will let, until he be taken out of the way. And then shall that Wicked be revealed, whom the Lord shall consume with the spirit of his mouth, and shall destroy with the brightness of his coming."

Notice that Paul says, "And now ye know...." In the Greek, the sentence could be better translated, *"Now, since I have already told you all these things, you ought to already know...."* This is important, for it tells us that Paul had already informed the Thessalonian believers about events that would occur in the last days.

Paul had only spent a mere matter of months with the Thessalonian church; we can therefore see from this passage of Scripture the importance he attached to their ability to understand end-time events. In the short time Paul was with the Thessalonian believers, he had instructed them so well on the events of the last days that he could now tell them, *"Since I have already told you all these things, you ought to already know...."*

Let me ask you this: If Paul used part of his brief stay with the Thessalonian church to teach them about the events that would occur in the last days, doesn't this tell us that our understanding of this subject should be a very high priority? We can't shut our eyes to these truths of Scripture. If Paul considered this theme so important that he would introduce it to a group of new believers, how much more do we who are seasoned believers need to grasp what the Bible teaches about the last days?

Paul told the Thessalonian believers that a Force "withholdeth" the antichrist from being revealed. Although the Greek doesn't specifically state the identity of the restraining Force in this verse, it seems to suggest that Paul is referring to the supernatural power of the Holy Spirit.

Think of it — what if the power of the Spirit of God was suddenly withdrawn or removed from the earth? It would be only a brief matter of time before the devil quickly consummated his dream of world domination. You see, the Holy Spirit is the Great Restrainer, and He is holding back this evil from coming to pass in the world today.

The *King James Version* uses the word "withholdeth" to describe this restraining work of the Spirit. In Greek, it is the word *katecho* and carries the idea of *holding something down* or *suppressing something*. It is clear that this is an evil so horrendous that it must be *held down, held back*, or *suppressed* lest it be loosed to release a wide range of wicked effects. The supernatural Force Paul refers to is *stalling, delaying*, and *postponing* the evil that is craving to be fully released and set into operation.

Peter tells us why the Spirit of God is stalling, delaying, and postponing this dreadful time at the end of the age. In Second Peter 3:9, he says that God is "…not willing that any should perish, but that all should come to repentance." God is holding back the ultimate day of evil to give unbelievers more time to come to Him in repentance. But a day is soon coming when the Great Restrainer will "…be taken out of the way" (2 Thessalonians 2:7).

When this day comes, the hindering Power that has continuously delayed the worldwide domination of evil and lawlessness will be removed. It will be as though He is suddenly lifted out of the middle of everything. At that moment, the evil forces that have long been suppressed will suddenly be freed, and their wicked plans, purposes, and desires will be abruptly energized. When the supernatural hindering Force is removed, these events will quickly come to pass with no hesitation, for the Restrainer will be out of the picture.

Once the Restrainer is gone, the antichrist will "be revealed." The word "revealed" is the word *apokalupto*. The Greek word *apo* means *away*, and the word *kalupto* refers to *something that is veiled, covered, concealed, or hidden*. When these two words are compounded, they form the word *apokalupto*, which depicts *a veil that has been removed, exposing what is behind the veil that was previously concealed or hidden from view*. When the Holy Spirit's restraining power has been withdrawn, there will no longer be any force present to hold back the evil forces. Therefore, this evil leader who has been concealed and hidden from public view will suddenly "appear." In that moment, it will seem as if a stage curtain has been pulled out of the way so that he can make his grand appearance to the world.

**Taking all these Greek words into consideration,
an interpretive translation of Second Thessalonians 2:6-8 could read this way:**

"Now in light of everything I've told you before, you ought to be well aware by now that there is a supernatural Force at work, preventing the materialization of this person and the disclosure of his identity.

"This restraining Force I'm referring to is so strong that it is currently putting on the brakes and holding back the unveiling of this wicked person, stalling and postponing his manifestation. But when the right moment comes, this evil one will no longer be withheld, and he will emerge on the world scene! The screen that has been hiding his true identity and guarding him from world view will suddenly be pulled back and evaporate — and he will step out on center stage to let everyone know who he is.

"These events have been covertly in the making for a long time, but the world doesn't realize that a secret plan is being executed right under their own noses. The only thing that has

kept this plan from already being consummated is the supernatural Force that has been holding it all back until now.

"But one day this Force will be removed from the picture — and when that happens, these events will quickly transpire. The removal of this restraining Force will signal the moment when the Lawless One will finally make his grand appearance to the world...."

Can you image how quickly evil would take over the world if the Spirit of God stopped restraining the presence of evil? Because God is holding back this force of evil to give men more time to repent, we are still living in a period of grace when men can call on the name of the Lord and be saved. We are truly living in a season of grace that God is extending to the world just before the worst evil in human history is manifested on the earth.

If you haven't been spending much time in prayer for your unsaved friends and loved ones, why don't you start making it a high priority today to pray for their salvation? Right now God is holding back evil so that your friends — and all mankind — may have one last opportunity to come to Him in repentance before the end of the age is consummated and all the prophecies of the Bible are fulfilled.

Which of your friends need to be saved? How often do you pray for them? What are you doing to ensure that they have an opportunity to hear the Gospel of Jesus Christ? If you possess the answers they need but don't share those answers with them, how do you think you will feel when you stand before the Judgment Seat of Christ?

If you do your best to introduce your loved ones to Jesus but they refuse to listen, at least your heart will be free of guilt on that day when you stand before Jesus. So why don't you begin to pray for them today? And while you're in that place of prayer, ask the Holy Spirit to give you another chance to share the Gospel with those whom you know and love!

MY PRAYER FOR TODAY

Lord, I thank You for holding back the evil forces that want to manifest in the world today. It's hard to imagine what the world would be like if Your Spirit no longer suppressed the evil in the hearts of men. I thank You for working in the world today, and I thank You for giving my friends, family, associates, and acquaintances one last chance to come to You. Please help me recognize divinely appointed moments when I can present the Gospel to those who are near me. And I ask You to help me formulate my words so they can understand what I am communicating to them. Holy Spirit, as I speak to people, I ask You to do the work of conviction in their hearts so they will have a desire to believe and to repent.

I pray this in Jesus' name!

MY CONFESSION FOR TODAY

I confess that I am sensitive to opportunities that God gives me to share the Gospel of Jesus Christ. I don't have a spirit of fear about witnessing. Because the power of the Holy Spirit lives inside me, I am brave, bold, and courageous when it comes to telling the Good News of Jesus Christ. People need the Gospel — and that means they need to hear what I have to tell them. When I speak, God's Spirit anoints me and people listen. As a result of my obedience, I am being used by God to bring many people to salvation in these last days!

I declare this by faith in Jesus' name!

1. Who are the unbelieving family members, friends, associates, or acquaintances you are most concerned about? Have you ever put them on a prayer list to help remind you to pray for their salvation every day?
2. Before you were saved, did anyone pray regularly for your salvation? Who was that person? After you came to the Lord, didn't it make you thankful that someone cared enough to pray for you? Have you ever taken the time to thank that person for making your salvation a high priority in his or her prayer time?
3. Is there someone you are going to see today who might be open if you shared the Good News that Jesus died for him or her? Who is that person?

NOVEMBER 29

The Annihilating Appearance Of Jesus Christ in Great Glory!

And then shall that Wicked be revealed,
whom the Lord shall consume with the spirit of his mouth,
and shall destroy with the brightness of his coming.
— 2 Thessalonians 2:8

When Jesus comes at the end of the age, He will come in *great* power and glory. In fact, when He comes, His glory will be so brilliant that it will totally annihilate the antichrist! This is why Paul told the Thessalonians, "And then shall that Wicked be revealed, whom the Lord shall consume with the spirit of his mouth, and shall destroy with the brightness of his coming" (2 Thessalonians 2:8).

After time runs out for the antichrist to do his work on the earth, Jesus will come. And Paul declares that when the Lord comes, He will "consume" this evil leader "with the spirit of his mouth." The Greek word translated "consume" is *anairo*, which means *to kill, to murder, to slay, to slaughter, to do away with,* or *to abolish.* The meaning here is clear: When the Lord comes, He will *obliterate* the antichrist. He will *wipe him out* and *permanently do away with him.*

How will the Lord do this? Paul says that "...the Lord shall consume [the antichrist] with the spirit of his mouth...." The word translated "spirit" is actually from the Greek word *pneuma,* which is normally translated *spirit.* Thus, the verse could be translated, *"BY the spirit of his mouth."* This means that even though Satan energizes the antichrist with all the power he possesses, this evil leader doesn't stand a chance in the Presence of Jesus. Paul lets us know that this demonized leader doesn't even have enough strength to withstand one puff from the mouth of the Lord!

The Greek word *stomos* describes the *mouth* of the Lord from which this obliterating power will come. You see, on that day the Lord will open his mouth and speak — and when He does, so much power will be released that it will permanently remove the antichrist from the world scene.

In fact, Paul says this final encounter with the Lord will "destroy" this evil leader. The word "destroy" is the Greek word *katargeo*. Paul uses this word twenty-five times in his New Testament writings, so we know exactly what he intends by using it. This word means *to bring to nothing; to reduce to waste; to render inactive; to abolish;* or *to put out of commission*. There is no doubt that when Jesus Christ comes, He will permanently put the antichrist out of commission! The rule of evil will come to an abrupt end when Jesus returns at the end of the age.

I want you to know what Paul is talking about when he uses the phrase "the brightness of his [Jesus'] coming." The word "brightness" is the Greek word *epiphaneia*. This word was used in classical Greece to describe *the sudden and occasional surprise appearance* of the Greek gods. When the fabled gods suddenly appeared, they were glorious and mighty in appearance. Now Paul reaches into classical literature and borrows a word that clearly means Jesus' coming will take many by surprise and will be accompanied by great splendor and glory.

The world, entrenched in evil, will think it has won the victory and is secure in its plans. But then the Lord will come and take them all by surprise! Before anyone realizes what is happening, God's glory will fill the sky, and Jesus will mightily appear in the sky overhead. His "coming" (from the word *parousia*, which describes *the Lord's strong Presence*) will take the world by surprise, overwhelming everyone as every evil system set in place by unregenerate man is suddenly obliterated!

An interpretive translation
of Second Thessalonians 2:8 could read:

"When the Wicked One steps onto the stage and makes his presence known, it won't be too long afterward that the Lord will come. And when He comes, His coming will be so grand, so glorious, and so overwhelming that He will totally obliterate the Lawless One by the mere breath of His mouth. Just one puff from the Lord, and this evil person will be incinerated! The very Presence of the Lord will eradicate him, permanently putting him out of commission."

You see, when you serve Jesus Christ, you have joined the greatest Champion in the universe. There is no power that can equal or surpass His power. There is no might on planet earth to compare with His awesome might. And just think — when you become a child of God, you become a joint heir with Him! Everything He possesses — including His power and His victory — becomes yours!

You should rejoice in the knowledge of what Jesus will do by His mighty power when He returns at the end of the age. However, don't overlook the fact that this same power is available to you today. Jesus has given you His power so you can use it in *this* life.

So if evil is resisting you in some area of your life right now, *open your mouth* and let the power of God be released to obliterate that attack! *Shock the devil with a sudden manifestation of God's power that permanently immobilizes him in every area of your life!*

MY PRAYER FOR TODAY

Lord, I thank You for Your awesome power that You have chosen to share with Your children. I don't ever have to let the devil run freely in my life. By opening my mouth and speaking the Word of God to my situation, Your power can be released to obliterate the enemy's work in my life. Thank You for making me Your joint heir and for investing Your great power in my life!

I pray this in Jesus' name!

MY CONFESSION FOR TODAY

I boldly declare that God's power resides in me. There is enough power inside me to obliterate any attack the devil would attempt to bring against my life. Rather than sit in fear and fret about what is happening to me, I will open my mouth, speak the Word of truth, and watch the power of God attack, overwhelm, and overcome the strategies that the devil has tried to use against me!

I declare this by faith in Jesus' name!

QUESTIONS FOR YOU TO CONSIDER

1. What are the areas of your life that seem to be under demonic assault right now?
2. What are you doing to resist these attacks? Are you foolishly shutting your eyes and hoping they will go away by themselves? Or are you opening your mouth to speak the Word of God and to release the power of God into your situation?
3. What scriptures should you be speaking over your life right now to bring a permanent solution to these assaults?

NOVEMBER 30

Are You Living Only for Today —
Or Living Also for Eternity?

Seeing then that all these things shall be dissolved,
what manner of persons ought ye to be
in all holy conversation and godliness?
— 2 Peter 3:11

One day I was standing at the foot of the Great Pyramid of Giza in Egypt with my wife and sons. We had spent that entire week floating down the Nile River, touring all the sites of ancient Egypt, many of which were more than 4,000 years old. We were amazed at how well the condition of these ancient locations had been preserved. Finally we stood at the foot of the ancient, massive Great Pyramid of Giza. It, too, was in marvelous condition, considering that it had been standing there for so many thousands of years. It was very evident that the Great Pyramid had been built solidly so it would stand as an eternal remembrance to the Egyptian king who built it.

As I stood there with my family, I told my sons, "This pyramid has stood here for thousands of years, but a day is coming in the future when it will be completely dissolved. When the final Day of the Lord comes, the Bible tells us that everything that exists on the earth will melt with fervent heat, and the earth and all its works will be burned up. Boys, that means a day is coming when none of these monuments will exist any longer. Everything built by man will vanish, including these monuments that have stood the test of time for thousands of years. The only thing that will last is what people have done for Jesus Christ."

The scripture I referred to as I talked to my sons was Second Peter 3:10. This verse says that when the Day of the Lord comes, "…the heavens shall pass away with a great noise, and the elements shall melt with fervent heat, the earth also and the works that are therein shall be burned up."

According to Peter, when the Day of the Lord comes at the very end of the age, everything we presently see and know will be changed. Even the heavens as we currently know them will pass away. The words "pass away" are from the Greek word *parerchomai*, which pictures *something that is temporary and will soon be passing away*. Peter says that the present heavens will pass away with a "great noise." The words "great noise" are from the Greek word *hroidzedon*. This word describes *a sound so loud that it is nearly deafening to those who hear it*. It further carries the idea of *a tremendous hissing, sizzling, cracking sound that rushes all about* or *a noise so thunderous that no one can escape it*.

When these events transpire, the heavens and all "the elements" shall melt with a fervent heat. The word "elements" is the Greek word *stoicheion*, and it refers to *everything that exists* — from the heavenly bodies in the sky overhead to the mountains, the earth, the buildings constructed by man, and even the smallest atomic particles. Absolutely nothing will survive the transforming, purifying fire that will melt everything.

The word "melt" in this verse is from the Greek word *luo*, which normally means *to loose*. But in this case, it pictures *the dissolving of matter* and *the complete dissolution of the earth's elements*.

This melting of the elements will occur because of a "fervent heat" that will be manifested on the Day of the Lord. The words "fervent heat" come from the Greek word *kausoomai*, which depicts *a fire so intense that nothing escapes its blaze*. It was used by medical writers to convey the idea of *a fever that consumed a victim*. This is an intense, raging, blazing, blistering, burning fire that *consumes* and hence *purges* everything it touches. Absolutely nothing will survive this fire when Jesus purifies this present world and creates a new heaven and a new earth.

I spoke these words to my sons because I wanted them to know that the only thing to survive this life will be what we do for Jesus Christ. We tend to think that our houses, buildings, and the things we construct in life will live forever. But the truth is, even the structures that are built to survive through the ages of time will eventually pass away. Since only that which is done for eternity will outlast this world, we can see why Peter asked the question, "Seeing then that all these things shall be dissolved, what manner of persons ought ye to be in all holy conversation and godliness?" (2 Peter 3:11).

A day is coming when all the material possessions you own and hold to be dear will be "dissolved." The word "dissolved" is from the Greek word *luo*, which is the same word mentioned above in Second Peter 3:10 to describe *the complete dissolution of everything that presently exists*. By using this word, Peter alerts us to the fact that nothing we presently own will last forever. In light of this truth, how should we view our material possessions, and how should we prioritize our lives?

Too often we devote the bulk of our time to our homes, gardens, cars, businesses, or other worldly affairs. Although we must give attention to the basic things that are necessary to life, we make a huge mistake if we focus on these temporal matters while neglecting the eternal spiritual issues that will pass from this life into the next. Only what is done for the Lord will last. Everything else will be left behind in a world that will one day be consumed with a fervent heat. Since everything will be dissolved, as Peter tells us, doesn't it make sense that we invest in our spiritual futures as well as in our present lives?

How should this knowledge affect the way you live? Peter asked, "Seeing then that all these things shall be dissolved, what manner of persons ought ye to be…?" In other words, since the heavens and the earth and everything in them are temporary and will one day pass away, what should have your greatest attention and devotion?

Unsaved men in today's world live for the present. Often they do great philanthropic works because they want their names to be remembered in future generations. Their desire is to have people revere them, place their names on buildings, name streets after them, and so forth.

However, every building that bears a person's name will one day evaporate. The pyramids that have stood before us for centuries will one day be gone. Those who live only for the present or to impress men will be the greatest losers of all, for everything they have lived for will burn up and pass away, never to be remembered again. On the other hand, those who live for eternity, walk by faith, and obey what the Word of God tells them to do will make a name for themselves that will be remembered in Heaven for all of eternity. *These are the biggest winners in life!*

The message I conveyed to my sons that day in front of the pyramids is the same message I want to impress upon you today: *Take the time to consider your priorities in life.* Are you investing in eternity, or are you consumed with natural things that won't survive that consuming fire, which will one day melt everything that exists? Since what you do for Jesus is the only thing that will survive, don't you think it would be wise to prayerfully consider your life to see if you are investing as much in eternity as you are investing in the present?

MY PRAYER FOR TODAY

Lord, please help me to live soberly and to invest not only in the present, but also in the eternity that is to come. I don't want to be among those who lived only for the present and therefore suffered loss because they forgot to invest in Heaven. Teach me how to manage and increase the material possessions You have given me so that I can use them to increase my wealth in Heaven. I am grateful for the things I own, but I am more thankful for the souls who are in Heaven because I used my resources to invest in eternity. Help me to use my life wisely and to live as I ought to live in light of eternity.

I pray this in Jesus' name!

MY CONFESSION FOR TODAY

I confess that I am living for eternity. Although I thank God for all the possessions He has given me, I realize that all of these are temporary blessings. The greatest investment I can make is in my spiritual future, so in addition to managing the physical blessings God has given me, I am a wise investor in my eternal destiny. I spend the bulk of my time, my money, my talents, and my energies on things that will further God's Kingdom and outlast this world!

I declare this by faith in Jesus' name!

QUESTIONS FOR YOU TO CONSIDER

1. In light of what you have read today, what changes do you need to make in your schedule and priorities in order to invest in things that will outlast this life?
2. Do you spend more time focusing on temporal matters that don't count for eternity,

or do you spend a healthy amount of your time, money, talents, and energies on doing what God's Word tells you to do?

3. If Jesus were to speak to you directly today, do you think He would tell you that you are living primarily for today, or that you are also investing wisely in your eternal future?

DECEMBER 1

Fortresses in Your Brain

(For the weapons of our warfare are not carnal,
but mighty through God to the pulling down of strong holds.)
— 2 Corinthians 10:4

*O*nce while I was ministering in southern England, I had a few free hours between services, so I asked the local church leaders to take me to see a famous old castle that was nearly one thousand years old. As I approached the castle, its tall, thick stone walls loomed upward overhead. After climbing to the top of the ancient tower, I stopped to enjoy a view of the entire valley below that was simply beautiful.

This particular castle was famous for its history because its lofty position on top of the small mountain had made it impenetrable for hundreds of years. Although many aggressors had attempted to attack and overtake it, its high position on top of the mountain, coupled with its tall, thick walls, had kept those who resided inside secure from outward attack. Over the years, enemies who tried to attack and conquer the fortress had been perpetually frustrated as a result of these advantages that prohibited such a victory.

As I stood in the top tower of that ancient fortress, looking down at the valley below and hearing the stories of all the foreign armies who had unsuccessfully tried to take this stronghold captive, I thought of Paul's words in Second Corinthians 10:4. He wrote, "(For the weapons of our warfare are not carnal, but mighty through God to the pulling down of strong holds.)"

What are the "strongholds" Paul is talking about in this verse? Whatever they are, Paul lets us know that they are so reinforced and resistant that they can only be eradicated by the power of God and the weapons supplied by the Holy Spirit.

The word "stronghold" comes from the Greek word *ochuroma*. It is one of the oldest words in the New Testament, originally used to describe a *fortress*, such as the one described above. It depicted *a fortress, a castle,* or *a citadel.* Ancient fortresses had exceptionally thick, very high, impregnable walls that were designed to keep outsiders from scaling the walls or from breaking inside. Such walls were intended to keep intruders *outside.*

But by the time of the New Testament, the word *ouhuroma* also came to be the very same Greek word used to describe *a prison.* Since the most secure, highly guarded prisons were usually constructed deep inside such fortresses, it makes sense that the word for *a fortress* or *stronghold* is the same identical Greek word used to picture *a prison.* Whereas a fortress keeps outsiders from getting *in*, a prison keeps insiders from getting *out*. Prisons are *places of detention* or *holding tanks*. They also have fortified walls, as well as bars of steel, that are designed to hold a prisoner in captivity.

The "strongholds" Paul refers to are lies that the devil has ingrained so deeply in your mind and in your belief system that they now exert power over certain areas of your life. Just as ancient rulers liked to build their castles perched high on a mountainside, the devil attempts to build strong lies in your mind so he can rule you from a lofty position in your thoughts and emotions. Although you may know logically that the lies the enemy speaks to your mind are untrue, these lies still wage war in your soul, attempting to sabotage your sense of self-worth and your self-image.

You see, when a person has a stronghold in his mind or emotions, he has thick, invisible walls around him that act like both a fortress and a prison in his life. Like the walls of a fortress, these lies insulate him from people who may try to break in to help him see the truth. Although others may want to help this person, they often find it impossible to break through the invisible barriers that surround his mind and emotions.

As a result, the person under mental and emotional assault is held captive like a prisoner to those lies. He sits behind mental and emotional bars, viewing life through the illusion of bondage that Satan has put into his mind. He looks at others, sadly wishing he could be free like them, not realizing that he has already been set free by the blood of Jesus Christ. The lies that operate in his soul keep him bound in an inner "prison" that he can't seem to break out of by himself.

So when you read Paul's words about "strongholds" in Second Corinthians 10:4, you need to picture both a fortress and a prison in your mind and then apply this picture to your own life. Are there any areas of your mind that are currently controlled by the enemy's lies of fear, doubt, and worry? Do you find yourself being repeatedly attacked in the areas of your self-worth and self-image? Are these attacks debilitating and crippling? Do you feel like a hostage to these areas of your mind and emotions? If you answered yes to any of these questions, you have probably allowed the devil to build strongholds in your mind and emotions that are hindering you from stepping out to do something God has purposed for you to do in your life.

If that's your situation, first recognize and repent for permitting those strongholds to develop in the first place. Then go back and see how the devil gained this foothold in your life. After you discover how the devil was able to work so deeply in your mind and emotions, ask the Lord to forgive you and to cleanse you from this devilish operation in your soul.

Once you have received this divine cleansing, it is time for you to arise in the power of the Spirit with the weapons of God and the name of Jesus Christ. Reject the devil's claim on your mind and emotions, and command him to leave in Jesus' name! Then get back on the path to right believing and right thinking by renewing your mind daily with the Word of God. If you truly want to be permanently set free from the lies that have controlled you for so long, you will have to use the weapons of the Spirit to pull down every stronghold the devil has erected in your life!

MY PRAYER FOR TODAY

Lord, I realize that the enemy has been attempting to control my self-worth and my self-image through lies that have been operating in my mind and emotions for a very long time. Because I allowed the devil access to my thought life in times past, I have been like a hostage held captive in an inner prison. I can see now how others have tried to help me, but they haven't been able to break through the strong walls of these mental lies that have surrounded my thinking. So today I am turning to You, Holy Spirit. I ask You for help as I learn to utilize the weapons of my warfare that You have supplied. Please help me uproot, tear down, and permanently walk free of every mental lie of the enemy for the rest of my life!

I pray this in Jesus' name!

MY CONFESSION FOR TODAY

I confess that I will no longer permit the devil to have a foothold in my mind and emotions. I am employing the use of the power of God, the weapons of the Holy Spirit, and the name of Jesus Christ, and I command the devil to withdraw his lies from my mind and emotions and to flee from me! The enemy has no right to operate inside my mind, and I refuse to allow his operation in my soul to continue. I will believe right, think right, and renew my mind daily with the Word of God. I am now permanently set free from lies that have controlled me for such a long time. From this moment forward, I am dominated by the truth of God's Word. Lies that have held me captive for so long have no more power over me!

I declare this by faith in Jesus' name!

QUESTIONS FOR YOU TO CONSIDER

1. Do you know of any areas of your mind and emotions that continually lie to you and try to hold you in some kind of spiritual captivity? What are those areas, and how long have they been exercising dominion in your life?
2. What are some of the steps you can start taking right now to step out of that bondage and into the liberty Jesus Christ wants to give to you?
3. Can you think of key scriptures you need to memorize and start confessing in order to renew your mind to the specific truths of God's Word that will help you think rightly about yourself? Why don't you write down those scriptures and put them in a visible place in your home to remind you about the truth God declares about you?

DECEMBER 2

The Lance of Prayer and Supplication

Praying always with all prayer and supplication in the Spirit,
and watching thereunto with all perseverance
and supplication for all saints.
— Ephesians 6:18

One of my favorite sections in museums is the one that displays armor used in the ancient world. I especially enjoy the section that displays the spears and lances that were used by the ancients. It is simply amazing to study the weaponry of the ancient soldier and discover how many different kinds of spears and lances were available to him. It becomes very evident that the spear and lance was one of the most important pieces of weaponry he possessed.

When Paul wrote his epistle to the Ephesians, he spoke extensively about the armor of God, urging believers to use their spiritual weaponry. However, as you study this full list of weaponry, it seems that the lance or spear, a key weapon, is missing. But although Paul didn't explicitly mention the lance, he did tell believers to take up the *whole* armor of God (Ephesians 6:11), implying a complete set of weaponry. We can therefore assume that Paul must have intended to include the lance or spear in this set of spiritual equipment.

The lance of our spiritual armor is found in Ephesians 6:18, where Paul says, "Praying always with all prayer and supplication in the Spirit...." I call this "the lance of prayer and supplication." Let's look more closely at this piece of weaponry so you can better understand why I say this.

The lances used by the large and diverse Roman army varied greatly in size, shape, and length. These weapons were devised to be used to attack an enemy from a distance. They were thrown with great force and hurled tremendous distances to strike the enemy from afar. Because different lances were thrown at different distances, they came in all sizes and shapes. The particular lance chosen by a soldier depended on how it was to be used.

By revelation, Paul begins to compare these various lances to the various kinds of prayer God has made available to us. This is why he said, "Praying always, with all prayer and supplication...." You see, when a believer effectively uses prayer, it becomes a lance that can be thrust forth into the spirit realm against the malevolent works of the adversary. By forcibly hurling this divine instrument of prayer into the face of the enemy, a believer can exert great spiritual power, literally attacking the devil from a distance in order to stop major obstacles from developing up close in his personal life.

I want you to especially notice the phrase "with all prayer." It is taken from the Greek phrase *dia pases proseuches* and would be better translated "with all kinds of prayer."

Do you understand the various forms of prayer that are available for you to use as you pray and wage spiritual warfare? Don't wrongly assume that all prayer is of the same kind. Just as Roman soldiers used all kinds of lances in battle, Paul lets you know that many forms of prayer are available for you to use in the fight of faith (*see* February 26). For instance, there is *the prayer of faith, the prayer of agreement, the prayer of intercession, the prayer of supplication, the prayer of petition, the prayer of consecration, the prayer of thanksgiving, united prayer,* and so forth.

Paul instructs us to use every form of prayer that has been made available to us as it is needed. No one kind of prayer is better than the others; each serves a different and necessary purpose in the life of faith.

Never forget that prayer is a vital piece of your spiritual weaponry. If you neglect this strategic piece of weaponry, you will find that the enemy keeps attacking you from up close. But as you learn to pray with authority, you will develop the ability to strike the enemy from a distance and therefore maintain a victorious position in your life.

God has placed the lance of prayer at your disposal so you can be assured of absolute and total victory. *As you use this lance of prayer and supplication in all its various forms, you will continually reinforce Jesus Christ's triumphant victory over Satan and gloriously demonstrate Satan's miserable defeat in every area of your life!*

MY PRAYER FOR TODAY

Lord, I thank You for entrusting me with all the weapons I need to keep the devil defeated in my life. Forgive me for not always taking advantage of the full weaponry You have provided.

Prayer is powerful — yet I admit that I have neglected this piece of weaponry in my life. Forgive me for allowing myself to get too busy to make time for prayer. Instead of ignoring this vital piece of weaponry, I want to learn how to use every form of prayer that is available to me so I can stop the devil from making up-close attacks in my life. Thank You for this vital weapon of warfare. Please teach me to use it powerfully, forcefully, and effectively against the works of the devil.

I pray this in Jesus' name!

MY CONFESSION FOR TODAY

I confess that prayer is a vital piece of my spiritual weaponry. Because I use this strategic piece of weaponry, I am able to stop the enemy from attacking me from up close. I pray with authority, and that authority gives me the ability to strike the enemy from a distance while maintaining a victorious position in my life. With the lance of prayer at my disposal, I can be sure of absolute and total victory. Although the devil tries to attack me, I overcome each of his attacks by striking him from a distance as I thrust the lance of prayer and supplication into the realm of the spirit. I commit myself to using the lance of prayer and supplication in all its various forms. As I do, I will continually reinforce Jesus Christ's triumphant victory over Satan and gloriously demonstrate Satan's miserable defeat in every area of my life!

I declare this by faith in Jesus' name!

QUESTIONS FOR YOU TO CONSIDER

1. Can you think of a time when you felt alerted in your spirit that an attack was coming from the enemy, and you disabled that attack by using your God-given authority in prayer? What was that occasion? How did your aggressive praying stop that attack in your life?
2. Looking back on your life, what do you think would have happened if you hadn't listened to the Spirit of God and hurled the lance of prayer and supplication into the spirit realm? If that attack against you had been successful, in what way would it have negatively affected your life? Have you taken the time to stop and thank God for alerting you to this potential spiritual attack?
3. Are you aware of the different kinds of prayer that are available for you to use? What are you doing to learn more about prayer and how to use prayer more effectively in your life?

Never forget that prayer is a vital piece of your spiritual weaponry. If you neglect this strategic piece of weaponry, you will find that the enemy keeps attacking you from up close. But as you learn to pray with authority, you will develop the ability to strike the enemy from a distance and therefore maintain a victorious position in your life.

DECEMBER 3

༄༅

The Servant of the Lord

And the servant of the Lord must not strive;
but be gentle unto all men, apt to teach, patient.
— 2 Timothy 2:24

Many years ago, we had a staff member who moaned and groaned all the time because he was working so hard and was making such great sacrifices for the Lord. It was true that he was working hard, but so were all the rest of us. I agreed with this staff member when he told me that he and his wife were facing hardships they had never faced before. However, I also knew they weren't alone in this predicament. We were all facing hardships because life in the former USSR was very difficult at that time.

The truth is, this man's family was living at a much higher level of comfort and privilege than his neighbors or fellow workers at the office. But because he complained so much, everyone on the team rallied to help his family get over the hump they were experiencing. But no matter how much people did for this staff member and his wife, they continued to moan and groan about how bad life was and how much they had sacrificed for the Lord — and they rarely ever thanked anyone for what he or she did to try to help them.

Remembering how difficult it had been when our family first moved to that part of the world, my wife and I felt a need to do everything we could to help this man and his family adjust. We tried to comfort this couple as they worked through their transition. We knew they were having to get used to some very difficult living conditions while dealing with the normal feelings of homesickness that almost everyone experienced who had just moved to that side of the world. But after a while, we also realized that no matter how much we comforted this couple, they just would *not* be comforted!

Finally, the entire staff began to run out of patience. Everyone was getting fed up with listening to this couple sing the same sad song every day at the office. I could see that feelings of resentment toward these two were growing among staff members as appreciation for the couple's work decreased. In the end, I knew I would have to sit down with this man and wife again to discuss their sour attitudes because they were adversely affecting so many people in our organization.

The day finally came when I pulled up my chair to the husband's desk and said, "I need to talk to you about your attitude." But before I could even get started, he had already put up a wall of defense that made it impossible for me to deal with him. Talking to that man was like talking to a brick wall! As he proceeded to be argumentative and defensive, I thought, *Wait a minute! I didn't come here to fight with him today! I came here to be a help and a blessing!*

After a few minutes, I could see that my attempt to speak a word of correction into this man's life was a total waste of both his time and my time. Had he opened his heart and allowed me to speak into his life, I could have helped him. But he wasn't open to receiving input from anyone and was therefore destined to go through a series of mishaps and serious mistakes of his own making. However, all those mistakes could have been avoided if only he had allowed someone to be a friend and speak the truth to him.

Speaking correction into someone's life isn't a responsibility any leader relishes. Nevertheless, it is something leaders are required to do from time to time. This was Paul's message to Timothy in Second Timothy 2:24. Paul wrote this letter to Timothy at a time when certain members of Timothy's team were apparently demonstrating a rebellious attitude toward him as their pastor and needed to be corrected. In Paul's letter, the apostle explained to Timothy how he was to bring correction to someone under his sphere of authority. This instruction is helpful to us as well for those times when we are required to speak correction into someone else's life.

In Second Timothy 2:24, Paul said, "And the servant of the Lord must not strive; but be gentle unto all men, apt to teach, patient." Notice that Paul called Timothy "the servant of the Lord." The word "servant" in this verse is the Greek word *doulos*. It describes *a bondslave who is bound to do what he is told to do, regardless of what he thinks about it*. This means that Timothy, as the bondslave of the Lord, was to hear what the Lord told him to do and then faithfully carry out His orders no matter what he felt or thought about them.

It is significant that Paul used this word when instructing Timothy to deal with problem-makers. It tells us that Timothy probably didn't want to do it and that Paul was therefore reminding the younger minister that as a servant of the Lord, he didn't have a choice regarding how he was going to handle such a situation.

Timothy was the chief leader of the church. Therefore, it was his responsibility to step into his leadership position and act with the authority and responsibility God had given him. No one else had the position or power to set things in order. Whether or not he wanted to do it, it was time for Timothy to step up to the plate and start playing according to God's rules.

Likewise, if God has chosen you to be a leader in your church, your business, your organization, or your family, you must learn to see yourself as a God-appointed leader and accept the responsibility that goes along with this position. This is not a responsibility that you can shirk or pass off to someone else.

If someone under your authority is acting wrongly, it is your job to deal with it. Rather than shut your eyes and hope the problem simply disappears, you must love that person enough to go to him and deal with him in the spirit of Jesus. Do what you can to bring correction into his life so he can be set free from a wrong attitude that will negatively affect both his present and his future.

If that person chooses to listen to you and to submit to your spiritual authority, he can be changed. But if he chooses to ignore you and to reject your helpful counsel, you must then make a choice about whether or not to let that person remain as a part of your team. One thing is for sure, however — ignoring the problem will not make it go away and, in fact, may make it even worse.

You may dread the moment you have to sit down with that person to discuss what is wrong in his attitude. But once you finally deal with the problem, you'll be so glad you did! The other team members will also be thankful that you took your leadership role seriously and refused to let a bad attitude negatively affect everyone else on the team. In the end, you'll bolster your own leadership position in the eyes of others because you did the right thing. Your willingness to confront a problem will cause your team to respect you more, and hopefully you will have helped that person whose attitude needed to be corrected.

So if you are a leader, accept the fact that bringing correction to people under your sphere of authority is part of your responsibility. As you pray and seek the mind of the Lord, the Holy Spirit will show you how to speak to people in this kind of situation. He will teach you how to help them see what they need to change in their lives and attitudes so they can move up higher in God.

Never forget that bringing people higher is one of the primary goals of a leader. So if you are entrusted with the care of others in any arena of life, do everything you can to lead them to a higher level of excellence — even if it means correcting them in love!

MY PRAYER FOR TODAY

First of all, Lord, I thank You for loving me enough to put people over me who were willing to bring correction into my life in the past. Although that correction was difficult to receive, I needed it and it ultimately benefited my life. For this, I am so thankful. Second, I ask You to help me now to be a blessing to those You have placed under my sphere of authority. When I see attitudes in them that need to be corrected, help me know how to approach them in a way that is positive and uplifting. I ask You to give me the wisdom I need to challenge those under my authority to a higher level in every area of their lives.

I pray this in Jesus' name!

MY CONFESSION FOR TODAY

I confess that those under my authority listen to me and submit to my spiritual authority; therefore, I am able to help them grow and mature in the Lord. I accept the fact that bringing correction to people under my sphere of authority is part of my responsibility. As I pray and seek the mind of the Lord, the Holy Spirit shows me how to correct people in love. He teaches me how to help them see what they need to change in their lives and attitudes so they can move up higher in God. I willingly make it my goal to bring the people under my care to a higher level in every area of their lives!

I declare this by faith in Jesus' name!

QUESTIONS FOR YOU TO CONSIDER

1. Can you think of a time when someone sat down with you and spoke words of correction to you that ultimately produced great and positive changes in your life?
2. Has there been a time in the past when you dreaded the moment you had to bring correction to someone, but afterward you were so glad you finally did it? What did your counsel produce in that person's life? Did he listen to you, or did he ignore your counsel?
3. Can you think of some positive ways you can speak words of correction to someone to make it a little easier for him or her to swallow?

If someone under your authority is acting wrongly, it is your job to deal with it. Rather than shut your eyes and hope the problem simply disappears, you must love that person enough to go to him and deal with him in the spirit of Jesus.

DECEMBER 4

If No One Else Will Stand by You,
The Lord Will Come to Your Assistance

At my first answer no man stood with me,
but all men forsook me:
I pray God that it may not be laid to their charge.
— 2 Timothy 4:16

*I*t is a heart-rending experience when friends let you down or when someone you thought to be faithful disappoints you. If this has ever happened to you, you know how upsetting this kind of situation can be. Yet this is precisely what happened to Timothy when he was serving as the senior pastor of the church in Ephesus. Leaders he thought would be faithful to the end had apparently walked out and left him in a moment of trouble. The hurt and pain Timothy felt from being abandoned by those he had trusted was so intense that he had written to Paul about it.

If you have ever felt betrayed by someone you loved, you should relate very well to the words the apostle Paul wrote in Second Timothy 4:16. Paul is referring to the time he stood before the Roman imperial court to be tried for the first time. In that moment when he needed friends to testify in his defense, Paul turned to see who would testify on his behalf — only to discover that every one of his friends had walked out and abandoned him.

Now as Paul writes to Timothy to encourage him to stand strong in his own ordeal, he recalls that extremely difficult time when those close to him chose to walk away. Paul says, "At my first answer no man stood with me, but all men forsook me: I pray God that it may not be laid to their charge."

The word "answer" is the Greek word *apologia*, which is a compound of the words *apo* and *logos*. In this case, the word *apo* means *back*, and the word *logos* is the Greek word for a *word*. When compounded, it means to *answer back* and depicts *a reply, a response,* or *an answer.* It was the old word used to describe *a court trial* where the accused was given an opportunity to respond to the charges brought against him.

Paul says, "At my first answer no man stood with me...." The word "stood" comes from the Greek word *paraginomai*. It is a technical term used to describe *a witness who stands forward in a court of law to support a prisoner.* By selecting this word, Paul makes his point clear: When he desperately needed the support of fellow believers, not one single friend stood forward to testify in his defense. When he turned and looked to see who would be his witness, all his friends were gone!

In fact, Paul goes on to say, "...But all men forsook me...." The word "forsook" in Greek is from the word *egkataleipo*, which is a compound of the words *ek, kata,* and *leipo*. The word *ek* means *out*; the word *kata* means *down*; and the word *leipo* means *to leave* or *to forsake.* But when all three of these words are joined to form a triple-compound word, the new word carries the idea of *walking out on someone; leaving someone in a terrible condition; abandoning a person at the worst possible moment;* and *deserting a person in the most terrible way.* In other words, it conveys the idea of *abandonment.* By using this wretched word, Paul is saying, *"Not only did they not come forward to support me and stand with me — they walked out on me and abandoned me at the worst possible moment!"*

You'd think these horror stories would have made Paul bitter; however, there isn't a trace of bitterness in the apostle. He has learned a marvelous secret: *When no one else will stand with you, the Lord will always come forward to stand alongside you, support you, and help you.*

Continuing in verse 17, Paul says, "Notwithstanding the Lord stood with me, and strengthened me; that by me the preaching might be fully known, and that all the Gentiles might hear: and I was delivered out of the mouth of the lion."

First, Paul says, "…The Lord stood with me…." This word "stood" is the Greek word *paristemi*, which means *to stand by one's side*. By using this word, Paul tells you that Jesus Christ is not ashamed of any faithful soldier. When no one else will come to your aid, Jesus Christ is always there to rescue you. Jesus will step forward to assist you and defend you when your friends and family have all bailed out!

Second, Paul says the Lord "strengthened" him. The word "strengthened" in the Greek is *endunamoo*, which always refers to *an empowerment* or *an inner strengthening*. It is a compound of the words *en* and *dunamis*. The word *en* means *in*. The word *dunamis* means *explosive strength, ability,* and *power*. It's where we get the word *dynamite*.

Thus, this word *endunamoo* presents the picture of *an explosive power that is being deposited into some type of container, vessel, or other form of receptacle*. The very nature of this word *endunamoo* means that there necessarily must be some type of *receiver* into which this *power* can be deposited.

What does this tell us? In that moment when Paul felt so abandoned, he received a supernatural infilling of divine power that literally super-charged him to bravely and victoriously face one of the most difficult times in his life. The moment Paul discovered he had no friends to lean on was the exact moment that the power of God filled him anew and made him supernaturally strong for the ordeal he was facing.

This was good news for Timothy — and for every other believer who ever feels abandoned and let down by friends. If anyone needed to be reminded that the Lord would stand by him and strengthen him in the midst of every crisis, it was Timothy. The young minister desperately needed a fresh infilling of God's power so he could victoriously walk through the ordeal that lay before him.

Just as God supernaturally strengthened Paul at a time when the apostle felt hurt and betrayed, God promised to do the same for Timothy in his hour of need. And God hasn't changed; He is still not a respecter of persons. If He did it for Paul and Timothy, He will do the same for you today!

Are you facing a disturbing situation today? Has something happened to make you feel lonely and abandoned by those you thought would be faithful to stand by your side? If this is the case, it's time for you to ask *Jesus* to stand by your side. If you will ask Him for help, He will step forward to assist you, befriend you, and fill you with the power you need to victoriously conquer this difficult time in your life. *So why don't you go ahead and ask the Lord to help you today?*

MY PRAYER FOR TODAY

Lord, I admit that I've been feeling pretty lonely in the situation I am facing right now. Even though my friends try to understand, they simply can't comprehend the emotional ordeal I am going through. But I know that You understand everything, Lord, so today I am asking You to step forward and assist me in my hour of need. Please stand at my side to help me, support me, and fill me with a fresh dose of the Holy Spirit's mighty power so I can victoriously overcome in the midst of this challenging trial. I know that with Your Presence and power at my side, I will win this fight of faith that I'm engaged in right now.

I pray this in Jesus' name!

MY CONFESSION FOR TODAY

I confess that Jesus loves me and understands me. Even though friends may desert me or fail to understand the dilemma I am facing in my life, Jesus completely comprehends the entire situation. Not only does He understand, but He is also my biggest Helper in my time of need. When I cry out to Jesus in faith, He responds by manifesting His strong Presence at my side. His Presence is with me to assist me, support me, and give me the strength I need to conquer all the attacks that come against my life. With Jesus, I can and will endure everything I face in life!

I declare this by faith in Jesus' name!

QUESTIONS FOR YOU TO CONSIDER

1. Can you think of several instances in your life when you felt extremely weak, but then Jesus Christ came alongside you and filled you with all the strength you needed to victoriously make it through the predicament you were facing?

2. Do you know a friend who is struggling right now and feeling very abandoned? If so, why don't you demonstrate your love to that friend today by taking the time to share how Jesus strengthened you in your past times of crisis? Your testimony may be the very thing that encourages your friend to let the Lord step forward as his Helper in his time of need.

3. When you were facing those hard times and the Spirit of God filled you with His power, how did you know that He had touched you? What was the immediate change you felt that let you know God had just given you a new infilling of His Spirit?

DECEMBER 5

You Still Have Room for Improvement!

When Jesus then lift up his eyes, and saw a great company
come unto him, he saith unto Philip,
Whence shall we buy bread, that these may eat?
And this he said to prove him: for he himself knew what he would do.
— John 6:5,6

When Jesus lifted up His eyes and saw the vast crowd coming toward Him on the mountainside, He turned to Philip and asked him a question that Philip may have perceived to be preposterous. Jesus asked him, "…Whence shall we buy bread, that these may eat?"

Let's talk about why this question could have seemed preposterous to Philip and to the rest of the disciples. In John 6:10, we find that there were five thousand men in the crowd that day. This word "men" is not a nonspecific term that includes men, women, and children; rather, it is the Greek word *andres*, which categorically means *male individuals*. Matthew 14:21 confirms that there were "…about five thousand men, beside women and children." Jewish tradition would have forbidden the women and children to sit down to eat with the men; thus, we can know that the women and children were seated separately from the men on the mountainside and were not included in the figure of five thousand.

If we add to that number of five thousand men all the women and children who accompanied them, we find that this easily could have been a crowd of thirty thousand or more. Just add five thousand husbands, five thousand wives, and approximately five children for each family, and you'll reach a sum of thirty thousand people.

Remember, the people of Israel believed that children were a blessing from the Lord and tried to have as many children as possible. Therefore, it is very likely that the number of children present in that crowd may have been even higher than this estimate of five per family. This makes the figure of thirty thousand people a very reasonable estimate. In fact, it is most likely an *under*estimation! The point, however, is this: This was not just a large crowd; a *very large multitude* of people had walked up that mountainside to see Jesus.

Now do you see why Jesus' question must have seemed so preposterous to Philip and the other disciples? Not one of them was prepared to throw a banquet for so many thousands of people. To make matters worse, they were out in the wilderness on top of a mountain, far from stores where massive amounts of food could be purchased. In fact, Matthew 14:15,16 tells us the disciples were so concerned about feeding the multitude that they told Jesus, "…This is a desert place, and the time is now past; send the multitude away, that they may go into the villages, and buy themselves victuals. But Jesus said unto them, They need not depart; give ye them to eat."

Jesus put the challenge to His disciples to quickly find food to feed this massive multitude. John 6:6 tells us that Jesus did this for the explicit purpose to "prove" them. The word "prove" is the Greek word *peiradzo*, a Greek word that was usually used to denote *a test to reveal the quality of a material substance.*

For instance, the word *peiradzo* was used to depict *the process of testing metal to discover whether its quality was superb or inferior*. As the metal was put through multiple degrees of intense fires, the fire caused the impurities in the metal that were hidden to the natural eye to rise to the surface. If no impurities surfaced, the metal was free of defects. But if impurities rose to the surface, the metal still needed future fires to make it pure and strong. Therefore, this testing by fire was a calculated, premeditated investigation, deliberately designed to *expose* any deficiency in the metal that would later cause it to fracture or fail.

This positively means that Jesus was deliberately testing the disciples, putting this challenge before them to expose the true level and quality of their faith. As a result, the disciples would discover whether or not they still had room for improvement in the faith realm.

As Jesus looked out at the crowd, John 6:6 tells us that He already knew exactly what He was going to do. He really didn't need His disciples' help; He just wanted them to recognize the true level of their own faith. Thus, Jesus asked them this question in order to "prove" them. He knew that there is just something about a new problem that exposes any deficiency in a person's faith and accentuates any weak area that remains in his life.

In verses 7 through 9, Andrew and Philip began to frantically search high and low through the crowd, rummaging around for whatever food they could find. In other words, they were seeking to solve this problem through natural means rather than to say, "Jesus, I know You can do all things. Speak the word, and this multitude will be fed."

Finally, Andrew found five loaves of bread and two fish — a tiny portion of food that was certainly not sufficient to feed a crowd of thirty thousand or more! But in this moment, Jesus revealed Himself as the Lord of Multiplication. Taking those five loaves of bread and two fish, Jesus showed His disciples that He was Lord even over impossible situations like this one.

Don't make the same mistake Philip did when a new problem or challenge arises in your life. Instead of fretting and failing to believe, stop to remember all the supernatural things you've already seen Jesus do in your life. Could the solution to this new dilemma possibly be any more difficult than any of the miracles you've already seen Him perform on your behalf?

And if the situation you're facing has exposed the fact that your faith level isn't what it should be, aren't you thankful this happened so you could see the true condition of your faith walk? Now you know that your faith still has room for improvement. It is a demonstration of God's mercy that He lets you find this out now rather than later in a critical moment when your faith might fracture or fail in a moment of great need. *Is it possible that God is trying to help by showing you that your faith life still has room for improvement?*

MY PRAYER FOR TODAY

Lord, I thank You for loving me so much that You help me discover the genuine level of my faith before I get into a situation where I seriously need it. To realize my need for improvement now is so much better than to find out when a difficult situation arises that my faith isn't sufficient for the challenge. So I thank You for the tender, loving care You have shown me by placing me in this challenging situation that reveals the true level of my faith. Help me to press forward and to grow in this area of my life!

I pray this in Jesus' name!

MY CONFESSION FOR TODAY

I confess that my faith is growing and getting stronger every day. I am thankful for the situations that have exposed my true faith level, for now I can work on improving the capacity of my faith. I know that faith comes by hearing the Word of God, so I purpose to baptize my spirit and soul in the truth of God's Word until my faith grows to a higher level than I've ever attained before! I want to possess mountain-moving faith, so I determine to press forward with my whole heart and soul toward the goal of increasing the capacity of my faith!

I declare this by faith in Jesus' name!

QUESTIONS FOR YOU TO CONSIDER

1. What past challenge comes to mind that exposed the true level of your faith and revealed that your faith still had room for improvement?
2. Are you facing a situation right now in your life, ministry, or business that is demanding more of your faith than you've ever experienced before?
3. What steps can you take to develop a daily plan to increase the capacity and strength of your faith?

DECEMBER 6

Take Up Your Shield of Faith!

Above all, taking the shield of faith,
wherewith ye shall be able
to quench all the fiery darts of the wicked.
— Ephesians 6:16

Many people wrongly assume that the shield of faith is the most important part of their spiritual weaponry because Paul said, *"Above all*, taking the shield of faith…" (Ephesians 6:16). But if you think about it for a moment, you see that the shield of faith *can't* be more important than the "loinbelt of truth" — the Word of God — because faith comes from God's Word (Romans 10:17).

So just what *did* Paul mean when he said, "Above all…."? The phrase "above all" is taken from the Greek phrase *epi pasin*. The word *epi* means *over*. The word *pasin* means *all* or *everything*. So rather than stating that the shield of faith is more important than the other pieces of armor, the phrase *epi pasin* describes the *position* faith should have over the other pieces of armor. It could be better translated, *"Out in front of all…."* or *"Covering all…."*

Therefore, the phrase "above all" emphatically tells you that your "shield of faith" is never meant to be held next to your side or timidly held behind your back. Faith is supposed to be *out front* where it can *completely cover* you and protect you from harm — especially when you are marching forward to take new ground for the Kingdom of God!

Just as Roman soldiers kept their shields out in front of them to defend them from deadly attacks and blows from their enemies, God wants you to tightly grip your shield of faith while keeping it out in front where it can protect and defend you. When your shield of faith is kept in this *out-front* and *covering* position, it can do what God intended for it to do! This is why Paul continues to say, "…wherewith ye shall be able to quench all the fiery darts of the wicked." (*See* September 6 to refresh your memory regarding what the Bible says about the fiery darts of the wicked.)

But it is also very important for you to notice that Paul says, "…*Taking* the shield of faith…." The word "taking" is from the word *analambano*, which is a compound of the Greek words *ana* and *lambano*. The word *ana* means *up*, *back*, or *again*; the word *lambano* means *to take up* or *to take in hand*. When compounded together, it means *to take something up in hand* or *to pick something back up again*. This plainly means your shield of faith can be either *picked up* or *laid down*. It places the responsibility on *you* as to whether you will use your shield of faith or allow yourself to go through life unprotected.

If you want to employ the use of your faith, you must make the choice to take it in hand and to place it in front of you. It will not assume its defensive position over your life by accident. Your faith will only operate in your life the way it was meant to do when you choose to pick it up and put it where it belongs — *out in front*.

If you ever go into battle without your shield of faith, you are making a mistake you will seriously regret. Keeping your shield of faith in position is not an option if you intend to overcome the enemy and win the battles that are before you.

Therefore, I urge you not to go into battle without this all-important piece of your spiritual armor. If you fail to keep that protective shield in front of you, you leave yourself exposed to the deadly strikes of your adversary, the devil.

On the other hand, as you choose to daily take up your shield of faith, holding it out in front of you so that it completely covers every part of your life, you put yourself in position to thwart every single attack that the enemy throws your way!

MY PRAYER FOR TODAY

Lord, I thank You for giving me a shield of faith that completely covers me from head to toe. I don't have to constantly succumb to the devil's attacks. By holding my shield of faith above all and out in front so that it covers me completely as You intended it to do, I can be protected from the attacks that the enemy would like to wage against me. Forgive me for the times I've let my shield lay at my side while I stayed busy complaining about the devil giving me fits. I realize now that it's up to me to pick up my shield of faith and put it where it belongs. So with Your help, Lord, I am reaching out right now to pick it up, to hold it out front, and to do my part to make sure the enemy has no access to me!

I pray this in Jesus' name!

MY CONFESSION FOR TODAY

I confess that God has given me a shield of faith that protects me against the works of the enemy. If I will hold my faith out front — and today I commit myself to doing just that — God's Word guarantees that this mighty shield will thwart the fiery darts that the enemy wants so desperately to throw at me. My shield will cause those darts to bounce off, thereby protecting me from being struck. I will walk with my shield of faith out in front so that it covers me as God intended for it to do. As long as I do that, I can be confident that I will move forward in life without the enemy winning any full-scale attack against me!

I declare this by faith in Jesus' name!

QUESTIONS FOR YOU TO CONSIDER

1. Can you say that your faith is alive and active and out in front of you as God intended for it to be, or have you allowed your faith to become inactive so that it lags behind?

2. Please answer these questions honestly, for a truthful answer may prevent future disaster in your life: Did you once walk in faith more consistently than you do today? Have you allowed your shield of faith to drop to your side instead of maintaining it in the forward position that allows it to defend you from the enemy's attacks?

3. What steps are you going to take to reignite your faith and return it to its position as the mighty shield of protection that God intended for it to be? What kind of plan are you going to follow to see your faith recharged, reenergized, and repositioned out in front of your life?

DECEMBER 7

❧❧❧

Is There Any Afflicted Among You?

Is any among you afflicted? let him pray....
— James 5:13

Did you ever notice that sometimes people really don't want to change or listen to counsel? Often they'd rather keep repeating all their struggles and problems to whoever will listen to them. Have you ever known a believer like this? Although you deeply loved that person, did it bother you to watch him habitually go from person to person, telling each about all his personal problems? Did he seem to relish every new chance he found to load down someone else with his troubles?

There is definitely a time when a person needs to have a friend in whom he can confide. Personally, I thank God for my friends who have allowed me to open my heart and talk to them about the various challenges this ministry has faced. But a spiritually mature person knows that in addition to pouring out all his aches and pains to a trusted friend, he must learn to stand up and take responsibility for himself in prayer.

A person who loads all his troubles on others and then expects them to do all his praying for him is revealing his own spiritual immaturity. A time eventually comes when every believer must learn to go to God in prayer and win some of his own victories by himself in the Presence of God.

Yes, it may seem so much easier to talk to people about your problems. However, if you talked only half as much to God as you do to others about those problems, He'd be able to give you the answers and solutions for every situation or dilemma that you're facing.

James addressed this truth in his famous New Testament epistle. It's important to note that the book of James possesses a unique quality, for it contains pastoral counsel that isn't included in other epistles. The reason for this is that James was a pastor, whereas the other New Testament writers were apostles. Therefore, James frequently addressed certain issues differently than the other writers, speaking from a pastor's perspective and giving the kind of counsel that can only come from a man who knows the needs and behavior of people.

It seems that some people to whom James was writing had discovered that their troubles could be used as a way to attract attention to themselves. So these people floated from person to person, repeating their story to anyone who would listen — probably in an attempt to fill an emotional deficit in their lives.

People who fit this description are like bees that extract all the pollen they can from one flower before moving on to do the same with the next flower and the next, etc. These individuals stay with one person as long as he will listen; then when that person has been drained dry, they move on to drain the next person. However, all they want to do is talk. They don't ever apply any wise counsel that good-hearted people try to give them.

Although there is a time to talk, there is also a time when you need to stop talking and start praying! This is why James says, "Is any among you afflicted? let him pray..." (James 5:13).

The word "afflicted" is from the Greek word *kakopatheo*, which is a compound of the words *kakos* and *pathos*. The first part of the word, *kakos*, describes *something that is evil*. In fact, it is so evil that it produces terribly negative effects in a person's life. It is often translated as the words *bad, evil, wicked,* or *vile,* and it frequently denotes *something that is hurtful or damaging,* such as the personal devastation that results from one's physical illness.

In Mark 1:32,34 and in Mark 2:17, the word *kakos* is actually translated as "disease" and "sick" to convey the idea of people who were not only sick but whose lives had been devastated as a result of their poor health. The people in these cited verses were bearing terribly negative consequences in numerous areas of their lives due to their continual ill health. But in James 5:13, the word *kakos* doesn't necessarily refer to sickness (although it could also include sickness). Instead, it refers to *a person who is harassed by some problem that is weighing him down and producing devastating results in his life.*

The second part of the word *kakopatheo* is the Greek word *pathos.* The *King James Version* generally translates this word as *suffering.* But although it can be used to picture a *physical suffering,* this word primarily conveys the idea of *a suffering that occurs in the mind.* It portrays a person who is *affected* by something that has happened and, as a result, *suffers mentally or emotionally.* Even if these troubles are tangible, material, concrete problems, the level of anguish produced in the mind and emotions as a result is a far greater strain than the actual problem itself.

When the words *kakos* and *pathos* are compounded to form the word *kakopatheo* that is used in James 5:13, it gives the idea of *a person who is intensely suffering — perhaps physically but definitely mentally — due to the evil events that have occurred in his or her life.*

There is no doubt, then, that James is speaking to people who have been through a bad experience or a series of bad experiences that have produced real trouble in their lives. Although they may need to initially share their pain with someone else, James says, "...Let him [the person with troubles] pray...." The strong Greek tense used in this verse means James isn't suggesting that people take this action; he is *commanding* them to do it.

The word "pray" is the Greek word *proseuche* — a compound of the words *pros* and *euche.* The word *pros* means *toward* and gives the idea of *closeness.* Nearly everywhere it is used in the New Testament, the word *pros* carries the meaning of *close, up-front, intimate contact with someone else.* The second part of the word *proseuche* is taken from the word *euche.* The word *euche* is an old Greek word that describes *a wish, desire, prayer,* or *vow.* It was originally used to depict *a person who made some kind of vow to God because of a certain need or desire in his or her life.* This individual would vow to give something of great value to God in exchange for a favorable answer to prayer.

In Greek culture, before people verbalized their prayer or offered a sacrifice to a "god," a commemorative altar was set up and thanksgiving was offered on that altar. Such offerings of praise and thanksgiving were called *votive offerings* (from the word "vow"). These votive offerings were similar to a pledge. The person would promise that once his prayer had been answered, he would be back to give thanks once more to God. These votive offerings of praise and worship were elaborate and well-planned. Giving thanks to a deity was a significant event, so it was done in a serious and grandiose manner to outwardly demonstrate a thankful heart.

All of this is included in the background of the word *proseuche,* the word used more than any other for "prayer" in the New Testament. Keep in mind, the majority of New Testament readers were Greek in origin and knew the cultural background of this word; hence, they understood its full ramifications.

The word *proseuche* tells us that prayer should bring us *face to face* and into *close contact* with God. Prayer is more than a mechanical act or a formula to follow; it is *a vehicle to bring us to a place whereby we may enjoy a close, intimate relationship with God.*

This is an especially meaningful message for those who are prone to talk incessantly to people but who fail to speak to God about their troubles. For such a person, there comes a time when he must stop looking for people to talk to and begin to draw as close as possible to God in order to find a permanent solution to his dilemmas.

But the idea of *sacrifice* is also associated with this word for "prayer." In this sense, it portrayed an individual who so desperately desired to see his prayer answered that he was willing to surrender everything he owned in exchange for an answer to his petition. Clearly, this describes an altar of sacrifice and an act of consecration in prayer whereby a believer's life is yielded entirely to God.

Thus, this particular word for prayer tells us of a place of decision and consecration, an altar where we freely vow to give our lives to God in exchange for His life. Because the word *proseuche* carries this meaning of surrender and sacrifice, we can know that God obviously desires to do more than merely bless us — He wants to change us! He wants to come to a place of consecration where we meet with Him face to face and surrender every area of our lives to Him; in exchange, He touches and transforms us by His power and Presence.

The tone used in James 5:13 reflects the idea of *urgency*, letting us know that James didn't want us to take a long time to get into God's Presence and allow Him to change us; rather, we are to get into this place of prayer as quickly as possible. You see, all the answers you and I need are found in the Presence of God. That is why it is so imperative that we come as close to His Presence as possible. And while we are in His Presence, He wants us to open our hearts to Him, tell Him what we feel, and be willing to surrender ourselves to Him completely. As we do this, God will give us the answers and the peace we need to victoriously face and conquer our various ordeals.

An interpretive translation
of this portion of James 5:13 could read:

"Is anyone among you going through an extremely difficult time in life that is causing him a lot of grief? I urge that person to draw near to God, to pour his heart out to Him, and to be willing to give up anything and to do anything God requires in order for his situation to be changed...."

As I noted earlier, there is definitely a time when you will need to confide in others about your problems. Thank God for real friends in whom we can confide! But there also comes a time when you must go to God for your solution and stop relying on your friends and associates to give you relief.

Is God's Spirit speaking to you today? Have you been going to people for your solutions instead of going first to God? *Why don't you take a little time today to quiet your heart and talk to the Lord about the things that are troubling you?*

MY PRAYER FOR TODAY

Lord, today I am asking You to forgive me for the times I've talked to people about my problems more than I've talked to You. I confess that I have leaned on people more heavily than I have leaned on You when facing difficult situations that required solutions. Now that I realize what I have done, I am making the decision to change the way I respond to challenges. I thank You, Lord, for the friends You have given me whom I can trust and confide in, but I know I will only find my real help and most permanent solutions as a result of being in Your Presence. Therefore, today I purpose to run to You first whenever the problems of life try to assault me. Only after I have received comfort and direction from You, my primary Source of help, will I consider turning to others whom You have given me for support.

I pray this in Jesus' name!

MY CONFESSION FOR TODAY

I confess that I run to the Lord whenever problems try to overwhelm me. He is my High Tower, my Strength, my Hiding Place, and the One in whom I trust. He has never failed me or forsaken me, and I know I can trust in Him. I thank God for the friends He has given me, but they can never take the place that only He has in my life. From this moment forward, I make the decision that before I pour out my heart to people, I will first pour out my heart to Him. I am willing to do whatever He asks and to give up anything He requires so that I may obtain the victory I need in my life.

I declare this by faith in Jesus' name!

QUESTIONS FOR YOU TO CONSIDER

1. Can you think of a person who habitually runs from person to person with his troubles but who never follows any suggestions that someone might give him to do? Does it seem that he just wants to spew his problems on everyone as a means of getting attention?
2. Have you ever been guilty of doing this same thing at some point in your past?
3. Are you presently spending time in the Presence of God on a daily basis? If not, is there a reason you have been avoiding the Presence of the Lord?

DECEMBER 8

Is There Any Merry Among You?

…Is any merry? let him sing psalms.
— James 5:13

Have you ever experienced something that thrilled you so deeply, you felt as if you'd explode if you couldn't express your joy about it? If you were alone when this happened, did it sadden you that you had no one to rejoice with you? Did it throw cold water on what you were feeling?

What should you do if you ever come to one of those moments when you're all alone, but you feel so elated that you just need to shout, dance, or sing to express yourself? I encourage you to go ahead and do it! The Lord is right there with you, and He'll be happy to share that moment of bliss with you. So don't waste time feeling sorry for yourself — just open your heart to the Lord and let out that shout! If you feel like screaming with joy, then scream! If you're so excited that you can't stand still, then throw off your shoes and start dancing! It's right for you to rejoice when something wonderful has happened in your life. That is precisely what James means when he says, "…Is any merry? let him sing psalms."

The word "merry" in this verse is the Greek word *euthumeo*, which is a compound of the Greek words *eu* and *thumos*. The word *eu* describes *a good feeling*, and it is where we get the word *euphoric*. It pictures a person who is absolutely *elated, thrilled,* or *ecstatic* about something. The word *thumos* is the idea of *swelling emotions* or *a strong and growing passion about something*. When these two are joined together to form the word *euthumeo*, the new word expresses the idea of *a person who is just about to explode with joy!* This person is so excited and overjoyed that he can hardly contain himself. He is so tickled about something that he can no longer restrain the happiness he feels!

James says that when you are filled with this kind of overflowing joy, you should express your exultation. Go ahead and let your heart sing! That is why he wrote, "…Is any merry? let him sing psalms." The words "sing psalms" comes from the single Greek word *psallo*, which first meant *to pluck*, as to pluck the strings of a harp or bow. Then later it meant *to play*, as a musician would play a stringed instrument. But by the time of the New Testament, it pictured *a person who sings a hymn or some other special heartfelt expression of music*. It is as if the strings of a person's heart are being plucked and played so he can fully express his heartfelt gratitude, praise, and worship to God.

In light of this, James 5:13
could be interpreted as follows:

"…Is there anyone among you who is so excited that he can hardly contain it and who feels as if he is about to burst with joy? If that person is so overjoyed and tickled that he can no longer restrain the happiness he feels, let him sing the song he feels in his heart."

Oh, how wonderful those moments are when your spirit is so filled with God's Presence that you feel a song arising from your heart! Why restrict the flow of life that is trying to emerge and refresh you at that moment? Remember, God gave your emotions to you. So when you're overflowing with joy because of something God has done for you or because of some wonderful event that has just transpired, don't hold back. It's healthy and good for you to *let your joy out*!

Also, don't let your rejoicing depend on whether or not people are present to do it with you. Have you forgotten that the Lord is always there with you? He will be happy to be a part of your celebration! In fact, it might even help you to express your joy if no one is there with you. If it's just you and the Lord, there is nothing to stop you from laying aside all your inhibitions so you can really throw your entire being into rejoicing!

MY PRAYER FOR TODAY

Lord, I needed this encouragement today, and I thank You for speaking to me through this Sparkling Gem. I do have something to shout about, so I make the decision today to go ahead and let out the joy that is in my heart! I thank You for being a part of my rejoicing and for the great and awesome things You are doing in my life!

I pray this in Jesus' name!

MY CONFESSION FOR TODAY

I confess that I don't need other people with me in order to truly rejoice in the Lord. When I feel the strings of my heart being plucked with joy, I am going to open my mouth and sing it out. When I feel so full of joy that I can't sit still, I am going to throw off my shoes and start dancing before the Lord. When I think I'm going to explode if I can't scream and yell with joy, I'm going to go somewhere where I can yell my head off without worrying about people who might be listening. God gave me emotions so I could rejoice — so I intend to rejoice with all my being whenever I am overflowing with the joy of the Lord!

I declare this by faith in Jesus' name!

QUESTIONS FOR YOU TO CONSIDER

1. Can you think of a time when you were so filled with joy that you started dancing and shouting? Did it feel like a volcano of joyous emotion was released from your spirit when you finally let your joy out?
2. How does it affect you when you see someone shouting and dancing for joy because of something good that has happened to him? Does it make you feel happy for that person, or does it make you want to tell him to be quiet?
3. If you find yourself getting upset when other people rejoice, what do you think lies at the root of this displeasure? Could it be that there is something inside you that the Spirit of God wants to remove so you can rejoice too?

DECEMBER 9

Is There Any Sick Among You?

Is any sick among you?
let him call for the elders of the church;
and let them pray over him, anointing him
with oil in the name of the Lord:
And the prayer of faith shall save the sick,
and the Lord shall raise him up....
— James 5:14,15

What should be done if a critically ill person is either bedfast, homebound, or immobile due to his illness yet deeply desires to have special prayer for his healing? Are there special cases when the elders of the church should go to a person's home to pray for him?

According to James 5:14 and 15, if a person is so extremely ill that he cannot come to church, the elders of the church should go to *him*. These verses give the scriptural procedure for how to pray for people who are in such a situation. Verse 14 begins by saying, "Is any sick among you? let him call for the elders of the church...."

The Greek word translated "sick" in James 5:14 does not describe people with minor ailments such as the common cold; rather, this Greek word *astheneo* refers to *people who are physically frail or feeble due to some bodily condition*. This deteriorated physical condition has rendered them unable to freely move about; hence, they are homebound by this infirmity and unable to come to church to receive prayer for healing.

In such situations, James says that the believer who is impaired by physical sickness has the right to "…call for the elders of the church…" to come to pray over him, "…anointing him with oil in the name of the Lord." James 5:15 promises that if faith is present when the elders pray, the Lord will raise up that believer from his bed of sickness.

Let's really look at this verse to understand the instructions that God gives for praying for such physically ill individuals. First, it says the sick believer should "call" for the elders of the church. The word "call" is the Greek word *proskaleo*, a compound of the words *pros* and *kaleo*. The word *pros* means *toward*, and the word *kaleo* means *to call, to invite,* or *to beckon.* When compounded together, it means *to summon to one's side.*

The tense used in this verse is so strong that it doesn't just picture a request for someone to come to one's side. Instead; it is an ardent plea, so intense that it could almost be perceived as a requirement. In other words, this person is *urgently* requiring the elders to come pray for him.

James instructs us that a believer in this physically impaired condition is to call for "the elders of the church." The word "elders" is the Greek word *presbuteros*, a word that appears no less than sixty-five times in the Greek New Testament. In the Gospels, the word *presbuteros* ("elders") was used to depict Israel's *most visible spiritual representatives of the people,* such as the ruling members of the local synagogues and the teachers and instructors of the Law who taught in the synagogues. The term itself expresses that these elders are not to be looked upon as common members of a local assembly; rather, they are deemed worthy of honor due to the position they hold.

In Acts 11:30, Luke uses the word *presbuteros* ("elders") to describe those who exercised authority and who formed the leadership of the Jerusalem church. In First Timothy 5:17,19 and in Titus 1:5, the apostle Paul uses the term *presbuteros* to depict *those who held officially appointed church offices.* In Titus 1:5, Paul instructs Titus to appoint elders in the church; then he follows up in Titus 1:7 by giving Titus the requirements for these elders. However, when Paul begins to list these requirements, he exchanges the word "elder" with the word "bishop." This is the Greek word *episkopos*, which definitely points to *the ordained leaders of a local assembly.* This means that the elders whom the sick believer is to call upon should be among the official or ordained ministers of the local church.

When these elders arrive on the scene to minister to the sick, James says they are to "…pray over him, anointing him with oil in the name of the Lord." The word "pray" is the Greek word *proseuchomai*, which represents *the act of drawing near to God and passionately petitioning Him to perform a specific act.* This is important, for it lets us know that this is not referring to a casual, token prayer but one that is deeply felt and passionately prayed. The tone in Greek again reflects the idea of *urgency.*

In addition to fervently praying for the sick person to be healed, the elders are also to anoint him with oil in the name of the Lord. The word "anoint" is the Greek word *aleipho*, and it refers to *the outward anointing of the body.* Although the exact type of oil is not the main topic of this verse, the Greek word *aleipho* usually referred to *olive oil.* We find this word used in Mark 6:13, where we discover that when Jesus sent the apostles forth to minister, "…they cast out many devils, and anointed with oil many that were sick, and healed them."

Oil itself has no healing properties, but in both the Old and New Testaments, it is used symbolically to depict the Presence of the Holy Spirit. By anointing the sick person with oil, the elder uses a tangible substance to declare that the Spirit of God is coming upon the infirmed to bring His healing power. Although the oil itself doesn't heal, the moment it is applied in prayer is the critical moment for the sick person to believe that God's Presence is coming upon him to bring healing to his sick body.

The elders are to perform this action in "the name of the Lord." The word "name" is from the Greek word *onomos*, and it represents *the full authority that exists in the person being named*. By praying in Jesus' name, a believer actually stands in the physical place of Jesus who is in Heaven, acting on His behalf and operating in the authority He has vested to that believer as His official representative.

Thus, this prayer is prayed by someone who understands he is standing by the bedside of the sick on Jesus' behalf. As the representative of Jesus Christ, this elder has the right to call on the power of God and to exercise all the authority that belongs to Jesus. What would Jesus do if He were physically present in the situation? That is precisely what this leader is to do as he ministers to the sick in the very stead of the Master.

But even if everything else is done according to this verse, the prayer must also be offered *in faith* if healing is the desired outcome. Too many pray with no feeling, fervor, or faith, and the results are therefore disappointing. For healing to result according to the promise of James 5:15, the prayer offered *must* be a "prayer of faith."

James goes on to say that when faith is present, the elders' prayer will "save the sick." The word "save" is the Greek word *sodzo*, which in this verse definitely describes a *physical healing* or *the restoration of one's health*. The word "sick" now switches from *astheneo*, which describes *a physical frailty or feebleness*, to the Greek word *kamno*, referring to *a person who has long suffered from this affliction and is extremely weakened from the effects of this disease*.

The next phrase confirms that this is no person with a head cold or minor ailment, for it says that after the oil is applied and the prayer of faith is prayed, "...the Lord shall raise him up...." The word "raise" is the Greek word *egeiro*, which means *to raise*, but it is also the root from which we get the word *resurrection*. This lets us know that the sick person is *gravely* ill, perhaps even close to death at the time of prayer. This would explain the urgency with which this prayer is to be offered.

James 5:14,15 could be interpreted to mean:

"Is there anyone among you who is extremely weakened due to illness? If there is such a person, let him urgently call for the ordained leaders of the local assembly to come and passionately petition God on his behalf. As the leaders pray, let them also anoint the sick person with oil, standing in the very place of Jesus — acting on Jesus' behalf and using the authority of His name. The prayer offered in faith will have definite results, for it will restore the sick person's health as the Lord raises him up from his bed of affliction."

It must be pointed out that it is "the Lord" who raises up the sick man from his bed of affliction. Although the elders actually anoint the person with oil and pray the prayer of faith, it is God who works with them and performs the miracle of healing. Here we see a beautiful picture of God and man working together to bring healing to those who are sick and disabled.

If you know anyone who is so gravely ill or weak that he is unable to come to church to receive prayer for his healing, let that person know he has a scriptural right to call for the elders of the local church to come anoint him with oil and pray the prayer of faith. As these elders stand at the sick person's bedside, acting and speaking on Jesus' behalf, James 5:15 promises that God's power will be ignited to raise him up from his bed of affliction!

MY PRAYER FOR TODAY

Lord, thank You for giving such clear instruction about how the critically ill are to call for the elders of the church to come pray for them. Please help me be an instrument of help to those who are gravely ill. Please alert me to the seriousness of their physical condition. Remind me to urge them to call for the local elders to come pray for them so that they might be restored to health. Help me to urgently press upon them the importance of exercising this God-given right. And, Lord, I ask You to raise them up by Your power so they can live a healthy life.

I pray this in Jesus' name!

MY CONFESSION FOR TODAY

I confess that I am quick to help the gravely ill remember that they have a right to call on the elders of their local church to come anoint them with oil and pray the prayer of faith for their recovery. The moment that the prayer of faith is prayed, God's power will be released — and that power will literally raise up the sick from the bed of affliction and out of the sickness that has disabled them. Jesus purchased healing for all believers. All they have to do is exercise their right to receive their healing by faith, and they will walk free of physical sickness and disease.

I declare this by faith in Jesus' name!

QUESTIONS FOR YOU TO CONSIDER

1. Have you ever been present when the elders of a local church came to anoint the sick with oil and pray the prayer of faith? When was that event, and what happened as a result of that time of prayer?
2. Can you think of anyone you know right now who is so sick that he or she cannot come to the church to receive prayer for healing? Have you suggested that this person call for the elders of the church to come pray for him or her?
3. Can you remember at least one time in your life when you witnessed the Lord literally raise up a person from the bed of sickness? When was that experience?

If you know anyone who is so gravely ill or weak that he is unable to come to church to receive prayer for his healing, let that person know he has a scriptural right to call for the elders of the local church to come anoint him with oil and pray the prayer of faith.

DECEMBER 10

Are You Resisting the Devil?

…Resist the devil, and he will flee from you.
— James 4:7

When the devil tries to assault your mind, telling you that your God-given dream will never come to pass, how do you resist those assaults? Do you stand firm against those lies and command them to leave? Or do you allow the devil to mentally assail your mind with untrue allegations?

In James 4:7, the Bible tell us, "…Resist the devil, and he will flee from you." The word "resist" is from the Greek word *anthistemi*, which is a compound of the words *anti* and *istimi*. The word *anti* means *against*, as *to oppose something*. The word *istimi* means *to stand*. When placed into one word, thus forming the word *anthistemi*, it means *to stand against* or *to stand in opposition*. It is a word that demonstrates *the attitude of one who is fiercely opposed to something and therefore determines that he will do everything within his power to resist it, to stand against it, and to defy its operation.*

By using this word, James plainly lets us know that we must be aggressively determined to stand against the work of the devil. Just shutting our eyes and hoping the enemy will withdraw won't work. We must dig in our heels, brace ourselves for a fight, and put our full force forward to drive him back and out of our lives. Our stand against Satan must be firm, unyielding, and steadfast if we want to successfully resist his bombardment of lies against our minds and emotions.

Notice that James says we are to resist the "devil." As noted in many other *Sparkling Gems*, the word "devil" is the translation of the word *diabalos*, which is more of a job description than it is a name. You see, if you understand the word "devil," you also know exactly how this sinister enemy works.

The word "devil" is a compound of the words *dia* and *balos*. The word *dia* has many meanings, depending on how it is used. However, in this particular case, it means *through*, as *to pierce something from one side all the way through to the other side*. The word *balos* means *to throw*, as when a person throws a ball, a rock, or some other object. When these two words are joined, it means *to repetitiously throw something — striking again and again and again until the object being struck has finally been completely penetrated.*

Now do you see why this word is a vivid job description for the devil? It tells us exactly how he operates. He comes to assault the mind — not once but many times. He strikes the mind and emotions again and again and again. He just keeps on striking until he wears down the resistance of the one being assaulted. Then as soon as the victim lets down his mental resistance, the devil gives one last firm punch that finally succeeds in penetrating his mind. Once the devil has gained access into that person's mind, he begins to deluge him with lies on top of lies. If the person listens to those lies and believes them, the devil can then successfully build a stronghold in his life from which he can begin to control and manipulate him.

Does this kind of mental attack sound familiar? Well, let me ask you a question: Instead of giving the devil the pleasure of filling your head with a barrage of lies, why don't you start to resist him? That's right — just tell the devil to shut up and to stop dropping those dim-witted religious thoughts of nonsense into your head! Tell him to hit the road!

It's time for you to resist the enemy of your soul. Let him know that you're not going to bite that bait anymore, so he may as well go fishing somewhere else. You're no longer going to be a sucker! You have just been informed that there is a deadly hook inside that bait that is designed to hook you, pull you into the devil's net, and turn you into dead meat for the devil to chomp on for a long time. *But he has hooked you with that bait for the last time!*

James 4:7 has good news for you. It says that if you will resist the devil, he will "flee" from you. The word "flee" in Greek is so exciting! It is from the word *pheugo*, which from the earliest times of Greek literature meant *to flee* or *to take flight.* It was used to depict *a lawbreaker who flees in terror from a nation where he broke the law.* The reason he flees so quickly is that he wants to escape the prosecution process. Remaining in the nation would most assuredly mean judgment; so rather than stay and face the consequences, the lawbreaker flees for his life.

This means the devil knows that he is a lawbreaker! He also knows that if a believer stands against him — in other words, if the believer resists the enemy by using his God-given authority in the name of Jesus and with the Word of God — it won't be long until that believer begins to rule and dominate the devil. Rather than allow this to happen, the devil begins to withdraw and look for a way to escape the prosecution process. Instead of sticking around and trying hopelessly to defend himself against the name of Jesus and the Word of God, the devil tucks his tail and runs! That is precisely what James means when he says that the devil will "flee."

An expanded and more contemporary interpretation of James 4:7 could read:

"Stand firmly against the devil! That's right — be unbending and unyielding in the way you resist him so that he knows he is up against a serious contender. If you'll take this kind of stand against him, he will tuck his tail and run like a criminal who knows the day of prosecution is upon him. Once you start resisting him, he'll flee from you in terror!"

Friend, the devil wants to make your life less-than-gratifying, unhappy, and uneventful. That's why he attacks your mind and tries to convince you that God's dream for your life will never come to pass. He desperately wants to convince you to settle for less than God's best in life. That's exactly why you *shouldn't* settle for anything less than God's best!

God has given you the name of Jesus and the promises of His Word, so it's time for you to close your ears to the devil's lies and start quoting the Word and commanding the devil to leave in Jesus' name. If you'll take this approach, the devil will not only shut up and stop telling you his lies, but he'll run from you in terror! *Don't you think it would be a good idea for you to get started quoting the Word of God and using the name of Jesus today?*

MY PRAYER FOR TODAY

Lord, because You have given me the promises of Your Word and the right to use Your name, I refuse to let the devil bombard my mind any longer. Right now I stand up to resist him, oppose him, and put him on the run. Devil, you will no longer have free access to my mind and emotions, for I am standing up to resist you. You better put on your running shoes, because if you stick around me, I intend to prosecute you with the full authority of God's Word! I tell you to GO in Jesus' name! And, Heavenly Father, I thank You so much for giving me the great privilege of using Your Word and the authority of Jesus' name!

I pray this in Jesus' name!

MY CONFESSION FOR TODAY

I confess that I am not a weakling! I have the power of God, the Word of God, and the name of Jesus Christ at my disposal. When I step into the full authority God has given me, the devil knows that he must flee. I will not submit to the devil's lies. If he tries to stick around and harass me, I will enforce God's authority upon him! That's why I know he will start to flee when I stand up to resist him in Jesus' name. So right now, I am taking charge over my mind and commanding the devil to take flight!

I declare this by faith in Jesus' name!

QUESTIONS FOR YOU TO CONSIDER

1. How do you respond when the devil tries to assault your mind with lies over and over again? Do you let him have free access to your thought life — or do you stand firm against those lies and command them to leave in Jesus' name?
2. Can you remember a time in your life when, after rising up and taking authority over Satan's mental bombardment in the name of Jesus, you could immediately tell that the mental assault had stopped and that Satan had indeed tucked his tail and run from you?
3. What steps can you take to prepare now before Satan launches the next mental assault? Wouldn't it be a good idea to build a strong arsenal of truth from God's Word by meditating on scriptures you can use as a sword against the enemy when taking authority over his attack?

DECEMBER 11

Abstain From Fleshly Lusts

Dearly beloved, I beseech you as strangers and pilgrims,
abstain from fleshly lusts, which war against the soul.
— 1 Peter 2:11

Does it seem like you have one temptation that you have to constantly fight more than others? What is that temptation? Is it a sexual temptation? Is it a temptation to eat something you shouldn't eat or to get upset with the same person again and again? Are you tempted to spend money you really don't have to spend? There are things you can do to make sure you don't give in to that temptation and let it conquer you. Along that line, I want to talk to you today about a scripture that will help you conquer temptation.

When Peter wrote to the Christians who lived in the first century, these believers had only recently come to the Lord. When they got saved, they were literally delivered from a lost Roman world that was filled with sin of all types, including a great host of sexual vices and different forms of carnality — all of which were considered to be acceptable in that society.

Now these believers were living for Jesus. Because they wanted to please Him, they were striving to live holy lives. The pagan environment in which they lived, however, caused them to feel the lure of sin very strongly.

The society these believers lived in celebrated carnality and flaunted their debauchery. This means the believers of the Early Church were constantly confronted by the very low standards of that world. Surrounded by sin, they had to constantly resist the lure of sin and not permit themselves to be pulled back into their old lifestyles.

To help them resist the temptation to fall back into sin, Peter told them, "Dearly beloved, I beseech you as strangers and pilgrims, abstain from fleshly lusts, which war against the soul" (1 Peter 2:11). The word "beseech" is the Greek word *parakaleo*, a compound of the words *para* and *kaleo*. The word *para* means *alongside*, as in *one who comes up close alongside another person*. The word *kaleo* means *to call, to beckon,* or *to beseech.* But when these two words are joined to form the word *parakaleo*, it presents the picture of *one who has something so important to say that he pulls right up alongside his listener, getting as close to him as possible; then he begins to literally plead with him to take some course of action.* This person urgently calls out, pleading with his listener to hear what he has to say and to do what he is suggesting.

So like a father in the faith, Peter pulls up alongside his readers and begins to call out to them — earnestly pleading with them to listen to the advice he is about to give them. When Peter's readers saw the word *parakaleo* ("beseech"), they understood that it was a flashing light to get their attention. They also undoubtedly understood that Peter felt very passionate about the urgent words he was about to speak to them and wanted them to carefully listen to what he had to say.

But as noted earlier (*see* January 14), the word *parakaleo* was also used as a military word. In the ancient Greek world, before military leaders sent their troops into battle, they would call them together to "beseech" them. Rather than hide the painful reality of war from the soldiers, the leaders would summon their troops together and speak straightforwardly with them about the potential dangers of the battlefield. These officers would also tell their troops about the glories of winning a major victory. They didn't ignore the dangers of battle; they came right alongside their troops and urged, exhorted, beseeched, begged, and pleaded with them to stand tall; throw back their shoulders; look the enemy straight on, eyeball to eyeball; and face their battles bravely.

Because the word *parakaleo* was widely used in this manner as well, Peter's readers also understood that he was now speaking to them as a general in the faith. The word "beseech" emphatically let them know that discipline and a rigid, committed warfare mentality would be required if they were going to accomplish what he was about to order them to do.

Peter goes on to tell his readers, "Dearly beloved, I beseech you as strangers and pilgrims, abstain from fleshly lusts, which war against the soul." Notice that Peter calls them "strangers" and "pilgrims." The word "stranger" is the Greek word *paroikos*, a word that describes *an individual who lives among the citizens of a nation but is not a citizen himself.* He is a *foreigner* or an *alien* in that nation. Even though he may have received the legal right to live there, he doesn't have the same right to participate in society as does a legal citizen.

By using this word, Peter reminds his readers (and us) that they are no longer citizens of the world. Even though they live in the midst of the world, they are now heavenly citizens and therefore cannot participate in the activities of a lost world as they once did. They must learn to live *among* those in the world without being *like* them.

To drive this point even deeper into the hearts of his readers, Peter also urges them to live as "pilgrims." The word "pilgrims" is the Greek word *parepidemos*. This word depicts the attitude that believers must have about their present lives in this world. It describes *a temporary traveler who is merely passing through a certain territory on the way to his final destination.*

Because this person is simply passing through, he doesn't allow himself to become attached but rather stays disconnected. Because he will soon break camp and move onward, he knows that it would be foolish for him to become entrenched in an environment where he cannot remain.

Now Peter uses this word to urge believers to live as if they are travelers who are only on this earth for a short stay. To help them stay free of the sinful environment that is in the world all around them, he implores them to "…abstain from fleshly lusts…."

The word "abstain" is the Greek word *apechomai*, which means *to deliberately withdraw from; to stay away from; to put distance between oneself and something else;* or *to intentionally abstain.* The word *apechomai* was a well-known word, so every person who read this word understood that Peter was telling them to put distance between themselves and the "fleshly lusts" that were raging all about them.

When Peter speaks of "fleshly lusts," he uses the word *sarkikos* for "fleshly." This word describes *the impulses, cravings, and desires of the carnal flesh* — those things that appeal to our lower side. The word "lusts" is the word *epithumia*, a compound of the words *epi* and *thumos*. The word *epi* means *over*, and the word *thumos* depicts *passion*. When compounded into the word *epithumia*, it pictures *a person so overcome by some passionate desire that he completely gives himself over to it.*

Let me stress something here that is imperative for you to understand: *Your flesh is never content until it has completely taken you over and consumed you.* Once you have given your flesh permission to have its way and to exercise even a small amount of power in your life, it will try to latch hold of you — and eventually it will wage war for total control of your life.

Please don't think you can participate in only a little taste of sin and then walk free of it. Once the flesh has been allowed to indulge in sin, the cry of the carnal nature to indulge in sin once more will become stronger and stronger, ferociously working against you in its attempt to pull you deeper and deeper into sin until you are completely conquered by it.

That is why Peter so firmly tells us to "…abstain from fleshly lusts, which *war against the soul.*" The word "war" is the Greek word *strateuomai*. This word is derived from the word *stratos*, from which we get the word *strategy*. But when it becomes the word *strateuomai* as used in this context, it pictures *a fiercely committed soldier who possesses a warring mentality.* Because he is so committed to waging war and destroying his resistance, he fights tactically, strategically, and aggressively. Furthermore, the Greek tense accentuates the fact that once the flesh has been allowed to express itself, it will wage *continual warfare* and its assault will be *unending*.

Peter's chief concern is that the flesh will wage continual warfare against the "soul." The word "soul" is the Greek word *psyche*, which describes *a person's mind, will, and emotions.* The New Testament writers clearly understood that the mind, will, and emotions are where Satan wages his greatest warfare against the saints. Therefore, Peter urges his readers not to open the door and invite this warfare to begin by deliberately participating in sinful activities. Instead, he tells them to abstain from fleshly lusts, thus keeping their mind, will, and emotions free of unnecessary battles.

Peter's words in First Peter 2:11
could be interpreted to mean:

"Dearly beloved, I sincerely beg and warn you to live as if you are travelers here in this world. Never forget that this is not your real residence and that you must not become too

attached to the environment around you. I urge you to refrain from any carnal, low-level desires that try to engulf you and thus drag you into a very long, protracted, strategic, and aggressive war in your mind, will, and emotions."

If you have one temptation that you have to constantly fight more than others, how did that fight begin? Did you look at something or allow your flesh permission to do something that you knew was wrong? Did you open the door to this attack yourself by not saying no to the flesh at a critical moment in your life? What are you going to do now to shut the door to the devil and drive this battle out of your head and flesh?

It is a whole lot easier to avoid fleshly temptations than it is to uproot them once they get deeply rooted inside your mind, will, and emotions. So if the world around you is crying out for you to participate in its sinful activities (just as it was probably doing to Peter's first-century readers), remind yourself that you are just a temporary traveler in this world with no rights to participate in such activities. Make the choice to refrain from the works of the flesh. *By making this decision, you can avoid horrific battles that others fight every day in their minds because they didn't say no to the temptations that were offered to them.*

MY PRAYER FOR TODAY

Lord, I ask You to help me say no to the temptations that are constantly assailing my mind and emotions. There are moments when my flesh screams to participate in sinful behavior. But I know that with the power of Your Spirit working inside me, I can resist and refuse to give in to these sinful impulses. Holy Spirit, I am leaning heavily on You to strengthen me so I can continue to abstain from fleshly lusts that wish to war against my soul and take me captive.

I pray this in Jesus' name!

MY CONFESSION FOR TODAY

I confess that I live like a stranger who is simply passing through this world. God has blessed me and made my journey comfortable, but I never forget that this is only a brief journey in my eternal destiny. When sin cries out for me to participate in its activities, I remind sin and the flesh that I am not a resident of this world and that I therefore do not have the right to enter into its activities. Because the Spirit of God lives in me, I am fully empowered to say no to sin and to remain free from its detrimental effects.

I declare this by faith in Jesus' name!

QUESTIONS FOR YOU TO CONSIDER

1. Can you think of a time in your past when you knowingly allowed yourself to dabble in a little sin? Did that one decision catch you and throw you into one of the biggest battles of your life?
2. If you were counseling someone else who was tempted to allow himself just a little taste of sin, what helpful advice would you give him to help him abstain from sin?
3. Is there one particular sin you are struggling with right now? Are there places or people you need to avoid in order to stay free?

DECEMBER 12

❧

Love Without Hypocrisy

Let love be without dissimulation....
— Romans 12:9

*H*ave you ever heard the words "I love you" from someone you really believed to be your friend, only to find out later that this same person talked behind your back, gossiped about you, and didn't treat you the way a real friend would? If you confronted that person about his actions, did he admit what he did and apologize for it? Or did he lie and try to cover up his deeds, even though you already knew the facts? Did it deeply disturb you to see him put on a fake face and pretend that he was your best friend and that none of the allegations were true, even though you knew he was lying?

If you have ever experienced a situation like this, you know how very hurtful it is when a "so-called" friend behaves this way. It shows a level of hypocrisy that is deeply disturbing. This type of behavior should never occur among believers, but unfortunately it does from time to time. To make sure *you* never fall into this kind of hypocrisy, the apostle Paul wrote and told you, "Let love be without dissimulation...."

Before we get to the word "dissimulation," which is our primary theme today, we must first look at the word "love." It is the Greek word *agape*, a word that describes *the highest, finest, and most noble kind of love*. In the New Testament, it is the single word that is used to describe *the love of God*. As noted earlier (*see* July 23), the word *agape* is so filled with deep emotion and meaning that it is one of the most difficult words to translate in the New Testament.

Agape occurs when an individual sees, recognizes, understands, or appreciates the value of an object or a person, causing the viewer to behold this object or person in great esteem, awe, admiration, wonder, and sincere appreciation. Such great respect is awakened in the heart of the observer for the object or person he is beholding that he is compelled to love it. In fact, his love for that person or object is so strong that it is irresistible.

In the New Testament, perhaps the best example of *agape* is found in John 3:16: "For God so loved the world, that he gave his only begotten Son, that whosoever believeth in him should not perish, but have everlasting life." In the phrase, "For God so loved the world," the word "love" is the word *agape*.

The human race was so precious to God and He loved man so deeply that His heart was stirred to reach out and do something to save him. In other words, God's love drove Him to action. You see, *agape* loves so profoundly that it knows no limits or boundaries in how far, wide, high, and deep it will go to show that love to its recipient. If necessary, *agape* love will even sacrifice itself for the sake of that object or person it so deeply cherishes. You can see from this description why *agape* is the highest, finest, and most noble form of love.

This is precisely the kind of love that should exist between believers. For instance, the apostle John wrote, "My little children, let us not love in word, neither in tongue; but in deed and in truth" (1 John 3:18). The word "love" in this verse is the word *agape*. The apostle John makes it very clear that real *agape* love is not merely a matter of speaking easy and empty words; rather, *agape* is accompanied by actions that are truthful. It is simply hypocritical to claim to possess such love while at the same time engaging in unfaithful behavior such as backbiting and gossiping. *Agape* would never behave in such a manner; rather, it is forgiving and helpful, willing even to sacrifice itself for the sake of someone else.

This is why Paul wrote, "Let love be without dissimulation...." The *King James Version* uses the old word "dissimulation," but the Greek word is *anupokritos*, and it describes *something that is pretended, simulated, faked, feigned, or phony.* It pictures *a person who deliberately gives a certain impression, even though he knows the impression he is giving is untrue.* In other words, this person is a *phony.*

So when the apostle Paul tells us to walk in love that is without dissimulation, he means this:

"If you are going to say you love someone, then make sure you really love them. Don't give an impression that isn't true. Don't say one thing and then do another. Your love should be without hypocrisy, so don't be phony when it comes to the subject of love."

Now let me ask you this question: Have you ever been two-faced with people who thought you were *their* friend? Did you say one thing to them but later talk behind their backs? Did you do exactly the same thing that someone else is doing to you right now? Is it possible that you are reaping what you have sown?

Instead of getting bitter and hardhearted toward someone who has acted hypocritically in his friendship with you, learn from this experience. Make a decision that you will not be phony or hypocritical in *your* relationships the way this person was to you.

Meanwhile, make sure you forgive those who have wronged you. Let it go, and do your best to overlook their inconsistencies. The Lord will probably deal with them about their actions, so if they come to you in repentance, let them know they are forgiven. But most importantly, let this be a time when you decide that *you* will not be guilty of giving a false impression to a friend. *Let your love be real. Don't be a phony.*

MY PRAYER FOR TODAY

Lord, I ask You to please forgive me for the times I've been an unfaithful friend. I know there have been times in my life when I gossiped and talked about people who were supposed to be my close friends. And I didn't stop there. Rather than confess what I did and ask for forgiveness, I tried to cover it up by acting like I hadn't done anything wrong. I am so sorry for what I have done. Please forgive me for lying. Please forgive me for being a phony in my relationships. I don't ever want to do this again, so I ask You to help me walk in truthfulness, integrity, and in genuine agape love.

I pray this in Jesus' name!

MY CONFESSION FOR TODAY

I confess that I walk in the agape love of God. I am a sincere, truthful, and dedicated friend. When I say that I love, I genuinely love. I don't talk behind people's backs. I don't gossip. I don't betray the friends God has brought into my life. If I do accidentally say something that is out of order, I quickly go to my friend to confess it and to ask for forgiveness. This truthfulness causes my friends to trust me and to know that I am truly a friend indeed.

I declare this by faith in Jesus' name!

QUESTIONS FOR YOU TO CONSIDER

1. Can you recall a time in your life when a friend was dishonest with you? How did it affect you when you discovered that this person had been two-faced?
2. Have you ever violated a relationship by being untruthful or by talking behind the back of another person? Who is that person? What do you think the Lord would have you to do to make things right in that relationship?
3. What has Jesus taught you through that past experience of violating a friendship? Why don't you get a notepad and write down the things you have learned from this experience that might later help a friend who is facing the same situation?

DECEMBER 13

Abhor That Which Is Evil

> ...Abhor that which is evil;
> cleave to that which is good.
> — Romans 12:9

*T*oday I want to talk to you about some of the detrimental things you have been tolerating in your personal life. First, let's look at the illustration of television as an example of what you must do to keep evil out of your life.

Our family rarely watches television or movies, but when we do, we are very careful about what we allow to be broadcast into our home. Denise and I know it is part of our God-given responsibility as parents to keep evil from gaining access, for God designed the home to be a godly sanctuary for the family. Because we don't want evil to affect our family, Denise and I carefully guard what is viewed on the television in our home. Some may say that our approach is narrow, but the apostle Paul clearly instructed all believers to "...abhor that which is evil..." (Romans 12:9).

The word "abhor" is the Greek word *apostugeo*, which is a compound of the words *apo* and *stugeo*. The word *apo* means *away*, and the word *stugeo* means *to hate*. It describes *an intense dislike, an aversion,* or *a repugnance to something.* When the words *apo* and *stugeo* are compounded together, the new word conveys the notion of *a person who hates something so extremely that he literally backs away from it in disgust.* Thus, the *King James Version* translates it as the word "abhor" to reflect the feelings of a person who is so repulsed by something that he shuns and avoids it at all costs.

This means God expects your tolerance level for sin and evil to be very low. In fact, you should have such a repugnance for evil that you actively and continually guard against it from ever invading your life or your family.

But when we speak of evil, exactly what do we mean? Since Paul is the one who told us to "...abhor that which is evil...," let's look at this word "evil" in the Greek text to see what he was talking about.

The word "evil" is the word *poneros,* and it conveys the notion of *anything that is full of destruction, disaster, harm, or danger.* It includes not only that which is dangerous to the physical body, but also that which is dangerous to the spirit or mind. So Paul is urgently telling us that we should have no tolerance at all for anything that would endanger our bodies or that would do any kind of damage to our minds or spirits.

As human beings, we are usually careful to take care of ourselves physically. However, Paul is telling us that we need to take care of our spirits and minds just as diligently as we watch over the natural care of our human bodies.

You see, if your spirit and mind are invaded by information or images that are evil, the entrance of those images into your mind and spirit can wreak havoc in your life for years to come. Your mind is like a movie screen — and what you allow into your mind lives in your imagination for a very long time.

So instead of watching, reading, or listening to a lot of evil garbage that will clog up your mind for years, why not take a safer and smarter route? In other words, don't allow that garbage to enter your mind in the first place!

What are you to do instead? Paul says you need to "...*cleave* to that which is good." The word "cleave" is the Greek word *kollao,* which is the old Greek word that means *to glue* or *to cement something together.* This word denotes *a permanent connection.* It is the picture of two things that have been glued or cemented together, so tightly joined and bonded that they are now permanently connected and cannot be separated.

Let me illustrate the strength of the word *kollao.* A form of this word is used in Ephesians 5:31, where Paul teaches that a man should leave his father and mother and "be joined" unto his wife. Just as it takes work for a man and wife to cleave to each other and to become one in mind and heart, it will take effort on your part to be joined unto that which is "good." That word "good" is the Greek word *agathos,* the Greek word that describes *anything that is good, beneficial, or profitable for you.*

So when you take these Greek word meanings into consideration, Romans 12:9 could be interpreted to mean:

"You need to abhor and be disgusted with anything that would bring evil and harm to your physical, mental, or spiritual life. Instead of giving place to those destructive things, why don't you put your whole self forward to become more joined with that which is good and profitable for you?"

As you've read this *Sparkling Gem* today, has God's Spirit been speaking to you about the things you've been tolerating in your life for which you should have *no* tolerance? If the answer is yes, it's time for you to get into the Presence of God and ask Him to forgive you for permitting wrong influences in your life or home. Then make a concrete, firm decision to remove those wrong influences, and deliberately turn your attention toward the things that will bring you closer to the Lord.

There are so many good things you could be watching, reading, and listening to. So make the quality decision to shun all that is evil as you cleave to that which is good!

MY PRAYER FOR TODAY

Lord, I ask You to help me be sensitive to the influences I allow in my home and life. I realize that You have given me the responsibility to watch over my life and that I need to be careful about the information and images I allow to pass into my spirit and mind. Please help me recognize the influences that are acceptable and those that are not. When I am quickened in my spirit that what I am watching, reading, or hearing is unprofitable, give me the strength of will to turn it off, lay it down, or walk away from it.

I pray this in Jesus' name!

MY CONFESSION FOR TODAY

I confess that I carefully guard what goes into my spirit and my mind because God has given me the responsibility to do so. Therefore, I will not permit any evil garbage into the domain of my life. By keeping my mind free of evil influences, I will protect my life and stop the devil from many of the attacks he would like to launch against me. I refuse to open the door and invite the enemy in by watching or listening to the wrong things. Instead, I will turn my attention to those influences that are good and profitable for me. I am going to put my whole heart and soul into meditating on that which will enrich my life and take me to a higher level.

I declare this by faith in Jesus' name!

QUESTIONS FOR YOU TO CONSIDER

1. What are you allowing in your thought life that you know is unhealthy for you? Has the Spirit of God been telling you to remove that evil influence before it affects your spiritual life and your mental health?
2. Are your children taking into their minds and spirits certain television programs or certain types of music and literature that are unhealthy for them? If yes, what are you going to do about it? Will you continue to tolerate and allow these evil influences until they eventually produce destructive fruit in the lives of your children? Or will you take the initiative to remove every evil influence in order to protect them?
3. What good things can you cleave to in order to bring a strong positive influence into the sanctuary of your home?

DECEMBER 14

Be Affectionate to One Another

Be kindly affectioned one to another with brotherly love;
in honour preferring one another.
— Romans 12:10

When my family and I first moved to the former Soviet Union, God connected us to some of the most wonderful people we've ever known. Although these people were from a completely different culture and background, they genuinely became a part of our family.

This was especially wonderful for our sons, who now lived so far from their own natural relatives. It was also wonderful for me, for I discovered a level of relationship I had never before known in the Christian community. Although no one could ever possibly replace our natural families, we were thankful to God for these brothers and sisters who truly became "family" to us on the other side of the world.

Unfortunately, in many parts of the Christian community, this level of relationship I am describing is sadly missing. It is unfortunate that people attend church week after week and hardly know the people they regularly sit next to in the church services. Life has become so busy with natural concerns that most believers suffer from a severe deficiency of relationships with their fellow believers. This was never God's plan for the local church, for He designed it to be a place where people's lives could be built together as living stones. His plan was and still is to have a people who demonstrate His covenant nature in their relationships with one another.

The apostle Paul talks about these types of covenant relationships in Romans 12:10 when he says, "Be kindly affectioned one to another with brotherly love; in honour preferring one another." When I read these words of Paul, I can't help but think of the spiritual family and the genuine brothers in Christ whom I love so much in the former Soviet Union. We love them so profoundly that we have literally laid down our lives for them — and they likewise love us and have laid down their lives for us.

The phrases "be kindly affectioned" and "brotherly love" are key to understanding the level of relationship that God intends for us to have with our Christian brothers and sisters. The phrase "be kindly affectioned" is from the Greek word *philostorgos*, which expresses the idea of *a love between friends that is authentic, sincere, tender, and warm*. This word *philostorgos* is a compound of the words *phileo* and *stergo*. The word *phileo* is the Greek word for *friendship*, and the word *stergo* is the Greek word that depicts *the tender love that should exist between the members of a family*. But because the words *phileo* and *stergo* are joined to form the word *philostorgos*, it represents *two or more friends who love each other just as deeply as if they were members of the same family*.

If Paul had stopped here, it would have already been enough to let us know that the members of the local church should be like family to us. But to further confirm this truth, Paul tells us that we are to have "brotherly love" between ourselves. The words "brotherly love" are translated from the Greek word *philadelphia*, a compound of *phileo*, which, as noted above, means *to love like a friend*. The second part of the word is *adelphos*, the Greek word for *a brother*. When compounded together, it becomes the word *philadelphia*, which means *to love dearly like a brother*.

By using both of these phrases, Paul is telling us that our relationships in the Body of Christ should carry the authenticity of family. We should indeed love each other as if we were genuinely blood brothers and sisters. In fact, our love for one another should be so profound that we hold one another in honor. This is precisely what Paul says next when he tells us, "Be kindly affectioned one to another with brotherly love; *in honour preferring one another.*"

The words "in honour" in Greek express the idea of *being appraised very highly* or *considered as very valuable or very precious*. It gives the idea of an appreciation so great that you would prefer to see the person you love succeed even more than you want to see your own success. You truly desire the very best for this person because you love him so deeply.

When the *King James Version* uses the word "preferring," it is the Greek word *proegeomai*, which means *to esteem, to admire, to highly respect, to consider,* and *to value very highly*. It represents the attitude of a person who values a friend so highly that he deeply desires the very best to come to pass for his friend — even if it means that his friend is blessed at his own expense. This means there is no room for jealousy or competition where this kind of love abounds.

**A fuller interpretive translation
of Romans 12:10 could read:**

"Love each other with the same love you have for your family. In fact, you should love each other with the same love that is shared between two brothers. The value you place on each other should be so high that it makes you desire to see those you love excel and achieve much in life, even if it means that they excel and achieve more than you do."

Do you have these kinds of relationships in the Christian community? I'm talking about precious relationships that you hold to be as dear to you as family. If so, you should count yourself very blessed, for the lives of many believers are vacant of such relationships. This is all the more reason to make sure you take the time to really express to these people whom you love as family just how deeply you love them!

God planned for the local church to be a place of covenant relationship. If you have such relationships, be careful to always treat them as a special gift from Heaven. And if your life lacks this blessing, ask the Holy Spirit to birth a God-given relationship that will bring a touch of Heaven into your life.

MY PRAYER FOR TODAY

Lord, I thank You for the incredible friendships You have placed in my life. I am immeasurably blessed to have such loving, faithful, and true relationships. When I think of all the people who live such lonely lives, it makes me want to stop and express my gratefulness to You for placing such precious people in my life. Lord, I also ask You to please help me see those who need to be loved so I can include them as a part of my life. I want to give to others the love and support that I have received. Holy Spirit, help me to start doing this today.

I pray this in Jesus' name!

MY CONFESSION FOR TODAY

I confess that God has given me a host of godly relationships. I am blessed with genuine friends who love me like family; who treat me like a brother (or sister); and who will walk in covenant with me for many years to come. This is God's will for my life. I will not be isolated or live in a way that is disconnected from God's family; rather, I will continually look for ways to grow closer and closer to His family. Also, just as God is blessing me with precious friends, I believe He is teaching me how to be a better friend to those who are near me.

I declare this by faith in Jesus' name!

QUESTIONS FOR YOU TO CONSIDER

1. Are some of your relationships so precious that you hold them to be as dear to you as family?
2. If so, have you taken the time to really express to them how much you love them?
3. What can you do to improve your skills to become a better friend?

DECEMBER 15

Be Not Slothful in Business

Not slothful in business;
fervent in spirit; serving the Lord.
— Romans 12:11

I'll never forget the time when, as I met with a head of government in a foreign nation, he looked me straight in the eyes and said, "I just don't understand many of the Christians I've met. To me, they seem to be some of the laziest people I've ever known in my life. I'm amazed that anyone would be satisfied to live with such low standards. Is this the way all Christians are?"

I was so embarrassed when I heard those words. I found myself wanting to apologize for the entire Christian community! But the truth is, I personally knew some of the Christians he was referring to — and I had thought the very same thing on many occasions! These people didn't seem to have enough gumption to get up and do something with their lives. It wasn't that they weren't talented, gifted, and knowledgeable. They were just satisfied with the level they had attained and had no desire to show any professionalism with their lives.

Honestly, it's a mystery to me how anyone can claim to be a Christian indwelt by the Spirit of God and yet be satisfied with such a low-level existence. Of course, I am very aware that many people weren't raised with the same high standard of excellence that my parents taught me. Perhaps some Christians grew up in an environment where low-level thinking was viewed as normal, and that's why they have accepted such a low standard for their own lives. However, other low-achievers can't claim a mediocre upbringing as an excuse. They just don't take advantage of opportunities to learn, adapt, and better themselves and therefore never experience needed change. This is usually a sign that these people have no inner desire to improve their lives.

You may send such individuals to school to educate them; you may even pay for them to fly halfway around the world to learn new and better techniques in their field of expertise. But if they don't possess the inner drive to improve themselves and to become more professional, it doesn't matter how much time or money you throw at them. It's all a waste unless they possess the desire to be diligent.

Such low-level standards should *never* be tolerated by a believer, a pastor, an employer, or an employee. Yet too often believers make excuses for their slothful attitudes and allow them to continue. As a result, the world frequently looks at the Church as a pathetic entity made up of a bunch of nincompoops who aren't serious about what they do or say.

I am certain that Paul's experience with low-achievers in the Church is one of the reasons he wrote the believers in Rome and told them to be "not slothful in business...." The word "slothful" is the Greek word *okneros*, a word that means *lazy* or *idle*. It carries the idea of *a person who has a do-nothing, lethargic, lackadaisical, apathetic, indifferent, lukewarm attitude toward life*. I find it very interesting that this word translated "slothful" is the identical Greek word used in Matthew 25:26 when Jesus tells of the "wicked" servant who was thrown into outer darkness because he produced nothing significant with the resources that had been entrusted to him. In these contexts, both "slothful" and "wicked" denote an attitude of apathy that should have no place at all in the life of a Christian.

But Paul goes on to say that we are not to be slothful "in business." The word "business" is the Greek word *spoudadzo*, and it means *to do something with eagerness* or *to do something with diligence*. It is the idea of *acting responsibly, quickly, and with attentiveness*. You could say that the word *spoudadzo* ("diligence") is exactly the opposite of a person who lazily strolls along with no passion or desire. Instead of being lazy and apathetic, a diligent person is excited and energetic, putting his whole heart into the project that has been given to him. He treats his responsibility as if it is important, and as a result of his excellent attitude, he does his job well.

Paul also says that we should be "...fervent in spirit...." The word "fervent" is the Greek word *zeo*, which originally meant *to boil*. This is the picture of a person so enthusiastic about his task that he can hardly contain his excitement. The desire to do his job with excellence and enthusiasm is *constantly boiling* inside the person who is diligent about his assignment. In fact, the Greek tense used here would be better translated, *"...Be constantly fervent in spirit...."* The word "spirit" does not refer to the Holy Spirit, but to the attitude of this believer. It means, *"...Be constantly fervent in your attitude...."*

Then Paul takes it another step by saying that we are to be "...fervent in spirit; serving the Lord." It is very plain what Paul is declaring here: *A right attitude is one of the most effective ways for a person to serve the Lord.* You see, when a believer does his job right and with an awesome attitude, it is a testimony to the name of Jesus. But when a believer does his work shabbily, he projects a sorry image of who Jesus is. This is exactly what happened in the case of that foreign head of government who asked me if all Christians were as mediocre as the ones he had encountered.

Paul uses the Greek word *douleuo* when he writes about "serving" the Lord. This word comes from the Greek word *doulos*, which means *a servant who does the bidding of his master*. The word *doulos* described a servant who was sold out, lock, stock, and barrel — totally committed to serving and pleasing his master. As a good servant, he would do his best to discover his master's desires and then explicitly do whatever was needed to fulfill those desires.

By using this word in this context, it is almost as if Paul is saying, *"If you really want to please the Lord and be a servant that brings Him satisfaction, then do these things...."* What things bring pleasure to the heart of Jesus? Let me repeat the qualities we've already discussed: having an attitude of excellence; doing your job with seriousness and responsibility; and being consistently fervent, committed, and enthusiastic in your attitude. When a believer steadfastly demonstrates these attributes in his life, he becomes a servant who truly brings satisfaction to the heart of Jesus Christ.

Don't misunderstand what I am saying. Your salvation is a free gift of God's grace, and nothing you do can buy you a special standing with Him. Nevertheless, how you serve God and the testimony that your life demonstrates to the world is very important to Jesus Christ.

So I urge you to take an honest look at yourself today. Ask yourself, *When people look at my life, do they come away with a positive idea of what a Christian is like, or does my example leave people unimpressed with Jesus Christ?* Then ask the Lord to show you any changes you need to make so you can move on up to a higher level of excellence in God!

MY PRAYER FOR TODAY

Lord, I am very convicted by what I have read today. I don't want to allow any area of my life to be a bad testimony of who Jesus is. Therefore, I am asking You to open my eyes and show me those areas of my life that need to come up to a higher level. Please forgive me for being tolerant of low standards that are not compatible with the excellence of Jesus' wonderful name.

Starting today, I want to move up higher. Holy Spirit, please help me as I start taking steps toward making serious changes in my life, my attitudes, and my actions.

I pray this in Jesus' name!

MY CONFESSION FOR TODAY

I confess that I will no longer be satisfied with living a low-level existence. God has something great planned for me, and I have made the decision to abandon the negligent attitudes that have dominated my life. Jesus has called me to be a servant that brings Him pleasure, so that is what I am going to do. I will not allow laziness or apathy to be a part of me any longer. I intend to start projecting continual enthusiasm and excitement about what Jesus has asked me to do!

I declare this by faith in Jesus' name!

QUESTIONS FOR YOU TO CONSIDER

1. Would you say that your life is a good testimony of who Jesus is, or does your example leave some people shaking their heads, wondering what is wrong with lazy, low-level Christians?
2. Perhaps you have a standard of excellence in some areas of your life but not in other areas. In your opinion, what areas of your life already portray excellence, and what areas do not?
3. Do you try to stay aware of how your attitudes, your dress, and your job performance are affecting people's opinions of Jesus? Are you continually striving to make sure your life gives an honorable impression of Jesus Christ to others?

DECEMBER 16

Meeting the Needs of Other Believers

Distributing to the necessity of saints....
— Romans 12:13

One of the most exciting things our ministry does is meet the needs of pastors who are leading congregations in the former Soviet Union. We feel a deep commitment to help these pastors because they haven't had the same opportunity for education that exists in Western countries. As a result of the revival that has swept across the former USSR since the collapse of communism, scores of pastors have found themselves leading congregations before they could receive any training to equip them for the job. These pastors are doing all they know to do in their leadership positions, but they are often ill-prepared for the task due to lack of teaching, training, and education.

Because of the work of our Church Association, pastors and leaders who formerly felt isolated and alone have now become spiritually "linked" to other pastors. Close friendships have formed as these pastors look to each other for support, fellowship, and spiritual encouragement. But in addition to providing this spiritual fellowship, our ministry has also become a channel through which designated offerings are routed to support many of these pastors whose income is not sufficient to support them full-time in the ministry.

You see, so many of these pastors live in villages that were economically devastated by the collapse of the Soviet Union. Because of this dire financial crisis, churches do not yet have the finances to support their pastor full-time, even though they desperately need a full-time pastor. Today many of these pastors are able to serve full-time because of the financial gifts that we channel to them each month. Because of the gifts of our ministry partners, we have been able to distribute funds to meet the needs of these saints.

It is very easy for us as believers to get so caught up in our own projects and plans that we forget about the needy people in the world who need our help. This is precisely why Paul encouraged us to be constantly "distributing to the necessity of saints..." (Romans 12:13). Especially at this time of the year when people are in a spirit of giving, I think it is important to look for ways to bless people who are less fortunate than ourselves. Every day we should pray and ask the Lord how He wants to use us to make a difference in someone else's life.

The word "distributing" is the Greek word *koinoneo*, which means *to share* or *to give some kind of contribution*. In the context of Romans 12:13, it means *to give a financial contribution*. However, the Greek tense suggests that this is not an occasional act but rather a *regular, consistent, habitual contributing of finances* for the "necessity of saints." That word "necessity" is the Greek word *chreia*, and it simply means *a need*. In other words, Paul is talking here about giving to meet the basic needs of the saints.

It is true that there are many humanitarian organizations to which we can give our money, but the apostle Paul loudly tells us that we are to first give to meet the needs of the "saints." Certainly it is right to meet the needs of fellow believers first; after all, they are our brothers and sisters. First John 3:17 asks us, "But whoso hath this world's good, and seeth his brother hath need, and shutteth up his bowels of compassion from him, how dwelleth the love of God in him?" When we know there is a need, it is time for us to act. This is why the apostle John goes on to say, "My little children, let us not love in word, neither in tongue; but in deed and in truth" (1 John 3:18).

Even if you have been struggling financially to make ends meet, I guarantee you that there are believers in other parts of the world — or perhaps even close to where you live — who are having a more difficult time than you are right now. Rather than be self-focused and feel sorry for yourself, why don't you take advantage of this special time of the year to go out of your way to do something special for someone else? Send an extra offering to a ministry that you support. Give a gift to help the poor and needy. Assess the needs of the saints as you become aware of them; then let the Holy Spirit lead you in distributing your financial gifts. Discover the joy of helping to meet the needs of fellow brothers and sisters who truly need any help you can give them!

MY PRAYER FOR TODAY

Lord, especially at this time of the year, I want to look beyond my own challenges and problems to see what I can do to meet the needs of brothers and sisters whose situations are more serious than mine. I don't want to be so self-focused on my own needs that I forget that there are others who are struggling more seriously than I am. In fact, even though I have been facing difficult times, I know that my life is much more blessed than some of my brothers and sisters who live in other parts of the world. Lord, please help me to always be grateful for what I have. Guide me as I seek to distribute a portion of my finances and make a difference in someone else's life. And please, Lord, multiply this seed that I am sowing by faith so that it comes back to meet the needs I am facing in my own life.

I pray this in Jesus' name!

MY CONFESSION FOR TODAY

I boldly declare that I am a giver! I refuse to allow the devil to make me focus so intensely on my own problems that I forget about the needs others are facing. Instead of taking care of only my own needs, I declare that I am going to give a portion of my finances to meet the needs of other believers who are in a more serious condition than I am right now. To the best of my ability, I will give from my resources to make a difference in someone else's life, especially during this holiday season. I also claim the promise of God that what I sow will be multiplied back to me again!

I declare this by faith in Jesus' name!

QUESTIONS FOR YOU TO CONSIDER

1. How long has it been since you gave a serious, significant gift during the holiday season to meet the needs of believers who are less fortunate in other parts of the world?
2. Do you know of believers living right in your own community who are struggling and could use an extra financial surprise to make their holidays more pleasant?
3. If you are facing a financial challenge yourself, why don't you figure out the size of harvest you need to receive and then sow a seed to match that kind of harvest?

DECEMBER 17

Learning To Be Hospitable

…Given to hospitality.
— Romans 12:13

During the time when the New Testament was being written, it is simply a fact that many Christians and church leaders were very mobile. First, many became mobile because they had been evicted from their homes and had lost their property due to persecution. Second, the early believers were mobile because they were moving like a spreading flame throughout the entire Roman world, carrying the Gospel to those who sat in darkness.

Because the Early Church was constantly on the move, it became necessary for believers to adopt an "open-home" mentality. In other words, they had to be willing to take in displaced Christians or missionaries who were passing through on their way to take the Gospel to a new region. This open-home mentality was so important that Paul included it in his list of requirements for church leaders. Paul wrote to Timothy that if a person wanted to be a leader, he had to be "…given to hospitality…" (1 Timothy 3:2).

In both Romans 12:13 and in First Timothy 3:2, Paul uses this phrase "given to hospitality." The word "hospitality" in both references is the Greek word *philoxenia*. This word is a compound of the words *philos*, which means *to love like a friend*, and the word *xenos*, the Greek word for *a stranger or foreigner*. There is no doubt that the word *xenos* doesn't refer to an acquaintance or associate; rather, it refers to one who is a complete stranger or a foreigner.

Therefore, when Paul tells the Early Church (and us) to be hospitable, he isn't telling us to be kind, friendly, or open-hearted with a known associate or a friend who is in need. He is telling us that we must show compassion and kindness to those we don't know at all. It is easy to open our homes and show kindness to someone we know, but it is a different thing altogether to be hospitable to those we *don't* know!

This would have been an especially important message to believers who lived in large metropolitan cities like Rome or Ephesus. Due to the size of their cities, people (including believers) were constantly arriving with a common need — finding a place to reside during their brief stay.

Modern-day Moscow fits this description quite well, and Denise and I do our best to be "given to hospitality." This city is like a magnet for all of Russia. Just as was true in the ancient cities of Rome and Ephesus, believers are constantly coming to Moscow for business and ministry. Often they need our help to find a place to stay. They need us to be hospitable and to help meet their needs, even if we don't know them.

For an early believer to be hospitable, he literally had to open his home to receive those Christians who had been displaced or who were traveling through the area. In that day, there were no hotels like there are in today's world, so opening one's home was the only way to show oneself hospitable.

In today's world, you could still take a traveler into your home. But it is also possible to show yourself hospitable by renting a hotel room to help out a traveler for several nights. You and the Lord must determine how you show hospitality; the important thing is that you are hospitable.

The real idea of the word *philoxenia* ("hospitable") is to be friendly or helpful to those who are strangers to you and to those who are in need. This word depicts that moment when you go outside your normal circle of friends and relationships to do something extra special for someone whom you do not know.

Romans 12:13 categorically states that we should be "given" to hospitality. The word "given" is from the Greek word *dioko*, which means *to aggressively pursue something; to ardently follow after something;* or *to hotly pursue something until you finally catch it*. In fact, the word *dioko* is so aggressive that it is usually translated in the New Testament as the word *persecution*.

It is significant that Paul used the word *dioko* in connection with becoming hospitable, because it tells us that we must aggressively set our hearts on attaining this goal. We must make the decision that we are going to develop this trait in our lives. Then we must put our whole hearts into learning how to be welcoming and helpful to believers in need — until finally we catch on to *God's* idea of hospitality and become genuinely hospitable people.

Romans 12:13 could be taken to mean:

"Hotly pursue and never stop pursuing the goal of becoming hospitable until you have caught on to the idea of hospitality and have genuinely become a hospitable person."

How long has it been since you opened the doors of your home to someone you didn't know? Do you mainly minister to people you know and enjoy, or do you have a heart to help those you don't know but who have legitimate needs in their lives? If you can't open the doors of your home to them, what else can you do to show them a hospitable heart?

Is this kind of hospitality a token service that you perform out of duty? Or have you been doing everything in your power to become a genuinely hospitable person in the way that you live and treat others? Even more importantly — what are you going to do *today* to start showing kindness to fellow believers in need?

MY PRAYER FOR TODAY

Lord, I ask You to please forgive me for only seeing the needs of my own social circle. The fact is, there are so many people who are in serious need, and I could be doing something to help at least one of them. I am asking You to help me take my eyes off myself and my little circle of friends and to start seeing the needs that are all around me. I don't want to be guilty of helping only those who bring a blessing to my life. I want to be a blessing even to those I don't know and who will never be able to return the favor to me themselves.

I pray this in Jesus' name!

MY CONFESSION FOR TODAY

I confess that I am a blessing to fellow believers who are in need. My heart is open; my home is open; my pocketbook is open; and I am willing and ready for the Lord to use me to help others. I thank God that He can use me to make an impact in other people's lives. I believe that He will bless me for stepping out of my limited little social circle to do a good deed for a fellow believer who really needs a helping hand. And I declare that I won't casually carry out an occasional act of mercy. Instead, I will aggressively pursue the attitude of hospitality until I catch it and become a genuinely hospitable person.

I declare this by faith in Jesus' name!

QUESTIONS FOR YOU TO CONSIDER

1. Was there a time in your past when someone took you in and showed you real hospitality? If so, what was that event, and what impact did that person make on your life?
2. Have you had an opportunity to be hospitable that you turned down because you didn't know the person or were afraid to open your home to a stranger?
3. How would you feel if you needed a place to stay and you couldn't find a single Christian who would open his or her home to you? On the other hand, how would it make you feel if you were a displaced Christian in need, and someone showed love and compassion to you?

DECEMBER 18

Blessing People Who Deliberately Try To Make Trouble for You

Bless them which persecute you:
bless, and curse not.
— Romans 12:14

*I*t is very easy to bless those who bless you and make you happy, but how are you going to respond to people who persecute you and try to deliberately injure you? Romans 12:14 says that you are to "bless them which persecute you...."

One day many years ago, my associate brought me the national newspaper of the country where we lived, and to my horror, there was a terrible article about me right on the front page! No one could miss the article because it was so huge — *and* it was filled with outrageous lies. The article contained nothing more than pure nonsense. However, I soon became very upset thinking about what people would think of me after reading that article. I knew that people tend to believe whatever is printed in the newspaper. The longer I thought about it, the more upset I became. I especially became infuriated with the female reporter who had written this barrage of nonsense and lies.

I wondered how I should respond. Should I put an advertisement in the newspaper to answer the allegations made about me and my ministry? Should I demand that the newspaper fire the woman who wrote this about us? What action should I take in response to this ugly development?

Adding to my shock regarding the article was the fact that the woman who wrote it had sat in my office and told me how blessed she was by our ministry. Only after reading what she wrote did I learn that she had completely lied to me. Nevertheless, rather than give in to my flesh and start ranting and raving about what she had done, I decided to obey the apostle Paul's instructions in Romans 12:13, where he says, "Bless them which persecute you...."

The word "bless" is the Greek word *eulogeo*, a compound of the words *eu* and *logos*. The word *eu* means *good* or *well* and depicts *any positive emotion*. It is where we get the word *euphoric*. The second part of the word *eulogeo* is the word *logos*, which simply means *words*. But when these two words are compounded into the word *eulogeo*, it means *to say good or positive things*. The word *eulogeo* is where we get the word *eulogy*, which is the sermon preached at a funeral. It is supposed to be a time when good words are spoken in remembrance of the person who died.

So when Paul tells us to "bless them which persecute you...," he is literally telling us that we are always to return a blessing for a curse, speaking only good words about those who wish to harm us. Taking this route must be hard on the flesh, for the Greek tense describes a *continual action*, implying that we must speak well of these people again and again and again. Our flesh may rise up to point the finger of accusation at someone and charge him with dishonest and wrong conduct. But that's when we have to tell our flesh to be quiet! Instead of falling into the mode of accuser in an attempt to defend ourselves, we are to take the more godly route of blessing those who persecute us.

Paul says that when we are in these situations, we are to "curse not." The word "curse" is the Greek word *kataraomai*, which simply means *to verbally curse*. In the ancient world, it was believed that when a person spoke good words about someone else, those words conveyed a blessing on that other person's life. Conversely, people believed that when someone spoke curses over another person, his very words caused curses to come upon that person's life.

This ancient belief in the power of words is actually borne out in the Scriptures. We should never forget the power that is contained in the words we speak. Proverbs 18:21 makes it very clear that the power of life and death is in the tongue.

So rather than get upset with the unbeliever who wrote that ugly article, I felt instructed of the Lord to start speaking blessings into her life. I realized that this journalist wrote that kind of article because she was lost and needed the Lord. So what good would it do if I allowed myself to speak curses over her life? It was time for me to rise to the occasion by deciding to "…bless, and curse not"!

So I started blessing this woman, thanking God for her and believing God to do something truly remarkable to make her life better and more blessed. As it turned out, that horrible article would be the last article of its kind about us to ever appear in that national newspaper. I am convinced that our decision to "…bless, and curse not" caused God's power to be released in the spirit realm, preventing any future negative press from being printed about us in that particular nation.

If someone has done something bad or injurious to you, I realize how tempting it is to retaliate by saying a lot of bad things about the offender. But in the end, this fleshly reaction won't help anyone. You never have to fall into this trap that causes you to be bitter and that releases a lot of negative words and curses on those who wronged you. You can take a redemptive approach — choose to speak only good about those who have sought to do you harm.

If you'll take the right approach to this hurtful situation, your actions can release enough supernatural power to keep this type of event from ever being replicated in the future. But if you respond wrongly, it probably won't be too long until you're facing the same situation again.

Never underestimate the importance of how you react to those who persecute you. Your words of blessing and forgiveness can put to bed forever all the past wrongs ever committed against you. On the other hand, your words of retaliation can reignite the fire of opposition so that the same kind of opposition keeps reoccurring again and again.

That's why it's so important that you never forget — you must continually be careful with your words!

MY PRAYER FOR TODAY

Lord, I want to forgive those who have done so much wrong by speaking lies and nonsense about me. I don't understand why they have spoken those lies, but now people are listening to the garbage they have told about me. Rather than respond in anger and speak a bunch of negative words that won't help anyone, I choose today to speak words of kindness and blessing over those who have tried to hurt me. Lord, I ask You to bless them, change them, help them, and lead them into a higher way of life. In the meantime, I am asking You to use this hurtful situation to bring about needed changes in me.

I pray this in Jesus' name!

MY CONFESSION FOR TODAY

I confess that I don't speak evil words about anyone — not even against those who seek to hurt me and to do harm to my life. My words are powerful, so I select the words I speak very carefully. I choose to bless and to curse not, and I declare that because I have taken this course of action, the strategies that the enemy is trying to use against me will be frustrated and stopped.

I declare this by faith in Jesus' name!

QUESTIONS FOR YOU TO CONSIDER

1. Can you recall a time when you were being verbally persecuted by someone who wanted to do you harm, but the Holy Spirit led you to refrain from speaking evil of that person and to speak only good about him or her?
2. If you do recall such an event in your life, what was the result when you obeyed the Spirit of God and stayed upbeat and positive about your accuser?
3. Can you think of a time when you said a lot of evil words about someone and those words eventually came to pass? Did you later regret that you had said those words?

DECEMBER 19

Learning To Rejoice And Learning To Weep

Rejoice with them that do rejoice,
and weep with them that weep.
— Romans 12:15

*I*t's such a big letdown when you experience something that gets you all excited, but you can't find anyone who will rejoice with you. Not so long ago, this happened to me.

After waiting a long time for a particular victory, it finally happened! I could hardly wait to tell it, so I summoned together the group I was with at the time to share this mighty victory. However, when I told these people the good news, they just stared back at me with expressionless faces, as if they hadn't heard a word I had said. When the meeting was dismissed, they left, barely acknowledging the great report I had told them. I was very disappointed because I wanted someone to rejoice with me!

Later that day as I thought about the group's lack of response to my exciting news, it made me wonder how many times I had done the same thing to people who shared their exciting news with me. As I pondered the expressionless faces I had seen earlier, I realized that the other members of that group may have been loaded down with their own cares or anxieties. Perhaps their own thoughts weighed so heavily on their minds that they weren't able to really grasp what I had told them.

We should never respond to someone's good report with a lack of enthusiasm. Regardless of what we're going through in our own lives, we need to get our focus off ourselves and learn to "rejoice with them that do rejoice...." (Romans 12:15). In this verse, the apostle Paul tells us about the importance of appropriate emotional responses. For instance, when a person rejoices about something wonderful that has happened in his life, then regardless of what we are personally feeling, it is appropriate for us to rejoice with him.

The word "rejoice" is from the Greek word *chairo*, and it means *to be glad, to be full of joy*, or *to be elated*. Furthermore, the word "rejoice" is a command, not a suggestion, which means Paul is ordering us to "rejoice *with* them that do rejoice...." The word "with" is the word *meta*. In this particular case, it means to rejoice *along with* those who are rejoicing and carries the idea of *joining on the same level* of rejoicing as "them that do rejoice."

The phrase "them that do rejoice" would be better translated as *"the rejoicing ones."* The Holy Spirit is instructing us that when people are thrilled and bubbling over with joy about something that has happened in their lives, we need to join right in with them and rejoice! If they are shouting, we need to shout with them. If they are laughing for joy, we need to laugh with them.

Therefore, this portion of Romans 12:15 presents this idea:

"When people are rejoicing, that's a time for you to join in the celebration and rejoice along with those who are rejoicing...."

You might say, "But it's hard for me to rejoice when I don't feel like rejoicing." Well, you just need to get over it and put your flesh out of the way for a few minutes! Let the other person enjoy his exciting news. Think how selfish it would be for you to throw cold water on his joy simply because you don't "feel like" rejoicing at the moment. What if you were in that person's shoes and someone responded to you with such a noticeable lack of enthusiasm? It would disappoint you, wouldn't it?

So rather than disappoint the person who is so excited, push your own emotional struggles out of the way for a few minutes and join in with those who are rejoicing! Besides, when you start to rejoice with a fellow believer, your deliberate rejoicing may be the very thing that sets you free from the emotional quandary that is trying to hold you down!

Paul goes on to tell us that we need to learn to "...weep with them that weep." The word "weep" is translated from the Greek word *klaio*, and it means *to weep, to wail, to sob*, or *to shed tears*. A very good example of this word is found in Mark 5:38 when Jesus went to Jairus' house and found "them that wept" because Jairus' daughter had died. This perfectly presents the idea of *weeping* and *sobbing* that is portrayed by the word *klaio*.

Just as it is appropriate for us to rejoice with those who are rejoicing, it is equally appropriate for us to weep with those who weep. We will all face times when people in our lives weep because of something that has happened or because of an event that has broken their hearts. When that happens, then no matter what we are personally feeling, it is fitting that we show softhearted tenderness toward those individuals, doing all that we can to comfort them.

Brokenhearted people usually need someone's arms wrapped about them. They also need to feel like they're not all alone. And sometimes they need a shoulder to cry on — not because that will make everything better, but simply because they need a tender touch in that moment of crisis. This is why Paul says we need to "...weep with them that weep."

Learning to respond with appropriate emotions is very important. A sullen frown during a time of rejoicing is not appropriate. A laughing and light-hearted spirit is often not appropriate in a room that is filled with brokenness and grief. As believers, we need to be sensitive to the needs of those around us, allowing the Holy Spirit to show us how to respond to the emotional climate in which we find ourselves. If we respond properly, we can be a blessing. But if we respond inappropriately, we can hurt people's feelings and either dampen their joy or deepen their sorrow.

Let the Holy Spirit be your Teacher and show you how to emotionally respond to the various situations of life. He knows exactly what response is needed and will make you a master of appropriate responses in every situation of life.

MY PRAYER FOR TODAY

Lord, I ask You to help me know how to respond appropriately to those who are around me. When they rejoice, help me put aside my own struggles and problems and enter into rejoicing with them. When people weep and I'm not feeling the pain they feel, help me set aside my own light-hearted mood so I can be the kind of friend they need in that vulnerable moment. Holy Spirit, I know You can teach me how to appropriately respond to the different situations I face in life. So I ask You to start teaching me how to be what I need to be in every type of circumstance.

I pray this in Jesus' name!

MY CONFESSION FOR TODAY

I confess that I am sensitive to the emotional climate around me. When people are rejoicing, I join in and rejoice with them. When people are weeping and feeling brokenhearted, I am careful to show love and compassion to them. Because the Holy Spirit is teaching me how to appropriately respond to the various situations that arise in life, I am becoming more fit to minister to people in any given circumstance.

I declare this by faith in Jesus' name!

QUESTIONS FOR YOU TO CONSIDER

1. Have you ever shared a great victory with a person or group of people who did not rejoice along with you? Was their lack of response a great letdown to you?
2. Have you ever seen someone respond inappropriately to a moment of crisis? When people were brokenhearted and weeping, did that person laugh and make jokes at a very serious moment? How did his or her insensitivity to the moment affect the other people in the room?
3. Are there people in your life right now who need you to rejoice with them or weep with them?

Brokenhearted people usually need someone's arms wrapped about them. They also need to feel like they're not all alone. And sometimes they need a shoulder to cry on — not because that will make everything better, but simply because they need a tender touch in that moment of crisis. This is why Paul says we need to "…weep with them that weep."

DECEMBER 20

What Is Your Attitude Toward People You Consider To Be Lower Than Yourself?

...Mind not high things,
but condescend to men of low estate....
— Romans 12:16

I'll never forget the time Denise and I were sitting in a restaurant with a well-known businessman, and this man embarrassed us so badly that we decided we would never go to dinner with him again. My wife and I had been regularly visiting this particular restaurant because we had met a waitress there whom the Lord had really put on our hearts. We didn't frequent that restaurant because we liked the food; we went there because we wanted to see this young lady come to a saving knowledge of Jesus Christ.

This businessman had contacted us and asked to visit with us. So we decided to take him to dinner at this restaurant where we had been sharing the message of Jesus with this waitress and with many of the other people who worked there.

All prospects for a nice dinner with our guest were soon shattered, however, because the man began to speak to the waiters and waitresses as if they were dogs! He kept brusquely ordering them to do this and that for him; meanwhile, the waitress — our friend whom we were trying to win to Jesus — looked over at us in shock! No one in that restaurant had ever received such horrible treatment from Denise or me.

As the evening wore on, the situation grew even worse. Our guest began to verbally abuse the waiters and waitresses. He told me, "I hope you don't mind how I talk to the servers, but they are here to serve me, and I intend to be served well."

With that, the man again started to rudely bark out more orders to the restaurant staff. Then he starting poking fun at their culture and laughing at them for being Russians. He flashed his Rolex watch and bragged to the servers about his luxury automobile and his massive residence back home. He did everything but say, "I'm better, smarter, and richer than any of you — and I don't want you to ever forget it."

Then this businessman asked the servers if they went to church anywhere. How I wished he had kept the Lord out of the conversation, because he was being such a poor example of Jesus Christ!

As dinner was served by fretful restaurant workers, Denise and I tried to turn the conversation to spiritual things. We endeavored to tell our guest about what God was doing in our lives and in our ministry, but it was obvious that he only wanted to talk about things that he thought would impress us. In reality, however, this man was consumed with himself, and we were completely unimpressed with him. He was rude and crude and a very poor example of a Christian businessman.

I excused myself to go to the restroom, but my real purpose in leaving the table was to get an opportunity to go directly to the kitchen and personally apologize for the offensive treatment the entire staff was enduring that night. I pushed open the double doors and walked into the kitchen as if I were a part of the staff; then I asked all the waiters and waitresses to come hear what I had to tell them.

Once they were gathered around me, I apologized profusely for what was happening at our table. They looked at me despondently and said, "Wow, that man is horrible. We are so thankful that you came back here to talk to us. We know that you and your wife are not like that man."

It simply breaks my heart when I see Christians like this businessman who think too highly of themselves. People like this "speak down" to others they perceive to be lower than they are. This prideful attitude should never be a part of a committed Christian's behavior. The apostle Paul told us, "...Mind not high things, but condescend to men of low estate...."

The word "mind" is from the Greek word *phroneo*. It means *to think, to consider,* or *to ponder*. It carries the idea of *intense reflection.* Furthermore, the Greek uses a negative, which makes this verse a strong prohibition. This means it could be better translated, *"...Stop fixating on high things...."* Paul is commanding us not to preoccupy ourselves with or be consumed by "high things." The words "high things" are from the Greek words *ta hupsela.* In this verse, they refer to the opinions and behavior patterns that accompany a person who has *an attitude of superiority.*

The apostle Paul tells us that instead of having this shameful attitude of superiority, we need to learn how to "...condescend to men of low estate...." The word "condescend" is the Greek word *sunapago.* This is a strange word to be used in this verse, for it is a compound of the words *sun* — which means *together with*; the word *apo* — which means *away*; and the word *ago* — which means *to be led.* A number of scholars say this word conveys the message that those who think too highly of themselves need to move away from (*apo*) such exalted thinking of themselves and be led (*ago*) to join or to associate with (*sun*) men of low estate. I believe that this is exactly what Paul had in mind when he chose to use the word *sunapago.*

But what does the Bible mean when it speaks of men of "low estate"? The Greek word for "low estate" is actually the word *tapeinos,* which is the Greek word that means *to be humble, modest, simple, and unpretentious.* In other words, the word *tapeinos* describes *common, ordinary, everyday, normal people.* It does *not* mean *poor.*

There are many proud and arrogant poor people, just as there are many humble wealthy people. The word *tapeinos* ("low estate" or "humble") doesn't refer to a person's financial status; rather, it refers to his attitude toward life, toward himself, and toward others. Regardless of his station in life, he has never allowed himself to think of himself as better than others.

Although there are several possible interpretations of this verse, this is the one I like the most:

"...Stop fixating on things that make you think too highly of yourself and that contribute to an attitude of superiority. You need to leave that snooty thinking behind and come back down to earth so you can learn how to associate with common, ordinary, everyday, normal people...."

I don't know if you have ever struggled with an attitude of superiority, but if you have, isn't it time for you to leave behind that way of thinking once and for all? *You are not any better than other people.* You came into the world the same way everyone else did, and you will leave exactly as everyone else leaves. You were purchased and washed with the same blood of Jesus that is available to every other soul on planet earth.

Even if you have more education, more money, and a higher status in society than most people, that doesn't make you better. In fact, these privileges make you more responsible, for God expects you to come down to a level where you can use your gifts, talents, and money to be a greater blessing to people!

Especially during this holiday season of the year when so many people are struggling to make ends meet, why don't you think of ways that you can minister to people in your life whom you normally wouldn't reach out to? Think of what a difference you can make in someone else's life by simply reaching out to bless him or her in some special way. Don't let yourself get away with thinking you're too busy or too high and mighty to do this, because you're not. Don't forget — someone once did this for you; now it is your time to do it for someone else.

MY PRAYER FOR TODAY

Lord, thank You for speaking to me today. Forgive me for the times I've acted like I was better than other people. I am sorry for that behavior, and I don't ever want to do it again. I ask You to convict me when I start to act this way and to show me how to quickly change my behavior. I really want to be an example that will make people want to know Jesus, so help me to change any part of my behavior that does not give a proper impression of Your holy character.

I pray this in Jesus' name!

MY CONFESSION FOR TODAY

I confess that I do not have a superior attitude about myself. I have the mind of Christ, and I demonstrate an attitude of love and acceptance to everyone I meet. When people walk away from me, they feel like they have been accepted, embraced, and treated with respect. Every day the Holy Spirit is teaching me more about how to give others a sense of value about themselves. I thank God that an attitude of superiority has no place in me and that each day I am getting better at reaching out to others to benefit and bless their lives.

I declare this by faith in Jesus' name!

QUESTIONS FOR YOU TO CONSIDER

1. Have you ever encountered a person like the one I described at the beginning of today's *Sparkling Gem?* How did that person's attitude of superiority affect you and others?
2. Have you ever been guilty of having such an attitude? Do you have this attitude in any area of your life right now? If the answer is yes, in what area of your life do you think of yourself as being better than other people?
3. Now that you know this attitude is not acceptable with the Lord, what are you going to do to change your attitude and actions? What steps can you take to start changing the way you relate to people whom you have previously treated as being "less" than you?

You came into the world the same way everyone else did, and you will leave exactly as everyone else leaves.

DECEMBER 21

❦

Don't Pay Evil Back for Evil!

Recompense to no man evil for evil....
— Romans 12:17

To oday's *Sparkling Gem* will be short, but pay close attention, because it's a very important one!

Most all of us have thought at one time or another, *Oh, how I want to get back at that person for what he did to me!* If *you* have had that thought in the past, or if you've been thinking such thoughts recently, then what we're going to talk about today should be very helpful to you!

In Romans 12:17, the apostle Paul told us, "Recompense to no man evil for evil...." The word "recompense" in this verse is the Greek word *apodidomi*, and it literally means *to give back* or *to pay back*. It carries the idea of *returning something to someone*. It is a compound of the words *apo*, which means *back*, as *to return back*, and the word *didomi*, which means *to give*. When compounded together, the new word gives the impression of *someone who wishes to retaliate, to get even, or to take revenge*. This person wants to pay someone back for what the other person did by doing the same thing to him; in other words, he wants to get even with the one who wronged him. In the Greek text, there is a negative in the verse, which means this action is strongly prohibited. *Paul is ordering us not to do this!*

Romans 12:17 goes on to say, "Recompense to no man *evil for evil*...." The word "evil" is the Greek word *kakos*. It describes *an action that is harmful, hurtful, or injurious* or *something done with an evil intent*. These are the actions of a person who intentionally acts to cause some kind of damage or ruin in someone else's life. But the Greek literally says *kakon anti kakou*, which means *evil for evil*. It is the idea of a person who thinks, *You did wrong to me, so now I'm going to do wrong to you. I'm going to do to you exactly what you did to me.* This is what the phrase "evil for evil" means in this verse.

A fuller interpretation of Romans 12:17 could read:

"Don't get even with people by retaliating and taking revenge. You should never get into the business of intentionally trying to hurt someone just because they hurt you."

The flesh loves to retaliate against those who have wronged us, but this is not the way Jesus teaches us to behave. Instead of retaliating, we must seek to walk in peace and to have pure hearts before God. It is impossible for us to be pure before God while we are at the same time devising mischief for those who have wronged us. We have to stay out of the mischief business and leave our offenders in the hands of God.

During the holiday season, people frequently get their feelings hurt, misunderstand each other, or simply get their wires crossed because there are so many people to deal with and so much to do. Stress is definitely a factor during this season, often adversely affecting relationships and changing the way people perceive situations.

So if you get upset about something that happens, don't give in to your emotions and end up in a fight. Rather than letting yourself get all stirred up or allowing yourself to imagine how you can get even with the person who has wronged you, get alone with the Lord and let Him fill your heart with peace. Once His peace is ruling in your heart, you'll see the situation from an entirely different perspective. Even if someone really did wrong you, God's peace will enable you to have a positive attitude toward that person. Meanwhile, you'll be able to walk on in peace with a pure heart before God, free from all bitterness, anger, and strife!

MY PRAYER FOR TODAY

Lord, I thank You for encouraging me to keep my heart free of strife during this extremely busy time of the year. There is so much to do, so many places I have to be, and so many people I need to see. I admit that the demands of this time of year put a lot of stress and strain on me. In the middle of all these activities, I don't want the devil to get the best of me, so I am asking You to fill me with Your peace. Let that divine peace rule me and my emotions so I don't let Satan get the upper hand in any of my relationships during this special time of year.

I pray this in Jesus' name!

MY CONFESSION FOR TODAY

I confess that I am free of strain and stress. My heart is filled with the peace of God, and that wonderful peace is ruling my heart, my mind, and my emotions. I am not quickly angered or offended. I walk in patience and kindness, and I am quick to forgive and to over-look the inappropriate actions of other people. Because God's peace is ruling in my heart, I will remain calm, peaceful, and undisturbed by anything that happens around me during this very busy holiday season.

I declare this by faith in Jesus' name!

QUESTIONS FOR YOU TO CONSIDER

1. By knowing what has happened in the past, are you now able to recognize the people or the circumstances that the devil uses to trigger your emotions and get you upset?

2. If your answer is yes, has the Holy Spirit shown you how to circumvent those moments so the devil can no longer ruffle your feathers and cause you to lose your peace? If your answer is no, have you asked the Holy Spirit to teach you to recognize those moments so they won't be repeated in your life?

3. When you are tempted to be upset, what helps you the most to be filled with the peace of God? Is it reading the Word for a few minutes, praying, or listening to praise and worship music?

If you get upset about something that happens, don't give in to your emotions and end up in a fight. Rather than letting yourself get all stirred up or allowing yourself to imagine how you can get even with the person who has wronged you, get alone with the Lord and let Him fill your heart with peace.

DECEMBER 22

You Have Jesus As Your Personal Intercessor!

Seeing then that we have a great high priest,
that is passed into the heavens,
Jesus the Son of God, let us hold fast our profession.
— Hebrews 4:14

*A*ccording to this verse, Jesus is your High Priest, and He lives forever to make intercession on your behalf (Hebrews 7:25). This means there is never a moment when Jesus Himself is not interceding for your victory and success. The devil may try to tell you that you're standing all alone in your walk of faith; he may tempt you to believe that no one is aware of the difficulties you are facing as you pursue God's call on your life. But that isn't true. Jesus is aware of everything you face, and He's making intercession for you *right now*.

No one wants you to succeed more than Jesus Himself. He knows the challenges you will face as you pursue what He has put in your heart. He knows the devil will try to abort your dream. He knows you will face moments when you are physically tired and mentally exhausted. Jesus understands every single emotion and temptation you will ever face. Remember, He also faced temptation during His own walk of faith.

Hebrews 4:15,16 says, "For we have not a high priest which cannot be touched with the feeling of our infirmities; but was in all points tempted like as we are, yet without sin. Let us therefore come boldly unto the throne of grace, that we may obtain mercy, and find grace to help in time of need."

This verse says that we are to come "…boldly unto the throne of grace…." The word "boldly" vividly portrays how much God wants you to come to Him, for it is the Greek word *parresia*, which gives the idea of *boldness*, *frankness*, *forthrightness*, and *outspokenness*. This clearly means God wants you to be very direct about telling Him when you need help! You never have to be timid or fearful about telling the Lord exactly what you are facing and what you need, because He encourages you to speak up and be bold!

When you come to this wonderful throne of grace, this verse promises that you will "…find grace to help in time of need." The word "time" is the Greek word *eukairos*, and it describes *a well-timed moment, the right time, a convenient time, a suitable time*, or *an appropriate time*. You see, there is no better time for you to approach the Lord boldly than when you have a need. That is an *appropriate time* for you to be bold with Him and to really express your heart.

As our High Priest, Jesus understands everything you and I will ever face. He can be touched with the feelings of our infirmities. As a father has pity on his children, so the Lord has pity on us (Psalm 103:13). He knows our frame and that we are made of dust (Psalm 103:14). Because Jesus is aware of our infirmities and limitations, He has assumed the role of our Intercessor. As our personal Advocate, Counselor, or Attorney, Jesus pleads our case before the Father and lays claim to our lawful rights.

You need never wonder if you are alone in your journey of faith. Jesus is right there with you, praying and interceding for you, for your calling, and for every need you are facing right now.

MY PRAYER FOR TODAY

Lord, I am so thankful that You beckon me to come boldly to Your throne of grace. It is so reassuring to know that You want me to not only come to You, but to speak up and boldly make my needs known. According to Your Word, there is no better time for me to be bold than when I am facing a need, so today I am going to be very bold and tell You what is on my heart and what I need. I thank You that Jesus is my High Priest and that He understands me and everything that affects my life.

I pray this in Jesus' name!

MY CONFESSION FOR TODAY

I confess that no one wants me to succeed more than Jesus Himself. He knows the challenges I face as I pursue what He has put in my heart. He knows I will face moments when I am physically tired and mentally exhausted. Jesus understands every single emotion and temptation I will ever face, and He is always right there to provide grace to help me in my time of need. God wants me to be very direct about telling Him when I need help, so today I come boldly before His throne to tell Him about the needs I am facing in my life. I never have to be timid or fearful about telling the Lord exactly what I need because He encourages me to speak up and be bold!

I declare this by faith in Jesus' name!

QUESTIONS FOR YOU TO CONSIDER

1. What is the single greatest need you are facing in your life?
2. Have you been bold to tell the Lord about your needs and what You need for Him to do on your behalf?
3. What is stopping you from going to the throne of grace right now? Don't you think it would be a good idea for you to take a little time to go before God's throne today and ask Him for an extra measure of grace to help in time of need?

As our High Priest, Jesus understands everything you and I will ever face. He can be touched with the feelings of our infirmities. Because Jesus is aware of our infirmities and limitations, He has assumed the role of our Intercessor. As our personal Advocate, Counselor, or Attorney, Jesus pleads our case before the Father and lays claim to our lawful rights.

DECEMBER 23

Made in the Likeness of Men

Who, being in the form of God,
thought it not robbery to be equal with God:
But made himself of no reputation,
and took upon him the form of a servant,
and was made in the likeness of men.
— Philippians 2:6,7

At this time of the year, believers all over the world celebrate the birth of Jesus Christ. His birth is one of the greatest miracles that has ever occurred, for it was a moment when God Almighty laid aside His glory and appeared on earth as a man. How wonderful, how marvelous to think that God would temporarily shed His divine appearance and actually take on the flesh of man! Yet this is precisely what happened the day Jesus was born in Bethlehem.

In Philippians 2:6 and 7, Paul wrote, "Who, being in the form of God, thought it not robbery to be equal with God: but made himself of no reputation, and took upon him the form of a servant, and was made in the likeness of men."

Paul begins by describing the preexistence of Jesus before He came to the earth as a man, saying, "Who, being in the form of God...." The word "being" is a translation of the Greek word *huparcho*, a compound of the words *hupo* and *arche*. In this case, the word *hupo* means *from*, and the word *arche* means *the first, original,* or *ancient*. When it becomes the word *huparcho*, it depicts *something that has always existed*.

By using this key word that means *to eternally exist*, Paul is declaring that Jesus had no beginning but always existed. This also explains Jesus' statement when He declared, "...Before Abraham was, *I am*" (John 8:58). Thus, Philippians 2:6 could be translated, *"Who, eternally existing in the form of God...."* In other words, Jesus' human birth in Bethlehem was not His beginning but merely *His manifestation to man,* a brief appearance in His eternal existence.

Paul writes that Jesus always existed in the "form" of God. The word "form" is the Greek word *morphe*. This word describes *an outward form,* which means that in Jesus' preexistence, He looked just like God. He was not just a component of God, nor a symbol of God; in reality, He *was* God. And as the eternal God Himself, Jesus possessed the very shape and outward appearance of God — a form that includes great splendor, glory, power, and a Presence so strong that no flesh can endure it.

God existed in glory more wonderful than the human mind can comprehend and more powerful than human flesh can endure. Yet He desired to come to earth to purchase redemption for man. Therefore, God had no choice but to reclothe Himself in a manner that could be tolerated by man. This is why He "...made himself of no reputation, and took upon him the form of a servant, and was made in the likeness of men." *This is the true story of Christmas!*

The phrase "made himself of no reputation" comes from the Greek word *kenos*, which means *to make empty, to evacuate, to vacate, to deprive, to divest,* or *to relinquish*. Because it was impossible for God to appear to man as God, He had to change His outward form. The only way He could make this limited appearance as a man was to willfully, deliberately, and temporarily let go of all the attributes we usually think of when we consider the characteristics of God. For thirty-three years on this earth, God divested Himself of all His heavenly glory and "…took upon him the form of a servant…" (Philippians 2:7).

The phrase "took upon him" perfectly describes that marvelous moment when God reached out to lay hold of human flesh and take it upon Himself so that He might appear as a man on the earth. The words "took upon him" are from the Greek word *lambano*, which means *to take, to seize, to catch, to latch on to, to clutch*, or *to grasp*. This word lets us know that God literally reached out from His eternal existence, reached into the material world He had created, and took human flesh upon Himself in "the form of a servant."

The word "form" in this phrase is exactly the same word that describes Jesus being in the form of God. It is the Greek word *morphe*. This means that just as Jesus in His preexistent form had all the outward appearance of God, now Jesus existed in the exact form of a man — appearing and living on this earth in exactly the same way as any other man. For a brief time in His eternal existence, Jesus emptied Himself of His divinity and literally became a man in every way.

Not only did God become man, but He took upon Himself the form of a "servant." This is the Greek word *doulos*, which refers to *a slave*. Paul now uses this word to picture the vast difference between Jesus' preexistent state and His earthly life.

Paul goes on to say that Jesus "…was made in the likeness of men." The phrase "was made" is the Greek word *ginomai*, which means *to become*, indicating that this was not Jesus' original form but it *became* His new form. This clearly describes the miracle that occurred when God *became* a man. Jesus had always existed in the form of God, not the form of man. But taking upon Himself human flesh, He was formed in the womb of the Virgin Mary and *became* a man.

God literally took upon Himself the "likeness" of a man. The word "likeness" is the Greek word *homoioma*, which refers to *a form* or *resemblance*. This refers not only to Jesus' being made in the *visible* likeness of men, but also in the *human* likeness of men. In other words, when Jesus appeared on this earth, He came in the actual form of a man and was just like man in every way.

Jesus was so completely made in the "likeness" of men that Hebrews 4:15 declares He was even tempted in every way that men are tempted. It says, "For we have not a high priest which cannot be touched with the feeling of our infirmities; but was in all points tempted like as we are, yet without sin."

So we see that when God the Father sent His Son into the world, Jesus left His heavenly home and took upon Himself human flesh. And because of this great exchange, He has stood in our place; He has felt what we feel; He is touched with the feeling of our infirmities; and He intercedes for us with great compassion as our High Priest.

At this time of the year, we are prone to think of Jesus as a little baby in a manger in a Bethlehem stable. Certainly this is true, but we should never forget that Bethlehem was *not* Jesus' beginning. It was merely a brief appearance in His eternal existence.

Out of His deep love for you and me, Jesus was willing to leave His majestic realms of glory to enter the realm of humanity. Shedding all His visible attributes that were too much for man's flesh to endure, He dressed Himself in the clothing of a human being and was manifested in the flesh. That little baby in Bethlehem was the eternal, ever-existent God Almighty, who dressed Himself in human flesh so that He could dwell among men and purchase our salvation.

God's great love for us drove Him to come down to our level so He could understand us better and later become an effective High Priest on our behalf. Think how wonderful it is that God loves us to such an extent!

When Paul started this text on God becoming a man, he started by saying, "Let this mind be in you, which was also in Christ Jesus" (Philippians 2:5). You see, God wants us to have the same mind or attitude that was demonstrated in Jesus Christ. Just as Jesus was willing to go this incredible distance to reach us, to love us, and to redeem us, we should desire to do the same for others!

This, then, is one of the primary messages of Christmas: We should be willing to divest ourselves of our privileges, such as the convenience and comfort of self-consumed living, and do whatever we can to reach out and help people. This is what Jesus did for us, so shouldn't we do the same for others?

MY PRAYER FOR TODAY

Lord, I thank You for loving me so much that You would leave Your realms of majestic glory to come dwell among men. If it had not been for Your great love that compelled You to come and redeem me, today I would still be lost in sin. Because You loved me so much, You were willing to come to this earth and purchase my salvation. You were born as a baby in Bethlehem, yet You always existed, and You came here with a definite plan to save me from an eternity separated from You. Thank You so much for coming, Lord. Thank You for loving me enough to temporarily shed Your glory and become a man so You could pay for my sin and save me to the uttermost!

I pray this in Jesus' name!

MY CONFESSION FOR TODAY

I confess that Jesus Christ is God come in the flesh! Before He was ever born as a baby in Bethlehem, Jesus always existed, for He is God Almighty. His birth in Bethlehem proves how vast His love is for me. He so desired to have me as His child that He was willing to make the ultimate sacrifice. And because He dressed Himself in flesh and lived as a man for thirty-three years, He understands everything I face and every temptation that comes my way. Oh, how wonderful it is to know that Jesus loves me!

I declare this by faith in Jesus' name!

QUESTIONS FOR YOU TO CONSIDER

1. When you think of Christmas and the birth of Jesus, do you ever think of how He existed before He was born in Bethlehem?
2. What do you think it was like for God to shed His glorious appearance and to take upon Himself the flesh of a human being?
3. How does this revelation of Jesus' act of ultimate humility affect you personally?

Jesus left His heavenly home and took upon Himself human flesh. And because of this great exchange, He has felt what we feel; He is touched with the feeling of our infirmities; and He intercedes for us with great compassion as our High Priest.

DECEMBER 24

⸎

The Real Reason for Christmas

And being found in fashion as a man,
he humbled himself, and became obedient unto death,
even the death of the cross.
— Philippians 2:8

Do you plan on taking the time this Christmas to tell your children or friends about the purpose of Christmas? If so, what will you tell them?

Although we usually meditate on the birth of Jesus at this time of the year, His purpose in coming to earth was *not* to give us the sweet picture of a baby in a Bethlehem manger. That little baby was born to die for you and for me and thus pay for the forgiveness of our sins. He was born to die on the Cross that we might be reconciled to God.

For this reason, I always told our sons when they were young, "Don't just think of a baby in a manger at Christmastime. Christmas is about much more than that. It is about God coming to earth in human flesh so He could die on the Cross to pay for your salvation and destroy all the works of the devil in your lives! That is what Christmas is all about!"

People rarely think of the Cross at Christmastime because it is the time set aside to celebrate Jesus' birth. But in Philippians 2, Paul connects the two thoughts. As Paul writes about God becoming a man, he goes on to express the ultimate reason God chose to take this amazing action. Paul says in verse 8, "And being found in fashion as a man, he humbled himself, and became obedient unto death, even the death of the cross." Because today is Christmas Eve, I want to use this *Sparkling Gem* to discuss the real reason for Christmas, which is contained in the truths found in this verse.

Philippians 2:8 says that Jesus was "...found in fashion as a man...." That word "fashion" is the Greek word *schema*. This is extremely important, for this was precisely the same word that was used in ancient times to depict *a king who exchanged his kingly garments for a brief period of time for the clothing of a beggar.*

How wonderful that the Holy Spirit would inspire the apostle Paul to use this exact word! When Jesus came to earth, it really was a moment when God Almighty shed His glorious appearance and exchanged it for the clothing of human flesh. Although man is wonderfully made, his earthly frame is temporal dust and cannot be compared to the eternal and glorious appearance of God. However, for the sake of our redemption, God laid aside all of His radiant glory, took upon Himself human flesh, and was manifested in the very likeness of a human being.

This is the true story of a King who traded His kingly garments and took upon Himself the clothing of a servant. But the story doesn't stop there. Jesus — our King who exchanged His royal robes for the clothing of flesh — loved us so much that He "...humbled himself, and became obedient unto death, even the death of the cross"!

The word "humbled" is the Greek word *tapeinao*, and it means *to be humble, to be lowly,* and *to be willing to stoop to any measure that is needed.* This describes the attitude God had when He took upon Himself human flesh. Think of how much humility would be required for God to shed His glory and lower Himself to become like a member of His creation. Consider the greatness of God's love that drove Him to divest Himself of all His splendor and become like a man. This is amazing to me, particularly when I think of how often the flesh recoils at the thought of being humble or preferring someone else above itself. Yet Jesus humbled Himself "…and became obedient unto death, even the death of the cross."

The word "obedient" tells me that this was *not* a pleasurable experience that Jesus looked forward to in anticipation. To humble Himself to this extent required Jesus' deliberate obedience.

As preexistent God, Jesus came to earth for this purpose. But as man dressed in flesh, He despised the thought of the Cross (Hebrews 12:2) and could only endure its shame because He knew of the results that would follow. For Jesus to be obedient as a man, He had to choose to obey the eternal plan of God.

The word "obedient" that is used to describe Jesus is the Greek word *hupakouo*, from the word *hupo*, which means *under*, and the word *akouo*, which means *I hear*. When these two words are compounded together, they picture someone who is *hupo — under someone else's authority*, and *akouo — listening to what that superior is speaking to him*. After listening and taking these instructions to heart, this person then carries out the orders of his superior.

Thus, the word *hupakouo* tells us that obedient people are 1) *under authority*, 2) *listening to what their superior is saying*, and 3) *carrying out the orders that have been given to them*. This is what the word "obedient" means in this verse, and this is what obedience means for you and me.

You see, even Jesus had to come to this place of obedience. Although He knew that He was the Lamb slain before the foundation of the world, that didn't mean His flesh was excited about dying as the Lamb of God on the Cross. According to this verse in Philippians 2:8, Jesus had to humble Himself and become "obedient" in order to follow God's plan. He wasn't looking forward to the experience of death on a Cross; He made a choice to humble Himself and to go to any measure in order to accomplish the Father's plan.

Part of the Father's plan was for Jesus to humble Himself "…unto death, even the death of the cross." The word "unto" is from the Greek word *mechri*, which is a Greek word that really means *to such an extent*. The Greek word *mechri* is sufficient in itself to dramatize the point, but the verse goes on to say that Jesus humbled Himself unto death, "…even the death of the cross." The word "even" is the Greek word *de*, which emphatically means *EVEN!* The Greek carries this idea: *"Can you imagine it! Jesus humbled Himself to such a lowly position and became so obedient that He even stooped low enough to die the miserable death of a Cross!"*

I heartily recommend that you take the time today to read the April 24 *Sparkling Gem* in order to refresh your memory on the full process of crucifixion. It was genuinely the worst death a person could ever endure. For Jesus to humble Himself to the point of death, *EVEN* the death of the Cross, demonstrates how much He was willing to humble Himself to redeem you and me.

Just think of it — Almighty God, clothed in radiant glory from eternity past, came to this earth formed as a human being in the womb of a human mother for one purpose: so that He could one day die a miserable death on a Cross to purchase our salvation! All of this required humility on a level far beyond anything we could ever comprehend or anything that has ever been requested of any of us. Yet this was the reason Jesus came; therefore, He chose to be obedient to the very end, humbling Himself to the point of dying a humiliating death on a Cross and thereby purchasing our eternal salvation.

So as you celebrate Christmas tonight and tomorrow, be sure to remember the real purpose of Christmas. It isn't just a time to reflect on the baby boy who was born in Bethlehem so long ago.

That baby was God manifest in the flesh. He was born to die for you and for me. Jesus was so willing to do whatever was required in order to redeem us from Satan and sin that He humbled Himself even unto death on a Cross! *That is what Christmas is all about!*

MY PRAYER FOR TODAY

Lord, I thank You for coming to earth so You could redeem me. When I think of the extent to which You were willing to go in order to save me, it makes me want to shout, to celebrate, and to cry with thankfulness. You love me so much, and I am so grateful for that love. Without You, I would still be lost and in sin. But because of everything You have done for me, today I am free; my life is blessed; Jesus is my Lord; Heaven is my home; and Satan has no right to control me. I will be eternally thankful to You for everything You did to save me!

I pray this in Jesus' name!

MY CONFESSION FOR TODAY

I confess that Jesus Christ loves me! He demonstrated His love to me by leaving behind Heaven's glory and taking upon Himself human flesh. And He did it for one purpose: so that one day He could go to the Cross and die for me and thus reconcile me unto God. There is no need for me to ever feel unloved or unwanted, because Jesus went the ultimate distance to prove that He loves me!

I declare this by faith in Jesus' name!

QUESTIONS FOR YOU TO CONSIDER

1. When you compare Jesus' ultimate act of obedience to God with your own willingness to obey God in every area of your life, are you satisfied with your level of obedience to Him? Or do you find yourself falling far short of what He requires?
2. What can you do on this Christmas Eve to more fully "let this mind be in you, which was also in Christ Jesus" (Philippians 2:5)? Are there specific ways you can show humility toward others or prefer someone else above yourself?
3. Now that you've read today's *Sparkling Gem*, what will change in the way you talk to your children or your friends about the real purpose of Christmas?

Here is the true story of a King who traded His kingly garments and took upon Himself the clothing of a servant. Jesus — our King who exchanged His royal robes for the clothing of flesh — loved us so much that He "...humbled himself, and became obedient unto death, even the death of the cross"!

DECEMBER 25

❧

Every Knee Will Bow To the Name of Jesus Christ!

Wherefore God also hath highly exalted him, and given him
a name which is above every name:
That at the name of Jesus every knee should bow,
of things in heaven, and things in earth,
and things under the earth;
And that every tongue should confess
that Jesus Christ is Lord, to the glory of God the Father.
— Philippians 2:9-11

*M*erry Christmas! I pray that this will be one of the most wonderful Christmases you have ever known in your entire life! And as you celebrate the first coming of Jesus Christ, don't forget to make sure your heart is ready for the second coming of Jesus Christ. In fact, I urge you to use today as a special reminder to tell everyone that Jesus is coming again soon!

Because Jesus came to earth the first time and became obedient unto death on the Cross, the Bible joyfully declares: "Wherefore God also hath highly exalted him, and given him a name which is above every name: that at the name of Jesus every knee should bow, of things in heaven, and things in earth, and things under the earth; and that every tongue should confess that Jesus Christ is Lord, to the glory of God the Father" (Philippians 2:9-11).

My friend, the first time Jesus came to this world, He came as a little baby boy that was born in Bethlehem. But the next time Jesus comes — and it could be at any time — He will come as the Lord of lords and the King of kings! According to the Bible, at that moment "…every knee should bow, of things in heaven, and things in earth, and things under the earth."

Notice it says that "every knee should bow." The word "bow" is the Greek word *kampto*, and it means *to bow low*. The same word is found in Romans 11:4, Romans 14:11, and Ephesians 3:14, where the apostle Paul uses it to picture *a person who bends his knee in acknowledgement of God's authority*. It is an action that expresses *honor*, *respect*, *humiliation*, and *worship*.

According to Philippians 2:10, a day is coming when those in Heaven, earth, and hell will bow their knees in honor, respect, humility, and worship of Jesus Christ! It is not a question of *if* people will bow their knees to Jesus; it is only a question of *when* and *how* they will do it. Will they freely do it while still living on this earth? Or will they do it from the vantage point of hell? *Everyone* will bow — including those who have already died and gone to Heaven; those who are still alive when Jesus comes; and even those who have died and are eternally separated from God. All will bow their knees in acknowledgement of Jesus Christ's Lordship!

And the bending of mankind's knees in acknowledgement of Jesus' Lordship will be no quiet affair, for Philippians 2:11 goes on to tell us, "…every tongue should confess that Jesus Christ is Lord, to the glory of God the Father."

The word "confess" is the Greek word *exomologeo*, which is a compound of the words *ek* and *homologia*. The word *ek* means *out*, and the word *homologia* refers to *a confession*. When taken as one word, it means *to audibly, vocally, and publicly declare a fact*. It also means *to speak it out, to yell it loudly*, or *to declare it out*. This means Heaven, earth, and hell will resonate and resound with the voices of all who have ever lived as they thunderously shout out and acknowledge: *"JESUS IS LORD!"*

Just as every knee shall bow, it is also a fact that every person will confess that Jesus Christ is Lord! If a person confesses Jesus to be his Lord right now in this life, it guarantees him a place in Heaven. If a person refuses to make that confession now, he will still do it later — only then it will be too late for him to gain a place in Heaven.

How tragic that people die without confessing Jesus as Lord, for a day is coming when even in death, they will be required to make this confession! If they confess Jesus as their Lord now, they reap the benefits of salvation and all the promises of God. If they do it later, it will be an acknowledgement that they were wrong and that Jesus was right; however, it will *not* change their eternal status.

This Christmas as you celebrate with family and friends, take a few minutes to remind everyone that Jesus is coming again, just as surely as He came the first time. And if anyone has never confessed Jesus as the Lord of his life, offer to take that person into a quiet room. After bowing your knees with him, lead him in a confession of Jesus' Lordship that brings him into the family of God. *Can you think of anything more important that could happen on Christmas Day?*

MY PRAYER FOR TODAY

Lord, I ask You to help me to be bold today when I see my family and friends. If I see people who I know are not saved, please give me the boldness I need to speak up and ask them to pray with me to make Jesus the Lord of their lives. I don't want this day to end without taking advantage of any opportunity that arises to present Jesus to someone who needs You and to lead that person in a prayer of salvation. Holy Spirit, I look to You for the wisdom and the boldness I need to be Your instrument in someone else's life on this special day.

I pray this in Jesus' name!

MY CONFESSION FOR TODAY

I confess that I am filled with the Holy Spirit. Right now He is giving me the boldness I need to tell my family and friends about Jesus Christ and His death on the Cross for them. There is no better gift I could give to anyone today than the message of the Gospel, so I am choosing to give an eternal gift in addition to all the other gifts that will be exchanged. The Holy Spirit is helping me recognize opportunities to witness and to pray with people who need to confess Jesus Christ as the Lord of their lives!

I declare this by faith in Jesus' name!

QUESTIONS FOR YOU TO CONSIDER

1. What family members and friends will you see today who are unsaved?
2. Have you thought about how you could talk to them privately to see if they would like to give their hearts to Jesus on this Christmas Day?

3. Before you go to Christmas festivities today, why don't you take a few minutes to pray for any unsaved people you will be seeing today, asking the Lord to open a door for you to speak to them about Jesus?

DECEMBER 26

The Power of Teamwork

For as the body is one, and hath many members,
and all the members of that one body,
being many, are one body: so also is Christ.
— 1 Corinthians 12:12

*A*lthough it may be possible to run a church, business, or organization single-handedly, it is certainly not the most efficient or effective method of operation. Nevertheless, countless people have tried to do so with minimal success. Inevitably, however, these same people eventually get so tired that they just can't run the whole show anymore. After a while, even the most stalwart become weary of carrying never-ending responsibility alone.

Doing things alone is a course of action that guarantees your venture will never be large. You may do a top-quality job that touches a very small market, but your lack of a team limits your ability to touch very many people at one time. You can run the operation single-handedly on a small scale, but you won't be able to build a larger church, business, or organization without the manpower needed to touch and serve many people. The philosophy of doing it all single-handedly limits the growth of any organization — not to mention the fact that it can physically wear you out and make you old at an early age!

In First Corinthians 12:12, the apostle Paul compared the Church to the human body, with different parts that are equipped to perform different functions. He says, "For as the body is one, and hath many members, and all the members of that one body, being many, are one body: so also is Christ."

Paul uses the word "many" to describe the various parts of the body. This word is translated from the Greek word *polus*, which describes *a huge quantity*. But the word *polus* not only accentuates the fact that there are *many* members; it also presents the idea that there is *great variety* among the members.

I like how *The Message* Bible says it:

You can easily enough see how this kind of thing works by looking no further than your own body. Your body has many parts — limbs, organs, cells — but no matter how many parts you can name, you're still one body. It is exactly the same with Christ. By means of his one Spirit, we all said goodbye to our partial and piecemeal lives. We each used to independently call our own shots, but then we entered into a large and integrated life in which *he* has the final say in everything.

As believers, we must say goodbye to our old, independent way of thinking and learn how to be *integrated* into a greater whole. We need each other, for without each other's input and gifts, we are incomplete.

When God's people come together as a team to achieve a common goal, their unified effort brings divine power and world-transforming moves of God to the earth! Doctrine, culture, language, and creeds will never bring unity to the Church. But when we become single-focused, working together as a team to win the world to Jesus Christ, that is when genuine *unity* will come to the Church. And unity is such a powerful force!

For some, *unity* is a vague, dream-like wish for a day when Christians sweetly smile at each other and sing in harmony; disagreements are resolved and eliminated; and we all say, think, and do the same identical things. But the Bible never promises that a day will come when we all agree about everything! This is a false concept of unity. It's a fantasy that will never be reached on this earth.

So what *is* unity? Unity occurs when people are *united in action and in passion for a common cause.* Their shared goal is so strong that it removes hostilities, puts away disagreements, and gives previously divided people a reason to take their place alongside each other. When this occurs, different gifts, talents, and anointings become connected together, and the result is an amazing river of divine power that achieves the supernatural and accomplishes the impossible.

I can tell you that in our own ministry organization, our leadership team is very gifted, very diverse, and from many different denominational and cultural backgrounds; yet we are extremely *united* as a ministry. But it is not our culture, language, or doctrine that unites us — it is our *common goal* to get the Gospel to as many people as we can by God's grace. This single purpose pulls our whole diverse staff together in phenomenal unity, which is one of the reasons we have had such powerful results. We may be many in number and diverse in gifts and talents, but *we are one in purpose.*

It is simply a fact that phenomenal results are reaped when concentrated attention is given to building this kind of teamwork. People who become cemented together by a common goal produce *unity*. And when this kind of chemistry is at work among your team members in your church, ministry, business, or organization, that team becomes a mighty force that helps you reach the goals and visions God has placed in your heart.

So don't try to fulfill your dream or run your church, ministry, business, or organization single-handedly. If you do, you'll only serve to physically, mentally, and spiritually exhaust yourself. Why don't you instead allow God to bring other team members to you who can help you fulfill your task? Don't settle for accomplishing your goal single-handedly on a small scale. Develop the manpower to build a larger church, business, or organization with enough hands to touch and serve *many* people!

As other members join your team and begin to use their gifts and talents to press toward the common goal, you'll find that their help greatly enhances both your effectiveness and your ability to impact this world for God. *So why don't you ask God today to bring you the individuals you need to help you fulfill your God-given assignment?*

MY PRAYER FOR TODAY

Lord, I want to thank You in advance for bringing me the team members I need to fulfill the vision You have put in my heart. I don't want to run this race by myself. I realize that even though I can do part of my assigned task alone, the greatest results can only be achieved with a team. Help me adjust my thinking so that I can think like a team member. Lead my team and me into a true sense of unity so that maximum power can be released through us to a world that desperately needs Jesus.

I pray this in Jesus' name!

MY CONFESSION FOR TODAY

I confess that God has made me a part of an awesome team. Every day we are becoming better and better, and as a result of the unity that exists between us, we are achieving more than we ever dreamed. So much power is released as we strive together to reach the common purpose God has given us. In fact, the impossible is possible, and the supernatural seems natural! With the help of the Holy Spirit, strife is removed and harmony is at work as we all reach toward our common, God-given goal!

I declare this by faith in Jesus' name!

QUESTIONS FOR YOU TO CONSIDER

1. Have you ever tried to run everything single-handedly and discovered that this was a very difficult way to operate the business, ministry, or department over which the Lord has placed you?
2. When you look around, can you see the gifted, talented people whom God has brought to help you fulfill your God-given dream? Are you allowing them to use their gifts to their full potential? Are you giving them the freedom to use the ideas, insights, and abilities God has given to them? If not, why aren't you tapping into the treasures God has placed within these important people in your life?
3. What is the single most important goal for your church, ministry, business, or organization? Do you have unity on your team regarding that goal? Does everyone on the team know it is your primary objective so they can rally around it?

DECEMBER 27

Why Jesus Compared Unforgiveness To the Sycamine Tree

...If ye had faith as a grain of mustard seed,
ye might say unto this sycamine tree,
Be thou plucked up by the root,
and be thou planted in the sea; and it should obey you.
— Luke 17:6

In Luke 17:1-6, Jesus taught His disciples about bitterness and unforgiveness and about how to remove these evil forces from one's life. As an illustration, Jesus likened these forces to the sycamine tree that was so well known in that part of the world. The word "sycamine" comes from the Greek word *sukaminos*, and it is the Greek word that refers to a tree that grew throughout the Middle East.

When you understand everything that is connected to the sycamine tree, you'll know exactly why Jesus chose to use this tree as an example of bitterness and unforgiveness in Luke 17:6. In that verse, Jesus told His disciples, "...If ye had faith as a grain of mustard seed, ye might say unto this sycamine tree, Be thou plucked up by the root, and be thou planted in the sea; and it should obey you." Notice that Jesus said, "...Ye might say unto this sycamine tree...." The word "this" indicates that Jesus was pointing out something very specific to them.

Keep in mind that Jesus was speaking of getting rid of bitterness and unforgiveness. In Luke 17:3, He told the disciples that they needed to forgive those who sinned against them. He then took it to the maximum in Luke 17:4 by saying that even if a brother does something wrong seven times in one day and is each time truly repentant, they were to keep on forgiving that offending brother.

Forgiving once is already a challenge for most people. But to forgive someone seven times in one day almost sounds impossible to many folks. It must have sounded preposterous to the disciples as well, for they said, "...Lord, Increase our faith" (Luke 17:5). This statement was the equivalent of their saying, *"Lord, we don't know if we have enough faith to forgive so many times in one day. You'll have to increase our faith if we're going to do this seven times in one day!"*

That is when Jesus began to teach His disciples about speaking to bitterness and unforgiveness. He said, "...If ye had faith as a grain of mustard seed, ye might say unto this sycamine tree...." When Jesus used the word "this," it was the equivalent of Jesus' telling them, *"Bitterness and unforgiveness are just like the sycamine tree — and if you really want to be free of these attitudes, you can speak to this menacing growth in your life and command it to be planted in the sea!"*

Before we can understand what Jesus taught about getting rid of bitterness and unforgiveness, we first need to see why He used the sycamine tree to illustrate these destructive forces. Was there a particular reason why He didn't use an oak tree, an apple tree, or a palm tree in this illustration? Why did He use the sycamine tree to symbolize the detrimental effects of bitterness and unforgiveness in a person's life?

As you look at the characteristics of the sycamine tree listed below, I believe you will comprehend why Jesus used this particular tree in this context.

1. The sycamine tree had a very large and deep root structure.

The sycamine tree was known to have one of the deepest root structures of all trees in the Middle East. It was a vigorous and robust tree that grew to a height of thirty feet or more. Because its roots went down so deep into the earth, it was very difficult to kill. Hot weather and blistering temperatures had little effect on this tree because it was tapped into a water source down deep under the earth. Even cutting it to its base would not guarantee its death because its roots, hidden deep under the ground, would draw from underground sources of water, enabling it to keep resurfacing again and again. In other words, this tree was *very* difficult to eradicate.

No wonder Jesus used this tree as an example of bitterness and unforgiveness! Like the sycamine tree, bitterness and unforgiveness must be dealt with clear to the roots, or they will keep springing up again and again. The roots of bitterness and unforgiveness go down deep into the human soul, fed by any offense that lies hidden in the soil of the heart. That hidden source of offense will cause these evil forces to resurface in a person's life over and over again. It will take a serious decision for that person to rip those roots of bitterness and offense out of his heart once and for all so they can't grow back in the future.

2. The sycamine tree's wood was the preferred wood for building caskets.

In Egypt and the Middle East, the sycamine tree was considered to be the preferred wood for building caskets and coffins. It grew quickly and in nearly any environment, making it accessible in many different places. It also grew best in dry conditions — the kind of conditions for which the

Middle East is famous. These are two reasons sycamine wood was used in so many places for building caskets and coffins.

Again, we can see why this illustration of the sycamine tree is so ideal for portraying bitterness and unforgiveness. Just as the sycamine tree grew very quickly, so does bitterness and unforgiveness. In fact, it doesn't take too long at all for these evil forces to get out of control and start taking over the whole place! When these fast-growing and ugly attitudes are allowed to grow freely, they not only spoil the condition of your own heart, but they ruin your relationships with other people.

Also, just as the sycamine tree grew easily in every environment, so does bitterness. It doesn't matter where people are from, where they live, what kind of cultural background they grew up in, or what level of society they belong to — bitterness and unforgiveness grow in human hearts everywhere, for they are universal in their scope of evil influence.

The sycamine tree grew best where little rain fell and water was sparse. Isn't this just like bitterness and unforgiveness? These negative attitudes flourish where spiritually dry conditions exist. You can almost count on finding bitterness and unforgiveness growing and blossoming where there is no repentance, no joy, and no fresh rain of the Spirit.

And don't forget that sycamine wood was the preferred wood for building caskets and coffins. What a powerful message this is! It tells us that bitterness and unforgiveness are *deadly*. Harboring bitterness will spiritually bury you more quickly than anything else! These attitudes are the materials that Satan uses to put you six feet underground!

Let me stress this point to you because it's so important: *If you permit bitterness and unforgiveness to grow in your life, it won't be long until these attitudes have killed your joy, stolen your peace, and canceled out your spiritual life!*

3. The sycamine tree produced a fig that was very bitter to eat.

The sycamine tree and the mulberry tree were very similar in appearance; the two trees even produced a fruit that looked identical. However, the fruit of the sycamine tree was extremely bitter. Its fruit looked just as luscious and delicious as a mulberry fig. But when a person tasted the sycamine fig, he discovered that it was horribly bitter.

Mulberry figs were delicious and therefore expensive. Because of the cost of this fruit, it was primarily eaten by wealthier people. But the sycamine fig was cheap and therefore affordable to poorer people. Because the poor couldn't afford the luscious mulberry fig, they munched on the sycamine fig as a substitute.

However, the sycamine fig was so bitter that it couldn't be eaten whole. In order to consume an entire sycamine fig, the eater had to nibble on it a little bit at a time. After a pause, the eater would return to nibble on it again, but he could never devour an entire piece of this fruit at one time; it was just too tart and pungent to eat at one sitting.

Jesus lets us know that like the sycamine fruit, the fruit of bitterness and unforgiveness is bitter, tart, and pungent. Like the fig, most people who are bitter and filled with unforgiveness chew on their feelings for a long time. They nibble on bitterness for a while; then they pause to digest what they've eaten. After they have reflected deeply on their offense, they return to the memory table to start nibbling on bitterness again — taking one little bite, then another little bite, then another. As they continue to think and meditate on their offense, they internalize their bitter feelings toward those who have offended them. In the end, their perpetual nibbling on the poisonous fruit of bitterness makes them bitter, sour people themselves.

And just as the primary consumers of the sycamine fruit were poor people, those who sit around and constantly meditate on every wrong that has ever been done to them are usually bound up with all kinds of poverty. Their bitter attitude not only makes them spiritually poor, but they are also frequently defeated, depressed, sick, and financially poor as well.

4. The sycamine tree was pollinated only by wasps.

It is very interesting to note that the sycamine tree was not naturally pollinated. The pollination process was only initiated when a wasp stuck its stinger right into the heart of the fruit. Thus, the tree and its fruit had to be "stung" in order to be reproduced.

Think of how many times you have heard a bitter person say: "I've been stung by that person once, but I'm not going to be stung again! What he did hurt me so badly that I'll never let him get close enough to sting me again!" It is likely that people who make such a statement have been "stung" by a situation that the devil especially devised to pollinate their hearts and souls with bitterness and unforgiveness. When a person talks like this, you can know for sure that *the wasp of bitterness got to them*!

Jesus said that in order to rid this nuisance from one's life, a person must have faith the size of "a grain of mustard seed." The word "grain" is the Greek word *kokkos*. It describes *a seed, a grain*, or *a very small kernel*. Jesus uses the example of a "mustard" seed in this example. The word "mustard" is the Greek word *sinapi*, which refers to *the small mustard plant that grows from a tiny, miniscule seed.*

By using this word, Jesus was telling His disciples that a great amount of faith is not needed to deal with bitterness and unforgiveness. Any person who has even a tiny measure of faith can speak to bitterness and unforgiveness and command them to leave — *if* that is really the desire of his heart.

So what is your desire today, friend? Do you genuinely wish to be free from the bitterness, unforgiveness, and offense that has festered in your soul for so long? Are you ready to rip those destructive roots clear out of your heart so they won't be able to resurface in your life again? Are you tired of those detrimental attitudes killing your joy, stealing your peace, and nullifying your spiritual life? If so, be sure to read tomorrow's *Sparkling Gem* so you can find out exactly how to permanently eradicate these attitudes from your life!

MY PRAYER FOR TODAY

Lord, thank You for speaking to my heart about getting rid of bitterness, unforgiveness, and offense. I know from experience that these attitudes are a killer to my spiritual life. When I am filled with bitterness and unforgiveness, I become a sour hostage to my memories. When I am consumed with offense, I lose my joy and peace and my relationships with other people are horribly affected. I thank You for giving me all the faith I need to deal with this issue, Lord. Today I am asking You to help me start the process of ripping those foul roots out of the soil of my heart and soul.

I pray this in Jesus' name!

MY CONFESSION FOR TODAY

I confess that I genuinely wish to be set free from bitterness, unforgiveness, and offense. I am weary of the way these poisonous roots have produced their deadly fruit in my life for so long. I am ready to do whatever is required to rip those roots clear out of my heart so they won't be able to resurface in my life again. By the power of the Holy Spirit and the authority God has given me, I repent of these detrimental attitudes that have been killing my joy, stealing my peace, and nullifying my spiritual life. By faith I am walking free from these enemies of my soul.

I declare this by faith in Jesus' name!

QUESTIONS FOR YOU TO CONSIDER

1. Have you been harboring ill feelings deep inside your soul that are now beginning to affect your spiritual life? Have you been feeling "dead" on the inside as a result of your tight hold on bitterness, unforgiveness, and offense?
2. Who is that person or group of people against whom you have been harboring these feelings? Did those who offended you do anything to you that you haven't been guilty of doing to someone else in the past?
3. Has it helped you to hold on so tightly to these feelings of unforgiveness? Has bitterness improved the quality of your life? Have your relationships become richer and fuller as a result of your clinging to offense? What fruit has been produced in your life because you've allowed these negative attitudes to fester and grow?

DECEMBER 28

It's Time for You
To Speak to Yourself!

...If ye had faith as a grain of mustard seed,
ye might say unto this sycamine tree,
Be thou plucked up by the root,
and be thou planted in the sea; and it should obey you.
— Luke 17:6

When Jesus taught His disciples about the evil effects of bitterness, unforgiveness, and offense, He also told them how to uproot and remove offenses and unforgiveness from the heart. Praise God that Jesus didn't just identify the problem and then leave us to figure out our deliverance by ourselves! He took it one step further and gave us the secret weapon for jerking those roots clear out of the ground and sending them to a place where they will *never again* produce their wicked fruit in us.

Jesus said, "...If ye had faith as a grain of mustard seed, ye might say unto this sycamine tree, Be thou plucked up by the root, and be thou planted in the sea; and it should obey you" (Luke 17:6). Notice Jesus said, "...Ye might *say* unto this sycamine tree...." In order to get rid of these destructive devices, you have to rise up and take authority over them!

Jesus specifically said that you must literally *speak* to the sycamine tree. The word "say" used in Luke 17:6 is the Greek word *lego*, which means *to speak*, but the tense that is used depicts *a strong, stern, serious, deeply felt kind of speaking.* In other words, this isn't a person who mutters thoughtless nonsense; this is a person who has made an inward resolution and now speaks authoritatively and with great conviction.

Your voice represents your authority; therefore, when you raise your voice, you *release* your authority. That is why you must *speak* to these attitudes and not just *think* about them. You can think all you want about removing those poisonous roots in your life, but your thoughts will not remove them. But when you get so tired of living under the stress and strain of bitterness, unforgiveness, and offense that you lift your voice and *command* these foul forces to go, they will finally begin to obey you!

I promise you, friend — if you wait until you feel like speaking to those ugly attitudes, you'll never do it! If you depend on your feelings and emotions to motivate you, you'll never be free of offense and unforgiveness. Your feelings and emotions will tell you that you have a right and a reason to feel the way you do. Your flesh will talk you into hanging on to those unprofitable, harmful attitudes. So make the choice not to listen to your negative emotions anymore; then start exercising your God-given authority by speaking to yourself!

It is time for you to accept personal responsibility for your inward condition. Stop blaming everyone else for all your bad attitudes, and acknowledge that there is something *inside you* that needs to be removed! Jesus said you must *speak* to that "sycamine tree" and tell it to *go*!

✦ *If you don't speak to your emotions, they will speak to you.*
✦ *If you don't take authority over your emotions, they will take authority over you.*
✦ *If you don't rise up and conquer your flesh, it will rise up and conquer you!*
✦ *So quit letting your emotions tell you what to think, what to do, and how to react.*
✦ *It's time for YOU to do the talking and to take command of your own thought life!*

You have to treat bitterness, resentment, and unforgiveness like they are enemies that have come to corrupt your soul. You must see them as bandits that have come to steal your joy, your peace, and your relationships. Would you throw open the door and allow a bandit to ravage your home? Of course not! In addition to using all the power available to you for removing that bandit, you'd probably command him to get out of your house! And I seriously doubt that you would whisper at him; most likely you would yell and scream as you *ordered* him out!

Likewise, you must decide not to tolerate this spiritual pestilence any longer, not even for a second. It's time for you to raise your voice of authority and declare to these attitudes that *they will no longer dominate you.* And if you must, speak to these attitudes and command them to go again and again and again and again and again — until they are finally uprooted and removed forever!

You have to go for the roots! If you want to be free, it's going to take an attitude that says, *"I'm going to get to the roots of this beast and yank them clear out of my soul, and I'm not going to stop until I'm totally free!"*

MY PRAYER FOR TODAY

Lord, I intend to exercise my God-given authority and to raise my voice to tell these attitudes that they will no longer hound and dominate me! Bitterness, I command you to leave me in Jesus' name! Unforgiveness, I refuse to be bound by you any longer, and I tell you to leave me right now! Offense, I will not be held hostage by you any longer, and I am telling you to flee from me in the name of Jesus! The Lord has redeemed me, and I refuse to allow you to operate in me any longer. I command you to go RIGHT NOW in Jesus' powerful name!

I pray this in Jesus' name!

MY CONFESSION FOR TODAY

I confess that I will not tolerate attitudes of bitterness and unforgiveness in my life anymore. I'm not going to just think about how bad these attitudes are and how I need to change. I'm going to lift my voice and speak to them like enemies of my soul that have come to destroy my life and ruin my relationships. I simply will not allow myself to be subjected to these hounding thoughts any longer. I proclaim that I am free of the memories of those who did wrong to me. I forgive them. I choose to let it all go. I am walking completely free from these attitudes and will not be controlled by them from this day forward!

I declare this by faith in Jesus' name!

QUESTIONS FOR YOU TO CONSIDER

1. Don't you agree that it's time for you to stop only thinking about changing and to start doing something about it? Don't you agree that you need to lift your voice and use your God-given authority to command bitterness and unforgiveness to release your mind and emotions?
2. How would you react if you knew a bandit was coming to ravage your house? Would you throw open the door, let him in, and watch him freely move about your house? Or would you summon all the power available to you to get rid of him?
3. Isn't it time that you start using your own authority to speak to the spiritual bandits that have been robbing you in so many areas of your life?

DECEMBER 29

Your Flesh Will Obey Your Commands!

...If ye had faith as a grain of mustard seed,
ye might say unto this sycamine tree,
Be thou plucked up by the root,
and be thou planted in the sea; and it should obey you.
— Luke 17:6

*J*esus said that when you finally decide to deal with the wrong attitudes that have stalked and hounded your life for so long, you must order them to "...be thou plucked up by the root, and be thou planted in the sea..." (Luke 17:6).

The words "plucked up by the root" are from the Greek word *ekridzoo*, which is a compound of the words *ek* and *ridzo*. The word *ek* means *out*, and the word *ridzo* is the Greek word for *a root*, like *the roots of a plant*. When joined into one word, the compound word means *to rip out by the roots*.

This is not a person who hopes the plant will be removed but does nothing to make it happen. Quite the contrary! This is the picture of a person who wraps his hands around the base of that plant, pulls with all his might, and rips the roots of that plant right out of the ground. He has made the determination that he is not going to stop until the ground he stands on is totally free from the roots of that nasty plant so that it will never produce life there again!

That's the way you have to deal with wrong attitudes that have been deeply rooted in your soul for a long time. I guarantee you that if those attitudes have been at work in you for a long time, they are now deeply rooted in the way you think and behave. At this point, the only way they are going to be ripped out of your soul is by your determined choice to do whatever is necessary to rip them out. There can be no accidental deliverance from these attitudes. If your heart is to be liberated, it will only happen as you choose to be liberated and then do something about it!

Once you've ripped those attitudes out of the soil of your soul, the Lord Jesus said that we need to command them to "be planted in the sea." The word "planted" is from the Greek word *phuteuo*, which would normally describe *the planting of a plant*. However, plants are not normally planted in the sea, so Jesus must have had something else in mind by using this word. The word *phuteuo* in this verse means to be permanently relocated to the "sea."

Isn't it interesting that Jesus said you have to command wrong attitudes to be planted in the sea? Why didn't He tell us to throw them into the garbage pile? Why did Jesus say to permanently relocate those wrong attitudes in the *sea*?

The sea is made of salt water. Salt water won't allow a plant to grow because the salt would kill the roots. So once a plant or tree is thrown into the seawater, it becomes a dead issue. No matter how hard you try, that plant will never grow again. Its life is gone forever! If you planted it in the garbage pile, it could reestablish its roots and grow again. But by throwing it into the sea, you have plunged those wrong attitudes into a place where they will never grow, never re-root, and never produce life again. Once in the sea, they are dead forever!

This is so very important in the context of this verse, for it tells us that Jesus doesn't want us to be just temporarily relieved of these destructive attitudes; He wants us to be *permanently* freed of them. He wants them to become dead issues that never stalk or hound us again.

This is precisely how you have to look at the dead issues that you've spoken to and commanded to *go*. Once you've told bitterness and unforgiveness to leave, don't ever allow them to take root in your life again! Even if your flesh would like to dwell on those old hurts again, don't allow that bitter tree to come back to life! Bury it in the sea of forgetfulness so its roots can *never* regain a foothold in your soul.

Jesus told us to say to the sycamine tree, "Be thou plucked up by the root, and be thou planted in the sea; and it should obey you." Notice the last phrase, "…and it should obey you." The word "obey" is the Greek word *hupakouo*, which means *to submit and to obey*.

Your out-of-control emotions are just like an out-of-control child. That child will rant, rave, and carry on all day long until you finally stand up and tell him to straighten up and act right! In the same way, the flesh will pout, throw a temper tantrum, and carry on to a ridiculous extent — until you finally decide that *enough is enough*! When you make that choice to rise up, speak to your emotions, and exert your authority in Jesus Christ, *your flesh WILL obey your commands*!

◆ *If you don't take authority over your flesh and emotions, they will continue to dominate and hound you.*

◆ *If you'll stand up to your emotions and plant them in the sea forever, they will obey you!*

So today I must ask, "Isn't it time for you to rise up and take charge of the situation in your soul?" Never forget that it is *your* soul, so you are responsible for what happens there. Even if others have wronged you, it is simply a fact that you are the only one who has the power to allow such a foul tree of bitterness to grow inside your soul. It is *your* responsibility to remove those bitter roots and be freed of that inner mess.

The Holy Spirit is present right now to help you make the choice to forgive, forget, and permanently walk free of the past wrongs that others have committed against you — or the wrongs you *think* they committed against you. Right now it doesn't matter who is right or wrong. What matters is that you uproot that tree of bitterness before it begins producing deadly fruit in your life.

So by faith, reach out and grab hold of the base of that ugly growth. Grip it tightly; pull with all your might; and *rip* those roots right of out of your heart. Then dump that gnarly tree of bitterness and unforgiveness permanently in the sea where it will never bother you again!

MY PRAYER FOR TODAY

Lord, I thank You that I don't ever have to be stalked and hounded by bitter attitudes and wrong thinking for the rest of my life. With the authority You have given me, I can speak to those attitudes and command them to go! I can speak to my flesh, and it will obey me. Rather than be conquered by my flesh, my negative emotions, and my wrong attitudes, I am asking You to help me rise up to take authority over my soul and clean up the mess that has been made inside my head. I know that with Your help, my whole perspective can change!

I pray this in Jesus' name!

MY CONFESSION FOR TODAY

I confess that it is time for me to rise up and take charge of the situation in my soul! It is my soul, so I am responsible for what happens there. Even if others did wrong to me, I choose to forgive, forget, and permanently walk free. Right now it doesn't matter who is right or wrong. What matters is that I uproot the tree of bitterness before it produces any more deadly fruit in my life. So by faith, I am reaching out to grab hold of the base of that ugly growth. I am gripping it tightly and pulling with all my might to rip those roots right out of my heart! Those old thoughts no longer have a right to operate inside me. They are now dead issues — cast once and for all into the sea where they can't hound me anymore!

I declare this by faith in Jesus' name!

QUESTIONS FOR YOU TO CONSIDER

1. Do you have a wrong attitude that has been deeply rooted in your soul for a long time?
2. If the answer is yes, are you ready and willing to rip that foul growth out of your soul today with the power of your spoken, faith-filled words and by your authority in the name of Jesus?
3. There will be no accidental deliverance from these attitudes, so what steps do you plan to take to see that your heart is fully liberated once and for all?

DECEMBER 30

Spiritual Rest

Come unto me, all ye that labour and are heavy laden,
and I will give you rest.
— Matthew 11:28

I am convinced that one reason the devil has access to people's emotions is that they keep flying through life without taking time to get renewed in the Presence of the Lord. They ignore their need to sit, to rest, and to wait upon the Lord. As a result, their perception of things around them gets blurred. Doing too much at too fast of a pace has worn them down, causing them to lose their focus and affecting their ability to see things the way they really are.

I know exactly what it's like to move at such a fast pace — to get the adrenaline flowing and then keep it flowing like a river for days at a time. When you're moving that fast, it's difficult to stop when you finally try to sit down and rest because your adrenaline is still racing. You may be sitting down physically, but you're still running emotionally!

There's a big problem with moving so fast. The demands of our schedule — job, family, church, friendships, and so forth — start piling up, each overlaying the other as we race from place to place. When this happens, we start becoming ineffective in every area of life. We're just trying to do too much, too fast. Eventually our busyness leads to a breakdown of everything. The body suffers. The mind suffers. The work suffers because we're too tired to perform at 100 percent and therefore can't do our job to our full potential. This then results in our having to battle feelings of condemnation for not doing a better job!

Let's face it — it's extremely difficult to do everything simultaneously. You may be able to swing it for a while, but in time, you'll start missing important details, forgetting what you said, missing appointments, messing up in your finances, and even getting emotional over unemotional issues because you've pushed yourself beyond your limit. If this is you, *slow down* and set aside some time to spend with the Lord.

I have to admit that sometimes I also fall into the trap of doing too many things too fast. At times, I feel like a locomotive that is racing down the track! It's not that I want to move so fast, but to get it all done correctly, I have to keep moving and stay on schedule. If I delay in one area, it throws everything else off schedule and creates a schedule crisis for many others in the ministry. For everyone else to do their jobs effectively, it means I must stay on schedule and keep on track every day of my life.

In moments when I feel overwhelmed, I hear Jesus speak to my spirit and say, "Come unto me, all ye that labour and are heavy laden, and I will give you rest" (Matthew 11:28). Notice that Jesus begins this verse, "Come unto me...." This is from the Greek word *deute*, and it is a greeting that literally means, *"Come — come now! I am inviting you to come!"* In Greek, it has the feeling of an exclamation, which lets us know that Jesus joyfully welcomes us to come to Him.

Jesus then says, "Come unto me, all ye that labour...." This implies that Jesus' invitation to come to Him is a special invitation directed to those who "labour." The word "labour" in Greek is from the word *kopiao*, which describes *a person who has become completely exhausted due to nonstop, continuous work.* This is obviously a person who has a lot of responsibility and is doing his best to do it all in a professional and excellent fashion. In order to do everything that is on his plate, this person is required to work hard all the time. That's why Jesus beckons this person to come to Him!

And Jesus doesn't beckon only the hard worker; He also calls out to those who are "heavy laden." These words are from the word *phortidzo,* depicting *a person who is carrying a very heavy load on his back.* Perhaps this load is his job, his family, his financial situation, or some personal burden. Regardless of what it is, Jesus pleads for the "heavy laden" person to come to Him!

To anyone who responds to this invitation and comes to Jesus, He promises that He will give them "rest." The word "rest" is the Greek word *anapauo,* the word that means *to refresh, to rejuvenate, to reinvigorate,* or *to revitalize.* You see, the Lord wants to refresh us so we can keep doing what He has called us to do. He wants us to be refilled so we can remain effective.

The only way we can remain continually effective is by making sure we spend time with the Lord. But in order to truly enter His Presence so we can hear the voice of the Holy Spirit, we must first quiet ourselves by getting away from the commotion of life and finding a quiet place to worship, pray, and read the Word. That's the only way we can quiet our soul enough to be able to hear God's voice speaking to our inner man. To think that we are going to run into the Lord's Presence and get everything we need in the space of five minutes just isn't realistic. *We must schedule time to be alone with God.*

Don't just run in and run out of the Lord's Presence. Plan to settle down and stay there long enough to get everything you need to carry on! Once you've stopped long enough to really rest in His Presence, you're finally in a position where you can start receiving from Him. Don't move too fast. Don't leave until you receive the refreshing you need. Just hang around in God's Presence as long as you possibly can! Tarry there awhile, and let the Holy Spirit give you peace, joy, strength, and direction.

Learn to rest in God's Presence. You see, there is a quiet place in Him, a place of refreshing, where you will find comfort, peace, and protection — every time. This is why Jesus said, "Come unto me, all ye that labour and are heavy laden, and I will give you rest." Notice that Jesus doesn't say He will come to *you.* He says that *you* must choose to go to *Him*! But if you will make the deliberate choice to wait upon the Lord, Jesus promises that you *will* find this promised rest!

This is your key to remaining steadfast and strong enough to keep on schedule and to stay on track with everything you need to do. And I promise you — if you will wait long enough in His Presence, He *will* speak to your heart to let you know if all your activities are ordained of Him or if there are some obligations or activities you need to eliminate.

Spending time with the Lord is not an option — it is the answer! So come into the Presence of God and allow Him to refresh you. As you do, the Holy Spirit will release His resurrection power and you will be quickened in your physical body. You will be strengthened, refreshed, recharged, and supernaturally empowered by God so you can get back out there with a fresh perspective and new energy to finish what you have started!

MY PRAYER FOR TODAY

Lord, I know that You have been calling out to me, beckoning me to spend time with You. But I've been so busy that I haven't made time in my schedule to come to You. Today I am making the choice to put everything else aside and to make my time with You the top priority in my day. I need Your strength; I need Your fellowship; I need Your tender touch; and I need to hear Your voice. Spirit of God, my schedule is very full, and I need special strength to make it through this busy time. So I am coming to You today to be refreshed so I can carry on!

I pray this in Jesus' name!

MY CONFESSION FOR TODAY

I confess that the only way I can remain continually effective is to spend time with the Lord. I will therefore quiet myself from the commotion of life and get into the Presence of Jesus. I will settle down and plan to stay there long enough to get everything I need from Him. Staying in His Presence is not an option! It is my key to remaining steadfast and strong enough to keep on schedule and to stay on track with everything I need to do. The Holy Spirit will release His resurrection power in me, and I will be strengthened, refreshed, recharged, and empowered by God. Then I can get back out there with a fresh perspective and new energy to finish what I've started!

I declare this by faith in Jesus' name!

QUESTIONS FOR YOU TO CONSIDER

1. When do you regularly spend time with the Lord? Is your time with Him more important to you than all the other things that you're scheduled to accomplish? If your time with Him really is that important, is there a reason you haven't planned it into your schedule?

2. When you spend time with the Lord, how long do you usually stay in His Presence? What do you do when you are there with Him? Do you read your Bible, pray, sing songs of worship?

3. How can you rework your schedule to make sure your time with God is the top priority? Why don't you look at your calendar and see what you can move around in order to accommodate your time with Jesus?

The only way we can remain continually effective is by making sure we spend time with the Lord. But in order to truly enter His Presence so we can hear the voice of the Holy Spirit, we must first quiet ourselves by getting away from the commotion of life and finding a quiet place to worship, pray, and read the Word. That's the only way we can quiet our soul enough to be able to hear God's voice speaking to our inner man. To think that we are going to run into the Lord's Presence and get everything we need in the space of five minutes just isn't realistic. *We must schedule time to be alone with God.*

DECEMBER 31

❧

A Special Message About Living in the Last Days

For God hath not given us the spirit of fear;
but of power, and of love, and of a sound mind.
— 2 Timothy 1:7

This is the greatest hour for the Church of Jesus Christ. A massive harvest is coming into the Church all over the world. Statistics prove that right now more people are coming to Jesus worldwide than at any other point in history. The Spirit of God is swinging the Gospel sickle, and millions upon millions of souls are being swept into the Kingdom of God. Praise the Lord! This is one of the greatest signs in evidence today that we are near to the coming of Jesus.

But right in the midst of all this, events have occurred throughout the earth that have shaken the nations of the world and filled men's hearts with fear. I am convinced that part of this worldwide assault has been the devil's attempt to put believers in fear so they will retreat from this worldwide Gospel advance. Although we need to be wise and do what we can to protect ourselves in times such as these, we do *not* need to react in fear. Fear is *never* the answer, for it results in blurred thinking and bad decisions.

God's Word promises us a sound mind *if* we will claim it. When Timothy was facing hard times, Paul told him, "For God hath not given us the spirit of fear; but of power, and of love, and of a sound mind" (2 Timothy 1:7).

This verse says that God has given us a "sound mind." This comes from the Greek word *sophroneo*, and it is a compound of the words *sozo* and *phroneo*. The word *sozo* is the Greek word for *salvation*. It means *deliverance, protection*, and *soundness*. The word *phroneo* is the root for the word *mind*. When these two words are put together as in this verse, the new word is translated *sound mind*. The idea presented by the word *sophroneo* is *a mind that is saved and protected* or *a mind that is sound*. It is just the opposite of a mind given to fear, panic, or unfounded and unreasonable thinking. This word describes a mind that is thinking correctly!

Because God has given us a "sound mind," we can think correctly about how to live in these last days — a time that Second Timothy 3:1 predicts will be "perilous." The word "perilous" in that verse is the Greek word *chalepos*, and it literally means *something that is difficult, dangerous, or filled with risk*. This is a prophetic warning to let us know that those who live in the very last of the last days will be confronted with a strange period of time like mankind has never seen before. It will be a time filled with difficulty, danger, and risk.

In this last *Sparkling Gem* of the year, I want to give you what Denise and I believe is a sensible approach to living in these last days. To ensure that we are doing all we can to remain in the blessings of God, these are the steps my wife and I apply to our own lives. These are the Holy Spirit's orders to Denise and me, and now I am passing them on to you as they've been given to us.

Living in the last days requires that we have a greater sensitivity to the Spirit of God. Romans 8:14 declares that one of the privileges of being a son of God is that the Spirit of God leads us. The word "led" is the Greek word *ago*. It is the picture of *someone extending his hand to you so he can gently lead you.*

In these last days, we must be led by the Holy Spirit. However, the Holy Spirit will lead us only if we give Him this right. Oh, how many times the Spirit of God has wanted to be our Leader, but we went our own way and ultimately suffered the consequences! He knew exactly how to lead us past every attack. He knew how to avoid each strategy of the devil.

Jesus said that the Holy Spirit would "...shew you things to come" (John 16:13). The word "shew" is the Greek word *odegeo* and is the word for *a guide who shows a traveler the safest course through an unknown country.* This means the Holy Spirit is our Guide. He knows the way we should go. He understands how to avoid every trap and obstacle along the way. When we are going into an area we've never been before, the Holy Spirit wants to show us how to take the safest route. *He knows exactly how to get us safely to our future point of destination.*

The Holy Spirit often stopped Jesus from going to certain regions because the Jews were waiting to trap Him. To avoid these traps, the Holy Spirit would *guide* Jesus another way. The Spirit also warned Paul not to go to certain places for the same reason. Also in the book of Acts, the Holy Spirit warned the Early Church *in advance* about persecution, famine, and other trials.

The Holy Spirit knows the future and wants to enlighten us with all the information we need in every situation. *This is part of His ministry to you and me.*

If the Holy Spirit speaks to you and tells you to do something specific, then obey Him! Do you remember when the death angel passed through Egypt and took the firstborn of all the Egyptians? The reason Israel was unaffected was that the Israelites obeyed the instructions God gave them to put blood on the doorposts of their houses. They brushed that lamb's blood on the doors of their homes just as God had ordered. Later when the death angel came, he passed by every home where he saw blood on the doorposts. In the end, not one of the Israelites was touched!

But what if Israel had disregarded God's instructions and tried to protect themselves another way? Would their efforts have worked? Of course not. God told them how to be protected. All they had to do was obey. If they did what God told them, they were guaranteed protection and blessing. They were untouched because they walked in obedience. Weeping, crying, and mourning were heard in Egypt, but not in the land of Goshen where the children of Israel lived. *They found protection in their obedience to the Word of God.*

As we obey the Word of God and listen to the Holy Spirit's leading, we will have wisdom to know every step we need to take in the days ahead. All we have to do is obey God's instructions, and He guarantees us blessing and provision even in difficult times. But if we try to take another approach, there is no guarantee for us to claim. *We must do what God says if we want to be assured of His divine blessing and protection.*

As a spiritual leader and friend, I want to encourage you to increase your level of faith, especially if you are facing challenging times. Stand on the Word of God; exercise your faith; listen to the Holy Spirit; and obey what He tells you to do. As you do these things, God's supernatural blessings will kick into action, and you will soon find a river of supernatural provision flowing to you.

There is no doubt that we are living in some of the most challenging days the world has ever seen. But you can face these times victoriously because God has given you a sound mind; He has given you the promises of His Word; and He has given you the leadership of His Spirit. Never has there been a more crucial time for you to operate in faith and not fear and to believe for a mighty move of God to take place on this earth!

MY PRAYER FOR TODAY

Lord, as an end-time believer, I need to be filled with faith and not with fear. Help me to fill my heart with Your Word, to stand on Your promises, to follow the leading of the Holy Spirit, and to exercise my faith more than ever before! I know that fear has blurred my thinking in times past, but it will NOT have any place in my life from this day forward! Instead, I release my faith and confidently expect to be a partaker in the last and greatest harvest of souls ever to be reaped for the Kingdom of God! Holy Spirit, help me rise to the occasion as I become an instrument God can use in these last days.

I pray this in Jesus' name!

MY CONFESSION FOR TODAY

I confess that I am filled with faith and not fear, and that I am excited to live in these last days. God has chosen for me to live in some of the most challenging days the world has ever seen, but I will face these times victoriously. He has given me a sound mind, the promises of His Word, and the leadership of His Spirit. Therefore, I will NOT retreat in fear or panic; instead, I am believing to be a part of the mightiest harvest of souls that history has ever seen!

I declare this by faith in Jesus' name!

QUESTIONS FOR YOU TO CONSIDER

1. Do you listen to the Holy Spirit when He nudges your heart and gives you direction?
2. As the calendar turns and the New Year begins, what instructions has the Holy Spirit already given you regarding the next twelve months?
3. Are you spending time with the Lord so He can speak to your heart? What changes do you need to make in your life so you can spend more quality time with the Lord during the next year?

As we obey the Word of God and listen to the Holy Spirit's leading, we will have wisdom to know every step we need to take in the days ahead. All we have to do is obey God's instructions, and He guarantees us blessing and provision even in difficult times. But if we try to take another approach, there is no guarantee for us to claim. *We must do what God says if we want to be assured of His divine blessing and protection.*

INDEX OF GREEK WORDS USED IN

SPARKLING GEMS FROM THE GREEK

English Index

bound (*desantes*) 243
bow (*gonupeteo*) 263
bow (*kampto*) 980
bowels (*splagchnos*) 772
brass (*chalkos*) 668
brethren (*adelphos*) 35, 36
brightness (*epiphaneia*) 914
bringing into captivity
   (*aichmalotidzo*) 629
broken in pieces (*suntribo*) 181
brother (*adelphos*) 35, 36
brotherly love (*philadelphia*) 525, 953
bruise (*suntribo*) 181
buffet (*kolaphidzo*) 237, 853
burden (*baros*) 354, 356
burden (*phortion*) 356
burn (*katakaino*) 476
business (*spoudadzo*) 956
buy (*agoradzo*) 344
by (*en*) 130, 131

C

call (*proskaleo*) 939
came in privily (*pareisago*) 814
care (*melei*) 325
careful (*merimnao*) 706
cares (*merimna*) 325, 706
cares of this life 706
carnal (*sarkos*) 107
cast (*ballo*) 257, 414
cast (*ekballo*) 390
cast (*epiripto*) 325
cast away (*apoballo*) 432, 433
cast out (*ekballo*) 475, 476
castaway (*adokimos*) 825
casting lots 271
caught (*sunarpadzo*) 530
change (*metamorphoo*) 644
charge (*parangelo*) 893
chaste (*agnos*) 745
chasten (*paideia*) 834
children (*tekna*) 367
choke (*sumpnigo*) 706

chosen (*eklego*) 384
cleave (*kollao*) 951
closet (*tameion*) 571
clothed 286
cloud (*nephos*) 98
co-laborers (*sunergos*) 565
come (*parousia*) 903, 914
come behind (*hustereo*) 306
come unto me (*deute*) 993
comforter (*paraklete*) 464
comfortless (*orphanos*) 53, 54
coming (*parousia*) 903, 914
command (*parangello*) 859
commit 518
commit (*paradidomi*) 234
commit (*paratithimi*) 163
common hall 262
communion (*koinonia*) 111, 112
compassed about (*peikeimenai*) 45, 46, 98
compassion (*eleao*) 392, 393
compassion (*splagchnos*) 772
compassion (*sumpathos*) 767, 777
compel (*aggareuo*) 266
comprehend (*katalambano*) 371
condemnation (*krima*) 551
condescend (*sunapago*) 968
confess (*ekzomologeo*) 725
confess (*exomologeo*) 981
confession (*homologia*) 314
confidence (*parresia*) 155, 156, 373, 433
confirm (*bebaioo*) 306
confound (*kataishuno*) 100, 382, 666
confound (*suncheo*) 478
confusion (*akatastasia*) 66
conqueror (*nikos*) 38
consider (*katanoeo*) 311, 443
consume (*anairo*) 913
conversation (*anastrophe*) 744
corrupt communication (*phaulos*) 453
counselor (*bouleutes*) 276
count not (*logidzomai*) 626
course (*aiona*) 119
course (*dromos*) 303
courteous (*tapeinophron*) 773

crave (*aiteo*) 277
creature (*ktisis*) 599, 868
crown (*stephanos*) 189, 263, 632
crucify (*staurao*) 269
cry (*epiphoneo*) 257
cry (*kradzo*) 587
curse (*kataraomai*) 962
cut off (*apokopto*) 223
cymbal (*kumbalon*) 669

D

dark (*skotos*) 273
dead (*nekros*) 286, 426
dead with him (*sunapothnesko*) 574
deadly (*thanasimos*) 484
death (*thanatos*) 484, 790, 867
deaths (*thanatoi*) 790
debate (*eris*) 454
deceive (*planao*) 555
decently (*euschemonos*) 173
decently and in order 172
deeds (*erga*) 631
deeds (*praksis*) 476
deep (*bathus*) 799
defile (*miaini*) 871
deliver (*paradidomi*) 244
deliver (*ruomai*) 450
delivered (*harpadzo*) 41
demonstration (*apodeiknumi*) 342
depart (*analusai*) 690
depart (*aphistimi*) 855
depth (*bathos*) 868
desire (*epithumia*) 690
desire (*orego*) 358, 832
desire (*thelema*) 490
desirous (*thelo*) 251
despair (*exaporeomai*) 424
despise (*exoutheneo*) 80
destroy (*apollumi*) 548
destroy (*katargeo*) 914
destroy (*luo*) 84, 85
devices (*neomata*) 128, 129, 629
devil (*diabalos*) 604, 839, 942

devilish (*daimoniodes*) 418, 419
devils (*daimonion*) 475
devour (*pino*) 653
diligently seek (*ekzeteo*) 102
disease (*kakos*) 934
disease (*nosos*) 487
disorderly (*atakeo*) 859
dissimulation (*anupokritos*) 949
dissolve (*luo*) 916
distributing (*koinoneo*) 958
do (*poieo*) 778
do (*prasso*) 514, 520
do good (*agathoergeo*) 898
doer (*poietes*) 27, 28
dog (*kunun*) 412
doing good (*euergeteo*) 536
door (*thura*) 295, 862
double-tongued (*dilogos*) 693, 694
doubt (*diakrinomai*) 447
draw back (*hupostello*) 578
drink (*pino*) 484
drop (*thrombos*) 202
drunkenness (*methe*) 511, 516
dwell (*enoikeo*) 61
dwell (*sunoikeo*) 757

E

ear (*otarion*) 223
earnestly (*ektenes*) 202
earth (*ges*) 274
earthen vessel (*ostrakinos*) 89, 90
earthly (*epigeios*) 418
earthquake (*seimos*) 285
easily 678
easy (*chrestos*) 543
effectual (*energeo*) 713, 862
elders (*presbuteros*) 939
elements (*stoicheion*) 916
emulation (*zelos*) 504, 515
endure (*anechomai*) 642
endure (*hupomeno*) 147, 685
endure hardness (*sunkakopatheo*)
  884, 885

G

gall 268
garden (*kepos*) 280
garment (*chiton*) 57
garment (*stole*) 286
gathering together (*episunagoge*) 904
gazingstock (*theatron*) 400, 401
gentle (*epios*) 317
gentleness (*chrestotes*) 534
gird up the loins (*anadzonnumi*) 445
give (*aponemo*) 760, 763
give (*didontos*) 738
give thanks (*eucharisteo*) 17
given (*dioko*) 960
glorify (*doxadzo*) 569
glory (*egkauchaomai*) 641
God (*theos*) 298
godliness (*eusebeia*) 874
good (*agathos*) 536, 778, 951
good (*eu*) 554
good (*kalos*) 898, 901
good cheer (*tharseo*) 792
goodness (*agathusune*) 536
gorgeous robe (*esthes lampros*) 254
gossip (*psithurismos*) 453, 457
grace (*charis*) 528, 848, 849
grain (*kokkos*) 987
gravity (*semnotes*) 367
great (*mega*) 49, 285, 862
great company (*polus ochlos*) 344
great earthquake 285
great multitude (*ochlos polus*) 208
great noise (*hroidzedon*) 916
great price (*poluteles*) 754
grieve (*lupete*) 9
grievous (*lupe*) 834
guile (*dolos*) 778

H

handle me (*psilaphao*) 296
harden (*skleruno*) 698
hate (*echthra*) 502, 503
hate (*miseo*) 57, 631
hatred (*echthra*) 515
heal (*iaomai*) 226, 261
heal (*kalos*) 487
heal (*therapeuo*) 881
heard (*akouo*) 478
hearers only (*akroates*) 13
heart (*kardia*) 751
heathen (*ethnos*) 808
heavy laden (*phortidzo*) 542, 994
height (*hupsuma*) 868
heirs together (*sunekleronomos*) 764
helmet (*perkephalaia*) 562, 563
helpeth (*sunantilambetai*) 565
herald (*kerux*) 469
heresies (*hairesis*) 508, 516
hewn (*laxeuo*) 281
hidden (*kruptos*) 751
high-minded (*hupsilophroneo*) 893
high things (*ta hupsela*) 968
highwaymen (*lestes*) 806
hinder (*egkopto*) 31, 32, 765, 783
hold fast (*katecho*) 170, 171
holy (*hagios*) 412
honor (*timao*) 760
honorable (*euschemon*) 276
hope (*elpidzo*) 251, 685
hospitable (*philoxenos*) 525
hospitality (*philoxenia*) 960
house (*oikos*) 619
humbled (*tapeinao*) 977
hunger (*limos*) 822
hurt (*adikeo*) 482
hurt (*blapto*) 484
husbandman (*georgos*) 890

I

I am (*ego eimi*) 219, 220
I follow after (*dioko*) 730
I put thee in remembrance
   (*anamimnesko*) 6
idle tale (*leros*) 287, 288
idolatry (*eidololatria*) 498, 514

M

made himself of no reputation (*kenos*) 974
made sure (*sphragidzo*) 282
making request (*deisis*) 845
mammon 436
man (*tis*) 887
manifest (*phaneros*) 493
many (*polus*) 882, 982
many others 882
mark (*skopos*) 691
marveled greatly (*thaumadzo*) 244,
   246, 479
master (*didaskalos*) 217
meek (*praus*) 754
meek and quiet spirit 754
meekness (*prautes*) 539, 540
melt (*luo*) 916
men (*andres*) 928
men of war (*strateuma*) 254
merry (*euthumeo*) 937
messenger (*angelos*) 852
might (*ischuos*) 349
mighty (*dunatoi*) 100
mind (*nous*) 623
mind (*phroneo*) 968
mine own countrymen (*genos*) 808
minister (*diakoneo*) 880
minister (*huperetas*) 421, 589, 590, 635
ministering to the saints 613
ministry (*diakonos*) 613, 614
miracle (*semeion*) 252
mock (*empaidzo*) 238, 239, 254, 264
mock (*mukteridzo*) 556
more than conquerors (*hupernikos*) 37, 38
mouth (*stomos*) 913
much more abound (*huperperisseo*) 545
multitude (*plethos*) 478
murder 510
must be (*dei*) 890
mustard (*sinapi*) 987
myrrh 279

N

name (*onomos*) 940
napkin (*soudarion*) 289
nations (*ethnos*) 466
necessity (*chreia*) 958
new (*kainos*) 281, 599
Nicanor 632
Nicolaitans (*nikolaos*) 631
Nicolas 633
nigh (*aggus*) 281
noble (*eugenes*) 380
nothing (*meden*) 707
novice (*neophutos*) 550

O

obedient (*hupakouo*) 978
obey (*hupakouo*) 991
obey not (*apeitho*) 744
obtain (*katalambano*) 187, 406, 407
of God (*para theou*) 737
offense (*skandalon*) 327
officer (*huperetas*) 207
often (*pollakis*) 802, 819, 822
old wives (*grauodes*) 837
one (*hen*) 846
one mind (*homophron*) 767
one who loves mankind (*philanthropia*) 525
one who loves money (*philarguros*) 525
one who loves strangers (*philoxenia*) 525
one who speaks falsehoods (*pseudologos*) 649
open (*anakalupto*) 644
open (*anoigo*) 862
openly (*parresia*) 75, 592
oppose (*antikeimai*) 907
order (*taksis*) 173
out of season (*akairos*) 553, 554
out of whom went (*exerchomai*) 881
outer darkness 390
over (*epi*) 91
overcome (*nikos*) 371, 792

P

painfulness (*mochthos*) 817

Parmenas (*para meno*) 632

partaker (*koinonia*) 582

partners (*koinonia*) 111, 112

partnership (*sudzao*) 574

pass away (*parerchomai*) 916

passeth (*huperecho*) 322

patience (*hupomeno*) 146, 147, 560, 578, 579, 641

patience (*makrothumia*) 533

patient (*aneksikakos*) 438

peace (*eirene*) 529, 531, 848

pearl (*margarites*) 415

pence (*denarius*) 610

perdition (*apoleia*) 578, 907

perfect (*teleo*) 730, 856

perilous (*chalepos*) 144, 996

perils (*kindunos*) 803, 805, 806 808, 811, 812, 813

perplex (*aporeo*) 286

persecution (*dioko*) 641

persuade (*peitho*) 867

Pharisee 277

Philip 632

philosophy (*philosophia*) 525

pilgrims (*parepidemos*) 946

pitiful (*eusplagchnos*) 771, 772

place (*topos*) 603, 840

plaiting of hair (*emploke*) 748

planted (*phuteuo*) 991

platted (*empleko*) 47, 263

plucked up by the root (*ekridzoo*) 990

poet (*poietes*) 28, 599

possible (*dunata*) 780

power (*dunamis*) 153, 868, 908, 927

power (*exousia*) 398, 598

power (*kratos*) 347, 348, 349, 540

pray (*proseuchomai*) 567, 939

prayer (*deisis*) 845

prayer (*proseuche*) 334, 335, 336, 709, 934, 935

preach (*kerusso*) 469, 470

preferring (*proegeomai*) 953

preparation (*etoimasin*) 158, 159

present (*paristimi*) 864, 865

press toward (*epekteinomai*) 691

pressed out of measure (*kath huperbole*) 423

principalities (*archai*) 398, 868

prison (*plulake*) 789

prize (*brabeion*) 691

Prochorus (*pro chorus*) 632

profession (*homologia*) 313, 314

profitable (*ophelimos*) 300

prove (*dokimadzo*) 696

prove (*peiradzo*) 345, 929

provoke (*paraxusmos*) 443

provoke (*paroxsuno*) 678

puffed up (*phusio*) 675

pull (*harpadzo*) 41, 42

put into (*ballo*) 200

put it upon (*epitithimi*) 263

put on (*enduo*) 533

put on him a scarlet robe (*chlamuda kokkinen*) 263

putting on of apparel 748

Q

quake (*seiso*) 274

quench (*sbennumi*) 96, 659

quicken (*zoopoieo*) 309

quicksand (*syrtis*) 530

quiet (*hisuchios*) 754

R

rabbi 278

race (*stadion*) 186

raise (*egeiro*) 940

ready to distribute (*eumetadotos*) 898

reap 556

reasonable service (*latreuo*) 499

rebuke (*epitimao*) 841

receive (*proslambano*) 720

reckon (*logidzomai*) 426

reckon (*sunairei logon meta*) 184

recompense (*apodidomi*) 970

recompense of reward (*misthapodosia*) 82, 155

redeem (*exagoridzo*) 121, 122

redemption (*lutroo*) 63, 64

refrain (*pauo*) 777

refresh (*sunanapauomai*) 452

refuse (*paraiteomai*) 404, 837

reign with him (*sumbasileuo*) 575

rejoice (*chairo*) 682, 965

rejoiceth not (*ou chairei*) 682

release 256

relief (*diakonos*) 613

remembrance (*mneia*) 175

render (*apodidomi*) 775

rent (*schidzo*) 275

reproach (*oneidismos*) 401

reprove (*elegcho*) 104, 430

request (*aiteo*) 178

request (*aitima*) 711

resist (*anthistemi*) 942

resist (*antitasso*) 437

rest (*anapauo*) 542, 994

rest (*anesis*) 142

reveal (*apokalupto*) 71, 907, 911

revelation (*apokalupsis*) 39, 851

revellings (*komoi*) 512, 516

richly (*plousios*) 43, 44, 624, 892, 893, 898

robber (*lestes*) 805, 806

rocks (*lithos*) 275

rocks (*petra*) 275

root (*ridzo*) 376, 732

rule (*brabeuo*) 2, 624

ruler (*archon*) 278

rulers of the darkness of this world (*kosmokrateros*) 398, 399

ruleth (*proistimi*) 619

run (*trecho*) 406

S

sat (*kathemai*) 285, 344

save (*sodzo*) 15, 73, 940

saw (*blepo*) 289

saw (*horao*) 251, 696

saw (*theaomai*) 344

say (*lego*) 988

scarlet (*kokkinos*) 263

scoffer (*empaidzo*) 904

scorpion 482

scourge (*phragello*) 259

seal (*sphragidzo*) 378

sedition (*dichostasia*) 507, 515

sedition (*stasis*) 256

see (*horao*) 252

see (*theaomai*) 289, 292

seed (*sperma*) 519

seek (*zelos*) 778

seek (*zeteo*) 678

sensual (*psuchikos*) 418

sentence (*apokrima*) 424

sentence (*krino*) 33, 34

serpent (*ophis*) 481, 661

servant (*diakonos*) 612, 613

servant (*doulos*) 59, 924, 975

serve (*doulos*) 436, 956

serve (*latreuo*) 498, 499

service (*diakonia*) 451

set him at nought (*exoutheneo*) 254

shake (*saleuo*) 622

shake (*seio*) 286

shall be able (*dunamai*) 868

shed abroad (*ekcheo*) 672

shew (*deigmatidzo*) 592

shield (*thureos*) 364

shine (*astrapto*) 286

shod (*hupodeomai*) 158

shook it off (*apotinasso*) 441

shortly 181

show (*apodeiknumi*) 908

show (*odegeo*) 646, 997

shut (*kleio*) 295, 772

sick (*arroustos*) 486, 487

sick (*astheneo*) 487, 938, 940

sick (*kakos*) 934

sick (*kamno*) 940

sick folk (*arroustos*) 487

sign (*semeion*) 472, 559, 908
signal (*sussemon*) 213
sin (*anomia*) 906
sing psalms (*psallo*) 937
sinneth 518
slothful (*nothros*) 133
slothful (*okneros*) 387, 389, 955
smote (*dero*) 239
smote (*epaio*) 223
so easily beset us (*euperistatos*) 51
soberly (*sophroneo*) 149, 607
soon (*tachus*) 622
soon shaken 622, 623
soul (*psyche*) 946
sound mind (*sophroneo*) 73, 996
sounding (*echo*) 668
sounding brass 668
sow (*speiro*) 556
speak (*lalouton*) 478
spikenard (*nardos*) 609
spirit (*pneuma*) 298, 299, 913
spoil (*apekduomai*) 592
spokesman (*kerux*) 469, 470
spot (*spilos*) 58
springing up (*phuoo*) 654
spue (*emeo*) 135
stand (*istemi*) 409, 553
stave (*zhulos*) 211
steadfast (*edraios*) 151, 167
Stephen (*stephanos*) 632
steward (*epitropos*) 882
stood (*paraginomai*) 926
stood (*paristemi*) 927
stood by (*epistemi*) 286
stooping down (*parakupto*) 289, 292
straight betwixt two (*sunecho*) 690
stranger (*paroikos*) 945
strength (*dunamis*) 856
strengthen (*endunamoo*) 927
strengthen (*enischuo*) 205
strife (*eritheia*) 66, 418, 454, 506,
    515, 722
strip (*ekduo*) 263
stripes (*molopsi*) 261

stripes (*plege*) 788, 789
strive (*athlesis*) 189, 887
strive (*machomai*) 317
strive together (*sunagonidzomai*) 450
strong (*endunamao*) 22, 153, 346, 347
stronghold (*ochuroma*) 918
struck (*paio*) 239
subjection (*doulagogeo*) 826
subjection (*hupotasso*) 332, 333, 740
substance (*huparchontos*) 880
suddenly (*tachus*) 581
suffer (*pascho*) 601
suffered them not (*ouk eiasen*) 729
suffereth long (*makrothumia*) 671
suffering (*kakopatheo*) 934
sufficient (*arkeo*) 856
supplication (*deisis*) 710
supply (*epichoregeo*) 4
sweat (*idros*) 202
swellings (*phusiosis*) 454
swift (*tachus*) 351
swine (*choipos*) 415
sword (*machaira*) 77, 211
sycamine (*sukaminos*) 984

T

take (*airo*) 543
take (*analambano*) 931
take heed (*blepo*) 409
take heed (*epecho*) 30
taken captive (*zoogreo*) 703
tame (*damadzo*) 459, 460
temperance (*enkrateia*) 540
tempest (*cheimadzoamai*) 530
tempestuous wind (*tuphonikos*) 530
temple (*naos*) 116, 907
tempt (*peiradzo*) 695
temptation (*peirasmos*) 617
testimony (*maturios*) 306
thanksgiving (*eucharistia*) 710
there arose (*ginomai*) 87
there was (*ginomai*) 273
they shall (*echo*) 487

they were instant (*epikeima*) 257
thief (*klepto*) 547
things present (*enistemi*) 868
things to come (*mello*) 868
think (*dokeo*) 409
think (*logidzomai*) 679
think of himself more highly
   (*huperphroneo*) 607
thirst (*dipsos*) 822
thorn (*skolops*) 852, 853
thoroughly furnished (*exartidzo*) 657
thought (*merimnao*) 706
time (*eukairos*) 972
time to come (*mello*) 901
Timon 632
tinkling (*alalazon*) 669
tinkling cymbal 669, 674
to call (*kaleo*) 26
to give (*didomi*) 39, 412
to kiss (*philema*) 123
to place (*tithimi*) 114
to the ground (*chamai*) 220
token (*sussemon*) 213
took upon himself (*lambano*) 975
torch (*phanos*) 210
touch (*aptomai*) 226
tradition (*paradidomi*) 859
tread (*pateo*) 482
treasure (*thesauros*) 89, 90
trespass (*hamartano*) 841
tribulation (*thlipsis*) 641, 642, 792
triumph (*triambeuo*) 75, 592
trouble (*thlipsis*) 142, 423
trouble you (*enochleo*) 655, 870
troubled (*throeo*) 623
trust (*elpidzo*) 893
tumults (*akatastasia*) 454
turned aside (*ektrepo*) 165, 166
two-edged (*distomos*) 109
two-edged sword 109

U

uncertain (*adelotes*) 893

uncleanness (*akatharsia*) 496, 514
understanding (*nous*) 322
unknown 479
unloose (*luo*) 85
unprofitable (*achreios*) 387, 390
unruly (*akatastatos*) 460
unseemly (*aschemoneo*) 676
unto (*mechri*) 978
unto me (*moi*) 862
upbraideth not (*oneididzo*) 738
upon (*epi*) 553

V

vainglory (*kenodoxia*) 722
variance (*eris*) 503, 515
vaunteth (*perpereuomai*) 674
vehemently (*eutonus*) 252, 253
very (*sphodra*) 285
very costly (*polutimos*) 609
vessel (*skeuos*) 760
vigilant (*gregoreo*) 652
vile (*raparian*) 20
vinegar (*oxsus*) 679
viper (*echidna*) 441

W

wait (*prosdechomai*) 276
walk (*peripateo*) 93, 119, 489, 490, 859
war (*strateuomai*) 946
warfare (*stratos*) 106, 107
was made (*ginomai*) 975
watch (*coustodia*) 282
watch (*tereo*) 271
watchings (*agrupvia*) 819
watchings often 819
waters (*potamos*) 803
waver (*aklines*) 337
we have (*echomen*) 89, 90
we shall also live with him (*sudzao*) 574
weak (*asthene*) 100
weaker (*asthenes*) 760
weakness (*astheneo*) 856

weapons (*hoplos*) 106, 210
wear (*perithesis*) 748
weary (*egkakao*) 718
weep (*klaio*) 965
weeping 292
weeping and gnashing of teeth 390, 391
weight (*ogkos*) 114
well (*kalos*) 619
well pleased (*eudokeo*) 771
went backward (*aperchomai*) 220
went forth 288
what (*ti*) 566
whatsoever (*ean*) 556
when they had taken up (*boetheia*) 530
wherein in time past 119
whisperings (*psithurismos*) 453, 454, 457
whole armor (*panoplia*) 319
whole band of soldiers (*spira*) 262
wicked (*okneros*) 387, 389, 955
wicked and slothful (*okneros*) 387, 389
wickedness (*poneros*) 399
wilderness (*eremia*) 811
wiles (*methodos*) 628, 629
will (*thelema*) 451
willing (*thelo*) 257
willing to communicate (*koinonikos*) 898
wind (*lalaipsi*) 87
wisdom (*sophias*) 39, 735
wise (*pronimos*) 661
wise (*sophos*) 342, 382, 596, 666
wise as serpents 661
witchcraft (*pharmakeia*) 499, 501, 515
with (*meta*) 965
with all (*en pase*) 908
with all prayer (*dia pases proseuches*)
   117, 921
withdraw (*stello*) 859
withhold (*katecho*) 911
without (*choris*) 700
won (*kerdeo*) 744
wonder (*teras*) 908
word (*logos*) 584, 585
word (*rhema*) 78, 109, 179, 584, 585
work (*energeo*) 59

worker (*ergos*) 884
workers together (*sunergos*) 565
workmanship (*poiema*) 28, 599
works (*ergos*) 493, 522, 559, 898
world (*kosmos*) 120, 467, 792
worship (*sebasma*) 907
wound (*plege*) 788, 789
wrap (*entulisso*) 289
wrath (*parorgismos*) 839
wrath (*thumos*) 454, 504, 505, 515
wrestle (*pale*) 395, 396
wrought (*katergadzo*) 559

Y

ye ought (*dei*) 361
ye shall be able (*dunamis*) 659
yoke (*zugos*) 543
young man (*neanikos*) 286

Greek Index

A

achreios (*unprofitable*) 387, 390
adelotes (*uncertain*) 893
adelphos (*brethren*) 35, 36
adelphos (*brother*) 35, 36
adikeo (*hurt*) 482
adikos (*iniquity*) 682
adokimos (*castaway*) 825
agape (*love*) 524, 525, 526, 527, 671, 675, 678, 680, 684, 685, 686, 687, 948
agathoergeo (*do good*) 898
agathos (*good*) 536, 778, 951
agathusune (*goodness*) 536
aggareuo (*compel*) 266
aggus (*nigh*) 281
agnoeo (*ignorant*) 128
agnos (*chaste*) 745
ago (*led*) 19, 462, 647, 997
agonidzo (*agony*) 202
agonidzo (*fight*) 303
agonidzo (*fought*) 303
agoradzo (*buy*) 344
agrupvia (*watchings*) 819
aichmalotidzo (*bringing into captivity*) 629
aiona (*course*) 119
airo (*take*) 543
aiteo (*ask*) 177, 711, 735, 738
aiteo (*crave*) 277
aiteo (*request*) 178
aitima (*request*) 711
akairos (*out of season*) 553, 554
akatastasia (*confusion*) 66
akatastasia (*tumults*) 454
akatastatos (*unruly*) 460
akatharsia (*uncleanness*) 496, 514

aklines (*waver*) 337
akoloutheo (*follow*) 587
akouo (*heard*) 478
akroates (*hearers only*) 13
alalazon (*tinkling*) 669
aleipho (*anoint*) 939
allos (*another*) 195, 196
ametakinetos (*immovable*) 167, 168
anadzonnumi (*gird up the loins*) 445
anairo (*consume*) 913
anakalupto (*open*) 644
anakrinas (*examine*) 256
analambano (*take*) 931
analusai (*depart*) 690
anamimnesko (*I put thee in remembrance*) 6
anapauo (*rest*) 542, 994
anastrophe (*conversation*) 744
andres (*men*) 928
anechomai (*endure*) 642
aneksikakos (*patient*) 438
anendektos (*impossible*) 327
anesis (*rest*) 142
angelos (*angel*) 867
angelos (*messenger*) 852
anoigo (*open*) 862
anomia (*sin*) 906
anthistemi (*resist*) 942
anti pas (*Antipas*) 250
antidikos (*adversary*) 652
antikeimai (*adversary*) 862
antikeimai (*oppose*) 907
antitasso (*resist*) 437
anupokritos (*dissimulation*) 949
apago (*led him away*) 232, 243
apechomai (*abstain*) 946
apeitho (*obey not*) 744

apekduomai (*spoil*) 592
aperchomai (*went backward*) 220
aphiemi (*forgive*) 843
aphistimi (*depart*) 855
aphthartos (*incorruptible*) 751
apo (*away*) 11, 113
apoballo (*cast away*) 432, 433
apodeiknumi (*demonstration*) 342
apodeiknumi (*show*) 908
apodidomi (*recompense*) 970
apodidomi (*render*) 775
apokalupsis (*revelation*) 39, 851
apokalupto (*reveal*) 71, 907, 911
apokopto (*cut off*) 223
apokrima (*sentence*) 424
apolausis (*enjoy*) 896
apoleia (*perdition*) 578, 907
apollumi (*destroy*) 548
apologia (*answer*) 926
aponemo (*give*) 760, 763
aporeo (*perplex*) 286
apostasia (*falling away*) 906
apostollos (*apostle*) 559
apostugeo (*abhor*) 950
apothesauridzo (*laying up*) 901
apotinasso (*shook it off*) 441
apotithimi (*lay apart*) 11, 21
apotithimi (*lay aside*) 113, 114
aptomai (*touch*) 226
archai (*principalities*) 398, 868
archon (*ruler*) 278
arkeo (*sufficient*) 856
arroustos (*sick*) 486, 487
arroustos (*sick folk*) 487
aschemoneo (*unseemly*) 676
aselgeia (*lasciviousness*) 497, 514
asotia (*excess*) 511
asthene (*weak*) 100
astheneia (*infirmity*) 565, 881
astheneo (*sick*) 487, 938, 940

astheneo (*weakness*) 856
asthenes (*weaker*) 760
astrapto (*shine*) 286
atakeo (*disorderly*) 859
athlesis (*fight*) 49
athlesis (*strive*) 189, 887

B

ballo (*against*) 530
ballo (*cast*) 257, 414
ballo (*put into*) 200
baptidzo (*baptism*) 330
baros (*burden*) 354, 356
bathos (*depth*) 868
bathus (*deep*) 799
bebaioo (*confirm*) 306
belos (*fiery darts*) 660
biblios (*book*) 476
biotikos (*life*) 706, 707
blapto (*hurt*) 484
blasphemeo (*blasphemy*) 239
blepo (*saw*) 289
blepo (*take heed*) 409
boetheia (*when they had taken up*) 530
bouleutes (*counselor*) 276
brabeion (*prize*) 691
brabeuo (*rule*) 2, 624

C

chairo (*joy*) 251, 682
chairo (*rejoice*) 682, 965
chalepos (*exceeding fierce*) 144
chalepos (*perilous*) 144, 996
chalkos (*brass*) 668
chamai (*to the ground*) 220
chara (*joy*) 451, 528, 529
charis (*grace*) 528, 848, 849
cheimadzoamai (*tempest*) 530
chiton (*garment*) 57
chlamuda kokkinen (*put on him
a scarlet robe*) 263

choipos (*swine*) 415
choris (*without*) 700
chreia (*necessity*) 958
chresteuomai (*kind*) 672
chrestos (*easy*) 543
chrestotes (*gentleness*) 534
chrio (*anoint*) 363
coustodia (*watch*) 282

egkataleipo (*forsook*) 926
egkauchaomai (*glory*) 641
egkopto (*hinder*) 31, 32, 765, 783
ego eimi (*I am*) 219, 220, 222
eidololatria (*idolatry*) 498, 514
eirene (*peace*) 529, 531, 848
ek hikanos chronos (*a long season*) 251
ekballo (*cast*) 390
ekballo (*cast out*) 475, 476
ekbasis (*escape*) 617
ekcheo (*shed abroad*) 672
ekduo (*strip*) 263
ekklino (*eschew*) 778
eklego (*chosen*) 384
ekluo (*faint*) 557
ekridzoo (*plucked up by the root*) 990
ektenes (*earnestly*) 202
ektrepo (*turned aside*) 165, 166
ekzeteo (*diligently seek*) 102
ekzomologeo (*confess*) 725
elaphron (*light*) 543
eleao (*compassion*) 392, 393
elegcho (*reprove*) 104, 430
elpidzo (*hope*) 251, 685
elpidzo (*trust*) 893
emeo (*spue*) 135
empaidzo (*mock*) 238, 239, 254, 264
empaidzo (*scoffer*) 904
empipto (*fall into*) 551
empleko (*entangle*) 47, 48
empleko (*platted*) 47, 263
emploke (*plaiting of hair*) 748
emprothen (*before*) 415
en (*by*) 130, 131
en panti kairo (*always*) 8, 117
en pase (*with all*) 908
endunamao (*strong*) 22, 153, 346, 347
endunamoo (*strengthen*) 927
enduo (*put on*) 533
energeo (*effectual*) 713, 862

energeo (*work*) 59
enischuo (*strengthen*) 205
enistemi (*things present*) 868
enkrateia (*temperance*) 540
enochleo (*trouble you*) 655, 870
enoikeo (*dwell*) 61
entulisso (*wrap*) 289
epaio (*smote*) 223
epecho (*take heed*) 30
epekteinomai (*press toward*) 691
ephistimi (*instant*) 553
epi (*in*) 893
epi (*over*) 91
epi (*upon*) 553
epi pasin (*above all*) 931
epichoregeo (*supply*) 4
epigeios (*earthly*) 418
epignosis (*acknowledge*) 714, 715
epignosis (*know*) 403
epikeima (*they were instant*) 257
epios (*gentle*) 317
epiphaneia (*brightness*) 914
epiphoneo (*cry*) 257
epipotheo (*lust*) 91, 92, 139
epiripto (*cast*) 325
episkopos (*bishop*) 638, 639, 829, 939
episkopos (*looking diligently*) 637, 639
epistemi (*stood by*) 286
episunagoge (*gathering together*) 904
epithumia (*desire*) 690
epithumia (*lust*) 490, 946
epitimao (*rebuke*) 841
epitithimi (*lay hands*) 487, 581
epitithimi (*put it upon*) 263
epitropos (*steward*) 882
epopteuo (*behold*) 745
eremia (*wilderness*) 811
erga (*deeds*) 631
ergos (*worker*) 884
ergos (*works*) 493, 522, 559, 898

eris (*debate*) 454

eris (*variance*) 503, 515

eritheia (*strife*) 66, 418, 454,
 506, 515, 722

eros (*love*) 524, 526

erotao (*beseech*) 903

eschatos (*last*) 144

esthes lampros (*gorgeous robe*) 254

ethnos (*heathen*) 808

ethnos (*nations*) 466

etoimasin (*preparation*) 158, 159

eu (*good*) 554

eucharisteo (*give thanks*) 17

eucharistia (*thanksgiving*) 710

eudokeo (*well pleased*) 771

euergeteo (*doing good*) 536

eugenes (*noble*) 380

eukairos (*in season*) 553

eukairos (*time*) 972

eulogetes (*blessing*) 775, 962

eulogia (*bless*) 962

eumetadotos (*ready to distribute*) 898

euperistatos (*so easily beset us*) 51

euprosdektos (*accept*) 451

euschemon (*honorable*) 276

euschemonos (*decently*) 173

eusebeia (*godliness*) 874

eusplagchnos (*pitiful*) 771, 772

euthumeo (*merry*) 937

eutonus (*vehemently*) 252, 253

exagoridzo (*redeem*) 121, 122

exaporeomai (*despair*) 424

exartidzo (*thoroughly furnished*) 657

exerchomai (*out of whom went*) 881

existimi (*amaze*) 479

exomologeo (*confess*) 981

exousia (*power*) 398, 598

exoutheneo (*despise*) 80

exoutheneo (*set him at nought*) 254

G

genos (*mine own countrymen*) 808

georgos (*husbandman*) 890

ges (*earth*) 274

ges (*land*) 273

ginomai (*be ye therefore*) 138

ginomai (*there arose*) 87

ginomai (*there was*) 273

ginomai (*was made*) 975

ginosko (*know*) 144

gnoridzo (*known*) 711

gnosis (*knowlege*) 403

gonupeteo (*bow*) 263

grauodes (*old wives*) 837

gregoreo (*vigilant*) 652

gumnadzo (*exercise*) 834, 838, 873, 874

H

hagios (*holy*) 412

hairesis (*heresies*) 508, 516

hamartano (*trespass*) 841

haploos (*liberally*) 738

harpadzo (*delivered*) 41

harpadzo (*pull*) 41, 42

hegeomai (*esteem*) 723

hen (*one*) 846

heteros (*another*) 195

himation (*apparel*) 748

hisuchios (*quiet*) 754

homoioma (*likeness*) 975

homologia (*confession*) 314

homologia (*profession*) 313, 314

homophron (*one mind*) 767

hoplos (*weapons*) 106, 210

horao (*saw*) 251, 696

horao (*see*) 252

hroidzedon (*great noise*) 916

hupakouo (*obedient*) 978

klepto (*thief*) 547
koinoneo (*distributing*) 958
koinonia (*communion*) 111, 112
koinonia (*fellowship*) 846
koinonia (*partaker*) 582
koinonia (*partners*) 111, 112
koinonikos (*willing to communicate*) 898
kokkinos (*scarlet*) 263
kokkos (*grain*) 987
kolaphidzo (*buffet*) 237, 853
kollao (*cleave*) 951
komoi (*revellings*) 512, 516
kopiao (*labor*) 993
kopos (*in weariness*) 816
kopos (*labor*) 542, 559, 786, 890
kosmokrateros (*rulers of the darkness of this world*) 398, 399
kosmos (*adorn*) 747
kosmos (*world*) 120, 467, 792
kradzo (*cry*) 587
kratos (*power*) 347, 348, 349, 540
kratos (*laid hold*) 232
krima (*condemnation*) 551
krino (*judge*) 588
krino (*judgment*) 588
krino (*sentence*) 33, 34
kruptos (*hidden*) 751
ktisis (*creature*) 599, 868
kumbalon (*cymbal*) 669
kunun (*dog*) 412

L

lalaipsi (*wind*) 87
lalouton (*speak*) 478
lambano (*took upon himself*) 975
lampas (*lantern*) 210
latreuo (*reasonable service*) 499
latreuo (*serve*) 498, 499
laxeuo (*hewn*) 281

lego (*say*) 988
leipo (*lack*) 734, 735
leros (*idle tale*) 287, 288
lestes (*highwaymen*) 806
lestes (*robber*) 805, 806
limos (*hunger*) 822
lithos (*rocks*) 275
logidzomai (*count not*) 626
logidzomai (*reckon*) 426
logidzomai (*think*) 679
logismos (*imagination*) 369
logos (*word*) 584, 585
loidoria (*evil*) 775
luo (*destroy*) 84, 85
luo (*dissolve*) 916
luo (*loose*) 85
luo (*melt*) 916
luo (*unloose*) 85
lupe (*grievous*) 834
lupete (*grieve*) 9
lutroo (*redemption*) 63, 64

M

machaira (*sword*) 77, 211
machomai (*strive*) 317
makrothumia (*longsuffering*) 533, 534, 671
makrothumia (*patience*) 533
makrothumia (*suffereth long*) 671
margarites (*pearl*) 415
maturios (*testimony*) 306
mechri (*unto*) 978
meden (*nothing*) 707
mega (*great*) 49, 285, 862
melei (*care*) 325
mello (*things to come*) 868
mello (*time to come*) 901
meno (*abide*) 578
merimna (*cares*) 325, 706
merimnao (*careful*) 706

merimnao (*thought*) 706
meta (*with*) 965
metamorphoo (*change*) 644
methe (*drunkenness*) 511, 516
methodos (*wiles*) 628, 629
miami (*defile*) 871
mimeomai (*follow*) 361
mimetes (*follow*) 137
mimetes (*follower*) 137, 160
miseo (*hate*) 57, 631
misthapodosia (*recompense of reward*)
  82, 155
mneia (*remembrance*) 175
mochthos (*in painfulness*) 817
mochthos (*painfulness*) 817
moi (*unto me*) 862
molopsi (*stripes*) 261
moraino (*foolish*) 381, 666
morphe (*form*) 974, 975
mukteridzo (*mock*) 556
muthos (*fable*) 837

N

naos (*a highly decorated shrine*) 116
naos (*temple*) 116, 907
nardos (*spikenard*) 609
neanikos (*young man*) 286
nekros (*dead*) 286, 426
neomata (*devices*) 128, 129, 629
neophutos (*novice*) 550
nephos (*cloud*) 98
nesteia (*fastings*) 822
nikolaos (*Nicanor*) 632
nikos (*conqueror*) 38
nikos (*overcome*) 371, 792
nosos (*disease*) 487
nothros (*slothful*) 133
nous (*mind*) 623
nous (*understanding*) 322

O

ochlos polus (*great multitude*) 208
ochuroma (*stronghold*) 918
odegeo (*show*) 646, 997
odoiporia (*journey*) 802
ogkos (*weight*) 114
oikos (*house*) 619
okneros (*slothful*) 387, 389, 955
okneros (*wicked*) 387, 389, 955
okneros (*wicked and slothful*) 387, 389
oneididzo (*upbraideth not*) 738
oneidismos (*reproach*) 401
onomos (*name*) 940
ophelimos (*profitable*) 300
ophis (*serpent*) 481, 661
orego (*desire*) 358, 832
orphanos (*comfortless*) 53, 54
ostrakinos (*earthen vessel*) 89, 90
otarion (*ear*) 223
othonion (*linen*) 279
ou chairei (*rejoiceth not*) 682
ouk eiasen (*suffered them not*) 729
oxsus (*vinegar*) 679

P

paideia (*chasten*) 834
paio (*struck*) 239
pale (*wrestle*) 395, 396
panoplia (*whole armor*) 319
pantote (*always*) 845
para meno (*Parmenas*) 632
para theou (*of God*) 737
para (*alongside*) 26
paradidomi (*commit*) 234
paradidomi (*deliver*) 244
paradidomi (*tradition*) 859
paraginomai (*stood*) 926
paraiteomai (*refuse*) 404, 837

parakaleo (*beseech*) 864, 903, 945

parakaleo (*besought*) 855

parakaleo (*exhort*) 26, 464

paraklete (*comforter*) 464

parakoloutheo (*follow*) 472

parakupto (*stooping down*) 289, 292

parangello (*command*) 859

parangelo (*charge*) 893

paraptoma (*fault*) 725

paratithimi (*commit*) 163

paraxusmos (*provoke*) 443

pareisago (*came in privily*) 814

parepidemos (*pilgrims*) 946

parerchomai (*pass away*) 916

paristemi (*stood*) 927

paristimi (*present*) 864, 865

paroikos (*stranger*) 945

parorgismos (*wrath*) 839

parousia (*come*) 903, 914

parousia (*coming*) 903, 914

paroxsuno (*provoke*) 678

parresia (*bold*) 156, 972

parresia (*confidence*) 155, 156, 373, 433

parresia (*openly*) 75, 592

pascho (*suffer*) 601

pateo (*tread*) 482

pathema (*afflictions*) 49

pauo (*refrain*) 777

peikeimenai (*compassed about*) 45, 46, 98

peiradzo (*assay*) 728

peiradzo (*prove*) 345, 929

peiradzo (*tempt*) 695

peirasmos (*temptation*) 617

peitho (*entice*) 342

peitho (*persuade*) 867

peri (*for*) 568

periballo (*array*) 254

perikalupto (*blindfold*) 239

periossos (*abundantly*) 548, 786

peripateo (*walk*) 93, 119, 489, 490, 859

perithesis (*wear*) 748

perkephalaia (*helmet*) 562, 563

perpereuomai (*vaunteth*) 674

petra (*rocks*) 275

phaneros (*manifest*) 493

phanos (*torch*) 210

pharmakeia (*witchcraft*) 499, 501, 515

phaulos (*corrupt communication*) 453

phaulos (*evil*) 66

phaulos (*foul*) 66

pheugo (*flee*) 617, 943

philadelphia (*brotherly love*) 525, 953

philadephia (*love as brethren*) 770

philanthropia (*one who loves mankind*) 525

philarguros (*one who loves money*) 525

philedonos (*lover of pleasure*) 512, 525

philema (*to kiss*) 123

phileo (*friend*) 123

phileo (*kiss*) 213

phileo (*love*) 524, 525, 526

philosophia (*love of wisdom*) 525

philosophia (*philosophy*) 525

philostorgos (*be kindly affectioned*) 953

philoxenia (*hospitality*) 960

philoxenia (*one who loves strangers*) 525

philoxenos (*hospitable*) 525

phobos (*fear*) 15, 41, 286, 745

phortidzo (*heavy laden*) 542, 994

phortion (*burden*) 356

photidzo (*illuminate*) 339

phragello (*scourge*) 259

phroneo (*mind*) 968

phroureo (*keep*) 322, 323

phthnos (*envy*) 140, 509, 510, 516

phuoo (*springing up*) 654

phusio (*puffed up*) 675

phusiosis (*swellings*) 454

phuteuo (*planted*) 991

pidzo (*root*) 732

pikria (*bitterness*) 732

pino (*devour*) 653
pino (*drink*) 484
pipto (*fail*) 687
pipto (*fall*) 220, 409
pisteuei (*believe*) 684
pisteuonti (*believe*) 781
pistis (*faith*) 537, 641
pistis (*faithful*) 537
planao (*deceive*) 555
plege (*stripes*) 788, 789
plege (*wound*) 788, 789
pleonadzo (*abound*) 545
pleonekteo (*advantage*) 127, 128
plethos (*multitude*) 478
plousios (*enrich*) 130, 131, 306
plousios (*richly*) 43, 44, 624, 892, 893, 898
plulake (*prison*) 789
pneuma (*spirit*) 298, 299, 913
poiema (*workmanship*) 28, 599
poieo (*do*) 778
poietes (*create*) 27, 28
poietes (*doer*) 27, 28
poietes (*poet*) 28, 599
pollakis (*often*) 802, 819, 822
polus ochios (*great company*) 344
polus (*many*) 882, 982
poluteles (*great price*) 754
polutimos (*very costly*) 609
poneros (*evil*) 951
poneros (*wickedness*) 399
porneia (*adultery*) 495, 514
porneia (*fornication*) 495
potamos (*waters*) 803
praksis (*deeds*) 476
prasso (*do*) 514, 520
praus (*meek*) 754
prautes (*meekness*) 539, 540
presbeuo (*ambassador*) 55
presbuteros (*elders*) 939

pro chorus (*Prochorus*) 632
proegeomai (*preferring*) 953
proistimi (*ruleth*) 619
pronimos (*wise*) 661
prosdechomai (*wait*) 276
prosechomai (*pray*) 567, 939
proseuche (*prayer*) 334, 335, 336, 709, 934, 935
proskaleo (*call*) 939
proslambano (*receive*) 720
proteron (*former days*) 340
psallo (*sing psalms*) 937
pseudadelphos (*false brother*) 649, 814, 815
pseudapostolos (*false apostle*) 649
pseudochristos (*false Christ*) 649
pseudodidaskalos (*false teacher*) 649
pseudologos (*one who speaks falsehoods*) 649
pseudomai (*lie*) 649
pseudomartureo (*false witness*) 649
pseudoprophetes (*false prophet*) 649
psilaphao (*handle me*) 296
psithurismos (*gossip*) 453, 457
psithurismos (*whisperings*) 453, 454, 457
psuchikos (*sensual*) 418
psyche (*soul*) 946
ptoma (*body*) 277

R

raparian (*filthiness*) 20
raparian (*vile*) 20
rhema (*word*) 78, 109, 179, 584, 585
ridzo (*root*) 376, 732
ruomai (*deliver*) 450

S

saleuo (*shake*) 622
sarkikos (*fleshly*) 946
sarkos (*carnal*) 107
sarx (*flesh*) 493

sbennumi (*quench*) 96, 659
schema (*fashion*) 977
schidzo (*rent*) 275
sebasma (*worship*) 907
seimos (*earthquake*) 285
seio (*shake*) 286
seiso (*quake*) 274
semeion (*miracle*) 252
semeion (*sign*) 472, 559, 908
semnotes (*gravity*) 367
sinapi (*mustard*) 987
skandalon (*offense*) 327
skeuos (*vessel*) 760
skleruno (*harden*) 698
skolops (*thorn*) 852, 853
skopos (*mark*) 691
skotos (*dark*) 273
sodzo (*save*) 15, 73, 940
sodzo (*save the sick*) 940
sophias (*wisdom*) 39, 735
sophos (*wise*) 342, 382, 596, 666
sophroneo (*soberly*) 149, 607
sophroneo (*sound mind*) 73, 996
soudarion (*napkin*) 289
speiro (*sow*) 556
sperma (*seed*) 519
sphodra (*very*) 285
sphragidzo (*made sure*) 282
sphragidzo (*seal*) 378
sphrodros (*exceedingly*) 530
spilos (*spot*) 58
spira (*band of men*) 207
spira (*whole band of soldiers*) 262
splagchnos (*bowels*) 772
splagchnos (*compassion*) 772
spoudadzo (*business*) 956
stadion (*race*) 186
stasis (*sedition*) 256
staurao (*crucify*) 269
stego (*bear*) 684

stello (*withdraw*) 859
stephanos (*crown*) 189, 263, 632
stephanos (*Stephen*) 632
stergo (*love*) 524, 526
stoicheion (*elements*) 916
stole (*garment*) 286
stomos (*mouth*) 913
strateuma (*men of war*) 254
strateuomai (*war*) 946
stratos (*warfare*) 106, 107
sudzao (*live with him*) 574
sudzao (*partnership*) 574
sudzao (*we shall also live with him*) 574
sukaminos (*sycamine*) 984
sumbasileuo (*reign with him*) 575
sumpathos (*compassion*) 767, 768
sumpnigo (*choke*) 706
sunagonidzomai (*strive together*) 450
sunairei logon meta (*reckon*) 184
sunanapauomai (*refresh*) 452
sunantilambetai (*helpeth*) 565
sunapago (*condescend*) 968
sunapothnesko (*dead with him*) 574
sunapothnesko (*if we be dead with him*) 574
sunarpadzo (*caught*) 530
suncheo (*confound*) 478
sunecho (*straight betwixt two*) 690
sunekleronomos (*heirs together*) 764
sunergos (*co-laborers*) 565
sunergos (*workers together*) 565
sunkakopatheo (*endure hardness*) 884, 885
sunoikeo (*dwell*) 757
suntribo (*broken in pieces*) 181
suntribo (*bruise*) 181
sussemon (*signal*) 213
sussemon (*token*) 213
syrtis (*quicksand*) 530

T

ta hupsela (*high things*) 968
tachus (*swift*) 351
tachus (*soon*) 622
tachus (*suddenly*) 581
taksis (*order*) 173
tameion (*closet*) 571
tapeinao (*humbled*) 977
tapeinophron (*courteous*) 773
tapeinoprosune (*lowliness of mind*) 723
tapeinos (*low estate*) 968
tekna (*children*) 367
teleo (*fulfill*) 490
teleo (*perfect*) 730, 856
teras (*wonder*) 908
tereo (*kept*) 303
tereo (*watch*) 271
thanasimos (*deadly*) 484
thanatephoros (*full of deadly poison*) 460
thanatoi (*deaths*) 790
thanotos (*death*) 867
tharseo (*good cheer*) 792
thaumadzo (*marveled greatly*)
   244, 246, 479
theaomai (*beheld*) 281, 293
theaomai (*saw*) 344
theaomai (*see*) 289, 292
theatron (*gazingstock*) 400, 401
thelema (*desire*) 490
thelema (*will*) 451
thelo (*desirous*) 251
thelo (*willing*) 257
themelios (*foundation*) 901
theopneustos (*inspiration*) 298, 299
theos (*God*) 298
therapeuo (*heal*) 881
thesauros (*treasure*) 89, 90
thlipsis (*affliction*) 401, 528
thlipsis (*tribulation*) 641, 642, 792

thlipsis (*trouble*) 142, 423
throeo (*troubled*) 623
thrombos (*drop*) 202
thumos (*anger*) 533
thumos (*wrath*) 454, 504, 505, 515
thuo (*kill*) 547
thureos (*shield*) 364
thura (*door*) 295, 862
ti (*any*) 484
ti (*what*) 566
timao (*honor*) 760
tis (*man*) 887
tithimi (*laid*) 281
tithimi (*to place*) 114
to loipon (*finally*) 567
to telos (*finally*) 767
topos (*place*) 603, 840
tou loipou (*finally*) 68
trecho (*free course*) 568
trecho (*run*) 406
triambeuo (*triumph*) 75, 592
tuphonikos (*tempestuous wind*) 530
tuphuo (*lifted up with pride*) 551

Z

zelos (*bitter envying*) 418
zelos (*emulation*) 504, 515
zelos (*envy*) 65, 454, 672
zelos (*seek*) 778
zeo (*fervent*) 956
zeteo (*seek*) 678
zhulos (*stave*) 211
zoe (*life*) 548, 867
zoogreo (*taken captive*) 703
zoopoieo (*quicken*) 309
zugos (*yoke*) 543

Scripture Index

John 19:25 — 882
John 19:28 — 270
John 19:30 — 273
John 19:38 — **276, 277**
John 19:39 — **276, 278, 279**
John 19:40 — **276, 279**, 289
John 19:41-42 — **280, 281**
John 20:1 — 882
John 20:3-4 — **288**
John 20:5 — 289, 292
John 20:6-7 — 289
John 20:8-10 — 290
John 20:11 — 289, **292**
John 20:12 — **292**
John 20:13 — **292, 293**, 882
John 20:14-17 — 293, 295, 882
John 20:18 — 293, 882
John 20:19 — 295, 296
John 20:21 — 296
John 20:22 — **295**, 290
John 20:25 — 296
John 20:26 — 295, 296
John 20:27 — 296
John 21:2-7 — 297
John 24:11 — 288
John 21:14 — 297
John 21:25 — 206, 208
Acts 1:3 — 297
Acts 10:3-4 — 175
Acts 10:38 — 111, 234, 536, 537
Acts 11:27-28 — 647
Acts 11:29 — 613, 647
Acts 11:30 — 939
Acts 12:4 — 789
Acts 13:5 — 404
Acts 13:8 — 808
Acts 13:13 — 404
Acts 13:45 — 808
Acts 13:50 — 808
Acts 13:51 — 802

Acts 14:2 — 808
Acts 14:6 — 802
Acts 14:19 — 796, 797, 808
Acts 14:20 — 797, 802
Acts 14:21 — 802
Acts 14:24-25 — 802
Acts 15:3-4 — 802
Acts 15:22 — 802
Acts 15:39-40 — 679
Acts 15:41 — 802
Acts 16:1 — 802
Acts 16:6 — 802
Acts 16:7 — 647, **727, 728**
Acts 16:8 — 802
Acts 16:9 — 647, 802
Acts 16:11 — 802
Acts 16:33 — 789
Acts 17:1 — 802
Acts 17:5-9 — 808
Acts 17:10 — 802
Acts 17:13 — 808
Acts 17:14-15 — 802
Acts 17:22 — 341, 342
Acts 17:23 — 341
Acts 17:28 — 341
Acts 17:32 — 341
Acts 17:34 — 342
Acts 18:1 — 802
Acts 18:3 — 407
Acts 18:12-16 — 808
Acts 18:18-19 — 802
Acts 18:22-23 — 802
Acts 19 — 783
Acts 19:1 — 802
Acts 19:14-15 — 94
Acts 19:18-19 — 476
Acts 2:1-5 — 478
Acts 2:6 — 478, 479
Acts 2:7-8 — 479
Acts 2:9-10 — 478

Bibliography

Abbott, T. K. *A Critical and Exegetical Commentary on the Epistles to the Ephesians and the Colossians*. Edinburgh: T. & T. Clark LTD., 1985.

Adkins, Lesley, and Roy A. Adkins. *Handbook to Life in Ancient Rome*. Oxford: Oxford University Press, 1994.

August, Roland. *Cruelty and Civilization*. New York: Barnes & Noble, 1994.

Bayraktar, Venbi. *Pergamon: Professional Guide*. Istanbul, Turkey: Net Turistik Yayinlar A. S., 1989.

Bigg, Charles. *A Critical and Exegetical Commentary on the Epistles of St. Peter and St. Jude*. Edinburgh: T. & T. Clark LTD., 1978.

Brooke, Canon A. E. *A Critical and Exegetical Commentary on the Johannine Epistles*. Edinburgh: T. & T. Clark LTD., 1980.

Brown, Colin. et al., eds. *The New International Dictionary of New Testament Theology*. 4 vols. Grand Rapids, Michigan: Regency Reference Library, 1971.

Bruce, F. F. *The Spreading Flame*. 1958; rpt. Grand Rapids, Michigan: Wm. B. Eerdmans Publishing Co., 1979.

Burckhardt, Jacob. *The Greeks and Greek Civilization*. Trans. Sheila Stern. New York: St. Martin's Press, October 1998.

Burton, Ernest De Witt. *A Critical and Exegetical Commentary on the Epistle to the Galatians*. Edinburgh: T. & T. Clark LTD., 1980.

Erdemgil, Selahattin. *Ephesus*. Istanbul, Turkey: Net Turistik Yayinlar A. S., 1990.

Eusebius, Pamphilus. *The Ecclesiastical History of Eusebius Pamphilus*. Trans. Isaac Boyle. Grand Rapids, Michigan: Baker Book House, March 1987.

Ferguson, Everett. *Backgrounds of Early Christianity*. Grand Rapids, Michigan: Wm. B. Eerdmans Publishing Co., 1987.

Fox, Robin Lane. *Pagans and Christians*. San Francisco: Harper & Row, 1986.

Grant, Michael. *Nero*. New York: Dorset Press, 1989.

Keppie, Lawrence. *The Making of the Roman Army*. New York: Barnes & Noble, 1984.

Maier, Paul. *Eusebeus: The Church History*. Grand Rapids, Michigan: Kregel Publications, 1999.

Malherbe, Abraham. *Moral Exhortation: A Greco-Roman Sourcebook*. Library of Early Christianity Series, Vol. 4. Philadelphia: The Westminster Press, 1986.

Meeks, Wayne. *The First Urban Christians*. New Haven: Yale University Press, 1983.

Moffatt, James. *A Critical and Exegetical Commentary on the Epistle to the Hebrews*. Edinburgh: T. & T. Clark LTD., 1986.

Plummer, Alfred. *A Critical and Exegetical Commentary on the Second Epistle of St. Paul to the Corinthians*. Edinburgh: T. & T. Clark LTD., 1985.

Poliakoff, Michael. *Combat Sports in the Ancient World: Competition, Violence, and Culture*. New Haven: Yale University Press, 1987.

Robertson, Archibald Thomas. *Word Pictures in the New Testament*. 5 vols. Nashville, Tennessee: Broadman Press, 1930-33.

Rogers, Cleon Jr., and Cleon Rogers III. *The New Linguistic and Exegetical Key to the Greek New Testament*. Grand Rapids, Michigan: Zondervan Publishing House, 1998.

Ropes, James Hardy. *A Critical and Exegetical Commentary on the Epistle of St. James*. Edinburgh: T. & T. Clark LTD., 1978.

Spicq, Ceslas. *Theological Lexicon of the New Testament*. Trans. James D. Ernest. 3 vols. Peabody, Massachusetts: Hendrickson Publishers, Inc., 1994.

Stowers, Stanley K. *Letter Writing in Greco-Roman Antiquity*. Library of Early Christianity Series, Vol. 5. Philadelphia: The Westminister Press, 1986.

Swaddling, Judith. *The Ancient Olympic Games*. Austin, Texas: University of Texas Press, 1980.

Tenney, Merrill. *New Testament Times*. Grand Rapids, Michigan: Wm. B. Eerdmans Publishing Co., 1965.

Vegetius Renatus, Flavius. *The Military Institutions of the Romans*. Trans. Lieutenant John Clark. Westport, Connecticut: Greenwood Press, 1944.

Vincent, Marvin R. *Word Studies in the New Testament*. 5 vols. 1887; rpt. Grand Rapids, Michigan: Wm. B. Eerdmans Publishing Co., 1977.

Walsh, Michael. *Roots of Christianity*. London: Grafton Books, 1986.

Wuest, Kenneth. *Wuest's Word Studies From the Greek New Testament*. 2nd ed. 3 vols. Grand Rapids, Michigan: Wm. B. Eerdmans Publishing Co., 1980.

Books by Rick Renner

Books in English

Seducing Spirits and Doctrines of Demons
Living in the Combat Zone
Merchandising the Anointing
Dressed To Kill
Spiritual Weapons To Defeat the Enemy
Dream Thieves
The Point of No Return
The Dynamic Duo
If You Were God, Would You Choose You?
Ten Guidelines To Help You Achieve
    Your Long-Awaited Promotion!
It's Time for You To Fulfill Your Secret Dreams
Isn't It Time for You To Get Over It?
Sparkling Gems From the Greek Daily Devotional
Insights on Successful Leadership
365 Days of Power

Books in Russian

How To Test Spiritual Manifestations
Living in the Combat Zone
Merchandising the Anointing
Dressed To Kill
Spiritual Weapons To Defeat the Enemy
Dream Thieves
The Point of No Return
The Dynamic Duo
Hell Is a Real Place
What the Bible Says About Water Baptism
What the Bible Says About Tithes and Offerings
Signs of the Second Coming of Jesus Christ
It's Time for You To Fulfill Your Secret Dream

Isn't It Time for You To Get Over It?
Ten Guidelines To Help You Achieve
   Your Long-Awaited Promotion!
The Death, Burial, and Resurrection of Jesus Christ
A Christian's Responsibility
If You Are Pursued by Failures
Insights on Successful Leadership

Books in German

Dream Thieves
The Point of No Return
Dressed To Kill
The Dynamic Duo

Audio Series by Rick Renner

Ministry and Servanthood (16 tapes)

The Anointing (4 tapes)

Miracles of Jesus Christ (8 tapes)

The Person, Power, and Work of the Holy Spirit (12 tapes)

Aggressive Worship (3 tapes)

Spiritual Armor (12 tapes)

Abraham, Father of Faith (10 tapes)

Samuel, Spokesman of Almighty God (10 tapes)

Prayers of the Apostle Paul (12 tapes)

Seven Messages to the Seven Churches
   In the Book of Revelation (10 tapes)

Supernatural Direction and Guidance (10 tapes)

Six Important Messages to Leaders Today (6 tapes)

Taking a Stand...in Difficult Situations (6 tapes)

Getting Rid of the Past (6 tapes)

How To Respond If You've Received the Judas Kiss (6 tapes)

Overthrowing Strongholds (6 tapes)

Keys to Winning the Race of Faith (6 tapes)

Healing the Mind and the Emotions of the Oppressed (3 tapes)

Fulfilling God's Divine Destiny for Your Life (3 tapes)

Seducing Spirits and Doctrines of Demons (3 tapes)

Pulling Down Strongholds (4 tapes)

Accomplishing Your Dreams Step-by-Step (3 tapes)

How To Survive Difficult Situations (3 tapes)

The Holy Spirit and You (3 tapes)

How To Improve Your Relationship With Your Spouse, Part 1 (6 tapes)

How To Improve Your Relationship With Your Spouse, Part 2 (6 tapes)

How To Protect You and Your Family in the Last Days (12 tapes)

If You're in a Trap, Here's How To Get Out (6 tapes)

The Greatest Miracles of Jesus Christ (6 tapes)

Wilt Thou Be Made Whole (2 tapes)

The Will of God, Key to Success (10 tapes)

Crossing the Bridge of Fear and Torment (2 tapes)

It's Time To Get Over Your Bad Attitudes and Fix Your Stinking Thinking (6 tapes)

The Person and Power of the Holy Spirit (6 tapes)

Videotapes by Rick Renner

The Communion of the Holy Spirit
The Supernatural Assistance of the Holy Spirit
For We Wrestle Not Against Flesh and Blood
Biblical Approach to Spiritual Warfare
Wilt Thou Be Made Whole
Spiritual Error in the Church, Part 1
Spiritual Error in the Church, Part 2
Spiritual Error in the Church, Part 3
Qualifications of Leadership, Part 1
Qualifications of Leadership, Part 2
Submission and Authority, Part 1
Submission and Authority, Part 2
Pulling Down Mental Strongholds, Part 1
Pulling Down Mental Strongholds, Part 2
Seven Messages to the Seven Churches —
    Overview of Seven Churches
Seven Messages to the Seven Churches —
    Rev. 2, John
Seven Messages to the Seven Churches —
    Ephesus
Seven Messages to the Seven Churches —
    Ephesus and Smyrna
Seven Messages to the Seven Churches —
    Pergamus
The Help of the Holy Spirit, Part 1
The Help of the Holy Spirit, Part 2
The Help of the Holy Spirit, Part 3
Right Foundations, Part 1
Right Foundations, Part 2
New Supply of the Spirit
The Power of the Tithe
How To Survive in Difficult Situations, Part 1
How To Survive in Difficult Situations, Part 2
Abusive Situations in Work and Marriage, Part 1
Abusive Situations in Work and Marriage, Part 2
Abusive Situations in Work and Marriage, Part 3
Proper Attitude for Pursuing Your Purpose, Part 1
Proper Attitude for Pursuing Your Purpose, Part 2
How To Make Every Minute Count

For Further Information

For all book orders, please contact:

TEACH ALL NATIONS

*A book company anointed to take God's Word
to you and to the nations of the world.*

A Division of
Rick Renner Ministries
P. O. Box 702040
Tulsa, OK 74170-2040
Phone: 877-281-8644
Fax: 888-281-4686
E-mail: tan@renner.org

*For prayer requests
or for further information about this ministry,
please write or call
the Rick Renner Ministries office
nearest you (see following page).*

All USA Correspondence:
Rick Renner Ministries
P. O. Box 702040
Tulsa, OK 74170-2040
(918) 496-3213
Or 1-800-RICK-593
E-mail: renner@renner.org
Website: www.renner.org

Riga Office:
Rick Renner Ministries
Unijas 99
Riga, LV-1084, Latvia
(371) 780-2150
E-mail: info@goodnews.lv

Moscow Office:
Rick Renner Ministries
P. O. Box 53
Moscow, 109316, Russia
7 (095) 727-1470
E-mail: mirpress@umail.ru

Kiev Office:
Rick Renner Ministries
P. O. Box 146
Kiev, 01025, Ukraine
380 (44) 246-6552
E-mail: mirpress@rrm.kiev.ua

Oxford Office:
Rick Renner Ministries
Box 7, 266 Banbury Road
Oxford, OX2 7DL, England
44 (1865) 355509
E-mail: europe@renner.org

NOTE:

To order a complete audio, video, and book catalog,
please contact our offices in Tulsa or Oxford.

About the Author

Rick Renner is a highly respected leader within the global Christian community. Rick ministered widely throughout the United States for many years before answering God's call in 1991 to move his family to the former Soviet Union and plunge into the heart of its newly emerging Church. Following an apostolic call on his life, Rick works alongside his wife Denise to see the Gospel preached, leadership trained, and the Church established throughout the world.

In a very real sense, the situation in these nations and in other countries still emerging from communist domination is very similar to the situation that existed in the book of Acts. The Church is growing; signs, wonders, and miracles are occurring; new churches are being started; and thousands of people are being saved. But because pastors have had insufficient training in practical areas of ministry and in theology, much has been done incorrectly in the effort to further God's Kingdom in this part of the world. Pastors have fire, desire, and a fervent call to reach their people for Christ. However, their lack of training often causes them to make mistakes that prove fatal to their churches or ministries.

Part of the mission of *Rick Renner Ministries* is to come alongside these pastors and ministers and to take them to a higher level of excellence and professionalism in the ministry. Therefore, since 1991 when the walls of communism first collapsed, this ministry has been working in the former USSR to train and equip pastors, church leaders, and ministers, helping them attain the necessary skills and knowledge to fulfill the ministries the Lord has given to them.

To this end, Rick Renner founded the *Good News Association of Pastors and Churches.* This church-planting and church-supporting organization has almost 800 pastors and churches in its membership. Rick Renner and his team meet once a quarter with all the members of the Association for the purpose of teaching the Word and ministering to the specific needs of the Association pastors and ministers.

Many pastors look to Rick Renner as a spiritual covering and mentor. Because they live in remote villages and feel forgotten, their relationship with Rick Renner and his team has become a vital link in their lives. Through this relationship, they receive the pastoral care they desperately need. Not only have the pastors and their families been strengthened, but many of their churches have grown significantly, even doubling and tripling in size. In this way, the *Good News Association* is making a significant impact in the local churches of the former Soviet Union.

In addition to the *Good News Association*, *Rick Renner Ministries* also owns and operates the *Good News Television Network*, the first and largest Christian television network in the territory of the former USSR. This network is a mighty instrument in God's hand that reaches 100 million potential viewers every day. Thousands of letters are received monthly from people who watch the programs broadcast on the *Good News Television Network*.

Since there are literally thousands of villages with no church in this region of the world, the television programs of the *Good News Television Network* serve as the only available "church" to millions of people in the former Soviet Union. These programs are a spiritual lifeline to these people, providing their only source for learning how to grow and mature in the Lord. More than two million people have committed their lives to Christ as a result of these broadcasts.

Rick Renner Ministries translates and publishes many books in the Russian language from its *Good News Distribution Department*. As a result, multiple tons of books have been delivered free of charge to people who have no church, no local Christian bookstore, and no other way to receive books and literature to help them grow in their relationship with God.

In addition to these already-mentioned outreaches of *Rick Renner Ministries*, Rick and Denise Renner are also pastors of the fast-growing *Moscow Good News Church*, located in the very heart of Moscow, Russia. Today the *Moscow Good News Church* is one of the largest Protestant churches in the city of Moscow with more than 2,000 people in active attendance.

Rick and Denise Renner are also founders of the *Good News Seminary*, a school that operates as a part of the *Moscow Good News Church* and specializes in training leaders to start new churches all over the former Soviet Union. Today students attend this seminary from many regions of Russia and other former Soviet Union republics.

We appreciate your prayers for Rick and Denise Renner and their entire ministry team as they fulfill their call to the former Soviet Union. If you are interested in become a partner with this ministry or if you would like to order a free product catalog, please call our Tulsa office at 1-800-RICK-593. Or if you wish, you can become a partner by filling out the proper form on our website at www.renner.org.

STUDY NOTES

STUDY NOTES